Arndt Bode   Mike Reeve   Gottfried Wolf   (Eds.)

PARLE '93
Parallel Architectures
and Languages Europe

5th International PARLE Conference
Munich, Germany, June 14-17, 1993
Proceedings

Springer-Verlag

Berlin Heidelberg New York
London Paris Tokyo
Hong Kong Barcelona
Budapest

Series Editors

Gerhard Goos
Universität Karlsruhe
Postfach 69 80
Vincenz-Priessnitz-Straße 1
D-76131 Karlsruhe, FRG

Juris Hartmanis
Cornell University
Department of Computer Science
4130 Upson Hall
Ithaca, NY 14853, USA

Volume Editors

Arndt Bode
Institut für Informatik, TU München
Arcisstr. 21, D-80333 München, Germany

Mike Reeve
European Computer-Industry Research Centre (ECRC)
Arabellastraße 17, D-81925 München, Germany

Gottfried Wolf
Deutsche Forschungsanstalt für Luft- und Raumfahrt (DFLR)
Rudower Chaussee 5, D-12489 Berlin Adlershof, Germany

CR Subject Classification (1991): C.1-4, D.1, D.3-4, F.1.3

ISBN 3-540-56891-3 Springer-Verlag Berlin Heidelberg New York
ISBN 0-387-56891-3 Springer-Verlag New York Berlin Heidelberg

Typesetting: Camera ready by author
Printing and binding: Druckhaus Beltz, Hemsbach/Bergstr.
45/3140-543210 - Printed on acid-free paper

Preface

PARLE is an international, European based conference which focuses on the parallel processing subdomain of informatics and information technology. Parallel processing is today recognized as an area of strategic significance throughout the world. As a result, many national, pan-European and world-wide initiatives are being planned or already exist to further research and development in this area.

Ever increasing demands are being made on computer technology to provide the processing power necessary to help understand and master the complexity of natural phenomena and engineering structures. Within human organizations ever more processing power is needed to master the increasing information flow. Many so-called "Grand Challenges" have been identified as being orders of magnitude beyond even the most powerful computers available today.

Although the microelectronics industry has made vast, impressive strides both in improving the processing power available from individual components and in dramatically reducing the cost of basic processing power, it is not in itself enough to satisfy even today's requirements.

Parallel processing technology offers a solution to this problem. By taking several basic processing devices and connecting them together the potential exists of achieving a performance of many times that of an individual device. However, it is still an important topic of research to discover how to do this optimally and then to be able to effectively exploit the potential power through real applications solving real-world problems. Some progress has been made, particularly in isolated applications, but building parallel application programs is today recognized as a highly complex activity requiring specialist skills and in-depth knowledge of both the application domain and the particular parallel computer to be used.

Many international conferences in the area of parallel processing focus on the now well-established technical areas broadly described as number-crunching. Although this area is also within PARLE's scope, it has tended to put more emphasis in its technical program on other areas, such as novel architectures, symbolic processing, parallel database technology,and functional and logic technology. These represent some of the most difficult challenges in making general purpose parallel computing a reality.

The PARLE Conference came into existence in 1987. It started its life as an initiative coming from the ESPRIT I programme and was financially supported by the Commission of the European Communities through that programme. Between 1987 and 1991 the conference was held biannually around Eindhoven in the Netherlands with Philips taking the responsibility for its organization.

In 1991 Philips decided that they no longer wished to continue organizing PARLE and so the future of the conference was reviewed. The conference Steering Committee members felt that PARLE had an important role to fulfil and so decided to continue, but with a revised format. PARLE is now focused on becoming *the* European conference with an international reputation in the domain of parallel architectures and languages.

A new conference organizational format has been adopted to emphasize this new commitment in a number of ways:

- the conference will be held annually,
- PARLE will be held exclusively within Europe,
- the conference venue will change country each year,
- the Steering Committee will represent various European countries,
- the Steering Committee should contain some of the most eminent European workers,
- the Programme Committee will represent most European countries,
- the Programme Committee will contain some important non-European experts,
- the Programme Committee will include specialists from industry as well as academia.

This format was first used for the 1992 conference held in June in a suburb of Paris and organized through the French Informatics Society, AFCET. It was judged to be a success in terms of the number of paper submissions received, the increased level of attendance, and the improved technical quality.

PARLE intends to become the European forum for interchange between experts in the parallel processing domain. It is intended to attract both industrial and academic participants with a technical programme designed to provide a balance between theory and practice. This role is an important function of PARLE and a consequence of its history.

The ESPRIT programme was partly conceived as an umbrella for collaborations involving industrial and academic participants. By working together and exchanging ideas, an important synergy can occur which profits both communities and can lead to extremely fast exploitation of innovative solutions in the market place. This promotes mutual understanding of important issues and prevents technology transfer barriers.

PARLE reflects this by promoting exchange between industry and academia, between practitioners and theoreticians, especially within the European context but also within the rest of the international community involved in the field of parallel processing systems. These different roles represent a key component of the strength and importance of PARLE.

Within Europe, the ESPRIT programme represents a significant research effort involving industrial and academic workers in, amongst other topics, the design and implementation of new computer architectures, theoretical work, parallel language design and development, tools to support parallel application construction, and, of course, the construction of prototype parallel applications. Considering the history and roles of PARLE, it is natural that the conference is supported by the Commission of the European Communities through the ESPRIT Programme and through representation at the level of the Steering

Committee. The European nature has also been emphasised through the support of CEPIS, the Council of European Informatics Societies, which represents over 200 000 Information Technology professionals in Europe.

PARLE'93 was organized in Munich by the European Computer-Industry Research Centre, ECRC, in cooperation with the Technical University of Munich and SIEMENS Central Research Laboratories. The conference was sponsored by the ESPRIT Programme of the Commission of the European Communities, ECRC, the Dresdner Bank, the city of Munich, AFCET, CEPIS, GI and ITG.

More than 200 papers were submitted and the best 52 were accepted as full papers. Additionally, the proceedings include short summaries of the papers accepted for presentation at the poster session and brief overviews of some of the CEC ESPRIT projects that provided support for PARLE'93.

An industrial exhibition was organized as part of the PARLE'93 conference. This provided an excellent opportunity for all attendees to gain first-hand experience of the newest products available. Considering this was the first time such an event has been held as part of a PARLE conference, it is gratifying that so many major international companies chose to participate. PARLE'93 also featured tutorials covering advanced parallel processing techniques. These two things have undoubtedly added an important new dimension to PARLE and we hope that next year's organizers will continue with them.

The programme chairmen are grateful to the authors, the members of the programme and steering committees, the referees, the supporting societies, and the organizing committee for their help in preparing PARLE'93 and the proceedings. We would also like to thank the following for their efforts in ensuring the smooth running of the conference: Uli Fuetterer, Christiane and Susanne Hollmayer, Isabelle Syre, and Ulrich Koschkar and family.

April 1993   Arndt Bode, Mike Reeve, Gottfried Wolf

PARLE 93 Organization

PARLE 93 Steering Committee

Werner Damm (U. of Oldenburg, D)   Jean Claude Syre (Bull SA, F)
Jose Delgado (INESC, P)   Jorgen Staunstrup (TU Denmark, DK)
Lucio Grandinetti (U. of Calabria, I) Mateo Valero (U. of Catalunya, E)
Constantin Halatsis (U. of Athens, GR) Thierry Van der Pyl (DGXIII, CEC)
Ron Perrot (U. of Belfast, UK)   Pierre Wolper (U. of Liege, B)
Martin Rem (TU Eindhoven, NL)

PARLE 93 Organizing Committee

Arndt Bode (T. U. Munich, D)	Joint Programme Chair
Werner Damm (U. of Oldenburg, D)	Steering Committee Liaison
Doug DeGroot (Texas Instruments / CSC, USA)	N. & S. American Co-ordinator
Ulrike Jendis (ECRC, D)	Treasurer
Peter Kacsuk (KFKI, H)	East European Co-ordinator
Masaru Kitsuregawa (U. of Tokyo, J)	Japan & Asian Co-ordinator
Rudi Kober (Siemens/ZFE, D)	Exhibition Chair
Michael Ratcliffe (ECRC, D)	Organizing Committee Chair
Mike Reeve (ECRC, D)	Joint Programme Chair
Gottfried Wolf (DLR, D)	Joint Programme Chair

PARLE 93 Programme Committee

PARLE 93 Sponsors

Contents

Paper Sessions

Architectures: Virtual Shared Memory

Functional Programming

Interconnection Networks: Embeddings

Architectures: Caches

Concurrency: Semantics

Tools

Neural Networks

Scheduling

Specification, Verification

Algorithms

Architectures: Fine Grain Parallelism

Databases

Poster Session

Regular Posters

ESPRIT Project Overvies

Simulation–based Comparison of Hash Functions for Emulated Shared Memory*

Curd Engelmann[1] and Jörg Keller[2]

[1] Universität des Saarlandes, Computer Science Department
Im Stadtwald, 6600 Saarbrücken, Germany
[2] Centrum voor Wiskunde en Informatica
Postbus 4079, 1009 AB Amsterdam, The Netherlands

Abstract. The influence of several hash functions on the distribution of a shared address space onto p distributed memory modules is compared by simulations. Both synthetic workloads and address traces of applications are investigated. It turns out that on all workloads linear hash functions, although proven to be asymptotically worse, perform better than theoretically optimal polynomials of degree $O(\log p)$. The latter are also worse than hash functions that use boolean matrices. The performance measurements are done by an expected worst case analysis. Thus linear hash functions provide an efficient and easy to implement way to emulate shared memory.

1 Introduction

Users of parallel machines more and more tend to program with the view of a global shared memory. Commercial machines (with more than 16 processors) however usually have distributed memory modules. Therefore the address space has to be mapped onto memory modules, memory access is simulated by packet routing on a network connecting processors and memory modules. This has to be done in a way that for (almost) all access patterns the requests are distributed almost evenly among the memory modules. The reason to demand this is obvious: if cases happen where the number of requests per module (the so called *module congestion*) is too high, then performance gets very poor.

Several kinds of hash functions have been proposed. But their theoretically provable properties are asymptotical results. As currently available machines are quite small (the number p of processors and memory modules usually is less than 1000) the actual behaviour of the chosen hash function can differ quite a lot from these theoretical properties. The lack of experimental data makes the selection of a particular hashing scheme difficult in practice. We are not aware of comparisons of hash functions based on simulated behaviour.

* This work was supported by the German Science Foundation (DFG) in SFB 124, TP D4, and by the Dutch Science Foundation (NWO) through NFI Project ALADDIN under Contract number NF 62-376. Part of this work was done while the second author was working at Universität des Saarlandes, Computer Science Department, Saarbrücken, Germany.

The goal of this investigation is to provide these data by comparing four kinds of hash functions by simulations. In Sect. 2 the most common kinds of hash functions are introduced. Section 3 describes the types of synthetic and real access patterns that were used as workloads. Section 4 sketches the experiments made and Sect. 5 presents and discusses the results.

2 Hash Functions

As already mentioned, a hash function serves to map a global address space onto distributed memory modules. More formally, for an address space M of size $m = 2^v$ and a set N of $p = 2^u$ memory modules, the mapping is a function $h : M \rightarrow M$ that maps addresses to memory cells. The function $mod : M \rightarrow N, mod(x) = x$ div m/p specifies the module of a memory cell x, the function $loc : M \rightarrow M', loc(x) = x$ mod m/p specifies the local address of cell x.

An optimal mapping function h should guarantee low module congestion for almost all possible access patterns (if all addresses of one pattern are distinct). This is achieved by using classes of functions in which each function has low module congestion for almost all patterns. A particular function is randomly chosen. This guarantees with very high probability that the current application does not exhibit the patterns on which the chosen function produces hot spots.

An additional problem consists in patterns with several processors concurrently accessing one cell. This problem cannot be solved by hashing. However there exist routing algorithms that perform *combining*. Requests that access the same cell are merged during routing, answers are duplicated. Ranade's emulation algorithm [10] is a good example. Therefore, concurrent access does not increase module congestion.

A class that restricts module congestion to $O(\log p)$ is

$$\mathcal{H} = \left\{ p(x) = \left(\sum_{i=0}^{\xi} a_i \cdot x^i \right) \bmod P \bmod m : 0 \leq a_i < P \right\} .$$

P is a prime larger than m, $\xi = O(\log p)$. A function of $\mathcal{H}$ is obtained by randomly choosing the values for a_i. This class was used in several theoretical investigations [6, 8, 10] to emulate shared memory on a processor network. The module congestion of $O(\log p)$ is sufficient because access from processors to memory modules across a constant–degree interconnection network needs time $\Omega(\log p)$ anyway.

However the functions in $\mathcal{H}$ are not bijective. This means that several addresses of the shared memory could be mapped onto the same cell. This requires secondary hashing on each memory module. Ranade [10] describes a method that performs secondary hashing in constant time and increases the size of the memory module only by a constant factor.

In practice however one should avoid secondary hashing and waste of memory because a constant factor of performance loss can destroy an asymptotically good result. Furthermore, the time to evaluate the hash function should be short. The functions in $\mathcal{H}$ require $\xi = O(\log p)$ multiplications and additions and a modulo division by a prime which needs a lengthy computation.

Therefore some alternatives were proposed:

1. For $\xi = 1$ one obtains a linear function. This reduces evaluation time to one multiplication, one addition and one modulo division. The function is still not bijective.
2. Furthermore if the modulo division by a prime is skipped and the coefficient a_0 is set to zero, the evaluation time is reduced to one multiplication. The operation modulo m is not counted because m is a power of two. If only odd values are chosen for a_1 the function also is bijective.
3. If the binary representation of an address is seen as a boolean vector, the hash function consists of multiplying this vector with an invertible boolean matrix. The time to evaluate this function is shorter than one multiplication.

Dietzfelbinger et. al. prove that the first alternative is asymptotically equivalent to the second [5]. Furthermore he proves that linear functions can result in a module congestion of $\Theta(\sqrt{p})$ for patterns with addresses of the form $b + s \cdot i$ where $i = 0, \ldots, n-1$ [4]. The constants b and s are called *base* and *stride*. This means that linear functions modulo a power of two are asymptotically worse than polynomials.

The third alternative was used in the design of the IBM RP3. Norton and Melton [9] introduce a class of boolean matrices where all matrices are invertible (which means bijectivity). Optimal distribution can be guaranteed for patterns with strides where s is a power of two and where in the binary representation of base b bits s to $s + \log n - 1$ are zero. For other bases the module congestion is at most 2. No theoretical results are given for other patterns, but their simulations hint that distribution is acceptable for other patterns, too. One particular matrix is obtained by randomly choosing several bits of the matrix and then computing all the other bits with respect to the above properties.

3 Workloads

The workloads are chosen to compare the hash functions with respect to known differences, especially behaviour on access patterns with strides, and with respect to patterns taken from applications. Therefore both synthetically generated patterns and application traces were taken.

The synthetic traces consist of randomly chosen patterns as a reference and strides with $s = 1, 13, 32$. The strides were chosen to compare matrix hashing and the other hash functions and to check whether linear functions get worse on these patterns. For $s = 32$ and $s = 1$ matrix hashing is optimal [9]. Theoretical results about the performance on the others are not known.

The traces were taken from three application programs: list ranking, matrix multiplication and connected components. The reasons for taking traces from applications are the variety of produced patterns and the structure of single patterns that often is more complex and less regular than in synthetical traces.

The three applications are chosen to represent a large variety of algorithms. Matrix multiplication is an example of a class of algorithms where the access patterns are regular and do not depend on the particular input values. Many other numerical algorithms behave that way, especially as many of them are originally designed to work on a processor network with a fixed interconnection structure (see e.g. [3]).

List ranking represents combinatorial algorithms where access patterns depend on the actual data. An example technique is pointer doubling. Processor i loads or stores $F[F[i]]$, where F is an array in the shared memory. Part of the accesses to shared memory still are regular. If processor i loads or stores $F[i]$, the access pattern is a stride with $s = 1$. Many PRAM algorithms working on lists and graphs are of this type (see e.g. [7]).

The connected components algorithm represents algorithms where access patterns depend on the actual data, but not all processors may participate in the access. This together with concurrent accesses to some cells, which get combined, makes module congestion smaller. Thus, connected components and similar algorithms are remarkable exceptions compared to list ranking type algorithms.

The list ranking algorithm is taken from a survey [7]. For a given linked list of n elements, the distance (or $rank$) to the end of the list is computed for each element. The algorithm needs n processors and $O(\log n)$ time. The list is represented as an array F, where $F[i]$ means successor of i in the list. For the last element of the list, $F[i] = i$. The rank is contained in array R. The PARDO code is shown in Fig. 1(a).The access patterns of this algorithm partly depend on the structure of the list and partly are strides with $s = 1$.

In the matrix multiplication algorithm $C = A \cdot B$, each processor computes one element of the destination matrix C. In order to avoid concurrent accesses, all processors start at different rows and columns of the matrices A and B. The PARDO code is shown in Fig. 1(b).Matrices A and C consist of $n = w2^{2z}$ elements and have dimension $2^z \times w2^z$, matrix B has dimension $w2^z \times w2^z$. The algorithm needs n processors and takes time $O(n^{1/2})$. The access patterns of this algorithm only depend on the dimensions of the matrices.

The connected components algorithm was adapted from Shiloach and Vishkin [11]. For a given undirected graph $G = (V, E)$, the connected components are computed. The algorithm needs $n = \max(|V|, 2|E|)$ processors and takes time $O(\log n)$. The graph is represented by two arrays HEAD and TAIL. For a given edge e, HEAD$[e]$ and TAIL$[e]$ contain the nodes to which e is adjacent. The components are represented by an array F. Two nodes u, v are in the same component if and only if $F[u] = F[v]$ after running the program. The PARDO code is shown in Fig. 1(c).The access patterns partly depend on the structure of the input graph and partly are strides with $s = 1$. Not all processors participate in every access.

```
(* Init rank R *)                         for u ∈ V pardo F[u] := u od;
for i := 1 to n pardo                     for t := 1 to 2 log |V| do
  if F[i] = i then R[i] := 0 else R[i] := 1   for u ∈ V pardo change[u] := 0 od;
od ;                                        starcheck;
(* Compute rank R *)                        for all (u, w) with {u, w} ∈ E pardo
for t := 1 to ⌈log n⌉ do                      if star[u] and F[w] < F[u] then
  for i := 1 to n pardo                          F[F[u]] := F[w];
    R[i] := R[i] + R[F[i]] ;                     change[F[u]] := 1;
    F[i] := F[F[i]] (* Pointer doubling *)       change[F[w]] := 1
  od                                          fi
od ;                                        od;
                                            starcheck;
(a) list ranking                            for all (u, w) with {u, w} ∈ E pardo
                                              if star[u] and not change[F[u]]
(* n = w2^{2z} *)                                  and F[w] ≠ F[u] then
k := 2^z; m := w2^z; l := w2^z;                  F[F[u]] := F[w]
for (i, j) := (1, 1) to (k, m) pardo          fi;
  C[i, j] := 0 (* Init C *)                    F[u] := F[F[u]]
od ;                                        od
for r := 1 to l do                        od.
  for (i, j) := (1, 1) to (k, m) pardo
    t := (i + j + r) mod l ;              proc starcheck ;
    C[i, j] := C[i, j] + A[i, t] · B[t, j]  begin
  od                                        for i ∈ V pardo
od ;                                          star[i] := true;
                                              if F[F[i]] ≠ F[i] then
(b) matrix multiplication                        star[F[F[i]]] := false
                                              fi;
                                              star[i] := star[F[F[i]]]
                                            od
                                          end;

                                          (c) connected components
```

Fig. 1. Code of applications

4 Experiments

To obtain the input data for the experiments, all applications are simulated by sequential programs, only the address traces are extracted. This frees us from considering a particular microprocessor instruction set and compiler. The address traces of the synthetic workloads are generated by a program, that simulates 4 steps of the machine. In the workloads with strides, the base b is increased each step by ns.

We are only interested in the resulting module congestion and not in the time to route the requesting packets from processors to memory modules. Therefore we can neglect the structure of the interconnection network. We only model it by a latency term because the processors perform latency hiding (see below).

All experiments are carried out for $m = 2^{22}$, the prime P is chosen closest to m. We simulate machines with $p = 2^u$, $u = 5, \ldots, 10$ processors. We run multiple processes per processor to hide the network latency from processors. The processes are executed in a round-robin manner, one instruction per turn. The exact number c of necessary processes per processor is depending on p, e.g. $O(\log p)$ in a butterfly network. We choose a fixed c to obtain comparable results and take $c = 5$ as an average from a machine size of $p = 128$ [2]. Therefore in each step $5p$ requests are made. Step in this context means synchronous execution of one instruction on each of the $5p$ processes.

As polynomials we used functions of degree $\xi = 2, 10, 20$. Each of the experiments was done 5 times with randomly chosen hash functions. More exactly, for each class five functions were randomly chosen and then used for all workloads and machine sizes.

As input for list ranking a list of length $n = 10p$ was randomly chosen. As input for connected components, a graph with $n = 10p$ nodes and $5p$ edges was randomly chosen. The problem size n is twice as large as the number of processes in these applications. Each process simulates two program processors step by step. A problem size larger than $5p$ is needed to obtain access patterns depending on the list or graph.

In matrix multiplication, the dimensions of the matrices are as follows: if $p = 2^{2z}$ then $w = c = 5$, if $p = 2^{2z+1}$ then $w = 2c = 10$.

In each experiment we measured for each step of the trace the maximum module congestion c_{max} and then computed the expected value of all c_{max} averaged over all steps. The analysis is a kind of (expected) worst case analysis. Each expected value was checked for significance by looking at the variance. The five values obtained by using five functions of one class for each experiment were checked against significant differences. In case there were none, the average was taken. In case there were some, ten additional hash functions were chosen and the average was taken from these 15 values. Significant differences appeared only for stride $s = 13$, $p = 2^7, \ldots, 2^9$ in both linear functions and for stride $s = 32$, $p = 2^9, 2^{10}$ in the linear function modulo power of two.

Because of mapping $5p$ requests per step onto p memory modules, $E(c_{max}) \geq 5$. The only exception is connected components, because not necessarily all processors make accesses in IF statements (see Sect. 3).

5 Results

The results of the experiments are presented in two ways. First we show the performance of the hash functions sorted by benchmarks. In Fig. 2 the performance on random patterns is given as a reference. The legend of the hash functions is shown in Fig. 3, which shows all other benchmarks. Second we show the performance sorted by hash functions in Fig. 4.

All figures are built as follows: the x–axis shows $\log p$ in range $5 \ldots 10$, the y–axis shows the expected value of the maximum module congestions in range $4 \ldots 14$.

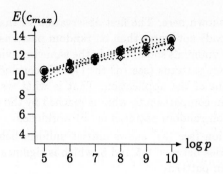

Fig. 2. Performance on random patterns

The performance on random patterns (see Fig. 2) is similar for all hash functions. Thus none of the hash functions is bad in an obvious way. The maximum module congestion rises from 10 for $p = 32$ to 12 for $p = 1024$. This will serve as a reference to analyse the performance on the other benchmarks.

5.1 Analysis of Benchmarks

The curves of Fig. 3 show similar shapes for all benchmarks: the polynomials of different degrees behave in a similar way and so do the three other hash functions. The behaviour of the polynomials furthermore is on all workloads worse than the behaviour of the simpler hash functions. Among the linear functions, the one modulo a prime always behaves a little bit worse than the linear function modulo a power of two. Thus the most interesting part is the comparison of our simple linear function with the boolean matrix hashing.

For strides that are a power of two, the boolean matrix hashes values optimally (see (a) and (c)) and reaches a module congestion of 6. The module congestion reached by the linear function lies between 6.5 and 7.5, so it is not far away.

A similar behaviour of linear function and boolean matrix can be seen in (d) and (f). This results from the fact that part of the accesses in these workloads are strides 1, when processors load or store values in arrays in the manner that processor i reads or writes $F[i]$.

However, as soon as we obtain other patterns, the boolean matrix hashing gets worse than the linear function (see (b) and (e)). Even for the matrix multiplication workload, where accesses always consist of $5 \cdot p^{1/2}$ strides with $s = 1$ and $p^{1/2}$ processors involved in each stride, the linear function is better.

5.2 Analysis of Hash Functions

Figure 4 shows the performance of the different hash functions. Because the connected components benchmark is not comparable to the others as explained in Sect. 3, it is not shown here. The first observation is, that all hash functions behave on all workloads not worse than on random patterns. The second observation is that the polynomials show roughly the same behaviour on all workloads as they do on random patterns (see (d) to (f)). We conclude that their performance is independent of the application. That is what we expected. But this performance is bad in comparison to what is reached by the other functions that behave better than on random patterns on all workloads.

The linear function (see (a)) shows almost uniform behaviour on all workloads, too, but it varies between 6.5 and 8, which is significantly better than the behaviour on random patterns.

The behaviour of the linear function modulo a prime is not uniform and varies between 6.3 and 10.

The behaviour of the boolean matrix hashing function can be divided in an expected optimal behaviour for strides with s a power of two and a significantly higher module congestion for other patterns, which is however still below the one produced by random patterns.

6 Conclusions

The above experiments show surprisingly that linear functions modulo a power of two and boolean matrix functions show best performance for practical use. Both have the additional properties of bijectivity and short evaluation time. The choice between these two depends on the expected user profile (if such exists) and the surrounding machine architecture. For machines that already contain a hardware multiplier this could be used to perform hashing in the case of the linear functions. Moreover, the use of matrix hashing is restricted by the fact that an implementation needs $(\log m)^2$ bit register hardware to store the boolean matrix. Therefore, if no user profile is known and chip area is restricted (or a multiplier already available), the use of the linear function is preferable.

The observations presented here lead to the use of linear hash functions in the prototype design of the SB–PRAM [1, 2] which emulates a synchronous shared memory machine with $p = 128$ physical processors and provides hardware support for hashing and packet routing including combining.

Unfortunately, some open questions remain. First, there is no theoretical framework to explain why simple hash functions work better than complex ones. Also, the exact relationship between linear functions with and without "modulo prime" is still unknown.

Acknowledgements

The authors would like to thank Martin Dietzfelbinger for helpful discussions.

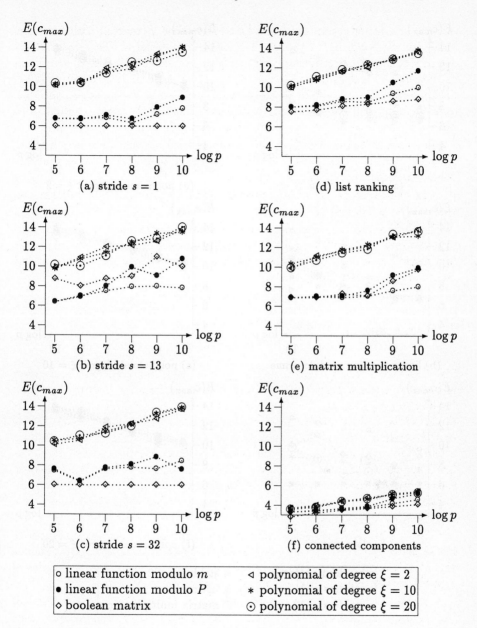

Fig. 3. Performance on benchmarks

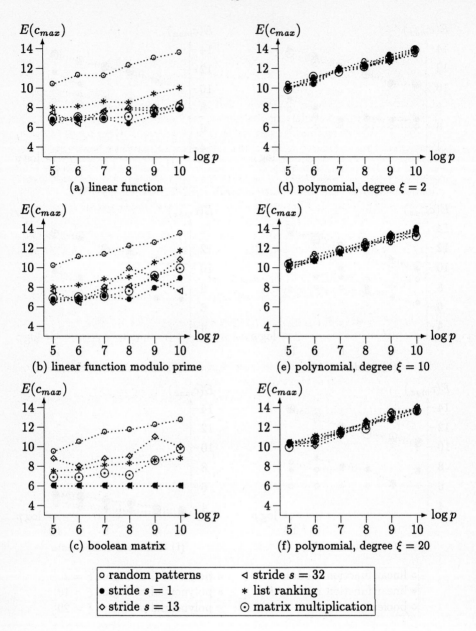

Fig. 4. Performance of hash functions

11

References

1. Abolhassan, F., Drefenstedt, R., Keller, J., Paul, W. J., Scheerer, D.: On the Physical Design of PRAMs. Informatik — Festschrift zum 60. Geburtstag von Günter Hotz (Teubner, 1992) 1–19
2. Abolhassan, F., Keller, J., Paul, W. J.: On the cost–effectiveness of PRAMs. Proc. 3rd IEEE Symp. on Parallel and Distributed Processing (1991) 2–9
3. Akl, S. G.: The Design and Analysis of Parallel Algorithms. (Prentice-Hall, 1989)
4. Dietzfelbinger, M.: On limitations of the performance of universal hashing with linear functions. Reihe Informatik Bericht Nr. 84 Universität–GH Paderborn (1991)
5. Dietzfelbinger, M., Hagerup, T., Katajainen, J., Penttonen, M.: A reliable randomized algorithm for the closest-pair problem. Manuscript (1992)
6. Karlin, A. R., Upfal, E.: Parallel hashing: An efficient implementation of shared memory. J. Assoc. Comput. Mach. **35** (1988) 876–892
7. Karp, R. M., Ramachandran, V. L.: A survey of parallel algorithms for shared–memory machines. Handbook of Theoretical Computer Science Vol. A (Elsevier, 1990) 869–941
8. Mehlhorn, K., Vishkin, U.: Randomized and deterministic simulations of PRAMs by parallel machines with restricted granularity of parallel memories. Acta Inform. **21** (1984) 339–374
9. Norton, A., Melton, E.: A class of boolean linear transformations for conflict–free power–of–two stride access. Proc. Internat. Conf. on Parallel Processing (1987) 247–254
10. Ranade, A. G.: How to emulate shared memory. Proc. 28th IEEE Symp. on Foundations of Computer Science (1987) 185–194
11. Shiloach, Y., Vishkin, U.: An $O(\log n)$ parallel connectivity algorithm. J. Algorithms **3** (1982) 57–67

Task Management, Virtual Shared Memory, and Multithreading in a Distributed Memory Implementation of Sisal

Matthew Haines* and Wim Böhm**

Computer Science Department
Colorado State University
Fort Collins, CO 80523

Abstract. This paper describes the design and initial performance of a runtime system for implementing Sisal [5] on a distributed memory multiprocessor. The runtime system provides support for task management and distribution, virtual shared memory, and multithreading. Tasks represent portions of code that can be executed in parallel, and we examine the performance effects of both flat and multi-level task distribution strategies. We introduce our virtual shared memory scheme, called VISA, and investigate a *block cyclic* mapping function using fixed and variable address translation. Finally, we study the effectiveness of *multithreading* in hiding latency for our current nCUBE/2-based implementation. In particular, we examine a machine-independent design for thread representation, thread switching, and split-phase transactions. We analyze the costs of multithreading and provide initial performance results.

1 Introduction

Today's distributed memory multiprocessors, with numbers of processors increasing into the thousands, provide a programmer with the potential for exploiting massive amounts of parallelism. However, programming these machines explicitly remains a difficult task at best. Firstly, there is the need to *detect* enough parallelism in an application to keep the machine resources busy. Secondly, once the parallelism in an application has been revealed, it needs to be *managed* for efficient utilization of the machine resources. Since most distributed memory multiprocessors have an order of magnitude difference in the time to access local memory versus the time to access remote memory, *managing latency* is tantamount to efficient execution. Latency can be *avoided* by keeping many memory accesses local, and *tolerated* by switching to other useful work that can be done in the time it takes to satisfy the remote reference (i.e. *multithreading*). Functional languages have demonstrated their ability to expose parallelism in an application as well as to simplify the task of parallel programming [6, 1]. This paper describes our attempt to exploit locality and tolerate latency on

* Supported in part by a grant from Sandia National Laboratories
** Supported in part by NSF grant MIP-9113268

conventional distributed memory multiprocessors using the functional language Sisal.

Sisal (Streams and Iterations in a Single Assignment Language) is a functional language that supports data types and operations for scientific computation [5]. The Sisal compiler consists of three parts: a frontend, a backend, and a runtime system. The *frontend* is responsible for ensuring the syntactic correctness of a Sisal program and translating the source program into intermediate dependence graph form. The *backend* is responsible for optimizing the intermediate representation and generating C code. The *runtime system* is responsible for providing the Sisal compiler with two main abstractions: task management and memory management. We describe the particular implementation of the Sisal runtime system for execution on the nCUBE/2 distributed memory multiprocessor. The rest of this paper is organized as follows. Section 2 outlines the process hierarchy used to support a wide range of processors and introduces the multi-level distribution scheme. Section 3 describes the Virtual Shared Memory system (VISA) used to provide the Sisal compiler with a single addressing space. Section 4 describes the multithreading design and its ability to hide remote memory reference latencies. We conclude and provide future directions in Section 5.

2 Task Management

2.1 Task Management Design

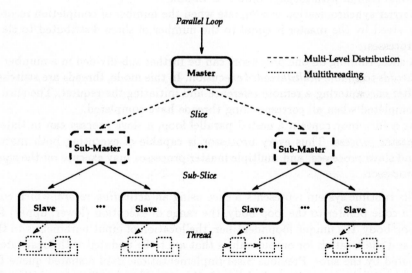

Fig. 1. Sisal Runtime System Process Hierarchy

Although Sisal allows extracting function-level and fine-grain instruction-level parallelism, the current runtime system is designed to handle only loop-level parallelism. This model provides an efficient paradigm for many scientific applications, where the major source of parallelism is in loops. Our system is intended to execute on a wide variety of distributed memory machines, with sizes ranging from tens to thousands of processors. We therefore have designed a flexible multi-level process hierarchy, where a process on each level represents a contiguous range of loop bodies (see Fig. 1). A program is executed in master/slave fashion as follows:

- The **master** process is responsible for dividing a parallel loop into *slices* which will then be executed by slave processes running in parallel. The distribution of slices among the slaves can be done in tree-fashion for a large number of slaves, thereby creating parallelism in the slice distribution phase. In this case, which we call *multi-level distribution (MLD)*, slices are created and sent to *sub-masters*, where they are further partitioned into *sub-slices* and distributed to the slaves in parallel. For a small number of slave processes, the master can create and distribute the slices directly among the slaves, avoiding the overhead of the intermediate stages in the multi-level distribution scheme. This is called *single-level distribution*. Once the slices have been distributed, the master must wait (using *barrier synchronization*) until all slices have been completed. Results of slices are reduced sequentially for single-level distribution, and in parallel for multi-level distribution.
- Each **slave** process continually checks its local work-list for slices to be taken off the work-list and executed. Upon completion of the slice, the slave process sends a completion message to its master or sub-master process and updates global results with locally-computed values.
- Barrier synchronization is complete when the number of completion records received by the master is equal to the number of slices distributed to slave processes.
- A slice, running on one processor, can be further sub-divided in a number of *threads* to enable *multithreaded* execution. In this mode, threads are switched after encountering a remote reference and initiating the request. The slice is completed when all corresponding threads have completed.
- As a slice may contain a nested parallel loop, a slave process can initiate a master process. Thus every processor is capable of executing both master and slave processes, and multiple master processes may execute on the same processor.

The runtime system represents a slice using an *activation record*, which contains a code pointer to the loop body, the range of execution (lower, upper) for the loop body, the unique loop identifier, the location of input parameters to the slice, and the location for output values that are to be updated with local values computed by the slice. Previous Sisal implementations used a shared queue for storing activation records, and although this provides an efficient solution for small shared memory multiprocessors, this centralized approach is disastrous for large distributed memory multiprocessors. Therefore each processor maintains a local activation record queue, and all activation records are now *distributed* by the master.

2.2 Task Management Evaluation

To compare the single-level and multi-level loop distribution schemes, we measure the performance of Purdue Parallel Benchmark #1, which computes $\int_0^\pi \sin(x)$ using the trapezoidal rule. Our test Sisal program computes $\sin(x)$ using a Taylor series to fourteen terms $(\frac{x^1}{1!} \ldots \frac{x^{27}}{27!})$ to match the precision of the nCUBE/2 system sin function.

Table 1 shows that the efficiency of this application using both single-level distribution and multi-level distribution is 100% up to 64 processors. For higher numbers of processors, the efficiency starts to decrease, getting much worse, especially for single-level-distribution, for 256 and 512 processors. Thus 64 processors is the point at which the overhead for sequentially distributing the loop slices and reducing the intermediate values starts to have a noticeable detrimental effect on the performance, and multi-level distribution is able to recapture some of the lost performance by parallelizing the distribution and reduction phases. For 256 and 512 processors, the gain is substantial: 5% and 10% efficiency, respectively.

Fan-out corresponds to the number of *sub-master* processes used in multi-level distribution, and *OFO* in Table 1 represents the optimal fan-out degree for each set of processors. Fan-out provides a means to control the amount of *overhead* of multi-level distribution, exemplified by the sequential loop in the master process that distributes the sub-tasks, versus the *gain* of having the sub-masters distribute the slices in parallel. Fig. 2 depicts this tradeoff for 512 processors, where a fan-out degree of 1 represents single-level distribution. In the fan-out region $1 \ldots 4$ there is not enough sub-master parallelism, whereas in the fan-out region $128 \ldots 512$ there is too much parallelism overhead. A fan-out degree about equal to the square root of the number of processors appears to be most effective for this application.

	single-level distribution			multi-level-distribution			
PEs	Time (s)	Speedup	Eff (%)	OFO	Time (s)	Speedup	Eff (%)
1	355.8472	1.00	100				
2	177.9336	2.00	100	2	177.9343	2.00	100
4	88.9698	4.00	100	2	88.9701	4.00	100
8	44.4940	8.00	100	2	44.4932	8.00	100
16	22.2639	15.98	100	4	22.2601	15.99	100
32	11.1649	31.87	100	4	11.1538	31.90	100
64	5.6461	63.03	98	8	5.6207	63.31	99
128	2.9484	120.69	94	8	2.8936	122.98	96
256	1.7236	206.46	81	16	1.6084	221.24	86
512	1.7582	202.39	40	32	1.3961	254.89	50

Table 1. Performance Numbers for Purdue 1, Single and Multi-Level Distribution

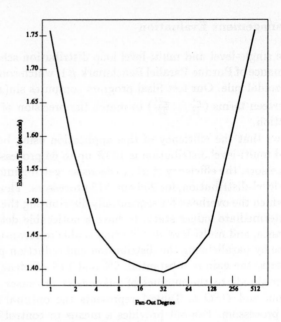

Fig. 2. Execution times for Purdue 1 on 512 processors for various Fan-Out Degrees

Table 1 also reflects the effect that the ratio of *computation time to communication time* can have on the performance of the application. As we double the number of processors, the computation time of each parallel slice is *halved*, since the same number of loop bodies are now distributed over twice the number of loop slices, and the communication time is *doubled*, since there are now twice the number of loop slices to be distributed and twice the number of intermediate values to be reduced. Thus the ratio of computation time to communication time, which determines the efficiency of an application, is reduced by a factor of four each time the number of processors is doubled. We can see the effect of this diminishing ratio in the efficiency for 256 and 512 processors. Multi-level distribution reduces the rate at which the communication time increases, thus decreasing the rate at which efficiency is lost.

3 Virtual Shared Memory

3.1 Virtual Shared Memory Design

Since the memory management abstraction in the Sisal compiler assumes a single addressing space, we have chosen to provide the compiler with a Virtual Shared Memory system (*VISA*) [4], supporting general data decompositions [2]. We also employ VISA in our parallel C programs used for baseline comparisons. VISA assigns a contiguous set of virtual addresses to each shared data structure. A *mapping function* then partitions the shared data structure among the participating memories such that each memory "owns" a unique portion of the original data structure. To create the single addressing space, each node reserves a portion of local memory that will store all locally-owned VISA variables. Each data structure may be distributed using a different mapping function, specified in the VISA allocation function, *visa_malloc*. Therefore, it is necessary to associate a descriptor with each data structure that is used in address translation. This descriptor, called a *range_map_entry* includes: the range (low, high) of virtual addresses, the number of elements and their size, distribution control parameters (*blocksize, start PE*, and *stride*), and a replication bit.

Address translation takes a VISA virtual address, and using the distribution control parameters in the *range_map_entry*, computes a *node, offset* pair. When the computed node id differs from the local node id (i.e. a remote reference), a message is sent to the remote node owning the datum, instructing the node to return the datum (*visa_get*) or place a value into its location (*visa_put*). The range_map_entries are replicated on each node since any node may access any VISA structure.

The **block cyclic** mapping function divides the data structure into blocks of size *blocksize*, and then assigns these blocks to memories in a round-robin fashion. Block cyclic mapping has different characteristics depending on the blocksize. If the blocksize is equal to the data structure size, the entire structure is allocated in one memory, which is useful for small structures or for sub-structures, such as the rows or columns of a matrix. However, allocating a data structure in one memory can become ineffective as parallelism is lost and excessive message passing is incurred. The other extreme, where the blocksize is one, is *interleaved* allocation, which can be useful if the amount of work to create each array element is unbalanced, or if the data structure being mapped is irregularly shaped and normal mapping techniques produce a highly imbalanced distribution. If the blocksize is equal to the data structure size divided by the number of memories, each memory node gets exactly one block of the data structure. In this case the data structure is distributed uniformly over the machine, which enhances the load distribution of the program.

A much simpler address translation scheme eliminates the need for a descriptor by having a fixed blocksize for all data structures. If the blocksize and number of processors are powers of two, the binary representation of the virtual address can be interpreted as consisting of three fields, *block-number, PE* and *offset*, which can be efficiently retrieved directly from the virtual address bits without having to consult a *range_map_table*. The disadvantage of this scheme is that uneven distribution can easily occur. Also, as we will see, this scheme can result in an excessive amount of remote references caused by unaligned loops and data structures.

3.2 Virtual Shared Memory Evaluation

To assess the advantages and disadvantages of the fixed and variable blocksize address translation schemes, we study a one-dimensional Successive Over-Relaxation (SOR) function running on a 64 processor nCUBE/2. The results are graphically displayed in Fig. 3. Three fixed blocksize mapping functions (*blocksize = 1*, *blocksize = c* for *c* = 8, 16, and 32, and *blocksize = n*) and one variable blocksize mapping functions (*blocksize = n/p* are examined.

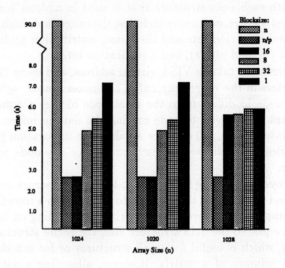

Fig. 3. Experimental Results: Execution Time Profiles for 1D SOR

The SOR program contains a nested loop. The outer loop performs array relaxations sequentially, whereas the inner loop computes $A[i]$ as the average of the previous iteration's $A[i-1]$, $A[i]$, and $A[i+1]$, and is distributed over the 64 processors in equal sized (n/p) loop slices. The *blocksize = n/p* variable address translation function *always* allocates the arrays in alignment with the loop slices, causing a minimal amount of message passing, but requires a more complex virtual to physical address translation. When combined with an array of size 1024, the fixed blocksize $c = 16$ provides an ideal distribution, keeping the loop slices and array blocks perfectly aligned. When the array size or the fixed blocksize is slightly altered so that the data distribution is no longer perfectly aligned with the data distribution in the fixed blocksize address translation function, the performance of the fixed-blocksize address translation function degrades significantly.

4 Multithreading

4.1 Multithreading Design

Since the nCUBE/2 multiprocessor provides no hardware support for multithreading, we have designed a *software multithreading* system, adapted from an idea obtained from Rob Pike at AT&T Laboratories [7], and based on the standard Unix system calls *setjmp*, which saves the state of the current computation, and *longjmp*, which restores a previously saved state. This provides machine-independent primitives for thread switching, assuming that the *setjmp* and *longjmp* routines are properly implemented so as to save and restore machine registers necessary to preserve the context of an activation.

The Sisal compiler creates and distributes independent, parallel slices to each of the participating processors in the system, who then further subdivide the tasks into *mt* threads, where *mt* is called the *degree of multithreading*. All threads are executed sequentially by a processor, and scheduled locally in a round-robin fashion. One *ThreadDescriptor* structure is allocated for each of the *mt* threads, and the ThreadDescriptors are linked together to form a circular list, which is then traversed by the thread scheduler.

Our threads contain a number of parallel loop bodies and consequently are still relatively large, as compared with other multithreading systems [3]. Since the threads are executed sequentially, the amount of parallelism we exploit *per processor* is equal to *mt*, the degree of multithreading. To simplify the synchronization process, our threads allow for only one outstanding remote request. We favor efficient sequential execution above exploiting maximal parallelism.

Multithreaded execution proceeds as follows. Before starting the first thread, a return address is saved using *setjmp*, so that after all the threads have completed, there is a place to return. The scheduler then selects a thread for execution, which continues until it either completes execution or begins a remote memory reference, implemented as a *split-phase transaction*. In the first phase, the thread sends a *visa_request* to the target processor that contains the desired value, then invokes the scheduler to start another thread. The scheduler selects the next thread from the circular list (if one exists) and begins its execution. The target processor will process the visa_request and send back an associated *visa_reply*, containing the requested remote value. When a visa_reply message arrives, a message handler stores the message in the storage buffer for the proper thread. A *presence bit*, indicating the arrival of the message, is also set.

When a thread is re-enabled by the scheduler, it examines the presence bit of its storage buffer to see if the visa_reply message arrived. If so, the message is removed from the buffer and the presence bit is reset, which completes the second phase of the split-phase transaction. If the message is not found in the buffer storage, the thread will wait for the message. Since threads are executed in a round-robin fashion, and the message start-up time for the nCUBE/2 (160 μs) is so high compared to the message transport time (2.6 μs per byte) [8], messages are received in order almost all of the time. Therefore, waiting for the outstanding message after the first thread switch will minimize the thread switching overhead without much loss of parallelism. This is clearly an architecture-dependent decision, and would have to be re-evaluated for a distributed system with different message passing timing characteristics.

Multithreading causes *each thread* (instead of a whole loop slice) to have to fetch input parameters. By replicating the parameter structures, these extra parameter fetches can be made local VISA references, but they still represent overhead for multithreading.

Now that we have detailed our design, we can analyze its cost. Multithreading incurs a *startup cost*, C_{start}, averaging 550 μs for creating the thread queue and message storage buffers. Fetching the extra thread input-parameters results in $C_{param} = 270\mu s$ per parameter. A *read* $A[i]$ fetches the blocksize, start processor, and processor stride from A's range map entry and computes the target processor number and local address. If the access is local, A[i] is fetched without further ado and the thread continues. This happens most of the time in programs with high locality and makes our threads much larger than threads that switch at any memory reference. If the access is remote, a read request package is created and sent off. The source processor spends an average of 200 μs to form the package and initiate the send, and this needs to be done whether multithreading or not. The round trip time for the remote read involves 170 μs message startup time and flight time through the net, 220 μs for the target processor to accept the message, fetch the data, form a reply package and initiate the send back, and 170 μs message startup time and flight time through the network back to the source processor. Therefore, the source processor has $C_{round} = 560\mu s$ to do other work. In this time, the source processor needs to do two context switches, one to another thread and one back, and it needs to accept the reply package and place it in the message buffer of the requesting process, which takes approximately 40 μs. Two context switches involve two *longjmps* and two *setjmps*, at a total cost of 2 * 90 μs = 180 μs. The difference $B_{switch} = 560 - 180 - 40 = 340\mu s$ is what is gained, but *only if there is useful work to do in the other thread*. When this is the case, this is called a *successful context switch*.

Multithreading profits if the total gain caused by successful context switches is larger than the initial costs of setting up the circular thread descriptor structure and fetching the extra input parameters. If we call H the number of successful context switches, and P the number of remote parameters needed by each thread, we get the following criterion for multithreading being effective:

$$\Delta Time \approx (H * B_{switch}) - C_{start} - (MT - 1) * (P * C_{param}) > 0 \qquad (1)$$

For MT=2 (default) and the above values for B_{switch}, C_{start}, and C_{param}, this implies:

$$H > (P * 270 + 550)/340 \qquad (2)$$

4.2 Multithreading Evaluation

Given the above analysis we evaluate the performance of the one-dimensional SOR program and compare the Sisal performance with an explicit parallel C version of the code, where the VISA runtime system is used to eliminate the need for explicit message passing. The initial performance data for a 16K element array and 10 iterations is given in Table 2, where *PEs* is the number of processors used, *No MT* represents the results without multithreading, and *MT* represents the results with multithreading turned on to a degree of *mt*.

	C		$Sisal$				
			No MT			MT	
PEs	Time (s)	Speedup	Time (s)	Speedup	mt	Time (s)	Sp
1	99.3485	1.00	111.5399	0.89			
2	52.9611	1.88	57.0005	1.74	2	56.9682	1.74
4	26.1242	3.80	28.5764	3.48	2	28.5649	3.48
8	12.7532	7.79	14.4006	6.90	2	14.3986	6.90
16	6.4087	15.50	7.4001	13.43	2	7.4048	13.42
32	3.2637	30.44	4.0764	24.37	2	4.0832	24.33

Table 2. SOR Timing Results, 16K Array Elements, 10 Iterations

An examination of the data in Table 2 reveals that the performance of Sisal without multithreading is very close to the C performance. Moreover, due to the locality of the data references in the program and the effectiveness of the mapping functions exploiting this, Sisal exhibits near linear speedup, leaving little room for improvement for multithreading. Two threads always provide the optimal multithreading performance. This conforms to numbers obtained from [8] which indicate that, for the nCUBE/2, the message start-up time is so large compared to message transmission time that, by the time the second thread sends a remote request, the reply from the first thread's request will have returned, and thus switching to a third thread is unnecessary and costly.

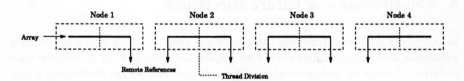

Fig. 4. Array distribution for SOR Program

Fig. 4 shows the distribution of the SOR array onto four nodes, and how the sub-arrays are again divided over the two threads per node. A down-arrow indicates a remote reference. The first node has zero successful switches as its first thread, which has no remote references, executes to completion before the second thread is started. The first node does not need to fetch thread parameters, as they are allocated locally. Still, multithreading only infers extra costs (P=0, H=0 in Eq. 2). Internal nodes have two successful context switches, which almost covers the costs of multithreading (P=2, H=2 in Eq. 2). The last node last node has only one successful switch, and therefore does not gain from multithreading either (P=2, H=1 in Eq. 2). Since barrier synchronization forces all nodes to wait for the slowest, this application does not benefit from multithreading.

Multithreading will only work if there are more remote references per thread, and if these remote references are surrounded by computations involving local references, so that when switching to another thread useful local work can be performed. In order to quantify this observation we examine the performance of a program performing a *Parallel Prefix* algorithm for computing the successive sums in an array. The parallel prefix algorithm successively iterates over an array, but unlike the SOR program, alters its remote reference pattern for each iteration. As the algorithm iterates, the distances become greater, and more remote references are incurred. The data in Table 3 confirms that this algorithm benefits from multithreading.

PEs	No MT			MT		
	Time (s)	Speedup	Eff (%)	Time (s)	Speedup	Eff (%)
1	113.6498	1.00	100			
2	71.3872	1.59	80	68.9103	1.65	82
4	39.3217	2.89	72	38.7369	2.93	73
8	21.3384	5.33	67	21.2796	5.34	67
16	11.6495	9.76	61	11.6435	9.76	61
32	6.6435	17.12	53	6.6349	17.13	54

Table 3. Timing Results for Parallel Prefix, 16K Array Elements

5   Conclusions and Future Directions

In this paper we have introduced the goal of our project, which is to study latency avoidance and latency tolerance for an implementation of Sisal on conventional distributed memory multiprocessors. Towards that end we are developing a run-time system that provides implicit support for both thread management and memory management.

We have presented a Multi-Level Distribution mechanism, which uses a tree approach to distributing the threads and retrieving their results. We have shown how this can improve the efficiency for programs such as Purdue Parallel Benchmark #1 on large numbers of processors.

We have introduced a virtual shared memory system, VISA, for Sisal. Mapping functions distribute data structures by mapping virtual addresses to a processor number and local address. We have evaluated various forms of the block-cyclic mapping function using both fixed and descriptor-based translation schemes. The flexible descriptor-based address translation mechanism is slightly more expensive than the optimal fixed blocksize translation mechanism, but performs well for all values of n since it can always use the optimal blocksize, whereas the fixed translation mechanism performs well only when the optimal blocksize and the fixed blocksize coincide. In all other cases, the fixed translation scheme performs very poorly.

We have introduced the design of a general-purpose, machine-independent software multithreading system and discussed its implementation within the VISA runtime system. We have shown that in the presence of only a few remote references, the multithreading does not improve the efficiency of the Sisal code over the non-multithreading case, because the overheads are greater than the gains. We have shown that in programs with more remote references, such as the parallel prefix program, multithreading does pay off, albeit not impressively. Multithreading would work better if the cost of local references could be brought down.

Conventional distributed memory multiprocessors are currently the most powerful machines in the world, in terms of raw processing power. However, exploiting this power requires the ability to avoid and tolerate remote memory latencies. It is our view that we must free the programmer from the details of explicitly programming distributed memory multiprocessors, but not at the expense of grave loss in performance. Clearly this is a challenging goal.

References

1. J. T. Feo D. C. Cann and R. R. Oldehoeft. A report on the SISAL language project. *Journal of Parallel and Distributed Computing*, 10(4):349–366, December 1990.
2. Michael H. Coffin. *PAR: An Approach to Architecture-Independent Parallel Programming*. PhD thesis, University of Arizona, Tuscon, Arizona, August 1990.
3. D. E. Culler, A. Sah, K. E. Schauser, T. von Eicken, and J. Wawrzynek. Fine-grain parallelism with minimal hardware support: A compiler-controlled threaded abstract machine. In 4th *International Conf. on Architectural Support for Programming Languages and Operating Systems*, 1991.
4. Matthew Haines and Wim Böhm. The visa user's guide. Technical Report CS-93-102, Colorado State University, Fort Collins, CO, February 1993.
5. J. R. McGraw, S. K. Skedzielewski, S. J. Allan, R. R. Oldehoeft, J. Glauert, C. Kirkham, W. Noyce, and R. Thomas. SISAL: Streams and iteration in a single assignment language: Reference manual version 1.2. Manual M-146, Rev. 1, Lawrence Livermore National Laboratory, Livermore, CA, March 1985.
6. R. S. Nikhil. Id (Version 90.0) Reference Manual. Technical Report CSG Memo 284-1, MIT Laboratory for Computer Science, 545 Technology Square, Cambridge, MA 02139, USA, July 1990. Supercedes: Id/83s (July 1985) Id Nouveau (July 1986), Id 88.0 (March 1988), Id 88.1 (August 1988).
7. Personal Communication with Rob Pike, AT&T Laboratories.
8. Thorsten von Eicken, David E. Culler, Seth Copen Goldstein, and Klaus Erik Schauser. Active messages: A mechanism for integrated communications and computation. In *Proceedings of the 19th Annual International Symposium on Computer Architecture*, pages 256–266, May 1992.

Simulating the Data Diffusion Machine

Erik Hagersten, Mats Grindal, Anders Landin, Ashley Saulsbury,
Bengt Werner, and Seif Haridi

Swedish Institute of Computer Science; Box 1263 ; 164 28 KISTA ; SWEDEN.

Abstract. Large-scale multiprocessors suffer from long latencies for remote accesses. Caching is by far the most popular technique for hiding
such delays. Caching not only hides the delay, but also decreases the network load. Cache-Only Memory Architectures (COMA), have no physically shared memory. Instead, all the memory resources are invested in
caches, enabling in caches of the largest possible size. A datum has no
home, and is moved by a protocol between the caches according to its
usage. Furthermore, it might exist in multiple caches. Even though no
shared memory exists in the traditional sense, the architecture provides
a shared memory view to a processor, and hence also to the programmer.
The simulation results of large programs running on up to 128 processors indicate that the COMA adapts well to existing shared memory
programs. They also show that an application with a poor locality can
benefit by adopting the COMA principle of no fixed home for data, resulting in a reduction of execution time by a factor three.

1   Introduction

Simulation is a core technology for research in the computer architecture field.
It is important to evaluate architectural ideas using large realistic programs and
problem sizes. This study presents a simulation study of one implementation of
the Data Diffusion Machine (DDM) [HLH92]. The DDM is a shared memory
multiprocessor, but its organization is quite different from other architectures in
that its memory system comprises of only caches.

In this study, we wanted to see how well the DDM adapted to existing shared
memory applications written with a completely different architecture in mind.
We developed an execution-driven simulation environment, which can run parallel programs written in C. The applications used in this study come from
the Stanford Parallel Applications for Shared Memory (SPLASH) [SWG91]. A
detailed architecture model describes the prototype DDM, currently being implemented at SICS. It allows us to study the behavior of the prototype and
to collect statistics one cannot gather in a real implementation. However, the
simulation model has a slowdown of approximately 2000 times, which limits the
practical problem size of the studied programs. To compensate for this, we varied the data set for the application, and found that the benefits from the DDM
architecture increased with the size of the data set.

The simulation of the DDM shows encouraging behavior for the studied programs. In this paper we present our simulation method, the performance of the
DDM, and some internal dynamic statistics.

2 Background

Existing architectures with shared memory are typically computers with one common bus connecting the processors to the shared memory, such as computers manufactured by Sequent, SUN and Encore, or with distributed shared memory, such as the BBN Butterfly and the IBM RP3.

Systems based on a single bus suffer from bus saturation and therefore typically have only some tens of processors, each one with a local cache. The contents of the caches are kept coherent by a cache-coherence protocol, in which each cache snoops the traffic on the common bus and prevents any inconsistencies from occurring [Ste90]. The architecture provides a uniform access time to the whole shared memory, and is therefore called uniform memory architecture (UMA).

In architectures with distributed shared memory, known as non-uniform memory architectures (NUMA), each processor node contains a portion of the shared memory; consequently access times to different parts of the shared address space can vary. NUMAs often have networks other than a single bus, and the network delay to different nodes might vary. The earlier NUMAs did not have coherent caches, and left the problem of coherence to the programmer. Research activities today are striving toward coherent NUMAs with directory-based cache-coherence protocols, e.g. Dash [LLG$^+$90] and Alewife [CKA91]. Programs can be optimized for NUMAs by statically partitioning the work and data. Given a partitioning where the processors make the most of their accesses to their part of the shared memory, a better scalability than for UMAs can be achieved.

In cache-only memory architectures (COMAs), the memory organization is similar to that of NUMA in that each processor holds a portion of the shared memory space. However, the partitioning of data between the memories is not static, since all distributed memories are organized as large (second-level) caches. The task of such a memory is twofold. Besides being a large (second-level) cache for the processor, it may also contain some data from the shared address space that the processor never has accessed, i.e., it is a cache and a virtual part of the shared memory at the same time. We call this intermediate form of memory *Attraction Memory* (AM). A coherence protocol will attract the data used by a processor to its attraction memory. The coherence unit, comparable to a cache-line, is moved around by the protocol and is called an *item*. On a memory reference, a virtual address is translated into an item identifier. The item identifier space is logically the same as the physical address space of conventional machines, but there is no permanent mapping between an item identifier and a physical memory location. Instead, an item identifier corresponds to a location in an attraction memory, whose address tag matches the item identifier. Actually there are cases where multiple attraction memories could have matching items.

COMA provides a programming model identical to that of shared-memory architectures, but does not require static distribution of execution and memory usage in order to run efficiently. Running an optimized NUMA program on a COMA architecture would result in a NUMA-like behavior, since the work spaces of the different processors would migrate to their local attraction memories.

However, a NUMA version of the same program would give a similar behavior, since the data is attracted to the using processor regardless of the address. A COMA will also adapt to and perform well for programs with a more dynamic, or semi-dynamic scheduling. The work space migrates according to its usage throughout the computation. Programs can be optimized for a COMA to take this property into account in order to create better locality.

2.1   The Data Diffusion Machine

The Data Diffusion Machine (DDM) [WH88] is a hierarchical COMA with its directory information distributed in the network. Between each level in the hierarchy sit state memories, called *Directories* (as shown in Figure 1). The directory is a set-associative status memory, which keeps information for all the items in the attraction memories below it, but contains no data. The directories can answer questions such as "Is this item below me?" or "Does this item exist outside my subsystem?" They guide *read requests* to a copy of the data and keep coherence traffic as local as possible. The lowest level bus in the hierarchy connects several DDM nodes. A DDM node contains one attraction memory and one or more processors.

The coherence protocol of the DDM [HHW90] attracts requested data to the attraction memories, controls the coherence among different copies of the same data, and makes sure that the last copy of a data is not lost on replacement.

The hierarchy as described here has a single top bus which easily could become the bottleneck of the system. This bottleneck can be widened by using several top buses, each one responsible for a specific address domain, e.g., even and odd. The topmost directories are also split into different address domains, and thus the transaction frequency is increased [Hag92].

The memory overhead, i.e., the extra memory required to implement the attraction memories and the directories, is surprisingly low. It has been calculated to 5 percent for a 32-processor DDM and 16 percent for a 256-processor DDM [HLH92].

2.2   A Protocol Example: Multilevel Read

Figure 1 shows an example of a multilevel read. Originally, the item studied existed in state shared (S) in the attraction memories of processors Py and Pz. The directories above them also had the item in state shared. The directory common to Py and Pz right underneath the top bus had the item in state exclusive (E), since its subsystem contained all existing copies of the item. All other directories and attraction memories had the item in state invalid (I).

At this point, a read request by processor Px cannot be fulfilled by its local local attraction memory, which puts the requested item in state Reading (R) and transmits the *read* request on the DDM bus. The *read* request cannot be satisfied by the subsystems connected to the bus, and the next higher directory retransmits the *read* request onto the next higher bus. The directory also changes the item's state to Reading (R), marking the outstanding request. Eventually, the request reaches a level in the hierarchy where a directory, containing a copy of the item, is selected to answer the request. The selected directory changes the state of the item to Answering (A), marking an outstanding request from above, and retransmits the *read* request on its lower bus. Transient states R and A in the directories mark the request's path through the hierarchy like unrolling a red thread while walking in a maze [HomBC]. When the request finally reaches an attraction memory with a copy of the item, its *data* reply simply follows the red thread back to the requesting node, changing all the states along the path to Shared (S).

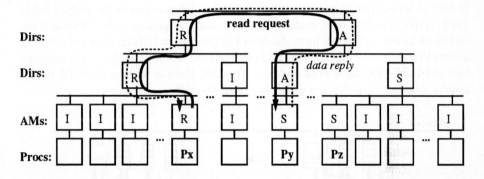

Fig. 1. A read request from processor Px has found its way to a copy of the item in the attraction memory of processor Py. Its path is marked with states Reading and Answering (R and A), which will guide the data reply back to processor Px.

3 DDM Prototype Overview

There are two projects currently working on DDM architectures. A link-based DDM based on Transputers is being developed at the University of Bristol [RW91]. This simulation study models a second, bus-based, DDM currently being built at the Swedish Institute of Computer Science based on Motorola MC88100 processors [HLH92]. The MC88100 has a combined cache and memory management unit (CMMU) chip MC88204 interfaced to a memory bus called M bus. The CMMU use a copy-back cache-coherence protocol similar to the write-once protocol [Goo83]. Each CMMU snoops all transactions on the M bus, and may stop a master by asserting a *retry* signal on the bus. The master immediately stops, backs off the bus, and turns into a slave with the need to arbitrate for the bus again. The CMMU that received the snoop hit is granted the bus and can update the memory during the next cycle.

3.1 Interfacing the DDM Node and the M bus

A DDM node contains the *memory below protocol* (MBP), and the *memory above protocol* (MAP) state machines, implementing the DDM protocol, and an associative state memory (ASM), containing the state and the address tag for each item in the node, as shown in Figure 2.

The MBP checks each transaction on the M bus for validity. If it is a *read* of an Invalid item, for example, the MBP asserts the retry signal. The retry signal makes the current CMMU bus master stop and release the bus, while the MBP initiates necessary actions for retrieving the requested item. The arbitration between the CMMUs is round-robin, allowing other CMMUs to access the memory while the data is being retrieved. The DDM node also hosts the *output above* FIFO (OA) for transactions bound for the DDM bus. The OA contains the transaction code and the item identifier of the transaction, but no data. The MAP can access the M bus by putting an M bus transaction in the *output below* FIFO (OB). The OB only contains address and transaction code. Transactions on the M bus from the OB have the data FIFOs *data in* (DI) or *data out* (DO) as an implicit source or destination. Data is retrieved from the node's data memory and put in the DO by a *read line* from the OB. Data is written from DI to the node's memory by putting a *write line* from the OB.

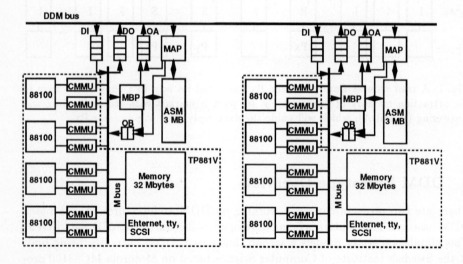

Fig. 2. DDM implementation consisting of two DDM nodes based on the 88000 family.

3.2 Implementing the Attraction Memory and its Protocol

There are several ways an AM and its protocol can be implemented based on the functionality of the retry signal.

Here, we describe a direct-mapped implementation of the AM, i.e., a one-way set-associative implementation. The location of data in the node's memory is determined by looking at the lower bits of its item identifier. The address space of the memory is mapped over and over again sequentially to cover the whole item identifier space. The higher order bits of the item identifiers are stored as address tags in the associative state memory (ASM).

A direct-mapped AM has a specific item always mapped to the very same location, so there is no need to compare tags before we know in which set an item should reside if it is there. We can assume that a transaction will succeed and start a *read line* before approval from the MBP is received. A CMMU that has already read three words can be forced to restart before reading the fourth, and last, word of a cache line. The MBP can therefore wait until the very last cycle before deciding whether to force a retry or not. This allows for state lookup and data transfer to overlap. In most situations, the delay of accessing the ASM will be completely hidden, adding no extra latency to the functionality of the AM, i.e., no wait states are inserted by the MBP.

The MBP compares the address tag bits stored in the ASM to the higher order bits of the item identifier on the M bus and the state stored in the ASM is checked; e.g., a *read* request to a present item in the Shared state is approved, resulting in no actions. If the transaction was not approved, e.g., a *read* request to state Invalid, the MBP:

1. asserts the retry signal, forcing the CMMU to release the M bus,
2. sets the address tag bits in the ASM to the higher bits of the item identifier,
3. changes the item's state to Reading, and,
4. puts a *read* request in the output above buffer.

When the *data* reply eventually comes back, the memory above protocol (MAP):

1. puts the data part of the transaction in the DI,
2. puts a *write line* transaction in the OB containing the item identifier, and,
3. changes the item's state to Shared.

The output below buffer has the highest priority on the M bus and gets the M bus next. It writes the contents of the DI to the item's location in the attraction memory. When the CMMU repeats its request again, it will not be interrupted by the memory below protocol. It can be noted that this method turns the M bus into a split-transaction bus, i.e., it is released between the original request and its completion. A write transaction on the M bus to an item in an inappropriate state is intercepted by a *retry* in a similar way by the memory below protocol, and necessary actions are taken. Therefore, from the viewpoint of the M bus, the rest of the DDM looks like yet another CMMU, only slower and noisier.

3.3 Building on Tadpole TP881V

In an attempt to save development effort and time, we searched for commercially available board systems implementing most of the desired functionality. We evaluated all known board systems based on the 88000 family. Most systems lacked the possibility of connecting yet another master board to the M bus. Tadpole Technology, U.K., had a design TP881V that suited us, marked with the dashed line in Figure 2. The TP881V consists of two VME-sized cards: a processor module card with four processors, their eight caches and 32 Mbytes DRAM, and a base module card with SCSI and Ethernet interfaces. The extra functionality required by a DDM node fits on one card designed at SICS. We can fit six DDM nodes with a total of 24 processors and 192 Mbytes attraction memory, power, and directory into a VME rack with 21 slots. The directories are yet not designed, but could be implemented using the described DDM design with small modifications. With an integration higher than the one used in our prototype, eight processor clusters will fit in a box rather than six. Up to a two-level DDM can rely on buses. The second-level split buses connecting eight clusters are 30 cm long. A DDM of three levels must rely on point-to-point connections at its top. Each point-to-point link is about 60 cm long.

3.4   Performance

We decided on a conservative bus design initially, since pushing bus speed is not a primary research goal. The DDM bus in the prototype operates at 20 MHz, with a 32-bit data bus and a 16-bit address bus. It uses drivers developed for the Future bus for all parallel signals, such as address and data. A new transaction starts every fourth cycle, i.e., a transaction frequency of 5 Mtransactions/s. It provides a moderate bandwidth of about 80 Mbytes/s.

A specified latency of a memory system is not necessarily equal to the number of cycles a processor has to stall. The scoreboard mechanism of the MC88100 makes the processor stall only if the register is read before the value of the load has arrived. Similarly, a slow write will not necessarily stall the processor. Here we specify the latency as the number of cycles elapsing between the issue of the load, and when the register can be read.

Read accesses from the CMMU to the attraction memory take seven cycles per cache line, and write accesses to the attraction memory take eleven cycles. To these numbers must be added an extra latency of four cycles for going through the processor caches. The best case latencies at no contention for different accesses can be found in the table below. Latencies for remote accesses are represented by two number: latency in a one level DDM / latency in a two-level DDM if the transaction has to go to the top bus.

Latency in the DDM Prototype [Processor Cycles]				
CPU access	Cache hit	Cache miss, AM in state:		
		Exclusive	Shared	Invalid
read	2	11	11	60/115
write	2	15	35/60	70/145

4 Simulation Technique

Inspired by the Tango simulator at Stanford [DGH90], we have developed an efficient execution-driven simulation method that models the parallel applications as if they were running on a real physical implementation of the architecture.

The parallel applications are developed in, or ported to, C to run on a SUN SPARC station as multiple processes sharing memory under SUN-OS. A modified gcc compiler, Abstract Execution (AE) [Lar90], is used to produce processes that not only execute the programs, but also produce a stream of information when doing so. The level of detail in the information stream is selectable, and for this study has been the full address trace of both instructions and data. AE was originally made to produce trace files from uni-processor execution. In our system the streams of information from the different processes are sent to different inputs of a simulation process, modeling the target architecture, as shown in figure 3. The streams serve as models of the processors. The execution speed of each process is determined by how fast the information in its stream is consumed by the simulated architecture, stalling the application process if necessary, making the relative execution speed between the processes that of their execution on the target architecture. Synchronization between the application processes is performed by ordinary shared-memory primitives, i.e., locks and barriers, in the shared memory.

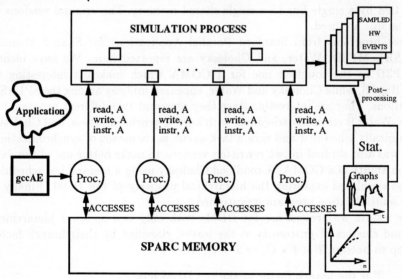

Fig. 3. The structure of execution-driven simulation.

Our simulation model is parameterized with data from our ongoing prototype project, and accurately describes its behavior. Part of the virtual memory system has been modeled, and MMUs make the translation from virtual to physical addresses. On a TLB fault, all necessary transactions from the MMU are sent to the DDM network. New translations from virtual pages to physical pages are created on demand from a randomized free list to make the behavior more realistic. No penalty is added for "reading from disk" since we assume that all pages are already in the machine when the simulation starts. The DDM initially has empty caches and AMs. The first read request for each datum is sent to a special AM, which makes all necessary transactions for returning the value.

The simulation model is instrumented with counters of hardware events, periodically sampled into a large statistics file. The technique has been used to simulate up to 128 processors running programs of up to 2 CPU minutes simulated time. The simulation currently runs the programs 2000 times slower than execution on a single SPARC station. The number of simulated processors has a small effect on the slow down if the application simulated has an ideal speedup, which allows for large machines running large applications to be studied.

5   Simulated Performance of the DDM Prototype

The SPLASH [SWG91] programs represent applications used in an engineering computing environment. They are written in C and use the synchronization primitives provided by the Argonne National Laboratory (ANL) macro package. They were developed for the Encore Multimax, a UMA architecture with small caches tied by a single bus to a single shared memory. The original versions of the programs are used.

Three programs from Stanford Parallel Applications for Shared Memory (SPLASH), MP3D, Water, and Cholesky are reported here. We have identified MP3D as the toughest one for a COMA which makes it interesting to study [Hag92], while Cholesky and Water, appeared midway among the SPLASH applications. They are interesting since they represent two different program behaviors. Water is statically scheduled with barrier synchronization, and Cholesky is dynamically scheduled and uses a task queue as its means of synchronization. MP3D was also studied in two rewritten versions to make better use of the data diffusion ability of a COMA. A modified Cholesky using a hierarchical scheduler was also simulated exploring the hierarchical property of the DDM. Finally, a matrix multiplication program was studied.

The results we present are for DDMs with only two or fewer hierarchical levels and clusters of processors at the leaves, classified by their branch factor from top to bottom $T \times I \times C$, or $T \times C$, where:

> T is the branch factor at the top DDM bus,
> I is the branch factor at the intermediate DDM bus, and,
> C stands for number of processor in one cluster, sharing an M bus.

Many different protocols for the DDM have been designed [HLH91, LHH91]. Here, we use the simplest protocol providing sequential consistency [HHW90].

For configurations 1×1 and 4×1, the DDM network has not been simulated. Instead, a 100 percent hit rate in the AM is assumed. The speedups presented in the graphs are self-relative, i.e., compared to the execution time for 1×1. A hit is defined as a read or write that can be completed without stalling the processor. The hit rates for instructions in the processor caches and the AMs are close to 100 percent for all configurations and applications. The numbers reported for the *data cache* (Dcache) and AM hits are for data only. The node miss rate, defined as the ratio of accesses missing in both the Dcache and the AM, is also for data only.

We present our results in graphs where speedup is a function of the number of processors. For comparison, we also show the linear speedup (*Speedup = #Processors*) and the algorithmic speedups (UNIT DELAY) reported by Singh et al. [SWG91], i.e., the maximum speedup on an ideal architecture.

The architecture modeled in this study differs slightly from the first DDM prototype. The processor caches in the simulator are 16 kbytes, compared to 64 kbytes in the prototype. This partly compensates for the small problem size in the simulation. The attraction memory modeled is two-way set-associative using the last-accessed-memory technique [Hag92], while the prototype implements a true two-way set-associative or direct mapped attraction memory. The associative state memory is modeled as if it was implemented by dual-ported memory rather than interleaved between the two buses. We do not model contention for writes back to the associative state memory.

For comparison, we also show the speedup for the DASH prototype [Len91] for cases where the numbers reported are for comparative problem sizes. Although these numbers are from real—not simulated—prototype hardware the problem size is about the same as for our simulations. The DASH prototype is built from clusters of four 33 MHz MIPS R3000 processors. Each processor has write-through 64 kbytes instruction and data caches and a unified second-level cache of 256 kbytes. The DASH prototype implements release consistency.

5.1 Application Performance

Water is an N-body molecular dynamics application that evaluates forces and potentials in a system of water molecules in the liquid state. It has a static scheduler and uses barriers for synchronization. Water is simulated running two time steps and 192/384 molecules.

The working set is only 320/640 kbytes. The execution time of this application is $O(n^2)$ to the number of molecules, so simulating a real-sized working set is difficult. The small working set results in an extremely good hit rate in the data cache. Misses in the data cache are caused mostly by invalidation misses [HS89], which the AM can do nothing about. The speedup shown for WATER in Figure 4 is almost ideal. Some statistics are presented in Figure 4. Note the difference in the AM hit rate between 64×1 and $2 \times 8 \times 4$. The processors in a cluster share data in their common AM, resulting in an increased hit rate for the four processors. Note, too, the decreased node miss rate when the data set is doubled to 384 molecules. Running this application with real-sized working sets will continue to provide impressive hit rates for large attraction memories.

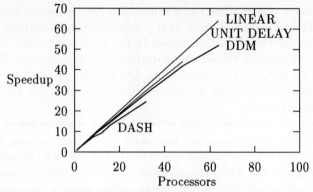

Data Set	192 molecules				384 mols.	
Topology	1×1	8×4	$2\times8\times4$	64×1	$2\times8\times4$	$4\times8\times4$
Hit rate Dcaches (%)	99	99	99	99	98.9	98.9
Hit rate in AM (%)	100	50	44	12	65	58
Node miss rate (%)	-	0.5	0.6	0.9	0.4	0.5
Busy rate:M bus (%)	2	21	31	32	26	37
Busy rate:DDM bus (%)	-	24	39	80	30	40
Busy rate:Top bus(%)	-	-	25	-	20	53
Speedup/#Processors	1/1	28.7/32	52/64	(39.5/64)	53/64	95/128

Fig. 4. The speedup for WATER with 384 molecules running two time steps. The unit delay is reported for 288 molecules and does not include cold-start effects. DASH simulates 512 molecules.

MP3D simulates the pressure and temperature around an object flying at high speed through the upper atmosphere. The primary data objects are particles (air molecules) moving around in a 3-dimensional "wind tunnel," represented by space-cell objects. The simulation is performed in discrete time steps, in which each molecule is moved according to its velocity and possible collision with other molecules, the flying object, and the boundaries. The algorithm is parallelized by statically dividing the particles among processors such that each processor moves the same particles each time.

Moving a particle involves updating the state of the particle and the state of the space cell where the molecule currently resides; in other words, all processors write to all space cells, resulting in poor locality. Between each move phase, some administrative phases are performed, like moving or removing particles from the entrance of the wind tunnel and calculating collision probabilities for each space cell. Simulating 75,000 particles and 14x24x7 space cells results in a total work space of about 4 Mbytes.

MP3D is normally run with the whole memory filled with data objects, mostly particles. The algorithm has poor locality, especially in its "move phase", resulting in poor scalability on the DDM, as well as for other architectures. MP3D is normally run for many simulation steps. To avoid cold-start effects in our tables, we present the steady-state behavior of the last four simulation steps.

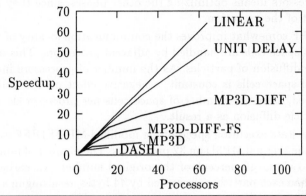

Application	MP3D		–DIFF-FS	–DIFF	
Topology	1×1	2×8×2	2×8×2	2×8×2	4×8×2
Hit rate Dcaches (%)	80	86	90	92	93
Hit rate in AM (%)	100	40	53	88	76
Node miss rate (%)	-	8.4	5.0	1	1.7
Busy rate: M Bus (%)	40	86	76	54	53
Busy rate:DDM bus (%)	-	88	83	24	29
Busy rate:Top bus(%)	-	66	60	13	36
Speedup/#Processors	1/1	6/32	13/32	19/32	27/64

Fig. 5. Speedup for MP3D with 75000 particles at steady state, i.e., the execution time of steps two through five. The unit-delay curve is for 3000 particles.

MP3D-DIFF is a modified version of the program, where a better hit rate is achieved [And91]. The distribution of particles over processors is based here on their current location in space [SWG91]; in other words, all particles in the same space cells are handled by the same processor. The update of both a particle's state and its space-cell state is now local to one processor. When a particle is moved across a processor border, its data is handled by a new processor; i.e., the particle data diffuses to the attraction memory of the new processor. This modification involves adding some 30 extra lines of code.

The move phase of MP3D is now optimized, since most operations are local to the processors. Only the diffusion of particles accross cells generates traffic. Efficiently supporting such a diffusion of the major data structure requires a COMA architecture. In a COMA, the particle data that occupy the major part of the physical memory are allowed to move freely among attraction memories.

Rewriting the same code for a NUMA involves adding one extra layer of indirection in accesses to the particle data and explicitly copying particle states between the local memories. The move phase now shows an improved speedup. The move phase that accounted for 93 percent of execution time on a uniprocessor now occupies around 50 percent of execution time on 32 processors. Improving speedup above 32 processors means optimizing the other phases, since they now are the dominant part of the execution.

MP3D-DIFF somewhat improves the communication locality of the application. Adjacent space cells are handled by adjacent processors. This improves the locality in the diffusion of particles. As the number of processors increase while the number of space cells is constant, a negative effect on the node miss rate can be expected, since the number of space cells per processor decreases, with increased particle diffusion as a result.

The steady-state execution speed of the modified MP3D-DIFF is about three times that of the original MP3D on 32 processors. The number of remote accesses is decreased to about 10 percent of the original number. An earlier version of MP3D-DIFF had each particle represented by 44 bytes, resulting in a fair amount of false sharing, so that two processors wrote to different parts of the same cache line and therefore appeared to share data, resulting in conflicting writes. The false sharing disappeared when each particle instead was made 48 bytes to better suit our 16-bytes cache line. The effect of false sharing can be studied as MP3D-DIFF-FS in Figure 5, where all the different runs are compared. Figure 6 compares the hit rates in the AM of the MP3D and MP3D-DIFF.

Work on improving the cache behavior for MP3D has also been reported by Cheriton et al. [CGM90]. In that study, machines with small caches were used. Such machines are not practical when applying this method to real-sized problems.

Reported speedups for MP3D-DIFF and MP3D-DIFF-FS are relative to the execution of the original MP3D on a single processor.

Cholesky factorizes a sparse positive definite matrix. The matrix is divided into supernodes that are put in a global task queue to be picked up by any processor. Locks are used for the task queue and for modifications in the matrix. We have used two input matrices as input to the program. The large matrix bcsstk15 occupies 800 kbytes unfactored and 7.7 Mbytes factored. Bcsstk 15 has a speedup of about 17 using 32 processors and seems to have potential for more speedup on larger DDMs (Figure 7). The smaller matrix bcsstk14, which yields a worse speedup, has been reported for the unit delay. Its input matrix occupies 420 kbytes unfactored and 1.4 Mbytes factored. Its speedup on 32 processors is 9.6.

From the numbers in Figure 7 it is interesting to note that the larger matrix not only has a better speedup, but also produces less traffic. It is divided into larger supernodes than the smaller matrix, resulting in more local execution per communication unit.

This application really highlights the danger of drawing general conclusions based on a small data set. Any architecture with small first-level caches would

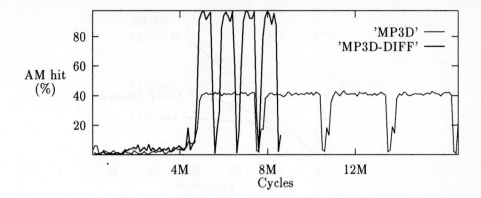

Fig. 6. Dynamic behavior of the hit rate in one attraction memory over time for the original MP3D and the modified version MP3D-DIFF on the topology 2x8x2. The move phases of the last four simulation steps can easily be identified by their higher hit rates. The first step includes the cold-start effect and takes longer time. The execution time of the last four steps represents the steady-state behavior of the simulation. The improvement of MP3D-DIFF by about three times comes partly from an increased hit rate in the processor caches from 86 percent to 92 percent (not shown here).

report good behavior for the small matrix because of a hit rate of 96 percent in the Dcache, a node miss rate of around 4 percent. However, simulating the larger matrix, usually neglected, would have resulted in an 11 percent node miss rate without a second-level cache instead of the achievable 2.8 percent.

Cholesky-H The scheduler part of Cholesky has been modified so that each cluster also has its own task queue, and task migration is hierarchical. Initially, all tasks reside in one global task queue. All processors retrieve jobs from the global queue and put newly created jobs in their local cluster queues. When the global queue is empty, the processors start retrieving tasks from their cluster queues. When the cluster queue is empty, a processor first looks for jobs in its binary brother cluster.[1] Secondly, the two binary cousins are checked for tasks, etc. Not only are tasks kept local to a bus this way, but the probability of retrieving a job related to one the clusters previously worked on is higher. The most notable difference between bcsstk14 and bcsstk14-H in Figure 7 is that the traffic on the top bus has decreased, even though the execution speed is about 10 percent faster. The reported speedup is relative to the execution of the unmodified program on a single processor.

Matrix is a program multiplying two 500-by-500 matrices using a blocking algorithm[LRW91]. The blocking algorithm is interesting, since it tries to make the most effective use of caches. Once a portion of a matrix (a block) has been read to a cache, it is used many times before being replaced with a new block.

---

[1] Calculated by toggling the least significant bit of the processor ID.

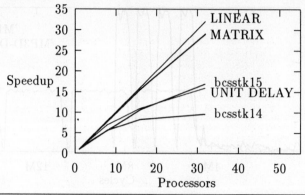

Application	Cholesky:bcsstk15 (large matrix)		bcsstk14 (small)	bcsstk14-H (hier.sched.)	MATRIX 500x500
Topology	1×1	8×2	$2\times8\times2$	$2\times8\times2$	$2\times8\times2$	8×4
Hit rate Dcaches (%)	87	88	89	96	96	92
Hit rate in AM (%)	100	81	74	6	24	98
Node miss rate (%)	-	2.3	2.8	3.8	3.2	0.16
Busy rate:M bus (%)	27	63	60	70	60	55
Busy rate:DDM bus (%)	-	57	66	80	70	4
Busy rate:Top bus (%)	-	-	49	70	41	-
Speedup/#Processors	1/1	10.6/16	17/32	9.6/32	11/32	29.1/32

Fig. 7. Statistics for matrix programs. The unit delay is for bcsstk14.

The blocking algorithm is yet another example of part of the working set being attracted and worked on locally, resulting in increased speedup and low communication. The algorithm has a block size larger than the data cache, resulting in extensive use of the AM. The work space is about 3 Mbytes. It shows a speedup close to ideal on a DDM (Figure 7), generating extremely little communication. An even more optimal design would be to do the blocking in two levels, with very large blocks kept in the AMs, and smaller blocks read to the data caches.

5.2 What About a Larger Problem Size?

We have used the largest problem sizes that our patience could bear, i.e., a simulation time of about one day per run. Still, the problem size was far from realistic in many cases. We tried to compensate for this by exploring what would happen to the architecture when the data set was increased. The nature of a COMA, with large resources for "second-level caches," makes the DDM less sensitive to the small-cache effect. Actually, it is first when a realistic problem size is used that a COMA really starts to pay off. Figure 8 shows the trends of cache-miss rates as the problem set is increased for the studied applications.

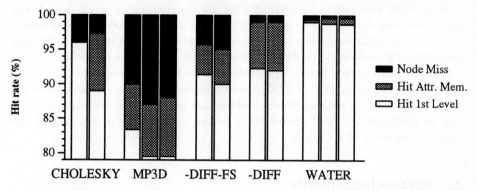

Fig. 8. The effects of the large attraction memories increase with the size of the data set. Here, the behavior of a small data set (to the left) is compared to larger data sets (to the right) for some applications. For the MP3D applications, the number of particles is increased while the number of space cells is held constant.

6 Related Work

The hierarchical DDM and its protocol have several similarities with the architectures proposed by Wilson [Wil86], and Goodman [GW88]. The problem of maintaining coherence in hierarchical systems is addressed in the Wilson. The Goodman proposal has a network built by a grid of buses. A node snoops two buses and has two assignments in that architecture. First it is a processing node and secondly it acts as a directory. The DDM is different in its use of transient states in the protocol, its lack of physically shared memory, and its storage of state information but no data in the network (higher level caches). It is also different in that it handles replacement in such a way that at least one copy of all the data in the caches is always guaranteed, and thus the shared memory is not needed. Recently, the commercial machine KSR1 was released [BFKR92]. It is similar to the DDM being a hierarchical COMA, but has a much larger item size and longer remote access delay than the DDM prototype.

7 Conclusion

A detailed execution-driven simulator of the DDM has been developed to study its behavior when executing real applications. Programs from the SPLASH suite, developed for a UMA architecture, with the largest bearable problem size were used to evaluate the DDM. Good speedup was reported for two of the three studied SPLASH applications, demonstrating a COMA's ability to adapt to static as well as dynamic scheduling. The poor locality of the third application, MP3D, resulted in a poor speedup for the DDM as well as for other architectures. This poor locality was tamed by restructuring its distribution of work from being static to being dynamic. The restructuring also increased MP3D's communication locality. Communication locality was also enhanced for Cholesky by adding hierarchical knowledge to its dynamical scheduler. Finally, the importance of the attraction memory was shown to increase with a larger data set.

The conclusion is that a COMA can successfully execute shared-memory applications written with a different architecture in mind. Further improvements can be obtained by small modification to the applications to better suit the unique properties of a COMA.

8   Acknowledgements

Part of the DDM work has been performed under the ESPRIT project 2741 PEPMA. We thank the many colleagues involved in or associated with the project. SICS is sponsored by Asea Brown Boveri AB, NobelTech Systems AB, Ericsson AB, IBM Svenska AB, Televerket (Swedish Telecom), Försvarets Materielverk FMV (Defense Material Administration), and the Swedish National Board for Industrial and Technical Development (Nutek).

References

[And91]   P. Andersson. Performance Evaluation of Different Topologies for the Data Diffusion Machine. Final work for Undergraduate Studies, KTH, November 1991.

[BFKR92] H. Burkhardt, S. Frank, B. Knobe, and J. Rothnie. Overview of the KSR1 Computer System. Technical Report KSR-TR-9202001, Kendall Square Research, Boston, 1992.

[CGM90] D.R. Cheriton, H.A. Goosen, and P. Machanick. Restructuring Parallel Simulation to Improve Cache Behavior in Shared-Memory Multiprocessor: A First Experience. Computer Science Department, Stanford, Internal paper, 1990.

[CKA91]   D. Chaiken, J. Kubiatowicz, and A. Agarwal. LimitLESS Directories: A Scalable Cache Coherence Scheme. In *Proceedings of the 4th Annual Architectural Support for Programming Languages and Operating Systems*, 1991.

[DGH90] H. Davis, S. Goldschmidt, and J. Hennessy. Tango: A Multiprocessor Simulation and Tracing System. Tech. Report No CSL-TR-90-439, Stanford University, 1990.

[Goo83]   J. R. Goodman. Using Cache Memory to Reduce Processor-Memory Traffic. In *Proceedings of the 10th Annual International Symposium on Computer Architecture*, pages 124–131, 1983.

[GW88]   J.R. Goodman and P.J. Woest. The Wisconsin Multicube: A New Large-Scale Cache-Coherent Multiprocessor. In *Proceedings of the 15th Annual International Symposium on Computer Architecture, Honolulu, Hawaii*, pages 422–431, 1988.

[Hag92]   E. Hagersten. *Toward Scalable Cache Only Memory Architectures.* PhD thesis, Royal Institute of Technology, Stockholm/ Swedish Institute of Computer Science, 1992.

[HHW90] E. Hagersten, S. Haridi, and D.H.D. Warren. The Cache-Coherence Protocol of the Data Diffusion Machine. In M. Dubois and S. Thakkar, editors, *Cache and Interconnect Architectures in Multiprocessors.* Kluwer Academic Publisher, Norwell, Mass, 1990.

[HLH91] E. Hagersten, A. Landin, and S. Haridi. Multiprocessor Consistency and Synchronization Through Transient Cache States. In M. Dubois and S. Thakkar, editors, *Scalable Shared-Memory Multiprocessors.* Kluwer Academic Publisher, Norwell, Mass, June 1991.

[HLH92] E. Hagersten, A. Landin, and S. Haridi. DDM – A Cache-Only Memory Architecture. *IEEE Computer*, 25(9):44–54, Sept. 1992.

[HomBC] Homer. *Odyssey.* 800 BC.

[HS89]   M. Hill and A.J. Smith. Evaluating Associativity in CPU Caches. *IEEE Transactions on Computers*, 38(12):1612–1630, December 1989.

[Lar90]   J. Larus. Abstract Execution: A Technique for Efficient Tracing Programs. Tech Report, Computer Science Department, University of Wisconsin at Madison, 1990.

[Len91]   D. Lenoski. *The Design and Analysis of DASH: A Scalable Directory-Based Multiprocessor.* PhD thesis, Stanford University, 1991.

[LHH91] A. Landin, E. Hagersten, and S. Haridi. Race-free Interconnection Networks and Multiprocessor Consistency. In *Proceedings of the 18th Annual International Symposium on Computer Architecture*, 1991.

[LLG⁺90] D. Lenoski, J. Laudon, K. Gharachorloo, A. Gupta, and J. Hennessy. The Directory-Based Cache Coherence Protocol for the DASH Multiprocessor. In *Proceedings of the 17th Annual International Symposium on Computer Architecture*, pages 148–159, 1990.

[LRW91] M.S. Lam, E.E. Rothberg, and M.E. Wolf. The Cache Performance and Optimizations of Blocked Algorithms. In *Proceedings of the 4th Annual Architectural Support for Programming Languages and Operating Systems*, pages 63–74, 1991.

[RW91]   S. Raina and D.H.D Warren. Traffic Patterns in a Scalable Multiprocessor through Transputer Emulation. In *International Hawaii Conference on System Science*, 1991.

[Ste90]   P. Stenström. A Survey of Cache Coherence for Multiprocessors. *IEEE Computer*, 23(6), June 1990.

[SWG91] J.S. Singh, W-D. Weber, and A. Gupta. SPLASH: Stanford Parallel Applications for Shared Memory. Stanford University, Report, April 1991.

[WH88]   D.H.D. Warren and S. Haridi. Data Diffusion Machine–a scalable shared virtual memory multiprocessor. In *International Conference on Fifth Generation Computer Systems 1988.* ICOT, 1988.

[Wil86]   A. Wilson. Hierarchical cache/bus architecture for shared memory multiprocessor. Technical report ETR 86-006, Encore Computer Corporation, 1986.

2DT-FP: An FP Based Programming Language for Efficient Parallel Programming of Multiprocessor Networks

Yosi Ben-Asher[1], Gudula Rünger[2] *, Assaf Schuster[3], Reinhard Wilhelm[2]

[1] Department of Mathematics, Haifa University, Haifa 32000, Israel
[2] FB 14 Informatik, Universität des Saarlandes, W-6600 Saarbrücken, Germany
[3] Computer Science Department, Technion IIT, Haifa 32000, Israel

Abstract. We propose a new paradigm for programming tightly coupled multicomputer systems, 2DT. 2DT-programs are composed of local
computations on linear data (columns) and global transformations on
2-dimensional combinations of the columns (2D-arrays). Local computations can be expressed in a functional or imperative base language; a
typed variant of Backus' FP, 2DT-FP, is chosen in this paper.
An interleaving semantics for 2DT-FP is given, exposing the potential
for parallel execution of 2DT-FP programs. The claim is proved that any
sequential and thus any parallel execution will deliver the same result.

Keywords: parallel language, operational semantics.

1 Introduction

Language design has to satisfy a set of requirements: The language has to be
expressive, i.e. it should allow the formulation of a sufficiently large set of relevant problem solutions. It should offer the right **level of abstraction** for the
problem area. And it should be **efficiently implementable** on available hardware. In the case of a parallel language, the following additional goals have to
be reached. It is desired to formulate the algorithms to be expressed in the language without loss of their inherent parallelism. This is called *maximal degree of
parallelism*. For the implementation, the following potential overheads of parallel
execution have to be avoided: too fine grained communication, too many costly
process creations, deletions and context switches, expensive data structures for
bookkeeping, and multiplexing of logical processors.

In the case of the 2DT-metaphor, we think to have satisfied the above requirements in the following way:

- Expressiveness : 2DT is adequate for programming algorithms that can be
  nicely mapped to 2-dimensional representations, e.g. graph algorithms and
  some numerical algorithms. For those algorithms, 2DT-programs preserve
  the degree of parallelism.

---

* supported by DFG, SFB 124

- Level of abstraction : In 2DT, the programmer can use *global transformations* on data representations instead of implementing these by low level communication primitives like message passing.
- Efficiency : Global transformations are implemented by message passing. The communication overhead can be greatly reduced by combining many small messages to few big ones. Efficient algorithms designed for an existing and realistic parallel hardware should exist for the chosen transformations. In an earlier work [BES92] efficient realizations are described for the introduced set of transformations (see sec.2) on the popular shuffle-exchange topology.

The only data-type of 2DT is the *2D-array*. A 2D-array consists of a set of local data objects, called *columns*, which are to be assigned to processes. Local computations on a column are associated with the *vertical* dimension, while manipulating data across columns is associated with the *horizontal* dimension. The terms column and 2D-array stem from these associations.

2DT supplies a set of operations on 2D-arrays.

- Local changes of columns: This is the result of local computations modifying all columns of the current 2D-array by the same operations. These operations are the instructions of the language which is chosen as the basis of a 2DT-language.
- Global transformations on a 2D-array: This serves as the communication mechanism between the columns (or processes) of a 2D-array. There are no transformations operating between different 2D-arrays, (see next item). This is a unique feature of 2DT, in contrast to shared memory or message passing oriented languages, where communication is not restricted by the language constructs. In addition, transformations have a synchronization effect between the processes they are executed on.
- Modification of the number of columns of a given 2D-array: This operation, namely *resize*, is connected with spawning (or terminating) processes.
- Splitting (and re-combining) of a 2D-array into several (effectively two) sub-2D-arrays: This transformation allows a "SPMD mode" of operations where different computations are associated with different 2D-arrays.

The communication transformations were chosen according to the following criteria: All columns of the current 2D-array ought to take part in every global transformation in order to increase the amount of data and size of messages manipulated by the transformation. A transformation uses the entire content of a column as its argument. This encourages the user to "collect" many data-items before using a transformation. Thus a massive communication takes place, and a possibility to create "big" messages is provided.

In 2DT the computations are triggered by data objects, such that processes are created for the columns. Thus *reshaping* a 2D-array results in creation and termination of processes. In this aspect 2DT can be classified as a *data-parallel* language [BS90]: processes are created in order to support parallel computations on data-objects.

Let $\mathcal{P}$ denote some 2DT program. $\mathcal{P} = T_k; \ldots T_2; T_1$ is the sequential composition of transformations T_i, $i = 1, \ldots, k$, each belonging to one of the four categories described above. The parallel execution of $\mathcal{P}$ on some input M, denoted $\mathcal{P}M$, can be viewed as a sequence of transformation applications on a (varying) set of 2D-arrays

$$\mathcal{P}M = T_k; \ldots T_2; T_1(M) = T_k(\ldots T_2(T_1(M)) \ldots)$$

The program starts its execution with a single column 2D-array containing the input. Figure 1 demonstrates a 2DT-program which computes the sum of n inputs $x_1, \ldots, x_n$ using some resize operations:

$$\mathcal{P}_{sum}[x_1 \ldots x_n] = T_{local\ sum}; T_{resize\ p\ to\ 1}; T_{local\ sum}; T_{resize\ 1\ to\ p}([x_1 \ldots x_n])$$

Assuming that there are at least p processors (for simplicity let p divide n), one process running on each processor, all local sums will be computed in parallel. Thus $\mathcal{P}_{sum}$ computes the sum of n inputs in $\frac{n}{p} + p$ local computation steps plus the time of the resize transformations.

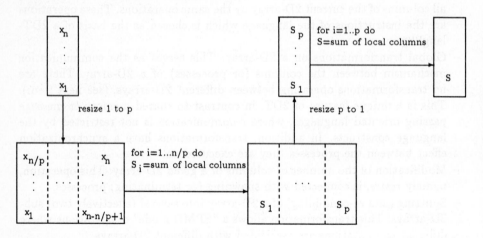

Fig. 1. *Summing program*

In this work the 2DT paradigm has been built on top of FP ([Bac78]), yielding a new language called 2DT-FP. 2DT-FP is geared towards tightly-coupled machines, working in cooperation on large input problems.

The remaining part of this paper is organized as follows: Section 2 describes the performance of the global transformations. In Section 3 an informal introduction to the components of the language 2DT-FP is given. Section 4 contains the description of syntax and formal semantics of 2DT-FP and the proof of "weak" determinism. Finally, section 5 presents detailed examples for parallel programs in 2DT-FP thus illustrating the "maximal degree of parallelism" offered by 2DT-FP.

1.1 Comparison of 2DT to other languages

2DT uses a fixed set of communication patterns and data-objects for spawning processes (in contrast to control driven parallelism). In this sense, it falls between two categories of parallel programming languages: At one end are languages for loosely coupled networks which use point-to-point message passing. These include OCCAM [Inm84], Ada [Uni83] and Pascal-Plus [Per87]. At the other end stand data-parallel languages such as Actus [PCM83] and C* [Ros87]. These languages, orientated to tightly coupled networks, have high-level parallel operations, supporting general communication patterns via array references [BS90]. 2DT does not allow arbitrary communication. Rather, for each 2D-array, a set of fixed, global communication patterns is used, involving all the processors. Communication results from the movement of data-items between columns of the 2D-array. Actus supplies shift operators as a global communication form. Other data-parallel languages such as C* offer more operations like *min*, *plus* and bit-wise operators. These are supported by 2DT as well, e.g. by using a one-dimensional restriction of the 2D-row-reduction transformation described in section 2.1. The set of global transformations provided by 2DT is larger, including *transpose*, *smoothing* and *duplication* which have to be simulated by library routines in languages like Actus or C*.

2DT operates on a mixture of a SIMD/MIMD mode. Even though all processors of a 2D-array execute the same code, different computations may be performed on different 2D-arrays. Thus 2DT can be classified as a SPMD language [Bel92] standing between SIMD languages (Actus) and MIMD languages (Ada).

2 The set of 2D-Transformations

In this section the global transformations and their time complexities are described. The choice of this particular set is a trial to include some of the most "basic" and "natural" operations for 2D-arrays:

- Equalize the heights of all the columns.
- Delete null elements.
- Exchange elements between rows and columns.
- General two dimensional permutations.
- Reshape the height and width of a 2D-array.

The transformations are illustrated in fig. 2 In each array the columns are numbered 0, 1 .... Each column holds four local elements denoted by four letters. ('@'s represent null elements.) The execution time for every transformation is expressed in terms of l - the maximum size of a local column, and p - the number of processors running one process each.

2.1 Description of the Transformations

The transpose operation has two versions: transpose columns to rows (**c2r**) moves the 2D-array elements from column-major into row-major order, while

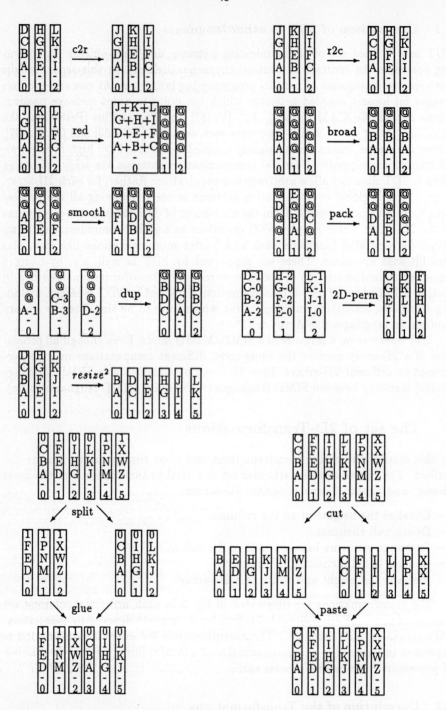

Fig. 2. Global transformations

transpose rows to columns (**r2c**) moves them from row-major into column-major order. Note that if A is a 2D-array, with p columns and of l elements each, such that $l \neq p$ then $c2r(A) \neq r2c(A)$, i.e. the transpose operation of 2DT is usually different from the matrix transpose. Intuitively, $c2r$ and $r2c$ allow a processor attached to a column to distribute its data to all other processors participating in the transformation. Thus $c2r$ and $r2c$ realize a multi-broadcast together with a multi-receive of data items.

Row reduction (red) of a 2D-array is done by combining all the elements of each row separately through an associative binary operation and storing the l results in the first column. An inverse operation can be defined for the row-reduction operation (see [BES92]). For reasons of simplicity we show only a simple version of this inverse transformation: a broadcast operation (**broad**) which copies the j'th element of the first column to all columns.

The smoothing transformations: As a result of local column modifications the sizes of columns may change. This may cause imbalance of the workload of processess for future operations. The **smooth** operation moves elements among columns, making the height of all the columns equal (up to a difference of one). Note that the order of the elements in the columns is not preserved. In [BES92] a **pack** operation which removes null elements while preserving a snake-like order of the 2D-array is presented, having efficiency similar to that of smooth.

Dup and 2D-permutation operations: The **dup** operation creates copies of data items while maintaining a load-balancing condition. A tag is attached to each item, indicating the number of required copies. During the operation these copies are produced while keeping all column sizes the same. If d denotes the total number of requested copies, then the size of each final column is $\leq 1 + d/p$. The copies may finally reside at any column. In a general permutation of data (**2D-perm**), each item in a column is sent to another location in the 2D-array. This can be implemented efficiently as described in [BSW89], where a 2D-permutation is based on the transpose operation. As demonstrated in fig. 2, each data-item has a tag number giving its destination column.

The resize operation may expand or shrink the 2D-array, together with the corresponding number of active (logical) processors. There are two variations: $resize^2$ doubles the number of columns by splitting each column into two new columns (containing half of the original column) and $resize^{-2}$ joins each pair of adjacent columns, thus halving the number of columns. In case that the number of columns is odd, the last column is not joined to any other column in $resize^{-2}$.

The Split&Glue and Cut&Paste constructors split a given 2D-array into two *son arrays*. A separate and parallel computation is performed on every son array. When both computations have terminated, their results (two new 2D-arrays) are joined back forming a single 2D-array. Split&Glue divides its 2D-array into two sets of columns, while Cut&Paste divide each column into two parts producing 2D-arrays with the same number of columns.

2.2 Performance evaluation and synchronization

A major motivation in the development of 2DT is to obtain highly efficient programs. A major contribution to this expected efficiency is a set of transformations having a corresponding set of efficient algorithms. Table 1 shows that all transformations (except the constructs) have performance which is nearly optimal on the shuffle-exchange topology (as described in [BES92]).

The global transformations described in the previous subsections require *synchronization*. We assume that a global 2D-transformation does not start until all processors reach some barrier. This may be achieved by a *sync* operation, paying $O(\log p)$ steps per application (on the shuffle-exchange). The *sync* is called before each application of a global transformation.

Table 1. Transformation times for a perfect shuffle exchange network

Operation	Perfect Shuffle Time	Lower Bound
Row-Reduction	$4(l + \log p)$	$l + \log p$
Broadcast	$4(l + \log p)$	$l + \log p$
Transpose (T_{rc} and T_{cr})	$1.5 * l * \log p$	$\Omega(l * \log p)$
Smoothing	$\frac{1}{3}l * \log p$	$\Omega(l * \sqrt{\log p})$
Packing	$l * \log p$	$\Omega(l * \log p)$
Dup	$d/p + O(l * \log p)$	d/p
2D-Perm	$2l + 6l * \log p$	$\Omega(l * \log p)$
Resize	$l * \log p$	$\Omega(l * \log p)$

3 2DT-FP Components

2DT-FP is a two level hierarchy, local FP-expressions are used to manipulate data inside columns, and global 2DT-FP expressions manipulate data across columns. The 2DT-FP syntax has a similar notation to that of FP, however, it contains additional data-sets and constructors. This section presents an informal introduction to 2DT-FP. Exact syntax and semantics, including type information, is given in the next section.

FP-objects are atoms, the bottom $\perp$ (for undefined computations) and sequences of objects $< x_1, \ldots, x_n >$ [Bac78]. All 2DT-FP components, including FP-sequences, are $\perp$-preserving, i.e. if one of their arguments contains $\perp$ then the result of their application is $\perp$.

A tuple of FP-objects $x_1, \ldots, x_n$ is denoted by $(x_1, \ldots, x_n)$, where each object x_i, $i = 1, \ldots, n$, corresponds to a column. A tuple of objects can be understood as a 2D-array in a "local" state, i.e. only FP computations can be performed separately and in parallel on each component of the tuple.

A column corresponds to a FP-object which is a component of a tuple of FP-objects. It represents the same data-information in a different shape possibly containing null elements @.

A 2D-array is a collection of columns denoted by $[c_1, \ldots, c_n]$. A 2D-array is in a "global" state, i.e. it has an appropriate shape for transformation application and only transformations can be applied to it.

FP-functions (user defined and primitive functions, see [Bac78]) compose the local part of 2DT-FP programs. A FP-function appears only once in a program but it is applied to all components of the current tuple of objects in parallel.

Transformations are operations which modify 2D-arrays. For 2DT-FP a set of deterministic transformations is chosen, i.e. *c2r*, *resize*,... (see sec. 2).

Conversions : there are two kinds of conversions denoted by $\uparrow$ and $\downarrow$. $\uparrow$ converts a tuple of objects into a 2D-array and $\downarrow$ performs the opposite. Typically $\uparrow$ will complete short columns with null elements such that transformations can be applied. A formal description of the conversions is a matter of implementation and is not included in the semantics of 2DT-FP.

2DT-FP functions compose the global part of a program which contains compositions of *transformations, local FP-functions, conversions* and *2DT-constructors*. For local computatons, also the operators ("#") and ("%%") are provided, which return the current column id and the number of columns of one 2D-array, respectively, and require the content of the whole array. The composition is done using the ';' operator. The syntax is designed such that it prohibits compositions of local FP-functions using the global ';' composition. Otherwise the proposed semantics would enforce synchronization between local computations.

Constructors: Split&Glue ($\xrightarrow{s\&g}$) and Cut&Paste ($\xrightarrow{c\&p}$) are constructors on 2DT-FP functions f, g using an auxiliary function p, with the syntax $p \xrightarrow{s\&g} \{f\|g\}$ and $p \xrightarrow{c\&p} \{f \times g\}$. Informally the semantics can be described as follows: A tuple $(x_1, \ldots, x_n)$ is divided into two tuples M_1, M_2, where the elements in M_1 satisfy the predicate p and those of M_2 do not. The 2DT-functions f and g are applied to M_1 and M_2 in parallel. Finally $M_1' = f(M_1)$ and $M_2' = g(M_2)$ are "glued" or "pasted" back to form a new tuple. Typically the $\xrightarrow{s\&g}$ -constructor is used to implement a global conditional function allowing the start and termination of parallel recursion. This possible usage of $\xrightarrow{s\&g}$ and $\xrightarrow{c\&p}$ will be discussed in the section explaining parallel programming in 2DT-FP.

4   2DT-FP semantics

2DT-FP functions are used to define a program, while tuples of objects and 2D-arrays only appear in the computation of a program as an argument or a result. The application of a function to an argument forms a 2DT-FP term. In order to distinguish local and global computations (and also different kinds of terms), we give a *type* to each 2DT-FP function.

In this section we present an overview on the exact syntax, 2DT-FP terms, types and the structural operational semantics. For the detailed versions of subsections 4.1 and 4.2 see [BRSW92].

4.1 Syntax of 2DT-FP

Basic types σ, τ, κ and μ are associated to FP-objects, tuples of objects, columns and 2D-arrays, respectively. The 2DT-FP functions may have one of the types:

$$\tau \to \tau \quad , \quad \mu \to \tau \quad , \quad \tau \to \mu \quad , \quad \mu \to \mu .$$

In order to combine 2DT with the underlying FP-language, we also introduce types of the lower level, i.e. FP-functions of type $\sigma \to \sigma$ and conversions of type $\sigma \to \kappa$ and $\kappa \to \sigma$. Both levels are separated syntactically. Notice that there will be no function of type $\kappa \to \kappa$ reflecting the fact that no explicit work on columns, the components of 2D-arrays, is possible. It is also possible to consider a set of 2D-arrays, implicitly created by the global level constructors (such as the 'split&glue'). However, the programmer can not explicitly use them and we need not to provide a type for it.

Definition 1. A program is a set of user defined 2DT-FP functions:

$$def \quad F_i \ = \ R_i \qquad\qquad i = 1, \ldots, n,$$

with a main function variable F_n. The function names F_i and the 2DT-FP function R_i are of the same type, i.e. F_i, $i = 1, \ldots, n$ are used as function names correctly. In the following the main function variable is denoted by $\mathcal{P}$.

4.2 Semantics of 2DT-FP

An operational semantics of 2DT-FP is given by defining a transition relation $t \longrightarrow t'$ between 2DT-FP terms on the structure of terms using a transition system [Plo81]. Intuitively, a transition $t \longrightarrow t'$ describes one term reduction step of a 2DT-FP term. The concurrent executions on different levels of 2DT-FP, i.e. computations on tuples of objects or sets of 2D-arrays, is modelled by interleaving rules like the following one for "local" computations.

For a local 2DT-FP function f and a tuple of objects $(x_1, \ldots, x_n)$ we have:

$$f(x_1, \ldots, x_n) \quad \longrightarrow \quad (f : x_1, \ldots, f : x_n)$$

Each $f : x_i$ is a regular FP application. However, different interleavings can take place according to the reduction rule for tuples of FP-applications:

$$\frac{f_i : x_i \ \longrightarrow \ t_i}{(f_1 : x_1, \ldots, f_i : x_i, \ldots, f_n : x_n) \ \longrightarrow \ (f_1 : x_1, \ldots, t_i, \ldots, f_n : x_n)}$$

where $f_i : x_i \longrightarrow t_i$, $i \in \{1, \ldots, n\}$, is an FP-reduction step.

We deem it proper to include also interleaving rules in the well known description of FP semantics. This is done so to provide different levels of parallelism so that a maximal degree of parallelism for the expression of algorithms can be achieved.

Definition 2. A *transition sequence* is a finite or infinite sequence of 2DT-FP terms t_i, $i \geq 0$, such that:

$$t_1 \longrightarrow t_2 \longrightarrow \ldots t_i \longrightarrow \ldots$$

A *computation* of $\mathcal{P}$ applied to the 2D-array M is a finite transition sequence starting with $\mathcal{P}M$ and ending with a 2D-array. A computation is *diverging* if the computation sequence is infinite. Let $\overset{*}{\longrightarrow}$ be the reflexive, transitive closure of the transition relation $\longrightarrow$. Then we define the *semantics of a program $\mathcal{P}$* as follows:

$$[\![\, \mathcal{P}\,]\!]\, M \;=\; \left\{\; M' \;\mid\; \mathcal{P}\, M \overset{*}{\longrightarrow} M', \quad M' \; is \; a \; 2D-array \;\right\} \; \bigcup$$

$$\{\; \infty \;\mid \exists an \; infinite \; computation \; sequence \; starting \; in \; \mathcal{P}M\}$$

4.3 Weak Determinism

The semantics of 2DT-FP describes nondeterminism in the sense that the execution of a program $\mathcal{P}$ applied to an argument M can create different computations. However, 2DT-FP programs have some kind of "*weak*" *deterministism* which means that all computations of $\mathcal{P}M$ produce the same result. For the proof the diamond property of the transition relation $\longrightarrow$ and some general results for binary relations are used.

Lemma 3 Diamond Property. *Let t be a 2DT-FP term and let $t \longrightarrow t_1$ and $t \longrightarrow t_2$ be two 2DT-FP transitions where $t_1 \neq t_2$. Then there exists a 2DT-FP term t_3 such that $t_1 \longrightarrow t_3$ and $t_2 \longrightarrow t_3$.*

Proof. Immediately following from checking all transition rules of all possible term structures. E.g. consider the tuple $t = (f_1 : x_1, \ldots, f_n : x_n)$ which is reduced according to the transition steps $f_k : x_k \longrightarrow y_k$, $k = i, j$, $i \neq j$:

$$t = (f_1 : x_1, \ldots, f_n : x_n) \longrightarrow \begin{cases} t_1 = (f_1 : x_1, \ldots, y_i, \ldots, f_j : x_j, \ldots, f_n : x_n) \\ t_2 = (f_1 : x_1, \ldots, f_i : x_i, \ldots, y_j, \ldots, f_n : x_n) \end{cases}$$

Then both terms can be reduced:

$$\left. \begin{matrix} t_1 \\ t_2 \end{matrix} \right\} \longrightarrow t_3 = (f_1 : x_1, \ldots, y_i, \ldots, y_j, \ldots, f_n : x_n)$$

□

Lemma 4. *For every 2DT-FP program $\mathcal{P}$ and for every 2D-array M there is a unique result of the computation $\mathcal{P}M$.*

Proof. Using Lemma 5.5 ([AO91] pp. 184) yields that $[\![\, \mathcal{P}\,]\!]M$ contains exactly one element.

□

5   Parallel Programming in 2DT-FP

The "utility" of a proposed language for parallel programming lies in its ability to directly code parallel algorithms for different types of applications. The execution time of the resulting program should correspond to the parallel complexity of the underlying algorithm or application. The *parallel execution time*, *pt*, is the time needed when the number of processors is sufficient to exploit all the potential parallelism. It is used to determine the complexities of the examples given in this section. The utility of a language can not be formulated theoretically. It should be tested through examples and experiments. In the following examples we use FP primitive functions such as *trans, distl, rotl, ...* as defined in [Bac78].

Assuming that the given 2D-array contains m vectors $v_1, \ldots, v_m$ of size n in row major order, and a special vector u, whose **inner product** with all v_i's is to be computed:

$$def \quad ip \; = \; T_{red}(+); \uparrow; (\propto *) \circ distr$$

The elements of u are distributed to all v_i then multiplied, finally $T_{red}(+)$ returns the inner product of every v_i with u. Thus m inner products are computed in $pt = 3m$ assuming that the reduction of one row takes just one step (which is a reasonable estimation, if there are n processors available; see table 1). [4]

The **matrix multiplication** can be computed in a similar manner using T_{red}. Assume that A and B are two matrices of size $n \times n$ given in a 2D-array with n columns, such that the $i'th$ column contains the i'th element from every row of A and the i'th element of every column of B, hence $column_i = \; << a_{1,i}, \ldots, a_{n,i} >, < b_{i,1}, \ldots, b_{i,n} >>$. Then

$$def \quad mm \; = \; T_{red}(+); \uparrow; flat \circ \propto ((\propto *) \circ distr) \circ distl$$

performs matrix multiplications in $5n^2$ steps, such that all n^2 results are stored in the first column of the 2D-array in column major order. The *flat* is used to remove inner $<,>$ from a sequence. Fig. 3 describes the stages in multiplying two matrices where $n = 2$.

Another possibility is to use $T_{transpose}$ and do local reductions instead of using T_{red}:

$$def \quad mm' \; = \; \propto (/+) \circ trans; \downarrow; T_{transpose}; \uparrow; \propto ((\propto *) \circ distr) \circ distl$$

In this case every column contains n elements of the result.

For a different kind of parallel paradigm consider the well known **divide and conquer method** where the **maximum** of an array with n elements is computed in $o(\log n)$ steps. The algorithm divides the array into two parts, the maximum of each part is computed in parallel by applying the algorithm to each of them recursively. The recursion halts when the array size is one. The divide and conquer method is directly applied in 2DT-FP using the $\xrightarrow{s\&g}$ constructor.

---

[4] *pt* counts the number of operations executed on every column, e.g. *distl* takes m steps to distribute the local element of u in every column .

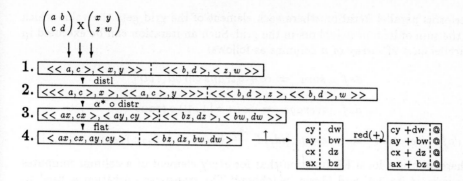

Fig. 3. Matrix multiplication stages

The input is given in a 2D-array with n columns, each containing one element, to which *pmax* is applied:

$$def \quad pmax \quad = \quad (eq \circ [\%\%, \bar{1}]) \xrightarrow{s\&g} \{id \parallel conquer; divide\}$$

$$def \quad conquer \quad = \quad (gt \longrightarrow [1]; [2]); \downarrow; T_{resize-2}; \uparrow$$

$$def \quad divide \quad = \quad (\leq \circ [\#, div \circ [\%\%, \bar{2}]]) \xrightarrow{s\&g} \{pmax \parallel pmax\}$$

The divide and conquer approach can also be used in non recursive manner which is more FP programming style: The **parallel prefix** *pp* of a $n \times n$ 2D-array is a common operation that returns the partial sums of an array. Let *ppl* denote the FP-function computing the local parallel prefix on columns:

$$def \quad ppfirst \quad = \quad eq \circ [\#, \bar{1}] \longrightarrow (rotr \circ ppl); id$$

$$def \quad padd \quad = \quad eq \circ [\#, \bar{1}] \xrightarrow{s\&g} \{id \parallel \downarrow; T_{resize2}; \uparrow; [\propto \bar{0}, id]\}$$

$$def \quad pp \quad = \quad ppl; \downarrow; T_{r2c}; \uparrow; ppfirst; \downarrow; T_{c2r}; \uparrow; padd \circ apndl \circ [/+, id]$$

The algorithm behind this program is rather simple:

1. compute the local sum at every column $S_i = \sum_{j=1}^{n} c_{i,j}$.
2. Compute the parallel prefix of the local sums $P_i = \sum_{j=1}^{i} S_j$.
3. add the sum of the sums of all previous columns to the first element of the current column $c_{i,1} = c_{i,1} + P_i$.
4. compute the parallel prefix at each column $c_{i,j} = \sum_{k=1}^{j} c_{i,k}$.

The above 2DT-FP program implements this algorithm, thus computing the pp of n^2 numbers in $pt = 7n + C$ where $C < 10$ and the time for transpose transformation is taken to be n. Note that *padd* demonstrates how to enlarge a 2D-array by one column, in fact arbitrary sizes can be achieved in this way.

Another common paradigm in parallel computations is the **finite grid elements method** used in numerical analyses to solve the Laplace equation . One performs parallel iteration where each element of the grid gets the value which is the sum of its four neighbors in the grid. Such an iteration can be executed in parallel on a 2D-array of n columns as follows:

$$def \quad sum \; = \; \alpha + \circ trans \circ [rotl, rotr]$$

$$def \quad average \; = \; \alpha \, (\div \circ [+, \bar{4}]) \circ trans$$

$$def \quad iteration \; = \; average; [id, id] \xrightarrow{c\&p} \{sum \times \downarrow; T_{r2c}; \uparrow; sum; \downarrow; T_{c2r}; \uparrow\}$$

where sum is a local FP-function that for every element of a column computes the sum of its 'up' and 'down' neighbors. The transpose operation is used to treat the 'right' and 'left' neighbors.

We conclude with a detailed program of **parallel quicksort** demonstrating the ability of 2DT-FP to reshape 2D-arrays. In this case the leader (and the elements with the same value) has to be glued left with the smaller elements and to be glued right with the bigger elements. Note that if the leader remains with one of the two 2D-arrays (of the smaller or bigger elements), then the recursion will not terminate since the leader will be re-elected at every iteration.

$$def \quad first \; = \; eq \circ [\#, \bar{1}] \longrightarrow [id, id]; [id, <>]$$

$$def \quad getleader \; = \; first \xrightarrow{c\&p} \{ id \times \downarrow; T_{broadcast}; \uparrow \}$$

$$def \quad divide1 \; = \; eq \circ [1, 2] \xrightarrow{s\&g} \{ 1 \parallel quicksort \circ 1 \}$$

$$def \quad divide \; = \; lt \circ [1, 2] \xrightarrow{s\&g} \{ quicksort \circ 1 \parallel divide1 \}$$

$$def \quad quicksort \; = \; gt \circ [\%\%, 1] \xrightarrow{s\&g} \{ divide; getleader \parallel id\}$$

6 Conclusion

A novel paradigm for efficient programming of multiprocessors network has been used to expand Backus FP to a parallel language. The 2DT-paradigm utilizes an implicit data type called the 2D-array, where separate computations performed on its columns are interpreted as processes. The program explicitly manipulates the elements of a single column, however implicitly this affects all columns of the same 2D-array. A set of transformations and constructors is used to reshape, split and join 2D-arrays. These operations realize the notion of spawning new processes and performing parallel recursion of computations.

In principle, the paradigm can be applied to other programming styles, such as imperative block structured languages (such as Fortran or C).

Currently we deal with implementation strategies of the language 2DT-FP. This includes useful exploitation of the different sources of parallelism (FP-, column- and 2D-array-parallelism), process management, communications pattern, simulation of processors. [BRSW93] contains first results.

7   Acknowledgments

We wish to thank Yoram Kornatzky and Gadi Aharoni for a review of subjects of FP. Special thanks are due to Itzik Nudler for his remarks in regarding other existing programming languages.

References

[AO91]   K. R. Apt and E. R. Olderog. *Verification of Sequential and Concurrent Programs.* Springer-Verlag, 1991.

[Bac78]   J. Backus. Can programming be liberated from the von Neumann style? A functional style and its algebra of programs. *Communication of the ACM*, 21(8):613–641, 1978.

[Bel92]   G. Bell. Ultracomputers: a teraflop before its time. *Communications of the ACM*, 35(8), 1992.

[BES92]   Y. Ben-Asher, D. Egozi, and A. Schuster. 2-D SIMD algorithms for perfect shuffle networks. *J. Parallel and Distributed Computing*, 16:250–257, 1992.

[BRSW92]   Y. Ben-Asher, G. Rünger, A. Schuster, and R. Wilhelm. 2DT-FP: An FP based programming language. Technical report, Universität des Saarlandes, SFB 124, 1992.

[BRSW93]   Y. Ben-Asher, G. Rünger, A. Schuster, and R. Wilhelm. Implementing 2DT-FP on a multiprocessor. 1993. submitted to ParCo93.

[BS90]   G.E. Blelloch and G.W. Sabot. Compiling collection-oriented languages onto massively parallel computers. *J. of Parallel and Distributed Computing*, 8(2):119–134, February 1990.

[BSW89]   Y. Ben-Asher, H. Seidl, and R. Wilhelm. The TRANSPOSE machine: A global implementation of a parallel graph reducer. In *Proc. of Tencon'89*, Bombay, 1989.

[Inm84]   Inmos Ltd. *Occam Programming Manual*, 1984.

[PCM83]   R.H. Perrott, D. Crookes, and P. Milligan. The programming language AC-TUS. *Software – Pract. & Exp.*, 13(4):305–322, April 1983.

[Per87]   R.H. Perrott. *Parallel programming.* Addison-Wesley, 1987. International Computer Science series.

[Plo81]   G. D. Plotkin. A structural approach to operational semantics. Technical Report DAIMI-FN 19, Department of Computer Science, Aarhus University, 1981.

[Ros87]   J.R. Rose. C*: a C++-like language for data parallel computation. *Usenix C++ Papers*, pages 127–134, December 1987.

[Uni83]   United States Department of Defense. *Reference Manual for the Ada Programming Language*, 1983.

The Data-Parallel Categorical Abstract Machine *

Gaétan Hains and Christian Foisy

Département d'Informatique et Recherche Opérationnelle, Université de Montréal,
Montréal, Québec, Canada, H3C 3J7,   email: {hains,foisy}@iro.umontreal.ca.

Abstract. Data-parallel ML is proposed for compilation to a distributed version (DPCAM) of Cousineau, Curien and Mauny's Categorical Abstract Machine. The DPCAM is a static network of CAMs which dynamically restrict the MIMD execution mode: nodes execute the same program and communicate only while executing the same function body. Programs violating this restriction or exhibiting unbounded spatial recursion abort or deadlock. The execution model thus defines a class of SPMD programs.

With respect to syntax and types, DPML is Mini-ML enriched with localization and remote evaluation functions. Its values are arrays of size matching the DPCAM network and containing ML values. Pointwise functions, data-parallel primitives and systolic algorithms are easily programmed. To improve the language's portability there is no automatic virtualization mechanism. Hence DPML is an intermediate target for more elaborate data-parallel languages, bridging the gap between direct source-language processor allocation and fully automatic allocation.

1   Introduction

This paper describes a data-parallel version (DPCAM) of the Categorical Abstract Machine of Cousineau, Curien and Mauny [9] with its programming language called data-parallel ML or DPML. The syntax of DPML is that of Mini-ML augmented with functions for localization: `local`, `first`, `last` and for remote evaluation: `get`. The Damas-Milner system is used for polymorphic type inference so that types convey no parallel information. Closed well-typed terms are compiled to DPCAM code which involves CAM instructions and operations for new communication structures. For the sake of portability, the DPCAM is a MIMD program with complete connectivity, but since programs are not *required* to use this flexibility, they may be optimized for an underlying topology.

Closed well-typed terms whose evaluation satisfies certain constraints are executed correctly, others deadlock or abort at run time. This constraint defines a class of SPMD programs by excluding full MIMD execution (unlimited asynchrony), process creation or nested parallelism. The abstract machine supports pointwise functions but also spatially recursive functions and pipelining for systolic algorithms.

---

* Work supported by FCAR and NSERC.

All DPML values are similar to POMPC's physical collections [16, 22]: global data structures whose size matches the abstract machine network. Virtualization mechanisms are thus excluded from the language's semantics, again for the sake of portability. A DPML term denotes both an array and its elements. This dual view microscopic/macroscopic was explained in [6]. Of course a useful data-parallel programming system should support virtualization and routing (e.g. CMLisp) so DPML is intended as intermediate target for more elaborate data-parallel languages, bridging the gap between direct processor allocation in the source language and fully automatic allocation. The DPCAM is portable and so are DPML programs which do not depend on the size of the network. However, programs which take advantage of a particular implementation by communicating along preferred channels may slowdown on other implementations.

We believe that complex compilers and interpreters can target DPML, and benefit from the safety of its type system and abstraction of ML programming. An advantage of data-parallel programming with ML should be the possibility of interactive program development, through an interpreter running on the parallel back-end computer.

2 Language Description

2.1 Syntax

The syntax (Table 1) is a simple extension of Mini-ML [8]. Readers unfamiliar with ML are referred to [18] for an introduction and to [21] for more details.

Specific to DPML are the *localization* constants: local, first, last of type integer. Their values are arrays of integers used to localize control. Assuming an $(n_2 - n_1 + 1)$-processor implementation of the DPCAM where processors are numbered n_1 to n_2, local evaluates to the integer $i \in \{n_1, \ldots, n_2\}$ on processor i. The value of first is n_1 and the value of last is n_2. The boolean constants first? and last? are syntactic sugar for local = first and local = last respectively.

Also specific to DPML is the remote evaluation operator get. The expression get (e', e) returns the value of e evaluated in the last *communication context* saved by processor i where i is the result of evaluating e' on the current processor. This notion will be made precise in Sec. 3.4. Together with the slogan *values are arrays* it determines the language's operational semantics.

For completeness DPML should have an imperative input procedure to load the network, but this has no effect on the rest of the language and will not be discussed here.

2.2 Types

The Damas-Milner type system [11] is used with minor extensions so types encode no parallelism-related information. In fact every object has an overloaded meaning microscopic/macroscopic as explained earlier. The type inference rules

Table 1. DPML syntax

$$P := (\ )\ |\ (P, P)\ |\ x$$

$$e := n\ |\ x\ |\ \text{true}\ |\ \text{false}\ |\ \text{fst}\ |\ \text{snd}\ |\ \text{and}\ |\ \text{or}\ |\ +\ |\ <\ |\ \cdots$$

$$|\ \text{get}\ |\ \text{local}\ |\ \text{first}\ |\ \text{last}\ |\ \text{first?}\ |\ \text{last?}$$

$$|\ e\ e\ |\ (e, e)\ |\ \text{fun}\ P\ \text{->}\ e\ |\ \text{let}\ P = e\ \text{in}\ e\ |\ \text{letrec}\ P = e\ \text{in}\ e$$

$$|\ \text{if}\ e\ \text{then}\ e\ \text{else}\ e$$

Syntactic categories: $n \in$ *Number*, $P \in$ *Pattern*, $x \in$ *Identifier*, $e \in$ *Expression*.

Table 2. DPML typing rules (partial list)

[INT]	$A \vdash n : \text{int}$	[LOCAL]	$A \vdash \text{local} : \text{int}$
[FIRST]	$A \vdash \text{first} : \text{int}$	[LAST]	$A \vdash \text{last} : \text{int}$
[,]	$\dfrac{A \vdash e : \tau \quad A \vdash e' : \tau'}{A \vdash (e, e') : \tau * \tau'}$	[GET]	$\dfrac{A \vdash e : \text{int} * \tau}{A \vdash \text{get}\,(e) : \tau}$

are taken from [8] with new axioms for the localization constants and a new rule for **get** (Table 2). Typing environments A are lists of assumptions $x : \sigma$ and τ, τ' are types. The **get** function is not curried because its compilation requires both of its arguments: the value of **get** alone is not defined. In other words, **get** is not a first-class function. This feature is in contrast with the first-class channels and communication events of MIMD functional languages like CML.

If left unrestricted, the interaction between polymorphism and communication would contradict the semantic soundness of ML types. A polymorphic communicating function could cause a type-related error at execution time. For example in what follows, polyscan is typed $(\alpha \to \alpha \to \alpha) \to \alpha \to \alpha$:

```
letrecpolyscan = fun f -> fun x ->
        if first? then x else (f get(local-1, polyscan f x) x)
in
        if first? then int-of-bool((polyscan or) true)
                    else polyscan add local
```

and this causes a dynamic error. The type variable α is instantiated to **bool** on some processors and to **int** on some others. Moreover, these processors communicate during their evaluation of **polyscan** and so exchange integers with booleans. To prevent this problem, the type inference phase of the compiler requires communicating functions to have a constant type. Future versions of the language should weaken this restriction.

2.3 Evaluation

The meaning of a DPML program can be defined without explicit reference to channels or communication events and is determined by its translation and execution on the stack machine, described in the next sections. The following remarks provide some insight into the operational semantics.

A pure ML program follows applicative order evaluation asynchronously on each node's local data. For example

```
letrec fac = fun n -> if n=1 then 1 else fac(n-1) * n in
fac (local - first + 1)
```

will evaluate faster on node i than node $i - 1$ of a homogeneous architecture. This aspect of the language extends SIMD execution to SPMD in the sense that it does not require global synchronization at each step. In fact, the DPCAM *must* be implemented on a MIMD architecture.

Values may be, like (`fun n -> 2 + n`) independent or, like `2 + local`, dependent on the node index. The value of $get(e, e')$ is node-independent if and only if either one of e, e' is.

The most important feature of expressions is their use of communications. The presence of conditional expressions makes it impossible to predict when evaluation will require communication:

$$\text{if} \langle \text{ any sequential program } \rangle \text{ then 2 else get(last, x)}.$$

However, since **get** is not a value, an expression which does not explicitly contain **get** will certainly not require communication.

For this reason, functions whose body contains **get** are called *communicating*. Communicating functions are detected and numbered by the compiler. This information will be passed to the DPCAM which will ensure that communicating nodes do so within the same communicating function. A linearly-recursive algorithm for the well-known scan operation can be programmed as:

```
letrec scan= fun x -> if first? then x else x*get(pred,scan x) (1)
```

where **pred** is syntactic sugar for `local - 1`. We may here explain why DPML's execution model is SPMD and not MIMD. A globally recursive function like (1) is executed semi-synchronously: all nodes evaluating its body push their local context on entry, lock some client or server state (defined later) while waiting for a remote evaluation, unlock it upon reception of the remote value, and pop the local context when leaving the function body.

Having defined **scan** as above, one might be tempted to compute the global product reduction **red** by:

```
letrec scan = ... in let red = fun x -> get(last, scan x)
```

but this would trigger n evaluations of **scan** in parallel, if it were not caught by the DPCAM as a case of nested communicating functions. The intended operational meaning should be instead: first evaluate one parallel scan and then broadcast its last element. This can be done by the following

```
letrec scan = fun x -> ... in
    let red = fun x ->
        (let scanres = scan x in get(last,scanres) )
```

Because of its linear communication structure, **scan** does not exploit any parallelism, except the possible overlapping with subsequent communicating functions.

As a parallel example we can write a segmented scan program **segscan** with static segment size. Here the localized result is the composition of two functions. The first one, **inscan** returns the product of the local segment's prefix ending locally. The second, **outscan** multiplies by the value found at the end of the previous segment, where there is one.

```
let k = ⟨ segment length ⟩  in let i = local - first
in letrec inscan = fun x ->
 (if (i mod k)=0 then x else x * get(pred, inscan x) )
in letrec outscan = fun x ->
 (if (i div k)=0 then 1 else get(i-(i mod k)-1, outscsan x) )
in let segscan = fun x ->
 let temp = inscan x in outscan temp
```

Thus programmed, the computation of prefix requires its binary scalar operation to be associative. This property being assumed, there is no reason not to seek further parallelism by nesting segments. In [14] we presented a functional notation called MOA for specifying such algorithms through array shape lists, implicitly communicating combinators and recursion on the shape lists. This notation should be directly compilable to DPML.

Our last example is taken from Quinton and Robert's book on systolic algorithms [23]. Let A and B be strings of length n and $L(i,j)$ the length of a longest substring (subsequence) common to $A[1..i]$ and $B[1..j]$. L is defined recursively by:

$$L(i,j) = \max \begin{cases} L(i-1,j) \\ L(i,j-1) \\ L(i-1,j-1) + [A(i) = B(j)] \end{cases}$$

The systolic algorithm is more or less directly programmed in DPML. A block version of the program is readily obtained from the one below, so for the sake of clarity we will assume a network of size n^2, **first** = 0 and **last** = $n^2 - 1$.

```
let n =  ⟨ square root of ⟩ last+1
in let row = fst in let col = snd in
let gamma = fun i ->  (n * (i div n), i mod n)
in let gammai = fun c ->   n * (row c) + (col c)
```

```
in let l-row = row (gamma local) in let l-col = col (gamma local)
in let north = gammai(lrow-1, lcol)
in let west = gammai(lrow, lcol-1)
in let corner = gammai(lrow-1, lcol-1)
in let is-north = (lrow = 0) in let is-west = (lcol = 0)
in let is-corner = is-north and is-west

in letrec L = fun dummy ->
    max3  (if is-north then 0
           else get(north, get(local, L 0)) )
          (if is-west then 0
           else get(west, get(local, L 0)) )
          (if (is-north or is-west) then 0
           else get(corner, get(local, L 0)) + intofbool(A=B)
```

For simplicity here *A* is assumed to be duplicated along each "row" and *B* along each "column". Also, the dummy argument to *L* carries no meaning. The most interesting dynamic property of the DPCAM (an improved version, not the "naive" one described below) is highlighted by this program's execution. The otherwise useless expression **get local** triggers sharing in the machine. Called through **get west, get north** and **get corner**, it is not evaluated as 3 distinct expressions, but as parts of the same communicating function L. The target node automatically reuses the value of L, thus preventing a combinatorial explosion of messages.

To manage placement, the **gamma** and **gammai** functions are used to convert between DPML's linear addresses and the two-dimensional addresses in *L*. Such code could be generated from MOA specifications, to abstract from the network topology.

3 The DPCAM

The DPCAM is a distributed abstract machine which evaluates a closed DPML expression by *localizing* it on each node of its network. Its structure is a fully-connected MIMD program of $2n$ processes. Half of them are sequential stack machines *clients* while the other half are processes called *servers* time-sharing n sequential machines each. There is also a controller process connected to all clients. There are in all n nodes, each one made of a client and a server.

3.1 Origins of the DPCAM

The Categorical Abstract Machine [9] is a sequential environment stack machine which has been used to compile CAML [18]. Its design originates in the work of Curien on categorical combinatory logic (CCL). The so-called static operators of CCL were found equivalent to very basic machine instructions (categorical combinators). Those instructions are considered as code acting on values. Their execution always returns a term in normal form with respect to the weak (dynamic) rules of CCL. A more detailed discussion is beyond the scope of this article and the interested reader is referred to [10].

The original CAM has the following state: a *term*, which is a structured value (a binary tree), a *code* (a categorical term which denotes a list of instructions), and a *stack* of environment terms. The configuration of a CAM is thus described by a triple (T, C, S). The article [9] describes all instructions as a transition table, complete with conditional and recursion.

The new machine only involves extensions to the original CAM: each node runs a full functional engine. To fully explain the structure of the DPCAM we must describe the synchronization mechanism which underlies its design.

3.2 Synchronization constraint

At the highest level, the DPCAM is the parallel composition of $n_2 - n_1 + 1$ CAMs running asynchronously. We can thus view the state of the whole machine as the union of n states, each state being indexed by the node index. If local is the next instruction in the code, the following CAM transition occurs on node j: $(T, \mathtt{local} :: C, S)_j \Rightarrow (j, C, S)_j$. first and last are treated just like ordinary constants. As expected, the state index has no effect on the original CAM instruction set.

The only instruction requiring synchronization between CAMs is get. Its operational semantics is defined through a corresponding DPCAM instruction, also called get, which takes as argument a code list. The distinction between the two instructions should be clear from the context. Let C be the compilation function as described in table 4. The meaning of $\mathtt{get}(e_1, e_2)$ is: evaluate e_1 in the current environment, and if the result i is a valid CAM address then evaluate e_2 in the environment (term) T_i. In terms of state transition:

$$(T, C(e_1) :: \mathtt{get}(C(e_2); \mathtt{reply}) :: C, S) \Rightarrow (i, \mathtt{get}(C(e_2); \mathtt{reply}) :: C, S) \qquad (2)$$

$C(e_2)$ is a list of CAM instructions plus our extensions: local, first, last, and get. Variable names in compiled expressions are replaced by their access code in the environment, a sequence of fst and snd instructions. This idea was already present in de Bruijn's abstract notation for λ-calculus. This is why during the compilation process a "dummy" environment is needed to keep track of variable occurrences.

Both sub-expressions e_1 and e_2 in $\mathtt{get}(e_1, e_2)$ are compiled with the same dummy environment P. This means that term T in equation 2 above has exactly the same shape as P. The evaluation of e_2 on remote CAM i thus needs an environment of the same shape P, otherwise e_2 would have no meaning. Table 4 reveals that there are only three constructions adding information into the environment, namely fun, let, and letrec. The compilation is then very simple: for every get in the program, identify the nearest enclosing fun, let, or letrec and parenthesize the sub-expression containing **get** with two new instructions: `pushct(i)` and `popct`.

3.3 Implementation

Client transitions Each client CAM (cCAM) has a dedicated server. $get(e_1,e_2)$ for a client CAM is just a value. Every time a cCAM executes a low-level **get**, it sends a request to the designated server which will process it with the help of other servers if necessary. The execution of `pushct(i)` by a cCAM has a threefold impact: 1) send to controller process the identification number i of the communicating function whose body follows in the code 2) upon reception of an acknowledge from the controller, send the current term (environment) to the local server 3) put the local mode register in *communication mode* (**comm(i)**). The execution of **popct** just resets the cCAM mode to *sequential mode* (**seq**). The mode register also prevents communicating function nesting: if the cCAM is in mode **comm(i)** and the next instruction is `pushct(j)` with $i \neq j$, then execution aborts (nesting error).

The state of a client CAM is given by a 5-tuple (m, cp, T, C, S) where m is either **seq** or **comm(i)**, cp is a port where responses from controller and servers will be sent (no queuing necessary). The remaining triple is a CAM state.

Controller transitions The acknowledge from the controller is broadcast to all cCAMs at the following condition: all cCAMs agree on the comm function number. If not, execution aborts (unbounded asynchrony error).

Server transitions Each server consists of a heap of $n_2 - n_1 + 1$ CAMs (heap CAM or hCAM), a mechanism to time-share those CAMs, and a queue for messages from clients and other server. Each remote cCAM is given a dedicated hCAM in every server. Each get request will be tagged with the cCAM address which initiated the chain of requests. Each time a server receives a new request associated with cCAM j, the dedicated hCAM j is initialized with the term (comm term) received from local client, the code of the request [2] and an empty stack. The execution of **reply**, inserted at compilation, by a hCAM sends the current term (answer) to the originator of the request.

The server queue contains two types of messages: new requests in transit from remote nodes to local hCAMs, and answers in transit from local hCAMs to remote nodes. Communication terms are received from the local client through a special port.

The server state is given by a a register with binary status (**busy** or **ready**), a port sp where the local cCAM will send the comm term, and the union of the states of all hCAMs. The **busy** status indicates that a unique hCAM is currently evaluating a request. The **ready** status indicates that either no request

---

[2] Just a pointer in a real implementation since each cCAM and server has a copy of the unique program.

was received or that all unfinished hCAMs are blocked because they are waiting for an answer. The state of a hCAM is given by (m, f, T, C, S) where m is the mode and f is a pair (i, j) where i is the address of the cCAM at the origin of the request chain, and j the address of the previous cCAM or hCAM in the chain. Table 3 summarizes both client and server transitions.

Table 3. Transition tables

Client transitions

client state $= (mode, port(cp), Term, Code, Stack)$

$\xrightarrow{[m]\|pq}$ means message m is sent to port or queue pq

$(seq, \emptyset, T, \text{pushct}(i) :: C, S)_j \xrightarrow{[i]\|contp} (sync(i), \emptyset, T, C, S)_j$

$(sync(i), [ok], T, C, S)_j \xrightarrow{[T]\|sp_j} (comm(i, 1), \emptyset, T, C, S)_j$

$(comm(i, k), \emptyset, \text{pushct}(i) :: C, S)_j \longrightarrow (comm(i, k+1), \emptyset, T, C, S)_j$

$(comm(i, k), \emptyset, T, \text{pushct}(1) :: C, S)_j \longrightarrow HALT$ (illegal nesting) $(i \neq l)$

$(comm(i, k), \emptyset, T, \text{popct} :: C, S)_j \longrightarrow (comm(i, k-1), \emptyset, T, C, S)_j$ $(k > 1)$

$(comm(i, 1), \emptyset, T, \text{popct} :: C, S)_j \longrightarrow (seq, \emptyset, T, C, S)_j$

$(comm(i, k), \emptyset, m, \text{get}(C1) :: C, S)_j \xrightarrow{[req(C1,j,Cj)]\|sq_m} (get(i, k), \emptyset, \bot, C, S)_j$

$(get(i, k), [rep(T)], \bot, C, S)_j \longrightarrow (comm(i, j), \emptyset, T, C, S)_j$

plus transitions of the original CAM when mode is seq or $comm$

Server transitions

server state $= (mode, port(sp), queue(sq))_l; (heap\ CAM\ state)_m$

heap CAM state $= (mode, from, Term, Code, Stack)$

$(ready, [CT], [req(C1, j, k)] :: sq)_l; (free, \bot, \bot, \bot, \bot)_j \longrightarrow$
$\quad (busy, [CT], sq)_l; (comm(i, 1), k, CT, C, [])_j$

$(ready, [CT], [rep(T, j)] :: sq)_l; (get(i, j), k, \bot, C, S)_j \longrightarrow$
$\quad (busy, [CT], sq)_l; (comm(i, j), k, T, C, S)_j$

$(busy, [CT], sq)_l; (comm(i, j), k, m, \text{get}(C1) :: C, S)_j \xrightarrow{[req(C1,j,Sl)]\|sq_m}$
$\quad (ready, [CT], sq)_l; (get(i, j), k, \bot, C, S)_j$

$(busy, [CT], sq)_l; (comm(i, j), ck, T, \text{reply}, [])_j \xrightarrow{[rep(T)]\|cp_j}$
$\quad (ready, [CT], sq)_l; (free, \bot, \bot, \bot, \bot)_j$

$(busy, [CT], sq)_l; (comm(i, j), sk, T, \text{reply}, [])_j \xrightarrow{[rep(T,j)]\|sp_k}$
$\quad (ready, [CT], sq)_l; (free, \bot, \bot, \bot, \bot)_j$

3.4 Compilation

Closed well-typed terms are compiled to DPCAM code. The compiler proceeds in two phases. The first phase identifies and numbers communicating functions. If the program passes successfully this first phase (without illegal nesting), the second phase generates DPCAM code involving **pushct** or **popct** to save and restore communication contexts. The compilation equations are given in Table 4 where $e_1?e_2$ evaluates to e_1 if this value is defined and to e_2 otherwise.

4 Related Work

Tail-recursive pointwise functions used in a communicating DPML program which terminates correctly for all its inputs, constitute a *contained program* in

Table 4. Translation from DPML to DPCAM code

$$[\![x]\!]_x = \mathtt{id} \qquad [\![x]\!]_{(p,x)} = \mathtt{snd} \qquad [\![x]\!]_{(x,p)} = \mathtt{fst}$$

$$[\![x]\!]_{(p_1,p_2)} = (\mathtt{snd};[\![x]\!]_{p_2})?(\mathtt{fst};[\![x]\!]_{p_1})$$

$$[\![(MN)]\!]_P = \mathtt{push};[\![M]\!]_P;\mathtt{swap};[\![N]\!]_P;\mathtt{cons};\mathtt{app}$$

$$[\![(M,N)]\!]_P = \mathtt{push};[\![M]\!]_P;\mathtt{swap};[\![N]\!]_P;\mathtt{cons}$$

$$[\![\mathtt{fun}\ p\ \mathtt{->}\ M]\!]_P = \mathtt{cur}(\mathtt{beg};[\![M]\!]_{(P,p)};\mathtt{end})$$

$$[\![\mathtt{if}\ e_1\ \mathtt{then}\ e_2\ \mathtt{else}\ e_3]\!]_P = \mathtt{push}[\![e_1]\!]_P;\mathtt{branch}([\![e_2]\!]_P,[\![e_3]\!]_P)$$

$$[\![\mathtt{let}\ p = e_1\ \mathtt{in}\ e_2]\!]_P = \mathtt{push};[\![e_1]\!]_P;\mathtt{cons};\mathtt{beg};[\![e_2]\!]_{(P,p)};\mathtt{end}$$

$$[\![\mathtt{let}\ \mathtt{rec}\ p = e_1\ \mathtt{in}\ e_2]\!]_P =$$
$$\mathtt{push};\mathtt{push};\mathtt{quote}();\mathtt{cons};\mathtt{push};[\![e_1]\!]_{(P,p)};\ \mathtt{twind};\mathtt{cons};\mathtt{beg};[\![e_2]\!]_{(P,p)};\mathtt{end}$$

$$[\![\mathtt{local}]\!]_P = \mathtt{local} \qquad [\![\mathtt{first}]\!]_P = \mathtt{first} \qquad [\![\mathtt{last}]\!]_P = \mathtt{last}$$

$$[\![\mathtt{get}(e_1,e_2)]\!]_P = [\![e_1]\!]_P;\mathtt{get}([\![e_2]\!]_P;\mathtt{reply})$$

the sense of Blelloch (Sec. 10.6.2 in [5]).

Known optimizations for compiling CAML to CAM can be reused for point-wise functions, so the work of Mauny and Suárez [19] is directly applicable.

The DP-CAM was described as a static MIMD program but it could also be implemented on a dataflow architecture (for example [1]) with bounded dynamic server creation.

MIMD functional languages like Concurrent ML (CML) [24] and FACILE [12] have unbounded asynchrony which is prevented by the DPCAM. For similar reasons Parallel SML [15] is not data-parallel. Para-ML [3] is related to CML by its explicit use of channels. However Para-ML is implemented for a massively parallel architecture and it is not clear how DPML compares with it.

The Planar Abstract Machine of [17] is strictly SIMD so it has no spatial recursion. A language of this type must have a fixed set of predefined functions for data-movement (map, reduce, scan etc.). An advantage of DPML is to remove this restriction while retaining bounded asynchrony. See also the parallel version of FP by Walinsky and Banerjee [26]. VCode [4] has complex instructions relative to the DPCAM. It's handling of parallelism through *segmented* instructions is different from ours.

Languages like $8\frac{1}{2}$ [13], Alpha [20] and Crystal [7] place restrictions on programs for statically-verified synchrony. For example Crystal prohibits second-order domain functions. This is similar to our non-nested monomorphic communicating functions.

The best-known language resembling DPML is perhaps CM-Lisp [25]. Types are a major but unessential difference. Dynamic scoping of variables forces run-time environment creation, causing unbounded asynchrony in the presence of nested xappings.

To our knowledge P-TAC [2] is closest to DPML. Its operational semantics is used to prove confluence and optimizations. In P-TAC, I-structures are used for sharing intermediate results. DPCAM states allow proofs of dynamic properties and optimizations. In DPML structure sharing is possible through **let**. Access to a node index for task allocation is a potential advantage.

Ongoing Work

Four successive refinements of the DPCAM described above have been designed, to account for successive optimizations related to sharing and pipelining. A first DPCAM has been written in Caml-light, tested on a network of Sun stations and will be ported to a Fujitsu AP-1000. The DPML $\rightarrow$ DPCAM compiler is being prototyped in Centaure. Future research should deal with denotational semantics, compiler writing in DPML, and compiler optimizations.

Acknowledgements

Luc Bougé and Jean-Luc Levaire for introducing us to POMPC and Centaure. INRIA's groupe Formel for providing us CAM programs. Gilles Kahn for suggestions concerning the use of Centaure. Alain Tapp for correcting one of the program examples.

References

1. M. AMAMIYA AND R. TANIGUCHI, *Datarol: A massively parallel architecture for functional languages*, in 2nd IEEE Symposium on Parallel and Distributed Processing, Dallas, Texas, Dec. 1990, IEEE Computer Society.

2. Z. ARIOLA AND ARVIND, *P-TAC: A parallel intermediate language*, in FPCA Functional Programming Languages and Computer Architecture, ACM Press, 1989, pp. 230–242.

3. P. BAILEY AND M. NEWEY, *Implementing ML on distributed memory multiprocessors*, in Boulder Workshop on Languages, Compilers and Run Time Environments for Distributed Memory Multiprocessors, Boulder, CO, October 1992, ACM. Appears in SIGPLAN Newsletter.

4. G. BLELLOCH AND S. CHATTERJEE, *VCODE: a data-parallel intermediate language*, in Third IEEE Symposium on the Frontiers of Massively Parallel Computation, J. JaJa, ed., 1990.

5. G. E. BLELLOCH, *Vector Models for Data-Parallel Computing*, MIT Press, 1990.

6. L. BOUGÉ, *On the semantics of languages for massively parallel SIMD architectures*, in PARLE-91, E. H. L. Aarts and J. van Leeuwen, eds., no. 505 and 506 in Lecture Notes in Computer Science, Eindhoven, The Netherlands, June 1991, Springer.

7. M. CHEN, *Transformations of parallel programs in Crystal*, Tech. Rep. YALEU/DCS/RR-469, Yale University, April 1986.

8. D. CLÉMENT, J. DESPEYROUX, T. DESPEYROUX, AND G. KAHN, *A simple applicative language: Mini-ML*, Rapport Technique 529, INRIA, Institut National de Recherche en Informatique et Automatique, 1991.

9. G. COUSINEAU, P.-L. CURIEN, AND M. MAUNY, *The categorical abstract machine*, in Functional Programming Languages and Computer Architectures, J.-P. Jouannaud, ed., no. 201 in Lecture Notes in Computer Science, Springer, 1985.

10. P.-L. CURIEN, *Categorical Combinators, Sequential Algorithms and Functional Programming*, Research Notes in Theoretical Computer Science, Pitman, 1986.

11. DAMAS AND MILNER, *Principal type-schemes for functional programs*, in Principles of Programming Languages. Annual ACM SIGACT–SIGPLAN Symposium, Association for Computing Machinery, New York, NY, 1982, pp. 207–212.

12. A. GIACALONE, P. MISHRA, AND S. PRASAD, *Facile: a symmetric integration of concurrent and functional programming*, International Journal of Parallel Programming, 18 (1989), pp. 121–160.

13. J.-L. GIAVITTO, *Un langage data-flow synchrone pour la simulation massivement parallèle*, in Secondes Journées Francophones des Langages Applicatifs, JFLA-92, C. Queinnec, ed., Tréguier, France, Février 1992, pp. 40–62. Revue Bigre no. 76-77.

14. G. HAINS AND L. M. R. MULLIN, *Parallel functional programming with arrays*, The Computer Journal, (1993).

15. K. HAMMOND, *Parallel SML: A Functional Language and its Implementation in Dactl*, Pitman– MIT Press, 1991.

16. P. HOOGVORST, R. KERYELL, P. MATHERAT, AND N. PARIS, *POMP or how to design a massively parallel machine with small developments*, in PARLE-91, E. H. L. Aarts, J. van Leeuwen, and M. Rem, eds., no. 505 in LNCS, Springer, 1991, pp. 83–100.

17. G. K. JOURET, *Compiling functional languages for SIMD architectures*, in Workshop on Abstract Machine Models for Highly Parallel Computers, P. M. Dew, T. Lake, and J. Davy, eds., University of Leeds, March 1991, British Computer Society. Two volumes.

18. M. MAUNY, *Functional programming using CAML*, Rapport Technique 129, INRIA, Institut National de Recherche en Informatique et Automatique, 1991.

19. M. MAUNY AND A. SUÁREZ, *Implementing functional languages in the categorical abstract machine*, in Conference on Lisp and Functional Programming, ACM, 1986.

20. C. MAURAS, P. GACHET, P. QUINTON, AND Y. SAOUTER, *ALPHA du CENTAUR: an environment for the design of regular algorithms*, tech. rep., IRISA - Rennes France, 1988.

21. R. MILNER AND M. TOFTE, *Commentary on Standard ML*, MIT Press, 1991.

22. N. PARIS, *Definition of POMPC (version 1.99)*, Publication 92-5-bis, Laboratoire d'Informatique de l'École Normale Supérieure, Paris, March 1991.

23. P. QUINTON AND Y. ROBERT, *Algorithmes et architectures systoliques*, Masson, 1989.

24. J. H. REPPY, *CML: A higher-order concurrent language*, in SIGPLAN'91 Conference on Programming Language Design and Implementation, ACM, June 1991.

25. G. STEELE AND W. HILLIS, *Connection Machine Lisp : A Fine Grained Parallel Symbolic Processing*, in ACM Conf. on Lisp and Funct. Progr., Cambridge MA, 1986, pp. 276–297.

26. C. WALINSKY AND D. BANERJEE, *A functional programming language compiler for massively parallel computers*, in Conference on Lisp and Functional Programming, Nice, France, June 1990, ACM.

Data Parallel Implementation of Extensible Sparse Functional Arrays

John T. O'Donnell

University of Glasgow, Glasgow G12 8QQ, U.K.

Abstract. Three important generalised array structures — extensible arrays, sparse arrays and functional arrays — are slow to access unless their use is severely restricted. All three can be combined in a powerful new active data structure called 'ESF arrays'. ESF arrays may grow or shrink dynamically, they can be searched quickly, and changes to them can be rolled back in a single operation. A new data parallel algorithm implements every operation on an ESF array in a small constant time, without placing any restrictions on the use of those operations. The algorithm is suitable both for massively parallel architectures and for VLSI implementation.

1. Introduction

Massively parallel architectures make possible active data structures that are infeasible to implement on conventional sequential machines. This paper applies massive parallelism to the design of active array data structures, and makes two original contributions:

1. The definition of a new data structure, the *ESF array*, combining the characteristics of three distinct data structures: extensible arrays, sparse arrays and functional arrays.

2. A fast data parallel implementation of ESF array operations. The algorithm is suitable both for massively parallel architectures and for custom VLSI implementation. The VLSI implementation is essentially an associative memory with an enhanced address decoder tree.

This algorithm is particularly significant because it performs ESF array operations *faster than possible* on a von Neumann machine, yet its VLSI complexity (both area and propagation delay) is *identical* to the complexity of a von Neumann machine.

2. Background

A crucial property of array operations is *constant time and space access*: the time and space to access or update an arbitrary element does not depend on the size of the array or the value of the index.

Many generalisations of arrays have been proposed to support the needs of diverse algorithms. Some are straightforward, such as multidimensional arrays and arrays of records. Here we are concerned with three important generalisations that are impossible to implement (on the von Neumann architecture) without losing the property of constant time and space access.

Extensible arrays. An extensible array does not have a fixed size; it can grow or shrink dynamically as a program runs. There is a function that returns the existing lower and upper bounds of an array, as well as an operation that changes the existing bounds, making the array larger or smaller. Extensible arrays are useful for algorithms that create or destroy information dynamically, including some database and graph algorithms.

It is very costly to implement such a dynamic data structure. If the extension is implemented by allocating a new (larger) block of memory and copying the array contents into it, then the extended array can still be accessed in constant time — but the extension itself is very slow. The extension can be performed in constant time by building a node with pointers to the previous array and the block of new elements, but then accesses become slower. During the 1960s Rosenberg developed more sophisticated algorithms that reduce the total cost of extensible arrays, although individual operations are still slowed down by the extensions.

Sparse arrays. In some applications, most of the elements of an array have a default value (typically 0). A sparse array saves space by representing only those elements with interesting, or non-default, values. More importantly, a sparse array provides a function $forward(i)$ that gives the index of the next interesting value beyond i, skipping over all the intervening default values. This makes traversal faster. For example, iterating from the lower to upper bound

> **for** $i := lb$ **to** ub **do**
>   **if** $a[i] \neq default$ **then** $Process\ (i)$;

requires $ub-lb+1$ iterations, but processing only the interesting elements of a sparse array requires fewer iterations:

> $i := lb$;
> **while** $i \leq ub$ **do**
>   **begin** $Process\ (i)$; $\ i := forward\ (i)$; **end**

Sparse arrays are usually represented with linked lists, where each node contains a non-default value and a pointer to the next one. This enables algorithms to traverse the interesting values quickly, but random access becomes slow.

An ideal implementation would perform all accesses — random as well as default-skipping ones — in constant time. Furthermore, its performance would not change anywhere along the continuum from fully dense arrays to fully sparse arrays. No such implementation is known for von Neumann architectures.

Dijkstra proposed *array variables* [1], combining some of the features of extensible arrays and sparse arrays. These are useful abstractions for deriving algorithms, but they are too inefficient for use in real programs.

Functional arrays. A functional array is immutable: it can be read, but never changed. Since no side-effecting operations are allowed, all accesses to such an array are performed by pure functions.

The application *lookup a i* gives the value of $a[i]$. Instead of modifying an old array, we must construct a new one by updating the old array with an index and new value. Thus *update a i x* constructs a new array identical to a, except that *lookup (update a i x) i = x*. The old array a is unaffected. Programs using functional arrays are constantly creating new arrays and discarding old ones.

Functional array updates are especially difficult to implement efficiently. In fact, nearly all past research on them has focused on methods for avoiding their use, rather than methods for making them fast!

The difficulty can be seen by considering two naïve implementations of *update*. The first idea is simply to copy the old array into a new block of memory which can then be updated destructively. This makes *lookup* fast, but *update* is prohibitively slow and wasteful of memory. The second idea, at the other extreme, is to record the updated value along with a pointer to the old array. This makes *update* fast but *lookup* becomes prohibitively slow. Various more sophisticated algorithms exist which amortise the costs between *lookup* and *update*, making both of them prohibitively slow.

The relationship between functional arrays and functional programming is surprisingly subtle. Since functional arrays are immutable, they satisfy referential transparency and equational reasoning, two of the cornerstones of functional languages. Nevertheless, functional arrays can be added just as easily to imperative languages. On the other hand, ordinary mutable arrays can be added to functional languages, as long as programs are restricted to single-threaded array access. This can be done using program analysis [2], structured access control [4] and expressive type systems [5]. Functional arrays are important because some algorithms require the facilities they provide — sharing, rollback and controlled access to alternative updates — not because of an illusory connection with functional languages.

3. ESF array operations

The last section described three important general array structures. It is conjectured to be impossible to implement any of them on a von Neumann architecture without paying a penalty, either in poor performance or in restricted access. *Extensible sparse functional (ESF) arrays* combine all three generalisations into a new data structure which is even more flexible but more difficult to implement.

The elements of an ESF array are assumed to have type *Value*. The array indices have type *Index* and an array itself has type *Array*. Some operations return a pair of indices with type *IndexPair*. The basic ESF array operations are described below, with the following naming conventions: a, a' : *Array*, i : *Index*, x : *Value*, and ip : *IndexPair*.

- *empty* : *Array* is a predefined constant array with the property that *lookup* (*empty*, i) is undefined for any index i.

- $a' := update\ (a, i, x)$ returns a new array a' exactly like a except that *lookup* $(a', i) = x$. The old array a still exists and is completely unaffected.

- $x := lookup\ (a, i)$ returns the value of array a indexed at i, like $a[i]$ in Pascal.

- $a' := remove\ (a, i)$ is similar to update. The result a' is exactly like a except that *lookup* $(a', i) = Undefined$, although a may be defined at index i. The old array a is unchanged.

- $ip := bounds\ (a)$ returns a structure ip containing the lower bound and the upper bound of a (i.e. the smallest/largest index at which a is defined).

- *forward* (a, i) returns the smallest index $j > i$ (if it exists) such that *lookup* (a, j) is defined. This is the index of the next interesting value in a starting from i.

- *backward* (a, i) returns the largest index $j < i$ (if it exists) such that *lookup* (a, j) is defined. This is the index of the previous interesting value in a starting from i.

- *size* (a) gives the number of defined (non-default) elements in a.

- *extent* (a) is the difference between the highest and lowest index of any defined value in a.

The data structure defined by these operations is purely functional since no operation modifies an existing object. The functions can only create new data structures or dispose of inaccessible ones. There is no restriction on the index used in an *update*, as with ordinary arrays, so ESF arrays are arbitrarily extensible. The *forward* and *backward* functions provide fast searching for non-default values in an array, supporting sparse arrays.

Besides the existing algorithms relying on the three generalised arrays, ESF arrays support several demanding new applications, and more are likely to be discovered.

Lambda calculus reduction illustrates the flexibility of ESF arrays. With ordinary data structures, there is no known way to implement the environment in a lambda calculus reducer so that both application and binding lookup take constant time. However, it is easy to do that with ESF arrays: each environment is represented by an array and each lambda variable is treated as an index. Thus $\rho' = \rho[E/x]$ becomes $p' = update\ (p, x, E)$ and $\rho\ x$ becomes $lookup\ (p, x)$. The ESF array algorithm ensures that application and binding lookup always take constant time, regardless of the amount of sharing present in the environment. This may lead to further complexity results for the lambda calculus.

There has been increasing activity in data parallel algorithms for time-critical database operations. ESF arrays appear ideal for databases, and they can probably be extended to supply powerful associative searching techniques. Further research is needed to assess the utility of this application.

Most algorithms using dynamic data structures with heap allocation are unsuitable for real time applications, since a garbage collection could occur at any time. Every ESF array operation takes constant time, and an update will never trigger a long garbage collection. An update will never fail unless memory is completely full of accessible data, and in that case update will signal a 'memory full' error in constant time. So a significant application of ESF arrays may be real time algorithms on dynamic data structures.

4. The key ideas

Before presenting the actual algorithms for ESF array operations, this section presents a sequence of key ideas required to understand the algorithm. The following section presents an example showing how these ideas work in practice.

Ordinary array representations use the memory address to associate an array element with its index. That won't work here because it interferes with sparse representations and sharing. Therefore we introduce an explicit representation of the association between indices and values, which are called *bindings*. The memory is organised into a sequence of *cells*, where each cell contains an `Index`, `Value`, and a flag `Full` indicating whether that cell contains an array element.

The primary difficulty with functional arrays is the massive sharing they produce. Suppose that `a' := update (a,i,x)` and `a` contains n elements.

- If `lookup (a,i)` is defined then `a'` will also contain n elements: (the $n-1$ elements of a at indexes other than `i`, and the `(i,x)` pair).

- If `lookup (a,i)` is not defined then `a'` will contain $n+1$ elements: all n elements from a plus the `(i,x)` pair.

The heart of ESF arrays is a mechanism for exploiting all the sharing without slowing down access to elements of any array.

The next step requires a significant change of perspective. Ordinary arrays use the address of an element to determine which array that element belongs to; in effect an array 'knows' what its elements are. ESF arrays turn that around. An object of type `Array` is nothing more than the *name* of an array; its only significant property is that two distinct arrays have distinct names. An array doesn't know what its elements are. Instead, each full cell contains the name of every array that contains the element stored in the cell; this is called the element's *inclusion set*. For example,

Operation	Index	Value	Inclusion set
$a_1 := update\ (empty, 1, 3.14)$	1	3.14	$\{a_1\}$
$a_2 := update\ (a_1, 2, 2.718)$	2	2.718	$\{a_2, a_1\}$
$a_3 := update\ (a_1, 3, 42.0)$	3	42.0	$\{a_3, a_1\}$

There is no bound on the size of an inclusion set, yet we must find a way to represent an arbitrary inclusion set in constant space — one cell. Furthermore, we must be able to evaluate $a \in S$ in constant time for arbitrary array a and inclusion set S. It is impossible to represent arbitrary sets in constant space, but inclusion sets are not arbitrary. They can only be generated by sequences of updates, and that forces inclusion sets to have certain structural properties which the algorithm can exploit.

So the key to ESF arrays is the efficient manipulation of inclusion sets. We start by introducing an array code for every array name. The reason is that array names must remain constant, but the codes will need to change frequently.

For every array name a:*Array* there is a corresponding code c:*Code* which is represented as a natural number. The function *encode* (a : *Array*) : *Code* returns the current code belonging to a. This is required to be a one to one correspondence, so we can refer to an individual array unambiguously using either its name or its code. The empty array always has code 0, so *encode* (*empty*) = 0.

An inclusion set S is represented by a pair (*lo*,*hi*) such that for any array a, $a \in S$ iff $lo \leq encode \ a \leq hi$. This is good because (1) S is represented in constant space (two binary numbers) and (2) the $a \in S$ predicate is implemented in constant time by two comparisons of binary numbers.

The compact representation of inclusion sets works because, after *any* sequence of updates, there exists a mapping from arrays to codes such that every inclusion set can be represented as above. However, whenever an update is performed it is necessary to adjust the mapping from arrays to codes and the inclusion sets of existing elements. This requires a small constant amount of arithmetic for every cell.

5. An extended example

The best way to get a feel for the ESF algorithm is by watching how the memory state changes as a sequence of updates is performed. This section gives an example showing how the inclusion sets change, and the next section gives the central parts of the algorithm.

Each step in the following example is illustrated with a picture showing (on the left) the history of updates so far; (in the middle) the dependency tree resulting from that history; (on the right) the array name/code mapping resulting from the history.

The example follows some notational conventions. The actual index/value bindings are irrelevant, so they are simply identified as b_i. A cell is pictured as a box containing a binding and an inclusion set represented by *lo–hi*, and annotated on the lower left corner with the name of the array whose update created that binding. The dependency relations among the cells are illustrated by drawing an explicit tree structure. It is important to understand, however, that there is no explicit tree structure in the machine; the only information actually present consists of the cell contents and the name/code mapping.

The following convention is used for array codes: newly created codes are in *italics*, old codes that were modified are in **boldface**, and old ones that remain unchanged are in roman type.

We must begin by updating **empty**. The code of **empty** is always 0, so the new binding has inclusion set 1–1 and the result a_1 is given code 1.

a_1 = update *empty* b_1

$$\begin{array}{|c|} \hline b_1 \\ \hline 1\text{--}1 \\ \hline \end{array}$$
a_1

a_1= *1*

The code of a_1 is 1, so when it is updated the result a_2 gets code 2. The new binding has inclusion set 2–2 representing $\{a_2\}$. The inclusion set of binding b_1 is changed: its lower bound remains the same since $1 \not< 1$, but its upper bound is incremented since $1 \leq 1$. Thus the inclusion set of b_1 becomes 1–2 which represents $\{a_1, a_2\}$.

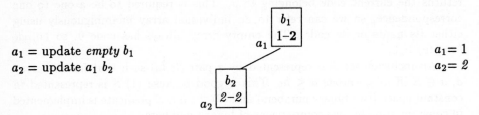

$a_1 = \text{update } empty \ b_1$

$a_2 = \text{update } a_1 \ b_2$

$a_1 = 1$

$a_2 = 2$

The next update illustrates the flexibility of functional arrays by making an alternative update to a_1. Since a_1's code is still 1, the new array a_3 receives code 2. But now the existing code of a_2 must be incremented, and a_2's binding b_2 must have its inclusion set adjusted. Notice how both the lower and upper bounds of b_2 are incremented (since $1 < 3$ and $1 \leq 3$) but only the upper bound of b_1 is changed (since $1 \leq 1$ but $1 \not< 1$). As a result, the *representation* of b_2's inclusion set has changed from 2–2 to 3–3, but its *value* remains $\{a_2\}$.

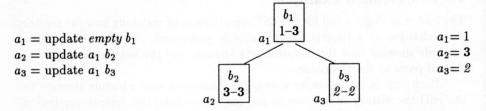

$a_1 = \text{update } empty \ b_1$

$a_2 = \text{update } a_1 \ b_2$

$a_3 = \text{update } a_1 \ b_3$

$a_1 = 1$

$a_2 = 3$

$a_3 = 2$

Now let's update something other than a_1! Notice how every binding above the new binding b_4 has its inclusion set adjusted, ensuring that a_4 contains all the bindings on the path from b_4 to the root of the dependency tree.

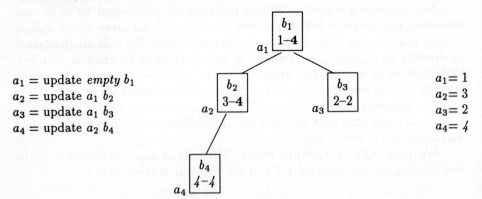

$a_1 = \text{update } empty \ b_1$

$a_2 = \text{update } a_1 \ b_2$

$a_3 = \text{update } a_1 \ b_3$

$a_4 = \text{update } a_2 \ b_4$

$a_1 = 1$

$a_2 = 3$

$a_3 = 2$

$a_4 = 4$

The next update is similar, and creates still more sharing.

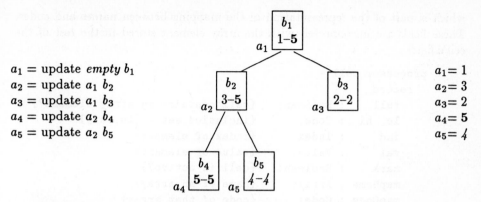

$a_1 = $ update *empty* b_1
$a_2 = $ update a_1 b_2
$a_3 = $ update a_1 b_3
$a_4 = $ update a_2 b_4
$a_5 = $ update a_2 b_5

$a_1 = 1$
$a_2 = 3$
$a_3 = 2$
$a_4 = 5$
$a_5 = 4$

Our final update demonstrates the massive quantity of computation required by update. Since we are updating a_3 whose code is currently 2, the following items must all be incremented: codes > 2; lower bounds > 2; upper bounds ≥ 2. As a result, at least one change is made to every nonempty cell in the machine! However, notice that the inclusion sets of b_2, b_4 and b_5 remain the same, while the inclusion sets of b_1 and b_3 have had the new binding b_6 added.

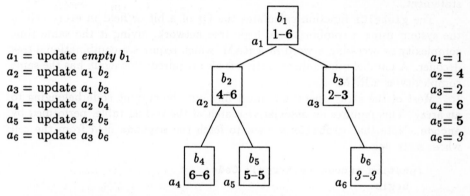

$a_1 = $ update *empty* b_1
$a_2 = $ update a_1 b_2
$a_3 = $ update a_1 b_3
$a_4 = $ update a_2 b_4
$a_5 = $ update a_2 b_5
$a_6 = $ update a_3 b_6

$a_1 = 1$
$a_2 = 4$
$a_3 = 2$
$a_4 = 6$
$a_5 = 5$
$a_6 = 3$

In this example, all the elements have belonged to the same family of arrays. There is no problem if a completely unrelated familiy is created by updating **empty**. That simply produces a new array with code 1, and all existing families have their codes incremented, moving them out of the way. There is no limit to the number of independent families of arrays, and there is never any conflict among them.

6. The data parallel ESF array algorithm

This section shows how *update* and *lookup* work. There is not space to give all the details, or a correctness proof, but the most important techniques are shown here.

Each array element is stored in a cell, which is a collection of fields along with a small arithmetic processor capable of incrementing, decrementing and comparison. The **mapName** and **mapCode** fields contain an array name–code pair, which is part of the representation of the mapping between names and codes. These fields are unconnected with the array element stored in the rest of the cell's fields.

```
processor cell =
  record
    full     : Boolean;    {cell contains an array element?}
    lo, hi   : Code;       {inclusion set = [lo..hi]}
    ind      : Index;      {index of element}
    val      : Value;      {value of element}
    mark     : Boolean;    {cell is active?}
    mapName  : Array;      {name of an array}
    mapCode  : Code;       {code of that array}
  end;
```

Several parallel constructs are used in the algorithm. The 'parallel S;' construct is a map function; it causes every cell processor to execute S in parallel. Field names used in S refer to fields within the local processor. In effect, the parallel construct combines parallelism, a Pascal for loop, and a Pascal with statement.

The globalOr function calculates the Or of a bit or field in every cell in the system using a combinational logic tree network, giving it the same time complexity as accessing a word in a RAM, which requires a combinational tree decoder. A parallel minimum operation is also required; this again has the same complexity as a RAM.

Most of the array operations must find out the current code belonging to an array. This requires an associative search of the coding table, performed by encode. Note that globalOr is used to fetch the mapCode field from the cell whose mark flag is 1.

```
function encode (a:Array): Code;
  begin
    parallel  mark := mapName=a;
    encode := globalOr mapCode
  end; {encode}
```

The update function must create a new array and its corresponding code; adjust the inclusion sets of existing cells; store the new binding into the newly allocated cell; and adjust the array name/code mapping.

```
function update (a:Array; i:Index; v:Value) : Array;
var c, c' : Code;
    a' : Array;
begin
```

First the code c of the old array is calculated, and the code of the new array is defined to be c+1. A new cell and array name are also allocated. The newName function generates a new array name using an associative search of the name–code mapping for an unused name, while newCell performs an associative search of the **full** fields of the cells. An important point is that allocation of names and cells always succeeds in constant time (or fails in constant time if the system is full).

```
c  := encode a;           {input array code}
c' := c+1;                {result array code}
newCell (x);              {allocate new cell}
a' := newName ();         {name of result}
```

The inclusion sets of existing cells must now be adjusted.

```
parallel
   begin
      if lo>c  then lo := lo+1;
      if hi>=c then hi := hi+1;
   end;
```

The next step is to put the new array element into the allocated cell. The code of the new array is `c'`, so the element has inclusion set `c'`—`c'`.

```
with x do
   begin  lo := c';  hi := c';  ind := i;  val := v;  end;
```

Finally, the name/code mapping is adjusted.

```
parallel
   if mapCode>c then mapCode := mapCode+1;
end; {update}
```

The **lookup** function marks every cell that meets two requirements: (1) its index matches the index being searched for, and (2) its inclusion set contains the array being accessed. Several cells may satisfy both constraints. For example, consider

```
a1 := update (empty, 5, 3.14);
a2 := update (a1, 5, 2.7);
x  := lookup (a2, 5);
```

Now both the cell containing the (5, 3.14) binding and the cell containing the (5. 2.7) binding have matching indices and inclusion sets. The (5, 3.14) binding is 'shadowed' by the more recent (5, 2.7) binding, so **lookup** has to find the most recent candidate cell. This can be performed either by representing the 'age' of a binding explicitly with a cell, or by using the location of a cell within the memory to encode the relative ages of two bindings. The details are straightforward, and omitted here.

```
function lookup (a:Array; i:Index): Value;
   var  c : Code;
   begin
      c := encode a;
      parallel   mark := ind=i and lo<=c and c<=hi;
```

```
found := globalOr mark;
if found then
   begin
      d := globalMin age;
      parallel   mark := mark and age=d;
      lookup := fetch
   end
   else lookup := Fail;
end; {lookup}
```

The **free** procedure decrements the bounds of inclusion sets just as **update** increments them. If the array being freed is the only array containing an element, then the inclusion set of that element becomes c—$c - 1$. This represents the empty set, enabling the system to reclaim the cell.

```
procedure free (a:Array);
   var  c : Code;
   begin
      c := encode a;
      parallel
         begin
            if c<=code then code := code-1;
            if lo>c   then lo := lo-1;
            if hi>=c then hi := hi-1;
            if lo>hi then dispose
         end
   end; {free}
```

7. Parallel machine models for ESF arrays

Every time an **update**, **lookup** or **free** is executed, every cell in the system has to perform a simple computation consisting of a few comparisons, increments and decrements. The calculations can be expressed by *mapping* a function over a set of cells in parallel, and the small amount of communication required can be implemented by *scanning* and *folding* associative functions over the cells.

The mapping operations (conditional incrementing and decrementing) require no communication so they take constant time. The scanning (global Or and finding minimum ages) can be performed by a combinational network in $O(\log N)$ time, *the same time it takes a random access memory (RAM) to access a word*. The usual convention is to count a RAM word access as $O(1)$. According to that convention *every operation on ESF arrays takes only constant time*. Several implementation techniques are feasible:

- *Simulation* on a sequential machine has been completed using the functional language Haskell to specify both the algorithm and the parallel architecture.

- *Emulation* using the massively parallel Connection Machine CM-200 has been partially completed.

- *Direct VLSI implementation* would give the fastest system. A VLSI architecture similar to Apsa [3] would be suitable. Such a memory circuit has the same chip area and speed characteristics as a RAM chip, yet it can perform the ESF array algorithms in a constant number of instructions. This approach would be much faster and cheaper than emulation on the Connection Machine, since the cell processors would be very simple and a general routing network is not required.

An interesting characteristic of the ESF algorithm is that it performs far more work than ordinary array accesses seem to, but it overcomes that extra work through massive parallelism. Every time an update or lookup is performed, the memory performs $\Theta(N)$ arithmetic operations, where N is the number of cells in the memory. However, each cell must perform only a constant number of operations, and the cells can all execute in parallel.

To put this in perspective, consider that a RAM memory containing N words also performs $\Theta(N)$ computations inside its address decoder as it accesses 1 word. The point is that the RAM wastes almost all of that work, while the ESF memory performs a trivial but useful computation in each cell. A common error is to ignore the wasted work performed by a RAM (giving $\Theta(1)$ access), while counting the useful work performed by ESF (giving $\Theta(\log N)$ access).

8. Conclusion

Massive parallelism makes it possible to combine three previously unrelated generalisations of arrays — extensible arrays, sparse arrays and functional arrays — into a powerful new data structure called the ESF array. The time, space and chip area complexity measures are exactly the same for ESF array operations as those of an ordinary array operations using RAM chip.

Various extensions to ESF arrays are possible, such as mapping, folding or scanning a function over the elements of an array in parallel. The massive sharing that is possible with functional arrays requires some of the extensions to be done carefully, and the details are a topic of future research.

References

1. E. W. Dijkstra, *A Discipline of Programming.* Prentice-Hall (1976).
2. P. Hudak, A. Bloss, The aggregate update problem in functional programming systems. *Proc. 12th ACM POPL* (1985).
3. J. T. O'Donnell, T. Bridges, S. W. Kitchel, A VLSI implementation of an architecture for applicative programming. *Future Generation Computer Systems*, 4(3) (Oct. 1988) 245–254.
4. S. L. Peyton Jones, P. L. Wadler, Imperative functional programming. *Proc. 20th ACM POPL* (1993) 71–84.
5. P. L. Wadler, Linear types can change the world! *Programming Concepts and Methods*, North-Holland (1990).

Embeddings of Tree–Related Networks in Incomplete Hypercubes *

Sabine Öhring[1] and Sajal K. Das[2]

[1] Department of Computer Science, Univ. of Würzburg, 8700 Würzburg, Germany
[2] Department of Computer Science, Univ. of North Texas, Denton, TX 76203, USA

An incomplete hypercube is a generalization of the well known hypercube network such that its number of nodes can be arbitrary as opposed to a strict power of two. The capability of the incomplete hypercubes to execute parallel programs using graph embedding techniques is studied in this paper. We present optimal (or near optimal) embeddings of various tree–related structures such as tree machines, mesh of trees, pyramids, and shuffle–trees into the optimum–sized incomplete hypercubes.

Keywords : Interconnection networks, graph embeddings, incomplete hypercubes, shuffle–trees, pyramids, mesh of trees.

1 Introduction

The power of a message passing parallel computer depends on the topology chosen for the interconnection network, which can be modeled as an undirected graph $G = (V, E)$ with V representing the processors and E representing the bidirectional links among them. Different graphs have been proposed as interconnection topology, such as complete binary trees, X-trees, meshes, hypercubes, de Bruijn networks, Stirling networks, recursive combinatorial networks, and so on [BP89, DM93, DGD92, Lei92, MS90].

The hypercube is widely used as an architecture for parallel machines (e.g. Intel iPSC or Ncube). Its popularity is due to modularity, symmetry, maximal fault–tolerance, logarithmic degree and diameter, simple routing scheme, and efficient simulation of important networks including trees and meshes [BI85, IJ87, SS88, Wu85]. However, a severe drawback of the hypercube topology is that its size has to be a power of two, whereas it is more interesting in practice to design a network with an arbitrary number of nodes. Furthermore, a hypercube becomes incomplete when several nodes are faulty.

Katseff [Kat88] first proposed the *incomplete hypercube*, consisting of two complete hypercubes – namely front and back cubes – which is further generalized by Tien and Yang [TY91] to incorporate an arbitrary number of nodes, and thus composed of several complete hypercubes. Sen [Sen89] defined the *supercube*, as another generalization of the hypercube with an arbitrary number of nodes but with more edges for higher

* This work is partially supported by Texas Advanced Research Program Grant under Award No. 003594003. The authors can be reached via E-mail at oehring@informatik.uni-wuerzburg.de and das@ponder.csci.unt.edu

fault-tolerance. Boals et al. [BGS92] have recently introduced a further generalization of incomplete hypercubes, called *composite cubes*.

Several tree–related networks such as mesh of trees, tree machines, pyramids, X–trees, or shuffle–trees are powerful networks for parallel computation that support algorithms for many important problems, e.g. sorting, routing, matrix and graph problems [Lei92]. To the best of our knowledge, only embeddings of complete or incomplete binary trees and grids into incomplete hypercubes have so far been developed [ARS92, BGS92, TCC90]. Embeddings of such graphs as pyramids, mesh of trees, tree machines, X–trees, and shuffle–trees are not known for (generalized) incomplete hypercubes, having an arbitrary number of nodes. This motivates the present paper which is organized as follows.

Section 2 gives various graph-theoretic terminology and definitions. Sections 3 through 6 are devoted to embeddings into the incomplete hypercubes. Section 7 provides a comparison of our embedding results with other hypercube–like hosts.

2 Definitions and Terminology

The binary *hypercube*, $Q_n = (V_n^Q, E_n^Q)$ of order n, consists of the node-set $V_n^Q = \mathbf{Z}_2^n$, the set of bit strings of length n. There exists an edge $\{x, y\} \in E_n^Q$ between two nodes x and y iff their binary representations differ exactly in one bit. Katseff [Kat88] proposed the *incomplete hypercube* I_k^n, $0 \leq k < n$, which consists of a *front* cube Q_n and a *back* cube Q_k, respectively denoted by $(0*^n)$ and $(10^{n-k}*^k)$, where $*$ is a don't care symbol, either 0 or 1. In I_k^n, a node is given by the $(n+1)$-bit string of the form $x = (x_n x_{n-1} \ldots x_0)$. Again an edge exists between two nodes of I_k^n iff they differ in exactly one bit. Fig. 1a) shows an incomplete hypercube, I_2^3.

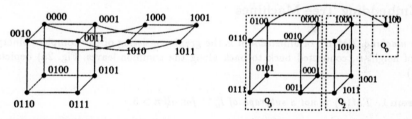

Fig. 1. a) Incomplete hypercube I_2^3 b) Incomplete hypercube $I(13)$ with 13 nodes

Tien and Yang [TY91] generalized *incomplete hypercubes*, $I(N)$ of an arbitrary size N, which is built from several complete hypercubes of different sizes. More precisely, nodes in an $I(N)$ have addresses from 0 to $N-1$. Let the bit string of N has α number of 1's in positions $n_1, \ldots, n_\alpha$ where $n_1 > \ldots > n_\alpha$. Then $I(N) = \{Q_{n_1}, \ldots, Q_{n_\alpha}\}$, is composed of α subcubes of distinct sizes. The subcube Q_{n_1} is built from the nodes numbered by β, for $0 \leq \beta \leq 2^{n_1} - 1$, and in general Q_{n_i} is built from the nodes $\beta = \sum_{j=1}^{i-1} 2^{n_j} + \gamma$, where $0 \leq \gamma \leq 2^{n_i} - 1$ and $2 \leq i \leq \alpha$. Thus the subcube Q_{n_1} consists of the nodes $0(*)^{n_1}$, Q_{n_2} of $1(0)^{n_1-n_2}(*)^{n_2}$, and Q_{n_i}, for $3 \leq i \leq \alpha$, of the nodes $1(0)^{n_1-n_2-1} \ldots 1(0)^{n_{i-2}-n_{i-1}-1} 1(0)^{n_{i-1}-n_i}(*)^{n_i}$. Fig. 1b) depicts $I(13)$.

Boals et al. [BGS92] proposed *composite cubes*, $CQ(N)$, as a generalization such that $I(N)$ is its special case. The *supercube* $S(N)$, for $N = 2^s + h$ nodes where $0 \leq h \leq 2^s - 1$, has the same node–set as the incomplete hypercube $I(N)$ but additional edges [Sen89], the so called *oblique* edges between the nodes $u = u_s u_{s-1} \ldots u_0$ and $v = v_s v_{s-1} \ldots v_0$, where $u_s \neq v_s$ (say $u_s = 1$), $dist(u,v) = 1$ and $u_s v_{s-1} \ldots v_0$ is not a node in the supercube. $dist(u,v)$ is the Hamming–distance between nodes u and v.

The power of a multiprocessor system depends on how efficiently the interconnection topology used can emulate other networks and how efficiently data and algorithm structures can be mapped onto the interconnection network. These mappings can be described more precisely as embedding of a *guest* graph G, with the nodes representing the parallel processes and the edges representing the communication requirements among them, into a *host* graph H which represents the multiprocessor network.

An *embedding* of a graph $G = (V_G, E_G)$ into $H = (V_H, E_H)$ is defined by the tuple (f, g) with a node mapping $f : V_G \to V_H$ and an edge routing $g : E_G \to \mathcal{P}_H$ (pathset of H), where $g(\{u,v\})$ connects nodes $f(u)$ and $f(v)$ in V_H, for all $\{u,v\} \in E_G$. The *dilation* of the embedding (f,g) is the maximum distance in the host between the images of adjacent guest nodes. The *expansion* is the ratio $\frac{|V_H|}{|V_G|}$. When the host graph H is chosen from a family of graphs of different sizes, then H is said to be an *optimum–sized* host, if no graph K in that family exists with $|V_G| \leq |V_K| < |V_H|$. The *load* of an embedding is the maximum, over all host vertices, of the number of guest nodes mapped to it. The *edge–congestion* is the maximum number of edges of G that are routed by g over a single edge of H. We seek to minimize the values for load, dilation, expansion, and edge–congestion in our embeddings that are additionally *modular*, in the sense that the embedding of a guest graph G of size (or dimension) $n + 1$ into the optimum–sized host is an extension of the embedding of G of size n into its optimum-sized host.

3 Embedding Tree Machines

A *tree machine*, $TM(n)$, of dimension n is the graph consisting of two complete binary trees of height n, connected back to back along the common leaves. Fig. 2a) depicts $TM(2)$.

Theorem 1. $TM(n)$ *is not a subgraph of* I_n^{n+1} *for all* $n > 3$.

Proof: The incomplete hypercube I_n^{n+1}, for $n \geq 1$, is bipartite in which the node–set can be divided in two equal–sized partitions each containing $2^n + 2^{n-1}$ nodes. One subset contains vertices having an even number of 1's in their bit addresses and the other having an odd number of 1's. The tree machine is also bipartite – the nodes at even levels belong to one partition, while those at odd levels in the other. For even n, the nodes of $TM(n)$ are partitioned in one set containing $\frac{5 \cdot 2^n - 2}{3}$ nodes and another set containing $\frac{4 \cdot 2^n - 4}{3}$ nodes. If n is odd, one partition contains $\frac{4 \cdot 2^n - 2}{3}$ and the other $\frac{5 \cdot 2^n - 4}{3}$ nodes. Since $\frac{5 \cdot 2^n - 2}{3} > 2^n + 2^{n-1}$ for even $n > 2$, and $\frac{5 \cdot 2^n - 4}{3} > 2^n + 2^{n-1}$ for odd $n > 3$, $TM(n)$ is not a subgraph of I_n^{n+1} for $n > 3$. For $n = 1, 2$, $TM(n)$ is a subgraph of I_n^{n+1} (cf. [OD92b]) $\square$

Theorem 2. *$TM(n)$ can be embedded in the optimum-sized incomplete hypercube I_n^{n+1} with load 1, dilation 2, edge-congestion ≤ 2 and expansion $\frac{2^{n+1}+2^n}{2^{n+1}+2^n-2} \doteq 1$.*

Proof: $TM(n)$ contains $2^{n+1} + 2^n - 2$ vertices. Therefore, the smallest incomplete hypercube with enough vertices to accommodate that structure is I_n^{n+1}. For the proof, we construct tree machines with tails or *metaroots* attached to each of the two roots. As a basis, $TM(1)$ can be embedded in I_1^2 with load 1, dilation and edge-congestion 2 as shown in Fig. 2b). (The white nodes and dashed lines give only the routing.)

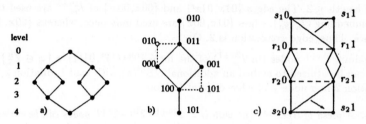

Fig. 2. a) Tree Machine $TM(2)$ b) $TM(1)$ in I_1^2 c) $TM(i+1)$ in I_{i+1}^{i+2}

Now assume as an induction hypothesis that $TM(i)$ can be embedded with load 1, dilation and edge-congestion 2 in I_i^{i+1} according to (f_i, g_i). Let the two roots of $TM(i)$ be mapped to the nodes r_1 and r_2, while the metaroots to s_1 and s_2. Then we embed $TM(i+1)$ in I_{i+1}^{i+2} by using two copies of $TM(i)$ embedded in I_i^{i+1} by (f_i, g_i). This is illustrated in Fig. 2c). In this mechanism, we add the bit 0 (after the rightmost position) to the vertices of the first copy, and the bit 1 to those of the second copy. In Figure 2c), $s_1 0$ and $s_2 0$ are the new roots, while $s_1 1$ and $s_2 1$ the new metaroots. □

4 Embedding Mesh of Trees

The *mesh of trees* [MS90] of dimension n, denoted by $MT(n)$, is the graph whose nodes are all pairs (x, y), where x and y are binary strings of length at most n and at least one of them has length exactly n. The edges in $MT(n)$ connect (x, y) with (xa, y), where $a \in \{0, 1\}$, when x is of length less than n, and (x, y) with (x, ya), when y is of length less than n. More informally, $MT(n)$ is constructed from an $2^n \times 2^n$ array of nodes with additional nodes and edges to form a complete binary tree in each row and column. It has a total of $N = 2^{2n+1} + 2^{2n} - 2^{n+1}$ nodes. Fig. 3 depicts $MT(2)$.

Theorem 3. *$MT(n)$ can be embedded in the optimum-sized incomplete hypercube I_{2n}^{2n+1} with load 1, expansion $\frac{2^{2n+1}+2^{2n}}{2^{2n+1}+2^{2n}-2^{n+1}} \doteq 1$, dilation 3 and edge-congestion 2.*

Proof: Let (f_n', g_n') denote the embedding of the complete binary tree, $CBT(n)$, of height n into the binary hypercube Q_{n+1} by inorder numbering of the vertices [BI85]. Also let $\Pi_{n,\dots,1}^{n+1}(x_n \dots x_0) = x_n \dots x_1$ be the projection of an $(n+1)$-bit string on the leftmost n bits. The nodes (x, y) of $MT(n)$ are embedded into I_{2n}^{2n+1} by the following mapping

$$f_n((x,y)) = \begin{cases} 01\Pi_{n,\ldots,1}^{n+1}(f'_n(x))\Pi_{n,\ldots,1}^{n+1}(f'_n(y)) & \text{if } 0 \le \text{level}(x) \le n-1, \text{level}(y) = n \\ 00\Pi_{n,\ldots,1}^{n+1}(f'_n(x))\Pi_{n,\ldots,1}^{n+1}(f'_n(y)) & \text{if level}(x) = n, 0 \le \text{level}(y) \le n-1 \\ 10\Pi_{n,\ldots,1}^{n+1}(f'_n(x))\Pi_{n,\ldots,1}^{n+1}(f'_n(y)) & \text{if level}(x) = \text{level}(y) = n. \end{cases}$$

The edge routing $g_n((x,y))$ equalizes the bits in $f_n(x)$ and $f_n(y)$ from the left to the right, using the mapping g'_n. The embedding f_n utilizes the fact that f'_n embeds the nodes of level i, for $0 \le i \le n-1$, of $CBT(n)$ to a string of the form $x1$ and the nodes of level n to a string $x0$, where $x \in \mathbf{Z}_2^n$. The edges in $MT(n)$ of the form $\{(x,y),(x',y)\}$ are mapped to a path of length ≤ 3, while the edges of the form $\{(x,y),(x,y')\}$ are mapped to a path of length ≤ 2. The edges $\{01x,01x'\}$ and $\{00x,00x'\}$ of I_{2n}^{2n+1} are used twice due to the embedding (f'_n, g'_n), edges $\{01x,00x\}$ are used only once, whereas $\{00x,10x\}$ are used twice. Thus, edge-congestion is 2. $\square$

The remaining 2^{n+1} nodes (in I_{2n}^{2n+1}) of the form $\{00x(1)^n, 01(1)^n x \mid x \in \mathbf{Z}_2^n\}$ not used by f_n, can be utilized to embed an additional $CBT(n)$ with load 1, dilation 2, and edge-congestion 2 in a node-and edge-disjoint fashion.

Theorem 4. *A mesh of trees $MT(n)$ with $N = 2^{2n+1}+2^{2n}-2^{n+1}$ nodes can be embedded in the optimum-sized incomplete hypercube $I(N)$ with expansion 1, load 1, dilation 3, and edge-congestion 2.*

Proof : The optimum-sized incomplete hypercube $I(N)$ for embedding $MT(n)$ has $N = 2^{2n+1} + \sum_{i=n+1}^{2n-1} 2^i$ nodes, which can be decomposed into $Q_{2n+1}, Q_{2n-1}, \ldots, Q_{n+1}$. Motivated by the size of these subcubes, we embed the nodes (x,y), with level$(x) = 1$ and level$(y) = n$ or vice-versa, into Q_{n+1} and generally the nodes (x,y) with level$(x) = i$ and level$(y) = n$ or vice-versa into Q_{i+n+1} for $0 \le i \le n-2$. The nodes (x,y) with level$(x) = n$ and level$(y) \in \{n-1, n\}$ or vise-versa are mapped into Q_{2n+1}. The subcube Q_{2n+1} can be identified by the nodes $0(*)^{2n+1}$, and the subcube Q_{2n-i}, $1 \le i \le n-1$, by the nodes $10(1)^{i-1}0(*)^{2n-i}$. For the embedding, we utilize the following code C_k^i, where $C_k = C_k^0$ and e denotes the empty string. Then $C_0 = \{e\}, C_1 = \{c_0, c_1\} = \{0, 1\}, \ldots, C_k = \{c_0, \ldots, c_{2^k-1}\}, C_{k+1} = \{0c_0, 1c_0, 0c_1, 1c_1, \ldots, 0c_{2^k-1}, 1c_{2^k-1}\}$ and $C_n^i = \{SR^i(c_0), \ldots, SR^i(c_{2^n-1})\}$. Thereby, $SR(x_{k-1} \ldots x_0) = x_0 x_{k-1} \ldots x_1$ and SR^i means that the operation SR is iterated i times. We can easily see that C_k^i is a bijective mapping of $\mathbf{Z}_2^k \to \mathbf{Z}_2^k$. It holds $C_{k+1}(x\nu) = \nu C_k(x)$ for $\nu = 0, 1$. The nodes (x,y) of $MT(n) = (V_n, E_n)$ are embedded due to the mapping f_n described in Table 1, where the leftmost $n+2-j$ bits, with $j = \min\{\text{level}(x), \text{level}(y)\}$, are called the *prefix* of the encoding, which decides to which subcube the node is mapped into.

The node-mapping f_n has load 1, since the coding C_k^i is an injective mapping and the prefixes of the bit strings, to which the nodes of $MT(n)$ are mapped to, are unique for any pair of level(x) and level(y). Furthermore, the dilation of f_n is 3 by considering the path on which an edge $\{(x,y),(u,v)\}$ of $MT(n)$ is mapped to (see Table 2). Here $u = x\nu$ and $v = y$, or $v = y\nu$ and $u = x$ with $\nu \in \{0, 1\}$. The notation *dist* in Table 2 denotes the Hamming-distance between nodes $f_n((x,y))$ and $f_n((u,v))$. If we use the routing function g_n such that all bits, in which $f_n((x,y))$ and $f_n((u,v))$ differ, are equalized from-left-to-right in Cases E1 to E5 and from-right-to-left in Case E6, it is guaranteed that the edge-congestion is 2. $\square$

Table 1. Node–mapping f_n

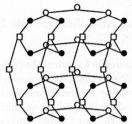

Fig.3. Mesh of trees $MT(2)$

Cases	$f_n((x,y))$
Case N1 level$(x) = j \leq n - 2$ level$(y) = n$	$10(1)^{n-2-j}01C_j(x)C_n(y)$
Case N2 level$(x) = n$ level$(y) = i \leq n - 2$	$10(1)^{n-2-i}00C_n^i(x)C_i(y)$
Case N3 level$(x) = n - 1$ level$(y) = n$	$001C_{n-1}(x)C_n(y)$
Case N4 level$(x) = n$ level$(y) = n - 1$	$000C_n^{n-1}(x)C_{n-1}(y)$
Case N5 level$(x) = n$ level$(y) = n$	$01C_n(x)C_n(y)$

Table 2. Edge-mapping

Cases	$f_n((x,y))$	$f_n((x\nu,y))$	dist
Case E1 level$(x) = j < n - 2$ level$(y) = n$	$10(1)^{n-2-j}01C_j(x)C_n(y)$	$10(1)^{n-3-j}01\nu C_j(x)C_n(y)$	≤ 3
Case E2 level$(x) = n - 2$ level$(y) = n$	$1001C_{n-2}(x)C_n(y)$	$001\nu C_{n-2}(x)C_n(y)$	≤ 3
Case E3 level$(x) = n - 1$ level$(y) = n$	$001C_{n-1}(x)C_n(y)$	$01\nu C_{n-1}(x)C_n(y)$	≤ 2
Case E4 level$(x) = n$ level$(y) = i < n - 2$	$10(1)^{n-2-i}00C_n^i(x)C_i(y) = 10(1)^{n-2-i}00\xi_{i-1}\ldots\xi_iC_i(y)$	$10(1)^{n-3-i}00C_n^{i+1}(x)\nu C_i(y) = 10(1)^{n-3-i}00\xi_i\ldots\xi_{i+1}\nu C_i(y)$	≤ 3
Case E5 level$(x) = n$ level$(y) = n - 2$	$1000C_n^{n-2}(x)C_{n-2}(y) = 1000\xi_{n-3}\ldots\xi_{n-2}C_{n-2}(y)$	$000C_n^{n-1}(x)\nu C_{n-2}(y) = 000\xi_{n-2}\ldots\xi_{n-1}\nu C_{n-2}(y)$	≤ 3
Case E6 level$(x) = n$ level$(y) = n - 1$	$000C_n^{n-1}(x)C_{n-1}(y) = 000\xi_{n-2}\ldots\xi_{n-1}C_{n-1}(y)$	$01C_n(x)\nu C_{n-1}(y) = 01\xi_{n-1}\ldots\xi_0\nu C_{n-1}(y)$	≤ 3

5 Embedding Pyramids

The *pyramid* of height n [MS90], denoted by $PR(n)$, is the graph with the node–set $V_n = \{(i,x,y) | 0 \leq i \leq n, 0 \leq x, y \leq 2^i - 1\}$ and edge–set $E_n = \{\{(i,x,y),(i+1,u,v)\} | 0 \leq i < n, u \in \{2x, 2x - 1\}, v \in \{2y, 2y + 1\}\} \cup \{\{(i,x,y),(i,u,v)\} | 0 \leq i \leq n, 1 \leq x, y \leq 2^i, (x,y)$

and (u, v) differ in exactly one coordinate by one}. In other words, $PR(n)$ is a 4-ary complete tree of height n with $N = \frac{4^{n+1}-1}{3}$ nodes, and the nodes at each level form a square mesh. Fig. 5b) shows a pyramid of height 2.

Theorem 5. *$PR(n)$ can be embedded in the optimum–sized incomplete hypercube I^{2n}_{2n-1} with load 1, dilation 2, edge–congestion 3, and expansion $\leq \frac{6}{5}$.*

Proof : Clearly, I^{2n}_{2n-1} is the optimum–sized incomplete hypercube to embed the pyramid $PR(n)$. Since I^{2n}_{2n-1} contains no cycle of length three, $PR(n)$ cannot be embedded as a subgraph or with dilation 1. This theorem can be proven by recursive construction, using an approach similar to that given in [MS90], pp. 270-271. Fig. 4b) shows that the pyramid $PR(1)$ with an alternate apex can be embedded with load 1, edge–congestion 3, and dilation 2 into the incomplete hypercube I^2_1. We prove in [ÖD92b] that any embedding of $PR(1)$ with an alternate apex in I^2_1 with load 1 and dilation 2 has edge–congestion 3. For the embedding (f_i, g_i) of $PR(i)$ into I^{2i}_{2i-1}, we claim that :

(a) f_i has load 1, dilation 2 and edge–congestion 3.
(b) f_i maps the apex of $PR(i)$ into a node of I^{2i}_{2i-1}, that has an unassigned neighbor, called the *alternate apex*, such that at most one edge is routed through the edge connecting the apex and the alternate apex.
(c) the embedding $\tilde{f}_i(x) = \begin{cases} f_i(alternate\ apex) & \text{if } x = \text{apex of } PR(i) \\ f_i(apex) & \text{if } x = \text{alternate apex of } PR(i) \\ f_i(x) & \text{otherwise} \end{cases}$
also fulfills the items (a) and (b).

Then the pyramid $PR(i+1)$, $1 \leq i \leq n-1$, is embedded into I^{2i+2}_{2i+1} as follows.

Step 1: I^{2i+2}_{2i+1} is partitioned into four subsets $I^{2i+2,y}_{2i+1}$ with the node–sets $\{xy \mid x$ is a node in I^{2i}_{2i-1} and $y \in \{00, 01, 10, 11\}\}$.
Step 2: Embed in $I^{2i+2,00}_{2i+1}$ and $I^{2i+2,01}_{2i+1}$ a copy of $PR(i)$ using the embedding f_i and embed in $I^{2i+2,10}_{2i+1}$ and $I^{2i+2,11}_{2i+1}$ a copy of $PR(i)$ using $\tilde{f}_i$ as defined above.
Step 3: The apex of $PR(i+1)$ is mapped into the alternate apex of $PR(i)$ embedded in $I^{2i+2,00}_{2i+1}$ and the edges are routed as sketched in Fig. 4.

□

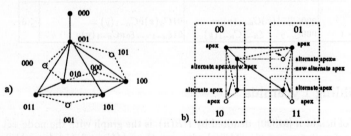

Fig. 4. a) $PR(1)$ with alternate apex in I^2_1 b) Embedding of $PR(i+1)$

Theorem 6. *The pyramid $PR(n)$ of height n with $N = \frac{4^{n+1}-1}{3}$ nodes can be embedded in the optimum–sized incomplete hypercube $I(N)$ with load 1, expansion 1, dilation 3 and edge–congestion 4.*

Proof : Since an incomplete hypercube $I(N)$ contains no cycle of length 3 for $N \geq 1$, $PR(n)$ cannot be embedded with dilation 1 into $I(N)$.

Also note that $PR(n)$ contains $N = \sum_{i=0}^{n} 2^{2i}$ nodes, where at each level i of the 4-ary tree, for $0 \leq i \leq n$, there is a $2^i \times 2^i$-mesh, denoted by $M(2^i)$. Thus, $I(N)$ consists of the complete hypercubes $Q_{2n}, Q_{2n-2}, \ldots, Q_2, Q_0$. We embed $PR(n)$ in $I(N)$ by mapping the subgraph $M(2^i)$ in Q_{2i}. Now the subcube Q_{2n} can be identified in $I(N)$ by the node–set $\{0(*)^{2n}\}$. Similarly, the subcube Q_{2n-2} can be identified by the node–set $\{100(*)^{2n-2}\}$, while Q_{2n-2k} by $\{(10)^k 0(*)^{2n-2k}\}$ and Q_0 by $\{(10)^n 0\}$.

As illustrated in Fig. 5a), $PR(1)$ can be embedded in $I(5)$ consisting of a Q_0 and a Q_2, with load 1, dilation 3 and edge–congestion 4. Now, assume that $PR(k)$ has been embedded using the node–mapping f_k in the generalized incomplete hypercube, $I(\sum_{i=0}^{k} 2^{2i})$ for $k \geq 1$. Then, to complete the proof by induction, the embedding f_{k+1} of $PR(k+1)$ can be given as follows.

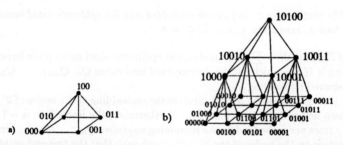

Fig. 5. a) Embedding of $PR(1)$ in $I(5)$ b) Embedding of $PR(2)$ in $I(21)$

The images of the nodes in levels 0 to k of $PR(k+1)$ are changed such that the bit string 10 is inserted in front of the leftmost bit. Furthermore, we have to embed the nodes in level $k+1$ of the pyramid. Each of these nodes is a son of a node v in level k. Let v be mapped on the node $100y$, i.e. $f_{k+1}(v) = 100y$ where $y \in \mathbf{Z}_2^{2k}$. Then the four sons of v are mapped to the nodes $000y$, $001y$, $010y$ and $011y$. These nodes have to be assigned to the sons such that the neighbored subsquares of the $2^{k+1} \times 2^{k+1}$ mesh become adjacent by using the induced embedding of $M(2^{k+1})$ in the subcube Q_{2k+2}. Fig. 5b) illustrates the embedding of $PR(2)$ in $I(21)$.

6   Embedding Shuffle–Trees

As alternative to the mesh of trees, Leighton [Lei92] proposed the *shuffle–trees*. The $N = 2^n$-sided shuffle-tree, $ST(n)$, has the node-set $V_n = V_n^1 \cup V_n^2$ with $V_n^1 = \{(x,y)|x,y \in \mathbf{Z}_2^n\}$ and $V_n^2 = \{(x,z)|x \in \mathbf{Z}_2^n, z \in \mathbf{Z}_2^k, 0 \leq k \leq n-1\}$ and the edge-set $E_n = E_n^1 \cup E_n^2$ with $E_n^1 = \{\{(x,y),(y,x)\}|x,y \in \mathbf{Z}_2^n\}$ and $E_n^2 = \{\{(x,z),(x,za)\}|x \in \mathbf{Z}_2^n, z \in \mathbf{Z}_2^k, 0 \leq k \leq n-1, a \in \mathbf{Z}_2\}$. The nodes in V_n^1 are the nodes of the $2^n \times 2^n$-grid of $ST(n)$ and those in V_n^2 are the nodes in levels 0 to $n-1$ of the complete binary trees involved. The root of the complete binary tree in column x is denoted by (x, e), where e is the empty string. The edges in E_n^1 are called the *rotation* edges and those in E_n^2 are the *tree* edges. Thus the shuffle-tree $ST(n)$ has $2^{2n+1} - 2^n$ nodes and $\frac{5}{2}N^2 - \frac{3}{2}N$ edges, and every node has degree 2 or 3. Fig. 6 shows $ST(2)$.

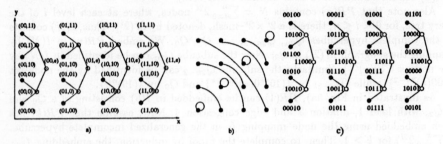

Fig. 6. $ST(2)$: a) tree edges   b) rotation edges   c) Embedding $ST(2)$ in $I(28)$

Theorem 7. *The shuffle-tree $ST(n)$ can be embedded into the optimum-sized incomplete hypercube with load 1, expansion 1, and dilation 6.*

Proof : Since $ST(n)$ has $N = \sum_{i=n}^{2n} 2^i$ nodes, the optimum-sized incomplete hypercube for its embedding is $I(N)$, which can be decomposed into cubes $Q_n, Q_{n+1}, \ldots, Q_{2n}$. Let φ denote the required embedding.

The general idea of embedding $ST(n)$ involves the embedding of the nodes of $2^n \times 2^n$-mesh (dark drawn nodes in Fig. 6) into Q_{2n}. Furthermore, the levels 0 to $n-1$ of all complete binary trees are embedded in the remaining subcubes $Q_n, \ldots, Q_{2n-1}$. First, we use a transformation on the nodes of the $2^n \times 2^n$-mesh such that the two end points of a rotation edge share the same y-coordinate. This transformation is accomplished by the mapping $f : Z_2^n \times Z_2^n \to Z_2^n \times Z_2^n$, satisfying $f((x, y)) = (x, (y + x) \bmod 2^n) = (x', y')$. After this mapping, the rotation edges can be drawn in a way depicted as in Fig. 7b, which is stated more formally in Lemma 8 that can be easily proved.

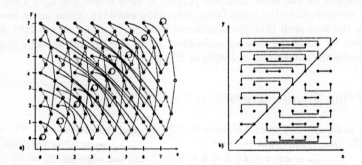

Fig. 7. Rotation edges of $ST(3)$ before and after the transformation

Lemma 8. *After using the transformation f on the nodes (x,y) of the $2^n \times 2^n$-grid, the rotation edges are of the form $\{(x,i),(i-x,i)\}$, for $x \leq i \leq 2^n - 1$, or of the form $\{(x,j-2^n),(j-x,j-2^n)\}$, for $2^n \leq x \leq j \leq 2^{n+1} - 2$.*

Following f, we use a second mapping ψ which maps the mesh–nodes finally to the nodes of the form $0(*)^{2n}$ in the subcube Q_{2n}.

Definition 9. [CS86] The m–bit *binary reflected Gray codes*, denoted by $\mathcal{G}_m$, is defined recursively as $\mathcal{G}_1 := \{g_0^{(1)}, g_1^{(1)}\} = \{0,1\}, \ldots, \mathcal{G}_k := \{g_0^{(k)}, g_1^{(k)}, \ldots, g_{2^k-1}^{(k)}\}$,
$$\mathcal{G}_{k+1} := \{0g_0^{(k)}, 1g_0^{(k)}, 1g_1^{(k)}, 0g_1^{(k)}, 0g_2^{(k)}, \ldots, 1g_{2^k-1}^{(k)}, 0g_{2^k-1}^{(k)}\}.$$

It holds that $g_i^{(m)}$ and $g_{(i+1) \bmod 2^m}^{(m)}$, $0 \leq i \leq 2^m - 1$, differ in exactly one bit, while $g_i^{(m)}$ and $g_{i+2^j}^{(m)}$, where $j > 0$ and $i + 2^j \leq 2^m - 1$, differ in exactly two bits.

Let $G_n(x) = \mathcal{G}_n(x \bmod 2^n)$. The y–coordinates of the nodes (x',y') are encoded by the binary reflected Gray codes. That is, $\Pi_{2n,\ldots,n}^{2n+1}(\psi(x',y')) = 0G_n(y')$ where $\Pi_{N_1,\ldots,N_2}^{N}(x_{N-1}\ldots x_0) = x_{N_1}\ldots x_{N_2}$ for $N-1 \geq N_1 \geq N_2 \geq 0$ is the projection of the bit string $x_{N-1}\ldots x_0$ of length N to the substring $x_{N_1}\ldots x_{N_2}$.

The x–coordinates of (x',y') are mapped by the binary reflected Gray codes where an offset (dependent on y') is added to the argument x'. More precisely, $\Pi_{n-1,\ldots,0}^{2n+1}(\psi(x',y')) = G_n(x' + \lfloor\frac{2^n-1-y'}{2}\rfloor)$. Thus, the embedding φ of the nodes (x,y), where $x,y \in \mathbb{Z}_2^n$, of the $2^n \times 2^n$-grid is given by $\varphi((x,y)) = 0G_n(x+y)G_n(x + \lfloor\frac{2^n-1-(x+y) \bmod 2^n}{2}\rfloor) = \psi \circ f((x,y))$, where $\circ$ is the composition operation.

Lastly, let us define the embedding φ for levels 0 to $n-1$ of the complete binary trees in columns 0 to $2^n - 1$ of the shuffle–tree starting with level $n-1$. For node (x,z) with level$((x,z)) = j$ such that $z \in \mathbb{Z}_2^j$, we define $\varphi((x,z)) = (1)^i 0\Pi_{n-1+j,\ldots,0}^{2n+1}\varphi((x,z\overline{x_{i-1}}))$ with $i = n-j$. Thereby, $x = x_{n-1}\ldots x_0$, and $\overline{x_i}$ is the complimentary bit of x_i. In other words, the string $(1)^{n-j}0$ is used as prefix for the node (x,y) in level j, $0 \leq j \leq n-1$, and the first $n+j$ bits of the encoding of the son $(x,z\overline{x_{n-1-j}})$ are used as suffix. Fig. 6 gives an example of our embedding φ of $ST(2)$ in $I(28)$. For detailed analysis of the cost–measurements, refer to [ÖD92b].

7 Comparison of Embeddings

The previous sections deal with embeddings of tree machines, meshes of trees, pyramids, and shuffle–trees into the incomplete hypercube of the type I_k^m, where $0 \leq k < n$, and the generalized incomplete hypercube $I(N)$ having an arbitrary number of nodes. In Table 3) we compare these results with embeddings in three other hypercube–like host networks – namely complete hypercubes, hyper Petersen networks HP_n, (defined as the cartesian product of binary hypercubes and the well-known Petersen graph [DB92]), and hyper-de Bruijn networks $HD(m,n)$, (defined as the cartesian product of binary hypercubes and de Bruijn networks [GP91]). The cost–measurements used for our comparison are dilation ($\mathfrak{D}$) and edge-congestion ($\mathfrak{E}$). Most of the results given in Table 3 are due to us, the detailed proofs of which are available in [DÖ92].

Table 3. Comparison of embedding results

Guest graph	I_k^n	$I(N)$	Q_n	HP_n	$HD(m,n)$
CBT(n) complete binary tree	CBT(n−1) in I_{n-1}^n as subgraph [TCC90] (optimal)	CBT(n−1) in $I(2^n-1)$ with $\mathfrak{D}=2$ and $\mathfrak{C}=2$ (optimal)	CBT(n−2) in Q_n as subgraph, CBT(n−1) in Q_n with $\mathfrak{D}=2, \mathfrak{C}=2$ [BI85] (optimal)	CBT(n−1) in HP_n as subgraph [DB92] (optimal) [DÖ92]	CBT(m+n−2) in $HD(m,n)$ as subgraph [GP91] CBT(n+m−1) in $HD(m,n)$ with $\mathfrak{D}=2, \mathfrak{C}=2$ [ÖD92a]
X(n) X-tree	X(n−1) in I_k^n with $0 \le k \le n-1$ $\mathfrak{D}=2$, $\mathfrak{C}=2$ (optimal)	X(n−1) in $I(2^n-1)$ with $\mathfrak{D}=2$, $\mathfrak{C}=2$ (optimal)	X(n−1) in Q_n with $\mathfrak{D}=2$, $\mathfrak{C}=2$ (optimal) [Ho90]	X(n−1) in HP_n with $\mathfrak{D}=2$ $\mathfrak{C}=2$ (optimal) [DÖ92]	X(n−1) in $HD(n-3,3)$ with $\mathfrak{D}=2$ $\mathfrak{C}=2$ [ÖD92a]
TM(n) tree machine	TM(n) in I_n^{n+1} with $\mathfrak{D}=2$, $\mathfrak{C}=2$ (optimal)	TM(n) in $I(2^{n+1}+2^n)$ with $\mathfrak{D}=2$, $\mathfrak{C}=2$	TM(n) in Q_{n+2} as subgraph [Efe91] (optimal)	TM(n) in HP_{n+2} with $\mathfrak{D}=2$, $\mathfrak{C}=2$ [DÖ92]	TM(m+n−2) in $HD(m,n)$ with $\mathfrak{D}=2$, $\mathfrak{C}=2$ [ÖD92a]
MT(n) mesh of trees	MT(n) in I_{2n}^{2n+1} with $\mathfrak{D}=3$, $\mathfrak{C}=2$	MT(n) with $\mathfrak{D}=3$, $\mathfrak{C}=2$ in $I(2^{2n+1}+2^{2n}-2^{n+1})$	MT(n) in Q_{2n+2} as subgraph [Efe91] (optimal)	MT(n) in HP_{2n+2} with $\mathfrak{D}=2$, $\mathfrak{C}=2$ [DÖ92]	MT($2^p, 2^q$) subgraph of $HD(m,n)$ $1 \le p \le m-2$ $1 \le q \le n-1$ [GP91]
PR(n) pyramid	PR(n) in I_{2n-1}^{2n} with $\mathfrak{D}=2$, $\mathfrak{C}=3$	PR(n) in $I((4^{n+1}-1)/3)$ with $\mathfrak{D}=3$, $\mathfrak{C}=4$	PR(n) in Q_{2n+1} with $\mathfrak{D}=2, \mathfrak{C}=2$ (optimal) [Sto86]	PR(n) in HP_{2n+1} with $\mathfrak{D}=2, \mathfrak{C}=2$ (optimal) [DÖ92]	PR(n) in $HD(2n-2,3)$ with $\mathfrak{D}=2, \mathfrak{C}=2$ [ÖD93]

8 Conclusions

In this paper we have presented (near) optimal embeddings of various tree-related topologies into incomplete hypercubes as the host. The guest networks include tree machines, mesh of trees, pyramids, and shuffle–trees. These results indicate that incomplete hypercubes are versatile (similar to complete hypercubes) in terms of their simulation capabilities. Due to the definition of composite cubes and supercubes – which are further generalizations of hypercubes with an arbitrary number of nodes – the embedding results proposed in this paper also carry over to these two host graphs.

Our comparison of incomplete and complete hypercubes, supercubes, and hyper Petersen networks by embedding one in another show that all these network topologies have nearly the same computational power [ÖD92b]. Currently, we are investigating dynamic embeddings of trees and grids into the incomplete hypercubes and their generalizations.

References

[ARS92] V. Auletta et al., On the fault tolerance and computational capabilities of the supercube. In *Proc. 4th Italian Conf. on Theoretical Computer Science*, pp. 38–52, 1992.

[BGS92] A.J. Boals, A.K. Gupta, and N. A. Sherwani. Incomplete hypercubes : Embeddings and algorithms. manuscript, September 1992.

[BI85] S.N. Bhatt and I. Ipsen. How to embed trees in hypercubes, Technical Report 443. Dept. of Computer Science, Yale Univ., New Heaven, CT, 1985.

[BP89]   J.C. Bermond and C. Peyrat. de bruijn and kautz networks : a competitor for the hypercube ? In *Hypercubes and Distributed Computers*, pp. 279–293, North–Holland, 1989.

[CS86]   T.F. Chan and Y. Saad. Multigrid algorithms on the hypercube multiprocessor. *IEEE Trans. on Computers*, vol. C–35, No. 11, pp. 969–977, November 1986.

[DB92]   S.K. Das and A.K. Banerjee. Hyper petersen network : Yet another hypercube–like topology. In *Proceedings of the 4th Symposium on the Frontiers of Massively Parallel Computation (Frontiers' 92)*, pp. 270 – 277, McLean, Virginia, USA, October 1992.

[DGD92]   S.K. Das, J. Ghosh, and N. Deo. Stirling networks : A versatile combinatorial topology for multiprocessor systems. *Discrete Applied Mathematics*, 37/38, special double volume on interconnection networks, pp. 119–146, July 1992.

[DM93]   S.K. Das and Aisheng Mao. Embeddings in recursive combinatorial networks. In *Lecture Notes in Computer Science*, vol. 657, pp. 184-204, 1993.

[DÖ92]   S.K. Das and S. Öhring. Embeddings of tree–related topologies in hyper petersen networks. Technical Report CRPDC-92-16, University of North Texas, University of Wuerzburg, September 1992.

[Efe91]   K. Efe. Embedding mesh of trees in the hypercube. *Journal of Parallel and Distributed Computing*, 11:222–230, 1991.

[GP91]   E. Ganesan and D.K. Pradhan. The hyper-de bruijn multiprocessor networks. In *Proceedings of the 11th Conference on Distributed Computing Systems*, pp. 492–499, Arlington, TX, May 1991.

[HJ87]   C.T. Ho and S.L. Johnsson. On the embedding of arbitrary meshes in boolean cubes with expansion two dilation two. In *Proc. 1987 Int. Conf. Parallel Processing*, 1987.

[Ho90]   C.-T. Ho. *Optimal Communication Primitives and Graph Embeddings on Hypercubes*. PhD thesis, Yale university, May 1990.

[Kat88]   H. P. Katseff. Incomplete hypercubes. *IEEE Trans. on Computers*, vol. 37, no. 5, pp. 604–608, May 1988.

[Lei92]   F.T. Leighton. *Introduction to Parallel Algorithms and Architectures : Arrays – Trees – Hypercubes*. Morgan Kaufmann Publishers, San Mateo, CA, 1992.

[MS90]   B. Monien and H. Sudborough. Embedding one interconnection network in another. In *Computational Graph Theory*, pages 257–282, Wien, 1990. Springer Verlag.

[ÖD92a]   S. Öhring and S.K. Das. On Dynamic and Modular Embeddings into Hyper de Bruijn Networks. Tech. Rep. TR 49, Univ. of Würzburg, Nov. 1992.

[ÖD92b]   S. Öhring and S.K. Das. Embeddings of tree–related networks in incomplete hypercubes. Technical Report CRPDC-92-20, University of North Texas, University of Wuerzburg, December 1992.

[ÖD93]   S. Öhring and S.K. Das. Dynamic embeddings of trees and quasi–grids into hyper-de bruijn networks. to appear in the *Proceedings of the 7th International Parallel Processing Symposium*, Newport Beach, California, April 1993.

[Sen89]   A. Sen. Supercube: An optimally fault tolerant network architecture. *Acta Informatica*, 26:741–748, 1989.

[SS88]   Y. Saad and M.H. Schultz. Topological properties of hypercubes. *IEEE Trans. on Computers*, vol. 37, no. 7, pp. 867–872, 1988.

[Sto86]   Quentin F. Stout. Hypercubes and pyramids. In V. Cantoni and S. Levialdi, editors, *Pyramidal Systems for Computer Vision*, pp. 75–89. Springer, Heidelberg, 1986.

[TCC90]   N.F. Tzeng, H.-L. Chen, and P.-J. Chuang. Embeddings in incomplete hypercubes. In *Proc. of the 1990 Int. Conf. on Parallel Processing, Vol. III*, pp. 335 – 339, 1990.

[TY91]   J.-Y. Tien and W-P. Yang. Hierarchical spanning trees and distributing on incomplete hypercubes. *Parallel Computing*, 17:1343–1360, 1991.

[Wu85]   A.Y. Wu. Embedding of tree networks into hypercubes. *Journal of Parallel and Distributed Computing*, 2:238 – 249, 1985.

Static and Dynamic Performance of the Möbius Cubes (Short Version)*

Paul Cull and Shawn M. Larson

Department of Computer Science, Oregon State University, Corvallis, OR, 97331
e-mail: pc@CS.ORST.EDU, larsons@CS.ORST.EDU

Abstract. The Möbius cubes are hypercube variants that give better performance with the same number of links and processors. We show that the diameter of the Möbius cubes is about 1/2 the diameter of the equivalent hypercube, and that the average number of steps between processors for a Möbius cube is about 2/3 of the average for a hypercube. We give an efficient routing algorithm for the Möbius cubes. This routing algorithm finds a shortest path and operates in time proportional to the dimension of the cube. We report results of simulation studies on the dynamic message-passing performance of the hypercube, the Twisted Cube of Hilbers *et. al.* [8], and the Möbius cubes. Our results agree with those of Abraham [2], showing that the Twisted Cube has worse dynamic performance than the hypercube. But our results show that the Möbius cubes and in particular the 1-Möbius cube have better dynamic performance than the hypercube.

1 Introduction

An interconnection network unites many processors to form a parallel computer. The topology of a network determines how well the processors can interact with each other to cooperatively solve a given problem.

The hypercube network has proved to be one of the most popular interconnection networks, and has been used in both Intel's and NCUBE's computers. Its popularity is due its small number of connections per processor and its relatively small diameter. If the communication time between processors dominates the computation time, then reducing the diameter of a network should improve the performance of a machine based on that network.

The hypercube does not have the smallest diameter possible for its resources. If we exchange or "twist" the endpoints of two edges of the 3-cube as in Fig. 1, the diameter of the network reduces from 3 to 2. This is the minimum diameter that can be obtained. To have a smaller diameter, the same number of nodes would require 16 edges.

This smaller diameter "cube" is mentioned in Seitz [9], who attributes it to Hillis [7]. In these references, there is no indication of how to generalize this construction to higher dimension cubes.

---

* A longer version is available upon request from authors - Tech. Rept. 93-20-02.

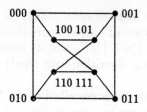

Fig. 1. A twisted 3-cube

In this paper, we produce our generalizations of the network in Fig. 1. We call our topologies the "Möbius cubes" – largely because the flattened 3-cube resembles the outline of a Möbius strip. Like the hypercube, the Möbius cubes of dimension n have 2^n nodes and n connections per node, but they have a much lower diameter and average internodal distance.

In Sect. 2, we discuss previous approaches to the idea of hypercube variants. In Sect. 3, we define the Möbius cubes and describe some of their basic properties. In Sect. 4 we present a routing algorithm for the Möbius cubes. In Sect. 5 we examine and compare the diameter and expected internodal distance of the Möbius cubes to the hypercube and Twisted Cube of Hilbers *et. al.* [8]. In Sect. 6 we compare the message latency and message arrival rates of the Möbius cubes and the other cubes.

2 Previous Work

Previous workers have considered variants of the hypercube. The simplest generalization of the Twisted 3-cube is the Twisted N-Cube of Estafahanian *et. al.* [6], which has only one crossed pair of edges. This twist gives a diameter of one less than the diameter of the hypercube of the same dimension. The Twisted N-Cube's routing algorithm is based on the hypercube's left-right bit correction algorithm, and has the same $O(n)$ runtime.

The Twisted Cube of Hilbers *et. al.* [8] of dimension n is constructed by joining four twisted cubes of dimension $n-1$, then applying "twists" to some of the communications links so that all four $(n-2)$-cubes are a distance of 1 apart. The Twisted Cube has a diameter of $\lceil (n+1)/2 \rceil$. The routing algorithm is more complicated than that of the hypercube, but still has the same $O(n)$ runtime. Abraham and Padmanabhan ([1] and [2]) compute the expected distance of the Twisted Cube, and compare the dynamic performance of the Twisted Cube and the hypercube. A stochastic simulation of the Twisted Cube in [2] shows that it has a performance comparable to the hypercube, but not quite what would be expected from the $\lceil (n+1)/2 \rceil$ diameter.

The Multiply Twisted Cube of Kemal [5] is a variation quite similar to the Twisted Cube, in that it joins 4 $(n-2)$-cubes together to form an n-cube. Its structure differs from the Twisted cube in that its connection rules cause communication links to be "twisted" across more than 2 dimensions. Its diameter, like the Twisted cube, is $\lceil (n+1)/2 \rceil$, and its routing algorithm is comparably simple. An optimal routing algorithm with $O(n^2)$ runtime and a broadcasting algorithm are given.

An entire family of networks is described by the MCube of Singhvi and Ghose [10]. This construction decomposes two MCubes of dimension k into 4 subcubes each, then joins each pair of subgraphs in a twisted connection to produce an MCube of dimension $k + 1$. This method produces a family of networks in that the decomposition of the two MCubes and the orientation of their subcubes is arbitrary. This does not prevent construction of a routing algorithm for all members of this network family, though this algorithm as presented has a $O(n^2)$ runtime even using precomputed routing tables. One particular MCube network, the "Flip MCube", has the orientation of its subcubes specified. The Flip MCube has diameter $\lceil (n+1)/2 \rceil$, and is shown in a dynamic simulation to have generally superior dynamic performance to the hypercube.

The Möbius cube networks continue the concept of twisted hypercubes. The diameter and average distance of the Möbius cubes are comparable to these measures in these other networks, and their dynamic performance shows marked improvement. They also show a much simpler processor connection rule.

3   Definition of the Möbius Cubes

A Möbius cube of dimension n has 2^n nodes. Each node has a unique n component binary vector for an address. For example, a node $\mathbf{X}$ has address $(X_1 X_2 \ldots X_n)$. The node $\mathbf{X}$ connects to n neighbors $\mathbf{Y}_1, \mathbf{Y}_2, \ldots \mathbf{Y}_n$, where each $\mathbf{Y}_i$ satisfies one of the following rules:

$$\mathbf{Y}_i = (X_1 \ldots 0\overline{X_i} \ldots X_n) \tag{1}$$

$$\mathbf{Y}_i = (X_1 \ldots 1\overline{X_i \ldots X_n}) \tag{2}$$

In the network graph, we define the edge between a node $\mathbf{X}$ and its i-th neighbor based on (1) as $(\mathbf{X}, \mathbf{X} + e_i)$, where e_i is the n-dimensional $(0, 1)$ vector with only its i-th element equal to 1. We define the edge between a node $\mathbf{X}$ and its i-th neighbor, based on (2) as $(\mathbf{X}, \mathbf{X} + E_i)$, where E_i is the n-dimensional $(0, 1)$ vector with the i-th through n-th components equal to 1.

More informally, a vector $\mathbf{X}$ connects to Y_i by complementing X_i if $X_{i-1} = 0$, or by complementing $X_i \ldots X_n$ if $X_{i-1} = 1$. The connection between $\mathbf{X}$ and $\mathbf{Y}$ along dimension 1 has X_0 undefined, so we can assume X_0 is either equal to 0 or equal to 1, which gives us slightly different network topologies. If we assume $X_0 = 0$, we call the network generated a "0-Möbius cube" and if we assume $X_0 = 1$, we call the the network a "1-Möbius cube."

Figure 2 illustrates the 0-Möbius and 1-Möbius cube of dimension 4. It also illustrates the expansibility of the Möbius cube networks. We can construct a 0-Möbius or 1-Möbius cube of dimension $n + 1$ from a 0-Möbius cube and a 1-Möbius cube of dimension n. We first create a new address $\mathbf{X}'$ from every

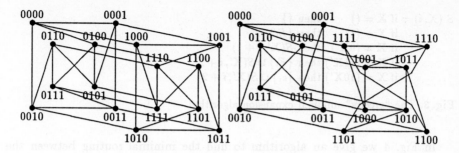

Fig. 2. 0-Möbius and 1-Möbius cubes of dimension 4.

address $\mathbf{X}$ by assigning $\mathbf{X}' = (0X_1 \ldots X_n)$ if $\mathbf{X}$ is in the 0-Möbius n-cube, or assigning $\mathbf{X}' = (1X_1 \ldots X_n)$ if $\mathbf{X}$ is in the 1-Möbius n-cube. We then construct the 0-Möbius $(n+1)$-cube by connecting all pairs of nodes that differ only in index 1, and the 1-Möbius $(n+1)$-cube by connecting all pairs of nodes that differ in index 1 through n.

4 Routing Algorithm

In this section we present our routing algorithm for the Möbius cubes. This algorithm takes two addresses $\mathbf{X}$ and $\mathbf{Y}$, and produces a shortest path between $\mathbf{X}$ and $\mathbf{Y}$. The proof of the algorithm depends on the idea of minimum expansions.

Any vector $\mathbf{X}$ over $\{\mathbb{Z}_2\}^n$ can be represented as:

$$\mathbf{X} = \sum_{i=1}^{n} (\alpha_i e_i + \beta_i E_i)$$

where the e_i's and E_i's are defined in Sect. 3 and the α_i's and β_i's are from $\{0, 1\}$. An expansion of $\mathbf{X}$ is minimal when it has the smallest weight, that is, the fewest non-zero coefficients.

The algorithm in Fig. 3 produces a minimal expansion of $\mathbf{X}$. Clearly from this algorithm the number of non-zero coefficients in a minimal expansion is at most $\lceil n/2 \rceil$. A vector $\mathbf{X}$ may have different minimal expansions from the one given by this algorithm. Luckily, a vector can have an alternate minimal expansion only in limited situations. Specifically, only when the minimum expansion $S(\mathbf{X}, 1)$ contains $\{e_i, e_{i+2}, \ldots, e_{i+2k-2}, E_{i+2k}\}$ can these elements be replaced by $\{E_i, e_{i+1}, \ldots, e_{i+2k-3}, e_{i+2k-1}\}$ without increasing the weight of the expansion, and only when $S(\mathbf{X}, 1)$ contains $\{E_i, e_{i+2}, \ldots, e_{i+2k-2}, E_{i+2k}\}$ can these elements be replaced by $\{e_i, e_{i+1}, \ldots, e_{i+2k-3}, e_{i+2k-1}\}$.

The weight of the minimal expansion of $(\mathbf{X} + \mathbf{Y})$ gives a lower bound on the distance between $\mathbf{X}$ and $\mathbf{Y}$ because the weight gives the distance when each processor has all $2n$ neighbors defined by (1) and (2), which constitute a superset of the n neighbors specified by the Möbius cubes.

$S(\mathbf{X}, i) =$ if $\mathbf{X} = ()$ then $\{\}$
         if $\mathbf{X} = (1)$ then $\{E_i\}$
         if $\mathbf{X} = (0\mathbf{X}')$ then $S(\mathbf{X}', i+1)$
         if $\mathbf{X} = (11\mathbf{X}')$ then $\{E_i\} \cup S(\mathbf{X}', i+2)$
         if $\mathbf{X} = (10\mathbf{X}')$ then $\{e_i\} \cup S(\mathbf{X}', i+2)$

Fig. 3. The "greedy" minimal expansion algorithm

In Fig. 4 we give an algorithm to find the minimal routing between the processor with address $\mathbf{X}$ and the processor with address $\mathbf{Y}$. The algorithm works by corresponding elements of the minimum expansion $S = S(\mathbf{X} + \mathbf{Y}, 1)$ to edges on a path between $\mathbf{X}$ and $\mathbf{Y}$.

Since not all elements in a minimal expansion correspond to edges of the Möbius cubes, the algorithm distinguishes between a "good" $t \in S$ and a "bad" $t \in S$ with repect to a vector $\mathbf{X}$, which indicates whether edge $(\mathbf{X}, \mathbf{X} + t)$ is present or not. The routing algorithm can immediately use a good e_i because its use will not affect the rest of the routing. Because E_i affects whether everything to its right is good or bad, good elements to E_i's right are handled first. When stuck with a bad element, the algorithm first checks to see if there is an alternate minimum expansion in which the bad element is replaced by a good one. If there is no alternate minimum expansion, the algorithm replaces the bad element with two good elements. Such a replacement occurs at most once, since after such a replacement (and taking care of at most one element), the algorithm will be faced with a leading good E_i. It will follow case 2, and take care of all the good elements to the right before using E_i. Any remaining elements to the right will be bad, but using E_i will convert them to good, and the good ones can be handled in one step each by the algorithm.

We have just given an informal proof for the following theorem. A more formal proof appears in the long version of the paper.

Theorem 1. *The routing algorithm given in figure 4 finds a minimal routing, from node $\mathbf{X}$ to node $\mathbf{Y}$. The number of routing steps is either $|S(\mathbf{X} + \mathbf{Y}, 1)|$ or $|S(\mathbf{X} + \mathbf{Y}, 1)| + 1$. The running time of the algorithm is $O(n)$ steps.*

5 Static Performance Measures

Static performance measures evaluate the performance of a network by examining graph-theoretic properties of the network. Static measures do not actually examine the behavior of messages in the network. Instead, by examining particular network properties, static performance measures place limits on the messages' behavior.

5.1 Diameter

The hypercube has a diameter of n, the maximum Hamming distance between any two nodes. Calculating the diameters of the Möbius cubes is slightly more

The input is a source address $\mathbf{X}$, a destination address $\mathbf{Y}$, and a set S which initially contains the "greedy" minimum expansion of $\mathbf{X} + \mathbf{Y}$:

```
Procedure ExactRoute(X, Y, S)
if S ≠ {} do
    i = min{j : t_j ∈ S}
    case 1: t_i = "good" e_i wrt X
        if ∃ ("good" t_{i+1} wrt X)S - {e_i})
            route along edge (Y - e_i, Y)
        else
            route along edge (X, X + e_i)
            call ExactRoute (X + e_i, Y, S - {e_i})
        end if
    case 2: t_i = "good" E_i wrt X
        if ∃ ("good" t_j wrt X, j > i) ∈ S} then
            route along edge (X, X + t_j)
            call ExactRoute (X + t_j, Y, S - {t_j})
        else
            route along edge (X, X + E_i)
            call ExactRoute (X + E_i, Y, S - {E_i})
        end if
    case 3: t_i = "bad" e_i wrt X
        if {e_i, e_{i+2}, ..., e_{i+2k-2}, E_{i+2k}} ⊆ S then
            call ExactRoute (X, Y, S ∪ {E_i, e_{i+1}, ..., e_{i+2k-3}, e_{i+2k-1}}
                -{e_i, e_{i+2}, ..., e_{i+2k-2}, E_{i+2k}})
        else
            call ExactRoute (X, Y, S ∪ {E_i, E_{i+1}} - {e_i})
        end if
    case 4: t_i = "bad" E_i wrt X
        if {E_i, e_{i+2}, ..., e_{i+2k-2}, E_{i+2k}} ⊆ S then
            call ExactRoute (X, Y, S ∪ {e_i, e_{i+1}, ..., e_{i+2k-3}, e_{i+2k-1}}
                -{E_i, e_{i+2}, ..., e_{i+2k-2}, E_{i+2k}})
        else
            call ExactRoute (X, Y, S ∪ {e_i, E_{i+1}} - {E_i})
        end if
    end case
end
```

Fig. 4. The Möbius cubes routing algorithm

complicated, due to the asymmetries of the network.

Theorem 2. *The diameter of the 0-Möbius cube is $\lceil (n/2) + 1 \rceil, n \geq 4$ and the diameter of the 1-Möbius cube is $\lceil (n+1)/2 \rceil, n \geq 4$ where n is the dimension of the cube.*

Proof. The greedy minimum expansion has at most $\lceil n/2 \rceil$ terms. The routing algorithm adds at most one more routing step, so the diameter is at worst $\lceil n/2 +$

1] steps. Routing from $(00\ldots0)$ to $(1(10)^{(n-1)/2})$, n odd, or to $(1(10)^{(n-2)/2}1)$, n even, requires this many steps on a 0-Möbius cube.

For a 1-Möbius cube, the greedy minimum expansion with the maximum number of terms falls under case 2 or the first part of case 3 in the algorithm, limiting the maximum number of steps to $\lceil(n+1)/2\rceil$. Routing from $(00\ldots0)$ to $(1(10)^{(n-1)/2})$, n odd, or to $(1(10)^{(n-2)/2}1)$, n even, requires this many steps. □

The 1-Möbius cube has the same diameter as the Twisted Cube. The 0-Möbius cube has a diameter 1 greater for any odd $n \geq 5$.

5.2   Expected Distance

The diameter represents the worst-case behavior of a single message travelling in the network. A measure of average-case behavior would be the expected distance, or the average number of routing steps between nodes. The asymmetries of the Möbius cubes make their expected distances difficult to calculate exactly. However, it is possible to bound them within values significantly below that of the hypercube's expected distance of $n/2$.

Theorem 3. *Let $E(n)$ be the expected distance for a Möbius cube of dimension n, then:*

$$\frac{n}{3} + \frac{1}{9}\left[1 - \left(-\frac{1}{2}\right)^n\right] \leq E(n) \leq \frac{n}{3} + \frac{1}{9}\left[1 - \left(-\frac{1}{2}\right)^n\right] + 1$$

Proof. We show the bounds by computing $D(n)$, the expected number of terms in the minimum expansion of any two vectors, since $D(n) \leq E(n) \leq D(n) + 1$. For a uniform distribution of source and destination address vectors, the mod 2 sums of the source and destination will be uniformly distributed over $\{\mathbb{Z}_2\}^n$, and from the minimum expansion algorithm:

$$D(n) = \frac{1}{2}D(n-1) + \frac{1}{2}(1 + D(n-2)),\ \ D(1) = 1/2,\ \ D(2) = 3/4$$

Solving this equation and substituting gives the bounds. □

Although the Möbius cubes have a diameter approximately half that of the hypercube, its expected distance is approximately $2/3$ the hypercube's expected distance.

A comparison of the expected distances of the hypercube, the Twisted cube and the Möbius cubes is shown in Fig. 5. For $n \leq 2$, all the cubes are identical. For $n \geq 3$, all three hypercube variants show an improvement on the hypercube's expected distance. The 1-Möbius cube has the smallest expected distance of all the cubes compared.

Though the Twisted Cube has the same diameter as the 1-Möbius cube, the expected distance demonstrates that the topologies of the two networks are distinct. For large n, the Twisted Cube has an expected distance of about $3n/8$ (derived from [2]), while the Möbius cubes have an expected distance of about $n/3$.

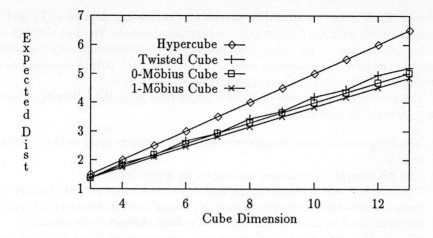

Fig. 5. Expected distances of the hypercube and variants

5.3 Fault Tolerance

The Möbius cubes and the hypercube show similar fault-tolerance behavior. The node-fault tolerance is the minimum number of nodes that must be removed to disconnect the network, minus one. Likewise, the edge-fault tolerance is the minimum number of edges that disconnect the network, minus one.

Theorem 4. *The node-fault and edge-fault tolerance of the Möbius cubes is $n-1$.*

Proof. We outline a simple inductive proof based on the construction of an n-dimensional Möbius cube from $(n-1)$-dimensional Möbius cubes. Briefly, if all the faults occur in one $(n-1)$-subcube, then the network is connected through the other subcube. If the faults are divided between the two subcubes, then by induction the two subcubes are each connected and joined together. □

6 Dynamic Performance

Dynamic performance measures go beyond static measures in evaluating a system's performance. They arise from the interaction of messages with not just the network, but with each other. Dynamic measures depend not only on the topology (or interconnections) of the network, but also the particular routing algorithm used and the distribution of messages in the network.

6.1 Model of Computation

To measure dynamic performance for a network, we simulated communications in the network. We used the model of Abraham [2] to represent each node in a network. Each node is assumed to consist of a processing element (PE) and a crossbar switch with $n+1$ input and $n+1$ output channels. The 1-st through n-th channels connect to the other crossbars by the interconnection network being studied. The $(n+1)$-st channels connect to the PE. Each output channel has a fixed-length buffer queue of messages, except the $(n+1)$-st.

The simulation is discrete-time. In a single time step, the following actions are performed by each node:

1. The PE generates zero or more messages and forwards them to the crossbar switch.
2. The PE accepts all messages waiting on its input channel.
3. The crossbar switch examines the buffers for each of its output channels; if there are messages waiting in an output channel's buffer, the crossbar switch forwards the first message through that output channel to its neighbor.
4. The crossbar switch takes all messages incoming on its input channels and places them in the buffer of the correct output channel.

For each network simulated, we use the algorithm currently published. the hypercube uses the standard L-R bit correction algorithm, the Twisted Cube uses the algorithm in [8], and the Möbius cubes use the algorithm demonstrated here, (which shows better performance than the algorithms given in [3] and [4]).

We assume that messages are generated from each PE with the destination selected uniformly from all other possible addresses. The messages are generated at a uniform message generation rate m_g. When $0.0 \leq m_g < 1.0$, each PE generates a message at each time step with probability m_g. When $1.0 \leq m_g < 2.0$, each PE generates at least one message every time step, and generates a second message with probabilty $m_g - 1.0$.

6.2 Message Latency

The mean message latency is the mean time a message spends travelling between its source and destination nodes. This is the expected internodal distance, plus the mean time spent waiting in buffer queues.

In Fig. 6, we compare the mean message latency for the hypercube, Twisted cube and both of the Möbius cubes of dimension 7, varying the message generation rate m_g from 0.1 to 1.975. For this particular simulation, we limited the simulation to 10000 time steps and to queues of 200 buffers. For the hypercube and the Twisted Cube, our simulation results are similar to Abraham's [2].

At low message generation rates, the number of conflicts for output channels is fairly low, so the mean internodal distance is the dominating factor in message latency. For this reason, the variant cubes show a smaller message latency. When the generation rate becomes high enough, the communications links begin to "saturate" – more messages arrive than the links can process and their queues lengthen without bound, causing the latency of messages using that link to be come increasingly longer. Because our simulation has finite length queues, messages begin to be lost as the crossbar buffer queues fill. This shows up on the

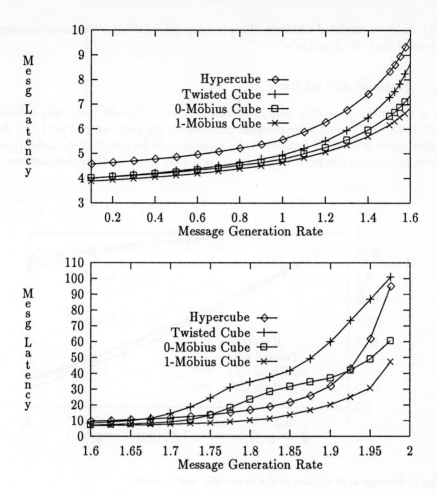

Fig. 6. Mean message latency of the hypercube and variants

graph as a "kink" in the plotted curves of the Twisted cube and the 0-Möbius cube.

The variant networks begin to saturate at different rates than the hypercube. In fact, the Twisted Cube performs considerably worse than the rest. The 0-Möbius cube and the Twisted cube have lower saturation rates than the hypercube, partly because their asymmetries cause their link saturation rates to vary considerably from the average.

However, asymmetries in networks will not always lead to worse dynamic performance. The 1-Möbius cube disproves this by saturating at a rate higher than that of the hypercube. We hypothesize that our routing algorithm for the 1-Möbius cube achieves fairly uniform utilization for all its links. When combined with its lower expected distance, this produces considerably lower mean message latencies than the hypercube.

6.3 Message Arrival Rate

In a real message-passing computer system, the nodes will have only a finite buffer space. If two or more message compete for the same output port and the buffer queue is filled, all but one of the messages will be lost. It then makes more sense to measure the percentage of messages that arrive at their destinations.

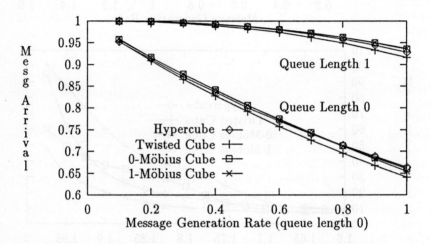

Fig. 7. Message arrival rates of the hypercube and variants

In Fig. 7, we compare the mean message arrival rates for the hypercube, the Twisted cube and both of the Möbius cubes of dimension 7, varying the message generation rate m_g from 0.1 to 1.0. We include the message arrival rates for buffer lengths of 0 and 1 on each output port. All of the networks perform with minimal differences in their behavior, though the Twisted cube consistently has the lowest message arrival rate. As with Abraham's simulation results, over 90% of the messages arrive when only a single buffer space per channel is included.

7 Conclusion

The Möbius cubes are interesting variants of the hypercube. Like the hypercube, the Möbius cubes are expansible, and have a logarithmic number of communication links per node, a uniform rule for node connections, and a simple and fast routing algorithm that has an $O(n)$ runtime. The Möbius cubes show superior static performance when compared to the hypercube: about 50% the diameter and about 66% the expected distance of the hypercube. The Möbius cubes show comparable dynamic performance to the hypercube, with the 1-Möbius cube showing the best message latency and message arrival rates. However, the Möbius cubes may be inferior to the hypercube in having less symmetry in their connections and in having a somewhat more complicated routing algorithm.

References

1. Abraham, Seth and Krishnan Padmanabhan, "An analysis of the twisted cube topology," *1989 International Conference on Parallel Processing*, Vol. 1, pp.116-120. Pennsylvania State Press.
2. Abraham, Seth, "Issues in the architecture of direct interconnection schemes for multiprocessors," *PhD thesis, CSRD Rpt. No. 977*, University of Illinois, 1990.
3. Cull, Paul and Shawn Larson, "The Möbius cube: an interconnection network for parallel processing," *OSU Technical Report 91-20-2*, Department of Computer Science, Oregon State University, 1991.
4. Cull, Paul and Shawn Larson, "The "Möbius cubes": improved cubelike structures for parallel computation," *6th International Parallel Processing Symposium*, pp. 610-613, IEEE Computer Society Press, 1992.
5. Efe, Kemal, "A Variation on the Hypercube with Lower Diameter," *IEEE Trans. Comput.*, vol. 40, no. 11, pp. 1312-1316, Nov. 1987.
6. Estafahanian, Abdol-Hossein, Lionel M. Ni, and Bruce Sagan. "The twisted n-cube with application to multiprocessing," *IEEE Transactions on Computers*, 40:1 (January 1991), pp.88-93.
7. Hillis, Daniel W., "The connection machine (computer architecture for the new wave)," *MIT AI Memo 646*, Sept. 1981.
8. Hilbers, Peter A. J., R.J. Marion Koopman and Jan L.A. Van de Snepscheut, "The twisted cube," *PARLE: Parallel Architecture and Languages Europe, Volume 1: Parallel Architectures*, pp. 152-158. deBakker, J., Numan, A. and Trelearen, P. (Eds.). Springer Verlag, Berlin, W. Germany, 1987.
9. Seitz, Charles L., "Concurrent VLSI Architectures, " *IEEE Transactions on Computers*, 33:12 (December 1984), pp. 1247-1264.
10. Singhvi, Nitin K., and Kanad Ghose, "The MCube, " *Technical Report No. CS-TR-91-10*, Dept. of Computer Science, State University of New York, Binghampton, 1991.

Optimal Mappings of m Dimensional FFT Communication to k Dimensional Mesh for Arbitrary m and k

Z. GEORGE MOU and XIAOJING WANG

Department of Computer Science and Center for Complex Systems
Brandeis University, Waltham, MA 02254, USA
{mou,wang}@cs.brandeis.edu

Abstract. The FFT communication patterns are important to not only FFT algorithms, but also many other algorithms over one or higher dimensional. The mapping of m dimensional FFT communication to k dimensional mesh has previously been considered only for the following special cases (a) $m = 1$ or 2, $k = 1$ or 2, (b) $m = 1$ or 2, $k = \log(n)$ where n is the size of the machine. In this paper, we present the optimal mappings of m dimensional FFT communication onto k dimensional mesh for arbitrary m and k. The mappings are optimal since the communication distances in the logarithmic steps sum to exactly the diameter of the mesh regardless of the dimension cr the shape of the mesh. An m-k shuffle permutation, which subsumes perfect shuffle, is introduced and used to derive some of the optimal mappings. As a by-product, an optimal broadcast algorithm over any dimensional mesh, including binary hypercube as a special case, is presented.

1 Introduction

The butterfly communication patterns found in FFT algorithms, which we will refer to as *FFT communications*, are important to not only the FFT algorithms but also many other divide-and-conquer algorithms for a broad class of numerical problems including reduction, scan, polynomial evaluation, linear difference equations, and bitonic sort. On the other hand, mesh is an important underlying topology for a wide range of parallel architecture, ranging from the one dimensional linear array to the binary hypercube which is no more than a mesh of logarithmic dimensional mesh. The study of the mappings from FFT communication to mesh architectures however has been very limited in the past. Let m be the dimension of the FFT communications, and k the dimension of the mesh, then the previous studies only cover the following special cases:

- $m = 1, 2, k = 1, 2$ [3, 1, 2].
- $m = 1, 2, k = \log(n)$ [11, 13, 5, 12, 10].
- $m = 1, 1 \le k \le \log(n)$ [7, 8].

For the case of $k = \log(n)$, we have included Stone's work on perfect shuffle [12] and Preparata's work on cube-connected-shuffle [10] since the well-known isomorphism between the two architectures and a binary hypercube [14]. It thus can be observed that the mapping has not been studied for high dimensional FFT and the meshes with the dimensionality between the two extremes – $k = 1$ and 2 and $k = \log(n)$. Moreover, there is a lack of general approach to the problem for different dimensions of the FFT and the mesh, and the inherent connections between the results for different dimensions cannot be easily seen.

In this paper, we study the mapping from m dimensional (m-d) FFT to k dimensional (k-d) mesh for arbitrary m and k. The main results generalize the previous work in [1, 3, 2, 11, 13, 7, 8] and include

- A unified framework to study the mapping for arbitrary m and k.
- A family of $(\log(n))!$ mappings for arbitrary dimensions of the FFT and the mesh with size n.
- Establish the lower bound of the communication cost, and prove the optimality of the family of mappings.

As a by-product of the proof in Section 3, we present optimal broadcast algorithms which can be used to (1) broadcast over k-d mesh for any k, including binary hypercube as a special case; (2) broadcast over a given dimension of an m dimensional array distributed over a k-d mesh for any m and k. This result thus generalizes the well-known result on broadcasting in [4].

This paper is organized as follows. We begin by introducing some basic notions about mesh and FFT communication in Section 2. In Section 3, we establish the lower bound of the FFT communication on mesh. Section 4 and 5 introduces two specific mappings from FFT communications to mesh for arbitrary dimensions, present the implementations of the communications on mesh, and prove their optimality. In Section 6 we introduce a family of optimal mappings for which the previous two are members. In Section 7, we generalize the results in previous sections to allow arbitrary shape of the FFT array and the mesh. Some of the related results that cannot be reported hear are mentioned in Section 8, where other comments are made as well.

2 Preliminary

2.1 k dimensional mesh

The topology of the mesh A k *dimensional mesh* with the *shape* $P_{k-1} \times \ldots, P_0$ consists of processors in the set P^k of the form

$$P = \{p = (p_{k-1}, \ldots, p_0) \mid 0 \le p_i \; P_{i-1}, \text{ for } i = 0 \text{ to } k - 1\}$$

where P_i is the size of the mesh along the ith *dimension*, p_i the coordinate of processors p along the ith dimension. Two processors $u, v \in P^k$ are *directly connected*, denoted by uLv, if only only if their coordinates differ along one dimension by one, namely

$$uLv \Leftarrow |u_i - v_i| = 1, \text{ and } u_j - v_j = 0 \le i, j < k - 1, j \ne i,$$

The total number of processors $s = |P| = \prod_{i=0}^{k-1}$ is referred to as the *size of the mesh*.

A *metric function* $\mathcal{D} : P^k \times P^k \to INT$ is introduced to measure the *distance between processors*. Given two processors $u = (u_0, u_1, \ldots, u_{k-1})$ and $v = (v_0, v_1, \ldots, v_{k-1})$ in P^k the function D is

$$\mathcal{D}(u, v) = \sum_{i=0}^{k-1} |u_i - v_i|$$

The *diameter* of a mesh is defined to be

$$Min\{\mathcal{D}(x,y) \mid x,y \in P\}$$

It follows from the definitions that

Theorem 1.

- the function D is a well-defined metric function over space P.
- when $k = 2$, D reduces to the Manhattan Distance over two dimensional grid space.
- when $k = log(n)$ D reduces to the Hamming Distance over the space of k-bit binary numbers.
- when the mesh is viewed as a graph, D is consistent with the length of shortest path between any two processors.
- The diameter of a k dimensional mesh is $\sum_{i=0}^{k-1}(P_i - 1)$ where P_i is the size of its ith dimension.

A mesh is *regular* if all of its dimensions has the same size. It follows that a regular k dimensional size has the diameter of $k(n^{1/k} - 1)$.

Communications over mesh A *communication between two processors* u and v denoted by $z(u, v)$ means that a message is sent from processor u to processor v. The communication is *symmetric* if at the same time a message is sent from processor v to processor u.

A *communication over the mesh* with processor set P^k with respect to binary relation R over P^k denoted by Z^R is the collection of communications between two processors

$$Z^R = \{z(u,v) | uRv\}$$

The communication Z^R is symmetric if all its members are symmetric. It is asymmetric if none of its members is symmetric [1].

A d-step communication over P^k is a sequence of d communications of the form

$$(Z^{R_0}, Z^{R_1}, \ldots, Z^{R_{d-1}})$$

such that Z^{R_i} is performed before $Z^{R_{(i+1)}}$ for $0 \le i < d - 1$

An asymmetric communication Z^R over a $k-d$ mesh is *uniform* if there exists a constant vector, referred to as the *communication vector*, $w = (w_0, \ldots, w_{k-1})$ such that pRp' if and only if $p' = p + w$. A symmetric communication is uniform if the relation R can be partitioned into two sub-relations R_1 and R_2 such that $R = R_1 \cup R_2$, and both Z^{R_1} and Z^{R_2} are uniform.

A special case of uniform communication is *single dimensional communication*, where the communication vector has the form of

$$(0, \ldots, w_i, 0, \ldots, 0)$$

In other words, the communication is sent from all the senders to all the receivers only along dimension i by distance w_i.

---

[1] A communication Z^R thus can be neither symmetric nor asymmetric by the above definition.

Cost of communications We measure the cost of a communication $z(u, v)$ between two processors (alone) denoted by $\mathcal{C}(z(u, v))$ by the distance between the two processors, namely

$$\mathcal{C}(z(u, v)) = \mathcal{D}(u, v)$$

The cost of a general communication over the entire mesh is difficult to determine because it depends on not only the distances the messages travel, but also the routing algorithms and if there is message congestion under the routing algorithm.

However the *cost of a uniform communication* with communication vector $w = (w_{k-1}, \ldots, w_0)$ is simply the norm of

$$|w| = \sum_{i=0}^{k-1} |w_i|$$

which reflects the minimum number of communication links that the messages go through. This cost is realistic under many possible routine algorithms. A straightforward one is that route the messages from dimension 0 by distance w_0, dimension 1 by distance $w_1, \cdots$, dimension $(k-1)$ by distance w_{k-1}. The communication cost along dimension i costs exactly w_k since all messages can travel with no interferences with each due to the uniformity. It follows that the cost of single dimensional communication with the communication vector $(0, \ldots, w_i, 0, \ldots, 0)$ is simply w_i.

Finally, the cost of a d-step communication over P^k is the sum of the cost of all the d steps, i.e.

$$\mathcal{C}(Z^{R_0}, Z^{R_1}, \ldots, Z^{R_{d-1}}) = \sum_{i=0}^{d-1} \mathcal{C}(Z^{R_i})$$

Note that although the order of the communication steps are generally important in computing, it is of no importance as far as the cost is concerned since addition is commutative. Therefore, two d-step communications

$$(Z_0^{R_0}, Z_0^{R_1}, \ldots, Z_0^{R_{d-1}}) \text{ and } (Z_1^{R_0}, Z_1^{R_1}, \ldots, Z_1^{R_{d-1}})$$

are *cost-equivalent* if and only if they contain the same set of constituents.

Communication instructions The above discussion is true for both MIMD and SIMD architectures. In the case of k-d SIMD architecture, we assume the *communication instruction*

$$d\,(w_{k-1}, \ldots, w_0)$$

which sends a message from each active processors processor $u = (u_0, \ldots, u_{k-1})$ to processor $v = (u_{k-1}+w_{k-1}, \ldots, u_{k-1}+w_{k-1})$. A uniform communication with communication vector $w = (w_{k-1}, \ldots, w_0)$ thus can be *implemented* by $d(z) = d(z_0, \ldots, z_{k-1})$ [2] Single dimensional communication on mesh can be expressed more concisely by the instruction

$$sd\,(i, w_i)$$

---

[2] Note that this implementation may cause messages sent between unrelated processors but will definitely deliver all the messages to be sent. The unwanted messages can be either prevented by a predicate over the processors or simply ignored after the reception, which is often the cheaper approach in practice

where the $0 \leq i < (k-1)$ is a dimension, $0 \leq w_i < P_i$ is the communication distance along that dimension i with size P_i.

Finally, we would like to emphasize that the discussions of this section applies to binary hypercube, which is no more than a regular k dimensional mesh with n processors where $k = \log(n)$.

2.2 M dimensional FFT communication

An m dimensional FFT communication is defined over an m *dimensional index set* I^m of the form

$$I^m = \{(i_0, i_1, \ldots, i_{m-1}) \mid 0 \leq i_j < A_j, \text{ for } j = 0 \text{ to } m\}$$

where A_j is the size along the dimension j. The *shape* of the index set is $A_0 \times \cdots A_{m-1}$, and the *size* of the index set is $n = \sum_{j=0}^{m-1} A_j$. The index set is said to be *regular* if all dimensions have the same size, namely, $A_j = A_i$ for all $0 \leq i, j < m$.

A communication between two indices $x, y \in I$, denoted by $c(i, j)$, means a value is sent from x to y. The communication is bidirectional if at the same time a message is sent from y to x.

A communication over an m dimensional index set I^m with respect to a binary relation over I^m denoted by C^R is a collection of communication between two indices $x, y \in I$ of the form

$$C^R = \{c(x, y) \mid xRy\}$$

A d-step communication over the index set I^m is a sequence of communications over I^m of the form

$$(C_{R_0}, C_{R_1}, \ldots, C_{R_{d-1}})$$

such that C_{R_i} is performed before $C_{R_{i+1}}$ for $0 \leq i < d-1$.

We next define a special binary relation over the index set I^m. Given two indices $x, y \in I^m$

$$x = (x_0, \ldots, x_p, \ldots x_{m-1}) \text{and} \quad y = (y_0, \ldots, x_p, \ldots, y_{m-1})$$

we say x and y are p-q *related* denoted by $x\, R_p^q y$ if and only the binary numbers of their pth dimensional index x_p and y_p differ in their qth least significant bits. Observe that this relation is symmetric by definition. It can be decomposed into two disjoint relations $R_p^q(0)$ and $R_p^q(1)$, where x is $R_p^q(0)((1))$ related to y if they are p-q related, and the qth bit of x_p is 0 (1), of y_p is 1 (0).

A *p-q communication* denoted by $C^R(p, q)$ over an index set is a collection of communications (to be performed in parallel) of the form

$$C^R(p, q) = C_p^{R^q} = \{c(x, y) \mid x R_p^q y\}$$

An m *dimensional FFT communication over* index set I^m with dimension size A consists of $(m \times \log(A))$-step p-q communications. The communication can be of *postmorphism* or of *premorphism* [9]. A postmorphism m dimensional communication is performed from the least significant bit to the most significant bit for each dimension

$$(C^R(0,0), \ldots, C^R(0, a_0 - 1),$$
$$C^R(1,0), \ldots, C^R(1, a_1 - 1),$$
$$\ldots, \ldots$$
$$C^R(m-1, 0) \ldots C^R(m-1, a_{m-1} - 1))$$
$$\text{where } a_j = \log(A_j)$$

In contrast, a premorphism m dimensional communication is performed from the most significant bit to the least significant for each dimension:

$$(C^R(0, a_0 - 1), \ldots, C^R(0, 0),$$
$$C^R(1, a_1 - 1), \ldots, C^R(1, 0),$$
$$\ldots, \ldots$$
$$C^R(m - 1, a_{m-1} - 1) \ldots C^R(m - 1, 0))$$

It should be pointed out that the m-d FFT communication is symmetric. More precisely, each step of the communication based on the relation R_p^q can be decomposed into two asymmetric communication, one is based on the relation $R_p^q(0)$, and another on the relation $R_p^q(1)$.

2.3 Mappings

Given an m-d index set I^m and the processor set P^k of a k dimensional mesh, a *mapping* $f : I^m \rightarrow P^k$ is an assignment from the set of indices to the set of processors. For the discussion of this section we assume the *mapping ratio* $R = |I^m|/|P^k| = 1$ and f is bijective.

A mapping f maps a communication c(x, y) between two indices $x, y \in I^m$ to a communication $z(f(x), f(y))$ between two processors $u, v \in P^k$ where u = f(x), and v = f(y), which we denote by $z(u, v) = f(c(x, y))$. Similarly, f maps a communication over an index set C^R to a communication Z^R over the mesh

$$Z_R = \{(z(f(x), f(y)) \mid xRy\}$$

which we denote by $Z^R = f(C^R)$.

The mapping f is a *uniform mapping* for a communication C^R over an index set if $Z^R = f(C^R)$ is uniform.

Given a d-step communication over an index set I^m

$$(C^{R_0}, C^{R_1}, \ldots, C_{R_{d-1}})$$

and a mapping f from I^m to P^k, we say f maps the d-step communication over I^m to a d-step communication over P^k

$$(f(C^{R_0}, f(C^{R_1}), \ldots, f(C_{d-1}^R))$$

The following proposition allows us to focus on the study of one instead of both of the two types of m-d FFT communications.

Theorem 2. *Let C and C' be respective the post- and pre- morphism FFT communications over the index set I^m, $Z = f(C)$ and $Z' = f(C')$ are the communications over P^k where f is a mapping function from I^m to P^k, then Z and Z' are cost equivalent.*

Proof Follows from the definitions.

Note that there was no notion of cost for communication over index set. With a mapping from index set to processors in meshes, we can now define the *cost of communications over index set under the mapping*. Given a mapping $f : I^m \rightarrow P^k$, the cost of a communication between two indices $x, y \in I^m$ is the cost of the communication between the two processors $f(x), f(y) \in P^k$, the cost of a communication C^R over I^m is the cost of the communication $f(C^R)$ over P^k, the cost of a d-step communication C is the cost of the d-step communication $f(C)$.

3   The lower bound of m-d FFT communication on k-d mesh

To show the optimality of the mappings, we need to establish the lower bound of the FFT communications on a k-d mesh. This section is to establish the lower bound for FFT communication through the problem of broadcast over m-d arrays, and show how broadcast can be reduced to the FFT communication.

Given an index set I^m, and an index $x \in I^m$, the problem of broadcast is to send a value associated with x to all other indices directly or indirectly. For simplicity of the discussion, we first assume $x = (0, \ldots, 0)$, the index with all 0's along all dimensions.

We next define a simpler problem over m-d index set called *broadcast along a given dimension*. Given an index set I^m, the problem of broadcast along its pth dimension is to send a value from each index x of the form

$$x = (x_{m-1}, \ldots, 0_p, \ldots, x0)$$

where $0 \leq x_j < A$ to the A indices in the set

$$\{x = (x_{m-1}, \ldots, X_p, \ldots, x0) \mid 0 \leq X < A\}$$

Lemma 3. *The problem of broadcast over I^m can be solved by solving m broadcasts along the m dimensions in any order.*

Proof Without loss of generality, we assume the m broadcast is done in the order of dimension 0, dimension 1, $\cdots$, and finally dimension $(m - 1)$.

After the first step, all indices in the following set

$$\{(0, \ldots, 0, X) \mid 0 \leq X < A\}$$

will have the value. And after the ith step, all indices in the index set of

$$\{(0, \ldots, X_{i-1}, \ldots, X_0) \mid 0 \leq X < A\}$$

will have the value. Therefore, after m steps, all indices will have the value.

In the following, we refer to the $\log(A)$-step communication based on the relation $R_{(p,q)}$ for a fixed p, and $q = 0$ to $(\log(A)-1)$ the m-d FFT communication (restricted) on the pth dimension.

Lemma 4. *The m-d FFT communication over I^m along the pth dimension can be used to achieve broadcast along the pth dimension.*

Proof The pth demensional FFT communication over array of shape A^m consists of A parallel FFT communications over vector of size A, each of them can be used to broadcast along one vector (see Figure 1 and [6].)

In order to complete the discussion of this section, we need to further establish the following fact

Lemma 5.

– *A one dimensional FFT communication can be used to broadcast from any index to all other in the vector.*

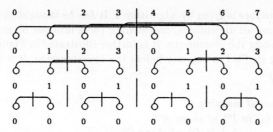

Fig. 1. A broadcast over vector with FFT communication

- *The m dimensional FFT communication can be used to broadcast from any index to all others in the array.*

Note that the second part of the lemma follows from the first. The first part can be proven by the construction of a algorithm with the FFT communication, which we omitted to save the space.

Theorem 6. *The lower bound for the m dimensional FFT communication over I^m on a k dimensional mesh P^k of shape $S_{k-1} \times \cdots, S_0$, where $|I^m| = |P^k|$, is the diameter of the mesh, i.e. $\sum_{i=0}^{k-1}(S_{k-1} - 1)$.*

Proof Since FFT communication can be used to broadcast any index to all others in I^m, no matter what the mapping $f : I^m \to P^k$ is, it can be used to send a value from a corner processor to a processor at the opposite corner with the distance equal to the diameter.

4   The Identical Mapping

The mapping f from an m-d index set I^m to a k-d mesh with processors P^k has the functionality of $f : I^m \to P^k$. In this section, we assume

- The mapping ratio is one, thus $|I^m| = |P^k|$.
- The mesh is regular, thus it has the shape of $S \times \cdots \times S = |P^k|$.

We introduce the following operations over binary numbers and integers:

Coding $B(i)$ where i is an integer returns i's binary number.
Decoding $B^{-1}(b)$ where b is a binary number returned the integer such that $B(B^{-1}(b)) = b$.
Concatenation $cat(b_{m-1}, \ldots, b_0) = b$, where b_i are binary numbers of w bits, b is a binary number of m*w bits whose first leftmost w bits are those of b_0, second leftmost w bits are those of b_1, and so on.
Decompose $dec(b, m) = (b_{m-1}, \ldots, b_0)$, the inverse of the concatenation operation cat.
Set $set(b, k, x) = b'$, where b, b' are binary numbers, k an integer, x a binary bit, b' is the same as b except that the kth least significant bit is set to x.
Quotient $Q(i, j)$ returns the quotient of the division i/j.
Remainder $R(i, j)$ returns the remainder of the division i/j.

The mapping we introduce is given by Algorithm 1. It can be thought as taking the bits from the indices along all dimensions, concatenate them into one binary number, and then take it apart along the dimensions. It is further illustrated in Figure 4. Since the bit positions are not shuffled in any way before the concatenation, it is referred to as the *identical mapping*.

Algorithm 1 *The identical mapping*
Input: index $(i_{m-1}, \ldots, i_0)$ *in* I^m *of shape* A^m.
Output: coordinate $(x_{k-1}, \ldots, x_0)$ *in* P^k *of shape* S^k.

$s = \log(S)$, $I = cat(B(i_{m-1}, \ldots, B(i_0))$ $(x_{k-1}, \ldots, x_0) = dec(I, s)$,
return $(x_{k-1}, \ldots, x_0)$

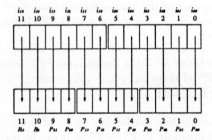

Fig. 2. An example of the identical mapping for n=12, m=2, k=3

The following proposition answers how the FFT communication is mapped to the communication on mesh under the identity mapping.

Theorem 7. *Let A and S be the dimension sizes of the index set I^m and mesh P^k respectively, $a = \log(A)$, $s = \log(S)$, then the identical mapping $f : I^m \Rightarrow P^k$ maps a step of FFT communication $C^R(p, q)$ over I^m to the single dimensional uniform mesh communication of the form $sd(i, w)$, where*

$$i = Q(p * a + q)/s \text{ and } w = 2^{R(p*a+q)/s}$$

Proof By the definition of relation $R(p, q)$, two communicating indices differ only in their qth bit of pth dimension. The identity mapping maps that bit to the wth bit of the ith dimension, the communication is thus sd (i, w).

We can then define a function $g_{id}(p, q) = (i, w)$ called the *translating function* associated with the mapping f from I^m to P^k, which takes p and q, returns p and w by the algorithm given in Theorem 7. The following algorithm then implement the postmorphism m-d FFT communication on a k dimension mesh under the identical mapping

Algorithm 2 *m-d FFT postmorphism communication under identity mapping with translating function*

for p = 0 to m-1
    for q = 0 to $\log(A) - 1$
        sd o g_{id} *(p, q)*

A disadvantage of the above algorithms is that the translating function is being computed for each value of p and p, and the computing is fairly expensive. The following algorithm exploit the regularity of the translation when p and q changes from one value to the next, and reduces the computation of the translation function to some simpler operations:

Algorithm 3 *m-d FFT postmorphism communication without translating function*

Max_Bit =$\log(P)$, *dim = 0, dis = 1 bit_ptr = 0;*
for i = 0 to $m * \log(A) - 1$
    sd (dim, dis)
    bit_ptr = bit_ptr +1
    if bit_ptr = Max_Bit then dim = dim +1, bit_ptr = 0, dis = 1
    else bit_ptr = bit_ptr +1, dis = 2 dis*

A similar program can be written for a premorphism m dimensional FFT communication.

We give an example in Figure 4 where a two dimensional postmorphism FFT communication is translated into the communications of communications on a three dimensional regular mesh for $n = 4k$ under the identical mapping.

	q = 0	q = 1	q = 2	q = 3	q = 4	q = 5
p = 0	sd(0,1)	sd(0,2)	sd(0,4)	sd(0,8)	sd(1,1)	sd(1,2)
p = 1	sd(1,4)	sd(1,8)	sd(2,1)	sd(2,2)	sd(2,4)	sd(2,8)

Fig. 3. The identical mapping for m = 2, k=3, and size = 4k

It can be easily verified the total communication distance in the 12 steps of the communication of the above example is

$$3 \times \sum_{i=0}^{3} 2^i = 3 \times 15 = 45$$

which exactly equal to the diameter of the three dimensional mesh of the shape of $16 \times 16 \times 16$, the mapping is thus optimal. More general, we have

Theorem 8. *The cost of the m-d FFT communication over index set of size n on a k-d regular mesh of the same size under the identical mapping is the diameter of the mesh -* $k(n^{1/k} - 1)$.

Proof: The cost is simply the sum of all the single dimensional communications, namely

$$k \times \sum_{x=1}^{\log(n/k)} 2^x = k(n^{1/k} - 1)$$

It follows from Propositions 8, 1, and 6 that

Theorem 9. *The identical mapping from m-d FFT communication over I^m to a k-d mesh P^k of the same size is optimal.*

5 The m-k Shuffle Mappings

In this section, we introduce another mapping from m-d FFT communication to k-d mesh of the same size based on what we call *m-k shuffle permutation*.

A *m-k* shuffle can be thought as a way of dealing n cards $0\ldots(n-1)$ from m dealers $M_0,\ldots,M_{m-1}$ to k gamblers $K_0,\ldots,K_{k-1}$. To begin, the n cards numbered from 0 to (n-1) are partitioned into m decks and dealer M_i holds the cards from $w_1 * i \, to \, w_1 * (i+1) - 1$. The dealing of the cards then proceeds as follows:

1. The dealer M_0 starts dealing the k cards on the top of his deck to the k gamblers, the ith card to gambler K_i.
2. After dealer M_j finishes his turn, dealer M_{j+1} deals his cards the same way to the k gamblers, for $j = 0$ to $m-1$.
3. After dealer M_{k-1} finishes his turn of dealing, dealer M_0 starts again.
4. The dealing stops when all the cards are given out.

Now there are w_2 cards in each of the k gamblers, and the cards are ordered by the time they are received. We then merge the k decks of cards from the k gamblers into one deck. So that the cards from gambler K_i proceeds the cards from gambler K_{i+1} from $i = 0$ to $(k-2)$. This process clearly maps each card from a position number x before the dealing to a new position number y in the merged pile. It should be pointed out that m-k shuffles are generalizations of the *perfect shuffle* permutation where $m = 2$ and $k = 1$. An example for $m = 2$, and $k = 3$ is given in Figure 4.

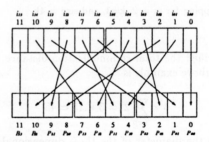

Fig. 4. An example of S_k^m for $n = 12, m = 2, k = 3$

Formally, an *m-k* shuffle S_k^m is a permutation over integers from 0 to $(n-1)$.

Theorem 10. *An m-k shuffle S_k^m over n integers, assuming that n is a multiple of m and k, n/m is a multiple of k, is the permutation over the integers $S_k^m(x) = y$ where*

$$y = R(x,k)w_2 + Q(R(x,w_1),k)m + Q(x,w_1)$$
$$\text{where } w_1 = n/m, w_2 = n/k$$

We next define a mapping of binary numbers based on m-k shuffle. Given a binary number $b = (b_{n-1}, \ldots, b_i, \ldots, b_0)$, the m-k shuffle of b is

$$S_k^m(b) = (b_{S_k^m(n-1)}, \ldots, b_{S_k^m(i)}, \ldots, b_{S_k^m(0)})$$

The m-k *shuffle mapping* from m-d FFT communication over index set I^m to k-d mesh with processors in P^k is different from the identical mapping only in that a m-k shuffle is performed over the concatenated binary number before it is partitioned into k dimensions:

Algorithm 4 *The m-k Shuffle Mapping*
Input: index $(i_{m-1}, \ldots, i_0)$ in I^m of shape A^m.
Output: coordinate $(x_{k-1}, \ldots, x_0)$ in P^k of shape S^k.

$s = \log(S)$, $I = cat(B(i_{m-1}), \ldots, B(i_0))$, $J = S_k^m(I)$, $(x_{k-1}, \ldots, x_0) = dec(J, s)$,
return $(x_{k-1}, \ldots, x_0)$

The following theorem answers how the FFT communication is mapped to the communication on mesh under the m-k shuffle mapping.

Theorem 11. *Let the m-k shuffle be the mapping from I^m of shape of shape A^m to mesh processor set P^k of shape S^k, $a = \log(A)$, $s = \log(S)$, $n = \log(|I^m|)$, $w_1 = n/m$, $w_2 = n/k$, then a step of FFT communication $C^R(p, q)$ over I^m is mapped to the single dimensional uniform mesh communication of the form $sd(i, w)$, where*

$$i = R(x, k)$$
$$w = Q(R(x, w_1), k)m + Q(x, w_1)$$

Proof Omitted.

The above theorem also defines the translating function for the m-k shuffle mapping, namely

$$g_{(m,k)}(p, q) = (i, w)$$
$$\text{where}$$
$$i = R(x, k), w = Q(R(x, w_1), k)m + Q(x, w_1)$$

The m-d FFT communication can then be implemented by the following algorithm

Algorithm 5 *m-d FFT postmorphism communication under m-k shuffle mapping with translating function*

for $p = 0$ to m-1
  for $q = 0$ to $\log(A) - 1$
    $sd \circ g_{m,k}(p, q)$

To take advantages of the regularity of the translation, a postmorphism, the algorithm can be rewritten as

Algorithm 6 *m-d FFT postmorphism communication under m-k shuffle mapping without translating function*

```
Max_Dim =k, dim = 0, dis = 1, bit_ptr = 0
for i = 0 to m * log(A) − 1
    sd (dim, dis), dim = dim + 1, bit_ptr = bit_ptr +2
    if bit_ptr = Max_Bit then dim = dim +1, bit_ptr = 0, dis = 1
    else bit_ptr = bit_ptr +1, dis = 2* dis
```

A similar program can be written for a premorphism m-d FFT communication.

We give an example in Figure 5 where a two dimensional postmorphism FFT communication is translated into communications on three dimensional regular mesh for $n = 4k$ under the m-k shuffle mapping.

	q = 0	q = 1	q = 2	q = 3	q = 4	q = 5
p = 0	sd(0,1)	sd(1,1)	sd(2,1)	sd(0,4)	sd(1,4)	sd(2,4)
p = 1	sd(0,2)	sd(1,2)	sd(2,2)	sd(0,8)	sd(1,8)	sd(2,8)

Fig. 5. The m-k shuffle mapping translation for m = 2, k=3, and size = 4k

To determine the cost the m-d FFT communication under the m-k shuffle mapping, we first show that

Theorem 12. *Let F be the m-d FFT communication over an index set I^m. f_{id} and $f_{(m,k)}$ respectively the identical mapping and the m-k shuffle mapping from I^m to a regular mesh of the same size, $f_{\text{id}}(F)$ and $f_{(m,k)}(F)$ the mapped mesh communications from the FFT communication. Then $f_{(m,k)})(F)$ and $f_{\text{id}}(F)$ are cost-equivalent.*

Proof Since they contain the same set of single dimensional communications, only in different orders.

It follows from Theorems 12 and 9 that

Theorem 13. *The m-k shuffle mapping from m-d FFT communication over I^m to a k-d regular mesh P^k of the same size is optimal.*

6 The bit-permuting family of optimal mappings

In the previous two sections we introduced two optimal mappings from m-d FFT communication to k-d mesh of the same size, and showed that both of them are optimal. In this section, we generalize the previous results by introducing a family of optimal mappings of which the two mappings – identical mapping and m-k shuffle mapping – are members.

Let I^m be an m-d index set of shape A^m, P^k the set of processors in a k-d regular mesh, $|I^m| = |P^k| = W, w = \log(W)$, Π a arbitrary permutation over w integers, and can also be applied to a w-bit binary number to obtain another w-bit binary number given by

$$\Pi(b_{w-1}, \ldots b_i, \ldots b_0) = (b_{\Pi(w-1)}, \ldots, b_{\Pi(i)}, \ldots, b_{\Pi(0)})$$

Algorithm 7 is a mapping based on the permutation Π, which we refer to as a *bit-permutation mapping based on Π*

Algorithm 7 *The bit-permuting mapping f_Π*
Input: index $(i_{m-1}, \ldots, i_0)$ in I^m of shape A^m.
Output: coordinate $(x_{k-1}, \ldots, x_0)$ in P^k of shape S^k.

$s = \log(S)$, $I = cat(B(i_{m-1}, \ldots, B(i_0))$, $J = \Pi(I)$, $(x_{k-1}, \ldots, x_0) = dec(J, s)$,
return $(x_{k-1}, \ldots, x_0)$

The following proposition tells how each step of FFT communication is translated into the mesh communications under the bit-permutation mapping.

Theorem 14. *Let the f_Π be the mapping from I^m of shape A^m to mesh processor set P^k of shape S^k, $a = \log(A)$, $s = \log(S)$, $\Pi(x) = y$, then a step of FFT communication $C^R(p, q)$ over I^m is mapped to the single dimensional uniform mesh communication of the form $sd(i, w)$, where i and w is the solution of the following linear equation group*

$$pa + q = x, \quad is + w = y$$

Proof Obvious.

We next show the above mapping is cost equivalent to identical mapping regardless of what the permutation Π is

Theorem 15. *Let F be the m-d FFT communication over an index set I^m. f_{id} and f_Π respectively the identical mapping and the mapping based on permutation Π from I^m to a regular mesh of the same size, $f_{id}(F)$ and $f_\Pi(F)$ the mapped mesh communications from the FFT communication. Then $f_{(m,k)})(F)$ and $f_{id}(F)$ are cost-equivalent.*

Proof Since they contain the same set of single dimensional communications in different orders.
It follows that for any permutation over $\log |I^m|$ integers we have

Theorem 16. *The mapping f_Π from m-d FFT communication over I^m to a k-d mesh P^k of the same size is optimal.*

Since an index set I^m of size N has $(\log(N))!$ different permutations we have

Theorem 17. *There are $(\log(N))!$ optimal bit-permutation mappings from an m-d FFT communication over I^m of size n to a k-d regular mesh P^k of the same size.*

Clearly, identical and m-k shuffle mappings are simply two members of the large family.

7 Generalizations

In the previous three sections, we have assumed the regularity of both index set and the mesh. In this section, we show that bit-permutation mappings can be generalized from arbitrarily shaped m-d FFT communication to arbitrarily shaped k-d mesh and are still optimal.
Let us first introduce an operation

$$dec2(b, i_{k-1}, \ldots, i_0) = (b_{k-1}, \ldots, b_0)$$

It takes a binary number b and k integers $i_{k-1}, \ldots, i_0$ as arguments, returns $k-1$ binary numbers, $b_{k-1}, \ldots, b_0$ such that b_0 contains the i_0 leftmost bits of b, b_1 the next i_1 leftmost bits of b, and so on. Clearly, the operation dec in Section 4 can be viewed as a special case of the operation dec2 where all the k integers take the same value.

We now define a mapping from the index set I^m of the shape $A_0 \times A_{m-1}$ to a k-d mesh with processors in P^k of the shape $S_0 \times S_{k-1}$ based on an arbitrary permutation over $\log(N)$ integers where $N = |I^m| = |P^k|$.

Algorithm 8 *The mapping for arbitrary shaped index set and mesh Input: index* $(i_{m-1}, \ldots, i_0)$ *in* I^m *of shape* A^m.
Output: coordinate $(x_{k-1}, \ldots, x_0)$ *in* P^k *of shape* S^k.
Notation: $a_i = \log(A_i)$ *for* $0 \le i < m$, $s_i = \log(S_i)$ *for* $0 \le i < k$, Π *a permutation over* $\left(\sum_{i=0}^m A_i\right)$ *integers.*

$s = \log(S)$, $I = cat(B(i_{m-1}, \ldots, B(i_0)))$, $J = \Pi(I)$, $(x_{k-1}, \ldots, x_0) = dec2(J, s_{k-1}, \ldots, s_0)$, *return* $(x_{k-1}, \ldots, x_0)$

We make the following claims about the the above bit-permutation mapping from I^m to P^k of arbitrary shape,

Theorem 18.

- *it maps each step of m-d FFT communication* $C^R(p, q)$ *over* I^m *to a single dimensional uniform communication over* P^k.
- *the cost of the m-d FFT communication under the mapping equal to the diameter of the k-d mesh, namely* $\sum_{i=0}^{k-1} S_i$, *and thus optimal.*

Proof It is easy to see that if the qth bit of pth dimension for an index in I^m is permuted to the jth bit of ith dimension in P^k, then a step of the FFT communication $C^R(p, q)$ is translated into the single dimensional communication sd $(i, 2^j)$ on the mesh. The second part follows from the fact that the each bit of each dimension will be mapped to exactly once, the total cost is thus

$$\sum_{i=0}^{k-1} \sum_{j=0}^{\log(S_j)} 2^j = \sum_{i=0}^{k-1} (S_j - 1)$$

in other words, the diameter of the mesh.

8 Conclusion

We have studied the mapping from m dimensional FFT communication to k dimensional for arbitrary m and k under a unified framework. We established the lower bound of the communication, and give $(\log(n))!$ bit-permutation mappings, all are optimal. The results in this paper thus generalizes the previous work in [1, 3, 2, 11, 13, 7, 8]. Our broadcast algorithms in Sec. 3 also generalized generalizes the well-known results on broadcasting in [4].

There are a number of related issues and results that can be further studied

- the applications of the mapping to algorithms other than FFT but use FFT communication patterns.
- array operations over specific dimension using FFT communication patterns, e.g., row-wise broadcast for $m = 2$.

Limited by the space, we will discuss the above issues elsewhere. It should be pointed out that the m-k shuffle subsumes that perfect shuffle ($m=2$, $k=1$), and the permutation used in [7, 8] ($m = 1, k$ arbitrary). Although the m-k shuffle mapping is cost-equivalent to the other mappings in the bit-permutation mapping family it can be shown that for operations over some but not all dimensions of an array, it outperforms other mappings such as the identical mapping, which is unfortunately widely used in implementations.

References

1. Peter M. Flanders. A unified approach to a class of data movements on an array processor. *IEEE Transactions on Computers*, C-31(9):809–819, September 1982.
2. Peter M. Flanders and Dennis Parkinson. Data mapping and routing for highly parallel processor arrays. *Future Computing Systems*, 2(2):184–224, 1987.
3. Donald Fraser. Array permutation by index-digit permutation. *Journal of ACM*, 23(2):298–309, April 1976.
4. S. Lennart Johnsson and Ching-Tien Ho. Spanning graphs for optimum broadcasting and personalized communication in hypercubes. *IEEE Trans. Computers*, 38(9):1249–1268, September 1989.
5. R. A. Kamin and G. B. Adams. Fast fourier transform algorithm design and tradeoffs on the cm-2. *International Journal of High Speed Computing*, 1(2):207–231, 1989.
6. Z. G. Mou. Divacon: A parallel language for scientific computing based on divide-and-conquer. In *Proceedings of the Third Symposium on the Frontiers of Massively Parallel Computation*, pages 451–461. IEEE, October 1990.
7. Z. G. Mou, C. Constantinescu, and T. Hickey. Divide-and-conquer on a 3-dimensional mesh. In *Proceedings of the European Workshops on Parallel Computing*, pages 344–355, Barcelona, Spain, March 1992.
8. Z. G. Mou, Cornel Costantinescu, and T. Hickey. Optimal mappings of divide-and-conquer algorithms to mesh connected parallel architectures. In *Proceedings of International Computer Symposium*, pages 273–284, Taiwan, December 1992.
9. Z. G. Mou and P. Hudak. An algebraic model for divide-and-conquer algorithms and its parallelism. *The Journal of Supercomputing*, 2(3):257–278, November 1988.
10. F. P. Preparata and J. Vuillemin. The cube-connected cycles: A versatile network for parallel computation. *Communications of the ACM*, 8(5):300–309, May 1981.
11. S.L.Johnsson, C-T Ho, M. Jacquemin, and A. Ruttenberg. Computing fast fourier transforms on boolean cubes and related networks. *SPIE Advanced Algorithms and Architectures for Signal Processing*, 826(II):223–230, 1987.
12. H. S. Stone. Parallel processing with the perfect shuffle. *IEEE Transactions on Computers*, C-20(2):153–160, February 1971.
13. C. Tong and P. N. Swarztrauber. Ordered fast fourier transforms on a massively parallel hypercube multiprocessor. *Journal of Parallel and Distributed Computing*, (12):50–59, 1991.
14. J. D. Ullman. *Computational Aspect of VLSI*. Computer Science Press, 1984.

Implicit Parallelism: The United Functions and Objects Approach

John Sargeant

Department of Computer Science
University of Manchester
Manchester U.K.
js@cs.man.ac.uk

Abstract. UFO is a general-purpose, implicitly parallel language designed to allow a wide range of applications to be implemented efficiently on a wide range of parallel machines while minimising the conceptual difficulties for the programmer. To achieve this, it draws on the experience gained in the functional and object-oriented "worlds" and attempts to bring these worlds together in a harmonious fashion.

This paper concentrates on examples which illustrate the various forms of parallelism available in UFO.

1 Introduction

Parallel programming today usually requires a significantly higher degree of skill and specialisation than ordinary sequential programming. This is unfortunate, since parallelism is rapidly becoming ubiquitous, from small-scale use in workstations to very large numbers of processors in massively parallel supercomputers. The difficulty stems from the explicit nature of most parallel programming; the application programmer has to map a particular problem onto a particular machine.

It is obviously desirable to have an implicitly parallel programming language, in which this mapping is done by the compiler and runtime system, and is not the responsibility of the application programmer. However, the various forms of implicit parallelism explored during the 80s (functional, And/Or parallel logic, concurrent object-oriented etc.[1, 2, 3, 4, 5, 6]) have, by and large, made little impact on real use of parallel machines. Fortran is enjoying a resurgence.

One problem has been lack of convincing demonstrations of performance. Efficient large-scale implicit parallelism is hard to achieve, but the UFO project will be able to build on a considerable body of research in this area, and on some promising results, such as those obtained for SISAL[7].

A more fundamental reason, in the author's view, is that many such languages have been too narrowly focussed, and have not incorporated the best of modern programming language technology. Functional languages, for instance, form a promising starting point, since they allow parallelism naturally, guarantee determinism, and are easy to reason about. However, pure functional languages seem inappropriate for some problems, which are more naturally expressed in terms of communicating objects, each of which manages its own local state. It *is* possible to have the benefits of both styles in one language, provided that careful attention is paid to the mechanisms for encapsulating state, and that certain safeguards are provided by a static type system.

The following are important characteristics of a realistic implicitly parallel language:

Parallelism by default. It seems inappropriate to merely enhance a sequential model of computation with a few parallel constructs in a world where computers are parallel. The design of UFO reduces sequencing to a minimum: data dependence and the queueing required to guarantee coherent access to stateful objects. The underlying computational model is (extended) dataflow, rather than communicating sequential threads, although an implementation may well use such threads.

Good abstraction and encapsulation facilities. The ability to write generic, reusable code is even more important than in a sequential environment, as some parallel algorithms are inherently more complex, and easier to get wrong, than sequential ones. UFO combines abstraction mechanisms normally found in functional languages, with others from object-oriented languages.

Amenability to reasoning. It should be relatively easy to reason about programs, both formally and informally, both by the programmer and the implementation. This is aided in UFO by the presence of a useful, statically determined, pure functional subset, and a static type system which ensures that programs are type-safe, and prevents various abuses of stateful objects.

No gratuitous inefficiency. Although some small constant factor in execution speed is a reasonable trade for expressiveness, serious inherent overheads will make the language unacceptable. UFO therefore avoids, for instance, lazy evaluation, and provides a mechanism to "switch off" dynamic binding when efficiency is critical.

UFO is a truly general-purpose programming language, and is perfectly suitable for use on machines with little parallelism.[1] The UFO project will write almost all its software in UFO; much of it - the compiler, programming support tools etc. - will probably not have a great deal of parallelism. However, this paper concentrates on the various forms of parallelism which can be exploited, through a series of small examples. The examples are chosen to illustrate language features rather than as "real" parallel applications.

The earlier examples are purely functional, namely a general framework for divide-and-conquer problems, an example of "data parallel" programming using functional arrays and loops, and a fragment of the compiler illustrating classes and inheritance. Stateful objects are then introduced and illustrated via some small examples, including a wavefront algorithm.[2]

---

[1] All machines have some parallelism nowadays.

[2] The reviewed draft of this paper contained several more examples, and more detail

122

2 Divide-and-conquer

A large subset of UFO (the subset which excludes the keyword "stateful") is a
higher-order pure functional language. The recommended style is to keep to this
subset unless there is a good reason to use stateful objects. In the functional
subset, determinism and deadlock-freedom are guaranteed, programs are generally much easier to reason about, and the implementation overheads associated
with stateful objects are avoided.

UFO has strong static generic typing, with mandatory type declarations for
function parameters. Type inference, as used in most modern functional languages, (e.g. Haskell[9]) would be very complex in the presence of inheritance,
and its benefits to the programmer would be outweighed (as it is in Haskell) by
the unhelpful type error messages which would result.

One simple form of parallelism is found in divide-and-conquer algorithms
which recursively split a problem into subproblems until the subproblems are
small enough to be solved directly.

The following general framework for divide-and-conquer programs[3] illustrates
a number of the features of UFO.

```
typevar Problem, Solution

dc( problem: Problem; primitive: Problem -> Bool;
    divide: Problem -> Array[Problem]; combine: Array[Solution] -> Solution;
    solve : Problem -> Solution ): Solution is
if problem.primitive
then problem.solve
else combine( map(problem.divide, dc(_, primitive, divide, combine, solve )))
fi
```

The divide-and-conquer function takes as arguments an arbitrary Problem, a
predicate to test whether a Problem is small enough to solve directly, a function
which divides a Problem into an array of smaller Problems, another which combines an array of Solutions into a single Solution, and finally the function which
turns a small Problem into a Solution. A particular divide-and-conquer problem
is expressed by providing **primitive**, **divide**, **combine**, and **solve** functions of
the appropriate types.

The body of a function is an expression, in this case a conditional expression.
If the problem is primitive, it is solved directly. Otherwise, it is split into an array
of subproblems by **divide**. Then **dc**, with the four functions wired-in, is mapped
across the array of subproblems (**map** simply applies a function to each element
of an array). The resulting array of solutions is combined to give the answer.

The reader may have noticed two different function call syntaxes: an OO-style
"message passing" syntax, e.g. **problem.primitive** and a conventional one, e.g.

in some areas. The severely reduced length limit on the real paper has forced these
to be omitted. Readers interested in more detail are encouraged to ftp[15].

[3] This formulation of divide-and-conquer is believed to be due to Ronan Sleep[8]

`combine( ... )`. These are interchangeable via a trivial syntactic transformation; the programmer is free to use whichever seems more natural for a particular call.

Another interesting aspect is the use of partial parameterisation in

`dc(_, primitive, divide, combine, solve )`

this gives a function of type Problem → Solution.

In a lazy functional language, extracting parallelism from `dc` requires strictness analysis to determine that `combine` must evaluate the whole of its input list. Failing this, serial, normal order evaluation will occur. This is one reason why UFO has strict evaluation; another is that there is a conflict between dynamic binding and lazyness, because in order to dynamically bind on an object, it is necessary to evaluate it. Lazy evaluation can be explicitly programmed, for those applications for which it is really useful.

3 Array/loop parallelism

A second form of parallelism is that generated from arrays and loops.[4] The array and loop constructs of UFO are largely inspired by SISAL[1]. The SISAL project has shown that functional arrays can be efficient, provided that suitable optimisations, particularly sharing analysis to avoid unnecessary copying, are performed by the compiler. Substantial numeric programs written in SISAL have been shown to run faster on multiprocessor Crays than Fortran versions[7]. The key to success is to avoid low-level programming in terms of individual updates, and instead to write loops which generate whole arrays at once.

The `map` function referred to above is written:

```
map( a: Array[T]; f : T-> U ): Array[U] is
    for x in a do y = f(x) return all y od
```

`for` loops are generated by arrays and create arrays. The effect of a loop ranging over integer indices, as in `for i in [1 to n]` is achieved by having syntax for arrays containing arithmetic progressions. [5] The keyword `all` indicates that the result is an array with one element for each value `y` for each loop cycle. The loop cycles are independent, so all the calls to f may be evaluated in parallel.

The following program , adapted from an example in the SISAL2 reference manual[10] "plays" Conway's "game of life". A colony of cells live on a grid. If a cell has more than 3 neighbours it "dies of overcrowding". If it has less than 2, it "dies of loneliness". If an empty square has exactly 3 neighbours, a cell is born there.

---

[4] often known as data parallelism, although that term usually means a rather more restrictive form than that which UFO provides.

[5] In practice, of course, such an array will not be stored by a good implementation.

```
type Cell = Int
type Grid = Array2[Cell]

dead is 0; alive is 1

newcell( g:Grid; i,j: Int ): Cell is
{
neighbours = G[i+1, j-1] + G[i+1, j] + G[i+1, j+1]
           + G[i,   j-1]              + G[i,   j+1]
           + G[i-1, j-1] + G[i-1, j] + G[i-1, j+1]
return
  if neighbours > 3 or neighbours < 2 then dead
  elseif neighbours == 3 then alive else G[i,j] fi
}

nextgrid( g: Grid ):Grid is
{ x = dimsize(g, 1); y = dimsize(g, 2)
return
  for i in [2 to x-1] cross j in [2 to y-1] do
  newg = newcell( g, i, j)
  return all newg
  od
}
```

UFO has true multi-dimensional arrays, rather than merely arrays of arrays. Arrays of specific dimensionality, such as the 2D arrays used here are regarded as subclasses of the general **Array** class. Some operations, such as **map** above, are defined on all arrays, others, such as the 2D indexing in this example, only on arrays of the appropriate dimensionality.

The **newcell** function simply calculates whether a cell will be dead or alive on the next iteration according to the rules. Nextgrid calculates the next version of the whole grid. An expression such as **all newg**, denotes an array, whose shape is determined by the generators, with one element for each instantiation of the loop. Combining two arrays in a **cross** product generator, as in this case, creates a result array whose dimensionality is the sum of the dimensionalities of the generating arrays, in this case 2D. Of course all the loop bodies may be evaluated in parallel.

The example is incomplete in two respects. Firstly, nextgrid returns a smaller grid than the one it's given; we need to put the boundary back on. Secondly, we need to set up the grid in the first place, preferably without having to "draw" the whole of it, or to do messy individual updates. This can be done as follows:

```
glider : Grid is
{ o = dead; x = alive
  return [2..4, 2..4 | o, o, x,
                       x, o, x,
                       o, x, x ]
}
```

```
iterate( n: Int) : Grid is
initially
  emptygrid = [1..100, 1..100 | all dead];
  i = 0;  grid = emptygrid # glider
while i < n do
  new grid = emptygrid # nextgrid(grid);
  new i = i + 1
return grid
od
```

The glider function sets up the standard "glider" example on a small grid. This is "stamped" onto a larger grid using the map overwrite operator, #. A # B is A except that where A and B intersect, the elements of B are substituted. The same technique is used to put the boundary back on the result of nextgrid. Sharing analysis can be expected to eliminate the extra arrays.

The body of function iterate is a loop controlled by a test rather than a generator. It shows how loop values (grid and i) can be used to express data dependence between loops. Note that, despite the presence of the imperative looking new i = i + 1 this is still pure functional, referentially transparent code. There is one new i for each instance of the loop; i cannot be reassigned, and neither can new i once it has been given its value. This *single assignment rule* is characteristic of dataflow languages. It will also have an important part to play in the semantics of stateful objects.

Array indexing is a special case of slicing, which can be used to select arbitrary (rectangular) subarrays of an array. For instance, an alternative way to calculate the number of neighbours is

```
neighbours = sum( G[i-1..i+1, j-1..j+1] ) - G[i,j]
```

Assuming sum is a function which sums the elements of an integer array.

4 Classes and inheritance

Good abstraction and encapsulation mechanisms will be vital to the success of any new parallel language. The use of higher-order functions in UFO was shown above. Another, complementary, set of mechanisms is provided in object-oriented languages, namely classes with inheritance and dynamic binding.

In UFO, classes with inheritance can be used even in pure functional programs. The prototype compiler is such a program and uses classes and dynamic binding extensively. Although it is not the main subject of this paper, there are potential benefits in doing selection by dynamic binding in a functional language, rather than by pattern matching and explicit conditional expressions. Dynamic binding gives better adaptation to change, since when a new subclass is added the additional methods required are localised within that subclass. Missing cases and broken patterns are not spread across the program. Using static typing along with dynamic binding ensures that there is always an appropriate method to call at runtime. This argument is eloquently argued by Meyer in[11].

A highly simplified fragment of the compiler will illustrate class definitions and inheritance:

```
deferred class Expression( spec: TypeSpec)
print: String is deferred
end

class IfExp( ... condexp, thenexp, elseexp : Expression ) inherits Expression
print is
   "if "   ++ condexp.print ++ "\n"
++ "then " ++ thenexp.print ++ "\n"
++ "else " ++ elseexp.print ++ "\nfi\n"
end
```

A deferred class[6], such as Expression, is one which serves as a superclass for other, concrete, classes but can't itself have instances. Individual methods of a deferred class may be deferred, like **print**, in which case the implementation is left entirely to subclasses, or a default implementation may be provided.

The parameters to a class (e.g. spec for Expression) are stored with the class as instance *values* (not variables; they cannot be updated). By default, these instance values can be accessed by code outside the class in the same way as parameterless functions, e.g. `t = some_exp.spec`. The instance values can be hidden, giving the effect of an ADT, by declaring them **private**. There is no separate interface definition because, as in Eiffel[12], the interface information can automatically be extracted by a simple tool.

IfExp is a concrete subclass of **Expression**. Typically, the class parameters for a subclass are an extension of those for its parent. This is indicated by the ... notation in the header.

print simply constructs a string representing the expression (**++** is append). This recursively calls other print functions on the component expressions. The appropriate print function is called at runtime by dynamic binding. The fact that there *is* an appropriate print function is guaranteed at compile time by static typing.

5 Asynchronous communicating objects

Some problems, particularly in a parallel environment, are not best expressed in the pure functional style. UFO therefore has stateful objects, and we have worked very hard in the design to minimise the problems this causes, both by the way the runtime behaviour of objects is defined, and in the type system.

5.1 A simple example

The following defines a random number generator class:

---

[6] Also known as a virtual class, or abstract class, in other object-oriented languages.

```
stateful class Random( private init_seed: Int ) is
  { initial seed = init_seed }

  ** Return a random real number between 0 and 1
  proc nextrand : Real is
  do
    new seed = (13849 + 27181 * seed) mod 65536;
    return new seed / 65536.0
  od
end ** Random
```

A stateful class typically has one or more *instance variables*. It may still have functions, which may refer to the current values of those variables, but it will also have *procedures* which may update them. The body of such a class starts with an *initialisation block*, which gives initial values for the instance variables.

Procedure calling is distinguished by the use of !, rather than the dot used for function calls. The body of a **proc** is similar to the body of a loop, and this similarity is deliberate. The single assignment rule applies, in that each procedure body may update each instance variable at most once. The distinction between **seed** and **new seed** is exactly that between **grid** and **new grid** in the loop example.[7] Of course, in this case, it does not maintain referential transparency, as calls to a **Random** object's **nextrand** procedure may occur from anywhere with a reference to that object, in a nondeterministic order. What it *does* do is to allow parallelism to be exploited within the body of a procedure, while maintaining internal consistency with respect to the instance variables; all references to **seed** within the same method invocation will see the same value. This scheme removes the need for any statement sequencing even within procedure bodies; *sequencing is still by data dependence only*.

This, of course, leaves the problem of how interference *between* method calls to stateful objects is prevented. This mechanism is as follows: such method calls (procedures and functions) are held in a FIFO queue. When it gets to the head of a queue, a method "locks" the object. To ensure coherence, a method starts by taking (reference) copies of instance variables to which it may refer, and uses these copies for all references. The values at the start of the method's execution are therefore seen, whether or not it (or some other method executing concurrently) updates them. Completion of the assignments triggers unlocking; the single-assignment rule ensures that the set of assignments to be made is statically obvious.

This very weak sequencing has several consequences. A function call locks the object only transiently, to take copies of the variables to which it refers. It therefore causes very little serialisation and cannot cause deadlock. Arbitrary numbers of functions can execute in parallel, and their execution does not prevent the execution of a procedure. A procedure call unlocks the object at the earliest

---

[7] This idea is not as novel as we first thought. Arvind's managers, dating from 1978, work the same way. However, he used explicit merging of input streams. The actor language HAL[16] also has single assignment update.

possible moment, when coherent access to the instance variables is guaranteed. The call may not return its result until much later. Conversely, it is possible for a method to return a result before it has terminated.[8] This and the previous property are usually considered characteristic of a "concurrent object-oriented" language.

The distinction between "synchronous" and "asynchronous" method calling/message passing is rather meaningless in this context, since we are not dealing with communicating sequential threads at the language level. In general, an implementation will need to ensure that it creates no spurious data dependencies which could cause deadlock; even a sequential implementation may need to operate in a pseudo-parallel manner. Finally, since locking exists only for long enough to ensure coherent access to instance variables, and sequencing is only by data dependence, it follows that the only way that deadlock can occur is by cyclic dependencies between instance variables. The hope is that this should be relatively easy to reason about.

5.2 Conditional message acceptance

The main problem with this approach is that it leaves the programmer with too little control over sequencing in some cases. This may be a problem if we want to ensure coherence of a whole substructure referred to from an object, not just the instance values. This is the traditional "granularity of locking" problem. Another case is if we want to ensure that one event "happens before" another, even if they are not data dependent, e.g. controlling the order of display in a user interface. Also, we might want to reason about some fairness property of an algorithm, not just termination/deadlock freedom.

One way to overcome this is to introduce additional data dependences, and UFO has some facilities for doing this. In particular, a caller may require an acknowledgement when a call has been queued, so that it can control the order of queuing. However, it is more in line with object-oriented philosophy to allow an object to control its own queue as far as possible. UFO, like other concurrent object-oriented languages, therefore has *conditional message acceptance* (CMA). A procedure may specify a new message acceptance list.[9] The next method to execute on the object will be the first in the queue which is on the list.

Consider the following, which behaves like a location in an I-store in a dataflow machine[13, 14], i.e. it is written once only, and reads queue until the write has occurred:

```
stateful class ILoc[T]( )
{ initial val = error:T;
  initial accept = << write >>
}
read is val;
```

---

[8] Since it may make procedure calls which do not return values necessary to produce the result.

[9] A function may not do so, because it would be altering the state of the object.

```
proc write( v: T ) : Void is
do new val = v; new accept = << read >> od
end
```

The pseudo-variable **accept** determines the current set of acceptable messages. Its type is a special type **Message_acceptance_list** (doing it this way ensures that updating the list has the same consequences as other updates - a function can't do it, for instance. It also allows the list to be set conditionally). Initially, only writes are accepted, so reads are blocked until a write has been done. In this very primitive I-store location subsequent writes are blocked for ever; more sophisticated versions can be obtained by inheritance. On a machine with hardware support for I-store style operations, such classes can still be transformed into something very efficient.

CMA provides a general conditional synchronisation mechanism, arguably cleaner than (for instance) semaphores. In doing so, it complicates the queuing mechanism, although research in implementing, for example, ABCL[4], suggests that this is not a serious problem.

5.3 A wavefront example

Some problems can only be formulated in a functional style if non-strict evaluation is assumed. An example is the "wavefront" problem, where a computation proceeds from the top left corner of a 2D array in a wavefront, where the value of each element is some function of its north, west, and northwest neighbours. Such a problem has O(n) parallelism for an n by n array. The I-store location shown above can be used to simulate such non-strict evaluation.

```
type Nonstrict_array = Array2[ILoc[Real]];
type func = ( Real, Real, Real ) -> Real;

wavefront( m,n: Int; initial: Real; f: func ): Array2[Real]
is
{
** Initialise the array
a =
  for i in [1 to m] cross j in [1 to n] do
  emptyij = ILoc[Real]
  return all emptyij
  od
return
** Do the wavefront, and convert to an ordinary array for function result
  for i in [1 to m] cross j in [1 to n] do
  if i == 1 or j == 1
  then { a[i,j]!write( initial ) }
  else { a[i,j]!write
  ( f(a[i,j-1].read, a[i-1,j-1].read, a[i-1,j].read)) }
  fi;
```

```
    aij = a[i,j].read
    return all aij
    od
}
```

However, this very fine-grain use of CMA is unlikely to be acceptably efficient except on machines with appropriate hardware support. On other machines, it is probably better to use ILocs and similar structures only for more traditional concurrent programming style problems, and to tackle problems such as the above by rewriting the algorithm.

Several other examples are given in [15], including a general-purpose "future" class, inheriting from ILoc, which can be used to build lazy data structures and suchlike.

6   The type system

UFO has static typing with genericity, overloading, and inheritance polymorphism. There are enough mandatory type declarations, and the rules about redefinition on inheritance are sufficiently conservative, to ensure that only relatively simple type checking (with only trivial inference) is required.

The type system is not the subject of this paper, but one aspect should be mentioned, namely the way in which it gives safeguards in the handling of stateful objects.

Two requirements are imposed statically:

1. **Any reference to an updatable object can be detected statically.** This requires a restriction that if a stateful class inherits from a stateless one, the stateful subclass is not type-conformant with its parent.
2. **A function may not modify its arguments.** This is not merely a parameter passing convention. We require that, if an object is passed to a function, no part of the structure referenced from that object can be modified by the function. This enables the programmer and the implementation to reason about functions much as in a pure functional language, even in the presence of stateful objects. It is enforced by a notion of Readonly types which are obtained from stateful class types by deleting the classes' procedures, thereby leaving them with no way to update their variables. Details are given in[15].

Although this is expected to make reasoning about functions easier, it does not provide full referential transparency. In particular, since functions can create and manipulate stateful objects, they may have nondeterministic behaviour. This is useful for some parallel algorithms, and there is no way that the type system can be expected to distinguish "reasonable" from "unreasonable" nondeterminism.

7   Current status

A subset of UFO (UFO0) has been implemented, and used to write its own compiler. This is being extended towards a full serial implementation of UFO1, the language described here. A good parallel implementation, together with the tools, libraries etc. necessary to make the language really usable, will involve a substantial effort. This effort should also include the definition of a formal semantics for the language, and a formal development methodology to allow proofs of correctness. Such an effort seems highly worthwhile given the limitations of current implicitly parallel languages.

A number of issues have deliberately not been addressed in the design of UFO1. These include exception handling and persistence. It is hoped that after a couple of years' experience with UFO1, a review will take place with the aim of defining a UFO2 which does address these matters, and any others which arise in the meantime.

References

1. J. R. McGraw, S. K. Skedzielewski, S. J. Allan, R. R. Oldehoeft, J. Glauert, C. C. Kirkham, W. Noyce, and R. Thomas: **SISAL: Streams and Iteration in a Single Assignment Language**, Reference Manual 1.2, Manual M-146, Rev. 1, Lawrence Livermore National Laboratory, 1985.
2. R.S. Nikhil: **ID Reference Manual**, CSG memo 284, MIT Laboratory for Computer Science, 1988.
3. G. Agha **Actors: A Model of Concurrent Computation in Distributed Systems** MIT Press series in artificial intelligence, 1986.
4. A. Yonezawa (ed.): **ABCL, an Object-oriented Concurrent System**, MIT press Computer Systems Series, 1990.
5. P. America: **POOL-T: A Parallel Object-Oriented Language**, in A. Yonezawa & M. Tokoro (eds) Object-Oriented Concurrent Programming, MIT Press computer systems series, 1987
6. K, Ueda, T. Chikayama: **Design of the Kernel Language for the Parallel Inference Machine** Computer Journal 33(6), 1990, pp494-500.
7. D. C. Cann **Retire Fortran? A debate rekindled** Communications of the ACM 35(8), August 1992, pp 81-89
8. M. R. Sleep, J. R. Kennaway, **The Zero Assignment Parallel Processor (ZAPP) project**, in D.A. Duce (ed.) Distributed Computing Systems Program, Peter Peregrinus, London, 1984, pp 250-267.
9. P. Hudak et. al.: **Report on the Programming Language Haskell, version 1.1**, Univerity of Yale tech. report, August 1991.
10. A. P. W. Böhm, D. C. Cann, J. T. Feo, R. R. Oldehoeft: **SISAL 2.0 Reference Manual**, tech. report CS-91-118, Computer Science dept. Colorado State University, 1991.
11. B. Meyer: **Object-oriented Software Construction**, Prentice Hall 1988
12. B. Meyer: **Eiffel the Language**, Prentice Hall 1992.
13. Arvind, R.E. Thomas: **I-structures: An efficient data type for functional languages** MIT/LCS/TM-178, Computer Science Laboratory, MIT., Cambridge, MA, 1981.
14. J. Sargeant, C.C. Kirkham: **Stored data structures on the Manchester Dataflow Machine** Proc. 13th Annual Symposium on Computer Architecture, 1986, pp 235-242
15. J. Sargeant: **United Functions and Objects: An Overview** Technical report UMCS-93-1-4, Department of Computer Science, University of Manchester, 1993. (Available by anonymous ftp from m1.cs.man.ac.uk)
16. C. Houck, G. Agha: **HAL: A High-level Actor Language and its Distributed Implementation** Proc. 21st International Conference on Parallel Processing, August 1992.

Detection of Recurrences in Sequential Programs with Loops

Xavier Redon and Paul Feautrier

Laboratoire MASI,
Université de Versailles-St. Quentin,
45, Avenue des Etats-Unis,
78000 Versailles, France
e-mail : redon@masi.ibp.fr, feautrier@masi.ibp.fr

Abstract. To improve the performances of parallelizing compilers, one must detect recurrences in scientific programs and subject them to special parallelization methods. We present a method for detecting recurrences which is based on the analysis of Systems of Recurrence Equations. This method identifies recurrences on arrays, recurrences of arbitrary order and multi-equations recurrences. We explain how to associate a SRE to a restricted class of imperative programs. We present a normalization of such SRE that allows the detection of recurrences by simple inspection of equations. When detected, a recurrence may be replaced by a symbolic expression of its solution. To iterate the process can lead to the identification of multi-dimensional recurrences.

1 Introduction

One of the most important challenges in present day computer science is the efficient compilation of programs for the newly emerging massively parallel architectures. In contrast of the situation for the last generation of supercomputers, which were mostly vector processors with a moderate degree of parallelism, now every last ounce of parallelism must be extracted in order to feed several hundred of vector microprocessors. It may be shown that potential parallelism exists as soon as the execution order of some operations may change without any consequence on the final result of the program. This kind of commutativity property may have two origins. The first one depends only on the pattern of use of memory cells. It is subsumed by Bernstein's conditions ([2]), and has been extensively exploited by present day parallelizing compilers. The second kind depends on algebraic properties of the operators which appears in the computation. The name "semantic parallelization" for the exploitation of these opportunities for parallelism has been coined by P. Jouvelot.

Example 1. Consider for instance the computation of the sum $\sum_{i=1}^{n} x_i$, its usual implementation is

```
s=0.
DO i=1,n
    s=s+x(i)
END DO
```

An ordinary parallelizing [1] compiler will say that this loop is sequential, due to a loop-carried dependence on s. As a consequence, the computation will take a time of the order of n. However, since addition is associative and commutative [2] one may divide the summation into segments of length $\frac{n}{p}$ (where p is the number of processors) then add the partial sums in a time of the order of $\frac{n}{p} + \log_2 p$. If the number of processors is very large (of the order of n) one may compute s in time $O(\log_2 n)$. Most programming languages lack a notation for expressing computations like $\sum_{i=1}^{n} x_i$. The main exception is APL, in which the name *reduction* was introduced.

It is thus seen that extracting expressions like the above sum from loops is a very important task for a parallelizing compiler. This is usually done in two steps. The first one consists in recognizing *recurrences* from their sequential expression. For instance the recurrence associated to the previous example is [3]

$$\left[\begin{array}{l} s_0 = 0 \\ \forall i \in \mathbb{N}_n^*, \, s_i = s_{i-1} + x_i \end{array} \right.$$

This is a purely algebraic task; it becomes very difficult when the sequential program gets complicated, and especially when arrays are involved. The second step consists in examining the recurrences to see whether the operators have the required properties. This is a pattern recognition step, whose performance will depend mainly on the size of the pattern base. Hence the interest of reducing this size by normalization of the recurrences.

The paper is organized as follows. The next section is a review of recent works on the subject. In section 3, we describe the basis on which our solution will be built, namely the translation of a sequential program into a System of Linear Recurrence Equations. In section 4 we discuss the pattern-matching process and describe a normal form for SLRE. Section 5 describes the normalization process and give a necessary and sufficient condition for the existence of a normal form. Section 6 describes the final step of our analysis, that is multi-dimensional recurrences detection. The conclusion includes some informations on an implementation of the method. In the interest of conciseness, most proofs have been omitted. They may be found in full in [10].

2 State of the Art

Some papers on reductions detection have already been published ([5] and [9]). The first presents a method based on symbolic stores and the last a method based on the dependence graph.

---

[1] some commercial compilers will recognize this form as an idiom and compile it efficiently.

[2] if one neglects rounding errors.

[3] Let $\mathbb{N}_n^*$ denote the set of natural integers $\{1, \ldots, n\}$.

2.1 Method Based on Symbolic Stores

The first step of this method is the analysis, by symbolic evaluation, of the bodies of the innermost loops of the program. A pattern matching step is then applied to the symbolic stores to recognize the reductions. Loop nests can be processed by propagation of the solutions of recurrences.

The principal advantage of these methods is that a normalization of the program occurs during the computation of the symbolic stores. Thus a method based on symbolic stores is somewhat indifferent to variations in the implementation of the algorithm. As against this the fact that values are considered as symbolic items is a substantial disadvantage. Indeed such a method cannot fully handle arrays (e.g. $a(i)$ and $a(i' + 1)$ are different symbols but may represent the same array cell if $i = i' + 1$). Therefore some recurrences on arrays cannot be detected. Moreover the imprecision due to the symbolic analysis can lead to wrongly replace a piece of code by a recurrence computation. To avoid this problem one must use an heuristic method to select loop bodies on which it is safe to apply the reduction detection. Consequently more recurrences will be missed.

2.2 Method Based on the Dependence Graph

For a detection of recurrences based on the Dependence Graph (DG) , one needs to represent loops. [9] presents a way to build such a DG. First, loops must be unrolled so as to reach normal form. A loop is in normal form when an iteration of the new loop uses only arrays cells and scalars computed in the same iteration or in the previous one. When the normal form is reached, a generic DG of the loop body is build. Since the loop is in normal form, the union of the DG of the initial iteration with the DG of an intermediate iteration and with the DG of the final iteration gives a DG for the whole loop. Then a pattern-matching step is applied to the loop DG, and for each sub-graph that involve recurrence an appropriate algorithm is generated.

Such a method allows better detection (e.g. it detects some cross-recurrences). A disadvantage is that this method does not include any normalization. This normalization must be done by classical transformations (e.g. substitution of temporaries, scalar expansion, loop interchange, etc.). Therefore this step can hardly be done without human control. Moreover, since the pattern-matching is applied to the whole graph, the time complexity increases quickly with the program size. Another limitation is that normal form for a loop exists only for the case of uniform dependences.

3 A New Method Based on SLRE Analysis

3.1 Motivation

The methods presented in the previous section all have some weak points. These are due to the lack of precision of the program representation (symbolic stores) or to the absence of normalization. An intermediate representation of programs by a System of Linear Recurrence Equations (SLRE) seems to be well adapted to the detection of recurrences. Indeed, a program written in an imperative language (e.g. FORTRAN) can be translated into a SLRE under certain usual assumptions (i.e. the Dataflow Graph of the program is computable, see below). Moreover we are able to normalize SLRE with a powerful tool: the forward substitution.

3.2 The Dataflow Graph

In order to translate the source program into SLRE, we use the algorithm described in [4] for computing the Dataflow Graph (DFG) of the source program. The DFG deals with *operations*. An operation is a pair build with an instruction and an occurrence of the iteration vector of the instruction. $(i, \mathbf{v})$ being an operation, the DFG gives, for each reference to a scalar or array element in this operation, the source operation (that is the operation in which the scalar or the array element is computed). When the DFG is build, it is easy to translate the source program into a Single Assignment program by renaming and expansion of variables.

Dataflow Analysis has been implemented, along the lines of [4] as part of the PAF project [4]. The present software for reduction detection uses the result of this analysis. It has the same range of application as the Dataflow Analysis module: static control programs with linear subscripts (see [4] for more informations on that point).

3.3 Representation for SLRE

Our detection is based on SLRE, thus we must give a precise definition of such systems and find out a way to represent them. Some languages (e.g. the Alpha language [8]) have already been designed to describe such equations. Alpha variables are spatial variables, i.e. triplets $< D, \phi, V >$ where the function ϕ associates to each point of the convex domain D a value in V. However, the Alpha notation has been designed more for automatic processing than for ease of use. Thus we prefer to deal with equations in the usual mathematical way.

We will work with LRE equations of the form

$$z \in D_i, \ U_i(z) = f_i(U_1(I_1(z)), \ldots, U_n(I_n(z))) \ ,$$

assuming that $(U_i)_{i \in \mathbb{N}_n^*}$ is the family of variables of the system. Moreover, we assume that D_i is a bounded convex. The I_i are linear subscripts functions and the functions f_i are conditional functions such that

$$f_i(x) = \begin{cases} Exp_i^1(x) \text{ if } x \in D_i^1 \\ \quad \vdots \\ Exp_i^m(x) \text{ if } x \in D_i^m \end{cases}$$

(The Exp_i^j are classical mathematical expressions and the D_i^j are bounded convexes). We say that f_i is an m clauses expression.

---

[4] PAF is a French acronym standing for Automatic Parallelization of FORTRAN.

3.4 Overview of the Method

Like every method for the detection of recurrences, our method consists of three parts. The first part is the conversion of the source program into SLRE. The second part is the normalization of the SLRE and the last part is the application of a pattern-matching on the SLRE. We want the pattern-matching phase, which is quite time consuming, to be as efficient as possible. Therefore, we apply the pattern-matching only one equation at a time. But we want an efficient method too, thus the normalization part try to break multi-equations systems into several systems with only one equation. Note that we are working with multi-dimensional arrays and loops. We begin to detect the recurrences relative to the highest dimension (i.e. the recurrences relative to the innermost loops). A detected recurrence is replaced by its symbolic solution and the analysis is applied to the next dimension. This allows the detection of multi-dimensional recurrences, that is recurrences relative to several nested loops.

4 Validity of Detection by Pattern-Matching

We use pattern-matching for the detection of recurrences. This section shows on which conditions this must be done to be valid. First we give some definitions about equations systems and about systems graphs.

4.1 Definitions

In this paper, we use definitions and results from graph theory. Our reference is [1]. First, we must precise the notion of equations system.

Definition 1 equations system. An equations system S is a set of LRE equations [5] such that

$$\forall(e, e') \in S^2, \ v_e = v_{e'} \Rightarrow D_e = D_{e'} \land \forall z \in D_e, \ Exp_e(z) = Exp_{e'}(z) \ .$$

To point out the dependences between equations we build the system graph (this graph is a sub-graph of the Dependence Graph of the original program).

Definition 2 system graph. Let S be an equations system, the graph of S (denoted by $\mathcal{G}_S$) is the graph whose vertices are the equations of S and whose edges are the couples (e, e') such that the variable $v_{e'}$ appears in the expression Exp_e.

We need to introduce the notion of depth into our graphs.

Definition 3 system p-graph. Let S be an equations system, the p-graph of S (denoted by $\mathcal{G}_S^p$) is a sub-graph of $\mathcal{G}_S$ such that (e, e') is an edge of $\mathcal{G}_S^p$ if and only if there exists $z \in D_e$ and $z' \in D_{e'}$ such that $v_{e'}(z')$ is used in expression $Exp_e(z)$ and p is the largest integer verifying $z[1..p] = z'[1..p]$.

---

[5] We will assume that an LRE equation e has the form $\forall z \in D_e, v_e(z) = Exp_e(z)$.

4.2 Conditions of Validity

A naive method to detect recurrences in a SLRE is to scan all the clauses of the equations and compare them with a general pattern. But this syntactic criterion does not suffice to characterize a recurrence. We need two additional conditions. First, the values needed for the computation of an element of the sequence must belong to the clause, except for the initial values of the recurrence. Second, the equation must not be part of a multi-equations recurrence. Indeed, in this case, a reference to an other equation can hide an auto-reference. A sufficient condition is that, if we are detecting recurrences in respect to dimension l, the graph $\mathcal{G}_S^{l-1}$ does not have any cycle (except loops) which include the equation. This condition presents the advantage of being easily verified.

Now we can present a two level characterization of a recurrence. At the equation level we must find the recurrent clauses:

Definition 4 recurrent clause. Let S be an equations system, e an equation of S and c a clause of Exp_e. The clause c is recurrent with order o and step k for the dimension p if and only if c matches the following pattern

$$F(v_e(\phi_{p,k}(z)), \ldots, v_e(\phi_{p,o.k}(z)))$$
$$\text{if } z \in D_e^c = \{a_1 \leq z_1 \leq b_1, \ldots, a_m(z_1, \ldots, z_{m-1}) \leq z_m \leq b_m(z_1, \ldots, z_{m-1})\}$$

where the vectors $\phi_{p,k'}(z)$ are of the form

$$\phi_{p,k'}(z) = (z_1, \ldots, z_p, z_p - k', x_1^{k'}(z), \ldots, x_{m-p}^{k'}(z))$$

and if and only if the images of D_e^c by the $\phi_{p,k'}$ auto-reference functions are included in D_e^c except for the initials values of the recurrence.

At the system level we must verify that equation level detection is valid:

Proposition 5 validity of pattern-matching. *Let S be an ordered system, e an equation of S and c a clause of Exp_e. If c is a recurrent clause with order o, step k and propagation function F^c for dimension l and if there is no cycle in $\mathcal{G}_S^{l-1}$ with length greater than or equal to 2 then c can be computed by a recurrence with order o, step k and propagation function F^c.*

5 System Normalization

The aim of systems normalization is to allow pattern-matching to recognize a maximum of recurrences. So, the condition of validity from the previous section must be fulfilled by a maximum of clauses. Therefore, we want to transform each system into a reduced one (i.e. a system whose graph does not have any cycle of length greater than 1). To be sure that the transformed system is equivalent to the original one we will use only *forward substitution* as a transformation tool.

First, we define the notions of substitution and transformation. Then we present the conditions on which a system can be transformed into a reduced one.

5.1 Definitions

Let us formalize the usual process of substitution in equations systems. Let e and $(e_i)_{i \in \mathbb{N}_n^*}$ be LRE equations. We denote by $e \odot \{e_1, \ldots, e_n\}$ the equation e in which all references to the variables $(v_{e_i})_{i \in \mathbb{N}_n^*}$ are simultaneously replaced by their respective expressions (i.e. the $(Exp_{e_i})_{i \in \mathbb{N}_n^*}$).

Our elementary transformation is the action of replacing one or more equations in a system S by new equations of the form $e \odot S'$ where e is the original equation and S' is a sub-system of S.

5.2 Criterion for System Reduction

The aim of this sub-section is to find the conditions on which a system is reducible (i.e. there exists a sequence of transformations such that the resulting system is a reduced system).

Proposition 6 reduction of a strongly connected system. *Let S be a strongly connected system* [6]. *Then S is reducible if and only if the cycles of $\mathcal{G}_S$ have a common vertex.*

In fact, when detecting recurrences with respect to the dimension l, the fulfillment of the validity condition only requires the reduction of the $(l-1)$-graph of the system. Therefore we just need to verify that the cycles of $\mathcal{G}_S^{l-1}$ have a common vertex. This criterion stands only for strongly connected systems. In the case of an arbitrary equations system one must try to reduce the system strong components. If each component is reducible then the system is reducible.

5.3 An Algorithm for Normalization

This section presents an efficient algorithm to reduce a system.

Algorithm 7 algorithm A. *let S be a strongly connected system.*
Initialization:
$$S_0 = C_0 = S$$
Propagation:
    If there exists, In set C_i, an e_i' only referenced by e_i
    Then /* Replace e_i by $e_i \odot e_i'$ and remove e_i' from C_i */
$$S_{i+1} = (S_i - \{e_i\}) \cup \{e_i \odot e_i'\}$$
$$C_{i+1} = (C_i - \{e_i, e_i'\}) \cup \{e_i \odot e_i'\}$$
    Else /* End of normalization */
$$S_{i+1} = S_i$$
$$C_{i+1} = C_i$$
    EndIf.
We denote by i_{final} the smallest i such as $S_{i+1} = S_i$. It is of no use to compute the sequence $((S_i, C_i))$ beyond i_{final}.

---

[6] A strongly connected system is a system whose graph is strongly connected. In the same way a strong component of a system is the vertex set of a strong component of the system graph.

For each strongly connected system S, this algorithm builds a system $S_{i_{\text{final}}}$. If S is reducible, $S_{i_{\text{final}}}$ is a reduced system. Moreover the complexity of $\mathcal{A}$ is linear in relation to the number of vertices of S. All these affirmations are proved in [10].

6 Symbolic Solutions for Recurrences

The major difficulty when detecting recurrences in a SLRE system is to deal with multi-dimensional sequences. We must detect recurrences relative to all dimensions. Moreover some recurrences can be relative to two or more dimensions. The first step to solve these problems is to detect recurrences from inside outward. The second step is to replace the clauses which represent a recurrence by its symbolic solution.

We can draw an analogy with differential equations: an equation $dy = f(x)dx$ may not have an algebraic solution but we always can say that y is equal to $y = \int f(x)dx$. The equation is not solved but we can work with y, for instance replace it by the integral in an expression. The symbol used to write a symbolic solution of a recurrence (i.e. the counterpart of the integral symbol) is called the recurrence operator.

We can summarize the algorithm of reduction detection by the following.

Algorithm 8. *Let S be a SLRE system extracted from an imperative program and let D be the maximal dimension of equation domains.*
For p=D − 1 Downto 0 Do
      p-reduce the system S.
      Recognize recurrences relative to the dimension $p + 1$ and replace
      them by a symbolic solution.
Done
In the final system, compose recurrence operators to obtain multidimensional recurrences.

6.1 Recurrence Operator

Definition 9 recurrence operator. An expression build with the recurrence operator is of the following form.

$$\text{Recur}(\,(o, k), \{(l, \lambda i_1 \ldots i_{l-1}.\alpha, \lambda i_1 \ldots i_{l-1}.\beta)\}, \tag{1}$$
$$\lambda i_1 \ldots i_l x_1 \ldots x_o.f, (\lambda i_1 \ldots i_l.g_s)_{s \in [1,o]}) \ .$$

Let us give the meaning of the different terms: o is the recurrence order, k is the recurrence step (see section 4.2). The recurrence is relative to dimension l, must iterate between the lower bound α and the upper bound β, its propagation function is f and the initial values are the $(g_s)_{s \in \mathbb{N}_o^*}$.

It is easy to rewrite a recurrent clause with the recurrence operator.

Example 2. For instance, the symbolic solution of the Fibonacci sequence

$$\left[\begin{array}{l} u_0 = 1 \\ u_1 = 1 \\ \forall i \in \mathbb{N} - \{0,1\},\, u_i = u_{i-1} + u_{i-2} \end{array} \right.$$

is

$$\left[\begin{array}{l} u_0 = 1 \\ u_1 = 1 \\ \forall i \in \mathbb{N} - \{0,1\},\, u_i = \mathrm{Recur}((2,1),\{(1,2,\infty)\},\lambda i x y.x + y,(\lambda i.1,\lambda i.1))(i) \end{array} \right.$$

Example 3. Let us process the following program to show how our method handle uni-dimensional recurrences.

```
x(0)=0                        (Ins1)
DO i=1,2*n
   save(i)=x(2*n-i+1)         (Ins2)
   x(i)=x(i-1)+save(i)        (Ins3)
END DO
```

The corresponding system is

$$\left[\begin{array}{l} \forall i \in \mathbb{N}_{2n}^*,\ \mathrm{Ins2}_i = \left\{ \begin{array}{ll} x_{2n-i+1} & \text{if } i \geq 1 \wedge i \leq n \\ \mathrm{Ins3}_{2n-i+1} & \text{if } i \geq n+1 \wedge i \leq 2n \end{array} \right. \\[2.5em] \forall i \in \mathbb{N}_{2n}^*,\ \mathrm{Ins3}_i = \left\{ \begin{array}{ll} \mathrm{Ins2}_1 & \text{if } i = 1 \\ \mathrm{Ins3}_{i-1} + \mathrm{Ins2}_i & \text{if } i \geq 2 \wedge i \leq 2n \end{array} \right. \end{array} \right.$$

(note that replacing the array reference `save(i)` by a scalar reference to `save` in instructions Ins2 and Ins3 would lead to the same system). The 0-graph of this system is not reduced, so the system must be normalized. Let us assume that the algorithm $\mathcal{A}$ choose to replace Ins2 by its value in Ins3 expression. The new system (Ins2 become useless and is removed) is

$$\left[\forall i \in \mathbb{N}_{2n}^*,\ \mathrm{Ins3}_i = \left\{ \begin{array}{ll} x_{2n} & \text{if } i = 1 \\ \mathrm{Ins3}_{i-1} + x_{2n-i+1} & \text{if } i \geq 2 \wedge i \leq 2n \\ \mathrm{Ins3}_{i-1} + \mathrm{Ins3}_{2n-i+1} & \text{if } i \geq n+1 \wedge i \leq 2n \end{array} \right. \right.$$

The final system (after recurrence detection) is

$$\left[\forall i \in \mathbb{N}_{2n}^*,\ \mathrm{Ins3}_i = \left\{ \begin{array}{l} \mathrm{Recur}((1,1),\{(1,1,n)\}, \\ \qquad \lambda i_1 y.y + x_{2n-i_1+1},(\lambda i_1.0))(i) \\ \quad \text{if } i \geq 1 \wedge i \leq n \\ \mathrm{Recur}((1,1),\{(1,n+1,2n)\}, \\ \qquad \lambda i_1 y.y + \mathrm{Ins3}_{2n-i_1+1},(\lambda i_1.\mathrm{Ins3}_{i_1-1}))(i) \\ \quad \text{if } i \geq n+1 \wedge i \leq 2n \end{array} \right. \right.$$

Applying some algebraic transformations on the final system give us the following result:

$$\mathrm{Ins3}_n = \sum_{i=1}^{n}(n-i+2)x_{2n-i+1}\ .$$

Hence the original program may be useful to compute a discrete random variable expectation. Moreover this sequential program is efficient since no multiplication is used. Note that classical methods do not handle this example. Indeed, the dependence $i \rightarrow 2n - i + 1$ prevent loop normalization as presented in [9] and cannot be exploited by symbolic analysis.

The recurrence operator is designed to allow substitutions, but some precautions must be respected. We distinguish two kinds of substitution in presence of recurrence operators.

The first kind is substitution *by* a recurrence operator. Since an expression build with such an operator is independent of the domain of its clause, this expression can be moved anywhere. Thus substitution by a recurrence operator is always valid. But since detection of recurrences is done in order to reduce computation time, we must not duplicate the symbolic solution of a recurrence. Therefore this kind of substitution will be allowed only if the symbolic solution is referenced once. As a result we will not be able to reduce some reducible systems since some substitutions are forbidden.

The second kind of substitution is substitution *into* a recurrence operator. In an expression of the form $\text{Recur}(a, b, c, d)$ the only terms in which doing substitutions make sense are c and d. A substitution in term c may lead to break the expression into severals symbolic solutions. There is no advantage in doing that, because we must re-compute the initial terms and because the new expressions must be computed sequentially, therefore the time complexity increases. But substitutions in term d are valid and useful. They do not involve modification in the other terms and they are necessary for multi-dimensional recurrences detection.

6.2 Multi-Dimensional Recurrences

As shown in algorithm (8) multi-dimensional recurrences are build in a final stage of recurrence operators composition. We first extend the definition of the recurrence operator to deal with multi-dimensional recurrence. Then we prove that, on certain conditions, two interlocked recurrence operators are equivalent to a recurrence operator with higher dimension.

Definition 10 extension of the recurrence operator. An expression build with a recurrence operator can also have the following form (the sequence of natural numbers $(l_s)_{s \in \mathbb{N}_n^*}$ is a strictly increasing one):

$$
\begin{aligned}
\text{Recur}(&(1, 1), \\
&\{ (l_1, \lambda i_1 \ldots i_{l_1 - 1}.\alpha_1, \lambda i_1 \ldots i_{l_1 - 1}.\beta_1), \ldots, \\
&\quad (l_n, \lambda i_1 \ldots i_{l_n - 1}.\alpha_n, \lambda i_1 \ldots i_{l_n - 1}.\beta_n) \}, \\
&\lambda i_1 \ldots i_{l_n} x.f, (\lambda i_1 \ldots i_{l_n}.g)) \ .
\end{aligned}
\tag{2}
$$

All the remarks of the previous sub-section about the incidence of the recurrence operator on equations substitution remain true with this new definition. Now we give the rule of composition for recurrence operators.

142

Proposition 11 composition of recurrence operators. *Let R be a valid expression which have the following form*

$$R = \text{Recur}((1,1), \{(l_1, \alpha_1, \beta_1)\},$$
$$\lambda i_1 \ldots i_{l_1} x . \lambda j_1 \ldots j_\omega . \text{Recur}((1,1), \{(l_2, \alpha_2, \beta_2), \ldots, (l_n, \alpha_n, \beta_n)\},$$
$$f, (\lambda k_1 \ldots k_{l_n} . x \, \Phi'(k_1 \ldots k_{l_n}))$$
$$) \, i_1 \ldots i_{l_1} \, \Phi(i_1, \ldots, i_{l_1}, j_1, \ldots, j_\omega),$$
$$(\lambda i_1 \ldots i_{l_1} . \lambda j_1 \ldots j_\omega . (h \, i_1 \ldots i_{l_1}))) \ ,$$

where Φ is a map from $\mathbb{N}^{l_1 + \omega}$ to $\mathbb{N}^{l_n - l_1}$ and Φ' a map from $\mathbb{N}^{l_n}$ to $\mathbb{N}^\omega$. If the expression f does not contain any symbol x and if the following condition is fulfilled

$$\forall I \in \mathbb{N}^{l_n}, \ I_{l_2} = (\alpha_2 \, I_1 \ldots I_{l_2 - 1}) - 1$$
$$\Phi(I_1 \ldots I_{l_1 - 1}(I_{l_1} - 1), \Phi'(I)) = max^{l_2}(I_1, \ldots, I_{l_1 - 1}, I_{l_1} - 1, I_{l_1 + 1}, \ldots, I_{l_n}) \ ,$$

where max^{l_r} is defined by recurrence: $\forall z \in \mathbb{N}^{l_n}, \ \forall l \in \mathbb{N}^*_{l_n}$,

$$max^{l_r}(z)_l = \begin{cases} \beta_l \, max^{l_r}(z)_1 \ldots max^{l_r}(z)_{l-1} \ if \, l \in \{l_r, \ldots, l_n\} \\ z_l \hspace{4.5cm} otherwise \end{cases}$$

then R is equivalent to

$$\lambda i_1 \ldots i_{l_1 + \omega} . \text{Recur}((1,1), \{(l_1, \alpha_1, \beta_1), \ldots, (l_n, \alpha_n, \beta_n)\},$$
$$f, (h)) \, i_1 \ldots i_{l_1} \Phi(i_1, \ldots, i_{l_1 + \omega}) \ .$$

Example 4. To illustrate the detection of multi-dimensional recurrences let us process the following program

```
s=0                    (Ins1)
DO i=1,n
  DO j=1,m
    s=s+a(i,j)         (Ins2)
  END DO
END DO
```

First we compute the system of the program

$$\left[\forall(i,j) \in \mathbb{N}^*_n \times \mathbb{N}^*_m, \ Ins2_{i,j} = \begin{cases} Ins2_{i,j-1} + a_{i,j} & if \, j > 1 \\ Ins2_{i-1,m} + a_{i,j} & if \, j = 1 \wedge i > 1 \\ 0 + a_{i,j} & if \, j = 1 \wedge i = 1 \end{cases} \right.$$

The 1-graph of the system is reduced, that allows us to detect recurrences relative to the second dimension. The system becomes:

$$\forall(i,j) \in \mathbb{N}^*_n \times \mathbb{N}^*_m,$$
$$Ins2_{i,j} = \begin{cases} \text{Recur}((1,1), \{(2,2,m)\}, \lambda i_1 i_2 x . x + a_{i_1, i_2}, (\lambda i_1 i_2 . Ins2_{i_1, i_2}))(i,j) \\ \hspace{3cm} if \, j > 1 \\ Ins2_{i-1,m} + a_{i,j} \ if \, j = 1 \wedge i > 1 \\ 0 + a_{i,j} \hspace{2cm} if \, j = 1 \wedge i = 1 \end{cases}$$

Then, we replace s_{i_1,i_2} by its value in the first clause. Thus the system is now:

$$\forall (i,j) \in \mathbb{N}_n^* \times \mathbb{N}_m^*,$$

$$\text{Ins2}_{i,j} = \begin{cases} \text{Recur}((1,1), \{(2,1,m)\}, \lambda i_1 i_2 x.x + a_{i_1,i_2}, (\lambda i_1 i_2.\text{Ins2}_{i_1-1,m}))(i,j) \\ \quad \text{if } j > 1 \wedge i > 1 \\ \text{Recur}((1,1), \{(2,1,m)\}, \lambda i_1 i_2 x.x + a_{i_1,i_2}, (\lambda i_1 i_2.0))(i,j) \\ \quad \text{if } j > 1 \wedge i = 1 \end{cases}$$

Since the 0-graph of this new system is reduced, we can detect recurrences relative to the first dimension:

$$\forall (i,j) \in \mathbb{N}_n^* \times \mathbb{N}_m^*,$$

$$\text{Ins2}_{i,j} = \begin{cases} \text{Recur}(\ (1,1), \{(1,1,n)\}, \\ \qquad \lambda j_1 y.\lambda j_2.\text{Recur}(\ (1,1), \{(2,1,m)\}, \\ \qquad\qquad \lambda i_1 i_2 x.x + a_{i_1,i_2}, \\ \qquad\qquad (\lambda i_1 i_2.y(m)))(j_1,j_2), \\ \quad (\lambda j_1 j_2.0))(i,j) \\ \quad \text{if } j > 1 \wedge i > 1 \end{cases}$$

In such a system the composition of recurrence operators is valid. The final system is:

$$\forall (i,j) \in \mathbb{N}_n^* \times \mathbb{N}_m^*, \ \text{Ins2}_{i,j} = \begin{cases} \text{Recur}(\ (1,1), \{(1,2,n),(2,1,m)\}, \\ \qquad \lambda i_1 i_2 x.x + a_{i_1,i_2}, \\ \qquad (\lambda i_1.0))(i,j) \\ \quad \text{if } j > 1 \wedge i > 1 \end{cases}$$

6.3 Comparison to Other Recurrence Operators

Some other recurrence operators already exist, namely the reduction operator in the Alpha language (see [6]) and the scan primitives also known as parallel prefix operations (see [3]). However we have introduced our own recurrence operator for the following motives. The Alpha operator is an operator on un-ordered set of values, which is thus restricted to reduction by associative and commutative operators. It only gives the final result of the reduction, while we need the partial results since they can be used in the original program.

Example 5. For instance the following expression build with the Alpha operator

$$\text{red}(+, \ (\text{i},\text{j} \ \text{->} \ ), \ \{\text{i},\text{j} \ | \ 1\text{<=}\text{i}\text{<=}\text{n}; \ 1\text{<=}\text{j}\text{<=}\text{m}\} \ : \ \text{a})$$

which computes the sum $\sum_{i=1}^{n} \sum_{j=1}^{m} a_{i,j}$ can be rewritten with the recurrence operator:

$$\text{Recur}((1,1), \{(1,1,n),(2,1,m)\}, \lambda ijx.x + a_{i,j}, (\lambda ij.0))(n,m)$$

But the set of values

$$(\text{Recur}((1,1), \{(1,1,n),(2,1,m)\}, \lambda ijx.x + a_{i,j}, (\lambda ij.0))(i,j))_{(i,j)\in \mathbb{N}_n^* \times \mathbb{N}_m^*}$$

cannot be expressed with the red operator.

The scan primitives are more adapted since they use ordered sets and compute all the terms of the recurrence. Indeed the one-dimensional form of our recurrence operator and the scan primitives are very similar.

Example 6. The expressions

$$\forall i \in \mathbb{N}_n^*, \mathrm{Recur}((1,1), \{(1,1,n)\}, \lambda i x.x + a_i, (\lambda i.0))(i)$$

and

$$scan(+, [a_1, \dots, a_n])$$

compute the same vector $[s_1, \dots, s_n]$ with $s_i = \sum_{k=1}^{i} a_k$.

But scan primitives are designed to describe one-dimensional recurrences. It is possible, by a change of variables, to transform any multi-dimensional recurrence into a one-dimensional one. However, when doing this, the subscripts functions become non-linear and the difficulty of system analysis increases.

7 Conclusion

In summary, our method of recurrences detection, when compared with other methods, presents the following advantages: our method is based on the DFG structure which allows us to fully handle arrays. Moreover, the representation of programs as equations systems give us a way to perform a strong normalization. As a consequence the detection is not sensitive to the algorithm implementation. Lastly the introduction of the recurrence operator allows us to detect multi-dimensional recurrences.

Note that conditionals can be easily handled by our method: the structural ones (i.e. conditionals whose predicate is a positive form, linear in the loop counters and parameters of the program) are inserted in the DFG structure. The non structural conditionals are transformed into guarded instructions.

We have realized an implementation of this method in Lisp (the size of this implementation is about 5000 lines). The program is mostly a symbolic manipulation of conditionals equations. These equations are defined on convex domains. As a consequence the forward substitutions leads us to deal with convex intersections and convex simplifications. The easiest way to simplify a convex is to use an algorithm for computing its vertices, like Chernikova's algorithm. We would like to thank H. Le Verge and D. Wilde for allowing us to use the particular implementation they developed at IRISA ([7]).

Due to the effectiveness of this algorithm the final systems (after recurrences detection) have a reasonable size (less than ten clauses per equations for small examples). Moreover the final systems are simplified by the elimination of useless equations. The execution time is function of the initial system complexity. Thus sample programs with classic uni-dimensional recurrences are processed quickly (a few seconds on a low end workstation). When composition of symbolic solutions of recurrences is necessary the execution time increases. Therefore a program computing a double sum needs 30s to be analyzed and we need 60s to process a triple sum program. The decomposition of the system into strong components allows us to deal with medium sized programs. But a real size program should be first analyzed by a front end program that finds out the portions of code where recurrences have to be detected.

The directions for future work are the following: since special recurrences can be implemented more efficiently than others in present day super-computers (i.e. reductions), we must point them out. Thus a dedicated pattern-matching phase must be developed. Moreover, in order to use the detected recurrences for parallel program construction, we plan to compute a schedule for the generated system (where recurrences are detected). Some adaptations to existing schedulers are needed since our symbolic solutions of recurrences may use unbounded fan-in operations.

References

1. C. Berge. *Graphes*. Gauthier-Villars, 1987.
2. A.J. Bernstein. Analysis of programs for parallel processing. *IEEE Trans. on El. Computers*, EC-15, 1966.
3. G.E. Blelloch. Scans as primitive parallel operations. *IEEE Trans. on Computers*, 38(11):1526–1539, 1989.
4. Paul Feautrier. Dataflow analysis of scalar and array references. *Int. Journal of Parallel Programming*, 20(1):23–53, February 1991.
5. Pierre Jouvelot and Babak Dehbonei. A unified semantic approach for the vectorization and parallelization of generalized reductions. In *Procs. of the 3rd Int. Conf. on Supercomputing*, pages 186–194. ACM Press, 1989.
6. H. Leverge. Reduction operators in alpha. In D. Etiemble and J.-C. Syre, editors, *Lecture notes in Computer Science No 605*, pages 397–411, 1992.
7. Hervé Leverge. A note on chernikova's algorithm. Technical Report 1992, INRIA, May 1992. Référence à vérifier.
8. Christophe Mauras. *Alpha : un langage équationnel pour la conception et la programmation d'architectures parallèles synchrones*. PhD thesis, Université de Rennes I, December 1989.
9. Shlomit S. Pinter and Ron Y. Pinter. Program optimization and parallelization using idioms. In *POPL'91*, 1991. to appear.
10. X. Redon. Détection des réductions. Technical Report MASI 92-52, Institut Blaise Pascal, September 1992.

Parallel Programming Using Skeleton Functions

J. Darlington, A.J. Field, P.G. Harrison,

P.H.J. Kelly, D.W.N. Sharp, Q. Wu

Dept. of Computing, Imperial College, London SW7 2BZ

email: {jd,ajf,pgh,phjk,dwns,wq}@doc.ic.ac.uk

R.L. While

Dept. of Computer Science, University of Western Australia,

Nedlands, Western Australia 6009

email: lyndon@cs.uwa.edu.au

Abstract

Programming parallel machines is notoriously difficult. Factors contributing to this difficulty include the complexity of concurrency, the effect of resource allocation on performance and the current diversity of parallel machine models. The net result is that effective portability, which depends crucially on the predictability of performance, has been lost.

Functional programming languages have been put forward as solutions to these problems, because of the availability of implicit parallelism. However, performance will be generally poor unless the issue of resource allocation is addressed explicitly, diminishing the advantage of using a functional language in the first place.

We present a methodology which is a compromise between the extremes of explicit imperative programming and implicit functional programming. We use a repertoire of higher-order parallel forms, *skeletons*, as the basic building blocks for parallel implementations and provide program transformations which can convert between skeletons, giving portability between differing machines. Resource allocation issues are documented for each skeleton/machine pair and are addressed explicitly during implementation in an interactive, selective manner, rather than by explicit programming.

1   Introduction

The main obstacle to the commercial uptake of parallel computing is the complexity and cost of the associated software development process. Programming parallel machines is more difficult than programming sequential machines in at least two fundamental ways: **predictability of performance** and **portability.**

Predictability of performance

Sequential programming languages, incorporating the von-Neumann model of computation, enjoy a simple one-to-one mapping between language constructs and their underlying machine implementation. Issues such as memory allocation are resolved by the compiler with no performance implications, allowing the programmer to concentrate on high-level aspects of the algorithm. The programmer can fairly confidently predict the performance of a program on a particular machine, whilst avoiding the burden and complexity of run-time resource allocation.

In contrast, the mapping of a parallel program onto a multiprocessor machine is typically a complex process involving decisions about the distribution of processes over the processors of the machine, scheduling of processor time between competing processes, communication patterns, etc. Often the only way for the programmer to achieve the desired level of performance is to take explicit control of these decisions in the program, with the obvious increase in program complexity and a corresponding deterioration in program reliability. Some predictability is retained with shared-memory multiprocessors, which attempt to sustain the von-Neumann model at low degrees of parallelism, but such machines are not scalable to the levels of performance required by many application areas.

Portability

The universality of the von-Neumann model guarantees portability of sequential programs at the language level, with no danger of an unforeseen degradation in performance. A sequential program moved to a machine with a faster processor will, almost certainly, run faster.

In the world of parallel machines the explicit nature of resource allocation means there is rarely any portability at all. Even where a high-level language can be compiled for different machines, the wide disparity in the architectures available means that the performance of a program can vary wildly and in unpredictable ways unless it is radically altered as part of the porting process.

The diversity of parallel machine architectures and the lack of a common model of computation has led the application development community to fragment into incompatible, machine-oriented camps with proprietary languages/language extensions predominating at the expense of a proper understanding of the field.

There appear to be two routes out of the current state of affairs.

- One approach is the development of a 'parallel von-Neumann machine', an abstract machine to which any useful programming model can be compiled with predictable (small) loss of performance, and which can itself be implemented on a scalable physical architecture, again at a known cost. This is the route taken by research into the parallel random-access machine (PRAM[17]) and distributed shared memory[12], which attempts to provide the illusion of a shared address space on a physically-distributed machine, in effect taking the shared-memory model to arbitrary degrees of parallelism.

- The second, perhaps more direct, approach is the development of a programming methodology for parallel machines which allows portability both of programs and their performance across the whole range of architectures. This is the approach taken in this paper.

Our approach involves abandoning the search for portability at the language level in favour of a structured decision-making process based on the use of high-level program forms, source-level program transformation and performance modelling.

2 An Overview of the Methodology

The central idea is to replace explicit parallel programming, using a parallel language, by the selection and instantiation of a variety of pre-packaged parallel algorithmic forms known as *skeletons*. The approach is similar to that taken by Cole[2] for imperative languages and follows Backus's principle[1] that the key to effective (functional) programming is the availability of a small fixed set of special operators (program-forming operations) which allow new functions to be created from old ones. The methodology can be broken down into three principal components: **skeletons**, **performance models** and **program transformation**.

Skeletons

A skeleton captures an algorithmic form common to a range of programming applications. In our work, skeletons have been developed as polymorphic, higher-order, functions in a non-strict functional programming language.

Each skeleton has a declarative *meaning*, established by its functional language definition. This meaning is independent of any particular implementation of the skeleton: this allows skeletal programs to be prototyped rapidly on sequential platforms and to be fully portable between different parallel machines. A skeleton also has specific *behaviours* on particular parallel machines on which it is known to be implementable. Of course, in principle, any skeleton can be executed on any machine: however, each skeleton is associated with a set of architectures on which efficient realisations are known to exist.

All parallelism in a program derives from the behaviour of its skeletons on the machine in question. Functions to which skeletons are applied are executed sequentially. All aspects of a skeleton's parallel behaviour, such as process placement or interconnectivity, are either clear from its definition or documented as issues to be addressed explicitly during implementation.

Performance models

Each skeleton/machine pair has associated with it a performance model which can be used to predict the performance of a program written using the skeleton on that machine. These models are used by the programmer, the transformation system and the compiler to guide decision-making at all levels of the program development process. Resource allocation in particular relies heavily on the use of these performance models.

Program transformation

Program transformation is used in the development process at all levels. At the topmost level, for example, it can be used to transform high-level problem specifications into initial skeleton forms. At the lower levels it can be used to convert programs from one skeleton form to another e.g. for the purposes of portability. At the lowest level, transformation can be used to fine-tune an architecture-specific program to a particular machine in that class. This may involve, for example, partial evaluation[4] to vary the grain-size used in an application or to configure the program for a particular machine size.

Wherever possible, the methodology aims to replace *(re)invention*, both of programs and transformations, by *selection* from a limited range of possibilities determined by context. The skeletons and associated transformations form a *decision-tree* that can be navigated by the programmer to map high-level specifications onto concrete machine architectures.

Portability of programs is provided by the high-level nature of the the original program specification and the ability to record, replay and alter the derivation process from specification to implementation. Resource allocation is tackled explicitly by addressing the important performance questions directly rather than implicitly by writing a program with the desired properties.

The next three sections of the paper discuss the three main aspects of the methodology in more detail. Section 6 discusses the implementation of the methodology and Section 7 concludes the paper.

3 Parallel Algorithmic Skeletons

3.1 Initial Skeletons

An initial set of skeletons has been defined to capture the most common forms used in parallel algorithms. These are listed below, all definitions are expressed in Haskell [8].

Simple linear process-parallelism is captured by the PIPE skeleton. A list of functions are composed together so that elements can be streamed through them.

Parallelism is achieved by allocating each function to a different processor. Note that this idea can easily be extended to higher dimensions.

$$\text{PIPE} :: [\alpha \rightarrow \alpha] \rightarrow (\alpha \rightarrow \alpha)$$
$$\text{PIPE} = \text{foldr1} (.)$$

The FARM skeleton captures the simplest form of data-parallelism. A function is applied to each of a list of 'jobs'. The function also takes an environment, which represents data which is common to all of the jobs. Parallelism is achieved by utilising multiple processors to evaluate the jobs (i.e. 'farming them out' to multiple processors).

$$\text{FARM} :: (\alpha \rightarrow \beta \rightarrow \gamma) \rightarrow \alpha \rightarrow ([\beta] \rightarrow [\gamma])$$
$$\text{FARM f env} = \text{map} . (\text{f env})$$

Many algorithms work by splitting a large task into several sub-tasks, solving the sub-tasks independently, and combining the results. This approach is known as *divide-and-conquer* and it is captured by the DC skeleton. Trivial tasks (t) are solved (s) directly on the home processor: larger tasks are divided (d) into sub-tasks and the sub-tasks passed to other processors to be solved recursively. The sub-results are then combined (c) to produce the main result.

$$\text{DC} :: (\alpha \rightarrow Bool) \rightarrow (\alpha \rightarrow \beta) \rightarrow (\alpha \rightarrow [\alpha]) \rightarrow ([\beta] \rightarrow \beta) \rightarrow \alpha \rightarrow \beta$$
$$\text{DC t s d c x} \mid \text{t x} \qquad = \text{s x}$$
$$\mid \text{not} (\text{t x}) = (\text{c} . \text{map} (\text{DC t s d c}) . \text{d}) \text{x}$$

Another common class of algorithms describes systems where each object in the system can potentially interact with any other object. Each individual interaction is calculated and the results are combined to produce a result for each object. This is described by the RaMP skeleton ('Reduce-and-Map-over-Pairs'). This skeleton is typically used for initial specification and implemented by transformation to an alternative form, for example by farming out the calculations for each object or by pipelining over the functions f and g.

$$\text{RaMP} :: (\alpha \rightarrow \alpha \rightarrow \beta) \rightarrow (\beta \rightarrow \beta \rightarrow \beta) \rightarrow [\alpha] \rightarrow [\beta]$$
$$\text{RaMP f g xs} = \text{map h xs}$$
$$\text{where h x} = \text{foldr1 g} (\text{map} (\text{f x}) \text{xs})$$

More dynamic algorithms are typified by the DMPA skeleton ('Dynamic-Message-Passing-Architecture'). Here any process can interact directly with any other process via message-passing, the actual connections being determined using run-time data. Each process has an internal state which records values local to the process: messages from other processes may modify the process's state and generate new messages to other processes. Parallelism arises from evaluating the processes on different processors.

$$\text{DMPA} :: \{\{\alpha\} \rightarrow \{(Int, \alpha)\}\} \rightarrow \{(Int, \alpha)\} \rightarrow \{\alpha\}$$

DMPA { P$_i$ initState$_i$ | $1 \leq i \leq n$ } initMess
  = filterms 0 mess
    where mess = P$_1$ initState$_1$ (filterms 1 mess) U $\cdots$ U
                  P$_n$ initState$_n$ (filterms n mess) U initMess
      filterms i ms = { conts | (j, conts) $\in$ ms, i == j }
      P$_i$ localState (c U cs) = replies U P$_i$ updState cs

All these skeletons describe MIMD modes of operation. The work described in [10] brings SIMD machines, such as the Thinking Machines' CM-2, within the range of our techniques. There a small set of higher-order primitives is defined corresponding to the basic computation and communication capabilities of such machines. There is a very natural fit between these primitives and the aggregate view of computation, providing both a congenial abstraction of SIMD machines and a basis for the efficient support of array operations in functional languages. These primitives provide a platform on which skeletons describing SIMD computations can be defined.

3.2 Example Applications

This section gives examples of the use of the skeletons in describing typical applications. Some functions which only perform low-level arithmetic or data manipulations are not fully specified.

As an example of the use of the PIPE skeleton the function compile below defines the general structure of a compilation route for a high-level programming language.

compile :: $[Char] \rightarrow [Char]$
compile = PIPE [writefile, genCode, typeCheck, parse, lex, readfile]

writefile, genCode, typeCheck, parse, lex, readfile :: $[Char] \rightarrow [Char]$
various stages in compiling a program

In the function exposedFaces, the FARM skeleton is used to determine which faces of a convex 3-dimensional body are visible from the origin of the co-ordinate system. Each face is checked individually by reference to a point which is inside the body. The co-ordinates of this point form the shared environment of the farm.

exposedFaces :: $[Face] \rightarrow [(Face, Bool)]$
exposedFaces fs = zip fs (FARM checkIfVisible (pointInBody fs) fs)

pointInBody :: $[Face] \rightarrow Point$
calculate a point which is inside the body fs (assumed convex)

checkIfVisible :: $Point \rightarrow Face \rightarrow Bool$
given a point p *inside the body, check if face* f *is visible*

An example application of the DC skeleton is mergesort. Given a function merge which combines two sorted lists whilst retaining their ordering, mergesort works by recursively splitting its argument into smaller sublists until the sublists are trivially sorted, then using merge to build a sorted permutation of the original list.

mergesort :: $(\alpha \rightarrow \alpha \rightarrow Bool) \rightarrow [\alpha] \rightarrow [\alpha]$
mergesort = (DC isSingleton id split) . foldr1 . merge
　　　　　　where isSingleton xs = length xs $\leq$ 1

split :: $[\alpha] \rightarrow [[\alpha]]$
split xs *into a list of its sublists*

merge :: $(\alpha \rightarrow \alpha \rightarrow Bool) \rightarrow [\alpha] \rightarrow [\alpha] \rightarrow [\alpha]$
merge two sorted lists into a sorted list

An example of the RaMP skeleton is the classical problem of nBody simulation. At each step of the simulation, the force between each pair of bodies is calculated and these are summed to determine the total force acting on each body and hence its new position and velocity.

nBody :: $[Planet] \rightarrow [[Planet]]$
nBody ps = ps : nBody (map newPos
　　　　　　　　　　　　　　(zip ps (RaMP calcF sumFs ps)))

newPos :: $(Planet, Force) \rightarrow Planet$
calculate the new position and velocity of planet p

calcF :: $Planet \rightarrow Planet \rightarrow Force$
calculate the force exerted by planet p_1 *on planet* p_2

sumFs :: $Force \rightarrow Force \rightarrow Force$
combine the effects of forces f_1 *and* f_2

The DMPA skeleton describes the most dynamic algorithms, where the interactions between processes are determined using run-time data. Interaction is via message-passing. The function database describes a dynamically-changing database whose contents are distributed over a network of processors. Each node has to be capable of handling requests for the whole database: requests which cannot be handled locally are forwarded to the relevant processor.

data Message = Query DataItem | Add DataItem | Del DataItem
　　　　　　| *other message-types*

```
database :: {(Int, Message)} → {Message}
database = DMPA { dbmanager_i initData_i | 1 ≤ i ≤ n }

dbmanager_i :: Localdata → {Message} → {(Int, Message)}
dbmanager_i dat ( Query info U ms )
        | DB == i = ( 0 , reply ) U dbmanager_i dat ms
        | DB /= i = ( DB , Query info ) U dbmanager_i dat ms
                where DB = whereStored info
dbmanager_i dat ( Add info U ms )
        | DB == i = dbmanager_i ( insert info dat ) ms
        | DB /= i = ( DB , Add info ) U dbmanager_i dat ms
                where DB = whereStored info
dbmanager_i dat ( Del info U ms )
        | DB == i = dbmanager_i ( delete info dat ) ms
        | DB /= i = ( DB , Del info ) U dbmanager_i dat ms
                where DB = whereStored info

whereStored :: DataItem → Int
where is data of the type of item stored?

insert, delete :: DataItem → Localdata → Localdata
insert/delete an item into/from the local database
```

Many other examples of the DMPA skeleton in action are described in [16], including a novel approach using dynamically-generated patterns of communication to maximise the potential of the network facilities of MIMD machines. Examples include a new algorithm for parallel quicksort of $O(\log n)^2$ and new algorithms for fractal generation and tesselation.

4 Performance Models

The ultimate aim of a parallel programmer is to write a program that will execute efficiently on the chosen target machine. With today's software technology targeted at non-uniform machines it is a difficult task to even predict the performance of a given parallel program, let alone to ensure that it will be optimal. We would characterise today's approach by the term *performance debugging*. The programmer writes a program that he hopes is reasonably efficient, executes it and observes its behaviour. The information gained from these observations is then used to modify the resource allocation decisions embodied in the program, and the modified program is executed again to see if any improvement ensues. Often the programmer is proceeding in the dark, as he may not even know what factors are important in determining the performance of the program.

Here we seek to develop a more scientific methodology based on the use of *performance models* which, given a program, can both predict its performance and suggest what may be done to improve that performance. Such a performance model is typically a set of analytical formulae parameterised by attributes of both the program and the machine. There has been an impressive body of work in producing such models for parallel hardware and software [7]. However, the state of the art is unable to provide practical methods to predict the performance of an arbitrary program executing on an arbitrary machine. By limiting our programs to instantiations of known skeletons, each targetted at a specific set of machines, the methodology becomes more practical.

A performance model is associated with each skeleton/machine pair and is used constructively in the programming process. A preliminary model is produced and verified and quantified experimentally. The model is adjusted until it is shown to be a reliable predictor of performance. This is equivalent to playing out the 'performance debugging' process once for each configuration and recording the result for future reference.

Consider as an example the Divide-and-Conquer skeleton, DC, targetted onto a distributed-memory machine. Such an architecture results in very non-uniform memory access times, with local store access being much cheaper than remote store access. The two most important factors governing program performance will thus be process granularity and data placement. The model, therefore, needs to take account of the complexity of each of the argument functions of DC and the speed of communication between processors. Taking all these factors into account, an application should be solved in parallel if the following condition holds (assuming a binary division function):

$$T_{sol_G} > T_{div_G} + T_{sol_{G/2}} + T_{comb_{G/2}} + T_{comms}$$

where T_{sol_x} is the time to solve a problem of size x on one processor, T_{div_x} is the time to split a problem of size x into two sub-problems, T_{comb_x} is the time to combine the results from two problems of size x and T_{comms} is the time to communicate problems and results between processors. The reasoning behind this formulae is that the right hand side represents the worst case involved in going parallel, i.e. there is no further gain to be made from further parallel execution and the two subproblems are solved sequentially. If this worst case is still less than the time to solve sequentially, T_{sol_x}, then it pays to keep dividing.

We can expand this to calculate the total time required to solve a problem of size G on M processors:

$$T_{sol_G} = \sum_{i=1}^{\log M} (T_{div_{G/2^{i-1}}} + T_{comb_{G/2^i}} + T_{comms}) + T_{sol_{G/M}}$$

Solving this equation for M will tell us the optimal number of processors to use in the evaluation. Note that further decisions will have to be made about whether shared data should be evaluated once and accessed remotely, evaluated once and copied to each processor or re-evaluated at each processor. [5] gives a performance model combining all these factors.

Many decisions in resource allocation can be expressed as source-level transformations, for example balancing the stages of a pipeline or matching the number of pipe-stages to the number of physical processors available. Decisions such as these can be implemented as transformation routines to be applied by the programmer after consultation with the performance model. Other decisions sit more naturally in the compilation process from the skeleton to the native code of the target machine. In particular, some skeletons will have multiple implementations on some machines, and the choice of the optimal one will be guided by the performance model.

We believe that this constructive use of performance models complements our structured approach to parallel programming. We consider it important that factors affecting performance are identified and quantified so they can be addressed explicitly and the relevant decisions documented, rather than being left unstated and accomplished indirectly as a side effect of a program with the appropriate behaviour.

5 Program Transformation

Transformation provides a natural route to portability in that a program written in terms of a skeleton which cannot be implemented easily on a given architecture can be re-expressed in terms of another skeleton which does have an efficient implementation on that architecture. This particularly applies to the higher-level skeletons which may not map easily onto any architectures.

As an example, a program written in terms of the RaMP skeleton can be implemented as a pipeline with length xs + 2 stages[11]:

$$\text{RaMP f g xs} \equiv (\text{ map snd . PIPE (map map (map g' xs))}$$
$$. \text{ map (pair unit}_g\text{)) xs}$$
$$\text{where g' b (a, c) = (a, g (f a b) c)}$$
$$\text{pair a b} = (b, a)$$

Alternatively it can be implemented on a distributed architecture as a FARM:

$$\text{RaMP f g xs} \equiv \text{FARM h (f, g, xs) xs}$$
$$\text{where h (f, g, xs) x = foldr1 g (map (f x) xs)}$$

Note that transforming a RaMP to a FARM leaves many implementation issues still to be resolved, in particular whether the environment is to be accessed remotely or passed to each processor.

An inter-skeleton transformation which relies heavily on fine-tuning is DC to PIPE. By assuming that an application of DC is overrun-tolerant[19], we can obtain the equivalence[18][6]

$$\text{map (DC t s d c) } \equiv \text{ PIPE (rept } q \text{ (map' n c)) . map s .}$$
$$\text{PIPE (rept } q \text{ (foldr1 (++) . map d))}$$

rept :: $Int \rightarrow \alpha \rightarrow [\alpha]$
rept n = take n . repeat

map' :: $Int \rightarrow ([\alpha] \rightarrow \beta) \rightarrow [\alpha] \rightarrow [\beta]$
map' n f xs | length xs $\geq$ n = f (take n xs) : map' n f (drop n xs)
            | length xs $<$ n = [ ]

where q is the number of levels in the evaluation tree and map' is a variation
of map which consumes its argument list in chunks of n elements. In the above
expression, n is the arity of each node in the evaluation tree, i.e. the length of
the result list of d. This transformation gives us a version of the application
which evaluates on a pipeline of length $2q + 1$ for arguments up to 'size' n^q.

For specific applications of DC we are often able to do much better, however.
Take the definition of mergesort from Section 3.2:

$$\text{mergesort = (DC isSingleton id split) . foldr1 . merge}$$
$$\text{where isSingleton xs = length xs } \leq 1$$

Unfolding the definition of mergesort once, and assuming the non-trivial case,
we can derive

$$\text{mergesort f } \equiv \text{ foldr1 (merge f) . map (mergesort f) . split}$$

This equivalence holds for any implementation of split which satisfies the property

$$\text{mergesort f . foldr1 (++) . split } \equiv \text{ mergesort f}$$

which is essentially the specification of split. We will choose a definition of split
which reduces its argument list to singletons in one pass (it is trivially shown to
satisfy the above property):

split :: $[\alpha] \rightarrow [[\alpha]]$
split = map mkSingleton
    where mkSingleton x = [x]

Applying the DC to PIPE transformation to the definition of mergesort gives us

$$\text{map (mergesort f) } \equiv \text{ PIPE (rept } q \text{ (map' n (foldr1 (merge f)))) .}$$
$$\text{map id}$$
$$\text{PIPE (rept } q \text{ (foldr1 (++) . map split))}$$

It is trivial to show that the expression foldr1 (++) . map split is idempotent,
so we have the equivalence

$$\text{PIPE} (\text{rept } q (\text{foldr1} (++) . \text{ map split})) \equiv \text{foldr1} (++) . \text{ map split}$$

for $q > 0$, together with the obvious equivalences

$$\text{map id} \equiv \text{id}$$

$$\text{f . id} \equiv \text{f}$$

The final pipeline for mergesort therefore has only $q + 2$ stages:

$$\text{map (mergesort f)} \equiv \text{PIPE} (\text{rept } q (\text{map' n} (\text{foldr1} (\text{merge f})))) .$$
$$\text{foldr1} (++) . \text{ map split}$$

This is clearly a significant improvement over the naive application of the transformation.

In short, transformation allows us to take a high-level, portable specification and target it onto any architecture which is at hand, and to fine-tune an instantiation of the specification to take advantage of the particular characteristics of an architecture without compromising program legibility and reliability. Portability arises directly from the ability to replay the transformation using different rules for different architectures.

6 Implementation

We have constructed an initial implementation of the skeletons using the functional language Hope+[15] as the source language and using C as the target language. This compiler makes extensive use of macros, giving us maximum flexibility to explore different implementation options, e.g. remote vs. local patterns of data access (e.g. FARM) and process placement options (e.g. DMPA).

The initial installation was carried out on a Meiko Transputer surface, using the CS Tools [13] library to provide flexibility in communication. Initial results, in terms of both speed-up and the usability of the methodology, have been promising although we have not, as yet, made direct comparisons with hand-coded versions of the same algorithms.. A subsequent, partial, implementation has been carried out on a Fujitsu AP1000 made available under Fujitsu Parallel Computing Centre Facilities programme. The AP1000 is of particular interest as its richer communication capabilities allow greater varieties of implementations to be considered. Further implementations of the skeletons on networks of workstations and a SIMD machine are planned.

7 Conclusions and Future Work

Implementation options

A preliminary study and implementation of compiler options has been carried out [9]. For each of the skeletons apart from DMPA two or three alternative implementation options were identified and the compiler extended to realise these options. Experiments showed that each of the options were more effective for some range of inputs than the general implementation.

Application-specific skeletons

Many potential application areas for parallel computing, for example databases and solid modelling, have their own characteristic high-level data and control structures. We plan to extend our skeleton-based methodology into these areas. We aim to construct domain-specific skeletons which would allow specialists to construct applications in these areas directly, without recourse to low-level programming. These initial system specifications could then be mapped onto the selected target machines by an extension of the program transformation and structured implementation techniques we have already developed. Preliminary studies in the area of solid modelling [14] and data bases have been encouraging.

'Languageless programming'

The ultimate goal of our work is to completely replace the requirement for invention or creation during application development by a process of selection from a range of possibilities determined by context. We aim to factor out all the decisions involved in creating an application and mapping it efficiently onto a machine and present them as a sequence of selections of appropriate skeletons, transformations and implementation options. Achieving this goal would have many benefits: simplifying application development; documenting the decisions made during the development of an application; and ensuring that the programmer addresses all the issues involved in the implementation process.

Given this framework, the system could be used via a menu-driven interface, with the skeletons and options presented visually. Visual programming is very attractive, but we feel that many current systems miss the point and simply present an unchanged programming paradigm in a visual manner. We consider that it is important to first convert the programming process from one of invention to one of selection, which lends itself well to the visual style of presentation.

8 Acknowledgements

We would like to thank all our colleagues at Imperial College for their inputs and assistance. The influence of and Backus's ideas on our work is obvious. The work reported here was initially developed in the UK SERC/DTI funded project 'The Exploitation of Parallel Hardware using Functional Languages and Program Transformation' and used equipment funded under the SERC's Parallel Equipment Initiative.We are also grateful to Fujitsu, Japan, for making the AP1000 machine available under the Fujitsu Parallel Research Centre Facilities programme.

References

[1] J. Backus, *Can Programming Be Liberated from the von-Neumann Style? A Functional Style and its Algebra of Programs*, CACM vol. 21, no. 8, pp. 613-41, 1978.

[2] M. Cole, *Algorithmic Skeletons: Structured Management of Parallel Computation*, Pitman/MIT Press, 1989.

[3] J. Darlington, Y-k. Guo and H.M. Pull, *A New Perspective on Integrating Functional and Logic Languages*, Conf. on Fifth Generation Computing Systems, Tokyo, June 1992.

[4] J. Darlington and H.M. Pull, *A Program Development Methodology Based on a Unified Approach to Execution and Transformation*, in Partial Evaluation and Mixed Computation, North-Holland, 1988.

[5] J. Darlington, M.J. Reeve and S. Wright, *Programming Parallel Computer Systems using Functional Languages and Program Transformation*, in Parallel Processing '89, Leiden, 1989.

[6] P.G. Harrison, *Towards the Synthesis of Static Parallel Algorithms: a Categorical Approach*, IFIP TC2 Working Conference on Constructing Programs from Specifications, Pacific Grove, California, May 1991 (published as *Constructing Programs from Specifications*, North-Holland).

[7] P.G. Harrison and N. Patel, *Performance Modelling: Application to Communication Networks and Computer Architecture*, Addison-Wesley, 1992.

[8] P. Hudak, S.L. Peyton Jones, P.L. Wadler, B. Boutel, J. Fairburn, J. Fasel, M. Guzmán, K. Hammond, J. Hughes, T. Johnsson, R. Kieburtz, R.S. Nikhil, W. Partain and J. Peterson, *Report on the Functional Programming Language Haskell*, SIGPLAN Notices 27(5), May 1992.

[9] C. A. Isaac, *Structural Implementations of Functional Skeletons*, MSc Project Report, Dept. of Computing, Imperial College 1992.

[10] G.K. Jouret, *Compiling Functional Languages for SIMD Architectures*, 3rd IEEE Symposium on Parallel and Distributed Processing, Dallas, December 1991.

[11] P.H.J. Kelly, *Functional Programming for Loosely-coupled Microprocessors*, Pitman/MIT Press, 1989.

[12] K. Li and P. Hudak, *Memory Coherence in Shared Virtual Memory Systems*, ACM Transactions on Computer Systems vol.7, no. 4, pp. 329-59, 1989.

[13] Meiko Ltd., *CS Tools for SunOS*, 1990 Edition: 83-009A00-02.02.

[14] G. Papachrysantou, *High Level Forms for Computation in Solid Modelling*, MSc Project Report, Dept. of Computing, Imperial College 1992.

[15] N. Perry, *Hope⁺*, Internal document IC/FPR/LANG/2.5.1/7, Dept. of Computing, Imperial College, 1989.

[16] D.W.N. Sharp and M.D. Cripps, *Parallel Algorithms that Solve Problems by Communication*, 3rd IEEE Symposium on Parallel and Distributed Processing, Dallas, December 1991.

[17] L.G. Valiant, *General Purpose Parallel Architectures*, in Handbook of Theoretical Computer Science, North-Holland, 1990.

[18] R.L. While, *Transforming Divide-and-Conquer to Pipeline*, Internal note, Dept. of Computing, Imperial College, 1991.

[19] J.H. Williams, *On the Development of the Algebra of Functional Programs*, ACM Transactions on Programming Languages and Systems vol. 4, pp. 733-57, 1982.

Data-Parallel Portable Software Platform: Principles and Implementation

V.B. Muchnick, A.V. Shafarenko and C.D. Sutton

Department of Electronic and Electrical Engineering
University of Surrey GU2 5XH England

A unified approach to the implementation of data-parallel programming languages on a variety of platforms is presented. It is based on a formally defined intermediate language (f-code), which was developed to represent the semantics of data-parallel processing in full as well as data management and control primitives inherent in the most widely used languages: Fortran, Pascal and C. Among the innovative features of f-code are a consistent set of nonscalar operations more generic than in APL yet easy to use and a semi-strong type system accounting for both strong typing as in Pascal and soft typing as in C and Fortran. The implementation principles of f-code and an example implementation for the i860 are discussed.

1   Basic Concepts

Concurrency: F-code is a Portable Software Platform (PSP) for parallel processing. The novelty of our approach to data parallelism is that it supports the whole conceivable variety of parallel operations by providing a rank coercion mechanism, which allows one to apply parallel operators to any combination of objects, no matter if they have matching ranks or not. This is done in a regular way and involves just one notion of operand *orientation*. Also, a reasonable default is provided for the case of shape mismatch. Wherever the ranks are same or coerced: f-code supplies a shape coercion rule.

Another sort of concurrency that f-code aims to accurately represent is functional parallelism, which manifests itself in the notion of expression. Typical assembly languages do not have this notion, so functional concurrency is only implicitly present in the assembler program. It is therefore desirable to preserve this concurrency in the PSP notation if the PSP is to support data parallelism. This is the reason that the syntax of f-code is made similar to that of Lisp: the f-program is a tree encoded in the form of list. Each vertex of the tree is a function (f-instruction) invocation with its subtrees executing in parallel for most of the vertex labels (or, f-instructions).

It should be emphasised that the support of functional concurrency in f-code does *not* mean that f-code is a functional language. A functional PSP would not be able to support imperative languages because of the principal divergencies in the two programming paradigms. Naturally f-code has to support actual variables and assignment, so it does not possess referential transparency.

Type and Sort: F-code types are subdivided into a fixed set of strong "basic" types which form a hierarchy in the sense of compatibility:

$$logical < character < integer < real < complex$$

and structural metatypes, or templates, which are user-defined and "soft" so that any pointer can be dereferenced using any metatype.

Every object is ascribed an attribute of *sort*, which can be *value*, *name*, or *target*. A target (which is indeed a target for assignment) is a strongly typed object each element of which refers to a value element whose type is equal to, or senior than, the type of the target (thus the compatibility of basic types is taken into account). Note that the type hierarchy for targets is reversed, because whereas one can raise a value from, say, integer to real or any higher type, an object of real type can be assigned values of integer or any junior type. The f-functions that provide access to variables can yield not only values but targets as well, which can be processed geometrically and still remain strongly typed even after they are mixed up with other targets to form the left-hand side of an assignment. Thus, f-code promotes a greater functional concurrency by allowing expressions on the left-hand side. Other PSPs for data-parallel processing, such as VSA [Jess90] were less neutral architecturally and therefore had to rely upon masked assignment only.

There are situations where a target is required not only for assignment, but also for dereferencing (which is the case with read/write variables). In that case a name is used which has a rigid (not coercible) type and which subsumes the functionalities of a value and a target.

Variables and Scopes: The main mechanism of memory scheduling in f-code is a stack, since this is the case in many of the top level languages. Also, stack scheduling in a functional type platform (which f-code actually is) is natural: evaluation of a program is effected through recursive function invocation, which uses a stack anyway.

Specifically, f-code supports a lazy function which creates a variable that exists during the lifetime of the function invocation. One of the arguments of this function (executed after the creation of the variable) is the scope of the variable. Access to the stack variable inside the scope is either through its identifier (similar to LISP, f-system maintains a dictionary of the active associations of all identifiers occurring in the f-program) or through a pointer to it.

F-code supports the traditional primitives to control heap memory as well.

Polymorphism and Inferrability: Generally speaking, the majority of f-instructions are polymorphic. For example, f-function DYADIC with operator ADD does integer addition when the operands are integer and real addition when they are real. It also works when the types of the operands differ from each other, in which case it coerces the data with the lower type. A more dramatical example of polymorphism is f-function COMPOSE which glues two objects. This function admits the operands of all sorts and types and works differently for values, names and targets.

Polymorphism drastically reduces the proliferation of f-functions thus facilitating interpretation of f-code. However, if an f-program is to be compiled, polymorphism may present a problem, since the f-compiler has to know for which type data the f-function should execute (in other words, data attributes have to be inferred). The solution suggested by f-code is to allow polymorphism inside an f-module only. Every identifier can therefore be retraced to the outmost environment where it is explicitly associated with some object. The variables that are essentially external parameters of the module do not have such an environment inside the module. To avoid the polymorphism caused by those parameters, there is a special f-function which coerces a variable to some specified attributes.

Control: The semantics of f-code is purely operational: there is neither predefined program structure nor restrictions whatsoever as to allowed combinations of instructions. Even the scoping of data is determined by lazy evaluation of f-functions, put another way, by the enforced ordering of argument evaluation for a function. The only way not to break the operational semantics and at the same time avoid an explicit instruction address space is to get the flow of data through the function calls that form the f-program to carry some control tokens which cause decision making at control vertices of the program graph.

2 Outline of F-code

This section details some specific features of f-code. It is included in the present paper in order to demonstrate the way f-code is defined as well as to show a few interesting solutions we have found to the problem of accurate representation of data-parallelism in architecture-neutral manner. This section does not therefore endevour to give a complete definition of f-code. The interested reader is referred to our internal report [Bol92] which contains such a definition.

Objects : The f-functions receive as operands, and return as results, *primitive* objects, which are homogeneous, scalar or data-concurrent nonscalar, aggregate of scalar elements having the following characteristics:

1. Type $t \in \{logical, character, integer, real, complex\}$. The types form an ascending hierarchy in the same order as they are listed above. For example, a character type is junior to the real type and senior to the logical type.

2. Sort $s \in \{value, target, name\}$. If an object is of sort value, it contains data of type t; if it is a name, every element of it contains a reference to

a value element of type t; if it is a target, every element of it contains either a reference to a value element of type $t' \geq t$ or a special dummy reference. Targets are used for element-wise movement of values in the course of assignment. A name can be used the same way as a target, but also admits data-parallel dereferencing, yielding a value of type t.

3. Shape $\mathbf{d} = \{d_i\}$ It is a vector of the extents of the object's dimensions d_i, each of which is a nonnegative integer number. The length of $\mathbf{d}$ is equal to the object's rank. In particular, if the object is scalar, vector $\mathbf{d}$ has zero length.

4. Contents c, which form an array of shape $\mathbf{d}$.

The f-program can manipulate heterogeneous aggregates of data as well, such as Pascal records or C structures. Characteristics of such *structured* objects are as follows:

1. *Template* (metatype) T, which is a tree whose leaves are types; all the nodes of this tree except the root one are labelled with shape vectors. Thus, at each level of hierarchy a template determines a sequence of fields. The number of the fields is equal to the number of successors of the node, while the types (or templates) and shape vectors of those fields are defined by the corresponding leaves (or subtrees) and their labels.

2. Shape $\mathbf{d}$.

3. Contents c, which form an array of shape $\mathbf{d}$ built up from structures of template T.

Structured objects can only consist of values. However, while accessing their homogeneous fields, primitive objects of any sort may arise. Such an access is effected through *pointers*, which are primitive objects of integer type. Pointers are also used for references to subroutines.

Representation of the F-program: The f-program is represented in a LISP-like list form as a system of nested lists. Two kinds of atoms are used:

1. Literals, which include function labels, keywords (which modify the semantics of f-functions), constants and bit masks, which are used to specify the operand orientation.

2. Identifiers, which are the only semantically variable entity of f-code. Identifiers are associated with primitive objects and templates.

Evaluation of the F-program: The evaluation rules are as follows:

1. The first item of the function list is a literal determining the function to be applied to the other items of the list.

2. Subsequent items are literals and identifiers the function needs to determine the activity it is to provide, or the arguments of the function, which are expressions that the f-system evaluates prior to the function invocation, unless otherwise stated in the function definition.

3. Any f-function that assumes its arguments to be evaluated before its invocation does not require any specific order of that evaluation, only requiring that all its argument objects should be available before it is activated. We call these *a priori* operands. The f-function deals with *a posteriori* operands, which are obtained from the a priori ones by applying an optional *type coercion*. The coercion changes the operand type: a value going up the hierarchy generalising the contents element-wise and a target going down with the contents preserved. A name can not be coerced.

The a posteriori type of each operand is determined by the semantics of the function. Some operations (for example, addition) can work with operands in a certain range of types $t^J \ldots t^S$ (integer...complex for this example); in such a case the common a posteriori type $\hat{t}$ of all operands is expressed in terms of their a priori type $t_1, \ldots, t_n$ as follows:

$$\hat{t} = \begin{cases} \min(t^S, \max(t^J, t_1, \ldots, t_n)) & \text{for values} \\ \min(t_1, \ldots, t_n) & \text{for names and targets} \end{cases}$$

If the a priori type of an operand happens to be different, then the coercion will normally take place. If the coercion is impossible, eg if it attempts to lower the type of a value or change the type of a name, this will result in an error.

Operations: We chose to define the effect of f-operations by providing formulas which evaluate the characteristics of the result from those of the operands. Here are some auxiliary formulas which we use in spatial juxtaposition of the operands and the result.

1. The contents array of a primitive object is indexed with a *multi-index*, which is a vector of nonnegative integers. Let us denote the length of $\mathbf{a}$ as $r(\mathbf{a})$ and introduce a partial ordering of such vectors. We will say that a vector $\mathbf{a}$ precedes a vector $\mathbf{b}$, and write $\mathbf{a} \prec \mathbf{b}$, if $r(\mathbf{a}) = r(\mathbf{b}) = r$ and $a_k < b_k$ for all $0 \leq k < r$. All the other operations with vectors that we will use below should be interpreted element-wise.

2. For a vector $\mathbf{a}$ of some length and and a mask m of the same length we define a *projector* as follows:

$$\mathbf{P} : (\mathbf{a}, m) \to \mathbf{b},$$

where $b_k = a_{x(k,m)}$, and $x(k, m)$ is the number of the k-th unity bit in the mask m. The length of the result vector is equal to the number of unity bits in the mask.

3. Let us introduce an *expander*:

$$E : (\mathbf{a}, m) \rightarrow \mathbf{b},$$

so that

$$b_k = \begin{cases} \infty & \text{if } m_k = 0 \\ a_{X(k,m)} & \text{otherwise} \end{cases},$$

where $X(k, m)$ is the number of mask bits $m_j = 1$ with $j < k$. Expander $E(\mathbf{a}, m)$ is determined only if m has the number of unity bits equal to the length of $\mathbf{a}$. The length of $\mathbf{b}$ is equal to the number of bits in mask m. Thus the following identity takes place: $P(E(\mathbf{a}, m), m) \equiv \mathbf{a}$.

In order to refer to a specific operand of the f-function, we use the operand's denotation as a superscript (for example, d^x is the shape vector of operand x). We also need the following shorthand notation:

$$\mathbf{p}^x(\mathbf{k}) = P(\mathbf{k}, m^x), \quad \bar{\mathbf{p}}^x(\mathbf{k}) = P(\mathbf{k}, \overline{m^x}), \quad \mathbf{e}^x = E(d^x, m^x),$$

where m^x is the mask preceding operand x and $\overline{m^x}$ is the complement of m^x:

$$\overline{m_i^x} = \begin{cases} 0, & m_i^x = 1 \\ 1, & m_i^x = 0 \end{cases}.$$

The meaning of this shorthand can be expressed verbally as follows: $\mathbf{p}^x(\mathbf{k})$ is the projection of the coordinate vector $\mathbf{k}$ on the mask of operand x, $\bar{\mathbf{p}}^x(\mathbf{k})$ is the projection on the complement of this mask, and $\mathbf{e}^x$ is the expansion of the shape vector of the operand x by its own mask.

Let us denote as $s^x(\mathbf{k})$ an array containing all the elements of some layer of the operand x contents. Its shape is $\mathbf{d} = \mathbf{p}^x(d^x)$ and its elements are determined by the following formula:

$$s^x(\mathbf{k})_\mathbf{l} = c^x_{\min(E(\mathbf{k}, \overline{m^x}), E(\mathbf{l}, m^x))}, \quad \mathbf{l} \prec \mathbf{d}.$$

In fact, this formula represents the contents of x as a family of layers, each of which is parallel to the coordinate axes marked by ones in the mask of this operand.

Data-Parallel Operations: F-code supports a vast set of data-parallel operators, which, apart from conventional arithmetic and logical operations, includes basic functions, bitwise operations and shifts. All of them are uniformly generalised to the nonscalar case with the help of f-functions MONADIC and DYADIC.

Function MONADIC has the following form:

```
( monadic <unary> EXPR.a )
```

where `<unary>` is a keyword denoting a specific unary operator, and `EXPR.a` is the f-expression that yields operand a. The result of function MONADIC is computed by data-parallel application to a of the operator $\odot$ determined by `<unary>`:

$$ d = d^a, \quad c_k = \odot a_k, \quad k \prec d. $$

Function DYADIC uses orientated operands:

(dyadic `<binary>` `<mask>` EXPR.1 `<mask>` EXPR.r)

Its result is computed as follows:

$$ d = \min(e^l, e^r), \quad c_k = c^l_{p^l(k)} \odot c^r_{p^r(k)}, \quad k \prec d, $$

where $\odot$ is the operator determined by the keyword `<binary>`.

The mechanism of orientation allows to freely combine operands of different ranks. For example, to compute a matrix as the tensor product of two vectors, one should specify mask `01` for one of the operands and mask `10` for the other one. Note that the formula for the shape vector of the result coerces the operand extents along coincident axes.

Other Computational Operations: Function REDUCE ensures both the complete reduction (to a scalar) of the operand, or a partial reduction (along any subset of the axes specified by the mask):

(reduce `<total>` `<mask>` EXPR.a)

Here `<total>` is a keyword which denotes a specific commutative, associative binary operator. F-code supports only that sort of reductions, since the parallel implementation is assumed. The result is computed as follows:

$$ d = \bar{p}^a(d^a), \quad c_k = \bigodot_{1 \prec p^a(d^a)} s^a(k)_1, \quad k \prec d. $$

where $\bigodot$ is the reduction corresponding to `<total>`.

The function POL evaluates a polynomial of an arbitrary number of nonscalar variables.

(pol EXPR.c {`<mask>` EXPR.v}...)

Operand c determines the coefficients of the polynomial, and operands v_i, $0 \leq i < n$, determine the values of variables on which to compute it. An equality $n = r(d^c)$ must be satisfied. The result is computed as follows:

$$ d = \min_{0 \leq i < n} e^{v_i}, \quad c_k = \sum_{1 \prec d^c} c^c_1 \prod_{0 \leq i < n} \left(c^{v_i}_{p^{v_i}(k)}\right)^{l_i}, \quad k \prec d. $$

Here the mechanism of orientation and shape coercion is the same as in function DYADIC.

Geometry: F-code supports a vast group of geometric operations that "cut out" fragments of the operand (SECT, SLICE, DIAG, GATHER), "glue" objects to one another (REPL, COMP), or rearrange the elements of the operand (TRANSP, PACK, TRANSFORM). All of these have the most general data-parallel semantics.

The most powerful geometric operation is TRANSFORM, which is a non-scalar indexing with the standard spatial juxtaposition of index aggregates:

(`transform EXPR.s {<mask> EXPR.t}... `)

Operands t_i, $0 \leq i < n$, are integer multi-indices. An equality $n = r(\mathbf{d}^s)$ must be satisfied. The result is computed as follows:

$$\mathbf{d} = \min_{0 \leq i < n} \mathbf{e}^{t_i}, \quad c_{\mathbf{k}} = c^s_{\mathbf{l}(\mathbf{k})}, \quad \mathbf{k} \prec \mathbf{d}, \quad l_i(\mathbf{k}) = c^{t_i}_{\mathbf{p}^{t_i}(\mathbf{k})}, \quad 0 \leq i < n.$$

3 Implementation

Although f-code — a functionally and geometrically parallel platform — favours computational models, such as [Jess91] and ETS Data Flow (which is an essentially unrestrained array-based data-flow model, see [Papa91]), it is an appropriate source for scalar hardware platforms, such as a vector processor. One should distinguish, however, between f-code related implementation issues ("front end") and those other issues arising from the code-generation/targeting process.

Selective Evaluation: If one is heedless of machine architecture and rather concentrates on data-concurrent semantics, we would like to be able to formulate the minimum extents of a parallel set of operations. We would like to evaluate *selectively,* in a spatial sense, so that if part of an intermediate object does not contribute to the result, this part should not be evaluated at all.

The inference stage of the compiler endows each *node* n with a type t_n, a rank r_n and a sort, s_n, in a primary tree T. In a bottom-up manner we construct at each node n an array of r_n f-code trees, which provide the extents of this particular operation. In the expression $B + C$, where B and C may be expressions, the extents of the operation are in terms of nodes lower down the tree: for example, if one adds a $5 \times 4 \times 6$ box to a $8 \times 6 \times 3$ box, one ends up with a $5 \times 4 \times 3$ box. The extents, $5, 4, 3$ have been evaluated from the minimum of the extents of its subordinates.

Selective evaluation is then very simple: we require three indices for the three dimensions of the result i, j, k which have ranges $i : 0..4, j : 0..3, k : 0..2$. However, B and C will not be evaluated for any other index than these, regardless of the apparent shape of the results of B, or C. This is lazy evaluation (the code will be executed eagerly) across sub-ranges of the operation.

Orientation: F-code provides an attractive mechanism of rank coercion, such that one may do operations between objects of different rank. Orientation is achieved in f-code by the use of masks. Example, adding a matrix to a box: $111B + 101C$. The 1's in the masks denote active dimensions. The result will also be a box, and will hence have three indices i, j, k. All three are active across B, akin to $B[i, j, k]$, whereas only two are active across C, akin to $C[i, k]$, since the bit corresponding to j is zero.

The rank of the result is the number of bits in the mask: for example one could create a 5 dimensional object (but no more from a matrix and a box) using $11100B + 00011C$; corresponding to

$$B[i, j, k] + C[l, m], i : 0..i_{max}, j : 0..j_{max}, k : 0..k_{max}, l : 0..l_{max}, m : 0..m_{max}$$

Orientations are then also important for evaluating the static extents of a data-parallel operation. Assuming B has extent trees b_0, b_1, b_2, respectively in each of its three dimensions, and C has extent trees c_0, c_1.

In the $111B + 101C$ example, the extent trees constructed for the addition will become

$$min(b_0, c_0), min(b_1, \infty), min(b_2, c_1), \text{ and hence } min(b_0, c_0), b_1, min(b_2, c_1)$$

where ∞ is used when a dimension is not active. If these were constants, they could be evaluated and folded as before.

Distributing Indices: Although it is not described thoroughly here, one should get a palpable impression of the extent trees which stand alongside the original tree, T. At every node of T we have an auxiliary array of trees providing extents. These trees are mainly disjoint from the original, except where an extent depends on some run-time value, where it will reference some of the original tree.

In the above example of $11100B + 00011C$, there are five general indices i, j, k, l, m corresponding to the five dimensions of the '+' operation and in the order of the masks specified. The '+' node will thus have five extent trees. If we choose to associate a particular extent tree with a particular index, and percolate the use of that index down it, the following will happen: i, j, k will be traced into the extent trees for expression B, as its three indices, l, m will be traced into expression C, as its two indices. If then, for example, the expression B happened to be $111D * 011E$, such that D is a box, and E is a matrix, the indices will be traced further, such that i, j, k will be traced into expression D, and indices j, k will be traced into expression E, and so on.

Eventually, tracing along extent trees, the index will reach an extent (sub)tree for a leaf of the original tree T. If this leaf happens to be a memory reference, for example, say E, C are variable matrices and D is a variable box, the full expression represents $(D[i, j, k] * E[j, k]) + C[l, m]$. Secondly, we have the extents, or range through which the indices pass.

Selective Evaluation and Geometric Operations: We should perhaps demonstrate that with the implementation of selective evaluation as it is, diagramatically.

SECT is a rank coercion mechanism in f-code to reduce the rank by one — in Fig 2, select a vector from a matrix, at position 2, along dimension 0. SLICE takes a selection of the matrix, in this case, along dimension 1, in positions 1, 2 and 3. (Defined by the RAMP). There are two representations which would result in the darkest, shaded area. That of

```
1. (Slice 1                2. (Sect 0
      (Sect 0                   (Slice 1
        ...                       ...
        (Const 2)                 (Ramp
      )                             (Const 1)
   (Ramp                           (Const 3)
      (Const 1)                    (Const 1)
      (Const 3)                  )
      (Const 1)                )
   )                         (Const 2)
)                          )
```

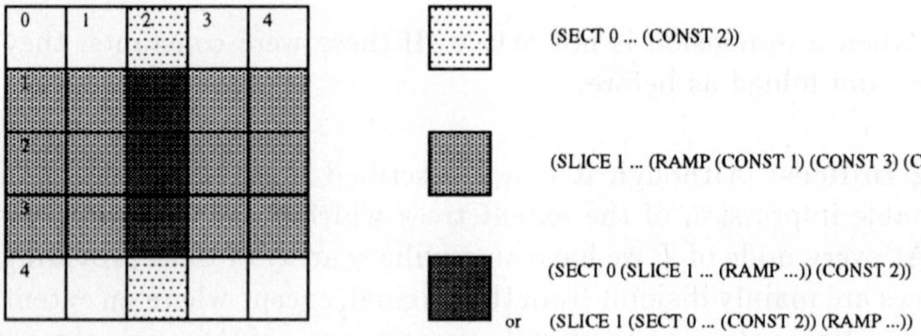

Figure 1: Slice of Sect / Sect of Slice

(SECT 0 ... (CONST 2))

(SLICE 1 ... (RAMP (CONST 1) (CONST 3) (CONST 1)))

(SECT 0 (SLICE 1 ... (RAMP ...)) (CONST 2))
or (SLICE 1 (SECT 0 ... (CONST 2)) (RAMP ...))

The first should logically do the SECT first, the second do a SLICE first. In a naïve implementation, it would seem that the first alternative would be the most efficient, because it results in a smaller shaded area at the intermediate stage, and hence it requires less memory references. If Sect were a hardware operation and slice not, this would indeed be true. If one considers only the indices which are used in performing this operation, the following is true:- If we have an index i for dimension 0, and an index j for dimension 1, i is always fixed at the value 2, by the SECT operation, and j always takes the series $1, 2, 3$ which is fixed by the SLICE operation. This does not depend on the order between SECT and SLICE. In a similar way, it is clear to say that a referentially transparent section of f-code will regardless of the ordering always be evaluated in the most selective way.

We say the most selective way, because it might not necessarily be the most efficient implementation. An f-code program must be rewritten in order to take advantage of, or to avoid parallel hardware features.

Rewrites: These are a few examples of optimization rewrites given for SECT, the idea of which is to propagate the SECT further down the tree towards the leaves. We would like to propagate SECT in instances where SECT is an available parallel hardware feature. There are rewrites for other functions in f-code.

Some rewrites are very straightforward

$$(SECT\ n\ (\alpha\ (...))\ i) \mapsto (\alpha\ (SECT\ n\ (...)\ i))$$

where $\alpha \in \{HOLD, CREATE, MONADIC, PART, COMMA, COERCE\}$

Other rewrites are more complicated. We define the application of $(SECT n...i)$ to an operand expression x with an orientation mask, m^x. Here n is the dimension to which the $SECT$ applies and i an expression which returns an integer value for the fixed index. This results in an operand expression $\hat{x}$ and a transfigured mask $\widehat{m^x}$, where

$$\hat{x} = \begin{cases} (SECT\ U(n,m)\ x\ i), & m_n^x = 1 \\ x, & otherwise \end{cases}$$

where $U(k,m)$ is the number of mask bits $k_j = 1$ with $j < k$.

$$\widehat{m^x_k} = \begin{cases} m_k^x, & k < n \\ m_{k+1}^x, & n \le k \le r(m^x) - 2 \end{cases}$$

$r(m)$ is the length of mask m; the length of the result mask is then $r(m^x) - 2$. We can then quite easily formulate more complicated rewrites for SECT:

$$(SECT\ n\ (DIADIC \odot m^l\ l\ m^r\ r)\ i) \mapsto (DIADIC \odot \widehat{m^l}\ \hat{l}\ \widehat{m^r}\ \hat{r})$$

$$(SECT\ n\ (REDUCE \odot m^a\ a)\ i) \mapsto (REDUCE \odot \widehat{m^a}\ \hat{a})\ ,\ m_n^a = 0$$

$$(SECT\ n\ (TRANSFORM\ s\ \{m^t\ t\}...)\ i) \mapsto (TRANSFORM\ s\ \{\widehat{m^t}\ \hat{t}\}...)$$

where $\{m^x\ x\}...$ means optional and repeated

$$(SECT\ n\ (SLICE\ k\ a\ e)\ i) \mapsto \begin{cases} (SLICE\ \hat{k}\ (SECT\ n\ a\ i)\ e), & k \ne n \\ (SECT\ n\ a\ (SECT\ 0\ e\ i)), & k = n \end{cases}$$

where

$$\hat{k} = \begin{cases} k, & k < n \\ k - 1, & k > n \end{cases}$$

The attempt of these rewrites is to propagate SECT as far down the tree as possible. One provides a hierarchy of rewrites, such that one might want SECT to be the function nearest the leaves, because it is the most selective, or it is a hardware operation. Of course, rewrites must be chosen such that they cannot occur indefinitely — but the most important thing to note is that they mainly occur within a referentially transparent area.

Code Generation: The following is a particular implementation for an i860; other machines may be treated differently. The general implementation is to produce a data-flow graph. The targeter deals with a graph, (using standard techniques) without the necessity to know anything about f-code at all.

In order to produce code, one first constructs a general acyclic, directed graph, for data dependencies, and control dependencies, providing a representation of the f-code program. It is again an intermediate representation of an abstract machine, however arcs on the graph are either pointers to blocks of memory (the start of a block of memory on a shared machine), or scalar entities. We do not lose, however, any representation of parallelism but the graph is low level and unsuitable for data-parallel optimization, and would be equally unsuitable for a high-level intermediate language.

The current abstract machine graph then includes the notion of nested *loops*, and *strides*. The intention is to remove complicated and inefficient multi dimensional indexing from memory referencing. For an implementation directed towards the i860, the intent is then to pipeline memory operations. Since we have a graph for an abstract machine, we then rewrite the graph into a graph representing machine instructions. This makes revamping the compiler for similar processors a more trivial procedure. The graph is arranged primarily for three address mode instructions. Each node in the graph is a tuple containing a destination and two sources; or three sources. The rewrites are from abstract instructions mulu, fdiv, fsqr (square root), etc to real i860 machine instructions, which are subsequently pipelined and consequently output.

One of the authors (AVS) is grateful to the Nuffield Foundation for financial support.

References

[Bol92]   Bolychevsky, A.B., Muchnick, V.B., Shafarenko, A.V. *Functional representation of a data-concurrent program*. Internal report, Department of Electronic and Electrical Engineering, University of Surrey.

[DRA91]   *TDF specification*, Defence Research Agency, RSRE Malvern, UK.

[Jess90]   Jesshope, C.R. The VSA: an abstract definition and interface for data-parallel program generation. *Computer and Artificial Intelligence*, 9, 441–459.

[Jess91]   Jesshope, C.R. Virtual shared memory for the ARAM model of compilation using the MP1 packet routing chip. *Parallel digital processors*, IEEE Publication number 334, 55–59.

[Papa91]   Papadopoulos, G.M. *Implementation of a general-purpose data-flow multiprocessor*, Pitman (London).

A Compositional Approach for Fault-Tolerance Using Specification Transformation

Doron Peled
AT&T Bell Laboratories
600 Mountain Avenue
Murray Hill, NJ 07974, USA

Mathai Joseph*
Department of Computer Science
University of Warwick
Coventry CV4 7AL, U.K.

Abstract

The incorporation of a recovery algorithm into a program can be viewed as a program transformation, converting the basic program into a fault-tolerant version. We present a framework in which such program transformations are accompanied by a corresponding *formula transformation* which obtains properties of the fault-tolerant versions of the programs from properties of the basic programs. Compositionality is achieved when every property of the fault-tolerant version can be obtained from a transformed property of the basic program.

A verification method for proving the correctness of formula transformations is presented. This makes it possible to prove just once that a formula transformation corresponds to a program transformation, removing the need to prove separately the correctness of each transformed program.

1   Introduction

A fault-tolerant program can be viewed as the result of superposing a recovery algorithm on a basic, non-fault-tolerant program. Thus, adding a recovery algorithm can be seen as a program transformation, producing a program that can recover from faults in its execution environment. The combined execution of the basic program and the recovery algorithm ensures that the fault-tolerant program achieves its goal despite the occurrence of specified faults. Many different recovery algorithms have been devised [6, 1] and these are often *generic* in the sense that they can be superposed over (or combined with) different basic programs. But it is important also to define the exact relation between the properties of a basic program and the properties of the fault-tolerant program obtained after the superposition of a recovery algorithm.

In this paper we describe a framework for reasoning about distributed fault-tolerant programs based on a transformational approach to representing faults and recovery algorithms. We define a criterion for correctness based on the use of a *formula transformation*, which transforms any property of the basic program into a property of its fault-tolerant version (i.e., after superposing the recovery algorithm).

This framework has an important practical advantage, as a (relatively complete) verification method is available to *verify* that a formula transformation corresponds to a

*Supported in part by SERC research grants GR/F 57960 and GR/H 39499.

program transformation. The formula transformation needs to be verified *only once* and can then be used to obtain properties of the transformed program from the properties of the basic program.

The method is compositional: the formula transformation can be embedded in a compositional proof rule so that proving the properties of a fault-tolerant version of a basic program can be performed by proving properties of the basic program. This makes it possible to deduce the properties of the fault-tolerant version of a program from the specification of the basic program and the properties of the recovery algorithm. Formula transformations also provide a means of *generically* specifying fault-tolerance in programs, rather than having to specify the behavior of each such transformed program separately. It may be observed that formula transformations corresponding to program transformations can be used for other applications of program superposition, such as for deadlock detection.

2 Representing Programs and their Properties

A program P is a triple $\langle \bar{y}, T, \Theta \rangle$, where $\bar{y}$ is a finite, ordered set of variables $y_1, y_2, \ldots y_m$, T is a finite set of atomic operations, and Θ is a (first order) initial condition. Each variable $y_i \in \bar{y}$ is defined over some domain. The Cartesian product S of these domains is called the *state space* of the program. A *state* s of a program is an assignment function from the set of variables to their appropriate domains. Let $s \models \varphi$ denote that the (first order) formula φ is satisfied by the state $s \in S$. In the sequel, first order formulas will have free variables from $\bar{y}$ (e.g., φ is actually $\varphi(\bar{y})$), unless denoted otherwise.

An operation $\tau \in T$ is defined using *transition formulas* that specify the effect of an operation in terms of the old values $\bar{y}$ and the new values $\bar{y}'$ of the set of program variables. For an operation α we write $[\mu_\alpha(\bar{y}, \bar{y}')]_{\bar{z}_\alpha}$, where $\mu_\alpha(\bar{y}, \bar{y}')$ is interpreted over pairs of states $\langle s, s' \rangle \models \mu_\alpha(\bar{y}, \bar{y}')$ such that the variables $\bar{y}$ are assigned values according to the state s, and $\bar{y}'$ according to the state s'. The variables $\bar{z}_\alpha$ are the only variables that may be changed by α, (i.e., if $x \notin \bar{z}_\alpha$, then $s'(x) = s(x)$). Then for any pair of states s, s' such that s' is obtained from s by executing α it holds that $\langle s, s' \rangle \models \mu_\alpha(\bar{y}, \bar{y}') \wedge \bigwedge_{y_i \in \bar{y} \setminus z_\alpha} y_i' = y_i$.

The initial states of the program are characterized by Θ. The enabling condition of an operation is a first order formula over free variables from $\bar{y}$ that holds for the states in which that operation can be executed, i.e., $en_\alpha = \exists \bar{y}' \, \mu_\alpha(\bar{y}, \bar{y}')$ where $\exists \bar{y}'$ is shorthand for $\exists y_1' \, \exists y_2' \, \ldots$.

Representing a concurrent program by a set of operations is convenient both for verification and for defining different kinds of program transformations. Examples of the translation of concurrent programs written in languages with shared variables and inter-process communication into set of operations can be found in [8].

Definition 2.1 *An execution sequence (or an* interleaving sequence*) of a program is an infinite sequence of states* $\sigma = s_0 \, s_1 \, s_2 \, \ldots$, *satisfying the following conditions: (1)* $s_0 \models \Theta$, *where* Θ *is the initial condition, (2) for each* $i \geq 0$, *either* $\sigma_i = \sigma_{i+1}$[1],

---

[1] 'Stuttering' is allowed in order to achieve compositionality.

or there exists some $\tau \in T$ *such that* $\langle s_i, s_{i+1} \rangle \models \mu_\tau(\bar{y}, \bar{y}')$, *and for each* $x \notin \bar{z}_\tau$, $s_i(x) = s_{i+1}(x)$, *(3)* $s_n \models \bigwedge_{\tau \in T} \neg en_\tau$ *iff for each* $m > n$, $s_m = s_n$.

The semantics of a program P is denoted by the function $\mathcal{M}[\![P]\!]$ and is the set of interleaving sequences of P.

'Fairness' conditions may further restrict the set of interleaving sequences that are considered to be executions of the program. Assume initially that there are no fairness restrictions. We shall use linear temporal logic (LTL) [8] as the specification language over the execution sequences of the program.

The LTL operators $\square$, U and $\mathcal{U}$ have their usual meanings. We allow quantification (i.e., $\exists z \, \varphi$, $\forall z \, \varphi$) over *rigid variables*, whose value is fixed over all states, and over *flexible variables*, whose value can change from state to state.

A *property* is either a temporal formula φ, or as the set of sequences $[\![\varphi]\!]$ that satisfy φ. Thus, a program φ has a property φ iff $\mathcal{M}[\![P]\!] \subseteq [\![\varphi]\!]$. This is also denoted by $P \models \varphi$.

Definition 2.2 *(cf [8]) An* exact specification Φ_P *of a program* P *is a formula that is satisfied exactly by the set of interleaving sequences of* P.

It is easy to see that for every formula φ, $P \models \varphi$ iff $\Phi_P \rightarrow \varphi$, i.e., $\mathcal{M}[\![P]\!] = [\![\Phi_P]\!]$.

3 Formalizing Recovery Algorithms with Formula Transformations

A *basic program* is designed to perform a computational task in a fault-free system and *generic* recovery program can be combined with various basic programs to give programs which execute 'correctly' when certain faults occur. Obviously, when a fault does occur, the combined program will not behave exactly as the original basic program behaves when no faults occur.

The executions of the combined program (in a fault-prone system) are related to the executions of the basic program (in a fault-free system) in a particular way that is guaranteed by the recovery algorithm. This relation will be formalized as a formula transformation, which takes a specification of the basic program and produces a specification of the combined program.

3.1 Program Transformations and Formula Transformations

The incorporation of a recovery algorithm into a basic program is a superposition which takes the union of the operations of the two programs and strengthens the enabledness conditions of some selected operations of the basic program [3]. Execution of operations is controlled by the superposed program. The superposition transformation enlarges the original state space S to a related space $\hat{S}$ which is the Cartesian product of more domains than are included in S.

Superposition is an example of a program transformation. A program transformation $\mathcal{T}$ is a function $\mathcal{T} : \mathsf{P} \mapsto \mathsf{P}$, where P is a domain of programs (e.g., programs written in a certain language, or programs given as sets of operations that satisfy certain syntactical conditions).

A formula transformation $\mathcal{F}$ is a function $\mathcal{F} : \mathcal{L} \mapsto \mathcal{L}$, where $\mathcal{L}$ is some specification language such as LTL.

Definition 3.1 *A formula transformation $\mathcal{F}$ corresponds to a program transformation $\mathcal{T}$ if it satisfies the condition that for each program P, if $P \models \varphi$, then $\mathcal{T}(P) \models \mathcal{F}(\varphi)$.*

Formula transformations can be used to verify properties of the transformed program $\mathcal{T}(P)$, from verified properties of the program P. Proving $\mathcal{T}(P) \vdash \psi$ is then reduced to proving a property of P, applying the formula transformation and doing some pure LTL verification. There is no need to use the actual code of $\mathcal{T}(P)$ in the verification. The proof uses the following proof rule:

$$
\begin{array}{ll}
1 & P \models \varphi \\
2 & \dfrac{\mathcal{F}(\varphi) \rightarrow \psi}{\mathcal{T}(P) \models \psi}
\end{array}
$$

Ideally, the transformation should make it possible to logically derive *every* property of the transformed program from the basic program (cf. Zwiers' *compositional completeness* [11]). In the following (relative) completeness definition, every property of the transformed program can be proved from the basic program and the transformation.

Definition 3.2 *A formula transformation $\mathcal{F}$ is* compositional complete *with respect to a program transformation $\mathcal{T}$ if for every program P, and every formula ψ such that $\mathcal{T}(P) \models \psi$, there exists a formula φ such that* (1) $P \models \varphi$ *and* (2) $\mathcal{F}(\varphi) \rightarrow \psi$.

A program transformation $\mathcal{T}$ is *monotonic* if for each pair of programs P_1, $P_2 \in \mathsf{P}$, if $\mathcal{M}[\![P_1]\!] \subseteq \mathcal{M}[\![P_2]\!]$ then $\mathcal{M}[\![\mathcal{T}(P_1)]\!] \subseteq \mathcal{M}[\![\mathcal{T}(P_2)]\!]$. Compositional completeness can be achieved iff the program transformation is monotone as shown in the full version of the paper [9].

3.2 Formula Transformation for Fault Tolerance

To represent failure and recovery, superposition can be done in two stages [7].

1. The recovery algorithm is superposed on the basic program.

2. A set of operations representing a 'fault program' is superposed on the program obtained in the first step.

There is no difficulty in seeing a recovery algorithm as a procedure which is superposed on a program, but it may be surprising that faults are also represented as pieces of code. However, faults can be considered as events that 'interfere' with the execution of a program [4] and represented by a set of specially constructed operations, avoiding the need to deal with particular kinds of faults at the semantic level (see [7] for a detailed discussion).

Let the basic (or fault-prone) program be denoted by P. Let the superposition of a recovery algorithm on a basic program P give $R = \mathcal{T}_1(P)$, and the superposition of the failure mechanism on R give $\mathcal{T}_2(R)$. Then the entire transformation is $\mathcal{T}(P) =$

$\mathcal{T}_2(\mathcal{T}_1(P))$. In the rest of this paper, we apply both transformations, namely the recovery algorithm and the failure mechanism, in this order, on basic programs.

The first step in formalizing a recovery algorithm is to specify those of its properties that are independent of the basic program. Such properties may include, for example, the guarantee that recovery will be eventually completed (perhaps conditional on the type and frequency of the faults), non–blocking of the basic program by the addition of the recovery actions, and the ability to overcome multiple faults. We call such properties the *fixed part* of the specification and include with them recovery actions (such as maintaining consistent checkpoints by taking periodical snapshots) that are executed when no failure occurs.

The second part of the formalization is a transformation $\mathcal{F}$ which converts properties of the basic program into properties of the fault-tolerant version. Given a basic program P which satisfies a certain property, applying the transformation $\mathcal{T}$ to P results in a *program* which satisfies a new specification. The transformation $\mathcal{F}$ is applied on *specifications*, so that for each φ satisfied by P, $\mathcal{F}(\varphi)$ is a specification of $\mathcal{T}(P)$ (i.e., $\mathcal{F}$ corresponds to $\mathcal{T}$). The fixed part of the specification may be embedded as a constant part of every formula obtained from the formula transformation.

Different behaviors can be guaranteed for different fault situations. For example, superposition of a particular recovery algorithm on a basic program might preserve some properties when assumptions are made to limit the repetitive occurrence of faults. If faults do occur during recovery, some weaker properties of the basic algorithm may be preserved. And some liveness properties may be maintained provided only a finite number of faults occurs.

In many cases, the internal details of the recovery algorithm are of less interest than the effect of the recovery on the basic program, so it is useful to suppress these details. In temporal logic, this can be defined using a state function $\mathcal{O}$ which filters out irrelevant parts of the state and a specification can then be given with respect to the filtered state space, rather than the original state space. For more complex kinds of program transformations, the filtering may need to be more complicated, e.g., filtering out the sending and receiving of control messages that are needed for the recovery but not for the basic program.

The state function $\mathcal{O}$ can be generalized in the obvious way to a function on sequences of states and on sets of sequences. If $\mathcal{M}[\![P]\!]$ is the semantic representation of program P as a set of interleaving sequences, then $\mathcal{O}(\mathcal{M}[\![P]\!])$ represents the result of applying the mapping $\mathcal{O}$ to conceal unwanted detail. Notice that it is possible that a program transformation is not monotone but becomes monotone under a given concealment.

If we ignore the internal details of the recovery part of the combined program, compositional completeness can be weakened and defined with respect to the concealment of the superposed program, i.e., by replacing $\mathcal{T}(P)$ with $\mathcal{O}(\mathcal{T}(P))$ in Definition 3.2.

4   An Example of Formula Transformations

A recovery algorithm must restore a program to a *consistent* state after a fault has occurred so that its execution can be resumed. A common way to achieve this is to preserve a *checkpoint* or a *snapshot*, which is a global state of the basic program P to which execution can be restored upon recovery. However, different recovery algorithms will have different ways of establishing the relation between this global state and the state in which the failure occurred. Some possible schemes are to permit recovery to either

1. A state in the past of the current interleaving sequence, i.e., *backward recovery*,

2. A state in a possible future of the last global state of the system before the most recent failure occurred, i.e., *forward recovery*.

Backward recovery allows a program suffering a failure to resume execution from a previously saved checkpoint. After recovery, a non-deterministic program will not necessarily repeat its previous execution in the interval between the time the checkpoint was established and the time the failure occurred. We shall illustrate the use of formula transformations for backward recovery using the example of a program subject to *fail-stop* faults during its execution.

Let the operations of the basic program be augmented by superposing an interrupt mechanism. The enabling condition en_τ of a basic program operation τ is strengthened by the addition of the boolean variable *main* to $en_\tau \wedge main$, which requires *main* to be T when there is no interrupt. On the occurrence of an interrupt, *main* is set to F to disable the basic program operations and enable the interrupt operations. When interrupt processing is over, *main* is reset to T.

Assume that during the normal execution of the program a timer interrupt periodically initiates the saving of consistent states of the program in a *non-volatile, non-destructive* stable memory. On the occurrence of a fail-stop fault [10], the contents of the main memory are assumed to be destroyed, and an interrupt triggers the execution of a failure interrupt handler.

Let the stable memory be partitioned into two segments, each having a dedicated area for every program variable. When an interrupt from the timer indicates that a new snapshot is to be taken, each basic program variable x is saved in either Area 1 or Area 2, according to the value of a special variable var_set. The value of this variable is altered only after the entire contents of memory have been saved, so that if a fault occurs while the memory is being saved it does not affect the last complete saved copy.

Timer Interrupt Handler		Failure Interrupt Handler	
on timer_interrupt do		on failure_interrupt do	
disable timer_interrupt;	% s=T	disable timer_interrupt;	% f=T $\wedge$ r=T
if var_set=2 then	% s=T	if var_set=1 then	% r=T
for each variable x do	% s=T	for each variable x do	% r=T
write x to area 1;	% s=T	read x from area 1;	% r=T
var_set:=1;	% c=T	else	% r=T
else	% s=T	for each variable x do	% r=T
for each variable x do	% s=T	read x from area 2;	% r=T
write x to area 2;	% s=T	enable timer_interrupt;	% r=T
var_set:=2;	% c=T	end handler;	
enable timer_interrupt;	% c=T		
end handler;			

The interrupt handler for a failure inhibits timer interrupts (so there is no saving of memory when a failure occurs) and copies back the contents of the last correctly saved segment of stable memory to the main memory. Notice that a failure can occur during the execution of the timer interrupt handler, or while recovering from a previous failure.

We define the following special state predicates. The specification transformation of the fault tolerant version of the program will conceal the internal variables of the interrupt handlers and the interrupt timer, revealing only the values of these predicates and the basic program variables.

f *(fault)* A fault occurs in this state (a single fault may hold through multiple states).

r *(recovery)* Recovery has begun following the occurrence of a fault, but is not completed.

s *(snapshot)* States in which a snapshot is taken.

c *(checkpoint)* A new checkpoint is established after a successful snapshot and execution of the basic computation is about to resume.

w *(wasted)* A fault will occur before the next checkpoint is reached and the present state of the computation will be wasted. Suffixes of an execution sequence from a w-state satisfy the temporal property $\neg r \wedge ((\neg c)\, \mathcal{U} \, r)$ and thus w can be seen as a shorthand for this formula.

Let a state in which the boolean state function x holds be called an x-*state* and a finite sequence of x-states be called an x-*interval*.

The transitions between states with different values of the state functions are shown in Figure 1. In each state, only state predicates with value T are listed; e.g., the state 'f, r' represents $\neg w \wedge f \wedge \neg c \wedge r \wedge \neg s$. The symbol '$\epsilon$' represents a state in which all the above predicates are F. Each node has a self loop (hence it is not possible to distinguish stuttering). In addition, no infinite sequence of states in any execution corresponds to an infinite path of dashed arrows (e.g., it is not possible that from some point in the computation '$x_7 : s$, w' will hold forever).

To present the fixed part of the specification of the recovery algorithm, i.e., the conditions of Figure 1, let x, x_i, y_i ... represent a boolean combination of all the above state predicates (e.g., $x_3 = \neg w \wedge \neg f \wedge c \wedge \neg r \wedge \neg s$).

A typical execution of the original program and of the fault-tolerant transformed program are also depicted in Figure 1. For each sequence in the basic program, there is a sequence in the transformed program that simulates its ϵ-intervals (corresponding intervals are shown with the same particular shading). Conversely, for every sequence of the transformed program there exists an execution sequence of the basic program in which everything but the ϵ-intervals are removed. Consider the following formulas:

- A state in which x holds can be changed only into a state in which one of $y_1, y_2, \ldots y_n$, hold: $\Box(x \rightarrow (x \, \mathsf{U} \, \bigvee_{i=1}^{n} y_i))$.

- From no point in the computation will all states satisfy one of $y_1, y_2, \ldots y_n$: $\Box\Diamond\neg \bigvee_{i=1}^{n} y_i$.

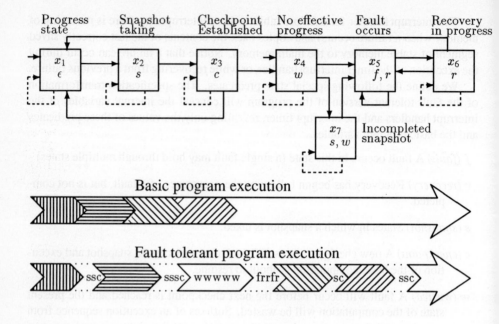

Figure 1: A non-instantaneous recovery

Then, the conditions imposed on the state predicates in Figure 1 can be written as:

$$FIXED = \quad \Box\Diamond\neg x_1 \wedge \Box\Diamond\neg x_2 \wedge \Box\Diamond\neg x_3 \wedge \Box\Diamond\neg x_4 \wedge \Box\Diamond\neg x_6 \wedge \Box\Diamond\neg x_7 \wedge$$

$$\Box(x_1 \rightarrow (x_1 \, \mathsf{U} \, x_2)) \qquad \wedge \quad \Box(x_2 \rightarrow (x_2 \, \mathsf{U} \, x_3)) \wedge$$

$$\Box(x_3 \rightarrow (x_3 \, \mathsf{U}(x_1 \vee x_4))) \quad \wedge \quad \Box(x_4 \rightarrow (x_4 \, \mathsf{U}(x_5 \vee x_7))) \wedge$$

$$\Box(x_5 \rightarrow (x_5 \, \mathsf{U} \, x_6)) \qquad \wedge \quad \Box(x_6 \rightarrow (x_6 \, \mathsf{U}(x_1 \vee x_5))) \wedge$$

$$\Box(x_7 \rightarrow (x_7 \, \mathsf{U} \, x_5))$$

In the second part of the transformation, defined below recursively as $l(\varphi, \neg r \wedge \neg w)$, the part of the execution that remains after taking away the intervals in which r or w hold behaves like the basic program with the addition of checkpointing actions.

The transformation is therefore $\mathcal{F}(\varphi) = FIXED \wedge l(\varphi, \neg r \wedge \neg w)$, where $l(\varphi, \eta)$ is defined inductively as

- $l(\varphi, \eta) = (\neg\eta \, \mathsf{U}(\eta \wedge \varphi))$, where φ is a classical (non-temporal) formula,

- $l(\Box\varphi, \eta) = \Box \, l(\varphi, \eta)$, $l(\varphi \, \mathsf{U} \, \psi, \eta) = l(\varphi, \eta) \, \mathsf{U} \, l(\psi, \eta)$,

- $l(\forall z \, \varphi, \eta) = \forall z \, l(\varphi, \eta)$, $l(\exists z \, \varphi, \eta) = \exists z \, l(\varphi, \eta)$,

- $l(\varphi \vee \psi, \eta) = l(\varphi, \eta) \vee l(\psi, \eta)$, $l(\varphi \wedge \psi, \eta) = l(\varphi, \eta) \wedge l(\psi, \eta)$, and

- negations are pushed inwards to stand adjacent to classical subformulas.

This transformation first pushes the negation symbol inside the formula as much as possible. This can be done using known LTL equivalences (e.g., $\neg \Diamond \varphi = \Box \neg \varphi$) and results in a formula in which negation symbols do not precede any temporal subformula. Then each classical (non-temporal) formula φ is replaced by $(\neg \eta \, U (\eta \wedge \varphi))$, which means that a state satisfying φ can be delayed by $(\neg \eta) = r \vee w$-states.

It is possible to be more accurate (at the expense of some elegance). Recall that more information is known about the w-intervals than is revealed in the transformation: any w-interval, together with all the previous $\neg r \wedge \neg w$-intervals, forms a prefix of a legal interleaving sequence of the basic program. Thus, each w-interval should be separately distinguished while the preceding w-intervals are ignored. The resulting temporal formula is omitted (see [9]).

In some cases, the environment may impose restrictions over the kind of recovery that is possible. Backward recovery assumes that the program is a *closed system* and that the recovery algorithm has the ability to control all parts of the system. But for program recovery in an *open* system, special care must be taken since the environment now includes other processes that might not be affected by the faults or the recovery algorithm. In this case, inputs from the environment must be stored in non-volatile memory to be used upon recovery and outputs to the environment that have been sent once must be blocked after recovery until real progress is being made.

Forward recovery, in which the system recovers from a fault by restarting the execution from a possible future global state can be treated in a way similar to backward recovery.

Recovery schemes are often based on establishing recovery points that do not necessarily belong to the same interleaving sequence, but merely to some *equivalent sequence* or, equivalently, a global state which is a 'slice' of a partial order execution [2]. For this reason, it is appropriate to extend the semantics by defining equivalence classes of interleaving sequences. This construction, related to partial order executions, leads to an elegant treatment of program and formula transformations when distributed programs are involved and is described in the full version of the paper.

5 Proving the Correctness of Formula Transformations

Verifying that a given program transformation corresponds to some formula transformation means that a whole class of properties is being verified at the same time, and with respect to a class of programs. Thus, a higher order logic verification method is needed. The verification of program transformations that preserve program semantics was studied by Huet and Lang [5] who used a second order language to verify program transformations that are used for code optimization of sequential programs. Our notion of correctness is more general as the transformations under discussion are not restricted to those that preserve the semantics of the transformed programs.

Since a recovery algorithm can be applied to an entire class of programs, we use a suitable representation of an *uninterpreted* basic program B written using uninterpreted relation and function symbols. A concrete program is obtained from the uninterpreted representation by instantiating the uninterpreted symbols.

For simplicity, assume that an uninterpreted program uses a single variable x to represent its entire state by an encoding of its variables. Each atomic program operation α can then be written using the transition formula $\mu_\alpha(x, x')$ (with $\bar{z}_\alpha = \{x\}$) and, because of the uniformity of the operations, the following single operation represents the entire program[2]

$$\mu(x, x') = ((x = x') \wedge \bigwedge_{\alpha \in T} \neg en_\alpha(x)) \vee \bigvee_{\alpha \in T} \mu_\alpha(x, x').$$

I.e., an uninterpreted program can be represented by a single operation $[\mu(x, x')]_{\{x\}}$. Let $\Theta(x)$ be a predicate that is true over the x's that are initial values of basic program. Then an exact specification of the program (with rigid variable y) is

$$\Phi_B = \Theta(x) \wedge \Box \exists y (x = y \mathcal{U} \mu(y, x)) \tag{1}$$

This formula is only partially interpreted, as μ and Θ are not given. When a concrete program P is given, the uninterpreted relation and function symbols of B are instantiated to the given relation and functions of P. At the same time, the occurrences of symbols in Φ_B can be instantiated similarly to form an exact specification Φ_P of P. Let B be an uninterpreted program. Apply T on B such that $T(B)$ is an uninterpreted fault-tolerant program. Let Ψ_B be an exact specification of $T(B)$.

Definition 5.1 *A formula transformation $\mathcal{E}$ is exact w.r.t. a program transformation T if for each property φ, $\mathcal{E}(\varphi)$ is a formula that is satisfied exactly by the execution sequences $\bigcup \{ \mathcal{M}[\![T(P)]\!] \mid \mathcal{M}[\![P]\!] \subseteq [\![\varphi]\!] \}$.*

Lemma 5.2 *If $\mathcal{E}$ is an exact formula transformation w.r.t. a program transformation T, and $\mathcal{F}$ is another formula transformation, then $\mathcal{F}$ corresponds to T iff for each LTL formula φ, $\mathcal{E}(\varphi) \rightarrow \mathcal{F}(\varphi)$.*

In order to verify that $\mathcal{F}$ corresponds to T,

1. formulate $\mathcal{E}$, an exact formula transformation w.r.t. T, and
2. prove that for each formula φ, $\mathcal{E}(\varphi) \rightarrow \mathcal{F}(\varphi)$.

The completeness of this method (which is a different completeness concept from the one defined in 3.2) is w.r.t. the expressiveness of the language used to formulate $\mathcal{E}(\varphi)$ in (1), and the ability to prove the implication in (2). A higher order logic for this purpose should at least allow expression of the properties of sets of infinite sequences that are expressible using LTL formulas.

Under the above (example of) abstract representation, there are only two relation symbols μ and Θ. Then, an exact formula transformation w.r.t. T can be formulated by

$$\mathcal{E}(\varphi) = \exists \mu \, \exists \Theta (([\![\Phi_B]\!] \subseteq [\![\varphi]\!]) \wedge \Psi_B) \tag{2}$$

where, as before, Φ_B and Ψ_B are the exact specifications of the uninterpreted programs B and of $T(B)$, respectively (the generality of the uninterpreted relations and functions

---

[2]This single operation allows further simplification of the exact specification of the program by representing program termination as infinite stuttering.

can be limited by adding some appropriate conjunct). The assertion $[\![\Phi_B]\!] \subseteq [\![\varphi]\!]$ is a high order formula that asserts that *any* sequence satisfying Φ_B also satisfies φ, i.e., that φ is a consequence of Φ_B. The formula (2) should be read as follows: an interleaving sequence σ satisfies $\mathcal{E}(\varphi)$ iff there exists a program P (i.e., an instantiation of the relation symbols μ and Θ) that satisfies φ, such that σ is an execution of $\mathcal{T}(P)$. That is, the formula $\mathcal{E}(\varphi)$ is satisfied exactly by execution sequences of programs obtained by the transformation $\mathcal{T}$ from programs satisfying φ.

Consider a simplified version of the algorithm in Section 4 which occasionally stops the basic computation, records the global state, and then allows the basic computation to continue. On the occurrence of a failure, the program is rolled back to the last saved state. It is assumed that taking snapshots and recovering are instantaneous.

Let the boolean state functions r, s and w (of states of the transformed program):

r *(affected)* A fault has occurred and recovery from it has not yet completed. Thus, part or all of the global state may be corrupted.

s *(snapshot)* A snapshot is taken of the state space.

w *(wasted)* There is effectively no progress of the basic computation, because the next fault will occur before the next checkpoint is reached. w is a shorthand for the formula $\neg r \land ((\neg s)\,\mathcal{U}\,r)$.

In the non-fixed part of the transformation, defined recursively as $l(\varphi, \neg w \land \neg r)$ (where $l(\varphi, \eta)$ is defined in Section 4), after taking away the intervals in which w holds, the part of the execution that remains behaves like the basic program (with the addition of checkpointing operations). With this simplified transformation, no claim is made about the basic program's behavior during the $w \lor r$-intervals.

Let B be an uninterpreted representation of the basic program using a single variable (as in the previous subsection), a single operation $\tau_{op} : [\mu(x, x')]_x$, and let the initial value of x satisfy $\Theta(x)$.

Assume a suitable definition of $\mathcal{T}(B)$. Let $\ll \eta \gg$ be a new temporal modal (actually, a family of modals) for each temporal formula η, such that $\ll \eta \gg \varphi$ is true iff the sequence obtained by keeping only the states that satisfy η also satisfies φ (or if it is finite, is a prefix of a sequence that satisfies φ). Then the following formula κ (with y a rigid variable) holds for $\mathcal{T}(B)$:

$$\kappa = w\,\mathcal{U}(\neg w \land \Theta(x)) \land \Box \exists y\,((w\,\mathcal{U}(\neg w \land x = y))\,\mathcal{U}(w\,\mathcal{U}(\neg w \land \mu(y, x))))$$

Hence, $\Psi_B \to \kappa$ holds. Using the axioms of $\ll \eta \gg$ below and other linear temporal logic axioms, it is possible to deduce that $\Psi_B \to \ll \neg w \gg (\Theta(x) \land \Box \exists y\,(x = y\,\mathcal{U}\,\mu(y, x)))$

Now consider the following higher order deduction for the correctness of the formula transformation $\mathcal{F}(\varphi) = \ll \neg w \gg \varphi$:

1. $\Psi_B \to \ll \neg w \gg \Phi_B$
2. $\mathcal{E}(\varphi) = \exists \mu \exists \Theta(([\![\Phi_B]\!] \subseteq [\![\varphi]\!]) \land \Psi_B)$ formulated in (2)
3. $\mathcal{E}(\varphi) \to \exists \mu \exists \Theta(([\![\Phi_B]\!] \subseteq [\![\varphi]\!]) \land \ll \neg w \gg \Phi_B)$ from 1 and 2.
4. $\mathcal{E}(\varphi) \to \exists \mu \exists \Theta(([\![\Phi_B]\!] \subseteq [\![\varphi]\!]) \land \ll \neg w \gg \varphi)$ from 3.
5. $\mathcal{E}(\varphi) \to ((\exists \mu \exists \Theta\,[\![\Phi_B]\!] \subseteq [\![\varphi]\!]) \land \ll \neg w \gg \varphi)$ from 4.
6. $\mathcal{E}(\varphi) \to \ll \neg w \gg \varphi$ from 5.

The next step is to get rid of the new modal $\ll \eta \gg$ so that $\mathcal{F}(\varphi)$ can be written in an equivalent form using only the traditional modal operators. The following axioms of $\ll \eta \gg$ enable this translation:

- $(\ll \eta \gg \varphi) \leftrightarrow (\neg \eta \, \mathsf{U}(\eta \wedge \varphi))$, when φ is a classical (non-temporal) formula.
- $(\ll \eta \gg \Box \varphi) \leftrightarrow (\Box \ll \eta \gg \varphi)$, $(\ll \eta \gg (\varphi \mathcal{U} \psi)) \leftrightarrow ((\ll \eta \gg \varphi) \mathcal{U} (\ll \eta \gg \psi))$
- $(\ll \eta \gg \forall z \, \varphi) \leftrightarrow (\forall z \ll \eta \gg \varphi)$, $(\ll \eta \gg \exists z \, \varphi) \leftrightarrow (\exists z \ll \eta \gg \varphi)$
- $(\ll \eta \gg \varphi \vee \psi) \leftrightarrow ((\ll \eta \gg \varphi) \vee (\ll \eta \gg \psi))$

These axioms reflect the fact that $\ll \eta \gg$ distributes with every other modal and connective except negation. The transformation $l(\varphi, \eta)$, given in Section 4 is easily obtained from these axioms.

Acknowledgements

We would like to express our gratitude to Liu Zhiming for his careful reading of this paper and his helpful comments.

References

[1] R. H. Campbell, B. Randell, Error recovery in asynchronous systems, IEEE Transactions on Software Engineering, SE-12, 1986, 811-826.

[2] K. M. Chandy, L. Lamport, Distributed snapshots: determining the global state of distributed systems, ACM Transaction on Computation Systems Vol. 3 (1985), 63–75.

[3] K.M. Chandy, J. Misra, Parallel Program Design: A Foundation, Addison-Wesley, 1989.

[4] F. Cristian, A rigorous approach to fault tolerant programming, IEEE Transactions on Software Engineering, SE-11(1), 1985, 23-31.

[5] G. Huet, B. Lang, Proving and applying program transformations expressed with second order patterns, Acta Informatica 11 (1978), 31-55.

[6] R. Koo, S. Toueg, Checkpointing and rollback-recovery for distributed systems, IEEE Transactions on Software Engineering, SE-13, 1987, 23-31.

[7] Z. Liu, M. Joseph, Transformations of programs for fault–tolerance, Formal Aspects of Computing, 4 (5), 1992, 442-469.

[8] Z. Manna, A. Pnueli, How to cook a temporal proof system for your pet language. Proc. ACM Symposium on Principles on Programming Languages, 1983, 141–151.

[9] D. Peled, M. Joseph, A Compositional Framework for Fault-Tolerance by Specification Transformation, submitted for publication.

[10] R. D. Schlichting, F. B. Schneider, Fail–stop processors: an approach to designing fault-tolerant computing systems, ACM Transactions on Computer Systems, 1, 1983, 222-238.

[11] J. Zwiers, Compositionality, concurrency and partial correctness, Springer-Verlag, LNCS 321, 1987.

Concurrent METATEM — A Language for Modelling Reactive Systems

Michael Fisher*

Department of Computer Science**
University of Manchester
Manchester M20 0GR
United Kingdom

Abstract. In this paper, a language based on the notion of concurrent, communicating objects is presented. Each object executes a specification given in temporal logic and communicates with other objects using asynchronous broadcast message-passing. In contrast to the notions of predicates as processes and stream parallelism seen in concurrent logic languages, Concurrent METATEM represents a more course-grained approach, where an object consists of a set of temporal rules and communication is achieved by the evaluation of certain types of predicate. Thus, Concurrent METATEM represents a combination of the direct execution of temporal specifications, together with a novel model of concurrent computation and, as such, it provides a new approach to the modelling of complex reactive systems.

1 Introduction

A wide variety of computer systems are *reactive*. Rather than simply reading a set of inputs and producing, on termination, a set of outputs, reactive systems typically consist of nonterminating, concurrent and distributed components, each of which continually interact with their environment [18, 13]. Such systems are widely used in complex real-life applications, yet they are notoriously difficult to characterise and model formally.

In this paper, a language for representing a subclass of reactive systems is described. This subclass contains reactive systems whose concurrently executing elements are self-contained entities that communicate through message-passing. These entities encapsulate both data and behaviour and, hence, can be termed *objects*. Such reactive systems are sometimes termed *concurrent object-based systems*.

The language described in this paper has been developed from the sequential execution of temporal formulae provided by METATEM, an executable temporal logic described in [4, 10]. Thus, individual objects execute temporal specifications and communicate with their environment at certain times by *broadcasting* information. This model of computation for executable temporal logics was initially outlined in [9] — here we describe the full language and present applications of this approach to the design and development of reactive systems.

Objects in Concurrent METATEM, while being logic-based, execute their logical specifications using a particular operational interpretation for temporal formulae. Certain predicates

---

* This work was supported by SERC under Research Grant GR/H/18449.
** Author's current address: Department of Computing, Manchester Metropolitan University, Manchester M1 5GD, U.K. (TEL: (+44) 61-247-1488, EMAIL: michael@uk.ac.mmu.com.sun).

represent messages to be broadcast from the object, while the object space itself is structured into *groups* in order to restrict the extent of this broadcast communication. Adopting this style of language not only gives the programmer a method of animating high-level specifications, but also provides a flexible way to model concurrent systems, where computation is carried out within groups of objects broadcasting, listening and executing asynchronously. Such executing objects are generally course-grained, with an object consisting of a set of logical rules which define constraints upon certain predicates. In particular, the temporal logic we use within each individual object has been shown to be useful in describing and implementing various properties of reactive systems [15, 4].

Concurrent METATEM is an instance of an abstract model of computation, called the *CMP Model*. Lack of space prevents us from exploring this model in full, but we note its links with coordination languages, such as Linda [12], where heterogeneous networks of objects can be constructed, and give a brief overview of its features in §2. An important aspect of this model, and hence of Concurrent METATEM, is the separation of each individual object's definition into its *interface definition* and its *internal definition*, described in §2.1 and §2.2 respectively.

In §3 the logical basis of the Concurrent METATEM language itself is introduced. This section includes an introduction to both temporal logic and the execution of temporal formulae, and provides sufficient details to enable us to develop a simple example in §4, while the more advanced features of Concurrent METATEM are described in §5. In §6, we briefly review some related work. Although lack of space prevents us from giving a full formal semantics of Concurrent METATEM systems, we outline the direction in which our formal framework is being developed and present our concluding remarks in §7.

2   The Computational Metaphor

The abstract model used here combines the two notions of *objects* and *concurrency*. Objects are considered to be self contained entities, encapsulating both data and behaviour, able to execute independently of each other, and communicating via message-passing.

The predominant approach to concurrent object-based systems is that of the *actor* model of computation [14, 2]. The metaphor used in the actor model is of a mail system, with messages being addressed and sent directly to individual actors. Thus, actor systems are based upon point-to-point message-passing and message-driven computation. Although objects in Concurrent METATEM are also concurrently executing entities communicating through message-passing, they have the following fundamental properties which contrast with the actor model.

1. The basic method of communication between objects is *broadcast* message-passing.
2. Objects are not message driven — they begin executing from the moment they are created and continue even while no messages are received.
3. An object can change its interface (i.e., the messages that it recognises) dynamically.
4. The object-space is structured by grouping appropriate objects together and by restricting communication across group boundaries.

So, rather than seeing computation as objects sending mail messages to each other, and thus invoking some activity, computation in a collection of Concurrent METATEM objects can be visualised as independent entities *listening* to messages broadcast from other objects.

As an analogy, consider a room full of people. All the people are thinking, but any person who speaks will be heard by everyone in the room. In such a group, each person continues his or her own thought processes in isolation until either that person decides to say something, or someone else says something on which the person wishes to act. Analogously, an object in Concurrent METATEM continues to execute even if it receives no input from its environment.

Thus, a Concurrent METATEM system consists of a set of concurrently executing objects which communicate through asynchronous broadcast message-passing. These objects are the basic computational entities in a system and each object has two components:

1. an abstract *interface definition*, and,
2. an *internal definition*.

The interface definition is abstract in the sense that the same definition can be used regardless of the object's internal definition. In contrast, though certain features are shared by all objects, the internal definition of an object is dependent upon the execution mechanism used within that object. In particular, we will use an executable temporal logic to implement individual objects (§3). First, however, we will describe, in more detail, the uses of interface and internal definitions.

2.1 Interfaces to Objects

Networks of objects communicate via broadcasting messages and individual objects only act upon certain identified messages. Thus, an object must be able to filter out messages that it wishes to recognise, ignoring all others. The definition of those messages that an object recognises, together with a definition of the messages that an object may itself produce, is provided by the *interface definition* for that particular object.

The interface definition for an object, for example 'stack', is defined as follows.

$$stack(pop, push) [popped, stackfull].$$

Here, {pop, push} is the set of messages the object recognises, while {popped, stackfull} is the set of messages the object might produce itself. These sets of messages need not be disjoint – an object might broadcast messages that the object itself recognises. Note also that many distinct objects may broadcast and recognise the same messages.

Each object in the system has, associated with it, a *message queue* representing the messages that the object has recognised, but has yet to process. The number of messages that an object reads from its message queue during an execution step is initially defined by the object's interface. The object may, for example, read one message at a time from the queue, or may, as in Concurrent METATEM (see §3), read sets of messages from the queue (see §5.2 for more details of the modification of this behaviour by the object itself). By default, the execution of an object is based on the set of messages received by the object since the last execution step it completed. Thus, objects process sets of messages, rather than enforcing some linearisation on the arrival order of messages.

2.2 Inside Objects

Given an object's interface definition, its internal definition can be defined in any way that is consistent with the interface, i.e., the internal definition represents a computation mechanism which recognises the appropriate incoming messages, computes accordingly, and broadcasts only the prescribed messages. Though this approach can be extended to heterogeneous objects, we here assume that all objects in the system are defined using Concurrent METATEM.

3 The Basic Features of Concurrent METATEM

The computation mechanism for a single object in the Concurrent METATEM system is provided by a METATEM-like computational engine, which is based on the execution of temporal logic formulae [4, 10]. We first give a brief overview of temporal logic together with an outline of the METATEM execution mechanism.

3.1 Temporal Logic

Temporal logic can be seen as classical logic extended with various modalities representing temporal aspects of logical formulae. The temporal logic we use is based on a linear, discrete model of time. Thus, time is modeled as an infinite sequence of discrete states, with an identified starting point, called 'the beginning of time'. Classical formulae are used to represent constraints within individual states, while temporal formulae represent constraints *between* states. As formulae are interpreted at particular states in this sequence, operators which refer to both the past and future are required.

The future-time temporal operators used in this paper are as follows.

- The *sometime in the future* operator, '$\Diamond$'.

    $\Diamond \varphi$ is true now if φ is true *sometime* in the future.
- The *always in the future* operator, '$\Box$'.

    $\Box \varphi$ is true now if φ is true *always* in the future.

Similarly, connectives are provided to enable formulae to refer to the *past*. The only past-time temporal operators needed for the examples below can be described as follows.

- The *since* operator, 'S'.

    $\varphi S \psi$ is true now if ψ was true in the past and φ was true from that moment until (but not including) the present moment.
- The *beginning of time* operator, 'start'.

    start is only true at the beginning of time.
- The *strong last-time operator*, '$\bullet$'.

    $\bullet \varphi$ is true if there was a last moment in time and, at the moment, φ was true.

There are many other temporal operators used in temporal logics in general, and in META-TEM in particular, though they will not be mentioned here (see [4, 10] for more details). It should be noted that the use of temporal logic as the basis for the computation rules gives an extra level of expressive power over the corresponding classical logics. In particular, operators such as '$\Diamond$' give us the opportunity to specify future-time (temporal) indeterminacy.

3.2 METATEM

METATEM is a programming and modelling language based on temporal logic and, as such, uses a set of 'rules', couched in temporal logic, to represent the object's internal definition. These rules are each of the form

'past and present formula' **implies** 'present or future formula'

Such rules are applied at every moment in time (i.e., at every step of the execution) and thus METATEM execution can be distinguished from the logic programming approach in that refutation is not involved in the computation process and the model for the formula representing the program is constructed by following the temporal rules *forwards* in time.

The operator used to represent the basic temporal indeterminacy within METATEM is the *sometime* operator, '$\Diamond$'. When a formula such as $\Diamond\varphi$ is executed, the system must try to ensure that φ *eventually* becomes true. Thus, such formulae are often called eventualities. As an example of a simple METATEM program, consider the following set of rules. (Note that these rules are not meant to form a 'meaningful' program – they are only given for illustrative purposes.)

$$\mathbf{start} \Rightarrow \text{popped(a)}$$
$$\mathbf{O}\text{pop(X)} \Rightarrow \Diamond\text{popped(X)}$$
$$\mathbf{O}\text{push(Y)} \Rightarrow \text{stackfull() } \vee \text{popped(Y)}$$

Note that the 'X' and 'Y' here represent universally quantified variables. Looking at these program rules, we see that popped(a) is made true at the beginning of time and whenever pop(X) is true in the last moment in time, a commitment to eventually make popped(X) true is given. Similarly, whenever push(Y) is true in the last moment in time, then either stackfull() or popped(Y) must be made true.

The basic predicates used in the logic are categorised as follows, with several categories of predicate corresponding to messages to and from the object.

- *Environment* predicates, which represent incoming messages.
  An environment predicate can be made true if, and only if, the corresponding message has just been received. Thus, a formula containing an environment predicate, such as 'push(Y)', is only true if a message of the form 'push(b)' has just been received (for some argument 'b', which unifies with 'Y').
- *Component* predicates, which represent messages broadcast from the object.
  When a component predicate is made true, it has the (side-)effect of broadcasting the corresponding message to the environment. For example, if the formula 'popped(e)' is made true, where popped is a component predicate, then the message 'popped(e)' is broadcast.
- *Internal* predicates, which have no external effect.
  These predicates are used as part of formulae participating in the internal computation of the object and, as such, do not correspond to external communication.
  This category of predicates may include various *primitive* operations.

Once the object has commenced execution, it continually follows a cycle of reading incoming messages, collecting together the rules that 'fire' (i.e., whose left-hand sides are satisfied by the current history), and executing one of the disjuncts represented by the conjunction of right-hand sides of 'fired' rules. For a more detailed description of the METATEM execution mechanism, see [10].

By default, predicates remain false unless otherwise constrained and each object executes asynchronously. The message-passing mechanism is asynchronous but does not guarantee that the order of arrival of messages is the same as the order of sending.

Objects may backtrack, with the proviso that an object may not backtrack past the broadcasting of a message. Consequently, in broadcasting a message to its environment, an object effectively *commits* the execution to that particular path. Thus, the basic operation of an object can be thought of as a period of internal execution, possibly involving backtracking, followed by appropriate broadcasts to its environment. The analogy with a collections of humans is of a period of thinking, followed by some (broadcasted) action, e.g. speech. Backtracking can occur during thinking, but once an action has been carried out, it cannot be undone.

We have outlined the logical basis of objects in Concurrent METATEM, together with their basic execution mechanism. We now postpone discussion of the more complex features of Concurrent METATEM until §5, and proceed to give a larger example of modelling using the system described so far.

4 Snow White and The Seven Dwarves — A tale of 8 objects

To give some idea of how Concurrent METATEM can be used, a simple example will be described in this section. This example is is a descendent of the 'resource controller' example which has been so overworked in previous papers on METATEM and, as such, is related to a variety of resource allocation systems. However, the individual objects can be specified so that they show a form of 'intelligent' behaviour, and so this example system is related to applications in Distributed AI. First, a brief outline of the properties of the leading characters in this example will be given.

4.1 The Scenario

Snow White has a bag of sweets. All the dwarves want sweets, though some want them more than others. If a dwarf asks Snow White for a sweet, she will give him one, but maybe not straight away. Snow White is only able to give away one sweet at a time.

Snow White and the dwarves are going to be represented as a set of objects in Concurrent METATEM. Each dwarf has a particular strategy that it uses in asking for sweets, which is described below[3].

1. eager initially asks for a sweet and, from then on, whenever he receives a sweet, asks for another.
2. mimic asks for a sweet whenever he sees eager asking for one.
3. jealous asks for a sweet whenever he sees eager receiving one.
4. insistent asks for a sweet as often as he can.
5. courteous asks for a sweet only when eager, mimic, jealous and insistent have all *asked* for one.

---

[3] The names and behaviours of the dwarves are different from the Fairy Tale!

6. generous asks for a sweet only when eager, mimic, jealous, insistent and courteous have all *received* one.

7. shy only asks for a sweet when he sees no one else asking.

8. snow-white can only allocate one sweet at a time. She keeps a list of outstanding requests and attempts to satisfy the oldest one first.
If a new request is received, and it does not occur in the list, it is added to the end. If it does already occur in the list, it is ignored. Thus, if a dwarf asks for a sweet *n* times, he will eventually receive at most *n*, and at least 1, sweets.

This example may seem trivial, but it represents a set of objects exhibiting different behaviours, where an individual object's internal rules can consist of both safety and liveness constraints, and where complex interaction can occur between autonomous objects.

4.2 The Program

The Concurrent METATEM program for the scenario described above consists of the definitions of 8 objects, given below. To give a better idea of the meaning of the temporal formulae representing the internals of these objects, a brief description will be given with each object's definition. Requests to Snow White are given in the form of an ask() message with the name of the requesting dwarf as an argument. Snow White gives a sweet to a particular dwarf by sending a give() message with the name of the dwarf as an argument. Finally, uppercase alphabetic characters, such as X and Y represent universally quantified variables.

1. eager(give)[ask] :
$$\text{start} \Rightarrow \text{ask(eager)}$$
$$\bigcirc \text{give(eager)} \Rightarrow \text{ask(eager)}$$
Initially, eager asks for a sweet and, whenever he has just received a sweet, he asks again.

2. mimic(ask)[ask] :
$$\bigcirc \text{ask(eager)} \Rightarrow \text{ask(mimic)}$$
If eager has just asked for a sweet then mimic asks for one.

3. jealous(give)[ask] :
$$\bigcirc \text{give(eager)} \Rightarrow \text{ask(jealous)}$$
If eager has just received a sweet then jealous asks for one.

4. insistent[ask] :
$$\text{start} \Rightarrow \Box \text{ask(insistent)}$$
From the beginning of time insistent asks for a sweet as often as he can.

5. courteous(ask)[ask] :
$$\begin{bmatrix} (\neg\text{ask(courteous)}) \, \mathcal{S} \, \text{ask(eager)} \, \wedge \\ (\neg\text{ask(courteous)}) \, \mathcal{S} \, \text{ask(mimic)} \, \wedge \\ (\neg\text{ask(courteous)}) \, \mathcal{S} \, \text{ask(jealous)} \, \wedge \\ (\neg\text{ask(courteous)}) \, \mathcal{S} \, \text{ask(insistent)} \end{bmatrix} \Rightarrow \text{ask(courteous)}$$
If courteous has not asked for a sweet since eager asked for one, has not asked for a sweet since mimic asked for one, has not asked for a sweet since jealous asked for one, and, has not asked for a sweet since insistent asked for one, then he will ask for a sweet.

6.   generous(give)[ask] :

$$\begin{bmatrix} (\neg \texttt{ask(generous)}) \, \mathcal{S} \, \texttt{give(eager)} \; \land \\ (\neg \texttt{ask(generous)}) \, \mathcal{S} \, \texttt{give(mimic)} \; \land \\ (\neg \texttt{ask(generous)}) \, \mathcal{S} \, \texttt{give(jealous)} \; \land \\ (\neg \texttt{ask(generous)}) \, \mathcal{S} \, \texttt{give(insistent)} \; \land \\ (\neg \texttt{ask(generous)}) \, \mathcal{S} \, \texttt{give(courteous)} \end{bmatrix} \;\Rightarrow\; \texttt{ask(generous)}$$

If generous has not asked for a sweet since eager received one, has not asked for a sweet since mimic received one, has not asked for a sweet since jealous received one, has not asked for a sweet since insistent received one, and, has not asked for a sweet since courteous received one, then he will ask for a sweet!

7.   shy(ask)[ask] :

$$\textbf{start} \Rightarrow \Diamond \texttt{ask(shy)}$$
$$\bullet \, \texttt{ask(X)} \Rightarrow \neg \texttt{ask(shy)}$$
$$\bullet \, \texttt{ask(shy)} \Rightarrow \Diamond \texttt{ask(shy)}$$

shy initially wants to ask for a sweet but is prevented from doing so whenever he sees some other dwarf asking for one. Thus, he only succeeds in asking for one when he sees no one else asking and, as soon as he has asked for a sweet, he wants to try to ask again!

8.   snow-white(ask)[give] :

$$\bullet \, \texttt{ask(X)} \Rightarrow \Diamond \texttt{give(X)}$$
$$\texttt{give(X)} \land \texttt{give(Y)} \Rightarrow \texttt{X=Y}$$

If snow-white has just received a request from a dwarf, a sweet will be sent to that dwarf eventually. The second rule ensures that sweets can not be sent to two dwarves at the same time by stating that if both give(X) and give(Y) are to be broadcast, then X must be equal to Y.

Note that, in this example, several of the dwarves were only able to behave as required because they could observe all the ask() and give() messages that were broadcast. The dwarves can thus be programmed to have strategies that are dependent on the behaviour of other dwarves. Also, the power of executable temporal logic is exploited in the definition several objects, particularly those using the '$\Diamond$' operator to represent multiple goals.

Sets of Concurrent METATEM objects representing 'standard' examples, such as the dining philosophers and producer/consumer problems can be similarly defined. Concurrent METATEM is being applied in a variety of areas, from the modelling of transport systems [8], to Distributed A.I. [9]. Systems based upon point-to-point message-passing, for example actor systems, can also be defined by ensuring that each message incorporates a destination address as one of its arguments.

Having seen how a non-trivial example containing a network of communicating objects can be defined in Concurrent METATEM, we will briefly describe some of the more advanced features of Concurrent METATEM.

5   Extensions of Concurrent METATEM

Although the features we will describe in this section can be categorised as *extra-logical*, the intention is that these extensions to the basic execution of temporal logic will be defined using meta-level techniques [5], rather than system primitives. Note that several of these capabilities have yet to be implemented fully.

5.1 Dynamic interfaces

The interface definition of an object defines the initial set of messages that are recognised by that object. However, the object may dynamically change the set of messages that it recognises. In particular, an object can either start 'listening' for a new type of message, or start 'ignoring' previously recognised message types. For example, given an original object interface such as

$$\texttt{stack(pop,push) [popped,stackfull]}$$

the object may dynamically choose to stop recognising 'pop' messages, for example by executing 'ignore(pop)'. This effectively gives the object the new interface

$$\texttt{stack(push) [popped,stackfull].}$$

This, together with broadcast message-passing, provides a powerful mechanism for the dynamic modification of a system's behaviour.

5.2 Manipulating message queues

An object is also able to dynamically modify its own behaviour regarding the manipulation of its message queue. The default behaviour of an object is for it to, at every execution step, read a sequence of messages from its input queue up to either the end of the queue, or the repetition of a message. For example, if the message queue is

$$\texttt{pop(a), push(c), pop(d), pop(e), push(c), pop(f), pop(a), ...}$$

then in one execution step the set of messages read in is

$$\texttt{\{ pop(a), push(c), pop(d), pop(e) \}}$$

and the message queue remaining is

$$\texttt{push(c), pop(f), pop(a), ...}$$

This behaviour can be modified dynamically so that, for example, objects read only one message at a time from their input queue, or read up to the second occurrence of either of several messages.

5.3 Synchronisation

Though objects execute asynchronously, provision for the *synchronisation* of objects is often useful. For example, an object might broadcast a request for something, then continue executing until a reply is received. While it is waiting for the reply, the object can process other messages. Alternatively, the object might broadcast its request, then *suspend* until an appropriate reply is received. In this case, it will not process any other messages in between the request being sent and the reply being received. This can be considered as a process of synchronising the object with the reply message. If we imagine that ask is a component predicate, while answer is an environment predicate, then we can represent such an object's rules as follows.

$$... \Rightarrow \texttt{ask}$$
$$\bullet\texttt{answer} \Rightarrow \texttt{doit}$$
$$\bullet\texttt{ask} \Rightarrow \texttt{answer}$$

If an ask message has been sent, then the only way to satisfy this last rule is to ensure that answer is received in the next state. Thus, the object cannot execute further until the required message arrives, and consequently it is suspended. In this way, objects in Concurrent METATEM can synchronise with selected messages. Note, however, that this approach might require some manipulation of the suspended object's message queue.

5.4 Rooms

One important extension currently being developed is the restriction of communication to certain groups. This method of structuring and partitioning the object space, called *rooms*, combined with objects that may occupy several rooms may alleviate some of the inefficiencies and security problems that occur with full broadcasting. Here, each object is a member of at least one room, and is able to 'hear' all the messages broadcast within those rooms. An object can selectively broadcast messages to particular rooms that it is a member of. This mechanism is related to the process group approach used in many distributed operating systems [6], and to the group model of computation described in [16].

6 Related Work

Due to lack of space we are only be able to briefly sketch the relationship between our work and others in the area of both executable logics and languages for distributed systems.

In [11], Gehani describes Broadcasting Sequential Processes (BSP) which is also based on the asynchronous broadcasting of messages. As in Concurrent METATEM, objects may screen out certain messages, but not only is the identity of the sender always incorporated into a message, but also objects cannot manipulate their message queue as is intended in Concurrent METATEM. One, more fundamental, difference between BSP and our approach is that objects in BSP are message driven.

The Linda model [12] has some similarities with this approach in that the shared data structures represented in the Linda tuple space can be seen as providing a broadcast mechanism for data. However, Linda is a general coordination language, while our computational model fixes much more than just the basic communication and distribution system, and provides more structuring of the object space. Having said this, it may be possible to use a suitable Linda system to implement Concurrent METATEM on a distributed architecture.

As mentioned earlier, our model has some similarities with the Actor model, the main differences being the ability to act in a non message-driven way, the object's definition using temporal logic, the ability to process sets of incoming messages, and the ability to synchronise with other objects. Maruichi et. al. [16] use a model of computation similar to ours for their investigation in DAI systems, while several distributed operating systems also use the notion of process groups (what we call 'rooms') in order to group processes (objects) together [6]. Though several of the above approaches have similarities with Concurrent METATEM, none are based on the direct execution of logical statements.

Related work on Concurrent Logic Programming has mainly been based on the execution of logic programs within the Linda and actor models, e.g. [19]. We again stress that although a (temporal) logic is executed directly, we do not use the logic programming approach. Various executable temporal logics have been developed, for example [17, 1], but few have incorporated the notions of concurrency and we know of none that are based upon a computational model similar to the one described here.

7 Conclusions

Concurrent METATEM not only provides a novel model for the simulation and implementation of a class of reactive systems, but also incorporates executable temporal logic to implement individual objects. Consequently, such components have explicit logical semantics and the behaviour of certain types of system is easily coded as temporal logic rules.

Concurrent METATEM has potential applications in a wide range of areas, for example simulation and programming in concurrent and distributed systems, the development of distributed algorithms, distributed process control, distributed learning/problem solving, and multi-agent AI. An advantage of this approach, at least when representing certain systems from Distributed AI, is that the model follows the way in which humans communicate and cooperate.

Although the use of broadcast message-passing has many advantages, particularly for developing flexible and fault-tolerant systems [7, 20, 3], the obvious drawback of this approach is that systems communicating in this may not scale up. Thus, the use of *rooms* to restrict the scope of the broadcasts, together with their representation as first-class objects, can be seen as an essential part of the development of efficient systems. We see systems being constructed in Concurrent METATEM which use broadcast locally (within rooms), but use point-to-point message-passing for non-local communication. Such point-to-point message-passing can always be defined on top of a broadcast message-passing, though this may involve some loss of efficiency.

A prototype interpreter for (propositional) Concurrent METATEM has been developed. This program provides a platform on which simple experiments into both synchronous and asynchronous systems can be carried out. Experience with this system will direct a future implementation of full (first-order) Concurrent METATEM. Future implementation work will include the development of efficient techniques for recognising and compiling both point-to-point message-passing and rooms via multi-cast message-passing.

On the formal side, we are developing a specification and development framework for Concurrent METATEM systems and have provided a semantics for such systems based upon *dense* temporal logic (unfortunately, due to lack of space we were unable to include this here). We are also investigating an algebraic semantics for Concurrent METATEM.

In summary, we believe that Concurrent METATEM provides a high-level language that is useful in the design, development and implementation of reactive systems.

References

1. M. Abadi and Z. Manna. Temporal Logic Programming. *Journal of Symbolic Computation*, 8: 277–295, 1989.
2. Gul Agha. *Actors - A Model for Concurrent Computation in Distributed Systems*. MIT Press, 1986.
3. Gregory R. Andrews. Paradigms for Process Interaction in Distributed Programs. *ACM Computing Surveys*, 23(1):49–90, March 1991.
4. H. Barringer, M. Fisher, D. Gabbay, G. Gough, and R. Owens. METATEM: A Framework for Programming in Temporal Logic. In *Proceedings of REX Workshop on Stepwise Refinement of Distributed Systems: Models, Formalisms, Correctness*, Mook, Netherlands, June 1989. (Published in *Lecture Notes in Computer Science*, volume 430, Springer Verlag).

5. H. Barringer, M. Fisher, D. Gabbay, and A. Hunter. Meta-Reasoning in Executable Temporal Logic. In J. Allen, R. Fikes, and E. Sandewall, editors, *Proceedings of the International Conference on Principles of Knowledge Representation and Reasoning (KR'91)*, Cambridge, Massachusetts, April 1991. Morgan Kaufmann.

6. Kenneth P. Birman. The Process Group Approach to Reliable Distributed Computing. Techanical Report TR91-1216, Department of Computer Science, Cornell University, July 1991.

7. A. Borg, J. Baumbach, and S. Glazer. A Message System Supporting Fault Tolerance. In *Proceedings of the Ninth ACM Symposium on Operating System Principles*, pages 90–99, New Hampshire, October 1983. ACM. (In ACM Operating Systems Review, vol. 17, no. 5).

8. M. Finger, M. Fisher, and R. Owens. METATEM at Work: Modelling Reactive Systems Using Executable Temporal Logic. In *Sixth International Conference on Industrial and Engineering Applications of Artificial Intelligence and Expert Systems (IEA/AIE-93)*, Edinburgh, U.K., June 1993. Gordon and Breach Publishers. (To appear).

9. M. Fisher and H. Barringer. Concurrent METATEM Processes — A Language for Distributed AI. In *Proceedings of the European Simulation Multiconference*, Copenhagen, Denmark, June 1991.

10. M. Fisher and R. Owens. From the Past to the Future: Executing Temporal Logic Programs. In *Proceedings of Logic Programming and Automated Reasoning (LPAR)*, St. Petersberg, Russia, July 1992. (Published in *Lecture Notes in Computer Science*, volume 624, Springer Verlag).

11. Narian H. Gehani. Broadcasting Sequential Processes. *IEEE Transactions on Software Engineering*, 10(4):343–351, July 1984.

12. D. Gelernter, N. Carriero, S. Chandran, and S. Chang. Parallel programming in Linda. In *International Conference on Parallel Processing*, August 1985.

13. D. Harel and A. Pnueli. On the Development of Reactive Systems. Technical Report CS85-02, Department of Applied Mathematics, The Weizmann Institute of Science, Revohot, Israel, January 1985.

14. Carl Hewitt. Control Structure as Patterns of Passing Messages. In P. H. Winston and R. H. Brown, editors, *Artificial Intelligence: An MIT Perspective (Volume 2)*, pages 433–465. MIT Press, 1979.

15. Z. Manna and A. Pnueli. *The Temporal Logic of Reactive and Concurrent Systems: Specification*. Springer-Verlag, New York, 1992.

16. T. Maruichi, M. Ichikawa, and M. Tokoro. Modelling autonomous agents and their groups. In Y. Demazeau and J. P. Muller, editors, *Decentralized A.I. (Volume 2)*, pages 215–234. Elsevier/North-Holland, 1990.

17. Ben Moszkowski. *Executing Temporal Logic Programs*. Cambridge University Press, Cambridge, U.K., 1986.

18. Amir Pnueli. Applications of Temporal Logic to the Specification and Verification of Reactive Systems: A Survey of Current Trends. *Lecture Notes in Computer Science*, 224, August 1986.

19. E. Shapiro and A. Takeuchi. Object Oriented Programming in Concurrent Prolog. In Ehud Shapiro, editor, *Concurrent Prolog–Collected Papers*, chapter 29, pages 251–273. MIT Press, 1987.

20. R. Strom and S. Yemini. Optimistic Recovery in Distributed Systems. *ACM Transactions on Computer Systems*, 3(3):204–226, August 1985.

Trace-Based Compositional Reasoning about Fault Tolerant Systems

Henk Schepers* and Jozef Hooman**

Department of Mathematics and Computing Science
Eindhoven University of Technology
P.O. Box 513, 5600 MB Eindhoven, The Netherlands

Abstract. In this report we present a compositional network proof theory to specify and verify safety properties of fault tolerant systems. Important in such systems is the fault hypothesis which specifies the class of faults that must be tolerated. In the formalism presented in this report, the fault hypothesis of a system is represented by a predicate which expresses how faults might transform the behaviour of the system. To reason about fault tolerant systems, we formulate a compositional proof method based on communication histories. Soundness and relative network completeness of the method is proven. Our approach is illustrated by applying it to the alternating bit protocol.

Key words: Compositional proof theory, fault hypothesis, fault tolerance, relative network completeness, safety, soundness, specification, verification.

1 Introduction

In fault tolerant systems, three domains of behaviour are distinguished: normal, exceptional and catastrophic (see [12]). Normal behaviour is the behaviour when no faults occur. The discriminating factor between exceptional and catastrophic behaviour is the *fault hypothesis* which stipulates how faults affect the normal behaviour. Relative to the fault hypothesis an exceptional behaviour exhibits an abnormality which should be tolerated (to an extent that remains to be specified). A catastrophic behaviour has an abnormality that was not anticipated (cf. [1], [11], [12], and [15]). In general, the catastrophic behaviour of a component cannot be tolerated by a system. Under certain fault hypotheses, the system is designed as if the hypothetical faults are the only faults it can experience and measures are taken to tolerate (only) those *anticipated* faults (see, e.g., [16] for some design examples). In fault tolerant systems, the normal and the exceptional behaviour constitute the acceptable behaviour.

In the Hoare style formalism of [5] Cristian deals with the effects of faults that have occurred by partitioning the initial state space into disjoint subspaces,

---

* Supported by the Dutch NWO under grant number NWI88.1517: 'Fault Tolerance: Paradigms, Models, Logics, Construction'. E-mail: schepers@win.tue.nl.
** E-mail: wsinjh@win.tue.nl.

and providing a separate specification for each part. In the formalisms for fault tolerance that have been proposed (cf. [3], [9], [14], [19]) in the more recent literature, the faults that cause exceptional behaviour are modeled explicitly, typically using the distinguished symbol '†'. In this report we propose a more abstract approach, in that we only describe the effect of faults on the observable behaviour of a process, i.e., the input and output behaviour on the visible channels. The fault hypothesis of a process is formalized by a predicate that expresses how the normal and the acceptable behaviour of that process are related.

We consider networks of processes that communicate synchronously via directed channels. Processes do not share variables. In this report we focus on the formalization of fault tolerance in relation to concurrency. Therefore, we abstract from the internal states of processes and concentrate on the input and output behaviour that is observable at their interface. So, in our proof theory we do not deal with the sequential aspects of processes and we use a simple SAT formalism to reason about the properties of networks of processes. Furthermore, we restrict ourselves to the specification and verification of *safety* properties of fault tolerant systems. Safety properties are properties that can be falsified by finite observations [21]. They are important for reliability because, in the characterization by Lamport [10], they express that 'nothing bad will happen'. Consider, for instance, a simple 1-place FIFO buffer B that has two observable channels *in* and *out*, with obvious interpretation. Typical safety properties of B are 'if there is a communication on *out* then the communicated value is equal to the most recently communicated value on *in*' and 'the number of *out* communications is equal to or one less than the number of *in* communications'.

We express properties by means of a first-order trace logic. To express that a process P satisfies a safety property ϕ we use a correctness formula of the form P sat ϕ. We use a special variable h to denote the trace, also called the history, of P. Such a history describes the observable behaviour of a process by recording the communications along the visible channels of the process.

A fault hypothesis χ of a process P is formalized as a predicate, whose only free variables are h and h_{old}, representing a reflexive relation between the normal and acceptable histories of a process. The interpretation is such that h_{old} represents a normal history of process P whereas h is an *acceptable* history of P with respect to χ. Such relations enable us to abstract from the precise nature of a fault and to focus on the abnormal behaviour it causes. For a fault hypothesis χ we introduce, similar to [17], the construct $(P \wr \chi)$ to indicate execution of process P under the assumption of χ. This construct enables us to specify *failure prone processes*. Consider again buffer B. Under the hypothesis that, due to faults, values in the buffer are corrupted, which is formalized by some fault hypothesis predicate *Cor*, we would like to prove that failure prone process $(B \wr Cor)$ still satisfies the property that 'the number of *out* communications is equal to or one less than the number of *in* communications'.

We present a proof theory to verify that a system tolerates the exceptional behaviour of its components to the desired extent. The proof theory is compositional to allow for the reasoning with the specifications of those components while ignoring their implementation details. Our method is illustrated by applying it to the alternating bit protocol, where, indeed, we only use the specifications of the components. Finally, we show that our proof theory is sound and obtain a completeness result by establishing preciseness preservation (see [20]).

The remainder of this report is organized as follows. Section 2 introduces our programming notation and the model of computation. In Section 3 we present the assertion language and correctness formulae. In Section 4 we incorporate fault hypotheses into this formalism. Section 5 contains the compositional network proof theory. In Section 6 we investigate the alternating bit protocol. We prove safety of this protocol to illustrate our method. In Section 7 we prove that the proof theory of Section 5 is sound and relatively complete. A conclusion and suggestions for future research can be found in Section 8.

2 Programs and Model of Computation

Let VAR be a nonempty set of program variables, $CHAN$ a nonempty set of channel names, and let VAL be a denumerable domain of values. $\mathbb{N}$ denotes the set of natural numbers (including 0). We assume given a programming language, e.g. CSP [7], which can be used to define networks of processes that communicate synchronously via directed channels. This language includes output statement $c!e$ to synchronously send the value of expression e on channel c, input statement $c?x$ to synchronously receive a value via channel c and assign this value to variable x, the construct $P_1 \parallel P_2$ to indicate parallel execution of processes P_1 and P_2, as well as, for $cset \subseteq CHAN$, the construct $P \setminus cset$ to hide the channels in $cset$.

Define $var(P)$ as the set of variables occurring in process P. Parallel processes do not share program variables, i.e., for $P_1 \parallel P_2$ we require $var(P_1) \cap var(P_2) = \emptyset$.

The set of visible, or observable, input channels of process P, notation $in(P)$, can be obtained by structural induction using $in(c!e) = \emptyset$ and $in(c?x) = \{c\}$. Then, $in(P_1 \parallel P_2) = in(P_1) \cup in(P_2)$ and $in(P \setminus cset) = in(P) - cset$. The set $out(P)$ of observable output channels of process P is defined likewise, using $out(c?x) = \emptyset$ and $out(c!e) = \{c\}$.

Definition 1 (Channels of a process) The set of channels of a process P, notation $chan(P)$, is defined by $chan(P) = in(P) \cup out(P)$.

To guarantee that channels are unidirectional and point-to-point, we require for $P_1 \parallel P_2$ that $in(P_1) \cap in(P_2) = \emptyset$ and $out(P_1) \cap out(P_2) = \emptyset$. To avoid programs such as $(c?x) \setminus \{c\}$, which would be equivalent to a *random assignment* to x, we require for $P \setminus cset$ that $cset \subseteq in(P) \cap out(P)$.

We represent a synchronous communication of value $\mu \in VAL$ along channel $c \in CHAN$ by a pair (c, μ), and define $ch((c, \mu)) = c$ and $val((c, \mu)) = \mu$. A history (also called a trace), typically denoted by θ, is a finite sequence of the form $\langle (c_1, \mu_1), \ldots, (c_n, \mu_n) \rangle$, where $n \in \mathbb{N}$, $c_i \in CHAN$, and $\mu_i \in VAL$, for $1 \leq i \leq n$. If $\theta = \langle (c_1, \mu_1), \ldots, (c_n, \mu_n) \rangle$, then the length of θ, notation $len(\theta)$, is defined by $len(\theta) = n$. A history represents the communications of a process along its observable channels up to some point in an execution. Let $\langle \rangle$ denote the empty history. The concatenation of two histories

$\theta_1 = \langle (c_1, \mu_1), \ldots, (c_k, \mu_k) \rangle$ and $\theta_2 = \langle (d_1, \nu_1), \ldots, (d_l, \nu_l) \rangle$, denoted $\theta_1{}^\wedge \theta_2$, is defined as $\langle (c_1, \mu_1), \ldots, (c_k, \mu_k), (d_1, \nu_1), \ldots, (d_l, \nu_l) \rangle$. We use $\theta^\wedge(c, \mu)$ as an abbreviation of $\theta^\wedge \langle (c, \mu) \rangle$. Let $TRACE$ be the set of traces.

Definition 2 (Projection) For a trace $\theta \in TRACE$ and a set of channels $cset \subseteq CHAN$, we define the *projection* of θ onto $cset$, denoted $\theta \uparrow cset$, as the sequence obtained from θ by deleting all records with channels not in $cset$.

Formally, $\theta \uparrow cset = \begin{cases} \langle\rangle & \text{if } \theta = \langle\rangle \\ \theta_0 \uparrow cset & \text{if } \theta = \theta_0{}^\wedge(c, \mu) \text{ and } c \notin cset \\ (\theta_0 \uparrow cset)^\wedge(c, \mu) & \text{if } \theta = \theta_0{}^\wedge(c, \mu) \text{ and } c \in cset \end{cases}$

Definition 3 (Hiding) Hiding is the complement of projection. Formally, the hiding of a set $cset$ of channels from a trace $\theta \in TRACE$, notation $\theta \setminus cset$, is defined as $\theta \setminus cset = \theta \uparrow (CHAN - cset)$

Definition 4 (Channels in a trace) The set of channels occurring in a trace θ, notation $chan(\theta)$, is defined by $chan(\theta) = \{c \in CHAN \mid \theta \uparrow \{c\} \neq \langle\rangle\}$

Notice that $\theta \uparrow cset = \theta$ iff $chan(\theta) \subseteq cset$, and that $\theta \uparrow \{c\} = \langle\rangle$ iff $c \notin chan(\theta)$.

Definition 5 (Prefix) The trace θ_1 is a prefix of a trace θ_2, notation $\theta_1 \preceq \theta_2$, iff there exists a trace θ_3 such that $\theta_1{}^\wedge \theta_3 = \theta_2$.

A set of traces $H \subseteq TRACE$ is prefix closed if every prefix of an element of H is also an element of H, i.e, for all $\theta_1 \in H$ we have that $\theta_2 \preceq \theta_1$ implies $\theta_2 \in H$. It is rather straightforward to define a semantic function $\mathcal{H}$ which assigns to each process P a prefix closed set $\mathcal{H}[\![P]\!]$ of finite traces. For infinite executions of P the set $\mathcal{H}[\![P]\!]$ contains all finite approximations, which is justified since we only deal with safety properties [21].

3 Assertion Language and Correctness Formulae

We use a correctness formula P **sat** ϕ to express that process P satisfies safety property ϕ. Informally, such a correctness formula expresses that any sequence of communications performed by P satisfies ϕ.

Conform the format of traces in the semantics of the previous section, we use communication records such as (c, μ), with $c \in CHAN$ and $\mu \in VAL$, in assertions. We have channel expressions, e.g. using the operator ch which yields the channel of a communication record, and value expressions, including the operator val which yields the value of a communication record and the length operator len. We use the empty trace, $\langle\rangle$, traces of one record, e.g. $\langle (c, \mu) \rangle$, as well as the concatenation operator $^\wedge$ and the projection operator $\uparrow$ to create trace expressions. Further, for a trace expression $texp$ and a value expression $vexp$ we have $texp(vexp)$ to refer to record number $vexp$ of $texp$, provided $vexp$ is a positive natural number less than or equal to $len(texp)$. To refer to the communication history of a process we use a special variable h. This variable is not updated explicitly by the process: it refers to a trace from the semantics, and consequently its value will in general change during the execution of the process. Then, we can write specifications such as $c!2$ **sat** $h{\uparrow}\{c\} = \langle\rangle \lor h{\uparrow}\{c\} = \langle(c,2)\rangle$. Let $VVAR$, with typical representative v, denote the set of logical value variables ranging over VAL, and let $TVAR$, with characteristic element t, be the set of logical trace variables ranging over $TRACE$. Assume that $VVAR \cap TVAR = \varnothing$.

Definition 6 (Abbreviations) Henceforth we use the following abbreviations, for trace expressions $texp$, $texp_1$, and $texp_2$, and channel expression $cexp$.

- $texp {\uparrow} cexp \equiv texp {\uparrow} \{cexp\}$
- $texp_1 \preceq texp_2 \equiv \exists t : texp_1{}^\wedge t = texp_2$
  This expresses that trace $texp_1$ is a prefix of trace $texp_2$.
- $texp_1 \preceq^n texp_2 \equiv \exists t : len(t) \leq n : texp_1{}^\wedge t = texp_2$
  To express that $texp_1$ is a prefix of $texp_2$ which is at most n records shorter.
- $texp_1 \trianglelefteq texp_2 \equiv$
  $$\begin{cases} \exists t : t^\wedge texp_1 \preceq texp_2 & \text{if } len(texp_1) \leq 1 \\ \forall i : \forall j > i : \exists t_1, t_2 : t_1{}^\wedge texp_1(i)^\wedge t_2{}^\wedge texp_1(j) \preceq texp_2 & \text{if } len(texp_1) > 1 \end{cases}$$
  To denote that $texp_1$ is a (not necessarily contiguous) subsequence of $texp_2$.

Definition 7 (Sequence of values) For a trace $texp$, define
$$Val(texp) = \begin{cases} \langle\rangle & \text{if } texp = \langle\rangle \\ Val(texp_0)^\wedge exp & \text{if } texp = texp_0{}^\wedge(c, exp) \end{cases}$$

Definition 8 (Channels in an assertion) For an assertion ϕ we inductively define the set $chan(\phi)$ of channels such that $c \in chan(\phi)$ iff a communication along c might affect the validity of ϕ. We only give the most interesting cases; the rest can easily be defined by structural induction.

- $chan(c) = chan(\mu) = chan(v) = chan(t) = chan(\langle\rangle) = \varnothing$
- $chan(h) = CHAN$
- $chan(texp {\uparrow} cset) = chan(texp) \cap cset$

An assertion is interpreted with respect to a pair (θ, γ). Trace θ gives h its value; environment γ interprets the logical variables of $VVAR \cup TVAR$. In [18] we formally define when assertion ϕ holds for trace θ and environment γ, notation $(\theta, \gamma) \models \phi$.

Definition 9 (Validity of an assertion) An assertion ϕ is *valid*, denoted by $\models \phi$, iff for all θ and $\gamma : (\theta, \gamma) \models \phi$

Definition 10 (Validity of a correctness formula) For a process P and an assertion ϕ a correctness formula P **sat** ϕ is *valid*, denoted by $\models P$ **sat** ϕ, iff for all γ and all $\theta \in \mathcal{H}[\![P]\!] : (\theta, \gamma) \models \phi$

4 Incorporating Fault Hypotheses

Based on a particular fault hypothesis, the set of behaviours that characterize a process is expanded. To be able to formulate a nice proof rule for such an expansion, a fault hypothesis χ of process P is formalized as a predicate, expressed in a first-order assertion language. Such a predicate χ represents a reflexive relation between the normal and acceptable histories of P. To express this relation, χ has two free variables h and h_{old}. The interpretation is such that h_{old} represents a normal history of process P whereas h is an *acceptable* history of P with respect to χ. Such relations enable us to abstract from the precise nature of a fault and to focus on the abnormal behaviour it causes.

Thus, the assertion language is extended with the term h_{old}. Sentences of the extended language are called *transformation expressions*, with typical representative ψ. Similar to assertions, we can easily define $chan(\psi)$ by structural induction, using $chan(h_{old}) = CHAN$. A transformation expression is interpreted with respect to a triple $(\theta_0, \theta, \gamma)$. Trace θ_0 gives h_{old} its value, and, in conformity with the foregoing, trace θ gives h its value, and environment γ interprets the logical variables of $VVAR \cup TVAR$ (a formal definition is given in [18]).

For a transformation expression ψ we also write $\psi(h_{old}, h)$ to indicate that ψ has two free variables h_{old} and h. We use $\psi(texp_1, texp_2)$ to denote the expression which is obtained from ψ by replacing h_{old} by $texp_1$, and h by $texp_2$.

Definition 11 (Fault hypothesis) A fault hypothesis χ is a transformation expression which represents a reflexive relation between h and h_{old}. Also, χ must be prefix closedness preserving. Formally, we require

- $\models \chi(h_{old}, h_{old})$
- $\models (\chi(h_{old}, h) \wedge t \prec h) \rightarrow \exists t_{old} \preceq h_{old} : \chi(t_{old}, t)$

Example 1 (Loss). Consider a communication medium M that accepts messages via channel m_{in} and delivers them via channel m_{out}. Assume M is a FIFO buffer with a capacity of one message, that is, M **sat** $Val(h \uparrow m_{out}) \preceq^1 Val(h \uparrow m_{in})$. To formalize the hypothesis that M may lose messages we define:

$$
\begin{aligned}
loss \;\triangleq\;\; & h \uparrow \{m_{in}, m_{out}\} \trianglelefteq h_{old} \uparrow \{m_{in}, m_{out}\} \\
\wedge\;\; & h \uparrow m_{in} = h_{old} \uparrow m_{in}
\end{aligned}
$$

Using P to denote a process expressed in the programming language mentioned in Section 2, the syntax of our extended programming language is given by:

Failure Prone Process $FP ::= P \mid FP_1 \| FP_2 \mid FP \setminus cset \mid (FP \wr \chi)$

We require, in $(FP \wr \chi)$, $chan(\chi) \subseteq chan(FP)$. Then, $chan((FP \wr \chi)) = chan(FP)$, $chan(FP_1 \| FP_2) = chan(FP_1) \cup chan(FP_2)$, $chan(FP \setminus cset) = chan(FP) - cset$.
The trace semantics of a failure prone process is inductively defined as follows:

- $\mathcal{H}[\![FP_1 \parallel FP_2]\!] = \{\ \theta\ |\ \text{for } i = 1, 2,\ \theta{\uparrow}chan(FP_i) \in \mathcal{H}[\![FP_i]\!],$
  $\text{and } \theta{\uparrow}chan(FP_1 \parallel FP_2) = \theta\ \}$

- $\mathcal{H}[\![FP \setminus cset]\!] = \{\ \theta \setminus cset\ |\ \theta \in \mathcal{H}[\![FP]\!]\ \}$

- $\mathcal{H}[\![(FP \wr \chi)]\!] = \{\ \theta\ |\ \text{there exists a } \theta_0 \in \mathcal{H}[\![FP]\!] \text{ such that,}$
  $\text{for all } \gamma, (\theta_0, \theta, \gamma) \models \chi, \text{ and } \theta{\uparrow}chan(FP) = \theta\ \}$

The set $\mathcal{H}[\![(FP \wr \chi)]\!]$ represents the *acceptable* behaviour of FP under fault hypothesis χ. Note that, $\mathcal{H}[\![FP]\!] = \mathcal{H}[\![(FP \wr (h{\uparrow}chan(FP) = h_{old}{\uparrow}chan(FP)))]\!]$, and that, because of the reflexivity of χ, $\mathcal{H}[\![FP]\!] \subseteq \mathcal{H}[\![(FP \wr \chi)]\!]$. Also, observe that the semantics is defined such that if $\theta \in \mathcal{H}[\![FP]\!]$ then $chan(\theta) \subseteq chan(FP)$. In [18] we prove that this semantics is prefix closed.

Definition 12 (Composite transformation expression) Let ψ_1 and ψ_2 be transformation expressions. Then, $(\psi_1 \wr \psi_2)$ is defined by

$$(\psi_1 \wr \psi_2) \triangleq \exists t : \psi_1(h_{old}, t) \wedge \psi_2(t, h)$$

Since the interpretation of assertions has not been changed, the validity of correctness formula FP **sat** ϕ is defined as in Definition 10, replacing P by FP.

5 A Compositional Network Proof Theory

In this section we present a compositional proof theory to prove safety properties of networks of processes. Since we focus on the relation between fault hypotheses and concurrency, we have abstracted from the internal states of the processes and do not give rules for atomic statements, nor sequential composition. Such rules could be formulated by using an extended assertion language which includes program variables and a denotation to indicate termination (see, e.g., [21]).

Rule 5.1 (Consequence)
$$\frac{FP \text{ sat } \phi_1,\ \ \phi_1 \rightarrow \phi_2}{FP \text{ sat } \phi_2}$$

Rule 5.2 (Conjunction)
$$\frac{FP \text{ sat } \phi_1,\ \ FP \text{ sat } \phi_2}{FP \text{ sat } \phi_1 \wedge \phi_2}$$

Rule 5.3 (Invariance)
$$\frac{cset \cap chan(FP) = \emptyset}{FP \text{ sat } h{\uparrow}cset = \langle\rangle}$$

Rule 5.4 (Parallel composition)
$$\frac{FP_1 \text{ sat } \phi_1,\ \ FP_2 \text{ sat } \phi_2}{FP_1 \| FP_2 \text{ sat } \phi_1 \wedge \phi_2}$$

provided $chan(\phi_i) \subseteq chan(FP_i)$, for $i = 1, 2$, that is, the assertion that holds for one process may only refer to a channel of the other process if this concerns a channel connecting the two processes (cf. [8], [21]). Note that, as a consequence of this restriction, any occurrence of h in specification ϕ_i of process FP_i should be projected onto a subset of $chan(FP_i)$.

Rule 5.5 (Hiding)
$$\frac{FP \text{ sat } \phi \ , \quad chan(\phi) \cap cset = \varnothing}{FP \setminus cset \text{ sat } \phi}$$

Finally, for the introduction of a fault hypothesis we have

Rule 5.6 (Fault hypothesis introduction)
$$\frac{FP \text{ sat } \phi}{(FP \wr \chi) \text{ sat } (\phi \wr \chi)}$$

Observe that since ϕ is an assertion, h_{old} does not occur in ϕ, and hence also $(\phi \wr \chi)$ is an assertion.

Example 2 (Loss). Consider medium M and fault hypothesis *loss*, both defined in Example 1. By (Fault hypothesis introduction),

$(M \wr Loss)$ **sat** $\exists t : \quad Val(t \uparrow m_{out}) \preceq^1 Val(t \uparrow m_{in})$
$$\wedge \ h \uparrow \{m_{in}, m_{out}\} \trianglelefteq t \uparrow \{m_{in}, m_{out}\} \ \wedge \ h \uparrow m_{in} = t \uparrow m_{in}$$

Now, by $h \uparrow \{m_{in}, m_{out}\} \trianglelefteq t \uparrow \{m_{in}, m_{out}\}$, we have, obviously, $h \uparrow m_{out} \trianglelefteq t \uparrow m_{out}$, which, since $Val(t \uparrow m_{out}) \preceq^1 Val(t \uparrow m_{in})$, implies $Val(h \uparrow m_{out}) \trianglelefteq Val(t \uparrow m_{in})$. Then, by $t \uparrow m_{in} = h \uparrow m_{in}$,

$(M \wr Loss)$ **sat** $Val(h \uparrow m_{out}) \trianglelefteq Val(h \uparrow m_{in})$.

6 Example: The Alternating Bit Protocol

The alternating bit protocol [2], extended with timers, is a simple way to achieve communication over a medium that may lose messages. Consider the duplex communication medium of Figure 1, where A and M are media with fault hypothesis *loss* as already discussed in Example 2. Sender S accepts via *in* data from the environment, appends a bit to it, and sends it via m_{in}; the value of the bit alternates for successive messages, starting with 1. Receiver R awaits a message via m_{out}, and sends the bit via a_{in} as an acknowledgement; R only passes the data via *out* to the environment if the value of the message's bit differs from the value of the previous message's bit, or if it is the first message. Consequently, messages along M consist of data-bit pairs (d, b), such that $dat((d, b)) = d$ and $bit((d, b)) = b$. Medium A transmits bits. Under the alternating bit protocol, S keeps sending a message via m_{in} until its acknowledgement arrives via a_{out}. The alternating bit ensures that R can identify duplicates.

In this section we will prove that $ABP \triangleq S \| (M \wr loss) \| (A \wr loss) \| R$ satisfies safety property $Val(h \uparrow out) \preceq Val(h \uparrow in)$. For a trace *texp* where the messages are data-bit pairs, $RDMsg(texp)$ denotes the subsequence of *texp* that is obtained by removing subsequent records of which the messages have the same bit. $Dat(texp)$ denotes the sequence of data, and $Bit(texp)$ denotes the sequence of bits appearing in *texp*. For a trace *texp* where the messages are bits only, $RDAck(texp)$ denotes *texp* without duplicates.

The informal description of sender S given above can be formalized as follows.

S **sat** $\quad Dat(RDMsg(h \uparrow m_{in})) \preceq^1 Val(h \uparrow in)$
$$\wedge \ Val(RDAck(h \uparrow a_{out})) \preceq^1 Bit(RDMsg(h \uparrow m_{in}))$$

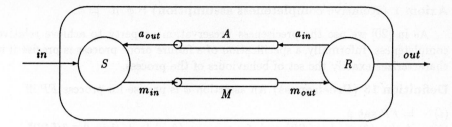

Fig. 1. Duplex communication medium

Similarly, we obtain the following specification for receiver R.

R **sat** $\quad Val(h{\uparrow}out) \preceq^1 Dat(RDMsg(h{\uparrow}m_{out}))$
$\quad\quad\quad \wedge\ Val(RDAck(h{\uparrow}a_{in})) \preceq^1 Bit(RDMsg(h{\uparrow}m_{out}))$

Then, by (Parallel composition) and (Consequence), we obtain:

ABP **sat** $\quad Dat(RDMsg(h{\uparrow}m_{in})) \preceq^1 Val(h{\uparrow}in)$ $\hfill (*)$
$\quad\quad\quad\quad \wedge\ Val(h{\uparrow}out) \preceq^1 Dat(RDMsg(h{\uparrow}m_{out}))$

In [18] we prove the following crucial property of the alternating bit protocol, using the results of Example 2.

Lemma 1 (Persistency)

ABP **sat** $\quad Val(RDAck(h{\uparrow}a_{out})) \preceq^1 Val(RDAck(h{\uparrow}a_{in}))$
$\quad\quad\quad\quad \wedge\ Dat(RDMsg(h{\uparrow}m_{out})) \preceq^1 Dat(RDMsg(h{\uparrow}m_{in}))$

Then, by (Consequence), we have

ABP **sat** $Dat(RDMsg(h{\uparrow}m_{out})) \preceq^1 Dat(RDMsg(h{\uparrow}m_{in}))$

which, by $(*)$, yields

ABP **sat** $Val(h{\uparrow}out) \preceq Val(h{\uparrow}in)$.

This shows that ABP tolerates loss of messages and acknowledgements.

7 Soundness and Relative Network Completeness

In [18] we prove that the proof theory of Section 5 is sound, that is, we prove that if a correctness formula is derivable then it is valid. Here we give the main steps of the proof that the proof system is complete, i.e., we prove that if a correctness formula is valid then it is derivable. As usual in such a completeness proof, we assume that we can prove any valid formula of the underlying (trace) logic (cf. [4]). Thus, using $\vdash \phi$ to denote that assertion ϕ is derivable, we add the following axiom to our proof theory.

Axiom 1 (Relative completeness assumption) $\vdash \phi$ if $\models \phi$

As in [20] we use the preciseness preservation property to achieve relative completeness. Informally, a specification of a failure prone process is precise if it characterizes exactly the set of behaviours of the process.

Definition 13 (Preciseness) An assertion ϕ is precise for process FP iff

(i) $\models FP$ **sat** ϕ.
(ii)   if $chan(\theta) \subseteq chan(FP)$ and, for some γ, $(\theta, \gamma) \models \phi$, then $\theta \in \mathcal{H}[\![FP]\!]$.
(iii) $chan(\phi) \subseteq chan(FP)$.

Let $\vdash P$ **sat** ϕ denote that correctness formula P **sat** ϕ is derivable. Note that no proof rules were given for the sequential aspects of processes, so our notion of completeness is relative to the assumption that for any sequential process there exists a precise assertion. This leads to the definition of *network* completeness.

Definition 14 (Network completeness) Assume that for every process P there exists a precise assertion ϕ with $\vdash P$ **sat** ϕ. Then, for any failure prone process FP and ϕ, $\models FP$ **sat** ϕ implies $\vdash FP$ **sat** ϕ.

The following lemma asserts that preciseness is preserved by the proof rules of Section 5. See [18] for the proof.

Lemma 2 (Preciseness preservation) Assume that for any process P there exists an assertion ϕ which is precise for P and $\vdash P$ **sat** ϕ. Then, for any failure prone process FP there exists an assertion ψ which is precise for FP and $\vdash FP$ **sat** ψ.

The following lemma asserts that any specification satisfied by a failure prone process is implied by the precise specification of that process. Since a precise specification only refers to channels of the process, and a valid specification might refer to other channels, we have to add a clause expressing that the process does not communicate on those other channels. The proof appears in [18].

Lemma 3 (Preciseness consequence) If ϕ_1 is a precise assertion for FP and $\models FP$ **sat** ϕ_2 then $\models (\phi_1 \wedge h{\uparrow}(chan(\phi_2) - chan(FP)) = \langle\rangle) \rightarrow \phi_2$

Now we can establish relative network completeness.

Theorem 1 Relative network completeness. The proof system of Section 5 is relatively network complete.

> *Proof*: Assume $\models FP$ **sat** ϕ. Further, assume that for every process P there exists a precise specification ϕ with $\vdash P$ **sat** ϕ. Then, by the preciseness preservation lemma, for any failure prone process FP there exists an assertion ψ which is precise for FP and $\vdash FP$ **sat** ψ (1).
> Since $(chan(\phi) - chan(FP)) \cap chan(FP) = \emptyset$, we obtain, by (Invariance), $\vdash FP$ **sat** $h{\uparrow}(chan(\phi) - chan(FP)) = \langle\rangle$ (2).
> By (1) and (2), $\vdash FP$ **sat** $\psi \wedge h{\uparrow}(chan(\phi) - chan(FP)) = \langle\rangle$, and thus, by the preciseness consequence lemma, the relative completeness assumption, and (Consequence), $\vdash FP$ **sat** ϕ.   □

8   Conclusions and Future Research

We have defined a trace-based compositional proof theory for fault tolerant systems. In this theory, the fault hypothesis of a process is formalized as a reflexive relation between the normal and acceptable behaviour of that process. With respect to existing SAT formalisms, only one new rule, namely the fault hypothesis introduction rule, is needed. We illustrated our method by proving a safety property of the alternating bit protocol. A related proof has been given in [13], also using traces. There, a less natural specification of the receiver evades the necessity to prove the property of persistency. In [18] we also prove properties of another well-known paradigm for fault tolerance, namely a triple modular redundant system.

In this report we only considered safety properties, ignoring liveness issues. Since the underlying trace logic is based on finite approximations, the proof theory we presented is not appropriate to deal with liveness properties. To reason about liveness properties, trace logic can be replaced by a more expressive logic, e.g. temporal logic. Then, instead of relating communication traces, a fault hypothesis relates normal and acceptable sequences of states. Consider, for instance, a system S whose state consists of 2 integers x and y, that is, $STATE_S = \{ \sigma \mid \sigma : \{x, y\} \to \mathbb{N} \}$. Let (μ_1, μ_2) denote a state σ with $\sigma(x) = \mu_1$ and $\sigma(y) = \mu_2$. Assume that in a sequence s of states a new state is recorded whenever the value of x or y changes. If transient memory faults occur, then it is possible that, instead of some intended sequence $s_{old} = (0, 0), (7, 0), \ldots$, we observe $s = (0, 0), (3, 0), (7, 0), \ldots$ because a fault affects the cell containing x before it is assigned the value 7. Observe that, in case the memory faults are transient, assigning 7 to x undoes the effect of the preceding fault.

We have also abstracted from the sequential aspects of processes. To reason about these aspects, often a proof system based on Hoare triples (see [6]) is more convenient. In such a proof system one reasons about correctness formulae of the form $\{p\}S\{q\}$ where S is a program, and p and q are assertions expressed in a first-order language. Informally, the triple $\{p\}S\{q\}$ means that if execution of S starts in a state satisfying p, and if S terminates, then the final state satisfies q.

Besides finding a logic to express fault hypotheses more elegantly, an obvious continuation of the research described in this report is the introduction of time into the formalism, to allow reasoning about properties of fault tolerant real-time systems. Then, the characterization that safety properties express that 'nothing bad will happen' and liveness properties express that 'eventually something good will happen' is, as indeed mentioned in [10], no longer appropriate. Consider, for instance, a communication medium that accepts messages via a channel *in* and relays them to a channel *out*. The property 'after a message is input to the medium via *in* it is output via *out* within 5 seconds' is a safety property, because it can be falsified after 5 seconds following an *in* communication. Note, however, that it expresses that something must happen. Hence, by adding time, the class of safety properties also includes progress properties.

Acknowledgements We would like to thank the referees for their useful remarks. Also, we would like to thank the members of NWO project 'Fault Tolerance: Paradigms, Models, Logics, Construction' for their comments.

References

1. Avižienis, A., Laprie, J.C.: Dependable Computing: From Concepts to Design Diversity, *Proceedings of the IEEE* **74**(5) (May 1986) 629–638.
2. Bartlett, K.A, Scantlebury, R.A., Wilkinson, P.T.: A Note on Reliable Full-Duplex Transmission over Half-Duplex Links, *CACM* **12**(5) (1969) 260–261.
3. Coenen, J., Hooman, J.: A Compositional Semantics for Fault Tolerant Real-Time Systems, *Lecture Notes in Computer Science* **571** (Springer, 1991) 33–51.
4. Cook, S.A.: Soundness and Completeness of an Axiom System for Program Verification, *SIAM Journal on Computing* **7**(1) (February 1978) 70–90.
5. Cristian, F.: A Rigourous Approach to Fault Tolerant Programming, *IEEE Trans. on Software Engineering* **SE–11**(1) (1985) 23 – 31.
6. Hoare, C.A.R.: An Axiomatic Basis for Computer Programming, *CACM* **12**(10) (1969) 576–580,583.
7. Hoare, C.A.R.: *Communicating Sequential Processes* (Prentice-Hall, 1985).
8. Hooman, J.: Specification and Compositional Verification of Real-Time Systems, *Lecture Notes in Computer Science* **558** (Springer, 1992).
9. Joseph, M., Moitra, A., Soundararajan, N.: Proof Rules for Fault Tolerant Distributed Programs, *Science of Computer Programming* **8** (1987) 43–67.
10. Lamport, L.: What Good is Temporal Logic, in: Manson, R.E., ed.: *Information Processing* (North-Holland, 1983) 657–668.
11. Laprie, J.C.: Dependable Computing and Fault Tolerance: Concepts and Terminology, *Proc. 15th Int. Symp. on Fault Tolerant Computing Systems* (IEEE Computer Society Press, 1985) 2–11.
12. Lee, P.A., Anderson, T.: *Fault Tolerance: Principles and Practice* (Springer, 1990).
13. Paliwoda, K., Sanders, J.W.: An Incremental Specification of the Sliding Window Protocol, *Distributed Computing* **5** (1991) 83–94.
14. Peleska, J.: Design and Verification of Fault Tolerant Systems with CSP, *Distributed Computing* **5** (1991) 95–106.
15. Randell, B., Lee, P.A., Treleaven, P.C.: Reliability Issues in Computing System Design, *ACM Computing Surveys* **10**(2) (June 1978) 123–165.
16. Schepers, H.: Terminology and Paradigms for Fault Tolerance, in: Vytopil, J., ed.: *Formal Techniques in Real-Time and Fault Tolerant Systems* (Kluwer Academic Publishers, 1993) 3–31.
17. Schepers, H.: Tracing Fault Tolerance, *Proc. 3rd IFIP Int. Working Conference on Dependable Computing for Critical Applications* (to appear).
18. Schepers, H., Hooman, J.: A Trace-Based Compositional Proof Theory for Fault Tolerant Distributed Systems, Eindhoven University of Technology, 1993.
19. Weber, D.G.: Formal Specification of Fault-Tolerance and its Relation to Computer Security, *ACM Software Engineering Notes* **14**(3) (1989) 273–277.
20. Widom, J., Gries, D., Schneider, F.B.: Trace-based network proof systems: expressiveness and completeness, *ACM TOPLAS* **14**(3) (July 1992) 396–416.
21. Zwiers, J.: Compositionality, Concurrency and Partial Correctness, *Lecture Notes in Computer Science* **321** (Springer, 1989).

A Kahn Principle for Networks of Nonmonotonic Real-time Processes

Robert Kim Yates[1]* and Guang Rong Gao[2]

[1] Lawrence Livermore National Laboratory, P.O. Box 808, Livermore CA 94551, USA
[2] McGill University, School of Computer Science, 3480 University St, Montreal
Quebec H3A 2A7, Canada

Abstract. We show that the input-output function computed by a network of asynchronous real-time processes is denoted by the unique fixed point of a Scott continuous functional *even though the network or its components may compute a discontinuous function*. This extends a well-known principle of Kahn to an important class of parallel systems that has resisted the traditional fixed point approach.

We present a fully abstract order-theoretic denotational semantics for networks of asynchronous real-time processes. The time-sensitive nature of the component processes allows them to compute functions which are not continuous, nor even monotonic, on the domain of timed message streams ordered by the usual prefix relation. Because of the discontinuous behavior of the components, the characterization of networks with nonmonotonic processes as fixed points of continuous functionals (the standard approach of denotational semantics, applied to untimed networks of monotonic processes by Kahn [6]) has been a much-sought but unattained goal. We show that the function computed by any timed network, even containing nonmonotonic processes, is identical to the unique fixed point of a continuous network functional whose construction is original.

1 Introduction

Complete partial orders[3] (cpos) and continuous[4] functions as used in the standard approach to denotational semantics embody a notion of finite approximation of infinite limits that is particularly appropriate for digital computation. Moreover, the Knaster-Tarski theorem and variants thereof guarantee the existence of fixed points to serve as solutions of sets of equations resulting from recursive programs or data types. In particular, if $f : D \rightarrow D$ is a continuous

---

* Work done while author Yates was a student at McGill University.

[3] A *partial order* $(D, \sqsubseteq)$ is a set D with reflexive, transitive and antisymmetric binary relation $\sqsubseteq$. Partial order $D, \sqsubseteq)$ is *complete* if every chain in D has a least upper bound in D. A *chain* is a nonempty subset $X \subseteq D$ with $x \sqsubseteq y$ or $y \sqsubseteq x$ for all $x, y \in X$. Element $u \in D$ is an *upper bound* of $X \subseteq D$ if $x \sqsubseteq u$ for all $x \in D$; u is the *least* upper bound of X $(u = \bigsqcup X)$ if $u \sqsubseteq z$ whenever z is an upper bound of X.

[4] Function f from cpo $(D, \sqsubseteq)$ to $(E, \leq)$ is *continuous* if $f(\bigsqcup_\sqsubseteq X) = \bigsqcup_\leq \{ f(x) \mid x \in X \}$ for any chain X. Then f is also monotonic, i.e., $f(x) \leq f(y)$ whenever $x \sqsubseteq y$.

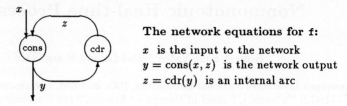

The network equations for f:

x is the input to the network

$y = \text{cons}(x, z)$ is the network output

$z = \text{cdr}(y)$ is an internal arc

Fig. 1. A network for program `f(x) = (cons x (cdr (f x)))`.

function on cpo $(D, \sqsubseteq)$ then $\mu f \overset{\text{def}}{=} \bigsqcup_{\sqsubseteq} \{ f^n(\bot) \mid n \geq 0 \}$[5] is guaranteed to be the least fixed point of f. That is, μf is the least element in D such that $\mu f = f(\mu f)$.

Consider the program `f(x) = (cons x (cdr (f x)))` in a lazy variant of a Lisp-like language. The denotation of `f` is the least function satisfying the recursive equation $f(x) = \text{cons}(x, \text{cdr}(f(x)))$, where functions are ordered pointwise by prefix.[6] To solve the equation, eliminate the recursion to obtain a nonrecursive functional, then take its least fixed point. Thus the meaning of `f` is given by function μF, for functional $F = \lambda f. \lambda x. \text{cons}(x, \text{cdr}(f(x)))$. Given any input x, the recursive equation for $f(x)$ will be satisfied by *any* list whose first element is x. This implies that there are many fixed points of F. The *least* fixed point is chosen as the denotation of `f` because it generates no gratuitous information, hence it corresponds to the input-output behavior expected from program `f`. E.g., if $x = a$ then $f(a) = a$ and $f(a) = ab^\infty$ are both valid solutions of equation $f(a) = \text{cons}(a, \text{cdr}(f(a)))$, but the least fixed point of F yields only the least solution: $[\mu F](a) = a$.

How do we know that functional F really has a fixed point? If F is continuous then the standard fixed point theorem of continuous functions on cpos guarantees that the least fixed point μF exists and is given by the equation $\mu F = \bigsqcup \{ F^n(\bot) \mid n \geq 0 \}$ (where $\bot$ here is the "everywhere empty" function that maps any pair of input streams to the empty stream Λ). But how do we know that F is continuous? The usual justification is that the components of F – cons, cdr and f – are continuous,[7] that application of a function to its arguments is continuous, and that function composition preserves continuity.

Kahn was the first to apply fixed point techniques to parallel programs. In [6], networks of determinate processes communicate asynchronously over unbounded FIFO channels, and the input-output function of any network is denoted by the least fixed point solution of the network's recursion equations. Program `f` could be a network of processes as shown in Fig. 1.

---

[5] Where $\bot$ is the least or so-called "bottom" element of D and f^n denotes repeated application of f n times.

[6] I.e., function f is less than or equal to g if $f(x)$ is a prefix of $g(x)$ for all inputs x.

[7] Dummy component f is known to be continuous because the functional F is defined to have the set of all continuous functions of the proper type as its domain.

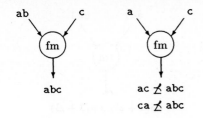

Input a is a prefix of ab and input c is a prefix of c, but neither of the possible outputs ac nor ca is a prefix of abc.

Fig. 2. Fair merge is not monotonic.

Kahn's principle is among the most important and elegant results in the theory of concurrency. However, in its original form it applies only to restricted programming models. In particular, a component process trying to read from one of its input ports must wait until a token is present before proceeding. This restriction precludes any problematic behavior by ensuring that the component processes compute continuous functions on the cpo of streams ordered by prefix.[8]

Some important stream operators are not so well behaved. Consider the *fair merge* operator which takes two possibly infinite streams of tokens and produces an interleaving of them, preserving the relative ordering of tokens from each individual input stream within the result. Clearly this requires the ability to check an input for the presence of data and continue on to do other things if none is present rather than blocking as in Kahn's formulation.[9] Fair merge mimics race conditions in concurrent systems and has been studied intensively. Keller [8] was the first to remark that fair merge is not monotonic in the cpo of streams ordered by prefix (Fig. 2).

We shall not deal here with non-determinate fair merge, but add a time tag to every token and let *timed merge* interleave them by their arrival order. The primary reason for this is a practical one: real-time systems are extremely important and we would like to contribute to the understanding of them.

We take a real-time network to be a fixed finite set of asynchronous determinate processes $A_1, \ldots, A_k$ that communicate by sending time-stamped tokens over unbounded FIFO channels. For each process or "node" A_a, $\mathbf{A}_a : \mathcal{S}^{i_a} \rightarrow \mathcal{S}^{o_a}$ denotes the function computed by A_a, where $i_a = \#(A_a^{in})$ is the number of input ports (channels) and $o_a = \#(A_a^{out})$ is the number of output ports of A_a. The set of all node output ports is denoted by A^{out}. Token values are chosen from a finite alphabet, and the sequence of tokens that appears on a channel forms a *stream*, with the time stamps strictly increasing and separated by a minimum temporal interval $\Delta > 0$. In this article we assume a single common alphabet, and denote the set of timed streams over this alphabet by $\mathcal{S}$. The time stamps are real values

---

[8] More precisely, the domain is the set of stream tuples ordered coordinatewise by prefix, i.e., $(x_1, \ldots, x_n)$ is less than or equal to $(y_1, \ldots, y_n)$ if and only if x_i is a prefix of y_i for all $i \in 1..n$.

[9] This intuition is proved valid by Panangaden and Stark in [14].

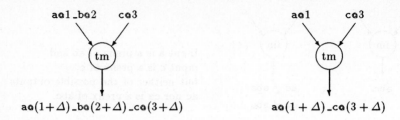

Input **ao1** (meaning token a arrives at time 1) is a prefix of **ao1_bo2** and **co3** is a prefix of **co3**, but output $ao(1+\Delta)\_co(3+\Delta)$ is not a prefix of $ao(1+\Delta)\_bo(2+\Delta)\_co(3+\Delta)$ (Δ is the time needed to transfer a token from input to output). Token sequence $co(3+\Delta)\_ao(1+\Delta)$ would not be a meaningful output because the times are not ascending.

Fig. 3. Timed merge is not monotonic.

and represent the time of appearance of a token as measured by a conceptual global clock. Each real-time processes executes a sequence of actions determined by its current state and the presence or absence of input tokens. A process may check one or more of its input channels for tokens and proceed to other things whether tokens are present or not. Every action consumes some determinate amount of time, greater than or equal to Δ. Communication between processes is instantaneous; delays can be modelled by interposing delay processes, with unpredictable delays modelled by providing the processes with extra inputs to control the amount of delay added between tokens. A network with i input and s output channels computes a function from i-tuples of streams to s-tuples of streams. Many real systems, from automated bank tellers to automated factories, can be described by such networks.

As shown in Fig. 3, timed merge is also nonmonotonic. It is easy to think of other real-time processes which compute nonmonotonic functions, e.g., the process which emits a token every cycle until it receives its first input token. It is this nonmonotonic (hence discontinuous) behavior that has made it difficult to extend Kahn's principle to networks containing merge nodes. In the traditional approach, the existence of the least fixed point of the functional for a set of recursive equations is guaranteed by the continuity of the components. *The functional of a real-time network can have nonmonotonic components, so how can the existence of the least fixed point be guaranteed?*

In the next section we review the traditional network functional for untimed networks of monotonic components. In section 3 we introduce the new network functional for real-time networks with nonmonotonic components. In section 4 we show that the new functional is continuous, and that its least fixed point describes the behavior of the network. Section 5 compares the results to previous work, and conclusions are drawn in the final section, 6.

2 The traditional functional for monotonic networks

In this section we aim to clarify the intuitions behind network functionals. Given a network N with i inputs and s outputs (one for every node output port[10]) composed of a collection of determinate blocking-read processes $A_1, \ldots, A_k$, Kahn's principle states that the network input-output function NetFun$_N$ computed by N operationally is described by the least fixed point $\mu\Phi$ of a functional Φ; i.e., NetFun$_N = \mu\Phi$, where the functional $\Phi : [\mathcal{S}^i \to \mathcal{S}^s] \to [\mathcal{S}^i \to \mathcal{S}^s]$ associated with network N is defined by the set of k equations

$$\Phi(f)(\sigma){\downarrow}A_a^{out} = \mathbf{A}_a((\sigma \otimes f(\sigma)){\downarrow}A_a^{in})$$

for all continuous functions $f \in [\mathcal{S}^i \to \mathcal{S}^s]$, inputs $\sigma \in \mathcal{S}^i$ and nodes $A_a \in A_1, \ldots, A_k$. The domain of functional Φ is the cpo $([\mathcal{S}^i \to \mathcal{S}^s], \overset{i \to s}{\preceq})$ of all continuous stream functions of i inputs and s outputs, with the functions ordered pointwise by prefix (i.e., $f \overset{i \to s}{\preceq} g$ if and only if $f(\sigma) \preceq^s g(\sigma)$ for all $\sigma \in \mathcal{S}^s$, where $\preceq^s$ is the coordinatewise prefix order: $(x_1, \ldots, x_s) \preceq^s (y_1, \ldots, y_s)$ if and only if $x_i \preceq y_i$ for all $i \in 1..s$ (each stream x_i is a prefix of the corresponding y_i)).

In the left side of the definition of the traditional Φ, expression $\Phi(f)(\sigma)$ denotes the s-tuple representing the value of all the output streams, in some canonical order, produced by function $\Phi(f) : \mathcal{S}^i \to \mathcal{S}^s$ given input $\sigma \in \mathcal{S}^i$; applying ${\downarrow}A_a^{out}$ then yields an o_a tuple by selecting only those streams representing the values at the output ports of node A_a, again in some canonical order. In the right side, $\sigma \otimes f(\sigma)$ denotes the tuple obtained by joining input $\sigma \in \mathcal{S}^i$ and output $f(\sigma) \in \mathcal{S}^s$ together into a single $i{+}s$-tuple; thus $\sigma \otimes f(\sigma)$ represents the contents of all the source ports of network N computing function f presented with input σ. Then applying ${\downarrow}A_a^{in}$ to $\sigma \otimes f(\sigma)$ yields an i_a-tuple by selecting only those streams representing the values at the input ports of node A_a. Finally, $\mathbf{A}_a : \mathcal{S}^{i_a} \to \mathcal{S}^{o_a}$ is the function computed by node A_a. The network functional is related to the *network equations* $H{\downarrow}A_a^{out} = \mathbf{A}_a(H{\downarrow}A_a^{in})$ $(\forall a \in 1..k)$, where unknown H is an $i{+}s$-tuple.

Because the node processes in the original Kahn principle are required to block on reads until data has arrived, every node function $\mathbf{A}_a$ is continuous in the coordinatewise prefix order, i.e., from domain $(\mathcal{S}^{i_a}, \preceq^{i_a})$ to codomain $(\mathcal{S}^{o_a}, \preceq^{o_a})$. Moreover, every function used in the definition of the network functional Φ is continuous, so Φ itself is continuous on cpo $([\mathcal{S}^i \to \mathcal{S}^s], \overset{i \to s}{\preceq})$ by the fact that composition preserves continuity. Then a standard theorem of semantic domain theory states that the least fixed point of Φ exists and is given by $\mu\Phi \overset{\text{def}}{=} \bigsqcup_{\substack{i \to s \\ \preceq}} \{ \Phi^n(\overset{i \to s}{\Lambda}) \mid n \geq 0 \}$ where $\overset{i \to s}{\Lambda}$ is the "everywhere empty" function defined by $\overset{i \to s}{\Lambda}(\sigma) = \Lambda^s$ for all $\sigma \in \mathcal{S}^i$, the bottom element of Φ's domain $([\mathcal{S}^i \to \mathcal{S}^s], \overset{i \to s}{\preceq})$. Since the application operator $\cdot(\sigma) : [\mathcal{S}^i \to \mathcal{S}^s] \to \mathcal{S}^s$

---

[10] In common with [10], we treat every node output as a network output even though it might only be attached to wires internal to the network.

is continuous by a standard theorem of semantic domain theory, we obtain $\mu\Phi(\sigma) = \bigsqcup_{\leq^s}\{\ \overset{i\to s}{\Lambda}(\sigma),\ \Phi(\overset{i\to s}{\Lambda})(\sigma),\ \Phi^2(\overset{i\to s}{\Lambda})(\sigma),\dots\}$. In other words, the least fixed point of network functional Φ is a function $\mu\Phi : S^i \to S^s$ whose value at any given input tuple σ is the "limit" (least upper bound) of the increasing sequence $\overset{i\to s}{\Lambda}(\sigma),\ \Phi(\overset{i\to s}{\Lambda})(\sigma),\ \Phi^2(\overset{i\to s}{\Lambda})(\sigma),\dots$.

To visualize this sequence, picture first the network N with the streams of input tuple σ placed on their individual network input wires, with all other wires holding the empty stream, represented by the $i+s$-tuple $\sigma\otimes\Lambda^s$; subtuple Λ^s is equal to $\overset{i\to s}{\Lambda}(\sigma)$, the first element of the sequence. To get the second element in the sequence, the definition of Φ instructs us to apply every node function, selecting the relevant input streams from tuple $\sigma\otimes\Lambda^s$ (the overall network trace generated by the previous application $\overset{i\to s}{\Lambda}(\sigma)$), then collect all the node outputs together into a new s-tuple of streams, call it θ, which is equal to $\Phi(\overset{i\to s}{\Lambda})(\sigma)$. Similarly, to get the third element in the sequence, apply every node function again, this time selecting the relevant input streams from $\sigma\otimes\theta$, the network trace generated by the previous application $\Phi(\overset{i\to s}{\Lambda})(\sigma)$, then collect all the node outputs together into yet another new s-tuple of streams, which is equal to $\Phi(\Phi(\overset{i\to s}{\Lambda}))(\sigma)$. Monotonicity of Φ ensures that $\Phi^n(\overset{i\to s}{\Lambda}) \overset{i\to s}{\preceq} \Phi^{n+1}(\overset{i\to s}{\Lambda})$, from which it follows that $\Phi^n(\overset{i\to s}{\Lambda})(\sigma) \preceq^s \Phi^{n+1}(\overset{i\to s}{\Lambda})(\sigma)$, i.e., for any given network output, the stream at that output in step n is always a prefix of the stream at that output in step $n+1$. Repeat the process until no change is seen on any of the wires. The least fixed point $\mu\Phi$ of network functional Φ is reached when no change is seen for *any* input $\sigma \in S^i$. Fig. 4 depicts an example of this scheme applied to a simple 1-input, 3-output network for the particular input point $\sigma = \mathrm{ac}$.

What happens if we use the traditional functional on a network containing nodes which compute nonmonotonic functions like timed merge? Fig. 5 shows a network similar to that of Fig. 4, but where all the tokens carry time tags and all the nodes impart a delay of one time unit; moreover, the blocking-read *alt* node has been replaced by a non-blocking timed merge node *tm*, which passes input tokens to the output in the order of their arrival, regardless of which input stream they belong to (with some rule for settling ties). Observe in Fig. 5 that in going from Φ^3 to Φ^4 the network output changes from $(\mathrm{a@2\_c@8, a@3, b@4})$ to $(\mathrm{a@2\_b@5\_c@8, a@3, b@4})$, wherein $\mathrm{a@2\_c@8}$ is not a prefix of $\mathrm{a@2\_b@5\_c@8}$, so set $\{\ \overset{i\to s}{\Lambda}(\sigma),\ \Phi(\overset{i\to s}{\Lambda})(\sigma),\ \Phi^2(\overset{i\to s}{\Lambda})(\sigma),\ \dots\}$ is not a chain in the coordinatewise prefix order $\preceq^3$, nor is $\{\ \overset{i\to s}{\Lambda},\ \Phi(\overset{i\to s}{\Lambda}),\ \Phi^2(\overset{i\to s}{\Lambda}),\ \dots\}$ a chain in the pointwise prefix order $\overset{1\to 3}{\preceq}$. Thus it is clear that when the network nodes are nonmonotonic, the traditional network functional Φ may itself be nonmonotonic. If the network functional is not monotonic then neither is it continuous, and the whole underpinning of the traditional Kahn principle collapses.

Alt takes input tokens from its left and right inputs in strict alternation, *hd* takes the first token from its input, and *suc* converts the value of every token to its successor in the alphabetic order (wrapping around from z to a).

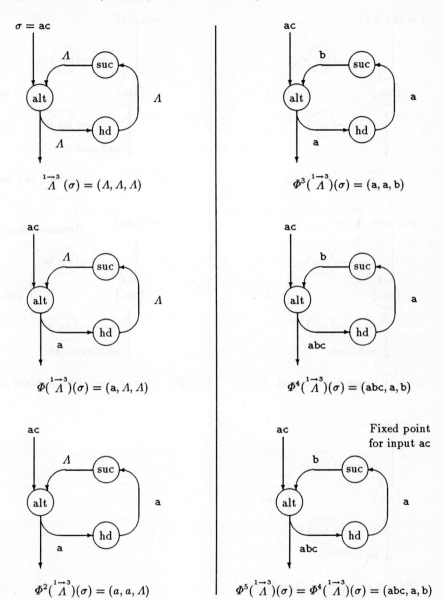

Fig. 4. Finding the traditional fixed point $\mu\Phi(\sigma)$.

Tm transmits tokens in order of their time of arrival, *hd* takes the first token from its input, and *suc* converts the value of every token to its successor in the alphabetic order (wrapping around from z to a). All three nodes impart a delay of one time unit.

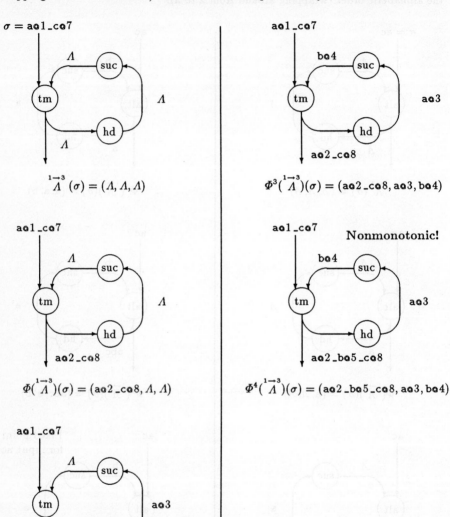

Fig. 5. Using the traditional functional on a nonmonotonic network.

The network is the same as in Fig. 5. *Tm* transmits tokens in order of their time of arrival, *hd* takes the first token from its input, and *suc* converts the value of every token to its successor in the alphabetic order. All impart a delay of one time unit.

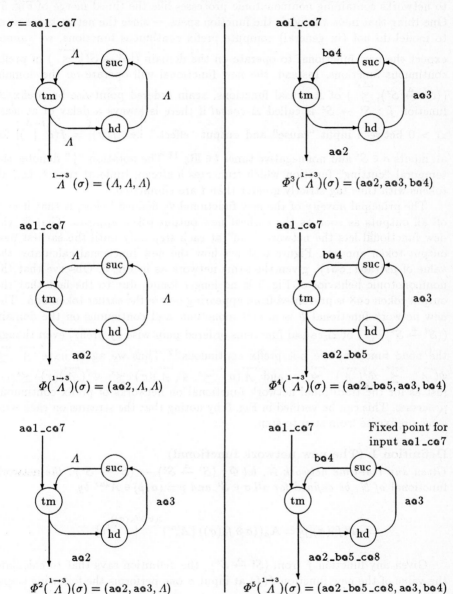

Fig. 6. Using the new functional Φ on a nonmonotonic network.

3   The new functional for real-time networks

How might one redefine the network functional to extend the Kahn principle to networks containing nonmonotonic processes like the timed merge of Fig. 5? One thing that must change is the function space — since the networks we want to model do not (in general) compute prefix continuous functions, we cannot expect the new functional to operate on the domain $([\mathcal{S}^i \to \mathcal{S}^s], \overset{i \to s}{\preceq})$ of prefix continuous functions. Instead, the new functional will operate on the domain $(\langle \mathcal{S}^i \overset{\Delta}{\to} \mathcal{S}^s \rangle, \overset{i \to s}{\preceq})$ of Δ-causal functions, again ordered pointwise by prefix. A function $f : \mathcal{S}^i \dashrightarrow \mathcal{S}^s$ is called Δ-causal if there is always a delay of at least $\Delta > 0$ between input "cause" and output "effect," i.e., $f(\sigma)\overset{t}{|} = f(\sigma \overset{t-\Delta}{|})\overset{t}{|}$ for all inputs $\sigma \in \mathcal{S}^i$ and nonnegative times $t \in \mathbb{R}_0$.[11] The notation "$\overset{t}{|}$" denotes the temporal "cutting" function which truncates a stream tuple at time t, i.e., all tokens with time tag strictly greater than t are eliminated.

The principal novelty of the new functional Φ, defined below, is that it cuts off all outputs as soon as the earliest new output token appears. That is, the new functional lets the network "run" at each step only until the earliest new output token appears. Figure 6 shows how the new functional calculates the value of $\mu\Phi(\text{a@1\_c@7})$, given the same network as in Fig. 5. Observe that the nonmonotonic behavior of Fig. 5 is no longer found, due to the fact that the output token c@8 is prevented from appearing before the earlier token b@5 . The new network functional Φ is in fact monotonic and continuous on the domain $(\langle \mathcal{S}^i \overset{\Delta}{\to} \mathcal{S}^s \rangle, \overset{i \to s}{\preceq})$ of Δ-causal functions ordered pointwise by prefix, even though the node functions are not prefix continuous.[12] Thus we again have $\overset{i \to s}{\Lambda} \overset{i \to s}{\preceq}$
$\Phi(\overset{i \to s}{\Lambda}) \overset{i \to s}{\preceq} \Phi^2(\overset{i \to s}{\Lambda}) \overset{i \to s}{\preceq} \cdots$ and $\overset{i \to s}{\Lambda}(\sigma) \preceq^s \Phi(\overset{i \to s}{\Lambda})(\sigma) \preceq^s \Phi^2(\overset{i \to s}{\Lambda})(\sigma) \preceq^s \cdots$
just as for the traditional network functional on networks of prefix continuous processes. This can be verified in Fig. 6 by noting that the streams on each wire grow prefixwise from step to step.

Definition 1 (The new network functional)
Given any real-time network N, let $\Phi : \langle \mathcal{S}^i \overset{\Delta}{\to} \mathcal{S}^s \rangle \to \langle \mathcal{S}^i \overset{\Delta}{\to} \mathcal{S}^s \rangle$, the network functional of N, be defined for all $\sigma \in \mathcal{S}^i$ and $p = (a, \dot{p}) \in A^{out}$ by

$$\Phi(f)(\sigma)[\dot{p}] = \mathbf{A}_a((\sigma \otimes f_N(\sigma)) \downarrow A^{in}_a)^{\natural(\sigma \otimes f_N(\sigma))} | [\dot{p}] .$$

Given any function f from $\langle \mathcal{S}^i \overset{\Delta}{\to} \mathcal{S}^s \rangle$, the definition says that to calculate the value of the new function $\Phi(f)$ at input σ one performs the following steps:

---

[11] Symbols $\mathbb{R}$ and $\mathbb{R}_0$ denote the reals and nonnegative reals, with $\mathbb{R}^\infty \overset{\text{def}}{=} \mathbb{R} \cup \{\infty\}$ and $\mathbb{R}_0^\infty \overset{\text{def}}{=} \mathbb{R}_0 \cup \{\infty\}$.

[12] The proof that Φ is continuous on cpo $(\langle \mathcal{S}^i \overset{\Delta}{\to} \mathcal{S}^s \rangle, \overset{i \to s}{\preceq})$ is long and tedious. An outline of the proof is given below; a full proof can be found in [17].

1. Convert f to f_N (this conversion is described in Def. 2 below).
2. Apply f_N to σ and weld input σ to the resulting s-tuple to get an $i+s$-tuple. This forms a new network snapshot $\sigma \otimes f_N(\sigma)$.
3. Project the new snapshot onto the set of ports A_a^{in}, picking out the inputs to node A_a. Do this for all the nodes $a \in 1..k$ in the network independently.
4. Apply the node function $\mathbf{A}_a$ to its inputs.
   Do this for all the nodes $a \in 1..k$ in the network independently.
5. Cut the results at time $\natural(\sigma \otimes f_N(\sigma))$.
   This allows no more than one new token to appear in any output stream.
   Function $\natural : \mathcal{S}_N^{i+s} \to \mathbb{R}_0^\infty$ is defined by $\natural(H) = \bigsqcup_{\leq} \{\, t \in \mathbb{R}_0 \mid \mathrm{Sat}_N(H, t)\,\}$.
   (See Defs. 4 and 2 below for the definitions of $\mathcal{S}_N^{i+s}$ and Sat_N.)
6. Put each new output stream in its proper place in the new output s-tuple, i.e., the $\dot{p}^{\text{th}}$ output stream of node A_a belongs in position $\dot{p}$, where $p = (a, \dot{p})$. For any node output port $p \in A^{out}$, integer $\dot{p}$ denotes the index of port p within a canonical total ordering of A^{out}.

All the components of Φ have already been defined, except for the *trimming functional* $\cdot_N$, which we now introduce.

Definition 2 *Given a TRTM network* $N = (A_1, \ldots, A_k, i, o, s, \mathrm{src})$, *let* $\cdot_N : \langle \mathcal{S}^i \xrightarrow{\Delta} \mathcal{S}^s \rangle \to \langle \mathcal{S}^i \xrightarrow{\Delta} \mathcal{S}^s \rangle_N$ *be the function defined by* $f_N(\sigma) = \bigsqcup_{\preceq^s} {}_f Y_\sigma$
for all $f \in \langle \mathcal{S}^i \xrightarrow{\Delta} \mathcal{S}^s \rangle$ *and* $\sigma \in \mathcal{S}^i$, *where*

$$
{}_f Y_\sigma \stackrel{\text{def}}{=} \{\, y \mid y \preceq^s f(\sigma) \wedge \mathrm{Sat}_N(\rho \otimes y,\, l)\, (\forall \rho \text{ s.t. } \rho \mid^{l-\Delta} = \sigma \mid^{l-\Delta}) \\ (\text{where } l = \mathrm{tlen}(y))\,\}
$$

$$
\langle \mathcal{S}^i \xrightarrow{\Delta} \mathcal{S}^s \rangle_N \stackrel{\text{def}}{=} \{\, f \in \langle \mathcal{S}^i \xrightarrow{\Delta} \mathcal{S}^s \rangle \mid \mathrm{Sat}_N(\sigma \otimes f(\sigma),\, \mathrm{tlen}(f(\sigma)))\ \text{for all } \sigma \in \mathcal{S}^i \,\}
$$

$$
\mathrm{Sat}_N(H, t) \stackrel{\text{def}}{=} H {\downarrow} A_a^{out} \mid^t = \mathbf{A}_a(H {\downarrow} A_a^{in}) \mid^t \ (\forall a \in 1..k)\ .
$$

Codomain $\langle \mathcal{S}^i \xrightarrow{\Delta} \mathcal{S}^s \rangle_N$ of functional $\cdot_N$ is a subspace of domain $\langle \mathcal{S}^i \xrightarrow{\Delta} \mathcal{S}^s \rangle$ wherein $f(\sigma)$ is a temporal prefix of the network solution for input σ, given $f \in \langle \mathcal{S}^i \xrightarrow{\Delta} \mathcal{S}^s \rangle_N$ and $\sigma \in \mathcal{S}^i$. Function $\mathrm{Sat}_N : (\mathcal{S}^{i+s} \times \mathbb{R}^\infty) \to \mathbb{T}$ is a predicate, where $\mathrm{Sat}_N(H, t)$ means that H satisfies the network equations through time t.

The purpose of the trimming functional $\cdot_N$ is to transform an arbitrary Δ-causal function $f \in \langle \mathcal{S}^i \xrightarrow{\Delta} \mathcal{S}^s \rangle$ into a function $f_N \in \langle \mathcal{S}^i \xrightarrow{\Delta} \mathcal{S}^s \rangle_N$ which is prefix-consistent with the network equations and is still Δ-causal. This is done because in taking an arbitrary function f from $\langle \mathcal{S}^i \xrightarrow{\Delta} \mathcal{S}^s \rangle$ there is no guarantee that f will have anything in common with the given network N other than being a Δ-causal function of i inputs and s outputs. The new function f_N is guaranteed to satisfy the network equations through its output length at every input point, i.e., $\mathrm{Sat}_N(\sigma \otimes f_N(\sigma),\, \mathrm{tlen}(f_N(\sigma)))$ for all $\sigma \in \mathcal{S}^i$. This is accomplished by taking the longest temporal cut of each output such that the desired result is achieved.

The trimming functional is a necessary "preprocessing" step of the network functional because without it Φ may be nonmonotonic when applied to "bad" functions, i.e., functions that are in $\langle \mathcal{S}^i \xrightarrow{\Delta} \mathcal{S}^s \rangle$ but not in $\langle \mathcal{S}^i \xrightarrow{\Delta} \mathcal{S}^s \rangle_N$. As shown in Fig. 7, the problem arises because of the presence of nonmonotonic

Let $\hat{\Phi}$ be like Φ but without the trimming functional, i.e., $\Phi = \hat{\Phi} \circ \cdot_N$, where

$$\hat{\Phi}(f)(\sigma)[\hat{p}] \;\stackrel{\text{def}}{=}\; \mathbf{A}_a\big((\sigma \otimes f(\sigma)) {\downarrow} A_a^{in}\big)^{\natural(\sigma \otimes f(\sigma))} \;|\; [\hat{p}] \qquad \forall\, \sigma \in S^i,\; p = (a, \hat{p}) \in A^{out}.$$

Let N be the network composed of node d and node $t1$ in sequence, where d delays every token by one time unit and $t1$ emits a z every cycle until it receives an input.

To demonstrate that $\hat{\Phi}$ is nonmonotonic it suffices to find two functions $f, g \in \langle S^1 \stackrel{\Delta}{\to} S^2 \rangle$ such that $f \stackrel{1 \to 2}{\preceq} g$ but $\textit{not}\ \hat{\Phi}(f) \stackrel{1 \to 2}{\preceq} \hat{\Phi}(g)$. Let $f(x) \stackrel{\text{def}}{=} (\Lambda, \Lambda)$ and $g(x) \stackrel{\text{def}}{=} (z{\otimes}1, a{\otimes}0)$ for all $x \in S$. Clearly f and g are Δ-causal since they are constant, and $f \stackrel{1 \to 2}{\preceq} g$ because $f(x) \preceq^2 g(x)$ for all $x \in S$. Note what happens on input $a{\otimes}0$.

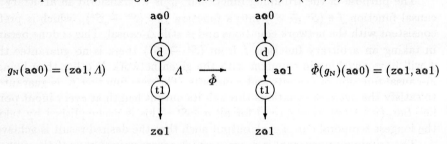

Since $\hat{\Phi}(f)(a{\otimes}0) = (z{\otimes}1, a{\otimes}1) \not\preceq^2 (\Lambda, a{\otimes}1) = \hat{\Phi}(g)(a{\otimes}0)$, $\hat{\Phi}$ is not monotonic. Note that the token $a{\otimes}0$ on the output arc of d is inconsistent with d's input $a{\otimes}0$. Functional $\cdot_N$ solves the problem by cutting g back to g_N, where $g_N(x) = (z{\otimes}1, \Lambda)$ for all $x \in S$.

Fig. 7. Without $\cdot_N$ the network functional is not monotonic.

components in real-time networks. The traditional functional for the networks of blocking-read processes treated in Kahn's theory does not need such a trimming step because all the network components compute monotonic functions.

4   The real-time Kahn principle

We shall show for any real-time network N that the functional Φ is continuous, and the least fixed point of Φ exactly describes the behavior of N.

The network functional Φ is continuous if and only if $\Phi(\bigsqcup F) = \bigsqcup F'$, where $F \subseteq \langle S^i \overset{\Delta}{\to} S^s \rangle$ is an arbitrary $\overset{i \to s}{\preceq}$-chain and $F' \overset{\text{def}}{=} \{ \Phi(f) \mid f \in F \}$. Since $\Phi(\bigsqcup F)$ and $\bigsqcup F'$ are functions in $\langle S^i \overset{\Delta}{\to} S^s \rangle$, to prove their equality we need to show

$$\Phi(\bigsqcup F)(\sigma)[\dot{p}] = (\bigsqcup F')(\sigma)[\dot{p}],$$

choosing arbitrary $\sigma \in S^i$ and port $p = (a, \dot{p}) \in A^{out}$.[13] By the definition of Φ,

$$\Phi(\bigsqcup F)(\sigma)[\dot{p}] = \mathbf{A}_a\big((\sigma \otimes (\bigsqcup F)_N(\sigma)) \downarrow A_a^{in}\big)^{\natural(\sigma \otimes (\sqcup F)_N(\sigma))} \mid \quad [\dot{p}].$$

Therefore, to prove Φ continuous we must show

$$\mathbf{A}_a\big((\sigma \otimes (\bigsqcup F)_N(\sigma)) \downarrow A_a^{in}\big)^{\natural(\sigma \otimes (\sqcup F)_N(\sigma))} \mid \quad [\dot{p}] = (\bigsqcup F')(\sigma)[\dot{p}]. \tag{1}$$

The definitions of F' and Φ and continuity of application[14] and indexing give

$$(\bigsqcup F')(\sigma)[\dot{p}] = \bigsqcup_{\preceq} \Big\{ \mathbf{A}_a\big((\sigma \otimes f_N(\sigma)) \downarrow A_a^{in}\big)^{\natural(\sigma \otimes f_N(\sigma))} \mid \quad [\dot{p}] \mid f \in F \Big\}.$$

Thus (1) is equivalent to the continuity of function $\mathscr{\Phi}_p : \langle S^i \overset{\Delta}{\to} S^s \rangle \to S$ given by

$$\mathscr{\Phi}_p(f) \overset{\text{def}}{=} \mathbf{A}_a\big((\sigma \otimes f_N(\sigma)) \downarrow A_a^{in}\big)^{\natural(\sigma \otimes f_N(\sigma))} \mid \quad [\dot{p}],$$

since if $\mathscr{\Phi}_p$ is continuous we have $\mathscr{\Phi}_p(\bigsqcup F) = \bigsqcup_{\preceq} \{ \mathscr{\Phi}_p(f) \mid f \in F \}$.

---

[13] That is, choose an arbitrary node output port p from A^{out}; call the first component a (the node number) and the second component $\dot{p}$ (the local output port number).

[14] In [17] it is proved that the application operator $\cdot(\sigma)$ that maps functions in cpo $(\langle S^i \overset{\Delta}{\to} S^s \rangle, \overset{i \to s}{\preceq})$ to output tuples in cpo $(S^s, \preceq^s)$ is continuous.

The proof is too long to include here, but in [17] the new network functional Φ is proven continuous by showing that $_\sigma\Phi_p$ is composed of continuous functions.

$$_\sigma\Phi_p \quad = \cdot[\dot{p}] \circ F_4 \circ F_3 \circ F_2 \circ \cdot_N$$

$$_\sigma\Phi_p(f) = \mathbf{A}_a((\sigma \otimes f_N(\sigma)) \downarrow A_a^{in}) \mid^{\natural(\sigma \otimes f_N(\sigma))} \quad [\dot{p}] \qquad \text{the definition of } _\sigma\Phi_p$$

$_\sigma\Phi_p \quad : \langle \mathcal{S}^i \xrightarrow{\Delta} \mathcal{S}^s \rangle \to \mathcal{S}$

ordered by $\overset{i \to s}{\preceq}$ and $\preceq$

$\cdot_N \quad : \langle \mathcal{S}^i \xrightarrow{\Delta} \mathcal{S}^s \rangle \to \langle \mathcal{S}^i \xrightarrow{\Delta} \mathcal{S}^s \rangle_N$

ordered by $\overset{i \to s}{\preceq}$ and $\overset{i \to s}{\preceq}$

Step 1: f_N is f stripped of all tokens inconsistent with N

$F_2(g) \quad = \sigma \otimes g(\sigma)$

$F_2 \quad : \langle \mathcal{S}^i \xrightarrow{\Delta} \mathcal{S}^s \rangle_N \to \mathcal{S}_N^{i+s}$

ordered by $\overset{i \to s}{\preceq}$ and $\sqsubseteq_N^{i+s}$

Step 2: $\sigma \otimes f_N(\sigma)$ is the net trace produced by f_N at σ

$F_3(H) \quad = (H, \natural(H))$

$F_3 \quad : \mathcal{S}_N^{i+s} \to \mathcal{S}_\tau^{i+s}$

ordered by $\sqsubseteq_N^{i+s}$ and $\sqsubseteq_\tau^{i+s}$

Step 3: $\natural(\sigma \otimes f_N(\sigma))$ is the time of the next new token

$F_4(H,t) = \mathbf{A}_a(H \downarrow A_a^{in}) \mid^t$

$F_4(\perp_\tau) = \Lambda^c$

$F_4 \quad : \mathcal{S}_\tau^{i+s} \to \mathcal{S}^c$

ordered by $\sqsubseteq_\tau^{i+s}$ and $\sqsubseteq^c$

where $c = \#(A_a^{out})$

Step 4: $\mathbf{A}_a(\sigma \otimes f_N(\sigma) \downarrow A_a^{in}) \mid^{\natural(\sigma \otimes f_N(\sigma))}$ run all nodes A_a until one of them emits a new token

$\cdot[\dot{p}] \quad : \mathcal{S}^c \to \mathcal{S}$

ordered by $\sqsubseteq^c$ and $\preceq$

Step 5: $\mathbf{A}_a(\sigma \otimes f_N(\sigma) \downarrow A_a^{in}) \mid^{\natural(\sigma \otimes f_N(\sigma))} \quad [\dot{p}]$ is the new stream at node A_a's p^{th} output port.

Definition 3 *For any $n \in \mathbb{N}$, let $\sqsubseteq^n$ be the relation on $\mathcal{S}^n$ defined by*

$$\rho \sqsubseteq^n \sigma \Leftrightarrow \rho = \sigma \mid^{tlen(\rho)}.$$

Definition 4 *Given a network $N = (A_1, \ldots, A_k, i, o, s, \mathrm{src})$, let*

$$\mathcal{S}_N^{i+s} \overset{def}{=} \{ \sigma \otimes \theta \mid \sigma \in \mathcal{S}^i \wedge \theta \in \mathcal{S}^s \wedge \mathrm{Sat}_N(\sigma \otimes \theta, tlen(\theta)) \},$$

and let $\sqsubseteq_N^{i+s}$ be the relation on $\mathcal{S}_N^{i+s}$ defined for all $\sigma, \rho \in \mathcal{S}^i$ and $\theta, \eta \in \mathcal{S}^s$ by

$$\sigma \otimes \theta \sqsubseteq_N^{i+s} \rho \otimes \eta \overset{def}{\Leftrightarrow} \sigma = \rho \wedge \theta \preceq^s \eta.$$

Definition 5 *Let* $S_\tau^{i+\bullet} = \{\, (\sigma \otimes \theta, t) \in S_N^{i+\bullet} \times \mathbb{R}_0^\infty \mid \theta \in S^s \wedge \text{tlen}(\theta) \le t \,\} \cup \{\bot_\tau\}$, *where* $\bot_\tau$ *is a new element not in* $S_N^{i+\bullet} \times \mathbb{R}_0^\infty$. *Let* $\sqsubset_\tau^{i+\bullet}$ *be the relation on* $S_\tau^{i+\bullet}$ *defined for all* $(\sigma \otimes \theta, t)$ *and* $(\rho \otimes \eta, u)$ *in* $S_N^{i+\bullet} \times \mathbb{R}_0^\infty$ *(* $\sigma, \rho \in S^i$ *and* $\theta, \eta \in S^s$ *) by*

$$\bot_\tau \sqsubset_\tau^{i+\bullet} (\sigma \otimes \theta, u)$$

$$(\sigma \otimes \theta, t) \sqsubset_\tau^{i+\bullet} (\rho \otimes \eta, u) \iff \sigma = \rho \wedge \theta = \eta\big\rceil^{<t} \wedge \text{tlen}(\theta) < \text{tlen}(\eta) \wedge t < u,$$

and let $\sqsubseteq_\tau^{i+\bullet}$ *be the reflexive closure of* $\sqsubset_\tau^{i+\bullet}$.

Proposition 6 *Sets* $S_N^{i+\bullet}$, $S_\tau^{i+\bullet}$ *and* S^c *ordered by* $\sqsubseteq_N^{i+\bullet}$, $\sqsubseteq_\tau^{i+\bullet}$ *and* $\sqsubseteq^c$ *are cpos. Functions* $\cdot_N$, F_2, F_3, F_4 *and* $\cdot[\check{p}]$ *described above are continuous. Functional* Φ *associated with real-time network* N *is continuous on cpo* $(\langle S^i \xrightarrow{\Delta} S^s \rangle, \overrightarrow{\preceq})$.

The next proposition states that Φ transforms every Δ-causal function into one that is guaranteed to be consistent with network N at every input, up through the last output token (but not necessarily beyond). In other words, the result of applying Φ is always a (pointwise) temporal prefix of the full solution of the network equations.

Proposition 7 *Let* N *be a real-time network, with network functional* Φ. *Then* $\Phi(f) \in \langle S^i \xrightarrow{\Delta} S^s \rangle_N$ *for all* $f \in \langle S^i \xrightarrow{\Delta} S^s \rangle$.

The Kahn principle will follow almost directly from the next proposition, which states that if applying Φ causes no change at a particular snapshot then we have reached the complete solution to the net equations for the given input.

Proposition 8 *Given real-time network* N, *let* f *be any function in* $\langle S^i \xrightarrow{\Delta} S^s \rangle_N$ *and* σ *be any tuple in* S^i. *If* $f(\sigma) = \Phi(f)(\sigma)$ *then* $\text{Sat}_N(\sigma \otimes f(\sigma), \infty)$.

A real network run certainly satisfies the network equations.

Proposition 9 *For any real-time network* N *and input* $\sigma \in S^i$, *the history* $\sigma \otimes \text{NetFun}_N(\sigma)$ *obtained by running the network on input* σ *satisfies the network equations of* N; *that is,* $\text{Sat}_N(\sigma \otimes \text{NetFun}_N(\sigma), \infty)$.

The delays imparted by causal functions ensure that any solution to the network equations is unique.

Proposition 10 *Let* N *be a real-time network. For any* $\sigma \in S^i$, $\theta \in S^s$ *and* $t \in \mathbb{R}^\infty$ *such that* $\text{Sat}_N(\sigma \otimes \theta, t)$, $\text{Sat}_N(\sigma \otimes \eta, t) \iff \theta\big\rceil^t = \eta\big\rceil^t$.

At last everything needed to prove the extended Kahn principle is assembled. We have tried to make it clear in the earlier examples and discussion just how repeated application of the network functional actually traces out, for any given network input, the same sequence of snapshots that would be produced by actually running the network. If the explanations have fulfilled their purpose, the validity of the Kahn principle for real-time networks should come as no surprise.

Theorem 11 (Kahn principle for real-time networks) *Let N be a real-time network, with functional Φ. Then* $\mathrm{NetFun}_N = \mu\Phi$, *the least fixed point of Φ.*

Proof. By Prop. 6, functional Φ is continuous on domain $(\langle \mathcal{S}^i \overset{\Delta}{\to} \mathcal{S}^s \rangle, \overset{i \to s}{\preceq})$, so the least fixed point $\mu\Phi = \bigsqcup_{\substack{i \to s \\ \preceq}} \{\, \Phi^n(\overset{i \to s}{\Lambda}) \mid n \geq 0 \,\}$ is well defined (where $\overset{i \to s}{\Lambda}$ is the "everywhere empty" function, the bottom element of Φ's domain).

We must show $\mathrm{NetFun}_N(\sigma) = \mu\Phi(\sigma)$ for all $\sigma \in \mathcal{S}^i$. By Prop. 9, $\sigma \otimes \mathrm{NetFun}_N(\sigma)$ satisfies the network equations, i.e., $\mathrm{Sat}_N(\sigma \otimes \mathrm{NetFun}_N(\sigma), \infty)$. We know by Prop. 10 that any two solutions to the network equations sharing the same network input are identical. Therefore to prove $\mathrm{NetFun}_N(\sigma) = \mu\Phi(\sigma)$ it suffices to show that $\sigma \otimes \mu\Phi(\sigma)$ satisfies the network equations, i.e., $\mathrm{Sat}_N(\sigma \otimes \mu\Phi(\sigma), \infty)$. In fact, we shall prove that $\sigma \otimes f(\sigma)$ satisfies the network equations given *any* fixed point $f = \Phi(f)$.

Let $f = \Phi(f)$ be an arbitrary fixed point of network functional Φ and σ be an arbitrary tuple from $\mathcal{S}^i$. Then we have

$$
\begin{aligned}
\Phi(f) &\in \langle \mathcal{S}^i \overset{\Delta}{\to} \mathcal{S}^s \rangle_N && \text{by Prop 7}\\
f &\in \langle \mathcal{S}^i \overset{\Delta}{\to} \mathcal{S}^s \rangle_N && \text{since } f = \Phi(f)\\
f(\sigma) &= \Phi(f)(\sigma) && \text{since } f = \Phi(f)\\
\mathrm{Sat}_N&(\sigma \otimes f(\sigma), \infty) && \text{by Prop 8}\\
\mathrm{Sat}_N&(\sigma \otimes \mathrm{NetFun}_N(\sigma), \infty) && \text{by Prop 9}\\
\mathrm{NetFun}_N(\sigma) \overset{\infty}{|} &= f(\sigma) \overset{\infty}{|} && \text{by Prop 10}\\
\mathrm{NetFun}_N(\sigma) &= f(\sigma) && \text{since } x = x \overset{\infty}{|} \text{ for any } x \in \mathcal{S}^n.
\end{aligned}
$$

$\square$ (End of proof of Theorem 11.)

In other words, the function computed by any real-time network is identical to the least fixed point $\mu\Phi$ of network functional Φ. In fact, $\mu\Phi$ is the *unique* fixed point of Φ.

The equivalence between denotation and operation means that the denotational semantics is fully abstract.[15] However, the identity $\mathrm{NetFun}_N = \mu\Phi$ does not capture the kind of equivalence we really are after, since the output of both NetFun_N and $\mu\Phi$ includes the contents of all the internal arcs of network N. As mentioned in the discussion of NetFun_N, the internal arcs of the network are treated as outputs because this simplifies the proof of the Kahn principle. However, we would in fact prefer two networks to be equivalent (both operationally and denotationally) if given the same input they produce the same streams on their true output ports, regardless of the number or contents of any internal arcs.[16] For instance, a network composed of two nodes in sequence each of which

---

[15] A semantics is *fully abstract* if any two program phrases behave identically whenever their denotations are identical. In the case of real-time networks, our semantics is fully abstract because $(\mathrm{NetFun}_{N_1} = \mathrm{NetFun}_{N_2}) \Leftrightarrow (\mu\Phi_{N_1} = \mu\Phi_{N_2})$, where Φ_{N_1} and Φ_{N_2} are the functionals associated with networks N_1 and N_2.

[16] By a *true output* we mean any arc that connects the output of a node to the environment, and by an *internal* arc we mean any arc that connects two nodes.

delays its input tokens by t ought to be equivalent to a network with a single node which delays its inputs by $2t$. We would like the internal arcs to be hidden. Let Hide : $(\mathcal{S}^i \rightarrow \mathcal{S}^s) \rightarrow (\mathcal{S}^i \rightarrow \mathcal{S}^o)$ be defined by $\text{Hide}(f)(\sigma) = f(\sigma){\downarrow}N^{out}$ for all $\sigma \in \mathcal{S}^i$. That is, Hide takes a function $f : \mathcal{S}^i \rightarrow \mathcal{S}^s$ and produces a function $\text{Hide}(f) : \mathcal{S}^i \rightarrow \mathcal{S}^o$ by discarding, for all inputs $\sigma \in \mathcal{S}^i$, all the streams of $f(\sigma)$ that correspond to internal arcs of the network N. By taking the denotation of a network to be $\text{Hide}(\mu\Phi)$ we get a fully abstract semantics in which the internal arcs are unobservable, as desired.

5 Related work

We find it interesting that there exists a continuous network functional suitable for extending the Kahn principle to nonmonotonic real-time networks, but acknowledge that the proof of continuity outlined here (and presented in full in [17]) is long and tedious. In [17] there is another, simpler proof of the same Kahn principle that uses the expansiveness[17] of Φ on the subdomain $\langle \mathcal{S}^i \overset{\triangle}{\rightarrow} \mathcal{S}^s \rangle_N$ of "good" functions in place of continuity. In later work [18] it is shown that iterating the traditional network functional (with the domain changed to $\langle \mathcal{S}^i \overset{\triangle}{\rightarrow} \mathcal{S}^s \rangle$ rather than $[\mathcal{S}^i \rightarrow \mathcal{S}^s]$) also produces the same unique fixed point; the technique used is that of contractive functions on complete metric spaces.

Other work in the theory of timed systems has centered on temporal logic ([4, 9], etc.) and algebraic-operational models like CSP and CCS ([12, 16] and others), with some work being done in automata theory ([1, 5, 11] and others). The literature on the semantics of networks with indeterminate untimed operators would easily fill a large book. We comment only on work most closely related to timed merge.

Hiaton theories [2, 7, 13, 15] make fair merge monotonic by inserting special tokens into streams to represent the absence of data. Hiaton theories are related to the semantics presented here in so far as hiatons are sometimes construed to signify the passage of an unspecified length of time.

Boussinot [2] was the first to employ hiatons in the semantics of networks with nonmonotonic merge operators. Hiatons, used together with oracles, do make merge continuous and solve the causality anomalies of Keller [8] and Brock and Ackerman [3]. However, Boussinot's semantics lacks full abstractness.[18] For example, the "identity" function id_τ on hiatonned streams must prepend a hiaton to the head of its output, with the effect that $\text{id}_\tau(x) = \tau x \neq \tau\tau x = \text{id}_\tau(\text{id}_\tau(x))$. Thus the denotational semantics distinguishes between a network composed of two id_τ nodes in sequence and the network composed of a single id_τ node, whereas operationally the networks are indistinguishable.

---

[17] A function f on partial order $(D, \sqsubseteq)$ is *expansive* if $x \sqsubseteq f(x)$ for all $x \in D$.

[18] To say that a semantics is *fully abstract* means that two program phrases behave identically (are interchangeable in any context) if and only if their denotations are identical. Full abstraction is considered a desirable property, since it means that the semantics has just the right information to be compositional, and no more.

Park [15] simplified and improved on Boussinot's theory. He presents a lucid discussion of the problematic nature of fair merge and shows why hiatons (or something similar) are needed if fair merge is to be continuous. Like [2], the result is a fixed point semantics lacking full abstractness, and for the same reasons.

In an unusual use of abstract interpretation justified by category theory, Panangaden [13] injects hiatons into streams to derive the meaning of a network, and then filters them out. In this theory hiatons are generated only when a poll operation detects that no input data is present; this is a marked advantage over the work of Boussinot and Park. The semantics might be fully abstract, but this is still an open question.

Kearney and Staples [7] make some technical improvements on Park's work by relaxing some of the rules on hiaton generation and by giving a compositional treatment of oracle inputs. However, the result is still not fully abstract.

Park says of hiatons that "[t]his device is displeasing, since it does not seem sufficiently 'abstract' " [15]. We would argue that hiatons are either too abstract or not abstract enough. If time delays are unobservable in the operational semantics then hiatons are not abstract enough, as seen by the lack of full abstraction in theories using them. On the other other hand, if time delays *are* to be observable in the operational model then hiatons are too abstract to carry much useful information. Hiatons could be *made* useful if they were to represent something concrete, like a failed poll as in [13] or a specific time delay. Hiatons are an abstraction of delays. Why not just put real delays into the semantics?

6 Conclusions

We have set forth a denotational semantics of real-time dataflow networks. To that end we described timed streams, their orderings and some operations upon them. A new network functional was defined and shown to be continuous, even when the network components are nonmonotonic. Subsequently it was shown that the least (in fact, unique) fixed point of the network functional is identical to the function computed by the network.

The method is successful because iterating the network functional starting from the everywhere-empty function traces out, input point-wise, the same sequence of snapshots that an observer would see traced out by a real network execution. The conclusion to draw is that it really doesn't matter whether the network components are monotonic or not. The continuity of the network functional is determined by what it does to chains of functions, not by what the component functions do to chains of input tuples.

There is much room for improvement in the design, construction and validation of parallel and real-time programs. The most successful methods for reasoning about concurrency have been the operational-algebraic methods typified by CSP and CCS. Might the ideas explored here be used to develop new or modify existing techniques for reasoning about parallel programs?

References

1. R. Alur and D. Dill. The theory of timed automata. In J.W. deBakker, C. Huizing, W.P deRoever, and G. Rozenberg, editors, *Real-Time: Theory in Practice*, pages 45–73. Springer-Verlag, LNCS 600, 1991. Proceedings of the REX Workshop.
2. F. Boussinot. Proposition de sémantique dénotationelle pour des réseaux de processus avec operateur de mélange équitable. *Theoretical Computer Science*, 18:173–206, 1982.
3. J. D. Brock and W. B. Ackerman. Scenarios: A model of non-determinate computation. In J. Diaz and I. Ramos, editors, *International Colloquium on Formalization of Programming Concepts*, pages 252–259. Springer-Verlag, LNCS-107, 1981.
4. E. Harel, O. Lichtenstein, and A. Pnueli. Explicit clock temporal logic. In *Proc. of the Fifth Annual IEEE Symposium on Logic in Computer Science*, pages 402–413, 1990.
5. T.A. Henzinger, Z. Manna, and A. Pnueli. Timed transition systems. In J.W. deBakker, C. Huizing, W.P deRoever, and G. Rozenberg, editors, *Real-Time: Theory in Practice*, pages 226–251. Springer-Verlag, LNCS 600, 1991. Proceedings of the REX Workshop.
6. G. Kahn. The semantics of a simple language for parallel processing. In *Information Processing 74*, pages 471–475, 1974.
7. P. Kearney and J. Staples. An extensional fixed-point semantics for nondeterministic data flow. *Theoretical Computer Science*, 91:129–179, 1991.
8. R. M. Keller. Denotational models for parallel programs with indeterminate operators. In E. J. Neuhold, editor, *Formal Descriptions of Programming Concepts*, pages 337–365, Amsterdam, 1978. North-Holland.
9. R. Koymans. Specifying real-time properties with metric temporal logic. *Real Time Systems*, 2(4):255–291, 1990.
10. N. A. Lynch and E. W Stark. A proof of the Kahn principle for input/output automata. *Information and Computation*, 82(1):81–92, 1989.
11. M. Merritt, F. Modugno, and M.R. Tuttle. Time-constrained automata. In J.C.M. Baeten and J.F. Groote, editors, *Proceedings of Concur '91*, pages 408–423. Springer-Verlag, LNCS 527, 1991.
12. F. Moller and C. Tofts. A temporal calculus of communicating systems. In J.C.M. Baeten and J.W. Klop, editors, *Proceedings of Concur '90*, pages 401–415. Springer-Verlag, LNCS 458, 1990.
13. P. Panangaden. Abstract interpretation and indeterminacy. In S. D. Brookes, A. W. Roscoe, and G. Winskel, editors, *Proc. of the Seminar on Concurrency*, pages 497–511. Springer-Verlag, LNCS-197, 1985.
14. P. Panangaden and E. W. Stark. Computations, residuals and the power of indeterminacy. In T. Lepisto and A. Salomaa, editors, *Proc. of the Fifteenth International Colloquium on Automata Languages and Programming*, pages 348–363. Springer-Verlag, LNCS-317, 1988.
15. D. Park. The fairness problem and nondeterministic computing networks. In J.W. de Bakker and J. van Leeuwen, editors, *Foundations of Computer Science IV, Part 2*, pages 133–161. Mathematical Centre, Tract #159, 1983.
16. G.M. Reed and A.W. Roscoe. A timed model for communicating sequential processes. *Theoretical Computer Science*, 58:249–261, 1988.
17. R.K. Yates. *Semantics of timed dataflow networks*. PhD thesis, McGill University, 1992.
18. R.K. Yates. Networks of real-time processes. Submitted for publication, 1993.

Adaptive Multicast Wormhole Routing in 2D Mesh Multicomputers

Xiaola Lin, Philip K. McKinley, and Abdol-Hossein Esfahanian

Department of Computer Science
Michigan State University
East Lansing, Michigan 48824-1027, USA

Abstract. We study the issues of adaptive multicast wormhole routing in 2D mesh multicomputers. Three adaptive multicast wormhole routing strategies are proposed and studied, which include minimal partial adaptive, minimal fully adaptive and nonminimal multicast routing methods. All the algorithms are shown to be deadlock-free. These are the first deadlock-free adaptive multicast wormhole routing algorithms ever proposed. A simulation study has been conducted that compares the performance of these multicast algorithms. The results show that the minimal fully adaptive routing method creates the least traffic, however, double vertical channels are required in order to avoid deadlock. The nonminimal routing algorithm exhibits the best adaptivity, although it creates more network traffic than the other methods.

1 Introduction

Efficient communication among nodes is critical to the performance of massively parallel computers. A *multicast* communication service is one in which the same message is delivered from a source node to an arbitrary number of destination nodes. Both *unicast*, which involves a single destination, and *broadcast*, which involves all nodes in the network, are special cases of multicast. Multicast communication has several uses in large-scale multiprocessors [1].

Efficient implementation of multicast communication services depends on the particular system architecture, which includes the network topology and underlying switching technique. Two-dimensional (2D) mesh direct networks have become a popular interconnection architecture for constructing large-scale distributed-memory multiprocessors. Networks with mesh topologies offer massive parallelism and are more scalable than many other approaches to multiprocessor interconnection. Formally, an $m \times n$ 2D mesh consists of $N = m \times n$ nodes; each node has integer coordinate (x, y), $0 \leq x < m$ and $0 \leq y < n$. Two nodes with coordinates (x_i, y_i) and (x_j, y_j) are connected if and only if channel $|x_i - x_j| + |y_i - y_j| = 1$. The 2D mesh topology is used in the Symult 2010, the Intel Touchstone DELTA, and the Intel Paragon.

Wormhole routing has become the predominant switching strategy in new generation parallel machines. In wormhole routing, a packet is divided into a number of *flits* for transmission. The header flit(s) of a packet governs the route, and the remaining flits follow in a pipeline fashion. The two salient features of wormhole routing are that (1) only minimal buffers are required and (2) the network latency is distance-insensitive when there is no channel contention. In wormhole-routed systems, each node contains a separate *router* to handle such communication-related tasks. For a survey of wormhole routing in direct networks, please refer to [2].

Because messages may hold some channels while waiting for others, wormhole routing is particularly susceptible to deadlock. Typically, deadlock is avoided in the routing algorithm, which determines the path followed by a packet in order to reach its destination(s). Routing can be classified as *deterministic* or *adaptive*. In deterministic routing, the path is completely determined by the source and destination addresses. A routing technique is adaptive if, for a given source and destination, which path is taken by a particular packet depends on dynamic network conditions, such as the presence of faulty or congested channels. Further, a routing algorithm is said to be *minimal* if the path selected is one of the shortest paths between the source and destination pair. Using a minimal routing algorithm, every channel visited will bring the packet closer to the destination. A *nonminimal* routing algorithm allows packets to follow a longer path, usually in response to current network conditions.

Several adaptive routing algorithms have been proposed for unicast communication in wormhole-routed networks [3, 4, 5]. We have previously developed deterministic deadlock-free multicast algorithms for wormhole-routed networks [6], and other researchers have studied adaptive, fault-tolerant multicast routing for networks using store-and-forward switching [7]. As will be explained in detail in next section, none of these methods alone can be used to provide deadlock-free adaptive multicast wormhole routing.

In this paper, we present three deadlock-free adaptive multicast routing algorithms for wormhole-routed 2D mesh networks. The fundamental concept behind the algorithms is that one or more worms is sent out from the source, each visiting a subset of the destinations. In Section 2, we discuss the issues involved in designing such algorithms so that they are both adaptive and deadlock-free. Section 3 presents a partially adaptive minimal multicast routing algorithm. In Section 4, a fully adaptive minimal multicast routing method is given; achieving full adaptivity requires additional channels in the network. In Section 5, we propose a nonminimal adaptive multicast algorithm based on node-labeling assignment used in our deterministic multicast algorithms [6]. Simulation results of all the proposed adaptive routing algorithms are presented in Section 6. Section 7 contains concluding remarks.

2 Deadlock and Adaptive Multicast Wormhole Routing

One of the most important issues in designing an adaptive multicast routing algorithm is how to guarantee freedom from deadlock. A deadlock occurs when two or more messages are delayed forever due to a cyclic dependency among their requested resources. In wormhole-routed networks, the critical resources are channels. Since blocked messages are not buffered at intermediate nodes and not removed from the network, one way to avoid deadlock is to guarantee that no cyclic dependency may arise in channel usage.

The deadlock problem in wormhole networks has long been studied, and various deadlock-free routing algorithms have been suggested for deterministic unicast communication [8, 6]. For example, deadlock can be easily avoided by assigning each channel a unique number and allocating channels to packets in strictly ascending (or descending) order. A channel numbering scheme often used in n-dimensional meshes is based on the dimension of channels. In such *dimension ordered routing*, each packet is routed in one dimension at a time, arriving at the proper coordinate in each dimension before proceeding to the next dimension. By enforcing a strictly monotonic order on the dimensions traversed, deadlock-free routing is guaranteed. Examples of dimension-ordered routing include XY routing for the 2D mesh and E-cube routing for the hypercube [2].

Several deadlock-free adaptive unicast routing methods have been proposed that are based on the use of virtual channels in the network. In the *virtual network model* [3], for example, there are two virtual channels for each physical channel in a 2D mesh. The network is divided into four acyclic subnetworks used to reach nodes to the northeast, southeast, southwest, and northwest, respectively, of the source node. This method produces a minimal deadlock-free routing algorithm. Actually, adding double channels in only one dimension of a 2D mesh is sufficient to produce a minimal *fully*-adaptive routing algorithm [4]. Providing deadlock-free, minimal, fully-adaptive routing algorithms for the hypercube, 2D-torus, or more general k-ary n-cube topologies requires more additional channels [4]. Non-minimal adaptive routing algorithms based on the use of additional channels have also been proposed [9].

Recently, another approach to adaptive wormhole routing has been proposed which does not require additional channels. The *turn model* [5] provides a systematic approach to the development of both minimal and nonminimal adaptive routing algorithms for a given network. The fundamental concept behind the turn model is to prohibit the smallest number of turns such that cyclic dependencies among channels are prevented.

Before discussing adaptive multicast routing, a brief review of deterministic multicast is in order. Currently, most multicomputers support only unicast communication in hardware. In these environments, multicast must be implemented in software by sending multiple unicast messages. One method is to send a separate copy of the message from the source to every destination. Depending on the number of destinations, this strategy may require excessive time because many systems allow a local processor to send only one message at a time. Although we have previously developed very efficient algorithms to support multicast in software [1], performance can be further improved by implementing multicast communication in hardware. In this paper, we are concerned only with hardware-supported multicast communication.

Hardware-supported wormhole multicast can be either *tree-based* or *path-based*. In *tree-based* routing, the destination set is partitioned at the source, and separate copies are sent on one or more outgoing channels. A message may be replicated at intermediate nodes and forwarded along multiple outgoing channels toward disjoint subsets of destinations. Unfortunately, tree-based routing, which is actually used to support a restricted form of multicast in the nCUBE-2, suffers from several drawbacks in multicomputers that use wormhole routing. Since there is no message buffering at routers, if one branch of the tree is blocked, all are blocked. Branches must proceed forward in lock step, which may cause a message to hold many channels for extended periods, thereby increasing network contention. More importantly, we have shown that tree-based routing is not deadlock free in hypercubes or 2D-meshes without using multiple channels per unidirectional channel [6].

We have developed a new approach to hardware-supported multicast, called *path-based* routing [6]. A *multicast path* for a set of destinations consists of a set of consecutive channels, starting from the source node and traversing each destination in the set. A multicast path can be represented by a list of addresses $(s, d_1, d_2, \ldots, d_k)$, where s is the source node and the d_i's are destinations in the order they are reached by the worm. Path-based multicasting may be implemented by placing the destination list in the header of the message; each destination address occupies one or more flits of the message header. When the flit(s) containing the first destination address, d_1, arrives at that node's router, the address d_1 is removed from the message header and the subsequent flits are forwarded both to the local host and to destination d_2. Eventually, the data component of the message will arrive at all the destinations. Path-based routing is applicable to many topologies, including hypercubes and meshes [6]. Most importantly, path-based routing is deadlock-free. Because multiple worms may proceed independently, path-based routing also avoids the branch-dependency problem of multicast trees. Due to its advantages over tree-based routing, we will continue to pursue path-based approaches in our study of adaptive multicast communication.

Two important issues must be accounted for in developing a path-based adaptive multicast routing algorithm. First, as with deterministic multicast communication, the degenerate cases of unicast and broadcast must use the same algorithm in order to guarantee freedom from deadlock. That is, the multicast algorithm is the *only* routing algorithm used in the network, thereby offering a comprehensive and consistent routing solution. An important property of our deterministic multicast path algorithms [6] is that a unicast message routed according to the algorithm will always follow a shortest path. The second issue involves the ordering of destinations in the path. Because of the pipelining characteristic of wormhole routing, it is not sufficient to simply order the destinations randomly and perform adaptive unicast routing between each pair, as deadlock may result. Ordering of destinations in such a way as to allow deadlock-free adaptive routing between the source and the first destination and between subsequent pairs of destinations is, in fact, a major task of this work.

In this paper, we will develop three deadlock-free multicast routing algorithms for different adaptive routing strategies. In order to describe and compare the three algorithms presented, we need to define terms describing the adaptivity of multicast routing. We will say that a multicast routing algorithm is *fully adaptive* if the message can take any path between each pair of nodes in the multicast path, that is, from s to d_1 and from d_j to d_{j+1}, for $1 \leq j \leq k-1$. An algorithm is *partially adaptive* if it can route messages adaptively only between some pairs of nodes in the multicast path. A multicast routing algorithm is *minimal* if it always follows a shortest path between each pair of nodes in the multicast path; otherwise, it is *nonminimal*.

3 Partially Adaptive Minimal Multicast Routing

The first algorithm studied, called the PM algorithm, is a partially adaptive minimal routing algorithm that does not require the use of virtual channels. The algorithm first selects a west-most destination d, that is, the one with smallest x-coordinate. If d has a smaller x-coordinate than that of the source node s, the message will be routed from s to d deterministically using XY routing. Any destination nodes in that path from s to d will be placed before d in the message header according to their positions in the path, so that these destinations can receive the message as it is forwarded from s to d. The message then is adaptively routed east towards other destination nodes, that is, the destination nodes are visited in ascending order according to their x-coordinates. If there is more than one node with the same x-coordinate, the message will be sent first north (in increasing y-coordinate order) then south (in decreasing y-coordinate order). It will be shown later that this routing strategy is deadlock-free. Figure 1 shows the algorithm for constructing the message header at the source node. The distributed routing algorithm for each node including the source node is given in Figure 2, which is a general path-based multicast routing algorithm.

Figure 3 shows an example of one of the multicast paths that may be created by the PM routing algorithm. Consider a multicast with source $(2,1)$ and destinations $(0,2)$, $(1,4)$, $(3,2)$, $(4,1)$, and $(5,4)$. At the source node $(2,1)$, the algorithm in Figure 1 is executed to order the destinations and construct the message header M_H. In the first iteration of Step 2, we have $(x_h, y_h) = (2,1)$. Since there is no destination (x, y) such that $x < x_h$ and $y = y_h$, Step 2(a) does not select any destinations. In Step 2(b), destination $(0,2)$ is selected. In the second iteration of Step 2, destination $(1,4)$ is selected by Step 2(b). In the third iteration, destination $(3,2)$ will be selected by Step 2(c), and so on. After the execution of the algorithm, the message header M_H is complete with $M_H = ((0,2), (1,4), (3,2), (4,1), (5,4))$. Note that if more than one destination has the same x-coordinate, the message will always be routed north then south. For example, if node $(4,3)$ were also a destination in the above example, it would be placed between $(3,2)$ and $(4,1)$ in the message header. Using the routing algorithm in Figure 2, the message will be sent to $(0,2)$ deterministically; it can then be sent adaptively between of each $(0,2)$ and $(1,4)$, and $(1,4)$ and $(3,2)$, $(3,2)$ and $(4,1)$, $(4,1)$ and $(5,4)$.

Next, we discuss the adaptivity and the deadlock-free properties of the PM

Algorithm: PM Message Header Algorithm: PM-H
Input: Destination set D, $D = \{(x_1, y_1), (x_2, y_2), \ldots, (x_k, y_k)\}$,
  and source address $u_0 = (x_0, y_0)$.
Output: Ordered list of destinations, M_H, placed in message header.
Procedure:
1. $K = D$; $(x_h, y_h) = (x_0, y_0)$; $i = 0$;
2. While $K \neq \emptyset$ do the following:
   (a) If there is an (x, y) in K, with $x < x_h$ and $y = y_h$, then select
       (x_j, y_j) such that $x_j = \max\{x_\ell | (x_\ell, y_\ell) \in K, x_\ell < x_h, y_\ell = y_h\}$, go
       to (d).
   (b) If there is an (x, y) in K, with $x = \min\{x_\ell | (x_\ell, y_\ell) \in K\}$ and
       $y \geq y_h$, then select (x_j, y_j) such that $x_j = \min\{x_\ell | (x_\ell, y_\ell) \in K\}$,
       and $y_j = \min\{y_m | (x_m, y_m) \in K, x_m = x_j, y_m \geq y_h\}$, go to (d).
   (c) If there is an (x, y) in K, with $x = \min\{x_\ell | (x_\ell, y_\ell) \in K\}$ and
       $y < y_h$, then select (x_j, y_j) such that $x_j = \min\{x_\ell | (x_\ell, y_\ell) \in K\}$,
       and $y_j = \max\{y_m | (x_m, y_m) \in K, x_m = x_j, y_m < y_h\}$;
   (d) $M_H[i] = (x_j, y_j)$; $i = i+1$; $K = K - \{(x_j, y_j)\}$; $(x_h, y_h) = (x_j, y_j)$;
3. Place M_H in the message header.

Fig. 1. PM algorithm for constructing the message header.

Algorithm: PM Algorithm for Message Routing
Input: A message with ordered destination list $M_H = (d_1, \ldots, d_k)$,
  a local address u, $u = (x, y)$.
Procedure:
1. If $u = d_1$, then $M_{H'} = M_H - \{d_1\}$ and the message is sent to the local
   host; otherwise, $M_{H'} = M_H$.
2. If $M_{H'} = \emptyset$, then terminate the message forwarding, but continue
   to deliver the remainder of the message to the local host (the last
   destination).
3. Let d be the first node in $M_{H'}$, $d = (x_d, y_d)$.
   (a) If $x_d \geq x$, select any channel (u, u') (u' is a neighboring node of
       u), that is along any one of the shortest paths from u to d_1;
   (b) If $x_d < x$, select the neighboring node u', $u' = (x - 1, y)$
4. The message is forwarded to node d' with address destination list $M_{H'}$
   in its header.

Fig. 2. PM algorithm for message routing.

234

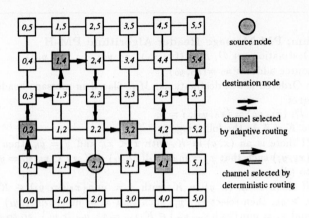

Fig. 3. An example of PM routing algorithm in a 6×6 mesh.

algorithm. Since the algorithm is a *minimal* adaptive algorithm, we will define the route between two nodes connected by a unique shortest path to be *adaptive*. Due to lack of space, the proofs of Theorem 1 and all subsequent theorems are omitted here and can be found in [10].

Theorem 1. *Suppose M_H is the message header for a multicast path created by the PM algorithm. A message with header M_H can be routed deterministically to at most one destination in M_H, and adaptively to each remaining destinations.*

Theorem 2. *The PM algorithm is deadlock-free.*

Given a multicast with k destination nodes, it is easy to see that the time complexity of the algorithm in Figure 1 is $O(k^2)$. Such an algorithm need be executed only once for a given set of destinations; in fact, this sorting may be done at compile time. If we do not consider the time for message copying at a destination node, the routing algorithm in Figure 2 requires $O(1)$ time, since each node in 2D mesh has at most four outgoing channels.

The PM algorithm sends a message using a single multicast path. The route from the source to the last destination node may be relatively long and use more channels than necessary. A simple optimization is to divide the destination set into subsets and use multiple multicast paths, one for each subset.

The algorithm for dual-path adaptive multicast routing, called PMD algorithm, divides the destination set into two subsets and copies of the message are routed independently along two multicast paths. The formal description of the algorithm is given in [10].

In the example shown in Figure 3, two multicast paths may be created as follows. At the source node (2,1), the set of destinations $\{(0,2), (1,4), (3,2), (4,1), (5,4)\}$ is divided into two subsets: $\{(0,2),(1,4)\}$; and $\{(3,2),(4,1),(5,4)\}$. In the first path with destination set $\{(0,2),(1,4)\}$, the message is delivered from the source node (2,1) to (0,2) deterministically and then from (0,2) to (1,4) adaptively. In the second path with destination set $\{(3,2),(4,1),(5,4)\}$, the message is forwarded to (3,2), from (3,2) to (4,1), and from (4,1) to (5,4), all adaptively. This PMD algorithm is also deadlock-free.

4 Fully Adaptive Minimal Multicast Routing

In the PM algorithm, a message is routed deterministically to at most one west-most destination node. For unicast communication in which the number of the destinations is one, this property implies that the message has to be delivered deterministically to any destination node west of the source node. Hence, only about half of the unicast communications can be adaptive. It can be easily shown that, without introducing virtual channels, it is impossible to have fully adaptive deadlock-free routing even for unicast communication. In order to support fully adaptive multicast routing, we double the vertical channels. Suppose one set of the vertical channels is C_{v1} and the other one is C_{v2}. We further divide the channels of the network into two disjoint sets C_W and C_E as follows,

$C_W = \{c | c$ is horizontal channel from east to west or $c \in C_{v1}\}$
$C_E = \{c | c$ is horizontal channel from west to east or $c \in C_{v2}\}$.

The proposed fully adaptive minimal routing algorithm, FM, divides the destination set into two subsets M_{HW} and M_{HE}. Basically, M_{HW} contains the destination nodes that are to the west (left) of the source, and M_{HE} the nodes to the east (right) of the source. The message will be delivered to M_{HW} and M_{HE} using the channels in C_W and the channels in C_E, respectively. The multicast routing for M_{HE} is the same as the PM routing described in the previous section; since there is no destination node to the west of the source node in M_{HE}, the message can be forwarded fully adaptively. The routing in C_W is similar to the routing in C_E but in opposite direction. Figure 4 gives the FM algorithm for constructing the message header. The algorithm first divides the set of the destination nodes into two subsets D_W and D_E, and then orders the nodes in D_E in exactly the same way as the PM algorithm in Figure 1. The nodes in D_W are ordered from east to west, that is, in descending order of their x-coordinates. Two independent multicast paths result, each delivering the message to one of subsets of the destinations and each using a different sets of the channels. The FM routing algorithm is similar to the one in Figure 2 except that no deterministic routing is required.

Figure 5 shows an example of the multicast paths that may be created by the FM routing algorithm. At the source node (2,1), the FM algorithm first divides the set of the destinations into two subsets: (0,2), (1,4); and (3,2), (4,1), (5,4). The message is forwarded to (0,2) and (1,4) adaptively using channels in C_W; the same message is sent to (3,2), (4,1) and (5,4), also adaptively, using channels in C_E.

Theorem 3. *The FM routing algorithm is deadlock-free.*

The algorithm in Figure 4 requires $O(k^2)$ time for a multicast with k destination nodes, but again may be executed once at compile time. As indicated in the previous section, the routing algorithm in Figure 2 takes $O(1)$ time.

Algorithm: FM Message Header Algorithm

Input: Destination set D and local address $u_0 = (x_0, y_0)$.

Output: Two ordered lists of destination nodes:
M_{HE} and M_{HW} placed in the message header.

Procedure:

1. Divide D into D_W and D_E such that $D_W = \{(x,y)|x > x_0 \text{ or } x = x_0 \text{ and } y > y_0\}$, and $D_E = D - D_W$.

2. Call PM-H(u_0, D_E) in Figure 1, which returns M_{HE}.

3. Suppose $D_W = \{(x_1, y_1), (x_2, y_2), \ldots, (x_k, y_k)\}$,

    (a) $K = D_W$; $(x_h, y_h) = (x_0, y_0)$; $i = 0$;

    (b) While $K \neq \emptyset$, do the following:

    - If there is an (x, y) in K, with $x = \max\{x_\ell | (x_\ell, y_\ell) \in K\}$ and $y \geq y_h$,

        then select (x_j, y_j) such that $x_j = \max\{x_\ell | (x_\ell, y_\ell) \in K\}$, and $y_j = \min\{y_m | (x_m, y_m) \in K, x_m = x_j, y_m \geq y_h\}$;

        else if there is an (x, y) in K, with $x = \max\{x_\ell | (x_\ell, y_\ell) \in K\}$ and $y < y_h$, then select (x_j, y_j) such that $x_j = \max\{x_\ell | (x_\ell, y_\ell) \in K\}$, and $y_j = \max\{y_m | (x_m, y_m) \in K, x_m = x_j, y_m < y_h\}$.

    - $M_{HE}[i] = (x_j, y_j)$; $i = i + 1$; $K = K - \{(x_j, y_j)\}$; $(x_h, y_h) = (x_j, y_j)$;

4. Construct two messages, one with message header M_{HE} and the other with message header M_{HW}.

Fig. 4. FM algorithm for constructing the message header.

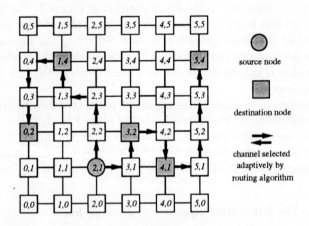

Fig. 5. An example of FM routing algorithm in a 6×6 mesh.

5 Nonminimal Adaptive Multicast Routing

In *nonminimal* adaptive routing, a message can be derouted in the presence of a blocked channel. As shown in [11], nonminimal adaptive routing has the potential to outperform minimal adaptive routing, especially under non-uniform traffic. In addition to the deadlock problem, a nonminimal multicast algorithm must also avoid livelock, in which a message fails to be delivered to its destinations due to its repeated derouting.

Our solution is to modify our deterministic dual-path method from [6] to support nonminimal adaptive routing. The method is based on a node-labeling scheme. First, we select a Hamiltonian path in the 2D mesh and assign integer numbers to the nodes according to their positions in the Hamiltonian path. We then divide the 2D mesh into two subnetworks, one called the *high-channel network*, containing all of the channels from lower labeled nodes to higher labeled nodes; the other called the *low-channel network* containing all of the channels from higher labeled nodes to lower labeled nodes. Figure 8 shows a label assignment for the nodes in 6×6 mesh. The label assignment function ℓ for an $m \times n$ mesh can be expressed as

$$\ell(x, y) = \begin{cases} x * n + y + 1 & \text{if } x \text{ is even} \\ x * n + n - y & \text{if } x \text{ is odd} \end{cases}$$

The destination node set is divided into two subsets, one containing destination nodes with labels higher than that of the source node, the other containing destinations with labels lower than that of the source node. The message is delivered to these two sets of the destinations using the high-channel and low-channel subnetworks, respectively.

Figure 6 and Figure 7 give, respectively, the message header algorithm and routing algorithm for the label-based, dual-path approach, collectively called the LD routing algorithm. The algorithm in Figure 6 divides the destinations into two subsets of the destinations as described above, and sorts the two subsets in ascending and descending order, respectively, using their labels as keys. The routing algorithm in Figure 7 is a general path-like routing algorithm that uses different set of the channels for different subsets of destinations.

Figure 8 shows an example of the two multicast paths that may be created by LD algorithm. The source node (2,1) has label $\ell(2,1)=14$, the destination nodes (0,2), (1,4), (3,2), (4,1), (5,4) have the labels 3, 8, 22, 26 and 32 respectively. At the source node, the destination node set is divided into two subsets: $\{(0, 2), (1, 4)\}$, whose labels are lower than that of the source node, and $\{(3, 2), (4, 1), (5, 4)\}$, whose labels are higher than that of the source node. The message will be delivered to the two sets of destinations using the low-channel network and high-channel network, respectively. For example, in high-channel network, message can be forwarded from the source node (2,1) with label 14 to destination (3,2) with label 22 by different paths, such as (14, 15, 22) or (14, 15, 16, 21, 22), or (14, 15, 16, 17, 20, 21, 22), etc. The message can be sent from node (3,2) with label 22 to destination (4,1) with label 26 by different paths, such as (22, 23, 26) or (22, 23, 24, 25, 26).

Algorithm: LD Message Header Algorithm

Input: Destination set D, local address u_0,
   and node label assignment function ℓ;
Output: Two sorted lists of destination nodes:
   D_H and D_L placed in the message header.
Procedure:
1. Divide D into two sets D_H and D_L such that D_H contains all the destination nodes with higher ℓ value than $\ell(u_0)$ and D_L contains the nodes with lower ℓ value than $\ell(u_0)$.
2. Sort the destination nodes in each of D_H and D_L, using the ℓ value as the key.
3. Construct two messages, one containing D_H as part of the header and the other containing D_L as part of the header.

Fig. 6. LD algorithm for constructing the message header.

Algorithm: LD Algorithm for Message Routing

Input: A message with sorted destination list $M_H = (d_1, \ldots, d_k)$,
   a local address u and node label assignment ℓ;
Procedure:
1. If $u = d_1$, then $M_{H'} = M_H - \{d_1\}$ and the message is sent to the local node; otherwise, $M_{H'} = M_H$.
2. If $M_{H'} = \emptyset$, then terminate the message forwarding, but continue to deliver the remainder of the message to the local host.
3. Let d be the first node in $M_{H'}$. Select any channel (u, u'), such that $\ell(u) < \ell(u') \leq \ell(d_1)$.
4. The message is sent to node u' with destination address list $M_{H'}$ in its header.

Fig. 7. LD algorithm for message routing.

Theorem 4. *The LD routing algorithm is deadlock-free.*

Because the message is routed in an increasing (or decreasing) order, no destination will be visited more than once in a multicast.

Theorem 5. *The LD routing algorithm is livelock-free.*

The time complexity of the algorithm in Figure 6 is $O(k \log k)$ for a multicast with k destination nodes since it is, in fact, a sorting algorithm. Also, the routing algorithm in Figure 7 only requires $O(1)$ time.

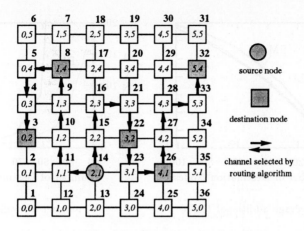

Fig. 8. An example of LD routing algorithm in a 6 × 6 mesh.

6 Performance Evaluation

We have conducted a simulation study of the performance of the proposed adaptive routing algorithms for different numbers of destination nodes in a 32 × 32 mesh. The performance metrics include the average traffic created by each routing algorithm and the number of the alternative paths, available to each routing algorithm. Randomly generated multicast sets with different number of destinations were tested in order to measure the performance of the routing algorithms. Each unit of traffic represents the transmission of a message over a channel. The traffic is defined as the total number of channels used for a given multicast communication.

A multicast with k destinations requires at least k units of the traffic. The additional traffic is defined as the total amount of traffic minus k. Figure 9(a) plots the amount of additional traffic generated by the PM, FM, and LD routing algorithms in 32 × 32 mesh. The PMD algorithm created almost the same amount of the traffic as the FM algorithm because both methods use dual-path minimal routing, which is not shown in the figures. Among the three routing algorithms, FM algorithm creates the least traffic. The LD algorithm produces the most traffic because it is a nonminimal routing algorithm. Although FM does not show a very significant improvement over the PM algorithm, since it uses double-vertical channel network, it would be expected to achieve a lower network latency than that of PM algorithm. Furthermore, both the PMD and FM methods produce routing paths that average approximately half the length from the source to the last destination as does the PM method, since the former methods use dual-path routing.

We also measured the adaptivity of the proposed algorithms by computing the average number of available paths from one node (initially from the source node) to the next destination in the multicast path. The PM, PMD and FM have very close numbers of available paths in terms of different numbers of destina-

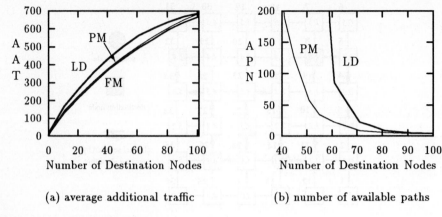

(a) average additional traffic   (b) number of available paths

Fig. 9. Comparison of multicast algorithms in a 32×32 mesh.

tions. This result occurs because the message is sent to at most one destination deterministically in PM. Although FM may not significantly outperform PM for adaptivity of multicast communication, as was explained before, only about half of the unicast communications can be performed adaptively in PM, while all of the unicast messages are adaptively routed in FM. Hence, FM exhibits much better performance if the percentage of the unicast communication is relatively high. As shown in Figures 9(b), LD exhibits much better adaptivity than the PM algorithm. This is because LD is a nonminimal routing algorithm, and thus more alternative paths are available for message transmission. However, when the number of destinations becomes large, the two algorithms have very close performance in terms of adaptivity.

7 Concluding Remarks

We have proposed three adaptive multicast wormhole routing algorithms for 2D mesh multicomputers. The algorithms include partially adaptive minimal routing, fully adaptive minimal routing, and nonminimal adaptive routing methods. The proposed adaptive routing algorithms are simple and deadlock-free. The minimal routing methods are livelock-free in nature, and the nonminimal routing method has been shown to be livelock-free. These routing strategies are the first adaptive multicast wormhole routing algorithms ever proposed. We have conducted a simulation study to compare the performance of the proposed adaptive routing algorithms. The results indicate that the minimal fully adaptive routing method creates the least traffic by using a double vertical-channel network. The nonminimal routing algorithm has the best adaptivity property, but it requires more channels for message transmission. The average traffic and adaptivity of the PM routing algorithm are close to those created by the PMD and FM routing algorithms, however, it has simpler control structure and does not require virtual channels. When the number of the destinations is relatively large, the PM algorithm also exhibits adaptivity close to that of the LD routing algorithm. The PM algorithm may be used when the percentage of unicast communication is relatively low. For unicast-intentive traffic, the FM routing algorithm may be the best choice. Finally, these routing methods for 2D mesh can be extended to mesh topologies with any dimension.

Acknowledgements

The authors would like to express their sincere appreciation to Professor Lionel M. Ni for his many contributions to this work. This work was supported in part by the NSF grants CDA-9121641, CDA-9222901, and MIP-9204066, and by an Ameritech Faculty Fellowship.

References

1. P. K. McKinley, H. Xu, A.-H. Esfahanian, and L. M. Ni, "Unicast-based multicast communication in wormhole-routed networks," in *Proc. of the 1992 International Conference on Parallel Processing*, vol. II, pp. 10–19, Aug. 1992.
2. L. M. Ni and P. K. McKinley, "A survey of wormhole routing techniques in direct networks," *IEEE Computer*, vol. 26, no. 2, pp. 62–76, Feb. 1993.
3. C. R. Jesshope, P. R. Miller, and J. T. Yantchev, "High Performance Communications in Processor Networks," in *Proceedings of IEEE 16th Annual International Symposium on Computer Architecture*, pp. 150–157, 1989.
4. D. H. Linder and J. C. Harden, "An adaptive and fault tolerant wormhole routing strategy for $k$ary n-cubes," *IEEE Transactions on Computers*, vol. 40, pp. 2–12, Jan. 1991.
5. C. J. Glass and L. M. Ni, "The turn model for adaptive routing," in *Proc. of the 19th Annual International Symposium on Computer Architecture*, pp. 278–287, May 1992.
6. X. Lin, P. K. McKinley, and L. M. Ni, "Deadlock-free multicast wormhole routing in 2D mesh multicomputers." accepted to appear in *IEEE Transactions on Parallel and Distributed Systems*.
7. Y. Lan, "Fault-tolerant multi-destination routing in hypercube multicomputers," in *Proceedings of the 12th International Conference on Distributed Computing Systems*, pp. 632–639, June 1992.
8. W. J. Dally and C. L. Seitz, "Deadlock-free message routing in multiprocessor interconnection networks," *IEEE Transactions on Computers*, vol. C-36, pp. 547–553, May 1987.
9. W. J. Dally and H. Aoki, "Adaptive routing using virtual channels," tech. rep., Massachusetts Institute of Technology, Laboratory for Computer Science, Sept. 1990.
10. X. Lin, P. K. McKinley, and A.-H. Esfahanian, "Adaptive multicast wormhole routing in 2D mesh multicomputers," tech. rep. MSU-CPS-ACS-77, Michigan State University, October 1992.
11. S. Konstantinidou and L. Snyder, "Chaos Router: Architecture and Performance," in *Proceedings of the 18th Annual Symposium on Computer Architecture*, pp. 222–231, 1991.

The Impact of Packetization in Wormhole-Routed Networks*

Jae H. Kim and Andrew A. Chien

kim@cs.uiuc.edu   achien@cs.uiuc.edu
Department of Computer Science
University of Illinois at Urbana-Champaign
1304 W. Springfield Avenue
Urbana, IL 61801

Abstract. Packetization is used in a variety of commercial multicomputers because of its potential performance advantages: higher throughput and a better distribution of message latencies. However, packetization has two significant drawbacks, 1) fragmentation and reassembly overhead and 2) increased traffic volume for routing and sequencing information. In this paper, we examine the performance benefits of packetization in existing dimension-order routed networks and in likely future router designs including adaptive routing and virtual lanes.

Our studies show that packetization has a mixed effect on performance in dimension-order routers. Packetizing uniform-sized traffic reduces network throughput dramatically. However, if the traffic is a bimodal distribution of sizes, packetization reduces the variance of latencies for short messages, and increases the network's overall throughput. On the other hand, packetization has no significant impact on the performance of advanced networks with adaptive routing and virtual lanes. Advanced routers without packetization give nearly identical performance to the corresponding packetizing networks under uniform-sized or bimodal traffic. Packetization may be unnecessary in such networks.

1 Introduction

In highly parallel machines, a collection of computing nodes works in concert to solve large application problems. The nodes communicate data and coordinate their efforts by sending and receiving messages through a routing network. Consequently, the achieved performance of such machines depends critically on that of their routing networks.

Many of recent multicomputer networks use cut-through or *wormhole routing* [9, 5], a technique which reduces message latency by pipelining its transmission over a number of channels along its path. However, channel coupling

---

* The research described in this paper was supported in part by NSF grants CCR-9209336 and MIP-92-23732, ONR grant N00014-92-J-1961, and NASA grant NAG 1-613. Additional support has been provided by a generous special-purpose grant from the AT&T Foundation.

in wormhole-routed networks makes efficient utilization of network channels difficult. Packetization, breaking large messages into sets of smaller messages for transmission, has been suggested as a technique for improving the performance of wormhole routed networks. A number of commercial systems incorporate some form of packetization [13, 4, 8].

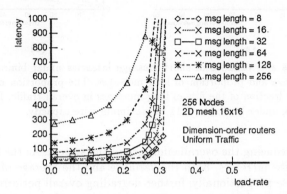

Fig. 1. Network latency versus load and message length. The load rate is normalized to the network's wire capacity.

There have been many studies evaluating the performance of wormhole-routed networks [6, 1, 11]. Both Mailhot [11] and Agarwal [1] found that network performance degrades as message length increases; closer examination shows that the performance decrease is caused by increased channel coupling due to longer messages. The results in Figure 1 illustrate this phenomenon. For large message sizes, network latency increases more rapidly, saturating network at lower load rates.

The superior throughput-latency characteristics of wormhole-routed networks for smaller message sizes motivate multicomputer system designers[2] to adopt packetization as a means of improving network performance. By splitting long messages into sets of short packets, the idea is to reduce the interchannel coupling, improving network performance.

Another potential advantage of packetization is an improvement in the distribution of short message latencies. Our simulations show that under bimodal traffic loads (short and long messages), long messages not only increase the average latency of short messages, but also disperse the latency distribution significantly[10]. This dependence is shown in Fig. 2. The dispersion is reflected in increased variance of short message latencies. Although only a fraction of the small messages experience increased delay (typically less than 30 %), even a single message suffering extremely long delays will slow tightly synchronized

---

[2] Designers of message passing libraries, system software, and application programmers may also fall into this category.

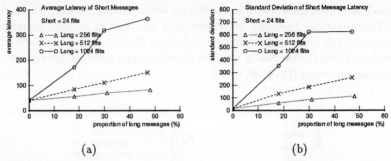

Fig. 2. Average and variance of short message latencies under bimodal traffic loads with different size and proportion of long messages. The proportion of long messages on x-axis is the fraction of the flits of long messages in overall traffic. Dimension-order routing network under load rate, 0.11 of maximum wire capacity.

applications, reducing the overall efficiency of the system. As the fraction or size of long messages increases, both the variance and the average of short message latency increase proportionally, further degrading overall performance. Packetization, by breaking long messages into short ones, reduces maximum blocking time due to another packet. Consequently, packetization may reduce the average latency and the variance in the latency for short messages in the network, potentially increasing overall network performance.

However, packetization has two significant drawbacks. First, packetization requires a mechanism for conversion between messages and packets. This requires packetization hardware (for outgoing messages) and reassembly hardware (for incoming messages). We consider hardware support to be a requirement because performing packetization and reassembly in software not only degrades processor performance, it also increases communication latency. For example, Chittor and Enbody's studies showed packetization overheads (24.6 μsec) for each packet, much larger than the typical routing delays (14.8 μsec) [3].[3] Second, packetization increases the network load; each packet must contain routing and sequencing information in its header. For smaller packet sizes, the overhead increases proportionally. For example, the Thinking Machines CM5 [8] uses five word packets, so one word of routing and sequencing overhead would imply a 25% increase in total network traffic.

In this paper, we examine in depth the question, *is packetization desirable in wormhole-routed networks?* For the remainder of the paper, we consider only k-ary n-cube networks. Within these networks, we examine impacts of packetization on two types of routers. First, we examine packetization in dimension-order routers, similar to those in most existing multicomputer networks. Second, we extend our study to next-generation networks which are likely to incorporate advanced routing techniques such as adaptive routing [12, 2] and virtual lanes [7].

---

[3] Chittor and Enbody studied the Symult 2010 system[13] in which long messages are split into packets of 256 bytes.

The remainder of the paper is organized as follows. In Section 2, we describe the simulation models and metrics used for the exploration. In Section 3, we evaluate the impact of packetization on dimension-order routing networks under two traffic models: uniform-sized traffic and bimodal traffic loads. In Section 4, we investigate the impact of packetization in networks with adaptive routing and virtual lanes. Finally, Section 5 concludes the paper, summarizing our results.

2 Methodology

Evaluation of a network's performance can be achieved through analytical modeling or simulation. Unfortunately, in networks supporting wormhole routing, nodes cannot be analyzed separately since their queues have strong interactions and coupled event transitions. Moreover, this study includes adaptive routers which have network status dependent behavior. Due to the difficulty of accurate analytic modeling, we present network performance evaluation based on simulation results.

Simulations are done at the register transfer level, using a simulator which is a 3000 line C program. The router latency and channel crossing requires one clock cycle. Throughout the study, simulations are performed on two-dimensional mesh networks with 256 nodes. All of the experiments in the paper use uniform traffic with randomly distributed sources and destinations.

All loads are normalized with respect to the network's maximum wire capacity, defined as all of the network channels transmitting simultaneously. Comparing packetized and nonpacketized workloads is a little tricky because a packetized workload induces a higher network load due to increased header overhead. Throughout, performance of packetizing networks is plotted using load figures for the corresponding nonpacketized traffic, yielding a fair comparison. Throughout, packetization and reassembly overheads are not considered (assumed to be zero).

When packetizing a message, some increase in size due to routing and sequencing overhead is inevitable. In all of our studies, the packetization header overhead is modeled as a single flit per packet for both routing and sequencing information. This conservative assumption favors packetizing networks, as for small flit sizes, the overhead might well be several flits.

The following simulations investigate the effects of packetization on the performance of wormhole-routed networks. The set of experiments were designed to evaluate the two supposed benefits of packetization: improved throughput/latency characteristics and improved latency distribution for other short messages.

Throughput/Latency Characteristics We explore if and how much packetization improves network performance by considering the effects of packetization in a variety of routing contexts. In all cases, the traffic load consists of uniformly-sized messages, and packetization implies that all messages are fragmented into sets of fixed size packets. The message latency is computed as the time from the sending of the first packet to receipt of the last packet for a message.

Latency Distribution for Other Short Messages We explore whether packetization improves the network performance experienced by other short message traffic by studying network performance under bimodal traffic loads. By using a bimodal distribution, short and long messages, we isolate the essential interaction between messages of different lengths. In this setting, we compare the performance of networks which use packetization and those that do not, focusing on the average latency and variance in latency experienced by the short message traffic. These comparisons, conducted in a variety of routing contexts, allow us to determine how packetization affects the network service of other short messages.

3 Packetization and Dimension-order Routers

In this section, we investigate the effect of packetization on the performance of a dimension-order router. The routers modeled are quite similar to those in the Intel Paragon [4] and the Symult 2010 [13]. In the nonpacketizing network, the messages are transmitted in the traditional fashion. In the packetizing network, each message is broken into packets of 16, 32, or 64 flits and queued in the network input queue. This produces highly correlated traffic, so the resulting performance is quite different from that reported by other researchers on comparable message sizes and uniform random traffic.

3.1 Packetization under Uniform-sized Traffic Loads

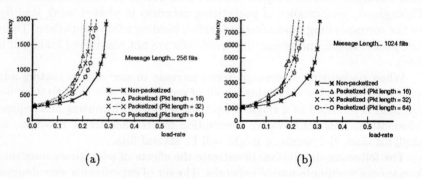

(a)   (b)

Fig. 3. Packetizing Dimension-Order Routers on (a) 256 flit messages and (b) 1024 flit messages. As packet size is reduced, network performance degrades further.

Packetization in a dimension order router does not improve performance; it actually reduces performance. The load-latency curves for a variety of message and packet sizes in Fig. 3 show that packetizing networks give significantly worse performance. Not only do the packetizing networks saturate at lower loads, for any load, the average latency is much worse. As the packet size is decreased, the performance degrades; the direct opposite to the behavior seen with uniform random traffic (see Fig. 1). The traffic correlation in the packetizing networks eliminates the advantages of short packet sizes. *Naive application of packetization to dimension order routers does not improve network latency or throughput.*

The poor performance of the packetizing networks can be explained by considering the relationship between the packets of a message. Because dimension-order routing allows only a single path, in the zero-load situation, the packetizing and non-packetizing network should have nearly identical performance. As the load rate is increased, each packet in a message sees an increased delay. However, the single path routing causes these delays to be cumulative; if leading packets are delayed, they delay all subsequent packets in the message. Decreasing the packet size increases the number of opportunities for delay to be introduced, increasing message latency.

Packetization also reduces network throughput in dimension-order routers. Because the packetizing network has higher latencies, at a given traffic load, more traffic is present in the network. The amount of traffic in the network determines the saturation point, so the net effect is to cause the network to saturate at lower loads. Adding actual packetization and reassembly overheads would further increase communication latency in an actual packetizing network, so the performance of real packetizing networks would be even worse. Thus, we must conclude that *packetization in dimension-order routed networks significantly degrades load-latency performance of the network under uniform-sized traffic.*

3.2 Packetization under Bimodal Traffic Loads

Though packetization reduces network throughput for uniform-sized traffic, it could still improve the latency distribution for short messages under bimodal traffic. When there is non-uniformly sized traffic in the network, the short messages, usually protocol or synchronization messages, may be blocked by a long message, producing extremely long latencies. As a result, both the average and the variance of short message latencies can increase dramatically.

Packetizing long messages into a set of short packets can reduce the interference of long messages on short ones by reducing the maximum blocking time. To explore the impact of packetization on the distribution of short message latencies, we use a bimodal distribution with short and long messages. Short messages are 32 flits, and the long messages are either 256 flits or 1024 flits, depending on the experiment. The fraction of long message traffic is 4 % and 1 % of the total number of messages for the respective long message sizes, keeping the volume of long message traffic constant at 30 % of the total flits. In nonpacketizing networks, long messages are routed as single packets. In packetizing networks, long messages are split into a set of short 32-flit packets, the same length as short messages. The resulting traffic is highly correlated, it so gives quite different results from uniform random traffic.

The distribution of short message latencies is sensitive to the choice of packetization size and network load rate. However, since we are primarily concerned

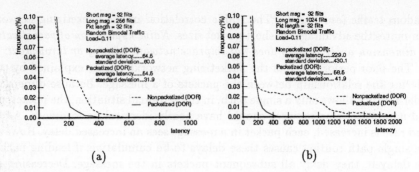

(a)   (b)

Fig. 4. Short message latency distribution for a bimodal traffic loads with 32 and (a) 256, (b) 1024 flit messages. Proportion is 70% short to 30% long by traffic volume.

with the shape of the distribution, we present results for a single packetization size, 32 flits, and load rate, 11% of wire capacity. The results for different packetization sizes and load rates are not qualitatively different.

Our simulation results show that *packetization reduces both the average latency and variance of the latency experienced by short messages*. In Figure 4, non-packetizing networks show dispersed latency distribution, giving large variance and average of short message latencies. The histogram buckets[4] are plotted along the x-axis, and the message frequency along y-axis. Packetization effectively eliminates short messages with large latencies. For longer messages sizes, the benefits of the packetization are more significant, giving a nearly identical distribution regardless of the size of long messages.

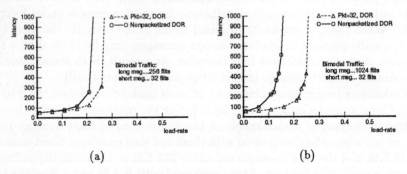

(a)   (b)

Fig. 5. Average latency vs. load rates of dimension-order routing networks under bimodal traffic loads. Long messages are (a) 256 flits and (b) 1024 flits long, respectively, and short messages are 32 flits for both (a) and (b).

Packetizing the long messages in dimension-order router, not only improves

---

[4] Each collects the messages for a range of 10 cycles. We have smoothed the curves using local averaging to improve their readability.

the distribution of short message latencies, it also improves overall network throughput (see Fig. 5). Because the bimodal traffic load used is predominantly short messages, 70% by volume, improving short message service improves overall throughput. The degree of this benefit depends critically on the fraction of long messages and their length. For the network traffic with more and larger long messages, packetization alleviates more blockage, increasing overall throughput.

In summary, packetization has a mixed effect on performance in dimension-order routers. Under uniform-sized traffic, packetization significantly reduces network performance. This is in direct contrast to previous studies which did not examine the correlated traffic produced by packetization. Despite this negative result, our results show that packetization improves the distribution of short message latencies, potentially increasing overall network throughout under bimodal traffic loads. The performance gains of packetizing networks are achieved by eliminating blocking by long messages. However, we know that advanced routing techniques such as adaptive routing and virtual lanes can also be used to reduce blocking by long messages. In the following sections, we investigate the impact of packetization on the performance of advanced routing networks.

4 Packetization and Multipath Networks

Several routing techniques that eliminate the intermessage interference in wormhole-routed networks have been proposed. For example, multipath routing techniques such as adaptive routing [12, 2] and virtual lanes [7] reduce intermessage interference by circumnavigating congestion and multiplexing resources respectively.

In this section, we investigate the impact of packetization on the advanced routing networks which incorporate both adaptive routing and virtual lanes. In such networks, much of the intermessage interference is eliminated, so packetization may not enhance network performance as much as in the dimension-order router.

For our studies, we use a planar-adaptive router [2], a minimal adaptive router. Its details are not important as for the two-dimensional networks considered, the planar-adaptive router is a fully adaptive, minimal router. The acronyms, DOR, PAR and VL are used for the dimension-order router, the planar-adaptive router and virtual lanes, respectively in the figures. As before, two traffic loads are used: uniform-sized traffic and bimodal traffic loads.

4.1 Packetization under Uniform-sized Traffic Loads

One problem with packetization in dimension-order routers is that single-path routing causes packet delays to be cumulative. The multipath routing techniques of adaptive routing, or multiplexing techniques such as virtual lanes can eliminate this effect. To investigate if packetization would allow messages to exploit this concurrency, we study packetizing and nonpacketizing networks with virtual lanes and adaptive routing.

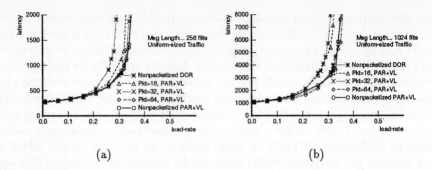

Fig. 6. Performance comparison of packetizing and nonpacketizing adaptive router with virtual lanes on (a) 256 flit messages and (b) 1024 flit messages. The performance of a nonpacketizing dimension-order router is shown for reference.

Fig. 6 compares the performance of packetizing and nonpacketizing networks which incorporate adaptive routing and virtual lanes. The advanced routing networks (PAR+VL) show essentially identical performance, regardless of packetization, in both cases giving much better performance than the dimension-order networks. *Under uniform-sized traffic loads, packetization has no significant impact on the performance of routing networks with adaptive routing and virtual lanes.* Most blocking can be avoided by using alternate paths, so packet blocking does not accumulate into message delay.

On the other hand, little overlap in transmission of successive packets in a single message is achieved. Packet injection speed is limited by the bandwidth of the network interface. This prevents a single message from exploiting multiple paths between source and destination. One possible future extension is to add multiple network input ports to increase the possibility of concurrent sub-packet transmission.

4.2 Packetization under Bimodal Traffic Loads

Packetization can improve the distribution of short message latencies in dimension-order routing networks, but can these improvements be achieved by other means as well? Though current generation routers are mostly deterministic, next generation routers are likely to incorporate adaptive routing and virtual lanes for a wide range of performance reasons such as more robust performance and higher throughput. Virtual lanes allow short messages to pass through channels previously blocked by long messages, improving the variance as well as the average latency of short messages. Adaptive routing allows short messages to get around blockage by selecting alternate paths. Since virtual lanes and adaptive routing both improve short message performance in very different ways, they complement each other to improve the short message latency distribution[10].

Fig. 7 shows that adaptive routing and virtual lanes can eliminate the effects of long messages on short messages almost completely. The distribution of short message latencies is improved dramatically. Comparing the advanced

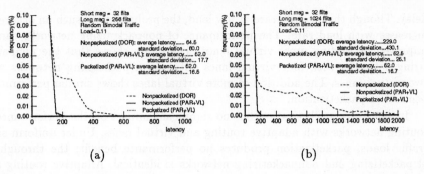

Fig. 7. Short message latency distribution for a bimodal traffic loads with 32 flit short messages and (a) 256, (b) 1024 flit long messages. Since the performance of the non-packetizing PAR+VL and packetizing PAR+VL is nearly identical, the graphs of the packetizing PAR+VL are hidden under those of nonpacketizing PAR+VL.

network (adaptive routing and virtual lanes) with and without packetization, there is virtually no difference in performance. Because most blocking by long messages are already eliminated by using virtual lanes and adaptive routing, the performance gains due to packetization are minimal. Hence, *packetization is not necessary for reducing average and the variance of short message latencies in routing networks with adaptive routing and virtual lanes.*

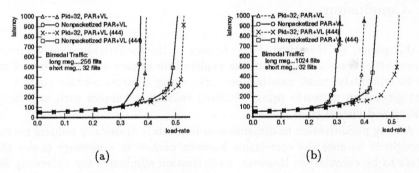

Fig. 8. Average latency vs. load rates of adaptive routing networks with virtual lanes under bimodal traffic loads. PAR+VL (444) indicates an adaptive router with twice as many virtual lanes.

We also evaluate overall network performance (throughput and latency) under bimodal traffic loads. Fig. 8 shows that the nonpacketizing networks exhibit lower throughput compared to corresponding packetizing networks. Though adaptive routing and virtual lanes reduce blocking by long messages, apparently two virtual lanes are not enough to eliminate the intermessage interference. For example, if a short message uses up its adaptivity and reaches a channel where all of the virtual lanes are monopolized by long messages, it will suffer a long delay. Though this is quite rare at low load, the probability of such an occurence increases with load rate. The performance of nonpacketizing networks can be improved by adding more virtual lanes. The figure shows that the nonpacketizing networks with four virtual lanes outperform packetizing networks with two virtual lanes. The addition of more virtual lanes shows similar performance benefits as packetization.

In summary, packetization has no significant impact on the performance of routing networks with adaptive routing and virtual lanes. Under uniform-sized traffic loads, packetization produces no performance benefit; the throughput of packetizing and nonpacketizing networks is identical. Adaptive routing and virtual lanes reduce intermessage coupling, eliminating the performance penalty for longer messages.

Under bimodal traffic loads, packetization also does not improve network performance. Adding packetization does not improve the distribution of short message latencies because adaptive routing and virtual lanes already allow short messages to avoid blocking by long messages. However, as the load increases, blocking by long messages can become significant, so it is important to ensure that a routing network design has enough virtual lanes. Overall, our results show no significant advantage for packetization in the advanced routing networks we studied. As a result, we must conclude that including adaptive routing and virtual lanes in a router eliminates the need for packetization.

5 Conclusion

In this paper, we investigated the impact of the packetization on wormhole-routed networks via simulation. We explored its impact on two classes of networks separately: most existing networks using dimension-order routers and next-generation networks using advanced routing techniques such as adaptive routing and virtual lanes.

Adding packetization to dimension-order routers drastically reduces network throughput because the correlation between packets in a message causes their delays to be cumulative. However, packetization eliminates the extremely long latencies, improving the latency distribution of short message latencies significantly. The improved short message latencies with packetization produce an increase in overall network throughput on bimodal traffic loads, despite the marked increases in the latencies of long messages.

Packetization shows different effects on networks with adaptive routing and virtual lanes. On uniform-sized traffic loads, packetizing and nonpacketizing networks show nearly identical performance. Under bimodal traffic loads, packetization does not improve the latency distribution of short messages. However, with bimodal traffic, packetization can increase network throughput. For networks with the same number of virtual lanes, the packetizing networks are able to sustain higher throughput. This is because the blocking by long messages cannot be eliminated completely, and the frequency of the blocking becomes substantial at high workloads. The undesirable blocking by long message can be mitigated by adding more virtual lanes.

Our results have a variety of practical applications. First, our experiments with packetization in a dimension-order router will help system software designers or message passing library designers to select appropriate packet sizes for existing multicomputers. Packetization clearly reduces performance for long messages in proportion to the packet size, while improving the performance for short messages. Second, designers of next generation networks considering the inclusion of adaptive routing and virtual lanes should understand that these features obviate the need for packetization. Consequently, hardware designs, performance studies, and performance models should not assume that traffic is packetized .

References

1. A. Agarwal. Limits on interconnection network performance. *IEEE Transactions on Parallel and Distributed Systems*, 2(4):398–412, 1991.
2. A. A. Chien and J. H. Kim. Planar-adaptive routing: Low-cost adaptive networks for multiprocessors. In *Proceedings of the International Symposium on Computer Architecture*, pages 268–77, May 1992.
3. S. Chittor and R. Enbody. Performance evaluation of mesh-connected wormhole-routed networks for interprocessor communication in multicomputers. In *Proceedings of Supercomputing*, 1990.
4. Intel Corporation. Paragon xp/s product overview. Product Overview, 1991.
5. W. Dally and C. Seitz. Deadlock-free message routing in multiprocessor interconnection networks. *IEEE Transactions on Computers*, C-36(5), 1987.
6. W. J. Dally. Performance analysis of k-ary n-cube interconnection networks. *IEEE Transactions on Computers*, 39(6), June 1990.
7. W. J. Dally. Virtual channel flow control. *IEEE Transactions on Parallel and Distributed Systems*, 3(2):194–205, 1992.
8. C. Leiserson et al. The network architecture of the connection machine cm-5. In *Proceedings of the Symposium on Parallel Algorithms and Architectures*, 1992.
9. P. Kermani and L. Kleinrock. Virtual cut-through: A new computer communications switching technique. *Computer Networks*, 3(4):267–86, 1979.
10. J. H. Kim and A. A. Chien. Evaluation of wormhole routed networks under hybrid traffic loads. In *Proceedings of the Hawaii International Conference on System Sciences*, January 1993.
11. John N. Mailhot. A comparative study of routing and flow control strategies in k-ary n-cube networks. B.S. thesis, Massachusetts Institute of Technology, 1988.
12. L. Ni and C. Glass. The turn model for adaptive routing. In *Proceedings of the International Symposium on Computer Architecture*, 1992.
13. C. L. Seitz, W. C. Athas, C. M. Flaig, A. J. Martin, J. Seizovic, C. S. Steele, and W. Su. The architecture and programming of the ametek series 2010 multicomputer. In *Proceedings of the Third Conference on Hypercube Computers*, pages 33–6. Association for Computing Machinery, ACM Press, January 1988.

Grouping Virtual Channels
for Deadlock-Free Adaptive Wormhole Routing

Ziqiang Liu[1], José Duato[2] and Lars-Erik Thorelli[1]
[1]Electrum 204, 164 40 Kista Sweden
[2]P.O.B. 22012, 46071 - Valencia, Spain

Abstract

Recently, intensive research has been done to develop adaptive deadlock-free wormhole routing strategies for interconnection networks. One effective method is to partition the physical network into several virtual networks such that there is no channel dependency cycle in each of them even if full or partial adaptive routing strategies are used. However, each physical channel can be split into more virtual channels than the number necessary to set up the virtual networks. The additional virtual channels can be considered as one *Resource Pool* for all virtual networks. It means the packet which is blocked in one virtual network can borrow one free valid virtual channel from the Resource Pool, returning it to the Resource Pool when it is released. We call this scheme the *grouping technique* and have applied it to *double-y* adaptive routing on a 2D mesh network, producing a new fully adaptive routing algorithm called *group-double-y*. The simulation results show that with heavily loaded network it can double/(increase 26%) the average physical channel utilization under uniform/matrix-transpose traffic pattern. We have also applied the grouping technique in the Turn model on a 2D mesh network, producing a fully adaptive, minimum and nonminimum routing algorithm called *group-turn-model*. Compared with *group-double-y*, the simulation results show that with heavily loaded network the *group-turn-model* increases/decreases the average physical channel utilization by (12%)/(2%) under matrix-transpose/uniform traffic pattern.

1 Introduction

In wormhole routing, a packet consists of a sequence of flits. A flit is the smallest unit of information that a channel can accept or refuse. Instead of storing a packet completely in a node and transmitting it to the next node, wormhole routing operates by advancing the head flit of the packet directly from incoming to outgoing channels. As flits are forwarded, the packet becomes spread out across the channels between the source node and destination. If an outgoing channel is not available, the packet will wait for it and block the progress of any other packet requiring the channels it occupies. This can produce deadlock. A way to determine whether a wormhole routing algorithm has a potential deadlock or not is to test whether its channel dependency graph is cyclic [DalSei87]. If the channel dependency graph has a cycle, a deadlock potential exists. Restricting the routing sequence over the channels can prevent such cycles and avoid the deadlock. For example, in a mesh-connected multiprocessor system, the XY-routing scheme always routes a packet through the X (horizontal) direction before the Y (vertical) direction. Dally [Dally92] has proposed a virtual channel flow control method to increase performance and avoid deadlock. In his method, each physical channel in the network is associated with several small queues, virtual channels, rather than a single deep queue. The virtual channels associated with one physical channel are allocated independently but compete with each other for physical bandwidth. A virtual channel dependency graph and a total order among them are established. Routing is restricted to visit channels in decreasing or increasing order to eliminate cycles in the channel dependency graph and avoid deadlock.

The restriction of routing, although avoiding deadlock, can increase traffic jams, especially in heavily loaded networks with long packets. In order to avoid congested regions of the network, an adaptive routing algorithm can be used. In the following section, several existing adaptive routing strategies will be briefly examined. In Section 3, the grouping technique is introduced, based on it several adaptive routing algorithms have been developed. Some simulation results of these routing algorithms are presented in Section 4. Section 5 gives some concluding remarks.

2   Deadlock-Free Adaptive Wormhole Routing Strategies

A general adaptive routing technique works by partitioning the channels into disjoint subsets. Each subset constitutes a corresponding subnetwork. Packets are routed through different subnetworks depending on the location of destination nodes. Jesshope, Miller and Yantchev [JMY89, JMY91] have proposed the virtual network method. In which, deadlock is avoided without imposing restrictions on routing by splitting the network into a number of acyclic virtual networks, either multiplexed onto the same channel resources or implemented directly in hardware. This allows packets to adapt to local traffic conditions, thus increasing the effective bandwidth of the network. They applied the virtual network idea to a 2D mesh and classify packets according to whether they need to be routed NE, SE, SW, or NW. A separate virtual network to route each class with full adaptivness is created.

Dally [Dally90] has proposed a different minimal path fully adaptive algorithm for 2D meshes. It requires two virtual channels per physical channel along only one of the two dimensions. We assume that this is the y dimension and the network can be called *double-y network*. The routing algorithm can be called the *double-y routing algorithm*. It routes an east-bound packet along the eastward physical channels and one set of y virtual channels and routes a west-bound packet along the westward physical channels and the other set of y virtual channels.

Glass and Ni have proposed the *Turn model* for designing adaptive wormhole routing algorithms [GlaNi92]. A unique feature of the model is that it is not based on adding physical or virtual channels to network topologies (though it can be applied to networks with extra channels). Instead, the model is based on analyzing the directions in which packets can turn in a network and the cycles that the turns can form. Prohibiting just enough turns to break all of the cycles produces routing algorithms that are deadlock free, livelock free, minimal or nonminimal, and maximally adaptive for the network. In an n-dimensional mesh, just a quarter of the turns must be prohibited to prevent deadlock. The remaining three quarters of the turns permit partial adaptiveness in routing. Applied to a 2D mesh network, the turn model can produce a partially adaptive routing algorithm: the *west-last routing algorithm:* route a packet first adaptively south, east and north, if necessary, and then west. The two turns prohibited are from west to north and from west to the south. The algorithm is fully adaptive if the packet destination is on the right-hand side (east) of the source; otherwise, it is deterministic.

José Duato has developed a theory for the design of deadlock-free adaptive routing algorithms based on virtual channel flow control [Duato91]. According to his theory, a connected and adaptive wormhole routing function R for an interconnection network I is deadlock-free if there exists a subset of channels $C_1 \subseteq C$ that defines a routing subfunction R_1 which is connected and has no cycles in its extended channel dependency graph D_E.

3   Grouping Technique in Adaptive Wormhole Routing

In [Dally90], when applying virtual channels to avoid deadlock in wormhole routing, Dally has pointed out that a physical channel can be split into more virtual channels then the ones needed to avoid the deadlock. In such case, the router can choose among several virtual channels associated with the same physical channel to send a packet, and can also allow active packets to pass blocked packets using network bandwidth that otherwise may be left idle. This reduces channel contention and the packet delay. The same idea can be used when applying virtual channels to produce adaptive wormhole routing, thus a physical channel can be split into more virtual channels than the ones needed to produce adaptive routing. One obvious way is to divide the additional virtual channels equally among each of the virtual networks. However, this method has a serious drawback, when the packet traffic in different virtual networks varies substantially. Virtual channels in the lower traffic virtual network are wasted, while there is shortage of virtual channels in the higher traffic virtual network. We suggest a new method, called the *grouping technique*. The basic idea is to put the additional virtual channels in a Resource Pool, from which they can be borrowed by the packets in different virtual networks. After the packet has released the borrowed virtual channel, it returns it to the Resource Pool. The same virtual channel can be borrowed again by another packet in any virtual network. If the routing algorithm in the virtual network is deadlock-free, adding more virtual channels to it and retaining the same routing algorithm will not cause any deadlock, but only improve the performance. We can apply Duato's adaptive routing theory to formally prove the routing algorithm developed from the grouping technique is deadlock-free [Duato91]. Let C_1 be the set of channels belonging to any virtual network. Let $C - C_1$ be the set of channels belonging to the Resource Pool. If routing is restricted to the virtual networks (C_1), the corresponding routing subfunction is obviously connected and has no cycles in its extended channel dependency graph. Effectively, it is obvious that there are only direct dependencies between channels inside each virtual network. Indirect dependencies appear when a message uses a channel belonging to a virtual network, then a channel from the Resource Pool and then a channel from the SAME virtual network again. Thus, indirect dependencies are also restricted to channels belonging to the SAME virtual network. Then the above routing algorithm is deadlock-free.

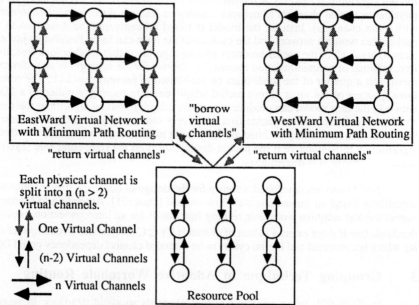

Figure 1: The virtual channel allocation in EastWard, WestWard virtual networks and the Resource Pool, when the Grouping Technique is applied in the double-y routing algorithm.

Applying the grouping technique to the double-y routing algorithm, the physical network is divided into two virtual networks: EastWard and WestWard, and one Resource Pool. In the EastWard virtual network, every node has n virtual channels in the east direction, and one virtual channel in both south and north directions. In the WestWard virtual network, every node has n virtual channels in west direction, and one virtual channel in both south and north. In the Resource Pool, every node has (n-2) virtual channels in both south and north directions. The virtual channel allocation in the EastWard, WestWard and Resource Pool is described in Figure 1. According to the packet's routing direction: EastWard-bound or WestWard-bound, the corresponding virtual network is chosen by the packet when it enters into the network. The routing in both virtual networks is shortest path and fully adaptive and we call the algorithm *group-double-y*. The virtual channels in the Resource Pool can be shared by packets in the EastWard and WestWard virtual networks.

The grouping technique can also be applied to adaptive routing with non-minimum paths. As in the above double-y routing algorithm, the packets in the EastWard or WestWard virtual network can use nonminimum paths in the south and north directions. If one virtual channel in west/east direction is added into EastWard/WestWard virtual network, the west-last/east-last partially adaptive routing algorithm developed by Glass and Ni from the Turn model can be applied [GlaNi92A]. Still according to the packet's routing direction: EastWard-bound or WestWard-bound, the corresponding virtual network is chosen. But in EastWard virtual network, packets can use the nonminimum path in each direction, as well as in WestWard virtual network. Example packet routing paths in EastWard and WestWard virtual networks are shown in Figure 2a and 2b. In these two figures, black squares represent nodes, and gray bars indicate blocked channels requiring that packets wait or take alternative paths. Note that both minimal and nonminimal paths are shown and the routing is fully adaptive. The routing algorithm can be called the *group-turn-model*.

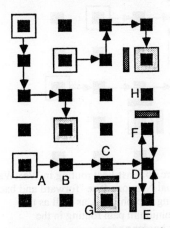 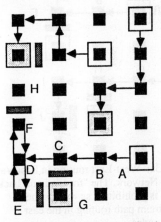

Figure 2a: West-Last routing in
EastWard Virtual Network

Figure 2b: East-Last routing in
WestWard Virtual Network

One important issue in adaptive routing with nonminimum paths is to avoid the "forward and back" routing. A packet routed from node 1 to node 2 should be prohibited from being routed back from node 2 to node 1. Also we have found that allowing the "forward and back" routing will introduce the deadlock situation as described in Figure 2a/2b. Consider a packet starting at node A and destinated to node G. Suppose that it is routed to node B, then node C, then node D, then node E. Suppose that the channel connecting the node E to G is busy. As the packet header is at a node located on the east/west border, the packet cannot go to the east/west. Also it cannot go to the west/east (west-last/east-last). Suppose it comes back to node D. Now, as the channel connecting to node E is busy (occupied by itself), the packet is routed to node F. Suppose that the channel connecting the node F to H is busy, the packet header can only go to the south, reaching node D again. From here, the only valid path to the destination node is occupied by itself, giving rise to a deadlock. This situation cannot appear if "forward and back" routing is prohibited.

However avoiding "forward and back" routing will cause deadlock in EastWard/WestWard virtual network with west-last/east-last routing as described in Figure 3a/3b. From the source node A, according to the packet's destination (node D) and the west-last routing following both minimum and nonminimum paths, the packet is routed to the node E. Because the node E is at the eastnorth corner, it has no channel in north or east direction. The packet cannot route in the west direction, because the packet has to finish routing in the south direction firstly. The packet cannot be routed back in south direction, because the "forward and back ack" routing is prohibited. So the packet cannot be forwarded any more and will never reach the destination. The whole network will get into the deadlock sooner or later. In order to avoid both "forward and back" routing and deadlock, more restricted routing in the edge nodes is necessary. In the east edge of EastWard virtual network, the routing with the nonminimum path should be prohibited as described in Figure 3a. In the west edge of WestWard virtual network, the routing with the nonminimum path should be prohibited as described in Figure 3b.

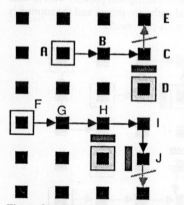

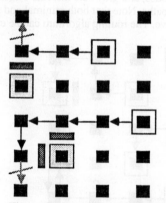

Figure 3a: West-Last routing in EastWard Virtual Network. The "forward and back" routing is prohibited, as well as the nonminimum path routing in the east border nodes.

Figure 3b: East-Last routing in WestWard Virtual Network. The "forward and back" routing is prohibited, as well as the nonminimum path routing in the west border nodes.

In a heavily loaded network the nonminimum path routing should be limited to increase the physical channel's efficient utilization. In the grouping technique, we can limit the nonminimum path routing by restricting it only to the virtual channels in the virtual networks. The virtual channels in the Resource Pool should only be used for minimum path routing. When a packet header, say in the EastWard virtual network, arrives at a node, four cases may occur. 1) According to the West-Last routing algorithm with the minimum path, at least one of the valid outgoing virtual channels in the EastWard virtual network is free.

The outgoing channel is randomly chosen between them. 2) case 1 does not occur, but still according to the West-Last routing algorithm with minimum path, at least one valid outgoing virtual channel in the Resource Pool is free. The outgoing channel is randomly chosen between them. 3) Neither case 1 nor 2 occurs, but according to the West-Last routing algorithm with the nonminimum path, there is at least one of the valid outgoing virtual channels in the EastWard virtual network is free. The outgoing channel is randomly chosen between them. Otherwise the header is blocked until case 1 or 2 or 3 occurs. It is possible to give another kind of restriction to the nonminimum path routing, for example, only on the virtual channel whose associated physical channel is idle.

4   Simulation Modeling and Results on a 2D Mesh Network

To route packets through a node of a 2D mesh network, channels entering a node must be "linked" to channels leaving the node or the delivery channels as described in Figure 4. Each node maintains a set of **translation tables** in the Matching Unit to perform this function. There is one translation table for each physical input channel and injection channel from the local processor. There is one entry in the table for each associated virtual channel. The entry contains three fields: an output physical channel, the number of associated output virtual channel and the free buffer space in it. When a flit arrives on, say, virtual channel 3 of east input physical channel, entry 3 of the associated translation table is read to yield the output physical channel and the number of the output virtual channel on which the packet´s flits are to be forwarded and buffered. The flit is then forwarded through the switch and put in the output virtual channel buffer. In case there is still free buffer space in the output virtual channel, an acknowledge signal will be sent to the sending node asking for transmitting the next flit.

Initially, all translation tables specify that flits are to be sent to the local **routing controller** as described by Reed and Fujimoto in their book [ReeFuj85]. When a header flit of one packet arrives at the incoming virtual channel or injection channel of a node, it is forwarded directly to the routing controller to request the service of the **router**. If the router is not free, the header flit is put in its waiting queue. Otherwise, a routing decision can be made that assigns the packet to some free valid output virtual channel or the delivery channel to the local processor, based on its destination and the routing algorithm in use. If there is no free valid channel, the packet is blocked and its header is put into the waiting queue at the router. The router is accessed by the packet headers in the waiting queue in round robin order [Duato92].

Once an output virtual channel is assigned to a packet, flit-level flow control is used to advance the packet across the physical channel and switch without intervention by the routing controller, as described in Figure 4. To advance from output buffer on the transmitting node (node A) to the output buffer on the receiving node (node B), a flit must first gain access to the physical channel to reach the input of node B, and then a path through the switch to reach the output buffer of node B. Typically either the switch is nonblocking (as described in Figure 4, multi-inputs and multi-outputs switch is used and there is no conflict when two flits are forwarded to the same output physical channel, but different virtual channels), and thus always available, or a few flits buffer is provided at the input of node B, so that switch and channel resources do not have to be allocated simultaneously [Dally92]. The overhead of the switch is ignored in the simulation experiment, because we are only interested to compare the relative performance of different routing algorithms and all of them have the same switch overhead. The transmit speed of the physical channel is defined as one flit per clock cycle, as well as the time slice to access the router. The buffer storage per physical channel is a constant (16 flits). The number of virtual channels per physical channel is varied from 1 to 16. If the number of virtual channels is increased, the buffer capacity of an individual virtual channel is proportionally reduced. All simulation experiments ran for 1000 clock cycles.

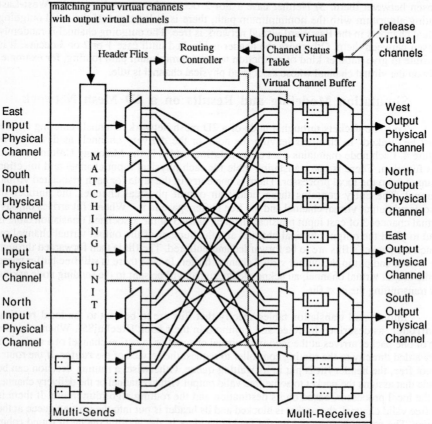

Figure 4: The diagram of a mesh routing chip. Dashed lines represent control signals and solid lines represent data paths.

The packet generation rate is the same for all nodes. If a new packet is generated before the tail of previous packet has left the node, it is queued. After generating a packet, each node waits a random number of clock cycles before generating the next one. The number of cycles is uniformly distributed between 0 and one positive simulation parameter M (100, 200, 400, 600, 800 or 1000). Changing the parameter will cause different packet generation rate (defined as 2 / M) and different network performance such as the average physical channel utilization. The physical channel utilization is defined as the average number of flits that have been transmitted on it per clock cycle. When the nonminimum path routing is involved, as described in Figure 3(a), flits transmitted on nonminimum path such as on physical channels H → I and I → J are not counted in their utilizations. The length of each packet is fixed at 16 flits. Except when specially specified, the network size in all simulation experiments is 32 × 32. Two network loads are considered: uniform and matrix-transpose (non-uniform). The uniform pattern sends each packet to any of the other processors with equal probability. The matrix-transpose pattern sends each packet from the processor at row i and column j to the one at row j and column i.

In the double-y routing algorithm, only the physical channels in the y-dimension are split into 2 virtual channels. In the following figures, the *double-y-n* scheme uses the same routing algorithm as the double-y, except that each physical channel is divided into n (n ≥ 2) virtual channels. In the EastWard/WestWard virtual network, each node has n virtual channels in the east/west direction and (n / 2) virtual channels in both south and north directions. The *group-double-y-n/group-turn-model-n* routing indicates that each physical channel is divided into n (n > 2) virtual channels and the virtual channel allocation in the EastWard, WestWard virtual networks and the Resource Pool is described in Figure 1/3, as well as the routing algorithm. In the *group-turn-model-I-n*, there is no restriction for the nonminimum path routing. In the *group-turn-model-II-n*, the nonminimum path routing is restricted to virtual channels in the virtual networks. In the *group-turn-model-III-n*, the nonminimum path routing is restricted to virtual channels whose associated physical channel is idle.

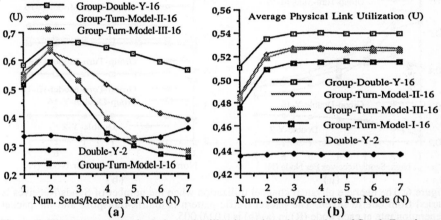

Figure 5: The average physical channel utilization when the number of Sends/Receives at each node is varied from one to seven. The packet traffic pattern is uniform and the packet generation rate at each node (R) in (a)/(b) is 0.02 /0.005.

Chittor and Enbody have suggested using multiple sends/receives between processor and router, instead of single send/receive to improve the performance of wormhole routing [ChiEnb90]. For example, in a 2D mesh network, four sends/receives can be used per node which is four times faster than single send/receive when each node is simultaneously sending one packet to each of its four neighbours. However, in many other previous simulation studies, it was assumed that there were one outgoing packet and unlimited number of incoming packets per node [LiuWu93, Duato92]. The reason to choose just one outgoing packet per node was to prevent a fast saturation of the network. The reason to choose unlimited number of incoming packets per node was to simplify the simulation experiment, even though it did not match reality. In a simulation experiment, we have compared the average physical channel utilization (U) with different number of sends/receives (N) when the packet traffic pattern is uniform/matrix-transpose as described in Figure 5/6.

As can be easily seen in Figure 5(a) where the packet generation rate (R) is high (0.02), varying parameter N does affect the performance. In the Group-Double-Y-16/Group-Turn-Model-II-16, changing N from 1 to 2, U is increased (7%)/(8%). Further increasing N, in the Group-Double-Y-16 and Group-Turn-Model-I/II/III-16, U is decreased. The reason is that with larger N, more packets are put into the network at a short period and make the network a fast saturation. U is decreased much quickly in Group-Turn-Model-I/II/III-16 than in Group-Double-Y-16, because more packets are forced to use the nonminimum path routing. The restricted nonminimum path routing algorithms (Group-Turn-Model-II/III-16) always have better performance than the one without restriction (Group-Turn-Model-I-16). When R is low (0.005) as described in Figure 6(b), increasing N from 1 to 3, which try to put more packets into a low traffic network increases U in all routing algorithms except the Double-Y-2. In the Double-Y-2, when R is low and high, increasing N does not change U very much. The reason is that the routing algorithm itself and the small number of virtual channels limit the number of packets entering into the network at the same time.

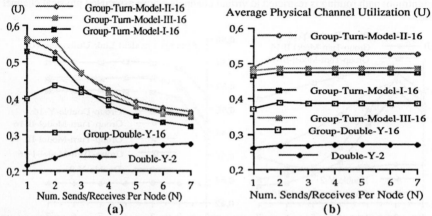

Figure 6: The average physical channel utilization when the number of Sends/Receives is varied from one to seven. The packet traffic pattern is matrix-transpose and the packet generation rate at each node (R) in (a)/(b) is 0.02/0.005.

In Figure 6, the nonminimum path routing in the Group-Turn-Model-I/II/III-16 avoids the traffic congestion which exists in the network when the traffic pattern is nonuniform. Thus U is increased dramatically even compared with Group-Double-Y. In Figure 6(a), where R is 0.02, the highest U in Group-Turn-Model-I/II/III-16 is achieved (about 55%) when N is one. The highest U in Group-Double-Y-16 is achieved (44%), when N is two. In Figure 6(b), where R is low (0.005), compared with Group-Double-Y-16, Group-Turn-Model-II-16 increases U by 10% in all range of N. Our conclusion is that multiple sends/receives (N) will not always lead to a fast saturation of the network and decrease U. Sometimes with a small value of N, U can even be increased. Considering the average performance of different routing algorithms with different N, in the rest of the simulation experiments, it is assumed that each node has two sends/receives. As also can be seen from both Figure 5 and 6, our grouping technique has relative better performance. In Figure 5(a), when N is two, in Group-Double-Y-16 the U is 66%, where as in Double-Y-2, U is only 33%. In Figure 6(b), compared with Double-Y-2, the Group-Turn-Model-II-16 always increase U at least by 20%.

Figures 7 and 8 show that initially, as expected, U increases with increased R. This increase stops when the network potential capacity (P) which is associated with both the routing algorithm and traffic pattern is approached. As with uniform traffic pattern, P is about 66% in Group-Double-Y-16, (58%)/(62%) in Group-Turn-Model-II/III-16 and 43% in Double-Y-2. With matrix-transpose traffic pattern, P is about 42% in Group-Double-Y-16, (49%)/(55%) in Group-Turn-Model-II/III-16 and 26% in Double-Y-2. Then U decreases with increased R. The reason is that a high traffic load lets the network saturate.

But U will not drop very much and soon approach a constant value, since all routing algorithms are deadlock free. For the whole range of R, both at uniform traffic and nonuniform traffic, our grouping technique has much better performance. In the Group-Double-Y-16/Group-Turn-Model-III-16, compared to the Double-Y-2, when the R is greater than 0.01, U is doubled in the uniform traffic pattern and (26%)/(38%) increased in the matrix-transpose traffic pattern. We have also observed that when applying the grouping technique to both Double-Y and Turn Model, increasing the number of virtual channels per physical channel from 8 to 16 will increase U, as described in Figures 7 and 8. In the Double-Y, where the virtual channels are statically allocated in two virtual networks, increasing n will dramatically decrease U, as we have claimed in the Section 3.

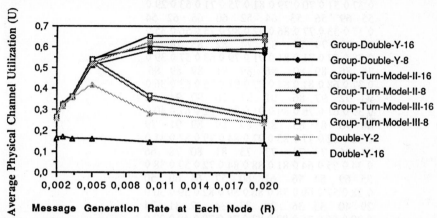

Figure 7: The average physical channel utilization when the packet generation rate at each node is varied from 0.002 to 0.02 and the packet traffic pattern is uniform.

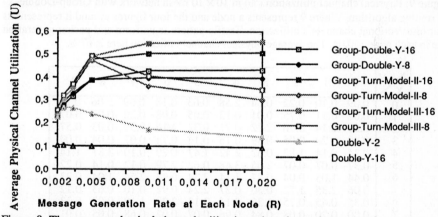

Figure 8: The average physical channel utilization when the packet generation rate at each node is varied from 0.002 to 0.02. The number of sends/receives per node is two and the packet traffic pattern is matrix-transpose.

In [DalAok92], Dally and Aoki have pointed out that with virtual channel flow control and adaptive routing, multicomputer networks may achieve performance approaching 90% of their physical capacity. In our simulation experiment, maximally about 70% of the physical capacity is reached. The reason is that the mesh is not a regular network, and the physical channel utilization is not uniform. As can be seen from Figure 9, in the middle of the 2D mesh network, where the node´s utilization is high as 97%. In the corners, the node´s utilization is very low, such as only 23% in the southeast corner. We have also observed that the average length of the waiting queue at each router (L) is not uniform, as described in Figure 10. For example, L is 4.16 at node (2,6), 1.14 at node (6,4) and zero at node (9,0). Generally speaking, there is a longer waiting queue in the middle than in the corners and it means that there is traffic congestion in the middle. Further research to avoid this problem is quite attractive.

```
◊ 22 ◊ 50 ◊ 75 ◊ 89 ◊ 93 ◊ 88 ◊ 76 ◊ 52 ◊ 29 ◊
  27  40  35  25  39  30  36  39  33  29
◊ 37 ◊ 51 ◊ 70 ◊ 79 ◊ 81 ◊ 75 ◊ 71 ◊ 53 ◊ 29 ◊
  55  69  56  53  64  52  60  66  62  54
◊ 37 ◊ 53 ◊ 77 ◊ 86 ◊ 92 ◊ 89 ◊ 75 ◊ 56 ◊ 35 ◊
  67  72  79  79  85  74  82  83  78  72
◊ 38 ◊ 57 ◊ 71 ◊ 81 ◊ 91 ◊ 79 ◊ 63 ◊ 57 ◊ 39 ◊
  76  86  89  80  86  89  91  89  89  86
◊ 37 ◊ 68 ◊ 81 ◊ 84 ◊ 87 ◊ 91 ◊ 75 ◊ 63 ◊ 36 ◊
  93  92  97  86  91  97  96  90  94  82
◊ 39 ◊ 61 ◊ 78 ◊ 89 ◊ 91 ◊ 88 ◊ 82 ◊ 67 ◊ 40 ◊
  88  90  85  85  88  89  89  89  91  79
◊ 38 ◊ 62 ◊ 77 ◊ 85 ◊ 92 ◊ 84 ◊ 79 ◊ 57 ◊ 31 ◊
  73  86  73  74  73  73  81  80  78  66
◊ 34 ◊ 55 ◊ 64 ◊ 81 ◊ 88 ◊ 84 ◊ 72 ◊ 59 ◊ 38 ◊
  55  69  54  56  61  60  57  64  60  50
◊ 28 ◊ 57 ◊ 69 ◊ 78 ◊ 86 ◊ 89 ◊ 82 ◊ 59 ◊ 30 ◊
  29  40  33  36  39  33  34  37  31  24
◊ 29 ◊ 56 ◊ 76 ◊ 83 ◊ 83 ◊ 76 ◊ 70 ◊ 49 ◊ 23 ◊
```

Figure 9: Physical channel utilization (%) in 10×10 mesh network with Group-Double-Y-16 routing algorithm. Where ◊ represents a node and the four figures around it represent its four bi-directional channels´s utilization. Traffic pattern is uniform and packet generation rate in each node is 0.04. The average physical channel utilization here is 67%.

X \ Y	0	1	2	3	4	5	6	7	8	9
0	0.09	0.10	0.22	0.34	2.58	0.63	0.18	0.09	2.06	0.19
1	0.02	0.11	0.75	0.01	0.13	0.05	0.08	0.22	0.02	0.07
2	0.87	0.14	0.96	2.22	0.71	0.32	4.16	0.32	0.03	0.57
3	0.40	0.20	0.05	0.89	0.16	0.14	0.74	0.07	0.04	0.09
4	0.34	0.14	1.82	0.62	2.42	1.47	0.20	0.10	3.81	1.14
5	0.37	0.07	0.07	2.05	3.48	0.62	2.79	0.12	0.14	0.22
6	0.44	1.05	0.04	0.87	1.14	2.34	0.98	2.64	1.04	0.33
7	0.06	2.35	1.72	0.30	0.27	2.24	0.92	0.10	0.63	0.12
8	0.35	0.45	0.25	1.26	0.14	2.13	2.20	1.19	0.02	0.13
9	0.00	0.20	0.08	0.84	0.96	0.07	0.02	0.68	0.05	0.01

Figure 10: Average length of waiting queue at each node´s router in 10×10 2D mesh with Group-Double-Y-16 routing algorithm. Traffic pattern is uniform and packet generation rate in each node is 0.04. The average of average length of waiting queue per router is 0.736.

Conclusion

In this paper, we have presented the grouping technique which can be applied to a normal adaptive routing algorithm based on the virtual network concept to further improve its adaptiveness and thus the network performance. Our simulation results of applying the grouping technique to double-y routing algorithm have confirmed it. We have also observed that in order to get good performance for a large 2D mesh network (32 × 32) with wormhole routing, each physical channel should be split into a large number of virtual channels (16) and the adaptive routing algorithm with grouping technique be applied.

Acknowledgement

Prof. Chris Jesshope at University of Surrey, UK has read the draft paper and given some important suggestion to improve the paper. Previous research works done in our group by Dr. Handong Wu and Abdel-Halim Smai in the interconnection network field are appreciated. Robert Rönngern has helped us to run the simulation program faster.

References

[AthSei88]   W.C. Athas, C.L. Seitz. "Multicomputers: Message-Passing   Concurrent Computers". *IEEE Computer*, Aug. 1988, PP. 9-24.

[ChiRic90]   Suresh Chittor, Richard Enbody. "Performance Evaluation of Mesh-Connected Wormhole-Routed Networks for Interprocessor communication in Multicomputers". *Proc. Supercomputing*, pp. 647-656, 1990.

[Dally90]   W. J. Dally. "Network and Processor Architecture for Message-Driven Computers". In Suaya and Birtwhistle, editors, *VLSI and Parallel Computation*. Morgan Kaufmann, 1990.

[DalAok92]   W. J. Dally and Hiromichi Aoki. "Adaptive Routing using Virtual Channels". tech. rep., MIT, Laboratory for Computer Science, Sept. 1990.

[Dally92]   W. J. Dally. "Virtual-Channel Flow Control". *IEEE Transactions on Parallel and Distributed Systems*, Vol. 3, No. 2, pp.194-205, March 1992.

[DalSei87]   W. J. Dally and C.L. Seitz. "Deadlock-free message routing in multiprocessor interconnection networks". *IEEE Trans. Computers*, Vol. C-36, No. 5, pp. 547-553, May 1987.

[Duato91]   José Duato. "On the Design of Deadlock-Free Adaptive Routing Algorithms for Multicomputers: design methodologies". In *Proc. Parallel Architectures and Languages Europe 91*.

[Duato92]   José Duato. "Improving the Efficiency of Virtual Channels with Time-Dependent Selection Functions". In *Proc. Parallel Architectures and Languages Europe*, pp. 635-650, 1992.

[GlaNi92]   Christopher J. Glass and Lionel M. Ni. "The Turn Model for Adaptive Routing". In *Porc. 19th International Symposium on Computer Architecture*, pp. 278-287. 1992.

[JMY89]   C.R. Jesshope, P.R. Miller and J.T. Yantchev. "High Performance Communications in Processor Networks". In *Proc. 16th Int. Symp. Computer Architecture*, pp. 150-157, 1989.

[JMY91]   C.R. Jesshope, P.R. Miller and J.T. Yantchev. The Mad-Postman Network Chip. *Proc. Transputing 91*.

[LiuWu93]   Ziqiang Liu and Handong Wu, "Performance Evaluation of Adaptive Wormhole Routing in 3D Mesh Networks". In *Proc. 26th Annual Simulation Symposium*, 1993.

[ReeFuj85]   Daniel A. Reed and Richard M. Fujimoto. *"Multicomputer Networks"*. The MIT Press 1985 Scientific Computation Series.

Monaco: A High-Performance Flat Concurrent Logic Programming System

Evan Tick

University of Oregon, Eugene OR 97403, USA

Abstract. This paper describes Monaco, a high-performance implementation of flat committed-choice languages such as Flat Guarded Horn Clauses. The compiler produces native code for linking to a runtime system on shared-memory multiprocessors. A reduced abstract-machine instruction set facilitates decision-graph code generation and traditional optimizations based on dataflow analysis. An inexpensive system-call interface is provided to lower the overhead of memory allocation and procedure invocation. Unification has been optimized to streamline the common cases. We report initial performance measurements of our current instantiation of the system, for the Sequent Symmetry, for a suite of benchmarks.

KEYWORDS: concurrent logic programming, compilation, dataflow analysis

1 Introduction

During language design and application development, compilation to intermediate (ready-for-emulation) instruction sets is most cost effective considering design time. However, as languages mature, the demand for well-balanced systems requires that we consider advanced compilation techniques to statically bind as much information as we can. This typical implementation scenario was played out, for several years, for the diverse family of logic programming languages. After initial forays into building logic programming machines based on the Warren Abstract Machine (WAM) [1], advanced compilers were built to better exploit conventional microprocessors (e.g., [22, 26]). Furthermore, a slew of more sophisticated optimization techniques have been in development (e.g., [5, 6, 12, 24]).

Specifically with respect to the development of committed-choice logic programming language [19] compilers, a combination of techniques are required to achieve high performance on conventional hardware. The compiler back-end can be viewed as a code generator and a code optimizer. My thesis in this paper is that for both phases, abstract machines based on the WAM, e.g., Parlog [4] and KL1 [11], must be discarded in favor of reduced instruction sets that allow fine-grain manipulations. This idea is not new — Asakawa *et al.* [2] developed a Prolog compiler based on an intermediate form of highly annotated graphs, producing PL.8 code for an industrial-strength optimizing compiler back-end. Their reliance on user declarations of type and mode information is no longer justified, given research over the years in dataflow analysis and abstract interpretation of logic programs. The application of these global techniques to concurrent logic programs has progressed more slowly because of the added complexities of dealing with concurrency, but the local analysis methods are directly applicable. For example, Kliger and Shapiro's decision-graph method for code generation [12] permits fast clause selection as an alternative to conventional indexing methods [1]. Dataflow analysis in the back-end facilitates common subexpression elimination of type checking and dereferencing among other things, that are impossible given WAM-like instruction sets.

An alternative is to macro-expand WAM-like instruction sets into native code or 'C', and then perform dataflow optimizations. The disadvantages of such a scheme are 1) native code optimizers may be nonexistent; 2) it will be machine dependent (even 'C' optimizations may depend on machine particulars), and 3) the analysis complexity is likely to be greater than analysis of an intermediate form.

With these issues in mind, we set about to build the Monaco compiler and runtime system, as a "second generation" implementation of concurrent logic programming languages, the first being emulator-based systems such as Panda [17] and JAM [4]. The Monaco compiler translates flat committed-choice logic programs into an abstract machine suitable for execution on shared-memory multiprocessor hosts. Our current implementation accepts Flat Guarded Horn Clause (FGHC) programs [19] and produces native Intel 80386 code for the Sequent Symmetry. A port to an SGI MIPS-based multiprocessor is in progress. Monaco's main purpose is to be a testbed for global optimization techniques such as type inferencing, mode analysis, sequentialization, and local memory reuse. Implementation and integration of these analyses are underway, although the focus of this paper is the kernel Monaco system and the locally-optimizing compiler only.

2 Monaco Abstract Machine

Efficient execution of concurrent logic programs requires: 1) fast selection of a committing clause; 2) fast active unification (effectively assignment); 3) efficient use of available memory (heap) bandwidth, and 4) sufficiently reduced frequency of process management (low concurrency overheads). The key design point in the Monaco abstract machine is the low-level instruction set, allowing dataflow analysis and optimization, and facilitating native-code generation. Secondly, a fast interface to system kernel functions is critical to a well-balanced implementation. Only with such a streamlined abstract machine can the true relative costs of the overheads summarized above be measured and tuned.

The Monaco abstract machine supports seven programmer-visible tagged data types: integers, immediates (symbolic atoms), reference pointers, logical variables, hooked variables, list pairs, and vectors. Abstractly, each of the first five simple objects occupies a machine *cell* consisting of a data field, tag, and lock. As in WAM, a compound object is represented as a pointer to a group of cells containing the list pair or vector. On Symmetry, we implement a cell in eight bytes, with a low-order 3-bit tag in the first word, and the second word currently devoted only to the lock (a scheme similar to that used in Panda, chosen for its simplicity and extensibility). For the SGI, we use a lock vector similar to that of JAM Parlog [4].

A logical variable cell is an uninstantiated location, with the data field pointing to the cell itself (as in WAM). When a variable becomes instantiated, its type changes to that of the value that the cell is instantiated with. A *hooked* variable cell is an uninstantiated location on which one or more process is blocked. The data field of the cell points to a list of suspended processes, as in Panda and JAM. If a hooked cell is bound, the processes hooked on the cell must be resumed. Tradeoffs concerning these design decisions are well documented [1, 4].

The Monaco abstract machine is a load-store architecture to facilitate mapping to RISC hosts. Other load-store instruction sets for logic programming languages exist (e.g., the BAM [26], PIM/i [18], PIM/p [21], and CARMEL-2 [10]), although they have been primarily designed for specialized hardware. A majority of the Monaco instructions are lightweight and can easily be translated into small sequences of instructions on the host. Most predicate and arithmetic instructions fall into this category. A few instructions are sufficiently complex that native code is avoided for portability considerations. These are implemented by an interface to the runtime system, called a *millicode call* (Section 3). The middle ground is covered by the data manipulators and constructors, currently implemented in native code, at some expense in code size, to minimize system-call frequency. Both active and passive unification are sufficiently complex to warrant implementation in millicode. Full passive unification in the head or guard is only needed in the rare case of shared variables, thus we do not review the algorithm [7] here. Active unification commonly occurs in the body. The unify instruction either returns, indicating success, or raises an exception, indicating failure (note that unlike logic programs, flat concurrent logic programs are not "complete," and thus immediately fail if any body goal fails).

The Monaco code for the quicksort procedure, written in FGHC, is shown in Figure 1 (part/4 not shown). The precise semantics of the instruction set [7] are not necessary to follow the example. Before entry to a procedure, the input arguments are loaded in to the abstract machine registers numbered from zero. The entry point to this procedure is labeled sort/3. Arguments are dereferenced before they are tested (1). Quicksort dispatches on its first (input) argument in a switch on tag instruction (2). If unbound, control flows to L1, where the argument is pushed on the suspension stack and suspension occurs (3-4). If an integer or vector, control flows to L2 where the suspension routine is called with no pushed arguments (4), resulting in failure. If an atom, control flows to L3, where the argument is compared to nil and either fails or commits to the first clause (5-9). If the first argument is a list, the second clause commits at L4 (10-35). The alloc instruction (10) allocates a 15-cell frame on the heap, because that many cells are required in the ensuing code. Two goal records are constructed for the two sort/3 goals in the body, and are enqueued (20,31). A call is made to the part/4 procedure (33), after setting up its arguments in appropriate registers (13,23,27,32), exploiting last-call optimization.

3 Compilation

The Monaco compiler follows a traditional pipeline organization, where the input is a source program and the output is an equivalent program in the abstract machine instruction set. The front-end parses the program and generates decision graphs with Kliger's algorithm [12]. Alternatively, "don't know" procedures (determinacy testing trees) in languages such as Pandora and Andorra can be generated [13]. These graphs and trees are fed to a code-generation phase which produces rudimentary

```
sort([],Rest,Ans) :- true | Rest = Ans.
sort([X|R],Y,T) :- true | part(R,X,S,L), sort(S,Y,[X|Y1]), sort(L,Y1,T).

sort/3:     deref      r0,r4              % r4 := deref(Argument 1)            1
            switch     [L1,L4,L3,L2,L2,L1,L1,L1],r4                           2
L1:         push       r0                 % No. Push Argument 1. Suspend.      3
L2:         suspend    sort/3             % Suspend                            4
L3:         mkconst    [],r3              % Argument 1 is []?                  5
            eq         r4,r3,r5                                                6
            br         z,r5,L2            % No, fail.                          7
            unify      r1,r2              % Yes. Rest = Ans                    8
            proceed                                                           9
L4:         alloc      15,r5              % Allocate 15 cells on heap.        10
            move       r5,r6                                                 11
            initgoal   sort/3,r6          % r6 -> goal sort/3                 12
            ref        r5,5,r3            % r3 := L                           13
            initvar    r3                                                    14
            sset       r3,1,r6            % 1(r6) := L                        15
            ref        r5,6,r8            % r8 := Y1                          16
            initvar    r8                                                    17
            sset       r8,2,r6            % 2(r6) := Y1                       18
            sset       r2,3,r6            % 3(r6) := T                        19
            enqueue    r6                 % enqueue sort(L,Y1,T)              20
            ref        r5,7,r9                                               21
            initgoal   sort/3,r9          % r9 -> goal sort/3                 22
            ref        r5,12,r2           % r2 := S                           23
            initvar    r2                                                    24
            sset       r2,1,r9            % 1(r9) := S                        25
            sset       r1,2,r9            % 2(r9) := Y                        26
            car        r4,r1              % r1 := X                           27
            ref        r5,13,r12                                             28
            initlist   r1,r8,r12          % r12 := [X|Y1]                     29
            sset       r12,3,r9           % 3(r9) := [X|Y1]                   30
            enqueue    r9                 % enqueue sort(S,Y,[X|Y1])          31
            cdr        r4,r0              % r0 := R                           32
            execute    part/4             % call part(R,X,S,L)                33
```

Fig. 1. Compiled Quicksort Procedure in Monaco

abstract machine code (assuming an infinite register set). Flow analysis proceeds by decomposing the program into a flow graph of basic blocks. Type and dereferencing information is propagated through the flow graph in the subsequent phase. At this point, macro-instructions are resolved, redundant computations are recognized and eliminated. Deadcode elimination and register allocation are performed as the final flow graph optimizations. The output from the register allocator is an abstract machine program instantiated with abstract register identifiers. A peephole stage removes dead blocks and branches.

A decision graph can be thought of as a tree of if-then-else and switch type nodes. Space is conserved by routing control to a "continuation" branch in certain cases, forming a graph rather than a full decision tree [12]. Returning to the Quicksort example in Figure 1, there are several interesting points about how code is generated from the decision graph (see Section 5 for empirical analysis).

– Originally we favored binary branches over switches, because we planned Monaco for a RISC target. However, the 80386, based on a condition-code register, is not conducive to branching on conditions stored in registers. Therefore we introduced the **switch** instruction, assembled into an indirect jump-on-tag table. We do not do optimal code generation as discussed in Debray [5].

- Structures are created on the heap by allocating space for the entire clause body, and then filling it in for each structure (including goal records). For each structure argument, a reference is built (with `ref`) pointing to the heap location where it will be constructed, and the storage is initialized (e.g., `initvar` and `initgoal`). Then the structure argument position is bound to the reference (with `sset`). This currently implies that variables reside outside of structures, which facilitates future optimizations concerning local memory reuse [20].

- The final Monaco code shown in Figure 1 is the result of extensive dataflow analysis and optimization. With no optimizations the procedure has 43 Monaco instructions, an increase of 30%. The primary savings in code size, and corresponding execution time, comes from common subexpression elimination and generation of tight control flow instructions. See [23] for the breakdown of performance gains due to optimizations.

- The compiler was purposely kept as modular as possible, with a minimum number of stages (no feedback), and therefore less than optimal code is produced. For example, we chose to do register allocation *after* common subexpression elimination. Thus if we have register spilling, the spill sequences will not be simplified. We also chose to abide by a code-generation policy wherein every pseudo register is defined at most once per procedure. Given this policy, which facilitates dataflow analysis, we need to assign *different* pseudo registers to passed parameters and tail-recursive (in general, some body goal chosen for direct execution after this thread) arguments. Those registers need to be coerced during register allocation. The result is poor allocation in the basic block containing the tail recursion because no constraints are present, during coloring of *previous* blocks, concerning tail-recursive register usage (recall, these final registers have been purposely aliased). A patch was added to scan the block in reverse, shorting out register-to-register moves, producing reasonable, but not excellent, code.

The macro assembler is the penultimate stage in the compilation process. It translates a Monaco assembly program into an 80386 assembly program, for final translation by the vendor assembler *as*. We do not globally reoptimize the assembly code, e.g., we do not optimally reallocate the 80386 registers. Of the eight programmable 80386 registers we do not use `%esp` and `%ebp` because they are used by 'C' calling protocols. In addition, we reserve one register for the suspension stack pointer, leaving five free registers. However, if we tried to do Monaco register allocation onto only five registers, significant spilling would occur. Another idea would be to map the first five allocated pseudo-registers onto the five actual registers. However, these are not general-purpose registers, so this scheme would require spilling around certain instructions to abide by usage constraints. We therefore chose a third approach wherein we allocate two general purpose 80386 registers as temporaries (aliased as `TMP0` and `TMP1`) to define the assembler templates corresponding to each Monaco instruction. The remaining three registers are currently used for noncritical purposes. The downside of this compromise is that `TMP0` and `TMP1` are not optimally allocated *among* the templates once they are spliced together.

Figure 2 gives a few examples of macro expansion of Monaco into 80386 assembly. The `move` instruction needs two assembly instructions, since the 80386 doesn't support memory-to-memory moves. In some cases, the first instruction of the template

```
        movl    Rs*4(REGS),TMP0      # move(Rs, Rd)
        movl    TMP0,Rd*4(REGS)

        movl    Rs*4(REGS),TMP0      # deref(Rs, Rd)
        movl    TMP0,TMP2            #   TrailPtr := t
L(k):   movl    TMP0,TMP1
        andl    $TAG_MASK,TMP1       #   while(TAG(t) == REF_TAG)
        jnz     L(k+1)               #   {
        movl    TMP0,TMP2            #      TrailPtr = t;
        movl    0(TMP0),TMP0         #      t = CELLREF(t);
        jmp     L(k)                 #   }
L(k+1): movl    TMP0,Rd*4(REGS)      # Rd = Result

                                     # punify(Rs1, Rs2, Rd)
        pushl   Rs2*4(REGS)          # push Rs2 on stack
        pushl   Rs1*4(REGS)          # push Rs1 on stack
        pushl   $LM_RET              # push return address
        jmp     *PUNIFY_OFF(REGS)    # indirect call to punify
LM_RET: addl    $8,%esp              # readjust stack
        movl    TMP0,Rd*4(REGS)      # Rd := punify(Rs1,Rs2)
```

Fig. 2. Examples of 80386 Macro Expansion on Symmetry

can be removed via peephole optimization. The **deref** instruction is one of the most complex expanded instructions. Instructions **unify, punify, enqueue, suspend,** and **execute** are sufficiently complex to warrant implementation within the runtime system as millicode. A millicode call is accomplished by means of an indirect jump table, with parameters passed in the usual 'C' style. This is illustrated by the **punify** expansion in Figure 2. The source operands and the return address are pushed onto the 'C' stack. The result is returned in **TMP0**, which is then stored in register **Rd**.

A final note about register allocation. It is somewhat pointless for the Symmetry host to go to the trouble of Monaco register allocation, only to implement Monaco registers in memory! However, Monaco is targeted for processors with healthy general-purpose register sets, so we chose to live with this inefficiency for now. Global allocation can be done once concurrent threads have been sequentialized, a static optimization we are now pursuing [15].

4 Monaco Runtime System

In this section, we review the Monaco runtime kernel, built from ideas borrowed from various other systems (JAM, Panda, Strand). The purpose of the review is to familiarize the reader with the functions performed by the runtime system and how they are are tuned for speed by "hedging" the code for the most frequent case.

Concurrent logic languages, due to the nature of the fine-grain tasks, single-assignment variables, and heap-based memory management, require extensive runtime support. The main objectives of the runtime system are to support fast process management, memory allocation, and runtime system calls, as described in this section. Like most WAM-based systems, the Monaco kernel is a set of *worker* processes that run as regular UNIX processes on all the processors. A worker process corresponds to one Monaco abstract machine processor. The number of workers can be specified when the system is invoked. We distinguish one of the workers as the *mas-*

ter, facilitating a simple user interface. The master accepts queries, outputs bindings, and detects termination and deadlock.

Computation in concurrent logic languages proceeds by selecting a goal for execution from a pool of ready-to-run goals. A goal reduction is carried out by executing the goal as a *light-weight thread*. A Monaco thread may be thought of as a goal in execution. The thread performs the clause try operations and if a clause commits, spawns child threads to represent the body goals of the clause. A goal does not always execute to completion: it may try to read the contents of an uninstantiated shared variable and will suspend. Any goal that instantiates that variable must *resume* all the goals suspended on the variable, adding them to the goal pool.

A worker operates in a loop: looking for reducible goals in the pool, finding one and reducing it, adding the body goals of that clause to the pool, and continuing to look for more work. To reduce synchronization, the goal pool is split among the workers — each has a private goal queue, implemented as a list. Thus we both enqueue and dequeue goals from the queue head, resulting in pseudo depth-first execution (not pure because idle workers steal goals from busy workers' queues). Depth-first evaluation has been shown to be relatively efficient [17], so we adopted it here. We also adopted the JAM scheduling strategy of a ring: an idle worker examines the private queues of successive clockwise neighbors until a goal is found. This scheme is efficient because the idle worker is responsible for finding work, affecting busy workers only when synchronizing on the queue. This scheme works effectively and produces reasonable load balancing, as shown in JAM and here (see Section 5). Our current research emphasis is an efficient instruction set and compilation procedure, so we have adopted standard techniques for thread management. Suspension and resumption is done with logical variables hooked to suspended goals via suspension slips, as in JAM Parlog [4] and KL1 [11] implementations.

Most goals allocate heap memory for creating data and body goal structures. We reduce the frequency of allocation by aggregating all heap requests within a clause into a single millicode call. The Monaco heap is split into equal-sized slices for each worker, avoiding synchronization. Each heap is initialized with two range pointers delimiting the unallocated area. All heap allocations, approximately one per reduction, manipulate and check these pointers accordingly. The overflow check is sufficiently frequent that we chose to generate it in native code. This naive heap implementation is sufficient for our initial evaluation of compilation techniques. The current version of Monaco does not have garbage collection (and so collection overheads are not accounted for in the empirical analysis given in Section 5).

The primary runtime operations are described in this section: variable dereference and binding, and active unification. For other support routines, see [7]. Both *soft* and *hard* dereferencing are implemented, listed in Figure 3. In the figure, input p is a tagged Monaco datum and CELLREF(p) is the contents of the cell at location p. Soft dereference corresponds to sequential Prolog dereferencing: the argument is not locked. The Monaco deref instruction is soft and native code is generated by the compiler. Hard dereferencing, used internally by active unification, is safe in the sense that the final dereferenced value is locked upon return if it is unbound. This prevents another writer from binding it. Although costly, hard dereferencing does not usually iterate because reference chains are short.

Any variable is potentially shared between multiple goals and needs to be locked

```
word soft_deref(word p) {          | bind(word X, word NewVal) {
  while (TAG(p) == #REF)           |   lock(X)
    p := CELLREF(p));              |   OldVal = X;
    return p;                      |   X = NewVal;
  }                                |   unlock(X);
-----------------------------------|   if (OldVal is bound)
word hard_deref(word p) {          |     unify(NewVal,OldVal);
  lock(p);                         |   else
  while (TAG(CELLREF(p)) == #REF) {|     if (goals suspended on X)
    unlock(p);                     |       wake goals on susp. list;
    p := CELLREF(p);               | }
    lock(p);                       |
  }                                |
  if ((TAG(CELLREF(p)) <> #VAR) and|
     (TAG(CELLREF(p)) <> #HOOK))   |
    unlock(p);                     |
    return CELLREF(p);             |
}                                  |
```

Fig. 3. Soft and Hard Dereference, and Bind Operations (Pseudo Code)

during binding. Several race conditions are possible. 1) Multiple writers may try to bind a variable, in which case they must synchronize on a lock, and only one may succeed. Fully-moded FGHC programs do not have this potential race. 2) A reader and writer may race to access a variable, in which case while the reader is deciding to suspend, the writer may bind the variable. The reader therefore must lock the variable before suspending, and noticing it has been bound, resume the goal. 3) A similar problem can occur when two readers are attempting to suspend on a variable — to prevent possible inconsistencies in the suspension-list data structure, suspend operations also must synchronize. 4) A goal may be suspended on multiple variables. If any of these variables is bound, the goal must be resumed. Multiple writers may race to resume the goal on different variables, in which case they must synchronize, to allow only one to resume the goal and remove its suspension list.

An algorithm solving these potential races when instantiating a variable is also shown in Figure 3. The algorithm is similar to that in JAM and other systems. bind(X,NewVal) assigns the value NewVal to X. Oldval is the old value in X, if X was bound. This algorithm minimizes the time a heap cell is locked. If X was already bound, then NewVal is assigned to X, but it is verified that OldVal and NewVal are unifiable. Normally, X is not already bound and the unify(NewVal,OldVal) operation is not executed. Since synchronization is enforced by the section of code where the old value of X is changed, races between multiple writers are eliminated.

General active unification is invoked as unify(a,b) where a and b are tagged Monaco objects. The code is sketched in the right half of Figure 4. In the general algorithm, operand a is soft dereferenced and a tag dispatch is performed. If a is bound, one of several specialized unification routines is called. If a is unbound, to avoid races, we hard dereference a and dispatch on tag again. The specialized routines are quite complex because races must be prevented if b is unbound. There are two additional complexities when binding two variables: avoidance of circular reference chains and deadlock. To solve these problems, we exploit the shared address space of the host to point the higher-address variable towards the lower-address variable. The

```
assign(word a, word b)           |  unify(word a, word b)
{word tmp;                       |  {word tmp;
  tmp = VALUE(a);                |    a = soft_deref(a);
  if(TAG(CELLREF(tmp))==VAR_TAG) {|    tmp = VALUE(a);
    lock(tmp);                   |    switch (TAG(a)) {
    if(TAG(CELLREF(tmp))==VAR_TAG) { |    case REF_TAG: return unify(a,b);
      a = tmp;                   |    /*FIX, IMM, PAIR, VECT similar*/
      *(CELLREF(a)) = b;         |    case VAR_TAG:
      unlock(tmp);               |    case HOOK_TAG:
      return SUCCESS;            |      a = hard_deref(tmp);
    }                            |      switch (TAG(a)) {
    else unlock(tmp);            |        case VAR_TAG:
  }                              |          return unify_var(a,b);
  unify(a,b);                    |          /* other tags similar */
}                                |        default: return FAILURE;
                                 |      }
                                 |    default: return FAILURE;
                                 |  }}
```

Fig. 4. Active Unification Algorithm

higher-address variable must be locked before attempting to lock the lower-address variable. These complications make unification slower than in Prolog or in sequential implementations of concurrent logic languages (e.g., [9]).

The full unification algorithm requires about 700 source lines, which is quite complex and difficult to optimize [7]. Through instrumentation, the most frequently-used path through the algorithm was identified: since the benchmark programs are fully moded, it is not surprising that dynamically 99% of the unifies are assignment to a variable. The other cases involve unification of hooked variables. The left of Figure 4 shows an optimized stub to quickly catch the most common case, or fall through to general unification. We test the tag of operand a, then lock it and test again, thereby preventing races. Operand b is constant, so need not be locked. Note that by using the CELLREF macro, we actually dereference operand a once, since the Monaco architecture can allocate variables on the heap only, referenced by register operands. The stub, as shown, assumes mode analysis has determined that operands a and b are output and input, respectively. If non-moded programs are permitted, operand b must be dereferenced and if it is not a constant, the general unifier must be invoked to avoid potential deadlock. Such seemingly minor details can drastically impact execution speed: the *queen* benchmark in the next section experiences a 14% slowdown if modes are not exploited. The stub has a major impact on performance [23], but still is inefficient with respect to binding in sequential implementations [9]. Without more powerful global analysis, we cannot safely remove the locking and rechecking of the LHS operand because it could be hooked by a concurrent goal.

5 Performance Evaluation

Performance evaluation of Monaco has focussed on measuring the uniprocessor execution time, speedups in parallel execution, and profiling of program execution. In this paper we present uniprocessor and preliminary multiprocessor performance results, and leave the detailed analysis to a companion paper [23].

For uniprocessor execution, Monaco is compared with Strand (Buckingham) [8], JAM V1.4 [4], PDSS V2.52.19 [3], Panda (using PDSS V0.8 compiler!) [17], and Janus [9]. For multiprocessor execution, comparison is made only with JAM because it is the fastest of the parallel systems with comparative scheduling. Empirical evaluation was conducted on a Sequent Symmetry S81 system with 16 MHz Intel 80386 microprocessors. Execution times (in milliseconds) are calculated as the elapsed time between starting the computation, until all the processors become idle. All measurements presented are the minimum of several runs.

Program	Monaco	Strand	JAM	Panda	PDSS	Janus
hanoi(14)	1.0	1.3	1.7	2.1	2.1	0.27
nrev(1000)	1.0	1.8	2.0	3.3	2.9	0.20
qsort(1000)	1.0	1.9	2.4	5.2	2.7	0.60
queens(10)	1.0	0.66	3.6	5.2	4.7	1.02
primes(5000)	1.0	3.0	3.7	5.8	3.7	0.48
pascal(200)	1.0	2.4	2.3	4.4	2.6	0.42
geo. mean	1.0	1.6	2.5	4.0	3.0	0.43

Table 1. Uniprocessor Execution Time Normalized to Monaco (Full Opt.) on Symmetry

Table 1 shows uniprocessor execution times, normalized to Monaco, for a benchmark suite. This is meant only as an approximate comparison: the systems offer different facilities (e.g., language capabilities, types of garbage collectors) that make a fair comparison difficult. For example, PDSS and Janus are sequential systems without any multiprocessor overheads. The other systems' times all include whatever overheads they incur for multiprocessor execution. *Queens* is the only program for which Monaco displays inferior performance with respect to a multiprocessor implementation (Strand), even though mode information is utilized. We believe this is due to somewhat naive code generation of arithmetic expressions on our part. For example, we currently do not do static type analysis, so that *queens* requires a great number of integer type checks. Janus shows high overheads enforcing its "two occurrence" rule with copying in *queens*.

These measurements satisfy us that our first instantiation of Monaco is on a performance par with alternative multiprocessor implementations. The measured system is largely untuned, with approximately 48% of execution time in user code and 52% in the kernel, on average. The benchmarks fall into two categories with respect to kernel time breakdown: 1) programs with frequent procedure invocations spend 29% of execution time in goal enqueue and dispatch functions; 2) programs with frequent unifications spend 36% of execution time in the unify stub. We need to streamline the worker goal management loop to reduce the former. The latter can be reduced by pulling the unify stub up into assembly code. We are also considering global analysis to determine that an output variable to be assigned cannot be hooked [27], thus obviating the need to lock and retest the tag. With general polishing of the kernel and assembler templates, significant speedup is expected. However, jc speeds will only be achieved with "real" register allocation.

As a first experiment with parallel execution, we measured execution speeds on increasing numbers of Symmetry processors (PEs), comparing Monaco with JAM Parlog. We found Monaco achieved speedups ranging from 8.5 (*hanoi*) to 14.9 (*queens*) on 16 PEs, whereas JAM achieved speedups of 3.9 (*qsort*) to 15.9 (*queens*). Over the benchmarks, the JAM/Monaco execution time ratio ranged from 1.1 (*nrev* on 16 PEs) to 5.9 (*qsort* on 16 PEs). Note that Monaco and JAM use almost identical scheduling algorithms, so similar results were expected. We conclude simply that Monaco is successfully exploiting fine-grain parallelism, even though its streamlined abstract machine achieved gains in absolute performance.

6 Related Work

Recent Japanese efforts in RISC-oriented committed-choice systems implementation include the PIM/i, PIM/p, and UNIRED-II microprocessors. To facilitate pipelining, these instruction sets are significantly lower level than previous WAM-based emulator designs. Sato [18] presents measurements of delayed branch characteristics in PIM/i, something we cannot measure with the current Monaco 80386 host. PIM/p [14] supports *macro-calls*, similar in function to Monaco's millicode calls. Macro-calls facilitate a quick switch to an "internal" instruction stream, for example defining unification. Monaco suffers in speed because of millicode calls must cross the 'C' interface. The FLENG optimizing compiler [27] for UNIRED-II includes global analysis, for instance to determine whether a variable can be hooked. The other PIM machines [21] have instruction sets similar to that of the early Panda system [17], an emulator-based FGHC implementation on shared-memory multiprocessors. The Panda compiler (PDSS [3]) utilizes an abstract machine instruction set similar to WAM [11], and is non-optimizing.

Jim's Abstract Machine (JAM) is a WAM-like emulator-based shared-memory implementation of Parlog [4], including support for Or-Parallel execution of *deep* guards. This introduces additional overheads for process management, since a process activation tree must be maintained. JAM exhibits higher performance than Panda because of more sophisticated memory and goal queue management. Strand [8] is a distributed-memory implementation of Flat Parlog, with *assignment* rather than unification. In this sense, the language is similar to *fully-moded* FGHC [25], where there is a single writer to a variable. This simplification facilitates fast binding. Other optimizations in the Strand implementation include simplified data structures to implement suspension, based on the observation that most goals suspend on only one variable at a time, and better compilation of process definitions. Thus Strand out-performs JAM. Both Strand and moded FGHC are of particular relevance to Monaco because we require the same restrictions within our mode analyzer [15].

Implementations of Flat Concurrent Prolog include the Logix system [19], the various Carmel microprocessors (e.g., [10]), and a more recent implementation, based on decision graphs, by Kliger [12]. The former is emulated, and the latter two are uniprocessor implementations, so direct comparison with Monaco is inappropriate. Monaco's decision-graph compilation method is borrowed from [12] — Monaco extends this locally with dataflow analysis, whereas [12] extends this globally with abstract interpretation to derive procedure bodies optimized for different call sites. Over an extensive set of benchmarks, Kliger reports speedups of 3.2 due to decision graphs over standard indexing, 1.2 due to his global optimizations, and 5.2 due to 68000 native-code compilation [12]. These results encourage us that Monaco is balanced in the sense of putting our effort where the highest payoffs occur.

A final related language is Janus [16], with the restriction that a stream can have one and only one producer and consumer, as annotated by the programmer. An experimental compiler jc has been developed [9] for uniprocessors, translating Janus into 'C'. Thus we consider jc the sequential baseline against which to compare Monaco efficiency.

Monaco is novel because it integrates an optimizing compiler with a real parallel system for concurrent logic programs. The runtime system adopts many features developed by previous researchers, paying heed to the engineering credo of simplifying the frequent cases. We believe that the sophistication of our local static analysis (and in fact of additional global analysis) is necessary to improve execution performance. This is supported by the uniprocessor performance measurements previously discussed, and strengthened by viewing individual speedups afforded by components of the compiler. For example, common subexpression elimination achieves a mean speedup of 15% across the benchmarks studied [23] — this is exactly the type of optimization that cannot easily be achieved in WAM-like architectures.

7 Summary and Future Work

We have presented Monaco, a native-code, shared-memory multiprocessor implementation of committed-choice logic programming languages. The novel attributes of the system are a low-level intermediate instruction set and a correspondingly sophisticated compiler. Decision-graph code generation followed by aggressive dataflow analysis demonstrates absolute speeds and speedups comparable to WAM-style emulator-based implementations of similar languages. These results have been achieved even with the severe handicap of an 80386 target, which forces us to access all our abstract machine registers from memory, and makes Monaco's register-based branches extremely inefficient.

With suitable reorganization, we believe Monaco can produce significantly better performance. One project we have started is sequentialization analysis to determine body goal ordering that guarantees deadlock-free sequential execution [15]. We have demonstrated this with a 'C' target, and achieved a speedup of 4.8 times over the current instantiation of Monaco, for the simple list *append* program on Symmetry. More complex procedures will achieve even greater speedup because multiple body goals execute on the stack rather than a heap-based pool of goal frames. We are currently exploring how to integrate the sequentialized code with concurrent code.

Acknowledgements

E. Tick was supported by an NSF Presidential Young Investigator award, with matching funds from Sequent Computer Systems Inc. The original Monaco team included C. Banerjee (performance analysis), S. Duvvuru (runtime system), L. Hansen (instruction set), M. Korsloot (indexer), and B. Massey (mode and sequentialization analysis).

References

1. H. Ait-Kaci. *Warren's Abstract Machine: A Tutorial Reconstruction.* MIT Press, 1991.
2. Y. Asakawa *et al.* A Very Fast Prolog Compiler on Multiple Architectures. In *Fall Joint Computer Conference*, pages 963–968. ACM and IEEE Computer Society, 1986.
3. T. Chikayama *et al.* Overview of the Parallel Inference Machine Operating System PIMOS. In *FGCS'88*, pages 230–251, Tokyo, November 1988. ICOT.
4. J. A. Crammond. The Abstract Machine and Implementation of Parallel Parlog. *New Generation Computing*, 10(4):385–422, August 1992.
5. S. Debray *et al.* Weighted Decision Trees. In *JICSLP'92*, MIT Press, 1992.
6. S. K. Debray, N.-W. Lin, and M. Hermenegildo. Task Granularity Analysis in Logic Programs. In *SIGPLAN PLDI'90*, pages 174–188, June 1990. ACM Press.
7. S. Duvvuru. Monaco: A High Performance Implementation of FGHC on Shared-Memory Multiprocessors. Master's thesis, University of Oregon, June 1992.
8. I. Foster and S. Taylor. Strand: A Practical Parallel Programming Language. In *North American Conference on Logic Programming*, pages 497–512. MIT Press, 1989.
9. D. Gudeman *et al.* jc: An Efficient and Portable Sequential Implementation of Janus. In *JICSLP'92*, pages 399–413. MIT Press, November 1992.
10. A. Harsat and R. Ginosar. CARMEL-2: A Second Generation VLSI Architecture for Flat Concurrent Prolog. *New Generation Computing*, 7:197–218, 1990.
11. Y. Kimura and T. Chikayama. An Abstract KL1 Machine and its Instruction Set. In *ISLP*, pages 468–477. IEEE Computer Society, 1987.
12. S. Kliger. *Compiling Concurrent Logic Programming Languages.* PhD thesis, The Weizmann Institute of Science, Rehovot, October 1992.
13. M. Korsloot and E. Tick. Compilation Techniques for Nondeterminate Flat Concurrent Logic Programming Languages. In *ICLP*, pages 457–471. MIT Press, June 1991.
14. K. Kumon *et al.* Architecture and Implementation of PIM/p. In *FGCS'92*, pages 414–424, Tokyo, June 1992. ICOT.
15. B. C. Massey. Sequentialization of Parallel Logic Programs with Mode Analysis. Master's thesis, University of Oregon, September 1992.
16. V. A. Saraswat *et al.* Janus: A Step Towards Distributed Constraint Programming. In *NACLP'90*, pages 431–446. MIT Press, October 1990.
17. M. Sato *et al.* Evaluation of the KL1 Parallel System on a Shared Memory Multiprocessor. In *IFIP Work. Conf. on Parallel Process.*, pg 305–318. North Holland, 1988.
18. M. Sato *et al.* Exploiting Fine Grain Parallelism in Logic Programming on a Parallel Inference Machine. Technical Report TR-676, ICOT, Tokyo, August 1991.
19. E. Y. Shapiro. The Family of Concurrent Logic Programming Languages. *ACM Computing Surveys*, 21(3), 1989.
20. R. Sundararajan *et al.* Variable Threadedness Analysis for Concurrent Logic Programs. In *JICSLP'92*, pages 493–508. Washington D.C., MIT Press, November 1992.
21. K. Taki. Parallel Inference Machine PIM. In *International Conference on Fifth Generation Computer Systems*, pages 50–72, Tokyo, June 1992. ICOT.
22. A. Taylor. LIPS on a MIPS: Results From a Prolog Compiler for a RISC. In *International Conference on Logic Programming*, pages 174–185. MIT Press, June 1990.
23. E. Tick and C. Banerjee. Performance Evaluation of Monaco Compiler and Runtime Kernel. In *Int. Conf. on Logic Programming*. Budapest, MIT Press, June 1993.
24. E. Tick and X. Zhong. A Compile-Time Granularity Analysis Algorithm and its Performance Evaluation. *New Generation Computing*, 11(3–4), June 1993.
25. K. Ueda and M. Morita. A New Implementation Technique for Flat GHC. In *International Conference on Logic Programming*, pages 3–17. MIT Press, June 1990.
26. P. L. Van Roy and A. M. Despain. High-Performace Logic Programming with the Aquarius Prolog Compiler. *IEEE Computer Magazine*, pages 54–68, January 1992.
27. K. Yanoo. An Optimizing Compiler for a Parallel Inference Language. In H. Tanaka, editor, *Annual Report of the Research on Parallel Inference Engine*, pages 71–94. University of Tokyo, April 1992. (in Japanese).

Exploiting Recursion-Parallelism in Prolog

Johan Bevemyr   Thomas Lindgren   Håkan Millroth

Computing Science Dept., Uppsala University
Box 311, S-75105 Uppsala, Sweden
Email: {bevemyr,thomasl,hakanm}@csd.uu.se

Abstract

We exploit parallelism across recursion levels in a deterministic sub-set of Prolog. The implementation extends a convential Prolog machine with support for data sharing and process managment. Extensive global dataflow analysis is employed to facilitate parallelization. Promising performance figures, showing high parallel efficiency and low overhead for parallelization, have been obtained on a 24 processor shared-memory multiprocessor.

1   INTRODUCTION

The Single Program Multiple Data (SPMD) model of parallel computation has recently received a lot of attention (see e.g. the article by Bell [1]). The model is characterized by each parallel process running the same program but with different data.[1] The attraction of this model is that it does not require a dynamic network of parallel processes: this facilitates efficient implementation and makes the parallel control-flow comprehensible for the programmer.

We are concerned here with the SPMD model in the context of logic programming. For recursive programs, the different recursive invocations of a predicate are all executed in parallel, while all other calls are executed sequentially. We refer to this variant of (dependent) AND-parallelism as *recursion-parallelism*. A recursive invocation minus the head unification and the (next) recursive call is referred to as a *recursion level*. Each recursion level constitutes a process, which gives the programmer an easy way of estimating the process granularity of a given program or call.

We implement recursion-parallelism by *Reform compilation* [6] (this can be viewed as an implementation technique for the Reform inference system [11]). This is a control-structure transformation that changes the control-flow of a

---

[1] This should not be confused with the Single Instruction Multiple Data or SIMD model, where processes are synchronized instruction by instruction.

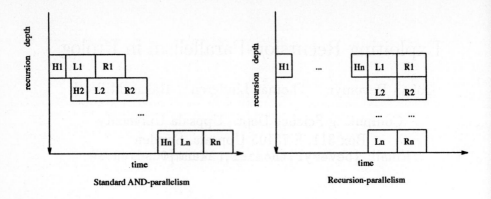

Figure 1: Executing a clause $H \leftarrow L, H', R$ with standard AND-parallelism and recursion-parallelism.

recursive program quite dramatically. When invoking a recursive program with a call of size n (corresponding to a recursion depth n) a four-phase computation is initiated:

1. A big head unification, corresponding to the n small head unifications with normal control-flow, is performed.

2. All n instances of the calls to the *left* of the recursive call are computed in parallel.

3. The program is called recursively. This call is known to match the base clause. Hence, in practice, this call is often trivially cheap.

4. All n instances of the calls to the *right* of the recursive call are computed in parallel.

The difference between standard AND-parallelism and recursion-parallelism is illustrated in Figure 1. The figure shows execution of a recursive clause $H \leftarrow L, H', R$, where H is the head, H' is the recursive call and L, R are (possibly empty) conjunctions. Note that the figure shows a situation where there are no data dependencies between recursion levels, and no unification parallelism.

This paper is organized as follows. In Section 2 we define Reform Prolog. We discuss some programming techniques and concepts in Section 3. An overview of the parallel abstract machine is presented in Section 4. Section 5 provides an overview of the compile-time analyses employed for parallelization. Extensions to the sequential instruction set are presented by means of an example in Section 6. Experimental results obtained when running benchmark programs on a parallel machine are presented and discussed in Section 7.

2 REFORM PROLOG

Reform Prolog parallelizes a deterministic subset of Prolog. This is similar to the approach taken in Parallel NU-Prolog [7]. However, Reform Prolog exploits recursion-parallelism when parallelizing this subset, whereas Parallel NU-Prolog exploits AND-parallelism.

With Reform Prolog, as with Parallel NU-Prolog, it is straight-forward to call parallel subprograms from a nondeterministic program. Thus, there is a natural embedding of parallel code in ordinary sequential Prolog programs. Since the entire call tree below a parallel call is not parallelized, some non-deterministic computations can be supported in a parallel context as shown below. This is not done in Parallel NU-Prolog.

Below we define the condition for when a recursive Prolog predicate can be parallelized, and how this condition can be enforced by the implementation. We need to define two auxiliary concepts:

- A variable is *shared* if it is visible from more than one recursion level. Note that a variable can be shared at one point of time and unshared (local) at another.

- A variable binding is *unconditional* if it cannot be undone by backtracking.

We say that a call in a parallel computation is *safe* if all bindings made to its shared variables are unconditional when the call is executed. The condition for when a predicate can be parallelized is then:

A recursive predicate can be parallelized only if all calls made in the parallel computation are safe.

Hence, limited non-determinism is allowed: when conditional bindings are made only to variables local to a recursion level, the computation is safe.

Safeness of a call is defined w.r.t. to the *instantiation* of the call (i.e., what parts of the arguments are instantiated). We can distinguish between the parallel instantiation and the sequential instantiation of a call. These might differ as a parallel call can 'run ahead' of the sequential instantiation: recursion levels that would execute after the current one sequentially, may already have bound shared variables.

We say that a call is *par-safe* when it is safe w.r.t. the parallel instantiation, and that it is *seq-safe* when it is safe w.r.t. the sequential instantiation.

The compiler is responsible for checking that programs declared parallel by the programmer are safe. For calls that can be proven par-safe at compile-time, there is no need for extra safeness checking at runtime. For calls that can be proven seq-safe at compile-time, but not par-safe, it is necessary to check safeness at runtime. If the call is not safe, then it is delayed until it becomes safe. This is done by suspending the call until:

1. The unsafe argument has become sufficiently instantiated by another recursion level; or

2. The current call becomes leftmost.

If neither par-safeness nor seq-safeness can be proven at compile-time, then parallelization fails.

3 RECURSION PARALLEL PROGRAMMING

Before describing the execution machinery, we briefly consider some programming techniques and concepts.

3.1 Machine utilization

The parallel programmer is concerned with utilizing the available parallel machine as efficiently as possible. In Reform Prolog, this means creating sufficient work and avoiding synchronization due to data dependences. A parallel machine where most of the workers are inactive due to lack of work is underutilized; a parallel machine where most workers are waiting for data is inefficiently used.

The number of processes available to the workers is precisely the number of recursion levels of the parallel call. To keep a large machine busy, there should consequently be many recursion levels – far more than the number of workers, ideally.

3.2 Safeness

To illustrate the concept of safeness, consider the following two programs:

```
split([],_,[],[]).
split([X|Xs],N,[X|Ys],Zs) :- X =< N, split(Xs,N,Ys,Zs).
split([X|Xs],N,Ys,[X|Zs]) :- X > N, split(Xs,N,Ys,Zs).

split*([],_,[],[]).
split*([X|Xs],N,Ys,Zs) :- X =< N, !, Ys = [X|Ys0], split*(Xs,N,Ys0,Zs).
split*([X|Xs],N,Ys,[X|Zs]) :- split*(Xs,N,Ys,Zs).
```

Assume that the third arguments of both predicates are shared, as might be the case if they were called from a parallel predicate. The predicate split/4 is then unsafe, since the third argument might be conditionally bound in the second clause, and then unbound again if the comparison $X \leq N$ fails. In contrast, the third argument of split*/4 is only bound in a determinate state and so split*/4 is safe for parallel execution (the binding of the fourth argument in the last clause does not affect safeness, since clauses are tried in textual order).

3.3 Suspension

The programmer would like to avoid suspension as far as possible. However, in the implementation described in this paper, cheap suspension and simple, efficient scheduling combine to lessen synchronization penalties considerably. Consider the following program:

```
nrev([],[]).
nrev([X|Xs],Zs) :- nrev(Xs,Ys), append(Ys,[X],Zs).

append([],Ys,Ys).
append([X|Xs],Ys,[X|Zs]) :- append(Xs,Ys,Zs).
```

The compiler detects that the first argument of append/3 is shared. Hence, indexing must suspend until the first argument Ys is instantiated by the previous recursion level. The third argument Zs is also found to be shared, but the situation is reversed: the next recursion level will wait for Zs to be bound.

The inner loop of append/3 is then: wait for the input to be instantiated; when this occurs, write an element on the output list and go back to the beginning again. Thus, there is considerable scope for overlapping computations. As can be seen in the benchmark section, speedups are almost linear on 24 processors.

We also ran a second version of nrev/2, where the data dependence of append/3 was removed by a simple transformation: the length of the first argument is known at call-time by an extra parameter. Every call to append/3 can then construct the list Ys asynchronously (the elements of the list will be filled in later) and there is no suspension under execution.

```
nrev*(0,[],[]).
nrev*(N+1,[X|Xs],Zs) :- nrev*(N,Xs,Ys), append*(N,Ys,[X],Zs).

append*(0,[],Ys,Ys).
append*(N+1,[X|Xs],Ys,[X|Zs]) :- append*(N,Xs,Ys,Zs).
```

Surprisingly, the nrev*/3 program is slower than the suspending nrev/2 program. Measurements show that this is because recursion levels of nrev/2 usually suspend very briefly, due to simple, fast suspension and straightforward scheduling of processes. For 16 processors, no processor was suspended more than 0.6% of the total execution time on the nrev/2 program; when run on 8 processors, the program suspended each worker less than 0.1% of the execution time.

On the other hand, the asynchronous nature of constructing the answer lists in nrev*/3 led to an increase in the number of general unifications, due to later recursion levels overtaking earlier ones. The cost is time and memory. (Note that nrev*/3 still exhibited a speedup of approximately 13 on 16 processors; nrev/2, however, was clocked at a speedup of over 15 on 16 processors.)

4 THE PARALLEL ABSTRACT MACHINE: OVERVIEW

The Reform engine consists of a set of *workers*, at least one per processor. Each worker is a separate process running a WAM-based [12] Prolog engine with extensions to support parallel execution. The Prolog engine is comparable in speed with SICStus Prolog (slightly faster on some programs, slightly slower on others).

The Reform engine alternates between two modes: sequential execution and parallel execution. One dedicated worker (the sequential worker) is responsible for the sequential execution phase. During this phase all other workers (the parallel workers) are idle. The sequential worker initiates parallel execution and resumes sequential execution when all parallel workers have terminated.

A common code area is used and all workers have restricted access to each others heaps. All other data areas are private to each worker. The shared heaps are used to communicate data created during sequential and parallel execution (an atomic exchange operation is employed when binding possibly shared heap variables). When there are several shared heaps it is no longer possible to use a simple pointer comparison for determining whether a binding should be trailed or not. We solve this problem by extending the representation of each variable with a timestamp.

The sequential worker's temporary registers can be read by the parallel workers. These registers are employed for passing arguments to the parallel computation (one such register contains the precomputed recursion depth, i.e., the total number of parallel processes).

Synchronization is implemented by busy-waiting, i.e., suspended processes actively check if they can be resumed. The drawback of this method is that a suspended process tie up a processor. The advantage is that non-suspended processes are not slowed down. In particular, very simplisitic and efficient approaches to process scheduling are possible. The Reform Prolog implementation currently supports *static scheduling* and *dynamic self-scheduling* [10]. With both approaches, the actual task switching amounts to a simple jump operation.

5 COMPILING RECURSION PARALLEL PROGRAMS

The compiler ensures the safeness of the computation, guarantees that time-dependent operations are performed correctly and employs suspending and locking unification when necessary.

These tasks depend on compile-time program analyses that uncover type, locality and determinacy information. The compiler then emits instructions based on this information, possibly falling back to more conservative code generation schemes when high-precision analysis results cannot be obtained.

5.1 Type analysis

The type inference phase employs an abstract domain based on the standard mode-analysis domain [5], augmented with support for lists and difference lists as well as handling of certain aliases.

The compiler distinguishes the parallel and sequential types of a predicate. The sequential type is the type that must hold when the current recursion level is leftmost, while the parallel type holds for any recursion level. The parallel type is the most frequently used for compilation.

5.2 Locality analysis

Locality analysis tries to find what terms are local to a process (recursion level), what terms are shared between processes and what terms contain variables subject to time-dependent tests. Consider the following program:

```
rp([],[]).
rp([X|Xs],[Y|Ys]) :- p(X,Y), rp(Xs).

p(a,X) :- q(X).                    p(b,c).

q(X) :- var(X),!,X = b.            q(c).
```

Given the call rp([a,b],[Y,Y]), we get two processes, p(a,Y) and p(b,Y). Both are safe and can thus proceed in parallel. Now assume p(b,Y) precedes p(a,Y), and binds Y to c. Then p(a,c) will reduce to q(c) which succeeds.

Sequential Prolog would have a quite different behaviour: first, p(a,Y) reduces to q(Y) and in turn to Y = b. Then p(b,b) fails. Hence, for this example, the parallel execution model is unsound w.r.t. sequential Prolog execution. This is due to the time-dependent behaviour of the primitive var/1.

Our solution to this problem is to mark, at compile-time, certain variables as being time-sensitive, or *fragile*. In the example, the argument of q/1 is fragile and the compiler must take this into account.

Furthermore, knowledge that a variable is *not* fragile, or *not* shared is extremely useful to the code generator. Using such information, operations with a very complex general case, such as unification, can in some cases be reduced to the same code as would be executed by a sequential WAM.

5.3 Safeness analysis

Safeness analysis aims to ensure that no conditional bindings are made to shared variables. In this respect, it is quite different from determinacy analysis: while determinacy analysis attempts to prove that a given call yields at most a single solution, safeness analysis instead proves no unifications with shared terms are made in a non-determinate, parallel state. Safeness analysis thus employs the results of type inference (to see whether the call is determinate or not) and locality analysis (only shared terms can be unsafe).

6 INSTRUCTION SET

The sequential WAM instruction set is extended with new instructions for supporting recursion-parallelism. Due to space limitations, we can only describe these by means of a simple example and refer to other sources for a full discussion [3, 2, 4]. Consider the program:

```
map([],[]).
map([A|As],[B|Bs]) :- foo(A,B), map(As,Bs).
```

The program is compiled into the following extended WAM code.

```
map/2:  switch_on_term Lv La L1 fail

Lv:     try La
        trust L1

La:     get_nil X0
        get_nil X1
        proceed

L1:     build_rec_poslist X0 X2 X3 X0   % first list
        build_poslist X1 X2 X4 X1       % second list
        start_left_body L2              % execute L2 in parallel
```

```
        execute map/2                    % call base case

L2:     initialize_left 1                % I := initial recursion level
L3:     spawn_left 1 X2 G2               % X2 := I++; while(I < N) do
        put_nth_head G3 X2 0 X0          %   X0 := G3[I]
        put_nth_head G4 X2 0 X1          %   X1 := G4[I]
        call foo/2 0                     %   call foo(G3[I],G4[I])
        jump L3                          % next iteration
```

The instructions `build_rec_poslist` and `build_poslist` employs a data structure called a *vector-list*. This is a list where the cells are allocated in consequtive memory locations, to allow constant-time indexing into the list. The instructions work as follows:

- `build_rec_poslist X0 X2 X3 X0` traverses the list in X0 and builds a vector-list of its elements, storing a pointer to it in X3, and storing the vector length in X2. The last tail of the list is stored in X0.

- `build_poslist X1 X2 X4 X1` traverses the list X1 to its X2'th element, and builds a vector-list of its elements in X4. If the list has fewer than X2 elements and ends with an unbound variable, then it is filled out to length X2. The X2'th tail of the vector-list is unified with the X2'th tail of the list in X1, and finally X1 is set to the X2'th tail of the vector-list.

The sequential worker's registers X2, X3 and X4 are referred to as G2, G3 and G4 in the parallel code.

The instruction `initialize_left` calculates the initial recursion level in static scheduling mode. In dynamic scheduling mode, this instruction is ignored.

7 EXPERIMENTAL RESULTS

In this section we present the results obtained when running some benchmark programs in Reform Prolog on a parallel machine.

7.1 Experimental methodology

Parallel machine. Reform Prolog has been implemented on the Sequent Symmetry multiprocessor. This is a bus-based, cache-coherent shared-memory machine using Intel 80386 processors. The experiments described here were conducted on a machine with 26 processors, where we used 24 processors (leaving two processors for operating systems activitites).

Evaluation metrics. The metric we use for evaluating parallelization is the speedup it yields. We present *relative* and *normalized* speedups.

Relative speedup expresses the ratio of execution time of the program (compiled with parallelization) on a single processor to the time using p processors.

Normalized speedup expresses the ratio of execution time of the original sequential program (compiled without parallelization) on a single processor to the time using p processors on the program compiled with parallelization.

7.2 Benchmarks.

Programs and input data. We have parallelized four benchmark programs. Two programs (Match and Tsp) are considerably larger than the other two. One program (Map) exploits independent AND-parallelism, whereas the other three exploits dependent AND-parallelism.

Map. This program applies a function to each element of a list producing a new list. The function merely decrements a counter 100 times. A list of 10,000 elements was used.

Nrev. This program reverses a list using list concatenation ('naive reverse'). A list of 900 elements was used.

Match. This program employs a dynamic programming algorithm for comparing, e.g., DNA-sequences. One sequence of length 32 was compared with 24 other sequences. The resulting similarity-values are collected in an sorted binary tree.

Tsp. This program implements an approximation algorithm for the Travelling Salesman Problem. A tour of 45 cities was computed.

Load balance. One way of estimating the load balance of a computation is to measure the finishing time of the workers. We measured the execution time for each worker when executing our benchmarks. Static scheduling was used in all experiments.

Map. This program displayed a very uniform load balance (less than 0.3% difference between workers). This is hardly surprising since the number of recursion levels executed by each worker is large, and there is no difference in execution time between recursion levels.

Nrev. The execution time of each worker only varied about 3% when executing this program. There is a slight difference in the execution time of each recursion level but the large number of recursion levels executed by each worker evens out the differences.

Match. When 16 workers were used, 8 workers executed 2 recursion levels each, while 8 workers executed a single recursion level. This explains the relatively poor speedup on 16 workers. When 24 workers were used the execution time varied less than 0.3% between workers. This is explained by the fact that each worker executed one recursion level, and that all recursion levels executed in the same time.

Match and Tsp. These program displayed an uniform load balance on all but three workers. This is explained by the fact that 45 recursion levels were executed in all; 21 workers executed 2 recursion levels each while 3 workers executed 1 recursion level each. Despite this the program displays good speedup (21.85). Using dynamic scheduling would not have improved the results in this case.

Sequential fraction of runtime. Each parallelized benchmark program has an initial part which is not parallelized. This includes setting up the arguments for the parallel call. It also includes head unification, and spawning of parallel processes.

According to Amdahl's law, the ratio of time spent in this sequential part of the program to that spent in the part which is parallelized (measured on a sequential machine) determines the theoretically best possible speedup from parallelization.

The following table shows for each benchmark program how large fraction of the execution time on a sequential machine is not subject to parallelization.

Map	Nrev	String	Tsp
0.3%	0.04%	0.003%	0.005%

We conclude from this data that the unparallelized parts represent negligible fractions of the total execution times. Another conclusion is that there is no point in parallelizing the head unification of parallelized predicates, since it represents such a tiny fraction of the computation.

7.3   Results

The results of the experiments are summarized in the tables below. In the tables P stands for number of workers, T for runtime (in seconds), S_R for relative speedup, and S_N for normalized speedup. The sequential runtime for each program is given below each table.

P	T	S_R	S_N	T	S_R	S_N
1	40.40	1.00	0.98	30.80	1.00	0.88
4	10.12	3.99	3.89	8.08	3.81	3.43
8	5.07	7.96	7.76	3.96	7.77	6.99
16	2.54	15.91	15.50	2.01	15.32	13.78
24	1.70	23.76	23.15	1.36	22.65	20.36

Map. (39.59 sec.)   **Nrev.** (27.70 sec.)

P	T	S_R	S_N	T	S_R	S_N
1	68.88	1.00	0.95	258.22	1.00	0.90
4	17.22	3.99	3.80	68.85	3.75	3.37
8	8.61	7.99	7.60	34.55	7.47	6.73
16	5.76	11.95	11.35	17.25	14.96	13.47
24	2.91	23.70	22.52	11.82	21.85	19.67

Match. (65.44 sec.)   **Tsp.** (232.40 sec.)

7.4   Discussion

From the above results we calculate parallel overhead and efficiency of parallelization and make a comparison with other systems.

We compare Reform Prolog with the only other Prolog systems, which supports deterministic dependent AND-parallelism, that we are aware of, Andorra-I [9] and NUA-Prolog [8]. The Andorra-I system is an interpreter written in C. NUA-Prolog is a compiled system using a WAM-based abstract machine.

It should be noted that these systems to some extent exploit different forms of parallelism. Reform Prolog and NUA-Prolog exploit deterministic dependent AND-parallelism (recursion parallelism in the case of Reform Prolog). Andorra-I exploits deterministic dependent AND-parallelism and OR-parallelism (here we are only interested in the AND-parallel component of the system).

Unfortunately, we can only make a very limited comparison with NUA-Prolog, since the published benchmark programs stress the constraint-solving capabilites of the system, rather than it potential for raw AND-parallel speedup. However, we have compared their result on the nrev benchmarks with ours.

Let us define

$$\text{parallel efficiency} = (\text{speedup on } N \text{ processors})/N$$

The table below displays the parallel efficiency of Reform Prolog on 24 processors. It also indicates the parallelization overhead on a single processor as compared to the sequential Prolog implementation.

Program	Relative efficiency	Normalized efficiency	Parallelization overhead
Map	99 %	96 %	2 %
Nrev	95 %	83 %	12 %
Match	99 %	94 %	5 %
Tsp	91 %	82 %	10 %

The Andorra-I system shows relative efficiency in the range of 47–83 % and normalized efficiency in the range of 35–61 % (assuming parallelization overhead of 35 %). We have excluded benchmarks that mainly exhibits OR-parallelism from this comparison. The figures are obtained on a Sequent Symmetry with 10 processors. NUA-Prolog shows a relative efficiency of 71 % and a normalized efficiency of 36 % on the nrev benchmark on an 11 processor Sequent Symmetry. (Note that the Reform Prolog figures were obtained using more than twice the number of processors the other systems used—using less processors improves the result.)

The Andorra-I system shows parallelization overheads in the range of 35–40 % on a set of benchmarks [9]. NUA-Prolog shows a parallelization overhead of 50 % on the nrev benchmark.

8 CONCLUSIONS

The developments and results discussed in this paper suggests that recursion-parallelism is an efficient method for executing Prolog programs on shared-memory multiprocessors. Our implementation exhibits very low overhead for parallelization (2–12 % on the programs tested).

We believe that the high parallel efficiency of Reform Prolog is due to efficient process management and scheduling. An important factor is that all parallel processes can be initiated simultaneously. These properties of the system are due to the static recursion-parallel execution model made possible by Reform compilation.

Acknowledgments

We thank the Swedish Institute of Computer Science (SICS) for making their 26 processor Sequent Symmetry available to us.

REFERENCES

[1] G. Bell, Ultracomputers: a Teraflop before its time, *Comm. ACM*, Vol. 35, No. 8, 1992.

[2] J. Bevemyr, *A Recursion-Parallel Prolog Engine*, PhL Thesis, Computing Science Department, Uppsala University, 1993.

[3] J. Bevemyr, T. Lindgren & H. Millroth, Reform Prolog: The Language and its Implementation, to appear in: *Proc. 10th Int. Conf. Logic Programming*, MIT Press, 1993.

[4] T. Lindgren, *The Compilation and Execution of Recursion-Parallel Prolog on Shared Memory Multiprocessors*, PhL Thesis, Computing Science Department, Uppsala University, May, 1993 (expected).

[5] S.K. Debray & D.S. Warren, Automatic Mode Inference for Logic programs, *J. Logic Programming*, Vol. 5, No. 3, 1988.

[6] H. Millroth, Reforming Compilation of Logic Programs, *Proc. Int. Symp. Logic Programming*, San Diego, Calif., MIT Press, 1991.

[7] L. Naish, Parallelizing NU-Prolog, *Proc. 5th Int. Conf. Symp. Logic Programming*, MIT Press, 1988.

[8] D. Palmer and L. Naish, NUA-Prolog: An Extension to the WAM for Parallel Andorra, *Proc. 8th Int. Conf. Logic Programming*, Paris, MIT Press, 1991.

[9] V. Santos Costa, D.H.D. Warren and R. Yang, The Andorra-I Engine: A Parallel Implementation of the Basic Andorra Model, *Proc. 8th Int. Conf. Logic Programming*, Paris, MIT Press, 1991.

[10] P. Tang and P.-C. Yew, Processor Self-Scheduling for Multiple Nested Parallel Loops, *Proc. 1986 Int. Conf. Parallel Processing*, 1986.

[11] S.-Å. Tärnlund, Reform, report, Computing Science Dept., Uppsala University, 1991.

[12] D.H.D. Warren, An Abstract Prolog Instruction Set, SRI Tech. Note 309, SRI International, Menlo Park, Calif., 1983.

Why and How in the
ElipSys OR-parallel CLP System

André Véron, Kees Schuerman, Mike Reeve, Liang-Liang Li

European Computer-Industry Research Centre
Arabellastrasse 17, 8000 Munich 81, Germany
Tel: +49 89 92699-0   Fax: +49 89 92699-170
e-mail:{kees,lll,mjr,veron}@ecrc.de

Abstract. ElipSys is a programming system supporting a constraint logic programming (CLP) language and OR-parallel execution. These two features complement each other: CLP programming eases the writing of efficient search programs while OR-parallelism allows one to attain quasi-linear or super-linear speed-ups when the programs are executed on parallel machines. The speed-ups come without significant additional programming effort. This paper gives the rationale behind this combination, explains how it influences the design of the language and the implementation, and gives results providing evidence for the synergy of these two paradigms.

1   Introduction

Most previous attempts to exploit the OR-parallelism inherent in logic programming systems have concentrated on the Prolog language and it has been shown, as expected, that OR-parallelism is most beneficial for search-based applications ([3, 19]). Unfortunately experience suggests that Prolog is not a satisfactory language for both stating and solving non-trivial search-based applications. Hence much of the research on OR-parallelism has somehow been biased towards Prolog without any convincing justifications. The ElipSys system has been built as an OR-parallel CLP system. In this paper we illustrate how this has influenced the design of the system and show that such a system can be effectively constructed.

Parallel logic programming and constraint logic programming have been two active fields of research in recent years ([15, 2, 4] and [7, 13, 9]). At the intercept of these two technologies is ElipSys the first logic programming system providing in one unified environment specialized computation domains, such as finite domains of integers or atoms, built-in arithmetic constraints, advanced coroutining and suspension mechanisms together with OR-parallel execution machinery and a complete garbage collector.

The motivation for building such a system is two fold. On the one hand it has been recognised that brute-force parallelism does not bring any change in the complexity of the problem to be solved and is therefore not enough by itself. On the other hand, if a problem is NP-complete, the designer of a CLP program is bound to come to a point where he does not know anymore how to refine any further the specification of how to proceed towards a solution. In other words, search or "don't know" exploration is mandatory. OR-parallelism and transformational CLP programming thus complement each other nicely. The assets and the realisability of such a combination have been highlighted in [12].

Parallel machines are now entering the mainstream. The availability of ElipSys on these new architectures has been a key issue in the design. This has had a major impact on the ElipSys execution model. ElipSys departs significantly from traditional OR-parallel execution models. It uses both the binding array technique and virtual shared memory to implement shared bindings. This alleviates the cost of data sharing while preserving scheduling flexibility.

The paper is built in three sections. The first section introduces the concepts underlying the ElipSys programming language. The second section gives an account of the implementation issues. The last section reports on some experiments with the parallelisation of CLP programs.

2 ElipSys: the user point of view

2.1 Rationale

Standard Prolog has failed as both a description and execution language for non-toy search problems ([11]). ElipSys aims at real-world search problems . Since ElipSys looks to the future and new applications, we have not striven for Prolog backwards compatibility.

The CHIP language ([8]) has been successfully applied to real-world applications and the ElipSys language bears much similarity to it. The seminal idea of CHIP was been to complement the SLD-resolution inference rule of Prolog with additional inference rules which can a priori remove branches of the search tree that lead only to failure nodes by using the information gathered along the search path ([11]). Thus dead-ends can be detected earlier and much backtracking can be avoided.

OR-parallelism and constraints are complementary means to attack search based problems. Because of the NP-completeness of the target problems, solutions cannot avoid search. They should mainly rely on the effective modelisation of the problem with the appropriate data structures and constraints, so as to have as low a complexity as possible. Search is then used to explore the remaining cases which have not been excluded. OR-parallelism is then a natural way to speed-up this phase of the computation. In other words, the computations after the "don't know point" inherent to the solving of NP-complete problems can be naturally supported by "don't know" parallelism.

2.2 Constraints

From its CHIP ancestor ElipSys has inherited finite domains, built-in arithmetic and symbolic constraints. It has been equipped with a flexible user level language integrating in one environment finite domains, builtin arithmetic constraints, advanced coroutining mechanisms and term manipulation primitives. While the first two items allow a CHIP programming style and expressive power, the last two make it possible to let users develop at user-level additional constraints or add new-inference rules. For instance, the generalised propagation of [17] has been implemented on ElipSys by using a meta-interpreter which delays and wakes up as the SLD-resolvent is updated by SLD-resolution steps.

2.3 Parallelisation

The ElipSys language is equipped with an annotation which enables the programmer to express where the search tree described by the program can be split into sub-search trees that it is appropriate to traverse in parallel. The annotation is a conservative hint to the underlying parallel system which is free to exploit it or not. No splitting can occur if no annotation is present.

2.4 Sources of parallelism in CLP programs

It must be noted that the size of a search tree depends both on the search tree initiated by a call and on the search trees initiated by subsequent calls in the continuation. Hence a simple predicate can be a good source of parallelism. This is especially true in CLP systems where branching is performed by an enumeration procedure. Labeling or enumeration steps trigger constraint propagation. Each propagation step is one sequential node in the search tree and increases the grain of the computation. Hence the enumeration procedures are first class candidates for a parallelisation annotation.

2.5 Linear and Super-linear speedups

Real-world combinatorial problems exhibit search spaces of considerable size. It follows from this that it is possible to make sure that sub-search trees created via the parallel annotation are themselves substantial enough to require a traversal time significantly more than the computation time needed to dispatch them to additional processors.

The immediate consequence is that for typical ElipSys applications parallelization introduces practically no overheads and that linear speed-ups can be routinely obtained. For instance the proof of optimality in non-trivial optimisation problems is often responsible for a major part of the total computation time. It requires the exhaustive traversal of a search tree in order to prove that it contains no solutions. These proofs can be linearly speeded-up by using OR-parallelism (see figure 2).

When a branch-and-bound search is used, an OR-parallel systems can find good solutions faster than a sequential system with a fixed search strategy and might thus bring super-linear speedups. As soon as not too simple search trees are to be traversed both kinds of speed-ups can be expected.

With respect to super-linear speed-ups it must be born in mind that they are by nature unpredictable. Whenever the programmer knows how to reach a good solution or how to constrain the search to avoid failure nodes he should program the search accordingly. One more time OR-parallelism is there to exploit *don't know* non determinism.

2.6 Pruning, side effects and parallelism

Practical experience with the parallelisation of various CHIP programs has shown that there was no need to have pruning operators and side-effects behave as in a sequential implementation. Decent enumeration routines tend not to use side-effects and pruning. This is primarily due to the very spirit of CLP programming which fosters the idea that constraints and enumeration are independent components of a search program. The constraints describe deterministically what the solutions are. The enumeration simply implements the traversal of a tree which bears all the solutions on its success leaves.

In traditional Prolog programming, side-effects and pruning operators are mainly used in search programs to control, awkwardly, the expansion of the search tree, to reject partially constructed solutions, to avoid re-traversing search trees, etc. Support for these techniques lose importance in a CLP system and have not been considered a hot topic in the design of ElipSys.

ElipSys is equipped with side-effects and cut to support the sequential Prolog-style code which typically surrounds a pure CLP piece of search code (which can use parallel execution) in real-world applications. During the parallel execution of the search-based core of the application, cuts behave like cavalier cuts. Side-effects are fully asynchronous. In the same spirit, collecting predicates such as bagof/3 and the like do not behave as in a sequential system and gather solutions in the order in which the system finds them.

2.7 Optimisation operators

Many combinatorial problems involve the optimisation of one criteria. Optimisation constructs are higher-order predicates which receive a goal and as cost function as arguments. Such predicates are solved when an answer substitution can be found which satisfies the goal and minimises the value of the cost function. The execution of the goal usually yields an annotated search tree. Hence the ElipSys version of these optimisation predicates do not behave as sequential ones. Any answer substitution for which the cost function is minimal can be returned. The value returned as the optimum of the cost function can be then used to enumerate all optimal solutions if needed.

Following [19] the presence of optimisation constructs in the ElipSys language can also be justified by the design choice not to model the sequential behaviour of pruning operators and side-effects. Well-packaged optimisation meta-predicates allow programmers not to resort to "acrobatic programming tricks" (made even more dangerous by the provision of OR-parallelism) and to increase the reliability of their programs (which is of paramount importance in decision-support systems).

2.8 Safe programs

Among all the programs which can be written with the ElipSys language, one can identify classes with interesting properties. The class of OR-parallel *safe* programs contains the programs whose answer set is invariant under OR-parallel execution. The subset of *decidably safe* programs of this class contains the programs for which there are compile-time analysis procedures which detect this property. Decidably safe programs are of special interest for they can be written and debugged in a sequential environment.

For the time being programmers can write safe programs by following sound programing principles such as avoiding reading the arguments of goals whose associated sub-search trees are annotated, avoiding making assumptions on the value or order of solutions gathered by collecting meta-predicates, avoiding the use of side-effects on global data structures for influencing the control, avoiding the use of cuts to implement deep guards. As programmers use more potentially non-safe features, the rules for sound programming get increasingly complex and difficult to master.

This "manual" approach is not satisfactory for the long term. The construction of tools to support compile-time analysis of the program is underway (for example in the ParForce ESPRIT Basic Research Action). These tools rely on abstract interpretation to detect in a conservative way potentially dangerous combinations of annotations, pruning operators and delayed goals, optimisation and collecting predicates.

One could argue that it would be better to model the sequential behaviour of the program. Without considering the increased complexity of the underlying parallel machinery and the corresponding overheads, this approach would probably do for all-solutions queries but would jeopardise the super-linear speed-ups which are expected in programs using programming techniques such as deep guards, branch and bound, or heuristics hybrisation (where for a given problem different search trees can be developed in parallel by using different branching heuristics).

3 Implementation issues

3.1 Abstract Machine

The ElipSys sequential abstract machine is a variant of the WAM. Extensions have been added to support coroutining and the connection to the OR-parallel scheduler. The needs for coroutining execution or interaction with the scheduler are tested at each CALL instruction. The binding scheme of ElipSys is binding array-based. No special optimisations in this respect have been made. The extensions introduce a 30 percent overhead on sequential execution of Prolog programs. This is similar to what has been reported in the Aurora system ([15]).

3.2 Binding Scheme

Much attention has been devoted to the management of bindings in OR-parallel systems. As far as we know, two schemes have emerged, the SRI model and the MUSE model ([21, 2]). The SRI scheme uses a binding array and a value trail stack. Each worker is equipped with a binding array. Bindings are performed through the binding array and reflected in the value trail stack. Hence once a segment of stack is shared, no workers will perform updates on it. Dereferencing a variable usually implies an access to the binding array to fetch the value of the binding. Untrailing is performed by reading the value trail backwards and resetting the binding array entries. Task switching between a **from** node and a **to** node is performed by backtracking and untrailing from the **from** node up to a common node on the ancestor paths of the two nodes and then by mimicking a downwards execution by reinstalling the bindings performed by building the path between the common node and the **to** node.

MUSE uses stack copying instead of stack sharing. Hence parallel sub-tasks can bind logically shared variables by physically updating stacks like in a standard Prolog system without having to maintain any additional binding machinery and incurring the value trailing overhead. Stacks are incrementally copied at task-switching time. Task-switching is performed by backtracking up to a common node and then copying the stacks down to the target node and finally undoing the updates performed by the task which has created the target node and which has dirtied the stacks after the creation of the node.

Overheads The SRI model introduces a 30 percent overhead compared with a sequential execution whereas the MUSE model overhead is about 5 percent ([15, 2]). The overhead of the SRI model, introduced by the more complex binding, trailing and dereferencing mechanisms, is expected to decrease as logic programming compilers improve and are able to remove more unnecessary dereferencing operations, and discover more opportunities for deterministic bindings and shallow backtracking.

Execution on non-shared memory machines The MUSE model has been shown to be more adapted than the SRI model for execution on non-shared memory machines than the SRI-model used for instance in Aurora ([3]). This stems from the fact that the SRI model does not perform caching of remote memory accesses whereas by default MUSE copies a priori the data it might need. The ElipSys execution model relies on Shared Virtual Memory to implement the sharing of stacks between tasks.

Shared virtual memory automatically manages the coherence of the shared parts of memory, caches transparently remote accesses, by relying on the MMU to perform its management operations. The assumption of the provision of shared virtual memory on the future hardware platforms is supported by the recent devlopments in parallel machine memory systems. The EDS machine at which ElipSys was initially targeted, the DASH multiprocessor, the DDM machine and the KSR-1 machine are examples of parallel systems where much emphasis has been put on shared virtual memory of one form or another ([10, 18, 14]).

With Shared Virtual Memory, ElipSys does not suffer from Aurora's liabilities. The ElipSys overhead compared to MUSE is not higher than the 30 percent overhead induced by the binding array.

Scheduling flexibility The MUSE model imposes some restrictions on the scheduling algorithms which can be used. Once a processor has been allocated sub-search tree, it cannot leave it unless other processors have already copied its stacks. While it might not be a really serious limitation, it has been decided not to restrict by an early design decision the range of possible scheduling algorithms that can be used in ElipSys.

For instance, best-first search might require the suspension of the exploration of one sub-search tree and the switching to a more promising sub-search located far away in the global search tree would be made problematic in a MUSE based system.

Consecutive Updates CLP systems make heavy use of data structures which are subject to consecutive backtrackable updates. Such structures are used for instance to implement specialised computation domains such as finite domains, and to manipulate coroutining data structures. These updatable data structures are readily available in sequential logic programming systems and therefore also available in MUSE based parallel systems.

In ElipSys, satisfactory techniques for the handling of these data structures in a binding-array-based system have been developed. They can cope with the joint requirements of garbage-collection and pruning operations ([20]).

Despite the constant overhead it introduces, the binding array scheme was preferred to a copying scheme as exemplified by MUSE. Scheduling flexibility was the determining factor in favor of the former, while the latter's advantage for execution on non-shared memory machine was foreseen to be equalised by the use of shared virtual memory.

3.3 Garbage collection

ElipSys is equipped with a garbage collector of comparable accuracy to those of sequential systems. It uses an independent garbage collection scheme ([1]) for the stacks and binding array and deals effectively with consecutive backtrackable updates ubiquitous in a CLP system ([20]). The provision of garbage collection gives users the opportunity to rely on coroutining as a routine programming technique for implementing user-level constraints and for monitoring executions via unification-sensitive handlers.

3.4 Scheduling

CLP programs typically have a three phase structure. The first phase transforms input into appropriate data structures. The second phase sets up constraints in a deterministic fashion. The final, enumeration, phase carries out the search. The predicates used to expand the search tree are first class candidates for parallelisation.

Because of the highly combinatorial nature of the target problems and the size of the associated search trees, it can be assumed that there is enough work to keep processors busy. Nevertheless dispatching search trees between processors has a cost which should be minimised. Hence the size of the sub-search trees and the grain of parallel computation should be maximised. The main search tree should be split as early as possible so as to load the processors with the largest possible sub-search trees.

The search trees generated by target applications of CLP programs are different from those generated by typical Prolog programs. Bottom-most scheduling has been found to be a reliable strategy for Prolog programs because they often exhibit small-grain parallel computations used to performing some local and small scope search. Typical CLP programs tend not to rely on local search. They rather rely on good formulations of the constraints to automatically prune and direct the search. CLP programs mostly make use of coarse-grain parallelism. Top-most scheduling is a priori felt to be more adequate for parallelising CLP programs for it minimises interaction with workers while speeding up local backtracking.

4   ElipSys is a practical tool

Real applications

An assessment of the ElipSys technology is being undertaken in the APPLAUSE (Assessment of Parallel Programming Using Logic)ESPRIT project (P6708). The project is applications oriented and aims at assessing the ElipSys technology for real-world applications. The fields of applications are pollution monitoring control, industrial planning and scheduling, tourist information systems and biology and protein engineering. First results with a protein structure prediction system are reported in [6].

Disjunctive scheduling

The bridge scheduling problem was first introduced in [5] and a CLP-based solution given in [11]. The problem is to minimise the time needed to erect a bridge. The construction can be decomposed into tasks for which an optimal schedule must be found. There are three kinds of constraints between the tasks:

precedence constraints e.g. Task1 must be completed before Task2.
distance constraints e.g. Task2 can start only three days after Task1 has been started.
disjunctive constraints e.g. when Task1 and Task2 share a resource and hence can not overlap in time.

The combinatorics stem from the use of disjunctive constraints corresponding to the scarcity of resources. Tasks sharing resources cannot be scheduled at the same time. Each pair of conflicting tasks must be ordered. This generates a binary search tree.

We have augmented the published program with a set of redundant constraints which enable the use of choices as constraints. We used a technique proposed in the integer programming community ([16]). Given a disjunction between tasks these constraints inforce one ordering of the tasks when the other ordering is discovered (after a constraint store consistency check) to be impossible. They significantly improve the backtracking behaviour of the system. Tasks are represented by a starting date implemented as a finite domain variable and a duration. The constraints and search related core of the program can be sketched as follows:

```
% StartI ranges over the possible starting dates of a task.
% DurationI is the (fixed) duration of a task.
% max_schedule is a constant greater than the starting date of any task

disjunctive_scheduling(Precedences,Distances,Disjunctions):-
        setup_precedences(Precedences),
        setup_distances(Distances),
        setup_disjunctions(Disjunctions),
        disjunctions_as_choices(Disjunctions).

setup_precedences([]).
setup_precedences([precedence(Start1,Duration1,Start2)| Precedences]):-
        Start1 + Duration1 #<= Start2,
        setup_precedences(Precedences).

disjunctions_as_constraints([]).
disjunctions_as_constraints([disjunction(Start1,Duration1,Start2,Duration2)|
        Precedences]):-
        disjunction_as_constraint(Start1,Duration1,Start2,Duration2),
        disjunctions_as_constraints(Precedences).

disjunction_as_constraint(Start1,Duration1,Start2,Duration2):-
        Aux :: 0 .. 1,  % a boolean variable
        Start1 + Duration1 + max_schedule*Aux #<= Start2 + max_schedule,
        Start2 + Duration2 #<= Start1 + max_schedule*Aux,

disjunctions_as_choices([]).
disjunctions_as_choices([disjunction(Start1,Duration1,Start2,Duration2)|
        Precedences]):-
        disjunction_as_choice(Start1,Duration1,Start2,Duration2),
        disjunctions_as_choices(Precedences).

?- parallel disjunction_as_choice/4.
disjunction_as_choice(Start1,Duration1,Start2,Duration2):-
        Start1 #>= Start2 + Duration2.
disjunction_as_choice(Start1,Duration1,Start2,Duration2):-
        Start2 #>= Start1 + Duration1.
```

We use this problem and algorithm to demonstrate how OR-parallelism can be effectively used to improve the average performance of search-based programs. To achieve this we do not take the usual approach consisting of timing the algorithm on different instances of the problem: in the real-world, solving algorithms should adapt to problems and not vice-versa.

We have assumed instead that we had reached the "don't know point" in the design phase of the algorithm where blind search is the only way out. We have then randomly generated different branching strategies and measured the timings they yield. The strategies differ in the order with which disjunctions are used to make choices. As in any branch-and-bound algorithms the enumeration order greatly affects performance. To be able to minimize the impact of a sub-optimal enumeration strategy is an important asset.

A good enumeration order is given in the original work. It is specially tuned to maximise the pruning effect of the branch-and-bound search procedure. It can be considered as the worst case for parallelisation for it exhibits the most effective pruning strategy; it is labelled with 1 in figure 1.

The diagonal lines identify the one, two, three and four orders of magnitude speed-up zones. The figure shows that all enumeration strategies are speeded up (although to different degrees) thus demonstrating that parallelism alleviates the costs of using a sub-optimal enumeration strategy and hence improves the average performance of search-based applications.

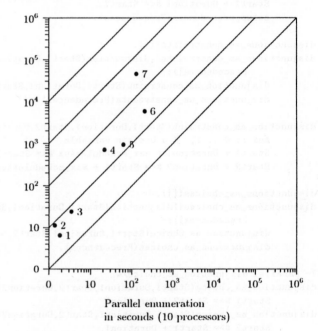

Fig. 1. Parallelisation of random Branch and Bound enumerations

Figure 2 shows how proofs of optimality (see section 2) can be linearly speeded-up by using parallelism. The search trees in those cases bear no solutions and an exhaustive traversal must be made. The labels correspond to the same enumeration strategies as those used in figure 1. Two typical curves are shown: one with a linear speed-up for sub-optimal enumeration strategy and one with a sub-linear speed-up for the good enumeration strategy. The difference in the two curves could have been expected after seeing figure 1. For this very problem the search strategy 1 is very effective and prunes the search tree so that no enough parallelism is available to exploit optimally ten processors.

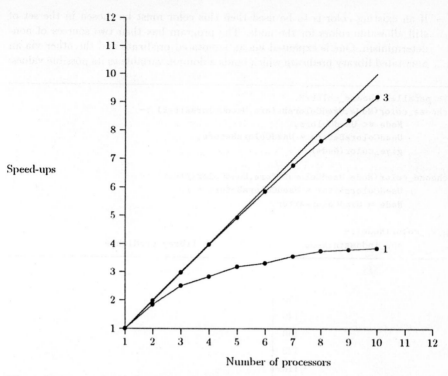

Speed-ups

Number of processors

Fig. 2. Linear speedups - Proofs of optimality

Graph Coloring The graph coloring problem is to find the minimum number of colors necessary to color the vertices of graph in such a way that no connected nodes have the same color. This problem is NP-complete and underlies many real-world situations such as the construction of time-tables, exhibition booths allocation. The graph coloring program is the one published in [11].

Nodes are represented as finite domain variables ranging over the set of possible colors. The program sets up a network of binary constraints between the nodes expressing that nodes which are adjacent should be colored differently. Once a node has been given a color all its neighbours have this color removed from their range by the constraints linking them:

```
new_node(X):- X :: 1 .. MaxColors.

link_nodes(Node1,Node):- Node1 ## Node2.
```

The search tree is built by considering nodes one by one and making the following choices:

- A node can be either colored with a color which is already used or with a new color.

– If an existing color is to be used then this color must be chosen in the set of still allowable colors for the node. The program has then two sources of non-determinism. One is exploited via an annotated predicate and the other via an annotated library predicate which binds a domain variable to its possible values:

```
?- parallel choose_color/3.
choose_color(Node,UsedColorsBefore,UsedColorsAfter) :-
        Node #< UsedColors,
        UsedColorsBefore = UsedColorsBefore,
        give_color(Node).

choose_color(Node,UsedColorsBefore,UsedColorsAfter) :-
        UsedColorsAfter = UsedColorsBefore + 1,
        Node = UsedColorsAfter.

give_color(Node):-
        par_indomain(Node).            % libray predicate
```

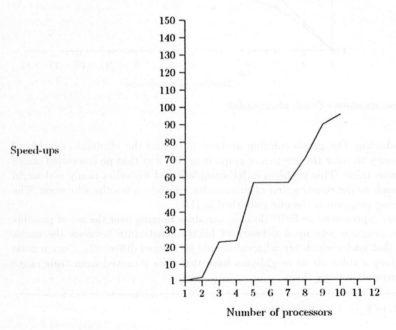

Fig. 3. Super-linear speedups - Graph coloring

Figure 3 shows how speedups can evolve with the number of processors used for the search. The coloring of this very graph (60 nodes, 50 percent density) is somehow ideal but is a good example of the potential synergies between OR-parallelism and branch-and-bound search techniques.

The more processors are used the more important is the "breadth-first" effect. As the number of processor increases, colorings (eventually using fewer colors)can be found earlier and thus improve the pruning effect of the branch-and-bound algorithm. The brutal jumps in the speed-up curve correspond to additional speculative work which succeeds at finding earlier new colorings and the horizontal segments to unsuccesful additional speculative work.

5 Conclusion

The ElipSys system demonstrates that OR-parallelism and CLP programming are complementary means to tackle large combinatorial problems. The support of a parallel CLP language leads to design decisions different from those which would be taken to implement a parallel Prolog system. The issues relating to the handling of un-pure features are simplified. First experiments and first practice have shown that the choices which have been made are viable and that the expected synergy between OR-parallelism and CLP programming was possible to achieve.

The next steps in the development of the ElipSys technology will be targeted at enlarging the set of applications. This will be done by integrating the latest developments in CLP programming (e.g. coming out of other ESPRIT projects such as CHIC EP2037), by enlarging the set of built-in search strategies and by porting the system to up-to-date multi-processors as they become commercially available.

Acknowledgments

This work was partially funded by the CEC as part of ESPRIT II project EP2025 EDS (European Declarative System) and as part of the of ESPRIT III project EP6708 APPLAUSE.

We are much indebted towards Michel Dorochevsky for its contribution to the building of ElipSys. We thank Jacques Noyé and Steven Preswitch for their comments on previous versions of this paper.

References

1. Khayri Ali. Incremental Gargage Collection for Or-parallel Prolog Based on WAM. In *Gigalips Workshop*, Stockholm, April 1989. SICS.
2. Khayri A.M Ali and Roland Karlsson. The Muse approach to OR-parallel Prolog. *International Journal of Parallel Programming*, 19(2):129–162, April 1990.
3. Khayri A.M Ali and Roland Karlsson. Or-parallel speedups in a knowledge based system: on muse and aurora. In ICOT, editor, *Fifth Generation Computing Systems*, pages 165–180, Tokyo, 1992. ICOT.
4. U.C. Baron, J. Chassin de Kergommeaux, M. Hailperin, M. Ratcliffe, P. Robert, J.C. Syre, and H. Westphal. The parallel ECRC Prolog system PEPSys: An overview and evaluation results. In *Proceedings FGCS'88*, Tokyo, November 1988. International Conference on Fifth Generation Computer Systems.
5. Martin Bartusch. Optimierung von NetzPlaenen mit Anordnungsbeziehungen bei knappen Betriesbmitteln. PhD Thesis, MIP-8618, Fakultaet fuer Mathematik und Informatik, Universitaet Passau (Germany), 1983.

6. Dominic Clark, Chris Rawlings, Mike Reeve, and André Véron. Protein structure prediction with parallel constraint logic programming. *Submitted to CABIOS, also available as ECRC Technical Report*, 1992.

7. Alain Colmerauer. An Introduction to PROLOG-III. *Communications of the ACM*, 33(7):69–90, July 1990.

8. M. Dincbas, H. Simonis, and P. Van Hentenryck. Solving Large Combinatorial Problems in Logic Programming. *Journal of Logic Programming*, 8(1-2):74–94, January-March 1990.

9. Mehmet Dincbas, Pascal Van Hentenryck, Helmut Simonis, Abderrahmane Aggoun, Thomas Graf, and Françoise Berthier. The Constraint Logic Programming Language CHIP. In *International Conference on Fifth Generation Computer Systems*, Tokyo, Japan, December 1988.

10. Erik Hagersten, Anders Landin, and Seif Haridi. DDM - A Cache-Only Memory Architecture. *IEEE Computer*, pages 44–54, September 1992.

11. Pascal Van Hentenryck. *Constraint Satisfaction in Logic Programming*. MIT Press, 1989.

12. Pascal Van Hentenryck. Parallel constraints satisfaction in logic programming: Preliminary results of CHIP within PEPSys. In Giorgio Levi and Maurizio Martelli, editors, *ICLP'89*, pages 165–180, Lisbon, June 1989. MIT Press.

13. Joxan Jaffar and Jean-Louis Lassez. Constraint logic programming. In *Proceedings of the 14th ACM Symposium on Principles of Programming Languages, Munich, Germany*, pages 111–119. ACM, January 1987.

14. Daniel Lenoski, James Laudon, Kourosh Gharachorloo, Wol f Dietrich Weber, Anoop Gupta, John Hennessy, Mark Horowitz, and Monica S. Lam. The Stanford Dash Multiprocessor. *IEEE Computer*, pages 63–79, March 1992.

15. Ewing Lusk, David H. D. Warren, Seif Haridi, and al. The Aurora Or-parallel Prolog system. *New Generation Computing*, 7(2):243–271, 1990.

16. Christos Papadimitriou and Kenneth Steiglitz. *Combinatorial Optimization*, pages 310–311. Prentice Hall, 1982.

17. Thierry Le Provost and Mark Wallace. Domain independent propagation. In *International Conference on Fifth Generation Computer Systems*, Tokyo, Japan, September 1992.

18. C.J. Skelton, C. Hammer, M. Lopez, M.J. Reeve, P. To wnsend, and K.F. Wong. EDS: A Parallel Computer System for Advanced Information Process ing. In *Proceedings of PARLE'92, Conference on Parallel Architectures and Languages Europe*, pages 3–20. Springer-Verlag, June 1992.

19. Peter Szeredi. Exploiting Or-parallelism in Optimisation Problems. In Krzysztof Apt, editor, *Joint International Conference and Symposium on Logic Programming*. MIT Press, 1992.

20. André Véron and Michel Dorochevsky. Binding Techniques and Garbage Collection for OR-parallel CLP systems. In *PLILP'92*, 1992.

21. D. H. D. Warren. The SRI model for or-parallel execution of Prolog - abstract design and implementation issues. In *Symposium of Logic Programming*, pages 92–102, 1987.

Skewed-associative Caches *

André Seznec, Francois Bodin
IRISA, Campus de Beaulieu
35042 Rennes Cedex
FRANCE
tel : (33) 99 84 73 36
FAX : (33) 99 38 38 32
e-mail : seznec@irisa.irisa.fr

Abstract. During the past decade, microprocessor peak performance has increased at a tremendous rate using RISC concept, higher and higher clock frequencies and parallel/pipelined instruction issuing. As the gap between the main memory access time and the potential average instruction time is always increasing, it has become very important to improve the behavior of the caches, particularly when no secondary cache is used (i.e on all low cost microprocessor systems). In order to improve cache hit ratios, set-associative caches are used in some of the new superscalar microprocessors.
In this paper, we present a new organization for a multi-bank cache : the skewed-associative cache. Skewed-associative caches have a better behavior than set-associative caches: typically a two-way skewed-associative cache has the hardware complexity of a two-way set-associative cache, yet simulations show that it exhibits approximatively the same hit ratio as a four-way set associative cache of the same size.
Keywords: microprocessors, cache, set-associative cache, skewed-associative cache.

1 Introduction

Performance of commercial microprocessors is increasing at a tremendous rate: 100 Mhz clocks were announced on the MIPS R4000 processor in september 1991, a 200 Mhz clock processor is offered by the end of 1992 by DEC, etc. At the same time, the architecture complexity of microprocessors is also increasing. First generation RISC microprocessors such as the MIPS R2000 or the first SUN Sparc microprocessors rapidly become obsolete. In association with technological advances which have allowed faster and faster clock speeds and larger and larger transistor counts, two major architectural techniques have been used in order to improve performance of the microprocessors: superscalar issuing of the instructions (IBM Power, SUN SuperSparc, Intel i860, etc) and "superpipelining" (i.e. increasing clock frequency by deepening the pipeline as in the MIPS R4000) [6, 15].

Most of the newly introduced commercial microprocessors have been designed to address a very large segment of the market: constructors generally claimed to address low cost embedded systems as well as high end file servers or workstations with the same basic microprocessor architecture.

In order to feed these new microprocessors with both instructions and data, a large memory is needed, and the effective performance of the whole system highly depends of the performance of the memory system. Unfortunately, over the last ten years, the main memory access cycle time has not decreased at the same rate as the processor cycle time. On a superscalar microprocessor such as the IBM Power e.g., the demand on memory instruction throughput may be up to 4 instructions per cycle and the demand on memory data throughput may be very close to one word of data per cycle. When the penalty for a cache miss is about 20 cycles, the performance may dramatically decreased when the number of cache misses increases even very smoothly (Amdhal's law).

Increasing the hit ratio of both data and instruction cache is a key issue in order to improve the effective performance of microprocessors and particularly for low-end systems.

---

* This work was partially supported by CNRS (PRC-ANM)

In section 2, we propose a new data mapping on a partially associative cache: the skewed-associative cache. Then some properties wished on skewing functions are characterized and a family of "good" skewing functions is presented.

Trace driven simulations results presented in section 3 shows that two-way skewed associative exhibits the same hit ratio as a four-way set associative cache of the same size, but at the hardware cost of a two-way set-associative cache.

2   Skewed-associative caches

2.1   Skewing on caches: principle

A set-associative cache is illustrated in Figure 1: a X way set-associative cache is built with X distinct banks of $\frac{L}{X}$ cache lines. Then a line of data with base address D may be physically mapped on physical line $f(D)$ in any of the distinct banks.

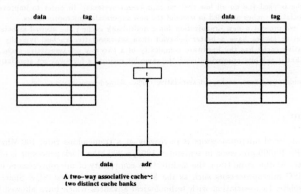

Fig. 1. An alternative vision of a two-way associative cache

We propose a very slight modification to this cache organization illustrated in Figure 2:

Different mapping functions are used for the distinct cache banks i.e., line of data with base address D may be mapped on physical line $f_0(D)$ in cache bank 0, in $f_1(D)$ in cache bank 1, etc. We call a multi-bank cache with such a mapping of the lines onto the distinct banks: a **skewed-associative cache**.

This hardware modification is very slight. It will induce a very marginal hardware upper cost when designing a new microprocessor with on-chip caches: we may choose f_i which may be implemented with a very few gates. But we shall see that this may help to increase the hit ratio of caches and then to increase the overall performance of a microprocessor using a multi-bank cache structure.

Note that skewed-associative caches may be used for internal primary caches as well as for external caches (primary or secondary).

Related works In 1977, Smith [12] considered set-associative caches and proposed to select the set by hashing the main memory address; this approach corresponds to figure 1: a *single* hashing function is used.

More recently Agarwal [2] (Chapter 6.7.2) studied hash-rehash caches.

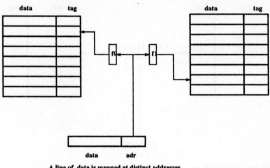

A line of data is mapped at distinct addresses
in the distinct banks of the cache

Fig. 2. A two-way skewed-associative cache

As, in a conventional cache, the address indexes into a cache set, and data is available to the processor if it is present in that set. This case is called a first time hit. On a miss, the address again indexes into the cache but using a different hashing function. If the second access is also unsuccessful then the data must be fetched from memory.

Hash-rehash caches present better overall hit ratios than direct-mapped caches approaching overall hit ratios for two-way set-associative caches, but Agarwal [2] shows that hash-rehash caches induces longer execution time than two-way set-associative caches.

In hash-rehash caches, the primary cache itself is used as a secondary cache after a first time hit, while in skewed-associative caches, different hashing functions are used for indexing *at the same time* the distinct cache banks.

2.2 Choosing skewing functions

In this section, we give some highlight on properties that might exhibit functions chosen for skewing the lines in the distinct cache banks in order to enable a good hit ratio. First we give some notations used:

- D is a line of data in main memory. For sake of simplicity, we shall also note D the address of the first byte in the line.
- f_i is the mapping function from S to CL_i.

Equitability First of all, for each line in the cache, the numbers of lines of data in the main memory that may be mapped on the cache line must be equal.

Inter-bank dispersion On classical associative set caches, when two lines of data would be mapped on the same set in the cache, they are conflicting for the same place in the X cache banks.

We have introduced skewed-associative caches to avoid this situation by scattering the data: we may chose mapping functions such that when two lines of data conflict for a single location in cache bank i, they have very low probability to conflict for a location in cache bank j.

These two situations are illustrated in figure 3 and figure 4.

Ideally, mapping functions may be chosen such as the set of lines that mapped on a cache line of bank i will be equaly distributed over all the lines of the other cache banks.

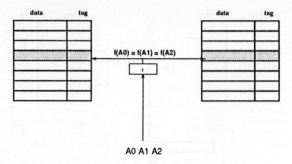

Fig. 3. 3 data conflicting for a single set on a two-way set-associative cache

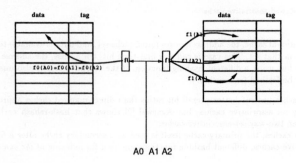

Fig. 4. Data conflicting for a cache line on bank 0 but not on bank 1

Local dispersion in a single bank Many applications exhibit spacial locality, then mapping functions must be chosen in order to avoid having two "almost" neighbor lines of data conflicting for the same physical line in cache bank i.

The different mapping functions must respect a certain form of local dispersion on a single bank; the mapping functions f_i must limit the number of conflicts when mapping any region of consecutive lines of data in a single cache bank i.

Simple hardware implementation A key issue for the overall performance of a microprocessor is the pipeline length. Using distinct mapping functions on the distinct cache banks will have no effects on the performance, if these computations can be added to a non critical stage in the pipeline and can be computed without lengthening the pipeline cycle.Let us notice that in most of the new generation microprocessors, the address computation stage is not the critical stage in the pipeline (e.g. in TI SuperSparc, two cascaded ALU operations may be executed a single cycle).

In order to achieve this, we have to chose mapping functions whose hardware implementation are very simple: a very few gates delay if possible.

2.3 A family of mapping functions

The family of mapping functions presented in this section exhibits most of the properties listed previously. The family of mapping is based on manipulations on bit strings in addresses of data.

From now, we consider that a cache bank is built with 2^n cache lines of 2^c bytes. We also suppose that the memory consists in 2^q bytes and that $q \geq 2*n+c$.

Let us consider the decomposition of a binary representation of an address A in bit substrings $A = (A_3, A_2, A_1, A_0)$, A_0 is a c bits string: the displacement in the line. A_1 and A_2 are two n bits strings and A_3 is the string of the $q - (2*n+c)$ most significant bits. Let $(y_n, y_{n-1}, .., y_1)$ be the binary representation of $Y = \Sigma_{i=1,n} y_i 2^{i-1}$. Let us consider the function H defined as follows:

$$H : \{0, .., 2^n - 1\} \longrightarrow \{0, .., 2^n - 1\}$$
$$(y_n, y_{n-1}, .., y_1) \longrightarrow (y_n \oplus y_1, y_n, y_{n-1}, .., y_3, y_2)$$

where $\oplus$ is the XOR (exclusive or) operation.

We consider the four mapping functions defined respectively by[2]:

$$f_0 : S \longrightarrow \{0, .., 2^n - 1\}$$
$$(A_3, A_2, A_1, A_0) \longrightarrow H(A_1) \oplus H^{-1}(A_2) \oplus A_2$$

$$f_1 : S \longrightarrow \{0, .., 2^n - 1\}$$
$$(A_3, A_2, A_1, A_0) \longrightarrow H(A_1) \oplus H^{-1}(A_2) \oplus A_1$$

$$f_2 : S \longrightarrow \{0, .., 2^n - 1\}$$
$$(A_3, A_2, A_1, A_0) \longrightarrow H^{-1}(A_1) \oplus H(A_2) \oplus A_2$$

$$f_3 : S \longrightarrow \{0, .., 2^n - 1\}$$
$$(A_3, A_2, A_1, A_0) \longrightarrow H^{-1}(A_1) \oplus H(A_2) \oplus A_1$$

Property 2.1 *As H is a bijection, the mapping of data using functions f_1, f_2, f_3 and f_4 is equitable.*

Property 2.2 *It is easy to prove that this set of functions f_1, f_2, f_3 and f_4 exhibits the dispersion property previously defined when the function $H^2 \oplus H \oplus Id$ is a bijection. $H^2 \oplus H \oplus I$ is a bijection for $n=3,4,6,7,9,10,12,13,15,16$[3].*

Property 2.3 *As H and $H \oplus Id$ are bijections, the local dispersion of data in a cache bank is quite optimum: for any cache line C, in any set L of $K * 2^n$ consecutive slices of data, there are at most $K + 1$ lines of data in L conflicting for the physical line C in the cache.*

Hardware implementation The hardware needed for implementing the proposed mapping functions is very simple:

each bit of $f_i(A)$ is deduced from the binary decomposition of A by XORing at most four bits!

Moreover, the four mapping functions may be implemented with similar hardware parts implementing $H(x) \oplus H^{-1}(y) \oplus z$ where x, y and z are chains of n bits (figure 2.3).

---

[2] a line in main memory is represented by the address of its first byte

[3] Using a slightly distinct basic function H allows to obtain the dispersion property for n= 5, 8, 11, 14.

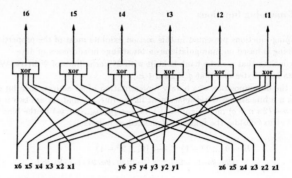

t6   t5   t4   t3   t2   t1

xor   xor   xor   xor   xor   xor

x6 x5 x4 x3 x2 x1   y6 y5 y4 y3 y2 y1   z6 z5 z4 z3 z2 z1

Fig. 5. Computing the skewing functions in hardware

2.4   An example

On a very simple example, we try to illustrate the benefits that can be expected when using a X-way skewed-associative cache in place of a X-way set-associative cache.

We give here an example with X=4 cache banks consisting of 8 lines. For sake of simplicity, a cache line of one word was assumed. A sequence of 32 addresses was randomly generated in $\{0, ..., 2^{20} - 1\}$. Let us assume that this set of data is the working set of an application.

The difference between the classical set-associative cache and the skewing mapping is illustrated in Figure 9^4:

1. **Data dispersion:**
   Let us consider that the sequence of references is issued only one time:
   - In the set-associative cache, on set 3, 8 data are conflicting, then four data must be rejected from the cache (cf Figure 6).
   - In the skewed-associative cache, 8 data are conflicting for location 1 in bank 1, but as the same data are not conflicting on the other banks, more data may be alive in the cache at the same time: 28 words after one reference to each data (cf Figure 7).
   A better dispersion of data among the cache lines is achieved on skewed-associative caches.
2. **Self data reorganization:**
   Let us now consider that the sequence of references is issued many times, as if this sequence corresponds to the working set of an application:
   - In the set-associative cache, during the whole application, only 25 words will be alive at the same time in the cache. In each set, there is no change to the number of alive cache lines compared with the Figure 6.
   - In the skewed-associative cache, the number of data present at the same time in the cache depends on the precise mapping of each data in the cache: among the other possible locations for a data D present in the cache at time t, there may be an empty location; the data D may be removed from the cache by a miss on an other data D'; in this case, the next time D will be referenced, D can be mapped in the empty location and thus the number of data alive at the same time in the cache can increase. In our example, all the data become alive at the same time after 22 references to each data (cf Figure 8).

---

[4] Number of data conflicting for a single location are indicated in bold for each set in the set-associative cache and for each location in the skewed-associative cache.

Set	Bank 0	Bank 1	Bank 2	Bank 3
0 (3)	311792	371000	590664	xx
1 (5)	869201	882529	411905	770697
2 (3)	696578	953178	324610	xx
3 (8)	544923	159243	76507	1007147
4 (2)	727204	749916	xx	xx
5 (1)	639421	xx	xx	xx
6 (5)	761790	298390	770462	234166
7 (5)	278911	1043919	246639	143631

Fig. 6. Mapping on a set-associative cache: after a single reference to each data

Address	Bank 0	Bank 1	Bank 2	Bank 3
0	770462 (2)	311792 (3)	411905 (3)	502185 (3)
1	544923 (5)	76507 (8)	546971 (6)	297638 (7)
2	278911 (3)	1043919 (5)	371000 (6)	810219 (7)
3	159243 (3)	727204 (2)	882529 (4)	xx (3)
4	696578 (7)	xx (1)	246639 (4)	937059 (2)
5	234166 (2)	761790 (5)	xx (2)	xx (4)
6	639421 (4)	953178 (3)	298390 (2)	590664 (5)
7	1007147 (6)	869201 (5)	143631 (5)	770697 (1)

Fig. 7. Mapping on a skewed-associative cache: after a single reference to each data

Address	Bank 0	Bank 1	Bank 2	Bank 3
0	770462 (2)	311792 (3)	696578 (3)	502185 (3)
1	544923 (5)	546971 (8)	953178 (6)	76507 (7)
2	278911 (3)	1043919 (5)	701631 (6)	1007147 (7)
3	159243 (3)	749916 (2)	882529 (4)	727204 (3)
4	761790 (7)	639421 (1)	246639 (4)	937059 (2)
5	297403 (2)	297638 (5)	234166 (2)	371000 (4)
6	411905 (4)	324610 (3)	298390 (2)	590664 (5)
7	810219 (6)	869201 (5)	143631 (5)	770697 (1)

Fig. 8. Mapping on a skewed-associative cache: after 22 references to each data

Fig. 9. An example of data mapping

The behavior of the skewed-associative cache, illustrated by the example, should enhance performance of blocked algorithms that iterate computations on small working set smaller than the cache size in which interference misses may degrade performance a lot [8].

2.5 Which replacement policy for skewed-associative cache

When a miss occurs in a X-bank caches, the line of data to be replaced must be chosen among X. Different replacement policies may be used. LRU replacement policy or pseudo-random replacement policy are generally used.

LRU replacement policy is generally considered as the most efficient policy. Implementing a LRU replacement policy on a two-way associative cache is quite simple. A single bit tag per cache line is sufficient: when a line is accessed, this tag is asserted and the tag of the second line of the set is deasserted. More generally a LRU replacement policy for a X-way associative is feasible with adding only X bit tags to each line.

Unfortunately, we have not been able to find concise information to associate with a cache line which would allow a simple hardware implementation of a LRU replacement policy on a skewed-associative cache: as the set of lines on which a line has to be replaced vary with the new line to be introduced, the information needed in order to determine the last referenced line in the set is the complete date of the reference.

Using a pseudo-random policy replacement generally induces more misses on caches than using a LRU replacement policy. We propose here a very simple replacement policy which requires only one tag bit per cache line and for which we have experimentally obtained very interesting behavior:

- The bit tag RU (Recently Used) is asserted when the cache line is accessed
- Periodically the bit tags RU of all the cache lines are zeroed: we experimentally determine that a good period is each $\frac{\text{cache size in bytes}}{4}$ accesses to the cache.

When a line misses in the cache, the replaced line is chosen among the X possible lines in the following priority order:

1. Randomly among the lines for which the RU tag is deasserted
2. Randomly among the lines for which the RU tag is asserted, but which have not been modified since they have been loaded in the cache[5]
3. Randomly among the lines for which the RU tag is asserted and which have been modified.

This replacement policy is quite simple to implement in hardware. An interesting property of this replacement policy is to limit the copy back of data on the main memory (or the secondary cache) and then to limit the traffic on memory.

We call this replacement policy: Not Recently Used Not Recently Written (NRUNRW).

3 Simulations

In the previous section, we have pointed out that there is a potential improvement on performance of multi-way caches when skewing addresses.

In order to verify that skewing addresses on multi-bank caches will improve the performance on effective applications, we have simulated the primary cache behavior on traces generated by 7 medium size applications (range from half a million data references to 12 millions references). This set was composed with :

1. OPACgen : a microcode generator for a hardware prototype of floating-point microcoded coprocessor
2. RESEAU : a simulator of a specific interconnection network
3. cptc : A Pascal-to-C translator
4. Cache : the cache simulator itself
5. Poisson : a Poisson solver
6. Sparse : a sparse matrix-vector multiply
7. Mulmat : a matrix multiply (60*60 by 60*60)

The first 4 applications are standard C applications. The last three applications are numeric applications.

The traces were generated by using the Abstract Execute software [9] targeted for a SPARC processor. Unfortunately system calls such as fprintf, fclose, etc, were not traced, neither exception managements, then the effective instruction miss ratios would certainly be higher than those obtained in our simulations (for results on influence of operating systems on cache performance see [1]).

---

[5] For the instruction cache, there no third choice

A single process execution was supposed : performance of caches in a time-sharing environment would be certainly worse than the results shown here [3, 10].

Simulations results have been normalized in order to give the same relative weight to each of the benchmarks. Only the geometric mean of all benchmarks is presented here since there is no significative dispersion of the results over the different programs. However it should be noted that numeric applications show, as expected, less different behaviors between set-associative cache and skewed-associative cache.

Some comments on simulations

Results presented in this paper are given for a cache line size of 64 bytes: other cache line sizes (16, 32 and 128 bytes) were also simulated, but 64 bytes was the size which gave globally the better results in terms of hit ratios on our set of benchmarks (this is coherent with results presented in [14]).

In [7], Jouppi pointed out that a significant improvement of the hit ratio of a direct-mapped cache may be obtained by adding a small fully associative cache (called a victim cache) in order to store the last lines rejected from the major primary cache.

In order to compare the results with on multi-bank caches with direct-mapped cache, such a victim buffer of two lines was simulated for all the configurations: as stated in [7], it improves significantly direct-mapped cache hit ratio. When a cache miss induces a hit in the victim cache, it does not induce any access to the main memory or secondary cache, they are not considered as misses in the rest of the paper.

Simulation results

Miss ratios on respectively the data cache and respectively the instruction cache on our benchmarks set are given respectively in Table 1 and Table 2. Cache sizes from 4096 bytes to 16384 bytes have been simulated; the replacement policies that were simulated are pseudo-random, LRU and NRUNRW (see section 2.5).

Cache Size (bytes)	4096	8192	16384
Direct-mapped	0.076040	0.062770	0.046019
LRU Standard 2 banks	0.063827	0.052571	0.040727
LRU Standard 4 banks	0.051429	0.041835	0.028765
LRU Standard 8 banks	0.048802	0.040838	0.027502
NRUNRW Standard 2 banks	0.065198	0.051921	0.040034
NRUNRW Standard 4 banks	0.053915	0.041629	0.028182
Random Standard 2 banks	0.065672	0.052012	0.039693
Random Standard 4 banks	0.055918	0.042340	0.028900
LRU Skewed 2 banks	0.050388	0.040764	0.027134
LRU Skewed 4 banks	0.048278	0.040066	0.025842
NRUNRW Skewed 2 banks	0.051740	0.040962	0.027514
NRUNRW Skewed 4 banks	0.049648	0.039819	0.026245
Random Skewed 2 banks	0.054219	0.042352	0.028633
Random Skewed 4 banks	0.053011	0.041384	0.027987

Table 1. Data cache miss ratio

These tables clearly show that a two banks skewed-associative cache has a behavior close to a four way set-associative cache. The behavior of a four banks skewed-associative cache is slightly better than the behavior of a four-way associative cache and seems close to the behavior of an eight-way set associative cache, but as pointed out previously the decreasing of the miss ratio obtained with an eight-way set-associative cache beside a four-way set-associative is quite marginal.

Cache Size (bytes)	4096	8192	16384
Direct-mapped	0.022611	0.008704	0.004133
LRU Standard 2 banks	0.016931	0.005847	0.001499
LRU Standard 4 banks	0.013598	0.006238	0.000538
LRU Standard 8 banks	0.011801	0.002425	0.000332
NRUNRW Standard 2 banks	0.016439	0.006238	0.001573
NRUNRW Standard 4 banks	0.013399	0.003748	0.000528
LRU Skewed 2 banks	0.012600	0.003378	0.001044
LRU Skewed 4 banks	0.011187	0.001726	0.000276
NRUNRW Skewed 2 banks	0.013893	0.003423	0.000968
NRUNRW Skewed 4 banks	0.012245	0.001983	0.000304
Random Skewed 2 banks	0.014433	0.003748	0.001158
Random Skewed 4 banks	0.013117	0.002562	0.000454

Table 2. Instruction cache miss ratio

Normalize execution time

In order to illustrate the influence of the miss ratio on the performance, we define the *normalized execution time* as the ratio of the effective execution time on the execution time which would have been reached if there was no time penalty on cache misses.

Definition 3.1 *For sake of simplicity to illustrate the stress on the caches, we shall assume that the nor-malized execution time T of an application is defined by:*

$$T = 1 + (1.5 * \tau_I + 0.5 * \tau_D) * LAT \qquad (1)$$

where τ_I is the miss ratio of the instruction cache and τ_D is the miss ratio of the data cache.

Formula 1 corresponds to an approximately realist execution on a superscalar microprocessor:

- an average of 1.5 instructions executed per cycle,
- an average of 1 load or store each 2 cycles.

The Figure 10 illustrates the potential benefit of using skewed-associative caches in terms of normalized execution times (see Definition 3.1) for different cache sizes and assuming equal sizes of the two caches:

- There is marginal performance benefit in using a partially associative cache organization when the main memory latency is small (e.g. 5 cycles), but when the memory latency becomes higher, using a partially associative cache organization allows very interesting performance improvement: for 8192 bytes and a 20 cycles memory latency, the normalized execution times vary from 1.46 to 1.89 for respectively a four banks skewed associative cache and the direct mapped cache [6].
- Using a four-way skewed associative cache in place of a classical four-way set associative cache improves performance: about 5% for a cache size of 8192 bytes and a 20 cycles memory latency.
- Using a two-way skewed associative cache seems very attractive: approximately equivalent performance as on a classical four way set-associative is obtained i.e. about 11 % performance improvement on a classical two-way set-associative for a cache size of 8192 bytes and a 20 cycles memory latency.

---

[6] A victim cache [7] of two lines is supposed for all configurations

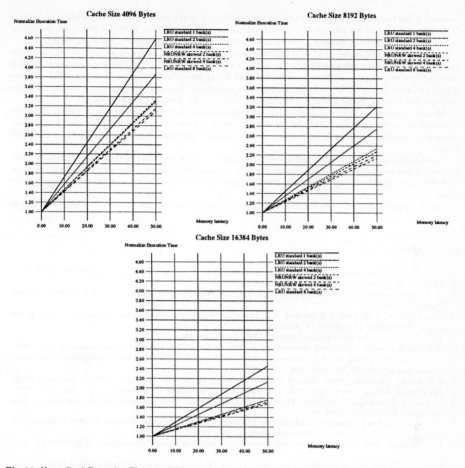

Fig. 10. Normalized Execution Times for different cache sizes

4 Conclusion

During the past decade, microprocessors potential performance has increased at a tremendous rate using RISC concept, higher and higher clock frequencies and parallel instruction issuing. On the other hand, larger and larger main memories are needed in order to feed microprocessors with both data and instructions. But the main memory access time has not decreased at the same rate. Then *effective* performance of a microprocessor on an application essentially depends on the behavior of the whole memory hierarchy: primary instruction and data caches, secondary caches (when available) and main memory system.

As the gap between the main memory access time and the potential average instruction time is always increasing, it has become very important to improve the behavior of the caches, particularly when no secondary cache is used (i.e on all low cost microprocessor systems). In order to improve cache hit ratios, set-associative caches are used in some of the new microprocessors (IBM Power, TI SuperSparc, Motorola 88110).

Set-associative caches are build with separate cache banks; a line of data may be mapped on any of the cache banks, but at the same address in the cache bank. The design of a X-way skewed-associative cache is obtained by a very slight modification of the design of X-way set-associative cache: each line of data has one possible location in any of the cache banks, but the addresses of these possible locations are different in the different cache banks. These different addresses are computed by skewing the addresses.

We have presented a family of skewing functions that exhibits interesting properties and particularly the dispersion property (lines conflicting for the same location in a cache bank are equitably distributed when mapped on another cache bank) and simple implementation hardware implementation (only a few XOR gates).

Simulations have shown that skewed-associative caches have a better behavior than set-associative caches: typically a two-way skewed-associative cache exhibits the same hit ratio as a four-way set-associative cache with the same number of cache lines, but has the same hardware complexity as a two-way set-associative cache.

Simpler skewing functions for the particular case of two-way skewed associative cache may be found in [11].

References

1. A. Agarwal, M. Horowitz, J. Hennesy "Cache performance of operating systems and multiprogramming workloads" ACM Transactions on Computer Systems, Nov. 1988
2. A. Agarwal *Analysis of Cache Performance for Operating Systems and Multiprogramming*, Kluwer Academic Publishers, 1989
3. T.E. Anderson, H.M. Levy, B.N Bershad, E.D. Lazowska "The interaction of architecture and operating system design" Proceedings of ASPLOS IV, April 1991
4. M.D. Hill, "A case for direct-mapped caches", IEEE Computer, Dec 1988
5. M.D.Hill, A.J. Smith "Evaluating Associativity in CPU Caches" IEEE Transactions on Computers, Dec. 1989
6. N.P. Jouppi, D.W. Wall "Available instruction-level parallelism for superscalar and superpipelined machines " Proceedings of ASPLOS III, April 1989
7. N.P. Jouppi, "Improving Direct-Mapped Cache Performance by the addition of a Small Fully-Associative Cache and Prefetch Buffers" Proceedings of the 17th International Symposium on Computer Architecture, June 1990
8. M. Lam, E. Rothberg and M. Wolf, "The Cache Performance and Optimizations of Blocked Algorithms", Proceedings of ASPLOS IV, April 91
9. J.R.Larus, "Abstract execution: a technique for Efficiently Tracing Programs" Technical Report, Computer Sciences Departement, University of Wisconsin-Madison, May 1990
10. J.C. Mogul, A. Borg "The effect of context switches on cache performance" Proceedings of ASPLOS IV, April 1991
11. A. Seznec, "A case for two-way skewed-associative caches", Proceedings of the 20th International Symposium on Computer Architecture, May 1993
12. A.J. Smith "A Comparative Study of Set Associative Memory Mapping Algorithms and Their Use for Cache and Main Memory" IEEE Transactions on Sofware Engineering, March 1978
13. A.J. Smith "Cache memories" ACM Computing Surveys, Sept. 1982
14. A.J. Smith "Line (block) size choice for CPU cache memories" IEEE Transactions on Computers, Sept. 1987
15. M.D. Smith, M. Johnson, M.A. Horowitz "Limits on multiple instruction issue" Proceedings of ASPLOS III, April 1989

Trace-Splitting for the Parallel Simulation of Cache Memory

Nicholas Ironmonger

Seminar for Applied Mathematics
ETH Zurich, 8092 Zurich, Switzerland
email: ndi@sam.math.ethz.ch

Abstract. This paper presents two techniques enabling the trace-driven simulation of a single cache memory to be performed in parallel. They are both based on splitting the trace into *sub-traces* which are then separately applied to suitably modified versions of the cache simulator. The two techniques are called *trace slicing* and *trace segmentation*, after the way the trace is split, and require only large-grain parallelism. While simple, slicing leads to poor speedup due to the unbalanced distribution of references in a trace. Segmentation provides good speedup, as equations and implementation results demonstrate. For each segment, *potential misses* due to the unknown initial contents are recorded; the true status of these is determined at the end of the simulation. The techniques may be applicable to forms of trace-driven analysis other than cache simulation.

1 Introduction

Cache memory plays a central part in the architecture of high performance computers, and has a large bearing on the performance attained. In designing such a computer, it is necessary to evaluate different cache architectures. Some analytic estimation techniques are of help with this task [1]; however for accurate and dependable evaluation it is still necessary to resort to simulation [14]. To evaluate an existing design, it is possible to make direct measurements of the hardware [5].

The usual approach is to obtain a *trace* of memory addresses accessed in the execution of a program, using one of a number of techniques [2, 3, 4, 10, 12, 13]. The trace is then used to drive a simulator that evaluates a cache design. With current techniques, the simulation is much slower (10 - 100 times) than the trace generation; furthermore, each trace is usually simulated many times with different cache designs. The primary item of interest in a simulation is to determine the number of *misses* (out of the total number of references) for a given cache design and program execution trace.

As hardware advances, cache sizes are increasing, requiring large traces for effective analysis [4], resulting in very long simulation times. This makes it valuable to explore the application of parallel processing to reduce the simulation time.

The parallel simulation of *multi-processor* traces is discussed in [9], using one processor for each cache driven by a separate trace and synchronising where required. For single-processor traces, a number of people have been working independently on this since around 1989-90 (the author included), but little has been published except for [6], which presents the essential idea of partitioning the trace, simulating in parallel, and then carrying out additional re-simulation steps to obtain the correct results.

Our work is based on the same basic principle, however we look more closely at the speedup equations and the practical limits that they impose; we describe a technique that is simpler, has better speedup limitations and is more suited to distributed memory multi-processors; and we present details and results of an implementation. We also make some additional observations on the second way of splitting traces. Some complementary and related work concerns the sampling of traces and estimation of miss rates [15, 8, 16], and the concurrent simulation of alternative cache organisations [11, 7]. These can in general be combined with parallel simulation.

We present two techniques to perform the simulation of a trace on a cache simulator in a parallel manner. They are both based upon splitting the trace up into *sub-traces* which are then separately applied to suitably modified versions of the cache simulator. The two techniques are *trace slicing* and *trace segmentation*. In a manner of speaking, they correspond to splitting the trace either along its entire length into slices, or by cutting it at intervals into separate segments. (In the terminology of [6], these correspond to *set partitioning* and *time partition-ing*.) The two methods of splitting result in significant differences in the overall approach, and have very different properties, which are discussed in detail later.

As well as describing the techniques, we give experimental results. These show that slicing has performance problems in practice. We explore segmentation in detail, presenting equations for the factors influencing the expected speedup, and describe an implementation. Results for the performance of segmentation on an 8-cpu multiprocessor are given. Finally we remark on some future research directions for parallel cache simulation.

2 Trace Slicing

In the first technique we describe, *Trace Slicing*, the trace is split length-wise into P slices, as shown in Fig. 1. Each slice is applied to a cache simulator running on a processor; thus the simulation is performed in parallel. The results (number of hits, misses, other detailed statistics) of each simulator are then combined (a trivial global summation) to produce the overall results.

Each slice contains references only to a particular set of addresses. The address space is thus partitioned uniquely into the P slices. The partitioning is chosen in accordance with the cache design, so that each slice corresponds uniquely to a particular group of lines in the cache. No two references in *different* slices can refer to the same cache line; hence their effect on the cache is independent - they can be applied in either order, and result in the same placement and the same misses or hits. Thus the different slices can be independently simulated

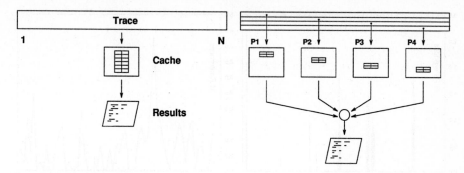

Fig. 1. *l:* Single processor trace simulation. *r:* Sliced trace parallel simulation

in parallel. Generally, low order address bits above the largest line size being simulated will be used to form the partitioning. The figure suggests a musical analogy: slicing is like selecting particular notes, while segmentation is like selecting different bars.

There is no overhead in the *simulation* of each slice; potentially a large degree of parallelism is attainable. The only overhead is the time required to partition the trace into slices. Unlike segmentation, described later, which can be done by simply addressing different file offsets in the trace file, slicing requires each reference to be examined and placed in the correct slice. This pre-processing can be done in parallel, slicing different time-segments in parallel and then concatenating the resulting slice-segments to form each full slice. The slices can be saved and used for multiple simulation runs of different cache configurations, provided that the addresses for any given line in a cache being simulated are all contained entirely in one slice.

2.1 Experimental results of Slicing

Unfortunately, experiments with slicing using a number of real traces have demonstrated very poor speedup, due to the lack of load-balancing with this technique. The underlying cause of this is illustrated by Fig. 2, which shows the number of references (instruction and data) made to each line (set) in a 2048 line cache, with a 16-byte line size. The distribution of references is extremely localised, with small clusters of peaks — some lines having millions of references — in a very flat landscape, mostly under a thousand references. This is from a trace of a small program which reads a file and calculates its entropy, thus the references are mainly confined to a few small procedures and heavily repeated loops. Admittedly, many programs are less extreme; however in general there is still considerable variation and hence reduction of speedup. Certainly many scientific programs will have such localised instruction references when they loop over large arrays.

When we take the most straightforward approach of using the lowest order bits (above the line-size boundary) to slice the trace, which would be expected

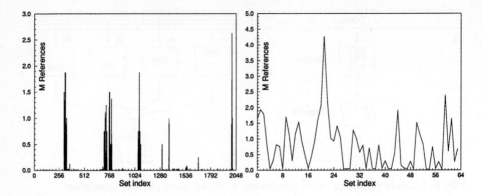

Fig. 2. Line reference distribution (2k and 64 lines).

to produce the most even distribution of references, the distribution is still extremely unbalanced, even for modest numbers of processors as shown in Fig. 2. This is the same data as the previous figure, but mapped down to a smaller number (64) of sets; for 64 processors, each would correspond to a slice. The tallest peak here has *many more* references than the tallest previously, since some of the peaks have mapped on top of one another.

It remains an open area of research to find some adaptation or extension of trace-slicing which exhibits good load balancing on real traces for even modest numbers of processors.

3   Trace Segmentation

In the second technique we describe, *Trace Segmentation*, the trace is split time-wise into P contiguous segments ts_i, as shown in Fig. 3. Each segment is applied to a cache simulator on each processor P_i. We call each of these a *segment cache*. This is performed in parallel. The results (number of hits, misses, other detailed statistics) of each simulator are then combined to produce the overall results. However, this alone is not sufficient to reproduce the simulation of the trace on a single cache; it will result in too many misses being recorded.

When a trace is applied to an empty (*cold*) cache, the first time each line in the cache is referenced, the entry is empty and a miss occurs. Such a miss is called a *cold miss*. With segmentation, for the first subtrace the misses produced correspond to real misses and must be counted, since the real cache is also empty. However, the second and succeeding subtraces are applied to a cold segment cache, whereas the real cache will contain valid entries at the times corresponding to the start of each subtrace, i.e., the real cache is *warm* at these points. Depending on the actual cache content at these points, these cold miss references may have in reality produced either a hit or a miss. We call these cold misses caused due to the segmentation of the trace *potential misses*, indicating that that they *may* give rise to a miss, but that at the time of the reference the result is unknown.

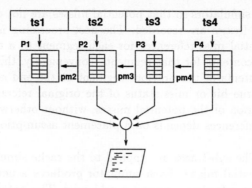

Fig. 3. Segmented trace parallel simulation.

The fundamental problem is to determine the true outcome of the potential misses for each subtrace. There several different approaches to this problem. They can generally be divided into the following three classes: 1. Approximation, 2. Pre-determining cache contents and 3. Post-processing potential misses.

3.1 Approximation

We observe that the real number of misses must lie between the number of (non potential) misses recorded, and this value plus the number of potential misses. This provides 100% confidence limits on the true results. However, since the overall miss rate (r) is quite small, it can be shown that for a cache of S lines, to obtain an accuracy a requires a segment length (N/P) of:

$$\frac{N}{P} > \frac{S}{a.r} \tag{1}$$

This is unreasonably long in practice; however, the limits are relaxed if assumptions are made about the misses, as is done in other work on trace sampling.

3.2 Pre-determining cache contents

The idea here is to initialise each of the segment cache simulators with the true contents corresponding to the time of the start of its sub-trace. This requires a (possibly backward) pre-processing scan of the trace segments; sufficient information may be generated once and stored to enable a range of different cache simulations to be performed. Due to a lack of space, this paper does not explore this idea any further.

3.3 Post-processing potential misses

The technique of trace segmentation we concentrate on for the remainder of this paper is based on post-processing the potential misses. The idea here is to apply the subtraces to the segment cache simulators as originally described, but to modify the simulators so that potential misses are not counted. Instead details of these addresses are recorded. The post-processing is carried out by applying the potential miss references for each segment to a cache containing the correct initial contents for that segment. Conveniently, this is the same as the final cache contents of the previous segment at the end of its simulation. This obtains the true hit or miss status of the original reference. The ability to defer the resolution of the potential misses, without otherwise affecting the outcome of later references depends on a placement assumption described in a later section.

To elaborate: The sub-traces are applied to the cache simulators, which do not count the potential misses. Each simulator produces a new potential-miss trace containing the references causing a cold miss. The potential-miss traces output by each segment cache are then fed in a pipe-like manner to the preceding segment caches, as shown by the arrows running to the left in Fig. 3. The details are best understood in reference to Fig. 4, which we explain in the next section.

3.4 Details of Segmentation

The data and timing dependencies for the segmentation scheme are illustrated in Fig 4, for the case with 4 processors. Note that it is not drawn to scale — in particular, the initial (white) segments will be many times longer than the (shaded) miss traces. The references *input* to a processor P_i are shown as the band running in time to the right across the page. The original trace is made up of the four white segments $ts_{1...4}$; these are numbered in chronological order, i.e., ts_1 *starts* with the *first* reference from the original trace, while ts_4 *ends* with the *last*.

The first processor P_1 starts with a true empty content; it produces no output trace. The remaining processors $P_{2...4}$ start with an unknown content; potential misses output by these segment caches are shown as a smaller band above the input producing them. We number these according to the number of the trace segment giving rise to them, namely $pm_{2...4}$. When each processor has completed reading its trace segment (at the time t_{seg}) the potential miss traces output are then read as input by the *preceding* processor, as indicated by the *shaded* input to each processor. If any further such misses are produced (pm_i' etc...), then this process continues, with the potential misses being passed back to preceding stages until they are all resolved. At this point (t_{end}), the simulation is complete and the statistics collected by each processor are gathered together and output.

The only synchronisation occurring is that represented by the dark vertical lines, where the processor completes reading the current input trace before reading any new input from the preceding processor. In rare cases it may complete the current input and have to wait for the preceding stage; however, note that it can read from the previous stage as soon as *any* misses are output, such as is shown for processor P_1, which starts reading pm_3' *before* P_2 has finished processing pm_3. Of course the last possible item of pm_3' is not known until the last item of pm_3 is processed (unless all lines in the cache have been accessed), as shown by the dark lines at the end of each segment.

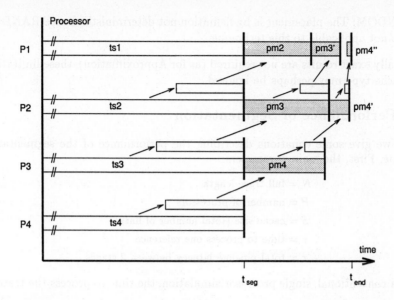

Fig. 4. Segmentation: data and timing dependencies

The statistics are accumulated where the status of references is resolved. If time-series statistics are being produced, it will be necessary to return the outcome of each potential miss to the place where the reference was made, in order to generate all statistics at the original reference point. This might best be implemented using a second pipeline in the opposite direction. Generation of, for instance, complete miss output traces for a cache simulation, can be similarly done using a post-processing stage to correct for any potential misses.

3.5 Placement assumption

There is an assumption behind the post-processing technique (and also for Approximation) that the cache exhibits a certain property, so that apart from the status of the cold misses, all other references produce the same result as the standard simulation. The property required is that the *placement* of a reference in the cache is deterministic, only depending on the particular reference, and not on the content of the cache, nor any other state variable. This is true for direct mapped caches. It is also true for (set-) associative caches which have a LRU replacement policy, but it is not true for FIFO nor for RANDOM policies. The reasons for this are as follows:

Direct: There is only one possible location to place each reference.
LRU: The reference is always placed at the head of the reference queue.
FIFO: The placement of a reference is different for a miss than for a hit. A miss results in the reference being placed at the head of the reference queue, but for a hit the reference remains at its current position. Thus the placement depends on the cache content, hence FIFO is not applicable to this technique.

RANDOM: The placement is by definition not deterministic, hence RANDOM is not applicable to this technique.

If totally exact results are not required (as for Approximation), these limitations on cache type may perhaps be ignored.

4   Performance of Segmentation

Here we give some equations describing the performance of the segmentation scheme. First, the main parameters:

$$N = \text{full trace length}$$
$$P = \text{number of processors}$$
$$S = \text{cache size (total number of lines)}$$
$$\tau = \text{time to process one reference}$$
$$L.\tau = \text{total pipeline latency between 2 stages}$$

For a conventional, single processor simulation, the time to process the trace is:

$$T_{\text{single}} = N\tau \tag{2}$$

For the parallel processor segmented-trace simulation, the time for simulating the original trace segments decreases in inverse proportion to the number of processors; however, additional time is required to process the resulting cold-miss references. This overhead reduces the performance, limiting the degree of parallelism sustainable with good efficiency. Fortunately the limits are quite reasonable in practice.

For each segment cache, the number of potential misses produced for *any* length of input is limited by the cache (tag) size S. Thus, the number of potential miss references *input* by each stage and hence the number of extra simulation steps needed by each processor to resolve these is also bounded by S. The processors operate in a pipeline manner, each continually processing its input and outputting any potential misses generated, with no synchronisation except to wait for input. Hence this extra simulation takes place concurrently on all processors, taking at most a time of $S\tau$.

This is in contrast to the scheme in [6]. Here, the re-simulation occurs in globally synchronised stages, copying the entire cache (tag) content from each processor to the next at each re-simulation stage, repeating this at most $P-1$ times. On a distributed memory processor, this copying alone will require a time of order $(P-1)S$. Even on a shared-memory processor, where such copying operations may be performed in unit time by exchanging pointers, these barrier synchronisations lead to poor performance, since in the worst case S potential misses output from the last segment, and resolved in the first will be resimulated in a block sequential manner on the one processor, taking $(P-1)S$ time steps.

Now, returning to our model for segmentation, in the ideal case, each reference is input and a potential miss, if produced, is passed on to the next processor in one time step. In a practical implementation, there may be some buffering and communication delays, leading to a *pipeline latency* of L time steps for each processor. Typically L may be expected to be around 10-100, much smaller than S. In the worst case, potential misses from the last segment may need to be resolved in the first segment cache incurring a total latency of $(P - 1)L\tau$. (In practice, most potential misses would be resolved by the previous stage, and hence with some small error, it may be sufficient not to resolve misses beyond one previous stage. This could be of advantage for implementations where the latency is significant.)

So, for the parallel segmented simulation, the total time is made up of three components: the parallel segment simulation, the parallel resolution of up to S potential misses per processor, and a pipeline latency delay, of up to (P-1) processors. Combining these components gives:

$$T_{par} = \frac{N}{P}\tau + S\tau + (P - 1)L\tau \tag{3}$$

Note that this is a *maximum*, assuming that for one or more segment-caches all S lines are referenced. Also, we are assuming that the communication times (included in τ) are the same for the initial trace as for the miss trace elements. Of course, depending on the I/O capacity of the computer, there will obviously be limits to how well the above pertains. Apart from the small time interval at the end when the cold-misses are processed, during which some processors may be idle, the load is balanced statically simply by the equal division of the trace into sub-trace segments. Now, the speedup efficiency η is simply the speedup divided by P and is given by:

$$\eta = \frac{\text{Speedup}}{P} = \frac{T_{single}}{PT_{par}} = \frac{1}{1 + P\frac{S}{N} + P(P-1)\frac{L}{N}} \tag{4}$$

Assuming for the moment that the contribution due to L is insignificant, we have:

$$P = (\frac{1}{\eta} - 1)\frac{N}{S} \tag{5}$$

The 90% efficiency point occurs at $P_{90\%} = \frac{1}{9}\frac{N}{S}$. This can be expressed another way, $\frac{N}{P_{90\%}} = 9S$, illustrating that the segment length $\frac{N}{P}$ must be kept above a significant multiple of the cache (tag) size to attain good speedup.

Alternatively, assuming for a moment that the cache size S is insignificant, but considering pipe-latency L, we see that:

$$P(P - 1) = (\frac{1}{\eta} - 1)\frac{N}{L} \tag{6}$$

Which, for $\eta = 90\%$, reduces to $P_{90\%} \approx \frac{1}{3}\sqrt{\frac{N}{L}}$. If N is very small, or L is very large, then this latency can have an impact on the overall performance or degree of usable parallelism. For instance, with a small *total* trace length $N = 10^7$, and a large latency of $L = 100$, then 90% η is surpassed for up to about 105 processors. Typically N will be larger than this and L smaller, so that usually S is the more important factor for modest numbers of processors $(S > (P - 1)L)$.

5 Implementation and Results of Trace Segmentation

In this section we briefly describe some results concerning the performance of an implementation of the segmentation scheme. An already existing trace filter and cache simulator was adapted for the purposes of this study. The flexible nature of this system meant that relatively few changes or additions were needed. For simplicity, this presently uses one Unix process per segment, connected by a standard Unix pipe. The experiments were performed on a Silicon Graphics SGI 4/D–380 computer; this has 8 MIPS R3000 processors on a shared bus, each with its own large cache. The measurements were made on an otherwise free machine (excepting unavoidable system processes), and all times reported are real times, as given by /bin/time, and thus include some overheads ($\sim 1\%$) only related to making the timing measurements.

The trace used was a basic-block trace produced by **pixie** from the simple 'entropy' program as described earlier and stored in a file. It contained both instruction basic-block addresses and data-reference addresses. The total trace length used was 20 M basic-block or data references and it was segmented equally at this level, before each basic-block reference was expanded into multiple single instruction references. Expanded, the total trace came to $N = 50.5$ M references; the variation in actual references in each segment was under 1%.

Figure 5 shows the results from one set of experiments using the above trace. The cache being simulated has 16k sets, each 2- way LRU associative, with a 16 Byte line-size. This corresponds to a total data size of 512 kByte, with the total number of lines (the term S in our equations) being 32k. The table shows the number of processors, P, the total trace length N (in 10^6 refs.), the segment length N/P, the total real time for the run, and the speedup.

P	$N(M)$	$N/P(M)$	$T_{real}(s)$	Speedup
1	50.5	50.5	468	$\equiv 1$
2	50.5	25.3	238	2.0
3	50.5	16.8	160	2.9
4	50.5	12.6	119	3.9
5	50.5	10.1	96	4.9
6	50.5	8.4	80	5.8
7	50.5	7.2	70	6.7
8	50.5	6.3	62	7.5

Fig. 5. Experimental Results for Segmentation on SGI 4D/380

The speedup obtained is very encouraging (7.5 for 8 processors), although less than the equations predicted for this segment length and cache size: since N/S is about 1500, practically linear speedup is expected. We suspect that the discrepancy is due to underlying system effects not introduced in the equations, such as limitations on the disk performance, and other factors, such as operating system overhead and bus-contention. Perhaps the latency of the Unix pipes is too large. All 8 processors are accessing the same file at different offsets; although the total bandwidth is less than the disk can supply for a single process, some degradation may be expected for such accesses. Other experiments using *pure* instruction and data traces (which do not benefit from the compression of basic-blocks) have resulted in a total bandwidth greater than the disk's maximum, with a serious impact on the speedup.

6 Properties and Conclusions

The two techniques, trace slicing and trace segmentation have quite different properties:

Trace *slicing* is in theory more attractive than segmentation for simple cache miss-ratio simulations, since it is simpler, requires no post-processing or modifications to the cache simulator, may be applied to large numbers of processors, requires less memory, and can be applied to a continuous trace stream rather that a stored trace file. However, at the stage of development as described, it has the single but overwhelming drawback that for real traces the slice lengths vary greatly, and hence the load balancing is poor, resulting in poor speedup.

Trace *segmentation* in practice is relatively simple to implement and demonstrates good speedup. The limitations on speedup due to cache size and segment length are quite favourable. Segmentation may also be used (with extensions we have only touched on this paper) for more complete simulation models, such as producing a trace output of memory references, or including the timing effects of a write buffer. This is not possible with slicing, since information about the ordering of references in different slices is lost.

Approximation - the use of segmentation without post-processing - requires extremely long trace-segments to achieve reasonable guaranteed error bounds, so is not usable in practice, unless reference properties are estimated.

7 Future Developments

The simulator is being adapted to two distributed memory multi-processors: an Intel i860 hypercube and a Thinking Machines CM5. Preliminary results have been good, with it working correctly on 64 processors, however some further tuning of the I/O operations of the program is needed to make full use of the potential disk bandwidth. Work remains, of course, to model the system-effects influencing the speedup. The biggest open challenge is to come up with a method of load-balancing for trace-*slicing* which is effective, but at the same time, efficient and simple. Further directions to explore with trace segmentation include:

(a) Extension to use trace streams for application on on-the-fly analysis, i.e. without requiring the complete trace to be first stored in a file.
(b) Producing complete memory reference output traces from the simulator.
(c) Extensions to analyse traces for purposes other than cache simulation.
(d) Any extra requirements or optimisations for use with complete system traces, which include context switches and the like.
(e) Extension of the ideas for use with the simulation of multi-processor traces.

8 Acknowledgements

I express thanks to Neil Gunther, Roland Rühl and the referees for their helpful comments on this paper, to Wilfred van Gunsteren for use of the SGI, and to Thinking Machines for access to the CM5.

References

1. A. Agarwal, M. Horowitz and J. Hennessy, "An Analytical Cache Model." ACM Trans. on Computer Systems, 7, 2, May 1989, pp. 184-215.
2. A. Agarwal, R. Sites and M. Horowitz, "ATUM: A New Technique for Capturing Address traces Using Microcode." The 13th Annual Symposium on Computer Architecture, IEEE June 1986, pp. 119-127.
3. W.G. Alexander and D. B. Wortman, "Static and Dynamic Characteristics of XPL Programs." Computer, 8, 11, Nov 1975, pp. 41-46.
4. A. Borg, R. E. Kessler and D. W. Wall, "Generation and Analysis of Very Long Address Traces." The 17th Annual Symposium on Computer Architecture, IEEE, June 1990, pp. 270-279.
5. D. Clark, "Cache Performance in the VAX 11/780." ACM Trans. on Computer Systems, 1, 1, Feb. 1983, pp. 24-37.
6. P. Heidelberger and H. S. Stone, "Parallel Trace-Driven Cache Simulation by Time Partitioning." Proceedings of the 1990 Winter Simulation Conference, IEEE, pp. 734-737.
7. M. D. Hill and A. J. Smith, "Evaluating Associativity in CPU Caches." IEEE Trans. on Computers, C-38, 12, December 1989, pp. 1612-1630.
8. S. Laha, J. H. Patel and R. K. Iyer, "Accurate Low-Cost Methods for Performance Evaluation of Cache Memory Systems." IEEE Trans. on Computers, C-37, 11, November 1988.
9. Y-B. Lin, J-L. Baer and E. D. Lazowska, "Tailoring a parallel trace-driven simulation technique to specific multiprocessor cache coherence protocols." Distributed Simulation 1989, The Society for Computer Simulation, pp. 185-190.
10. A. Lunde, "Empirical Evaluation of Some Features of Instruction Set Processor Architectures." CACM, 20, 3, Mar. 1977, pp. 143-153.
11. R. L. Mattson, J. Gecsei, D. R. Slutz and I. L. Traiger, "Evaluation Techniques for Storage Hierarchies." IBM Systems Journal, 9, 2, 1970, pp. 78-117.
12. G. McDaniel, "An Analysis of a Mesa Instruction Set Using Dynamic Instruction Frequencies." Proc. Symp. Architectural Support for Programming Languages and Operating Systems, ACM, Mar. 1982, pp. 167-176.
13. MIPS Computer Systems Inc., "Pixie", MIPS Language Programmer's Guide. 1986.
14. A. J. Smith, "Cache memories." ACM Trans. on Computer Systems, 14, 3, Sep. 1982, pp. 473-530.
15. H. S. Stone, "High-Performance Computer Architecture." Addison-Wesley Publishing Co. 3rd. edition, 1993.
16. D. A. Wood, M. D. Hill and R. E. Kessler, "A Model for Estimating Trace-Sample Miss Ratios." Proc. ACM SIGMETRICS Conference on Measurement and Modeling of Computer Systems, May 1991, pp. 79-89.

Locality and False Sharing in Coherent-Cache Parallel Graph Reduction

Andrew J. Bennett and Paul H. J. Kelly

Department of Computing,
Imperial College of Science, Technology and Medicine,
London SW7 2BZ

Abstract. Parallel graph reduction is a model for parallel program execution in which shared-memory is used under a strict access regime with single assignment and blocking reads. We outline the design of an efficient and accurate multiprocessor simulation scheme and the results of a simulation study of the performance of a suite of benchmark programs operating under a cache coherency protocol that is representative of protocols used in commercial shared-memory machines and in more scalable distributed shared-memory systems. We analyse the influence of cache line size on performance and expose the relative contributions of spatial, temporal and processor locality and false sharing to overall performance.

1 Background

Parallel graph reduction (PGR) is a well-known technique which uses a shared graph structure to manage and synchronise the parallel execution of a functional program. It provides a simple model of communication and synchronisation between processors with distinctive properties of importance in the design and optimisation of multicache implementations of shared-memory. The performance of parallel programs under this regime depends critically on the provision of access to the shared heap with very high average performance.

The most successful implementations of PGR (e.g. Goldberg's Buckwheat system [8] and Augustsson and Johnsson's $\langle \nu, G \rangle$-machine [3]) have used general-purpose shared-memory multiprocessors based on well-known bus-based snooping cache coherency protocols. For modest numbers of processors these systems implement a shared heap with near-ideal performance, but their size is limited by contention for the snooping bus.

Shared-bus multiprocessors now have relatively high-latency communication (i.e. the latency of a memory reference that requires use of the bus is now many times greater than one that does not), and the number of processors that can be supported by the bus is very small. A solution is to use a more complex network, but such networks favour the transmission of larger messages, and require directories to store copy sets because broadcast is no longer available.

There are three important issues to be addressed:

1. How does cache line size affect the performance of parallel graph reduction operating with invalidation based protocols?

2. How much of a performance impact does false sharing (i.e. contention for write access to a cache line) have?
3. How significant is the effect of invalidation traffic on performance, particularly when broadcast is not available?

This paper describes simulation work aimed at determining the performance of PGR operating with a multicache implementation of shared-memory, and builds on our earlier work in which performance under an ideal shared-memory was studied [5].

2 Parallel Graph Reduction

The essence of PGR is that in a function application

```
f e1 e2
```

we may mark one or more of the parameters for possible parallel execution — as with e1 here, for example:

```
f #e1 e2
```

At runtime a heap-based representation of how e1 is to be computed is built and added to a pool of available tasks for distribution to other processing elements (PEs) — the node is *sparked*. In the body of the function f where the parameter is used, code is emitted to check whether the parameter has yet been evaluated — the node is *demanded*. If another PE has accepted the task, this PE will block; otherwise it will evaluate e1 itself.

Once a parameter has been evaluated, it is not changed.

Without going into a great deal more detail, it should be clear that this mechanism requires shared-memory, but that it uses shared-memory in a disciplined fashion: each cell is marked with a tag indicating whether it contains an evaluated result, or if not whether it is being computed by some PE. A cell is not written to without first gaining exclusive access to the cell, and setting the tag appropriately.

3 Cache Coherency Protocols

We simulate the Berkeley Ownership [12] protocol, similar to that used in commercial bus-based shared-memory machines such as the Sequent Symmetry.

The shared-memory region is divided into a number of cache lines of some constant size. Each line has an owner (either a PE or main memory); ownership changes dynamically according to coherency transactions. When a PE attempts to read a line which it does not have a copy of, a read request is broadcast, and the owner of the line responds by broadcasting a copy of the line. The requesting PE adds the line to its cache (expelling another line if the cache is full) and proceeds to use it. In this way, multiple copies of lines come into existence in the system. A write to a line that is cached locally but not remotely can take place without using the network.

The difficulty occurs when a write to a line that has multiple copies occurs: either the new data can be broadcast enabling other caches to update their copies, or the remote copies can be invalidated before the write is allowed to proceed. The relative performance of update and invalidation protocols is determined by the data sharing behaviour and by the network characteristics: update protocols offer better performance when significant contention for shared data exists and the network has low latency [2] but we adopt an invalidation protocol since we are interested in higher latency networks. The requesting PE becomes the new owner of the line when the write has completed.

The same protocol can be used on non-broadcast networks provided directories are used to record which caches have copies of each line and a mechanism to locate the owner of lines is adopted — see for example Li's fixed distributed manager algorithm [14], a basic distributed shared-memory (DSM) protocol.

3.1 False Sharing

Networks with large latencies tend to favour the transmission of relatively large messages which in turn tend to favour the use of large line sizes. However a large line size will cause false sharing [6] in which several data objects located on the same line are used independently by different PEs but any write will cause copies of the line to be invalidated. This effect is referred to as *line stealing*. This additional communication and serialisation is due to contention for ownership of the cache line.

4   Experimental Design

Our objective was to produce repeatable and reusable results, and so at several points we have chosen a simplified approach rather than a more optimised implementation in which the issues might be obscured. Our simplifications are described in Sects. 4.2 and 4.3.

4.1   Source Language and Compiler

The source language is a lazy, higher-order functional language in the tradition of SASL, Miranda and Haskell. The primary objective in building an optimising compiler for a lazy functional language is to reduce the frequency at which claims and references are made to the heap. It is therefore of great importance that the compiler used in our experiments should perform reasonably well. Although comparing compilers is difficult, we have some confidence that the system is competitive with the state of the art [11]. It also, conveniently, generates C, making generated code very easy to instrument and modify.

4.2   Process Management

Parallel computation is coordinated via the heap where graph nodes are allocated. Work is allocated to processors via a work pool, which in the current system is a simple queue. The heap is accessed by the processors in order to determine what needs to be evaluated, and processes synchronise using a blocking read operation.

4.3   Garbage Collection

When storage allocated from the shared heap becomes free, it should be recycled for reuse. In a parallel system a parallel garbage collector is needed, and the area is the subject of intensive research. The behaviour of the garbage collector may interfere with normal program execution in two ways: firstly, it may change the relative timing of processes, depending on when it is activated, and whether all processors collect in synchrony. Secondly, garbage collection may substantially change the pattern in which store is allocated.

We have made an important simplification here: we have no garbage collection at all. Instead, each processor is allocated a large contiguous segment of the shared address space, and it allocates space from it starting from the base.

The motivation for this decision is as follows: to introduce a garbage collector into the simulation we would have to choose one of the available algorithms, and our results would then be applicable only when a similar collector is in use. Unfortunately, there is no obvious candidate: there is no consensus on how garbage collection should be done in large shared-memory systems. However, any copying collector would finish by handing the application program a contiguous segment of free store. Thus, there is a significant period during which heap cell allocation proceeds in precisely the simple pattern we assume. We simply assume this is the case all the time.

This assumption illuminates an important point: our objective is to learn general lessons about a large class of systems. We are less concerned that the experiments predict the actual performance of some production system, as to do so we would have to introduce many factors which are orthogonal to the issues we intend to study.

4.4   Example Functional Programs

The complete suite of programs we have been using are as follows:

pfib   compute the nth Fibonacci number
nqueens compute a safe arrangement of queens on an $n \times n$ chess board
matmult multiply two $n \times n$ matrices
quad   find the integral of a cubic function using adaptive quadrature

Less trivial example programs are available, but the programs in this suite are simple enough to offer the possibility that their behaviour might be understood, while covering a variety of parallel program structures. The programs were used in Goldberg's Alfalfa and Buckwheat experiments, and are fully described in his thesis [8]. Marking of expressions for parallel evaluation is introduced manually.

5   Cache Simulation

Trace-driven simulation has been employed in simulating shared-memory systems. However, there are problems with the validity of such studies since the relative timing of processes depends on the behaviour of the memory system. For this reason, we have chosen execution-driven simulation. It is slower than trace-driven simulation, since the object code is reexecuted for each experiment, but it eliminates the validity problems of trace-driven simulation since the simulated processors read the data as it is at the simulated time at which the reference is made.

For these experiments, the simulator models the state and copy set of each cache line in the shared-memory in order to determine the latency of each heap reference. Further information is also associated with each cell and cache line to enable the performance of the cache system to be closely monitored. The simulation scheme is more fully described in [4].

5.1   Architectural Model

We basically assume a 32-bit non-pipelined load-store architecture, with the following assumptions:

- The stack, private data and code regions of each process are served by a separate, perfect cache system; each read or write to these regions has a latency of one cycle
- The heap cell allocation method used is incremental, consequently the allocation of a cell on a cache line that has not been used before, although a write-miss, can be treated as a write-hit using a "direct write" instruction [9] since the old contents of the line will not be used
- We assume that infinite sized, fully associative caches are used, so cache capacity effects do not occur. The extra overheads caused by using non-fully associative caches is unlikely to be significant [13]. Adopting infinite sized caches allows the main memory unit to be removed entirely and all shared data resides in a cache

Although each assumption is invalid on a real machine, they prevent the results from being obscured by other effects. In addition, these assumptions reduce the number of global events produced, improving simulation time.

The network model determines the latency of coherency transactions. For ease of comparison, a model very similar to those used in several related cache performance studies is used (for example [1]). Note that these latencies remain fixed when the cache line size is altered. We make no claim that the figures are accurate or realistic; essentially they apply an arbitrary weighting to network activity. In analysing our results we count the events themselves, thus avoiding this bias. Network contention is not directly modeled since we are primarily interested in a network in which contention effects are more complicated than a bus.

6 Simulation Results

Many simulation runs were made of the benchmark set, using the simplified invalidation protocol and the architectural model described above. Simulation parameters were the number of PEs (1, 2, 4, 8, 16 and 32) and cache line size (1, 2, 4, 8, 16, 32, 64, 128 and 256 cells). Line sizes are specified in units of heap cells (a cell is 24 bytes in the current implementation).

Simulated execution times indicate that each program is highly parallel. Due to the architectural assumptions made, the simulated execution time of each program for a single processor is independent of cache line size. However, when more than a single PE is simulated, cache line size does have an influence, but the magnitude is dependent upon the details of the architectural model.

6.1 Spatial Locality and Line Stealing

It is apparent that line size does affect performance, but the contributions of spatial locality and line stealing are not clear. The simulator uses monitoring information to enable these effects to be measured separately. A classification of heap references is produced, allowing any gains from spatial locality and losses due to line stealing to be quantified. Monitoring information associated with each heap node records the elapsed simulated time when the cell was last written, a list of PEs that have accessed the cell since that time and the last PE to write to the cell. Information stored with each cache line describes the elapsed simulated time at which each PE last took a copy of that line.

Heap read references are classified as follows:

Simple-read: the PE has accessed an up-to-date copy of the cell before, and has a coherent copy of the associated cache line

Mandatory-read: the PE has never had an up-to-date copy of the cell in its cache, and communication must take place. Either the PE has not accessed the cell before, or the cell has been updated by a remote PE since it did

Gain-read: the PE has not accessed an up-to-date copy of the cell before, but has a coherent copy of the cache line, i.e. a gain from spatial locality

Loss-read: the PE had an up-to-date copy of the cell in its cache at some time in the past, but the line has been invalidated, i.e. a loss from line stealing caused by false sharing

The classification scheme for write references concentrates on relating line sharing to cell sharing, and the effect this has on whether an invalidation needs to be issued on a write, and is described in terms of "active sharing". An object (heap cell or cache line) is said to be actively shared if an up-to-date copy of it has been accessed by more than one PE. Therefore multiple copies of an actively shared cache line exist in the system.

Allocation-write: a write-miss caused by allocating a new cell on an as yet unused cache line. It can be treated as a write-hit using a direct write instruction

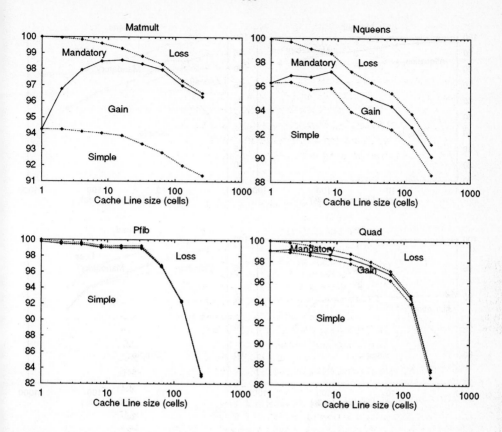

Fig. 1. Classification of read references as a function of cache line size for 32 PE simulations

Simple-write: a write-hit, neither the cell nor the line is actively shared
Mandatory-write: a write-miss or a write-hit and both the cell and the line are actively shared, i.e. an invalidation must be issued
Gain-write: the cell is actively shared, but the line is not, i.e. no invalidation is needed
Loss-write: the cell is not actively shared, but the line is, i.e. an invalidation is needed although the cell is not actively shared

Graphs showing percentage composition of read and write heap references for matmult, pfib, quad and nqueens with 32 PEs are shown in Figs. 1 and 2.

The graph of read references for nqueens shows some interesting trends. The solid line separates read references not requiring network use (simple-reads and gain-reads below) from those that do (mandatory-reads and loss-reads above):

- When the line size is 1 cell, clearly there is no opportunity to exploit spatial locality, but also false sharing cannot occur. Therefore all reads are

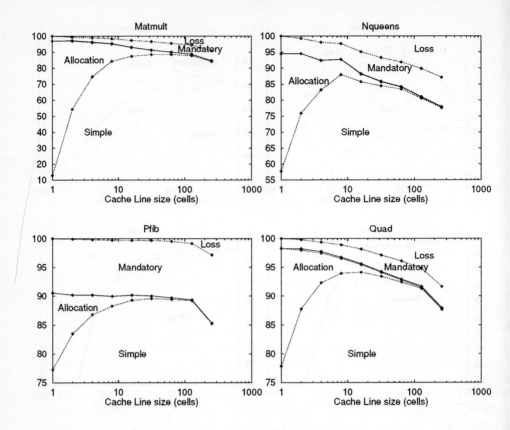

Fig. 2. Classification of write references as a function of cache line size for 32 PE simulations

either simple-reads or mandatory-reads (only about 4% of references are mandatory-reads)

- As the line size is increased, spatial locality gains are made, reducing the number of mandatory-read accesses. This trend continues for larger line sizes until the mandatory-reads are almost eliminated
- Line stealing occurs even when the line size is 2 cells, and increases steadily for larger line sizes
- Read references not requiring network use peak at a line size of 8 cells, after which it drops away rapidly. So it is clear that spatial locality is being exploited. However, losses due to false sharing outweigh gains when the line size exceed 16 cells

The corresponding graph for writes shows that, at line size 1, more than 35% of writes cause fresh lines to be allocated. This demonstrates the importance of a "direct write" instruction which allows previously unused cache lines to be used immediately. The majority of writes are classified as simple-writes. Mandatory-write references are roughly constant across line sizes. The loss effect steadily increases until it is about 13%. The percentage of writes requiring use of the network (above the solid line) increases from the smallest line size.

Read and write graphs for matmult, pfib and quad are broadly similar, although the magnitude of each region varies greatly. Pfib reads are almost entirely simple-reads for line sizes less than 64 cells, and so the potential gain is correspondingly small. The contention for lines when line size exceeds 32 cells for pfib can be clearly seen to be due to line stealing. For write references, the simple-write versus allocation-write variation is seen again, and mandatory-writes are also largely insensitive to line size. Mandatory-writes are particularly high because such a high percentage of cells are actively shared [5].

Heap read references for matmult are approximately 5.5% mandatory-reads when the line size if 1 cell, larger than for any other program, and therefore matmult offers the best opportunity to benefit from spatial locality. This is indeed achieved: reads not requiring the network peak at a line size of 16 cells, after which false sharing reverses the effect. Write references show similar trends to the other programs.

Although the programs show different behaviour with varying line size, significant similarities in the graphs are apparent. The graphs for write accesses are particularly similar in form: each shows that the vast majority of writes are simple-writes or allocation-writes (and therefore of low latency). For small line sizes, many fresh lines can be allocated cheaply using a direct write instruction. It might be expected that many writes to large lines would require invalidations, but the burstiness of writes is such that this is not a significant problem. Burstiness is particularly apparent when an unevaluated node is demanded, causing the node to be locked, several fields to be updated, and then unlocked. Although the first write of a burst may require an invalidation, there is a high probability that the line will not be accessed by other PEs during the rest of the burst, and therefore no extra invalidation traffic will be required. Consequently there is a high degree of processor locality (at least for relatively small line sizes). The solid line on each write graph separate low latency from high latency actions: in all cases this line falls with increasing line size, and so (for writes alone) the minimum line size is desirable.

The read graphs are also fairly similar in general form, but differences in the heap cell reference characteristics of the programs are more apparent here. In each case, the mandatory-reads at the minimum line size are virtually eliminated at large line sizes, and a steadily increasing proportion of reads are loss-reads due to false sharing. Mandatory-reads can never be eliminated since some represent the minimum communication that is required for parallel execution. Nqueens and matmult which both use constructed data have optimum line sizes of 8 and 16 cells respectively, whereas for pfib and quad it is 1, although little is lost by using a line size as large as 16 or 32 cells.

7   More Realistic Networks

The network model adopted is simple enough that the influence of varying line size on performance can be accurately measured and attributed to the simulation parameters of line size and number of PEs. A more realistic network model would differ in two significant ways: contention would increase latencies under heavy loads, and broadcast may not be available requiring the protocol to be modified so that the copy set of each cache line is explicitly stored. Graphs showing the distribution of invalidations required for invalidating writes (not shown here) indicate that, under reasonable conditions, less than two invalidations are required, enabling small directories to be used.

8   Discussion and Related Work

There are many studies of the cache behaviour of parallel imperative programs in the literature, but few related to declarative languages.

A short study of the cache behaviour of parallel functional programs on shared bus architectures is given as an example of the use of the MiG execution-driven simulator in [15]. The parallel evaluation strategy is a modified form of graph reduction in which shared nodes are only ever read, greatly simplifying the coherency problem, and making direct comparisons with our work difficult.

A related study of caching effects in a sequential functional language implementation [13] found significant locality which was attributed to the misses caused by the incremental allocation strategy, the LIFO behaviour of the graph reducer stack and the evaluation of suspension (in which multiple fields are read in a burst). Our stacks are not shared and we assume they are dealt with by a separate perfect cache, but this work does support the adoption of a "direct write" instruction. Cache associativity was also studied, with the conclusion that little is to be gained by increasing from 2 to 4-way set associativity since little interference occurs. This supports our decision not to include associativity effects in our cache model.

A simulation study of a coherent cache shared-bus architecture to support parallel logic languages is reported in [9]. The design uses the Illinois protocol as a base (essentially the same as our protocol) with several instructions added to support various communication patterns that commonly occur. Examples of new instructions are "read-purge" which removes cache lines from the cache, and direct-write. The latter is the only instruction that is used in heap references and yielded simulated execution time improvements of between 38% and 45%. These figures are high since the cache line size is only four words (approximately our minimum line size). The language does not have arrays and little spatial locality was found — this corresponds with our results showing that programs without constructed data did not show gains from spatial locality when large cache lines were used.

9 Conclusions

This paper has presented the design of an efficient and accurate event-driven multiprocessor simulator based on an optimising functional language compiler. A simplified architectural model is used in which processor pipeline, cache capacity and network contention effects are ignored. This loses low-level accuracy but allows us to identify object reference patterns which affect performance and to separate the conflicting effects of spatial locality and false sharing.

The simulator has been used to study the performance of a benchmark set of parallel functional programs operating under an invalidation-based cache coherency protocol. Our results include the following:

- Cache line size can have a significant effect on performance, limited only by the number of PEs
- Each program displays significant processor locality which is vital for an invalidation protocol, but contention for lines reduces this and greatly harms performance with particularly large line sizes
- Programs which did not use constructed data did not benefit from large line sizes at all, but were not greatly harmed by line sizes up to at least 8 cells. Programs which use constructed data (nqueens and matmult) can benefit from large line sizes due to spatial locality: matmult shows peak performance for line sizes of 8 or 16 cells
- Write behaviour is broadly similar for all the programs dues to the burstiness of writes. Contention for lines is so great when large sizes are used with many PEs that each burst may produce several invalidating writes. Delayed consistency [7] could solve this problem
- Not surprisingly, we found that our results are very different from those derived from shared-memory programs written in conventional languages. We have observed greater processor locality and less invalidation traffic for large lines when compared to simulations of the Splash suite for example [10]
- The use of a fast cache line allocation instruction (such as direct-write) is important when using small cache lines since a high proportion of write references are used to allocate new heap cells
- The use of a single global task pool has not appeared as a bottleneck, but it does mean that we fail to make full use of locality and this deserves further study

Future work will include more PEs, a wider range of example programs and a more thorough study of network contention. Directions for further study include affinity scheduling (in which scheduling decisions are influenced by the location of data), automatic compile-time parallelisation (following [8]) and the effect of garbage collection and compaction. Other ideas include the development of performance debugging tools based on data sharing measurements and the use of high-level data distribution annotations.

References

1. Anant Agarwal, Richard Simoni, John Hennessy, and Mark Horowitz. An evaluation of directory schemes for cache coherence. *15th Annual International Symposium on Computer Architecture, Honolulu, May, in Computer Architecture News*, 16(2):280–289, May 1988.

2. James Archibald and Jean-Loup Baer. Cache coherence protocols: Evaluation using a multiprocessor simulation model. *ACM Transactions on Computer Systems*, 4(4):273–298, November 1986.

3. Lennart Augustsson and Thomas Johnsson. Parallel graph reduction with the $\langle \nu, G \rangle$-machine. In *Fourth International Conference on Functional Programming Languages and Computer Architecture, London, September*, pages 202–213, 1989.

4. Andrew J. Bennett. *Parallel graph reduction for shared-memory architectures.* PhD thesis, Department of Computing, Imperial College, London, 1993.

5. Andrew J. Bennett and Paul H. J. Kelly. Simulation of multicache parallel graph reduction. In *Workshop on Parallel Implementations of Functional Languages, Aachen, Sept*, 1992.

6. Lothar Borrmann and Petro Istavrinos. Store coherency in a parallel distributed memory machine. In Arndt Bode, editor, *European Distributed Memory Conference, Munich, April 1991*, volume 487 of *Lecture Notes in Computer Science*, pages 32–41, Berlin, 1991. Springer-Verlag.

7. Michel Dubois. Delayed consistency. In Michel Dubois and Shreekant S. Thakkar, editors, *Workshop on Scalable Shared Memory Multiprocessors, Seattle, May*, pages 207–218, Boston, 1992. Kluwer Academic Publishers.

8. Benjamin F. Goldberg. *Multiprocessor Execution of Functional Programs.* PhD thesis, Yale University, New Haven, 1988.

9. Atsuhiro Goto, Akira Matsumoto, and Evan Tick. Design and performance of a coherent cache for parallel logic programming architectures. *16th Annual International Symposium on Computer Architecture, Jerusalem, May, in Computer Architecture News*, 17(3):25–33, June 1989.

10. Anoop Gupta and Wolf-Dietrich Weber. Cache invalidation patterns in shared-memory multiprocessors. *IEEE Transactions on Computers*, To appear, 1992.

11. Pieter H. Hartel and Koen G. Langendoen. Benchmarking implementations of lazy functional languages. In *Proceedings of the Conference on Functional Programming Langauges and Computer Architecture, Copenhagen, June*, 1993.

12. R. H. Katz, S. J. Eggers, D. A. Wood, C. L. Perkins, and R. G. Sheldon. Implementing a cache consistency protocol. *12th Annual International Symposium on Computer Architecture, Boston, June, in Computer Architecture News*, 13(3):276–283, June 1985.

13. Koen Langendoen and Dirk-Jan Agterkamp. Cache behaviour of lazy functional programs. In *Workshop on Parallel Implementations of Functional Languages, Aachen, Sept*, 1992.

14. Kai Li and Paul Hudak. Memory coherence in shared virtual memory systems. *ACM Transactions on Computer Systems*, 7(4):321–359, November 1989.

15. H. L. Muller, K. G. Langendoen, and L. O. Hertzberger. MiG: Simulating parallel functional programs on hierarchal cache architectures. Technical Report CS-92-04, Department of Computer Systems, University of Amsterdam, 1992.

SLiD — A Cost-Effective and Scalable Limited-Directory Scheme for Cache Coherence

Guoying Chen *

Ultracomputer Research Laboratory, New York University
715 Broadway, 10th Floor, New York, NY 10003 (chenguo@nyu.edu)

Abstract. In this paper, we propose a hybrid scheme — dubbed SLiD (*Scalable Limited Directory*) that combines the good features of the *chained directory* and *limited directory* schemes and minimizes the effect of the weak points of each individual scheme, namely the performance penalty in the limited directory when pointer overflow occurs, and the linear latency in the chained directory scheme when performing invalidations due to a write. Moreover, the hybrid scheme provides designers with three structural options for different requirements of performance and implementation cost.

Simulation studies demonstrate that the SLiD scheme is promising. Compared with other related schemes, the SLiD scheme is scalable and cost-effective.

1 Introduction

Designing a cost-effective and scalable cache coherence protocol has been one of the major issues in building large-scale multiprocessors. Numerous cache coherence schemes have been proposed in the past few years. Directory-based schemes [4] are currently among the most promising solutions because they rely only on point-to-point interconnects rather than on broadcast mechanisms. In such schemes, a directory entry is maintained for each memory block to keep track of those caches in which a copy of the block resides. The directory-based protocol ensures the coherency by either invalidating or updating the cached copies of the block.

Theoretically, the full-map directory protocol proposed by Censier and Feautrier [3] produces the optimal performance among all existing cache coherence schemes. However, the memory overhead of the full-map directory is quadratic with the number of processors in the system, and is therefore prohibitively expensive for large-scale systems. More current research has focused on the reduction of the storage overhead while approximating the performance of the full-map scheme. The two representatives of such schemes are *limited directory* and *chained directory*. The limited directory scheme, although favorable to those programs with a small degree of data sharing, suffers a big performance penalty when the degree of sharing reaches beyond a certain point. The chained directory is effective in managing read and replacement operations, but the writes can incur long latency in invalidations.

In this paper, we propose a hybrid scheme, dubbed SLiD (*Scalable Limited Directory*). It combines the good features of the chained directory and limited directory schemes

---

* Supported by U.S. Department of Energy under grant number DE-FG02-88ER25052.

and minimizes the effect of the weak points of each individual scheme, namely the performance penalty in the limited directory when pointer overflow occurs, and the linear latency in the chained directory scheme when performing invalidations due to a write. Furthermore, the SLiD scheme framework provides designers with three structural options for different performance requirements and implementation cost.

The remainder of this paper is organized as follows. An overview of the background of this study is given in section 2. The SLiD cache coherence scheme is presented in section 3, including a basic SLiD protocol and its two extensions to improve the performance. The comparison and evaluation of the SLiD scheme with other related schemes are covered in section 4, followed by the conclusion in section 5.

2 Background: Limited and Chained Directories

The *limited directory* [2] was proposed to solve the severe memory overhead problem arising from the full-map directories [3], where each memory block contains a *presence flag vector* with n-bits, each indicating the sharing status of one cache/processor. In a limited directory, only certain pointers (say i) are stored in each entry. Each pointer is a unique identifier of the processor, occupying $log_2 N$ bits. If most of the time no more than a few caches share a given memory block, most of the presence flag bits in the full-map directory are not actively set. In such cases, using limited pointers is more efficient than using a presence flag vector. In terms of memory overhead, the limited pointers has only $O(log N)$ in the directory width, comparing to the full-map's $O(N)$.

For convenience, throughout this paper we adopt the notation of $Dir_N X$ appeared in [2] by Agarwal et al. The limited directory is denoted as $Dir_i X$, while the full-map $Dir_N X$, where N is the total number of processors, and X represents invalidation mechanisms such as broadcast ($X = $ B) or non-broadcast ($X = $ NB).

The $Dir_i X$ [2] is attractive because only a few processors usually access a given memory block before it is written. This leads to the conclusion that most of the time only a few pointers are required in the directory for managing the coherent data of a memory block. However, this brings the pointer exhaustion problem. Since i is constant, other mechanisms must be resorted when no pointers remain. Dir_iB (with *broadcast*) and Dir_iNB (*non-broadcast*) are two such alternatives. In the Dir_iB, a *broadcast bit* is set when a pointer is attempted to add into the directory that is already full. When a write occurs in this situation, an invalidation broadcast must be sent to all caches. The broadcasting mechanism, however, generates excessive traffic to the interconnection network and increases contention. Unless the number of extra invalidations is minimized, the broadcast scheme is not a viable option for designing large-scale systems.

Alternatively, the Dir_iNB tackles the pointer exhaustion problem by invalidating one of the i pointers previously stored so that a new read request can be satisfied. The advantage of this strategy is that it never has to broadcast an invalidation message to all caches in the system. The disadvantage is that the read misses may lead to an invalidation that would not have been necessary if sufficient cache pointers had been available. As a result, the network traffic increases. Moreover, the copy just invalidated might be read before it is written. This read could have been a hit had the invalidation not occurred.

Therefore, the Dir_iNB has a negative impact not only on the network traffic but on the miss rate as well.

The *chained directory* ($Dir_1\cdot$) is organized by linking all caches who share the same memory block with a linked list, rather than storing the cache identities in memory modules. Therefore, the cost of an update operation in the chained directory is very different than the cost in a full-map directory or in a limited directory scheme because the consistency commands are traversed along the list (singly linked or doubly linked).

The chained directory scheme has an advantage in that it never runs out of cache pointers, although the operation in the linked list is more complicated than that in the limited directory. The weakest point of the chained directory, however, is the performance penalty of invalidations upon a write request. Because of the linear linkage, the invalidation would incur $O(n)$ latency if the sharing set is of size n.

Although some other interesting approaches will be discussed later, the doubly linked-list directory has been adopted by IEEE SCI (Scalable Cache Interface) Standard P1596 [10] and a variant of the limited directory scheme, called *LimitLESS*, has been proposed by MIT Alewife group[5].

3 The SLiD Scheme

We discovered that the combination of the limited directory and the chained directory can eliminate the pointer overflow problem of $Dir_i X$. In such a combined scheme, it is also possible to explore other techniques to reduce the cost of linear invalidations.

In this section, we begin with describing a basic SLiD protocol. Then, we extend it and enhance its performance by reorganizing the linked list, while not significantly increasing its complexity in hardware. Throughout the paper, we assume that a sequential memory consistency model is used.

3.1 Basic SLiD Protocol ($Dir_{i+1}\cdot$)

An entry of the basic SLiD directory contains i base pointers, a link pointer (*linkp*), and a counter (*count*), as shown in Fig. 1. The *linkp* extends the limited directory by heading a linked list of extra pointers that the Dir_iNB can not support. In other words, the linked list headed by the *linkp* is used to emulate a full-map directory when i base pointers are exhausted.

The states and state transitions of the generic SLiD protocol for a memory block are shown in Fig. 2.

Similar to the full-map scheme, the SLiD scheme has four major states for a given memory block: (1) *Not-Cached*: no cache holds the memory block. (2) *Read-Exclusive*: only *one* cache holds the block exclusively and it has not been modified. (3) *Clean-Shared*: more than one cache share the block and it has not been modified. If more than i pointers are sharing the block, it is in *Clean-Shared SLD* (scalable limited mode); otherwise, it is in *Clean-Shared LD* (limited mode). (4) *Dirty-Exclusive*: only one cache holds the memory block and it has been modified.

The state transitions in Fig. 2 can be summarized as follows: The initial state of a given memory block is with *Not-Cached*. A read or a write operation will generate a

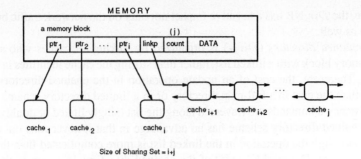

MEMORY

Fig. 1. SLiD protocol: basic directory structure

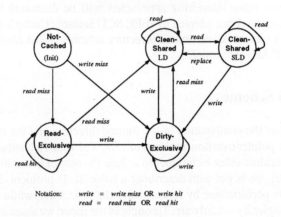

Notation: write = write miss OR write hit
read = read miss OR read hit

Fig. 2. SLiD protocol: state transition diagram of a memory block

miss in this state. Upon a read miss, the memory state is changed into *Read-Exclusive*, implying that only one cache exclusively accesses the block without modification. Upon a write miss, however, the memory state becomes *Dirty-Exclusive*, implying that only one cache updates the memory block exclusively.

If the current state is either *Read-Exclusive* or *Dirty-Exclusive*, a read miss by any other cache will transform the state into a *Clean-Shared*. For the *Dirty-Exclusive* state, the most recent value must be updated in the memory block upon a read. However, due to the limitation of the i base pointers, the *Clean-Shared* state is split into two parts (in two modes): *LD* and *SLD*. It is in *LD* mode when less than or equal to i pointers are required (i.e. when $count = 0$); it is in *SLD* when $count > 0$. An interesting transition case is when one (or several) of the i base pointers is replaced or invalidated, the linked list must transfer one (or several) of its elements to fill the vacancy (or vacancies). Accordingly, the $count$ is decreased. Whenever $count = 0$, the state is back to *LD*.

Similarly, a cached copy under the SLiD scheme is in one of the following four states (see Fig. 3): (1) *Invalid* — the copy is stale; (2) *Read-Exclusive* — the copy is read exclusively and it has not been modified; (3) *Clean-Shared* — the copy is shared by other caches and it has not been modified; (4) *Dirty-Exclusive* — the copy is the only valid copy in the system and it has been exclusively updated. Note that in Fig. 3, a dashed line denotes the consistency command induced by other caches, while a solid line represents its own action.

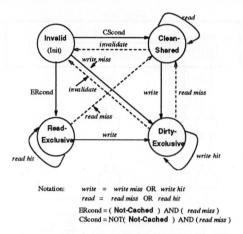

Notation: write = write miss OR write hit
           read = read miss OR read hit
           ERcond = (**Not-Cached**) AND (read miss)
           CScond = NOT(**Not-Cached**) AND (read miss)

Fig. 3. SLiD protocol: state transition diagram of a cached copy

Initially, the cache line is in *Invalid* state. Upon a read request, two cases are possible: (1) If an "exclusive read" is requested, meaning that the memory block is not fetched in any cache, the "ERcond" condition is satisfied and a read miss is thus generated. The memory block is then set in *Read-Exclusive* state, and so is the cached copy. (2) If the associated memory block is not in *Not-Cache* state, implying that at least one other caches access the block, the "CScond" condition is therefore met and a read miss is generated, with the state being changed into *Clean-Shared*. Upon a write request in the initial state, a write miss is produced, and its state is set to *Dirty-Exclusive*.

A read hit by the cached copy in *Read-Exclusive* state does not change anything, while an induced read miss (or a write operation) in that state will change the state into *Clean-Shared* (or *Dirty-Exclusive*). An invalidation command will transform a *Clean-Shared* or *Dirty-Exclusive* state into the *Invalid* state. However, an induced read miss from the *Dirty-Exclusive* state will enforce the updated values to be written into the memory block before proceeding the actual read, and consequently the new state becomes *Clean-Shared*.

It is noteworthy that the *Read-Exclusive* state is used to optimize the protocol for programs with relatively large percentage of *read-only* operations by a single processor. In this state, no global communication is necessary. But if more than one processor read the block, the cached copy will be in the *Clean-Shared* state and stays there without invoking invalidations until a write request.

3.2 Enhancements

Multiple Links ($Dir_{(i+\sum_{j=1}^{i} k_j)}$). The first enhancement, the SLiD with multiple links, extends the limited directory by i *linked lists*, each headed by one of the i base pointers. As shown in Fig. 4, in addition to the i base pointers, i counters $(c_1, \cdots, c_i)$ are attached to them respectively. Also shown in Fig. 4 is a field (called ML mode) that designates the operation mode (0 for the *limited* mode, and 1 for the *multi-links* mode).

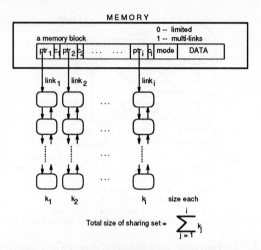

Fig. 4. SLiD protocol: directory of multiple links

Initially, the ML mode is set to 0, the protocol is actually a limited directory. When all i base pointers are exhausted and the ML mode is set to 1, their semantics is changed: i base pointers become the pointers to i linked lists. Then, the next sharing cache is inserted into one of the multiple links. The insertion algorithm is very simple: it is inserted into a linked list that has the *smallest* number of elements. Thus, the multiple linked lists are well balanced in size, no matter when the insertion is made. It is easy to see that the read latency has no substantial change compared to the chained scheme. For an invalidation operation, unlike one-by-one "gossip" in the SCI, the SLiD can perform it efficiently in the *limited* directory mode, and in the *multi-links* mode as well. In the latter case, the invalidation can be carried out in parallel among i linked lists. As for a replacement operation, it can be done in constant time because of the deletion algorithm on the doubly linked list.

In summary, the SLiD with multiple links can reduce memory latency in constant factors. This enhancement is the result of the compromise between performance improvement and reasonable implementation cost.

Multiple Trees $(Dir_{(i+\sum_{j=1}^{i} T_j)})$. To reduce the memory latency with no linear invalidation phenomenon, the basic SLiD can be further optimized by a *multiple-tree* structure (see Fig. 5). Similarly as in the STP (Scalable Tree Protocol) proposed in [11], each of the multiple links can always be maintained with an *optimal tree*. In other words, for each tree the nodes in the lth level can be inserted only after all nodes in the $(l-1)$th level are completely filled.

Besides requiring K children pointers, each node of the optimal tree is constructed by adding 3 more pointers (*predecessor, successor, and parent*, not shown in Fig. 5)

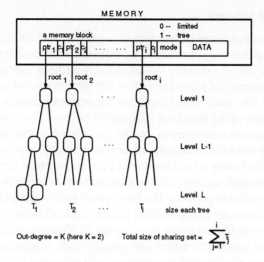

Fig. 5. SLiD protocol: directory of multiple trees

in each cache line. In such a configuration, the read latency has no substantial change and coherence actions for a read operation can be overlapped with local computations. The replacement operation can be done in constant time because of the availability of predecessor and successor pointers. More details about the optimal tree can be found in [11].

In contrast to other chained directory schemes, the SLiD with multiple trees has the invalidation latency of only $O(logN)$ (with a smaller constant factor than the STP), since the invalidation command is sent to each root of the optimal trees and the operation can be distributed in each tree in $O(logN)$ steps. This can be done simultaneously because all i trees are independent each other.

Similar to the mode field in the *multiple links*, the SLiD with multiple trees distinguishes the base *limited* directory mode with the multiple *tree* mode. The mode status can be computed directly from the counters $(c_1, c_2, ..., c_i)$. The tree mode is set if all i base pointers are used up and at least one of the counters exceeds 1. The size of the trees is perfectly balanced as it does in the multiple links.

In summary, the SLiD protocol with multiple trees might have the best performance among three structures, since it eliminates the long latency of the chained directories and certain parallelism can be obtained during the process of invalidation. Of course, it is accomplished by adding some more hardware to the scheme, particularly a number of optimal trees having to be maintained.

4   Comparison with Other Related Schemes

In this section, we first briefly describe some other schemes related to the SLiD. Then, we compare them by analyzing and evaluating the memory and cache storage requirements. Finally, we describe some of our simulation results.

4.1 Other Related Schemes

Several interesting proposals are closely related to our work. (1) the LimitLESS scheme [5]: where a full-map directory is emulated by software when the directory runs out of pointers. The scheme allows a memory module to interrupt the processor for the software to handle the "exceptions" of pointer overflow; (2) the schemes of *coarse vector* and *sparse directory* [9]: the *coarse vector* combines the broadcast strategy with a bit vector used to limit the scope of the broadcast (also called *regional invalidations*), while the *sparse directory* organizes a directory as a cache (i.e., each directory entry is associated with several memory blocks) to reduce the memory overhead; (3) dynamically allocating pointers [12]: instead of using a fixed number of pointers per entry, the *dynamic pointer allocation* scheme allocates automatically as many pointers as needed by memory blocks from a free pool of available pointers. The free pointer pool is actually memory-based, and the allocated pointers are joined together to keep track of the cached copies; (4) the STP scheme [11]: it is suggested in this paper for the SLiD protocol with multiple trees; (5) the primary-node scheme[7]: where one primary node is associated with a given memory block and rest of other sharing copies are with secondary nodes. Unfortunately, we do not have enough space here to describe and compare them each other. The interested reader may consult [6] and [7] for details.

4.2 Implementation Cost Comparison

Table 1 shows a comparison of all related schemes in terms of memory overhead for each memory block and each cache line, where C, M, N, i denote respectively the total number of cache lines, memory blocks, processors/caches, and base limited pointers. The memory consumption is expressed asymptotically. The directory residency and the pointer overflow handling strategy of each scheme are also listed in the table. (Note that the d in the dynamic pointer allocation scheme is not a constant number. Its value varies on program dynamic executions and the applicational characteristics.)

Table 1. Memory overhead of different schemes

Scheme	Notation	Memory Overhead	Dir Residence	Overflow Handling
Full-map	Dir_N	MN	Mem	Never
Limited	Dir_i	$iM\,Log_2\,N$	Mem	Inv or B
LimitLESS	Dir_i'	$iM\,Log_2\,N$	Mem	Software Emulate
Coarse	Dir_iCV	$iM\,Log_2\,N$	Mem	Regional Inv
Dynamic	Dir_d	$dM\,log_2\,N$	Mem	Inv
Chained	Dir_{1*}	$(C+M)log_2\,N$	Cache	Link Grow
SLiDbasic	Dir_{i+1*}	$(C+iM)log_2\,N$	Mem & Cache	Link Grow
SLiDmlinks	$Dir_{(i+\sum_{j=1}^{i}k_j)}$	$(C+iM)log_2\,N$	Mem & Cache	Links Grow
SLiDmtrees	$Dir_{(i+\sum_{j=1}^{i}T_j)}$	$(C+iM)log_2\,N$	Mem & Cache	Trees Grow

From Table 1, we can see that the SLiD schemes consumes relatively more memory than the limited pointers but much less than the full-map scheme in large-scale multiprocessors. But, the SLiD scheme has no problem of pointers overflow and all pointers are expected to be actively in use all the time.

4.3 Sample Systems

Our sample system is a 512-processor machine with 16MB of main memory and 256KB of cache memory associated with each processor. The memory block is of 32 bytes in size, so is each cache line. Associated with each memory block are 1 dirty bit and 3 protocol state bits. For schemes with limited pointers, $i = 4$ is considered [2]. The memory overhead for different schemes in such a system configuration is shown in Table 2.

Table 2. Storage requirement in a sample system for different schemes

Scheme	Memory Used in %	Total Memory Used (in million bits)	Cache Used in %	Total Cache Used (in million bits)
Full-map	66.84	132096	—	—
Limited Dir	13.51	10240	—	—
Chained Dir	4.83	3328	6.57	72
SLiDbasic	18.47	14848	6.57	72
SLiDmlinks	20.99	17408	6.57	72
SLiDmtrees ($K = 2$)	20.99	17408	14.95	180
SLiDmtrees ($K = 3$)	20.99	17408	17.42	216
SLiDmtrees ($K = 4$)	20.99	17408	19.75	252

From Table 2, we can see that the full-map is the most expensive scheme for large-scale systems (in this particular case of 512 processors, it takes 66.84% of whole memory). The limited directory and the chained directory have a low overhead, consuming 13.51% and 4.83% of main memory respectively. The SLiD schemes consumes around 18% – 21%, relatively more than the limited directory and the chained directory, but affordable in such and even a larger system.

All three SLiD structures are well scalable in large-scale machines. Fig. 6 and Fig. 7 respectively show the directory storage overhead of main memory and cache memory in systems with different number of processors, ranging from 128 to 4096. (Note that the x axis scales up with the logarithm of the number of processors.)

The trend indicated in Fig. 6 demonstrates in another way the directory storage overhead in main memory for different schemes. For storage overhead in cache lines (see Fig. 7), the SLiD with multiple trees have a higher overhead than other three schemes (the chained scheme, the basic SLiD, and the SLiD with multiple links), while the latter three have the same cache storage overhead due to the fact that their cache line maintains same number of pointers for the linked list. As shown in Fig. 7, the larger the out-degree (K), the more overhead in cache memory. This is because more pointers are required for each cache line as K increases.

In summary, the results in different sample systems show that the SLiD structures generally have a relatively more storage overhead than the limited and chained directories. But the cost still grows approximately linearly with the number of processors in the system. It is thus affordable to implement them for the machines with thousands or even more processors.

---

[2] Here 4 is not a guessing number. In fact, the MIT Alewife group has implemented 4 – 5 pointers [1] in its LimitLESS scheme for the prototype targeted up to 512 processors.

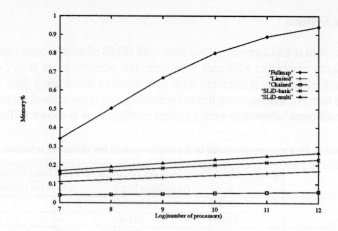

Fig. 6. Directory *memory storage* with different number of processors

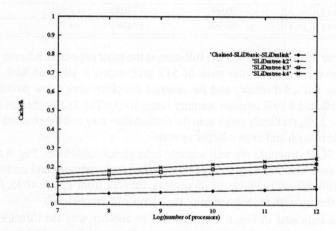

Fig. 7. Directory *cache storage* with different number of processors

4.4 Simulation Results

With our simulator *habakkuk* [8], we simulated the SLiD scheme and three representatives (full-map, limited and chained directories) of related schemes based on four 64-processor traces provided by MIT [4]. The four traces were collected from applications of FFT, SIMPLE, SPEECH and WEATHER, the characteristics of which are listed in Table 3. (The size of traces is of that in their compressed form.) Due to space limitation, in this section we can only briefly explain why the SLiD scheme is promising in extending the limited directories. Much more simulation work and results are presented in a separate paper [8] and [7].

Table 3. Trace information summary

Application	Lang.	Size	Trace Length	What application does
FFT	Fortran	16MB	7.465M	do a radix-2 Fast Fourier Transform
SIMPLE	Fortran	22MB	27.175M	model the behavior of fluids with equations
SPEECH	Mul-T	66MB	11.772M	decode state of spoken lang. understanding sys.
WEATHER	Fortran	76MB	31.780M	partition the global atmosphere and solve its PDE

In terms of processor utilization, simulation results show that the performance of the SLiD scheme [3] is very close to that of the full-map directory and superior to that of the chained and limited directories. The SLiD does a good job particularly for applications that the limited directory does poorly (see Table 4).

From table 4, we can see that the basic SLiD scheme improves the performance over limited directory by 49.72%, 142.31% and 127.22% respectively for SIMPLE, SPEECH and WEATHER, while by only 1.99% for FFT. This is due to the fact that for FFT the average time between writes by different processors to one share block is low (in other words, there are very few cases in FFT application sharing one block by more than i (here, $i = 4$) processors). For FFT, even the full-map directory does not perform significantly better than the limited directory. On the contrary, it is different for other three applications. For them, the SLiD scheme performs much better than the limited directory and almost as well as the full-map scheme.

Table 4. Performance of different schemes

Application	fullmap	limited	chained	basic SLiD	SLiD vs. limited	SLiD vs. chained
FFT	.4152	.4067	.3820	.4148	1.99%	8.59%
SIMPLE	.4562	.2703	.3900	.4047	49.72%	3.77%
SPEECH	.4934	.2009	.4568	.4868	142.31%	6.57%
WEATHER	.6164	.2700	.5949	.6135	127.22%	3.13%

Compared to chained directory (doubly-linked), the SLiD scheme still performs better (by from 3.13% to 8.59%), though not so significantly as over the limited directory.

The performance penalty of the SLiD scheme is also small. In all four application simulations, the probability of a shared reference being in-SLiD-mode is very small (FFT 0.0242%, SIMPLE 2.8110%, SPEECH 1.0463% and WEATHER 0.0869%). This leads to our belief that managing the pointer overflow with the basic SLiD protocol or the SLiD with multiple links may be enough in most cases, which would incur moderate and tolerable latency in the process of invalidation.

The experimental results convince us that the limited directory is useful *and* the SLiD scheme is necessary and effective to handle pointers overflow.

---

[3] We here only cite the data simulated by the basic SLiD protocol. The enhancements with multiple links and multiple trees exhibit better performance results.

5 Conclusion

The objective of this study has been to find a cost-effective and scalable scheme for maintaining cache coherency. The SLiD framework achieves such a goal. It provides us with three structural options that depend on the demands of the performance, the hardware complexity, and the cost of implementation. Although they differ each other, all three options are based on (but not constrained by) the limited directory. In addition, they will never run out of pointers and are well scalable.

More efforts are being undertaken to investigate the SLiD scheme in a simulation environment with larger number of processors.

Acknowledgments: Thanks go to Allan Gottlieb, Eric Freudenthal and Jan Edler for their reading and commenting on earlier drafts of this paper. David Chaiken of MIT kindly provided the 64-processor traces for this study.

References

1. Anant Agarwal, David Chaiken, Guoying Chen, and Allan Gottlieb. *Private Communications*, November 1992.
2. Anant Agarwal, Richard Simoni, John Hennessy, and Mark Horowitz. An evaluation of directory schemes for cache coherence. In *Proceedings of the 15th Annual International Symposium of Computer Architecture*, pages 280–289, May 1988.
3. L. M. Censier and P. Feautrier. A new solution to coherence problems in multicache systems. *IEEE Trans. on Computers*, C-27(12):1112–1118, December 1978.
4. David Chaiken, Craig Fields, Kiyoshi Kurihara, and Anant Agarwal. Directory-based cache coherence in large-scale multiprocessors. *Computer*, 23(6):49–58, June 1990.
5. David Chaiken, John Kubiatowics, and Anant Agarwal. LimitLESS directories: A scalable cache coherence scheme. In *Proceedings of the 4th International Conference on Architectural Support for Programming Languages and Systems*, pages 224 – 234, April 1991.
6. Guoying Chen. SLiD — A cost-effective and scalable limited-directory scheme for cache coherence. Ultracomputer Note 186, Courant Institute, NYU, November 1992.
7. Guoying Chen. *Design and Simulation Analysis of Directory-Based Cache Coherence Schemes for Large-Scale Multiprocessors*. PhD thesis, Courant Institute, NYU, New York, 1993. (In preparation).
8. Guoying Chen. An evaluation of the SLiD and its related cache coherence schemes. Ultra-computer note, Courant Institute, NYU, March 1993. (submitted for publication).
9. Anoop Gupta, Wolf-Dietrich Weber, and Todd Mowry. Reducing memory and traffic requirements for scalable directory-based cache coherence schemes. In *Proceedings of the 1990 International Conference on Parallel Processing*, pages I312 – I321, Auguest 1990.
10. David V. James, Anthony T. Laundrie, Stein Gjessing, and Gurindar S. Sohi. Distributed-directory scheme: Scalable coherent interface. *Computer*, 23(6):74–77, June 1990.
11. Håkan Nilsson and Per Stenström. The scalable tree protocol – a cache coherence approach for large-scale multiprocessors. In *Proceedings of the Fourth IEEE Symposium on Parallel and Distributed Processing*, November 1992.
12. Richard Simoni and Mark Horowitz. Dynamic pointer allocation for scalable cache directories. In *Proceedings of 1st International Symposium on Shared Memory Multiprocessing*, pages 309–318, April 1991.

FORMAL DEVELOPMENT OF ACTOR PROGRAMS USING STRUCTURED ALGEBRAIC PETRI NETS

Didier BUCHS
CUI, University of GENEVA,
24, rue du Général Dufour
1211 Genève
email : BUCHS@cui.unige.ch

Nicolas GUELFI
LRI, URA 410 CNRS,
Bât. 490, University of PARIS XI
91405 ORSAY FRANCE
email : GUELFI@lri.lri.fr

ABSTRACT[*]

This paper provides an actor semantics using a formalism called CO-OPN (Concurrent Object Oriented Petri Nets) which is modular and incorporates both concurrency and data structuring features. Actor languages are the main model of concurrent object-oriented languages, but they are rarely well formalized. CO-OPN is a structured extension of Petri nets and algebraic abstract data types. A CO-OPN specification is composed of a set of objects (algebraic abstract data types and Petri nets), and of a synchronous communication mechanism. This synchronization mechanism is defined in order to keep object state encapsulation, allowing the independent specification of each object. The translation of an actor program into a CO-OPN specification is done by building objects for actors. The adequacy of CO-OPN in describing the semantics of concurrent object-oriented languages is shown by this formal semantic description of actor languages. Some particular implementations are suggested, improving the concurrent execution of actor programs.

Keywords : Formal program development, modular specification, actor languages semantics, high-level Petri nets, algebraic abstract data types.

1. INTRODUCTION

Actor languages [AGHA 86] is a model used to introduce concurrency in object-oriented programming. The actor model has many features such as encapsulation, asynchronous communication and dynamic creation of actors that are well suited to object programming. The semantics of concurrent object-oriented languages are generally not well-defined (for instance, Concurrent Smalltalk [YOKO 86]), because such semantics must incorporate operational semantics for the concurrent aspects and algebra for the manipulated data. In this paper we propose a semantics of actors in which implementation choices are as delayed as possible. The data structure part of actors is described by means of algebraic specifications. The modular aspects of actors are modeled with specific structuring primitives. The semantics proposed in the paper can then express true concurrency of the modeled actor system. The specification formalism used is CO-OPN [B&G 91], which provides both concurrency and data description. Such a formalism puts minimal

---

[*] This work has been supported by the "Fond National Suisse de la recherche Scientifique" and by the "ESPRIT" basic research action,"DEMON", n° 3148.

constraints on the concurrency and on the data structure aspects. It allows us to analyze concurrency without having to choose a model for the data structures.

A CO-OPN specification consists of a set of objects described by algebraic Petri nets [VAUT 87] [REIS 91] (a class of high-level nets) that are connected through a synchronous communication mechanism integrating sequential and concurrent conditions over the communications. Some work has been done [B&G 91] on the semantic description of CO-OPN and the analysis of CO-OPN specification such as object equivalencies, object replacement and change of algebraic abstract data type models. These results as well as the semantics of CO-OPN cannot be fully detailed here but some basic ideas are presented, especially on the semantics of CO-OPN and on the analysis of the concurrency in an actor system. The aim of this paper is to use a simple model of actors, in which all important concepts of actors can be found, and to model it by CO-OPN. We first discuss related work, then we informally introduce CO-OPN, and we present the translation of actor programs into the CO-OPN formalism with an example and discuss some particularities of our translation, especially on the concurrency aspects. In [GUEL 90] a complete and formal description of the semantics of actors is given. Beyond this case study, we show the software engineering interest of CO-OPN in the modeling and development [B&F&R 92] of concurrent programs and in the complex specification of programming languages or computer programs.

1.1. Work on semantic description of Actors

Here we present related work on the semantic description of actor languages and the formalism used. The actor model has first been introduced in [HEWI 73]. This model has been the subject of much research. Formal work can be found in [CLIN 81], [AGHA 86] and [JANS 89]. The following are quite recent semantic approaches near CCS [MILN 89] and net theory.

- In [HOPK 89] a theoretical model consisting of an extension of CCS including dynamicity (DCCS) is studied for the description of actor programs.
- Yield another variant [NIER 90]: CCS augmented with a pattern mechanism in order to be more expressive in the description of the data structures. The semantics of this language is an interleaving semantics but no real description of data structures is given.
- Another model called POTS (Parallel Object based Transition System) is introduced in [ENGE 90]. It imposes an additional structure on the place of a Predicate/Transition net. Objects in a given state are represented by places and events by transitions. The structure of the objects is defined by three functions mapping places to the represented objects, their states (unborn, alive, or dead) and their acquaintances.
- A modeling of an actor program by one colored net is done in [V&S 90] without data types and modularity.

Neither data structure nor modularity of actors are expressed by these semantics. Our aim is to show how our formalism, CO-OPN fulfill these two requirements.

2. CO-OPN

A CO-OPN specification is composed of objects described by algebraic Petri nets and a synchronization mechanism linking these nets together. This synchronization mechanism is defined in order to keep object state encapsulation, allowing us to specify independently each object. Some examples for the use of CO-OPN can be found in [B&G 92A] and [B&G 92B] .

2.1. Algebraic abstract data types

Since the algebraic specification approach is well-known (see for instance [E&M 85]), only the key points are summarized here. All of our specification examples are written using the PLUSS language [BIDO 89]. The approach consists of describing a class of objects, usually called the sorts, by defining the set of functions which operate on that class. These functions are described syntactically by their names and domains. Their semantic content is defined by a set of axioms expressed by conditional equations on terms. The functions can be grouped into categories called generator functions (**"generated by"** part) and operators (**"operations"** part). The finite set of axioms (**"axioms"** part) can only contain operations (functions) on the defined sort or on other previously defined sorts (**"use"** part), universally quantified variables (**"where"** part), and conditional tests.

2.2. Algebraic Petri nets

The Petri nets, $PN=<P,T,In,Out,M0>$, are generally used to model the dynamic behavior of discrete systems [REIS 85]. The relation between the model and the system is easily established using the *places* (P) representing the states of the system and the *transitions* (T) for the actions that can occur in it. Oriented links between places and transitions indicate preconditions (In) and post-conditions (Out) of an action. Petri nets have a nice graphical representation : circles represent the places, boxes represent the transitions and oriented arcs link nodes of different kinds. A particular state of the net is defined by the notion of *marking* where each place contains *tokens*. The particular marking M0 is the initial state of the system. The Petri net has a model of execution, namely the evolution of the *tokens*. This provides a description of the dynamic behavior of the system.

Algebraic Petri nets $APN=<Spec,P,T,Cond,In,Out,M0>$ present two levels:
- the algebraic abstract data types (Spec) describing the data structures,
- the net providing the description of the behavior of the control structure.

The resulting net is therefore a kind of colored Petri net [JENS 81]. The expressiveness of Petri nets is improved by associating instances of algebraic abstract data types to the places instead of anonymous tokens [VAUT 87]. A place is a multi-set. A predicate is attached to each transition (Cond). A transition is fired only if all input places contain the values defined in its input arcs and if the predicate is verified. Once a transition occurs, the values are consumed by the transition and removed from their places and put in variables and used to compute the output values according to the term attached to its output places. The semantics is directly described by means of concurrent transition systems [B&G 91], the semantics of APN is the concurrent transition system $CTS_A(APN)$, for a given algebra $A \in MOD(Spec)$, which is a transition system with concurrent firing of actions. The notation: [] indicates the empty multi-set; and [succ(zero),succ(succ(zero))] indicates a multi-set containing the numbers 1 and 2.

2.3 The CO-OPN Objects

A CO-OPN specification $SPEC_O=<Spec,O,T_{ext},T_{int},P,AX>$ is composed of a set of objects O. Each object is an APN with two kinds of transitions: the first ones are 'external' transitions called 'methods' (in the set T_{ext}), the second ones are the 'internal' transitions (in T_{int}). The methods are parametered transitions and they are the only way to modify object states (the content in the places of the net) from the outside of an object and thus reflect the object behavior in the semantics. The internal transitions are non-parametrized transitions used to model the evolution of an object independently from the outside. The object states are the states of the places. The behavior of the net is described in the axioms. An axiom ax=<t,Cond,In,Out,SE> corresponds to the flow relation of the net transition 't' extended with the notion of synchronization SE (see next paragraph).

Example: We would like to describe an object called 'Buffer' (figure 1 text & 2 graphical form) which is a FIFO manager built over the 'fifonat' sort. Two methods compose this object, 'get' and 'put', each method having as parameter the sort 'nat'. For each transition we give an axiom of the form: *"transition_name_with_its_ parameters : boolean_condition ⇒ input_relation → output_relation"*

```
object :      Buffer ;
use :         Nat,FifoNat,Bool;
methods :     get,put : nat;
places :      buffer : fifonat;
var :         b:fifonat; m:nat;
axioms : get(next(b)) : not(is-empty(b))
   ⇒ buffer ([b]) → buffer([del(b)]);
put(m): buffer([b])→buffer ([cat(b,m)]) ;
init_marking:    buffer([empty]);
end;
```

Figure 1

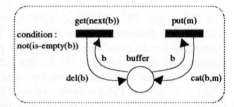

Figure 2

2.4. Synchronizations between objects

To construct a system from a set of objects, we have to link them in a specific way. Instead of using a classical message passing mechanism, the links between objects are defined as a synchronization expression "SE" composed with the binary operators 'sim' (for simultaneous), 'seq' (for sequence), the unary operator 'id' and the 'empty' synchronization. For example, the construction 'a with sim(b,c)' where 'a','b','c' are methods and means that the method 'a' can be fired if the methods 'b' and 'c' can be fired simultaneously. In the same way 'a with seq(b,c)' means that the method 'a' can be fired if the methods 'b' and 'c' can be fired in sequence. The synchronization 'a with id(b)' means that the method 'a' can be fired if the methods 'b' can be fired (abbreviated to 'a with b'). Finally, the empty synchronization does not need any synchronization condition to fire a transition.

The simultaneous condition makes sense because the semantic of CO-OPN for a particular algebra A ∈ MOD(Spec) is given by means of concurrent transition systems $DTS_A(SPEC_O)$ expressing concurrency of actions. Moreover, to define the semantics of the object system it is necessary that the synchronization links between objects constitute a partial order (no cycles as in figure 3). To show a CO-OPN object system we add to the previous object "buffer", two objects, "consumer" and "producer", using synchronization expressions represented by symbolic links (stripped arrows fig 3). The relation between the objects is created by method calls.

```
object :        Producer ;
use :  Nat,Buffer,Bool;
methods :   send : nat;
places :        counter : nat;
var :  m,n:nat;
axioms :
send(m) with  put(m) : counter([n])
→counter([add(succ(zero),n)]);
init_marking: counter([zero]);
end;
```

```
object :           Consumer ;
use :  Nat,Buffer;
methods :    receive;
var :  m:nat;
axioms :
receive with get(m);
init_marking:
end;
```

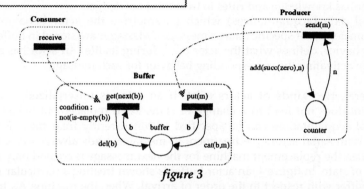

figure 3

The semantics of a CO-OPN specification (given in **[B&G 91]**) is described by means of inference rules. The object system states are the states of all objects, the labels of the transition are multi-sets of concurrent actions, with one multi-set for each object. Then the semantics of an object system $SPEC_O$ is defined by the concurrent distributed transition system $DTS_A(SPEC_O)$ where A is a model of the algebraic specification considered.

Parametrized Objects

A parametrized object is an object that uses particular objects called parameter objects and special algebraic abstract data types called parameter specification.

Properties of CO-OPN formalism.

Some properties are formalized within the CO-OPN framework.
- The equivalence for an algebra A by the notion of concurrent bisimulation.
- One object can be replaced in an object system by an other one which is equivalent, producing a new object system bisimilar to the initial one.
- If two observationally equivalent algebras are used in the same object system, then the two different object systems are equivalent by bisimulation.

These properties allow us to refine an abstract CO-OPN specification by progressively replacing abstract object or specification with more concrete ones.

3.   ACTORS MODELING USING CO-OPN

In this section our method for the modeling of actor programs is described. First, the general model for actors is introduced. Then the basic concepts of our method are presented. Finally, an example is given and the corresponding CO-OPN specification is built with respect to the method described. A formal and complete description of our method is given in [GUEL 90] [B&G 92C].

3.1 The general model of actors

Actors languages are parallel languages in which it is possible to create more actors to increase the parallelism. The general idea is to split information and control as much as possible. In an actors system the dynamic creation of actors is allowed, communication is done by asynchronous point-to-point message passing. To summarize, the actor model is a distributed model where knowledge and behavior are distributed between actors which concurrently compute the tasks.
An actor has knowledge and rules to treat this knowledge:
- Local data (acquaintances) which parametrize the actor behavior and a parameter list of specific data as messages. Messages are stored in buffers.
- A behavior, defines what the actor does during its life. An actor has a unique script activating the corresponding behavior for each message.

In general, two kinds of actors exist. If an actor is unserialized, a message treatment does not lead to a change of state. Then replacement behavior with identical acquaintances can be specified to concurrently treat messages in the buffer. With serial actors the treatment of messages leads always to a change of state. Then the replacement machine for the next message is created only after the change of state. In figure 4, an actor buffer is shown treating a particular message of the buffer with respect to the order of arrival. When the machine A_n treats the nth message, messages can be sent to other actors, new actors can be created and an other machine (A_{n+1}) must be created to treat the $(n+1)^{th}$ message. Machine operations can be processed before and after creating its replacement .
To integrate all these features, actor grammars must include three basic primitives : the 'send' command for message passing, the 'new' command for the creation of actors and the 'become' command for the specification of the actor replacement .

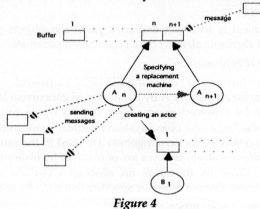

Figure 4

3.2. General concepts of the construction

The three important characteristics of actor languages are the concurrency aspects, which are modeled by Petri nets, the data structures, modeled using algebraic specification, and modularity modeled using CO-OPN objects structuring features. The construction of the CO-OPN system of an actor program is twofold:

1) the construction of the algebraic specifications in the PLUSS language;

2) the construction of the object system in the CO-OPN language.

3.2.1. Construction of the algebraic specification

The specification of the algebraic abstract data type is required to model the data structures in actor programs. Then the terms of these sorts can be used in the actor program. The algebraic specifications for the data structures defined for our construction (actors and buffers) are needed. An algebraic specification named #ActorNameBuffer must be defined for: the actor structures ('act#ActorName') for the states, the message ('#ActorNameMethod')and the buffer (sort 'buffer#ActorName' and sort 'methodList#ActorName'). The construction of the algebraic specifications is performed by parsing the actor programs (We use the '#' notation to indicate textual variables).

3.2.2. Construction of the CO-OPN system

An actor class description can be divided into two parts: an object for each method and an object for the interface of the actor class. The interface is an object which synchronizes all the evolutions of these actors. The interface contains transitions for the creation of a new actor, for the reception of messages, for the treatment of messages and for the actor replacement. Places containing the buffers of the actor instance and the the actor instances are added to the interface object. The synchronizations are induced by the method objects. For example, if in a method 'j' of an actor 'i' the code is " send a message k to an actor l ", the object corresponding to the method 'j' has to be synchronized with the interface of the actor l. When the objects specifying an actor 'Actor$_i$' are built, all instances of such actors have their own behavior simulated by the same group of objects. The places of the set of objects representing a class of actor 'Actor$_i$' contain all actors of type 'Actor$_i$' already created. All instances are distinguished by their own address, memorized in the tokens. Note that a CO-OPN object simulates concurrently the behavior of all actors of same class. A list of actor declarations has the following representation:

> **BegActor** #Actor$_i$ (...... parameter list ......)
> • • • ;
> [#Method$_j$ (...... parameter list ......) • • •];
> • • •
> **EndActor;**

For each actor "Actor$_i$" the following objects are built (figure 5):
- an object for each method 'Method$_k$' to model the behavior of this method.
- an object 'IActor$_i$' representing the interface of the 'Actor$_i$'.

The first layer corresponds to the interfaces object of the actors. All the method objects of the actors are defined in the second layer. The central object 'NewAddress' (figure 6) manages the creation of new addresses. The synchronization between actors is always from a method object to an interface object or to the 'NewAddress' object.

360

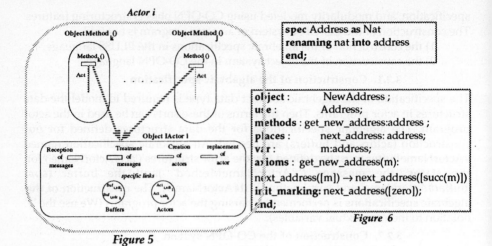

Figure 5

spec Address as Nat
renaming nat into address
end;

Figure 6

object :   NewAddress ;
use :   Address;
methods : get_new_address:address ;
places :   next_address: address;
var :   m:address;
axioms : get_new_address(m):
next_address([m]) → next_address([succ(m)])
init_marking: next_address([zero]);
end;

The method object

A method object is associated with each method 'Method$_j$' declared in an actor program. This object is composed by a transition 'Method$_j$ ()' linked to a place with an arc labeled by the the actor executing the method. This place is linked with the same kind of arc to a transition 'END' representing the end of the method 'Method$_j$' (fig. 7(a)). For each instruction of the method, a transition is added (fig. 7(b)) and specific links are established with corresponding labels. Six kind of transitions, one for each kind of expression, are allowed by our grammar. They are described by our example in the next section.

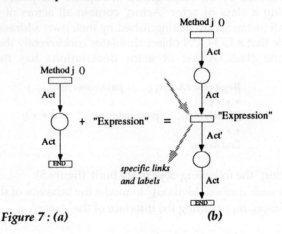

Figure 7 : (a)   *(b)*

The interface object

The interface objects have the same design for each actor (figure 8):

- The transition 'receive(M,adr(B))' receives a message 'M' in the buffer 'B' of an actor of type $actor_i$ with address 'adr(B)'.
- The transition 'Treat(next(B),Act)' modeling the message treatment, is synchronized with the first transition of each method object '$Method_j$' of the actor '$Actor_i$'.
- The transition 'create(Act,Adr)' creates a new actor of class '$Actor_i$' with a new address 'Adr'.
- The transition 'replace(Act)' is called by an execution of a '$become(Actor_i)$' command. Then the actor '$Actor_i$' is put in the place 'Actors'. The become command is used in an actor of class '$Actor_i$' to specify the replacement actor for the treatment of the next message in the buffer.
- The place 'Buffers' containing all the buffers of each instance of the class of actors '$Actor_i$' (in the figure 8 'Buf_{i,adr_k}' and 'Buf_{i,adr_l}' are included in the place 'Buffers', they are, respectively, the buffer of address 'adr_k' and 'adr_l'.
- The place 'Actors' containing all the actor structures of the instances of the class of actors '$Actor_i$' (figure 8 'Act_{i,adr_k}' and 'Act_{i,adr_l}' are included in the place 'Actors', they are respectively the structures of actor of address 'adr_k' and 'adr_l'.

Object IActor i

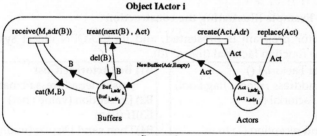

figure 8

We give (fig. 9) the generic specification of the object $IActor_i$ and its parameter.

```
par :   BufferActorᵢ ;
use :   Address, MethodListActorᵢ ;
sorts :       bufferActorᵢ, methodListActorᵢ, ActorᵢMethod, actActorᵢ ;
generated by :
        bufferActorᵢ : address * methodListActorᵢ → bufferActorᵢ;
        empty: → methodListActorᵢ ;
        cat : ActorᵢMethod * methodListActorᵢ → methodListActorᵢ;
operations : adr: bufferActorᵢ → address ;
        del: methodListActorᵢ → methodListActorᵢ ;
end;
```

362

```
gen object :        IActorᵢ (BufferActorᵢ);
use :               Address ;
methods:            receive: ActorᵢMethod * address ;
                    treat : ActorᵢMethod * actActorᵢ ;
                    create : actActorᵢ * address ;
                    replace : actActorᵢ ;
places :            Buffers : bufferActorᵢ ;
                    Actors : actActorᵢ ;
var :               M : ActorᵢMethod ;        (sort def. in ActorᵢTerm)
                    B : bufferActorᵢ ;         (sort def. in BufferActorᵢ)
                    Act : actActorᵢ ;          (sort decf. inActorᵢTerm)
                    Adr : address ;
axioms :            receive (M,adr(B)) : Buffers([B]) → Buffers([cat(M,B)]) ;
                    treat(next(B)),Act) : not(is-empty(B))
                         ⇒ Buffers([B]) , Actors([Act]) → Buffers([del(B)]) ;
          create(Act,Adr):→Buffers([bufferActorᵢ(Adr,EmptyList)]) ,Actors([Act]);
                    replace(Act) :         → Actors(Act) ;
InitMarking : Buffers([]), Actors([]) ;
end;
```

Figure 9

3.3.   Example illustrating the construction

A simple actor program is presented, and its CO-OPN object system, which
computes the function factorial (figure 10).

```
A1) BegActor Factorial ()
A2)[do-it(m:address , n:nat , flag:bool)
A3)become Factorial () ;
A4)If (n = 1)
A5)Then send reception (1) to m
A6)Else let x:=newFactCust (m,n,flag)
A7)     send do-it (x , n-1 , false)
          to MyAdr
fi ]; EndActor;
```

```
B1) BegActorFactCust
     (customer:address,nb:nat, flag:bool)
B2) [ reception (value : nat)
B3)If (flag)
B4)Then send Display(mult(nb,value))
        to customer
B5)Else send reception(mult(nb,value) )
        to customer
fi ]; EndActor;
```

```
C1)   BegActor Global ()
C2)        [ Init ( )
C3)             let p := new Factorial ()
C4)             let q := new Factorial ()
C5)             send do-it (MyAdr , 4 , true) to p
C6)             send do-it (MyAdr , 6 , true) to q];
C7)        [ Display (value : nat) Screen(value);];
      EndActor;
```

Figure 10

This actor program is made of three actors which are 'Factorial','FactCust' and
'Global'. The computation of factorial is done with the following steps (4! fig. 11):
-   Actors 'FactCust' with 'nb' to the value 'n' , 'n-1', ... '1' are created by 'Factorial'.

- After the creation of the last actor 'FactCust' with 'nb'=1, this starts the process where the ith actor sends back the product of i by the product coming from the previous actor whose results are equal to (i-1)!
- The first actor sends the result to the actor 'Global'.

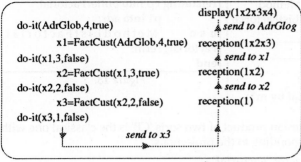

One can note that this computation is quite sequential. But, in the actor 'Global' two computation can be started concurrently (for instance 4! and 6!).

figure 11

Algebraic specifications associated to actor 'Factorial'

The examination of the actor programs permits the enumeration of the sorts address, nat and bool used in the actor 'Factorial' (directive 'use : Address,Nat,Bool'). The new sorts which are declared in 'Factorial_Term' are 'actFactorial' representing the data structure associated to the actors 'Factorial' and 'factorialMethod' representing the possible messages for the actor 'Factorial'. The generators of the sort 'actFactorial' is '<_,_,_,_,_>: address * address * nat * bool * address → actFactorial', representing this actor data structure. The first element is the address of the actor and the others are the variables of the actor 'Factorial'. The second is 'm' (sort address), the third 'n', the fourth 'flag' (sort bool) and the fifth 'x' (sort address). For example, if an actor has the address 5 and if the value of (m,n,flag,x) is (6,2,true,7), then the actor is <5,6,2,true,7> in the sort 'actFactorial'. The generators of the sort 'factorialMethod' is the name of the methods declared in the actor 'Factorial'. The operations associated with this sort are the projections (P1_,P2_,..) giving the parameters of the n-tuple of values. Only one method 'do-it' is declared in this actor by 'do-it_ _ _ : address * nat * bool → factorialMethod'.

```
spec :      Factorial_Term;
use :       Bool, Nat, Address;
sort :      actFactorial,factorialMethod;
generated by :<_,_,_,_,_> : address*address*nat*bool*address→ actFactorial;
            do-it _ _ _: address * nat * bool → factorialMethod ;
operations :    P1_: actFactorial → address;    (* first value *)
                P2_ : actFactorial → address ;   (* second,etc*)
                P3_ : actFactorial → nat ;
                P4_ : actFactorial → bool ;
                P5_ : actFactorial → address ;
axioms :    Proj1 : P1(<adr₁,adr₂,n₁,b₁,adr₃>) = adr₁ ;
            Proj2 : P2(<adr₁,adr₂,n₁,b₁,adr₃>) = adr₂ ;.........
where :     adr₁,adr₂,adr₃: address; n₁ : nat;,b₁ : bool; end;
```

Figure 12

Each actor has a buffer which is a FIFO structure 'BufferFactorial'.

```
spec MethodListFactorial
as FIFO (Elem ⇒ Factorial_Term by  m)
where m : elem ⇒ factorialMethod
renaming Fifo into methodListFactorial
end;
```

```
where m1 : e1 ⇒ address;
where m2: e2⇒ methodListFactorial;
renaming cp into bufferFactorial;
         p1 into adr;
u s e        M e t h o d L i s t F a c t o r i a l,
Factorial_Term;
end
```

```
spec BufferFactorial
as CP (E1 ⇒ Address by m1,
    E2 ⇒ MethodListFactorial by m2)
```

Figure 13

The specification of the cartesian product of two sorts 'CP' is the classical one with two operations P1,P2 corresponding to the projections.

Object specification of the actor 'Factorial'

The CO-OPN specification of the actor 'Factorial' is made of the specification of the method 'do-it' and of the interface 'IFactorial' obtained as an instance of 'IActor¡'.

```
object :   IFactorial as IActor¡ (BufferActor¡ => BufferFactorial by morph);
where :   morph:       bufferActor¡ => bufferFactorial;
                       Actor¡Method => factorialMethod;
                       actActor¡ => actFactorial;
end;
```

```
1)    object :      do-it ;
2)    use :         IFactorial , IGlobal, IFactCust,
                    Factorial_Term, Global_Term, Fact_CustTerm, Address,Nat,Bool ;
3)    methods :     do_it : address * nat * boolean;
4)    internal :    t2,t3,t4,t5,t6,t7,end;
5)    places :      pl1,pl2,pl3,pl4,pl5,pl6: actFactorial;
6)    var :         x,cpt : address; p:nat;fl : bool;
      axioms :
7)         do_it with treat(do_it(x,p,fl),Act): → pl1([<P1(Act),x,p,fl,P4(Act)>])
8)         t2    with replace(Act)  : pl1([Act]) → pl2([Act])
9)         t3    : P3(Act) ≠ zero ⇒ pl2([Act]) → pl4([Act])
10)        t4    : P3(Act) = zero ⇒ pl2([Act]) → pl3([Act])
11)        t5    with receive(reception(1),P2(Act)): pl3([Act]) → pl6([Act])
12)        t6    with
sim(create(<cpt,P2(Act),P3(Act),false,zero>,get_new_address(cpt)),P2(Act))
                       :pl4([Act]) → pl5([Act])
13)        t7 with receive(do-it(x,n-1,false),P1(Act)) pl5([Act]) → pl6([Act])
14)        end    : pl6([Act]) →
15)    init_marking:
      end;
```

Figure 14

Following, we explain some CO-OPN declarations of the object 'do-it' (figure 14):

2) The actor 'Factorial' must declare the algebraic specification used by its related actors ('Factorial_Term' , 'FactCust_Term', 'Global_Term'). Furthermore, the interfaces corresponding to the actor used by 'Factorial' are declared ('IFactorial', 'IFactCust', 'IGlobal').

3) The methods are shown in the transitions system of the CO-OPN system.

4) The internal transitions are not shown in the transition system.

5) The place sort s is 'ActFactorial' containing the actors of class 'Factorial'.

7) The method 'do-it', is synchronized 'with' the method 'treat' of the object 'IFactorial'. The parameters of the method 'treat' indicate that the place 'Buffers' must have a message 'do-it(m,n,flag)' and the place 'Actors' must contain the associated actor (i.e the actor to which the buffer belongs). If such synchronization is possible then the transition is fired, corresponding to the beginning of the method 'do-it' and the actor variables are updated.

12) The new address needed by the creation of a new actor is given with the method 'get_new_address'.

4.   DISCUSSION ABOUT THE MODELING OF ACTORS USING CO-OPN

In this section the concurrency aspects of our modeling of actor languages are discussed and some improvement are suggested.

Concurrency between actors: All instances of actors allow concurrent behavior. This is modeled by the possibly concurrent firing of the interface methods expressed by the CO-OPN semantics. But these firings can be sequentialized by the message treatment. Note that the dynamics of the actors creation is modeled by the creation of tokens in the interface objects.

Concurrency on address creation: A sequencing appears in the creation of actor address, because the object 'NewAdress' cannot be accessed concurrently. Two solutions appear: The first consists of keeping a centralized address manager which can be concurrently accessed by several actors. The second consists of distributing the address manager on the actor class.

Concurrency inside a method: The execution of the instructions of one method are sequentialized. This is due to our kind of actor language. The data structures dependencies allow one to parallelize the method code. This can be modeled by CO-OPN using the appropriate Petri net design.

Serial actor and unserial actor: Our actor model is a serial actor model. If unserial actors are considered, our semantics should allow concurrent access to buffers. This is done by the concurrent firing of the transitions 'receive' or 'treat'. The messages have to be in the multiset of a place instead of in the FIFO structure.

Fairness: A condition for the right execution of actor program is that the execution of transitions should be fair. This condition is an unusual property of Petri nets.

Actor replacements, actor equivalence: Within the framework of CO-OPN formalism it is possible to describe the actor method replacement with CO-OPN object replacement. To insure an actor replacement, the old actor method and the related interface object have to be equivalent (w.r.t the definition of bisimulation [B&G 91]) to the newest one with the same interface object. This replacement can be used to implement such actor programs using CO-OPN refinements.

5. CONCLUSION

Our modeling of actors using CO-OPN takes into account both data structures and modularity. The data structures are modeled using algebraic specifications, the modularity using CO-OPN objects and communication between actors through CO-OPN synchronization expressions and actors ' interfaces.

The contribution of our formalism to the modeling of actors is new, crucial and twofold: (1) The ability to obtain a semantics of actors including data structures, modular aspects, and true concurrency. (2) The possibility of modeling concurrent object-oriented languages.

BIBLIOGRAPHY

[AGHA 86] G. Agha: "Actors: a model of concurrent computation in distributed systems", The MIT Press (1986)

[B&F&R92] D. Buchs, J. Flumet, P. Racloz "Producing prototypes from CO-OPN specifications", 3rd IEEE International workshop on Rapid system Prototyping, USA, June 1992.

[B&G 91] D. Buchs, N. Guelfi "CO-OPN : A Concurrent Object Oriented Petri Net Approach for System Specification", 12th International Conference on Application And Theory of Petri Nets, Aarhus 1991.

[B&G 92A] D. Buchs, N. Guelfi "Distributed System Specification using CO-OPN", 3rd IEEE Int. workshop on Futur trends of Distributed Computing Systems, Taipei 1992.

[B&G 92B] D. Buchs, N. Guelfi "Open distributed programming using the object-oriented specification formalism CO-OPN", 5th International conference on Putting into Practice Methods and Tools for information system Design, Nantes 1992.

[B&G 92C] D. Buchs, N. Guelfi "A Semantic Description of Actor Languages using CO-OPN", Abstract in the 14th Int. Conference On Software Engeeniring, Melbourne, 1992

[BIDO 89] M. Bidoit "PLUSS, un language pour le developpement de spécification algébrique modulaires" Thèse de doctorat d'Etat, LRI UPS Orsay

[CLIN 81] W.D. Clinger "Foundations of actors semantics", AI-TR-633, MIT artificial intelligence laboratory, (1981).

[E&M 85] H.Ehrig, B.Mahr "fundamentals of algebraic specification 1: equations and initial semantics,Springer Verlag 1985."

[ENGE 90] J. Engelfriet, G. Leih, G. Rozenberg " Parallel object-based systems and Petri nets", Technical Reports 90-04 and 90-05, Leiden University, 1990.

[GUEL 90] N.Guelfi "Classes de réseaux structurés : étude, utilisation et modification." Rapport de stage de DEA 90, LRI UPS Orsay (1990)

[HOPK 89] R.P. Hopkins, M. Koutny, B.Randell"Some results on dynamically structures communicating systems", research report, Univ. of Newcastle upon Tyne (1989)

[JANS 89] D.Janssens & G.Rozenberg "Actors grammars", Math. syst. Th. 22, 75-107, (1989).

[JENS 81] K. Jensen "Coloured Petri Nets and the invariant method", TCS 14 , pp 317-336, North Holland Pub.Co (1981)

[MILN 89] R. Milner "Communication and Concurrency". Prentice Hall, 1989.

[NIER 90] O. Nierstrasz "A guide to Specifying Concurrent Behaviour with Abacus", in Object Management (ed) D. Tsichritzis, University of Geneva, 1990.

[REIS 85] W. Reisig "Petri Nets" Springer Verlag (1985)

[V&S 90] G. Vidal-Naquet, Y. Sami "Formalisation of the behavior of actors by colored Petri nets and some applications", PARLE 91, LNCS N°506.

[VAUT 87] J.Vautherin "Parallel systems specification with coloured Petri nets and algebraic specification" LNCS ICPN 87

[YOKO 86] Y.Yokote, M.Tokoro The Design and Implantation of Concurrent Smalltalk, SIGPLAN Notices, Vol 21, No 11, 1986.

A Parallel Programming Style and Its Algebra of Programs

Chris Hankin[1], Daniel Le Métayer[2], David Sands[3]

[1] Department of Computing, Imperial College
180 Queen's Gate, London SW7 2BZ, UK. (e-mail: clh@doc.ic.ac.uk)
[2] IRISA, Campus Universitaire de Beaulieu
35042-Rennes Cédex, FRANCE. (email:lemetayer@irisa.fr)
[3] Department of Computer Science, University of Copenhagen
Universitetsparken 1, DK-2100 Copenhagen Ø, DENMARK. (e-mail: dave@diku.dk)

Abstract. We present a set of primitive program schemes, which together with just two basic combining forms provide a suprisingly expressive parallel programming language. The primitive program schemes (called *tropes*) take the form of parameterised conditional rewrite rules, and the computational model is a variant of the *Gamma* style, in which computation proceeds by nondeterministic local rewriting of a global multiset.
We consider a number of examples which illustrate the use of tropes and we study the algebraic properties of the sequential and parallel combining forms. Using the examples we illustrate the application of these properties in the verification of some simple program transformations.

1 Introduction

In his Turing Award lecture, John Backus [Bac78] advocated the design of programming languages in terms of a fixed set of high-level constructors, or combinators, capturing common computation patterns. In this paper we follow Backus' programme in the context of parallel programming languages. This approach has two main benefits: it leads to more hierarchical and more structured programs; The set of combinators can be associated with a rich algebra of programs giving rise to useful program transformations. Backus exemplified his recommendations with the FP language. FP is a functional language based on a single data structure, the sequence. A set of combining forms is provided as the only means of constructing new programs from primitive functions. Examples of combining forms are:

$$\alpha f :< x_1, ..., x_n > \; = \; < f : x_1, ..., f : x_n > \qquad (f \circ g) : x = f(g : x)$$

Where : denotes application. The following is a typical law of the FP algebra:
$\alpha(f \circ g) = (\alpha f) \circ (\alpha g)$.

---

[1] Partially funded by ESPRIT WGs 6345 (SemaGraph) and 6809 (Semantique).
[2] Partially funded by SERC Visiting Fellowship GRH 19330.
[3] Partially funded by ESPRIT WG 6809 (Semantique) and the Danish Natural Sciences Research Council

Most existing functional languages do not follow such a radical approach and allow the programmer to define his own combining forms as higher-order functions. Nevertheless the extensive use of higher-order functions is a main feature of the functional programming style because it favours readability, modularity and program reuse [Hug89].

Functional languages have also been claimed as attractive candidates for programming parallel machines. This belief is based on the fact that functional programs are free of side-effects. However functional languages encourage the use of recursion both for defining data structures and programs. In fact recursion is the only means of defining new data structures in functional languages. The problem with recursion is that it introduces an inherent sequentiality in the way data structures can be processed. For example if lists are defined as *list* α = *nil* | *cons* α (*list* α) then any list manipulating program must access the elements of the list sequentially. It may be the case that this sequentiality is not relevant to the logic of the program; so even functional languages can impose the introduction of unnecessary sequentiality in a program. This drawback is also identified in [Maa92] where a range of "parallel" datatypes are introduced.

To avoid this flaw, we propose a programming style based on multisets because the multiset (or bag) is the least constraining data structure possible. Starting with a recursively built data structure on a base type α (for example *list* α) and removing all the structure, produces a multiset of elements of type α (not a set because the same element can occur several times in the structure). If the structure of the data is relevant to the logic of the program then it can be maintained in the multiset through a systematic encoding. For example a list $(x_1, ..., x_n)$ can be represented as a multiset of pairs (i, x_i). The important point is that this does not introduce any hierarchy between the values in the structure; all the values are still available and accessible at the same level.

For similar reasons, we do not allow recursion in programs since this encourages sequential hierarchy between computations. We focus in this paper on a collection of parameterised rewriting rules which form the counterpart of Backus's combining forms for multiset rewriting. These rules arise from previous work on the Gamma formalism [BM93]. We show the usefulness of these rules in terms of parallel program construction and we study their algebra of programs.

Section 2 is an informal introduction to the program schemes presented in this paper. Their semantics are defined formally in Section 3. Section 4 is a study of the confluence and termination of these schemes, describes the associated algebra of programs, and presents some examples of their use. The conclusion is a discussion of related works and avenues for further research.

2   Tropes: an Informal Introduction

We use a notation of the rewriting systems literature to denote multiset rewriting. The rule:

$$x_1, ..., x_n \rightarrow A(x_1, ..., x_n) \Leftarrow R(x_1, ..., x_n)$$

can be interpreted informally as the replacement into the multiset of elements $x_1, ..., x_n$ satisfying the condition $R(x_1, ..., x_n)$ by the elements of $A(x_1, ..., x_n)$. Viewed as a single program the (in general nondeterministic) result is obtained when no more rewrites can take place. A and R are functions. For example the program: $x_1, x_2 \rightarrow x_1 \Leftarrow (x_1 = x_2)$ computes the underlying set of a multiset by replacing pairs of equal elements by a single one until there are no further duplicate elements.

We consider only the rewriting of a single multiset in this paper and programs are not strongly typed (elements of different types can coexist in the multiset). When $R(x_1, ..., x_n) = True$, we omit the condition and write:

$$x_1, ..., x_n \rightarrow A(x_1, ..., x_n)$$

Similarly if $A(x_1, ..., x_n) = \emptyset$ we write: $x_1, ..., x_n \rightarrow \Leftarrow R(x_1, ..., x_n)$

We use two operators for combining programs, namely sequential composition $P_1 \circ P_2$ and parallel combination $P_1 + P_2$. Their semantics are defined formally in the next section. Not surprisingly, the intuition behind $P_1 \circ P_2$ is that the result of P_2 is passed as an argument to P_1. On the other hand, the result of $P_1 + P_2$ is obtained by performing the rewrites of P_1 and P_2 in parallel. For example, the following program returns the number of positive values in the initial integer multiset: $(x_1, x_2 \rightarrow x_1 + x_2) \circ ((x \rightarrow 1 \Leftarrow x > 1) + (x \rightarrow \Leftarrow x < 0))$.

The interested reader can find more examples of the relevance of multiset rewriting for parallel programming in [BM93]. We focus in this paper on five parameterised rewrite rules called *tropes* for:

Transmuter, Reducer, OPtimiser, Expander, and Selector.

The tropes are defined in terms of multiset rewrites in the following way:

$$
\begin{aligned}
\mathcal{T}(C, f) &= x \rightarrow f(x) \Leftarrow C(x) \\
\mathcal{R}(C, f) &= x, y \rightarrow f(x, y) \Leftarrow C(x, y) \\
\mathcal{O}(<, f_1, f_2, S) &= x, y \rightarrow f_1(x, y), f_2(x, y) \Leftarrow (f_1(x, y), f_2(x, y)) < (x, y) \\
&\quad \text{and } S(x, y) \text{ and } S(f_1(x, y), f_2(x, y)) \\
\mathcal{E}(C, f_1, f_2) &= x \rightarrow f_1(x), f_2(x) \Leftarrow C(x) \\
\mathcal{S}_{i,j}(C) &= x_1, ..., x_i \rightarrow x_j, ..., x_i \Leftarrow C(x_1, ..., x_i) (\textbf{where } 1 < j \leq i + 1)
\end{aligned}
$$

Notice that the reducer and the selector strictly decrease the size of the multiset; the expander increases its size; the transmuter and the optimiser keep its size constant. We first provide the intuition behind each of these tropes, then we present examples of composition of tropes and suggest the algebraic laws that they should satisfy.

Transmuter: The transmuter applies the same operation to all the elements of the multiset until no element satisfies the condition C. For example the following program returns, for each initial triple $(n, m, 0)$, a triple whose third component records the number of times m is a multiple of n.

$$
\begin{aligned}
nt = \mathcal{T}(C, f) \textbf{ where } C((n, m, k)) &= multiple(m, n) \\
f((n, m, k)) &= (n, m/n, k + 1)
\end{aligned}
$$

Note the standard use of pattern matching in the definitions of C and f.

Reducer: This trope reduces the size of the multiset by applying a function to pairs of elements satisfying a given condition. The counterpart of the traditional functional *reduce* operator can be obtained with an always true reaction condition. For instance: $add = \mathcal{R}(True, +)$ returns the sum of the elements of a multiset.

Expander: The expander is used to decompose the elements of a multiset into a collection of basic values. For example *ones* decomposes positive values n into n occurrences of 1s.

$$ones = \mathcal{E}(C, f_1, f_2) \text{ where } C(x) = x > 1$$
$$f_1(x) = x - 1 \quad f_2(x) = 1$$

A multiset version of *iota*, which in FP generates a sequence from 1 to n, can be defined as:

$$iota(n) = (\mathcal{T}(C_1, f_1) + \mathcal{E}(C_2, f_2, f_3))\{(1, n)\} \quad \text{where}$$
$$C_1((x, y)) = (x = y) \quad f_1((x, y)) = x$$
$$C_2((x, y)) = (x \neq y)$$
$$f_2((x, y)) = (x, y - 1) \quad f_3((x, y)) = y$$

Selector: The selector acts as a filter, removing from the multiset elements satisfying a certain condition. For example: $max = \mathcal{S}_{2,2}(\leq)$, $rem = \mathcal{S}_{2,2}(multiple)$. So *max* returns the maximum element of a multiset and *rem* removes any element that is the multiple of another element ($multiple(x, y)$ is true if x is a multiple of y). The multiset of prime numbers smaller than n can be computed as:

$$primes = rem \circ \mathcal{S}_{1,2}(isone) \circ iota \text{ where } isone \; x = (x = 1)$$

Optimiser: $\mathcal{O}(<, f_1, f_2, S)$ optimises the multiset according to a particular criterion (expressed through the ordering $<$) while preserving the structure of the multiset (described by the relation S). Consider for example the sorting of a sequence $(x_1, ..., x_n)$. The sequence is represented as a multiset of pairs (i, x_i) and the program proceeds by exchanging ill-ordered values:

$$sort = \mathcal{O}(\ll, f_1, f_2, S) \quad \text{where}$$
$$f_1((i, a), (j, b)) = (i, b), \quad f_2((i, a), (j, b)) = (j, a)$$
$$((i, a), (j, b)) \ll ((i', a'), (j', b')) \equiv (b < b')$$
$$S((i, a), (j, b)) = (i > j)$$

Let us now take a few examples involving various combinations of tropes to suggest the transformations that we will study in the rest of the paper. The *primes* program defined above can be used to compute the prime factorization of a natural number.

$$pf(n) = (gen + del) \circ nt \circ int \circ primes(n)$$

$gen = \mathcal{E}(C, f_1, f_2)$ where	$del = \mathcal{S}_{1,2}(C)$ where	$int = \mathcal{T}(C, f)$ where
$C((x, y, k)) = (k > 0)$	$C((x, y, k)) = (k = 0)$	$C(x) = integer(x)$
$f_1((x, y, k)) = (x, y, k - 1)$		$f(x) = (x, n, 0)$
$f_2((x, y, k)) = x$		

The transmuter *nt* defined earlier in this section computes the number of times *n* is a multiple of each prime number. The transmuter *int* acts as an interface between *primes* and *nt*, transforming each prime number x into a triple $(x, n, 0)$. The parallel combination *gen* + *del* decomposes each triple (x, y, k) into k occurrences of x. For example if $n = 2^3 * 3 * 11^2$, then $pf(n) = \{2, 2, 2, 3, 11, 11\}$. We will show in the next sections that *gen* + *del* can be transformed into *del* $\circ$ *gen*, which means that the deletion of unnecessary elements can be postponed until the end of the computation. We also have that *nt* $\circ$ *int* $\sim$ *nt* + *int* showing that both transmuters can be executed concurrently.

As a final illustration of the use of tropes, let us consider an image processing application: the edge detection problem [Sed88]. Each point of the image is originally associated with a grey intensity level. Then an intensity gradient is computed at each point and edges are defined as the points where the gradient is greater than a given threshold T. The gradient at a point is computed relative to its neighbours: only points at a distance d less than D are considered for the computation of the gradient. The gradient at a point is defined in the following way:

$$G(P) = maximum(neighbourhood) - minimum(neighbourhood)$$
$$\textbf{where } neighbourhood = \{intensity(P') \mid distance(P, P') < D\}$$

We use a multiset of quadruples (P, l, min, max). P is the coordinates of the point, l is its intensity level and *min* and *max* are the current values of respectively $minimum(neighbourhood)$ and $maximum(neighbourhood)$. The initial value of *min* and *max* is l. The evaluation consists in decreasing *min* and increasing *max* until the limit values are reached. This is achieved by two optimisers *decmin* and *incmax*. The selector *disc* discards the points where the gradient is less than the threshold and the transmuter *rf* removes unnecessary fields from the remaining elements.

$$
\begin{aligned}
&edges(n) = (disc + rf) \circ (decmin + incmax) \\
&decmin = \mathcal{O}(\ll, f_1, f_2, S) \ \textbf{where} \\
&\quad f_1(X, Y) = (X.P, X.l, Y.l, X.max), \quad f_2(X, Y) = Y \\
&\quad (X', Y') \ll (X, Y) \equiv (X'.min < X.min) \\
&\quad S(X, Y) = distance(X.P, Y.P) < D \\
&incmax = \mathcal{O}(\prec, f_1, f_2, S) \ \textbf{where} \\
&\quad f_1(X, Y) = (X.P, X.l, X.min, Y.l), \quad f_2(X, Y) = Y \\
&\quad (X', Y') \prec (X, Y) \equiv (X'.max > X.max) \\
&\quad S(X, Y) = distance(X.P, Y.P) < D \\
&disc = \mathcal{S}_{1,2}(C) \ \textbf{where} \\
&\quad C(X) = quadruple(X) \ and \ ((X.max - X.min) < T) \\
&rf = \mathcal{T}(C, f) \ \textbf{where} \\
&\quad C(X) = quadruple(X) \ and \ ((X.max - X.min) \geq T) \\
&\quad f(X) = (X.P, X.l)
\end{aligned}
$$

The algebra of programs developed in the rest of the paper allows us to perform the following transformations:

$$disc + rf \implies disc \circ rf$$
$$disc + rf \implies rf \circ disc$$
$$decmin + incmax \implies decmin \circ incmax$$
$$decmin + incmax \implies incmax \circ decmin$$

These transformations can be used to tune a program to a particular architecture by increasing or decreasing its potential for parallelism. In the next section we provide a formal account of the semantics of tropes. Then we come back to the transformations suggested above and present their conditions of application.

3 Semantics of Combining Forms for Tropes

In this section we consider the operational semantics of programs consisting of tropes, together with the two *combining forms* introduced in the last section: sequential composition, $P_1 \circ P_2$, and parallel combination, $P_1 + P_2$

$$P \in \text{Programs} ::= \text{Tropes} \mid P \circ P \mid P + P$$

To define the semantics for these programs we define a single step transition relation between *configurations*. The terminal configurations are just multisets, and the intermediate configurations are program/multiset pairs written $\langle P, M \rangle$.

We define the single step transitions first for the individual tropes. For each instance of the tropes $t : \bar{x} \to A\bar{x} \Leftarrow R\bar{x}$ define

$$\langle t, M \rangle \to \begin{cases} \langle t, M - \bar{a} \cup A\bar{a} \rangle & \text{if } \exists \bar{a} \subseteq M.R\bar{a} \\ M & \text{otherwise} \end{cases}$$

So a program consisting of a single trope terminates when there are no applicable reactions in the multiset. Since no program defined using sequential composition can terminate in one step, single step terminal transitions are only defined for programs not containing sequential composition; thus the remaining *terminal* transitions are defined by the following rule:

$$\frac{\langle P, M \rangle \to M \quad \langle Q, M \rangle \to M}{\langle P + Q, M \rangle \to M}$$

The remaining transitions are defined using the concept of *active contexts*. An *active context*, $\mathbf{A}$ is a term containing a single hole $[\,]$:

$$\mathbf{A} ::= [\,] \mid P + \mathbf{A} \mid \mathbf{A} + P \mid P \circ \mathbf{A}$$

Let $\mathbf{A}[P]$ denote active context $\mathbf{A}$ with program P in place of the hole.

The idea of active contexts is that they isolate parts of a program that can affect the next transition, so that for example, the left-hand side of a sequential composition is not active (but it can become active once the right-hand side has terminated). The remaining transition rules are defined by the following two rules:

$$\frac{\langle t, M \rangle \rightarrow \langle t, M' \rangle}{\langle \mathbf{A}[t], M \rangle \rightarrow \langle \mathbf{A}[t], M' \rangle} \qquad \frac{\langle Q, M \rangle \rightarrow M}{\langle \mathbf{A}[P \circ Q], M \rangle \rightarrow \langle \mathbf{A}[P], M \rangle}$$

The first says that if there is a possible reaction in an active context then it can proceed, while the second says that if the right hand side of a sequential composition can terminate, then it can be erased. As usual, we use $\rightarrow^*$ to represent the reflexive and transitive closure of $\rightarrow$. Notice that since a program does not uniquely factor into a sub-program in an active context, the one-step transition relation is not deterministic, but it should not be difficult to see that it is total on non-terminal configurations (under the assumption that the transition relation on single tropes is total).

Inspection of the semantics shows that "programs" are not fixed. This leads us to the notion of the *residual* part of a program – the program component of any configuration that is an immediate predecessor of a terminal configuration (multiset). The *residual part* of a program P, written $\underline{P}$, is defined by induction on the syntax:

$$\underline{t} = t \qquad \underline{P_1 \circ P_2} = \underline{P_1} \qquad \underline{P_1 + P_2} = \underline{P_1} + \underline{P_2}$$

This provides us with a simple (ie. weak) postcondition for programs. We define a predicate Φ on a program and a multiset to be true if and only if the residual part of the program is terminated with respect to the multiset.

Definition 1 (The postcondition Φ) $\Phi(P, M) \Leftrightarrow \langle \underline{P}, M \rangle \rightarrow M$

Intuitively, $\Phi(P, M)$ holds if M is a possible result for the program P. The significance of this is that the predicate $\Phi(P, \_)$ can be constructed syntactically by considering (the negations of) the reaction conditions in $\underline{P}$.

We can now define an ordering on programs. Intuitively, $P_1 \sqsubseteq P_2$ whenever, for each possible input M, if P_1 can diverge (i.e. rewrite forever, written $\langle P_1, M \rangle \uparrow$) then so can P_2, and if P_1 can terminate producing some multiset N then so can P_2.

Definition 2

$$P_1 \sqsubseteq P_2 \Leftrightarrow \forall M.(((\langle P_1, M \rangle \uparrow \Rightarrow \langle P_2, M \rangle \uparrow)$$
$$\wedge (\forall N.\langle P_1, M \rangle \rightarrow^* N \Rightarrow \langle P_2, M \rangle \rightarrow^* N))$$

We write $P \sim Q$ if $P \sqsubseteq Q$ and $Q \sqsubseteq P$.

Without further ado, we present a key result from [HMS92] which establishes when sequential composition correctly implements parallel combination.

Theorem 1. $(\forall M.(\Phi(Q, M) \wedge \langle P, M \rangle \rightarrow^* N) \Rightarrow \Phi(Q, N)) \Rightarrow P \circ Q \sqsubseteq P + Q$

This theorem can be used to remove parallel combinations, replacing them by sequential compositions. The reverse transformation is only applicable under more stringent conditions. Given that $P \circ Q \sqsubseteq P + Q$, then $P \circ Q$ is a correct "interleaving" of the steps involved in executing $P + Q$; if we know that $P + Q$ always terminates (is *strongly normalising*, written $(P + Q) \downarrow_{must}$) and that it is confluent (deterministic) then all interleavings have the same effect and $P + Q \sqsubseteq P \circ Q$. This is the second key result from [HMS92] which allows us to parallelise sequential programs. Before presenting the theorem, we formally define confluence.

Definition 3 P *is* confluent, *written* $Con(P)$, *iff* $\forall M.Con(P, M)$ *where* $Con(P,M)$ *is the predicate:*

$$\langle P, M \rangle \rightarrow^* \langle P_1, M_1 \rangle \wedge \langle P, M \rangle \rightarrow^* \langle P_2, M_2 \rangle \Rightarrow$$
$$\exists \langle P_3, M_3 \rangle.(\langle P_1, M_1 \rangle \rightarrow^* \langle P_3, M_3 \rangle \wedge \langle P_2, M_2 \rangle \rightarrow^* \langle P_3, M_3 \rangle)$$

Theorem 2. $(P \circ Q \sqsubseteq P + Q \wedge Con(P + Q) \wedge (P + Q) \downarrow_{must}) \Rightarrow P + Q \sim P \circ Q$

We close this section which a theorem that collects together a number of properties first presented in [HMS92].

Theorem 3. *1. $+$ is associative and commutative, $\circ$ is assoc., $\circ$ is monotone.*
2. $(P_1 + P_3) \circ P_2 \sqsubseteq (P_1 \circ P_2) + P_3$
3. $(P_1 + \underline{P_3}) \circ (P_2 + P_3) \sqsubseteq (P_1 \circ P_2) + P_3$
4. $(P \sqsubseteq \overline{P + P}) \wedge (P \sim \underline{P} \Rightarrow P \sim P + P)$
5. $(P_1 + P_2) \circ (Q_1 + Q_2) \sqsubseteq (P_1 \circ Q_1) + (P_2 \circ Q_2)$
6. $P_1 \circ (P_2 + P_3) \sqsubseteq (P_1 \circ P_2) + (P_1 \circ P_3)$

4 Properties

We show in this section how some general results, including some of those presented above, can be specialised to derive useful properties of tropes. We first study the conditions under which a program is confluent and terminating. Then we prove a number of laws concerning compositions of tropes.

4.1 General Confluence and Termination Properties

The computation model of Gamma is closely related to conditional term rewriting. We call a program *simple* if it does not contain any sequential compositions. One property of the semantics defined earlier is that for any simple program P, if $\langle P, M \rangle \rightarrow \langle Q, N \rangle$ then $P = Q$. Consequently, a simple program P can be viewed as defining a multiset rewriting relation which is an associative, commutative, conditional rewriting system. Arbitrary programs may not be viewed in this way because of the combinations of $+$ and $\circ$ that are allowed. There are, however, some general results for Abstract Reduction Systems [Klo90] which are useful.

For simple programs confluence may be proved using one of the standard decompositions, such as *Newman's Lemma* (see eg. [Klo90]). A most useful method for proving the termination of Gamma programs (see [BM90]) is the Dershowitz-Manna multiset ordering [DM79] in which a well-founded multiset ordering can be derived from a well-founded ordering on the elements of the multiset.

We now consider how these properties interact with the combinators that we have introduced. It is easy to verify that the sequential composition of two programs which are confluent (strongly normalising) will result in a combined program which is confluent (resp. strongly normalising). Now we consider programs of the form $P_1 + P_2$ where P_1 and P_2 are simple. We call the multiset-rewriting relations associated with the two sub-programs $\rightarrow^*_1$ and $\rightarrow^*_2$, respectively, and we will say that they *commute* if they satisfy a diamond property of the following form:

$$\exists M_3.\, M_1 \,{}^*_1\!\!\leftarrow M \rightarrow^*_2 M_2 \Longrightarrow M_1 \rightarrow^*_2 M_3 \,{}^*_1\!\!\leftarrow M_2.$$

Now if $\rightarrow^*_1$ and $\rightarrow^*_2$ are individually confluent and they commute, then the combined rule system is also confluent; this a consequence of the *Hindley-Rosen Lemma* which is proved by a simple diagram chase. Termination, however is not necessarily preserved - we require a stronger condition than commutativity. If we add the condition that $\rightarrow_2$-rewrites cannot create $\rightarrow_1$-redexes, then termination of the combined rule system follows from the separate termination of the two programs.

The generalisation of these last two paragraphs to arbitrary programs constructed from the combinators is a matter for further investigation.

4.2 Confluence and Termination of Tropes

Transmuter: For termination we require a well-founded ordering, $<$, on the multiset such that: $C(x) \Rightarrow f(x) < x$. Since a transmuter only selects one element at a time, it is trivially confluent.

Reducer: Termination follows trivially from cardinality considerations. In turning to confluence, we consider the reducer $\mathcal{R}(C, f)$. We require the following notion: the symmetric predicate C is *f-preserved* iff:

$C(x, y) \wedge C(x, z) \Rightarrow C(f(x, y), z) \wedge C(y, f(x, z)).$

A sufficient condition for a reducer to be confluent is that f is associative and commutative and that C is f-preserved.

Optimiser: The detailed consideration of the optimiser is omitted from this paper due to lack of space. It has proved difficult to derive general conditions for termination and confluence of this trope but we have identified two special cases which are useful in program development. These will be described elsewhere.

Expander: We consider the expander, $\mathcal{E}(C, f_1, f_2)$ applied to a multiset S. Define S_C to be the subset of S whose elements satisfy the predicate C. Suppose that we have a well-founded ordering, $<$, on S_C. We say that a function, f, is *reductive* on S_C if for all $x \in S_C$, either $f(x) \notin S_C$ or $f(x) < x$. A sufficient condition for termination of an expander is that the two functions f_1 and f_2 are reductive on S_C. Since an expander has a single variable on the left hand side, there are no overlapping redexes and confluence is trivial.

Selector: Termination of this rule follows trivially by cardinality considerations. Given the generality of the rule, it is difficult to give conditions for confluence. Restricting ourselves to rules of the form $S_{2,2}(C)$, a sufficient condition is that C is antisymmetric and transitive.

4.3 Laws

We start with some definitions of derived relations which will provide us with some useful notations. Given R, a reaction condition of arity n, we define:

$$\overline{R}_M(x) \Leftrightarrow \forall \bar{a} \subseteq M . x \in \bar{a} \Rightarrow \neg R(\bar{a})$$

Informally, $\overline{R}_M(x)$ says that element x is unable to partake in a reaction within multiset M. If this holds for arbitrary M, we just write $\overline{R}(x)$, with the intuition that x cannot partake in any reaction for which R is the associated reaction condition. We say that two reaction conditions are *exclusive* if the sets of elements that satisfy them are guaranteed to be disjoint:

$$Exclusive(R, R') \Leftrightarrow \forall x.(\overline{R}(x) \vee \overline{R'}(x))$$

We can now start to list some properties of tropes. The first set are general laws, expressed in terms of individual reactions written abstractly as condition/action pairs (R, A):

Theorem 4. *1. $Exclusive(R, R')$ and $(\forall a \in A(x_1, \ldots, x_n).\overline{R'}(a))$ implies*
   $(R, A) + (R', A') \sim (R, A) \circ (R', A')$
2. If $\langle(R, A), M\rangle \rightarrow \langle(R, A), N\rangle$ and $\forall x \in M \backslash N . \overline{R'}_M(x)$ imply that[4]
   $\forall y \in N \backslash M . \overline{R'}_N(y)$, then $(R, A) + (R', A') \sqsupseteq (R, A) \circ (R', A')$

The first part is quite intuitive, since the condition expresses complete interference-freedom of R and R'. The second part has a somewhat stronger precondition which can be informally read as: if all the removed elements of a (R, A)-reaction were R'-stable for the original multiset then all the new elements will be stable for the resulting multiset. This is sufficient to guarantee that after termination of (R', A') subsequent reactions by (R, A) could not generate any elements that enable R', and hence the refinement.

The next theorem states some properties of particular tropes and their interactions obtained by specialising the above properties:

Theorem 5. *1. $(C'(x) \wedge \overline{C}(x) \Rightarrow \overline{C}(f'x)) \Rightarrow$*
   $S_{i,j}(C) + T(C', f') \sqsupseteq T(C', f') \circ S_{i,j}(C)$
2. $S_{i,j}(C_1 \vee C_2) \sim S_{i,j}(C_1) + S_{i,j}(C_2)$
3. $(\neg C(x) \wedge C'(x) \Rightarrow \neg C(f'(x))) \Rightarrow$
   $T(C', f') + \mathcal{E}(C, f_1, f_2) \sqsupseteq T(C', f') \circ \mathcal{E}(C, f_1, f_2)$
4. $(\neg C'(x) \wedge C(x) \Rightarrow \neg C'(f_1(x)) \wedge \neg C'(f_2(x))) \Rightarrow$
   $T(C', f') + \mathcal{E}(C, f_1, f_2) \sqsupseteq \mathcal{E}(C, f_1, f_2) \circ T(C', f')$
5. $\forall P.S_{i,j}(C) + P \sqsupseteq S_{i,j}(C) \circ P$

---

[4] Notation: $M \backslash N$ is multiset difference, so, eg. $\{1, 1, 2\} \backslash \{1, 3\} = \{1, 2\}$.

Now we use the various properties to prove some of the transformations mentioned in Section 2.

Lemma 6. *1. $gen + del \sim del \circ gen$*
2. $nt + int \sim nt \circ int$
3. $disc + rf \sqsupseteq disc \circ rf$
4. $disc + rf \sqsupseteq rf \circ disc$
5. $decmin + incmax \sqsupseteq incmax \circ decmin$
6. $decmin + incmax \sqsupseteq decmin \circ incmax$

Proof. 1. Then we have that the two reaction conditions are exclusive, and therefore, since *del* has an empty action, we have the desired result by Theorem 4 (1).
2. Since the two tropes consume elements of different types, we have that their conditions are exclusive. Moreover, elements produced by *nt* are stable for *int*. Consequently the result follows by Theorem 4 (1).
3. Follows immediately from Theorem 5 (5).
4. Suppose that $(quadruple(X) \wedge (X.max - X.min) \geq T$. Then we have $\overline{C}(X)$ and $\overline{C}(f(X))$ thus, we have the required result by Theorem 5 (1).
5. and 6. follow by application of Theorem 4 (2). The verifications of the preconditions are straightforward.

5 Concluding Remarks

The programming style defined and studied in this paper stemmed from previous work on program construction in the Gamma formalism [BM93]. The main achievements of this paper are:

- The formal definition of the tropes and their semantics.
- The study of their algebra of programs.

A collection of examples illustrating the relevance of the programming style advocated in this paper can be found in [BM93].

Our main objectives are closely related to those of the Unity designers [CM88]. In contrast with their approach we have emphasized the development of a calculus of program transformation whereas they have focussed on logical aspects of program refinement. The use of the multiset as a basic data structure for parallel programming (and subsequent program transformation) has also been investigated in the functional programming setting by Roe [Roe91]. Conditional rewriting as a general model of parallel programming has been advocated by Meseguer [MW91] who shows how various computational formalisms can be expressed in this framework.

In [HMS92] we developed a formal semantics for a Gamma variant and studied its properties (some of which appear as Theorem 3). The weakness of our earlier work was that we did not specify the details of the primitive rewrites, the (R, A)-pairs; as a consequence our calculus was restricted to quite general transformations. In this paper we have introduced five primitive program forms, the tropes, as a basis for parallel programming. We have shown how many of the examples can be recast using the tropes and the two combining forms. Being specific about the primitive forms allows us to develop a much richer calculus; the new rules are summarised in Theorems 4 and 5. We have shown how these rules may be used to transform some of the earlier examples.

The multiset rewriting paradigm has also been applied in the context of reactive systems [MW91] [BM93]. Further work will include the study of the tropes in that context. The semantics of the tropes in section 3 involves two different kinds of rewritings: *active steps* which rewrite the multiset and *passive steps* during which the program is modified. The latter does not have any obvious analogy in the term rewriting approach. The work reported here will form the starting point for a deeper study of the similarities and differences with commutative and associative term rewriting systems.

Acknowlegement Thanks to T. Mogensen for comments on an earlier draft.

References

[Bac78] J. Backus. Can programming be liberated from the von Neumann style? A functional style and its algebra of programs. *Communications of the ACM*, 21(8):613–641, August 1978.

[BM90] J.-P. Banâtre and D. Le Métayer. The Gamma model and its discipline of programming. *Science of Computer Programming*, 15:55–77, 1990.

[BM92] J.-P. Banâtre and D. Le Métayer, editors. *Research Directions in High-level Parallel Programming Languages*. Springer-Verlag, LNCS 574, 1992.

[BM93] J.-P. Banâtre and D. Le Métayer. Programming by multiset transformation. *CACM*, January 1993.

[CM88] K. M. Chandy and J. Misra. *Parallel Program Design: A Foundation*. Addison-Wesley, 1988.

[DM79] N. Dershowitz and Z. Manna. Proving termination with multiset orderings. *Comm. ACM*, 22:465–476, 1979.

[HMS92] C. Hankin, D. Le Métayer, and D. Sands. A calculus of Gamma programs. Research Report DOC 92/22, Department of Computing, Imperial College, 1992.

[Hug89] J. Hughes. Why functional programming matters. *The Computer Journal*, 2(32):98–107, April 1989.

[Klo90] J.W. Klop. Term rewriting systems. Technical Report CS-R9073, CWI, 1990.

[Maa92] A. Maasen. Parallel programming with data structures and higher-order functions. *Science of Computer Programming*, 18:1–38, 1992.

[MW91] J. Meseguer and T. Winkler. Parallel programming in Maude. In *[BM92]*, 1991.

[Roe91] P. Roe. *Parallel Programming using Functional Languages*. PhD thesis, Glasgow University, 1991.

[Sed88] R. Sedgewick. *Algorithms*. Addison-Wesley, 1988.

$B(PN)^2$ – a Basic Petri Net Programming Notation

Eike Best
Institut für Informatik
Universität Hildesheim, Germany

Richard P. Hopkins
Department of Computing Science
University of Newcastle upon Tyne, UK

Abstract This paper presents the syntax of a concurrent programming notation which integrates a variety of process interaction techniques, its compositional Petri net semantics via the Box calculus, and an example of using the semantics for program verification.
Keywords Concurrent Programming Notation, Petri Nets, Peterson's Mutual Exclusion Algorithm

1 Introduction

The practical applications of Petri nets to date have mainly been in high level design and verification [13], for which a wide variety of (semi)automated tools (some of them in commercial use) have been developed [5]. Our concern in this paper is with applying Petri nets in the more intricate task of verifying the properties of concurrent algorithms (as in e.g. [17]), and thus also in the semantics of the languages needed to express them. A substantial body of research (e.g., [3, 6, 14, 18, 24]) addresses the compositional Petri net modelling of the abstract control structure of programs. However, comparatively little has been done to also express data structures adequately, which in our understanding means: compositionally.

The Box calculus [1], a syntactic superstructure built on top of (labelled) Petri nets, has been developed partially in order to address the compositional semantics of programming languages, and to provide the basis for semantics-driven programming language design. It has been successfully employed [9] in the semantics of an existing language, namely occam [15]. In this paper we describe $B(PN)^2$, the first definition of a Petri net based programming notation intended to: (A) Have a perspicuous and compositional Petri net semantics, allowing the application of Petri net indigenous proof methods, to complement other techniques; (B) Have more flexibility than, say, occam, in particular in the smooth integration of a variety of process interaction techniques, whilst being sufficiently conventional such that traditional programmers can feel at ease with it.

2 The Box calculus

The Box calculus comprises 'Box expressions' E which can be seen as a controlled extension of process terms of CCS [16], and their compositional semantics, $Box(E)$, in terms of a class of labelled place/transition nets referred to as (Petri) Boxes.

Table 1 specifies the subsyntax of Box expressions as needed here. Some concepts are familiar: sequential composition (;), choice ▯, corresponding to

$$E ::= \alpha \mid E; E \mid \mathbb{I}\{E_i \mid i \in I\} \mid E\|E \mid [\alpha : E] \mid [E * E * E]$$

Table 1: Fragment of the Box expression syntax

CCS' $+$ and COSY's comma [14] (written $E_1 \mathbb{I} \ldots \mathbb{I} E_n$ for finite choice); and iteration:

$$[\texttt{entry} * \texttt{body} * \texttt{exit}]$$

which is behaviourally equivalent to the recursive expression

$$\texttt{entry}; \mu X.((\texttt{body}; X) \mathbb{I} \texttt{exit}),$$

but in contrast yields a cyclic Petri net structure and preserves finiteness. The more unusual features are multi-actions α, concurrent composition $\|$ and scoping [:] over an action set α, which we shall explain in the context of their use in semantics for shared variables. This use is based on the technique in [16] where the declaration of a shared variable yields a process (here a Box (expression), referred to as a 'Data Box') which interacts with processes ('User Boxes') accessing the variable.

The Box formalism assumes a set A of action names. A multi-action α is a finite multiset over A. The empty multiset, $\emptyset$, plays the same role as τ in CCS. A carries a bijection called conjugation $\hat{} : A \rightarrow A$ satisfying $\hat{a} \neq a$ and $\hat{\hat{a}} = a$ for all $a \in A$. This setup gives the PBC some resemblance to SCCS [16]. However, the idea is that two multi-actions α_1 and α_2 can only synchronise over pairs a and $\hat{a}$ (perhaps repeatedly so), the resulting multi-action being the multiset sum $\alpha_1 + \alpha_2$ minus the set $\{a, \hat{a}\}$. Thus, the PBC is asynchronus while SCCS is synchronous.

A typical element of A is the data action x_{01} produced by a User process for the change of x's value from 0 to 1 (resulting from say $x := 1$). This has conjugate $\widehat{x_{01}}$, also denoting that change, but as part of the behaviour of the Data Box for x. The following Box expression illustrates the interplay of multi-actions, concurrent composition and scoping. It corresponds to a possible execution of

$$(x, y) := (z + y, z - y)$$

with all variables of type $\{0, 1\}$; which requires synchronisation of four participants, one each for x, y, z, and an additional one for the assignment.

$$[\{x_{01}, y_{01}\} : \\ \{\widehat{x_{01}}\} \| \{\widehat{y_{01}}\} \| \{\widehat{z_{11}}\} \| \{x_{01}, y_{01}, z_{11}\}]$$

Figure 1 shows the Petri net semantics of this Box expression, and how it is obtained compositionally: (a) shows the concurrent composition of, from left to right, parts of the Data Boxes for the three declarations and part of the Box for the assignment (note that there is concurrent execution with no implicit synchronisation - a significant difference between the PBC and other process calculi). The scopings to give (b) (scoping over x) and then (c) (scoping over y) each introduce synchronisations on the scoped action names and remove any transitions having the scoped actions. This example exhibits the partial synchronisation which is crucial for the compositional semantics of blocks, since x, y and z could be declared in different blocks.

As shown in Figure 1, there are distinguished entry (e) and exit (x) places which establish the initial marking (as shown) and the termination, and drive various compositions; for example, for sequential composition the exit places of the first Box are combined with the entry places of the second [1, 2, 21, 25].

3 Syntax of $B(PN)^2$

Table 2 describes the syntax of $B(PN)^2$. Syntactic metavariables are printed in teletype font while keywords are printed in bold. Other elements of the notation are printed in italic. Some of the constructs are familiar from traditional programming languages: identifiers (variable names) w (for plain variables) or c (for channels); sequential composition (;) and parallel composition $\|$; (Boolean and integer) constants; unary/binary operations op; and variable declarations. For instance, the clause **var** $w : \{\mathbf{F}, \mathbf{T}\}$ declares a Boolean variable w, and the clause **var** $w : \mathbf{Z}$ declares an integer variable. (A complete program, as usual, is a block for which all variables have been declared.) The more novel constructs are:

(1) The clause **var** c: **chan** b **of** s declares a channel (FIFO buffer) c of capacity b that may carry values within s. This may be of: unbounded capacity (ω); zero capacity in which case it gives handshake communication as in CSP [11] or occam; or any capacity in between.

(2) The command **do** ... **od** combines the traditional **if** command (in its **exit** clauses) with the traditional **while** command (in its **repeat** clauses). There can be zero or more iterations, each being the execution of one of the repeat clauses; followed by execution of one of the exit clauses.

(3) The command $\langle \mathtt{expr} \rangle$ denotes the atomic execution of the expression **expr**. A variable w can appear as $'w$ and as w' denoting, respectively, its value just before and just after execution of the command; and (redundantly but conveniently) as just w, denoting both and implying $'w = w'$. Communication, over a channel c, is also incorporated in this framework, with $c!$ performing an 'output' communication, and $c?$ a 'input' communication; in both cases the expression yields the value communicated.

Each expression allows such executions which yield the value $\mathbf{T}$; and which may alter the values of its free variables but no others (differing in this respect from the related approach of [10]). For instance: $\langle y' = y' \rangle$ allows the setting of y to any value and thus differs from $\langle x' = x' \rangle$ and from $\langle \mathbf{T} \rangle$; the commands $\langle 3 \rangle$ or $\langle \mathbf{F} \rangle$ have no terminating executions.

Table 3 gives a correspondence between this notation and some traditional style expressions, illustrating its considerable flexibility (including unbounded nondeterminism). On the Petri Box semantic side, this flexibility does not have to be paid for, since the definition is no more complicated - in fact, simpler - than it would be for the special cases usually considered (such as occam-like synchronisation). When

382

(a) $Box(\{\widehat{x_{01}}\}\|\{\widehat{y_{01}}\}\|\{\widehat{z_{11}}\}\|\{x_{01}, y_{01}, z_{11}\})$

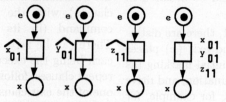

(b) $Box([\{x_{01}\} : \{\widehat{x_{01}}\}\|\{\widehat{y_{01}}\}\|\{\widehat{z_{11}}\}\|\{x_{01}, y_{01}, z_{11}\}])$

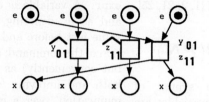

(c) $Box([\{x_{01}, y_{01}\} : \{\widehat{x_{01}}\}\|\{\widehat{y_{01}}\}\|\{\widehat{z_{11}}\}\|\{x_{01}, y_{01}, z_{11}\}])$

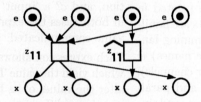

Figure 1: An example of multi-way synchronisation and scoping

block	::=	begin scope end	
scope	::=	com | decl; scope	
decl	::=	var var − name : type | decl;decl	
type	::=	set | chan b of set	$(b \in \{0, 1, 2, \ldots, \} \cup \{\omega\})$
com	::=	⟨expr⟩ | com; com | com ‖ com | block | do alt − set od	
expr	::=	′w | w | w′ | c? | c! | const | expr op expr | op expr	
alt − set	::=	com; repeat | com; exit | alt − set ☐alt − set	

Table 2: Syntax of $B(PN)^2$

Traditional notation / explanation	$B(PN)^2$
$x := 4$	$\langle x' = 4 \rangle$
await $x = 4$ **then skip end**	$\langle x = 4 \rangle$ or $\langle ('x = 4) \wedge (x' = 4) \rangle$
$c!(x+y)$ (**occam** / CSP)	$\langle\, c! = (x + y)\, \rangle$
$(x + y < 9); c?x$ (CSP input guard)	$\langle\, ('x + y < 9) \wedge x' = c?\, \rangle$
$P(s)$ on an n-ary semaphore s	$\langle\, 's > 0 \wedge s' = 's - 1\, \rangle$
set x (nondeterministically) to 1 or to 2	$\langle x' = 1 \vee x' = 2 \rangle$
set x to any value (leave others unchanged)	$\langle x' = x' \rangle$

Table 3: Examples of atomic commands

$B(PN)^2$ is considered as a basis for an actual programming language, rather than for algorithm design/verification, implementability becomes an issue, for which the generality presents potential difficulties. One may draw from existing work on abstract data types and unification (e.g., [20]) in order to obtain feasible, albeit inefficient, implementations; or restrict the syntax of expressions appropriately for a more easily implemented subset, with some possibility of behaviour-preserving transformations to this from the general syntax.

4 $B(PN)^2$ semantics

In this section, we define a semantic function E which associates to every $B(PN)^2$ program P a Box expression $E(P)$, and hence, by the results of [1], a Petri net $Box(E(P))$, compositionally. There is a rich set of algebraic laws for Box expressions, which give rise to such laws for the programming notation, but we will not deal with these here.

The semantics of the command combi-

nators, i.e., sequence, parallel composition and choice/iteration are straightforward using the corresponding constructs of Box expressions, as shown in Table 4. In the case of choice/iteration, we use two supplementary semantic functions - R which extracts the 'Repeat' components, and X which extracts the 'eXit' components, so that these can be appropriately placed in the Box iteration construct.

The remaining constructs depend on the action sychronisation. Let VAL denote the full set of possible values, i.e., all constants and all other elements of the possible types of the variables. Let x be a plain variable and c a channel variable. First we define the sets of actions which could possibly pertain to x or c:

$$act(x) = \{x_{uv} \mid u, v \in VAL\} \cup \{x\}$$
$$act(c) = \{c!v, c?v \mid v \in VAL\} \cup \{c\}$$

In the set A of actions we collect all elements of $act(x)$ where x is a plain variable of P, all elements of $act(c)$ where c is a channel variable of P, as well as their conjugates $\widehat{x_{uv}}$, $\hat{x}$, $\widehat{c!v}$, $\widehat{c?v}$ and $\hat{c}$. The forms x_{uv} and $\widehat{x_{uv}}$ were discussed previously. The forms using ?

$$
\begin{aligned}
E(\mathsf{com}_1; \mathsf{com}_2) &= E(\mathsf{com}_1)\ ;\ E(\mathsf{com}_2) \\
E(\mathsf{com}_1 \| \mathsf{com}_2) &= E(\mathsf{com}_1)\ \|\ E(\mathsf{com}_2) \\
E(\mathbf{do}\ \mathsf{alt} - \mathsf{set}\ \mathbf{od}) &= [\emptyset * R(\mathsf{alt} - \mathsf{set}) * X(\mathsf{alt} - \mathsf{set})\,] \\
R(\mathsf{alt} - \mathsf{set}_1\ \square\mathsf{alt} - \mathsf{set}_2) &= R(\mathsf{alt} - \mathsf{set}_1)\ \square R(\mathsf{alt} - \mathsf{set}_2) \\
X(\mathsf{alt} - \mathsf{set}_1\ \square\mathsf{alt} - \mathsf{set}_2) &= X(\mathsf{alt} - \mathsf{set}_1)\ \square X(\mathsf{alt} - \mathsf{set}_2) \\
R(\mathsf{com};\ \mathbf{repeat}) = X(\mathsf{com};\ \mathbf{exit}) &= E(\mathsf{com}) \\
X(\mathsf{com};\ \mathbf{repeat}) = R(\mathsf{com};\ \mathbf{exit}) &= \square\emptyset \qquad\qquad (= \mathbf{stop},\ \text{cf. Fig. 4})
\end{aligned}
$$

Table 4: Semantics of command combinators

and ! are analogous with ! denoting the sending of a value over a channel and ? standing for the receiving of a value. The elements of the form x or c and their conjugates are block termination actions to be explained shortly.

Table 5 (second line) shows the declaration of a plain or channel variable z and the construct comprising its scope. The expression $E(\mathbf{decl})$ produces the required Resource (Data or Channel) Box for z which is placed in parallel with the Box for its scope, with the latter being followed by the termination action for the declaration (which matches a conjugate action $\hat{z}$ of the Resource Box).

The Resource Boxes are here just illustrated by appropriate Petri net structures giving the required behaviour. Figure 2 shows the Resource Box for a variable w of type $\{0, 1\}$; and Figure 3 for a channel c of capacity 0 and a channel d of capacity 1, each of type $\{0, 1\}$. These Figures should allow the reader to infer the necessary generalisations (arbitrary type / arbitrary capacity). A Channel Box of infinite capacity is described in [12]. For a 0-capacity channel we a use a channel Box rather than the direct synchronisation of $\widehat{c!v} = c?v$, one reason being for consistency with the cases of non-zero capacity. Also, it is not difficult to modify the Resource Boxes we have defined, to allow several accesses at the same time (e.g. concurrent read), or to allow other synchronising data structures.

When a sequential predecessor of some block passes control to it, all e-places of any Resource Boxes declared at the beginning of the block receive an initial token; the first access to, say, a Data Box for w, moves that token to a specific value place ($w = 0$ or $w = 1$ in the case of Figure 2); subsequent accesses move the token between those places; and block termination moves it to the x-place from which it is removed by a sequential successor of the block (which could be the same block if it is within a loop). This semantics satisfies the requirement that Boxes be 'self-cleaning', and also avoids any intialisation action, to give a proper semantics for choice over blocks.

Every atomic command of the form $\mathsf{com} = \langle \mathbf{expr} \rangle$ gives rise to an alternative composition of multi-actions, say $\alpha_1\ \square\alpha_2\ \square\alpha_3\ \square \ldots$ Every α_i corresponds to one particular setting of the

$$E(\textbf{begin scope end}) \quad = \quad E(\textbf{scope})$$
$$E(\textbf{decl}(z); \textbf{scope}) \quad = \quad [\; act(z) \; : \; E(\textbf{decl}) \,\|\, (E(\textbf{scope}) \,; \{z\}) \;]$$

Table 5: Semantics of blocks and declarations

$Box(\; \textbf{var } w : \{0,1\} \;)$

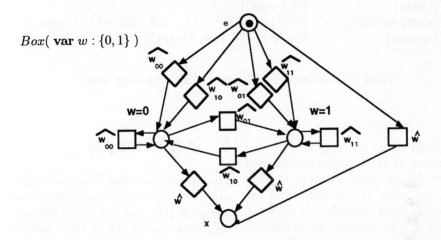

Figure 2: A Data Box

$Box(\textbf{var } c\colon \textbf{chan } 0 \textbf{ of}\{0,1\})$ $\quad$ $Box(\textbf{var } d\colon \textbf{chan } 1 \textbf{ of}\{0,1\})$

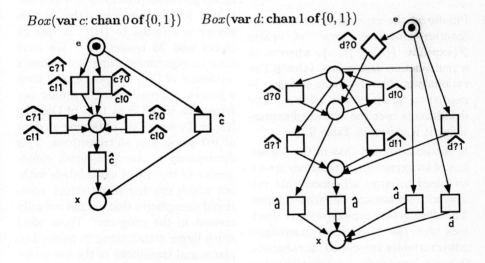

Figure 3: Two Channel Boxes

$$
\begin{aligned}
\mathcal{F}('x) &= \{(\{x_{uv}\}, u) \mid u, v \in VAL\} \\
\mathcal{F}(x') &= \{(\{x_{uv}\}, v) \mid u, v \in VAL\} \\
\mathcal{F}(x) &= \{(\{x_{vv}\}, v) \mid v \in VAL\} \\
\mathcal{F}(c?) &= \{(\{c?v\}, v) \mid v \in VAL\} \\
\mathcal{F}(c!) &= \{(\{c!v\}, v) \mid v \in VAL\} \\
\mathcal{F}(\texttt{const}) &= \{(\emptyset, \texttt{const})\} \\
\mathcal{F}(\texttt{expr}_1 \, op \, \texttt{expr}_2) &= \{(\alpha_1 \cup \alpha_2, v_1 \, op \, v_2) \mid i = 1, 2 : \ (\alpha_i, v_i) \in \mathcal{F}(\texttt{expr}_i)\} \\
\mathcal{F}(op \, \texttt{expr}) &= \{(\alpha, op \, v) \mid (\alpha, v) \in \mathcal{F}(\texttt{expr})\}
\end{aligned}
$$

Table 6: The semantics $\mathcal{F}(\texttt{expr})$ of an expression $\texttt{expr}$

pre-/post-values of the plain variables occurring in $\texttt{expr}$, and communicated values for its channel variables, such that the value of the expression becomes $\mathbf{T}$. Some examples are shown in Figure 4. In general, we define the Box expression of a command $\texttt{com}$ as a choice construct as follows:

$$
E(\langle \texttt{expr} \rangle) = \Box \{\alpha \mid (\alpha, \mathbf{T}) \in \mathcal{F}(\texttt{expr})\}
$$

Finally, at the expression level, the semantics involves sets of pairs $\mathcal{F}(\texttt{expr}) = \{(\alpha, v) \mid \ldots\}$, where α is a multi-action and v is a value. The rationale is that the multi-action α is needed to 'produce' the value v. The definition is over the syntax of expressions; it is shown in Table 6.

It should be noted that in the semantics of an expression, transitions are introduced to cover *all* conceivable values, with no account of variable types. The effect is that type errors give deadlock due the removal of transitions when variables are scoped. It enhances, in our understanding, compositionality and conceptual simplicity; for instance, no concept of 'environment' is necessary.

5 An example

This section discusses Peterson's algorithm for the mutual exclusion of two processes [19], and the use of elementary structure theory of Petri nets in order to prove the mutual exclusion property of the system. Figure 5 shows the algorithm expressed in $B(PN)^2$.

Space prohibits presenting the Box obtained for this program (the curious reader is referred to [1]). It has 26 places and 35 transitions. We have done an experiment using first Milner's semantics of [16], Chapter 8, and then a generic approach using a similar net semantics for CCS as that of Olderog [18] or Taubner [24], obtaining a count of 107 places and 55 transitions. This discrepancy in size is a direct consequence of the use of multi-labels without which one has to introduce additional semaphores that are not actually present in the program. These yield much larger translations; in particular, places and transitions in the net sometimes have no natural correspondence to the program text. However, a natural correspondence, what we call the 'perspicuousness' of our semantics, is

$B(PN)^2$	Box expression	Petri Box
$\langle x' = {}'y$ $\wedge y' = {}'x \rangle$	$\{x_{00}, y_{00}\} \; \square \{x_{01}, y_{10}\}$ $\square \{x_{10}, y_{01}\} \; \square \{x_{11}, y_{11}\}$	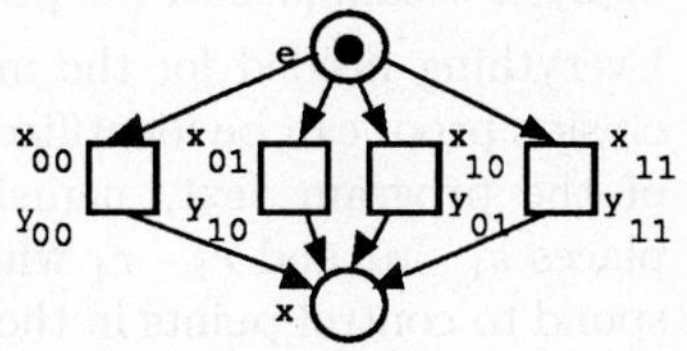
$\langle c?x'$ $\wedge y' = 1 \rangle$	$\{c?0, x_{00}, y_{01}\} \; \square \{c?0, x_{10}, y_{01}\}$ $\square \{c?0, x_{00}, y_{11}\} \; \square \{c?0, x_{10}, y_{11}\}$ $\square \{c?1, x_{01}, y_{01}\} \; \square \{c?1, x_{11}, y_{01}\}$ $\square \{c?1, x_{01}, y_{11}\} \; \square \{c?1, x_{11}, y_{11}\}$	Analogous (8 transitions)
$\langle \mathbf{T} \rangle$	$\emptyset$	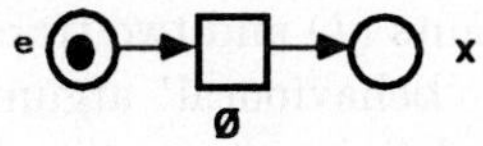
$\langle \mathbf{F} \rangle$	$\text{stop} = \square \emptyset$	

This assumes the declaration **var** $x, y : \{0, 1\}$; $c : $ **chan** 0 **of** $\{0, 1\}$.

Figure 4: Some examples of the translation of atomic commands

$$
\begin{aligned}
&\textbf{begin var } i^1, i^2 : \{0,1\} \textbf{ init } 0; \; t : \{1,2\} ; \\
&\quad \textbf{do} \quad \langle i^{1'} = 1 \rangle \; ;_{s_1} \; \langle t' = 2 \rangle \; ;_{s_2} \; \bigg\| \; \textbf{do} \quad \langle i^{2'} = 1 \rangle \; ;_{r_1} \; \langle t' = 1 \rangle \; ;_{r_2} \\
&\qquad \textbf{do} \langle i^2 = 0 \vee t = 1 \rangle \; ;_{s_3} \qquad\quad \textbf{do} \langle i^1 = 0 \vee t = 2 \rangle \; ;_{r_3} \\
&\qquad CS_1 \; ;_{s_4} \textbf{ exit} \qquad\qquad\qquad\quad CS_2 \; ;_{r_4} \textbf{ exit} \\
&\qquad \textbf{od} \; ;_{s_4} \qquad\qquad\qquad\qquad\quad \textbf{od} \; ;_{r_4} \\
&\qquad \langle i^{1'} = 0 \rangle; \textbf{ repeat} \qquad\qquad\quad \langle i^{2'} = 0 \rangle; \textbf{ repeat} \\
&\quad \textbf{od} \qquad\qquad\qquad\qquad\qquad\quad \textbf{od} \\
&\textbf{end}
\end{aligned}
$$

Figure 5: A $B(PN)^2$ program of Peterson's algorithm

of great benefit in applying Petri net analysis techniques to the program.

Everything needed for the mutual exclusion proof can be identified in terms of the program text, namely: some places s_1 - s_4 and r_1 - r_4 which correspond to control points in the program as indicated by annotating the semicolons; and the places $t = 1$ etc., which derive from the Data Boxes for the variables (t^0 is the entry place). We employ the following sets of places, three S-invariants (I) and two traps (Q) [22] and, as 'behavioural' arguments, use only the defining properties: 'the token count on an S-invariant remains constant' and 'a trap cannot be emptied of tokens'.

$$
\begin{aligned}
I_t &= \{t^0, t = 1, t = 2\} \\
I_s &= \{i^1 = 0, s_1, s_2, s_3, s_4\} \\
I_r &= \{i^2 = 0, r_1, r_2, r_3, r_4\} \\
Q_1 &= \{i^1 = 0, s_1, t = 2, r_2\} \\
Q_2 &= \{i^2 = 0, r_1, t = 1, s_2\}.
\end{aligned}
$$

I_t stems from a Data Box, and is therefore syntactically derivable from the structure of the Box. I_s and I_r are 'local' in the sense that each of them comprises a sequential process together with its local variable; this corresponds to what is otherwise known as a 'local assertion'. The necessary 'global' reasoning is achieved by means of the two traps Q_1 and Q_2.

Proof of the mutual exclusion property, by contradiction. Suppose a state (marking) M is reachable from the initial state M_e and $M(s_3) = 1 = M(r_3)$ (i.e., the mutual exclusion property is violated at M). By the S-invariants I_s and I_r, by the fact that both have exactly one token under M_e and by the S-invariant property, it follows that

$M(i^1 = 0) = 0 = M(i^2 = 0)$. The S-invariant I_t tells us that either $M(t = 1) = 0$ or $M(t = 2) = 0$ (or both). In the first case, the trap Q_2 is unmarked under M, and in the second case, the trap Q_1 is unmarked under M. Using the trap property, this contradicts the fact that none of the two traps is unmarked under M_e. ∎

This example illustrates some points about Petri net indigenous proof techniques, particularly the use of local states in the net model, and the use of deriving general behavioural properties from analysis of the net structure; and also the ability to apply Petri net methods without the need to visualise the net involved (although the net can be helpful). In this case the traps and invariants came from an understanding of the intent of the algorithm, and they are easily checked on the Box for the program. However there are well-established Petri net tools [23] to automatically identify invariants and traps, or to check those which might be hypothesised. It is generally important that this is done purely on the structure of the net, without the combinatorial explosion of checking all possible behaviours which is prohibitive when larger programs are considered. Also such proofs can be guided by an exploitation of the fast automatic model checking technique described in [4].

6 Discussion

The Box calculus has been developed in order to make Petri nets amenable to composition / decomposition, and in order to bring their general programming language semantics capabilities to the fore. $B(PN)^2$ is an experimental superstructure built on top of the Box calculus which has been designed with two aims in mind:

(1) To flexibly allow the expression of a variety of different algorithms designed for various different architectures, without deviating too much from traditionally known programming.

(2) To guarantee a semantics which is firmly based on Petri nets, but still has all the nice properties (for instance compositionality) one expects (and we would add: are necessary) of a semantics useful for verification.

The latter is particularly to facilitiate the application to programs of Petri net analyis techniques, as illustrated by the example which gives an new correctness proof for Peterson's algorithm. In another piece of work, an indigenous Box calculus proof method has been applied to a new algorithm for Triple Modular Redundancy systems which makes essential use of the capability for multiple synchronisation at the programming language level, as in e.g. $\langle a? = x' \wedge b? = x' \rangle$, to only accept a value from a source if two sources provide it [12]. In future work, $B(PN)^2$ needs also to be provided with an indigenous logic, for which we hope to be able to resort to recent work on partial order based temporal logics [7].

Despite the fact that, as we claim, our translation yields a 'perspicuous' semantics, the size of the net to which a program is translated becomes an issue if one wishes to use the translation with automated Petri net tools. While the translation given here will for some programs yield an infinite net[1], there is also a high level Petri net version of the Box calculus [8] which can alternatively be used and yields a finite (but possibly unbounded) net for all Box expressions produced by the language semantics, even if recursion is included in the language.

Our immediate plans for $B(PN)^2$ is for it to be the high-level input language for a programming environment which comprises (a) a semantical tool to create the Box associated with a $B(PN)^2$ program; (b) tools to create its partial order and other semantics; and (c) a model checker. These developments are planned to be carried out within the coming two years in the framework of a DFG project called *PEP* (*P*etri net based *E*nvironment for *P*rogramming).

Acknowledgements

The authors would like to thank the anonymous reviewers for their detailed comments. This work has been done within the Esprit BR-A 3148 DEMON (Design Methods Based on Nets) and the Esprit BR-WG 6067 CALIBAN (Causal Calculi Based on Nets).

References

[1] E.Best, R.Devillers and J.G.Hall: The Petri Box Calculus: a New Causal Algebra with Multiway Communication. Advances in Petri Nets 1992 (ed. G.Rozenberg), 21-69, Springer-Verlag Lecture Notes in Computer Science Vol.609 (1992).

---

[1] if there is a variable with infinite type or a channel with infinite capacity or infinite type.

[2] L.Cherkasova and V.Kotov: Descriptive and Analytical Process Algebras. Advances in Petri Nets 89 (ed. G.Rozenberg), Springer-Verlag Lecture Notes in Computer Science Vol. 424, 77-104 (1989).

[3] P.Degano, R.De Nicola and U.Montanari: A Distributed Operational Semantics for CCS Based on C/E Systems. Acta Informatica 26 (1988).

[4] J.Esparza: Fast Model Checking Using Branching Processes. Hildesheimer Informatikbericht 14/92 (October 1992). An abridged version appears in Proc. of TAPSOFT-93 (1993).

[5] F.Feldbrugge: Petri Net Tool Overview 1989. Advances in Petri Nets 1989 (ed. G.Rozenberg), Springer-Verlag Lecture Notes in Computer Science, Vol.424, 151-178 (1990).

[6] U.Goltz: On Representing CCS Programs by Finite Petri Nets. Proc. MFCS-88, Springer-Verlag Lecture Notes in Computer Science Vol.324, 339-350 (1988).

[7] U.Goltz, R.Kuiper and W.Penczek: Propositional Temporal Logics and Equivalences. Proc. of CONCUR-92,Springer-Verlag Lecture Notes in Computer Science, 222-236 (1992).

[8] J.G.Hall: Petri Boxes and General Recursion. In: DEMON Final Report, appears as GMD-Studie Nr.217 (1993).

[9] J.G.Hall, R.P.Hopkins and O.Botti: A Basic-Net Algebra for Program Semantics and its Application to occam. In 'Advances in Petri Nets 1992' (ed. G.Rozenberg), 179-214 (1992).

[10] E.C.R.Hehner: Predicative Programming Part I. Comm. of the ACM, Vol.27(2), 134-152 (February 1984).

[11] C.A.R.Hoare: Communicating Sequential Processes. CACM 21(8), 666-677 (1978).

[12] R.P.Hopkins: The TMR and Concurrent Queue Case Studies. In: DEMON Final Report, appears as GMD-Studie Nr.217 (1993).

[13] K.Jensen: Coloured Petri Nets. Springer-Verlag Lecture Notes in Computer Science Vol.254, 248-299 (1986).

[14] R.Janicki and P.E.Lauer: *Specification and Analysis of Concurrent Systems. The COSY Approach.* Springer-Verlag, EATCS Monographs on Theoretical Computer Science Vol. 26 (1992).

[15] D.May: occam. SIGPLAN Notices, Vol.18(4), 69-79 (April 1983).

[16] R.Milner: *Communication and Concurrency.* Prentice Hall (1990).

[17] T.Murata, B.Shenker and S.M.Shatz: Detection of ADA Static Deadlocks Using Petri Net Invariants. IEEE Transactions on Software Engineering, 15(3), 314-326 (1989).

[18] E.R.Olderog: Nets, Terms and Formulae. Habilitation (1989). Cambridge Tracts in Theoretical Computer Science (1991).

[19] G.Peterson: Myths about the Mutual Exclusion Problem. IPL Vol. 12/3, 115-116 (1981).

[20] U.Pletat: Algebraic Specifications of Abstract Data Types and CCS: an Operational Junction. Proc. of: 6th IFIP International Workshop on Protocol Specification, Testing and Verification, Montreal (1986).

[21] V.Pratt: Modeling Concurrent Systems with Partial Orders. Int. Journal of Parallel Programming, Vol.15(1), 33-71 (1986).

[22] W.Reisig: *Petri Nets: an Introduction.* EATCS Monographs on Theoretical Computer Science Vol.4, Springer Verlag (1988).

[23] P.H.Starke: PAN - a Petri Net Analyser (1992). Described in [5] as part of PSI-tool.

[24] D.Taubner: *Finite Representation of CCS and TCSP Programs by Automata and Petri Nets.* Springer-Verlag Lecture Notes in Computer Science Vol. 369 (1989).

[25] G.Winskel: A New Definition of Morphism on Petri Nets. Proc. STACS-84, Springer-Verlag Lecture Notes in Computer Science Vol.166, 150-150 (1984).

A CALCULUS OF VALUE BROADCASTS

K. V. S. PRASAD

March 15, 1993

ABSTRACT. Computation can be modelled as a sequence of values, each broadcast by one agent and instantaneously audible to all those in parallel with it. Listening agents receive the value; others lose it. Subsystems interface via translators; these can scramble values and thus hide or restrict them. Examples show the calculus describing this model to be a powerful and natural programming tool. Weak bisimulation, a candidate for observational equivalence, is defined on the basis that receiving a value can be matched by losing it.

1. INTRODUCTION

This paper presents a new version of a calculus of broadcasting systems, CBS [Pra91b], a CCS-like calculus [Mil89] with broadcast communication instead of handshake. No knowledge of older versions of CBS[1] is necessary, but familiarity with CCS will be helpful. [Pra91b] should be consulted for motivation of the communication model, discussion of design decisions, and comparison with CCS.

1.1. Preview. CBS agents evolve by transmitting (i.e., broadcasting), receiving, or losing data values. The expression o denotes the agent that transmits nothing, and whose only response to transmissions by others is to lose the transmitted value.

$$o \xrightarrow{5:} o$$

The expression $x? P$ denotes an agent that is *listening*. It *receives* any value v transmitted by the environment, and subsequently acts like the agent $P[v/x]$.

$$x? P \xrightarrow{5?} P[5/x] \qquad\qquad x? x! o \xrightarrow{6?} 6! o$$

The expression $5! Q$ denotes an agent that transmits the value 5 and subsequently acts like Q. This agent *loses* all values transmitted by others.

$$5! Q \xrightarrow{5!} Q \qquad\qquad 5! Q \xrightarrow{6:} 5! Q$$

Key words and phrases. Broadcast, parallel computation, distributed computing, process calculi, CCS, communicating processes, bisimulation, observational equivalence.

CR classification. F3.2 Semantics of Programming Languages—operational semantics; algebraic approaches to semantics; F3.1 Logics of programs

Author's address: Department of Computer Sciences, Chalmers University of Technology, S-412 96 Gothenburg, Sweden. *E-mail:* prasad@cs.chalmers.se.

[1] The version of [Pra91b] is referred to as Channelled CBS. The Patterned CBS that has been privately circulated is an intermediate version.

Transmission is *autonomous*, while reception and loss are both *responses* to transmissions by the environment, and are therefore controlled. Thus 5! 6! o will transmit 5 and then 6, while $x?(x+1)!$ o is stuck until its environment transmits (8, say), when it will reply (9).

There is no prefix corresponding to loss—there is no agent $v\!:\!P$.

Transmitted values are received or lost instantaneously by each of the agents composed in parallel with the transmitter. CBS uses synchronous cooperation in that every agent has to transmit or respond at every step. But transmissions cannot be combined, only interleaved. The expression $x?\,P\,|\,5!\,Q\,|\,y?\,y!$ o denotes a system of three agents in parallel. The derivations below show two possible evolutions, the first being a transmission by the system, and the second a response.

$$x?\,P\,|\,5!\,Q\,|\,y?\,y!\,\text{o} \xrightarrow{5!} P[5/x]]\quad Q|5!\,\text{o}$$
$$x?\,P\,|\,5!\,Q\,|\,y?\,y!\,\text{o} \xrightarrow{4?} P[4/x]|5!\,Q|4!\,\text{o}$$

Communication is synchronous: it takes place only if transmission and reception are performed simultaneously. But the transmitter does not wait for the receiver.

The composition of independently designed components is facilitated by *translation* and by *noise*. A translator ϕ is a pair of functions, $\phi^{\uparrow}$ and $\phi_{\downarrow}$. The agent ϕP transmits the value $\phi^{\uparrow}5$ if P transmits 5, and receives or loses 4 according as P receives or loses $\phi_{\downarrow}4$. Values are hidden and restricted by translation to noise by $\phi^{\uparrow}$ and $\phi_{\downarrow}$ respectively. Noise, denoted by the distinguished value τ, is always lost.

$$x?\,P \xrightarrow{\tau} x?\,P$$

$\tau?\,P$ is not part of the syntax of agents. Translating functions must map τ to τ.

2. THE SYNTAX AND OPERATIONAL SEMANTICS OF CBS

Assume a set $\mathbb{E}$ of data expressions containing a set of values $\mathbb{V}$ and a set of variables $\mathbb{X}$. Let v range over $\mathbb{V}$, x over $\mathbb{X}$, and e over $\mathbb{E}$. Let $\tilde{v}$ and $\tilde{x}$ be finite sequences of values and variables respectively. Let $e[\tilde{v}/\tilde{x}]$ denote the result of substituting $\tilde{v}$ for $\tilde{x}$ in e. Assume also that $\mathbb{E}$ contains a syntactic category of boolean expressions ranged over by b and taking values in $\{\text{tt}, \text{ff}\}$.

Assume $\tau \in \mathbb{E}$ but $\tau \notin \mathbb{V}$, and let $\mathbb{V}_{\tau} = \mathbb{V} \cup \{\tau\}$. Let w, w' range over $\mathbb{V}_{\tau}$. Let ϕ be a pair of functions $\phi^{\uparrow}$, $\phi_{\downarrow}: \mathbb{V}_{\tau} \to \mathbb{V}_{\tau}$ satisfying $\phi^{\uparrow}\tau = \tau$ and $\phi_{\downarrow}\tau = \tau$.

Let A range over agent constants. Then CBS agent expressions are given by

$$P ::= \text{o} \;\Big|\; x?\,P \;\Big|\; e!\,P \;\Big|\; P + P \;\Big|\; \text{if } b \text{ then } P \text{ else } P \;\Big|\; A\,(\tilde{v}) \;\Big|\; \phi P \;\Big|\; P\,|\,P$$

Occurrences of x in P become *bound* in the prefix term $x?\,P$, and the scope of x in $x?\,P$ is P. Bound variables are assumed to be renamed as necessary to avoid clashes under substitution. Let $fv(P)$ denote the set of free variables in P. For example, $fv(x!\,\text{o}) = \{x\}$. An agent P is *closed* if $fv(P) = \emptyset$. Thus $x?\,x!\,\text{o}$ is a closed agent but $x!\,\text{o}$ is not. The set of all agents is denoted $\mathbb{P}$, and the set of closed agents $\mathbb{P}_{cl}$. The substitution of data expressions for data variables extends from $\mathbb{E}$ to $\mathbb{P}$ in the evident way.

Agent constants are declared in definitions of the form

$$A\,(\tilde{x}) \stackrel{\text{def}}{=} P$$

Operator	Transmit	Receive	Lose[1]
$\circ$			$\circ \xrightarrow{w:}$
Listen		$x? P \xrightarrow{v?} P[v/x]$	$x? P \xrightarrow{\tau:}$
Transmit	$w! P \xrightarrow{w!} P$		$w! P \xrightarrow{w':}$
Sum[2]		$\dfrac{P_1 \xrightarrow{w\natural} P_1'}{P_1 + P_2 \xrightarrow{w\natural} P_1'}$	$\dfrac{P_1 \xrightarrow{w:} \quad P_2 \xrightarrow{w:}}{P_1 + P_2 \xrightarrow{w:}}$
Branch[3]		$\dfrac{P_1 \xrightarrow{w\natural} P_1'}{\text{if tt then } P_1 \text{ else } P_2 \xrightarrow{w\natural} P_1'}$	$\dfrac{P_1 \xrightarrow{w:}}{\text{if tt then } P_1 \text{ else } P_2 \xrightarrow{w:}}$
Define $A(\tilde{x}) \overset{\text{def}}{=} P$		$\dfrac{P[\tilde{v}/\tilde{x}] \xrightarrow{w\natural} P'}{A(\tilde{v}) \xrightarrow{w\natural} P'}$	$\dfrac{P[\tilde{v}/\tilde{x}] \xrightarrow{w:}}{A(\tilde{v}) \xrightarrow{w:}}$
Translate	$\dfrac{P \xrightarrow{w!} P'}{\phi P \xrightarrow{\phi^\uparrow w!} \phi P'}$	$\dfrac{P \xrightarrow{\phi_\downarrow w\flat} P'}{\phi P \xrightarrow{w\flat} \phi P'}$	

Operator	Transmit	Receive	Lose[1]
Compose[4]	$\dfrac{P_1 \xrightarrow{w\natural_1} P_1' \quad P_2 \xrightarrow{w\natural_2} P_2'}{P_1 \mid P_2 \xrightarrow{w(\natural_1 \bullet \natural_2)} P_1' \mid P_2'} \quad \natural_1 \bullet \natural_2 \neq \bot$		$\begin{array}{c|ccc} \bullet & ! & ? & : \\ \hline ! & \bot & ! & ! \\ ? & ! & ? & ? \\ : & ! & ? & : \end{array}$

[1] $P \xrightarrow{w:}$ is an abbreviation for $P \xrightarrow{w:} P$.

[2] There is a symmetric $\natural$ rule. Note that $\natural \in \{!, ?\}$, $\sharp \in \{!, ?, :\}$, and $\flat \in \{?, :\}$.

[3] There are similar rules for if ff then P_1 else P_2.

[4] $\bot$ means "undefined" in the synchronisation algebra (boxed) for $\bullet$.

TABLE 1. Transition rules for closed agents

where $\tilde{x} = x_1, \ldots, x_n$ and it is assumed that $fv(P) \subseteq \{x_1, \ldots, x_n\}$. The scope of the parameters $\tilde{x}$ is P. In these definitions, assume that A does not occur in P except as a prefixed subexpression: that is, assume that recursion is guarded. Definitions may be mutually recursive. An *agent* is a term containing no undefined agent names. Dealing with such agent variables is standard, and is largely ignored in this paper. An *open* agent here is one with free data variables.

The actions of transmitting, receiving and losing the value w are denoted by $w!$, $w?$ and $w:$ respectively. It is convenient to use variables that range over punctuation. Let $\natural$ range over $\{!, ?\}$, $\sharp$ over $\{!, ?, :\}$ and $\flat$ over $\{?, :\}$. Punctuation variables are treated in the same way as other variables: thus if $v\natural$ and $v'\natural$ both occur in the same context, they can stand for $v?$ and $v'?$, or for $v!$ and $v'!$ but not for $v!$ and $v'?$. This last pair is an instance of $v\natural_1$ and $v'\natural_2$.

The operational semantics of closed agents is presented in Table 1. Open agents perform no actions. The first two sum rules, the first branch rule, and the first define rule apply to both transmission and reception. The second translate rule applies to both reception and loss, and the compose rule to all three kinds of action. Note that $\phi^\uparrow w\sharp$ and $\phi_\downarrow w\sharp$ mean unambiguously $(\phi^\uparrow w)\sharp$ and $(\phi_\downarrow w)\sharp$.

2.1. Properties of the transition system. Let $\equiv$ denote syntactic equality. Let $P \xrightarrow{w\natural}$ abbreviate "there exists P' such that $P \xrightarrow{w\natural} P'$", and let $P \xrightarrow{w\natural}\!\!\!\!\!/$ abbreviate "there is no P' such that $P \xrightarrow{w\natural} P'$". The first proposition below has been anticipated by the abbreviation $P \xrightarrow{w:}$ for $P \xrightarrow{w:} P$.

PROPOSITION 1. *If* $P \xrightarrow{w:} P'$ *then* $P \equiv P'$. $\square$

PROPOSITION 2. $P \xrightarrow{w:}$ *iff* $P \xrightarrow{w?}\!\!\!\!/$. $\square$

The proofs are by induction on the structure of P. Note that neither $P \equiv P_1 \mid P_2$ nor $P \equiv P_1 + P_2$ can lose a value unless both P_1 and P_2 can. Also, $x? \, P \xrightarrow{\tau?}\!\!\!\!/$.

Replacing losses by the predicate "cannot receive a" yields essentially the same calculus. A transition system with negative premises is well defined if these can be derived first, independently of the positive transitions [Gro90]. Losses are similar.

PROPOSITION 3. *The relation* $\xrightarrow{w:}$ *is independent of* $\xrightarrow{w'!}$ *and* $\xrightarrow{v?}$. $\square$

PROPOSITION 4. $\forall P$, *the set* $\{w \mid P \xrightarrow{w!}\}$ *is finite.*

Proof. By induction on the structure of P. There are only finite sums in CBS. $\square$

PROPOSITION 5 (IMAGE FINITE). $\forall P, w$, *the set* $\{P' \mid P \xrightarrow{w\natural} P'\}$ *is finite.*

Proof. By induction on the structure of P. The result has already been proved for losses. Again, it is important that sums are finite. For $P_1 \mid P_2$, there are several cases to consider. For example, $w!$ can be the result of $P_1 \xrightarrow{v!} P_1'$ and $P_2 \xrightarrow{v?} P_2'$. There are only finitely many P_1' and P_2', by induction hypothesis.

For $\phi P \xrightarrow{w!} \phi P'$, we have to consider all v such that $\phi^\dagger v = w$. But there are only finitely many such v's, by the previous proposition. $\square$

Design notes. Let $A \stackrel{\text{def}}{=} x? \, A$. Then the usual recursion rule, if used also for losses, would allow $A \xrightarrow{\tau:} x? \, A$. The new rule, like that for conditional, prevents changes of state upon loss. The restriction to guarded recursion disallows $X \stackrel{\text{def}}{=} X$. Here X would do neither $v?$ nor $v:$.

Synchronisation between actions is possible only when they refer to the same transmission. $\mid$ is commutative and associative because $\bullet$ is. Interleaving is expressed as synchronisation between a $\natural$ action and a loss. Since any agent can do exactly one of $w:$ and $w?$, reception is enforced whenever possible.

3. STRONG BISIMULATION

The rest of this paper assumes that $\mathbb{V}$ does not contain $\mathbb{P}$, thereby restricting attention to a first order version of CBS.

DEFINITION 6 (STRONG BISIMULATION FOR CLOSED AGENTS). $\mathcal{R} \subseteq \mathbb{P}_{cl} \times \mathbb{P}_{cl}$ is a strong bisimulation if whenever $P\mathcal{R}Q$,
(i) if $P \xrightarrow{w\natural} P'$ then $\exists Q'$ such that $Q \xrightarrow{w\natural} Q'$ and $P'\mathcal{R}Q'$,
(ii) if $Q \xrightarrow{w\natural} Q'$ then $\exists P'$ such that $P \xrightarrow{w\natural} P'$ and $P'\mathcal{R}Q'$ $\square$

As in CCS, the largest strong bisimulation is an equivalence, denoted $\sim$.

The next lemma says that losses can be ignored when proving strong bisimulation. Thus losses are only significant in derivations when they contribute to transmission or reception.

LEMMA 7. *If* $\mathcal{R} \subseteq \mathbb{P}_{cl} \times \mathbb{P}_{cl}$ *is a relation such that whenever* $P\mathcal{R}Q$,
(i) if $P \xrightarrow{w\natural} P'$ *then, for some* Q', $Q \xrightarrow{w\natural} Q'$ *and* $P'\mathcal{R}Q'$,
(ii) if $Q \xrightarrow{w\natural} Q'$ *then, for some* P', $P \xrightarrow{w\natural} P'$ *and* $P'\mathcal{R}Q'$
then $\mathcal{R}$ *is a strong bisimulation.*

Proof. Suppose $P\mathcal{R}Q$ and $\mathcal{R}$ satisfies (i) and (ii). Now if $P \xrightarrow{w:} P$, then by Proposition 2, $P\xrightarrow{w?}\!\!\!\not\rightarrow$. Then $Q\xrightarrow{w?}\!\!\!\not\rightarrow$. Otherwise $P\xrightarrow{w?}$, since receptions are covered by the conditions on $\mathcal{R}$. By another application of Proposition 2, $Q \xrightarrow{w:} Q$. Similarly for the other direction. $\square$

DEFINITION 8 (STRONG BISIMULATION FOR OPEN AGENTS). Let $P, Q \in \mathbb{P}$ contain free variables $\tilde{x}$ at most. Then $P \sim Q$ if for all indexed sets $\tilde{v}$ of values, $P[\tilde{v}/\tilde{x}] \sim Q[\tilde{v}/\tilde{x}]$. $\square$

It is now possible to state that $P \sim Q$ implies $x?\,P \sim x?\,Q$. In fact,

PROPOSITION 9. $\sim$ *is a congruence for CBS*

Proof. By adapting the corresponding proof in [Mil89]. $\square$

DEFINITION 10. For any $\mathbb{L} \subseteq \mathbb{V}$, if the transmissions $w!$ of P and all its derivatives are such that $w \in \mathbb{L} \cup \{\tau!\}$ then P *has sort* $\mathbb{L}$, written $P:\mathbb{L}$. $\square$

Translating functions $\phi^\uparrow$, $\phi_\downarrow: \mathbb{V}_\tau \to \mathbb{V}_\tau$ can be extended to $\mathbb{E}$ in the evident way. Define $\phi \circ \psi$ to be the pair $\langle \phi^\uparrow \circ \psi^\uparrow, \psi_\downarrow \circ \phi_\downarrow \rangle$.

PROPOSITION 11 (STRONG BISIMULATION LAWS).
(1) *(a)* $(\mathbb{P}/\sim, +, o)$ *is a commutative monoid.*
    (b) $P + P \sim P$
(2) $(\mathbb{P}/\sim, |, o)$ *is a commutative monoid.*
(3) *(a)* $\phi\psi P \sim \phi \circ \psi P$
    (b) $\phi\ e!\,P \sim \phi^\uparrow e!\,\phi P$
    (c) $\phi(P_1 + P_2) \sim \phi P_1 + \phi P_2$
    (d) $\phi(P_1 \mid P_2) \sim \phi P_1 \mid \phi P_2$ *if* $\forall v \in \mathbb{L}_1 \cup \mathbb{L}_2$, $\phi_\downarrow \phi^\uparrow v = v$, *where* $P_1:\mathbb{L}_1$, $P_2:\mathbb{L}_2$
$\square$

3.1. Axioms for finite agents. The equations 1(a) and 1(b) of Proposition 11 constitute a complete axiom system for strong bisimulation, as they do for CCS. For pure CBS, the proof is identical to that of [Mil89]; this reflects the fact that strong bisimulation ignores the communication model. Value passing CBS needs in addition an inference system for reasoning about data [Hen91], but the process content of the proof is essentially the same. The standard form is

$$P \equiv \sum_{i=1}^{k} x?\,P_i + \sum_{i=1}^{l} w_i!\,P_i$$

where each P_i is also in standard form. By convention, the empty sum is o.

PROPOSITION 12 (EXPANSION THEOREM). *For* $r \in \{1,2\}$ *let*

$$P_r \equiv \sum_{i=1}^{k_r} v_{ir}! \, S_{ir} + \sum_{i=1}^{l_r} \tau! \, T_{ir} + \sum_{i=1}^{m_r} x? \, U_{ir}$$

Now let $r, s \in \{1,2\}$ *and* $r \neq s$. *Then*

$$P_1 \mid P_2 \sim \sum_{r,i,j} v_{ir}! \, (S_{ir} \mid U_{js}[v_{ir}/x]) + \sum_{r,i} \tau! \, (T_{ir} \mid P_s) + \sum_{r,i,j} x? \, (U_{ir} \mid U_{js})$$

where i *ranges from 1 to* k_r, l_r, *and* m_r *respectively in the three sums, and* j *ranges from 1 to* m_s. *If* $m_s = 0$ *then* j *takes the value 0. The convention is that* $U_{0s} = U_{0s}[v_{ir}/x] = P_s$. $\square$

4. WEAK BISIMULATION

DEFINITION 13 (WEAK BISIMULATION FOR CLOSED AGENTS). $\mathcal{R} \subseteq \mathbb{P}_{cl} \times \mathbb{P}_{cl}$ *is a weak bisimulation if whenever* $P\mathcal{R}Q$,
(i) *if* $P \xrightarrow{v!} P'$ *then* $\exists Q'$ *such that* $Q \xrightarrow{\tau!^* v! \tau!^*} Q'$ *and* $P'\mathcal{R}Q'$,
(ii) *if* $P \xrightarrow{\tau!} P'$ *then* $\exists Q'$ *such that* $Q \xrightarrow{\tau!^*} Q'$ *and* $P'\mathcal{R}Q'$,
(iii) *if* $P \xrightarrow{vb_1} P'$ *then* $\exists Q'$ *such that* $Q \xrightarrow{\tau!^* vb_2 \tau!^*} Q'$ *and* $P'\mathcal{R}Q'$
and similarly with P *and* Q *interchanged.* $\square$

The largest weak bisimulation is an equivalence, denoted $\approx$. Note that $v?$ and $v:$ match each other; both are silent responses to a $v!$ by the environment. In Law 1 below, the responses to a 5! are $o \xrightarrow{5:} o$ and $x? o \xrightarrow{5?} o$. Law 2 complements Proposition 11. If $\phi_\downarrow v = \tau$, a $v:$ on the left is matched by a $v?$ on the right.

PROPOSITION 14 (SOME WEAK BISIMULATION LAWS).

(1) $o \approx x? o$
(2) $\phi \, x? \, P \approx X$ *where* $X \stackrel{\text{def}}{=} x? \, if \phi_\downarrow x = \tau \, then \, X \, else \, \phi P[\phi_\downarrow x/x]$
(3) $\tau! \, v! \, P \approx v! \, P$
(4) $P \approx \tau! \, P + P$
(5) $\tau! \, P \approx \tau! \, P + P + x? \, P$
(6) $w! \, (P + \tau! \, Q) + w! \, Q \approx w! \, (P + \tau! \, Q)$ *and* $x? \, (P + \tau! \, Q) + x? \, Q \approx x? \, (P + \tau! \, Q)$

$\square$

$\tau!$'s are autonomous and unobservable as in CCS. But note that $\tau! \, P \not\approx P$ in general. See Ex. 6 in Table 2, which also gives other examples of $\not\approx$. Law 3 generalises to $\tau! \, P \approx P$ for any P with no $v?$ actions. This is the closest CBS gets to the CCS law $\tau. P \approx P$. Laws 4 and 5 are the closest to the second CCS τ law, $P + \tau. P \approx \tau. P$. Only the third CCS τ law holds for CBS (Law 6).

4.1. Weak congruence. $\approx$ is preserved by all the operators of CBS except $+$. Law 6 above is a congruence, but not Laws 1—5 (see Ex. 1, 7, 8 of Table 2). The largest congruence in $\approx$, denoted $\approx^c$, can be characterised operationally as for CCS by restricting matching options for the first transitions. This congruence is of questionable use, since no axiomatisation has been found yet. As with CCS, $\approx$ is often enough in practice, since specifications usually require a $|$ context, not a $+$ context. Further, if $P \approx Q$ then $w! \, P \approx^c w! \, Q$ and $x? \, P \approx^c x? \, Q$. But most important are the developments of [Pra93b], which suggest that $\approx^c$ is a non-issue.

	A	$\not\approx B$	Test	A	B
1.	$x?\,o + 3!\,o$	$\not\approx 3!\,o$	$1!\,3?\,\top$	*fails*	*may*
2.	$x?\,\text{if } x = 1 \text{ then } 3!\,o \text{ else } o \not\approx$ $x?\,\text{if } x = 2 \text{ then } 3!\,o \text{ else } o$		$1!\,3?\,\top$	*must*	*fails*
3.	$x?\,3!\,P$	$\not\approx 3!\,P$	$3?\,\top$	*fails*	*must*
4.	$1!\,2!\,o + 1!\,3!\,o$	$\not\approx 1!\,(2!\,o + 3!\,o)$	Equal by de Nicola-Hennessy testing $1?\,(2?\,\top \wedge 3?\,\top)$	*fails*	*may*
5.	$1!\,x?\,o + 1!\,3!\,o$	$\not\approx 1!\,(x?\,o + 3!\,o)$	$1?\,3?\,\top$ $1?\,(3?\,\bot \vee 2!\,3?\,\top)$	*may* *may*	*must* *fails*
6.	$\tau!\,x?\,x!\,o$	$\not\approx x?\,x!\,o$	$3!\,3?\,\top$	*may*	*must*
7.	$1!\,P + x?\,2!\,Q$	$\not\approx \tau!\,1!\,P + x?\,2!\,Q$	$1?\,\bot \vee 3!\,1?\,\top$	*fails*	*may*
8.	$x?\,x!\,o + 5!\,o + \tau!\,5!\,o$	$\not\approx x?\,x!\,o + 5!\,o$	$5?\,\top \wedge 3!\,3?\,\top$	*may*	*must*
9.	$x?\,x!\,o + \tau!\,x?\,x!\,o$	$\not\approx \tau!\,x?\,x!\,o$	$5!\,5?\,\top$	*must*	*may*

The atomic tests are $\top$ (success), $\bot$ (failure), $v!$ (may fail if the tested agent diverges, i.e., does an infinite sequence of transmissions), and $v?$ (succeeds if the tested agent does a $v!$, possibly preceded and followed by $\tau!$'s, and fails if it transmits any other value first, or diverges, or deadlocks).

TABLE 2. Examples of testing for $\not\approx$

4.2. Hennessy-Milner Logic.

The modal characterisation theorem [Mil89] of weak bisimulation in terms of Hennessy-Milner Logic goes through with the following definition of satisfaction for the $\langle w \sharp \rangle$ operator.

$$P \models \langle v! \rangle A \quad \text{iff for some } P', \quad P \xrightarrow{\tau!^* v!\tau!^*} P' \quad \text{and } P' \models A$$
$$P \models \langle \tau! \rangle A \quad \text{iff for some } P', \quad P \xrightarrow{\tau!^*} P' \quad \text{and } P' \models A$$
$$P \models \langle v\flat_1 \rangle A \quad \text{iff for some } P', \quad P \xrightarrow{\tau!^* v\flat_2\tau!^*} P' \quad \text{and } P' \models A$$

4.3. Alternative definitions of $\approx$.

The weak bisimulation of [Pra91a] allows τ's only before a matching transmission, and none surrounding a matching response. $\approx$ then differs from the present relation in some cases (e.g., Laws 5 and 6 fail), but agrees in most. The advantage is that losses can be ignored in the reasoning (e.g., in Ex. 6 of Table 2). But are Laws 3 and 5 desirable? Characterising weak bisimulation as a testing equivalence [Abr87] would settle the issue formally. This is yet to be done. Table 2 is a start.

5. CHANNELS, GUARDS AND SUMS

Let π_i be patterns, and v/π be the substitution that results from matching v against π. Then the construct

$$x?\,\text{case } \pi_1 \colon P_1 \text{ or } \pi_2 \colon P_2 \text{ or } \ldots \text{ else } P \text{ end}$$
$$\stackrel{\text{def}}{=} x?\,\text{if } x \text{ matches } \pi_1 \text{ then } P_1[x/\pi_1] \text{ else if } x \text{ matches } \pi_2 \text{ then } P_2[x/\pi_2] \text{ else } \ldots P$$

approximates the $\sum_i \pi_i?\,P_i$ of Patterned CBS, where $\pi?\,P$ is a primitive.

$$\pi?\,P \xrightarrow{v?} P[v/\pi] \text{ if } v \text{ matches } \pi \qquad \pi?\,P \xrightarrow{v:} \pi?\,P \text{ if } v \text{ does not match } \pi$$

Examples below show that the approximation is only $\approx$, not $\approx^c$ or $\sim$, but the greater expressive power of Patterned CBS seems not to be necessary for programming.

Channelled CBS [Pra91b] offers only the patterns $\langle a, v \rangle$ where a is a channel, and v a value. Pure CBS restricts further to patterns a; [Pra91b] interprets these traditionally as channels without values. A better interpretation is that $3? P$ awaits a 3 on a single (unnamed) channel, and loses everything until then.

EXAMPLE 15. [Input guards] Below, $X (3, P) \approx 3? P$ and $Y \approx 3? P + 4? Q$.

$$X (v, p) \stackrel{\text{def}}{=} x? \text{ case } v : p \text{ else } X (v, p) \text{ end}$$

$$Y \stackrel{\text{def}}{=} x? \text{ case } 3 : P \text{ or } 4 : Q \text{ else } Y \text{ end}$$

But $3? P + 4? Q \xrightarrow{3?} R$ implies $R \equiv P$, whereas $X (3, P) + X (4, Q) \xrightarrow{3?} X (4, Q)$. Also $Y + 2! \circ \xrightarrow{5?} Y$ but $3? P + 4? Q + 2! \circ \xrightarrow{5?}$. The approximation is not $\approx^c$. □

EXAMPLE 16. [Channels] Suppose $\mathbb{V}$ consists of two types of integers, "ordinary" $\langle \text{Ord}, n \rangle$ and "tagged" $\langle \text{Tag}, n \rangle$. Y below is a Patterned CBS agent.

$$Y \stackrel{\text{def}}{=} \langle \text{Tag}, x \rangle? \langle \text{Tag}, 2 * x \rangle! Q$$

$$X \stackrel{\text{def}}{=} x? \text{ case } \langle \text{Tag}, n \rangle : \langle \text{Tag}, 2 * n \rangle! Q \text{ else } X \text{ end}$$

$P \stackrel{\text{def}}{=} x? (2 * x)! Q'$ $\phi \uparrow \stackrel{\text{def}}{=} \{ n \mapsto \langle \text{Tag}, n \rangle \}$ $\phi \downarrow \stackrel{\text{def}}{=} \{ \langle \text{Tag}, n \rangle \mapsto n, \langle \text{Ord}, n \rangle \mapsto \tau \}$

Then $X \approx Y$. The agent ϕP offers a better solution under a constraint: $\phi P \sim Y$, but only if $\phi Q' \sim Q$. Translating functions are specified by their graphs. They are taken to leave values unchanged except if otherwise specified. □

5.1. A simplified CBS. [Pra93b], which deals with an implementation of CBS, also replaces $+$ by a guarded sum construct with the input pattern $x?$ and a finite number of output guards. This permits loss and reception to be identified. The $x?$ case end construct then approximates a sum of patterns up to $\sim$. Further, the definition of $\approx$ is then exactly that of CCS, and Laws 1 and 6 of Proposition 14 hold for $\sim$. Lastly, $\approx$ is preserved by guarded sums, and is a congruence.

These radical advantages depend on the assumption, supported by experience with CBS so far, that $x? P + v! Q$ (timeout) is the only kind of sum needed in programming. Sums of output guards are still needed for reasoning; consider the expansion of $3! P | 4! Q$. The non-determinism in $3! P | 4! Q$ can be seen as arising from different speeds of computation in parallel components. By contrast, the non-determinism in $x? P + y? Q$ seems hard to motivate. It is not clear whether both are needed in a specification language.

6. PROGRAMMING EXAMPLES

6.1. Milner's scheduler. Agents P_i, $i \in 1 .. n$, each perform a task repeatedly, and are to be scheduled cyclically by signals $\langle \text{Go}, i \rangle$. The end of each task is signalled by $\langle \text{Done}, i \rangle$. The specification of the scheduler is

$$S (i, X) \text{ if } i \in X \stackrel{\text{def}}{=} x? \text{ case } \langle \text{Done}, j \rangle : S (i, X - \{ j \}) \text{ else } S (i, X) \text{ end}$$

$$S (i, X) \text{ if } i \notin X \stackrel{\text{def}}{=} x? \text{ case } \langle \text{Done}, j \rangle : S (i, X - \{ j \}) \text{ else } S (i, X) \text{ end}$$
$$+ \langle \text{Go}, i \rangle! S (i + 1, X \cup \{ i \})$$

Here i says whose turn it is, and X is the set of active agents; $i + 1$ and $i - 1$ below are calculated modulo n. This is close to Milner's specification [Mil89].

The scheduler can be implemented as a set of cells A_i, which schedule their respective wards and then wait for $\langle \text{Done}, i \rangle$ and $\langle \text{Go}, i-1 \rangle$ to happen in either order. To start with, only A_1 is ready to schedule its ward; the others wait for scheduling signals. Since no agents are active as yet, there cannot be any termination signals.

$$A_i \stackrel{\text{def}}{=} \langle \text{Go}, i \rangle! \, B_i$$

$$B_i \stackrel{\text{def}}{=} x? \, \textsf{case} \, \langle \text{Done}, i \rangle: D_i \, \textsf{or} \, \langle \text{Go}, i-1 \rangle: C_i \, \textsf{else} \, B_i \, \textsf{end}$$

$$C_i \stackrel{\text{def}}{=} x? \, \textsf{case} \, \langle \text{Done}, i \rangle: A_i \, \textsf{else} \, C_i \, \textsf{end}$$

$$D_i \stackrel{\text{def}}{=} x? \, \textsf{case} \, \langle \text{Go}, i-1 \rangle: A_i \, \textsf{else} \, D_i \, \textsf{end}$$

$$Sched \stackrel{\text{def}}{=} \phi \left(A_1 \mid \textstyle\prod_{i \neq 1} D_i \right) \text{ where } \phi_1 \stackrel{\text{def}}{=} \{ \langle \text{Go}, v \rangle \mapsto \tau \}$$

$\prod_{i \in I} P_i$ is a standard abbreviation for the parallel composition of P_i for $i \in I$. The difference from the CCS implementation is that the $\langle \text{Go}, i \rangle$ can be heard both by P_i and by B_i or D_i, so there is no need to relay the information by new signals. The following relation is a strong bisimulation, and so $Sched \sim S(1, \emptyset)$.

$$\left\{ \left\langle S(i, X), \phi \left(C_i \mid \textstyle\prod_{j \in X, j \neq i} B_j \mid \textstyle\prod_{j \notin X} D_j \right) \right\rangle \, \middle| \, i \in X \right\}$$
$$\cup \, \left\{ \left\langle S(i, X), \phi \left(A_i \mid \textstyle\prod_{j \in X} B_j \mid \textstyle\prod_{j \notin X, j \neq i} D_j \right) \right\rangle \, \middle| \, i \notin X \right\}$$

Because of the relaying, CCS has weak bisimulation here, and a proof by bisimulation upto bisimulation.

6.2. Broadcast sort. The specification for a sorting machine below is given in terms of lists xs of numbers. $\top$ is the end marker for the input list.

$$S(xs) \stackrel{\text{def}}{=} x? \, \textsf{if} \, x = \top \, \textsf{then} \, H(xs) \, \textsf{else} \, S(sort(x::xs))$$

$$H([]) \stackrel{\text{def}}{=} S([])$$

$$H(xs) \stackrel{\text{def}}{=} (hd \, xs)! \, H(tl \, xs)$$

$$S([]) \xrightarrow{5?} S([5]) \xrightarrow{8?} S([5,8]) \xrightarrow{7?} S([5,7,8]) \xrightarrow{\top?}$$
$$H([5,7,8]) \xrightarrow{5!} H([7,8]) \xrightarrow{7!} H([8]) \xrightarrow{8!} S([])$$

We consider only the case where all the numbers input by the user are distinct. The more general case needs a little more detail but is almost as easy.

$$Sorter \stackrel{\text{def}}{=} \phi(In(\bot, \top)) \text{ where } \phi^\uparrow = \{ \langle \text{out}, u \rangle \mapsto u \} \text{ and } \phi_\downarrow = \{ \langle \text{out}, u \rangle \mapsto \tau \}$$

$$In(l, u) \stackrel{\text{def}}{=} x? \quad \textsf{if} \, x = \top \, \textsf{then} \, Out(l, u) \, \textsf{else}$$
$$\textsf{if} \, l < x \, \textsf{and} \, x < u \, \textsf{then} \, In(l, x) \mid In(x, u) \, \textsf{else}$$
$$In(l, u)$$

$$Out(\bot, \top) \stackrel{\text{def}}{=} In(\bot, \top)$$

$$Out(\bot, u) \stackrel{\text{def}}{=} \langle \text{out}, u \rangle! \, o$$

$$Out(l, u) \stackrel{\text{def}}{=} x? \, \textsf{case} \, \langle \text{out}, l \rangle: Out(\bot, u) \, \textsf{else} \, Out(l, u) \, \textsf{end}$$

Broadcast sort is a parallelised insertion sort. The input so far is held in a sorted list, maintained by cells each holding a number u and a "link" l, the next lower number. Let $\bot$ and $\top$ be sentinel values, respectively less than and greater than all numbers. There is always exactly one cell with $l = \bot$, and exactly one with $u = \top$.

The next input number splits exactly one cell into two. At the end of input, output is initiated by the cell with $\bot$ transmitting its u. Each cell (l, u) changes to $(\bot, u)$ when it hears l, thus continuing output.

Let $augxs = [x_0, x_1, \ldots, x_n, x_{n+1}]$ be any list with at least two elements, and

$$Inaug(augxs) \stackrel{\text{def}}{=} \phi(In(x_0, x_1) \mid In(x_1, x_2) \mid \ldots \mid In(x_n, x_{n+1}))$$
$$Outaug(augxs) \stackrel{\text{def}}{=} \phi(Out(x_0, x_1) \mid Out(x_1, x_2) \mid \ldots \mid Out(x_n, x_{n+1}))$$
$$aug(xs) \stackrel{\text{def}}{=} [\bot] \mathbin{+\!\!\!+} sort(xs) \mathbin{+\!\!\!+} [\top]$$

where $\mathbin{+\!\!\!+}$ is list concatenation. The function aug sorts a list of numbers and decorates it with $\bot$ and $\top$. Then the relation

$$\{\forall xs, \langle S(xs), Inaug(aug(xs)) \rangle\} \cup \{\forall xs, \langle H(xs), Outaug(aug(xs)) \rangle\}$$

is a strong bisimulation. It proves that $S([]) \sim Sorter$.

6.3. The alternating bit protocol. Signals can be lost in CBS if the intended receiver is not listening. An alternating bit protocol can be used to achieve a measure of synchronisation between agents that do not wait for each other, rather than to deal with lossy media. In the CCS formulation, agents wait for a while and then timeout autonomously. In CBS, this is the natural behaviour of competing transmissions. The program below is a simplified version of that in [Mil89]—no media or timeouts—but the sequences of (re)transmission and acknowledgement are similar. Further, the sender manufactures the messages itself, rather than receive them from outside.

$$S(b, n) \stackrel{\text{def}}{=} \langle b, n \rangle! \, S(b, n)$$
$$+ x? \text{ case } b: \langle \bar{b}, n + 1 \rangle! \, S(\bar{b}, n + 1) \text{ else } S(b, n) \text{ end}$$

$$R(b) \stackrel{\text{def}}{=} b! \, R(b)$$
$$+ x? \text{ case } \langle \bar{b}, n \rangle: \langle relay, n \rangle! \, b! \, R(b) \text{ else } R(b) \text{ end}$$

$$SYS(b, n) \stackrel{\text{def}}{=} \phi(\langle b, n \rangle! \, S(b, n) \mid \bar{b}! \, R(\bar{b})) \text{ where } \phi^\uparrow \stackrel{\text{def}}{=} \{\langle relay, n \rangle \mapsto n, x \mapsto \tau\}$$
$$\text{and } \phi_\downarrow \stackrel{\text{def}}{=} \{x \mapsto \tau\}$$

$$Spec(n) \stackrel{\text{def}}{=} n! \, Spec(n + 1)$$

Then $SYS(parity(n), n) \approx Spec(n)$. This is an easy exercise, with the system settling down rapidly into a 4-state loop.

7. Conclusions, Related work, Future work

[Pra91b] had ports (channels), input guards, summation, restriction/hiding distinct from translation, and dealt with value passing only by encoding to the pure calculus. These concepts, carried over from CCS, are foreign to the physical model underlying CBS. [Pra91b] therefore gave unsatisfactory accounts of hiding/restriction; worse, it failed to discover the programming power in CBS.

This paper uses the natural model for broadcast that eludes [Pra91b], the single unnamed channel. This makes for elegance of notation: $e! \, P$ and $\pi? \, P$. Channels are seen as special kinds of structured values, and Pure CBS as the sub-calculus that uses only constant patterns $(3? \, P)$. More general patterns, and sums of input guards (i.e., $3? \, P + 4? \, Q$), can be mimicked up to $\approx$ by case analysis following the single pattern x?. Thus the absence of channels as a basic concept enables a smooth interface to functional programming. Other benefits are a natural generalisation to a higher order calculus (yet to be studied), and the formulation of hiding and restriction as translation to τ, thus simplifying the calculus.

[Pra93b], as yet seen as experimental, completes the development, permitting only sums with one input summand, $x? P$, and a finite number of output summands. This permits loss and reception to be identified. $\approx$ is then defined exactly as for CCS, and is a congruence. General patterns $\pi? P$ can be mimicked up to $\sim$.

CBS is natural and powerful; it expresses concisely several programs that would be tedious in CCS. It can handle problems, such as sorting, not tailor made for process calculi. More, it suggests a new paradigm of programming, though its range is unclear. [Pra93b] reports several other examples. Shortage of space precludes a comparison of CCS and CBS. Please see [Pra91b].

[Pra91b] had no definition of weak bisimulation. This has now been defined, and produces testing results that justify describing $\approx$ as observational equivalence.

Implementations. Several implementations for CBS exist [Pet93, Pra93b, Jon92]. Several examples, including those in this paper, have been run on them. All the implementations are small, and none need any change to the language they use, Lazy ML [AJ92]. That of [Pra93b] is less than two pages long, and seems capable of parallel implementation. It types the calculus simply but satisfactorily, within the ML type system. CBS thus compares well with the many other attempts [Hol83, GMP89, BMT92] to combine functional and concurrent programming.

Message priority. CBS separates autonomous actions from controlled ones, rather than manufacture autonomous τ's out of controlled actions as in CCS. Because of this, a prioritised version of CBS is easy to develop [Pra93a]. This compares favourably with the difficulty of putting priority into CCS [CH88].

I/O Automata. Input/output automata [LT87] use a model of computation tantalisingly similar to that of CBS. One difference is that I/O automata are *input enabled.* So are agents in [Pra93b], so that paper provides a process calculus formulation of I/O automata [Vaa91]. A technical difference is that models of I/O automata use quiescent and fair traces, not bisimulation.

Process calculi. The handshake model predominates overwhelmingly even though it appears incapable of distributed implementation [Sjö91] and is a low level primitive entailing very detailed code. Nor has it proved a fruitful paradigm for new algorithms. There is increasing willingness to look at other models. CBS offers one.

Algorithms. Broadcast has almost always been treated as something to be implemented rather than to be used. This is true of literature on hardware, on distributed systems and on algorithms. Even literature that describes it as a primitive [BC91] gives no examples of use. I had therefore re-invented the sorting algorithm in this paper, and several others, when I saw [HT92] and then discovered [YLC90] and [DK86]. This is clearly only a small field of research, but its neglect is sobering.

Future work. More examples are needed to establish the applicability of CBS and to test whether the language of [Pra93b] suffices. A parallel implementation has to be explored. Theoretical work includes the formulation of bisimulation as testing, efficient methods for checking bisimulation, axiomatisations, a study of higher order CBS and timed CBS, and the relation to other models such as I/O automata.

Acknowledgements. CBS has been developed over several years, and owes something to almost everyone I know in the field of concurrency, particularly at Chalmers.

REFERENCES

[Abr87]   Samson Abramsky. Observation equivalence as a testing equivalence. *Theoretical Computer Science*, 53, 1987.

[AJ92]   Lennart Augustsson and Thomas Johnsson. Lazy ML user's manual. Technical report, Department of Computer Science, Chalmers University of Technology, 1992.

[BC91]   Kenneth Birman and Robert Cooper. The ISIS project: Real experience with a fault tolerant programming system. *Operating Systems Review*, 25(2), April 1991.

[BMT92] Dave Berry, Robin Milner, and David Turner. A semantics for ML concurrency primitives. In *Symposium on Principles of Programming Languages*. ACM, 1992.

[CH88]   Rance Cleaveland and Matthew Hennessy. Priorities in process algebras. In *Symposium on Logic in Computer Science*. IEEE, 1988.

[DK86]   Rina Dechter and Leonard Kleinrock. Broadcast communications and distributed algorithms. *IEEE Trans. on Computers*, 35(3):418, Mar 1986.

[GMP89] Alessandro Giacalone, Prateek Mishra, and Sanjeev Prasad. Facile: A symmetric integration of functional and concurrent programming. *International Journal of Parallel Programming*, 18(2), 1989.

[Gro90]   J.F. Groote. Transition system specifications with negative premises. In *CONCUR '90*, 1990. Springer Verlag LNCS 458.

[Hen91]   Matthew Hennessy. A proof system for communicating processes with value-passing. *Formal Aspects of Computer Science*, 3:346–366, 1991.

[Hol83]   Sören Holmström. PFL: A functional language for parallel programming. Technical Report 7, Dept. of Computer Sciences, Chalmers Univ. of Tech., 1983.

[HT92]   Tzung-Pei Hong and Shian-Shyong Tseng. Parallel perceptron learning on a single-channel broadcast communication model. *Parallel Computing*, 18:133–148, 1992.

[Jon92]   Simon Jones. Translating CBS to LML. Technical report, Department of Computer Science, University of Stirling, 1992.

[LT87]   Nancy Lynch and Mark Tuttle. Hierarchical correctness proofs for distributed algorithms. Technical Report MIT/LCS/TR-387, Laboratory for Computer Science, Massachusetts Institute of Technology, 1987.

[Mil89]   Robin Milner. *Communication and Concurrency*. Prentice Hall, 1989.

[Pet93]   Jenny Petersson. Tools for CBS. Licentiate thesis, Department of Computer Science, Chalmers University of Technology, 1993. In preparation.

[Pra91a]   K. V. S. Prasad. Bisimulations induced by preorders on action sequences. In *Chalmers Workshop On Concurrency*, May 1991.

[Pra91b]   K. V. S. Prasad. A calculus of broadcasting systems. In *TAPSOFT'91 Volume 1: CAAP*, April 1991. Springer Verlag LNCS 493.

[Pra93a]   K. V. S. Prasad. Broadcasting with priority. Technical report, Department of Computer Science, Chalmers University of Technology, 1993.

[Pra93b]   K. V. S. Prasad. Programming with broadcasts. Technical report, Department of Computer Science, Chalmers University of Technology, 1993.

[Sjö91]   Peter Sjödin. *From LOTOS specifications to distributed implementations*. PhD thesis, Uppsala University, December 1991.

[Vaa91]   Frits Vaandrager. On the relationship between process algebra and input/output automata. 6th Annual Symposium on Logic in Computer Science, 1991.

[YLC90]   Chang-Biau Yang, R. C. T. Lee, and Wen-Tsuen Chen. Parallel graph algorithms based upon broadcast communications. *IEEE Trans. on Computers*, 39(12):1468, Dec 1990.

TRAPPER:
A Graphical Programming Environment
for Industrial High-Performance Applications

Christian Scheidler, Lorenz Schäfers
Daimler-Benz Research
Alt-Moabit 91b, D-1000 Berlin 21
scheid@b21.de, ljs@b21.de
Tel: (030) 39982-258
FAX: (030) 39982-107

Ottmar Krämer-Fuhrmann
GMD, German National Research Center for Computer Science
Schloss Birlinghoven, D-5205 Sankt Augustin
ok@gmdzi.de

Abstract

We present a graphical programming environment called TRAPPER™ (TRAffonic[1] Parallel Programming EnviRonment). TRAPPER supports the development of industrial applications which require high computing power. The programming environment is based on the programming model of communicating sequential processes. TRAPPER contains tools for the design, mapping, visualization and optimization of parallel systems. The *Designtool* supports a hybrid program development, where the parallel process structure is described using a graphical representation and the sequential behavior is described using textual representations. The configuration of the target hardware and the mapping of the application onto the configured hardware is supported by the *Configtool*. During run-time, the *monitoring-system* records software events like interprocess-communication and measures the computation and communication loads of the underlying hardware. The run-time behavior of the software is animated by the *Vistool*, the load behavior of the hardware is displayed by the *Perftool*. The first target systems are Transputer-based systems.

Keywords: Programming Environments, Industrial Applications, Scheduling, Run-Time Systems

1. Introduction

Parallel computing is accepted as the only technology which offers a long term possibility of improving the performance of computer systems. Parallel processing has been widely accepted in the field of numerical computing, but will also have a great impact in technical systems. To fulfill the ever increasing demands of a technological marketplace, the next generation of many products of the Daimler-Benz group will require high computing power.

In this paper we describe TRAPPER, a graphical programming environment that assists the programmer in developing application software for systems which use parallel

---

1. TRAFFONIC™ is a Daimler-Benz research program concerned with the use of electronics in traffic systems.

processing as a key technology for high computing power. The TRAPPER philosophy is to have the programmer explicitly specify the parallel structure of the application and to aid the programmer as much as possible in the various phases of the development life-cycle. TRAPPER is based on the programming model of communicating sequential processes, which is suited to a large class of industrial applications. A typically embedded system consists of sensors, a processing unit and some output devices. The sensor gathers data from the the outside world. The processing unit consists in general of cascaded processing blocks, which execute various operations on the data. The computation results are delivered to the output devices.

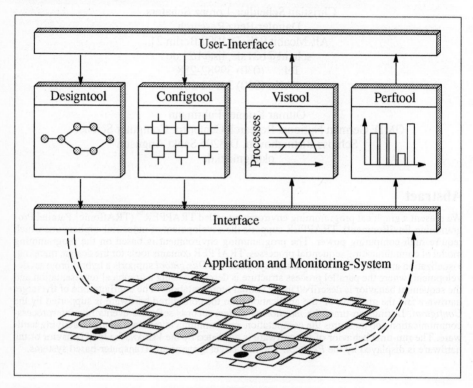

Fig. 1. TRAPPER components

Figure 1 shows the various TRAPPER components. With the *Designtool* the programmer specifies the process graph, where the nodes in the graph represent processes and the edges denote communication channels. The process graph describes the parallel structure of the application, independent from the target hardware. Each process is a sequential task having access to local memory only. Processes can communicate with each other by message passing constructs. The *Configtool* allows the user to specify the configuration of the hardware system and determines the mapping of the process graph onto the hardware. The *monitoring-system* collects run-time information about software-events like inter-process-communication and measures the computation and communication loads of the target hardware. All events are time stamped automatically and are stored in monitor files. Two different tools allow the visualization of the program execution. The *Vistool* enables program animation, i.e. the graphical display of execution phases, variable contents and application specific information. It is therefore useful during the debugging phase. The *Perftool* displays information about the hardware, i.e. load characteristics and scheduling information. It is especially suited during the optimization phase. Both tools allow not only on-line animation but also off-line animation, with stepping and backtracing facilities. Furthermore, they support the snapshot concept, which displays actual system states, as well as the visualization of dependencies between events on a time scale. The tool components reside on the host, currently a Sun Sparcstation. The tools are implemented in C++, using the InterViews [11] graphics library, which is based on the XWindow system. The monitoring-system is the only TRAPPER component running on the target hardware. The monitoring-system is implemented in C using the Inmos ICC-TOOLSET.

TRAPPER is under development within the Daimler-Benz research program TRAF-FONIC™ in cooperation with the GMD. In one of the TRAFFONIC projects, a parallel processor is being developed which can be embedded into vehicles. The machine will be based on Inmos T9000 and C104 technology, which enables parallel processing with virtual fully-connected networks. Peripheral boards realize the interface to a video system and the CAN-Bus. The TRAFFONIC system has a hardware driven central clock, which is important for the monitoring, i.e. time-stamped events. The tools developed in the context of TRAPPER will be used on this parallel processor. TRAPPER together with the parallel processor will be used as a universal development platform in a broad spectrum of high-tech applications covering the range from image and signal processing to control systems and artificial intelligence.

The current version of TRAPPER supports parallel embedded systems based on the avaiable Transputer technology (T2xx, T4xx, T8xx). A first release has been delivered to Mercedes-Benz vehicle research center and to other members of the Daimler-Benz group.

1.1 Related Work

Since the existence of parallel computers researchers have investigated the difficulties associated with the programming of parallel computers. Different architectures like SIMD and MIMD-machines make the situation even harder. Tools for parallel computers can be classified into systems which support *implicit* or *automatic* parallelization and systems which support *explicit* or *non-automatic* parallelization. SUPERB [16] is an example of a tool which supports automatic parallelization. In the SUPERB-project program transformation techniques applied on vector machines, are extended for distributed-memory MIMD-machines. TRAPPER belongs to the class of tools supporting explicit parallelism.

Tools supporting explicit parallelization can be further classified by their underlying programming model. Languages like C* or FORTRAN 9x are based on the *data-parallel* programming model and are well suited to numerical applications with regular data-structures. The benefit of the data-parallel programming model is the absence of multiple control flows, which leads to an easy but inflexible programming model. Currently, TRAPPER does not support the data-parallel programming model. The *process-parallel* programming models is more flexible, but the existence of multiple control flows raises new problems in the various program development tasks. There are several research activities dealing with design [1][2][13], mapping[3], debugging [9][10], animation [4][7] and optimization [5][9][14] [15] of parallel programs.

At the *design phase* the programmer has to describe the parallelism of the application. Text-oriented programming languages reflect the parallel structure of a program very poorly. Therefore, tools like HeNCE [1], Millipede [2], MP [13] and TRAPPER use graphical representations instead of textual representations to describe the parallelism. The tools differ in their graphical representations. In HeNCE graphs, nodes represent subroutines and arcs represent data-dependencies between subroutines. HeNCE graphs also include pipeling and conditional constructs and loops. MP, Millipede and TRAPPER use process graphs, where nodes represent processes and arcs represent communication channels.

The *mapping* of the application onto the target hardware is a task which does not exist in the traditional development cycle of sequential programs. A lot of research has been done in this area, a good survey is given in [3]. A comprehensive presentation of the Poker environment is given including algorithms for partitioning, placement and routing. TRAPPER supports automatic mapping. The underlying algorithm searches partitions of the process graph with a well distributed computation load and a small communication load between the partitions. The computation and communication loads have to be specified by the programmer.

The *debugging* of a parallel program with multiple control flows is difficult, because the traditional breakpoint approach cannot be applied. A breakpoint in one process can lead to different program behavior, thus hiding synchronization errors like deadlocks. LeBlanc [10] suggested a method called Instant Replay to overcome these difficulties. Events relevant to synchronization of processes are recorded in a tracefile. The tracefile is then used for a deterministic replay of the parallel program. In the replay phase, breakpoint debugging is possible, because the program is executed under control of the tracefile. Currently, Instant Replay is not supported by TRAPPER. The recording mechanism could be easily integrated into the TRAPPER monitoring-system, but it is questionable, how useful Instant Replay is in the context of embedded systems. A typical embedded system like a control application has real-time conditions, which makes breakpoint debugging nearly impossible.

Monitoring of the application and the underlying target hardware by the *monitoring-system* is necessary for the animation and optimization task. The monitoring-system is the only TRAPPER component running on the target hardware. Monitoring-systems can be implemented in hardware [4], software [12] and as a hybrid system [6]. Hardware monitors are inflexible and expensive, the main advantage is the minimal pertubation of the application software. Hybrid monitoring-systems use software routines to generate the monitoring data, collecting and storing of the monitoring data is carried out by extra hardware. Therefore, hybrid monitoring-systems are still very costly, if the target system is a parallel computer with a large number of nodes. The TRAPPER monitoring-system is a software monitoring-system. The monitoring-system is flexible, gathers events happening inside the transputer chip, which are not visible for a hardware monitor (e.g. process scheduling), requires no extra hardware and therefore, consumes less electric power[2].

Animation is crucial for the understanding of the run-time behavior of a parallel program. Parallel activities are better understandable if they are presented in a graphical way. ParaGraph [7] is a very popular visualization tool which can display trace data in different graphical forms including Gantt-Charts, Kiviat diagrams, communication diagrams and space-time diagrams. TRAPPER offers similar graphical features. It extends ParaGraph by using the process graph developed with the Designtool as the main animation surface. Thus, the animation is based on a structure which is familiar to the programmer.

Optimization is the last step in the software development cycle. It plays a major role in parallel processing, because performance is the main reason for parallel programming. An inefficient, but correct program, is of no practical use for execution on a parallel computer. Sequential profilers are of little help, because in a program with multiple control flows not all pieces of code are significant to the total execution time of the application. Therefore Miller [15] suggested a method called Critical Path Analysis (CPA) to find the parts of a parallel program, which are significant to the total execution time. CPA will be integrated into the TRAPPER environment. We believe, that CPA is also very helpful in

---

2. Electric power is a critical resource in the experimental car containing the TRAFFONIC parallel processor, although a second electric generator is provided. The number of nodes is only constraint by the available electric power.

the context of real-time programs, where deadlines should not be exceeded by the application. Relevant work in this area is also described [5][9][14].

2. The TRAPPER components

2.1 The Designtool

The *Designtool* supports a hybrid program development: The *parallel* structure of the application is described by a *graphical* representation (process graph), whereas the *sequential* components are described by *textual* representations (process code). The process graph consists of nodes and edges, where nodes represent processes and edges represent communication channels. Each process consists of a unique process identifier, a process type denoted by the process name and dedicated communication interfaces called ports. A port has name and a direction, possible directions are "bidirectional", "input" or "output".

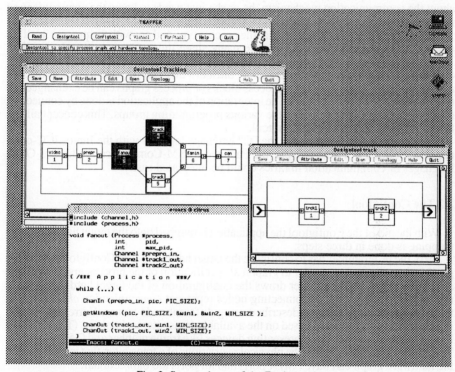

Fig. 2. Screen dump of the Designtool.

Large process graphs can be designed hierarchically as a composition of *subsystems*. A subsystem is a graphical building block and can be viewed as a black box, which contains a subgraph of the process graph. A subsystem itself can contain other subsystems. A process graph can be either designed top-down or bottom-up. Using the top-down approach, the application engineer describes the system as a composition of subsystems. Subsystems are split until they can be described as a composition of sequential processes. Using the bottom-up approach the application engineer first describes the sequential processes. Processes are then assembled to form subsystems.

A screen dump of the Designtool is given in figure 2. The upper left window shows the main TRAPPER control panel. The window under the control panel shows the activated Designtool with the (simplified) process graph of a TRAFFONIC-application "autonomous vehicle guidance ". In this example, the data in the process graph flows from left to right. Normal processes are represented by boxes with one frame and subsystems are represented by boxes with double frames. The right window shows an opened subsystem consisting of two processes. Ports are represented by squares lying at the frame of the subsystems.

The behavior of a process is described textually by the process code. The programmer selects a process in the process graph and activates a text editor. TRAPPER checks whether the associated code file exists and generates a process frame, if no process code exists. Then TRAPPER opens a text editor with the associated code file. In figure 1, the process code of the process `fanout` is showed in the lower left window. The `include`-statements and the parameter list are generated by the Designtool. The parameter list contains the channel parameter `prepro_in, track1_out, track2_out,` which correspond to the ports of the `fanout`-process box. The suffix `_in/_out` shows the direction of the corresponding port. The programmer does not need to know much details about the communication mechanism, he or she just needs to know the communication routines of the selected communication library.

The process code is associated with the process type and not with the process itself. In other words, processes having the same name share the same process code. By that, TRAPPER implicitly supports the single program multiple data (SPMD) approach. Additionally, each process has an "editable" attribute that can be used to lock processes against further editing. Pre-coded process blocks or process graphs can be exchanged between users in a software project. The integration of the application is done by connecting the process graphs, developed by the various programming groups. This concept allows to use TRAPPER as an integration tool.

Currently, TRAPPER supports the "C" language together with the Inmos ICC-communication library or alternatively, the Parsytec RTSM-Communication library. Other languages or communication libraries could be integrated easily.

2.2 The Configtool

With the aid of the Configtool the application is mapped onto the target hardware. The mapping is done in three steps.

First, the programmer has to configure the target hardware. The Configtool supports a graphical configuration similar to graphical specification of the process graph. With the aid of a graphics editor the user draws the configuration of the target hardware. Nodes represent *processors*, edges connecting nodes represent *communication channels*. Different processor types can be described using different node names. Currently, TRAPPER can configure systems based on the available transputer technology (T80x, C004). Predefined node types exist representing devices like frame grabber and CAN-Interface. The graphics editor considers the physical restrictions of a transputer, that is each node in the hardware graph can have only 4 ports and all ports are bidirectional.

In the second step, the application is mapped onto the configured hardware. The process graph builds the user-interface of the Configtool. The mapping can be done *manually* or *automatically*. In the manual mode, the programmer clicks on a node in the process graph and specifies the node number of the target processor. The mapping is visualized by coloring the process graph, where each color is associated with a dedicated processor. Subsystems can be mapped onto the same processor or distributed over different processor nodes. In the automatic mode, TRAPPER computes a mapping of the process graph. The TRAPPER mapping algorithm searches a partitioning of the process graph with a well distributed computation load and a small communication load between partitions. The computation and communication load has to be specified by the programmer by adding weights to the nodes and edges of the process graph. In general, only sub-optimal solutions can be found, because the underlying optimization problems (e.g. graph partitioning) belong to the class of NP-problems. The solution is displayed by coloring the process graph, processes mapped onto the same processor have the same color. The mapping computed by TRAPPER can be modified by the user if required.

In the third step, the monitoring-system has to be configured. The programmer specifies which software events (communication events, variable access events) and which hardware events (computation load, communication load) have to be monitored. By that, the programmer can control the overhead caused by the monitoring-system. The third step can be skipped, if no monitoring-system is required.

After finishing the previous steps, TRAPPER generates the configuration file needed by the underlying system software. Currently, TRAPPER generates configuration files for the Inmos ICC-TOOLSET and Parsytec's RTSM. For both systems, TRAPPER generates:

- the Inmos configuration file (cfs-file) , which textually describes the process graph, the hardware graph and the mapping,
- stub-files, which connect the process code with the Inmos cfs-file and
- the makefile, which can be finally activated to compile, link, collect and load the application.

The RTSM system software needs some additional configuration files which are also generated by the Configtool.

2.3 The Monitoring-System

The *monitoring-system* provides run-time information as input to the Vistool and the Perftool. The former needs information about the state of the application and the latter needs information about the state of the underlying hardware. The monitoring-system is the only component running on the target hardware and is therefore not as portable as the other TRAPPER components.

Currently we are developing a software monitoring-system for transputer-based systems (T80x, C004). It is based on the Inmos ICC-TOOLSET and the RTSM system software. As soon as the next transputer generation is available, the monitoring-system will be ported to the new target hardware (T9000, C104). A software monitoring-system is preferred to a hardware monitoring-system because:

- a software monitoring-system is more flexible than a hardware monitor
- a software monitoring-system can gather events (e.g. process scheduling) happening inside the transputer chip, which are not visible for a hardware monitor,
- a software monitor does not require extra hardware and consumes less electric power.

The main disadvantage of a software monitoring-system is intrusion. The monitoring-system consumes resources like CPU time and memory space. The application is slowed down and, even worse, the run-time behavior of the application is changed. Both effects are crucial in time-critical applications, where an activation of the monitoing-system may lead to a violation of timing constraints.

To cope with the slow-down effect, we chose a pragmatic approach by making the monitoring overhead controllable by the user. This is achieved by configuring the monitoring-system with respect to the granularity of observation. There is a direct relation between the level of detail in observation and the resulting costs. The more details the user wants to monitor, the more processor time has to be spent.

A configurable monitoring-system does not provide a solution to the second problem since even a slight degree of intrusion may change the application's run-time behavior. Instant Replay is a possible solution if the application has no real-time constraints. Events relevant to synchronization of processes are recorded in a tracefile. The tracefile is then used for a deterministic replay of the parallel program. In the replay phase, a detailed monitoring of the application is possible, because the program is executed under control of the tracefile. This mechanism is of no help if the application has real-time constraints. A violation of a deadline in the replay phase has to be interpreted as a erroneous program behavior.

The events are forwarded to the host by a subsystem of the monitor called *transport system*. The transport system can operate in synchronous and asynchronous mode. In synchronous mode the events are steadily passed on to the host, whereas in asynchronous mode they are buffered at the target nodes. Buffering is especially suitable for short monitoring periods and/or rarely occurring events. It can minimize network intrusion to zero. On the host, data is either directly used as input to the visualization- and Perftool (on-line animation) or written into a monitoring-file for off-line animation.

The implementation of the monitoring-system should not rely on the underlying hardware to provide portability. We chose different implementation levels for the different monitor parts:

- *Software-events,* like interprocess communication and variable access, are monitored using *source code instrumentation*, a language dependent implementation technique.
- *Systemload* like CPU and link load are measured by the system software (RTSM), which is a operating system dependent implementation technique.
- *Hardware-events* like process scheduling is implemented using a spy-process. The spy-process manipulates the process queue ("ready queue") of the transputer and records information about the next process to be executed. It then alters the queue links and thus is executed again, as soon as the next application process is descheduled. Monitoring using the spy-process is a hardware-dependent implementation.

2.4 The Vistool

The *Vistool* aids the observation of the run-time behavior of the application. It is integrated with the Perftool in such a way that a consistent view on the states of hardware and software components is offered. The Vistool supports the programmer in the analysis of the parallel algorithm by displaying run-time data of the application. This helps the user to understand the dynamics of distributed systems, gives debugging information, allows the detection of errors (i.e. deadlocks by the visualization of cycles of outstanding communication requests) and gives important information for code optimization.

The Vistool has on-line and off-line mode. In most real-time applications, the off-line mode is preferable. The events are collected in a monitoring-file which is read by the animation system. This decoupling of the animation from the execution allows the observation of the software events with a selectable time behavior. Additional features, like single stepping and backtracing are offered by TRAPPER, so that the programmer can drive the animation to the interesting program phases.

The Vistool has two different views, one which is based on the process graph and a second one which is based on the time scale. The process graph view is based on the graphical representation developed with the Designtool. The programmer can select between a variety of different animation features like coloring of nodes or edges, textures on nodes or edges, changing the line width or drawing arrows on the edges,displaying plots, histograms or rastered squares in the process boxes. The process graph animation can be used to display the process state, variable values or interprocess-communication. The time scale animation shows the same events in relation to a time scale. For a set of processes which can be selected interactively by the user, the states are displayed either as a moving curve or by a colored time bar. This animation represents communication operations also as arrows between processes at different time instants. This feature allows a very detailed insight to the cooperation of distributed processes and therefore enables the programmer to debug and optimize his program.

2.5 The Perftool

The *Perftool* supports the user in the optimization phase, which completes the software development after the design and debugging phases. The software developer gets hints on possible bottlenecks that are due to load imbalances. Use of the Perftool is tightly coupled to the use of the Vistool. An important task of the Perftool is then to find a relation between the behavior of the hardware and the software, e.g. to relate a non-satisfactory CPU load and a specific code segment which causes it.

Like the Vistool, the Perftool offers two different views: the first is based on the hardware graph, which has been designed using the Configtool, the second is based on time scaled charts. Within the hardware graph the CPU load and link load are shown by coloring the node symbols and link symbols. Animation of the hardware graph shows the whole parallel machine and gives a first, rough impression of its behavior. A more detailed insight can be gained with animations based on time scaled charts. Each chart shows the temporal behavior of the selected component. Included are visualization of CPU load, link load, scheduling information (Gantt chart) and Critical Path Analysis. Performance statistics are also provided. They include run-time, CPU utilization, communication overhead, speedup and efficiency of the application.

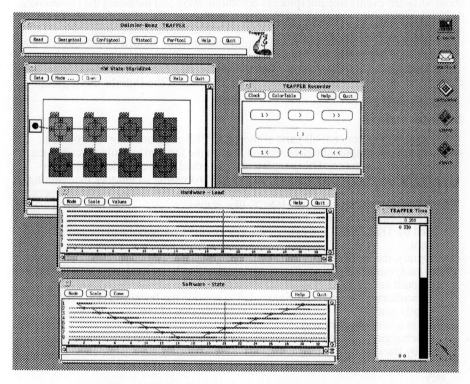

Fig. 3. Screen dump of the Perftool

Figure 3 shows the appearance of the Perftool. The upper right window shows the animation controller with interface similar to a tape recorder. Every display of the Vistool and the Perftool is controlled by this component. The animation controller supports single-stepping, normal replay and fast forward in both directions. The middle left window shows the animated hardware graph. The computation load is visualized by coloring the nodes and the computation load is animated by coloring edges. Below the hardware graph window, the computation load is additonaly displayed in a time scale chart. The vertical line shows the current time. Finally, the the lowest window represents the communication behavior of the application software in a message sequence chart.

3. Summary

We presented TRAPPER, a programming environment for industrial high performance applications. The TRAPPER philosophy is to have the programmer explicitly specify the parallel structure of the application. TRAPPER supports a hybrid program development, where the process structure is described using a *graphical representation* and the sequential behavior is described using *textual representations*. The process structure is specified by process graphs, where the nodes represent processes and edges represent communication channels. TRAPPER consists of tools which support the design, mapping, monitoring, animation and optimizing of parallel applications. With the aid of the *Designtool* the programmer specifies the process graph. The *Configtool* allows the user to specify the configuration of the hardware system and determines the mapping of the process graph onto the hardware. The *monitoring-system* collects run-time information about software-events like interprocess-communication and measures the communication and communication loads of the target hardware. The *Vistool* enables program animation, i.e. the graphical display of execution phases, variable contents and application specific information. The *Perftool* displays information about the hardware, i.e. load characteristics and scheduling information.

TRAPPER is an active research project. A first release has been delivered to the Mercedes-Benz vehicle research center and other members of the Daimler-Benz group.

4. Future work

Future activities concern all parts of the TRAPPER programming environment:
- Currently, the graphical representation used in the Designtool only describes the static process structure. Other representations could be used to describe the dynamic behavior of processes. Typical parallel processing techniques like farming, pipelining, etc. could be integrated as graphical building blocks. Possible representations could be Petri-Nets or HeNCE-like graphs.
- Other hardware platforms like Texas Instruments 320C40 systems will be supported by TRAPPER. The extensions concern the Configtool and the monitoring-system.
- Currently, the input data for the mapping algorithm (computation and communication load) has to be specified by the programmer. Alternatively, the load information could be extracted from the monitoring-file of a previous execution.
- The monitoring-system can be extended to provide the Instant Replay [10]. Therefore, all events which determine the synchronization of processes have to be monitored in a very efficient way.
- The debugging features of the visualization have to be extended. This could be done by integrating existing debuggers or by extending the on-line features of the Vistool. In both cases, the integration of the Instant Replay mechanism is necessary.
- Other forms of support like phase-behavior analysis [14] will be provided by the Perftool.

5. References

[1]   Adam Beguelin, Jack J. Dongarra, G.A. Geist, Robert Manchek and V.S. Sunderam. "Graphical Development Tools for Network-Based Concurrent Supercomputing". *Proc. of Supercomputing 1991*, Albuquerque.

[2]   M. Aspnäs, R.J.R. Back, T. Langbacka. "Millipede - A Programming Environment Providing Visual Support for Parallel Programming". *Proceedings of EWPC 1992, the European Workshops on Parallel Computing*, Barcelona, Spain.

[3]   Francine Berman. "Experience with an Automatic Solution to the Mapping Problem". In *The Characteristics of Parallel Algorithms*, MIT Press, 1987, pp. 307–334.

[4]   Thomas Bemmerl and Arndt Bode. "An Integrated Environment for Programming Distributed Memory Multiprocessors". In *EDMCC2, Proc. of the 2nd European Distributed Memory Computing Conference*, Munich, April 1991, LNCS 487, Springer-Verlag.

[5]   Cynthia A. Funk-Lea, Tasos D. Kontogiorgos, J.T. Robert, and Larry D. Rubin. "Interactive Visual Modeling for Performance". *IEEE Software*, Vol. 8, No. 5, Sep. 1991, pp. 58–68.

[6]   Dieter Haban and Dieter Wybranietz. "A Hybrid Monitor for behaviour and Performance Analysis of Distributed Systems". *IEEE Transactions on Software Engineering*, Vol. 16, No. 2, February 1990, pp. 197-211.

[7]   Michael T. Heath and Jennifer A. Etheridge. "Visualizing the Performance of Parallel Programs". *IEEE Software*, Vol. 8, No. 5, Sep. 1991, pp. 29–39.

[8]   L. Lamport. "Time, Clocks and the Ordering of Events in a Distributed System". *Communications of the ACM*, 21(7), 1978.

[9]   Thomas J. LeBlanc, John M. Mellor-Crummey, and Robert J. Fowler. "Analysing Parallel Program Executions Using Multiple Views". *Journal of Parallel and Distributed Computing*, Vol. 9, No. 2, June 1990, pp. 203–217.

[10]   Thomas J. LeBlanc and John M. Mellor-Crummey. "Debugging Parallel Programs with Instant Replay". *IEEE Transactions on Computers*, Vol. C 36, No. 4, April 1987, pp. 471–482.

[11]   Mark A. Linton, John M. Vlissides, and Paul R. Calder. "Composing User Interfaces with InterViews". *Computer*, 22(2):8–22, February 1990.

[12]   E. Maehle and W. Obelöer. "DELTA-T: A User-Transparent Software Monitoring Tool for Multi-Transputer Systems". *Proc. EUROMICRO '92*, Paris, Sept. 15-17, 1992.

[13]   Jeff Mangee and Narakner Dulay. "MP: A Programming Environment for Multicomputers". In *Proc. of the IFIP WG 10.3 on Programming Environments for Parallel Computing*, Edinburgh, Scotland, 6-8 April 1992.

[14]   Barton P. Miller et al. "IPS-2: The Second Generation of a Parallel Program Measurement System". *IEEE Transactions on Parallel and Distributed Systems*, Vol. 1, No. 2, April 1990, pp. 206–217.

[15]   C. Q. Yang, and B. P. Miller. "Critical path analysis for the execution of parallel and distributed programs" *Proceedings of the 8th International Conference on Distributed Computing Systems*, June 1988, pp. 366–375.

[16]   Hans Zima. "Supercompilers for Parallel and Vector Computers". ACM Press, Frontier Series, 1990.

Control and Data Flow Visualization
for Parallel Logic Programs
on a Multi-window Debugger HyperDEBU

Junichi TATEMURA, Hanpei KOIKE, Hidehiko TANAKA

{tatemura,koike,tanaka}@mtl.t.u-tokyo.ac.jp

Department of Electrical Engineering, The University of Tokyo

7-3-1 Hongo, Bunkyo-ku, Tokyo, 113 JAPAN

Abstract. A fine-grained highly parallel program has many threads of execution. The first task to debug it is comprehending the situation of the execution. For this task, it is important to visualize the execution. Our debugger HyperDEBU for a parallel logic programming language Fleng visualizes control / data flows of execution of a Fleng program according to a user's intention. Breakpoints are introduced as information which represents a user's intention or points of view. HyperDEBU uses this information to visualize execution of a program. HyperDEBU enables efficient debugging by its visual examining / manipulating facilities.

1 Introduction

When a program shows unexpected behavior, the first task for a programmer to debug it is comprehending the situation of the execution of this erroneous program. A programmer can debug a sequential program by tracing one thread of execution through some event filters. However, it is very difficult to trace a complicated structure composed of a large number of control and data flows of a highly parallel program. Even if he tries to trace some threads of these flows through an event filter, it is a hard problem to determine what should be extracted from such an enormous amount of data, and, furthermore, he can not comprehend their relationship with each other. That is to say, it is very much more difficult to comprehend a global situation of the execution of a highly parallel program than of a sequential program.

To solve this problem, a debugger is required to provide a macroscopic view abstracted from the information of the execution in order to help a programmer to comprehend the situation of the erroneous program.

There are two types of program visualization researched; a visual debugger for sequential programs, and an algorithm animation to enable a user to understand an algorithm. They have different levels of abstraction. A visual debugger displays an execution at the abstract level with primitives of programming languages, and enables users to examine the precise behavior of the program. An algorithm animation system [1] displays an execution at the abstract level with an individual algorithm. Some codes are inserted as "probes" into each part of a program to call animation program dedicated to the program (or an algorithm).

However, for debugging highly parallel programs, they can not apply directly. If a debugger uses only the low level abstraction of the visual debugger, it is hard to comprehend the global situation of the program. On the other hand, the high level abstraction of the algorithm animation is not applicable directly because it requires complete specification for visualization, which may be a heavy load on a programmer and a cause of additional mistakes. Moreover, to find a bug, it must visualize unexpected behavior and provide the lower view for bug locating.

To realize a debugger for highly parallel programs, we need a visualizing technique using a proper abstraction for what we expect at that time. The debugger needs to visualize execution of a program according to a user's intention which varies during the debugging.

In this paper, we propose a method of visual debugging in which a debugger makes efficient use of a user's knowledge given in addition to source codes. This knowledge represents the user's intention or points of view. The debugger uses this information to visualize execution of a program. It does not require complete information about the program; it provides low abstraction level debugging when it has no information from a user, and, as it is given information, enables the user to debug the program at higher abstraction level.

We developed a multiwindow debugger HyperDEBU for a Committed-Choice Language Fleng which is one of the parallel logic programming languages. HyperDEBU visualizes execution of a Fleng program and enables users to comprehend the global situation of the execution. An execution history of a Fleng program comprises of a large amount of control flow and data flow information. This debugger visualizes these flows according to a user's intention on global and local views. In this paper, we describe the multiwindow debugger HyperDEBU and the methods and facilities of its visualization of control / data flows.

2 Committed-Choice Language Fleng

Committed-Choice Languages (CCLs) [4] such as Guarded Horn Clauses (GHC) ,Concurrent Prolog and PARLOG are parallel logic programming languages which introduce a control primitive "guard" for synchronization. Fleng [2] is a CCL designed in our laboratory. We are developing the Parallel Inference Engine PIE64 [3] which executes Fleng programs. Fleng is a simpler language than other CCLs ; Fleng has no guard goal, and only a head realizes guard mechanism.

A Fleng program is a set of horn clauses like:

$$H:-B_1,\cdots,B_n.\quad n\geq 0$$

The side to the left of :- is called the *head*, and the right side is called the *body* whose item B_i is called a *body goal*.

Execution of Fleng program is repetition of rewriting a set of goals in parallel. For each goal, one of the clauses whose head can match with the goal, is selected, and then the goal is rewritten into the body goals. The new goals are added to the set of goals. The execution begins when an initial goal is given and is completed when no goal remains. The rewriting operation is called *reduction*, and the matching operation is called *unification*.

Unification is an algorithm which attempts to substitute values for variables such that two logical terms are made equal. To realize communication and synchronization in concurrent logic programs, unification in CCL is divided into two classes : *guarded unification* and *active unification*. Guarded unification is applied in a head part of a clause and variables in a goal are prevented from being substituted. Such unification is *suspended* until these variables have values. Active unification is applied in a body part of a clause and is able to substitute values for variables of goals. The synchronization mechanism of guarded unification prevents reading a variable before it is bound to value, and eliminates many nondeterministic bugs due to synchronization.

Therefore, a clause in a Fleng program defines control flows with *goal reduction* and data flows with *active / guarded unification*.

3 HyperDEBU : a Multi-window Debugger for Fleng Programs

We developed a multiwindow debugger HyperDEBU which provides a multi-dimensional interface.

A sequential program has only one thread of execution, which can be debugged with a sequential interface. On the other hand, a parallel program has multiple complicated control/data flows which are considered to be multi-dimensional information. If a sequential interface is used to debug a parallel program, the bottleneck between a programmer and the program makes it difficult to examine and to manipulate the execution of the program. Therefore, a multi-dimensional interface is necessary to debug a parallel program.

Since a user compares a model represented by a debugger with the expected behavior of the program when he/she debugs a program, the debugger must provide a view of the kind he/she wants. Accordingly, the debugger must provide views which have flexible levels and aspects of abstraction.

Most conventional multiwindow debuggers use a window as a sequential debugger assigned to one of the processes. However, multi-dimensional information cannot be handled well in this way. HyperDEBU provides windows flexible enough for programmers to examine and manipulate complicated structures composed of multiple control/data flows. Tracing links on a window which displays information of a program execution, a user can get an expected window.

The conventional notion of process for CCL is associated with one goal or one sequence of goals. The process model for our debugger is equivalent not to one goal but to all of its subgoals generated by reduction. Let G be a goal and P be a set of goals which are derived from G. We call P *"the process with respect to G"*, and call G *"the topgoal of P"*. Since a subgoal can be a topgoal, a process consists of some subprocesses. This hierarchy of processes makes the debugger applicable to highly parallel programs.

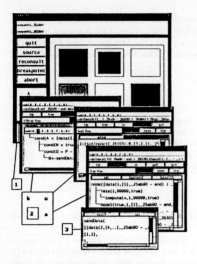

Fig. 1. Overview of HyperDEBU

HyperDEBU consists of the following windows : (1) toplevel-window, (2) process-windows ((a) TREE view (b) I/O tree view (c) GOAL view), and (3) structure-windows. Figure 1 shows an overview of HyperDEBU.

HyperDEBU has these features which cooperate with each other to aid a user to find a bug.

1. **Various views for bug locating.** Since it is necessary to zoom gradually in on the location of the bug as the breadth of a view is kept properly, a debugger's view is required to have the flexibility of views from global to local. A toplevel-window provides a global view. A user can get a process-window to examine detail of any process displayed on the toplevel-window. A process-window enables examination and manipulation of the process. To locate bugs, a user can get a subprocess as another window from this process. The process-window has three views of the process. Moreover, HyperDEBU has a structure-window which provides a data-level view.
2. **Visualization.** The global view of the toplevel-window visualizes execution of a Fleng program. This function helps a user to comprehend the global situation of the execution, and makes bug locating more efficient.
3. **Breakpoints for parallel execution.** Since a parallel program has multiple threads of control flow, a new mechanism to control the execution is needed in order to debug a highly parallel program. We extend "breakpoints" as a debugger's knowledge given by a user before the execution of the program. The debugger uses this information to control the execution, visualization and static debugging.
4. **Browsing program code.** To comprehend static information of Fleng programs, HyperDEBU has a prototype of the program code browser. This function helps a user to set breakpoints, make static debugging, and correct a source code.

4 Program Visualization on HyperDEBU

4.1 Basic Approach

To visualize execution of a highly parallel program, a debugger must deal with a large amount of control flow and data flow information. A Fleng program can be represented by visualizing *goal reduction* as control flow and *guarded / active unification* as data flow. However, visualizing all goals and data is hard to comprehend.

HyperDEBU visualizes these flows using proper abstraction according to a user's intention which is given as additional information. The debugger provides low level abstraction for debugging when it has no information from a user, and, as it is given information, enables the user to debug the program at higher level abstraction.

We introduce "breakpoints" as information which represents a user's intention or points of view.

4.2 Breakpoints for Parallel Execution

Breakpoints are specified as pairs of "point" and "direction". They are regarded as additional knowledge about a program to be debugged. The following places in a program can be specified as a point : (1) predicate (a set of clauses which have the same name), (2) clause, (3) body goal, and (4) argument of goal.

There are directions as follows :

- pause : This directs to stop a goal there.
- process : This directs to visualize a process with respect to a goal.
- notree : This directs not to keep execution history.
- stream : This directs to visualize a data as a stream.

The "process" breakpoint and the "stream" breakpoint are regarded as a user's information to visualize control flows and data flows, respectively. These details are described later.

4.3 Local and Global Views

HyperDEBU provides *local* views with low level abstraction to locate bugs, and *global* views with high level abstraction to comprehend the global situation. Each type of views represents control and data flows of execution of a program.

Local Views with Low Level Abstraction : A user can examine and manipulate execution of a program through process windows of HyperDEBU. The process window has multiple views to show control and data flows; TREE view and I/O tree view. These views use the abstraction at the level with goals and data within a process. The TREE view visualizes a tree of goal reduction to represent control flows. The I/O tree view visualizes a tree of guarded /active unifications to represent data flows. These *local* views are helpful to zoom in on the location of the bug, and to examine detailed behavior of the erroneous part of the program.

Global Views with High Level Abstraction : The toplevel window of HyperDEBU provides a global view with high level abstraction. After a user comprehends situation of execution using this global view, he can get a process window from the toplevel window as a local view to locate bugs. To realize this visualization facility, we introduced (1) a set of visualized objects to represent processes and streams, (2) a method to decide visualized objects from program code and user's intention, and (3) a method to arrange visualized objects on a display. Note that one of problems on the visualization of Fleng program execution is the need for dynamic location of display objects since goals and data themselves are created dynamically.

In the following two sections, we describe details of our visualization technique for control and data flows.

5 Visualizing Control Flows

5.1 Visualized Objects

HyperDEBU visualizes creations and state transition of processes. Since a process is defined as a set of goals derived from a goal, each goal in the execution history has corresponding process. HyperDEBU visualizes only processes with respect to some particular goals.

Figure 2 shows an overview of the toplevel window. Each process is displayed as a rectangle.

- A color of the rectangle indicates the state of the process (white, light gray and dark gray indicate active, suspend,and terminated respectively)
- A nest of rectangles indicates the relation between a process and its subprocess.
- A topgoal of a process is displayed when the mouse cursor enters the corresponding rectangle.
- Clicking a rectangle generates a new process-window for this process.

Contents of all the windows are updated reflecting the state of the execution dynamically. By observing creations and state transition of processes, and by observing modification of data in the arguments of topgoals, a user can comprehend the execution of Fleng program correctly and easily.

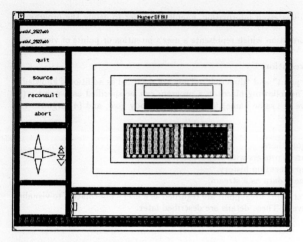

Fig. 2. Visualizing Control Flows

5.2 Breakpoints

HyperDEBU visualizes a process as a rectangle only if "process" breakpoint is specified at its top goal. Other processes are abstracted as internal goals in their parent processes, and not visualized as rectangles.

Since a rectangle may have a large number of goals as its elements, this visualization facility is applicable to a realistic highly parallel application composed of modules in which many goals are executed in parallel.

Even when the same execution of a program is visualized, a user can get various display from different view points according to he selects where breakpoints are set.

5.3 How to Display

As processes are created, HyperDEBU arranges rectangles dynamically using the following policy.

Let P be a process to be visualized. Then we introduce the following terms:

- $Sub(P, n)$: n-th sub-process of a process P.
- $D(P)$: depth in the hierarchy of rectangles $(D(Sub(P, n)) = D(P) + 1, D(P) = 0, 1, 2, \cdots)$.

The rectangle of P is divided into $X \times Y$ areas (X lines and Y columns) and each area is called $a(i, j)$ $(i = 1, \cdots, X, j = 1, \cdots, Y)$. $Sub(P, n)$ is placed at $a(i, j)$. (i, j, X, Y) is decided as follows : if $D(Sub(P, n)) = 2k$ $(k = 0, 1, 2, \cdots)$,

$$(i, j, X, Y) = \begin{cases} (m, n - m(m-1), m, m) & \text{if } m^2 \leq n < m(m+1) \\ (n - m^2, m+1, m, m+1) & \text{if } m(m+1) \leq n < (m+1)^2 \end{cases}$$

if $D(Sub(P, n)) = 2k + 1$ $(k = 0, 1, 2, \cdots)$,

$$(i, j, X, Y) = \begin{cases} (n - m(m-1), m, m, m) & \text{if } m^2 \leq n < m(m+1) \\ (m+1, n - m^2, m+1, m) & \text{if } m(m+1) \leq n < (m+1)^2 \end{cases}$$

where $m = 1, 2, 3, \cdots$.

As n increases in the execution, rectangles are arranged as in Figure 3 $(D(Sub(P, n)) = 2k)$. This method to arrange displayed objects has the following features:

- efficient use of area in a rectangle
- applicable to animation since it is easy to understand the relationship between the adjacent states of placements
- simple incremental arrangement algorithm (easy to implement for dynamic visualization)

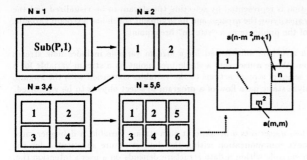

Fig. 3. Arranging Visualized Objects of Control Flow

6   Visualizing Data Flows

6.1   Visualized Objects

HyperDEBU visualizes particular *streams* which make main global data flows of the computation. The stream-based communication is a essential programming technique in CCL which enables a continual communication between processes. It is realized using shared variables as follows.

1. One of goals which have a shared variable writes some data structure into this variable (stream output).
2. When the value of the variable is bound, the other goals read it (stream input).
3. The data structure includes new variables which are shared by goals and used to continue the communication.

To represent the stream-based communication, a debugger must visualize its *"stream variables"* and its *"stream actions"*. A *"stream variable"* is a variable which is shared by some goals and used for communication as described above. *"Stream actions"* are operations of these goals to the stream variable, and include creation of the stream, distribution of the stream, and input/output of the stream. These actions are visualized as Figure 4.

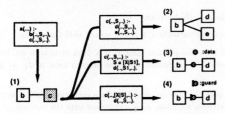

Fig. 4. Creation, Distribution, Input and Output of Stream

Figure 4-(1) is the object visualized when the body goals b and c, which share a new stream variable S, are created. This figure represents the creation of a new stream. Figure 4-(2) is the object visualized when the goal c is reduced into d and e and the number of goals which have a reference to the stream variable S is increased. This figure represents the distribution of the stream. Figure 4-(3) is the objects visualized when a data structure [X|S1] is substituted for the variable S. S1 is a new stream variable for the next communication. This figure represents the stream output. Figure 4-(4) represents the objects visualized when c is reduced into d after waiting for a data structure [X|S] which is displayed as a "guard". This figure represents the stream input.

To visualize a stream, the places corresponding to the stream actions as represented in Figure 4 must be specified in the program codes. Since many clauses have the stream actions to the same stream, these places are too many for a user to specify. A debugger is required to show essential information using as less specification from a user as possible. To realize this requirement, we should make clear (1) what a user wants to see, (2) how the user tells it to a debugger, and (3) what the debugger selects to visualize.

User's Point of View : A stream can be examined from various points of view. As a point of view, a user selects one of processes, and tries to examine: (1) its companions for the stream-based communication, and (2) its stream actions.

User's Specification : A user's intention is represented by selecting the stream to be visualized and the process as a point of view, that is, by specifying the process and its argument which has a stream variable. The user can specify the argument of the predicate as a "stream" breakpoint.

Objects to be Visualized : The data structure substituted for a stream variable includes new stream variables for the next communication. While a user sets a single breakpoint on a stream variable for a stream, a debugger must visualize a series of stream actions to the variables concerned with the stream. Accordingly, the debugger must analyze static data flow of a program to select objects to be visualized.

6.2 Breakpoints

Specifying "stream" Breakpoint : When a user sets a breakpoint on a stream variable, a debugger must find new stream variables for the next communication within the data structure substituted for the variable. Since the place of a stream variable within a data structure depends on a user's intention (i.e. what is a stream to be visualized), the user must specify not only a place of a stream variable in an argument of a process, but also where are next stream variables in the data of the stream variable. For this reason, we introduce "*types*" of streams which are sets of data substituted for a stream variable :

$$S = s_1(S) + s_2(S) + \cdots + s_m(S) + t_1 + \cdots + t_n$$

where $s_i(S)$ is a term (i.e. pattern of data) including stream variable S and any other variables; the term represents a set of data which are unifiable to it by substituting any data for their variables. Only the same type of data can be substituted for S, which is a stream variable for the next communication. t_i is a term which has no stream variables. This is used for termination of a stream. The operator "+" represents the union of sets.

In most cases, a sequence of list is used for a stream in a Fleng program. This type of stream is represented as:

$$S = [X|S] + []$$

This is the default stream type in the current implementation of HyperDEBU. Although a visualization mechanism supports general types of the stream, a user can specify only the list as a type through the current user interface. We need a new interface which enables a user to specify general types easily.

Selecting Visualized Objects : The debugger analyzes static data flows of the program with the information from the user, and selects the objects to be visualized. The debugger takes the following steps :

1. find all the stream variables concerned with the specified stream :

   (a) If a stream breakpoint is specified to a stream variable s, s is *concerned with* the stream.

   (b) When s_1 is a stream variable *concerned with* the stream, and T is a data structure unified with s_1, if T includes a next stream variable s_2 specified with the stream type of s_1, s_2 is *concerned with* the stream.

   (c) When s_1 is a stream variable *concerned with* the stream, and T is data structure unified with a variable s_2, if T includes s_1 as a next stream variable, s_2 is *concerned with* the stream.

2. judge stream actions to be (or not to be) visualized :

   (a) If a stream breakpoint is specified to a stream variable s, a stream action to s is visualized.

   (b) If a body goal is a predicate which has a stream action to be visualized, a stream action of its head is to be visualized.

The step 2 provides proper information for the user's point of view. The debugger visualizes a series of actions *from* the creation of the stream variable shared with companions of the specified process *to* the action of the process, and abstracts the other stream actions. For example, stream actions of a goal as a subroutine for sending messages, and ones of companions for communication with the specified process are not visualized if these goals have no stream breakpoint. These goals are still visualized as goals even if they are reduced into subgoals.

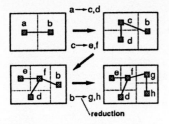

Fig. 5. Arranging Visualized Objects of Data Flow

6.3 How to Display

The debugger must visualize graphs composed of links of stream and nodes such as goals, data, and guards. To visualize such graphs for debugging, a method to arrange nodes on a display needs to satisfy the following requirements :

- To avoid additional tasks, a user does not have to specify the arrangement.
- Since graphs grow dynamically, the method should be incremental and suitable for animation.

Our method is as follows:

- **grouping nodes:** The nodes linked with streams each other are gathered as a group, and placed on the rectangle area in the same way to arrange processes.
- **arrangement in a group:** A rectangle area is divided into rectangles as many as nodes in the group. Each node is placed at the center of a rectangle. When a node is divided into new nodes, its rectangle is also divided and supplied for these nodes. The dividing line is vertical to the line which has created the rectangle for the node. Adjusting borders between rectangles, all the rectangle are kept the same size with each other. Figure 5 shows how to display a graph growing as nodes are generated.a,···,h are nodes to be visualized such as goals, data, and guards. For example, the upper two graph show that a is divided into c and d by a stream action.

A user can specify both "process" and "stream" breakpoints to visualize control and data flows. A rectangle of process is also regarded as a node of the data flow graph. Data flow within a process is displayed in its rectangle.

7 Implementation and User Interface

HyperDEBU is written in Fleng itself, and runs on a Fleng system in parallel. It provides dynamic and interactive visualization and manipulation; since a user program and HyperDEBU run in parallel, a user can examine the state of the program and manipulate the execution at a run time.

In this section, we describe the visualization facility installed on HyperDEBU, by showing examples of displays.

7.1 Example of Data Flow Visualization

For an example of the data flow visualization on HyperDEBU, a program "primes" in Figure 6 is visualized.

This program generates a list of prime numbers. **gen/3** generates a list of integer from 2 to **Max**. **sift/2** gets this data and generates a filter which removes multiples of the integer **P**. We take up a stream which passes through these filters and generates prime numbers as the global data flow, and visualize it from two points of view.

According as points of view, we specify two different combination of breakpoints:

(1) Stream breakpoints are specified at the second and third arguments of **filter/3**.
(2) A stream breakpoint is specified at the first argument of **sift/2**.

The stream type of the breakpoint is a default type "*list*". The results are displayed in Figure 7-(1) and (2), respectively.

```
primes(Max, Ps) :- gen(2,Max,Ns), sift(Ns,Ps).
gen(N,Max,Ns) :- less_eq(N,Max,LE), gen1(LE,N,Max,Ns).
gen1(true,N,Max,Ns) :- Ns = [N|Ns1], add1(N,N1),
                         gen(N1,Max,Ns1).
gen1(false,N,Max,Ns) :- Ns = [].
sift([P|Xs],Zs) :- Zs = [P|Zs1], filter(P,Xs,Ys),
                     sift(Ys, Zs1).
sift([], Zs) :- Zs = [].
filter(P,[X|Xs],Ys) :- mod(X,P,Mod), eq(Mod,0,Eq),
                         filter1(Eq,P,X,Xs,Ys).
filter(P, [], Ys) :- Ys =[].
filter1(true,P,X,Xs,Ys) :- filter(P,Xs,Ys).
filter1(false,P,X,Xs,Ys) :- Ys = [X|Ys1], filter(P,Xs,Ys1).
```

Fig. 6. Example Program to be Visualized

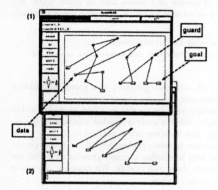

Fig. 7. Example of Data Flow Visualization

User Interfaces : The execution of the program "primes" is visualized as a graph on the toplevel window of each HyperDEBU in Figure 7. The elements of the data flow graph are as follows:

- data : a small square is output data of the stream.
- guard : a node composed of a circle and a line segment is a "guard", which gets input data from the side with the line segment.
- goal : a rectangle named by characters is a goal.
- stream : a line connecting nodes is correspond with a stream variable and shows the flow of data.

This data flow graph grows and changes its shape as the program is executed, and shows the situation of the execution dynamically by animation.

A user can manipulate objects interactively. When the mouse cursor points each node, the contents of the node is displayed at a sub window of the toplevel window. Clicking a node generates a structure window for this node. A user can examine the data more in detail with this window.

User's Point of View : The two toplevel windows (1) and (2) in Figure 7 provide different views. The former shows stream actions and companions of **filter**, and the latter shows ones of **sift**. In Figure 7-(1), a stream starts with the goal **gen** at the left side, goes through four guard objects, and gets at the goal **filter**. This indicates **filter** gets data through these guards from **gen**. Then the stream continues going to the next **filter** through two data objects and two guard objects. This indicates the **filter** outputs these data and the next **filter** gets them. In Figure 7-(2), stream actions of **filter**s are not visualized. HyperDEBU visualizes only the creation of **filter** to represent stream actions of the goal **sift**. Although the stream actions of **gen** are not visualized in both views, selecting a breakpoint at **gen** makes them visualized.

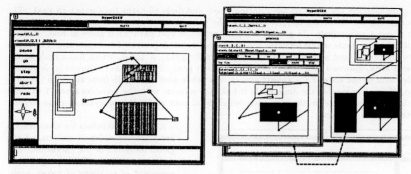

Fig. 8. Example of Control and Data Flow Visualization

7.2 Example of Control and Data Flow Visualization

The left side of two displays in Figure 8 shows an example of control and data flow visualization with "process" and "stream" breakpoints. The process breakpoints are specified at gen/3 and filter/3. The gray rectangles are the "filter" processes, one of which has its stream actions in its own rectangle. Since data flow graphs within a process are visualized in the rectangle of the process, the visualized data flows are made layered and easy to understand.

HyperDEBU supports the magnification of the display and zooming by process windows in order to help a usr's comprehension of complicated control and data flow graphs. The right side of Figure 8 shows an example of complicated graphs. The view of toplevel window is magnified and one of visualized processes is opened as a process window, in which the control and data flows of the process is visualized. The process window can also display the local view to show detailed information.

8 Example of Debugging

In this section, we will demonstrate the effectiveness of HyperDEBU by showing an example of debugging using HyperDEBU.

The following example is a program to solve "good-path problem".

```
path(A) :- token(start,[],A,[]).

token(Node,History,H,T) :- eq(Node,goal,F),
                           token1(F,Node,History,H,T).
token1(true,Node,History,H,T) :- H = [[goal|History]|T].
token1(false,Node,History,H,T) :-
    next(Node,Next), checknext(Next,[Node|History],H,T).

checknext([],History,H,T) :- H = T.
checknext([N|Ns],History,H,T) :-
    member(N,History,Result),
    gonext(Result,N,History,H,T1),
    checknext(Ns,History,T1,T).

gonext(true,_,_,H,T) :- H = T.
gonext(false,Node,History,H,T) :- token(Node,History,H,T).

next(start,Next) :- Next = [a,d].
next(a,Next) :- Next = [start,b].
next(b,Next) :- Next = [a,c,goal].
next(c,[b,d,goal]).                          %erroneous
%next(c,Next) :- Next = [b,d,goal].          %correct
next(d,Next) :- Next = [start,c,e].
next(e,Next) :- Next = [d,goal].
```

This program searches the paths on the directed graph and finds all paths from **start** to **goal**. The **next** clauses specify the directed graph; for example, the first clause tells the node **start** has two arrows directed to **a** and **d** respectively. To get the solution, an initial goal **path(X)** is given at first. Then it matches with the first clause of this program and a new goal **token** is generated and spawned. The **token** goals spawn themselves and search the paths from **start** for **goal**. A **token**, which has a node as the first argument **Node**, spawns a goal **checknext** if **Node** is not **goal**. The **checknext** spawns goals **gonext** for the nodes next to the **Node**. Each **gonext** generates a **token** goal if the path from **start** to the node has no loop. If a **token** reaches the node **goal**, it links the solution with the variables **H** and **T** to make the list of the solutions. However, the erroneous definition of **next** makes this program suspend illegally without returning the solutions.

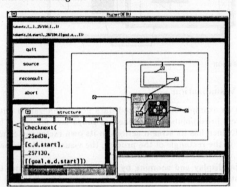

Fig. 9. Visualizing the Erroneous Program : Scene 1

At first, breakpoints for visualization are placed in order to understand the global situation of the execution. The main control flows of this program are composed of creations of **token** goals, and the main data flows are considered as the stream which links all the solutions with a list. So a "process" breakpoint is specified at **token**, and "stream" breakpoints are specified at the third and fourth argument of **token**. Figure 9 shows the visualization of control and data flows on the toplevel window. The nested rectangles represent the processes with respect to **token** goals. These process are linked with a stream in sequence. They searches for solutions in parallel, and when a process finds a solution, it is linked with the stream. However, a process represented as a gray rectangle is suspended and a goal is still linked with the stream in the rectangle. A structure window is opened by clicking this goal, and shows the goal **checknext** is suspended waiting for the data of its argument. This goal stops data flow of the list of solutions.

Then a process window is opened from the gray rectangle in which **checknext** is suspended. Figure 10 shows the opened process window. The rectangle of the process turns to black in the toplevel window. The process window displays I/O tree View to visualize detailed data flows.

This view tells that **checknext** is waiting for the data from **next** which is suspended illegally. Finally, we can detect a bug in the definition of **next**.

In this example, we visualize the global data flow which is used to collect solutions, and find a bug in the other local data flow. Visualizing main global control and data flows helps a user to comprehend the situation of the execution. Then, after zooming in on the location of the bug with a process window, a user can find bugs in its local views of control and data flow.

9 Related Works

As several recent works for the visualization of CCL programs, VISTA [5], Pictorial Janus [6], etc. are researched. They have different policies for visualization from our debugger.

VISA is a performance visualization tool which displays control flows of a CCL program as a colored tree. This tool does not deal with data flow visualization.

Pictorial Janus unifies the program visualization and the visual programming. The execution of a program is fully visualized. Oppositely, when the visualized program is given, the program runs visually. However, to use this system for debugging, a proper abstraction method according to a user's intention and a interactive manipulation facility are required.

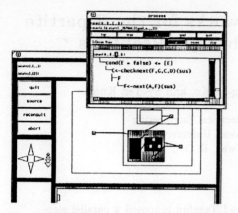

Fig. 10. Visualizing the Erroneous Program : Scene 2

10 Future Work

For more improvement, we have some subjects as follows:

- more sophisticated algorithm to arrange visualized objects.
- grouping visualized data flow objects to reduce complexity of data flow graphs.
- applying the information from a user to static debugging.
- enhancement of functions to display objects, for example, using colors.

11 Conclusion

In this paper, we described the control and data flow visualization facility of a multiwindow debugger HyperDEBU for parallel logic programs. It provides proper information according to a user's intention, and helps to comprehend the situation of the execution. Applying the debugger to examples, we demonstrated that this function is useful to find a bug efficiently.

HyperDEBU is runnable on any Fleng systems since it is written in Fleng itself. Currently, it is running on the Fleng interpreter on UNIX sequential workstations and Mach parallel workstations. Being used in development of application programs, it is being evaluated and improved .

References

[1] Brown,M.H.: Exploring Algorithms Using Balsa-2, IEEE Computer, Vol.21 No.5,pp.14-36 (May 1988).
[2] Nilsson, M. and Tanaka, H.: *Massively Parallel Implementation of Flat GHC on the Connection Machine*, Proc. of the Int. Conf. on Fifth Generation Computer Systems, p1031-1040 (1988).
[3] Koike, H. and Tanaka, H. : *Parallel Inference Engine PIE64*, in *Parallel Computer Architecture*, bit, Vol.21,No.4,1989, pp.488-497 (in Japanese).
[4] (Ed.) Shapiro, E. : *Concurrent Prolog : Collected Papers* , (Vols. 1 and 2), The MIT Press (1987).
[5] Tick,E.: Visualizing Parallel Logic Programs with VISTA, International Conference on Fifth Generation Computer Systems 1992, pp.934-942 (1992).
[6] Kahn, K.M. : Concurrent Constraint Programs to Parse and Animate Pictures of Concurrent Constraint Programs, International Conference on Fifth Generation Computer Systems 1992, pp.943-950 (1992).

Artificial Neural Networks for the Bipartite and K-partite Subgraph Problems *

Jenn-Shiang Lai, Young-Ja Ko, and Sy-Yen Kuo

Department of Electrical Engineering
National Taiwan University
Taipei, Taiwan, R. O. C.

Abstract. In [1], Lee, Funabiki and Takefuji proposed a parallel algorithm for solving the bipartite subgraph problem with the maximum neural networks. In this paper, we present a new algorithm based on the discrete Hopfield network to deal with the same problem. Compared with the previous maximum neural network algorithm, our method can find solutions of same quality or better with half of neurons and much less computation time. Furthermore, for the general K-partite subgraph problem, a novel interactive Hopfield network system is devised to solve it effectively. The algorithm has been implemented and the experimental results indeed demonstrate the effectiveness of our approach.

1 Introduction

The aim of the bipartite subgraph problem is to remove minimum number of edges in a given graph such that the remaining graph is bipartite. Since the bipartite subgraph problem is NP-complete, heuristics and relaxation of constraints have been used to find acceptable solutions in reasonable time [2, 3, 4]. Recently, Lee, Funabiki, and Takefuji [1] proposed a parallel algorithm based on the maximum neural network to solve this problem. Although their algorithm can achieve some good results, the number of neurons required and the amount of execution time are both quite large. In this paper, we will present an improved algorithm to deal with the bipartite subgraph problem using the discrete Hopfield network, and obtain same or better results by using half of neurons and much less simulation time than the previous approach.

Since Hopfield and Tank [5] proposed a neural network for solving combinatorial optimization problems, the Hopfield network has been widely applied to solve many difficult problems. The Hopfield network is a system constructed by a large number of processing elements (neurons). Each neuron can be in one of two possible states, either 1 or 0. All links between neurons are bidirectional. The weight w_{ij} characterizes the link connecting neurons i and j; the external input to neuron j is I_j, and the state V_j of a neuron j is determined by [6]

---

* This research was supported by the National Science Council, Taiwan, R. O. C., under Grant NSC 81-0404-E002-105.

$$V_j = 1 \text{ if } \sum_i w_{ij} V_i + I_j > 0$$

$$V_j = 0 \text{ if } \sum_i w_{ij} V_i + I_j < 0$$

$$V_j \text{ is unchanged if } \sum_i w_{ij} V_i + I_j = 0$$

If we initialize the states of all neurons, the Hopfield network will stablize into a final state corresponding to the minimum energy of the Lyapunov function

$$E = -\frac{1}{2} \sum_i \sum_j w_{ij} V_i V_j - \sum_j I_j V_j$$

For this reason, it has been widely used to solve a combinatorial optimization problem whose cost function can be expressed as this quadratic Lyapunov energy function.

The rest of this paper is organized as follows: In Section 2, we introduce the method to solve the bipartite subgraph problem by the Hopfield network. Section 3 presents the architecture, the algorithm and properties of the interactive Hopfield network system. Section 4 explains how to solve the K-partite subgraph problem with the interactive Hopfield network system. In Section 5, experimental results for the bipartite subgraph problem are discussed. Concluding remarks are given in Section 6.

2   Bipartite Subgraph Problem

Given a graph $G = (V, E)$, the goal of the bipartite subgraph problem is to find the subset $E' \subseteq E$ such that $G' = (V, E')$ is bipartite and $(|E| - |E'|)$ is minimized. Assume that (a_{ij}) is the adjacency matrix of graph G, then the bipartite subgraph problem can be mathematically stated as finding the minimum of the following objective function

$$E = \frac{1}{2} \sum_i \sum_j a_{ij} \overline{V_i \oplus V_j}$$

where $\oplus$ is the logical XOR, $\overline{X}$ means the complement of X, and $V_i \in \{0, 1\}$ indicates the state of neuron i.

If any two adjacent vertices are in the same set after partition (that is, the states of two adjacent vertices are identical), the system energy will be increased by 1, and the edge connecting these two vertices should be deleted to form a bipartite graph. Since there is no coefficient tuning problem (such as that for graph partitioning [7]), the converged state will be the valid solution. Also, when E reaches the minimum, the number of deleted edges is minimized.

As illustrated in Table 1, the Boolean function of logical variables can be represented by the related arithmetic function. Hence, the former objective function can be expanded as

$$E = \frac{1}{2} \sum_i \sum_j a_{ij} \overline{V_i \oplus V_j}$$

$$= \frac{1}{2} \sum_i \sum_j a_{ij} (2V_i V_j - V_i - V_j + 1)$$

Table 1. The Boolean and arithmetic representations for four typical functions.

Logic Function	Boolean Representation	Arithmetic Representation
NOT X	$\overline{X}$	$1\text{-}X$
X AND Y	$X \wedge Y$	XY
X OR Y	$X \vee Y$	$X + Y - XY$
X XOR Y	$X \oplus Y$	$X + Y - 2XY$

If the constant $\frac{1}{2} \sum_i \sum_j a_{ij}$ is neglected, then the energy function can be rearranged into

$$E = -\frac{1}{2} \sum_i \sum_j (-2a_{ij}) V_i V_j - \sum_j \left(\sum_i a_{ij} \right) V_j$$

This is in the form of Lyapunov function for the Hopfield network, and therefore, we can obtain the values of connection weights and external inputs ($w_{ij} = -2a_{ij}$ and $I_j = \sum_i a_{ij}$).

Figure 1(a) shows the original graph of a 30-vertex graph problem, and Figure 1(b) is a solution derived by our method, where black circles and white circles represent two disjoint sets of vertices.

3 Interactive Hopfield Networks

In this section, we will propose a novel neural network system for the general K-partite subgraph problem. The proposed interactive Hopfield network system is shown in Figure 2. It is composed of two (interactive) Hopfield networks, U-network and V-network, and the energy function for this system is

$$E = \frac{1}{2} \sum_i \sum_j \Psi(U_i, U_j, V_i, V_j)$$

where U_i and U_j are states of neurons i and j of the U-network; V_i and V_j are states of neurons i and j of the V network.

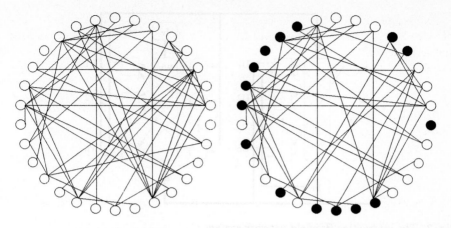

Fig. 1. The 30-vertex bipartite subgraph problem. (a) Original graph with 50 edges. (b) One of the Hopfield network solutions with 42 edges embedded.

Because the state variables, U_i, U_j, V_i, and V_j have to be either 0 or 1, any high-order (second-order or more) element in $\Psi(U_i, U_j, V_i, V_j)$ with respect to a state variable can be reduced into the first-order form with respect to that variable. For example,

$$U_i^3 = U_i$$
$$U_j V_i^2 = U_j V_i$$
$$U_i^2 U_j^4 V_i V_j^3 = U_i U_j V_i V_j$$

Henceforth, this energy function can be formulated as

$$E_{U-\text{network}} = -\frac{1}{2}\sum_i\sum_j (w_{ij}^U) U_i U_j - \sum_j I_j^U U_j + C_U$$

or

$$E_{V-\text{network}} = -\frac{1}{2}\sum_i\sum_j (w_{ij}^V) V_i V_j - \sum_j I_j^V V_j + C_V$$

where $w_{ij}^U = \psi_w^U(V_i, V_j)$, $I_j^U = \psi_I^U(V_i, V_j)$, $w_{ij}^V = \psi_w^V(U_i, U_j)$, and $I_j^V = \psi_I^V(U_i, U_j)$; C_U and C_V are constants for each network, respectively.

Since a Hopfield network will always evolve toward a minimum of its energy function, if the weights and external inputs of one network are determined by the present state of the other network, then any change (at arbitrary time) in the state of a neuron will reduce the network energy. Eventually, both networks will stablize into the minimal energy states. Also, since $E_{U-\text{network}} = E_{V-\text{network}} = E$, the whole system will reach the stable state corresponding to the minima of the energy function E. As a result, if the cost function of a given problem is in the form of $E = \frac{1}{2}\sum_i\sum_j \Psi(U_i, U_j, V_i, V_j)$, we can solve that problem with the interactive Hopfield network system.

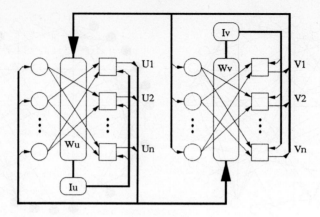

Fig. 2. The interactive Hopfield network system.

4 K-partite Subgraph Problem

The K-partite graph is a graph where the vertices are partitioned into K-disjoint sets and no edge exists between two vertices in the same set [1]. Similar to the bipartite subgraph problem, the goal of the K-partite subgraph problem is to remove minimum number of edges for a given graph such that the remaining graph is K-partite.

Consider the quadripartite subgraph problem. Assume that the state of vertex i in the graph G is (U_i, V_i) and the 4 disjoint sets for the quadripartite subgraph problem are S_0, S_1, S_2 and S_3, where

$$S_0 = \{i \,|\, (U_i, V_i) = (0, 0)\}$$
$$S_1 = \{i \,|\, (U_i, V_i) = (0, 1)\}$$
$$S_2 = \{i \,|\, (U_i, V_i) = (1, 0)\}$$
$$S_3 = \{i \,|\, (U_i, V_i) = (1, 1)\}$$

Hence, we can also formulate the quadripartite subgraph problem as finding the minimum of the objective function

$$E = \frac{1}{2} \sum_i \sum_j a_{ij} \left(\overline{U_i \oplus U_j} \wedge \overline{V_i \oplus V_j} \right)$$
$$= \frac{1}{2} \sum_i \sum_j a_{ij} (2U_i U_j - U_i - U_j + 1)(2V_i V_j - V_i - V_j + 1)$$

Similarly, the number of removed edges for the quadripartite subgraph problem will be minimized when this energy function is minimized. A system of this energy function consists of two interactive Hopfield networks. These two networks have the following energy functions respectively

$$E_{U-\text{network}} = \frac{1}{2} \sum_i \sum_j [a_{ij}(2V_iV_j - V_i - V_j + 1)](2U_iU_j - U_i - U_j + 1)$$

$$= -\frac{1}{2} \sum_i \sum_j (-2a_{ij}\rho_{ij})U_iU_j - \sum_j \left(\sum_i a_{ij}\rho_{ij} \right) U_j + C_U$$

$$E_{V-\text{network}} = \frac{1}{2} \sum_i \sum_j [a_{ij}(2U_iU_j - U_i - U_j + 1)](2V_iV_j - V_i - V_j + 1)$$

$$= -\frac{1}{2} \sum_i \sum_j (-2a_{ij}\sigma_{ij})V_iV_j - \sum_j \left(\sum_i a_{ij}\sigma_{ij} \right) V_j + C_V$$

where $\rho_{ij} = 2V_iV_j - V_i - V_j + 1$, and $\sigma_{ij} = 2U_iU_j - U_i - U_j + 1$. C_U and C_V are constants for each network. Also, we can get the weights and external inputs for each network ($w_{ij}^U = -2a_{ij}\rho_{ij}, I_j^U = \sum_i a_{ij}\rho_{ij}, w_{ij}^V = -2a_{ij}\sigma_{ij}$, and $I_j^V = \sum_i a_{ij}\sigma_{ij}$).

Because any change in the state of a neuron will reduce the energy of the corresponding Hopfield network and $E_{U-\text{network}} = E_{V-\text{network}} = E$, eventually this system will reach a minimum energy state and stop. The algorithm for the quadripartite subgraph problem is shown as follows:

procedure Quadripartite_Subgraph_Problem
    Randomly generate the initial state of each neuron;
    repeat
        Calculate the weights and external inputs for the U-network;
        for each neuron j of U-network
            if $\sum_i w_{ij}^U U_i + I_j^U > 0$ **then**
                $U_j = 1$;
            if $\sum_i w_{ij}^U U_i + I_j^U < 0$ **then**
                $U_j = 0$;
        end;
        Calculate the weights and external inputs for the V-network;
        for each neuron j of V-network
            if $\sum_i w_{ij}^V V_i + I_j^V > 0$ **then**
                $V_j = 1$;
            if $\sum_i w_{ij}^V V_i + I_j^V < 0$ **then**
                $V_j = 0$;
        end;
    until the state of this network is stable;
end;

Figure 3 shows one of the quadripartite subgraph solutions for the 30-vertex graph problem in Figure 1(a), where black circles, white circles, gray circles, and double-circles represent the four disjoint sets of vertices. Clearly, algorithms for other 2^l-partite subgraph problems can also be deduced from a system of l interactive Hopfield networks in a similar way.

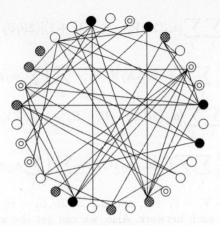

Fig. 3. One of the quadripartite subgraph solutions with 50 edges embedded.

In addition, this method can also be applied to the K-partite subgraph problem when $K \neq 2^l$. Suppose that the state of vertex i for the tripartite subgraph problem is (U_i, V_i); the 3 disjoint sets for this problem are

$$S_0 = \{i \mid (U_i, V_i) = (0, 0)\}$$
$$S_1 = \{i \mid (U_i, V_i) = (0, 1)\}$$
$$S_2 = \{i \mid (U_i, V_i) = (1, 0) \text{ or } (1, 1)\}$$

then the energy function for the tripartite subgraph problem can be written as

$$E = \frac{1}{2} \sum_i \sum_j a_{ij} ((U_i \wedge U_j) \vee (\overline{U_i \oplus U_j} \wedge \overline{V_i \oplus V_j}))$$

$$= \frac{1}{2} \sum_i \sum_j a_{ij} [U_i U_j + (2U_i U_j - U_i - U_j + 1)(2V_i V_j - V_i - V_j + 1)]$$

Thus, we can obtain a system similar to that for the quadripartite subgraph problem except $w_{ij}^U = -a_{ij}(2\rho_{ij} + 1)$. Figure 4 shows one of the tripartite subgraph solutions for the same 30-vertex graph problem.

In general, for the K-partite subgraph problem, the state of each vertex can be represented by $(V_i^{(l-1)}, V_i^{(l-2)}, \cdots, V_i^{(0)})$ and the disjoint K sets are $S_0, S_1, \cdots,$ and S_{K-1}, where

$$l = \lceil \log_2 K \rceil$$

$$S_k = \left\{ i \left| \sum_{j=0}^{l-1} V_i^{(j)} 2^j = k \right. \right\} \quad \text{for } k = 0, 1, 2, \cdots, K - 2$$

$$S_{K-1} = \left\{ i \left| \sum_{j=0}^{l-1} V_i^{(j)} 2^j \geq K - 1 \right. \right\}$$

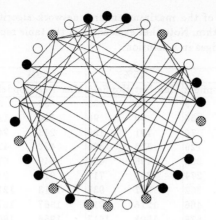

Fig. 4. One of the tripartite subgraph solutions with 49 edges embedded.

and formulate the cost function as

$$E = \frac{1}{2} \sum_i \sum_j a_{ij} \Gamma(V_i^{(l-1)}, V_i^{(l-2)}, \cdots, V_i^{(0)}, V_j^{(l-1)}, V_j^{(l-2)}, \cdots, V_j^{(0)})$$

where

$$\Gamma(V_i^{(l-1)}, V_i^{(l-2)}, \cdots, V_i^{(0)}, V_j^{(l-1)}, V_j^{(l-2)}, \cdots, V_j^{(0)}) = \begin{cases} 1, & \text{if vertices } i \text{ and } j \text{ are} \\ & \text{in the same set} \\ \\ 0, & \text{otherwise} \end{cases}$$

Using a system consists of l interactive Hopfield networks of n neurons, we can solve the n-vertex problem by this technique.

5 Experimental Results

The algorithm for the bipartite subgraph problem was implemented in C on SUN SPARCstation 2. Table 2 shows the comparison of the solution quality between the maximum neural network algorithm and our algorithm, where the 5%, 15%, 20%, and 25% density graph problems with up to 300 vertices are examined. Note that the density of the randomly generated n-vertex graph is defined by the ratio between the number of given edges and $n(n-1)/2$, and each instance was simulated 100 times.

Generally, when the edges of a graph are not dense, or the number of vertices are small, our method can find a solution of the same quality as that obtained by the maximum neural network algorithm. However, when the density or the problem size increases, our method can find a better solution than the maximum neural network algorithm.

On the other hand, the simulation results depicted in Figures 5, 6, 7, and 8 show that our algorithm always converges to a solution within 20 iterations,

Table 2. Comparison of the maximum neural network algorithm and the discrete Hopfield network algorithm. Note that each entry in the table represents the maximum number of embedded edges in a solution.

Node Size	5%		15%		20%		25%	
	Max Net	Hopfield	Max Net	Hopfield	Max Net	Hopfield	Max Net	Hopfield
20	9	9	25	25	32	32	37	37
40	36	36	90	90	114	114	142	142
60	76	76	191	190	243	242	290	290
80	131	129	326	326	422	420	517	517
100	201	202	495	496	640	638	778	780
120	276	274	706	711	916	916	1097	1094
140	363	362	937	936	1213	1211	1471	1473
160	467	466	1216	1214	1567	1571	1914	1912
180	576	578	1503	1517	1956	1965	2385	2392
200	713	704	1858	1845	2395	2402	2924	2936
220	856	840	2231	2220	2874	2879	3523	3529
240	993	989	2621	2636	3394	3390	4152	4172
260	1151	1161	3051	3057	3960	3955	4854	4865
280	1320	1318	3509	3507	4570	4586	5634	5601
300	1505	1506	4025	4027	5240	5245	6386	6421

which is not sensitive to the problem size and converges to a stable state much faster than the maximum neural network does.

For solving n-vertex bipartite subgraph problem, the maximum neural network algorithm needs $2n$ neurons, but our algorithm requires only n neurons. Since the discrete Hopfield neural network is used, our method can be simulated with integer computations rather than floating-point computations in the maximum neural network.

If the continuous model of the Hopfield network is applied to our method, then the input activation u_j of neuron j is governed by the motion equation

$$\frac{du_j}{dt} = \sum_{i \neq j} w_{ij} V_i - \frac{u_j}{\tau} + I_j$$

where $V_i = [1 + \tanh(\lambda u_i)] / 2$ is the output of neuron i, I_j is the external input to neuron j, and the parameter λ is the constant gain. In this way, this algorithm can be implemented by hardware [5]. Since the hardware for the Hopfield network is presently available, the bipartite subgraph problem can be solved in parallel. In addition, by removing the decay term u_j/τ in the motion equation, it can also be simulated by software [1].

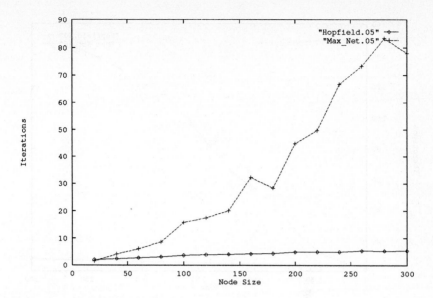

Fig. 5. The relationship between the convergence iteration steps and the number of vertices with edge density 5%.

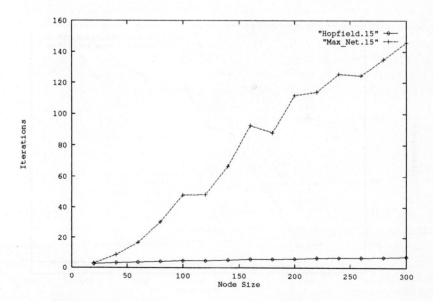

Fig. 6. The relationship between the convergence iteration steps and the number of vertices with edge density 15%.

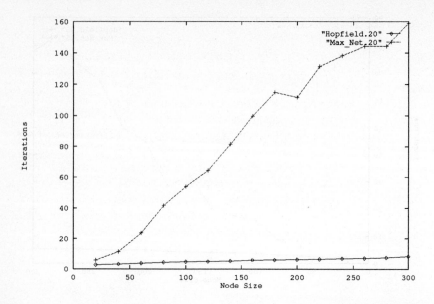

Fig. 7. The relationship between the convergence iteration steps and the number of vertices with edge density 20%.

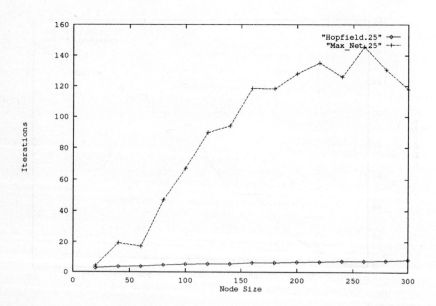

Fig. 8. The relationship between the convergence iteration steps and the number of vertices with edge density 25%.

6 Concluding Remarks

In this paper, we have presented an efficient algorithm for the bipartite subgraph problem based on the discrete Hopfield network, and developed the architecture of a novel interactive Hopfield network system to solve the K-partite subgraph problem. Our algorithm can find solutions of the same quality or better as those obtained by Lee, Funabiki and Takefuji's algorithm, and the number of iterations required for convergence is significantly reduced. Moreover, in contrast to floating-point computation, integer computation is used in our method. Since the hardware for the Hopfield network is presently available, the bipartite subgraph problem can be solved in parallel. Furthermore, for the n-vertex K-partite subgraph problem only $\lceil \log_2 K \rceil n$ neurons are required by our algorithm. Hence, compared to the maximum neural network algorithm which requires Kn neurons, our method can be implemented more efficiently.

References

1. K. C. Lee, N. Funabiki, and Y. Takefuji, "A parallel improvement algorithm for the bipartite subgraph problem," *IEEE Trans. Neural Networks*, Vol. 3, No. 1, January 1992, pp. 139-145.
2. J. A. Bondy and S. C. Locke, "Largest bipartite subgraph in triangle free graphs with maximum degree three," *J. Graph Theory*, Vol. 10, 1986, pp. 477-504.
3. F. Barahona, "On some weakly bipartite graphs," *Oper. Res. Lett.*, Vol. 2, No. 5, 1983, pp. 239-242.
4. C. P. Hsu, "Minimum-via topological routing," *IEEE Trans. Computer-Aided Design*, Vol. 2, October 1983, pp. 235-246.
5. J. J. Hopfield, and D. W. Tank, "Neural computation of decisions in optimization problems," *Biolog. Cybern.*, Vol. 52, 1985, pp. 1-25.
6. J. J. Hopfield, "Neurons with graded response have collective computational properties like those of two state neurons," *Proc. Nat. Academy of Science*, Vol. 81, No. 10, May 1984, pp. 3088-3092.
7. D. E. Van den Bout and T. K. Miller, III, "Graph partitioning using annealed neural networks," *IEEE Trans. Neural Networks*, Vol. 1, No. 2, June 1990, pp. 192-203.
8. Y. Takefuji, and K. C. Lee "Artificial neural networks for four-coloring map problem and k-colorability," *IEEE Trans. Circuits Syst.*, Vol. 38, March 1991, pp. 326-333.
9. S. Chakradhar, M. Bushnell, and V. Agrawal, "Toward massively parallel test generation," *IEEE Trans. Computer-Aided Design*, Vol. 9, September 1990, pp. 981-984.
10. G. A. Tagliarini, J. F. Christ, and E. W. Page, " Optimization using neural networks," *IEEE Trans. Computers*, Vol. 40, No. 12, December 1991, pp. 1347-1358.
11. R. L. Lippmann, "An introduction to computing with neural nets, " *IEEE ASSP Mag.*, Vol. 4, 1987, pp. 4-22.
12. Philip D. Wasserman, "Neural Computing, Theory and Practice," Van Nostrand Reinhold, 1989.

HOMOGENEOUS NEURONLIKE STRUCTURES FOR OPTIMIZATION VARIATIONAL PROBLEM SOLVING

Kalyayev I.A.

Scientific Research Institute of Multiprocessor Computing Systems, Taganrog, Russia.

The wide class of optimization problems requiring the selection of a single optimal solution among a set of possible variants falls into the category of variational problems. The mismatch between the parallel nature of variational problems and the serial way of information processing on standard computers makes great dificalties in solving this problems by computer, espessially when the task must be solved quickly in real time. The method of solving the different types of variational problems with the help of homogeneous neuronlike structure (HNS) using the parallel information processing is presented in this work. By that a high speed in working out of the solution is achieve. One of the variational problems, requiring the solution in real time is the problem of planning the collision-free robot movement to the target. The solution of given problem by the HNS is presented in the paper. The high homogeneity and simplicity of the HNS cells allowed to construct the VLSI of HNS fragments and the HNS microassemby which are described in this paper. Some examples the applications of HNS in autonomous transport robot-planetcars control systems are given too.

INTRODUCTION

It's known that serial computers which are widely used at present time are not effective in solving a set of complicated problems. A wide class of optimization problems requiring to find of a single optimal solution that satisfies some criteria among several possible variants fall into this category of problem. That is due to mismatch between parallel nature of optimal problems and serial way of information processing in computers. This paper deal with the method of solving an optimization problem by means of

parallel type homogeneous neuronlike structures (HNS) which provide
both fast solution and compact VLSI - based implementation.

PROBLEM FORMALIZATION

The apparatus of variational calculus allows to formalize a
wide class of optimization problems. Generally, the variational
problem is formulated by following way /1/: it is necessary to
define the functions $y_i(S)(i=1,2,...,n)$ realizing the extremum of the
functional

$$J = \int_0^{S_K} f(y_1, y_2, ..., y_n, y_1', y_2', ..., y_n') \, ds \qquad (1)$$

under the boundary conditions

$$\alpha_j (y_1(0), y_2(0), ..., y_n(0)) \leq 0 \quad (j=1,2,...,m_1) \qquad (2)$$

$$\beta_j (y_1(S_K), y_2(S_K), ..., y_n(S_K)) \leq 0 \quad (j=1,2,...,m_2) \qquad (3)$$

and following constraints

$$\varphi_j (y_1, y_2, ..., y_n) \leq 0 \qquad (j=1,2,...,m_3) \qquad (4)$$

$$\psi_j (y_1, y_2, ..., y_n, y_1', y_2', ..., y_n') \leq 0 \quad (j=1,2,...,m_4) \qquad (5)$$

where ds - is the metric of n - dimensional functional space $\{Y\}^n$
is formed by the sought functions $y_i(S)$ ($i=1,2,...,n$) . In
application problems the sought functions $y_i(S)(i=1,2,...,n)$
typically define the states of an object or a process whose
transfer to the target states should be done in optimal way.

The known digital solving methods of variational problems
require a great number of calculations /2/ which makes it difficult
to use digital method for quick solving the variational problem in
real time. This failure can be avoided using the graph method of
representation of variational problems which is described by
following way.

The functional (1) is substituted by the integral sum in form:

$$J \approx \sum_{j=0}^{K} f(y_1^j, y_2^j, ..., y_n^j, \frac{\Delta y_1^j}{\Delta S_j}, ..., \frac{\Delta y_n^j}{\Delta S_j}) \cdot \Delta S_j \qquad (6)$$

where $\Delta y_i^j = y_i^{j+1} - y_i^j$ ($i=1,2,...,n$).

As a result the initial problem reduces to the problem of the

definition of discrete values $y_i^j (i=1,2,...,n; j=0,1,...,K)$ realizing
the extremum of integral sum (6) and satisfying the boundary
conditions (2), (3) and constraints (4), (5). The last problem can
be represented as the graph. For this purpose the function space
$\{Y\}^n$ is covered by the regular graph whose vertices $q_j \in Q$ are
matched to discrete points $Y_j = \langle y_1^j, y_2^j, ..., y_n^j \rangle$ of the space $\{Y\}^n$.
The weight γ equal to

$$\gamma(q_j, q_{j+1}) = f(y_1^j, y_2^j, ..., y_n^j, \frac{\Delta y_1^j}{\Delta S_j}, ..., \frac{\Delta y_n^j}{\Delta S_j}) \cdot \Delta S_j$$

is assigned to the arc $x(q_j, q_{j+1}) \in X$ connecting the vertices
corresponding to the neighbour discrete points Y_j and Y_{j+1}
of the space $\{Y\}^n$ (Fig.1).

Besides, on the graph $G(Q,X)$ necessary to define a sets
of the initial vertices $Q_o \subseteq Q$, final vertices $Q_K \subseteq Q$ and allowed
vertices $Q_A \subseteq Q$ satisfying the systems (2), (3) and (4),
respectively, as well as a set of the allowed arcs $X_A \subseteq X$ satisfying
the system (5) when substituting $y_i = y_i^j$ and $y_i' = \Delta y_i^j / \Delta S_j$.
As a result of such a graph representation the problem of
definition of values $y_i^j (i=1,2,...,n; j=0,1,...,K)$, which
realize the extremum of the integral sum (6), is reducing to the
problem of construction the path between one of the sets of the
initial vertices Q_o and one of the sets of the final
vertices Q_K . This path has to come only through a set Q_A
of the allowed vertices and a set X_A of the allowed arcs and has
the extremum sum weight of the arcs appertaining to this path.

By using the graph method of the variafional problem solving
two problems appeare:
1. how to select the graph-model $G(Q,X)$ topology?
2. how much the variational problem solution had been gotten with
the help of the graph model differs from the accurate solution?
This queslions had been investigated carefully in paper /3/.

PRINCIPLES OF ORGANIZATION THE HOMOGENEOUS NEUROLIKE STRUCTURE (HNS)

The fact that variational problems of various types may be reduced
to the standard task of the extreme path construction on the graph
model, allows to use neuronlike structures with parallel

information processing to solve them.

Let's suppose that we have a structure topologically similar to the graph-model $G(Q,X)$ of the functional space $\{Y\}^n$ of the variational problem which mast be solved. The structure cell is corresponded to each vertex q_j of the graph $G(Q,X)$, moreover, if two vertices q_j and q_{j+1} of the graph are connected by the arc $x(q_j,q_{j+1})$ then the cells corresponding to them are connected by the link going from the q_j cell output to the q_{j+1} cell input.

Besides, let's demand that the delay of the signal passing between the q_j cell input and its output, connected with the cell q_{j+1} is to be proportional to the weight γ of the arc $x(q_j,q_{j+1})$. If the arc $x(q_j,q_{j+1})$ belongs to the set $X \setminus X_A$, where X_A is the set of allowed arcs, then the signal passing through the link connecting the cells q_j and q_{j+1} is blocked. Similarly, all the links, connecting the cell corresponding to the vertex q_j with the neighour cells are blocked too, if $q_j \in Q \setminus Q_A$, where Q_A – is the set of the allowed vertices.

If in such a structure we generate a signal in the cell, corresponding to some vertex q_j then this signal, passing from cell to cell will be spread along the whole structure. In this case the time, during which this signal will reach the inputs of cell, corresponding to the vertex q_e, will be proportional to the weight of the minimum path in the graph $G(Q,X)$, between the vertices q_e and q_j. Moreover, the link, by which the first of the signals came to the cell q_j, will define the initial arc $x(q_e,q_{e+1})$ of this path.

Thus, if the signal is to be formed in the cell $q_K \in Q_K$ HNS and is to be registered in the cell $q_o \in Q_o$ the link via which the first signal has income, we will determine initial arc $x(q_o,q_1)$ of minimum path on the graph $G(Q,X)$ between vertices q_o and q_K. If to repeat the procedure of signal propagation in HNS from cell q_K, fixing the first of incomming signals in the cell q_1, then we will determine the next arc $x(q_1,q_2)$ of the minimum path. Repeating analogous procedure K times, we will determine the whole minimum path on the graph $G(Q,X)$ between vertices q_o and q_K. This path determines in its turn desired decision of the variational problem.

Similarly, the variational problem on the maximum of the

functional (1) may be solved with the help of the HNS, mapping the graph $G(Q,X)$. The difference will be in the fact, that it is necessary to estasblish the delay time on the links between the HNS cells proportionally to the value $\gamma_{max}-\gamma$, where γ_{max} - is the maximum possible value of the weight γ , γ - is the value of weight the ars $x(q_j,q_{j+1})$.

In this case the time delay on some path between the cells q_0 and q_K will be proportional to the value

$$\sum_{e=0}^{K-1} (\gamma_{max} - \gamma_e) = K \cdot \gamma_{max} - \sum_{e=0}^{K-1} \gamma_e$$

where γ_e - is the weight of the l-th arc, belonging to this path. In other words if the more the value $\sum_{e=0}^{K-1} \gamma_e$ is, the less the time delay will be on this path. So if we form the signal in the cell q_K , then the first signal which will reach the cell q_0 will be signal, arrived along the path, having the maximum total weight of the arcs belonged to it.

Analyzing the above procedure of the variational problem solving we may define the following functions that the HNS cell have to realize.
1. If the cell corresponds to the vertex $q_K \in Q_K$ then the signal is formed in it.
2. If the signal has come to the cell q_j then it is transferred to the neighbour cell q_{j+1} with the time delay proportional to the weight γ of the arc $x(q_j,q_{j+1})$ in case when $q_j \in Q_A$ and $x(q_j,q_{j+1}) \in X_A$. Otherwise it is not transfered.
3. In the cell $q_0 \in Q_0$ the link is fixed along which the first signal has come to it.

The cell design in Fig 2 answers to all these functions.

The important feature of the proposed HNS organization is the fact that this structure allows to get legal solutions when some cells or the links between them break down. In fact, we may consider the breaking down of some cells or the links simply as the introduction of extra constraints, putting on the sought functions $y_i(s) (i=1,2,\ldots, n)$. In this case the solution, got on the rest part of the cells and links of the HNS, will be optimal with the account of these extra constraints. This fact allows to come to the conclusion of the high HNS vitality.

METHODS OF SOLUTION OF HIGH DIMENSION VARIATIONAL PROBLEMS ON THE HNS.

One of the failure of the proposed method is the rapid increase of the hardware expences of the HNS realization with the growth dimension of the functional space . The author had proposed a number of methods, allowing to solve this problem /4/. Let's consider two them.

The method of spliting the tasks into the subtasks is the widely spread approach to solve the problem of complex multidimentional tasks . This approach may be used also in the variational problems solving by the graph method. The main idea here is that: with the help of an integrated (rough) model of the functional space to split the initial task into the sequence of subtasks, each of which may be solved with the help of the HNS of small size.

Let we have the HNS consisting of M cells. Let's form the functional space model in the form of such graph $G(Q,X)$ that $|Q| \leqslant M$. As a result we get the model of the first level. Let,s distinguish the verteces q_o and q_K on this model, that are defined by the boundary conditions of the task and build the extreme path between these vertices with the help of the HNS available. As a result we'll get the sequence of points $Y_o^1, Y_1^1,..., Y_K^1$ of the functional space $\{Y\}^n$, defined by the extreme path vertices.

Each pair of points Y_j^1, Y_{j+1}^1 $(j=0,1,...,K-1)$ of this sequence define some transition in the functional space $\{Y\}^n$ (Fig.3). Taking into account that each part of the extreme solution must be also extreme, then the transition between the points Y_j^1 and Y_{j+1}^1 must be done along the extreme path. In other words the original task of determining the extremum functional J with the boundary conditions $y_i(0) = y_i^o$ and $y_i(S_K) = y_i^K$ reduces to the solution of K tasks of determining the extremum functional J with the boundary conditions $y_i(0) = y_{ij}^1$ and $y_i(S_K) = y_{ij+1}^1$, where $< y_{1j}^1, y_{2j}^1,..., y_{nj}^1 >$ and $< y_{1j+1}^1, y_{2j+1}^1,..., y_{nj+1}^1 >$ are the coordinates of the points Y_j^1 and Y_{j+1}^1 respectively. Besides, as the points Y_j^1 and Y_{j+1}^1 are in same subspace $\{Y\}_j^n$ of the functional space $\{Y\}^n$, then to solve the subtask we may use the HNS mapping this subspace, but not the whole space $\{Y\}^n$. Let's form the graph - model $G_2^j(Q_2^j, X_2^j)$ of this subspace, while $|Q_2^j| \leqslant M$, and with the help of the HNS let's built the extreme path on this graph between the vertices q_{oz}^j and q_{Kz}^j, which are defined by the coordinates of the points Y_j^1 and Y_{j+1}^1. Similarly it is necessary to solve all of the K subtasks. In this case the total solution of the variational problem will be recieved as a result of the sequential "stitching" of all the subtasks K solutions.

The process of spliting may be extended, taking the neighbour pairs of points of the functional space recieved at the previous stage as the boundary conditions of the variational subtask.

Another approach is based on the heuristic supposition that the sought solution of the variational problem is near the straight line, connecting the points $Y_o = \langle y_1^o, y_2^o, \ldots, y_n^o \rangle$ and $Y_K = \langle y_1^K, y_2^K, \ldots, y_n^K \rangle$. The main idea of this approach is to distinguish in n-dimensional functional space one m - dimentional subspace (m<n), to which the straight lihe between the points Y_o and Y_K belongs and then to find the solution in this subspace with the help of m - dimentional HNS. For simplicity let's consider the method working for m=2.

Let's built a straight line in the functional space $\{Y\}^n$ passing through the points Y_o and Y_K and connect it with the axis $\mathcal{V}_1$ of the two - dimentional coordinate system $\mathcal{V}_1 O \mathcal{V}_2$ the beginning of which coincide with the point Y_o (Fig.4). Let's assume a straight line passing through the point Y_o and perpendicular to the axis $\mathcal{V}_1$ as the axis $\mathcal{V}_2$ of the system $\mathcal{V}_1 O \mathcal{V}_2$. As a result we get a two-dimensional subspace $\{Y\}^2$ of the n-dimentional space $\{Y\}^n$. Hereafter we'll call the subspace $\{Y\}^2$ as the solution plane.

Since the points Y_o and Y_K simultaneously belong to the subspace $\{Y\}^2$, then some set of paths between these points that will define possible solutions of the variational problem may be defined in it. If among this set we choose the path where the variational functional takes the extreme value, then we'll define some approximate solution of the task. This may be done with the help of the HNS mapping the graph model of the subspace $\{Y\}^2$. It should be noted that since the direction of the axis $\mathcal{V}_2$ of the system $\mathcal{V}_1 O \mathcal{V}_2$ is not set rigidly, then by changing this direction it is possible to change also the solution plane $\{Y\}^2$. It is possible to study various plane solutions and choose the extreme solution among them with the help of the same HNS.

THE ORGANIZATION OF SYSTEMS PLANNING THE TRANSPORT ROBOTS MOVEMENT ON THE BASIS OF THE HNS.

Proposed HNS were used for creation of control systems of autonomus transport robots (TR) intended for functioning complex environment, information about which is unknown before. That is why robot's route cannot determine before but has to be built and corrected at the rate of receipt of new environment information i.e. in real time. For all this, as a rule robot has a big number of different alternatives of the movement routes to the target among which it is necessary to select optimal one. Decision of the last problem may be performed effectively by HNS /4/.

Formally the problem of planning robot's optimal movement to the target can be represented as the following variational problem (Fig.5): to determine the functions $y_1(s)$ and $y_2(s)$ minimizing the functional

$$ J = \int_0^{S_K} T(y_1, y_2, y_1', y_2', \rho_1, \ldots, \rho_n) \, ds \tag{7} $$

under boundary conditions $y_i(0) = y_i^o$ and $y_i(S_K) = y_i^K$ $(i=1,2)$ and constraints

$$ Y = \langle y_1, y_2 \rangle \notin \{Y\}_f^2 \tag{8} $$

$$ \Psi_j(y_1, y_2, y_1', y_2', \rho_1, \ldots, \rho_e) \leq 0 \ (j = 1, 2, \ldots, m) \tag{9} $$

where $Y = \langle y_1, y_2 \rangle$ - are the coordinates of the TR state in the environment; $\langle y_1^o, y_2^o \rangle$ and $\langle y_1^K, y_2^K \rangle$ are the coordinates of the current and target TR statement in the environment; $\{Y\}_f^2$ is a set of forbidden TR states in which it meets obstacles; $T(y_1, y_2, y_1', y_2', \rho_1, \ldots, \rho_e)$ is a function defining the difficulty of the robot passing through elementary trajectory section; $\Psi_j(y_1, y_2, y_1', y_2', \rho_1, \ldots, \rho_e)$ is a system of constraints defined by the environment and the characteristics of the TR shassi; $\rho_1, \ldots, \rho_e$ are the parameters of environment defined by means of TR sensor systems;

As a result of application of above approach to the last problem we obtain HNS reflected two-dimensional functional space $\{Y\}^2$. The procedure of decision problem of optimal ATR route constraction with application such HNS is decomposed by two phases. At the first phase programming process of HNS performs which consists in the programming of time delays proportional to weight

$$\gamma(q_j, q_{j+1}) = T\left(y_1, y_2, \frac{\Delta y_1}{\Delta S_j}, \frac{\Delta y_2}{\Delta S_j}, \rho_1, \ldots, \rho_e\right) \cdot \Delta S_j$$

of corresponding arcs $x(q_j, q_{j+1})$ and blocking of cells and links between them, corresponding to sets $Q \setminus Q_A$ and $X \setminus X_A$ which are determined by constraints (8) and (9). On the second stage in HNS cell, corresponding to $\langle y_1^K, y_2^K \rangle$ coordinates of robot's target, the signal is formed. In the cell, corresponding to $\langle y_1^o, y_2^o \rangle$ coordinates of the current position of the robot, the link is registered, via which the first of the signals incomes. This link in its turn determines the direction of current optimal movement of the robot towards the target with avoiding of obstacles.

After processing of robot movement step in the given direction HNS programming procedures and decision making are repeated all over again, with new information on the environment and new current position of the robot in the environment, e.c. up to achieving the target by the robot.

HNS was used for building of two ATR control systems. The first of this systems provided for ATR collision-free functioning in natural environment with dimensions 50 x 50m. HNS, which was used in this system, consisted of 16x24 cells. The HNS programming was carried out on the basis of the information got with the help of the scanning range-finder. The range-finder determines the function of the difficulty of robot passing through the area of environment (this function is dependent on the slope of this area relatively to the horizon).

The second system based on the HNS having 4096 cells. As in the previous system the HNS programming is accomplished with the help of the scanning range-finder.

The peculiarity lies in the fact that the ideas of method of task spliting into the subtasks are used in the second system that allows to solve the planning task in the environment of size

256x256 metres. Besides, in contrast to the first system here the HNS is not rigidly linked with some fixed area of the environment, but at each cycle of solution the graph-model of the environment, surrounding the robot at the current moment, is mapped in it. The latter allows the robot to function practically in an unlimited environment.

This two systems were tested in the real environments.

MICROELECTRONIC IMPLEMENTATION OF HNS

High homogeneity and simplicity of HNS cells best of all answering the modern microelectronic technology open wide perspectives for implementation of HNS in the form of VLSI. Stimulus to perform these works was necessity for building of small-scale control systems of TR functioning in real complex environment. Accomplished analysis allowed to formulate the following fundamental principles of HNS VLSI design /5/:

1. Each VLSI has to realize the HNS fragment. It is necessary to provide for possibility of VLSI HNS fragments "stitching" with each other for the purpose to increase the structure size.

2. Because of constraints limitation on the number of VLSI external contacts the information exchange between HNS fragment has to organize through sequence channels or two-directional buses.

3. For the purpose of increasing of VLSI survability it is necessary to provide for localization circuites of defective cells generating false signals.

On the base of the given principles the VLSI of the HNS fragment were designed and constructed orientated towards the task solution problem of planning robot movement to the target in the environment with obstacles. The structural scheme of the given VLSI is shown in Fig.6. It contains the HNS fragment, array decoder (AD) and a set of two-dimentional transfer designs (TTD). The HNS fragment presents an array of 16x8 cells, each of which is constructed according to the design given in Fig.2.
The VLSI operates in two modes - the mode of programming and the mode of the signal wave propagation. In the mode of programming the cell addresses are consecutivly driven to the address inputs of the

VLSI. Besides, along with the address of the cell, the code carrying the information about the weight γ of the corresponding graph-model arcs and about the belonging of the corresponding graph-model vertex to the set of the allowed verteces, is driven to the program input of VLSI. This information is written to the cell distinguished by the decoder. Similarly, all HNS cells are consecutively programmed.

After this the second, the main mode of the VLSI operation is started. To do this it is necessary to drive the address code of the target vertex q_K of the graph $G(Q, X)$ to the address inputs and to drive the signal allowing the VLSI work to the input S. As a result the signal, which is spread along the whole HNS, is formed in the cell distinguished by the decoder.

The HNS fragment VLSI is realized on the basis of the base array chip having 3000 gates by K-MOS technology.

The microassembly of the HNS was desighed and constructed on the basis of the HNS fragment VLSI. The microassembly consists of 8 chips of the HNS fragment VLSI united into the common HNS of size 32x32 cells (1024 cells). Microassemblies may be "stiched" with each other to increment the HNS to the desized size.

CONCLUSION

So the research allows to conclude that the given approach can be effectively applied to the construction of small-scale computers of autonomous robots and similar devices operating under conditions requiring the selection of extreme solving, among multiple possible variants in real time.

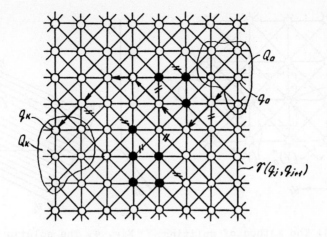

● —the vertices of the set $Q \backslash Q_A$

⚡ — the arcs of the set $X \backslash X_A$

Fig.1. The graph model of the functional space

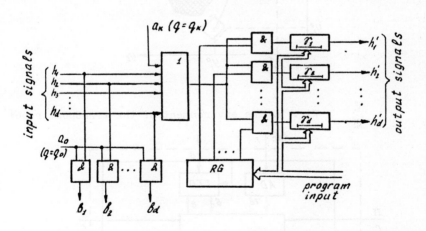

Fig. 2. The scheme of the HNS cell

450

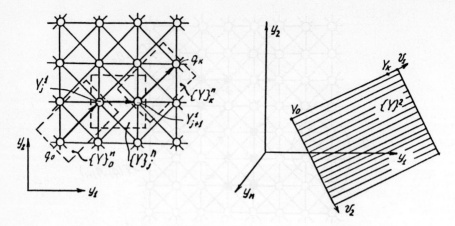

Fig. 3. The method of spliting
the task into subtasks

Fig. 4. The solutio plane

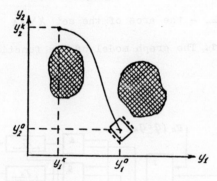

Fig. 5. The environment of the transport robot

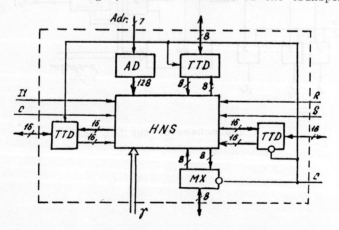

Fig. 6. The scheme of the HNS fragment VLSI

REFERENCES

1. Alsgoltss L.лe. Differential equations and calculus of variations.- Moscow, 1969, 424p.

2. Moisejev N.N. Elements of the optimal system theory. - Moscow 1975, 525p.

3. Kalyayev I.л., Kapustyan S.G. Homogeneous structures for aptimization and planning variational problems solving. - L'vov, 1991, 88p.

4. Kalyayev л.V., Chernychin J.V., Noskov V.P., Kalyayev I.л. Homogeneous control structures of adaptiv robot - Moscow, 1989, 147p.

5. Kalyaev л.V., Chernukhin J.V., Kalyaev I.A. et al. Construction of homogeneous control structures of adaptive autonomus robots, Microprocessor software and systems, - Moscow, 1985, N 4, pp.68-71

Effectiveness of Heuristics and Simulated Annealing for the Scheduling of Concurrent Tasks — An Empirical Comparison

Christophe COROYER†   and   Zhen LIU‡

† I3S–LISAN, CNRS, Bât. 4, rue A. Einstein, 06560 Valbonne, France
‡ INRIA, Centre Sophia Antipolis, 2004 route des Lucioles, 06565 Valbonne, France

Abstract: It is well-known that the scheduling of concurrent tasks with precedence constraints in parallel systems in order to minimize the makespan is NP-complete. We study both the average effectiveness and the average efficiency of 27 heuristics and 7 simulated annealing algorithms used for the minimization of makespan. It is shown, by a computational experiment, that the simulated annealing algorithms are very effective compared with the heuristics, provided these algorithms converge. It turns out that some heuristics are quite effective on the average, and that the heuristics, provided they are used together, have a qualitative behavior not much worse than that of the simulated annealing and are much more efficient.

Keywords: Scheduling, heuristics, simulated annealing, makespan, empirical comparison, parallel processing, precedence constraints.

1   Introduction and Problem Description

Consider the following scheduling problem: there are N tasks and K parallel processors, indexed from 1 to N and 1 to K, respectively. A processor can execute at most one task at a time, and a task can only be assigned to one processor. The execution of the tasks is nonpreemptive, and is constrained by some precedence relations which can be described by a task graph $G = (V, E)$, where $V = \{1, 2, \cdots, N\}$ is the set of vertices corresponding to the tasks, and E the set of directed edges representing precedence relations between tasks. For all $i, j \in V$, relation $(i, j) \in E$ implies that task j can only start after task i has finished. The objective is to minimize the makespan, i.e. the total processing time of the tasks, by assigning the tasks to the processors and by ordering the execution. The task assignment may have constraints, viz. a task may only be assigned to a subset of processors. Two extreme cases are considered in this paper: 1) the assignment of the tasks is predefined so that each task can only be assigned to a predefined processor; 2) the task assignment has no constraints so that each task can be assigned to any of the processors.

Studies on the optimal scheduling have been carried out for particular cases. Hu [8] studied the problem with in-tree structure, i.e. a task has at most one successor, and there is only one task (root of the tree) without a successor. It is shown that the HLF (Highest Level First) policy is optimal. Coffman and Graham [2] found an efficient optimal algorithm for scheduling identical tasks with arbitrary precedence constraints on two parallel processors. Coffman and Liu [3] analyzed the out-forest structure and found optimal scheduling when all the subtrees in the out-forest have an embedding relation.

Algorithms leading to optimal solutions of the general model can also be found in the literature (e.g. Ramamoorthy et al. [14]). However, it is well known that optimal solutions are NP-complete [11]. In fact, when there are no precedence relations, this boils down to the classical job-shop problem in the theory of operations research.

Various heuristics have been proposed in the literature, see e.g. Ramamoorthy et al. [14], Liu and Labetoulle [13]. Worst-case analysis of the heuristics (see Graham [5] and Liu

[12]) shows that the ratio of the makespan of any priority-based heuristic to the optimal solution is bounded by $2 - 1/K$.

The technique of Simulated Annealing (SA), which is an extension of the Monte Carlo method, is used to find approximate solutions to combinatorial optimization problems [9, 10]. In particular, this can also be applied to our scheduling problem.

In this paper, we are interested in the average effectiveness (i.e. the average quality of the solutions) and the average efficiency (i.e. the average time complexity) of the heuristics and the SA algorithms, as well as the comparison of their effectiveness and efficiency. We carry out a computational experiment on 27 heuristics and 7 homogeneous and inhomogeneous SA approaches. It is shown, by a computational experiment, that the SA algorithms are very effective compared with the heuristics, provided the temperature is decreasing slowly enough so that these algorithms converge. It turns out, unlike the bound provided by the worst case analysis, that some heuristics are quite effective on the average. Another observation is that the heuristics, when they are used together, i.e. for every problem all the heuristics are tried and the best solution is chosen, have a qualitative behavior not much worse than that of the SA and are much more efficient.

Earlier empirical comparisons of heuristics were performed by Adam et al. [1] where five heuristics were tested. Our investigation differs from that of Talbot et al. [16] where the heuristics for minimizing the number of processors were considered.

The paper is organized as follows. In Section 2, we describe the heuristics that are considered in the paper. In Section 3, we discuss how the technique of SA are used for solving the scheduling problem. In Sections 4 and 5, we present empirical comparison results among heuristics and between heuristics and SA algorithms, respectively.

2 Priority-Based Heuristics

We consider a class of priority-based heuristic algorithms for the scheduling problem. Since the tasks that we deal with have precedence constraints, it is natural to consider the tasks to be scheduled according to the partial order defined on them. Hence in our scheduling algorithm, only those tasks which have no predecessors in the task graph, or whose predecessors have already been scheduled by the algorithm, will be taken into consideration as candidates for scheduling.

The basic idea of priority-based heuristic approach consists of choosing tasks one by one from the candidates according to their priorities. As soon as a processor is idle, we assign the candidate task with the highest priority onto it, provided the task has access to the processor. If there is no candidate, the processor remains idle. More precisely, let C denote the set of candidate tasks, P_i the processing time of task i, and T_j the available time of processor j, i.e. the time when processor j finishes the tasks already assigned on it, and can begin to process another task. This schema can be written in a PASCAL-like language as follows.

Generic Priority-Based Heuristic

C = set of tasks without predecessors;
for $k = 1, \cdots, K$ do $T_k = 0$;
repeat
    $H = \min_{1 \leq k \leq K} T_k$;
    repeat
        $S = \{j \mid T_j = H\}$;
        for all $j \in S$:
            if the last finished task of processor j has successors which have
                no unfinished predecessors at time H

then put these successors into C;

    if C is empty then

$$H = \min_{1 \leq k \leq K} \max(H, T_k);$$

      for all $j \in S$ do $T_j = H$;

  until C is not empty;

  for all $j \in S$:

    assign the task i onto processor j such that i has the highest priority

      among the tasks in C which have access to processor j;

    remove i from C;

    update T_j by $T_j + P_i$;

until all the tasks are scheduled.

Different heuristics can be obtained by using this schema together with some priority criteria. In general, one can distinguish two types of priorities: static and dynamic rules. Static rules consist of associating with each task a priority which can be determined before the scheduling process, while dynamic rules determine the priorities of tasks during the scheduling process. When a tie occurs, more priority criteria can be used, so that one can construct hybrid priorities.

The simplest example of static priority rule is Largest Processing Time, which requires that the task whose processing time is the largest among the candidates be scheduled first. A simple example of dynamic rule is Earliest Enabled, which requires that the first enabled task, i.e. the one whose predecessors are complete earliest, be scheduled first.

In this paper, we analyze 27 heuristics (cf. Table 1). The reader is referred to [4] for the precise definitions of these heuristics.

3 Simulated Annealing

The technique of Simulated Annealing (SA) is often used to find approximate solutions to combinatorial optimization problems [10]. This method is used here for solving the task scheduling problem.

The basic idea of the SA algorithms is as follows: one starts with an initial solution and an initial temperature (which is a control parameter) and iterates the improvement procedure. In each iteration, one decreases, when necessary, the temperature and generates a new solution by perturbing the configuration of the old one. If the cost of the new solution is lower than the old one, the new solution is accepted. Otherwise, this solution is accepted with a certain probability.

We distinguish two types of the SA algorithms according to the temperature decrease procedure:

- homogeneous algorithm: the temperature is decreased when some equilibrium state of the solutions is reached.
- inhomogeneous algorithm: the temperature is decreased at each iteration.

These two schemas are illustrated below, where T, S and C denote the temperature, the solution and the cost of the solution, respectively.

Homogeneous algorithm

    T=initial temperature;

    S=initial solution;

    C=cost of the initial solution;

    repeat

        repeat

```
        S'=PERTURB(S);
        C'=cost of S';
        if C' < C then accept S'
        else accept S' with probability exp((C - C')/T);
        if accept then update S and C;
    until equilibrium is reached;
    update temperature T;
until stopping criterion is fulfilled.
```

Inhmogeneous algorithm

```
    T=initial temperature;
    S=initial solution;
    C=cost of the initial solution;
    repeat
        S'=PERTURB(S);
        C'=cost of S';
        if C' < C then accept S'
        else accept S' with probability exp((C - C')/T);
        if accept then update S and C;
        update temperature T;
    until stopping criterion is fulfilled.
```

In terms of a Markov chain, a solution is a state and an iteration represents a state transition. The homogeneous and the inhomogeneous algorithms correspond to the homogeneous and the inhomogeneous Markov chains, respectively.

We refer the reader to [10] for a detailed discussion on the convergence and implementation issues of the algorithms. We discuss below how these algorithms are used for solving our scheduling problem.

The initial solution is arbitrarily chosen.

The initial temperature should be determined in such a way that all the transitions at this temperature are accepted. However, in practice, we define an acceptance ratio χ_0, which equals the number of accepted solutions over the number of proposed solutions, and we determine the initial temperature in such a way that the acceptance rate at the initial temperature is not less than χ_0. One of the possible ways to do that is to generate several new solutions and compute the average increase of cost ΔC, and set $-\Delta C / \ln \chi_0$ as the initial temperature.

The perturbation of a solution is implemented by either moving a task from one processor to another or permute the execution order of two tasks on the same processor.

The equilibrium is reached when the probability distribution of the solution equals the Boltzman distribution given by : $P(S) = \exp(-C(S)/T)/Q(T)$, where S, T and $Q(T)$ are the solution, the temperature and the normalizing constant, respectively. In the implementation, we approach this equilibrium state by, according to the recommendations of Ramanujam et al. [15], setting the number of internal iterations (cf. homogeneous algorithm) as a multiple of the number of neighbors of a solution. In accordance with the above perturbation function, we define two measures of the number of neighbors in a problem:

$$\alpha = n(m - 1) \quad \text{and} \quad \beta = \sum_{i=1}^{n} n_i/2,$$

where n is the number of tasks, m is the number of processors, and n_i is the number of tasks which have no precedence relation with task i in the task graph.

The **temperature update** function is geometric for homogeneous algorithms. As for inhomogeneous algorithms, it is shown (see [6, 7, 10]) that the convergence to a globally minimal solution is ensured when the temperature tends to zero not faster than $O([\log k]^{-1})$. In our experiments, it turns out that such a decreasing speed is too slow for most of the problems. Thus we have chosen decreasing functions of orders $O(q^k)$ $(q < 1)$ and $O(1/k)$.

Two **stopping criteria** are used in our implementations: The annealing process is stopped either when the temperature is lower than certain threshold or when consecutive solutions are identical for a certain number of times.

4 Comparison between Heuristics and Simulated Annealing

The comparison has been carried out for about 700 problems. We have randomly generated 100 task graphs by fixing the precedence ratio to be 1/8, and by varying the number of tasks from 20 to 100, and the execution times of the tasks from 1 to 100. For each task graph and each heuristic and simulated annealing, experiments are performed for the number of processors being equal to $2, 3, \cdots$, until the makespan reaches the *theoretical minimum makespan*, i.e. the length of the critical path of the task graph.

4.1 Scheduling with a Given Assignment

Consider first the case where the assignment of the tasks is predefined. The heuristics are used to obtain the execution order on each of the processors. We have generated $J = 700$ problems and for each of them, the assignment is randomly defined.

We have implemented a homogeneous SA algorithm. The initial solution is randomly generated. The initial temperature is computed in order to have an initial acceptance ratio not less than 0.95. The number of internal iterations equals β (cf. Section 3). The temperature updating function is geometric with ratio 0.95. The algorithm is stopped when the temperature is lower than 10^{-6}. The comparison results are summerized in Table 1. The results are obtained by computing the solutions of all the heuristics and the simulated annealing algorithm for each of the problems.

Denote by π an arbitrary scheduling policy. For each problem i, $i = 1, \cdots, J$, denote by $M_i(\pi)$ the makespan of problem i given by policy π, and denote by M_i the makespan of the best solution of the problem found by the policies under investigation, viz. $M_i = \min_\pi M_i(\pi)$. The data provided in the table indicate:

- column **A**: the rate at which a policy yields the best solution: $100 \times \sum_{i=1}^{J} 1(M_i(\pi) = M_i)/J$.
- column **B**: the average relative difference between the solution of a policy and the best solution: $\sum_{i=1}^{J} (M_i(\pi) - M_i)/M_i$.
- column **C**: the average of relative qualities of the solutions of a policy with respect to the best solutions: $\sum_{i=1}^{J} (M_i(\pi)/M_i)/J$.
- column **D**: the relative quality of the average of the solutions of a policy with respect to the best solutions: $\sum_{i=1}^{J} M_i(\pi)/ \sum_{i=1}^{J} M_i$.

One might have observed that among the heuristics, the **Least Schedule Flexibility** policy as well as the hybrid policies based on it are the best among this set of heuristics. Note also that the policies based on the notion **Most Descendants** are also very effective. According to these results, the **Largest Processing Time** policy is the poorest within this set of heuristics.

It turns out that in 55% of the cases, the SA algorithm strictly overperforms the heuristics, whereas in 6% of the cases, the heuristics strictly overperform the SA algorithm, and

457

Table 1. Comparison between the heuristics and the SA algorithm with a given assignment

	A	B	C	D
Largest Processing Time	2.00	22.73	1.23	1.22
Smallest Processing Time	6.14	14.60	1.15	1.14
Highest Level	32.00	5.00	1.05	1.04
Most Sons	16.00	11.40	1.11	1.11
Most Descendants	31.57	4.96	1.05	1.04
Longest Path	23.57	5.66	1.06	1.05
Successors' Weight	6.71	15.71	1.16	1.15
Descendants' Weight	28.57	4.97	1.05	1.04
Earliest Enabled	8.86	12.68	1.13	1.12
Least Schedule Flexibility	34.86	4.34	1.04	1.04
Highest Level Essential Task	31.00	5.10	1.05	1.05
Highest Level Largest Processing Time	26.57	5.92	1.06	1.05
Highest Level Smallest Processing Time	31.43	4.87	1.05	1.04
Most Sons Longest Path	16.43	10.73	1.11	1.11
Most Descendants Longest Path	32.00	4.83	1.05	1.04
Most Descendants Least Schedule Flexibility	33.86	4.70	1.05	1.04
Longest Path Largest Processing Time	23.57	5.74	1.06	1.05
Longest Path Smallest Processing Time	23.43	5.67	1.06	1.05
Longest Path Most Sons	23.57	5.69	1.06	1.05
Longest Path Most Descendants	23.57	5.68	1.06	1.05
Longest Path Least Schedule Flexibility	23.43	5.67	1.06	1.05
Least Schedule Flexibility Highest Level	34.86	4.32	1.04	1.04
Least Schedule Flexibility Descendants' Weight	34.43	4.34	1.04	1.04
Least Schedule Flexibility Longest Path	33.00	4.41	1.04	1.04
Least Schedule Flexibility Most Descendants	34.71	4.33	1.04	1.04
Most Sons Longest Path Successors' Weight	16.57	10.72	1.11	1.11
Most Sons Longest Path Descendants' Weight	16.43	10.73	1.11	1.11
Simulated Annealing	94.29	0.16	1.00	1.00

in 39% of the cases the best solution found by the heuristics has the same makespan as the SA algorithm. The average difference of makespan between heuristics and the simulated annealing is 17.20.

We thus conclude that when there is a given task assignment, the SA algorithm is effective. Moreover, it finishes within a reasonable time. In Table 2, we provide the average execution times of the heuristics and the SA algorithm applied to these 700 problems on a DEC-5400.

4.2 Scheduling without Assignment Constraints

Consider now the case where the task assignment has no constraints. The heuristics as well as the simulated annealing algorithms have to assign the tasks and schedule their executions.

When the task assignment has no constraints, the SA algorithms are much more time-consuming. Indeed, the scheduling process now consists of two steps: assigning the tasks and

Table 2. Average execution times when the assignment is given

Largest Processing Time	0.02s
Smallest Processing Time	0.02s
Highest Level	0.02s
Most Sons	0.02s
Most Descendants	0.02s
Longest Path	0.02s
Successors' Weight	0.02s
Descendants' Weight	0.02s
Earliest Enabled	0.02s
Least Schedule Flexibility	0.13s
Highest Level Essential Task	0.02s
Highest Level Largest Processing Time	0.02s
Highest Level Smallest Processing Time	0.02s
Most Sons Longest Path	0.02s
Most Descendants Longest Path	0.02s
Most Descendants Least Schedule Flexibility	0.13s
Longest Path Largest Processing Time	0.02s
Longest Path Smallest Processing Time	0.02s
Longest Path Most Sons	0.02s
Longest Path Most Descendants	0.02s
Longest Path Least Schedule Flexibility	0.13s
Least Schedule Flexibility Highest Level	0.13s
Least Schedule Flexibility Descendants' Weight	0.13s
Least Schedule Flexibility Longest Path	0.13s
Least Schedule Flexibility Most Descendants	0.13s
Most Sons Longest Path Successors' Weight	0.02s
Most Sons Longest Path Descendants' Weight	0.02s
Simulated Annealing	1m8.19s

ordering the executions. For each step, either SA algorithms or heuristics can be applied. We thus implement two "mixed" SA algorithms with the annealing process for the task assignment step and the heuristics for the execution scheduling, three two-step SA algorithms with annealing processes for both steps. In addition, we also implement a single step SA algorithm, which, at each perturbation, chooses with a certain probability a perturbation of task assignment or a perturbation of execution order. In all these annealing processes, the initial solution is randomly generated and the initial temperature is determined by the acceptance ratio 0.95.

1. IISA (.95, Random): We first implement an algorithm with a homogeneous simulated annealing for the task assignment step and a random policy for the execution ordering step.
   - Homogeneous annealing for the task assignment with the number of internal iterations equals α (cf. Section 3). The temperature updating function is geometric with ratio 0.95. The annealing process is stopped when the temperature is lower than 0.01.

- The scheduling of task executions is done randomly subject to the precedence constraints.

2. HSA (.95, LSF):
   - Homogeneous annealing for the task assignment with the number of internal iterations being α and a geometrical temperature decrease of ratio 0.95. The annealing process is stopped when the temperature is lower than 0.01.
   - The Least Schedule Flexibility policy for the scheduling of task executions.

3. HSA (.5, .5): Homogeneous annealings for both the task assignment and the task execution scheduling. For both annealing processes, the number of internal iterations equals α, the temperature updating function is geometric with ratio 0.5, and the processes are stopped when the temperature is lower than 0.01 or when the last 5α consecutive solutions are identical.

4. IHSA (.98, .98):
   - Inhomogeneous annealing for the task assignment with a geometrical temperature decrease of ratio 0.98. The annealing process is stopped when the temperature is lower than 0.01.
   - Inhomogeneous annealing for the scheduling of task executions with a geometrical temperature decrease of ratio 0.98. The annealing process is stopped when the temperature is lower than 0.001.

5. IHSA ($1/n$, $1/n$):
   - Inhomogeneous annealing for the task assignment with the temperature updating function given by T_0/n, where T_0 is the initial temperature and n is the index of the current iteration. The annealing process is stopped when the temperature is lower than 0.01 or when the last 5α consecutive solutions are identical.
   - Inhomogeneous annealing for the scheduling of task executions with the temperature updating function given by T_0/n. The annealing process is stopped when the temperature is lower than 0.001 or when the last 5β consecutive solutions are identical.

6. HSA (.98): This is a one-step Homogeneous Simulated Annealing algorithm. At each perturbation, with probability p, we modify the task assignment by moving a task from one processor to another, and with probability $1 - p$, we modify the scheduling of the tasks by interchanging the execution order of two tasks on a processor provided there is no precedence constraint between these two tasks. The probability p is determined in such a way that $p/(1 - p) = \alpha/\beta$. The temperature updating function is geometric with ratio 0.98. The number of internal iterations equals $p\alpha + (1 - p)\beta$. The annealing process is stopped when the temperature is lower than 0.01.

Note that in the two-step annealing processes, we have chosen the above parameters in order to make possible the comparison between heuristics and the SA algorithms. However, with these parameters, the annealing processes will not converge. Thus, in the implementations of IHSA($1/n$, $1/n$) and HSA(.5, .5), we take the best solution encountered during the execution of the algorithms as the final solution.

In Table 3, we provide the comparison results over a set of $J = 115$ problems, where the number of tasks varies from 20 to 30.

Note that in this case, the best heuristics are those based on the notion of **Longest Path**. The poorest one now becomes the **Smallest Processing Time**.

It can be seen from the table that on the average the simulated annealing algorithms are effective. However, they are much more time-consuming. In Table 4, we provide the average execution times of the heuristics and the SA algorithms applied to these 115 problems on a DEC-5400. The symbol ϵ indicates that the execution time is smaller than 0.01s. Observe that the HSA(.98) is the most effective and also the most time-consuming.

Table 3. Comparisons of heuristics and SA algorithms without assignment constraints

	A	B	C	D
Largest Processing Time	20.00	8.89	1.09	1.09
Smallest Processing Time	11.30	11.41	1.11	1.11
Highest Level	53.04	2.28	1.02	1.02
Most Sons	39.13	3.82	1.04	1.04
Most Descendants	50.43	2.25	1.02	1.02
Longest Path	69.57	0.58	1.01	1.01
Successors' Weight	43.48	4.46	1.04	1.04
Descendants' Weight	62.61	0.75	1.01	1.01
Earliest Enabled	19.13	8.89	1.09	1.09
Least Schedule Flexibility	33.04	6.24	1.06	1.06
Highest Level Essential Task	53.91	1.93	1.02	1.02
Highest Level Largest Processing Time	66.96	0.64	1.01	1.01
Highest Level Smallest Processing Time	49.57	3.06	1.03	1.03
Most Sons Longest Path	54.78	1.43	1.01	1.01
Most Descendants Longest Path	58.26	0.94	1.01	1.01
Most Descendants Least Schedule Flexibility	51.30	2.33	1.02	1.02
Longest Path Largest Processing Time	70.43	0.56	1.01	1.01
Longest Path Smallest Processing Time	68.70	0.57	1.01	1.01
Longest Path Most Sons	68.70	0.54	1.01	1.01
Longest Path Most Descendants	68.70	0.56	1.01	1.01
Longest Path Least Schedule Flexibility	71.30	0.56	1.01	1.01
Least Schedule Flexibility Highest Level	44.35	6.27	1.06	1.06
Least Schedule Flexibility Descendants' Weight	45.22	6.35	1.06	1.06
Least Schedule Flexibility Longest Path	45.22	6.32	1.06	1.06
Least Schedule Flexibility Most Descendants	45.22	6.35	1.06	1.06
Most Sons Longest Path Successors' Weight	55.65	1.41	1.01	1.01
Most Sons Longest Path Descendants' Weight	54.78	1.43	1.01	1.01
Homogeneous SA (.95, Random)	66.96	0.98	1.01	1.01
Homogeneous SA (.95, LSF)	80.87	0.23	1.00	1.00
Homogeneous SA (.5 .5)	67.83	0.51	1.01	1.00
Inhomogeneous SA (.98 .98)	69.57	0.85	1.01	1.01
Inhomogeneous SA (1/n, 1/n)	78.26	0.39	1.00	1.00
Homogeneous SA (.98)	93.91	0.08	1.00	1.00

It is worthwhile noticing that if these heuristics are used together for each of the problems, i.e. for each problem we try all the heuristics and take the best solution, they have quite a similar effectiveness as "best" SA algorithms. Such a fact is illustrated in Table 5, where the experimental results are obtained for the above 115 problems. One observes that the total execution time of the heuristics is over 100 times smaller than those SA algorithms which have a similar effectiveness. As a consequence, the heuristics, provided they are used together, are not only efficient but also very effective.

Table 4. Average execution times without assignment constraints

Largest Processing Time	ϵ
Smallest Processing Time	ϵ
Highest Level	ϵ
Most Sons	ϵ
Most Descendants	ϵ
Longest Path	ϵ
Successors' Weight	ϵ
Descendants' Weight	ϵ
Earliest Enabled	ϵ
Least Schedule Flexibility	0.02s
Highest Level Essential Task	ϵ
Highest Level Largest Processing Time	ϵ
Highest Level Smallest Processing Time	ϵ
Most Sons Longest Path	ϵ
Most Descendants Longest Path	ϵ
Most Descendants Least Schedule Flexibility	0.02s
Longest Path Largest Processing Time	ϵ
Longest Path Smallest Processing Time	ϵ
Longest Path Most Sons	ϵ
Longest Path Most Descendants	ϵ
Longest Path Least Schedule Flexibility	0.02s
Least Schedule Flexibility Highest Level	0.02s
Least Schedule Flexibility Descendants' Weight	0.02s
Least Schedule Flexibility Longest Path	0.02s
Least Schedule Flexibility Most Descendants	0.02s
Most Sons Longest Path Successors' Weight	ϵ
Most Sons Longest Path Descendants' Weight	ϵ
Homogeneous SA (.95, Random)	1m12.04s
Homogeneous SA (.95, LSF)	5m50.27s
Homogeneous SA (.5 .5)	10m37.81s
Inhomogeneous SA (.98 .98)	3m45.37s
Inhomogeneous SA (1/n, 1/n)	10m19.59s
Homogeneous SA (.98)	25m19.02s

5 Conclusions

In this paper, we have evaluated, by means of computational experiment, the effectiveness of 27 heuristics and 7 SA schemas used for the minimization of makespan. Our experiment has shown that efficient algorithms exist for finding optimal or near optimal solutions.

In case the task assignment is predefined, the Least Schedule Flexibility policy is on the average the most effective among the 27 heuristics. The homogeneous SA algorithm finishes within a reasonable time and yields quite good results for most of the problems. When the heuristics are used together for problem resolution, the homogeneous SA algorithm still overperforms the heuristics on the average. However, for about 40% of the cases, the heuristics, provided they are used together, have the same solution as the SA algorithm.

Table 5. Heuristics vs. SA algorithms

	average difference of makespan between heuristics and SA	overperformance rate of heuristics	overperformance rate of SA	equal performance rate
HSA (.95, Random)	-0.73	27.83	8.70	63.48
HSA (.95, LSF)	0.01	10.43	15.65	73.91
HSA (.5 .5)	-0.27	22.61	12.17	65.22
HHSA (.98 .98)	-0.60	25.22	7.83	66.96
HHSA (1/n, 1/n)	-0.15	13.04	15.65	71.30
HSA (.98)	0.17	5.22	20.87	73.91

Moreover, the heuristics are much faster.

In the case where the task assignment has no constraints, the Longest Path policy is the most effective among the 27 heuristics on the average. We have implemented two "mixed", three two-step and a one-step SA algorithms. We have compared these SA algorithms with the 27 heuristics. We have shown that the one-step homogeneous SA algorithm is the most effective among the six annealing processes and that all the annealing algorithms overperform the heuristics. Nevertheless, when the heuristics are used together, they provide the same solutions as the SA algorithms for about 70% of the cases. Moreover, the total execution time of the heuristics is more than 100 times smaller than those SA algorithms which have a similar effectiveness.

In the implementation of the two-step annealing processes, in order for the empirical comparison be feasible, we have chosen the parameters of the algorithms which do not guarantee the convergence of the algorithms. This may explain the fact that these algorithms appear to be less effective than the one-step SA algorithm. However, if the parameters are appropriately chosen so that the convergence is ensured, one may expect that, at the expense of the execution time, they provide optimal or near-optimal solutions.

References

1. T. L. Adam, K. M. Chandy, J. R. Dickson, "A Comparison of List Schedules for Parallel Processing Systems", *Comm. ACM*, Vol. 17, pp. 685-690, 1974.
2. E. G. Coffman Jr., R. L. Graham, "Optimal Scheduling for Two-Processor Systems", Acta Informatica Vol. 1, pp. 200-213, 1972.
3. E. G. Coffman Jr., Z. Liu, "On the Optimal Stochastic Scheduling of Out-Forests", *Operations Research*, Vol. 40, Supp. No. 1, pp. S67–S75, Janvier 1992.
4. C. Coroyer, Z. Liu, "Effectiveness of Heuristics and Simulated Annealing for the Scheduling of Concurrent Tasks — An Empirical Comparison," Rapport de Recherche INRIA, No. 1379, Jan. 1991.
5. R. L. Graham, "Bounds on Multiprocessing Timing Anomalies", *SIAM J. Appl. Math.*, Vol. 17, No. 2, pp. 416-429, 1969.
6. B. Hajek, "Cooling Schedules for Optimal Annealing", *Mathematics of Operations Research*, Vol. 13, No. 2, may 1988.
7. B. Hajek, G. Sasaki, "Simulated Annealing - to cool or not", *Systems and Control Letters*, Vol. 12, pp. 443-447, 1989.

8. Y. C. Hu, "Parallel Sequencing and Assembly Line Problems", *Operations Research*, Vol. 9, 841-848, 1961.

9. S. Kirkpatrick, C. D. Gellat Jr., M. P. Vecchi, "Optimization by Simulated Annealing", *Science*, Vol. 220, pp. 671-680, 1983.

10. P. J. M. van Laarhoven, E. H. L. Aarts, "Simulated Annealing: Theory and Applications", *D. Reidel Publishing Company*, 1987.

11. J. K. Lenstra, A. H. G. Rinnooy Kan, "Complexity of Scheduling under Precedence Constraints", *Operations Research*, Vol. 26, No. 1, pp. 22-35, 1978.

12. Z. Liu, "A Note on Graham's Bound." *Information Processing Letters*, Vol. 36, pp. 1-5, 1990.

13. Z. Liu, J. Labetoulle, "A Heuristic Method for Loading and Scheduling Flexible Manufacturing Systems", *Proc.of the Intern. Conf. Control 88*, London, IEE Conference Publication, No. 285, pp. 195-200, 1988.

14. C. V. Ramamoorthy, K. M. Chandy, M. J. Gonzalez Jr., "Optimal Scheduling Strategies in a Multiprocessor System", *IEEE Transactions on Computers*, Vol. C-21, No. 2, pp. 137-146, 1972.

15. J. Ramanujam, F. Ercal, P. Sadayappan, "Task Allocation by Simulated Annealing", *Proceedings of the Third Intern. Conf. on Supercomputing*, Vol 3, 471-480, 1988.

16. F. B. Talbot, J. H. Patterson, W. V. Gehrlein, "A Comparative Evaluation of Heuristic Line Balancing Techniques", *Management Science*, Vol. 32, No. 4, pp. 430-454, 1986.

Task Scheduling with Restricted Preemptions

K. Ecker, TU Clausthal[1], R. Hirschberg, pdv-Systeme[2]

Abstract One of the basic problems in time sharing systems and multiprocessing operating systems is to find an optimal schedule for a given set of tasks. In this paper we analyze the complexity of a restricted version of the general preemptive scheduling problem. We introduce a scheduling model that guarantees that preemption of a task is only possible after a reasonable part of the task has been processed. It turns out that this problem is *NP*-hard in general, but very good approximation algorithms can be found and special cases can be solved exactly in polynomial time.

1. Motivation

We consider preemptive task scheduling under the restriction that processor assignment should happen only in certain minimum portions of time, hence task preemptions occur only after some "granularity" time. This is motivated from the fact that preemptions are usually costly, and hence the aim is to avoid processing of a task for only a very short time before preemption. In many situations such as computations or time sharing systems and parallel operating systems it is obvious that the computation should proceed to a definite step before it is preempted.

Two kinds of preemption costs have to be considered: time and finance. Time delays originating from preemptions are less crucial if the delay caused by a single preemption is small compared to the time the task continuously spends on the processor. Financial costs connected with preemptions, on the other hand, reduce the total benefit gained by the task execution; but again, if the profit gained from tasks is large compared to the losses caused by their preemptions the schedule will be more useful and acceptable.

These circumstances suggest the introduction of a scheduling model where task preemptions are only allowed after the tasks have been executed continuously for some given amount k of time. The value for k (preemption granularity) should be chosen large enough so that time delay and cost overheads connected with preemptions are negligible. In addition, upper bounds on the preemption overhead can easily be estimated since the number of preemptions for a task of processing time p is limited by $\lfloor p/k \rfloor$.

2. The Model

In this paper we consider deterministic scheduling problems of type[3] $P \parallel C_{\max}$ where the elements of a set $\mathcal{T}$ of tasks are to be scheduled on a given set $\mathcal{P}$ of m identical

---

[1] K. Ecker,   Institut für Informatik, TU Clausthal, Erzstr. 1, 3392 Clausthal, Germany.
Tel +49-5232-72-3554, Fax +49-5323-72-3575,
e-mail: ecker@decst.in.tu-clausthal.de

[2] R. Hirschberg, pdv-Systeme Gesellschaft für Systemtechnik mbH, Bornhardtstr. 3, 3380 Goslar, Germany. Tel. +49-5321-80761, Fax +49-5321-8924.

[3] See [BESW93] for a detailed description of the three-field notation of scheduling problems.

processors, and the aim is to find a schedule of minimum makespan. The problem of preemptive scheduling was investigated by various authors, e.g. [BLRK83, BLLRK83, BRH90, CG91, CS81, FG86, GS78, HLS77, Law82, LL78, LLLRK84, MC69, MC70, Sah79, Slo78, Wer84]. These papers discuss the problem under different assumptions such as precedence constraints, resource constraints, task release times or due dates, uniform or unrelated processors. Results on these different types of preemptive scheduling can also be found in [BESW93].

In this paper the tasks of $\mathcal{T}$ are assumed to be pairwise independent and, for practical reasons, integer processing times are assumed. We restrict preemptions by introducing a *granularity* $k \in \mathbb{N}$ which means that the execution of each task $T_j \in \mathcal{T}$ has to obey the following condition: if the processing time p_j of T_j is less than or equal to k, then preemption is not allowed; otherwise preemption may take place after the task has been continuously processed for at least k units of time. For the remaining portion of a preempted task the same condition is applied. This ensures that a "long" task is processed in portions of lengths $\geq k$, except possibly the last part. We refer to this type of scheduling problem as the *k-restricted preemptive scheduling* problem, and the notation $P \mid k\text{-}pmtn \mid C_{max}$ is introduced where k is understood to be an input parameter of the problem. Notice that for $k = 0$, this problem reduces to the classical preemptive scheduling problem. On the other hand, if for a given instance the granularity k is larger than the longest processing time among the given tasks, then no preemption is allowed and we end up with nonpreemptive scheduling.

We illustrate k-restricted preemptive scheduling by means of a simple example: Let $\mathcal{T} = \{T_1, T_2, T_3, T_4\}$ and let all tasks have the same processing time $p_j = 6$. Suppose that 3 processors are available and $k = 4$. Fig. 1 compares classical preemptive scheduling and 4-restricted preemptive scheduling: Fig. 1(a) shows a schedule where no restrictions on preemptions are imposed, whereas the one in fig. 1(b) is a feasible 4-restricted preemptive schedule. Notice that the schedule in fig. 1(a) is not feasibly 4-restricted because task T_3 is preempted already after two time units. Obviously the schedule of fig. 1(b) is of minimum makespan for the 4-restricted scheduling problem.

We will also discuss an even more restricted version of the k-restricted scheduling problem where task preemptions are only allowed at those moments, when the task has been processed exactly an integer multiple of k time units. That is, each task T_j of processing time $p_j > k$ is partitioned into portions of length k, except for the last portion which may be shorter than k. We refer to this problem as the *exact-k-preemptive scheduling*, for which the notion $P \mid exact\text{-}k\text{-}pmtn \mid C_{max}$ will be used.

In this paper we first consider the k-restricted scheduling problem for $m = 2$ processors. Then we prove that both, the k-restricted scheduling problem and the exact-k-preemptive scheduling problem, are *NP*-hard for $k > 0$ and $m > 2$. Approximate algorithms are discussed, and an upper bound is derived for the performance ratio of one of the approximation algorithms.

In the following analysis we replace each task T_j by a chain of l subtasks $T_j^1, \cdots, T_j^{l-1}, T_j^l$ where $l := \lceil p_j/k \rceil$, and the processing times of the subtasks T_j^i are: p_j^i

$= k$ for $i < l$, and $p_j^{\,l} = p_j$ mod k. For notational reasons, we denote the last subtask of the chain belonging to T_j by T_j'', and refer to T_j'' as the *final subtask* of T_j. If p_j mod k $= 0$, there is no final subtask of T_j. In that way the original scheduling problem is replaced by a problem where the task set is partially ordered by a chainlike precedence relation; task processing times are equal except that of the last task in each chain which is always smaller than k.

(a)   (b)

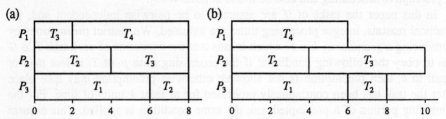

Fig. 1. (a) A preemptive example schedule without restriction, (b) A 4-restricted preemptive example schedule

In some situations, however, we don't need such a refined decomposition of tasks. We then replace the given task set $\mathcal{T}$ by the set $\mathcal{T}'$ where each task T_j of $\mathcal{T}$ with processing time $p_j > k$ and p_j mod $k \neq 0$ is partitioned into two subtasks, T_j' and T_j'' of processing times $p_j' = (l-1)k$ (where l is defined as before) and $p_j'' = p_j$ mod k, respectively.

3. The Two-Processor Case

Before we start with a detailed analysis of the two-processor case we give a simple enumerative algorithm which can be useful in case of small numbers of tasks.

Algorithm *Enumeration*
```
begin
C* := max {p₁, p₂, ..., pₙ, (1/2)Σ pᵢ};
for all permutations (T_α₁, T_α₂, ..., T_αₙ) do
   begin
   Assign tasks in order T_α₁, T_α₂, ... to processor P₁, preempt at C*, and continue
      with processor P₂;
   if the schedule thus obtained is feasible
   then exit
   else
      if the reversed schedule is feasible
      then begin reverse schedule; exit; end
      else    -- both subtasks of the preempted task have length < k
         begin
         Correct the schedule by preempting the last task of P₁ (the first task of P₂)
            properly;
            -- enlarge the larger subtask until its length is k
         Reverse schedule, if necessary;
            -- this happens only if the subtask assigned to P₁ is enlarged to k
```

```
        if the schedule length is shorter than the shortest schedule found so far
        then Store this schedule;
        end;
    end;
Print the schedule stored last;
end;
```

Clearly, the time complexity of algorithm *Enumeration* grows exponentially in the number of tasks. Though - as we will see - this algorithm turns out to be useful in certain special situations, we can present a fast algorithm for the problem of scheduling independent tasks k-preemptively on $m = 2$ processors. Therefore we consider three different cases of problem instances, (a) where there is a task T_i with $p_i \geq 2k$, (b) all tasks have processing times $< 2k$, and there is a task T_i with $p_i \leq k$, and (c) $k < p_j < 2k$ for all tasks T_j. Let $C^* := \max\{p_1, p_2, ..., p_n, (1/2)\Sigma\, p_i\}$, which is a lower bound for the minimum makespan of a feasible schedule.

Case (a): If T_i has processing time $p_i \geq 2k$, then first assign tasks in arbitrary order to processor P_1, so that T_i is started before time C^* and ends at a time $\geq C^*$. Preempt T_i at C^* and continue assigning the remaining tasks to P_2. This schedule is of the length C^* and, as $p_i \geq 2k$, one of its subtasks has length $\geq k$. If necessary, reverse the order in which the tasks are assigned to the processors to get a feasible schedule.

Case (b): Replace the given task set T by a set T' where each task T_j of T with processing time $p_j > k$ is replaced by a chain of subtasks as described in the preceeding section. Notice that now each long task of T contributes two subtasks to T', one of length k (*nonfinal* subtask), and one of length $< k$ (*final* subtask). Let T'' $\subset T'$ be the set of all the nonfinal subtasks of T' together with the 'short' tasks of T (i.e. those tasks of T whose processing times are $\leq k$). Without considering subtask dependencies solve the 2-partition optimization problem for the elements of T''. This can be done in time $O(n\log k)$ [GJ79]. Let $\{T_1'', T_2''\}$ be the resulting 2-partition. Then assign the subtasks of T_i'' arbitrarily and without preemption to processor P_i ($i = 1, 2$). Since all the (sub)tasks of T_i'' are pairwise independent, conflicts cannot occur. Let C_1 and C_2 be the finishing times of processors P_1 and P_2, respectively. Suppose w.l.o.g. that $C_1 \geq C_2$. Note that $C_1 - C_2 \leq k$ since otherwise the solution of the 2-partition problem was not optimal. Now two different situations have to be distinguished:

– If task T_i is assigned P_1 (see fig. 2) then the subtasks not yet scheduled (i.e. those of $T' - T''$) can be scheduled between times C_1 resp. C_2 and C^* without conflicts using McNaughton's wrap around rule. Then, at most one of these subtasks, say T_l, will be preempted. As T_l is the final subtask of a 'long' task, one of the preempted parts of T_l can be recombined with the previously scheduled subtask of T_l of length k. It can easily be seen that the resulting schedule is feasible.

– If, however, T_i is assigned to processor P_2 (see fig. 3), conflicts may occur if we try to schedule the remaining subtasks using the wrap around rule. Let T_l be the subtask assigned last to P_1. As $C_1 - C_2 \leq k$ and each remaining subtask is of integer length ≥ 1, we conclude that if there are more than k remaining subtasks, up to k of them can be scheduled during times C_2 and C_1 without conflict. When scheduling the final subtask T_l'' of T_l, it might happen that bound C^* would be exceeded so that T_l'' needs to be preempted in order to meet the total length C^*. But thus a conflict between parts of T_l'' would be introduced. Since the length of T_l'' is less than k, this situation is only possible if $C^* < C_1 + k$. But now we can easily estimate the total number of tasks: The total number of final subtasks is then limited by $C^* - C_2$ which is less than $2k$. Hence $C_1 \leq 2k^2$. The number of short tasks is limited by C_2 which is also less than $2k^2$. Thus we get the bound $2k + 2k^2$ for the total number of tasks in the original task system $\mathcal{T}$, and we can apply the algorithm *Enumeration*. This solves the problem in constant (independent of n) time.

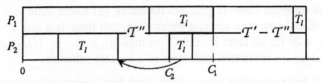

P_1 $\qquad$ T_i $\qquad$ T_l

$-\mathcal{T}''-$ $\qquad$ $-\mathcal{T}' - \mathcal{T}''-$

P_2 $\qquad$ T_l $\qquad$ T_l

0 $\qquad$ C_2 $\quad$ C_1

Fig. 2. Case (b): Recombination of subtasks of T_1 to get a feasible k-preemptive schedule

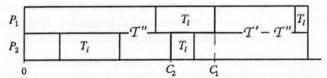

P_1 $\qquad$ T_l $\qquad$ T_l

$-\mathcal{T}''-$ $\qquad$ $-\mathcal{T}' - \mathcal{T}''-$

P_2 $\qquad$ T_i $\qquad$ T_l

0 $\qquad$ C_2 $\quad$ C_1

Fig. 3. Case (b): Recombination of task T_1 may not be possible

If the number of remaining subtasks is $\leq k$ (in fact, if the sum of their processing times is less than or equal k), a conflict with T_l might occur. But in that case we know that there are less than $k + 1$ 'long' tasks in $\mathcal{T}$, and hence $C_1 \leq k(k + 1)$; the number of 'short' tasks is limited by $C_2 < C_1$. So the total number of tasks in that special situation is bounded from above by $k(k + 2)$, and we can again apply the algorithm *Enumeration*.

Case (c): If the processing time of each task is between k and $2k$, then set $\mathcal{T}'$ has two subtasks for each task of $\mathcal{T}$, a nonfinal of length k and a final of length $< k$. Let $\mathcal{T}''$ be the set of subtasks of length k. Notice that these subtasks are pairwise independent. The way we proceed is to schedule first the subtasks of $\mathcal{T}''$ and then try to assign the remaining subtasks in wrap around manner. If the number of subtasks in $\mathcal{T}''$ is even, the final subtasks (which are again pairwise independent) can be assigned wrap around without problem; as in case (b), if a final subtask is preempted, one of its parts has to be combined with its nonfinal subtask in order to guarantee a feasible schedule (see fig. 4). On the other hand, if the number of non-final subtasks is odd, we can apply the same idea as in the second part of case (b) (see also fig. 5). If the number of final subtasks is larger than k, at least k of them are not in conflict with the last scheduled nonfinal subtask and then the finals can be assigned using wrap around without problem. If, however, the number of finals is less than or equal to k, this may be impossible. But then the total number of tasks in $\mathcal{T}$ is also limited from above by k and the algorithm *Enumeration* does the job.

Let us mention that in cases (b) and (c), the call of algorithm enumeration can be avoided; a very careful and lengthy analysis of the corresponding situations would show that optimal schedules can also be constructed directly.

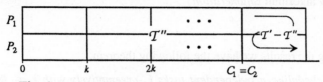

Fig. 4. Case (c): Assigning final subtasks with wrap around

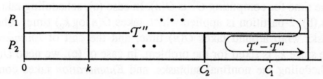

Fig. 5. Case (c): Assigning final subtasks with wrap around

Combining the results of the above three cases we propose the following algorithm for the 2-processor case:

Algorithm
```
begin
C* := max {p₁, ..., pₙ, (1/2)Σ pᵢ} ;
if  T has a task Tᵢ with pᵢ ≥ 2k
then       -- case (a)
   begin
   schedule tasks so that Tᵢ is preempted;
        -- this or the reversed schedule is feasible
   exit;      -- the schedule is of length C*
   end;
if  T has a task Tᵢ with pᵢ < k
then       -- case (b)
   begin
   For the nonfinal subtasks and the short tasks generate a nonpreemptive schedule
          by applying 2-partition;
   Assign remaining tasks with wrap around so that the total schedule length is C*;
   if  no conflicts occur
   then  Reorder the subtasks so that a feasible schedule results
   else      -- the total number of tasks in T is ≤ 2k(k + 1)
      Apply algorithm Enumeration;
   exit;
   end
if       -- case (c) remains
   begin
   Assign nonfinal subtasks optimally and without preemption to the processors;
   Assign final subtasks following the wrap around rule;
```

```
if no conflicts occur
then  Reorder the subtasks so that a feasible schedule results
    else       -- the total number of tasks in T is ≤ k
        Apply algorithm Enumeration;
    end
end;
```

Summarizing the results we have the following theorem.

Theorem. *Scheduling n independent tasks k_0-preemptively with $k_0 \in \mathbb{N}$, fixed, on two processors can be performed optimally in $O(n)$ time.*

Proof. The time for computing C^* is $O(n)$. In case (a), scheduling takes also $O(n)$ time. In case (b), 2-partition is applied which takes $O(n \log k_0)$ time; scheduling the remaining tasks wrap around takes $O(n)$ time, and the call of *Enumeration* takes constant time since k_0 is fixed for the problem. In case of (c), we need $O(n)$ time for optimally scheduling the nonfinal subtasks, and *Enumeration* takes constant time. So altogether, since solving the 2-partition problem in case (b) is dominating, we get the total time complexity $O(n)$ for the algorithm. $\square$

Example 1. Consider scheduling of three tasks, T_1, T_2, and T_3, with processing times 6, 6, 6, respectively; $k = 4$. Clearly, $C^* = 9$, C_1, and $C_2 = 4$, and we are faced with the situation sketched in fig. 4. The analysis of case (b) shows that we have to call *Enumeration*. The resulting schedule is shown in fig. 6.

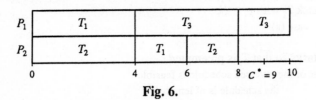

Fig. 6.

Example 2. Let there be given tasks $T_1, \cdots, T_5$ with processing times 5, 6, 7, 7, 7; $k = 4$. Now we have case (c), and the algorithm generates the schedule shown in fig. 7(a). This schedule is not feasible because of the preemtion of T_4 at time 13. But reordering subtasks as indicated in fig. 7(a) leads to the final solution (fig. 7(b)).

4. *NP*-hardness

It can easily be seen that the problem $P \mid k\text{-}pmtn \mid C_{max}$ with no restriction for the value of k is *NP*-hard. Any instance Π of the problem $P \mid\mid C_{max}$ can be polynomially transformed to an instance Π' of $P \mid k\text{-}pmtn \mid C_{max}$ by chosing k as the maximum value of the processing times of tasks belonging to Π. As $P \mid\mid C_{max}$ is known to be *NP*-hard even for two processors [Kar72], the same is valid for the corresponding k-restriced preemption problem and obviously also for the class $P \mid exact\text{-}k\text{-}pmtn \mid C_{max}$. So provided that the classes $\mathcal{P}$ and $\mathcal{NP}$ are not identical, only pseudo-polynomial algorithms can be found for these problems. On the other hand, since the problem $P \mid 0\text{-}pmtn \mid C_{max}$ is polynomially solvable with McNaughton's wrap-around rule, the question arises if it is possible to find a threshold value $k_0 \in \mathbb{N}$ so that $P \mid k_0\text{-}pmtn \mid$

$C_{\max}$ is polynomially solvable whereas $P \mid (k_0 + 1)\text{-}pmtn \mid C_{\max}$ is *NP*-hard.

(a)

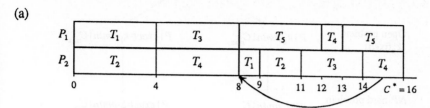

(b)

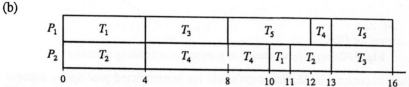

Fig. 7. (a) A schedule where task T_4 is unfeasibly preempted, (b) A correct schedule for the problem of example 2

Lemma. *If problem $P \mid k_0\text{-}pmtn \mid C_{\max}$ is polynomially solvable for some fixed integer value $k_0 > 0$ then the problem is solvable in polynomial time for any fixed preemption granularity.*

Proof. Let k_0 be fixed and suppose $P \mid k_0\text{-}pmtn \mid C_{\max}$ is polynomially solvable. For every $k_1 > 0$ any problem in $P \mid k_1\text{-}pmtn \mid C_{\max}$ can be transformed to a problem belonging to $P \mid k_0\text{-}pmtn \mid C_{\max}$ by multiplying all processing times with k_0/k_1. Solving this problem with the polynomial algorithm and multiplying the task processing times in the resulting schedule with the inverse factor leads to a feasible schedule for the original problem with minimum makespan. $\square$

The dependencies between complexity classes are illustrated in fig. 8.

5. Approximate Algorithms for the *m*-Processor Case

In this section we present two simple approximation algorithms that can be applied in the case of m ≥ 2 processors. The first algorithm is a generalization of McNaughton's wrap around rule.

Algorithm *McNaughton-modified*
```
begin
```
Compute $C^* := \max \{p_1, ..., p_n, (1/2)\Sigma\, p_i\}$;
Decompose the task set $\mathcal{T}$ into two subsets, $\mathcal{T}_1$ and $\mathcal{T}_2$, where $\mathcal{T}_2$ contains $m-1$ of the longest tasks of $\mathcal{T}$;
Schedule tasks of $\mathcal{T}$ using the wrap around rule. Each time a preemption occurs at C^*, take a task from set $\mathcal{T}_2$;
```
if``` an infeasible preemption occurs
 -- i.e. a processor starts with a subtask $T_j''$ of length $< k$
```then``` enlarge $T_j''$ so that its length is $k$ or, if $p_j \leq k$, $T_j'' = T_j$ ;
```end;```
```

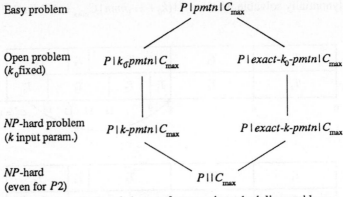

Fig. 8. Complexity of classes of preemptive scheduling problems

Notice that, in contrast to McNaughton's rule for nonrestricted preemptive scheduling, the modified algorithm for the k-preemptive scheduling is no longer optimal in general.

The second algorithm is a modification of the LPT (largest processing time) algorithm. This algorithm may also be regarded as a modification of HU's level algorithm. We present both algorithms to show this conjecture.

Algorithm *LPT-modified*
```
begin
Sort tasks in LPT order;
while the task list is not empty do
    begin
        Let T_i be the next task from the list;
        if p_i ≤ k
        then  assign T_i to the next processor that becomes idle
        else
            begin
                Assign part of T_i of length k to the next processor that becomes idle;
                Insert the remaining part of T_i to task list according to LPT;
            end;
    end;
end;
```

For applying Hu's level algorithm [Hu61], we replace long tasks by chains of subtasks of length k, followed by a final subtask of length $< k$. By doing this the original task system changes into a set of dependent subtasks with chain-like task dependencies. A well-known result for scheduling tasks with tree-like precedences is: If tasks have unit processing times, Hu's level algorithm allows to construct m-processor schedules of minimum makespan. The following heuristics uses the main ideas of this algorithm. Define for each subtask T_j^i a *level* as the sum of processing times of this subtask and that of all the subtasks following in the chain T_j^i belongs to. As Hu's algorithm is defined for in-trees we have to add a dummy task of processing time 0 that is an immediate successor of the final subtasks of the chains.

Notice that the level introduced here is the same as Hu's level if the processing times of all subtasks (including final subtasks) are the same. Then the algorithm is as follows.

Algorithm *Hu-modified*
begin
Calculate levels of the subtasks;
repeat
 Construct list L consisting of all the subtasks without predecessors;
 Sort L in nonincreasing order of subtask levels;
 Any time a processor becomes idle assign the first subtask of L to the processor;
 Remove the assigned subtask from the list;
until all subtasks have been scheduled;
end;

The algorithm can be implemented to run in $O(n)$ time. Notice that the level algorithms from Muntz and Coffman [MC69 and MC70] and Horvath et al. [HLS77] are not applicable for k-pmtn problems because these algorithms do not allow preemption at any time.

Example. Decomposing the tasks of the above example 1 results in 5 chains, each consisting of two subtasks; in each chain, the first subtask is of length $k = 4$, and the second subtasks have lengths 1, 2, 3, 3, 3 respectively. Fig. 9 shows these chains with levels of subtasks, together with a final dummy task of processing time 0.

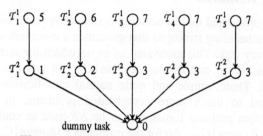

dummy task

Fig. 9. Replacing tasks by chains of subtasks

Theorem. *The algorithm Hu-modified generates schedules of length*
$$C_{\text{Hu}} \le C^* + (k-1)(m-1)/m.$$
This bound cannot be improved.

 Proof. Recall that if there are no final subtasks (i.e. all processing times are integer multiples of k) then Hu's algorithm generates an optimal schedule. If there are final subtasks, then the schedule constructed by the algorithm must end with some final subtask T_i''. Let C be the time this subtask is finished. Now consider the following two situations: If $p_i = C$ then at every time some part of T_i is processed, and the schedule is obviously optimal. If $p_i < C$, then we claim that all processors are busy at least until time $C - (k-1)$. To see this consider the last interval $[l_1, l_2)$ where no subtask of T_i is processed, and let T_i' be the subtask of T_i started at time l_2.

Notice that both values, l_1 and l_2, are integer multiples of k: no final subtask can be processed before time l_2 since the subtask T_i' of higher priority was started at time l_2. All subtasks started at time $l_2 - k$ have a level greater than or equal to $C - l_2$, the level of T_i'. This allows us to calculate the average of the finishing times of all processors except the one processing T_i''. The workload w of all the subtasks started at time $l_2 - k$ or later is $w \geq (m+1)(C - l_2)$. On the other hand, this workload must coincide with the processing capacity used for these subtasks which is given by $C - (l_2 - k) + (m-1)(t - (l_2 - k))$. From this we get the condition

$$(m+1)(C - l_2) \leq C - (l_2 - k) + (m-1)(t - (l_2 - k)),$$

or $t \leq m/(m-1)(C-k) > C-k$.

A lower bound for the makespan of an optimal schedule can furthermore be calculated as $C^* \geq (1/m)(C + (m-1)t)$ from which we get $C^* \geq C - (k-1)(m-1)/m$.

The proof that the above bound is tight can be seen from the following example: Scheduling of $n = 3$ tasks, each with processing time 5 on $m = 2$ processors, and $k = 2$. A lower bound for the schedule length is $C^* = 7.5$. A feasible schedule of this length can be obtained from McNaughton's rule, whereas a schedule generated with Hu-modified is of length $C^* + (k-1)(m-1)/m = 8$. $\square$

An immediate consequence is:

Theorem. *For the problem $Pm \mid exact\text{-}k\text{-}pmtn \mid C_{max}$ we get: If task processing times are integer multiples of k, then both algorithms, LPT-modified and Hu-modified, are optimal.* $\square$

6. Concluding Remarks

In time sharing systems and multiprocessing operating systems there is obviously an essential need in scheduling strategies that guarantee a minimum span of continuous processing for every task. This motivated us to introduce the restricted preemption problems $P \mid k\text{-}pmtn \mid C_{max}$ and $P \mid exact\text{-}k\text{-}pmtn \mid C_{max}$ in order to avoid inefficient task preemptions. These simple and quite natural modifications of the problem $P \mid pmtn \mid C_{max}$ lead to much more complicated problems. In fact the general restricted preemption problem turned out to be NP-hard in contrast to the easily solvable problem $P \mid pmtn \mid C_{max}$. So for the problems $P \mid k\text{-}pmtn \mid C_{max}$ and $P \mid exact\text{-}k\text{-}pmtn \mid C_{max}$ there is little hope for finding polynomial time algorithms. Only if k is fixed to some integer value k_0 or if the number of processors is restricted there might be a chance to find fast algorithms. In particular, we discussed an exact algorithm for the special case $P \mid k_0\text{-}pmtn \mid C_{max}$. Despite the fact that the general case is hard to solve we showed that very fast and very good approximation algorithms with asymptotic performance ratio equal 1 can be found. Nevertheless we had to leave the question open if the problem $P \mid k_0\text{-}pmtn \mid C_{max}$ is polynomially solvable and even if the same problem with only 3 processors is polynomially solvable.

References

BESW93   J. Błażewicz, K. Ecker, G. Schmidt, J. Węglarz, *Scheduling in Computer and Manufacturing Systems*, Springer-Verlag, 1993.

BLLRK83   K. R. Baker, E. L. Lawler, J. K. Lenstra, A. H. G. Rinnooy Kan, Preemptive scheduling of a single machine to minimize maximum cost subject to release dates and precedence constraints, *Oper. Res.* 31, 1983, 381-386.

BLRK83   J. Błażewicz, J. K. Lenstra, A. H. G. Rinnooy Kan, Scheduling subject to resource constraints: classification and complexity, *Discrete Appl. Math.* 5, 1983, 11-24.

BRH90   S. K. Baruah, L. E. Rosier, R. R. Howell, Algorithms and complexity concerning the preemptive scheduling of periodic, real-time tasks on one processor, *Real-Time Systems* 2, 1990, 301-324.

CG91   E. G. Coffman, Jr., M. R. Garey, Proof of the 4/3 conjecture for preemptive versus nonpreemptive two-processor scheduling, Report Bell Laboratories, Murray Hill, 1991.

CS81   Y. Cho, S. Sahni, Preemptive scheduling of independent jobs with release and due times on open, flow and job shops, *Oper. Res.* 29, 1981, 511-522.

FG86   A. Federgruen, H. Groenevelt, Preemptive scheduling of uniform machines by ordinary network flow techniques, *Management Sci.* 32, 1986, 341-349.

GJ79   M. R. Garey, D. S. Johnson, *Computers and Intractability: A Guide to the Theory of NP-Completeness*. W. H. Freeman, San Francisco, 1979.

GS78   T. Gonzalez, S. Sahni, Preemptive scheduling of uniform processor systems, *JACM* 25, 1978, 92-101.

HLS77   E. C. Horvath, S. Lam. R. Sethi, A level algorithm for preemptive scheduling, *JACM* 24, 24, 1977, 32-43.

Hu61   T. C. Hu, Parallel sequencing and assembly line problems, *Oper. Res.* 9, 1961, 841-848.

Kar72   R. M. Karp, Reducibility among combinatorial problems, in: R. E. Miller, J. W. Thatcher (eds.), *Complexity of Computer Computations*, Plenum Press, New York, 1972, 85-104.

Law82b   E. L. Lawler, Preemptive scheduling in precedence-constrained jobs on parallel machines, in: M. A. H. Dempster, J. K. Lenstra, A. H. G. Rinnooy Kan (eds.), *Deterministic and Stochastic Scheduling*, Reidel, Dordrecht, 1982, 101-123.

LL78   E. L. Lawler, J. Labetoulle, Preemptive scheduling of unrelated parallel processors by linear programing, *J. Assoc. Comput. Mach.* 25, 1978, 612-619.

LLLRK84   J. Labetoulle, E. L. Lawler, J. K. Lenstra, A. H. G. Rinnooy Kan, Preemptive scheduling of uniform machines subject to release dates, in: W. R. Pulleyblank (ed.), *Progress in Combinatorial Optimization*, Academic Press, New York, 1984, 245-261.

MC69   R. Muntz, E. G. Coffman, Jr., Optimal preemptive scheduling on two-processor systems, *IEEE Trans. Comput.* C-18, 1969, 1014-1029.

MC70   R. R. Muntz, E. G. Coffman, Preemptive scheduling of real-time tasks on multiprocessor systems, *JACM* 17, 1970, 324-338.

Sah79   S. Sahni, Preemptive scheduling with due dates, *Oper. Res.* 5, 1979, 925-934.

Slo78   R. Słowinski, Scheduling preemptible tasks on unrelated processors with additional resources to mionimize schedule length, in G. Bracci, R. C. Lockemann (eds.), Lecture Notes in Computer Science, vol 65, Springer Verlag, Berlin, 1978, 536-547.

Wer84   D. de Werra, Preemptive scheduling linear programming and network flows, *SIAM Journal Algebra and Discrete Mathematics* 5, 1984, 11-20.

Effects of Job Size Irregularity on the Dynamic Resource Scheduling of a 2-D Mesh Multicomputer*

Dugki Min and Matt W. Mutka

Department of Computer Science
Michigan State University
East Lansing, MI 48824-1027

Abstract. Irregularities of the shapes and sizes of jobs are important factors affecting the performance of a resource scheduling algorithm in a 2-D mesh multicomputer. We examine the performance effect of irregularity, by examining a dynamic scheduling system that schedules jobs with requests that range from regular-shaped partitions of a multicomputer to irregular-shaped partitions. In order to evaluate the effect of irregularity, we examine a job scheduling algorithm called the *BWQ-search algorithm*, which uses multiple queues for ordering jobs to be placed on a 2-D mesh multicomputer. We find that the performance is similar when the system schedules jobs that request various types of irregular-shaped partitions. A large improvement in performance occurs if all jobs scheduled on the multicomputer request very regular-shaped partitions.

1 Introduction

The rapid progress in the evolution of multicomputer systems focuses the attention of many researchers on defining and solving new resource management problems. An important issue for multicomputer systems is scheduling concurrent jobs. Innovative job scheduling and processor allocation policies exist for several different architectures, applications, and performance requirements. Job scheduling and processor allocation policies may be classified as either static or dynamic. Static schedulers strive to determine for a given job list and multicomputer architecture the order that jobs should be processed and how should the jobs be allocated to the processors so that the completion times of all jobs are minimized. Static schedulers must know the characteristics of all jobs, which include their computing and communication demands. Many researchers have proposed solutions to static scheduling problems for general purpose multicomputer systems [8, 13]. Certain special purpose static schedulers, such as those designed for hard real-time systems [10, 11], optimize the schedules of the jobs on multicomputers such that all jobs complete before their specified deadlines.

* This research was supported in part by the NSF grant no. CCR-9010906, CDA-9121641 and CDA-9222901.

In contrast to static schedulers, dynamic schedulers assume jobs arrive according to a stochastic process. The scheduler has no prior knowledge of the characteristics of the jobs to be scheduled. Dynamic schedulers are important components in general purpose multicomputer systems where jobs composed of cooperating tasks are executed. The design of a dynamic scheduler strives to provide short job turnaround times while maintaining high processor utilization. As described by Krueger *et al* [6], a dynamic job scheduler has two components: a *job-scheduling policy* that selects jobs to execute on the available processors in the system and the *processor allocation policy* that partitions the available processors in the system into subsystems that are allocated to jobs.

Much of the research of dynamic scheduling for multicomputers has focused on scheduling jobs that require regular-shaped partitions from a multicomputer. For example, when researchers considered dynamic scheduling for hypercube multicomputers, the question of job scheduling was concerned with finding a subcube of the appropriate size [2, 6]. Due to the special structure of a hypercube system, the number of processing nodes is assumed to be 2^k, where $k \geq 0$ and the shapes of partitions are assumed to be hypercube. The number of processors assigned to a job should depend on the number of processors that provide the best performance for the job. The absolute execution time for a given application will decrease until the optimal number of processors are allocated to the application. Due to the communication overhead, any additional processors assigned to the application will increase the execution time. For example, if an application optimally requires 50 processors, a hypercube will allocate a subcube of 64 processors, effectively wasting the computing power of 14 processors.

The regular structure of hypercubes and the method for determining the number of processors to assign to a job may affect the relative importance of the job scheduling and processor allocation algorithms. Krueger *et al* [6] have found that the choice of the job scheduling algorithm is more important for the overall performance of the system than the choice of the processor allocation strategy. An effective class of scheduling algorithms for a hypercube system is the *scan* discipline. In this discipline, job arrivals are placed in queues corresponding to the size of the subcube requested. Jobs are scheduled by scanning through the non-empty queues, similar to the c-scan algorithm for disk scheduling [14]. A simple processor allocation strategy such as *buddy* allocation performs as well as more sophisticated strategies under all but a few of the extreme conditions for a hypercube system [6]. On the other hand, there has been little research conducted detailing the effect of the shape and size of a submesh on the performance of job scheduling and processor allocation policies for a mesh multicomputer systems. The motivation for studying policies for two dimensional (2-D) mesh multicomputer systems is the increasing pace of the development of these systems. The regular and simple structure of the 2-D mesh multicomputer systems can be implemented at a low cost, while many algorithms implemented for the structure exhibit good performance. Examples of implementations of mesh computing systems include the Intel Touchstone Project [15], the Symult 2010 [12], and the Tera Computing System [1].

One approach for processor allocation in a mesh computer is to arbitrarily select processors at any location in the multicomputer. For example, the Symult 2010 uses a greedy algorithm for allocating processors to a job, so that it is likely that the processors allocated to a job will not be located within a contiguous region. With such a strategy, the communication traffic between processors allocated to one job may contend for network resources with the communication traffic between processors of a different job. It is an important research topic to characterize contention that can occur between jobs to determine whether it is necessary to eliminate inter-job contentions by requiring processor allocations in contiguous regions of the multicomputer [9]. We concentrate on job scheduling and processor allocation strategies in this paper with the assumption that jobs are allocated in contiguous regions to avoid inter-job contentions.

Processor allocation strategies for mesh multicomputers that avoid inter-job contentions have followed a generalization of the traditional binary buddy strategy for memory management. Using these strategies, partitions allocated to jobs have a square submesh geometry, with the lengths of the sides of the submesh equal to $2^k, k \geq 0$ [8]. These assumptions of the geometry of the shapes of jobs are not appropriate when we consider a general mesh system. For a general system, jobs may request irregular-shaped partitions as well as square-shaped partitions, such that the lengths of the sides of a partition might not equal 2^k. Large internal fragmentation occurs if a traditional binary buddy strategy is used for jobs with irregular sizes and shapes. A general recognition strategy is needed to identify available submeshes of arbitrary sizes at any location in a mesh. One strategy proposed is based on *frame sliding* [3]. In this strategy, a submesh is allocated that matches the shape and size requested by an incoming job. Therefore internal fragmentation is completely avoided. As a result of its matching capability, this scheme can be used for general sizes and shapes. However, due to the irregular sizes of jobs, it is still difficult to avoid large external fragmentation. The irregularities are inherent in general 2-D mesh systems and cause significant system fragmentation that degrades system performance.

In order to evaluate the effects of irregularity of job shapes and sizes, we study a job scheduling strategy in which similar types of requests are served in groups by means of a multiqueue scheduling algorithm. Our strategy, called the *BWQ-search algorithm*, is explored for managing a 2-D mesh multicomputer system that adapts to the demands that confront a general purpose system. By means of this algorithm, we identify important components of a multiqueue job scheduling strategy and evaluate the relative benefit of the components. If the job scheduler is blocked by a large job that cannot be assigned immediately, our strategy provides additional opportunities for allocation of resources to jobs that require smaller submeshes. The effect is a reduction in fragmentation and an improvement in the response time in comparison to conventional algorithms that do not exploit the concept of grouping similar sizes of jobs. We have analyzed our strategy for four classes of jobs that represent different amounts of variability in size and shape.

A simulation model of a system on which our approach is analyzed is presented in Section 2. Section 3 includes a description of the job scheduling strategy. The results of a study of the performance is given in Section 4. Based on the simulation results, we discuss effects of the variability in the size and shape of an incoming job on the performance of the job scheduling algorithm. A summary and conclusions are given in Section 5.

2 Simulation Model

An important design issue for a resource scheduling strategy is to study the amount of performance degradation with respect to the amount of irregularity of the size of a job or the irregularity of the shape of the partition of processors the job will occupy. The average amount of system fragmentation may vary and depends on the freedom that the shape of jobs may assume and sizes that a job can request. Greater freedom in the variations of shapes may cause larger system fragmentation. For this purpose, we study the performance effects of four representative cases of jobs, which can be described in terms of the shapes of the perimeter of the required partitions. The shapes are chosen with the restriction that processors are allocated in contiguous regions in which the routing technology of the multicomputer will not overlap one job's message traffic with the message traffic of other jobs. For example, assume a multicomputer is wormhole-routed and uses XY routing [5, 4]. For our study, the length of the sides of a partition will determine the shape of the jobs. The following job shapes are considered:

- *Square-2^k*: each side length is equal, and the length is 2^k, where $k \geq 0$.
- *Square-var*: each side length is equal, but can be any integer value in the range from 1 to the maximum side length of the mesh system.
- *Rectangular-restricted*: side lengths of a job partition can be different, but the difference should not be larger than a given constant.
- *Rectangular-unrestricted* : each side length can be any integer value from 1 to the maximum size of a side of the mesh system.

We model a dynamic scheduling system in which job arrivals follow a Poisson process. An incoming job consists of a number of interacting tasks that communicate via messages and specifies the geometry of a submesh it will need to occupy. The job will be allocated to a submesh of the requested geometry to avoid internal fragmentation. The hold time for each job is assumed to be exponentially distributed and independent.

Since little information is available about the computing time demands required for jobs on mesh multicomputers, we consider the case that jobs are executed on a multicomputer in order to increase the throughput produced by a job, which is described as *uncorrelated* workloads by [6, 7]. Therefore, the amount of work done by each processor is independent of the submesh size. A job that consumes a large submesh will hold the submesh relatively the same length of time as a job requiring a small submesh. The larger submesh will have a greater computational throughput.

Our model of a multicomputer system consists of a control processor and a number of general-purpose processors that are interconnected by a 16*16 2-D mesh network. The goal of the control processor is to decrease the average job turnaround time and to increase the system utilization. The control processor is divided into two parts: the job scheduler and the processor allocator. The job scheduler selects jobs for the processor allocator while the processor allocator assigns jobs to appropriate partitions of unoccupied processors. In our study we consider only the allocation of processors to a job in a contiguous region. If jobs could be allocated to processors that are dispersed across a multicomputer, the system fragmentation can be removed completely. However, the communications of a job may be affected by the communications of other jobs, and therefore increase communication delays. These contention delays between job may become severe if the average amount of communication of a job is large. In order to allocate processors to a job in a contiguous region, we used the frame sliding (FS) method[3], which was developed for a general 2-D mesh system and allocates jobs in contiguous regions in an efficient way of minimizing system fragmentation. For evaluating components of job scheduling algorithms, a group-based strategy, called *BWQ-algorithm*, is used and described in the next section. The algorithm is studied for its ability to increase system utilization by reducing system fragmentation and improve the mean job turnaround time.

3 The BWQ Searching Algorithm

We propose a nonblocking multiqueue-based job scheduling algorithm, called the BWQ algorithm. This job scheduling algorithm is divided into two parts: the *Between Queue (BQ) policy* and the *Within Queue (WQ) policy*. The BQ policy controls the order that a scheduler selects queues. The WQ policy controls the order that jobs are selected from a queue. Each queue has its own *Within Queue(WQ) policy*. In general, the WQ policy for each queue reorders the jobs within the queue so that in some situations a smaller job can be allocated before a larger job for which a partition is not available. However, the WQ policy is simply FIFO if all jobs in a queue have the same size.

3.1 Between Queue (BQ) Policy

The BQ Policy controls the order that queues are considered for selecting jobs to allocate. Queues are ordered according to the size of the jobs they contain, ranging from the smallest to largest jobs as illustrated in Fig. 1.

Initially, the scheduler searches the queue that holds the smallest jobs and schedules its jobs according to the WQ policy of the queue. If the queue is empty, the scheduler moves to the next non-empty queue in circular-right pattern and tries to schedule the jobs of the queue with the WQ policy. When all jobs are scheduled and assigned without blocking, the BQ policy moves to the next non-empty queue. If no jobs within the queue can be scheduled for allocation, the job

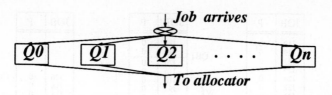

Fig. 1. Multi-queue based job scheduling.

scheduler moves back to a non-empty queue that holds smaller jobs. The scheduler is not necessarily blocked from assigning jobs for which partitions do exist. Therefore, an additional opportunity for resource allocation is given to smaller jobs that require smaller submeshes. This non-blocking property may decrease the turnaround times of the smaller jobs and reduce the external fragmentation in the system. Depending on the scheduling policy, the scheduler may move to the queue with the smallest jobs or to the previous non-empty queue. The policy needs a limit on the number of times the scheduler can return to queues holding smaller jobs to avoid starvation of larger jobs. Every time the scheduler passes a large job, the priority of the job is increased by 1. If the priority reaches the *Between Queue Search Limit (BQSL)*, then the scheduler is blocked to schedule the "starving" job. Initially the priority of each job is set to zero. The BQSL is a design parameter with performance implications that we will discuss later in this section.

3.2 Within Queue(WQ) policy

The WQ policy is controlled by a *lookahead window* that provides an additional allocation opportunity for smaller jobs within a queue. When a job or multiple jobs are ready to be scheduled within a single queue Q_j, the jobs that are chosen from the queue for scheduling come from the set of jobs within the *lookahead window* of the queue. Initially the set of jobs in the lookahead window are the n jobs at the head of the queue, where n is the lookahead window size. If n is greater than one and the first job of the queue cannot be allocated, then the job scheduler considers jobs in the queue within the lookahead window to find a job that is allocatable. If it finds such a job, it schedules the job and looks to the next n jobs. Otherwise, the job scheduler moves to another queue according to the BQ policy. A large lookahead window size increases the probability of finding a job that can be scheduled, but also increases the cost to search for a job. The window size needs to be bounded depending on the type of jobs assigned to a particular queue. The window size of each queue is a design parameter that is discussed later in this section.

Figure 2 shows the state of a queuing system of an job scheduler that has 3 queues. The first queue (Q0) is a FIFO queue, i.e. the size of the lookahead window is 1 and the BQSL is fixed to 0. Jobs in the queues have priority P set to 0. Notice that $J5$ and $J7$ in queue Q1 have $P > 0$, which means that these jobs were not able to be scheduled in previous attempts.

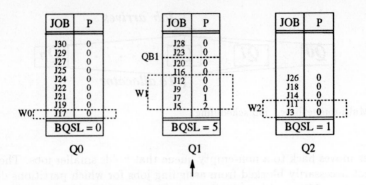

Fig. 2. An illustration of job scheduling of three queues.

The second and third queues, Q1 and Q2, are general lookahead window queues. Each has a BQSL given as a design parameter. After scheduling the jobs in Q0, the scheduler is currently working in Q1. Some jobs have been assigned and the scheduler searches within the lookahead window of Q1. Notice that Q1 has a dotted-line that is called the *Qboundary*. This parameter is discussed in the next subsection.

3.3 Design Parameters

In this subsection, three design parameters are studied to maximize system performance. To isolate the effect of each parameter, we fix the other parameters at specific values. Experiments were conducted for all four job types. Since some of our studies produce similar results, only the results of the rectangular-unrestricted input are displayed when they are similar.

Number of queues The number of queues used is an important design parameter that can have a significant effect on the system performance. In a hypercube multicomputer system, the number of queues used is the number of possible subcubes whose sizes are powers of 2 [6]. For the 2-D mesh system we cannot apply the same method if jobs have irregular sizes. This parameter depends on factors such as the allocation strategy, job arrival rates, distribution of job sizes and system size.

Figure 3 presents the effect of increasing the number of queues on the performance of BWQ job scheduling algorithm in our simulation model of mesh system. We could use hundreds of queues due to the variability of the possible sizes for all types of jobs. However, the number of queues was limited to six or less in order to study the effect of increasing the number of queues. The simple case of using only one queue implies a FIFO queue. The BQSL of each queue is set to 30. Thresholds that establish the sizes of jobs placed in each queue are defined in order to balance the number of jobs that arrive at each queue. When the number of queues is increased from one to three, the mean turnaround time decreases significantly. However, for more than 3 queues the mean turnaround time does not improve. Consequently, with a certain number of queues we obtain a system performance that is near the maximum. The appropriate number of queues may change, depending on the allocation strategy, distribution of job sizes, and the size of the mesh system. Larger mesh systems with incoming jobs that have greater variability in sizes may need more queues. For our simulation model, 3 queues are enough.

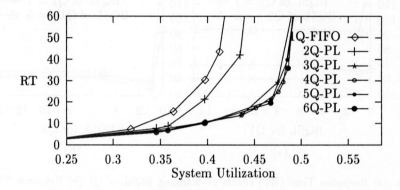

Fig. 3. Response Time (RT) effect of increasing number of queues on the performance of job scheduling policy: BQSLs = 30, Input type = Rectangular-unrestricted.

Between Queue Search Limit(BQSL) Another important design parameter is the BQSL of each queue. Any queue with a BQSL equal to zero becomes a scheduling bottleneck. Large jobs in a queue that cannot be scheduled immediately block all other jobs in the system, which may result in an increased mean turnaround time. Therefore, the BQSL of each queue should be tuned in relation to the BQSLs of the other queues. Results providing information about the tuning of the BQSL are displayed in Fig. 4. Three queues were used and incoming jobs of the unrestricted rectangular type were generated with the arrival rate set to result in 50% system utilization. Because Q0 is designed as a FIFO queue, the BQSL for Q0 was set to 0. The simulation results show that mean turnaround times are much higher when at least one of the BQSLs is zero. Therefore, a significant improvement in performance occurs when the BQSL of each queue is larger than zero. These results imply that providing an additional scheduling opportunity for smaller jobs when blocking would occur (i.e. non-blocking) has a profound effect on the mean turnaround time. However, it is inappropriate to set the BQSL to a value that is too large. If the BQSL is greater than or equal to 5, then the mean turnaround time increased significantly since large jobs can wait too long. Another interesting aspect is the relative effect of the BQSL of one queue on the performance of the jobs in another queue. When we compare Fig. 4(a) and 4(b), the effect of the value assigned to the BQSL of Q2 is more significant than the value assigned to Q1.

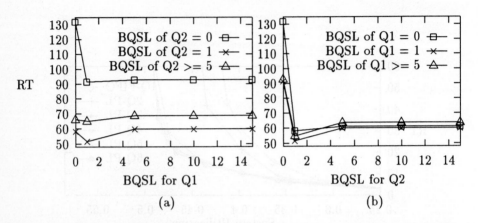

Fig. 4. (a) Response Time (RT) effects of changing BQSL of Q1 (b) Response Time (RT) effects of changing BQSL of Q2: 3 Queues with both window sizes = 1, Input type=Rectangular-unrestricted.

Lookahead Window The lookahead window of each queue is used to reorder jobs within a queue. The size of the lookahead window is another factor that should be tuned appropriately for system performance. At a high level of system utilization, as illustrated in Fig. 5, large lookahead windows improve the performance. The diamond plot of Fig. 5 shows the simulation results when the lookahead window size of queues 1 and 2 is one (WS=1). The cross plot of Fig. 5 shows the improved performance for larger window sizes. We have found that the performance improvement due to the lookahead window is sensitive to the type and characteristics of the incoming job stream. An incoming job stream with a wide variation in the sizes of jobs benefits much more from a larger lookahead window size than an incoming job stream with uniform sizes of jobs.

Qboundary The purpose of the boundary is to avoid starvation of jobs. Only the current queue for which the scheduler is selecting jobs has a Qboundary. It is established when the scheduler first considers a queue and remains until all jobs below the Qboundary have been scheduled. Jobs arriving after the Qboundary has been established will not be considered candidates during the current scheduling phase of the queue. Suppose there is no Qboundary established for

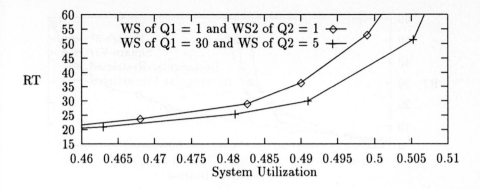

Fig. 5. Response Time (RT) effects of lookahead windows: 3 queues, BQSLs of Q1 and Q2 = 30, Input type=Rectangular-unrestricted, FS-allocator.

a queue, e.g. Q1. Further suppose all new jobs are placed in Q1. Therefore, the scheduler will only select jobs from Q1, which results in the other jobs starving.

4 Performance Effects of Variability in Size and Shape

Once we obtain parameters for the BWQ algorithm, we are ready to examine the effects of the variability of sizes and irregularity of shapes of jobs on the dynamic scheduling system. Figure 6 shows results that demonstrate these effects. The four curves show the mean job turnaround times of BWQ scheduling algorithm for the four different types of inputs described in Section 2. An important feature is the difference between the curves for Square-2^k input and the other inputs. The mean job turnaround time of Square-2^k is stable up to 60% system utilization. In contrast, the other inputs become unstable before 45% system utilization. This fact implies that a variability of input sizes has a dramatic effect on the performance of a job scheduling policy.

One of the key factors that contributes to the difference in the results is the system fragmentation. As the system utilization increases to 80%, the external fragmentation due to Square-2^k input decreases to 12%. However, the other types of inputs cause the system to become unstable at lower system utilizations, resulting in a high external fragmentation (38% external fragmentation at 45% utilization). Although our job scheduling algorithm tries to reduce system fragmentation by allowing non-blocking for the other types of inputs, the processor allocator has difficulty in assigning jobs efficiently because the sizes of inputs vary greatly. While the variability of input size has a profound effect on the performance of job scheduling algorithms, irregular input shapes do not make a significant difference in the system performance, as illustrated in Fig. 6. The performance for the input types Square-var, Rectangular-Restricted, and

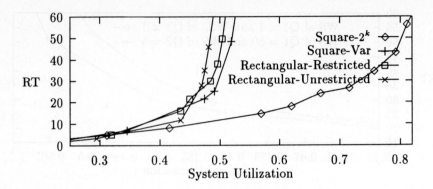

Fig. 6. Response Time (RT) effects of variability in size and shape on job turnaround times of BWQ algorithm: Q1 with BQSL = 10 and Q2 with BQSL = 1.

Rectangular-Unrestricted are similar as the system utilization increases. As a result, we have the freedom to change input shapes when assigning jobs. Nevertheless, the "less-regular" jobs (i.e. Rectangular-Unrestricted) display a little poorer result than the "more regular" jobs (i.e. Square-var). From the above analysis, we can conclude:

- The type of input has significant effects on the performance of a job scheduling algorithm. A regular-shaped job – regular-shaped (2^k) cluster – can be scheduled with significantly better performance in comparison to other input shapes that have less regularity.
- If the geometry of job partitions are allowed to be arbitrary shapes, then differences between separate classes of irregular jobs (*e.g.* Square-Var, Rectangular-Restricted, Rectangular-Unrestricted) are insignificant.

5 Conclusion

We discussed the performance effects of arbitrary sizes of jobs in 2-D mesh system and proposed a job scheduling strategy. We simulated jobs of several different types with job scheduler and processor allocator developed to reduce system fragmentation. The job scheduling algorithm used is a nonblocking multiqueue-based job scheduling algorithm that is efficient and suitable for general 2-D mesh multicomputer systems. In the strategy, external fragmentation is minimized to decrease job turnaround time and to increase system utilization by reordering the scheduling of jobs. The simulation results showed that the amount of inherent system fragmentation of a 2-D mesh system depends on the amount of irregularity of the sizes and shapes of job requests. There is a large performance improvement between very regular-shaped partitions and the other types of partitions. The results were analyzed in the context of developing a processor allocation strategy for wormhole-routed 2-D mesh systems.

References

1. Alverson, R., and et. al.: The Tera Computer System. In Proc. 1990 International Conference on Supercomputing (Jun 1990), pp. 1–6
2. Chen, M.-S., and Shin, K.: Processor Allocation in an N-Cube Multiprocessor Using Gray Code. IEEE Trans. on Computers C-36, 12 (Dec 1987), 1396–1407
3. Chuang, P.-J., and Tzeng, N.-F.: An Efficient Submesh Allocation Strategy for Mesh Computer Systems. In Proceedings of the 1991 International Conference on Distributed Computing Systems (May 1991), IEEE
4. Dally, W. J.: Performance Analysis of k-ary n-cube Interconnection Networks. IEEE Transactions on Computers 39, 6 (1990), 775–785
5. Dally, W. J., and Seitz, C. L.: The Torus Routing Chip. Journal of Distributed Computing 1, 3 (1986), 187–196
6. Krueger, P., Lai, T.-H., and Radiya, V. A.: Processor Allocation vs. Job Scheduling on Hypercube Computers. In Proceedings of the 1991 International Conference on Distributed Computing Systems (May 1991), IEEE
7. Leutenegger, S. T., and Vernon, M. K.: The Performance of Multiprogrammed Multiprocessor Scheduling Algorithms. Proc. of the 1990 ACM Conf. on Measurement and Modeling of Computer Systems (May 1990), ACM, pp. 226–236
8. Li, K., and Cheng, K. H.: A Two Dimensional Buddy System for Dynamic Resource Allocation in a Partitionable Mesh Connected System. In Proceedings of the ACM Computer Science Conference (1990), pp. 22–28
9. Min, D., and Mutka, M. W.: A Framework for Predicting Delay Due to Job Interaction in a 2-D Mesh multicomputer. In Proc. of the 7th International Parallel Processing Symposium (Apr 1993), IEEE
10. Peng, D.-T., and Shin, K. G.: Static Allocation of Periodic Tasks with Precedence Constraints in Distributed Real-Time Systems In Proc. of Intl. Conf. on Distributed Computing Systems (1990), IEEE, pp. 190–198
11. Ramamritham, K.: Allocation and Scheduling of Complex Periodic Tasks. In Proc. of 1990 Int. Conference on Distributed Computing Systems (1990), IEEE, pp. 108–115
12. Seitz, C. L., and et. al.: The Architecture and Programming of the Amtek Series 2010 Multicomputer. In Proc. of the Third Conference on Hypercube Concurrent Computers and Applications, 1 (Jan 1988), ACM, pp. 33–36
13. Shirazi, B., and Wang, M.: Analysis and Evaluation of Heuristic Methods for Static Task Scheduling. Journal of Parallel and Distributed Computing (Oct 1990), 222–232
14. Silberschatz, A., Peterson, J., and Galvin, P.: Operating System Concepts, 3rd ed. Addison Wesley, 1991.
15. Zorpette, G.: Technology 1991: Minis and Mainframes. IEEE Spectrum (Jan 1991), 40–43

Static Allocation of Tasks on Multiprocessor Architectures with Interprocessor Communication Delays

Sylvie NORRE
Université BLAISE PASCAL - Clermont-Ferrand II
Laboratoire d'Informatique
F63177 AUBIERE Cedex - FRANCE
Tel: (33) 73 40 74 43   Fax: (33) 73 26 88 29
E-mail: glm@libd1.univ-bpclermont.fr

Abstract:
   This paper deals with the problem of task allocation, subjected to precedence constraints, on multiprocessor architectures with interprocessor communication delays. Two kinds of scheduling are distinguished: the deterministic scheduling (the duration of each task and the duration of each communication delay are known and are constant) and the stochastic scheduling (the duration of each task and the duration of each communication delay is modelled by a probability law).
   For each of these two scheduling problems, we propose several scheduling methods and we build several models in order first to estimate the efficiency of the obtained schedules and second to evaluate the multiprocessor architecture performances, such as the busy percentage of processors. These methods are based on the coupling between priority list algorithms and neighbourhood methods. Because neighbourhood methods are not suitable for stochastic scheduling problem, we have modified the simulated annealing algorithm in order to solve stochastic optimization problems.
   For the deterministic scheduling, we use finite deterministic simulation models. In the case of stochastic scheduling, we built several models: a markovian model, a stochastic simulation model and a hybrid model (markovian analysis and simulation).
   Although this scheduling problem is NP-complete, these methods compute satisfactory solutions in reasonable computing times. The mean improvement compared with classical list scheduling methods is about 10% in the deterministic case as well as in the stochastic case.

Keywords: Stochastic scheduling, Deterministic scheduling, Task allocation on multiprocessor architectures.

1. Introduction

The elaboration of parallel programs can be divided in two consecutive parts:
- the first part concerns the program specification. The precedence constraints between tasks must be deduced from the data dependence analysis,
- the second part consists in task scheduling, subjected to precedence constraints, among the processors in order to minimize the total execution time.

In this paper, we deal with the problem of task allocation on multiprocessor architectures with interprocessor communication delays. We suppose that the parallel tasks have been determined and that the precedence constraints between tasks are specified on a precedence graph. Two kinds of scheduling problems are considered: the deterministic scheduling and the stochastic scheduling. Several scheduling methods are proposed for each of these two scheduling problems. We specially describe how stochastic methods, such as the simulated annealing algorithm, can solve, in reasonable calculation durations, the task allocation problem. We also build several models in order to estimate on one hand the efficiency of the obtained schedules and on the other hand the performances of the multiprocessor architecture.

Some simplifying assumptions are introduced because of the complexity of the studied systems:

-the number n of tasks and the number p of processors are finite,

-the processors are identical: a task can be executed on any processor,

-the duplication of tasks is not allowed,

-the tasks are not preemptive,

-a task T_i $(1 \leq i \leq n)$ can only be executed if all its predecessors are completed and have transferred data necessary for executing this task T_i (communication delays),

-at a given time, a processor executes at most one task,

-the task allocation is static.

2. Deterministic scheduling

This problem can be formulated as follows:

Let $G=(T,X)$ be a directed acyclic graph (DAG) such that:

-$T=\{T_i\}_{i=1,n}$ represents the set of tasks,

-X represents the set of precedence constraints between tasks (an arc weighted by c_{ij} and located between two tasks T_i and T_j $(i \neq j)$ can only start c_{ij} units of time after the end of the task T_i (we note $T_i << T_j$).

A schedule O is defined as a set of triples $\{(T_j, P(T_j), S(T_j)), j=1,n\}$ which satisfies the precedence constraints and the communication delays (the task T_j is assigned to the processor $P(T_j)$ at time $S(T_j)$). The completion time $C(T_j)$ of a task T_j is equal to $C(T_j)=S(T_j)+d(T_j)$ where $d(T_j)$ represents the execution duration of the task T_j. In consequence of the precedence constraints and of the communications delays, the following inequality must be satisfied: If $T_i << T_j$ then $S(T_j) \geq C(T_i)+c_{ij}$

The makespan $C(O)$ of a schedule O is the largest completion time of all the tasks:
$$C(O) = max\ C(T_j)$$
$$j=1,n$$

So, the objective is to determine a schedule S whose makespan is minimal i.e.
$$C(S) = min\ C(O) \quad \text{where } \mathcal{O} \text{ is the set of schedules}$$
$$O \in \mathcal{O}$$

Unlike classical scheduling problems, relaxing the resource limitations does not make the scheduling problems with interprocessor delays easy [Garey 83]. Most of them remain NP-hard even when severe restrictions are made on the precedence graph or on the values of the communication and/or processing times [Picouleau 92]. Some particular cases are however polynomial [Chrétienne 89], [Chrétienne 92].

In this paper, we are interested in the determination of an approximated solution. The approximation scheduling methods that we propose are based on priority list algorithms and on the simulated annealing algorithm. In order to build a schedule and to estimate its makespan, we build a deterministic simulation model.

2.1. Principle of the scheduling methods

2.1.1. List scheduling algorithms

The list scheduling heuristics are essentially devoted to scheduling problems without building a list of tasks sorted on the descending priority. When a processor is available for execution, the list is scanned from left to right and the first free task is scheduled (a task is free if all its predecessors have completed execution).

When communication costs are zero, a good choice for a priority list is the CP (Critical Path) or HLFET (Highest Level First with Estimated Times) method [Adam 74]. The priority of a task is its bottom up level i.e. the length of the longest path from it to an exit node. The CP list scheduling possesses many nice properties when communication cost is zero [Hu 61], [Coffman 72], [Adam 74], [Coffman 76]. Unfortunately, these nice properties do not carry over to the case of nonzero communication costs.

Many modifications of the CP algorithm have been proposed in order to take into account scheduling problems where communication costs are not zero [Hwang 89], [Gerasoulis 92]. In this paper, we have retained the ELS heuristic [Hwang 89] because of its small execution time and low complexity. This heuristic is composed of two successive steps. In the first step, the communication times are ignored in order to compute a solution from classical list scheduling. In the second step, necessary communication delays are added to the schedule obtained in the first step. This list algorithm permits to build rapidly feasible schedules. However, the makespan of such schedules is often far from the optimum. So, in order to obtain schedules with smaller makespan, we propose the coupling of one of these list algorithms with a neighbourhood method, such as the simulated annealing algorithm.

2.1.2. Coupling of the simulated annealing algorithm with the ELS heuristic

Principle of the simulated annealing algorithm [Siarry 88],[Van Laarhoven 89]

The simulated annealing algorithm is a stochastic algorithm which can be formulated as follows. Starting off at a given configuration OC, a sequence of iterations is generated, each iteration consisting of a possible transition from the current configuration OC to a configuration OV selected from the neighbourhood of the current configuration. If this neighbouring configuration OV has a lower cost, the current configuration is replaced by this neighbour. Otherwise, the neighbouring configuration is accepted with a probability π depending on a control parameter named temperature and on the difference between the costs of OV and OC.

Several variants of the simulated annealing algorithm have been proposed:

-The *iterative improvement* : the probability π is equal to zero.

-The *kangaroo method* [Fleury 93] is based on iterative improvement and consists in accepting a wrong transition, which corresponds to an increase in the cost function, if no amelioration has been done during a given number of iterations.

-The *method of repeated iterative improvements*: several independent iterative improvements are applied on different initial configurations.

Simulated annealing algorithm is a generalization of iterative improvement in that it accepts deteriorations in the cost function. So, by definition, this algorithm does not terminate in a local minimum.

The coupling of all these stochastic methods with the ELS heuristic are studied. The generation mechanism, identical for all theses methods, is described subsequently.

In [Norre 93], we study the problem of task allocation on a multiprocessor architecture without interprocessor communication delay. We propose in particular several stochastic methods based on the simulated annealing algorithm whose generation mechanism is the following one:

Let OC be a current schedule. This schedule is composed of n triples $(T_i, P(T_i), S(T_i))$ $(1 \leq i \leq n)$ which are sorted on the increasing starting date (if $i < j$ then $S(T_i) \leq S(T_j)$).

The generation of a neighbouring configuration OV is carried out as follows:

-A triple $E = (T_e, P(T_e), S(T_e))$ $(1 \leq e \leq n)$ is randomly chosen.

-All the triples in OC that are anterior to the triple E are retained in the schedule OV.

-The schedule OV is then completed according to one of the two following strategies:

Strategy 1: • A task T_j, randomly chosen among all the tasks that can be executed at time $S(T_e)$, is put in place of the task T_e.

• the schedule of the $(n-e-1)$ other tasks is obtained by applying the CP method.

Strategy 2: • the processor $P(T_e)$ is set idle during a delay. Several delays can be applied: they correspond to the difference between the ending execution time of tasks which are executed on the other processors and the time $S(T_e)$. One of these delays is randomly chosen.

• the schedule of the $(n-e)$ other tasks is obtained by applying the CP method.

If the retained strategy can not be applied, its alternative is chosen. If none of these two strategies is suitable, this process is repeated using a new triple E.

This generation mechanism is retained in the present study and is used as indicated hereafter. The generation of a schedule is always decomposed in two steps : in the first step, the communication times are ignored and a schedule is computed, in the second step, the necessary communication delays are added to the schedule obtained in the first step. The generation mechanism that we proposed is applied during the step 1. The acceptance criteria of a neighbour is based on the makespans of the schedules computed in the step 2.

The reversibility condition, which is required by the theorem of [Hajeck 88] in order to guarantee the theoretical convergence of the simulated annealing algorithm, is not checked. The accessibility condition is however checked, and it is sufficient to prove the theoretical convergence of the kangaroo method [Fleury 93].

Three stopping criteria are defined:

-the maximal number of iterations is reached,

-the obtained schedule has a makespan equal to the critical path of the precedence graph,

-the obtained schedule has a makespan equal to the ratio between the sum of the execution duration of all the tasks and the number of processors.

If one of these two last conditions is true, the iterative process is stopped because an optimal solution is found. So, the maximum of these two criteria defines a lower bound of the makespan. We point out that this lower bound, named B, will be reached very infrequently because it does not include communication costs.

2.2. Application

Random graph generation

In order to generate graphs, we have developed a random graph generating program which accepts as input:

-the total number of tasks,

-the minimum and maximum number of initial (resp. final) tasks,

-the minimum and maximum number of successors (resp. predecessors) of a vertex,

-the minimum and the maximum value of the task execution duration,
-the minimum and the maximum value of the communication cost.

For each vertex, its duration, its number of successors and its number of predecessors are picked from an uniform distribution whose parameters are input data. The communication cost of each arc is determined alike.

In our case, we generate twenty graphs whose task duration ranges from 5 to 10 and whose number of tasks is equal to 5, 10, 15 or 20. For each graph, we consider three variation ranges for the communication costs: from 1 to 5, from 5 to 10 and from 10 to 15.

Scheduling method implementation

Several scheduling methods have been tested on these random graphs:

-the *ELS heuristic*: during the first step of this heuristic, the schedule is computed by the CP algorithm. In the second step, communication costs are added.

-the *iterative improvement algorithm*: the initial solution is generated by the ELS heuristic. The maximal number of iterations is 5000, a greater number does not induce improvement.

-the *simulated annealing algorithm*: the initial solution is generated by the ELS heuristic. The initial temperature is equal to the difference between the makespan of the initial solution and the lower bound B. The rate of convergence is not faster than $O(1/\log(k))$ where k is the number of iterations.

-the *kangaroo method*: the initial solution is generated by the ELS heuristic. The maximal number of iterations is equal to 50000 and a wrong solution is accepted when no improvement has occurred after 3000 iterations.

-the *repeated iterative improvement algorithm*: the maximal number of iterations is equal to 50000 and the generation of a new solution is performed when no improvement has occurred after 5000 iterations. The new solutions are computed by the ELS heuristic where the schedule in the first step is computed by the RANDOM heuristic [Adam 74]. This heuristic is a list algorithm which consists to choose randomly the task to be executed among all the executable tasks.

Two models are built for each of these scheduling methods. The first one is written in the Fortran programming language. The second one is written with the Qnap2 package (Queueing Network Analysis Package) [Qnap2 91]. This package offers an interface language, which is object-oriented and particularly well suited for modelling parallel tasks, synchronization mechanisms and resource sharing problems. These two models validate themselves. They use the same random number generator [Lewis 73]. So, schedules that are computed are identical although model implementations are different.

Results

The stochastic methods have been applied on the twenty graphs described previously. The results are presented in figure 1. For each stochastic method, that we propose, we compute the mean improvement G compared with the ELS heuristic. Let S be a solution. Let SII be the solution computed by the ELS heuristic. The improvement of the solution S compared with the solution SII is defined as:

$$G=100*(C(SII)-C(S))/C(SII).$$

The mean improvement G of a stochastic method compared with the ELS heuristic is defined as the mean of the improvements for the twenty graphs.

The number of processors is equal to two. However, all the proposed scheduling methods have also been applied on a greater number of processors.

Communication cost range	Iterative Improvement	Rep. Iterative Improvement	Simulated annealing	Kangaroo
[1,5]	+2,94	+ 3,24	+ 3,45	+ 3,39
[5,10]	+6,77	+ 7,00	+ 7,23	+ 7,05
[10,15]	+ 10,16	+ 12,54	+ 13,47	+ 12,56

Fig. 1. mean improvement of the stochastic methods compared with the ELS heuristic

All these stochastic methods permit to improve solutions computed by the ELS heuristic. The best method seems to be the simulated annealing algorithm but the difference between all these stochastic methods is not significant.

When communication costs are smaller than task execution durations, the mean improvement compared with the ELS heuristic is low (about 3%). In this case, communication costs are not very influential and the ELS heuristic computes solution which are not far from the optimum. During the first step, the ELS heuristic ignores communication costs and computes a solution from the CP method. The experimental results obtained by [Adam 74] show that the CP heuristic gives solution whose makespan is near the optimum in practice in the sense that it is within 5% of the optimum in 90% of randomly generated DAGs. The schedule, obtained in the first step, is not modified a lot when communication costs are added to it because these costs are small compared with the task execution duration. So, the makespan does not increase a lot and remains closed to the optimal solution.

The mean improvement compared with the ELS is more important (about 13%) when communication costs are greater than task execution durations. In this case, the ELS heuristic does not give good solutions because during the building of the schedule, it ignores communication costs, which have in fact a greater influence than task execution durations.

All these methods permit to compute solutions in short CPU times, about a few minutes for the Fortran model (on UNIX workstations with processor 68040 clocked at 25 MHz). Qnap2 models induce CPU times which are superior than those induce by Fortran models. Qnap2 models are however interesting because they permit to validate Fortran models and because they will be very easily adjustable to the stochastic case.

3. Stochastic scheduling

The set of assumptions is the same as in the deterministic case expected those concerning the task execution durations and the communication delays. These durations are no more constant but are now modelled by a probability law. This assumption will be introduced when:

- the operating system induces some variations on these durations,
- these durations are dependent on the input parameters of the program. For example, a task may contain a loop whose number of iterations can be one, ten, thousand or more.

The problem is to determine a schedule which minimizes the mean execution duration of all the tasks (quantity named makespan). A schedule is now defined as a set of triples $(T_j, P(T_j), I(T_j))$ $(1 \leq j \leq n)$ which satisfies the precedence constraints and the communication delays (the task T_j is assigned to the processor $P(T_j)$; the introduction order of the task T_j on the processor $P(T_j)$ is $I(T_j)$).

3.1. Stochastic evaluation of a schedule

We suppose that a scheduling method has computed a feasible schedule. So, for each task, we know its assigned processor and its introduction order on this processor. The aim is to build models which permit to evaluate this schedule when the communication costs and the execution durations are modelled by a probability law. We propose two models: a stochastic simulation model and a markovian model.

3.1.1. The simulation model

Using a finite stochastic simulation model, several independent simulations are successively executed. Each simulation describes one behaviour of the model. The starting and ending execution times of each task differ from one simulation to another because of the probability law. As the study concerns the transient state, the number of simulations must be high enough to ensure a good statistical sampling of the stochastic behaviour of the model.

3.1.2. The markovian model

The growing interest in markovian solvers concretized recently in several new proposals in the area of queueing network models [Mueller 85] and stochastic Petri nets [Natkin 80]. Many authors have been interested in the automatic generation of the state space, such as [Paul 85]. The work of [Stewart 78] served as a starting point for the development of the markovian solver of the Qnap2 package [Potier 85].

In our case, the *state of the system E* is represented by four, two by two disjointed, set of tasks:

$E=A \cup B \cup C \cup X$ with $A \cap B=\emptyset$, $A \cap C=\emptyset$, $A \cap X=\emptyset$, $B \cap C=\emptyset$, $B \cap X=\emptyset$, $C \cap X=\emptyset$, $Card(A)+Card(B)+Card(C) = n$ (number of tasks) and $Card(X)=m$ (number of arcs).

-A is the *set of tasks that are being executed*:
$A = \{ k_i, i = 1,2,...,K \mid k_i \in T\}; Card(A) = K$ and $1 \leq K \leq p$.

-B is the *set of tasks that are not yet executed*:
$B = \cup B_i$ with $B_i = \{ l_j, j=1,2,...,L_i \mid l_j \in T, P(l_j)= i, \forall 1 \leq j \leq n, I(l_j)<I(l_{j+1})\}$;

$i=1,p$
$Card(B_i) = L_i$ and $1 \leq L_i \leq n; Card(B) = L = \sum L_i$ and $1 \leq L \leq n$.

$i=1,p$

B_i is the ordered set of tasks that must be assigned to the processor i.

- C is the *set of tasks that are achieved*:
$C = \{ m_k, k = 1,2,...,K \mid m_k \in T\}; Card(C) = M$ and $1 \leq M \leq n$.

-X is the *set of arcs (or communication costs)*:
$X=X_1 \cup X_2 \cup X_3$ with:

- $Card(X_1)+Card(X_2)+Card(X_3)=m$
- X_1 is the *set of communication costs that are not yet executed*:

$X_1 = \{e_i, i = 1,2,...,d_1 \mid e_i \in X\}; Card(X_1) = d_1$ and $1 \leq d_1 \leq m$.
- X_2 is the *set of communication costs that are being executed*:

$X_2 = \{f_j, j = 1,2,...,d_2 \mid f_j \in X\}; Card(X_2) = d_2$ and $1 \leq d_2 \leq m$.
- X_3 is the *set of communication costs that are achieved*:
$X_3 = \{ g_k, k = 1,2,...,d_3 \mid g_k \in X\}; Card(X_3) =d_3$ and $1 \leq d_3 \leq m$.

$X_3 = \{ g_k, k = 1,2,....,d_3 \ / \ g_k \in X \}; Card(X_3) = d_3$ and $1 \leq d_3 \leq m$.

The *state change* is due to the end of a task or to the end of a communication.
Case 1: suppose that task k_t $(1 \leq t \leq K)$ ends
-The task k_t is moved from the set A to the set C i.e.
$$A = A \setminus \{k_t\}; \ C = C \cup \{k_t\}.$$
-The communication costs between k_t and its successors must start:
Let $Csucc1(k_t)$ be the output arcs (k_t,s) $(s \in T)$ of the task k_t such that $P(k_t) = P(s)$ (the communication cost is equal to zero: the arc is moved from the set X_1 to the set X_3).
Let $Csucc2(k_t)$ be the output arcs (k_t,s) $(s \in T)$ of the task k_t such that $P(k_t) \neq P(s)$ (the communication cost is not equal to zero: the arc is moved from the set X_1 to the set X_2).
Let $Csucc(k_t)$ be the output arcs of the task k_t $(Csucc(k_t) = Csucc1(k_t) \cup Csucc2(k_t))$.
$$X_3 = X_3 \cup Csucc1(k_t); \ X_2 = X_2 \cup Csucc2(k_t); \ X_1 = X_1 \setminus Csucc(k_t)$$
-For each idle processor z $(z \notin \{P(k_i), k_i \in A \setminus \{k_t\} \})$, we check that all the predecessors of the task $l_1 \in B_z$ are achieved (l_1 is the next task to be executed on this processor z) and that all the communication costs between l_1 and its predecessors are achieved (i.e. all the data required for the execution of the task l_1 are available). If these two conditions are true, the task l_1 is moved from the set B_z to the set A. Otherwise, nothing is done (a task l_j $(j>1)$ can eventually be executable on the processor z but the introduction order of tasks does not allow that the task l_j is executed before the task l_1. So, the processor is set idle although some tasks may be executed)
Let $D(k_t)$ the set of such tasks (this set can be empty).
$$D(k_t) = \cup \ (l_1 \ / \ P(l_1)=z, Pred(l_1) \subset C, Cpred(l_1) \subset X_3)$$
$$z \notin \{P(k_i), k_i \in A \setminus \{k_t\} \}$$
with $Pred(l_1)$ the set of predecessors of the task l_1,
$Cpred(l_1)$ the set of input arcs of the task l_1.
$$B=B \setminus D(k_t); \ A=A \cup D(k_t).$$
So, when the task k_t ends, the new system state is:
$$E_t=A_t \cup B_t \cup C_t \cup X_t=(A \cup D(k_t) \setminus \{k_t\}) \cup (B \setminus D(k_t)) \cup (C \cup \{k_t\}) \cup ((X_3 \cup Csucc1(k_t)) \cup$$
$$(X_2 \cup Csucc2(k_t)) \cup (X_1 \setminus Csucc(k_t))).$$
The transition rate from state E to state E_t is equal to the inverse of the mean execution time of the task k_t $(1/d(k_t))$.

Case 2: suppose that the communication cost f_c $(1 \leq c \leq d_2)$ ends
-The communication cost f_c is moved from the set X_2 to the set X_3 i.e.
$$X_2 = X_2 \setminus \{f_c\}; \ X_3 = X_3 \cup \{f_c\}.$$
-Let s $(s \in B)$ be the task which has f_c as input arc. If $s \in B_i$ and $s=l_j$ with $j \neq 1$ then nothing is done. If $s \in B_i$ and $s=l_j$ with $j=1$, we check if the processor $i=P(l_1)$ is idle and if the task can be executed (i.e. all its predecessors and all the communication costs between l_1 and its predecessors are achieved). If it is true, the task l_1 is moved from the set $B_{P(l1)}$ to the set A. Otherwise, nothing is done.
Let $E(f_c)$ be the set of tasks which are moved from B to A in consequence of the ending of f_c (this set is either empty, either composed of the unique task $\{s\}$).

So, when the communication cost f_c ends, the new system state is:
$$E_c = A_c \cup B_c \cup C_c \cup X_c = (A \cup E(f_c)) \cup (B \backslash E(f_c)) \cup C \cup ((X_3 \cup \{f_c\}) \cup (X_2 \backslash \{f_c\}) \cup X_1 \, .$$

The transition rate from state E to state E_c is equal to the inverse of the mean communication cost of f_c $(1/d(f_c))$.

Since there are K tasks and d_2 communication costs being executed, there are $K+d_2$ states accessible from the state E.

The initial state (we choose for convenience sake) is:
- $M=0$ (there is no achieved task)
- $d_1 = m$, $d_2 = 0$, $d_3 = 0$ (all the communication costs are not yet executed)
- $K=min(k,p)$, $L=n-min(k,p)$ if there are k tasks that are initially executable.

This model is implemented with the Qnap2 package which offers a Markovian solver [Potier 85]. This Markovian solver transforms a model described with the language of Qnap2 into a first order markovian process and then computes the steady-state solution of this process. Whatever the task graph is, the Markov chain is automatically built and steady state performances are computed. The mean execution duration of the schedule is deduced as well as the mean busy percentage of each processor. We can note that this modelling process is closed to [Molloy 82] and [Marsan 86] which principle is first to model the system with a stochastic Petri Net, and second to build the homogeneous Markov chain associated to the reachable marking graph of the Petri Net in order to deduce the performance criteria.

3.1.3. Results
These two models have been tested on different set of tasks. The figure 2 presents the results obtained for four examples when communication costs range from 5 to 10.

For each set of tasks, the mean execution duration of three schedules, obtained in the deterministic case, are evaluated: those computed by the ELS heuristic, the iterative improvement method and the simulated annealing algorithm.

For the markovian model, we indicate the Markov chain number of states.

For the simulation model, a confidence interval of the mean execution duration is computed by the regenerative method [Qnap2 91].

Ex.	Method	MARKOVIAN		SIMULATION		
		number of states	makespan	makespan		confidence interval
1	ELS	51	63,94	64,03	±	0,1287
	Iter. Improv.	118	57,48	57,56	±	0,1225
	Simul. annealing	118	57,48	57,56	±	0,1225
2	ELS	141	62,02	62,12	±	0,1209
	Iter. Improv.	141	62,02	62,12	±	0,1209
	Simul. annealing	141	62,02	62,12	±	0,1209
3	ELS	1090	105,4	105,4	±	0,1626
	Iter. Improv.	2058	102,2	102,3	±	0,1489
	Simul. annealing	612	98,69	98,70	±	0,1519
4	ELS	229	143,9	143,9	±	0,2091
	Iter. Improv.	410	135,6	135,7	±	0,2122
	Simul. annealing	332	133,1	133,2	±	0,2047

Fig. 2. Comparison between the markovian model and the simulation model

The results given by the simulation and the markovian analysis are identical within a range of few percents. The markovian model returns values that are included in the confidence intervals of the stochastic simulation model. So, we can consider that these models validate themselves. The markovian analysis is interesting because on one hand, it gives exact results at the steady state and on the other hand, it is faster than the simulation when the number of states is not too high. The markov chain number of states and its steady-state computation time increases drastically when the number of tasks and the number of processors grow. Moreover, in opposition to the simulation model, the markovian model is no more suitable when the probability laws are general.

These models also permit to estimate the steady state performances of the multiprocessor architectures: it gives the mean busy percentage of the processors.

3.2. The hybrid method

This method adjusts the simulated annealing algorithm to stochastic problems in order to minimize the mean execution duration of schedules. It uses both iterative improvement, simulation and markovian analysis. The principle consists in generating several feasible schedules using the generation mechanism described in the part 2.1.2. The mean execution duration of the schedules are evaluated by the markovian model presented in the part 3.1.2. A neighbouring schedule is then accepted if its mean execution duration is lower than the current one.

More precisely, an iteration of this method can be described as follow:

-Let OC be the current schedule whose mean execution duration is equal to $C(OC)$.

-A neighbouring schedule OV is generated according to the generation mechanism described in the part 2.1.2. So, for each task, we know the assigned processor and the order of introduction on this processor.

-The mean execution duration $C(OV)$ of the neighbouring schedule OV is computed using the markovian model.

-If $C(OV) \leq C(OC)$ then the schedule OC is replaced by the schedule OV.

This method has been applied on ten sets of tasks when communication costs range from 10 to 15. The figure 3 presents the mean execution duration of the schedules obtained by the ELS heuristic and by the hybrid method. The hybrid method number of iterations is equal to 1000 (no improvement is obtained for a larger number).

Example	ELS	Hybrid method
1	80,38	67,65
2	91,19	79,79
3	79,43	69,17
4	79,27	75,27
5	99,25	88,01
6	123,00	97,86
7	125,70	110,60
8	119,70	115,10
9	147,70	138,10
10	169,40	134,90
Mean Improvement / ELS		+ 12,08

Fig. 3. Mean execution duration of schedules (communication costs range from 10 to 15)

The hybrid method induces a mean improvement of 12,08% compared with the ELS heuristic. In all events, the mean execution duration of the schedule computed by the hybrid method is lower than the mean execution duration of the schedule computed by the ELS heuristic. The mean improvement compared with the ELS heuristic depends on the granularity of the task set (ratio between transfers and computations). The more the communication costs are important compared with task durations, the more the mean improvement is high. This mean improvement is about 3% (resp. 8%, 12%) when the communication costs range from 1 to 5 (resp. 5 to 10, 10 to 15). This method is interesting because it works on exact results at the steady state (markovian model). However, for 10 tasks (resp. 20 tasks), CPU times are about 2 hours (resp. 7hours) on UNIX workstations with processor 68040 clocked at 25 MHz.

Since the iterative improvement converges only on local minima, it seems to be interesting to put another stochastic methods, such as simulated annealing, in place of this method. Although this modification is easy and attractive, it has not been applied because such methods require a greater number of iterations and consequently higher CPU times.

Since markovian models induce high CPU times, it will be interesting to substitute simulation models to them. When using simulation models, it is unfortunately difficult to know the time at which steady state is reached. So, it will be necessary to compute confidence intervals in order to decide to accept or not a neighbouring schedule, as mentioned in [Bulgak 88].

4. Summary

We have proposed in this paper several scheduling methods dedicated to the problem of task allocation on a multiprocessor architecture with interprocessor communication delays. These methods are based on the coupling of the ELS heuristic with the simulated annealing algorithm.

Two kinds of scheduling problems are distinguished: the deterministic scheduling and the stochastic scheduling). Several models have been built in order first to estimate the efficiency of the obtained schedule and second to evaluate the multiprocessor architecture performances such as the busy percentage of each processor. Among these models, we distinguish deterministic and stochastic simulation models, a markovian model and a hybrid model (markovian analysis and simulation).

Our methods improve always the solution computed by the ELS heuristic. In the deterministic case, the mean improvement is about 3% (resp. 7%, 13%) when communication costs range from 1 to 5 (resp. from 5 to 10, from 10 to 15). In the stochastic case, the mean improvement is about 12% when communication costs range from 10 to 15. These methods can be applied on other optimization problems. Our actual interests consist in extending our methods in order to take into account more real scheduling problems (communication channel capacity, unequal processor distance, ...).

References

[Adam 74] T.L. Adam, K.M. Chandy, J.R. Dickson, "A comparison of list schedules for parallel processing systems", Communications of the ACM, Vol 17 (n°12), Dec 1974.

[Bulgak 88] A.A. Bulgak, J.L. Sanders, "Integrating a modified simulated annealing algorithm with the simultion of a manufacturing system to optimize buffer sizes in automatic assembly systems", Proceedings of the 1988 Winter Simulation Conference, pp. 684-690.

[Chrétienne 89] P. Chrétienne, "A polynomial algorithm to optimally schedule tasks on a virtual distributed system under tree like precedence constraints", EJOR 43, 225-230, 1989.

[Chétienne 92] P. Chrétienne, C. Picouleau, "The basic scheduling problem with interprocessor communication delays", Ecole d'été sur la théorie de l'ordonnancement et ses applications, 28 Sept-20 Octobre 1992, Château de Bonas (Gers), France, pp. 81-100.

[Coffman 72] E. G. Coffman, R.L. Graham, "Optimal scheduling for two processor systems", Acta Informatica, Vol 1, pp.200-213,1972.

[Coffman 76] E.G. Coffman, "Computer and jobshop scheduling theory", John Wiley and sons,1987.

[Fleury 93] G. Fleury, "Quelques méthodes de résolution de problèmes NP-complets", Thèse d'université, Université Blaise Pascal, Clermont-Ferrand II, à paraître, 1993.

[Garey 83] M.R. Garey, D.S. Johnson, "Computers and intractability: a guide to the theory of NP-completeness", Freeman, New-York, 1983.

[Gerasoulis 92] A. Gerasoulis, T. Yang, "A static macro-dataflow scheduling tool for scalable parallel architecture", Ecole d'été sur la théorie de l'ordonnancement et ses applications, 28 Sept-20 Octobre 1992, Château de Bonas (Gers), France, pp. 382-417.

[Hajeck 88] B. Hajeck, "Cooling schedules for optimal annealing", Mathematics of Operations Research, 1988, pp.311-329, 1988.

[Hu 61] T.C. Hu, "Parallel sequencing and assembly line problem", Operational Research, Vol 9, pp. 841-843, Nov. 1961.

[Hwang 89] J.J. Hwang, Y.C. Chow, F.D. Anger, C.Y. Lee, "Scheduling precedence graphs in systems with interprocessor communication times",SIAM JComp,18,2,April 1989,pp.244-257.

[Lewis 73] T.G. Lewis, W.H. Payne, "Generalized feedback shift register pseudo random number algorithm", J. ACM, Vol 20, n°3, pp.456-468, July 73.

[Marsan 86] M.A. Marsan, G. Balbo, G. Conte, "Performance models of multiprocessor systems", The MIT Press, USA, 1986.

[Molloy 82] M.K. Molloy, "Performance analysis using Petri Nets", IEEE Transactions on Computers, Vol C31, September 1984, pp.913-917.

[Mueller 85] B. Mueller, "NUMAS: a tool for the numerical modelling of computer systems", in Modelling Techniques and Tools for Performance Analysis, North-Holland, 1985.

[Natkin 80] S. Natkin, "Réseaux de Petri stochastiques", Thèse de Docteur-Ingénieur, Cnam Paris, 1980.

[Norre 93] S. Norre, "Affectation de tâches sur une architecture multiprocesseur - Méthodes stochastiques et évaluation des performances", Thése de doctorat,Université Clermont-Ferrand II.

[Paul 85] D.W. Paul, "An approach toward a universal specification language for discrete stochastic systems", in Modelling Techniques and Tools for Performance Analysis, North-Holland, 1985.

[Picouleau 92] C. Picouleau, "New complexity results on the UET-UCT scheduling problems", Ecole d'été sur la théorie de l'ordonnancement et ses applications, 28 Sept-20 Octobre 1992, Château de Bonas (Gers), France, pp. 487-502.

[Potier 85] D. Potier, M. Véran, "The markovian solver of Qnap2 and applications", Rapport Technique INRIA n°49, Mars 1985, France

[Qnap2 91] Qnap2 version8, manuel de référence, Société Simulog, 1991.

[Siarry 88] P. Siarry, G. Dreyfus, "La méthode du recuit simulé: théorie et applications", ISDET, Paris, 1988.

[Stewart 78] W.J. Stewart, "A comparison of numerical techniques in markov modelling", C. ACM 21, 2, 1978, pp.144-152.

[Van Laarhoven 89] P.J.M. Van Laarhoven, "Simulated annealing: theory and applications", Kluwer Academic Publishors, The Netherlands, 1989.

PEI : a Single Unifying Model to Design Parallel Programs

E. Violard and G.-R. Perrin

University of Franche-Comté, Laboratoire d'Informatique
F-25030 Besançon cedex
e.mail : violard@comte.uucp perrin@comte.uucp

Abstract

A lot of programming models have been proposed to deal with parallelism in order to express program transformations and refinements. This justifies to introduce an unifying theory to abstract different concepts. The aim of this paper is to introduce such a theory. This theory includes the definitions of problems, programs and transformation rules. It is founded on the simple mathematical concepts of multiset and of an equivalence between their representations as data fields. Program transformations are founded on this equivalence and defined from a refinement relation. Due to the unifying aspect of this theory, solutions that can be reached by these transformations are relevant to various synchronous or asynchronous computing models.

Introduction

It is now admitted that reliable parallel programming techniques should be founded on formal transformations of programs. To manage these transformations safely, a convenient model has to be defined, to express the successive statements, and the transformation rules. Concerning these transformations the art conditions show two complementary philosophies : the stepwise refinement of programs from a specification and the synthesis of programs from a set of recurrence equations.

If a program F' satisfies any specification that a program F satisfies, F' is called a *refinement* of F [Mor90]. This approach requires a logic in order to reason on programs. UNITY [CM88] is a fundamental contribution in this domain. UNITY allows to express specifications and solutions in the same formalism. UNITY models programs as transition systems. GAMMA [Cre91] uses the same approach as UNITY, but is founded on a different model : a program GAMMA is a multiset transformer. These two formalisms associated with a refinement calculus are characterized by a non-deterministic computing model which allows to introduce only necessary sequentiality.

Due to the results of Karp, Miller and Winograd [KMW67], the second philosophy lies on a convenient abstract expression of programs in terms of *recurrence equations*. Indeed, prefiguring architecture evolutions, the introduction of the uniform recurrence equations defines a formal framework where the classical notions of data dependencies, potential parallelism and computation scheduling can be presented. Since this presentation many proposals have generalized this abstract modeling. Affine recurrences on integral convex domains are mainly studied for systolic synthesis (see for example [Qui89], [CMP92], etc.). ALPHA [Mau89] and CRYSTAL [CCL91] are the main formalisms using this approach. These languages are founded on a deterministic computing model and transformation rules depending on the properties of some data structures.

So, different ways have been explored now-adays about parallel programming : expression of data dependencies, transformation rules, refinements, etc. This fully justifies to introduce an unifying theory which supposes an abstraction of the different concepts. This paper is devoted to such a theory.

This theory is founded on the simple mathematical concept of multiset, represented as a *data field*. In this theory a program is a function on data fields which is denoted as a set of un-oriented equations. Then the two sides of any equation define two equal data fields. This expression generalizes classical recurrence equations.

On an other hand, transformations on these equations are founded on a mathematical data fields equivalence referring to the same multiset. This equivalence induces an equivalence of programs which is defined from a refinement relation between programs that *satisfy* a given problem.

We present this theory in the following way. Section 1 is devoted to the definitions of data fields and operations on data fields set. In section 2, we define programs from the concept of data field, and we introduce their notation. A refinement relation between programs is presented in section 3. This relation is the foundation of our transformations which introduces an operational definition of programs. Last, section 4 is an illustration of the program derivation process with the Gaussian elimination problem.

1 Multisets and Data Fields

1.1 Definition

Intuitively, a multiset is a set in which an element can appear more than once. This is its formal definition :

Definition 1 *Let E be a set. A* multiset M on E *is a function from E to N, which associates with any element x of E, the number $M(x)$ of occurrences of x in M.*

The set of multisets will be denoted as $\mathcal{M}$. The set of multisets on E will be denoted as $\mathcal{M}(E)$. A multiset can be denoted between $\prec$ and $\succ$.

Example: The multiset M on $\{1, 2, 3, 4, 5\}$ defined as :

$$M : \quad \{1, 2, 3, 4, 5\} \quad \rightarrow \quad N$$
$$x \quad \mapsto \quad \begin{array}{l} 0, \text{if } x = 1 \\ 3, \text{if } x = 2 \\ 1, \text{if } x \in \{3, 4, 5\} \end{array}$$

can be written $M = \prec 5, 2, 2, 4, 3, 2 \succ$.

This notion is adequate to represent the data and results of (parallel) problems. But, a (parallel) program has to set values geometrically, that is, in space and time. Therefore, we introduce the concept of *geometrical representation* of a multiset. A geometrical representation associates a geometrical coordinate in Z^n with any value. This is its definition :

Definition 2 *Let M be a multiset on E. A geometrical representation v of M is a function from Z^n to E, $n \in N$ such that :*

$$M = \prec v(z), z \in D_v \succ$$

where D_v, the domain of v, is called the drawing *of the representation.*

Figure 1 presents a geometrical representation in Z^2 of the previous multiset.

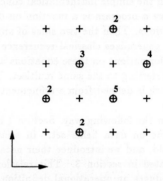

Fig. 1. A geometrical representation of a multiset

The set of functions from Z^n to E, $\forall n \in N$, will be denoted as $\mathcal{A}(E)$.

Theorem 1 *The binary relation $\mathcal{R}$ on $\mathcal{A}(E)$, which is defined as :*

$$(v, v') \in \mathcal{R} \Leftrightarrow \exists h \text{ a bijection, } v' = v \circ h$$

is an equivalence relation.

The word "representation" is justified by this equivalence relation on $\mathcal{A}(E)$, since the *quotient set* $\mathcal{A}(E)/\mathcal{R}$ is isomorphic to $\mathcal{M}(E)$.

There are an infinity of geometrical representations for a given multiset. They differ one another by a bijection. This is expressed by the concept of *data field*. Intuitively, a data field is a geometrical representation defined *within a bijection*. Formally, it is the association of a geometrical representation v and a bijection σ. The image of v by σ is an other geometrical representation for the same multiset.

Definition 3 *Let E be a set. A* data field *on E is defined by a function v from Z^n to E and a bijection σ from $D_\sigma \subset Z^n$ to Z^m with $D_v \subset D_\sigma$.*

A data field will be denoted as $[v]_\sigma$. The set of data fields will be denoted as $\mathcal{C}$. The set of data fields on E will be denoted as $\mathcal{C}(E)$. The set of data fields on E of bijection σ will be denoted as $\mathcal{C}_\sigma(E)$.

Definition 4 *Let $X = [v]_\sigma$ be a data field.*
We call drawing *of X, denoted as D_X, the drawing of v.*

Definition 5 *Let $X = [v]_\sigma$ be a data field.*
We call multiset associated *with X, the multiset $M_X = \prec v(z), z \in D_v \succ$.*

Figure 2 represents an example of data field associated with the previous multiset.

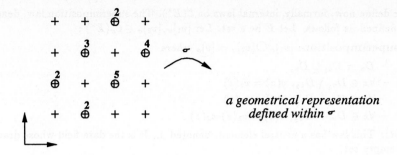

Fig. 2. An example of data field

1.2 Internal Operations on Data Fields

Internal operations on the set of data fields are based on a binary *superimposition* operation. This operation is so called because resulting data field drawing is the union of used data field drawings, and because this operation is not commutative.

This operation is schemed on figure 3. This figure represents a data field obtained by applying the superimposition operation on two data fields. An opaque motif represents a value in a data field drawing point : circles are first field values, triangles are second field values. So, resulting data field drawing is the union of the two data fields drawings. The resulting data field value in an intersection point, depends on the order used to superimpose the two data fields.

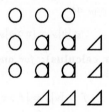

Fig. 3. Superimposition operation

The values of a resulting data field are sequences of values which are obtained by successively superimposing data fields. As any data field can be obtained by superimposition, we define operations on $\mathcal{C}(E^\star)$ instead of $\mathcal{C}(E)$, where $E^\star$ is the set of the not empty sequences of elements in E.

Definition 6 *Let E be a set. $E^\star$ is the set built from an associative operation on E denoted as $\cdot$, in the following way :*

- $\forall x \in E, x \in E^\star$
- $\forall x, y \in E^\star, x \cdot y \in E^\star$

The elements of $E^\star$ are called sequences of elements in E. The classical functions *head* and *tail* are defined on sequences.

We define now, formally, internal laws on $\mathcal{C}(E^\star)$. The superimposition law, denoted $\bigcirc$, is defined as follows. Let E be a set. Let $[v_1]_\sigma, [v_2]_\sigma \in \mathcal{C}_\sigma(E^\star)$:

- **superimposition:** $[v_1]_\sigma \bigcirc [v_2]_\sigma = [v]_\sigma$ *where*
    - $D_v = D_{v_1} \cup D_{v_2}$
    - $\forall z \in D_{v_1} \setminus D_{v_2},\ v(z) = v_1(z)$
    - $\forall z \in D_{v_2} \setminus D_{v_1},\ v(z) = v_2(z)$
    - $\forall z \in D_{v_1} \cap D_{v_2},\ v(z) = v_1(z) \cdot v_2(z)$

Note: This law has a neutral element, denoted $\perp$. It is the data field whose drawing is the empty set.

The following binary laws are restrictions of the superimposition law, called sum and product operations (of superimposition). We denote them respectively $\oplus$ and $\odot$. Let E be a set. Let $[v_1]_\sigma, [v_2]_\sigma \in \mathcal{C}_\sigma(E^\star)$:

- **sum:** $[v_1]_\sigma \oplus [v_2]_\sigma = [v]_\sigma$ *where*
    - $D_v = (D_{v_1} \cup D_{v_2}) \setminus (D_{v_1} \cap D_{v_2})$
    - $\forall z \in D_{v_1} \setminus D_{v_2},\ v(z) = v_1(z)$
    - $\forall z \in D_{v_2} \setminus D_{v_1},\ v(z) = v_2(z)$

- **product:** $[v_1]_\sigma \odot [v_2]_\sigma = [v]_\sigma$ *where*
    - $D_v = D_{v_1} \cap D_{v_2}$
    - $\forall z \in D_v,\ v(z) = v_1(z) \cdot v_2(z)$

Theorem 2 $\bigcirc$ *is associative and* $\forall X, Y \in \mathcal{C}_\sigma(E^\star)$, $X \bigcirc Y = (X \oplus Y) \oplus (X \odot Y)$

1.3 External Operations on Data Fields

We introduce, here under, two external laws on $\mathcal{C}(E^\star)$. Let E and F be two sets. Let $[v]_\sigma \in \mathcal{C}_\sigma(E^\star)$ where $D_\sigma \subset Z^n$:

- **geometrical operation (or routing):** *for any function g from Z^n to Z^n ($D_g \subset D_\sigma$), we define data field $g\,[v]_\sigma$ as:*

$$g\,[v]_\sigma = [v \circ g]_\sigma$$

- **functional operation (or calculus):** *for any function f from $E^\star$ to $F^\star$, we define data field $f \triangleright [v]_\sigma$ as:*

$$f \triangleright [v]_\sigma = [f \circ v]_\sigma$$

Notice that the drawing of data field $g\,[v]_\sigma$ is, by definition, the domain of the function $v \circ g$, that is, the set $\{z, z \in D_g \wedge g(z) \in D_v\}$. Similarly, the drawing of data field $f \triangleright [v]_\sigma$ is, by definition, the domain of the function $f \circ v$, that is, the set $\{z, z \in D_v \wedge v(z) \in D_f\}$. Moreover, this field is an element of $\mathcal{C}_\sigma(F^\star)$.

Intuitively, geometrical operation allows to move some values of a data field, while functional operation allows to compute some values of a data field.

Examples:

1. Figure 4 represents a data field and the resulting data field by applying of the geometrical operation defined as :

$$\begin{aligned}
\{(i,j) \in Z^2, i < j\} &\rightarrow Z^2 \\
(i,j) &\mapsto (i-1, j+1)
\end{aligned}$$

Values above diagonal are moved in the direction $(1, -1)$, while others values are cleared because they don't occur in the function domain. The geometrical representation of resulting data field is still defined within bijection σ.

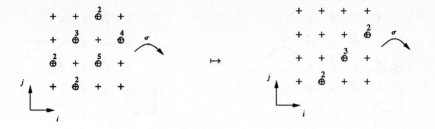

Fig. 4. An example of geometrical operation

2. Figure 5 represents a data field and the resulting data field by applying of the functional operation defined as :

$$\begin{aligned} \{x \in \mathbb{N}, x \bmod 2 = 0\} &\to \mathbb{N} \\ x &\mapsto x/2 \end{aligned}$$

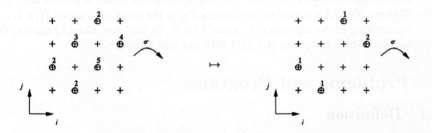

Fig. 5. An example of functional operation

Odd values are divided by two, while others values are cleared because they don't occur in the function domain. The geometrical representation of resulting data field is still defined within bijection σ.

Moreover, we define a change of basis operation, in the following way. Let E be a set. Let $[v]_\sigma \in \mathcal{C}_\sigma(E^\star)$ with $D_\sigma \subset \mathbb{Z}^n$:

- **change of basis operation**: *for any bijection h from $D_h \subset \mathbb{Z}^n$ to $\mathbb{Z}^p$, we define data field $[v]_\sigma : h$ as :*

$$[v]_\sigma : h = [v \circ h^{-1}]_{\sigma \circ h^{-1}}$$

Intuitively, this operation allows to change the representation of a given multiset. The resulting data field is not defined within bijection σ, but within bijection $\sigma \circ h^{-1}$. The drawing of resulting data field is the image by h of the initial drawing.

Examples:

1. Figure 6 represents a data field and the resulting data field by applying the change of basis operation defined as :

$$\begin{aligned} \mathbb{Z}^2 &\to \mathbb{Z}^2 \\ (i,j) &\mapsto (3-i,j) \end{aligned}$$

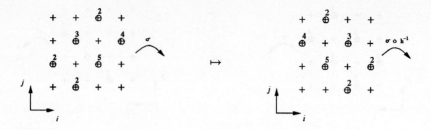

Fig. 6. An example of change of basis operation

2. *the Packing Function.* Considering any data field X, whose drawing D_X is a subset of Z, we introduce a canonical change of basis operator which packs this drawing in an interval of N, whose length is the cardinality of D_X. Associated with any field X, this operator is defined as the result of the predefined function *tilda*, applied on X.

More formally, for any field X, whose drawing D_X is a subset of Z, *tilda*(X) denotes the increasing bijection from D_X to N, whose image is [0..card D[.

For example, if X is a field whose drawing D_X is the set of odd natural $\{1, 3, 5, ...\}$, the drawing of the expression X : *tilda*(X) is N. In this case, *tilda*(X) denotes the function which associates $(i - 1)/2$ with any odd natural i.

2 Problems and Programs

2.1 Definition

A problem defines a relation between some inputs and some outputs. In the parallel programming point of view, inputs and outputs can be represented by some multisets. So, a (parallel) problem can be considered as a relation between the input multisets of values and the output multisets of values, that is, as a multiset transformer.

Programming activity consists in associating a data field with each of these multisets. We will say that a program is a function from input data fields to output ones.

Definition 7 *A problem $\mathcal{P}$ is a subset of $\mathcal{M}^n \times \mathcal{M}^p$. A program F is a function from $\mathcal{C}^n$ to $\mathcal{C}^p$. A program F satisfies a problem $\mathcal{P}$ (we note F sat $\mathcal{P}$) iff :*
$\forall (D, R) \in \mathcal{P}$,

- $\exists \overline{X} \in D_F,\ M_{\overline{X}} = D$
- $(\overline{X} \in D_F \wedge M_{\overline{X}} = D) \Rightarrow M_{F(\overline{X})} = R$

where the overlined names denote n-uples of data fields and the concept of multisets associated with a data field is generalized to n-uples. So, $\overline{X} = (X_i)_{i=1..n}$ and $M_{\overline{X}} = (M_{X_i})_{i=1..n}$.

2.2 Notation

In this section, we introduce a notation for programs to formalize our transformations. We choose to describe a program as an equations set. This arbitrary choice has the advantage of showing how the concept of recurrence equations set can be inserted in the context of a problem defined as a relation between multisets. If we denote as $X_i, i \in 1..n$, the input data fields and $Y_j, j \in 1..p$, the output data fields, a program F is written as a system of m equations and p unknowns $Y_j, j \in 1..p$, equivalent to the equation $(Y_j)_{j \in 1..p} = F((X_i)_{i \in 1..n})$. We will write the program F as follows :

$$F : (X_i)_{i \in 1..n} \mapsto (Y_j)_{j \in 1..p}$$
$$\{ \ \hat{E}_k = \check{E}_k, k \in 1..m$$

where each equation $\hat{E}_k = \check{E}_k$ denotes the equality of two data fields, and where the two hands $\hat{E}_k$ and $\check{E}_k$ of any equation are expressions built from the input fields $X_i, i \in 1..n$, the output fields $Y_j, j \in 1..p$ and possibly some other intermediate fields (expressing the recursivity of F) by using the operations on data fields.

Remark: These equations connect two data field expressions, while in classical recurrence equations langages, the left expression is reduced to a variable. In the following, we will see the expression and the interest of such a generalization in the construction and statement transformations steps. In [Mis90], such equations connecting two expressions are used to describe non-deterministic process networks (a non-deterministic process is a process whose outputs can not be expressed as functions of inputs).

Lambda-Calculus Use. Any external operation on data fields which can appear in a program, has a function as argument. These functions have to be defined in the context of the program. To simplify the definition of these functions, we use some notations derived from the lambda-calculus. Applications will be denoted, as follows.

When no ambiguity exists, we will denote any function f of domain $D_f = \{x, P(x)\}$ as the following lambda-expression :

$$f = \lambda x \mid P(x) . f(x)$$

Moreover, we introduce the following simplifications of notation :

- if $\forall x \in D_f$, $f(x) = x$, the function f can be denoted as $\lambda x \mid P(x)$
- if $\forall x$, $P(x)$, the function f can be denoted as $\lambda x . f(x)$

The expression $f(x)$ can be reduced to a simple arithmetical expression $e(x)$ or a *selection* of such simple expressions $e_1(x), e_2(x), \ldots, e_r(x)$ according to r cases defined by r subdomains of D_f. Such a selection will be denoted in the following way :

$$f = \lambda x \mid P(x) . \left\{ \begin{array}{ccc} P_1(x) & \mapsto & e_1(x) \\ P_2(x) & \mapsto & e_2(x) \\ \vdots & \vdots & \vdots \\ P_r(x) & \mapsto & e_r(x) \end{array} \right\}$$

where the $P_i(x)$ are predicates which form a partition of $P(x)$.

2.3 Example

We present a trivial example of program. This program satisfies a problem $\mathcal{P}$ which unformally consists in computing the product of the elements of a given multiset. We formally define this problem in the following way :

$$(M, N) \in \mathcal{P} \Leftrightarrow M = \prec x_1, \ldots, x_n \succ \ \wedge \ N = \prec \prod_{i=1}^{i=n} x_i \succ$$

To write a program that satisfies the problem, we choose to represent the multiset M by the drawing $\{i, 1 \leq i \leq n\}$. So, values are set on a line (fig. 7). We will denote as X, the data field which represents M and Y, the data field which represents N.

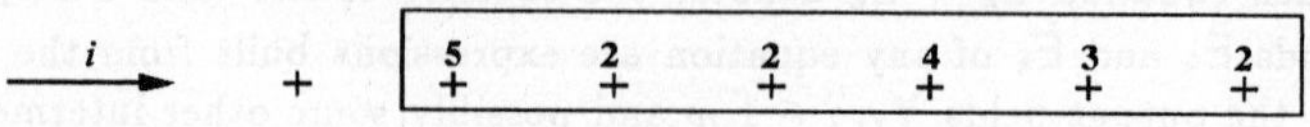

Fig. 7. A drawing for the multiset M

To define an iterative computation of the product, we build a sequence of values of X. This can be realized in superimposing the values using the product operation and shifting values with a routing operation pre which moves values one unit to the right. Figure 8 shows the series $(Z_j)_{j=0..n-1}$ of obtained fields. The last element of this series is the field X' which contains the sequence of all values of X.

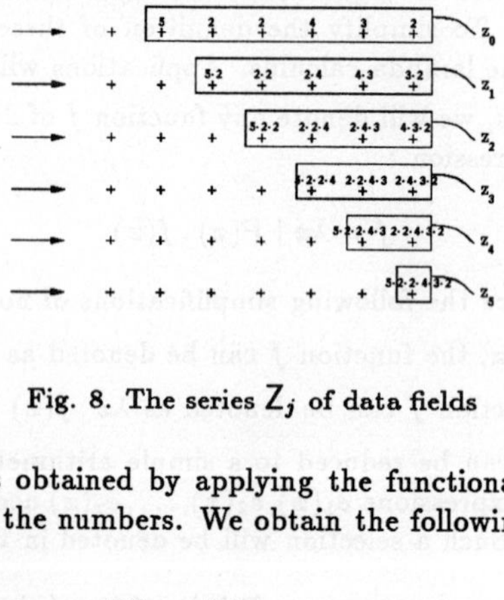

Fig. 8. The series Z_j of data fields

The output field Y is obtained by applying the functional operation prod, which computes the product of the numbers. We obtain the following iterative definition for the problem $\mathcal{P}$:

$$Product_0 : (\mathsf{X}) \mapsto (\mathsf{Y})$$
$$\left\{ \begin{array}{lll} Z_0 & = & \mathsf{X} \\ Z_j & = & \text{pre } Z_{j-1} \odot \mathsf{X}, \quad j \in 1..n-1 \\ \mathsf{X}' & = & Z_{n-1} \\ \mathsf{Y} & = & \text{prod} \triangleright \mathsf{X}' \end{array} \right.$$

where :

$$\text{prod} = \lambda x . \left\{ \begin{array}{lll} x = tail(x) & \mapsto & x \\ x \neq tail(x) & \mapsto & head(x) \times \text{prod}(tail(x)) \end{array} \right\}$$
$$\text{pre} = \lambda i . i - 1$$

Here is an other more significant example of program. This program satisfies the Gaussian elimination problem, whose formal definition can be found in [Vio92]. This is the initial statement for the program :

$$Gauss_0 : (\mathsf{A}, \mathsf{B}) \mapsto (\mathsf{A}', \mathsf{B}')$$

$$
\left\{
\begin{array}{l}
\mathsf{X} = \ \lambda(i,j,k) \mid (k{+}1 \leq i \leq n \ \wedge \ k{+}1 \leq j \leq n{+}1 \ \wedge \ k{>}0) \\
\qquad\qquad \lambda(a{\cdot}b{\cdot}c{\cdot}d) \, . \, a{-}b{\times}c/d \, \triangleright \\
\qquad\qquad\qquad\qquad (\text{pre } \mathsf{X} \odot \text{shift } \mathsf{X} \odot \text{move } \mathsf{X} \odot \text{lie } \mathsf{X}) \\
\quad \oplus \ \ \mathsf{A} \oplus \mathsf{B} \\
\mathsf{A}' \oplus \mathsf{B}' = \lambda(i,j,k) \mid (k{=}i{-}1) \ \mathsf{X}
\end{array}
\right.
$$

where :

$$
\begin{array}{lcl}
\text{pre} & = & \lambda(i,j,k)\,.\,(i,j,k{-}1) \\
\text{shift} & = & \lambda(i,j,k)\,.\,(i,k,k{-}1) \\
\text{move} & = & \lambda(i,j,k)\,.\,(k,j,k{-}1) \\
\text{lie} & = & \lambda(i,j,k)\,.\,(k,k,k{-}1)
\end{array}
$$

Some other equivalent programs which satisfy the same problems, may be written. The formal definition of the program equivalence is now introduced.

3 Program Equivalence

3.1 Definition

We define an equivalence of data fields and programs, denoted by $\equiv$. It is the foundation for our transformational approach to derive solutions from a program statement.

Intuitively, we will say that two data fields are equivalent if they represent the same multiset.

Definition 8 *Let* $\mathsf{X}, \mathsf{X}' \in C$. *By definition,*

$$\mathsf{X} \equiv \mathsf{X}' \Leftrightarrow M_{\mathsf{X}} = M_{\mathsf{X}'}$$

Intuitively, we will say that two programs are equivalent if the input data fields and the output data fields are equivalent. In other words, two programs are said equivalent if the multisets associated with output data fields are the same for some identical multisets associated with the input data fields. This notion of equivalence is defined from a refinement relation.

Definition 9 *A program* F' *is a refinement of a program* F *(we note* $F \sqsubseteq F'$*) iff* F' *satisfies any problem* $\mathcal{P}$ *that* F *satisfies.*

From this classical definition of refinement, and by considering definition 7, we have the following theorem :

Theorem 3 *A program* F *is refined by a program* F' *iff :*

- $\overline{\mathsf{X}} \in D_F \Rightarrow (\exists \overline{\mathsf{X}'} \in D_{F'}, \ \overline{\mathsf{X}} \equiv \overline{\mathsf{X}'})$
- $(\overline{\mathsf{X}} \in D_F \ \wedge \ \overline{\mathsf{X}} \equiv \overline{\mathsf{X}'} \ \wedge \ \overline{\mathsf{X}'} \in D_{F'}) \Rightarrow F(\overline{\mathsf{X}}) \equiv F'(\overline{\mathsf{X}'})$

where the concept of equivalence of data fields is generalized to n-uples. So, $\overline{\mathsf{X}} \equiv \overline{\mathsf{X}'}$ means $\forall i \in 1..n, \mathsf{X}_i \equiv \mathsf{X}'_i$.

Definition 10 *Programs* F *and* F' *are equivalent (we note* $F \equiv F'$*) iff* $F \sqsubseteq F'$ *and* $F' \sqsubseteq F$.

In the following sections, we present rules which allow to transform a program into an equivalent one.

3.2   Transformation Rules

These transformation rules are partitioned in three sets : the first rules are derived from operator properties, the following ones are derived from equations systems and the last ones are equivalence rules.

Operator Properties Rules. These rules consist in substituting a data field expression for an other one, that can be proved equal from some operator property or from the mathematical structure of data fields set. These rules maintain the equality of programs.

$$f \triangleright (f' \triangleright X) = f \circ f' \triangleright X \tag{1}$$

$$g\,(g'\,X) = g' \circ g\,X \tag{2}$$

$$(X:h):h' = X:h' \circ h \tag{3}$$

$$g\,(f \triangleright X) = f \triangleright (g\,X) \tag{4}$$

$$(f \triangleright X):h = f \triangleright (X:h) \tag{5}$$

$$(g\,X):h = h \circ g \circ h^{-1}\,(X:h) \tag{6}$$

$$f \triangleright (X \oplus X') = f \triangleright X \oplus f \triangleright X' \tag{7}$$

$$g\,(X \odot X') = g\,X \odot g\,X' \tag{8}$$

Equations Systems Rules. These rules maintain the equality of programs. Let us cite, for example, the substitution rule. For any program F, denoted as :

$$F : (X_i)_{i \in 1..n} \mapsto (Y_j)_{j \in 1..p}$$
$$\{ \ \hat{E}_k = \check{E}_k, k \in 1..m$$

the substitution of an equation side with the other one leads to :

$$F' : (X_i)_{i \in 1..n} \mapsto (Y_j)_{j \in 1..p}$$
$$\left\{ \begin{array}{l} \hat{E}_1 = \check{E}_1[\hat{E}_2 \setminus \check{E}_2] \\ \hat{E}_k = \check{E}_k, k \in 2..m \end{array} \right.$$

where $\check{E}[\hat{F} \setminus \check{F}]$ denotes the expression obtained by replacing any occurrence of expression $\hat{F}$ with expression $\check{F}$ in expression $\check{E}$.

Equivalence Rules. These rules are more general than the preceeding ones. They transform a program into an equivalent one. The first of these rules is a classical one which allows to change representation of inputs and outputs. We give here under its formal definition.

For any n-uple of bijections $(d_i)_{i \in 1..n}$ such that $\forall i \in 1..n$, $D_{X_i} \subset D_{d_i}$

For any p-uple of bijections $(r_j)_{j \in 1..p}$ such that $\forall j \in 1..p$, $D_{Y_j} \subset D_{r_j}$

$$\begin{array}{c} F : (X_i)_{i \in 1..n} \mapsto (Y_j)_{j \in 1..p} \\ \{ \ \hat{E}_k = \check{E}_k, k \in 1..m \end{array} \equiv \begin{array}{c} F' : (X'_i)_{i \in 1..n} \mapsto (Y'_j)_{j \in 1..p} \\ \{ \ \hat{E}'_k = \check{E}'_k, k \in 1..m \end{array}$$

where :

- $\forall k \in 1..m$, $\hat{E}'_k = \hat{E}_k[[X_i \setminus X'_i : d_i]]_{i \in 1..n}[[Y_j \setminus Y'_j : r_j]]_{j \in 1..p}$

- $\forall k \in 1..m,\ \check{E}'_k = \check{E}_k[[X_i \setminus X'_i : d_i]]_{i \in 1..n}[[Y_j \setminus Y'_j : r_j]]_{j \in 1..p}$

and $E[[X \setminus Y]]$ *denotes the expression which is obtained by replacing all occurrences of name* X *by expression* Y *in expression* E.

A second rule allows to transform a recurrent definition of data fields interpreted as a *path*. To explain this rule and the concept of path, let us consider the trivial example in section 2.3. Let us consider the data field series which is formed to build the sequence of values (fig. 8). We obtain this new recurrent definition from the iterative one, by forming the data field Z, drawn on the plane, which groups the terms of this series.

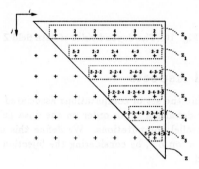

Fig. 9. The data field Z

The field Z is the sum of field X and the product of fields diag Z and init Z. diag Z is the field Z moved in the direction $(1,1)$. The field init Z is obtained by broadcasting the values for $j = 0$ of field Z along the dimension j.

$$Product_1 : (X) \mapsto (Y)$$
$$\begin{cases} Z &= X \oplus (\text{diag } Z \odot \text{init } Z) \\ X' &= \text{last } Z \\ Y &= \text{prod } \triangleright X' \end{cases}$$

where :

$$\text{diag} = \lambda(i,j).(i-1, j-1)$$
$$\text{init} = \lambda(i,j).(i,0)$$
$$\text{last} = \lambda(i,j) \mid (j = n - 1)$$

In such a recurrent definition, we can interpret the routings diag and init as dependencies between the defined data field points. In the present case, this dependencies are the vectors $(1,1)$ and $(0,j), j > 0$, corresponding to routings diag and init. Figure 10 represents the dependencies of field Z. For a given computation point, here the point $(n, n-1)$, the set of dependencies form a *path* in Z^2 which defines data routing to that point.

Other paths could be defined for this example. They would define equivalent programs but impose different partial orders, which determine the operational behaviour of programs.

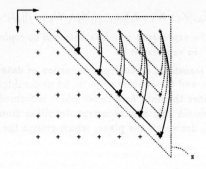

Fig. 10. The dependencies of data field Z

3.3 Operational Aspects

Operational aspects define the set of computations associated with any data field definition. This means the definition of an order on the data field elements. This order is a partial order for parallel computations. We define this order, denoted as $\vdash$, for some given partial order $<$ on Z^m, by considering the bijection σ from Z^n to Z^m which characterizes a data field.

Definition 11 *Let* $X = [v]_\sigma$ *a data field where* σ *is a bijection from* Z^n *to* Z^m,

$$\forall z, z' \in D_X, \; v(z) \vdash v(z') \Leftrightarrow \sigma(z) < \sigma(z')$$

The choice of the order relation $<$ on Z^m predetermines the operational definition of a program. In fact, the aim of the transformations is to make explicit or to build a "nice" bijection σ which introduces the "convenient" order to define a "nice" operational behaviour of the program. These transformations lie on the change of basis operation. It is shown in the following section devoted to program derivations.

Examples: Let us consider a bijection σ from Z^n to Z^m such as $\sigma(z) = (p(z), t(z))$, where p is a function from Z^n to Z^{m-1} and t a function from Z^n to N. Note that such a definition is a classical way to define a scheduling and a mapping of the computations on a processor set.

- Let $<$ an order on Z^m such that $\sigma(z) < \sigma(z')$ iff $t(z) < t(z')$ on N. The induced operational definition only defines computations scheduling.

- Let $<$ an order on Z^m such that $\sigma(z) < \sigma(z')$ iff $p(z) = p(z') \wedge t(z) < t(z')$. The induced operational definition defines computations mapping and the scheduling of the processors.

4 Programs Derivation

Programs derivation is illustrated here under with the Gaussian elimination problem. We present the first step to design a systolic solution for the problem whose initial statement was previously given. The first step consists in applying a change of basis, called time, which explicits a scheduling of the computations by definining a part of the bijection σ. Applying a change of basis leads to operate this change of basis on all data fields names.

The following program $Gauss_0'$ is obtained from the initial statement by using a transformation rule which applies the change of basis time, on the two sides of an equation.

$$Gauss_0' : (A, B) \mapsto (A', B')$$

$$
\left\{
\begin{array}{l}
X : time \\
\quad = \ (\lambda(i,j,k) \mid (k+1 \leq i \leq n \ \wedge \ k+1 \leq j \leq n+1 \ \wedge \ k > 0) \\
\qquad \lambda(a \cdot b \cdot c \cdot d) . \, a - b \times c/d \ \triangleright \\
\qquad\qquad\qquad (\text{pre } X \odot \text{shift } X \odot \text{move } X \odot \text{lie } X) \\
\quad \oplus \ A \oplus B) : time \\
(A' \oplus B') : time = (\lambda(i,j,k) \mid (k = i-1) \ X) : time
\end{array}
\right.
$$

where :

$$time \quad = \quad \lambda(i,j,k) . \, (i, j, i+j+k)$$

This second program, $Gauss_0''$ is obtained by expanding this change of basis in the second equation and by applying property 6. In this last equation, time is now applied on all data field names.

$$Gauss_0'' : (A, B) \mapsto (A', B')$$

$$
\left\{
\begin{array}{l}
X : time \\
\quad = \ (\lambda(i,j,k) \mid (k+1 \leq i \leq n \ \wedge \ k+1 \leq j \leq n+1 \ \wedge \ k > 0) \\
\qquad \lambda(a \cdot b \cdot c \cdot d) . \, a - b \times c/d \ \triangleright \\
\qquad\qquad\qquad (\text{pre } X \odot \text{shift } X \odot \text{move } X \odot \text{lie } X) \\
\quad \oplus \ A \oplus B) : time \\
A' : time \oplus B' : time = \lambda(i,j,t) \mid (t = 2i+j-1) \ X : time
\end{array}
\right.
$$

This new program is obtained by still processing the application of change of basis until its last phase : time is then applied on all data fields names.

$$Gauss_0''' : (A, B) \mapsto (A', B')$$

$$
\left\{
\begin{array}{l}
X : time \\
\quad = \ \lambda(i,j,t) \mid (t-i-j+1 \leq i \leq n \ \wedge \ t-i-j+1 \leq j \leq n+1 \ \wedge \ t > i+j) \\
\qquad \lambda(a \cdot b \cdot c \cdot d) . \, a - b \times c/d \ \triangleright \\
\qquad\qquad\qquad (\text{pre}' \ X : time \odot \text{shift}' \ X : time \\
\qquad\qquad\qquad\quad \odot \text{move}' \ X : time \odot \text{lie}' \ X : time) \\
\quad \oplus \ A : time \oplus B : time \\
A' : time \oplus B' : time = \lambda(i,j,t) \mid (t = 2i+j-1) \ X : time
\end{array}
\right.
$$

where :

$$
\begin{array}{lll}
\text{pre}' & = & \lambda(i,j,t) . \, (i, j, t-1) \\
\text{shift}' & = & \lambda(i,j,t) . \, (i, t-i-j, 2t-2j-i-1) \\
\text{move}' & = & \lambda(i,j,t) . \, (t-i-j, j, 2t-2i-j-1) \\
\text{lie}' & = & \lambda(i,j,t) . \, (t-i-j, t-i-j, 3t-3i-3j-1)
\end{array}
$$

This last program is obtained by applying the equivalence rule which permits to change the representation of data and results : so, $A : time$ is renamed as A, $A' : time$ is renamed as A' ... Instead of defining the intermediate field $X : time$, we call it X, by using the substitution rule. At this step, the index t identifies the temporal component of the solution.

$$Gauss_1 : (A, B) \mapsto (A', B')$$

$$
\left\{
\begin{array}{l}
X \\
\quad = \lambda(i,j,t) \mid (t-i-j+1 \leq i \leq n \ \wedge \ t-i-j+1 \leq j \leq n+1 \ \wedge \ t > i+j) \\
\qquad \lambda(a \cdot b \cdot c \cdot d) \cdot a - b \times c/d \ \triangleright \\
\qquad\qquad\qquad (pre' \ X \odot shift' \ X \odot move' \ X \odot lie' \ X) \\
\quad \oplus \ A \oplus B \\
A' \oplus B' = \lambda(i,j,t) \mid (t = 2i+j-1) \ X
\end{array}
\right.
$$

The following program is the last in the derivation chain. It is obtained by applying an other change of basis which defines the mapping of the computations. By decomposing the functional operation by introducing the intermediate field Y and by "uniformizing" the dependencies, a scheduling and a mapping are determined, which describe the systolic array drawn on figure 11 (for $n = 4$).

$$Gauss_n : (A, B) \mapsto (A', B')$$

$$
\left\{
\begin{array}{l}
X = \ \lambda(x,y,t) \mid (y+1 \leq x \leq n \ \wedge \ y > 0 \ \wedge \ t \geq x+2y+1) \\
\qquad \lambda(a \cdot b \cdot e) \cdot a - b \times e \ \triangleright \\
\qquad\qquad\qquad (high \ X \odot high \ init \ X \odot Y) \\
\quad \oplus \ A \oplus B \\
Y = \ \lambda(x,y,t) \mid (x-y=1) \ right \ high \\
\qquad \lambda(c \cdot d) \cdot c/d \ \triangleright (X \odot init \ X) \\
\quad \oplus \ \lambda(x,y,t) \mid (x-y>1) \ right \ Y \\
A' \oplus B' = \lambda(x,y,t) \mid (x = y+1) \ X
\end{array}
\right.
$$

where :

$$
\begin{array}{rcl}
high & = & \lambda(x,y,t) \cdot (x, y-1, t-1) \\
init & = & \lambda(x,y,t) \cdot (x, y, x+2y+1) \\
right & = & \lambda(x,y,t) \cdot (x-1, y, t-1)
\end{array}
$$

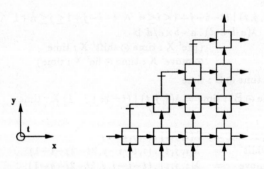

Fig. 11. A systolic array for the Gaussian elimination problem

Some other examples are developped in [Vio92]. Part of them lead to asynchronous solutions. Asynchronism of programs is defined from the packing function *tilda*.

5 Conclusion

The theory we have presented in this paper is founded on the simple mathematical concepts of multiset and of an equivalence between their representations as data fields. Program transformations are founded on this equivalence and defined from a refinement relation. Due to the unifying aspect of this theory, solutions that can be reached by these transformations are relevant to various synchronous or asynchronous computing models.

This theory is the foundation of the langage PEI. A first version of this language is presented in [VP92]. A new design of PEI is currently in progress. The mathematical basis of this language leads to a elegant implementation in CENTAUR [INR91] of an environment whose purpose is to transform parallel programs (fig. 12).

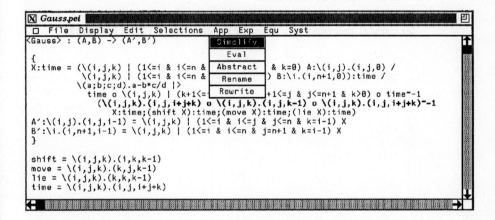

Fig. 12. The PEI environment

References

[CCL91] M. Chen, Y. Choo, and J. Li. *Parallel Functional Languages and Compilers.* Frontier Series. ACM Press, 1991. chapter 7.

[CM88] K.M. Chandy and J. Misra. *Parallel Program Design :* A foundation. Addison Wesley, 1988.

[CMP92] P. Clauss, C. Mongenet, and G.-R. Perrin. Synthesis of size-optimal toroidal arrays for the algebraic path problem : A new contribution. *Parallel Computing*, 18:185–194, 1992.

[Cre91] C. Creveuil. *Techniques d'analyse et de mise en oeuvre des programmes* GAMMA. PhD thesis, Université de Rennes 1, Décembre 1991.

[INR91] INRIA Sophia-Antipolis, Valbonne. *Centaur 1.1*, 1991.

[KMW67] R.M. Karp, R.E. Miller, and S. Winograd. The organization of computations for uniform recurrence equations. *Journal of ACM*, 14(3):563–590, Juillet 1967.

[Mau89]   C. Mauras. ALPHA : *un langage équationnel pour la conception et la programmation d'architectures parallèles synchrones*. PhD thesis, Université de Rennes 1, Décembre 1989.

[Mis90]   J. Misra. Equational reasoning about nondeterministic processes. *Formal Aspects of Computing*, 2:167–195, 1990.

[Mor90]   C. Morgan. *Programming from specifications*. C.A.R. Hoare. Prentice Hall Ed., Endlewood Cliffs, N.J., 1990.

[Qui89]   P. Quinton. The mapping of linear recurrence equations on regular arrays. *Journal of VLSI Signal Processing*, 1, 1989.

[Vio92]   E. Violard. *Une théorie unificatrice pour la construction de programmes parallèles par des techniques de transformations*. PhD thesis, Université de Franche-Comté, Octobre 1992.

[VP92]   E. Violard and G.-R. Perrin. PEI : a language and its refinement calculus for parallel programming. *Parallel Computing*, 18:1167–1184, 1992.

Correctness of Automated Distribution
of Sequential Programs

Cyrille Bareau, Benoît Caillaud, Claude Jard, René Thoraval*

IRISA, Campus de Beaulieu, F-35042 RENNES Cedex FRANCE,
E-mail: jard@irisa.fr, Tel: (+33) 99 84 71 93, Fax: (+33) 99 38 38 32

Keywords: distributed memory parallel machines, formal program development methodologies, parallel language constructs and semantics.

Abstract

In this paper, we prove that the data-driven parallelization technique, which compiles sequential programs into parallel programs for distributed memory parallel computers, is correct. We define a model based on labeled transition systems, and we prove, in spite of nondeterminism due to communications asynchronism, the confluence of all the possible behaviours of parallel programs obtained from the compilation rules.

We also show that this model is powerful enough to prove the correctness of various optimizations of the basic compilation mechanism.

1   Introduction

1.1   The Problem

Large scale parallelism promises high performance computing, using the power of distributed memory parallel computers. Unfortunately, it is now clear that difficulties in correctly and efficiently programming them limit their use. Indeed, current programming techniques are often based on communicating sequential processes, the definition of which is application dependent and requires a strong participation by the programmer.

To resolve this problem, one radical answer is to hide parallelism from the programmer. That is, his programming model: imperative sequential programming, is left unchanged, but a compiler is required to express his work in terms of a distinct execution model: asynchronous parallelism allowed by distributed memory machines.

Currently, the main parallelization technique in this area is the "data-driven parallelization" approach which consists in automatically creating communicating processes from sequential code plus data decomposition specifications [6, 14, 1, 12].

The most usual code transformation is based on the *Single Program Multiple Data* (SPMD) principle and on the standard notion of "refresh" of remote variables. We call it the "basic refresh transformation". All the generated processes execute identical code with respect to the control structure, but each assignment is only replicated on processes that own the left-hand-side variable. Moreover, communication code is generated in order to implement access to remote variables: a copy of each referenced variable is to be sent by its owner towards the process that needs it (see figure 1).

This transformation has solely been considered with respect to the "minimal" following property: given corresponding initial data, either the source sequential code and the parallel generated one produce corresponding results, or both of them diverge. That is, programs are only considered in terms of an "input-output" semantics. Notice that such a semantics remains

---

* Université de Nantes, Section Informatique, 2 rue de la Houssinière F-44072 Nantes cedex 03

quite implicit, for, to our knowledge, the aforementioned correctness property has never been given a formal proof so far.

1.2   Our Goal

To be used as an automatic parallelization method, the data-driven approach needs to be extended. This especially means that:

- more elaborate transformations have to be designed.
- more complex properties have to be considered (interaction with an environment, resource management: memory and communication channels, etc).
- transformations and properties require unambiguous definitions.
- properties of transformations must be proven.

All these issues are being addressed by a growing number of European research groups, for instance the Esprit-Prepare project.

They clearly require a formal treatment. This is why the data-driven parallelization approach has to be given a solid theoretical foundation. The major goal of this paper is to give this foundation a first contribution.

1.3   Problem Complexity

The basic refresh transformation is very simple. Its correctness seems obvious. It is thus rather surprising to find out that a correctness proof is so intricate when conducted from scratch.

Let us point out the real difficulty of such a proof. Applied to a fragment of sequential code that may be executed in one step, the transformation is clearly correct. Unfortunately, one cannot a priori generalize this result to an entire sequential program. Indeed, the execution of the parallel counterpart of one sequential step may be not completed when embarking on the execution of the counterpart of another step. This is due to nondeterminism which results from unpredictable process speeds and communication asynchronism.

In other words, the intended verification appears to a priori be as complex as the verification of any nondeterministic parallel program. This complexity is abundantly illustrated throughout the literature.

1.4   Our Approach

In this paper, we construct a model in order to precisely describe the data-driven parallelization approach and to reason about it. Our construction is similar to that of confluent systems in [9] and in [10] (chapter "Determinacy and Confluence"). This model enables us to characterize the limited nondeterminism that has to be taken into account in the data-driven parallelization approach.

This characterization has a crucial corollary: a correctness proof technique of compilation function that is valid in a deterministic world (see for instance [11]), is also valid in the nondeterministic world we consider. Indeed, we show that it is sufficient to prove the correctness of one particular behaviour of a generated parallel program in order to establish the correctness of all its behaviours. Thus, when considering such a particular behaviour, one can proceed for instance by inference on the compilation rules and by induction on the number of computation steps. Clearly, the benefit of the aforementioned corollary is in a drastic simplification of the verification.

Therefore, our model provides a formal framework for designing other asynchronous parallelizing or optimizing transformations, and for proving their correctness.

1.5   Paper Organization

The paper is organized as follows.

We first present the theoretical model, based on products of labeled and partially deterministic transition systems [3]. This enables us to compare a behaviour of a sequential source program

519

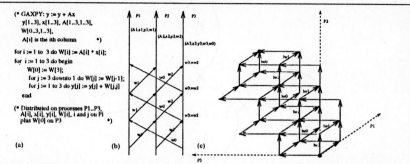

We deal with a sequential source program (a), annotated with a data distribution which assigns program variables to processes (here on the three processes P1 to P3). The principle is that the owner of a variable is responsible for its assignment (local writes), and thus the distant variables belonging to the right part of the assignment must be exchanged. Figure (b) shows the message exchanges obtained by running the parallel generated code. Figure (c) shows the corresponding transition system which will serve as a model: we observe the classical explosion of the possible behaviours due to asynchrony and parallelism, but with a regular structure due to confluence. Some particular snapshots are circled (when communication channels are empty): these states will be connected with the source program states.

Fig. 1. (a) source program, (b) its execution, (c) the resulting transition system

with the corresponding parallel ones. One key semantic property of the resulting transition systems is the diamond property that reduces the combinatorics of all the parallel behaviours to a single significant behaviour easily connected to the source program. We also prove that some properties of the communication medium are required, and that they are provided, for example, by the usual point-to-point Fifo channels.

Then we propose a simplified sequential language, given by a syntax and an operational semantics. We define the notations for the distribution of data, basis of the program generation in an SPMD model. We formally describe the basic refresh transformation. Finally we prove its correctness (based on the same approach as in [5]).

The last part of the paper shows that our formal model and proof methodology can be used to design other transformations. We use as examples an optimization of the refresh mechanism and the anticipation of message send.

2 Models and Theoretical Basis

2.1 Transition Systems

A transition system P is denoted by $\langle q_P, Q_P, A_P, \rightarrow_P \rangle$, where q_P is the initial state, Q_P is the set of states, A_P is the action alphabet and $\rightarrow_P \subseteq Q_P \times A_P \times Q_P$ is the transition relation. The usual product on transition systems is denoted by $\prod$ or $\times$.

A distributed program over processors $I = 1 \ldots n$ is hereafter modeled by a vector $(P_i)_{i=0\ldots n}$ of transition systems (figure 2), where P_0 models the communication medium, and $\forall i \in I$, P_i models the ith process of the program. Communications between processes take place through P_0 which captures the communication asynchronism.

The set $\mathcal{D}$ denotes the collection of all data values that can be sent or received. The alphabet of P_0 (denoted by Σ) is the set of communication actions and is the disjoint union of send (!) and receive (?) actions of a value $e \in \mathcal{D}$ from $i \in I$ to $j \in I$: $\Sigma = \bigoplus_{i,j \in I} (\Sigma^!_{i,j} \oplus \Sigma^?_{i,j})$, where $\forall i, j \in I$, $\Sigma^!_{i,j} = \{!e_{i \rightarrow j}\}_{e \in \mathcal{D}}$ and $\Sigma^?_{i,j} = \{?e_{j \rightarrow i}\}_{e \in \mathcal{D}}$.

Any process that performs a receive action is non-deterministic since it accepts several data values — i.e. several receive events. However this nondeterminism is particular since it can be

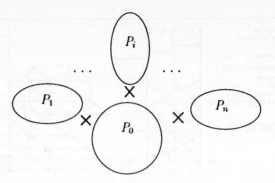

Fig. 2. Architecture of a parallel program

discarded by an abstraction of data values. We define for that purpose an equivalence relation $\rho = \{(?e_{i\rightarrow j}, ?f_{i\rightarrow j})\}_{i,j \in I \, e, f \in \mathcal{D}}$. The data abstraction is then formalized using the notion of quotient of a transition system by an equivalence relation:

Definition 1 Quotient Transition System. Let P be a transition system and ξ an equivalence relation over A_P. The quotient transition system P/ξ is defined by:

$$P/\xi = \langle q_P, Q_P, A_P/\xi, (1_{Q_P} \times \varphi_\xi \times 1_{Q_P})(\rightarrow_P)\rangle$$

where $\varphi_\xi : A_P \longrightarrow A_P/\xi$ is the mapping which associates to a letter $\alpha \in A_P$ the class of α modulo ξ, and $1_{Q_P} \times \varphi_\xi \times 1_{Q_P} : (q, \alpha, q') \longmapsto (q, \varphi_\xi(\alpha), q')$.

We now define two predicates:

Definition 2. Let P be a transition system, and $B \subseteq A_P$.

$$\begin{cases} \det^{ext}(P, B) \iff \forall q \in Q_P \; |\{\alpha \mid \exists q' \in Q_P, (q, \alpha, q') \in \rightarrow_P\} \cap B| \leq 1 \\ \det^{int}(P) \iff \forall \alpha \in A_P, \forall q \in Q_P, |\{q' \mid (q, \alpha, q') \in \rightarrow_P\}| \leq 1 \end{cases}$$

The predicate $\det^{ext}(P,B)$ means that the transition system is externally deterministic over B: for each state of P, at most one action of B can be performed. And $\det^{int}(P)$ means that the transition system is internally deterministic, which corresponds to the usual meaning of determinism.

In the sequel, distributed programs under hypotheses 3 and 5 are considered.

Hypothesis 3. *The distributed program matches the following predicates:*

$$\begin{cases} \forall i \in I & \det^{ext}(P_i/\rho, A_{P_i}/\rho) \\ \forall i, j \in I & \det^{ext}(P_0, \Sigma_{i,j}^?) \\ \forall i \in I \cup \{0\} & \det^{int}(P_i) \end{cases}$$

Hypothesis 3 ensures that nondeterminism in P_i arises only when P_i performs a receive action from a given process, but with an unknown value. Since P_0 is deterministic over the receive actions of messages from j to i, the product $P_i \times P_0$ is deterministic over the actions of P_i.

Definition 4 Diamond Property. Let P be a transition system and $B \subseteq A_P^2$. P has the diamond property over B iff $\forall q \in Q_P, \forall (\alpha, \beta) \in B, \forall q_1, q_2 \in Q_P, q_1 \neq q_2$:

$$\begin{cases} q \xrightarrow{\alpha}_P q_1 \\ q \xrightarrow{\beta}_P q_2 \end{cases} \implies \exists q' \in Q_P \begin{cases} q_1 \xrightarrow{\beta}_P q' \\ q_2 \xrightarrow{\alpha}_P q' \end{cases}$$

Hypothesis 5. P_0 has the diamond property over $\Sigma^2 \setminus \bigcup_{i,j \in I} \left(\Sigma'_{i,j} \right)^2$

The following theorem is established in [2].

Theorem 6. *A transition system that has the diamond property has the following properties:*
1. *There is at most one maximal state (sink state).*
2. *The transition system has a maximal state if and only if it has no infinite computation.*

Notice that, thanks to Newman's theorem, a transition system that has the diamond property is confluent (see figure 1), the confluence property implying the first part of the previous theorem [2].

We can now state our first main theorem:

Theorem 7. *Let* $(P_i)_{i=0...n}$ *be a distributed program verifying hypotheses 3 and 5. The product transition system* $P = \prod_{i=0}^{n} P_i$ *has the diamond property over* A_P^2 *and is internally deterministic, i.e.* $det^{int}(P)$.

The sketch of the proof of theorem 7 is as follows: every pair of distinct actions that can occur from any state of the distributed program should be considered. Furthermore for each pair it should be shown that the diamond property is verified : hypothesis 3 ensures the diamond property for any pair of actions that are not both communications, and hypothesis 5 ensures the diamond property for any pair of communication actions.

2.2 Implementation of P_0

We hereafter use unbounded point-to-point Fifo communication channels. We give in this section a model of Fifo channels in terms of a transition system.

Definition 8. Let $P_0^F = \left\langle (\emptyset, \ldots, \emptyset), (\mathcal{D}^\star)^{n^2}, \Sigma, \rightarrow_F \right\rangle$ be a transition system, where $\rightarrow_F$ is defined by the following axiomatic:

$$\frac{q_{i,j} \xrightarrow{\alpha} q'_{i,j}}{(\ldots, q_{i,j}, \ldots) \xrightarrow{\alpha} (\ldots, q'_{i,j}, \ldots)} \qquad e \cdot q_{i,j} \xrightarrow{?e_{i \rightarrow j}} q_{i,j} \qquad q_{i,j} \xrightarrow{!e_{i \rightarrow j}} q_{i,j} \cdot e$$

The transition system P_0^F is a model of a complete network of point-to-point Fifo channels over I.

Theorem 9. P_0^F *verifies hypotheses 3 and 5*

The proof follows the lines of theorem 7. However it is worth considering a particular case, one message send and receive on the same queue:

$$
\begin{array}{ccc}
q_{0,0}, \ldots, e \cdot q_{i,j}, \ldots, q_{n,n} & \xrightarrow{?e_{i \rightarrow j}} & q_{0,0}, \ldots, q_{i,j}, \ldots, q_{n,n} \\
\downarrow !f_{i \rightarrow j} & & \downarrow !f_{i \rightarrow j} \\
q_{0,0}, \ldots, e \cdot q_{i,j} \cdot f, \ldots, q_{n,n} & \xrightarrow{?e_{i \rightarrow j}} & q_{0,0}, \ldots, q_{i,j} \cdot f, \ldots, q_{n,n}
\end{array}
$$

It should be noted that the Fifo assumption is crucial, since desequencing communication channels do not fit the requirements of hypotheses 3 and 5.

2.3 Distribution Proof Bases

Correspondence between Sequential and Distributed Program States. Let us now consider programs in a language $\mathcal{L}$ computing over variables. The set of variables is denoted by $\mathcal{V}$ and each variable ranges over $\mathcal{D}$.

The state of a process $P_i, i \in I$ is represented by $q_i = \langle S_i, \sigma_i \rangle$ where $S_i \in \mathcal{L}$ is the continuation program and $\sigma_i : \mathcal{V} \longrightarrow \mathcal{D}$ is an environment.

The communication medium of a parallel program is assumed to be a complete network of point-to-point Fifo channels, modeled by P_0^F.

Given a distribution mapping and a compilation function, the state correspondence connection $\leadsto$ is defined as follows:

Definition 10. Let $\pi : \mathcal{V} \longrightarrow 2^I \setminus \{\emptyset\}$, $[\![\cdot]\!] : \mathcal{L} \longrightarrow \mathcal{L}^I$ be respectively a distribution mapping and a compilation function.

The connection $\rightsquigarrow \subseteq Q_P \times Q_{P_0^F} \times \prod_{i \in I} Q_{P_i}$ associates to any sequential state some particular parallel states (see figure 1). It is defined as follows:

$$< S, \sigma > \rightsquigarrow (q_0, (< S_i, \sigma_i >)_{i \in I}) \iff \begin{cases} q_0 = (\emptyset, \ldots, \emptyset) \\ (S_i)_{i \in I} = [\![S]\!] \\ \forall v \in \mathcal{V}, \forall i \in \pi(v), \ \sigma(v) = \sigma_i(v) \end{cases}$$

Principle of the Correctness Proof. The aim of the correctness proof is to show that the semantics of programs is preserved by compilation. The semantics we consider in definition 11 is an "input-output" semantics in which only initial and maximal states are meaningful.

Definition 11. The meaning of a transition system P is a mapping which associates to an initial state q, the following set:

$$\mathcal{M}_P(q) = \{q' \mid q \longrightarrow^*_P q', \ q' \text{maximal}\} \cup \{\perp \mid q \longrightarrow^\omega_P\}$$

The symbol $\perp$ denotes the divergence of the transition system.

Assuming that $\perp \rightsquigarrow \perp$, the correctness of the compilation function is defined as follows:

Definition 12. The compilation function $[\![\cdot]\!] : \mathcal{L} \longrightarrow \mathcal{L}^I$ is correct if and only if for any sequential program P:

$$\forall q_1 \in Q_P, \ \forall q_2 \in Q_Q, \ \forall q'_1 \in \mathcal{M}_P(q_1), \ \forall q'_2 \in \mathcal{M}_Q(q_2), \ q_1 \rightsquigarrow q_2 \implies q'_1 \rightsquigarrow q'_2$$

where $Q = P_0^F \times \prod_{i \in I} [\![P]\!]_i$.

It should be noted that the meaning of a program which has the diamond property is reduced to one element: either $\perp$ or a unique final state (theorem 6).

So, the correctness of a compilation function becomes:

Lemma 13. *Let assume that the language $\mathcal{L}$ verifies hypotheses 3 and 5. The compilation function $[\![\cdot]\!] : \mathcal{L} \longrightarrow \mathcal{L}^I$ is correct if and only if for any program $S \in \mathcal{L}$ and any initial environment $\sigma : \mathcal{V} \longrightarrow \mathcal{D}$.*

1. If $\mathcal{M}(\langle S, \sigma \rangle) \neq \{\perp\}$, the following diagram holds:

$$\begin{array}{ccc} \langle S, \sigma \rangle & \rightsquigarrow & \langle q_0, (\langle S_i, \sigma_i \rangle)_{i \in I} \rangle \\ \downarrow_* & & \downarrow_* \\ \langle S', \sigma' \rangle & \rightsquigarrow & \langle q'_0, (\langle S'_i, \sigma'_i \rangle)_{i \in I} \rangle \end{array}$$

with $\langle S', \sigma' \rangle$ and $\langle S'_i, \sigma'_i \rangle$ maximal.
2. If $\mathcal{M}(\langle S, \sigma \rangle) = \{\perp\}$, then :

$$\begin{array}{ccc} \langle S, \sigma \rangle & \rightsquigarrow & \langle q_0, (\langle S_i, \sigma_i \rangle)_{i \in I} \rangle \\ \downarrow_\omega & & \downarrow_\omega \end{array}$$

Since $\mathcal{L}$ verifies hypotheses 3 and 5, theorem 7 applies and the meaning of a program, sequential or parallel, is reduced to a single element. Therefore lemma 13 is straightforward from definition 12 and theorem 6.

We can show either correspondence by induction on an elementary diagram which associates a finite, non-empty parallel computation to a single step of the source sequential program. That is, for one step of the sequential program, there exists a particular non-empty finite computation of the parallel program that preserves the state correspondence. This can be formalized by the following diagram:

$$\begin{array}{ccc} \langle S, \sigma \rangle & \rightsquigarrow & \langle q_0, (\langle S_i, \sigma_i \rangle)_{i \in I} \rangle \\ \downarrow & & \downarrow_+ \\ \langle S', \sigma' \rangle & \rightsquigarrow & \langle q'_0, (\langle S'_i, \sigma'_i \rangle)_{i \in I} \rangle \end{array}$$

This property relies on the semantics of the language $\mathcal{L}$ and on the compilation function $[\![\cdot]\!]$. It will be proved by inference on the rules of the operational semantics of $\mathcal{L}$ and on the axiomatic definition of $[\![\cdot]\!]$.

3 Parallelization

3.1 Language Syntax and Semantics

We present the process language $\mathcal{L}$ (the sequential language being the same one, but restricted to one processor). It is a simple language, containing all the features of a usual sequential language with respect to the control structure.

Syntax. A parallel program is defined as a collection $(P_i)_{i \in I}$ of processes generated by the following grammar in BNF notation:

$$\mathcal{L} ::= statement^*$$
$$statement ::= \quad v := expr$$
$$\mid \text{if } expr \text{ then } \mathcal{L} \text{ else } \mathcal{L} \text{ fi}$$
$$\mid \text{while } expr \text{ do } \mathcal{L} \text{ od}$$
$$\mid \, !v_{i \to j}$$
$$\mid \, ?v_{j \to i}$$

We assume that the domain of values $\mathcal{D}$ contains an undefined value $\bot$, which enables to deal with runtime errors. For a matter of readability, we ignore the question of types, which presents no difficulties.

In the sequel we will use ε and b to range over $expr$, S over $\mathcal{L}$ and s over $statement$.

Operational Semantics. The operational semantics of the process language defines for each process i a transition relation $\longrightarrow_i \subseteq Q_{P_i} \times A_i \times Q_{P_i}$, where A_i is the disjoint union of internal actions ($v := \varepsilon$ and b) and communication actions related to i. Inference rules are given in figure 3.

Verification of the Deterministic Hypotheses. The transition system defined by the operational semantics of $\mathcal{L}$ verifies hypothesis 3. The proof is straightforward. Moreover, lemma 13 can be used since P_0^F verifies hypotheses 3 and 5.

3.2 The Basic Refresh Transformation

This section presents the compilation of a sequential program into a parallel one, both in $\mathcal{L}$. We first define the notations for the distribution of data, basis of the program generation in an SPMD model. Then we describe the compilation rules, relying on the notion of *refresh* of remote variables, as it was implemented for instance in the PANDORE compiler [1].

Data Distribution. A distribution is a tuple $< I, \pi, \varphi >$ where:

- I is the set of processors.
- $\pi : \mathcal{V} \longrightarrow 2^I \setminus \{\emptyset\}$ is a mapping that associates to each variable v a set of processors such that $\forall i \in \pi(v)$, i owns v.
- $\varphi : \begin{array}{l} \mathcal{V} \times I \longrightarrow I \\ \forall i \notin \pi(v), \varphi(v,i) \in \pi(v) \end{array}$

  φ is a mapping which, to each couple made of a variable v and a processor i that does not own v, associates a processor owning v, which is responsible for the refresh of v on i (updated values of v are sent from $\varphi(v,i)$ to i).

From now on, we will implicitly consider a given data distribution (the implementation of the mappings π and φ being left to the compiler writer).

We also introduce a notion of context: a context is any mapping from I to $2^{\mathcal{V}}$. For instance, μ is the context which associates to each processor i the set of variables it owns:

$$\mu(i) = \{v \in \mathcal{V} \mid i \in \pi(v)\}$$

$$< v := \varepsilon, \sigma_i > \xrightarrow{\ v := \varepsilon\ }_i < nil, \sigma_i[\sigma_i(\varepsilon)/v] >$$

$$\frac{<s_i, \sigma_i > \xrightarrow{\ a\ }_i <S'_i, \sigma'_i >}{<s_i\,;\,S_i, \sigma_i > \xrightarrow{\ a\ }_i <S'_i\,;\,S_i, \sigma'_i >}$$

$$\frac{\sigma_i(b)}{< \text{if } b \text{ then } S^t_i \text{ else } S^f_i \text{ fi}, \sigma_i > \xrightarrow{\ b\ }_i < S^t_i, \sigma_i >}$$

$$\frac{\neg\sigma_i(b)}{< \text{if } b \text{ then } S^t_i \text{ else } S^f_i \text{ fi}, \sigma_i > \xrightarrow{\ b\ }_i < S^f_i, \sigma_i >}$$

$$\frac{\sigma_i(b)}{< \text{while } b \text{ do } S_i \text{ od}, \sigma_i > \xrightarrow{\ b\ }_i < S_i\,;\, \text{while } b \text{ do } S_i \text{ od}, \sigma_i >}$$

$$\frac{\neg\sigma_i(b)}{< \text{while } b \text{ do } S_i \text{ od}, \sigma_i > \xrightarrow{\ b\ }_i < nil, \sigma_i >}$$

$$< !v_{i \to j}, \sigma_i > \xrightarrow{\ !\sigma_i(v)_{i \to j}\ }_i < nil, \sigma_i > \qquad < ?v_{j \to i}, \sigma_i > \xrightarrow{\ ?e_{j \to i}\ }_i < nil, \sigma_i[e/v] >$$

Fig. 3. Operational semantics rules

Compilation Rules. Let $\Delta : expr \longrightarrow 2^V$ and $\xi_i : statement \longrightarrow 2^V$ be two mappings giving respectively the set of variables occurring in an expression, and the variables to be refreshed on the processor i for any statement:

$$\forall i \in I \begin{cases} \xi_i(v := \varepsilon) = \begin{cases} \Delta(\varepsilon) \setminus \mu(i) & \text{if } i \in \pi(v) \\ \emptyset & \text{otherwise} \end{cases} \\ \xi_i(\text{if } b \text{ then } S^t \text{ else } S^f \text{ fi}) = \Delta(b) \setminus \mu(i) \\ \xi_i(\text{while } b \text{ do } S \text{ od}) = \Delta(b) \setminus \mu(i) \end{cases}$$

and finally ξ is the mapping: $statement \longrightarrow (I \longrightarrow 2^V)$ such that

$$\xi(s)(i) = \xi_i(s)$$

In order to properly define the *refresh* construction, we now need a mapping which associates to a context a sequence of communication statements. The execution of this sequence achieves the transmission of the values of every variable in the context. Any transmission takes place from one owner of the variable to a processor which needs it.

Let $F = \{!v_{j \to k}, ?v_{j \to k}\}_{j,k \in I, v \in V}$ and $\gamma : (I \longrightarrow 2^V) \longrightarrow F^*$.

The mapping γ associates to any context c a word $\gamma(c)$ in which no letter appears twice[2]. Moreover the totally ordered set $(\Gamma(c), <_{\Gamma(c)})$ of its successive letters satisfies the following conditions:

$$\Gamma(c) = \{!v_{\varphi(v,j) \to j}, ?v_{\varphi(v,j) \to j}\}_{j \in I, v \in c(j)}$$

and

$$\forall\, !v_{i \to j}, ?v_{i \to j}, !u_{i \to j}, ?u_{i \to j} \in \Gamma(c) \begin{cases} !v_{i \to j} <_{\Gamma(c)} ?v_{i \to j} \\ !u_{i \to j} <_{\Gamma(c)} !v_{i \to j} \iff ?u_{i \to j} <_{\Gamma(c)} ?v_{i \to j} \end{cases}$$

---

[2] The choice of a particular γ is a question of implementation.

The order $<_{\Gamma(c)}$ is such that each send statement of a variable v occurs "before" the corresponding receive statement, and the order between the emissions of two variables is coherent with the order of their receptions. Therefore, deadlocks and inconsistencies are avoided.

The function pr_i is the projection of a communication sequence $\gamma(c)$ on each processor i, defined as follows:

$$\left\{ \begin{array}{ll} pr_i(nil) = nil \\ pr_i(!v_{i \to j}.r) = !v_{i \to j}; pr_i(r) \\ pr_i(?v_{j \to i}.r) = ?v_{j \to i}; pr_i(r) \\ pr_i(!v_{k \to l}.r) = pr_i(r) & \text{if } k \neq i \\ pr_i(?v_{k \to l}.r) = pr_i(r) & \text{if } l \neq i \end{array} \right.$$

We can now define the refresh function:

$$refresh_i = pr_i \circ \gamma$$

Finally, $exec_i$ is a projection which ensures the execution of an assignment only on the processors owning its left-hand side variable:

$$exec_i (v := \varepsilon) = \left\{ \begin{array}{ll} v := \varepsilon & \text{if } i \in \pi(v) \\ nil & \text{otherwise} \end{array} \right.$$

Nil:	$[\![nil]\!]_i = nil$
Concatenation:	$[\![s; S]\!]_i = [\![s]\!]_i ; [\![S]\!]_i$
Assignment:	$[\![v := \varepsilon]\!]_i = \left[\begin{array}{l} refresh_i\,(\xi\,(v := \varepsilon)); \\ exec_i\,(v := \varepsilon) \end{array} \right.$
Conditional:	$[\![\text{if } b \text{ then } S^t \text{ else } S^f \text{ fi}]\!]_i = \left[\begin{array}{l} refresh_i\,\left(\xi\,(\text{if } b \text{ then } S^t \text{ else } S^f \text{ fi})\right); \\ \text{if } b \text{ then } [\![S^t]\!]_i \text{ else } [\![S^f]\!]_i \text{ fi} \end{array} \right.$
Iteration:	$[\![\text{while } b \text{ do } S \text{ od}]\!]_i = \left[\begin{array}{l} refresh_i\,(\xi\,(\text{while } b \text{ do } S \text{ od})); \\ \text{while } b \text{ do} \\ \quad [\![S]\!]_i ; \; refresh_i\,(\xi\,(\text{while } b \text{ do } S \text{ od})) \\ \text{od} \end{array} \right.$

Fig. 4. Compilation rules

The compilation of a sequential program S results in a parallel program $([\![S]\!]_i)_{i \in I}$. The function $[\![.]\!]_i : \mathcal{L} \longrightarrow \mathcal{L}$ is defined by the rules of figure 4.

3.3 Correctness Proof of the Compilation

Theorem 14. Let $q = <s; S, \sigma>$, $q' = <S'; S, \sigma'>$ and $\tilde{q}$ be such that $q \rightsquigarrow \tilde{q}$ and $q \to q'$, then $\exists \tilde{q}'$ such that the following diagram holds:

$$\begin{array}{ccc} q & \rightsquigarrow & \tilde{q} \\ \downarrow & & \downarrow + \\ q' & \rightsquigarrow & \tilde{q}' \end{array}$$

Proof

Let $\tilde{q} = (q_0, (< [\![s; S]\!]_i, \sigma_i >)_{i \in I})$.

For all $i \in I$, let us note χ_i such that:

$$[\![s; S]\!]_i = refresh_i\,(\xi(s)); \chi_i(s); [\![S]\!]_i$$

The activation of the refreshment sequence $\gamma\,(\xi(s))$ corresponds to a first (possibly empty) sequence of $\longrightarrow$-transitions, such that,

$$\tilde{q} \longrightarrow^* \tilde{q}'' = (q_0, (< \chi_i(s); [\![S]\!]_i, \sigma_i'' >)_{i \in I})$$

The definition of γ ensures that this computation can be achieved. From $q \rightsquigarrow \tilde{q}$ and from the definition of *refresh*, we obtain

$$\forall v \in \mathcal{V}, \forall i \in \pi(v), \; \sigma_i''(v) = \sigma(v) \tag{1}$$

$$\forall i \in I, \forall v \in \xi_i(s), \; \sigma_i''(v) = \sigma_{\varphi(v,i)}''(v) \tag{2}$$

and from 1 and 2 we deduce
if $s = v := \varepsilon$

$$\forall i \in \pi(v), \; \sigma_i''(\varepsilon) = \sigma(\varepsilon) \tag{3}$$

and if s is a conditional or an iteration,

$$\forall i \in I, \; \sigma_i''(b) = \sigma(b) \tag{4}$$

There is at least one $\chi_i(s)$ which is different from nil, therefore the execution of one step of each $\chi_i(s) \neq nil$, in any order, produces a non-empty sequence:

$$\tilde{q}'' \longrightarrow^+ \tilde{q}' \; = \; (q_0', (< S_i''; [\![S]\!]_i, \sigma_i' >)_{i \in I})$$

Let us show that $q' \rightsquigarrow \tilde{q}'$.

a) Queues are empty in state $\tilde{q}''$, because each message has been received, and so they remain empty, therefore $q_0' = q_0$.

b)

$$\forall v \in \mathcal{V}, \forall i \in \pi(v), \; \sigma_i'(v) = \sigma'(v) \tag{5}$$

The proof, by inference on the compilation rules, is straightforward. The only case in which the environment is modified is the assignment: in this case we have immediately 5 from 3.

c)

$$\forall i \in I, S_i'; [\![S]\!]_i = [\![S'; S]\!]_i \tag{6}$$

By inference on the compilation rules and thanks to the trivial property of the compilation function: $[\![S']\!]_i; [\![S]\!]_i = [\![S'; S]\!]_i$, we have:

− $s = v := \varepsilon$.

Then $S' = nil$ and $\chi_i(s) = exec_i(s)$ is rewritten into $S_i' = nil$.

− $s = $ if b then S^t else S^f fi.

Then if $\sigma(b)$ holds, we have $S' = S^t$. From 4 we deduce that $\chi_i(s) = $ if b then $[\![S^t]\!]_i$ else $[\![S^f]\!]_i$ fi is transformed into $[\![S^t]\!]_i$, i.e. $S_i' = [\![S^t]\!]_i = [\![S']\!]_i$. The case $\neg\sigma(b)$ is similar.

− $s = $ while b do S'' od.

Then if $\sigma(b)$ holds, we have s rewritten into $S' = S''; s$. From 4 we deduce that $\chi_i(s) = $ while b do $[\![S'']\!]_i$; $refresh_i(\xi(s))$ od is transformed into $S_i' = [\![S'']\!]_i$; $refresh_i(\xi(s)); \chi_i(s) = [\![S'']\!]_i; [\![s]\!]_i = [\![S''; s]\!]_i = [\![S']\!]_i$.

If $\neg\sigma(b)$ then s becomes nil and so, from 4, $\chi_i(s)$ also becomes nil, i.e. $S_i' = nil$.

□

As an immediate consequence of lemma 13 and theorem 14, we have the main result of this paper:

Theorem 15. *The compilation function* $[\![.]\!] : \mathcal{L} \longrightarrow \mathcal{L}^I$ *is correct.*

4 Illustrations of the Generality of the Approach

This section shows that our model can also be used as a tool for exploring other, more complex, translation techniques. These techniques are informally explained; a formal treatment, including detailed proofs, is available in [4].

Note that it is possible to extend our language with arrays; then a slightly more complex refresh must be defined. This extension is also presented in [4].

4.1 Optimization of the Refresh Mechanism

Introduction. The basic refresh mechanism is not optimal in terms of communications. Consider the following example:

$$z := 0;$$
$$x := z + 1;$$
$$x := z + x$$

Clearly, if x and z are mapped on distinct processors, the compilation induces two refresh of z, but the second one is useless: the value of z is unchanged.

In other words, the refresh mechanism ensures the causality between assignments that cannot be swapped. For instance the assignments $z := 0$ and $x := z + 1$ do not commute, therefore they must be causally ordered. However the second communication pair is useless since $z := 0$ and $x := z + x$ are already causally related by transitivity.

Principle. The principle of the optimization is to delete refresh statements that are known at compile time to be useless. An optimal refresh mechanism can be achieved in this way, at the expense of an exponential code inflation. The optimization we deal with is a compromise between the "raw" refresh and an optimal one: it does not produce a great amount of code but is far better than the raw refresh.

We associate a "compile time" context with each control point of the source program, i.e. with each point before or after a statement. The context related to a given point associates to each process i the set of remote variables that can be known at compile-time to have updated values on i at that point. The compilation function takes into account such contexts: at any point before the evaluation of an expression, it only produces refresh statements of the variables that are not in the context associated with the point. These refreshed variables are then put in this context, whereas any modified variable is removed from it. The approximation lies in the conditional and iteration rules. The context assumed after the execution of a conditional statement is the intersection of contexts obtained by execution of the then and else parts; for an iteration, we keep as resulting context the intersection between the context before the loop body and the context at the end of this body.

Proof Principle. The correctness of this optimization is proved by defining an extended state correspondence, that takes into account the context of refreshed variables. In the same way, we extend the operational semantics by adding the context of updated variables to each state of the program.

Thanks to this correspondence, the correctness proof exactly follows the lines of the basic refresh proof (cf paragraph 3.3). Although it is more tricky because of the complexity of handling the contexts.

4.2 Anticipation of Message Send

Introduction. Here we consider a post-compilation optimization. One should notice that message exchanges are placed as late as possible, i.e. right before the expression that requires the refresh of variables. However, it is worth anticipating as much as possible message sending, in order to reduce idle times during the execution of receive statements.

Principle. The optimization principle is to swap each send statement with the preceding statements, as far as some consistency rules are respected. These rules are quite obvious: they prohibit from exchanging a statement $!v_{i\rightarrow j}$ with any statement an execution of which could affect either v or the channel from i to j.

Proof Principle. We use the diamond property of both parallel programs, and establish a correspondence between states of the source parallel program and states of the optimized one. This correspondence is defined "modulo" the transiting messages (i.e. the channel queues) of both programs. Thanks to this correspondence relation it is possible to associate an equivalent particular execution of the optimized program to any execution of the source program.

5 Conclusion

We have presented a formal explanation of automated distribution of sequential programs. Although the data-driven parallelization technique is widely accepted, the formal description of its associated compilation rules, the semantic properties to be preserved and the correctness proofs turn out to be quite difficult to establish. We think however such a theoretical foundation is necessary to allow further development in this field.

The main technical contributions of the paper are:

- a formal model based on products of labeled and partially deterministic transition systems, allowing the comparison of the sequential source behaviour with the corresponding parallel ones.

- a proof technique based on the diamond property, which avoids the combinatorics of considering all the parallel behaviours.

- a complete example of treatment of a simplified sequential language. Compilation rules were detailed enough to permit a straightforward prototype implementation in ML (CAML [13]), generating a distributed code written in ESTELLE [7] (an ISO language to describe communicating processes) and experimented with a prototyping distributed environment [8].

By dealing with optimizations of the refresh mechanism, we have also tried to show that our contribution may serve as a basis for designing and proving other (and new) parallelizing rules.

References

1. Françoise André, Jean-Louis Pazat, and Henry Thomas. Pandore: a system to manage data distribution. In *ACM International Conference on Supercomputing*, June 11-15 1990.

2. K.R. Apt and E.-R. Olderog. *Verification of Sequential and Concurrent Programs*. Springer-Verlag, 1991.

3. A. Arnold. Transition systems and concurrent processes. *Mathematical Problems in Computation Theory, Banach Center Publications*, 21, 1988.

4. Cyrille Bareau, Benoît Caillaud, Claude Jard, and René Thoraval. *Correctness of Automated Distribution of Sequential Programs*. Technical Report 665, Institut de Recherche en Informatique et Systèmes Aléatoires, June 1992.

5. Luc Bougé. *On the semantics of languages for massively parallel Simd architectures*. Research report 91-14, LIP/ENS Lyon, April 1991.

6. David Callahan and Ken Kennedy. Compiling programs for distributed-memory multiprocessors. *The Journal of Supercomputing*, (2):151–169, 1988.

7. ISO 9074. *Estelle: a Formal Description Technique based on an Extented State Transition Model*. ISO TC97/SC21/WG6.1, 1989.

8. C. Jard and J.-M. Jézéquel. ECHIDNA, an Estelle-compiler to prototype protocols on distributed computers. *Concurrency Practice and Experience*, 4(5):377–397, August 1992.

9. Robert M. Keller. A fundamental theorem of asynchronous parallel computation. In T. Y. Feng, editor, *Parallel Processing*, pages 102–112, Springer Verlag, 1975. Lecture Notes in Computer Science 24.

10. R. Milner. *Communication and Concurrency*. Prentice Hall, 1989.

11. H. R. Nielson and F. Nielson. *Semantics with Applications: a Formal Introduction*. Wiley, 1992.

12. Edwin M. Paalvast, Henk J. Sips, and A.J. van Gemund. Automatic parallel program generation and optimization from data decompositions. In *International Conference on Parallel Processing*, August 1991.

13. P. Weis, M.V. Aponte, A. Laville, M. Mauny, and A. Suárez. *The CAML reference manual*. Rapport Technique 121, INRIA, septembre 1990.

14. Hans P. Zima, Heinz-J. Bast, and Michael Gerndt. Superb: a tool for semi-automatic mimd/simd parallelization. *Parallel Computing*, (6):1–18, 1988.

Compositionality Issues of Concurrent Object-Oriented Logic Languages

E. Pimentel and J.M. Troya

Dpto. de Lenguajes y Ciencias de la Computación
Universidad de Málaga
Pza. El Ejido, s/n. 29013 Malaga - SPAIN

Abstract

We define the operational and denotational semantics for $L^2||O^2$, a language incorporating the typical mechanisms of object oriented programming into concurrent logic languages. Our proposal allows the exploitation of two kinds of parallelism in the object-oriented paradigm: inter-objects and intra-objects parallelism. On the other hand, the communication among objects is asynchronous. The operational semantics of the language is given in terms of a transition relation, but it presents a problem: it is not compositional. To solve this lack of compositionality, we define a denotational semantics, which is correct with respect to the operational one. We have chosen complete metric spaces as the mathematical framework to develop this semantic, by using contractions on them.

1. Introduction

One of the more significant proposals to incorporate parallelism in logic programming was concurrent logic languages [Shapiro 89], but they are difficult to use for programming in the large, because of the absence of modularization mechanisms. However, their computational model supports the object-oriented paradigm [Shapiro and Takeuchi 83]. In this sense, a number of object-oriented extensions of concurrent logic languages have been proposed: Vulcan [Kahn et al. 87], Polka [Davison 89], Mandala [Ohki et al. 89], $L^2||O^2$ [Pimentel and Troya 91]. All these proposals use the logic component in the integration to obtain very expressive object-oriented programming languages. The intrinsic parallelism of concurrent logic languages allows the exploitation of two kinds of parallelism in the object-oriented paradigm: inter-objects and intra-objects parallelism. Generally, the parallel object-oriented languages incorporate an inter-objects parallelism (objects can proceed in parallel) but the behavior of each object usually is sequential. On the other hand, communication among objects is synchronous: a message can only be processed by an object when it is explicitly waiting for it. However, in $L^2||O^2$ the objects are parallel processes waiting for messages, and although they must be consumed sequentially, they can proceed in parallel.

The need to formally define the computational models of the object-oriented languages is obvious. In this sense, a number of operational and denotational semantics for some mechanisms and languages have been proposed [Cook and Palsberg 89; Yelland 89; Agha 86]. The parallelism in object-oriented computing has been studied by America and Rutten (1989) by defining the POOL language. However, in this language the objects are sequential and communication is synchronous. The semantic aspects of concurrent object-oriented logic languages have been dealt in [Pimentel and Troya 92], by defining an operational and a declarative semantics, but they are not compositional. Our aim is to define a compositional semantics for $L^2||O^2$ in the same way as [America and Rutten 89], but taking into account that communication in our proposal is asynchronous, and it incorporates intra-objects parallelism.

In Section 2 we introduce an object-oriented view of the concurrent logic languages and we consider an operational and a declarative semantics for a version of the Parlog language. In Section 3 we define the $L^2\|O^2$ language. Later, in Section 3, a subset of $L^2\|O^2$ is considered, and its operational semantics, based on a transition relation, is defined. As a consequence, we obtain all computed answer substitutions corresponding to all successfully terminating computations of a given goal. We apply the category of complete metric spaces to define the denotational semantics in order to achieve compositionality. The two semantics are related by giving an equivalence between them in terms of an abstraction operator.

2. Concurrent logic languages.

The commited choice logic languages, whose more outstanding representatives are Parlog [Clark and Gregory 86], Concurrent Prolog [Shapiro 83] and GHC [Ueda 85], are characterized by the appearance of guards in the clauses, such that the general aspect of one of them is:

$$H<-G_1,G_2,...,G_n : B_1,B_2,...,B_m.$$

where the goals G_i form the guard of the clause, and B_j its body.

Another characteristic of these languages is the distinction between input and output arguments; either with a mode declaration (Parlog), adding '?' after the variable (Concurrent Prolog), or including the input constraint in the execution model (GHC).

The reduction of an atomic goal is made choosing a clause from the candidates nondeterministically, and substituting it by the clause body. When a choice is done, it cannot be undone (commit). The candidate clauses set for a given goal are composed of those clauses whose input variables in the head match the corresponding variables in the goal, and whose guard is successfully evaluated.

The concurrence is obtained due to AND-stream parallelism. Thus, the goal

```
?- producer(S),consumer(S).
```

where the arguments of *producer* and *consumer* are input and output variables, respectively, can be solved by suspending the evaluation of *consumer(S)* until *producer* produces a value for S. But the concurrence is effective due to the *partial binding*, that is, a predicate will generate a list incrementally, and it will be consumed in the same way.

Finally, another significant characteristic of our proposals is back communication (*incomplete messages*). For example, the clause:

```
p(success(Ok),V) <- c(V) : Ok = ok.
```

will return *ok* on the *Ok* variable, if V satisfies c, although the first argument of p is declared as input.

3. The $L^2\|O^2$ Language

The syntax, semantics and implementation of the $L^2\|O^2$ language which we define are based on those of Parlog++ and Polka, although they present significant differences [Pimentel and Troya 92].

The syntactic outline of a class definition in the language proposed is:

```
<class> [<channels>] [; <channels>]
[inherit <classes>]
[state <state_variables_and_supplier_objects>]
messages
EGHCs
end.
```

where EGHCs are a sequence of extended guarded Horn clauses whose syntax and semantics we will study below.

The interface of a class instance will be given by their input and output channels. They are declared after the class name (the output channels appear after ;). A class always will have an input channel (self) in addition to those appearing in the declaration. The state of an object will be determined by the structures in the state clause. They can be state variables or instances of some other classes. The encapsulating and hiding information issues related with the instance variables will be similar to Smalltalk; in our context, it means that the accessing to the state will be made using incomplete messages. Message processing will be determined by the extended guarded clauses. These clauses have the following syntax:

```
[[I] ?] H <- G : B.
```

where I will be an input channel of the class or an output channel of an object in state section. If I is not present, we consider the self channel. The non-extended guarded Horn clauses correspond to private predicates, and they have the same syntax that Parlog clauses, with mode declaration. There can appear in B primitives of message passing as $O \ ! \ m$, m being a term, and O either an output channel of the class, an input channel of some instance in state, or the keyword self. The message m can be also a sequence of messages. Additional characteristics to make easier the programming are included in $L^2 \| O^2$: sending of messages along the keyword super, the name of any inherited class, or an argument of the head. However, in order to simplify the semantics definition they will not be considered.

The behavior of a point can be described in $L^2 \| O^2$ as follows:

```
point
state X,Y
messages
    ? init(A,B)     <- nonvar(A),nonvar(B) : X is A, Y is B.
    ? x(A)          <- var(A) : A is X.
    ? x(A)          <- nonvar(A) : X becomes A.
    ? y(B)          <- var(B) : B is Y.
    ? y(B)          <- nonvar(B) : Y becomes B.
    ? move(A,B)     <- nonvar(A),nonvar(B) : X,Y becomes X+A,Y+B.
    ? module(M)     <- module(X,Y,M).
    mode module(?,?,^).
    module(A,B,D) <- D1 is A*A+B*B, sqrt(D1,D).
end.
```

Because of there are no variables after the class name, the only input channel will be the self channel. The variables X and Y will determine the state of an instance, and they are updated with the becomes primitive [Davison 89]. Note that private predicates, as *module*, will be defined by Parlog clauses.

The class instances are created from the state clause of a class or by means of a query. The queries will be made from that which we will call *top* (T), and this will be considered a special class, whose state section will contain the part of the query creating instances, and whose messages section will be composed of non-extended guarded Horn clauses. For example, the next query:

```
?- point(P1),point(P2),
   P2!init(2,0), P1!(init(1,2),move(1,0),x(A),y(B)).
```

will be made in the frame of the class *top* where the state section will contain: point(P1), point(P2). The rest of the calls will be considered the goal to solve.

4. Operational semantics

The operational semantics that we present here is based on the semantics of the underlying concurrent logic language, i.e. Parlog. In this sense, we will assume a transition relation $\rightarrow_{\text{Parlog}}$ for the Parlog language as that defined in [Boer et al. 89].

Let's suppose the general description of a class is:

```
c  i₁,i₂,…,iₙ;o₁,o₂,…,oₘ
inherit c₁,c₂,…,cₕ
state x₁,x₂,…,xₛ,d₁(j̄₁,p̄₁),d₂(j̄₂,p̄₂),…,dᵤ(j̄ᵤ,p̄ᵤ)
messages
   Mᴄ
end
```

where $c, c_k, d_k \in \Sigma^c$ (class names); $i_k, o_k \in Ch$ (set of channels); $x_k \in SVar$ (state variables); $\overline{j_k}, \overline{p_k} \in Ch^+$ (sequences of channels); and M_c is a set of EGHCs. Variables occurring in the clauses of M_c can be state or logical; we will denote each kind by SVar and LVar, respectively. So, a class $c \in \Sigma^c$ will be characterized by:

$$I_c = i_1 \cdot \ldots \cdot i_n \in Ch^+,$$
$$O_c = o_1 \cdot \ldots \cdot o_m \in Ch^+,$$
$$S_c = \{x_i\}_{i=1\ldots s} \in \mathscr{P}_{\text{fin}}(SVar),$$
$$H_c = \{c_i\}_{i=1\ldots h} \in \mathscr{P}_{\text{fin}}(\Sigma^c),$$
$$U_c = \{d_k(\overline{j_k},\overline{p_k})\}_{k=1\ldots u} \in \mathscr{P}_{\text{fin}}(At(Ch,\Sigma^c)),$$

and M_c. $At(Ch,\Sigma^c)$ denotes the set of atoms composed by functors of Σ^c, and arguments of Ch. A program will be given by a set of class definitions. We define on the set H_c an order relation $<_c$ given by the order in which the classes appear in the inherit section. Although in $L^2\|O^2$ the inheritance graph is ordered with respect to this relation, the present work has not considered any order on the class hierarchy. To simplify the semantics, we have supposed all classes in the graph have the same priority to solve any message or predicate. For this reason H_c is modeled by a set. The class hierarchy associated to a class c will be represented by the set:

$$\overline{H_c} = \{c,T\} \cup \left(\bigcup\nolimits_{a \in H_c} \overline{H_a} \right).$$

From now, we will consider all becomes operations in a EGHC grouped at the end of its body, and it will not be used this primitive in the Parlog clauses. That is, EGHCs will have the following aspect:

```
[I]?H <- G:B, x becomes t.
```

In addition, state variables only will be used in extended clauses.

An instance is identified by its class name and its channels. In fact, when an object is created, we use a call as $c(i_0,i_1,\ldots,i_n,o_1,o_2,\ldots,o_m)$, where $c \in \Sigma^c$ and $i_k,o_j \in Ch$. However, to make easy the object representation we assume a set Obj containing names for active objects, and a function

$$T : Obj \rightarrow \Sigma^c,$$

which assigns to each object $\alpha \in Obj$ the class to which it belongs. Furthermore, we consider the function

$$v : \mathscr{P}(Obj) \times \Sigma^c \rightarrow Obj,$$

such that $v(X,c) \notin X$ y $T(v(X,c))=c$, for finite $X \subseteq Obj$ and $x \in \Sigma^c$. The v function gives for a finite set X of object names and a class name c a new name for an instance of c.

We will base the operational semantics of the language on the transition systems. The execution of a program will be modeled by a configuration sequence with transitions among them.

4.1. Configurations

To describe the state of an object we need to consider different aspects. Firstly, it is necessary to know the current values of its state variables. So, one of the state components of an object $\alpha \in Obj$ (with $a=T(\alpha)$) is the mapping

$$\overline{S_a} \to Tm,$$

where $\overline{S_a} = \bigcup_{d \in \overline{Ha}} S_d$, and Tm is the set of terms. In general, the state of a system of objects can be modeled by:

$$St_{var} = Obj \to Svar \to Tm,$$

But the state of an instance is also dependent on its connection with other objects of the system by means of its channels. It can be expressed by

$$St_o = Obj \to Ch \to Obj.$$

For each $\alpha \in Obj$ $(a=T(\alpha))$, an element $\sigma \in St_o$ will determine the correspondence between its output channels and the objects taking them as input channels. That is,

$$\sigma(\alpha) : \overline{O_a} \cup \overline{OU_a} \to Obj,$$

where

$$\overline{O_a} = \begin{cases} \overline{O_{a_1} \cdot O_{a_2} \cdots O_{a_h}} \cdot O_a & \text{if } H_a = \{a_i\}_{i=1..h} \text{ and } a_i <_a a_{i+1} \\ O_a & \text{if } H_a = \emptyset \end{cases}$$

$$\overline{OU_a} = \bigcup_{c \in \overline{Ha}} \{j \in Ch : \exists\, d(\overline{j}, \overline{p}) \in U_c, \text{con } j \in \overline{j}\}$$

Here, we are using the sequence $\overline{O_a}$ as a set containing all output channels defined in the class a and its ancestors. Similarly, $\overline{OU_a}$ denotes the output channels corresponding to the suppliers. So, St_o determines the receivers associated to each output channel of an object, but it does not exist information about what input channel will be used to make the connection. To cover this aspect, we define:

$$St_i = \{r \in Obj \to Ch \to Ch : supp(r(\alpha)) \cap ran(r(\alpha)) = \emptyset \wedge r(\alpha) \text{ injective } \forall\, \alpha \in Obj\},$$

where *supp* and *ran* represent the support and the range, respectively, of a mapping. An element $r \in St_i$ represents, for each object α $(a=T(\alpha))$, a renaming of channels:

$$r(\alpha) : \overline{I_a} \cup \overline{IU_a} \to Ch,$$

where $\overline{I_a}$ and $\overline{IU_a}$ are defined in a similar way to $\overline{O_a}$ and $\overline{OU_a}$, respectively. Given an object, a renaming can be expressed by the set of pairs $\{p/r(\alpha)(p) : p \in supp(r(\alpha))\}$, and this notation can be extended to sequences; so that if $\overline{o} = o_1, \ldots, o_k$ and $\overline{p} = p_1, \ldots, p_k$, the renaming $\{\overline{o}/\overline{p}\}$ will represent $\{o_1/p_1, \ldots, o_k/p_k\}$.

Until now, we only have modeled the functional aspects of the objects. The logical component will be given by substitutions. Let Subst be the set of substitutions. A substitution is a total function from logical variables to terms, $\theta : LVar \to Tm$, such that $supp(\theta)$ is finite. The empty substitution will be denoted by ε. The composition of substitutions and the most general unifier (mgu) of terms are defined as usual.

Finally, we need to maintain a set containing the active objects of the system.

Definition 1 (State)

We define the set of states St by:

$$St = St_{var} \times Subst \times St_o \times St_i \times \mathscr{P}(Obj)$$

We denote each component of $\sigma \in St$ by $(\sigma_1, \sigma_2, \sigma_3, \sigma_4, \sigma_5)$. We shall use the following variant notation. By $\sigma\{\alpha, x \to t\}$ (with $\alpha \in Obj$, $x \in SVar$ and $t \in Tm$) we shall denote the state σ' that is as σ but for the value of $\sigma'_1(\alpha)(x)$, which is t. Similarly, we denote by $\sigma\{\alpha, o \to \beta\}$ ($\alpha \in Obj$, $o \in Ch$ and $\beta \in Obj$) the new state σ', equal to σ but for $\sigma'_3(\alpha)(o)$, which is β. Likewise, by $\sigma\{\alpha, r_\alpha\}$ ($r_\alpha \in Ch \to Ch$) we represent the state σ' that is as σ but for the value of $\sigma'_4(\alpha)$, which is r_α. This notation can be extended to sequences: if $\overline{x} = x_1 \cdot \ldots \cdot x_s$, $\overline{t} = t_1 \cdot \ldots \cdot t_s$, and $\overline{o} = o_1 \cdot \ldots \cdot o_m$,

$$\sigma\{\alpha,\overline{o} \to \beta\} = \sigma\{\alpha,o_1 \to \beta\}\ldots\{\alpha,o_m \to \beta\}, \text{ and}$$
$$\sigma\{\alpha,\overline{x} \to \overline{t}\} = \sigma\{\alpha,x_1 \to t_1\}\ldots\{\alpha,x_s \to t_s\}.$$

Also, by $\sigma\theta$ ($\sigma\in$ St, $\theta\in$ Subst) we denote $(\sigma_1,\sigma_2\theta,\sigma_3,\sigma_4,\sigma_5)$.

Definition 2 (Configurations)

A configuration will be composed of a set of pairs and a state. Each pair will model the pending goals for each active object. So, the set of configurations will be

$$\Gamma = \mathcal{P}(\text{Obj}\times\mathcal{P}(\text{At})) \times \text{St}.$$

Given a configuration $(X,\sigma)\in \Gamma$, when an object α is created the set of goals to solve is empty. In this case, the pair $(\alpha,\emptyset)$ will belong to X. But the absence of goals can be produced because all goals have been solved. In fact, a pair $(\alpha,\{\text{true}\})\in X$ represents that situation. We will identify the true atom with the symbol $[]$. So, we will distinguish the situation $(\alpha,\emptyset)$ from $(\alpha,[])$. The first one corresponds to an object α recently created, and the second one to an object without pending goals.

A configuration $(X,\sigma)\in \Gamma$ is terminal if and only if $\forall (\alpha,G_\alpha)\in X$, $G_\alpha=\emptyset \vee G_\alpha=[]$.

4.2. Transition rules

Before to describe the transition relation, we will explain when a clause is candidate to solve a goal or to process a message, in a similar way to concurrent logic languages. For the rest of the section let W denote a fixed program. Given a set of logical variables V, W_V denotes the program whose clauses are variants, with respect to V, of the clauses of W. The set of variables occurring in a term t is indicated by var(t). Similarly, if $p\in$ At, ivar(p) denotes the set of variables corresponding to input arguments of p. We introduce the notions of input and output mgu's of two predicates by considering the mgu restricted to input and output arguments, respectively. To simplify the aspect of transition rules, we will not use brackets to denote sets if they are not necessary.

Definition 3 (Candidate clauses)

Given a class c and an atom g, a clause $C\equiv(h \leftarrow F:B)\in (M_d)_{ivar(g)}$ $(d\in \overline{H_c}\cup\{T\})$ is *candidate* to solve the goal g, if and only if:
$$\exists \theta=mgu_i(g,h) : \langle F,\theta\rangle \overset{*}{\to}_{Parlog} \langle [],\theta'\rangle \wedge \theta'_{|ivar(g)}=\varepsilon$$
Let $M_c(g)$ be the candidate clauses set, in the context of c, to solve g. $\theta_C(g)$ denotes θ'.

Likewise, given an evaluation $\xi\in$ Eval, an extended clause $C\equiv(i?h \leftarrow F:B)\in (M_d)_{var(m)}$ $(d\in H_c)$ is *candidate*, in the environment (c,ξ), to process the message m along the channel i, if and only if:
$$\exists \theta=mgu(m,h\xi) : \langle F\xi,\theta\rangle \overset{*}{\to}_{Parlog} \langle [],\theta'\rangle \wedge \theta'_{|var(m)}=\varepsilon$$
Let $M_{c,\xi}(m,i)$ be the set of candidate clauses, and $\theta_{C\xi}(m)$ the substitution θ'.

Now, we can define $\to \subseteq \Gamma \times \Gamma$ as the smallest relation verifying:

4.2.1. Creation of instances

$$d\in \Sigma^c, \beta=\nu(\sigma_5,d)$$
$$\sigma'=\sigma\{\alpha,\overline{i} \to \beta\}\{\beta,\overline{o} \to \alpha\}\{\alpha,\overline{o}/\overline{O_d}\}\{\beta,\text{self}\cdot\overline{I_d}/\overline{i}\}, \text{ with } \sigma'_5=\sigma_5\cup\{\beta\}$$
$$\overline{\langle\{(\alpha; d(\overline{i},\overline{o}))\}, \sigma\rangle \to \langle\{(\alpha;[]),(\beta;\emptyset)\}, \sigma'\rangle}$$

The creation of an instance is made by a goal whose functor is a class identifier (d). A new object is created (β) without goals to solve, by considering its input channels as output channels of α ($\alpha,i_0\cdot\overline{i} \to \beta$), and vice versa ($\beta,\overline{o} \to \alpha$). Also, the channels are conveniently linked in each object: $\{\alpha,\overline{o}/\overline{O_d}\}\{\beta,\text{self}\cdot\overline{I_d}/\overline{i}\}$.

4.2.2. Private predicates

The reduction of a goal depends of the environment in which it must be solved:

$$\frac{\exists\, C\equiv(h \leftarrow F:B)\in M_{T(\alpha)}(g\sigma_2)}{\theta=\theta_C(g\sigma_2)}$$

$$\langle\{(\alpha;\, g)\},\sigma\rangle \rightarrow \langle\{(\alpha;\, \text{outunif}(g\sigma_2,h\theta,B)\},\sigma\theta\rangle$$

To solve the goal g in the object α, we choose a candidate clause C. The second component of σ is modified by the substitution θ, and the new goals generated are the body of the clause and the output unification of the original goal and the head of the clause. The output unification is given by:

$$\exists\, \theta=mgu_o(g,h)$$

$$\langle\{(\alpha;\, \text{outunif}(g,h),B)\},\sigma\rangle \rightarrow \langle\{(\alpha;\, B)\},\sigma\theta\rangle$$

4.2.3. Messages on an output channel

The sending messages can be made along `self` or an output channel, including the channels corresponding to input channels of suppliers (objects defined in the `state` section). The message processing along output channels is modeled in a similar way to private predicates.

$$\sigma_3(\alpha)(o)=\beta,\, \sigma_4(\beta)(p)=o,\, b=T(\beta),\, \eta=\sigma_1(\beta)$$
$$\exists\, C\equiv(p?h \leftarrow F:B,\, \bar{x}\text{ becomes }\bar{\iota})\in M_{b,\eta}(m\sigma_2,p)$$
$$\theta=\theta_{C\eta}(m\sigma_2),\, \sigma'=\sigma\{\beta,\bar{x}\rightarrow\bar{\iota}\}$$
$$B'=\begin{cases} B\cup U_b \text{ si } G=\emptyset \\ B \text{ si } G\neq\emptyset \end{cases}$$

$$\langle\{(\alpha;\, o!m),(\beta;\, G)\},\sigma\rangle \rightarrow \langle\{(\alpha;\, [\,]),(\beta;\, G,B'\eta)\};\sigma'\theta\rangle$$

In this case, the clause C is chosen from the candidates to process the message m after to substitute its logical variables. The clause body is added to the list of pending goals in the object β, and if β has been recently created (P=$\emptyset$) the goals in U_b are also added. So, the creation of objects declared in the `state` section is made when the current object receives the first message. All these goals must be solved in the new environment given by η. For this reason, the state variables occurring on B are evaluated by η. In the previous rule it was not necessary because the private clauses does not include state variables. The global state is modified by the `becomes` primitive ($\sigma\{\beta,\bar{x}\rightarrow\bar{\iota}\}$) and the substitution θ.

4.2.4. Messages on self

Another way to send messages is by using the special variable `self`. When we use the send primitive with this one, the messages are put on the first channel. The candidate clauses are considered from $M_{a,\eta}$. So, if the message is sent to `self` whole inheritance graph is used to find a convenient clause. The transition is produced in a similar way to the previous rule:

$$a=T(\alpha),\, \eta=\sigma_1(\alpha)$$
$$\exists\, C\equiv(?h \leftarrow F:B,\, \bar{x}\text{ becomes }\bar{\iota})\in M_{a,\eta}(m\sigma_2,\text{self})$$
$$\theta=\theta_{C\eta}(m\sigma_2),\, \sigma'=\sigma\{\beta,\bar{x}\rightarrow\bar{\iota}\}$$

$$\langle\{(\alpha;\, \text{self}!m)\},\sigma\rangle \rightarrow \langle\{(\alpha;\, B\eta)\},\sigma'\theta\rangle$$

4.2.5. Interleaving

The parallel execution will be modeled by interleaving. Firstly, the objects can progress in parallel (inter-objects parallelism), as it is showed by the following rule:

$$\frac{\langle X, \sigma\rangle \to \langle X', \sigma'\rangle}{\langle X\cup Y, \sigma\rangle \to \langle X'\cup Y; \sigma'\rangle}$$

The goal conjunction will be modeled by the following rule, and it illustrates the intra-objects parallelism:

$$\frac{\langle\{(\alpha;P)\}\cup Y, \sigma\rangle \to \langle\{(\alpha;P')\}\cup Y', \sigma'\rangle}{\langle\{(\alpha;P\cup Q)\}\cup Y, \sigma\rangle \to \langle\{(\alpha;P'\cup Q)\}\cup Y',\sigma'\rangle}$$

4.3. Operational semantics

Let, for $St_\partial^\infty = St^+ \cup St^* \cdot \{\partial\} \cup St^\omega$ and ∂ denoting fail (or deadlock), the function

$$O_1 : \mathcal{P}(Obj \times \mathcal{P}(At)) \to St \to \mathcal{P}(St_\partial^\infty)$$

be given as follows:

$s \in O_1[X](\sigma)$, with $(X,\sigma) \in \Gamma$ iff one of the following conditions is satisfied:

(i) $s = \sigma_0 \cdot \sigma_1 \cdot \ldots \cdot \sigma_n$ ($n \geq 0$) and $\exists X_0, X_1, \ldots, X_n$ such that

$\langle X, \sigma\rangle = \langle X_0, \sigma_0\rangle \to \langle X_1, \sigma_1\rangle \to \ldots \to \langle X_n, \sigma_n\rangle$, and $\langle X_n, \sigma_n\rangle$ is terminal.

(ii) $s = \sigma_0 \cdot \sigma_1 \cdot \ldots \cdot \sigma_n \cdot \partial$ ($n \geq 0$) and $\exists X_0, X_1, \ldots, X_n$ such that

$\langle X, \sigma\rangle = \langle X_0, \sigma_0\rangle \to \langle X_1, \sigma_1\rangle \to \ldots \to \langle X_n, \sigma_n\rangle \nrightarrow$, and $\langle X_n, \sigma_n\rangle$ is not terminal.

(iii) $s = \sigma_0 \cdot \sigma_1 \cdot \ldots$ and $\exists X_0, X_1, \ldots$ such that $\langle X, \sigma\rangle = \langle X_0, \sigma_0\rangle \to \langle X_1, \sigma_1\rangle \to \ldots$

Note that each case corresponds to one of the three parts of St_∂^∞. If $s \in St^+$ (case i), it stands for a finite normally terminating computation; if $s \in St^* \cdot \{\partial\}$ (case ii), it reflects a finite abnormally terminating computation, which is indicated by the symbol ∂ (fail or deadlock); and if $s \in St^\omega$ (case iii), it represents an infinite computation.

Definition 4 (Operational semantics)

We define $O : \mathcal{P}(At) \to \mathcal{P}(St_\partial^\infty)$ by

$$O[G] = O_1[\{(v(\emptyset,T); G)\}](\emptyset,\varepsilon,\emptyset,\emptyset,\{v(\emptyset,T)\}).$$

The first, third and fourth components of initial substitution correspond to functions with empty support, that is, totally undefined.

5. Denotational semantics

The operational semantics O defined before presents a problem: the lack of compositionality. In fact, let's suppose the following two definitions of the class c:

```
c                                         c

messages                                  messages
    ? m(x)  ←  self!m1(x).                    ? m(x)  ←  self!m1(x).
    ? m(x)  ←  self!m2(x).                    ? m1(a).
    ? m1(a).                                  ? m1(b).
    ? m2(b).                              end

end
```

If we consider two programs W_1 and W_2 containing the first and second class definitions, respectively, the goal $\leftarrow c(i)$ will not obtain any answer substitution, and the operational semantics O w.r.t. the programs W_i will be the same: $O[c(i)] = \{\sigma\}$, where $\sigma_1 = \emptyset$, $\sigma_2 = \varepsilon$, $\sigma_3(\alpha)(i) = \beta$, $\sigma_4(\beta)(self) = i$, $\sigma_5 = \{\alpha,\beta\}$, $T(\alpha) = T$, and $T(\beta) = c$. However, if we extend the goal with an atom $i!m_1(a)$, thus yielding the goal $\leftarrow c(i), i!m(a)$, then we get different operational meanings. In W_1 the goal can fail (choosing the wrong clause to process m), whereas in W_2 it cannot. In fact,

$$O_{W_1}[c(i), i!m(a)] = \{\sigma, \sigma \cdot \partial\}, \text{ and } O_{W_2}[c(i), i!m(a)] = \{\sigma\}.$$

In order to obtain compositionality, we will define a denotational semantics of $L^2||O^2$ by means of reflexive domains equations solved in the category of complete metric spaces. We will use an approach similar to that presented in [America and Rutten 89]. Then we will prove that the denotational semantics is correct with respect to the operational semantics.

Definition 5 (Semantic process domain)

Let $\bar{P}$ be a complete ultra-metric space satisfying the reflexive domain equation:
$$\bar{P} = \{p_o\} \cup id_{1/2} (St \to \mathcal{P}_{co}(Step\bar{p})),$$
where $Step\bar{p} = (St\times\bar{P}) \cup (Obj\times Ch\times At\times\bar{P}) \cup (Obj\times Ch\times At\times\mathcal{P}(At)\times\bar{P})$.

The sets $\{p_0\}$, St, Obj, Ch, and At become complete ultra-metric spaces by supplying them with the discrete metric. America and Rutten (1988) describe how to find a solution for such an equation. The operation $id_{1/2}$ is only necessary to guarantee that the equation is solvable by defining a contracting functor on the category of complete metric spaces. If (M,d) is a metric space, $id_{1/2}(M,d)$ represents (M,d/2).

A process $p\in\bar{P}$ is either p_o or a function from St to $\mathcal{P}_{co}(Step\bar{p})$, the set of all compact subsets of $Step\bar{p}$. The process p_o is the terminated process. For $p\neq p_o$ the process p can be, depending on the current state σ, a different step $p(\sigma)$. If $p(\sigma)=\emptyset$, then no further action is possible, which is interpreted as abnormal termination (failure or deadlock). For $p(\sigma)\neq\emptyset$, each $\pi\in p(\sigma)$ consists of some action (a change of the state σ or an attempt at communication), and the remaining actions to be taken after this action. There are two different types of steps. First, a step, $\pi\in p(\sigma)$, may be an element of $St\times\bar{P}$, say $\pi=\langle\sigma',p'\rangle$. In this case, the only action is a change of state, σ'. The process p' represents the remaining actions process p can do. When $p'=p_o$ no steps can be taken after step π. Second, π might be a send step, $\pi=\langle\alpha,o,m,p'\rangle$. The action involved here consists of an attempt at communication, in which a message m is sent to the object α, along the channel o. The process p' also represents the remaining actions of p. Finally, π may represent an answer step, $\pi=\langle\alpha,i,m,G,p'\rangle$, where p' represents the action to be taken when the message m arrives at object α by channel i, and guard G is satisfied upon the transition relation $\to_{Parlog}$.

We now define a semantic operator for the parallel composition of two processes, for which we shall use the symbol $||$.

Definition 6 (Parallel composition)

Let $|| : \bar{P} \times \bar{P} \to \bar{P}$ be such that it satisfies the equation:
$$p||q = \lambda\sigma.(p(\sigma)\underline{||}q \cup q(\sigma)\underline{||}p \cup p(\sigma)|_\sigma q(\sigma))$$
for all $p,q\in\bar{P}\backslash\{p_o\}$, and such that $p_o||p=p||p_o=p$. The operators $\underline{||}$ and $|_\sigma$ are defined by:
$$X\underline{||}q = \{\pi\hat{||}q : \pi\in X\}$$
$$X|_\sigma Y = \{\pi|_\sigma\rho : \pi\in X, \rho\in Y\},$$
for $X,X'\in\mathcal{P}_{co}(Step\bar{p})$, and where $\pi\hat{||}q$ is given by:
$$\pi\hat{||}q = \begin{cases} \langle\sigma,p||q\rangle & \text{if } \pi=\langle\sigma,p\rangle \\ \langle\alpha,o,m,p||q\rangle & \text{if } \pi=\langle\alpha,o,m,p\rangle \\ \langle\alpha,i,h,G,p||q\rangle & \text{if } \pi=\langle\alpha,i,h,G,p\rangle \end{cases}$$
and $\pi|_\sigma\rho$ by
$$\pi|_\sigma\rho = \{\langle\sigma\theta',p||q\rangle\} \text{ if } \{\pi,\rho\}=\{\langle\alpha,o,m,p\rangle,\langle\alpha,i,h,G,q\rangle\}, \sigma_4(\alpha)(i)=o,$$
$$\exists\; \theta=mgu(m\sigma_2,h), \langle G,\theta\rangle\to^*_{Parlog} \langle [],\theta'\rangle, \theta'|_{livar(m\sigma_2)}=\varepsilon$$
$$\pi|_\sigma\rho = \emptyset \text{ otherwise}$$

Since we intend to model parallel composition by interleaving, the merge of two processes p and q consist of three parts. The first one contains all possible first steps of p followed by the parallel composition of the rest of actions of p and q. The second part is similar. The last part contains the communication steps that result from two matching communication steps taken simultaneously. For $\pi \in$ Step$\overline{p}$ the definition of $\pi \| q$ is straightforward, but the definition of $\pi |_\sigma \rho$ is more complicated. If the steps π and ρ do not match, it is the empty set. When they do match, that is, one of them is a send step and the other one is the corresponding answer step, the result is a new state given by the substitution derived from unification and guard evaluation, together with the parallel composition of the remaining actions that each step can do.

To model the denotational semantics, we need to define the following function:

$$\mathcal{D}_1 : \mathcal{P}(At) \cup \{answer\} \to Obj \to \overline{P}$$

given by:

(1) $\mathcal{D}_1[true](\alpha) = p_o$

(2) $\mathcal{D}_1[c(i_0, \overline{i}, \overline{o})](\alpha) = \lambda\sigma.\{\; \langle \sigma', \mathcal{D}_1[answer](\beta) \| \mathcal{D}_1[d_1](\beta) \| ... \| \mathcal{D}_1[d_n](\beta) \rangle :$
$\sigma' = \sigma\{\alpha, i_0 \cdot \overline{i} \to \beta\}\{\beta, \overline{o} \to \alpha\}\{\alpha, \overline{o}/\overline{O_d}\}\{\beta, \{self \cdot \overline{I_d}/\overline{i}\},$
$\sigma'_5 = \sigma_5 \cup \{\beta\}, \beta = \nu(\sigma_5, c), d_i \in U_{T(\alpha)}\}$

(3) $\mathcal{D}_1[g](\alpha) = \lambda\sigma.\{\; \langle \sigma\theta_C(g\sigma_2(\alpha)), \lambda\sigma'.\{\langle\sigma'mgu_o(g\sigma_2(\alpha),h), \mathcal{D}_1[B](\alpha)\rangle\}\rangle :$
$(h \gets F{:}B) \in M_{T(\alpha)}(g\sigma_2(\alpha))\}$

(4) $\mathcal{D}_1[o!m](\alpha) = \lambda\sigma.\{\; \langle\sigma_3(\alpha)(o), o, m, p_o\rangle\}$

(5) $\mathcal{D}_1[answer](\alpha) = \lambda\sigma.\{\; \langle\alpha, i, h, F\sigma_1(\alpha), q\rangle :$
$q = \lambda\sigma'.\{\langle\sigma'\{\alpha, \overline{x} \to \overline{t}\}, q'\rangle\},$
$q' = \mathcal{D}_1[B\sigma'_1(\alpha)](\alpha) \| \mathcal{D}_1[answer](\alpha),$
$(?h \gets F{:}B, \overline{x} \text{ becomes } \overline{t}) \in \bigcup_{c \in \overline{H}_{T(\alpha)}} M_c\}$

(6) $\mathcal{D}_1[G_1, G_2](\alpha) = \mathcal{D}_1[G_1](\alpha) \| \mathcal{D}_1[G_2](\alpha)$

Each equation gives a denotation to a different atom in the context of an object. The denotation of a goal in an object is represented by a mapping from states to compact subsets of Step$p$. So, the denotation of a goal creating an instance of a class c (2) is given by the parallel composition of the denotation of each instance in the state section of that class, and a special sentence, *answer*, which is not included in the language definition. Each state σ is modified by linking the input and output channels.

A goal will be denoted (3) by all possible reductions by using all candidate clauses. A substitution, for each candidate clause, is first modified by the input unification with the head and the guard evaluation, and then by the output unification. Finally, the remaining processes are given by the body of the candidate clause. To send a message, we use an intermediate step (4), including the receiver object, the output channel, the message, and the terminated process. The fourth component will be necessary to express the interleaving with other processes.

The *answer* sentence (5) expresses that the object is willing to accept any message defined in a class from the inheritance hierarchy. When a message is consumed by an object, that is, when a clause has been chosen to process it, the object will continue waiting for more messages. Note that it is not necessary the whole processing of the message to consume another one. The body of the clause and the answer action are executed in parallel.

Finally, the equation (6) defines a conjunction of goals as the parallel composition of each goal. The compositionality is achieved by this equation, and the second one (2).

Definition 7 (Denotational semantics)
We define $\mathcal{D}: \mathcal{P}(At) \to \overline{P}$ by
$$\mathcal{D}[G] = \mathcal{D}_1[G](\nu(\emptyset, T))$$

5.1. Semantic correctness of $\mathcal{D}$

The operational and denotational semantics for $L^2 \| O^2$ have been defined by using the two following semantic universes:

$$P = St \to \mathcal{P}_{nco}(St_\partial^\infty),$$
$$\overline{P} = \{p_o\} \cup id_{1/2}\,(St \to \mathcal{P}_{co}(Stepp))$$

P is the metric space corresponding to $St \to \mathcal{P}(St_\partial^\infty)$ that was used to define O_1 ($\mathcal{P}_{nco}(St_\partial^\infty)$ represents the set of non-empty compact subsets of St_∂^∞). We observe the second universe is more involved than the first one. So, the denotational semantics $\mathcal{D}$ distinguishes more situations than the operational one, O. But, we would wish that $\mathcal{D}$ distinguishes at least the same situations as O, i.e. $\mathcal{D}$ is correct with respect to O. In fact, we will define an *abstraction* operation,

$$abstr : \overline{P} \to P,$$

which relates the two semantic universes.

Definition 8 (Abstraction operation)

Let $p \in \overline{P}$, $\sigma \in St$, and $\omega \in St_\partial^\infty$. Then,

(i) ω is a *finite stream* in $p(\sigma)$ if there exist $\langle \sigma_i, p_i \rangle$, $1 \le i \le n$, such that
$$\omega = \sigma_1 \cdot \ldots \cdot \sigma_n, \langle \sigma_1, p_1 \rangle \in p(\sigma), \forall\, 1 \le i < n\ [\langle \sigma_{i+1}, p_{i+1} \rangle \in p_i(\sigma_i)], \text{ and } p_n = p_o,$$

(ii) ω is a *infinite stream* in $p(\sigma)$ if there exist $\langle \sigma_i, p_i \rangle$, $1 \le i$, such that
$$\omega = \sigma_1 \cdot \sigma_2 \cdot \ldots, \langle \sigma_1, p_1 \rangle \in p(\sigma), \forall\, i \ge 1\ [\langle \sigma_{i+1}, p_{i+1} \rangle \in p_i(\sigma_i)],$$

(iii) ω is a *deadlocking stream* in $p(\sigma)$ if there exist $\langle \sigma_i, p_i \rangle$, $1 \le i \le n$, such that
$$\omega = \sigma_1 \cdot \ldots \cdot \sigma_n \cdot \partial, \langle \sigma_1, p_1 \rangle \in p(\sigma), \forall\, 1 \le i < n\ [\langle \sigma_{i+1}, p_{i+1} \rangle \in p_i(\sigma_i)], p_n \ne p_o,$$
and $p_n(\sigma_n) \cap (St \times \overline{P}) = \emptyset$.

Now we define a function $abstr : \overline{P} \to P$ by:

$$abstr(p_o) = \lambda\sigma.\{\tau\},$$
$$abstr(p) = \lambda\sigma.\ \{\omega : \omega \text{ is a stream in } p(\sigma)\},$$

for $p \ne p_o$, and τ being the empty sequence.

Theorem (Correctness)

$$O' = abstr \cdot \mathcal{D},$$

where $O' : \mathcal{P}(At) \to P$ is given by: $O'[G] = O_1[\{(\nu(\emptyset, T); G)\}]$.

To prove this theorem we need to characterize the function O' as the fixed point of a suitable contraction, and to show that also $abstr \cdot \mathcal{D}$ is a fixed point of this contraction. Then, Banach's theorem implies that $O' = abstr \cdot \mathcal{D}$.

6. Conclusions and future work

Formal definitions of object-oriented computing can provide a clear specification of the more relevant mechanisms of this paradigm and establish a more solid basis for the design of object-oriented languages. This is particularly important for parallel programming. In this sense, we have shown how the complete metric spaces can be used to formally define a parallel object-oriented logic language, $L^2 \| O^2$, which incorporates an intra-objects parallelism, and an asynchronous communication model.

We are interested in the relation of the semantics presented here, and the declarative semantics defined as the least fixpoint of an immediate consequences operator [Pimentel and Troya 92], by making use of an extended notion of Herbrand base and interpretations, enriched with variables and with annotations.

6. References

Agha, G. 1986. Actors: A Model of Concurrent Computation in Distributed Systems. MIT Press.

America, P.H.M., de Bakker, J.W., Kok, J.N. and Rutten, J.J.M.M. 1986. A denotational semantics of a parallel object-oriented language, Technical Report, CS-R8626, Centre for Mathematics and Computer Science, Amsterdam.

America, P.H.M. and Rutten, J.J.M.M. 1988. "Solving reflexive domain equations in a category of complete metric spaces", in M. Main, A. Melton, M. Mislove and D. Schmidt (eds), Proc. of Third Workdhop on Mathematical Foundations of Programming Languages Semantics, LNCS 298, Springer-Verlag, pp. 254-288.

America, P.H.M. and Rutten, J.J.M.M. 1989. "A Parallel Object-Oriented Language: Design and Semantic Foundations", in J.W. de Bakker (ed), Languages for Parallel Architectures. Design, Semantics, Implementation Models. Wiley, pp. 1-49.

Boer, F.S., Kok, J.N., Palamidessi, C. and Rutten, J. 1989. "Semantic models for a version of PARLOG", in G. Levi y M. Martelli (eds), Proc.of Sixth Int. Conf. on Logic Programing, MIT Press, pp. 621-635.

Cook, W and Palsberg, J. 1989. "A denotational semantics of inheritance and its correcteness", in N. Meyrowitz (ed), Proc. OOPSLA'89. SIGPLAN Notices, vol. 24, nº 10, ACM Press/Addison-Wesley, pp. 433-443.

Clark, K. and Gregory, S. 1986. "PARLOG: Parallel Programming in Logic", in ACM Transactions on Programming Languages and Systems, vol. 8, 1, pp. 1-49.

Davison, A. 1989. Polka: A Parlog Object-Oriented Language. PhD. thesis. Univ. of London.

Kahn, K., Tribble, E.D., Miller, M.S. and Bobrow, D. 1987. "Vulcan: Logical Concurrent Objects", in E. Shapiro (ed). Concurrent Prolog: Collected Papers, vol. 2, MIT Press, Cambridge (Mass), pp. 274-303.

Ohki, M., Takeuchi, A. and Furukawa, K. 1987. "An Object-oriented Programming Language Based on the Parallel Logic Programming Language KL1", in Proc. of the Fourth Int. Conf. on Logic Programming, MIT Press, pp. 894-909.

Pimentel, E. and Troya, J.M. 1991. "A Concurrent Object Oriented Logic Language", in Atti del Sesto Convegno sulla Programmazione Logica. Pisa. pp. 227-240.

Pimentel, E. and Troya, J.M. 1992. "$L^2||O^2$: Operational and Declarative Semantics", in Proc. of ALPUK'92. Springer-Verlag.

Shapiro, E. 1983. "A subset of Concurrent Prolog and its interpreter". Technical Report, TR-003. ICOT, Tokyo.

Shapiro, E. 1989. "The Family of Concurrent Logic Programming Languages", in ACM Computing Surveys, vol. 21. nº3. ACM. pp. 413-510.

Shapiro, E. and Takeuchi, A. 1983. "Object Oriented Programming in Concurrent Prolog", in New Generation Computing, 1. pp. 25-48.

Ueda, K. 1985. "Guarded Horn Clauses". Technical Report, TR-103. ICOT, Institute for New Generation Computer Technology, Tokyo.

Yelland, P.M. 1989 "First Steps Towards Fully Abstract Semantics for Object Oriented Languages", in Proc. of the Third European Conf. on Object-Oriented Prog. Cambridge Univ. Press.

Using State Variables for the Specification and Verification of TCSP Processes

Luis M. Alonso

Departamento de Lenguajes y Sistemas Informáticos

Universidad del Pais Vasco

E-20080 San Sebastian, Spain

e-mail: alonso@si.ehu.es

R. Peña Mari

Departamento de Informática

Universidad Complutense de Madrid

E-28.040 Madrid, Spain

e-mail: ricardo@mat.ucm.es

Abstract

A technique for the specification of TCSP processes based upon the concept of states and state variables is presented. It is shown how safety and liveness properties can be proved for processes specified in this way. Parallel composition of specifications is defined, preserving the failures semantics. A technique related to bisimulations is proposed to prove refinements correct. The technique is extended to handle the concealment of events in the implementing process.

1 Introduction

In [3] a technique for the specification and verification of concurrent systems was presented. There, processes were considered to be objects in the *failures model* or *TCSP* [2]. A process specification was given by a family $(\xi_t)_{t \in \mathcal{I}}$ of mutually recursive equations. The index $\mathcal{I}$ of this family was the set of all valid traces, defined by means of partial abstract types. For every trace t, the equation ξ_t was a TCSP term with a fixed syntactic structure. In a sense, the trace of a process was considered as defining its state. It is clear that one can consider other abstract types for states, much in the same way as many models are eligible for the algebraic specification of traces. In this paper, we present another approach to TCSP process specification, more amenable in our opinion for proving properties. Now *state variables* are used to define the possible states of processes. The semantics of process specifications is given in terms of *acceptance automata,* a particular case of labelled transition systems [1].

The organization of the paper is as follows. Section 2 summarizes the concepts referring to acceptance automata that will be used in the rest of the paper. In Section 3 we introduce the concept of *process specification with state variables.* Section 4 is dedicated to explain how safety properties and some liveness properties of a process, can be proved on process specifications. In Section 5 we define the parallel composition of process specifications. In Section 6 we characterize the notion of refinement of a process specification by another. Finally, section 7 provides a review of tha main proposals and results achieved in the paper.

2   Acceptance Automata

Full details of acceptance automata might be found in [1]. In this section we include the kernel ideas for the purposes of this paper. Roughly speaking, an acceptance automaton is a labelled transition system plus a *menu relation* showing the sets of events that the process might be willing to engage in for every state. This relation is used to represent the internal non-determinism in the system. After performing some sequence of actions, the process reaches some state; in this state it is allowed to chose one out of several sets of events, called *menus.* Then it will engage in any one of those events, as decided by its environment, so going on to some next state. This is formally expressed in the following definition.

Definition 1 An *acceptance automaton* is given by a tuple $\mathcal{A} = (\mathcal{L}, \Sigma, i, \mathcal{M}, \longrightarrow)$, where:

- $\mathcal{L}$ is a non-empty *alphabet* of events

- Σ is a set of states

- $i \in \Sigma$ is *the* initial state

- $\mathcal{M} \subseteq \Sigma \times \mathcal{P}(\mathcal{L})$ is a *menu relation* that will be denoted $m \in \mathcal{M}(\sigma)$

- $\longrightarrow \subseteq \Sigma \times \mathcal{L} \times \Sigma$ is a *transition relation* that will be denoted $\sigma \xrightarrow{e} \sigma'$

$\mathcal{M}$ and $\longrightarrow$ shall be defined so that:

- $\mathcal{M}$ is total in its domain, i. e. : $\forall \sigma \in \Sigma. \exists m \in \mathcal{P}(\mathcal{L}).m \in \mathcal{M}(\sigma)$

- $\forall \sigma \in \Sigma. \forall m \in \mathcal{M}(\sigma). \forall e \in \mathcal{L}.e \in m \Rightarrow (\exists \sigma' \in \Sigma. \sigma \xrightarrow{e} \sigma')$

- $\forall \sigma, \sigma' \in \Sigma. \forall e \in \mathcal{L}. \sigma \xrightarrow{e} \sigma' \Rightarrow (\exists m \in \mathcal{M}(\sigma).e \in m)$

We say that an acceptance automata is *unambiguous* if it there is a mapping from traces to states. It is *saturated* if the family of menus in every state is saturated, i. e. :

$$\forall m', m'' \in \mathcal{M}(\sigma). \forall m \in \mathcal{P}(\mathcal{L}).m' \subseteq m \subseteq m'' \Rightarrow m \in \mathcal{M}(\sigma)$$

We use the term *standard acceptance automata* when referring to unambiguous, saturated acceptance automata, without non-reachable or junk states. In [1] the failures semantics $[\![\mathcal{A}]\!]$ and operators on acceptance automata are defined. The more general form of definition 1 is needed to define the parallel composition and hiding operators. Since the resulting process might be divergent and acceptance automata do not model divergent processes, hiding is defined as a partial operator. For the purposes of this paper, only the notion of divergence free automata is needed.

Definition 2 Given an acceptance automaton $\mathcal{A} = (\mathcal{L}, \Sigma, i, \mathcal{M}, \longrightarrow)$, and a set of events $\mathcal{L}_h \subseteq \mathcal{L}$, we say that $\mathcal{A}$ is *divergence free* with respect to $\mathcal{L}_h$, if the following condition holds:

$$\forall s \in traces(\mathcal{A}).\exists n \in N.\forall t \in \mathcal{L}_h^*.s\,{}^\frown t \in traces(\mathcal{A}) \Rightarrow \sharp t \le n$$

where $traces(\mathcal{A})$ denotes the set of event sequences corresponding to possible executions from the initial state.

With the following facts, the refinement relation among TCSP processes is characterized in terms of acceptance automata. To this end, we suppose given standard acceptance automata

$$
\begin{aligned}
SPEC &= (\mathcal{L}_{spec}, \Sigma_{spec}, i_{spec}, \mathcal{M}_{spec}, \longrightarrow_{spec}) \\
IMP &= (\mathcal{L}_{imp}, \Sigma_{imp}, i_{imp}, \mathcal{M}_{imp}, \longrightarrow_{imp})
\end{aligned}
$$

Fact 3 Let $SPEC$ and IMP standard acceptance automata, with $\mathcal{L}_{spec} = \mathcal{L}_{imp}$, $[\![IMP]\!]$ is a refinement of $[\![SPEC]\!]$ iff there exists a relation $\Phi \subseteq \Sigma_{imp} \times \Sigma_{spec}$ satisfying:

1. $(i_{imp}, i_{spec}) \in \Phi$

2. $\forall (\sigma_{imp}, \sigma_{spec}) \in \Phi.\forall m \in \mathcal{M}_{imp}(\sigma_{imp}).m \in \mathcal{M}_{spec}(\sigma_{spec})$

3. $\forall (\sigma_{imp}, \sigma_{spec}) \in \Phi.\forall \sigma_{spec} \xrightarrow{e}_{spec} \sigma'_{spec}.\forall \sigma_{imp} \xrightarrow{e}_{imp} \sigma'_{imp}.(\sigma'_{imp}, \sigma'_{spec}) \in \Phi$

We shall use the term *refinement relation* when referring to Φ.

The following fact relates a given acceptance automaton IMP with any acceptance automaton $SPEC$, such that $\mathcal{L}_{spec} = \mathcal{L}_{imp} - \mathcal{L}_h$ and:

$$[\![SPEC]\!] \sqsubseteq [\![IMP]\!]\backslash\mathcal{L}_h$$

Fact 4 Let $SPEC$ and IMP standard acceptance automata, with $\mathcal{L}_{spec} = \mathcal{L}_{imp} - \mathcal{L}_h$. Provided that IMP is divergence free with respect to $\mathcal{L}_h$, then $[\![IMP]\!]\backslash\mathcal{L}_h$ is a refinement of $[\![SPEC]\!]$ iff there is a relation $\Phi \subseteq \Sigma_{imp} \times \Sigma_{spec}$ satisfying:

1. $(i_{imp}, i_{spec}) \in \Phi$

2. $\forall (\sigma_{imp}, \sigma_{spec}) \in \Phi.\forall m \in \mathcal{M}_{imp}(\sigma_{imp}).m - \mathcal{L}_h \subseteq next(\sigma_{spec})$

3. $\forall(\sigma_{imp}, \sigma_{spec}) \in \Phi. \forall m \in \mathcal{M}_{imp}(\sigma_{imp}).(m \cap \mathcal{L}_h = \emptyset) \Rightarrow m \in \mathcal{M}_{spec}(\sigma_{spec})$

4. $\forall(\sigma_{imp}, \sigma_{spec}) \in \Phi. \forall e \in \mathcal{L}_{spec}. \forall \sigma_{spec} \xrightarrow{e}_{spec} \sigma'_{spec}. \forall \sigma_{imp} \xrightarrow{e}_{imp} \sigma'_{imp}.$

$$(\sigma'_{imp}, \sigma'_{spec}) \in \Phi$$

5. $\forall(\sigma_{imp}, \sigma_{spec}) \in \Phi. \forall \sigma'_{imp} \in \Sigma_{imp}. \forall e \in \mathcal{L}_h. \sigma_{imp} \xrightarrow{e}_{imp} \sigma'_{imp} \Rightarrow$

$$(\sigma'_{imp}, \sigma_{spec}) \in \Phi$$

where

$$next(\sigma_{spec}) \triangleq \bigcup_{m \in \mathcal{M}(\sigma_{spec})} m$$

We shall use the term *abstraction relation* when referring to Φ.

3 Process specification using state variables

In this section we present a formalism for describing non-divergent TCSP processes. Let $\mathcal{A}$ be an acceptance automaton representing the non-divergent process $\mathbb{P}$. We will use a tuple $x_1 \ldots x_n$ of *state variables* to represent the set of states Σ. With an appropiate choice of state variables, any state $\sigma \in \Sigma$ may be seen as an assignment of values to state variables. Likewise, the transition relation may be described giving an expression $E_{(e,x)}$ for every pair of event e and state variable x. Finally, the menu relation $\mathcal{M}$ is described with a set of menu names $\mathbf{N} = \{n_1 \ldots n_k\}$, and a boolean expression $B_{(e,n)}$ defined for every pair of menu name n and every event e. For any state $\sigma \in \Sigma$, let m_n be the set of those events e such that the value of $B_{(e,n)}$ is true in σ. Then, in $\mathcal{M}(\sigma)$ we simply have all those sets m_n, for $n \in \mathbf{N}$. This is formally expressed in the following definition:

Definition 5 A *process specification using state variables*, in short *process specification*, is given by a tuple $(\mathcal{L}, \mathcal{V}, \sigma_0, \mathbf{T}, \mathbf{N}, \mathbf{M})$ where:

- $\mathcal{L}$ is a non-empty *alphabet* of events

- $\mathcal{V} = \{x_1 \ldots x_n\}$ is a finite set of typed variables, called *state variables*

- σ_0, is the *initial assignment*,

- $\mathbf{T}$ is a $\mathcal{L}$-indexed family of *transition rules*, $(\mathbf{T}_e)_{e \in \mathcal{L}}$. A transition rule $\mathbf{T}_e$ associates to every state variable x a properly formed expression, denoted $E_e(x)$, with free variables in $\mathcal{V}$

- $\mathbf{N}$ is a non-empty set of *menu names*

- $\mathcal{M}$ is a $\mathcal{L} \times \mathbf{N}$-indexed family of boolean expressions with free variables in $\mathcal{V}$. We will use the term *menu rule* when referring to such expressions.

Let us now introduce some terminology and notation that will be used hereafter. Given a set of state variables $\mathcal{V} = \{x_1, \ldots, x_n\}$, we will denote by $\Sigma(\mathcal{V})$ the set of all possible assignments of values to variables in $\mathcal{V}$. If it is made clear by the context, we will simply write Σ. Let $\sigma \in \Sigma(\mathcal{V})$ and let $E(\mathcal{V})$ be an expression with free variables in $\mathcal{V}$. We will denote by $\overline{\sigma}(E(\mathcal{V}))$, in short $\overline{\sigma}(E)$, the evaluation of the expression E after assigning values to variables by σ. Let $\mathbf{T}_e = \{E_1 \ldots E_n\}$ be a transition rule, we will denote by $\mathbf{T}_e \circ \sigma$ the following assignment:

$$\mathbf{T}_e \circ \sigma = \{x_i \leftarrow \overline{\sigma}(E_i), x_i \in \mathcal{V}\}$$

Last, given a predicate $\mathcal{P}$ with free variables in $\mathcal{V}$, we will denote by $\mathbf{T}_e(\mathcal{P})$ the predicate obtained by substituting $E_e(x_i)$ for every occurence of variable x_i in $\mathcal{P}$.

We shall use some syntactic sugar when writing process specifications, avoiding the definition of transition rules for those state variables that remain unchanged.

Example 6 A *Flag* is capable of engage sequentially in two events *set*, and *reset*:

```
process Flag
    alphabet set, reset
    menu names default
    state variables ok : bool := true
    transition rules
        on set  ⇒ ok := false
        on reset ⇒ ok := true
    menu rules
        when ok then set in default
        when ¬ok then reset in default
end process Flag
```

Example 7 A *Non-deterministic counter* may be incremented or decremented, whenever it is positive, but in this case it may reject further incrementing, so that the only possible action could be decrementing the counter:

```
process Counter⊥
    alphabet incr, decr
    menu names Stop, noStop
    state variables n : nat := 0
    transition rules
        on incr ⇒ n := n + 1
        on decr ⇒ n := n - 1
    menu rules
        when n = 0 then incr in Stop
        when true then incr in noStop
        when n > 0 then decr in Stop, noStop
end process Counter⊥
```

We end this section with the definition of $[\![SP]\!]$, the failures semantics of a process specification $SP = (\mathcal{L}, \mathcal{V}, \sigma_0, \mathbf{T}, \mathbf{N}, \mathbf{M})$.

Definition 8 The *acceptance automaton defined by* SP, denoted $\mathcal{A}(SP)$, is the tuple $\mathcal{A} = (\mathcal{L}, \Sigma, i, \mathcal{M}, \longrightarrow)$ where:

- Σ, the set of states, is the set of assignments $\Sigma(\mathcal{V})$

- i, the initial state, is the initial assignment σ_0

- $\mathcal{M} \subseteq \Sigma \times \mathcal{P}(\mathcal{L})$, the menu relation, is the smallest relation satisfying:

$$\forall n \in \mathbf{N}.\forall \sigma \in \Sigma.\exists m \in \mathcal{M}(\sigma).\forall e \in \mathcal{L}.\overline{\sigma}(B_{(e,n)}) = true \Leftrightarrow e \in m$$

- $\longrightarrow \subseteq \Sigma \times \mathcal{L} \times \Sigma$, the transition relation, is the smallest relation satisfying:

$$\forall \sigma \in \Sigma.\forall e \in \mathcal{L}.\sigma \xrightarrow{e} \sigma' \Leftrightarrow (\exists n \in \mathbf{N}.\overline{\sigma}(B_{(e,n)}) = true)$$

where $\sigma' = \mathbf{T}_e \circ \sigma$

4 Proving properties of process specifications

It is not a good practice trying to write out directly the specification of a process with state variables. A more advisable approach would start with the statement of the properties that the behaviour of the process should meet. Once it has been proved that the behaviour described by a specification exhibits some desired characteristic, it can be taken for granted that any valid implementation, say a network of processes, will also exhibit that property. This is a very valuable fact from a methodological point of view, since it allows us to discuss about the desired properties of the system at an abstract level.

It is generally admitted the existence of two kinds of properties, concerning the behaviour of a concurrent system:

- *safety properties*, stating that nothing bad ever happens in the system,

- *liveness properties*, stating that something good will eventually happen in the system.

In the failures model, safety properties take the form of a predicate over the process traces. On the other hand, it is a well known fact that only a restricted class of liveness properties can be expressed and reasoned upon in this model. For instance, to prove that *at least one* of the events in the set $\{e_1 \ldots e_k\}$ will be offered by process $\mathbb{P}$, after traces satisfying predicate $P(tr)$, the following predicate $S(tr, ref)$ must hold:

$$S(tr, ref) \triangleq P(tr) \Rightarrow \{e_1 \ldots e_k\} \not\subseteq ref$$

for any $(tr, ref) \in \mathbb{P}$.

We will discuss now the analysis of properties when dealing with state variables. To prove a safety property it must be shown that it holds for all values of state variables corresponding to legal traces of the process. The assignments corresponding to reachable states must then be properly characterized. This motivates our following definition.

Definition 9 A predicate *Inv*, with free variables in $\mathcal{V}$, is a *SP*-invariant if it meets the following conditions:

- $\overline{\sigma}_0(Inv) = true$

- $G_e \wedge Inv \Rightarrow \mathbf{T}_e(Inv)$, holds for all $e \in \mathcal{L}$.

where:
$$G_e \triangleq \exists n \in \mathbf{N}.B_{(e,n)}$$

is the *guard* of event e.

The proof of any safety property *Safe* of a process specification *SP* reduces to prove that the following implication holds universally:

$$Inv \Rightarrow Safe$$

for some *SP*-invariant *Inv*.

It is clear that any *SP*-invariant is also a safety property, although the opposite is not valid in general. We may conclude that, in order to prove some safety property *Safe*, we will first try to show that it is an invariant in the sense of definition 9. This will be the case in many problems but if it were not so, *Safe* shall be strenghten in order to carry out its proof. Our experience shows that this strenghtening process is simple.

To prove *deadlock freedom* in a given specification, we have to test whether all the menu rules can be falsified for some menu name. From the preceding arguments, it is clear that what has to be shown is that:

$$Inv_{SP} \Rightarrow \forall n \in \mathbf{N}.\exists e \in \mathcal{L}.B_{(e,n)}$$

for some *SP*-invariant *Inv*. Likewise, to prove that some of the events in the set $\{e_1 \ldots e_k\}$ will be offered in those states satisfying predicate $\mathcal{P}$, the following condition must hold:

$$Inv_{SP} \wedge \mathcal{P} \Rightarrow \forall n \in \mathbf{N}.B_{(e_1,n)} \vee \ldots \vee B_{(e_k,n)}$$

The simplicity of the translation of both safety and liveness properties from the traces domain to that of state variables suggests that process specifications be written according to the following steps. First, establish the family of state variables $\mathcal{V}$ to be used; in this way the relevant issues in the evolution of the process are fixed. Then, establish the guards G_e, for every event defining when every event *could* be offered. Last, define which are the *liveness requirements* for the process, this is to say, define when an event taken from a set of events *should* be offered. For the vast majority of practical situations, liveness requirements are suitably formulated by predicates of the form:

$$P(\mathcal{V}) \Rightarrow M(\mathcal{V})$$

where $P(\mathcal{V})$ denotes a predicate with free variables in $\mathcal{V}$, and $M(\mathcal{V})$, denotes an expression, also with free variables in $\mathcal{V}$, whose value is a set of events. A liveness requirement of this form is satisfied by a process specification SP if:

$$Inv_{SP} \wedge \mathcal{P} \Rightarrow \forall n \in \mathbf{N}. \exists e \in M.B_{(e,n)}$$

holds, for some SP-Invariant Inv_{SP}. Once the liveness requirements have been defined, the set of menu names and the menu rules are easily obtained. The set of menu names must obviously be chosen to accomodate the greatest number of menus that could be offered by the system in any state.

5   Parallel composition of process specifications

In this section, we define the parallel composition SP of specifications with state variables SP_1 and SP_2. Following TCSP, events common to SP_1 and SP_2 are synchronized in the whole system, i.e. a common event is performed by the system if that event is simultaneously performed by the subsystems. We shall consider that SP_1 and SP_2 do not share any state variable, using renaming of variables when necessary.

In view of the definition of parallel composition for acceptance automata, every state variable in SP_1 and SP_2 is a state variable in SP. Neglecting the synchronization aspects, if we consider states σ_1, with menus m_1, m_1', in $\mathcal{A}(SP_1)$, σ_2, with menus m_2, m_2', in $\mathcal{A}(SP_2)$, and (σ_1, σ_2) in $\mathcal{A}(SP_1)\|\mathcal{A}(SP_2)$, the menus offered in this state, according to the definition of $\mathcal{A}(SP_1)\|\mathcal{A}(SP_2)$ are: $m_1 \cup m_2, m_1' \cup m_2, m_1' \cup m_2, m_1' \cup m_2'$. There are four possible choices for SP, so the set of menu names in SP may be taken to be the cartesian product of menu names in SP_1 and SP_2.

Definition 10 Given two process specifications SP_1 and SP_2 with disjoint sets of state variables, the *parallel composition* of SP_1 and SP_2, denoted by $SP_1\|SP_2$, has $\mathcal{L}_1 \cap \mathcal{L}_2$ as synchronization alphabet and is defined as follows:

- $\mathcal{L} = \mathcal{L}_1 \cup \mathcal{L}_2$

- $\mathcal{V} = \mathcal{V}_1 \cup \mathcal{V}_2$

- $\sigma_0 = \sigma_{0_1} \cup \sigma_{0_2}$

- $\mathbf{T}$ is the $\mathcal{L}$-indexed family of transition rules, defined by:

$$E_e(x) \triangleq \begin{cases} E_{1_e}(x) & \text{if } e \in \mathcal{L}_1 \wedge x \in \mathcal{V}_1 \\ E_{2_e}(x) & \text{if } e \in \mathcal{L}_2 \wedge x \in \mathcal{V}_2 \\ x & \text{if } (e \notin \mathcal{L}_1 \wedge x \in \mathcal{V}_1) \vee (e \notin \mathcal{L}_2 \wedge x \in \mathcal{V}_2) \end{cases}$$

- $N = N_1 \times N_2$

- M is a $\mathcal{L} \times$ N-indexed family of boolean expressions defined by:

$$B_{e,(n,m)} \triangleq \begin{cases} B_{1_{(e,n)}} & \text{if } e \in \mathcal{L}_1 \wedge e \notin \mathcal{L}_2 \\ B_{2_{(e,m)}} & \text{if } e \in \mathcal{L}_2 \wedge e \notin \mathcal{L}_1 \\ B_{1_{(e,n)}} \wedge B_{2_{(e,m)}} & \text{if } e \in \mathcal{L}_1 \wedge e \in \mathcal{L}_2 \end{cases}$$

The discussion in the begining of the section shows that this definition preserves failures semantics:

Proposition 11

$$\mathcal{A}(SP_1 \| SP_2) = \mathcal{A}(SP_1) \| \mathcal{A}(SP_2)$$

6 Refinements

The initial specification of the intended system should be as non-deterministic as possible. For instance, in example 7 we do not impose any lower or upper bound on the size of the counter: this implies that any counter suffices for our purposes. Definition 8 along with the notion of refinement defined in TCSP, allows us to state this concept for specifications with state variables. In the rest of this section, we suppose given process specifications

$$\begin{aligned} SPEC &= (\mathcal{L}_{spec}, \mathcal{V}_{spec}, \sigma_{0spec}, \mathbf{T}_{spec}, \mathbf{N}_{spec}, \mathbf{M}_{spec}) \\ IMP &= (\mathcal{L}_{imp}, \mathcal{V}_{imp}, \sigma_{0imp}, \mathbf{T}_{imp}, \mathbf{N}_{imp}, \mathbf{M}_{imp}) \end{aligned}$$

with different sets of state variables.

Definition 12 Given specifications with state variables $SPEC$ and IMP, both having the same alphabet, we say that IMP is a *refinement of $SPEC$*, denoted by $SPEC \sqsubseteq IMP$, if $\mathcal{A}(SPEC) \sqsubseteq \mathcal{A}(IMP)$.

Using fact 3 we can also develop proofs by comparing the menus offered in equivalent states, i.e. in states reached after the same trace. As it is shown in fact 3, verifying correctness in this way forces us to establish some *refinement relation* between states. This relation must be preserved by transitions and takes the form of a predicate with free variables in $\mathcal{V}_{spec}$ and $\mathcal{V}_{imp}$. Now, we formalize this, proposing a verification technique to prove correctness of refinements.

Definition 13 Given process specifications $SPEC$ and IMP, and given predicates Inv_{SPEC} and Inv_{IMP}, which are $SPEC$-invariant and IMP-invariant respectively, a predicate $\mathcal{P}$, with free variables in $\mathcal{V}_{spec} \cup \mathcal{V}_{imp}$, is a *refinement relation* with respect to $SPEC$ and IMP if:

- $\sigma_0(\mathcal{P}) = true$, with $\sigma_0 = \sigma_{0spec} \cup \sigma_{0imp}$

- the following universally quantified implication holds:

$$Inv_{SPEC} \wedge Inv_{IMP} \wedge G_{spec_e} \wedge G_{imp_e} \wedge \mathcal{P} \Rightarrow \mathbf{T}_e(\mathcal{P})$$

where $e \in \mathcal{L}$ and $\mathbf{T}_e = \mathbf{T}_{spec_e} \cup \mathbf{T}_{imp_e}$.

Proposition 14 Given process specifications $SPEC$ and IMP, $[\![IMP]\!]$ is a refinement of $[\![SPEC]\!]$ if there are predicates Inv_{SPEC} and Inv_{IMP}, which are $SPEC$-invariant and IMP-invariant respectively, and a predicate $\mathcal{P}$ which is a refinement relation with respect to $SPEC$ and IMP, such that whenever the conjunction

$$Inv_{SPEC} \wedge Inv_{IMP} \wedge \mathcal{P}$$

holds, so do the following conditions, for every event $e \in \mathcal{L}$:

- **safety** $\forall e \in \mathcal{L}.G_{imp_e} \Rightarrow G_{spec_e}$
- **liveness** $\forall n \in \mathbf{N}_{imp}.\exists m \in \mathbf{N}_{spec}.\forall e \in \mathcal{L}.B_{spec_{(e,m)}} \Rightarrow B_{imp_{(e,n)}}$

This proposition may be justified observing that definition 13 ensures points 1 and 3 in fact 3. Also, point 2 is given by the two clauses in the proposition. Although fact 3 is a necessary and sufficient condition, proposition 14 provides only a sufficient condition because, in general, the desired refinement relation may not be expressed in first order logic. The reader can use this proposition to prove that process $Flag$, as defined in example 6, is a refinement of process $Counter_1$ defined in example 7.

When refining some specification by another, we introduce new state variables, or define a more deterministic system more amenable for system implementation but the alphabet of the system remains to be the same. After some refinement steps of this kind, we will reach to the point where the task of decomposing the system into communicating subsystems has to be done. Then we shall prove that, abstracting from internal activities, the external behaviour is correct. Divergence may appear if we abstract internal communication in a network when there is the possibility for an infinite chattering to occur. Then, when considering a network of processes, it must be shown that divergence can not happen, before we proceed to show the correctness of the external activity. The technique to show divergence freedom is established now:

Definition 15 Given a process specification SP, with alphabet $\mathcal{L} \cup \mathcal{L}_h$, SP is *divergence free* with respect to $\mathcal{L}_h$ if $\mathcal{A}(SP)$ is divergence free with respect to $\mathcal{L}_h$.

Proposition 16 Given a process specification SP, with alphabet $\mathcal{L} \cup \mathcal{L}_h$, SP is *divergence free* with respect to $\mathcal{L}_h$ if there exist a SP-invariant Inv, and an integer expression Ω, with free variables in $\mathcal{V}$, satisfying:

$$\forall v_i \in \mathcal{D}_i.Inv \quad \Rightarrow \quad \Omega \geq 0$$
$$\forall s \in \mathcal{L}_h.Inv \wedge G_s \quad \Rightarrow \quad \mathbf{T}_s(\Omega) < \Omega$$

(This proposition follows directly from a similar result stated in [1] for acceptance automata.)

Once we have proved that *IMP* is divergence free with respect to the set of events $\mathcal{L}_h$ ($\mathcal{L}_{spec} = \mathcal{L}_{imp} - \mathcal{L}_h$,) we can use fact 4, to prove that the external behaviour agrees with that described by *SPEC*. In order to carry out this proof, some *abstraction relation* among states must first be established. Then, it must be shown that, for any values of state variables satisfying the abstraction relation, every external event offered by *IMP* may be offered by *SPEC*. Besides this, the set of events associated to every menu name in *IMP* must contain the set of events associated to some menu name in *SPEC*, in every stable state, i.e. in every state where no internal event is enabled. This leads us to the following definition and result:

Definition 17 Given process specifications *SPEC* and *IMP*, with $\mathcal{L}_{spec} = \mathcal{L}_{imp} - \mathcal{L}_h$, and given predicates Inv_{SPEC} and Inv_{IMP}, which are *SPEC*-invariant and *IMP*-invariant respectively, a predicate $\mathcal{P}$ with free variables in $\mathcal{V}_{spec} \cup \mathcal{V}_{imp}$, is an *abstraction relation* with respect to *SPEC*, *IMP* and $\mathcal{L}_h$ if:

- $\sigma_0(\mathcal{P}) = true$, with $\sigma_0 = \sigma_{0_{spec}} \cup \sigma_{0_{imp}}$

- The following universally quantified implication holds, for all $e \in \mathcal{L}$:

$$Inv_{SPEC} \wedge Inv_{IMP} \wedge G_{spec_e} \wedge G_{imp_e} \wedge \mathcal{P} \Rightarrow \mathbf{T}_e(\mathcal{P})$$

  where $\mathbf{T}_e = \mathbf{T}_{spec_e} \cup \mathbf{T}_{imp_e}$.

- The following universally quantified implication holds, for all $s \in \mathcal{L}_h$:

$$Inv_{SPEC} \wedge Inv_{IMP} \wedge G_{imp_s} \wedge \mathcal{P} \Rightarrow \mathbf{T}_{imp_s}(\mathcal{P})$$

Proposition 18 Given process specifications *SPEC* and *IMP*, with $\mathcal{L}_{spec} = \mathcal{L}_{imp} - \mathcal{L}_h$, $[\![SPEC]\!] \sqsubseteq [\![IMP]\!] \backslash \mathcal{L}_h$ if *IMP* is divergence free w.r.t. $\mathcal{L}_h$ and there are predicates *SPEC*-invariant, Inv_{SPEC}, *IMP*-invariant, Inv_{IMP}, and abstraction relation $\mathcal{P}$ with respect to *SPEC*, *IMP*, and $\mathcal{L}_h$, such that whenever the conjunction

$$Inv_{SPEC} \wedge Inv_{IMP} \wedge \mathcal{P}$$

holds so do the following conditions: $n \in \mathbf{N}_{imp}$:

- **Safety**
$$\forall e \in \mathcal{L}.G_{imp_e} \Rightarrow G_{spec_e}$$

- **Liveness**

$$(\forall s \in \mathcal{L}_h.B_{imp_{(s,n)}} = false) \Rightarrow (\exists m \in \mathbf{N}_{spec}.\forall e \in \mathcal{L}.B_{spec_{(e,m)}} \Rightarrow B_{imp_{(e,n)}})$$

  for every menu name $n \in \mathbf{N}_{imp}$.

The reader can use this proposition to prove that abstracting from internal communications, a network of two flags is divergence free and also that it is a refinement of the counter defined in example 7.

7 Conclusions

A technique for the specification and verification of communicating processes has been presented. It is based on the theory of the failures model, providing a systematic approach for writing specifications. The basic stages in the verification procedure are also standarized.

The approach to system specification is based upon the concept of state variables, which are used to mirror the relevant aspects in the history of the system. In order to handle system complexity, state variables are intoduced in a stepwise fashion, as we are getting closer to the description of the intended implementation. In the last stage of the design process, we deal with the specification of the subsystems used and so, the design process is re-started for the components of the system. Subsystem implementations are verified independently one of each other, establishing a hierarchical structure in the development process.

Verification techniques are based in first order logic, invariants, with respect to the occurrence of events, and well-founded orders. This has the practical advantage of being familiar to programmers, since they are widely known ideas used in sequential programming for the verification of loops. The authors have tried the approach proposed in this paper in more sophisticated examples. It has been applied to the specification of the most common and difficult synchronization problems, and also to the verification of several implementations by means of networks of processes. Although the complexity of concurrent systems can not be under-estimated, the experience gained is seen as very satisfactory, both for the expresiveness of the technique and for the complexity of the proofs. A remarkable fact is that, after every process in the system is described in a deterministic form, its translation to some suitable programming language, such as OCCAM, is immediate.

References

[1] L.M. Alonso and R. Pena. Acceptance Automata: A Framework for Specifying and Verifying TCSP Parallel Systems. In E.H.L. Aarts, J. van Leeuwen, and M. Rem, editors, *PARLE'91: Parallel Architectures and Languages Europe*, volume LNCS 506, pages 75–91. Springer-Verlag, 1991.

[2] C.A.R. Hoare. *Communicating Sequential Processes*. Prentice-Hall, London, 1985.

[3] R. Pena and L.M. Alonso. Specification and Verification of TCSP Systems by means of Partial Abstract Types. In E.H.L. Aarts, J. van Leeuwen, and M. Rem, editors, *TAPSOFT'89: Theory and Practice of Software Engineering*, volume LNCS 352, pages 328–244. Springer-Verlag, 1989.

A Parallel Reduction of Hamiltonian Cycle to Hamiltonian Path in Tournaments

E. Bampis, M. El Haddad, Y. Manoussakis and M. Santha*
L.R.I., Bât. 490,
Université de Paris-Sud (Orsay)
91405 Orsay Cedex, France

Abstract

We propose a parallel algorithm which reduces the problem of computing Hamiltonian cycles in tournaments to the problem of computing Hamiltonian paths. The running time of our algorithm is $O(\log n)$ using $O(n^2/\log n)$ processors on a CRCW PRAM, and $O(\log n \log \log n)$ on an EREW PRAM using $O(n^2/\log n \log \log n)$ processors. As a corollary, we obtain a new parallel algorithm for computing Hamiltonian cycles in tournaments. This algorithm can be implemented in time $O(\log n)$ using $O(n^2/\log n)$ processors in the CRCW model, and in time $O(\log^2 n)$ with $O(n^2/\log n \log \log n)$ processors in the EREW model.

Introduction. A *tournament* $T(V, A)$ is a directed graph with vertex set $V(T)$ and arc set $A(T)$ such that between each pair of vertices there is precisely one arc. Two well known results due respectively to Redei [8] and Camion [3], state that every tournament has a Hamiltonian path and that every strongly connected tournament has a Hamiltonian cycle.

The fastest sequential algorithm for finding Hamiltonian paths in tournaments is of complexity $O(n \log n)$. Algorithms of such complexity were obtained by Hell and Rosenfeld [6] and by Soroker [9]. Camion's standard proof [3] gives an obvious $O(n^3)$ sequential algorithm for finding Hamiltonian cycles in tournaments. Recently, Manoussakis [7] presented a new sequential algorithm of complexity $O(n^2)$ for this problem. This algorithm is optimal since, as it has been proved by Soroker in [9], there is no sequential algorithm solving the Hamiltonian cycle problem in tournaments in time less than $O(n^2)$.

The parallel complexity of these problems is also well studied. Bar-Noy and Naor [1] presented a parallel algorithm which uses sorting techniques for the Hamiltonian path problem in tournaments. The running time of their algorithm is $O(\log n)$ using $O(n)$ processors in the CRCW model, and therefore it is of optimal speed-up with respect the best sequential algorithm. Their algorithm

*Centre National de la Recherche Scientifique, URA 410, Université Paris-Sud Orsay, France.

can be implemented by generic techniques in an EREW PRAM in parallel time $O(\log^2 n)$ with $O(n)$ processors. For the Hamiltonian cycle problem in tournaments Soroker [10] has designed a parallel algorithm of running time $O(\log^2 n)$ using $O(n^2/\log n)$ processors in the EREW PRAM model.

In this paper we present a parallel algorithm which reduces the problem of computing Hamiltonian cycles in tournaments to the problem of computing Hamiltonian paths in the following sense: Given a Hamiltonian path in a tournament as input, the algorithm constructs a Hamiltonian cycle. The parallel running time of our algorithm is $O(\log n)$ using $O(n^2/\log n)$ processors in the CRCW model. We also give an implementation of the algorithm in time $O(\log n \log \log n)$ on an EREW PRAM using $O(n^2/\log n \log \log n)$ processors. Putting together the algorithm of Bar-Noy and Naor [1] for computing Hamiltonian paths and our reduction, we obtain a new parallel algorithm for finding Hamiltonian cycles in tournaments. The running time of this new algorithm is $O(\log n)$ using $O(n^2/\log n)$ processors in the CRCW model, and therefore it achieves an optimal speed-up with respect to the sequential complexity of the problem. It is faster than the algorithm of Soroker [10], but it uses a more powerful PRAM model. In the EREW model the algorithm runs in time $O(\log^2 n)$ and uses $O(n^2/\log n \log \log n)$ processors. Therefore it reduces the number of processors with a factor $O(\log \log n)$ with respect to Soroker's algorithm and also with respect to the generic transformation of our CRCW algorithm into an EREW one.

We say that a vertex x *dominates* vertex y in T if the arc (x, y) is in $A(T)$. By definition, *the merge* of two paths in a tournament is a path in which the relative order of the vertices in the original paths remains the same.

We describe now the key idea of the algorithm. Let $H = (x_1, x_2, ..., x_n)$ be the Hamiltonian path given as input. For each arc (x_i, x_j) we define x_i as the *source-coordinate* and x_j as the *destination-coordinate* of the arc. For the purpose of the algorithm we call an arc (x_i, x_j) *backward* if $j \le i - 2$. The algorithm is based on the following claim:

A Hamiltonian cycle exists in T if and only if there is a set S of backward arcs such that:

1. For each i and j, if (x_i, x_j) belongs to S, then for each $i' < i$ and $j' > j$ the arcs $(x_{i'}, x_j)$ and $(x_i, x_{j'})$ do not belong to S.

2. If we order the arcs of S decreasingly according to their source-coordinate, then the destination-coordinate of every arc is between the coordinates (or equal to the source-coordinate) of the next arc.

3. The source-coordinate of the first arc of the ordered set S is the vertex x_n of H, and the destination-coordinate of the last arc in S is x_1.

The algorithm first finds such a set S (if there is one). The properties of the set S imply that for every pair of consecutive arcs (x_i, x_j) and (x_k, x_l) of S, the arc (x_l, x_{i+1}) always exists. Using this fact, we can find a cycle C_1 and a path Q_1 covering together all the vertices of the tournament T. More precisely, Q_1

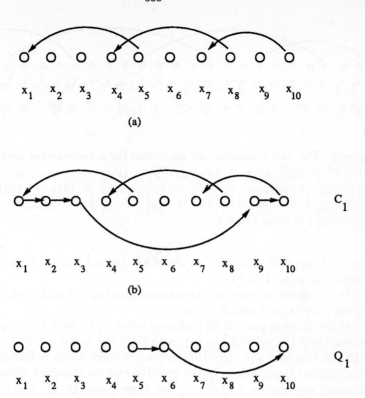

Figure 1: *We illustrate the method of finding the cycle C_1 and the path Q_1 for a tournament of 10 vertices. (a) The set $S = \{(x_{10}, x_7), (x_8, x_4), (x_5, x_1)\}$, (b) the cycle C_1, (c) the path Q_1.*

and C_1 have two common vertices z_1 and z_2, where $z_1 \neq z_2$. We illustrate the method of finding C_1 and Q_1 in the example of the figure 1. Finally, we merge Q_1 and the cycle C_1 and we obtain the desired Hamiltonian cycle.

The Algorithm.
Input: A tournament T on n vertices, and a Hamiltonian path $H = (x_1, x_2, ..., x_n)$ in T.
Output: A Hamiltonian cycle, if any, in T.
The algorithm consists of 6 steps.

(1) In parallel, for each vertex x_i, $3 \leq i \leq n$, we search the vertex with the smallest index j, if any, such that the backward arc (x_i, x_j) exists. Then we delete all backward arcs (x_i, x_r) for which $j < r$.

(2) For each vertex x_j, $1 \leq j \leq n - 2$, we determine in parallel the largest

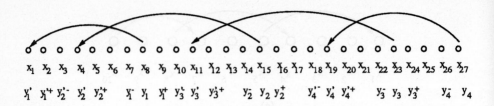

Figure 2: *The new notations are illustrated for a tournament with 27 vertices.*
Here, $P_1' = \{y_1'^+, y_2'^-\} = \{x_2, x_3\}, P_2' = \{y_2', \cdots, y_1\} = \{x_4, \cdots, x_8\}, P_3' = \{y_3', \cdots, y_2\} = \{x_{11}, \cdots, x_{15}\}, P_4' = \{y_4', \cdots, y_3\} = \{x_{19}, \cdots, x_{23}\}$ and $P_1 = \{y_1^+, \cdots, y_3'^-\} = \{x_9, x_{10}\}, P_2 = \{y_2^+, \cdots, y_4'^-\} = \{x_{16}, x_{17}, x_{18}\}, P_3 = \{y_3^+, \cdots, y_4^-\} = \{x_{24}, x_{25}, x_{26}\}.$

index i, if any, such that the backward arc (x_i, x_j) exists. Then we delete all backward arcs (x_r, x_j), for $r < i$.

(3) We delete in parallel all backward arcs (x_k, x_l) such that there exists a backward arc (x_i, x_j) with $k < i$ and $j < l$.

(4) We delete in parallel all backward arcs (x_r, x_s) such that there exists two backward arcs (x_i, x_j) and (x_k, x_l), with $l < s < j \leq k < r < i$.

(5) In this step the algorithm decides if there exists a Hamiltonian cycle in the original tournament. In the positive case we construct three linked lists containing respectively a cycle C_1 and three paths Q_1, Q_2 and Q_3 in the remaining graph. The paths Q_2 and Q_3 form a partition of C_1, that is they are disjoint, and their union is C_1. These paths will be used in the construction of the Hamiltonian cycle.

Let $S = \{(y_m, y_m'), (y_{m-1}, y_{m-1}'), (y_{m-2}, y_{m-2}'), \ldots, (y_1, y_1')\}$ be the set of the remaining backward arcs after Step 4, where y_i is an descendent of y_j for $i > j$ on the Hamiltonian path H.

Claim. *There exists a Hamiltonian cycle in T if and only if the following three conditions are satisfied:*

- $y_m = x_n$,

- $y_1' = x_1$,

- *for each i, $1 \leq i \leq m - 1$, we have $y_i \geq y_{i+1}'$.*

We will prove this claim when we justify the algorithm.

If one of these three conditions is not met then the algorithm declares that there is no Hamiltonian cycle in the tournament T. Otherwise let y_i^+ (respectively y_i^-) denote the successor (the predecessor) of y_i on H (see fig. 2). First we define two types of subpaths P_i and P_i' of H:
For $1 \leq i \leq m - 2$, let P_i be the segment of H from vertex y_i^+ to $y_{i+2}'^-$. Also, let P_{m-1} be the segment from vertex y_{m-1}^+ to y_m^-. For $2 \leq i \leq m$, we define P_i' to

be the segment of H from vertex y_i' to y_{i-1}. Finally let P_1' be the segment from vertex $y_1'^+$ to $y_2'^-$.

Now we define the cycle C_1 and the path Q_1. If m is even, then we set

$$C_1 = (y_m, P_m', P_{m-1}', \cdots, P_2', y_1', P_1', P_2, \cdots, P_{m-4}, P_{m-2}, y_m),$$

and

$$Q_1 = (y_1, P_1, P_3, P_5, \ldots, P_{m-1}, y_m).$$

If m is odd, then we set

$$C_1 = (y_m, P_m', P_{m-1}', \ldots, P_2', y_1', P_1', P_2, \ldots, P_{m-3}, P_{m-1}, y_m),$$

and

$$Q_1 = (y_1, P_1, P_3, P_5, \ldots, P_{m-2}, y_m).$$

It is easy to check that these sequences of vertices do indeed constitute a cycle or a path. Most of the necessary arcs exist trivially by definition. The only non trivial points are that the arc (y_i^-, y_i^+), for $2 \le i \le m - 1$, exists because otherwise the arc (y_i, y_i') would have been deleted in Step 3, and also the arc $(y_m'^-, y_m)$ exists because otherwise the arc (y_m, y_m') would have been deleted in Step 1.

C_1 and Q_1 together cover all the vertices of the tournament. Also, they have exactly two vertices in common, y_1 and y_m. We define Q_2 as the subpath of C_1 which goes from y_1 to y_m. The path Q_3 is defined as the rest of C_1. We create a successor relation for Q_1 and Q_2, and finally compute the rank of the elements in these lists. This is needed for the merging procedure of the final step.

(6) We compute Q_4, the merge of the paths Q_1 and Q_2 in the original tournament T. The paths Q_3 and Q_4 together form a Hamiltonian cycle in T.

Justification of the algorithm. The algorithm constructs a Hamiltonian cycle in Step 6 if and only if the three conditions of the Claim in Step 5 are satisfied. Clearly, when the algorithm finds a Hamiltonian cycle then such a cycle does exist in T since during the algorithm arcs were only deleted. Therefore its correctness follows from the only if part of the claim, which we prove now. If some of the conditions of Step 5 are not satisfied then the graph after Step 4 is not strongly connected. An easy analysis shows that the graph after Step 4 is strongly connected if and only if the original tournament is strongly connected. Therefore T is not strongly connected in this case and by the result of Camion it does not have a Hamiltonian cycle.

Implementation of the algorithm on a CRCW PRAM. We show how to implement the algorithm in time $O(\log n)$ on a CRCW PRAM using $O(n^2/\log n)$ processors. The algorithm will make repeated use of the following procedures which find the greatest (smallest) index among the non zero elements of a binary sequence.

Procedure MAXINDEX (MININDEX) (B):
Input: A binary sequence $B = b_1, b_2, \ldots, b_n$.
Output: The maximum (minimum) index k, $1 \le k \le n$, such that $b_k = 1$.

The procedure MAXINDEX was implemented by Bar-Noy and Naor [1] in time $O(1)$ with $O(n)$ processors in a CRCW PRAM.

We suppose that the tournament T is stored in the adjacency matrix M which respects the order of the vertices on the Hamiltonian path $H = (x_1, x_2, ..., x_n)$, that is the ith row and column correspond to the vertex x_i. In the first 4 steps of the algorithm we work only with the lower triangular part M' of M which corresponds to the backward arcs. For each i, $3 \leq i \leq n$, we denote by $j(i)$ the smallest index j, if any, such that the backward arc (x_i, x_j) exists. Similarly, for each j, $1 \leq j \leq n - 2$, let $i(j)$ denote the largest integer i, if any, such that the backward arc (x_i, x_j) exists after Step 1.

In Step 1, we use procedure MININDEX for each row i, in order to determine $j(i)$. This can be done in time $O(1)$ using $O(n^2)$ processors. The deletion of the arcs can also be done in constant time.

Step 2 is the same as Step 1, except that we use MAXINDEX instead of MININDEX. Notice that after Step 2, in each row i and each column j of M' there is at most one non zero element, respectively of index $j(i)$ and $i(j)$.

In Step 3, first we create in parallel for each k a binary sequence $A^k = a_1^k, ..., a_n^k$. By definition $a_{j(i)}^k = 1$ if $k < i$ and the arc $(x_i, x_{j(i)})$ exists. These sequences can be created in constant time with $O(n^2)$ processors. Then using the procedure MININDEX we determine in parallel for each k the smallest index (if any) $l(k)$ such that $a_{l(k)}^k = 1$. This can be done in time $O(1)$ using $O(n^2)$ processors. The arc $(x_k, x_{j(k)})$ will be deleted exactly when $l(k) < j(k)$, which can also be checked in constant time.

In Step 4, first we determine in parallel for each r the smallest index $j(i)$ (if any) such that $r < i$ and the arc $(x_i, x_{j(i)})$ exists. If $r > j(i)$ then we determine the maximum index $i(l)$ (if any) such that $l < j(r)$ and the arc $(x_{i(l)}, x_l)$ exists. All this can be done like in Step 3. The arc $(x_r, x_{j(r)})$ will be deleted exactly when $j(i) \leq i(l)$.

In Step 5, by previous techniques it can be decided in time $O(1)$ with $O(n^2)$ processors if the three conditions are satisfied. Now we define the successor relations SUC_1 and SUC_2 for the paths Q_1 and Q_2.

$$SUC_1(x_k) = \begin{cases} x_n & \text{if } i(k+1) = n, \\ x_{i(k+1)+1} & \text{if } i(k+1) \neq n \text{ and } (x_{i(k+1)}, x_{k+1}) \text{ exists}, \\ x_{k+1} & \text{otherwise}. \end{cases}$$

The definition of SUC_2 is identical except that $SUC_2(x_{i(1)}) = x_1$. These relations also can be computed in time $O(1)$ with $O(n^2)$ processors. Finally the rank of the elements can be computed in time $O(\log n)$ with $O(n)$ processors [11].

For Step 6 we can use the CRCW PRAM algorithm of Bar-Noy and Naor which computes in a tournament the merge of two paths of length $O(n)$ in time $O(\log \log n)$ with $O(n)$ processors.

Clearly all of these steps can also be implemented in time $O(\log n)$ using $O(n^2 / \log n)$ processors.

Implementation of the algorithm on an EREW PRAM. We now implement the algorithm on an EREW PRAM in time $O(\log n \log \log n)$ using

$O(n^2/\log n \log\log n)$ processors. For the implementation we use the following Simulation Principle between different PRAMs [4]: Any algorithm on a CRCW PRAM in time t using p processors can be simulated by an EREW PRAM in time $O(t \log p)$ with the same number of processors.

The list ranking problem in Step 5 can also be implemented on an EREW PRAM in time $O(\log n)$ with $O(n)$ processors [11]. The CRCW implementation of the merging in Step 6 gives rise by the Simulation Principle to an EREW implementation in time $O(\log n \log\log n)$ with $O(n)$ processors. Everything else in the CRCW implementation of the algorithm (in the first 5 steps) was computed in time $O(1)$ with $O(n^2)$ processors. In fact, this part of the algorithm consists of n independent, analoguous computations, each of which was implemented in time $O(1)$ with $O(n)$ processors in the CRCW model. We show now how these independent computations can be implemented on an EREW PRAM in time $O(\log n)$ with $O(n)$ processors, and that Brent's Principle [2] then can be applied to do the implementation also with only $O(n/\log n)$ processors. Hence the n independent computations can be done in time $O(\log n)$ with $O(n^2/\log n)$ processors, and therefore also in the claimed bounds.

The crucial part of these computations is the procedure MAXINDEX. The following EREW implementation computes this procedure in time $O(\log n)$ with $O(n)$ processors. For simplicity we suppose that number n of elements in the binary sequence B is a power of two, and we denote $\log n$ by l.

begin

for $i := 0$ **to** $n - 1$ **do in parallel**

$\qquad a_{0,i} := b_{i+1}$

for $i := 1$ **to** l **do**

$\qquad$ **for** $j := 0$ **to** $2^{l-i} - 1$ **do in parallel**

$\qquad\qquad a_{i,j} := a_{i-1,2j} \bigvee a_{i-1,2j+1}$

$\{$ *We have now for every i that if $a_{i,j}$ is the leftmost 1 among $a_{i,0}, \ldots, a_{i,2^{l-i}-1}$ then $a_{i-1,2j}$ or $a_{i-1,2j+1}$ is the leftmost 1 among $a_{i-1,0} \ldots a_{i-1,2^{l-i+1}-1}$.* $\}$

if $a_{l,0} = 0$ **then** all the entries in B are 0.

else

$\qquad k := 0$

$\qquad$ **for** $i := l - 1$ **downto** 0 **do**

$\qquad\qquad$ **if** $a_{i,2k} = 1$ **then** $k := 2k$

$\qquad\qquad$ **else** $k := 2k + 1$

end

This implementation uses $O(n)$ processors and time $O(\log n)$, and the total number of its primitive operations is $O(\sum_{i=1}^{\log n} 2^{\log n - i}) = O(n)$. Therefore Brent's principle can indeed be applied, and using careful processor allocation it can be executed in the same time with $O(n/\log n)$ processors.

Remark: After a slight modification, our algorithm works also in the case where T is *not connected*. In this case, for each connected component of T, we obtain a Hamiltonian cycle and so we have a collection of disjoint cycles covering the vertices of T. Also, this algorithm works in the case of *semi-complete digraphs*, i.e. digraphs without no non-adjacent vertices.

References

[1] A. Bar-Noy and J. Naor, *Sorting, minimal feedback sets, and Hamiltonian paths in tournaments*, SIAM J. Disc. Math Vol.3 No1 (1990), pp. 7-20.

[2] R. Brent, *The parallel evaluation of general arithmetic expressions*, J. ACM 21 (1974), pp. 201-206.

[3] P. Camion, *Chemins et circuits Hamiltoniens des graphes complets*, C.R. Acad. Sci. Paris (A) 249 (1959), pp. 2151-2152.

[4] R. Cole and U. Vishkin, *Approximate and exact parallel scheduling, part 1: the basic technique with applications to optimal parallel list ranking in logarithmic time*, SIAM J. Comput. 17 (1988), pp. 128-142.

[5] A. Gibbons and W. Rytter, *Efficient Parallel Algorithms*, Cambridge University

[6] P. Hell and M. Rosenfeld, *The complexity of finding generalized paths in tournaments*, J. of Algorithms 4 (1982), pp. 303-309.

[7] Y. Manoussakis, *A linear-time algorithm for finding Hamiltonians cycles in tournaments*, Discrete Applied Mathematics 36 (1992), pp. 199-201.

[8] L. Redei, *Ein Kombinatorischer satz*, Acta Litt. Sci. Szeged (1934), pp. 39-43.

[9] D. Soroker, *Fast parallel algorithms for graphs and networks*, Ph.D Thesis, Rept UCB/CSD87/390, Computer Science Division, University of California, Berkeley, CA (1987).

[10] D. Soroker, *Fast parallel algorithms for finding Hamiltonian paths and cycles in a tournament*, Journal of Algorithms 9 (1988), pp. 276-286.

[11] U. Vishkin, *Implementation of simultaneous memory address access in models that forbid it*, J. Algorithms 4 (1983), pp. 45-50.

A Unifying Look at Semigroup Computations on Meshes with Multiple Broadcasting

D. Bhagavathi S. Olariu W. Shen L. Wilson

Department of Computer Science, Old Dominion University, Norfolk, VA 23529, U.S.A.

Abstract. Semigroup computations are a fundamental algorithmic tool finding applications in all areas of parallel processing. Given a sequence of m items $a_1, a_2, \ldots, a_m$ from a semigroup S with an associative operation $\oplus$, the semigroup computation problem involves computing $a_1 \oplus a_2 \oplus \ldots \oplus a_m$. We consider the semigroup computation problem involving m ($2 \leq m \leq n$) items on a mesh with multiple broadcasting of size $\sqrt{n} \times \sqrt{n}$. Our contribution is to present the first lower bound and the first time-optimal algorithm which apply to the entire range of m ($2 \leq m \leq n$). First, we show that any algorithm that solves the semigroup computation problem must take at least Ω ($\max\{\min\{\log m, \log \frac{n^{\frac{2}{3}}}{m^{\frac{1}{3}}}\}, \frac{m^{\frac{1}{3}}}{n^{\frac{1}{6}}}\}$) time. Second, we show that our bound is tight by designing an algorithm whose running time matches the lower bound. These results unify and generalize all semigroup lower bounds and algorithms known to the authors. ...

1 Introduction

Semigroup computations are a fundamental algorithmic tool, with numerous applications to all branches of parallel processing [2, 12]. Formally, the *semigroup computation* problem [2, 12] is defined as follows: given a sequence $a_1, a_2, \ldots, a_m$ of items from a semigroup S with an associative operation $\oplus$, compute $a_1 \oplus a_2 \oplus \ldots \oplus a_m$. The purpose of this paper is to propose a unifying look at semigroup computations on meshes with multiple broadcasting, that is, mesh-connected computers enhanced by the addition of row and column buses.

The semigroup computation problem has been well studied in the literature. Aggarwal [1] and Bokhari [7] have studied the problem in the context of mesh-connected computers augmented by a global bus. Kumar and Raghavendra [11] showed that on a mesh with multiple broadcasting of size $\sqrt{n} \times \sqrt{n}$ the semigroup computation problem with $m = n$ has a lower bound of $\Omega(n^{\frac{1}{6}})$. At the same time, they exhibited an $O(n^{\frac{1}{6}})$ and therefore optimal algorithm for semigroup computation. Later, Chen et al. [8] and Bar-Noy and Peleg [3] have shown that semigroup computations can be performed faster on a *rectangular* mesh with multiple broadcasting. Specifically, they show that the semigroup computation of n items can be solved in $O(n^{\frac{1}{8}})$ time on a mesh of size $n^{\frac{3}{8}} \times n^{\frac{5}{8}}$. Chen et al. [8] also showed that if every processor can hold $n^{\frac{1}{9}}$ items from the input sequence, then the computation can be performed in $O(n^{\frac{1}{9}})$ time on a mesh of size $n^{\frac{1}{3}} \times n^{\frac{5}{9}}$.

Quite recently, Lin et al. [13] have exhibited a number of lower bounds for meshes with multiple broadcasting. In particular, they show that semigroup computations involving $m \leq \sqrt{n}$ items stored consecutively in the first column of a mesh with multiple broadcasting of size $\sqrt{n} \times \sqrt{n}$ take $\Omega(\log m)$ time.

To put existing results in perspective, we shall refer to semigroup computations involving $m \in O(\sqrt{n})$ items as *sparse*, while the case $m \in O(n)$ will be referred to as *dense*. Finally, the case corresponding to $2 \leq m \leq n$ will be termed *general*. In this terminology, up to now, lower bounds and matching algorithms for semigroup computations have been obtained only for the sparse and dense cases, but nothing is known about the general case.

The present work was motivated by an attempt to remove the artificial limitation of the problem to the sparse and dense cases. The goal of this paper is to present a time-optimal algorithm for the semigroup computation in the general case. This algorithm unifies the previous special case results. We propose to attack the problem over its entire range rather than considering individually the two special cases which have been previously studied on this architecture. In this context, we first derive a lower bound for semigroup computations in the general case. More precisely, we show that every algorithm that solves the semigroup computation involving m ($2 \leq m \leq n$) items must take at least $\Omega(\max\{\min\{\log m, \log \frac{n^{\frac{2}{3}}}{m^{\frac{1}{3}}}\}, \frac{m^{\frac{1}{3}}}{n^{\frac{1}{6}}}\})$ time on a mesh with multiple broadcasting of size $\sqrt{n} \times \sqrt{n}$. As expected, our result matches the known lower bounds for the sparse and dense cases.

Next we show that the lower bound that we derived is tight by providing an algorithm that solves the general case semigroup computation in time proportional to $\max\{\min\{\log m, \log \frac{n^{\frac{2}{3}}}{m^{\frac{1}{3}}}\}, \frac{m^{\frac{1}{3}}}{n^{\frac{1}{6}}}\}$. Our algorithm contains the algorithms in [8, 11, 13] as special cases. Further, we establish that the semigroup algorithms in [3, 8] remain optimal even if "slightly" more processors are available.

The remainder of the paper is organized as follows: Section 2 presents the model of computation used throughout this paper; Section 3 gives the lower bound arguments for the general case; Section 4 discusses the details of a time-optimal algorithm for semigroup computation; finally, Section 5 summarizes the results and poses a number of open problems.

2 The model of computation

The mesh-connected computer architecture has emerged as one of the natural choices for solving a large number of computational tasks in image processing, computational geometry, and computer vision [2, 12, 15]. Its regular structure and simple interconnection topology makes the mesh particularly well suited for VLSI implementation [10, 17, 20]. However, the mesh tends to be slow when it comes to handling data transfer operations over long distances. In an attempt to overcome this problem, mesh-connected computers have recently been enhanced by the addition of various types of bus systems [1, 7, 11, 14, 17, 19].

For example, Aggarwal [1] and Bokhari [7] consider meshes enhanced by the addition of a single global bus. Yet another such system has been adopted by the DAP family of computers [17], and involves enhancing the mesh architecture by the addition of row and column buses. In [11] an abstraction of such a system is referred to as mesh with multiple broadcasting.

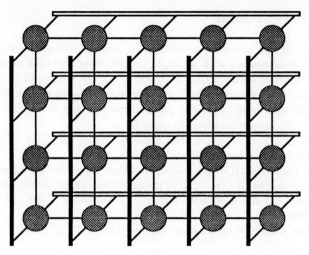

A 4 × 5 mesh with multiple broadcasting

A mesh with multiple broadcasting of size $M \times N$, hereafter referred to as a *mesh* whenever no confusion is possible, consists of MN identical processors positioned on a rectangular array overlaid with a bus system. In every row of the mesh the processors are connected to a horizontal bus; similarly, in every column the processors are connected to a vertical bus (refer to Figure 1). The processor located in row i and column j $(1 \leq i \leq M; 1 \leq j \leq N)$ will be referred to as $P(i, j)$. Throughout this paper we assume that the mesh with multiple broadcasting operates in SIMD mode: in each time unit, the same instruction is broadcast to all processors, which execute it and wait for the next instruction. Each processor is assumed to know its own coordinates within the mesh and to have a constant number of registers of size $O(\log MN)$; in unit time, every processor either performs some arithmetic or boolean operation, communicates with one of its neighbors using a local link, broadcasts a value on a bus or reads a value from a specified bus. These operations involve handling at most $O(\log MN)$ bits of information. For practical reasons, only one processor is allowed to broadcast on a given bus at any one time. By contrast, all the processors on the bus can simultaneously read the value being broadcast. In accord with other researchers [1, 3, 7, 8, 11, 14, 17, 19], we assume that communications along buses take $O(1)$ time. Recent experiments with the YUPPIE multiprocessor array system seem to indicate that this is a reasonable working hypothesis [14].

As pointed earlier, the mesh with multiple broadcasting closely models commercially available architectures. It is not surprising, therefore, that a number of efficient algorithms to solve computational problems on this model have been proposed in the literature. These include image processing [17, 18], computational geometry [5, 6, 11, 16], semigroup computations [3, 8, 11], and selection [4, 8, 11], among others.

3 The lower bound

The purpose of this section is to establish a non-trivial lower bound on semigroup computations on meshes with multiple broadcasting. For this purpose, consider a mesh with multiple broadcasting $\mathcal{R}$ of size $\sqrt{n} \times \sqrt{n}$ storing m $(2 \leq m \leq n)$ items $a_1, a_2, \ldots, a_m$ from a semigroup S with an associative operation $\oplus$. The items are stored in column-major order one per processor in the first $\lceil \frac{m}{\sqrt{n}} \rceil$ columns of the mesh. We shall distinguish several ranges for m.

First, in case $2 \leq m < \sqrt{n}$, the lower bound of $\Omega(\log m)$ of [13] applies. For further reference we state the following result.

Lemma 0. (Lin *et al.* [13]) Any algorithm that solves the semigroup computation problem involving m $(2 \leq m < \sqrt{n})$ items stored consecutively, one per processor, in the first column of a mesh with multiple broadcasting of size $\sqrt{n} \times \sqrt{n}$ must take $\Omega(\log m)$ time.

Therefore, from now on we shall assume that $m \geq \sqrt{n}$, which implies

$$\frac{n^{\frac{2}{3}}}{m^{\frac{1}{3}}} \leq \sqrt{n}. \tag{1}$$

For the remainder of the lower bound argument, we assume for simplicity that $\frac{m}{\sqrt{n}}$ is an integer.

Lemma 1. Any algorithm that solves the semigroup computation problem involving m $(\sqrt{n} \leq m \leq n)$ items stored one per processor in the first $\frac{m}{\sqrt{n}}$ columns of a mesh with multiple broadcasting of size $\sqrt{n} \times \sqrt{n}$ must take at least $\Omega(\log \frac{n^{\frac{2}{3}}}{m^{\frac{1}{3}}})$ time.

Proof. We construct a sequence of m items as follows. The first group consists of $\frac{n^{\frac{2}{3}}}{m^{\frac{1}{3}}}$ items that we place consecutively in the first column of the mesh. Note that by virtue of (1) this is always possible. The remaining items are chosen to be the null element with respect to $\oplus$ (note that even if the semigroup has no null element, we can augment the structure, for lower bound purposes, by adding such an element). Now the result of the semigroup computation is known as soon as the partial result involving the $\frac{n^{\frac{2}{3}}}{m^{\frac{1}{3}}}$ items in the first column is available, and conversely. The lower bound of [13] applies, guaranteeing that $\Omega(\log \frac{n^{\frac{2}{3}}}{m^{\frac{1}{3}}})$ time is needed to complete the computation.

We shall complement the result of Lemma 1 by presenting a different lower bound argument of *information transfer* type [12]. Our argument can be seen as a generalization of lower bound arguments in [1, 3, 7]. The semigroup computation terminates at the end of t computational steps, when some processor in $\mathcal{R}$ has enough information to compute $a_1 \oplus a_2 \oplus \ldots \oplus a_m$.

We view the information available to a processor as consisting of two distinct types: on the one hand, the processor may have access to information that has been broadcast on buses and, on the other, the processor may have access to information received from local communication only. To make this statement precise, let $\mathcal{B}(i)$ be the *set* of input items that have contributed to any information which has been broadcast on some bus at the end of time unit i, and write $b(i) = |\mathcal{B}(i)|$. Further, for each processor P of the mesh, let $\mathcal{L}(i, P)$ be the *set* of all input elements initially stored in processors whose Manhattan distance from P is at the most i. It follows that $\mathcal{L}(0, P) = \{$item stored initially by $P\}$. The following result follows directly from the definition of Manhattan distance.

Lemma 2. With $l(i)$ standing for $\max_{P \in \mathcal{R}} |\mathcal{L}(i, P)|$ we have

$$\begin{cases} l(i) \leq 1 + 2i(i+1) \text{ for } i \geq 1 \\ l(0) = 1 \end{cases}$$

Lemma 3. Let t be the least integer for which $b(t) + l(t) \geq m$. Then t is a lower bound on the number of computational steps needed by any algorithm to correctly solve the semigroup problem.

Proof. Suppose not; let $j < t$ be the number of computational steps after which some processor P of the mesh $\mathcal{R}$ has enough information to know the result of the semigroup computation.

Note, however, that the number of input items that have contributed to the information known by P is bounded by $b(j) + l(j)$. By our choice of t, it must be that $b(j) + l(j) < m$, implying that P can complete the semigroup computation without having all input items contribute. But now we have reached a contradiction since one may change the items that have not contributed, invalidating the algorithm.

Lemma 4. For all i ($i \geq 0$),

$$\begin{cases} b(i) \leq b(i-1) + 2\sqrt{n} * l(i-1) \text{ for } i \geq 1 \\ b(0) = 0 \end{cases}$$

Proof. First, the fact that $b(0) = 0$ follows from the definition of $\mathcal{B}(0)$. Further, observe that by definition, the set of input items that have contributed to the information that has been broadcast on any bus of the mesh can only be enriched by having some processor broadcast, in the i-th time unit, information that it has received locally by the end of the first $i - 1$ computational steps. Since there are $2\sqrt{n}$ buses available for broadcasting, the conclusion follows.

We are now in a position to state the following result that provides yet another component of the overall lower bound.

Lemma 5. Any algorithm that solves the semigroup computation problem involving m ($\sqrt{n} \leq m \leq n$) items stored one item per processor in the first $\frac{m}{\sqrt{n}}$ columns of a mesh with multiple broadcasting of size $\sqrt{n} \times \sqrt{n}$ must take at least $\Omega(\frac{m^{\frac{1}{3}}}{n^{\frac{1}{6}}})$ time.

Proof. Let t denote the least number of steps needed for any semigroup algorithm to terminate. The recurrence of Lemma 4 along with Lemma 2 yields:

$$\sum_{i=1}^{t} b(i) \leq \sum_{i=1}^{t} b(i-1) + 2\sqrt{n} \sum_{i=1}^{t} (1 + 2i(i-1))$$

which telescopes to

$$b(t) \leq 2t\sqrt{n} + 4\sqrt{n} \frac{t(t+1)(2t+1)}{6} - 4\sqrt{n} \frac{t(t+1)}{2}.$$

Now after appropriately upperbounding the right hand size of this inequality we obtain

$$b(t) \leq \frac{4}{6} \sqrt{n} t(t+1)(2t+1) \leq 4\sqrt{n} t^3.$$

Now Lemma 2 and Lemma 3 combined with the above inequality guarantee that

$$m \leq b(t) + l(t) \leq 4\sqrt{n}t^3 + 1 + 2t(t+1).$$

By suitably upperbounding the right hand side, we get

$$m \leq 4\sqrt{n}t^3 + 2t^3 \leq 8\sqrt{n}t^3$$

and so,

$$t \geq \frac{1}{2}\left(\frac{m}{\sqrt{n}}\right)^{\frac{1}{3}}$$

which completes the proof of Lemma 5.

To unify the results in Lemma 0, Lemma 1, and Lemma 5, we make the following observation, whose justification is routine.

Observation 6. Let m be an arbitrary integer in the range $2 \leq m \leq n$. Then

- for $2 \leq m < \sqrt{n}$, $\frac{m^{\frac{1}{3}}}{n^{\frac{1}{6}}} < \log m < \log \frac{n^{\frac{2}{3}}}{m^{\frac{1}{3}}}$;

- for $\sqrt{n} \leq m \leq n$, $\log \frac{n^{\frac{2}{3}}}{m^{\frac{1}{3}}} \leq \log m$.

Thus, by Lemma 0, Lemma 1, Lemma 5, and Observation 6 combined we have the following lower bound result for semigroup computations on meshes with multiple broadcasting.

Theorem 7. Any algorithm that solves the semigroup problem involving m ($2 \leq m \leq n$) items n column-major order in the first $\lceil \frac{m}{\sqrt{n}} \rceil$ columns of a mesh with multiple broadcasting of size $\sqrt{n} \times \sqrt{n}$ must take at least $\Omega(\max\{\min\{\log m, \log \frac{n^{\frac{2}{3}}}{m^{\frac{1}{3}}}\}, \frac{m^{\frac{1}{3}}}{n^{\frac{1}{6}}},\})$ time.

4 The algorithm

The purpose of this section is to exhibit an algorithm for semigroup computation whose running time matches the lower bound derived in the previous section.

Consider a mesh $\mathcal{R}$ with multiple broadcasting of size $\sqrt{n} \times \sqrt{n}$. The m ($2 \leq m \leq n$) data items are stored in the first $\lceil \frac{m}{\sqrt{n}} \rceil$ columns of $\mathcal{R}$, in column-major order. At various steps of the algorithm, the mesh $\mathcal{R}$ may be dynamically partitioned into submeshes to suit computational needs. We will describe these partitions as they become necessary. Our algorithm consists of the following sequence of computational steps. In case $m < \sqrt{n}$, Step 0 below is executed and the algorithm terminates. Otherwise, Steps 1 through 3 are executed. The details of these steps follow.

Step 0. In case the number m of input items is less than $\sqrt{n}$ we proceed recursively. Consider the submesh $\mathcal{M}$ determined by the first m rows and m columns of $\mathcal{R}$.

We partition the submesh $\mathcal{M}$ into submeshes of size $\frac{m}{2} \times \frac{m}{2}$ each, and recursively solve the semigroup computation problem. Specifically, the semigroup computation involving the first half of the input is solved in the north-western submesh of $\mathcal{M}$, while the semigroup computation involving the second half of the input is solved in the south-eastern submesh of $\mathcal{M}$. Clearly, this is possible and no broadcasting conflict will arise. Furthermore, it is easy to confirm that the running time of this step is bounded by $O(\log m)$.

Step 1. We shall refer to the submesh consisting of the first $\frac{m}{\sqrt{n}}$ columns[1] as $\mathcal{R}'$. To make the presentation easier to follow we let

$$x = \frac{m^{\frac{1}{3}}}{n^{\frac{1}{6}}}. \tag{2}$$

In this notation, we view the mesh $\mathcal{R}'$ as consisting of submeshes $R_{i,j}$ ($1 \leq i \leq \frac{\sqrt{n}}{x}, 1 \leq j \leq \frac{m}{x\sqrt{n}}$) of size $x \times x$, with each $R_{i,j}$ involving processors $P(r,s)$ with $1+(i-1)x \leq r \leq ix, 1+(j-1)x \leq s \leq jx$. The leftmost processor in the top row of every such submesh is termed the *leader* of the submesh.

For the sake of simplicity, we assume that $\frac{m}{x\sqrt{n}}$ and $\frac{\sqrt{n}}{x}$ are integers. In each of the submeshes $R_{i,j}$, perform the semigroup computation in $O(x)$ time, using local communication only [12], and store the partial result in the leader of the submesh, that is, processor $P(1+(i-1)x, 1+(j-1)x)$.

To summarize, at the end of Step 1 the leader of every submesh $R_{i,j}$ contains the partial result $\alpha_{i,j}$ of the semigroup computation involving the items in $R_{i,j}$. Furthermore, Step 1 takes $O(x)$ time.

Step 2. We now view the mesh $\mathcal{R}'$ as a collection of submeshes R_i ($1 \leq i \leq \frac{\sqrt{n}}{x}$), with R_i containing the submeshes $R_{i,1}, R_{i,2}, \ldots, R_{i,\frac{m}{x\sqrt{n}}}$. The objective of this step is to perform the semigroup computation on the partial results in each of the submeshes R_i. The new partial result will be stored by processor $P(1+(i-1)x, 1)$, the leader of the submesh R_i.

The idea is to compact the $\alpha_{i,j}$'s in R_i into the first $\frac{m}{x^2\sqrt{n}}$ columns of R_i and to perform the semigroup computation after compaction. Note that by virtue of (2), $\frac{m}{x^2\sqrt{n}} = x$ confirming that the data movement is feasible. The details are presented next.

Partition the $R_{i,j}$'s into x groups such that the rth group involves submeshes $R_{i,1+(r-1)x}, \ldots, R_{i,rx}$.

Next, compact all the $\alpha_{i,j}$'s in the rth group into column r of R_i. To avoid broadcasting conflicts, every processor $P(1+(i-1)x, 1+(j-1)x)$ ($1 \leq i \leq \frac{\sqrt{n}}{x}; 1 \leq j \leq \frac{m}{x\sqrt{n}}$), sends the value $\alpha_{i,j}$ it contains vertically to processor $P(1+(i-1)x, 1+(j-1)x + j \bmod x)$, using local links only. This can be done in $O(x)$ time. Finally, in each R_i, groups of x $\alpha_{i,j}$'s are moved horizontally to their final destination. Note that by virtue of (2) the data movement described above is completed in (x) time.

As a result of the previous data movement the partial results of Step 1 are contained in the first x columns of the mesh. Now in every $R_{i,1}$ perform the semigroup computation using local communications only. Clearly, (2) guarantees that this can be done in $O(x)$ time. Once computed, the new partial results are stored in the leader of every submesh R_i ($1 \leq i \leq \frac{\sqrt{n}}{x}$).

Step 3. We now have one partial result per submesh R_i. To complete the algorithm, we need to perform the semigroup computation on these $\frac{\sqrt{n}}{x}$ partial results.

---

[1] For simplicity we assume that $\frac{m}{\sqrt{n}}$ is an integer

We begin by compacting the partial results in the first $\frac{\sqrt{n}}{x}$ positions in the first column of $\mathcal{R}$. This is done as follows: every processor $P(1 + (i-1)x, 1)$ that holds a partial result β_i at the end of Step 2, broadcasts β_i horizontally to processor $P(1 + (i-1)x, i)$, which in turns broadcasts β_i vertically to $P(i, i)$, and finally to $P(i, 1)$.

Clearly, the above data movement takes $O(1)$ time. Finally, using the optimal algorithm of Lin *et al.* [13], we perform the semigroup computation on the β_i's in $O(\log \frac{\sqrt{n}}{x})$ time, and store the final result in processor $P(1,1)$.

To analyze the running time of our algorithm, note that in case $m < \sqrt{n}$ only Step 0 is executed and the running time is bounded by $O(\log m)$. In case $m \geq \sqrt{n}$, Steps 1 through Step 3 are executed. By (2), Step 1 and Step 2 are performed in $O(\frac{m^{\frac{1}{3}}}{n^{\frac{1}{6}}})$ time, while Step 3 takes $O(\log \frac{n^{\frac{2}{3}}}{m^{\frac{1}{3}}})$ time.

Finally, the analysis of the running times of Steps 0 through 3, combined with Observation 6, allow us to state the following result.

Theorem 8. The semigroup computation involving m $(2 \leq m \leq n)$ items stored in column-major order in the first $\lceil \frac{m}{\sqrt{n}} \rceil$ columns of a mesh with multiple broadcasting of size $\sqrt{n} \times \sqrt{n}$ takes $O(\max\{\min\{\log m, \log \frac{n^{\frac{2}{3}}}{m^{\frac{1}{3}}}\}, \frac{m^{\frac{1}{3}}}{n^{\frac{1}{6}}}, \})$ time being, therefore, time optimal.

5 Conclusion and open problems

In this paper we addressed the semigroup computation problem involving m $(2 \leq m \leq n)$ items on a mesh with multiple broadcasting of size $\sqrt{n} \times \sqrt{n}$. Our contribution is to have presented the first lower bound and the first time-optimal algorithm which apply to the entire range of m $(2 \leq m \leq n)$. We provided a unifying look at semigroup computations on meshes with multiple broadcasting by solving the problem for the *general* case rather than treating only the *sparse* and *dense* cases. First, we provided a lower bound by showing that any algorithm which solves the semigroup computation problem must take at least $\Omega (\max\{\min\{\log m, \log \frac{n^{\frac{2}{3}}}{m^{\frac{1}{3}}}\}, \frac{m^{\frac{1}{3}}}{n^{\frac{1}{6}}}, \})$ time. Second, we have shown that our lower bound is tight by designing an algorithm whose running time matches the lower bound. These results generalize all semigroup algorithms known to the authors.

In [3, 8] it was argued that rectangular meshes lead to faster algorithms for semigroup computations than square meshes. It is interesting to note that our lower bound implies that the semigroup algorithms in [3, 8] are optimal *even* if a larger number of processors are available. Specifically, our result shows that semigroup computations involving n items stored one item per processor in a mesh of size $n^{\frac{5}{8}} \times n^{\frac{5}{8}}$ takes as long as the same computation on a rectangular mesh of size $n^{\frac{3}{8}} \times n^{\frac{5}{8}}$. Therefore, in this case, the additional processors cannot speed up the computation.

A number of important problems remain open. Similar unifying results are desirable for other important algorithmic problems on meshes with multiple broadcasting. Candidate problems include, prefix computation, selection, sorting, and list ranking among many others.

References

1. A. Aggarwal, Optimal bounds for finding maximum on array of processors with k global buses, *IEEE Trans. on Computers*, C-35, 1986, 62–64.
2. S. G. Akl, The design and analysis of parallel algorithms, Prentice-Hall, Englewood Cliffs, New Jersey, 1989.
3. A. Bar-Noy and D. Peleg, Square meshes are not always optimal, *IEEE Trans. on Computers*, C-40, 1991, 196-204.
4. D. Bhagavathi, P. J. Looges, S. Olariu, J. L. Schwing, and J. Zhang, A fast selection algorithm on meshes with multiple broadcasting, *Proc. International Conference on Parallel Processing*, 1992, St-Charles, Illinois, III-10-17.
5. D. Bhagavathi, S. Olariu, W. Shen, and L. Wilson, A Time-Optimal Multiple Search Algorithm on Enhanced Meshes, with Applications, *Proc. Fourth Canadian Computational Geometry Conference*, St-Johns, August 1992, 359-364.
6. D. Bhagavathi, S. Olariu, J. L. Schwing, and J. Zhang, Convex Polygon Problems on Meshes With Multiple Broadcasting, *Parallel Processing Letters*, to appear.
7. S. H. Bokhari, Finding maximum on an array processor with a global bus, *IEEE Trans. on Computers* vol. C-33, no. 2, Feb. 1984. 133-139.
8. Y. C. Chen, W. T. Chen, G. H. Chen and J. P. Shen, Designing efficient parallel algorithms on mesh connected computers with multiple broadcasting, *IEEE Trans. Parallel and Distributed Systems*, vol. 1, no. 2, Apr. 1990.
9. S. A. Cook, C. Dwork, and R. Reischuk, Upper and lower time bounds for parallel random access machines without simultaneous writes, *SIAM Journal on Computing*, 15 (1986) 87–97.
10. J. L. Hennessy and D. A. Patterson, Computer Architecture, A Quantitative Approach, Morgan Kaufmann Publishers, San Manteo, 1990.
11. V. P. Kumar and C. S. Raghavendra, Array processor with multiple broadcasting, *Journal of Parallel and Distributed Computing*, vol 2, 1987, 173-190.
12. F. Thomson Leighton, Introduction to Parallel Algorithms and Architectures: Arrays, Trees, Hypercubes, Morgan Kaufmann Publishers, San Mateo, 1992.
13. R. Lin, S. Olariu, J. L. Schwing, and J. Zhang, Simulating enhanced meshes, with applications, *Parallel Processing Letters*, to appear.
14. M. Maresca and H. Li, Connection autonomy and SIMD computers: a VLSI implementation, *Journal of Parallel and Distributed Computing*, vol. 7, 1989, 302-320.
15. D. Nassimi and S. Sahni, Finding Connected Components and Connected Ones on a Mesh-Connected Parallel Computer, *SIAM Journal on Computing*, 9 (1980), 744-757.
16. S. Olariu, J. L. Schwing, and J. Zhang, Time-Optimal Sorting and Applications on $n \times n$ Enhanced Meshes, *Proc. IEEE Internat. Conf. on Computer Systems and Software Engineering*, The Hague, May 1992.
17. D. Parkinson, D. J. Hunt, and K. S. MacQueen, The AMT DAP 500, 33rd *IEEE Comp. Soc. International Conf.*, Feb. 1988, 196-199.
18. V. K. P. Kumar and D. I. Reisis, Image Computations on Meshes with Multiple Broadcast, *IEEE Trans. Pattern Analysis and Machine Intelligence*, vol. 11, No. 11, (1989) 1194-1202.
19. J. Rothstein, Bus automata, brains, and mental models, *IEEE Trans. on Systems Man Cybernetics* 18, 1988.
20. H. S. Stone, High-Performance Computer Architecture, Second, Edition, Addison-Wesley, Reading, MA, 1990.

A Fast, Simple Algorithm to Balance a Parallel Multiway Merge

Rhys Francis[1*], Ian Mathieson[1] and Linda Pannan[2]

[1] CSIRO Division of Information Technology, 723 Swanston St., Carlton, VIC 3053, Australia

[2] RMIT Computer Science Department, Bundoora Campus, Plenty Rd., Bundoora, VIC 3083, Australia

Abstract. This paper addresses the problem of constructing a work load balanced parallel multi-way merge. While a balanced multi-way merge provides an ideal component for multiprocessor sorting algorithms, the general problem concerns the merge of N elements from k ordered segments using p processors. To achieve balanced parallel execution all processors must merge appropriate sections of these source segments into distinct but equal sized sections of the result array.

This paper presents the simplest published algorithm which solves this partitioning problem, enabling all processors to perform independent merges in a completely balanced manner. The partitioning algorithm is asynchronous, suited to implementation on multiprocessors and has a time complexity of $O(k \log(k) \log(N/k))$ which is independent of data distribution and includes a data access component of $O(k \log(N/k))$. In this study, p and k are unrelated but smaller than the problem size N.

1 Introduction

There has been a long running interest in the problem of applying multiple processors to the merge operation. Work in the area can be roughly divided into theoretical and practical results. The theoretical results have as their focus algorithmic performance under the assumption that the number of processors can be a function of the data set size. Such algorithms are typically analysed in terms of operation counts on synchronous PRAM models. The surveys of Lakshmivarahan et al. (1984) and Bitton et al. (1984) and the more recent text by Akl (1989) contain many examples of these algorithms and their analysis. The more practical results concern the application of a configuration of processors in an actual system implementation to achieve improved merge times, often within the context of sorting. This paper addresses the issue of balancing the work per processor within a multi-way merge executing on shared memory multiprocessor architectures.

A balanced multi-way merge provides an ideal component for practical multiprocessor sorting algorithms. In the first phase of such sorts, the data set is

---

* Dr. Francis can be contacted via email as Rhys.Francis@mel.dit.CSIRO.AU

split into distinct segments and separate simultaneous sorts are performed on each segment. In the second phase, the sorted segments are combined in some fashion to form a final result. The appeal of this two phase strategy is that for $p << N$, sorting the independent segments represents a significant amount of the total work in the problem, all of which is completed asynchronously, only involves access to separable data, employs a standard sequential sort algorithm and yet is fully parallel. Hoare's QuickSort (1962) is often used for this first phase due to its expected $O(n \log(n))$ running time and the efficient implementation derived by Sedgewick (1978). The technical difficulties all occur in the second, combining phase.

The fundamental properties which give rise to parallel merging were identified by Valiant (1975) and also Gavril (1975). The particular property of importance is that two ordered array segments, A and B, can each be divided into an equal number of distinct sections in such a way that the elements of the corresponding sections of A and B will find final placement in a contiguous section of the merged result array. Hence, if a suitable partitioning can be identified, each pair of corresponding sections could be merged into the appropriate section of a result array independently of the merge of other sections. The independence of the processing of each section provides the parallelism. To implement this idea, an algorithm is required which can derive the partitioning of A and B. Apart from correctly identifying corresponding sections, the partition should also create equal work for each merge.

The more general problem concerns the merge of k ordered segments using p processors. As in the two segment case, there must exist a partitioning of the k segments into sections in which the elements of corresponding sections will find final placement in a contiguous section of the merged result array. For balanced parallel execution, the sections generated in the final merged result should be equal in size. Consequently, the problem is one of finding a partitioning of the source segments which can be independently merged into equal sized sections of the result array. This paper gives an algorithm which finds the required partitioning.

This new algorithm is an asynchronous shared memory multi-way merge capable of merging k ordered segments using p processors with a time complexity independent of data distribution. In this study, p and k are unrelated and much smaller than the problem size N. The relevant measure is the speedup of the algorithm compared to linear speedup when running on p processors. The experimental results presented in the paper give practical evidence of the correctness of the algorithm and show its performance against the sequential multi-way merge.

2   Basis of the Algorithm

The multi-way merge takes N values in the form of k ordered segments of total size N, and merges them into a single ordered array using p processors. This section introduces an algorithm which partitions the source segments so that each processor performs $1/p$ of the merge operations. The algorithm is described by considering the role of each of the p processors during the partitioning.

Briefly, each processor is allocated one of p equal-sized destination segments within the final ordered result array. Each then searches for the elements within the source segments which will find placement within that destination segment; these are distributed across the k source segments (Fig. 1). This search is effected by each processor finding the largest element in every source segment that must be included within its destination segment. These elements constitute the upper boundaries of this processor's partitioning of the source segments. The lower boundaries are the upper boundaries of the partition belonging to the next lower destination segment. When all sets of partition boundaries are available each processor can perform an independent k-way merge across its partitions into the corresponding destination segment within the result array.

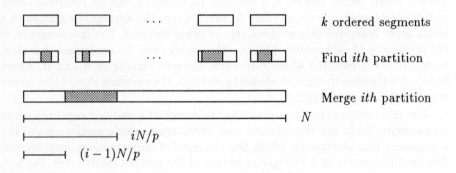

Fig. 1. Actions of processor i in parallel multi-way merge

To simplify the discussion, we may assume that all values in the source segments are distinct. In this way, the ordering relation need only consider the value of each element in order to achieve the unique partitioning solution. For the case where repeated values do occur, we redefine the ordering relation to take account of both the value and the index so that elements with the same value are ordered by the values of their indices. This preserves all required ordering relations, all elements are distinct, and the algorithm continues to apply.

Definitions

In the following discussion, statements containing the free variables i and j are universally quantified over $i, j \in \{1..k\}$, subranges of arrays represent the set of elements indexed by the subrange, and universal quantification of a relation over an empty subrange is taken to be true.

The array segment limits, L and H, are defined so that k disjoint source segments of an array, $A[1..N]$, can be described by

$$\mathcal{A}_i \equiv A[L_i..H_i] \quad \text{where} \quad \sum_{i=1}^{k}(H_i - L_i + 1) = N$$

and N is the number of elements in the merged result array. Source segments are ordered, and contain distinct values, so that

$$(\forall s, t : s, t \in \{L_i..H_i\} \wedge s < t : A[s] < A[t])$$

and

$$(\forall s, t : s \in \{L_i..H_i\} \wedge t \in \{L_j..H_j\} : A_i[s] \neq A_j[t]) \ .$$

Indices $\mathcal{L}_i$, $\mathcal{S}_i$ and $\mathcal{H}_i$ are introduced into the source segment $\mathcal{A}_i$ such that

$$\mathcal{L}_i, \mathcal{S}_i, \mathcal{H}_i \in \{L_i..H_i + 1\} \quad \text{and} \quad \mathcal{L}_i \leq \mathcal{S}_i \leq \mathcal{H}_i \ ,$$

where $\mathcal{L}_i..\mathcal{H}_i$ are the bounds on the search space for $\mathcal{S}_i$. The left and right parts of each $\mathcal{A}_i$ are identified such that

$$LEFT_i = A[L_i..\mathcal{S}_i - 1] \quad \text{and} \quad RIGHT_i = A[\mathcal{S}_i..H_i] \ .$$

The solution partition is denoted by indices $\mathcal{S}'_i$ and the left and right parts of each $\mathcal{A}_i$ at the solution are $LEFT'_i$ and $RIGHT'_i$. We refer to $LEFT'_i$ as the *included* set of elements, that is those elements which when merged will have result indices less than or equal to that of the Dth element (Fig. 2). The $RIGHT'_i$ are the *excluded* elements. Also, $Left_i = A[L_i..\mathcal{L}_i - 1] \subseteq LEFT'_i$ and $Right_i = A[\mathcal{H}_i..H_i] \subseteq RIGHT'_i$. Any elements remaining between $Left_i$ and $Right_i$, being $A[\mathcal{L}_i..\mathcal{H}_i - 1]$, may be called *undecided* elements.

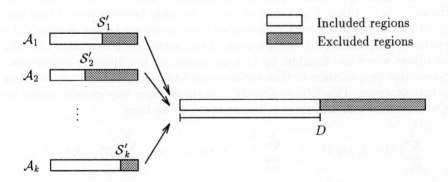

Fig. 2. Basic properties giving rise to partitioning of source segments

Requirements

Each processor performs a partitioning to find all $\mathcal{S}'_i$ in the source segments where the elements to the left of these $\mathcal{S}'_i$ will be merged into the section left of D in the result array (Fig. 2). This constitutes the processor's *solution partitioning*, since D is the upper boundary of the processor's allocated destination segment. This solution partitioning must satisfy two requirements.

The *ordering requirement* is that all elements lying to the left of all $\mathcal{S}'_i$ must have values less than or equal to all values to the right of all $\mathcal{S}'_i$, that is

$$LEFT'_i < RIGHT'_j \ .$$

The *distance requirement* is that the number of included elements must be D, that is

$$\sum_{i=1}^{k} (\mathcal{S}'_i - L_i) = D \ .$$

Note that once the merge has been performed, a *Dth* element will exist. The value of the *Dth* element could then be used to search the source segments for its insertion point. These insertion points would correspond to the partitioning indices $\mathcal{S}'$ which satisfy the ordering and distance requirements. Thus a partitioning which satisfies these requirements must also exist before the merging is performed, and it is unique provided all elements are made distinct. The problem is therefore one of finding the $\mathcal{S}'$ without prior knowledge of the value of the *Dth* element of the merged result.

Searching

To find the partitioning of the source segments, each processor repeatedly proposes and tests its own set of partition boundaries, which eventually converge on the solution partition. Fig. 3 depicts the relationship between sets of trial partition points and the correct partition solution, as shown by the shading. This relationship is the key to the operation of the partitioning algorithm. All trial partitions which are feasible, by at least satisfying the distance requirement, must either be a solution or their indices must be distributed about the solution indices as shown. This follows directly from the distance requirement, where for a trial partition $\mathcal{S}_i$ and the solution partition $\mathcal{S}'_i$ we have

$$\sum_{i=1}^{k} (\mathcal{S}'_i - L_i) = D \ \wedge \ \sum_{i=1}^{k} (\mathcal{S}_i - L_i) = D \ \Rightarrow \ \sum_{i=1}^{k} (\mathcal{S}'_i - \mathcal{S}_i) = 0 \ .$$

Either the trial is the solution and $\mathcal{S}_i = \mathcal{S}'_i$, or at least one segment's index is too low, $\mathcal{S}_\alpha < \mathcal{S}'_\alpha$, and one too high, $\mathcal{S}'_\beta < \mathcal{S}_\beta$.

Ordering of the source segments and the various definitions give us that

$$\mathcal{S}_\alpha < \mathcal{S}'_\alpha \ \Rightarrow \ A[\mathcal{S}_\alpha] < RIGHT'_j \ \Rightarrow \ A[\mathcal{S}_\alpha] \in LEFT'_i$$

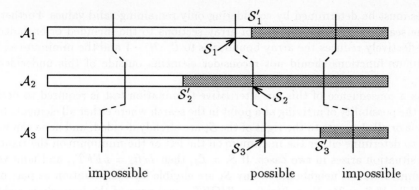

Fig. 3. Possible and impossible trial partitions of source segments

and

$$\mathcal{S}'_\beta < \mathcal{S}_\beta \quad \Rightarrow \quad LEFT'_i < A[\mathcal{S}_\beta] \quad \Rightarrow \quad A[\mathcal{S}_\beta] \in RIGHT'_j$$

Now, if the trial is not the solution partitioning then the smallest value in the trial set, $A[\mathcal{S}_{min}]$, is identified as an element of $LEFT'_i$ and the largest, $A[\mathcal{S}_{max}]$, is an element of $RIGHT'_i$. Neither they, nor their left and right neighbours, respectively, need therefore be considered further.

In this way the algorithm is seen to make progress for each trial partition which is not a solution since the search space can be refined for the segments containing $A[\mathcal{S}_{min}]$ and $A[\mathcal{S}_{max}]$. The refinement is achieved by setting $\mathcal{L}_{min} = \mathcal{S}_{min}$ and trialing a new $\mathcal{S}_{min}$ between the old $\mathcal{S}_{min}$ and $\mathcal{H}_{min}$, and by setting $\mathcal{H}_{max} = \mathcal{S}_{max}$ and trialing a new $\mathcal{S}_{max}$ between the old $\mathcal{S}_{max}$ and $\mathcal{L}_{max}$. By ensuring that the $\mathcal{S}_{min}$ and $\mathcal{S}_{max}$ change by the same amount the distance requirement can be maintained and a new trial partition established with all other indices held constant.

Termination

The above search step is repeated until the solution partitioning is achieved, and the algorithm is terminated. At that point both the ordering and distance requirements must be satisfied. The distance requirement is used as a loop invariant throughout each search step iteration, as already described. Consequently, the test for termination need only consider the ordering requirement.

The obvious test for $LEFT_i < RIGHT_j$ is to show that all immediate left neighbours of all $\mathcal{S}_i$ boundary points are smaller than all of their immediate right neighbours. So, if the maximum left boundary point value, $max(A[\mathcal{S}_i-1])$, is less than the minimum right boundary point value, $min(A[\mathcal{S}_i])$, then the ordering requirement holds and termination is appropriate.

During the search, $\mathcal{S}_i$ ranges in value from L_i to $H_i + 1$. As a result, if $\mathcal{S}_\gamma = L_\gamma$ for some $\mathcal{S}_\gamma$, access to $A[\mathcal{S}_\gamma - 1]$ is invalid and if $\mathcal{S}_\gamma = H_\gamma + 1$ the element $A[\mathcal{S}_\gamma]$ is inaccessible. In such cases the $max(A[\mathcal{S}_i - 1])$ and $min(A[\mathcal{S}_i])$

values must be determined by considering only remaining valid values. Further, as the search progresses addition of array sections to the included or excluded sets effectively reduces the array boundaries to $\mathcal{L}_i..\mathcal{H}_i - 1$ and the minimum and maximum functions should not reconsider elements outside of this undecided range.

As a consequence of this, an alternative termination test is required to deal with the possibility of arriving at a point in the search where either all elements to the left or all elements to the right of the $\mathcal{S}_i$ are already decided, and none can be used to determine either the maximum on the left or the minimum on the right. This situation arises in two cases. If $\mathcal{S}_i = \mathcal{L}_i$, then $Left_i = LEFT_i$, and none of the immediate left neighbours of any $\mathcal{S}_i$ are eligible for consideration as part of $RIGHT_j$. If $\mathcal{S}_i = \mathcal{H}_i$, then $Right_j = RIGHT_j$, and none of the immediate right neighbours can be considered for $LEFT_i$. When one of these situations occurs, either the combined included element set, or the combined excluded element set, must be of the required size. Since each of the constituent $Left_i$ sets, or $Right_i$ sets, were developed in accordance with the ordering requirement, the partitioning is a solution and the search may be terminated.

3 Implementation

Discussion of the partition algorithm in the previous section used general terms such as boundary points within arrays and elements at, or either side of, those points. An actual implementation must deal with the effects of array indices and boundaries. Pseudocode of the complete partition algorithm is provided in Fig. 4 and corresponds to the outline in the previous section. It can be seen that the implementation takes the form of a single simple search loop which is performed in parallel by separate processors probing the k data segments independently. Several points are worth noting.

1. The algorithm assumes that each processor, i, has access to the result array, the number of processors taking part in the merge, the value of i, and all the source segments.

2. Initially, processor i determines the upper boundary of the ith destination segment within the result array, at iN/p, shown as D in Fig. 2. It then makes a first guess at the partition solution by selecting trial upper boundaries within the source segments so that each segment contributes approximately the same number of elements for trial *inclusion* to the partition. This gives trial partition points at positions iN/kp elements along every source segment in accordance with the distance requirement.

3. The search loop maintains the distance requirement while testing for achievement of the ordering requirement on each iteration. Hence, the trial boundaries within the *max* and *min* segments are continually decremented and incremented, respectively, by equal amounts so that the sum of elements in all $LEFT_i$ remains constant at D. Maximum and minimum functions return the maximum of the immediate left neighbours of $\mathcal{S}_i$ and the minimum of the immediate right neighbours, respectively. These $max(A[\mathcal{S}_i-1])$ and $min(A[\mathcal{S}_i])$

```
Procedure Partition ( S, P, Id, K, A, D, B )

{ Params :                                                            }
{       S[1..K] = computed indices into segments for this partition   }
{       K = number of segments, A = data array, D = partition length  }
{       B[0..K-1] = index of first element of each sorted segment in A }
{       B[K] = one more than the index of the last element in A       }
{ Locals :                                                            }
{       k = ranges over 1..K, DeltaMax, DeltaMin, Delta = changes to S }
{       lmax, lmin, SegofMax, SegofMin = indices into min/max segments }
{       L[1..K], R[1..K] = reducing bounds on S in each segment       }

{ initialise segment pointers }

forall k in 1..K do
        L(k) = B(k-1)
        R(k) = B(k)
        S(k) = L(k) + D / K + ( if ( k <= D mod K ) then 1 else 0 )
end {forall}

{ partition the values }

loop
        { find maximum of all values at S(k)-1 and minimum at S(k),
          considering only those S(k)-1 and S(k) bounded by L(k)..R(k) }

        lmax = maximum over k of A[ S(k)-1 ] where S(k) > L(k)
        rmin = minimum over k of A[ S(k) ] where S(k) < R(k)

        SegofMax = segment containing lmax
        SegofMin = segment containing rmin

    exitif ( invalid(lmax) or invalid(rmin) or lmax < rmin )

        { eliminate excluded regions from further consideration }

        R(SegofMax) = S(SegofMax) - 1
        L(SegofMin) = S(SegofMin) + 1

        { reposition S(k) in SegofMax and SegofMin }

        DeltaMax= ( R(SegofMax) - L(SegofMax) ) / 2
        DeltaMin= ( R(SegofMin) - L(SegofMin) ) / 2

        Delta= MIN( DeltaMax, DeltaMin )

        S(SegofMax) = R(SegofMax) - Delta
        S(SegofMin) = L(SegofMin) + Delta

end {loop}
```

Fig. 4. Algorithm to balance the partitions

values are used both to test for achievement of the ordering requirement and to reduce the search space in the *max* and *min* segments containing these values, as described earlier and illustrated in the pseudocode.

Repeated values

The code of Fig. 4 uses simple comparisons between the values of elements and hence requires all values to be distinct. In order to apply this partitioning step in cases where values repeat within the data, an ordering relation must be defined to make all values distinct. If this is not done, repeated values permit many possible partitioning solutions and it becomes impossible to guarantee equal work loads in the merge step. Elements with the same value can be distinguished by their index within the array A. This definition maintains all necessary ordering relationships.

In terms of the code, the changes required are that the search for the minimum must find the first smallest value and the search for the maximum must find the last largest. In addition, the test for termination becomes

```
exitif ( invalid(lmax) or invalid(lmin)
         or lmax < rmin or ( lmax = rmin and SegofMax < SegofMin ) )
```

4   Analysis and Related Work

The balanced multi-way merge presented here exhibits a two part complexity due to the partitioning algorithm and the merge step. Assume that all segments are equal in size, N/k, and recall that each processor merges N/p of the result. The partitioning effectively performs a binary search on each of the k segments and during each iteration of the search finds the segments with the current maximum and minimum boundary values. As the cost of finding the maximum or minimum of a slowly changing set is logarithmic, each partitioning has a complexity of $O(k \log(k) \log(N/k))$. The p partitionings required for the merge can be performed simultaneously. The merge process requires that the minimum of k values be determined for each of N/p values merged giving a complexity of $O(k + \log(k)N/p)$. Finally, barrier synchronisation between the partition and merge steps adds a further complexity of $O(p)$.

Most related work involves sorting where k is assumed equal to p. In that case, the time complexity of our multi-way merge becomes $O(p + p\log(p)\log(N/p) + \log(p)N/p$. In comparison, a multi-way merge previously implemented used a tree of two-way merges. Since a single two-way merge can be executed in parallel on a shared memory multiprocessor with p processors in $O(\log(N) + N/p)$ time (Francis and Mathieson 1988; Varman et al. 1990a), a tree of two-way merges can be implemented in $O(\log^2(p) + \log(p)\log(N) + \log(p)N/p))$ time, with an additional $O(p\log(p))$ term for synchronisation.

Unfortunately, these complexities mask the multiprocessor performance effects by focussing on comparisons rather than accesses. For the tree of merges, the number of data accesses required in searching is $O(log(p)\log(N))$ and for merging $O(\log(p)N/p)$. In the multi-way merge, assuming sufficient registers or cache to hold the p values used in forming each minimum and maximum, the equivalent costs are $O(p\log(N/p))$ and $O(N/p)$, respectively. Thus the performance benefit in the multi-way merge over a tree of two-way merges accrues from the reduction in the number of data accesses. This is of real benefit where bus saturation can occur in multiprocessors.

Several parallel multi-way merge algorithms have been reported previously within the context of multiprocessor sorting. Of these, Quinn's partitioning algorithm (1988) is unbalanced and Evans' algorithm (1990) extends the range for which balancing is reasonable, but does not guarantee balancing. Shi and Schaeffer (1992) reported the use of regular sampling to guarantee load balancing within a factor of two of ideal.

Very recently, we have become aware of Varman et al. (1990b) in which an iterative algorithm gives a balanced merge. This algorithm trials subsets of the data to determine a partitioning of the subset into left and right parts which obeys the ordering requirement and then adjusts the balance between the left and right parts to correct for the distance requirement. The algorithm extends the subset in such a way as to keep the costs of maintaining the ordering and distance requirements within tight bounds. Their paper proposes the use of a complex kth smallest selection algorithm which, for very large k, may produce executions faster than the algorithm reported here. However, for practical cases, their algorithm has the same formal complexity in time and accesses as this algorithm, with a more involved structure.

The contribution of this work is a new, simple, easily implemented algorithm, which balances the multi-way merge step of practical multiprocessor sorts. The algorithm tolerates repeated values and exactly partitions the destination array.

5 Performance

The following results were obtained by executing the balanced multi-way merge on a Sequent S27 multiprocessor[3] using two datasets. The runs used the partitioning algorithm described in Fig. 4. Due to the small number of processors in the machine, simple loops were used to determine the maximum and minimum values when required. For larger machines strategies yielding logarithmic costs could be used.

The two datasets illustrate performance effects for selected combinations of N, k and p. The INORDER dataset consists of k equal sized non-overlapping ordered sets of integers. INORDER shows the performance effects where the segments to be merged have no values in common. The RANDOM dataset consists of k equal sized ordered segments. RANDOM shows the typical case where the range of the values in the segments overlap each other and may contain repeated values.

---

[3] The machine (located at Argonne National Laboratories) contains 32 Mb of shared memory and 26 16-MHz Intel 80386 32-bit CPUs, each with a 64 Kb 2-way set-associative copy-back cache.

The timing programs first generate the appropriate datasets and then repeatedly execute a merge of the k segments until timing with 3 digits of precision can be calculated. The cost of the algorithm is computed by comparing the cost per merge with the cost computed in the same way, but with the call to the parallel merge replaced by a call to an empty routine. Hence, the results have three figure accuracy, represent the time to partition and merge the data, and factor out the overheads of fork-join parallelism. The graphs show speedup computed with respect to a sequential k-way merge of the same datasets.

The results graphed in Figs. 5(a) and 5(b) show speedups where $k = 12$ for three sizes of datasets $N = 1024$ (1k), $N = 16$k and $N = 128$k for both RANDOM and INORDER data. The small dataset (1k) shows the performance loss expected for such small workloads per processor and the increase in parallel overheads (synchronisation, contention, etc) as p increases. This imbalance is no longer significant in the medium and large datasets (16k and 128k), which illustrate near linear speedup for the numbers of processors used ($p = 1$ to $p = 25$). These results are typical of the algorithm's performance.

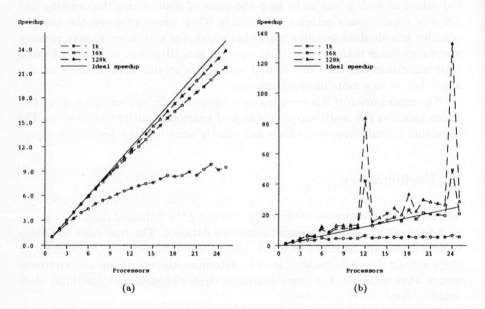

Fig. 5. Speedup vs. number of processors for parallel multiway merges of $k = 12$ segments from datasets (a) RANDOM and (b) INORDER.

The particular construction of the multi-way merge explains the spectacular superlinearity evident when k is a factor of p. The first stage of the multi-way merge repeatedly finds the smallest value in two or more remaining partitions, and transfers that value to the destination segment. When only one source partition remains, the second stage is executed to transfer that remaining partition into the destination segment. The copy operation is much faster than the merge operation. When k is a factor of p for INORDER, each processor calculates a partition entirely contained in a single segment. As a result, the processors immediately fall into the copy loop. The sequential algorithm transfers all but one of the segments using a merge loop and performs far more operations in total than are executed by all the processors in the parallel version. A similar but less dramatic effect occurs when p and k share a large common factor.

6 Conclusion

This paper demonstrates an algorithm which partitions the work in a multi-way merge to provide perfect balancing of workload in a multiprocessor implementation. The algorithm has been implemented and validated on a multiprocessor with speedups near linear. The algorithm is simple, readily implemented, and provides the basis for a solution to the practical multiprocessor sorting problem.

References

S. G. Akl (1989): "The Design and Analysis of Parallel Algorithms", *Prentice Hall*.

D. Bitton, D. J. Dewitt, D. K. Hsiao and J. Menan (1984): "A Taxonomy of Parallel Sorting", *ACM Computing Surveys*, **16**, 287–318.

D. J. Evans (1990): "A parallel sorting-merging algorithm for tightly coupled multiprocessors", *Parallel Computing*, **14**, 111–121.

R. S. Francis, and I. D. Mathieson (1988): "A Benchmark Parallel Sort for Shared Memory Multiprocessors", *IEEE Trans. on Computers*, **37**, 1619–1626.

F. Gavril (1975): "Merging with Parallel Processors", *Comm. ACM*, **18**, 588–591.

C. A. R. Hoare (1962): "Quicksort", *Computer J.*, **5**, 10–15.

S. Lakshmivarahan, S. K. Dhall and L. L. Miller (1984): "Parallel Sorting Algorithms", *Advances in Computing*, **23**, 295–354.

M. J. Quinn (1988): "Parallel sorting algorithms for tightly coupled multiprocessors", *Parallel Computing*, **6**, 295–357.

R. Sedgewick (1978): "Implementing Quicksort Programs", *Comm. ACM*, **21**, 847–856.

H. Shi and J. Schaeffer (1992): "Parallel Sorting by Regular Sampling", *J. Parallel and Distributed Computing*, **14**, 361–372.

L. G. Valiant (1975): "Parallelism in comparison problems", *SIAM J. Computing*, **4**, 348–355.

P. J. Varman, B. R. Iyer, D. J. Haderle and S. M. Dunn (1990a): "Parallel merging: algorithm and implementation results", *Parallel Computing*, **15**, 165–177.

P. J. Varman, B. R. Iyer, and S. D. Scheufler (1990b): "A Multiprocessor Algorithm for Merging Multiple Sorted Lists", *Proc. Int. Conf. on Parallel Computing, Vol. III*, 22–26.

M. Wheat and D. J. Evans (1992): "An efficient parallel sorting algorithm for shared memory multiprocessors", *Parallel Computing*, **18**, 91–102.

Some Design Aspects for VLIW Architectures Exploiting Fine–Grained Parallelism

Wolfgang Karl*

Institut für Informatik, Technische Universität München,
Arcisstr. 21, D–8000 München 2,
Tel.: +49+89-21058278, email: karlw@informatik.tu-muenchen.de,

Abstract. Very Long Instruction Word Architectures (VLIW architectures) can exploit the fine–grained (instruction level) parallelism typically found in sequential–natured program code. A parallelizing compiler is used to restructure the program code. Sophisticated global compaction techniques have emerged that can effectively extract fine–grained parallelism from ordinary sequential natured program code.
In this paper we propose an effective mechanism for multiway branches and introduce a generalized conditional execution model for VLIW architectures. For the evaluation of VLIW architectures and their parallelizing compilers we use a simulation environment. This simulation environment comprises a parallelizing compiler and a highly configurable simulator for VLIW architectures. With this simulation environment the architectural enhancements proposed in this paper can be evaluated. Our studies are directed in finding high performance combinations of VLIW architectures and parallelizing compilers.

1 Introduction and Motivation

Very Long Instruction Word Architectures (VLIW architectures) and super-scalar architectures can issue more than one instruction per cycle and therefore they exploit the fine–grained (instruction–level) parallelism typically found in sequential–natured ordinary programs. Preferably in superscalar machines conflict resolution and instruction scheduling are performed dynamically at run–time. Using techniques like reservation stations or scoreboarding fine–grained parallelism can be extracted to some extend [18] [17]. For VLIW architectures parallelizing compilers are necessary for the reordering of the program code. Compile–time scheduling allows the utilization of sophisticated analysis and transformations that would be too expensive at run–time. In the last few years parallelizing and optimization techniques have emerged that can effectively extract fine–grained parallelism form ordinary programs [13] [11] [22] [3] [15].

* This work is part of the SFB 0342, founded by the DFG. Within the project C2, there is a cooperation with the Siemens AG, Munich. The VLIW simulator and parts of the VLIW compiler have been developed by G. Böckle and his group. We could adopt their work for our own research activities. I would like to thank G. Böckle and the members of hid group for their support and their helpful comments.

Our studies are directed in finding high performance combinations of VLIW architectures and compilation techniques. For our experiments evaluating VLIW architectures and their parallelizing compilers we use a simulation environment now being developed at the University of Technology Munich. This simulation environment comprises a parallelizing compiler and a highly configurable simulator for VLIW architectures. The parallelizing compiler performs a thorough analysis of the source code determining the dependences between machine operations. Then, the machine operations are scheduled into wide instruction words taking into account data precedence, optimal scheduling of functional units, register usage and memory access. Our parallelizing compiler targeted to VLIW architectures is based on a modified version of the percolation scheduling approach [22]. New scheduling strategies and software–pipelining techniques have been developed and evaluated using the the first version of our simulation environment [20]. These new global compaction and software–pipelining techniques are focused on the extraction of fine–grained parallelism in general purpose and system code.

Global compaction algorithms in parallelizing compilers for VLIW architectures generally produce wide instructions packed with multiple tests along with data operations. Depending on the results of parallel tests a multiway branch mechanism selects the next instruction from many targets. In this paper we present an efficient hardware–implemented *multiway branch mechanism* that speeds up the execution of multiple conditional jumps.

Additionally, our studies on high performance combinations of VLIW architectures and parallelizing compilers comprises alternative execution models for VLIW architectures. As an architectural improvement for VLIW architectures we propose the *conditional execution* of operations. For VLIW architectures supporting the conditional execution of machine operations both paths emanating from a conditional branch may be compacted into one wide instruction word. While issuing the operations in the wide instruction word the corresponding condition codes are evaluated, and only the operations on the taken path, i. e. the ones for which the condition codes evaluate to "true", may write their results to the destination registers. For this special kind of speculative execution we can show that it supports the exploitation of a high degree of fine–grained parallelism on VLIW architectures. Our simulator for VLIW architectures allows operations to be executed conditionally so that this architectural feature can be evaluated.

For the conditional execution model presented in Sect. 4 additional transformations of the program code are necessary before instruction scheduling can take place. These new transformations are integrated in the percolation scheduling framework and described in Sect. 7.

2 VLIW architectures

A VLIW architecture is characterized through a wide instruction word providing enough control bits to directly and independently control the action of every functional unit. There is one control unit issuing a wide instruction every cycle, a large number of data paths and functional units which can be used in parallel. Figure 1 shows an VLIW–machine and the wide instruction word with the fields controlling the different functional units.

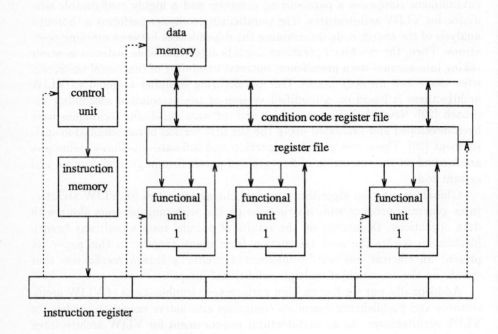

Fig. 1. Block diagram of a VLIW architecture

For our studies we use an "idealized" model of a VLIW architecture [9] with N_{FU} uniform functional units connected to a central register file. Each functional unit has two read and one write port to the register file and the register file has enough memory bandwidth to balance the operand usage rate of the functional units. The central register file simplifies code generation. When scheduling instructions the selection of the functional unit would be unimportant and the code generation only has to worry about when the operations have to be scheduled. Separate read/write ports for all functional units would guarantee the independence of the operations.

The first VLIW architecture was proposed by J. Fisher at Yale University around 1982 [14] as a scheme for extracting parallelism from scientific code. The VLIW architecture, called ELI–512, has 8 fixed–point and 8 floating point "clusters" each of which has separate register banks, ALUs, multipliers etc. The instruction is 512 bit wide. The ELI–512 architecture has a crossbar connection within a cluster but timid interconnections between clusters so that extra cycles are required moving data between clusters. The multiway branch mechanism is of the form: **if** $test_1$ **then goto** $target_1$; **if** $test_2$ **then goto** $target_2$ ...; **else goto** $target_n$.

Multiflow corp. introduced the first commercial VLIW architectures. The TRACE machines, inspired from the ELI–512, have i–boards for integer operations and f–boards for floating point operations, each of which have separate register banks and ALUs. The TRACE 28/200 includes architectural design decisions which are targeted to the parallelization of scientific program code. The lack of a global register file, pipelined memory access and a branching mechanism that allows the parallel execution of conditional branches that must lie on a single path through the program and a compilation technique whose performance heavily relies on the assumption that a program will follow one path than another are evidently intended to achieve good performance more on scientific code than on non–numerical code where assumptions about which path will be taken are less reliably.

K. Ebcioğlu at IBM in Yorktown Heights has proposed an VLIW architecture with 8 uniform processing elements [10]. The communication delays between the processing elements are minimized via a single central register file with a large number of ports. To perform well on programs with unpredictable branches the architecture features decision–tree shaped instructions that allow multiple branching and that allow operations to be executed conditionally depending on where the instruction branches to. The IBM VLIW architecture is intended to achieve good performance not only on scientific, but also on sequential natured non–numerical program code.

Several proposals for VLIW architectures have been derived from the IBM–VLIW–machine. The architecture synthesis of high performance application–specific processors described in [7] is based on the IBM–VLIW–machine's execution model. In [1] a VLIW architecture has been proposed which is also derived from IBM–VLIW–machine. This VLIW architecture supports a 3–way branch mechanism and allows operations to be executed conditionally depending on where the instruction branches to.

Philips Research in Palo Alto proposed a microprocessor with a wide instruction word, called LIFE–VLIW–processor [21] [23]. The VLIW–microprocessor has two ALUs for arithmetic, and logical operations, an interface to the data memory and a central register file. The functional units are controlled from a 200 bit wide instruction word. To reduce the costs of branches the VLIW–microprocessor supports conditional execution of operations as proposed in [16].

These examples show a rapidly growing interest in VLIW architectures. The trend goes to conditional execution models for VLIW architecture because it seems to be a promising approach in exploiting a high degree of fine–grained parallelism in general purpose applications. Our studies described in this paper evaluate VLIW architectures and parallelizing compilers supporting this architectural feature.

3   A Hardware Mechanism for Multiway Branches

Global compaction techniques for VLIW architectures generate code with wide instruction words packed with multiple tests along with other data operations. The VLIW architecture must be capable of executing multiple tests in parallel. An efficient multiway branch mechanism is necessary in selecting the next instruction to be executed from many targets.

The derivation of our multiway branch mechanism starts with the following example consisting of nested if–statements:

```
if    cc1
    then if  cc2
            then if  cc4
                    then goto L1
                    else goto L2
            else if  cc5
                    then goto L3
                    else goto L4
    else if  cc3
            then if  cc6
                    then goto L5
                    else goto L6
            else if  cc7
                    then goto L7
                    else goto L8.
```

These 7 dependent tests should be packed from compaction algorithms into one wide instruction word. Dependent tests in a wide instruction word form a decision tree. A decision tree is a rooted acyclic graph (dag). The leaf nodes are marked with the targets and the nodes which are not leaf nodes are the tests with the condition codes. Each node with a condition code has two successors. The edge marked with "t" points to the left successor and the node marked with "f" points to right successor. A node's successor can be a condition code or a leaf node. Figure 2 shows a decision tree with 7 tests and 8 targets. A decision tree with $n-1$ nodes has n leaves. Hence, a multiway branch based on a decision tree with n targets has $n-1$ tests (condition codes).

Evaluating a decision tree consists in determining an unique path from the root to a leaf node. Starting at the root the left successor have to be selected if the condition evaluates to "true", else the right successor have to be selected. The leaf node reached by this way provides the address of the instruction to be executed next. The target marked with $L1$ would be chosen if the condition codes $cc1$, $cc2$ and $cc4$ evaluates to "true".

Effective handling of multiway branches have a direct impact on the performance of a VLIW–machine. The evaluation of the condition codes and the determination of the target have to performed rapidly so that the next instruction can be fetched and executed in the next cycle.

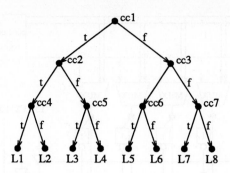

Fig. 2. Decision tree for a multiway branch

From the decision tree with 7 condition codes in Fig. 2 one can see that a target is uniquely determined by three condition codes:

- target $L1 \iff cc1 \wedge cc2 \wedge cc4$;
- target $L2 \iff cc1 \wedge cc2 \wedge \overline{cc4}$;

$$\vdots$$

- target $L7 \iff \overline{cc1} \wedge \overline{cc3} \wedge \overline{cc7}$.

Hence, for every target only three condition codes have to be connected over a logical AND. For example, if condition code $cc1$ evaluates to "true", condition codes $cc3$, $cc6$ and $cc7$ can be ignored. The form of the decision tree results in eight mutually exclusive combinations of three condition codes which have to be connected over a logical AND. Only one of the eight combinations results to "true" so that a target can be determined uniquely. Figure 3 shows the hardware implementation of a multiway branch based on a decision tree.

The implementation consists of logical AND–array as used in a PLA (programmable logical array). The condition codes defining a target are connected over a logical AND marked with a point on the cross points. The address of a target can be provided only if the corresponding line supplies a "1", i. e. the corresponding AND results to "true". The "1" opens the corresponding gate of the address line realized through a tri–state. The OR–circuit consists of a logical OR of the i-th address line ($0 \leq i \leq m-1$, with m : number of the address lines) of the eight targets so that only such address will be provided which is switched by the tri–state. For each of the seven condition codes a multiplexer selects one condition code register. There are seven fields in the instruction word controlling the multiplexers with $\lceil \log_2 N_{CR} \rceil$ bits, where N_{CR} is the number of the condition code registers. The target addresses are also coded in the instruction word.

Our scheme of a multiway branch described above corresponds to a fixed hardware implementation of a decision tree. Each arbitrary form of a decision tree can be transformed in the correct form as shown in Fig. 4.

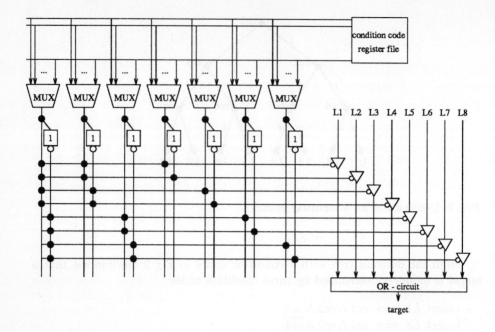

Fig. 3. Hardware implementation of a multiway branch

4 Conditional Execution of Operations

As shown in Sect. 2 modern VLIW architectures have the capability to execute operations conditionally. In the following section we introduce a generalized *conditional execution model* for VLIW architectures. Conditional execution of operations on a VLIW–machine is a technique in which operations of several program branches are issued concurrently. An operation to be issued conditionally has the form

$$op_i \mid c_i,$$ (1)

where op_i is an operation and c_i is a condition code. A condition code function $c_i : \mathcal{CR} \times \mathbb{B} \longrightarrow \mathbb{B}$ is assigned to each condition code, where $\mathcal{CR}$ is set of condition code registers. The condition code function compares the content of the condition code register with its second argument and provides the Boolean value "true" only if the content of the condition code registers is equal to its second argument:

$$c_i(cr_i, t) = \begin{cases} t & \text{if} \quad \langle cr_i \rangle = t \\ f & \text{if} \quad \langle cr_i \rangle = f \end{cases}$$ (2)

$$c_i(cr_i, f) = \begin{cases} t & \text{if} \quad \langle cr_i \rangle = f \\ f & \text{if} \quad \langle cr_i \rangle = t \end{cases}.$$ (3)

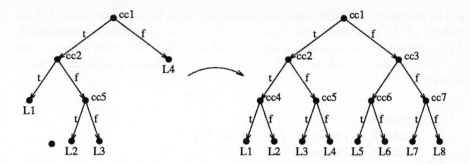

Fig. 4. Conversion of an arbitrary tree in a decision tree

An operation which has to be executed conditionally will change the state of the machine only if the condition code function results to t ("true"). An operation can depend on several condition codes. The operation op_i with

$$op_i \mid c_{i_1}, c_{i_2}, \ldots, c_{i_l} \tag{4}$$

will complete execution only if

$$c_{i_1} \wedge c_{i_2} \wedge \ldots \wedge c_{i_l} = t. \tag{5}$$

At compile time the code generator decides which operations have to be executed conditionally. An operation which has to be executed conditionally will be issued on the VLIW–machine. In the same cycle the condition code function will be evaluated whereas their result must be available in time to prevent the machine to change their state. If the condition code function results to "true" the operation completes execution, if the condition code function results to "false" the operation has the effect of a noop–operation.

For arithmetic or logical operations such a behavior will be reached through inhibit writing the destination register. For load and store operation it must also be inhibited to write a register or a memory cell.

The motivation for the introduction of the conditional execution model can be shown with the following example. The code sequence with RISC–like operations

P1:

```
        cmpl cr1, r1, r2   /* cr1 = r1 < r2 */
        bc cr1, L1         /* if cr1 goto L1 */
        sub r3, r1, r2     /* op1_1^f */
        jmp L2
    L1: sub r3, r2, r1     /* op1_1^t */
    L2: ...
```

will be executed on a RISC–machine where execution branches to label $L1$ if the content of the condition code registers $cr1$ is "true" or continues sequentially if the content of the condition code register is "false". The code sequence can be reordered for a machine which supports the conditional execution model as follows:

P1':

          cmpl $cr1, r1, r2$
          sub $r3, r1, r2 \mid cr1 = f$ /* op_1^f */
          sub $r3, r2, r1 \mid cr1 = t$ /* op_1^t */
  L2: ...

The condition codes $cr1 = t$ and $cr1 = f$ assigned to the operations op_1^t and op_1^f, respectively, cannot be fulfilled concurrently. Only one of the two subtractions can write its result to the destination register. The other operation has the effect of a noop–operation. Hence, both operations can be issued in parallel on a VLIW architecture supporting the conditional execution model. Therefore, the program code above can be transformed:

P1":

          cmpl $cr1, r1, r2$
          sub $r3, r1, r2 \mid \overline{cr1}$ $\parallel$ **sub** $r3, r2, r1 \mid cr1$
  L2: ...

As shown in the example with the capability of executing operations conditionally the VLIW architecture's parallelism can be exploited to a higher degree. But there are additional bits necessary in the instruction word coding the condition codes. In every field controlling a functional unit the condition codes have to be coded together with the operation. There are several possibilities in coding the condition codes in the instruction word. The coding can consist of the address of a condition code register and a bit for the corresponding Boolean value to be tested so that $1 + \lceil \log_2 N_{CR} \rceil$ bits are necessary. If an operation can be dependent on l conditions every field controlling a functional unit needs $l * (1 + \lceil \log_2 N_{CR} \rceil)$ bits for the coding of the conditions. This can be viewed as a vertical coding of the conditions.

The other possibility is to assign every condition code register a fixed place in the field controlling a functional unit. There are two bits necessary for every condition code register, one bit for the Boolean value to be tested and one bit which shows whether the condition code register have to be tested, i. e. whether the operation depends on the content of the corresponding condition code register. Hence, there are $N_{CR} * 2$ bits necessary in every field of the instruction word. This can be viewed as a horizontal coding of the conditions. Between these two forms of coding conditions several intermediate forms exists.

Running a program with operations to be executed conditionally on a VLIW architecture every condition code function for each operation to be executed conditionally must be evaluated independently. The VLIW architecture must be capable to compare the content of a condition code register with the condition codes coded in the instruction word in every cycle.

The evaluation of the condition code functions must take place at the beginning of a machine cycle so that writing a result to a destination register can be stopped if the corresponding condition code function results to "false". The decision whether an operation have to be executed conditionally or not takes place at compile–time. The program transformations required by the conditional execution model are described in Sect. 7. The described conditional execution model for VLIW architectures is a generalized scheme compared to the examples mentioned in Sect. 2. An operation can depend on several condition codes and operations to be executed conditionally can be compacted in an instructions with operations to be executed unconditionally.

5 A Compiler for VLIW architectures

The compiler for our experiments has to translate a program written in C into a highly parallel wide instruction word code. The compiler has to detect fine–grained parallelism throughout any application especially in general purpose code. There are several compaction and software–pipelining techniques to be evaluated and compared for their suitability and efficiency in generating code for a VLIW–machine. Therefore, an important requirement for the VLIW–compiler is the possibility in integrating and applying different approaches during the course of our experiments.

Our compiler is divided into a front end and a back end. These phases are shown in Fig. 5. The front end includes the phases for the lexical, syntactic and semantic analysis, the creation of the symbol table and the generation of intermediate code (rtl–code). For this task the *VPCC*–Compiler is used. The VPCC–Compiler being developed at the University of Virginia is a highly portable optimizing C–compiler [4] [5]. The rtl–representation is the starting point for instruction selection, data flow analysis and the parallelization, the phases of the back end of our compiler.

The instruction selection consists of assigning machine operations to the rtl–lines. The target operation set is based on the MIPS R2000 instruction set [19]. For each operation within the R2000 instruction set using an immediate operand there is an additional operation that uses long immediates. Long immediates are 32 bit long and will be placed in special fields of the long instruction word. Because of the assumption that there exists a condition code register file, branches are taken in dependence of the contents of condition code registers as described above. These registers are set by compare instructions and branches (multiway branches) check the contents of the condition code registers.

The data flow analysis determines data flow information needed for data dependency analysis which is a precondition for parallelization. The data flow analysis relies on iterative data flow algorithms described in [2]. Liveness information has to computed as well. Data flow analysis is performed interprocedurally applying the approach proposed in [8] to get more precise data flow informations.

The parallelization and generation of wide instruction word code will be achieved by applying the transformations defined within the percolation schedul-

592

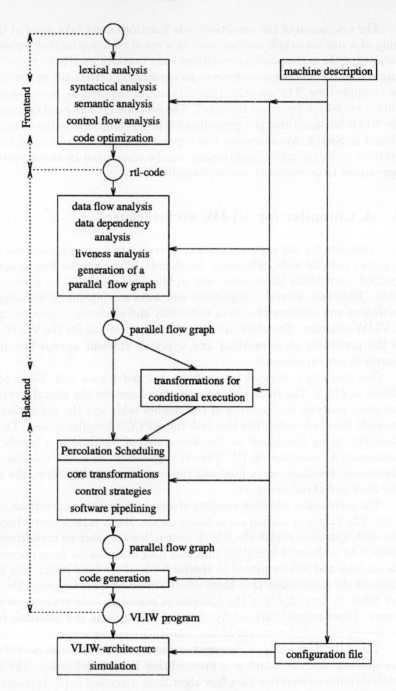

Fig. 5. The phases of our VLIW-compiler

ing framework [22]. The core transformations require the existence of a so–called parallel program graph that represents the program's control flow. Therefore, for each function a parallel program graph will be constructed from a control flow graph generated before by a control flow analysis. Each node within the parallel program graph corresponds to an instruction word of a VLIW–machine. In the initial parallel program graph each node contain exactly one operation. The operations can roughly divided into two classes: the assignments and the tests. The assignments change the content of some store and tests affect the control flow. Execution starts with the top node (root) and continues sequentially from one node to its successor. When execution reaches a node the assignments of that node will be issued concurrently. The tests of that node provide the name (label) of a node to be executed in the next cycle applying the multiway branch mechanism described above.

6   Automatical Parallelization on Instruction Level

Our system for automatical parallelization on instruction level is based on the percolation scheduling approach. With percolation scheduling a set of transformation rules is given by which a program graph can be restructured. The rules within the percolation scheduling framework allow the operations to move from one node to its predecessors thus increasing the parallelism in the predecessor nodes. As a consequence some nodes will become empty so that they can be removed from the program graph. This shortens the path through the program graph, thus decreasing the total execution time. Operations in the program graph can only be moved if no data dependencies are violated. In [22] four core transformations are defined: move-op, move-cj, unify and delete. Code motions are accomplished with move-op (for moving assignments) and move-cj (for moving branches). The move-op and move-cj transformations preserve the program's semantic by generating copies of that node whose operations are being moved across basic block boundaries. Therefore, the unify transformation defines how several copies of an operation can be moved to a common predecessor node. Delete removes nodes which are empty due to the application of the move-op or move-cj transformations. Following the modified version of percolation scheduling by A. Aiken [3] our implementation of the core transformation combines the move-op and the unify transformation.

The core transformations are the building blocks of the parallelization system. An efficient control strategy is necessary which guides the application of the core transformations. Several control strategies have been developed and implemented for our experiments evaluating which of them is best suited for the different kinds of applications. For the scope of this paper is beyond the detailed description of these control strategies we rely on [20].

For the experiments described in this paper we use the compact–tree strategy after which the core transformations have to be applied. The method is leant to the technique mentioned in [12]. The nodes in the parallel program graph are selected in a breadth–first order. The depth of a node is given by the maximum number of nodes on any path from the root to it. Migrate moves operations of those nodes with the same depth as far as possible. The nodes closest to the root will be chosen first.

Loops have an important impact on the runtime of a program. Approaches speeding up loops are of great interest for parallel architectures especially for VLIW architectures. For our parallelizing system we have first implemented loop–unrolling combined with global register renaming based on the parallel program graph. After unrolling loops compacting the resulting program graph can be performed using one of the methods described above.

7 Compile–time Transformations for the Conditional Execution Model

As mentioned above, the compiler has to transform the parallel program graph when targeted to a VLIW architecture supporting the conditional execution model. These transformations comprise the elimination of branches (tests) and the assignment of the condition codes to the operations which depend on the branch to be eliminated.

An essential property of the conditional execution model introduced above is that the conditional and unconditional execution of operations are not mutually exclusive. Only those branches with properties to be described next will be eliminated. Therefore, only a subset of the program's operations will be executed conditionally.

The transformations require a parallel program graph constructed from a reducible control flow graph. Structured programming results in programs from which regular structures can be recognized in the corresponding parallel program graph. The subgraph derived from an *if*–statement consists of a node with two successors and the paths originated in that node reach a common destination node. This subgraph can be represented as a *rhomb*. The elimination of the branch in a node of a subgraph representing a rhomb leads to a linearization of that subgraph.

Formally a rhomb can be defined as follows. Given a parallel program graph. A *rhomb* is a subgraph of a parallel program graph with the following properties:

1. node n_i is the *root* of the rhomb and has two successors.
2. Every node on a path starting at n_i has at most one successor or the node is the root of a rhomb.
3. Every path starting at n_i reaches an unique node $n_j, n_j \neq n_i$, which is the only node with more than one predecessors and which can be reached from every path starting at n_i. The node n_j is called destination node of the rhomb.

After this recursive definition of a rhomb, a rhomb can be nested corresponding nested if–statements. A rhomb does not have a back edge to a node on a path starting at n_i, because then more than one node exist which can be reached from all paths starting at the root of the rhomb or there is no node with more than one predecessor which can be reached from all paths starting at the root. The definition above allows a back edge from the destination node of the rhomb to the root. Nested rhombs can have a common destination node. The destination node can have at most $k + 1$ predecessors if k is the number of nodes with two successors on paths starting at the root and reaching the destination node.

The algorithm for finding rhombs in a parallel program graph searches a node with two successors. A recursive procedure *find-rhomb* with the root as argument is called. This procedure traverses the parallel program graph in a breadth–first manner and searches for a node with more than one predecessor. If all paths of the subgraph reaches this destination node then a rhomb have been found. If a node is reached which has two successors *find-rhomb* is called recursively.

Each rhomb in a parallel program graph has to be determined. Using a heuristic one can decide which rhombs have to be linearized. For each rhomb to be linearized the test operation in the root will be eliminated. For each operation on the true path and for each operation on the false path the corresponding condition codes are assigned. The root's right successor (false path) becomes the successor of the left predecessor of the destination node and the edge from the root to its right successor will be removed. Inner rhombs will be linearized first.

After the linearization the resulting program graph can be compacted applying the percolation scheduling approach described above. Only the move-op core transformation has been changed in checking first whether the operation to be moved and all operations in the node where the operation has to be moved to have complemented condition codes. Two operations with complemented condition codes can be packed in one instruction word regardless the data dependencies. For all other cases data dependencies have to be checked as usual.

Several researches proved that optimal solution can be achieved in parallelizing loops without branches. With the transformations described above branches in loops can be eliminated. Therefore, for parallelizing loops with operations to be executed conditionally good results can be expected. The transformations described above lead to control flow graphs (parallel program graphs) with enlarged basic blocks. As a consequence no code explosion will arise.

In the next section we present the first results obtained by the first version of our simulation environment.

8 Some Preliminary Results

Our parallelizing compiler takes as an input a C program and generates a sequence of long instruction words applying loop unrolling, register renaming and percolation scheduling as described above. Depending on the switch chosen the transformations required by the conditional execution model are applied before compaction. The parallelized code can run on a simulator for VLIW architectures. The main purpose of the simulator is to model the hardware configuration of a variety of VLIW architectures and to provide some information about the performance of a chosen VLIW architecture under a work load generated by the compiler. Programs generated with operations to be executed conditionally can also run on the simulator. The statistics about the performance comprise the simulation time (number of cycles executed) the statical number of operations executed (noops included), informations about the instruction fetches and data access, call and branch statistics. A detailed description of the simulator for VLIW architectures can be found in [6]. While our VLIW–compiler assumes a VLIW architecture with enough resources exploiting the fine-grained parallelism extracted by the parallelization the first version of our simulator is restricted to VLIW architectures with 16 processing elements only.

For the experiments demonstrating the impact of the conditional execution model on the performance of a VLIW architectures some short sequential natured programs have been selected. The minmax.c program finds the minimum and the maximum of an array of integers, sieve.c computes primes and quicksort.c sorts a field of integers applying the quicksort algorithm.

Table 1 compares the results optained running the parallelized programs on the simulator. In column "Orig." the runtime (in cycles) is given for the sequential program. A sequential program consists of a sequence of long instruction words. Each long instruction word contains only one useful operation. In column "PS" the number of cycles required by the execution of the compacted program is given. Column "C+PS" indicates the number of cycles the program with operations to be executed conditionally takes on the corresponding simulated VLIW architecture. The speedup is computed by dividing the number of cycles the sequential program takes on the simulated VLIW architecture through the number of cycles the compacted program takes on the simulated VLIW architecture.

Table 1. Runtime (in cycles) and speedup

	Orig.	PS	C+PS	S_{PS}^{Orig}	S_{C+PS}^{Orig}
minmax.c	430	278	215	1,55	1,93
qsort.c	1564	1236	1190	1,27	1,31
sieve.c	18423	15352	15323	1,20	1,20

Table 2 shows that loop unrolling before compaction has an high impact on the performance of the VLIW architecture. For the program minmax.c a speedup of 4.19 can be achieved when unrolling the loop two times. Also sieve.c speeds up to 1.80 when unrolling each loop one time.

The results shown in Table 1 and 2 have been optained by the first version of our parallelizing compiler and the simulator for VLIW architecture. Although preliminary, they show that a high degree of fine–grained parallelism can be extracted by the VLIW–compiler and exploited by VLIW architectures.

When compacting unrolled loops code explosion arises. This is the reason why fields in Table 2 remain empty. When unrolling the loop one time and compacting the unrolled loop the resulting parallel program contains long instructions with more than 16 operations. When compacting a program with tests to be elimi-

Table 2. Cycles and speedup

	Unroll	Orig.	PS	C+PS	S^{Orig}_{PS}	S^{Orig}_{C+PS}
minmax.c	0	402	156	157	2,57	2,56
minmax.c	1	–		112	–	3,59
minmax.c	2	–		96	–	4,19
sieve.c	0	18019	14617	14892	1,23	1,21
sieve.c	1-0		12439	10987	1,45	1,64
sieve.c	2-0		11716	10585	1,54	1,70
sieve.c	1-1		10939	9989	1,65	1,80

nated no code explosion can arise. Code explosion arises when operations will be moved across basic block boundaries because copies have to be generated. Therefore, when eliminating tests in a loop by the transformations described above code explosion can be prevented. Table 3 shows the number of instructions for each of the test programs. The unrolled and compacted version of the program minmax.c contains 188 instructions while the program with operations to be executed conditionally contains only 24.

Table 3. number of instructions

	Unroll	Orig	PS	PS+ C
minmax.c	0	60	33	17
minmax.c	1	–	118	22
minmax.c	2	–	188	24
qsort.c	0	102	55	44
sieve.c	0	39	25	22
sieve.c	1	–	23	17
sieve.c	2	–	24	18
sieve.c	1-1	–	35	25

9 Conclusion

In this paper we have presented an effective mechanism for multiway branches. Additionally, we introduced a generalized conditional execution model for VLIW architectures. For the evaluation of these architectural enhancements we can use a simulation environment currently being developed. This simulation environment is primarily intended to be a testbed for a number of VLIW architecture models and parallelization techniques. Our intention is to find high performance combinations of VLIW architectures and parallelizing compilers. Different parallelization techniques can be integrated and evaluated with our simulation environment. Optionally, the parallelizing compiler can generate code for VLIW architectures supporting the conditional execution of operations.

The results of our first experiments show that a high degree of fine–grained parallelism can be extracted and exploited on VLIW architectures, especially on those supporting the conditional execution model. There seems to be a good potential in this kind of computer architecture and there are improved compilation and parallelization techniques for it. With our simulation environment we can investigate and prove the usefulness and effectiveness of VLIW architectures and their parallelization techniques for scientific code as well as for sequential natured code. As indicated by the examples, the conditional execution model for VLIW architectures is well suited in exploiting fine–grained parallelism in sequential natured program code.

Much more work has to be done to improve the parallelization techniques by a more thorough data dependency analysis, memory disambiguation and other methods. With more sophisticated software–pipelining techniques we estimate that the results can be improved by a factor of 3 to 5. In addition, resource constrained parallelization has to be considered too, to get much more realistic results.

References

1. Abnous, A., Potasman, R., Bagherzadeh, N., Nicolau, A.: A Percolation Based VLIW Architecture. Proceedings of the 1991 International Conference on Parallel Processing (1991) I-144–I-148. CRC Press
2. Aho, A. V., Sethi, R., Ullman, J. D.: Compilers – Priciples, Techniques and Tools. Addison Wesley Publishing Company, Reading Massachusetts (1986)
3. Aiken, A.: Compaction–Based Parallelization. PhD thesis, Department of Computer Science, Cornell University, Ithaca, New York 14853-7501 (1988)
4. Benitez, M. E., Davidson, J. W.: A Portable Global Optimizer and Linker. Proceedings of the SIGPLAN '88 Symposium on Programming Language Design and Implementation, SIGPLAN Notices, (1988) 329–338, Atlanta, Georgia
5. Benitez, M. E., Davidson, J. W.: Code Generation for Streaming: an Access/Execute Mechanism. ASPLOS–IV Proceedings, Fourth International Conference on Architectural Support for Programming Languages and Operating Systems (1991) 132–141, Santa Clara, California
6. Böckle, G., Trosch, S.: A Simulator for VLIW Architectures. SFB–Bericht 342/16/90 A, Institut für Informatik, Technische Universität München, (1990)
7. Breternitz, M.: Architectural Synthesis of High Performance Application–Specific Processors. PhD thesis, Carnegie Mellon University (1991)
8. Callahan, D.: The Program Summary Graph and Flow–sensitive Interprocedural Data Flow Analysis. Proceedings of the SIGPLAN '88 Conference on Programming Language Design and Implementation, SIGPLAN Notices, (1988) 47–56, Atlanta, Georgia
9. Colwell, R. P., Nix, R. P., O'Donnell, J. J., Papworth, D. B., Rodman, P. K.: A VLIW Architecture for a Trace Scheduling Compiler. IEEE Transactions on Computers, C-37(8), (1988) 967–979

10. Ebcioğlu, K.: Some Design Ideas for a VLIW Architecture for Sequential Natured Software. Proceedings of IFIP WG 10.3 Working Conference on Parallel Processing, (1988) 3–21, Pisa, Elsevier Science Publishers B. V.

11. Ebcioğlu, K., Nakatani, T.: A New Compilation Technique for Parallelizing Loops with Unpredictable Branches on a VLIW–Architecture. Proceedings 2nd Workshop on Compilers and Languages for Parallelism, University of Illinois, (1989)

12. Ebcioğlu, K., Nicolau, A.: A Global Ressource Constrained Parallelization Technique. International Conference on Supercomuting, (1989) Crete, Greece

13. Fisher, J.: Trace–Scheduling: A Technique for Global Microcode Compaction. IEEE Transactions on Computers, C-30(7) (1981) 478–490

14. Fisher, J.: Very Long Instruction Word Architectures and the ELI–512. Proceedings of the 10th Symposium on Computer Architecture (1983) 140–150

15. Gasperoni, F.: Compilation Techniques for VLIW–Architectures. Research Report RC 14915, IBM Research Devision, T. J. Watson Research Center, Yorktown Heights, (1989) New York

16. Hsu, P. Y. T., Davidson, E. S.: Highly Concurrent Scalar Processing. Proceedings of the 13th Annual Symposium on Computer Architecture, (1986)

17. Johnson, M.: Superscalar Microprocessor Design. Prentice Hall, (1991) Englewood Cliffs, New Jersey 07632

18. Jouppi, N. P., Wall, D. W.: Available Instruction Level Parallelism for Superscalar and Superpipelined Machines. ASPLOS–III Proceedings, Third International Conference on Architectural Support for Programming Languages and Operating Systems, (1989) 272–282, Boston, Massachusetts

19. Kane, G.: Mips RISC Architecture. Prentice Hall, (1987) Englewood Cliffs, NY 07632

20. Karl, W. Architektureigenschaften und Parallelisierungsmethoden für Rechner mit Funktionspipelining. Dissertation, Institut für Informatik, Technische Universität, München, (1992) (to appear in B. I. Wissenschaftsverlag, Mannheim)

21. Labrousse, J., Slavenburg, G. A.: A 50 MHz Microprocessor with a Very Long Instruction Word. IEEE International Solid–State Circuit Conference (1990)

22. Nicolau, A.: Percolation Scheduling: A Parallel Compilation Technique. Technical Report TM 85-678, Department of Computer Science, Cornell University, (1985) Ithaca, New York 14853

23. Slavenburg, G. A., Huang, A. S., Lee, Y. C.: The LIFE Family of High Performance Single Chip VLIWs. HOT CHIPS Symposium (1991)

Load Balanced Optimisation of Virtualised Algorithms for Implementation on Massively Parallel SIMD Architectures[1]

C. A. Farrell   *D. H. Kieronska*
Department of Computer Science
Curtin University of Technology
Perth, Western Australia
craig@cs.curtin.edu.au   dorota@cs.curtin.edu.au

Abstract

Load balancing on parallel machines is rarely considered in the context of SIMD architectures. In some SIMD algorithms, specifically in a class of tree-based reduction algorithms, where the number of active processors varies with each step of the algorithm, load balance can be poor. This problem becomes magnified if an algorithm needs to be virtualised, ie. the required number of processors is being simulated by a smaller number of real processors.

In this paper we discuss the issue of load balancing virtualised algorithms for implementation onto massively parallel SIMD architectures. We show how a programmer's prior knowledge of an algorithm can be used to optimise the virtualised implementation of that algorithm.

1 Introduction

When implementing algorithms on parallel architectures, optimal performance is achieved by distributed load balancing and by reducing the amount of interprocessor communication required during execution. To an extent these two goals are somewhat contradictory especially on distributed memory architectures where the more processors there are, the further apart the data can be spread. This problem was highlighted in [11, 1] where it was found that the location of data (rather than efficient load balancing) should be the primary determining factor when scheduling execution of parallel threads on shared memory multiprocessors.

Massively parallel machines (as opposed to multiprocessor machines) are characterised by large numbers of processors, sometimes called processing elements or PEs, and well developed communication mechanisms. The individual PEs on massively parallel machines are generally not as powerful as the ones available on more coarsely grained architectures, but far more numerous [7, 2]. On some massively parallel machines, communication costs can be independent of the distance between PEs and the amount of data being transferred [2]. Massively parallel machines tend to be more balanced between communication speed and processor speed, meaning that the processing

---

[1] This research was partially supported by an external research grant from Digital Equipment Corporation.

potential lost during interprocessor communication is relatively small when compared to more coarsely grained architectures.

Commercially available massively parallel machines are divided into two classes: Multiple Instruction Multiple Data (MIMD) and Single Instruction Multiple Data (SIMD). In this paper we are concerned with the SIMD model where all the processors are executing the same instruction at any given point in time. The key to improving performance on massively parallel SIMD machines, is to minimise the amount of interprocessor communication [8, 9, 10] but not at the expense of SIMD load balance.

The concept of load balancing is not usually associated with SIMD models. In its broadest sense, it involves distributing the work among processors in such a way that every processor has approximately the same amount of work to do. On a SIMD machine, where all processors are executing the same instructions (synchronously), the balance is lost when some processors become non-active.
Consider a general step in a parallel algorithm

```
while(more data to process) do
    process_data(iproc);
```

where each PE is processing its own data, be it stored in global shared memory or local PE memory. Load imbalance on SIMD machines occurs when some processors are called upon to do more processing than other processors. Since all processors execute in step, the total time (cost) of this code can be expressed in terms of the time taken (cost) by the processor with the most data to process. SIMD load imbalance may be caused by the size of the problem being smaller than the number of processors available, or by an uneven distribution of data to be processed.

Load balance on massively parallel SIMD machines is a critical factor in machine performance. Since all the processors are executing the same instruction, if only one processor is active the load is very poorly balanced and machine performance suffers. In this paper we investigate the relative performance improvements that can be gained for virtualised algorithms on massively parallel SIMD architectures by maintaining a good SIMD load balance. The key to the power of massively parallel SIMD machines, like the Connection Machine[7] and the Maspar MP1[2], lies in the ability to keep most of the PEs active most of the time. Interprocessor communication is still an important performance factor on massively parallel machines. However, with the better balance between processor speed and communication, interprocessor communication is not as critical to overall performance as it is on more coarsely grained parallel architectures.

Load balancing on SIMD machines is also an important problem to be considered when the algorithm is being virtualised. Virtualisation is the concept of making the available processors repeatedly execute the same code in order to simulate the number of virtual processors (VPs) assumed by an algorithm. Virtualisation is required on any parallel machine where the number of processors assumed by an algorithm is larger than the number of PEs available on the machine. The concept of virtualisation is built into many parallel implementation environments [3,6,13] as well as being implemented by automatic virtualisation schemes like [5,12,14]. On the Connection Machine using the Parallel Instruction Set [14] virtualisation is supported in hardware. The programmer defines a *virtual machine size*, that is a virtual-to-physical ratio which determines the number of virtual processors to be simulated on each physical one.

In contrast to the Connection Machine is the approach taken on the MasPar MP1, where virtualisation, rather than be supported in hardware, is a compile time problem. Using this approach, data structures, variables as well as processors need to be virtualised. Although this approach seems to put the onus for virtualisation with the applications programmer or language designer, it has some distinct advantages [4]. For the rest of this paper we will be using the MasPar MP1 approach to virtualisation which means we can show, in source code form, how algorithms are virtualised. We present our algorithms in a language close to the MasPar MPL language. MPL is a superset of C with only a few extra constructs to support parallelism, but importantly, the virtualisation is not hidden from the programmer.

Consider the following tree based reduction summation algorithm designed to be implemented on a parallel SIMD machine.

```
int  answer[N];
...
p_add()
{
        for (L=0; L< log2(N); L++)
            if (( iproc % 2^(L+1) ) == 0)
                answer[iproc] = answer[iproc] + answer[iproc + 2^L];
}
```

Algorithm 1
Tree based summation algorithm assuming a one dimensional array of processors.

In MPL *iproc* is a constant defined on each PE which specifies its unique PE number. This algorithm assumes all the initial data is loaded in the *answer* array. The sum of all the values in the *answer* array will finish up in the first element of this array (ie. answer[0]) at the end of the summation. This algorithm assumes N processors and takes $log_2(N)$ steps to calculate the sum of all the data.

In this algorithm we see that after the first step half the processors become inactive. After another step three quarters of the processors become inactive and so on $log_2 N$ times. The number of processors inactive at any given level L is:

$$\text{number inactive} = \sum_{i=0}^{L} N / (2^{i+1})$$

Algorithm 1 clearly exhibits poor SIMD load balancing properties. Processor 0 does $log_2(N)$ additions while processor 1 does none. The problem of poor load balancing exhibited by this algorithm is magnified if the algorithm needs to be virtualised. Using the parallel implementation environments currently available [3, 6, 13] or an automatic virtualisation scheme [5, 12, 14] not only will PEs be inactive, but some simulated VPs will also be inactive. This problem is made worse still by the fact that some of the automatic virtualisation systems require the number of virtual processors to be simulated be a power of 2 [12, 14]. This often results in the value of N being "padded" out to a power of 2 and hence even more inactive VPs may be simulated.

2 The Problem

Consider running Algorithm 1 on a machine where N was larger than the number of PEs available (*real_procs*); the algorithm would need to be virtualised. On the Connection Machine this would involve increasing the virtual-to-physical ratio to some value larger than 1. On the MasPar MP1 we would need to apply some virtualisation technique to the algorithm at compile time. By applying the rules for automatic implementation of cut and stack virtualisation for parallel algorithms on SIMD machines [5] and assuming the *answer* array is stored in global shared memory, a virtualised form of this algorithm would be produced as follows:

```
#define viproc (( real_procs  * vtick) + iproc)
int answer [N];
plural int L;
...
p_add()
{
```
$$\text{for(L=0;L<}\log_2\text{(N\_prime);L++)} \quad \dots\dots\dots\dots\dots\dots\dots\dots\dots(1)$$
$$\text{for(vtick=0; vtick} < \text{(N +real\_procs)/ real\_procs; vtick++)} \dots(2)$$
$$\text{if((viproc } \% \ 2^{L+1}) == 0)$$
$$\text{if((viproc} + 2^L) < N)$$
$$\text{answer[viproc]} = \text{answer[viproc]} + \text{answer[viproc+}2^L]$$
```
}
```

Algorithm 2
Virtualised solution to the tree based parallel reduction summation.

In order to make this a more general algorithm, and be able to sum arbitrary values of N (not just powers of 2) we have changed the loop bound(1) to be *N_prime*. *N_prime* is defined to be the smallest power of 2 that is greater than or equal to N. This does not mean that this virtualised algorithm simulates *N_prime* VPs. This is only done to make the $log_2(N\_prime)$ loop (1) iterate enough times to compute the correct result.

The number of VPs simulated is defined by the *vtick* loop(2) and it is certainly not true that the number of simulated VPs will be a power of 2. The keyword *plural* is an MPL keyword which defines a variable (in this case L) on every processor. In Algorithm II L is defined to be plural for simplicity. L could have been defined to reside in global shared memory and Algorithm 2 would have executed in the same manner.

As can bee seen from Algorithm 2 the virtualisation process has done nothing for the underlying poor SIMD load balancing properties of the Algorithm 1. The virtualisation process has in fact magnified the inefficiency. Not only are PEs inactive when the size of the problem is smaller than *real_procs*, but also when N is larger than *real_procs* VPs are being simulated even though they are inactive.

In order to illustrate this consider Figure 1 which shows the execution of Algorithm 2 on a machine with 3 PEs (ie. *real_procs* = 3) and $N=8$. The boxes represent the state of all the PEs at each *vtick* iteration. Each box is *real_procs* wide and shows the PE numbers (*iproc*) as well as the simulated VP number (*viproc*). Active VPs at each level are denoted with "X" while inactive ones are denoted by "O". The different Levels in this diagram represent different iterations of the $log_2(N\_Prime)$ loop (1) and show how at each level the *vtick* loop will simulate the N processors assumed by the algorithm. On most optimised systems some of the *vtick* loops will be skipped since no processors will be active, for example on level 2 when *vtick* equals 2 and on level 3 when *vtick* equals both 1 and then 2. These are sometimes called *skipped steps*.

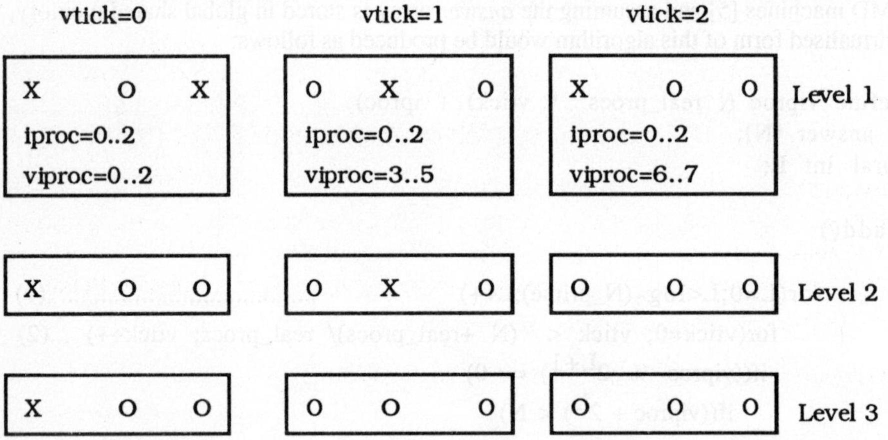

vtick=0	vtick=1	vtick=2	
X O X iproc=0..2 viproc=0..2	O X O iproc=0..2 viproc=3..5	X O O iproc=0..2 viproc=6..7	Level 1
X O O	O X O	O O O	Level 2
X O O	O O O	O O O	Level 3

X = Active Processor

O = Inactive Processor

Figure 1

Execution of virtualised parallel summation algorithm on a machine with 3 PEs and $N=8$

In this example 3 virtual clock ticks (*vticks*) are required for the 3 PEs to simulate all 8 VPs. Thus *vtick* ranges from 0 through to 2 simulating the N VPs during each iteration of the $log_2(N\_prime)$ loop. The actual algorithm requires 4 active VPs at level 1, 2 at level 2 and 1 at level 3. Given that 3 PEs are available, an optimal solution would require 2 *vticks* to simulate level 1, while level 2 and 3 should take one *vtick* each. Instead, redundant *vtick* iterations are performed at some levels, simulating inactive VPs. Processor 0 is still required to do $log_2(N\_prime)$ additions while processor 1 is required to do no additions. These inefficiencies would be even worse when using a parallel implementation environment or virtualisation technique which required the number of VPs to be simulated be a power of 2. Under these systems when $N=2^i + 1$, the number of simulated VPs would be 2^{i+1}. The technique for virtualisation we have used for our work [5] does not suffer from this power of 2 inefficiency.

However, no matter which virtualisation technique or parallel implementation environment is used the underlying inefficient load balancing properties of algorithm 1 will be magnified by the virtualisation process.

3 An Optimised Solution

The key to improving the virtualised algorithm's efficiency for massively parallel SIMD machines is to only simulate VPs that are active. This may result in extra interprocessor communication but on the massively parallel model, with its balance between processor speed and communication speed, this is not such a limiting barrier as it would be on a more coarsely grained parallel architecture. The number of active processors at each level of the algorithm is given by:

$$N / 2^{i+1}$$

With this insight into the load balancing characteristics of the algorithm, it becomes possible to optimise its virtualised equivalent. By substituting an expression representing the id of an active VP for each occurrence of *viproc* in Algorithm 2, it is possible to make the virtualised implementation of the algorithm only simulate active VPs at each level of the tree, thus maximising the load balance. To put this in the context of Figure 1, if only 4 VPs are active at some arbitrary level i, then only 4 VPs will be simulated, instead of all N VPs as would have previously occurred. This also means that the *vtick* loop can be reduced from $((N + real\_procs) / real\_procs)$ to $(((N/2^L) + real\_procs) / real\_procs)$ to reflect the smaller number of *vtick* iterations required at each level.

```
#define viproc (( real_procs  * vtick) + iproc)
int  answer [N];
plural int  L;
...
p_add()
{
        for(L=0; L <  log2(N_prime); L++)
            for(vtick=0; vtick <  (N/2^(L+1) + real_procs)/real_procs; vtick++)
                if((((viproc * 2^(L+1)) % 2^(L+1)) == 0)
                    if((((viproc* 2^(L+1)) + 2^L) < N)
                        answer[viproc* 2^(L+1)] = answer[viproc* 2^(L+1)] +
                                              answer[(viproc* 2^(L+1)) + 2^L]
}
```

Algorithm 3
Optimised Virtualised solution to the tree based parallel reduction summation

Algorithm 3 shows the optimal form of the virtualised reduction summation algorithm. In this algorithm we can see the reduced *vtick* loop as well as the new expression for *viproc*. Each virtual processor *viproc* now simulates virtual processor $viproc*2^{L+1}$, which is an expression that reflects the active VPs at level L. In this way only active VPs are simulated at each level. The limit of the *vtick* value ensures that the minimal number of iterations occur in order to simulate the number of active processors at each level.

4 Results

The increased performance gained from this technique as a result of a better SIMD load balance is independent of the parallel memory model used. By virtualising Algorithm I, using the rules for automatic virtualisation [5] assuming either a distributed PE memory or a global shared memory model we always saw improved execution times for the parallel reduction summations. Tables 1 and 2 show the results of running these virtualised algorithms (Algorithms 2and 3) on a DEC MPP12000 (Maspar MP1 equivalent) under both the global shared memory and distributed PE memory models.

N	2048	5000	20,000	25,000	27,000
real_procs 2048					
Non-Optimised	0.3	0.5	1.8	2.3	2.5
Optimised	0.3	0.5	1.7	2.1	2.2
real_procs 1024					
Non-Optimised	0.3	0.5	2.0	2.5	2.7
Optimised	0.3	0.5	1.7	2.1	2.3
real_procs 512					
Non-Optimised	0.3	0.6	2.3	2.8	3.1
Optimised	0.3	0.4	1.8	2.1	2.3

Table 1

Results of executing algorithm II (Non-Optimised) and Algorithm III (Optimised) on different sized SIMD machines[*] assuming global shared memory

N	2048	5000	100,000	500,000	1,000,000
real_procs 2048					
Non-Optimised	0.1	0.1	0.5	3.4	4.2
Optimised	0.2	0.2	0.4	1.2	2.3
real_procs 1024					
Non-Optimised	0.1	0.1	0.5	3.3	6.7
Optimised	0.2	0.3	0.4	1.8	3.4
real_procs 512					
Non-Optimised	0.1	0.1	1.3	6.3	12.7
Optimised	0.2	0.2	0.8	3.8	6.3

Table 2

Results of executing Algorithm II (Non-Optimised) and Algorithm III (Optimised) on different sized SIMD machines[*] assuming distributed PE memory

---

[*] Machines with less than 2048 PEs were simulated on a DEC MPP12000Sx (MasPar MP1 equivalent) using the specified number of PEs.

Figure 2 shows the relative performance for Algorithms 2 and 3 on a massively parallel SIMD machine using 512 PEs.

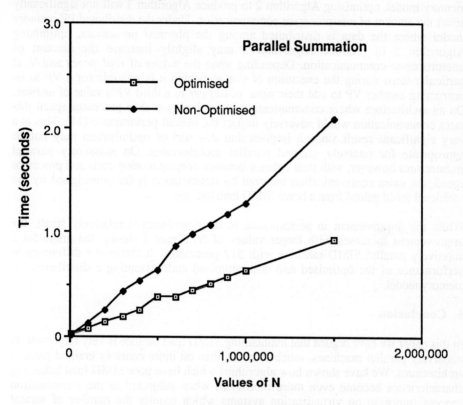

Figure 2
Performance of the optimised and non-optimised versions of the parallel summation
algorithm on a SIMD machine using 512 PEs

5 Discussion

By using our prior knowledge of how an algorithm works we have produced an improved virtualisation of the algorithm which yields a better SIMD load balance during execution (we have not altered the algorithm itself). To the best of our knowledge this type of intelligent virtualisation cannot currently be done by any of the parallel implementation or automatic virtualisation systems available. It requires knowledge and understanding of how the original algorithm works and how the properties of that algorithm can be exploited when that algorithm is virtualised.

This improved virtualised algorithm will also perform better under systems which assume the number of VPs to be simulated be a power of 2. Under these systems Algorithm 3 will produce more *skipped steps* (steps where no processors are active). This is also what would occur if we did not reduce *vtick* loop in Algorithm 3

This SIMD load balanced optimisation will have an effect on interprocessor communication which should not be ignored at this point. Under the global shared memory model, optimising Algorithm 2 to produce Algorithm 3 will not significantly affect the amount of interprocessor communication. Under the distributed PE memory model where the data is distributed among the physical processors, optimising Algorithm 2 to produce Algorithm 3 may slightly increase the amount of interprocessor communication. Depending upon the values of *real_procs* and N, at particular steps during the execution of this algorithm it is possible for a VP to be instructing another VP to add their value of *answer* to a third VP's value of *answer*. On an architecture where communication is much slower than processor speed this extra communication would adversely impact the overall performance [11]. This is a very significant result since it implies that this sort of optimisation may not be appropriate for coarsely grained parallel architectures. On massively parallel architectures however, with their balance between communication costs and processor speed, the extra communication incurred by optimisation is far outweighed by the additional speed gained from a better SIMD load balance.

While the improvement in performance in these statistics is relatively small, the improvement increases with larger values of N. Figure 2 shows the graph for a massively parallel SIMD machine with 512 processors. It shows the difference in performance of the optimised and non-optimised code assuming a distributed PE memory model.

6 Conclusion

In this paper we have argued that maintaining SIMD load balance is very important on massively parallel machines, much more so than on more coarsely grained parallel architectures. We have shown how algorithms which have poor SIMD load balancing characteristics become even more inefficient when subjected to the virtualisation process (more so on virtualisation systems which require the number of virtual processors to be a power of 2). We have shown by example how it may be possible to improve the virtualisation of a particular algorithm for implementation on to a massively parallel machine. This may involve some *a priori* knowledge about a particular algorithm, which is used to modify the virtualised form of the algorithm to maintain a better SIMD load balance. On massively parallel machines our results show that this can be done even at the expense of introducing some additional interprocessor communication. We have also shown that improvements gained by maintaining an optimal SIMD load balance are independent of the parallel memory model being used by the underlying parallel architecture.

References

[1]   Anderson T.E., Lazowska H.M and Levy H.M., "The Performance Implications of Thread Management Alternatives for Shared Memory Mulitprocessors" IEEE Transactions on Computers, 38(12): pp. 1631-1644, December 1989.

[2]   Blank T., "The Maspar MP-1 Architecture", Proceedings of the IEEE Compcon Spring 1990, IEEE, February 1990.

609

[3]   Braunl T., "Structured Programming in Parallaxis", Structured Programming, 10/3, pp121-132, 1989.

[4]   Christy P., "Virtual Processors Considered Harmful", Proceedings of the Sixth Distributed Memory Computing Conference, Portland, Oregon, April 28 - May 1, 1991.

[5]   Farrell C. A. and Kieronska D. H. "On Implementation of Automatic Virtualisation of Parallel Algorithms for SIMD Architectures", Technical Report Number 17, Department of Computer Science, Curtin University, 1992.

[6]   Foster I. and Tucke S., "Parallel Programming with PCN", ANL-91/32, Argonne National Laboratories, Argonne, Illinios 60439, April 1991.

[7]   Hillis W. Daniel, "The Connection Machine", MIT Press, 1985.

[8]   Huang C.-H. and Sadayappan P., "Communication-Free Hyperplane Partitioning of Nested Loops", Languages and Compilers for Parallel Computing Fourth International Workshop Santa Clara, California, USA, August 1991.

[9]   Knobe K, Lukas J. D and Steele G L., "Data Optimisation: Allocation of Arrays to Reduce Communication on SIMD Machines", Journal of Parallel and Distributed Computing 8, pp. 102-118, 1991.

[10]   Li J. and Chen M., "The Data Alignment Phase in Compiling Programs for Distributed-Memory Machines", Journal of Parallel and Distributed Computing 13, pp. 213-221, 1991.

[11]   Markatos E.P and LeBlanc T.J, "Load Balancing vs Locality Management in Shared-Memory Mulitprocessors", Technical Report 399, Dept. of Computer Science University of Rochester, Rochester, NY 14627, October 1991.

[12]   NASA Goddard Space Flight Center, "Automatic virtualisation package for the Maspar", Available for anonymous ftp at gsfc.nasa.gov. NASA Goddard Space Flight Center Greenbelt, Maryland, USA.

[13]   Rose J.R and Steele G., "C*: An extended C Language for Data Parallel Programming", Thinking Machines Corporation, Cambridge Massachusetts.

[14]   Thinking Machines Corporation, "Introduction to Programming in C/Paris" Thinking Machines Corporation Cambridge Massachusetts, June 1991.

Performance evaluation of WASMII: a data driven computer on a virtual hardware

Xiao-ping Ling and Hideharu Amano

Faculty of Science and Technology
Keio University, Japan
{ling,hunga}@aa.cs.keio.ac.jp

Abstract. The virtual hardware has proposed to realize a large digital circuit with a small real hardware by using an extented Field Programmable Gate Array(FPGA). Several configuration RAM modules are provided inside the FPGA chip, and the configuration of the gate array can be rapidly changed by replacing the active module. Configuration data is transferred to an unused configuration RAM module from an off-chip backup RAM.

A novel computation mechanism(WASMII), which executes a target dataflow graph directly, is proposed based on the virtual hardware. A WASMII chip consists of the expended FPGA on virtual hardware and the additional mechanism to replace configuration RAM modules in the data driven manner. Configuration data is preloaded by the order which is assigned in advance with a static scheduling. By connecting a number of WASMII chips, a highly parallel system can be easily constructed.

1 Introduction

Research of data driven computing has been continued for decades. Although it has been expected to remove faults of stored programming style computers, it has failed to have an impact on mainstream computing because of its architectural problems. If we can connect infinite hardware resources freely, we can construct a dataflow machine with a lot of operational units directly reflecting a dataflow graph like old analog computers. Of course, this method is not realistic because of the limitation of resources. A lot of architectural techniques have been introduced in order to make the dataflow model realistic, and some of experimental dataflow machines are operational.However, the advanced techniques require complicated structures/controls for implementation. As a result, dataflow machines tend to become complex and expensive.

Recently, technologies around the FPGA (*Field Programmable Gate Array*) have been developed rapidly. A FPGA LSI chip can be used as various kinds of hardware because the configuration of the chip is fully programmable. Recent automatic cell placement and routing techniques enable the quick programming and configuration of them.

Here, we extend structure of the current FPGA, and propose a concept of the virtual hardware. Using this technique, a large digital circuit is realized with a small amount of real hardware.

Next, using this mechanism, a data driven computation mechanism called the WASMII is introduced. A scheduling algorithm and initial evaluation results are also presented.

2 The virtual hardware

The FPGA(Field Programmable Gate Array) is an integrated circuit whose configuration can be determined not by a mask pattern but by external information. Technologies around the FPGA has been rapidly established in the recent few years. Now, various types and size of FPGA are available. For example, Xilinx XC3000 family[1] is one of the most popular FPGAs.

If configuration information can be quickly changed, a hardware function realized with the FPGA is also changed quickly. However, the current FPGA requires a long time ($\mu secs$ or $msecs$) for inserting configuration information from the off-chip ROM. This problem can be solved by the extension shown in Figure 1.

A certain number(n) of configuration RAM units are prepared inside the chip and they can be connected with elements (ex. function units, bonding matrices) in the FPGA through a multiplexor. Here, each configuration RAM unit can control all elements in the FPGA. By switching internal RAM units, configuration of the FPGA is quickly replaced. The internal RAM units are also connected with an external backup RAM. When a RAM unit is not used (not connected with elements of the FPGA), new configuration information can be carried from the backup RAM. By replacing pages and preloading the configuration information from the backup RAM, a large scale hardware can be realized with a single FPGA chip.

We call this mechanism the **virtual hardware**, and use terms according to the terminology in the virtual memory. An internal configuration RAM unit is called an internal **page**, and loading the information from backup RAM is called the **preloading**. When a page is connected to elements in the FPGA and forms the real circuit, the page is called **activated**.

3 The structure of the WASMII

The virtual hardware is effective to emulate a digital circuit which is large but works partially at a time. A kind of CPU structure[2] can be realized efficiently by using this mechanism. However, applications of the virtual hardware are limited with the following reasons. First, it is hard to select an appropriate part of hardware when a circuit works. Next, it is impossible to save data which is stored in elements (flip-flops, registers or memory) of the FPGA. Configuration RAM only stores information for configuration. Data stored in configured elements disappear when the page is replaced.

A data driven computation is one of the most hopeful applications of the virtual hardware. A dataflow graph is divided into the size of FPGA and allocated to pages of the virtual hardware. Since the computation of each node in the target dataflow graph is driven by tokens, a page can be activated when all tokens for nodes in the page are ready. A page can be replaced when all tokens are flushed out of the page. There is no memory in nodes of a dataflow graph because a dataflow machine has essentially no side effect. Moreover, in most programs, only a part of dataflow graph is activated at a certain time.

Here, a chip structure for dataflow machines based on the virtual hardware is proposed first. We call this computation mechanism the **WASMII**(*What A Stupid Machine It Is!*), and a chip structure for this mechanism the **WASMII chip**. Then, a parallel system using WASMII chips is introduced.

3.1 Single-chip WASMII

The structure of the WASMII chip is shown in Figure 3. The token router and input token registers are attached to the virtual hardware shown in Figure 1.

- **The token router** is a packet switching system for transferring tokens between pages. It receives tokens from the activated page and sends them to the input token registers. A high speed multistage packet switching network[3] can be utilized.
- **Input token registers** store tokens outside pages. A set of registers is required to every page of the WASMII chip.

Outside the WASMII chip, a scheduler is prepared. A small microprocessor system may be connected with a host workstation can be used as a acheduler. It carries configuration data from the backup RAM to internal pages according to the order decided by the static scheduling. A target dataflow graph is divided into subgraphs, each of which is mapped to a page. Here, we assume that several nodes of a dataflow graph can be executed with a FPGA chip.

When all required input tokens arrive at the input token registers, the corresponding page is ready to be activated. After all tokens are flushed out of the current activated page, one of ready pages is activated by the order assigned in advance. In an activated page, all nodes and wires are realized with a real hardware on the FPGA. Each node starts its computation completely in the data driven manner. Tokens transferred out of the activated page are sent to the input registers through the token router, and they enable the other pages to be ready.

3.2 Multi-chip WASMII

WASMII chips can be easily connected together and form a highly parallel system, called the **multi-chip WASMII**, by extending the token router so as to transfer tokens between pages in different WASMII chips. Figure 2 shows one of the simplest structures of the multi-chip WASMII.

In this structure, each WASMII chip has its own backup RAM, and subgraphs are statically allocated to each chip. Here, we adopt a simple nearest neighbor mesh connection topology. In the multi-chip WASMII, relatively large latency

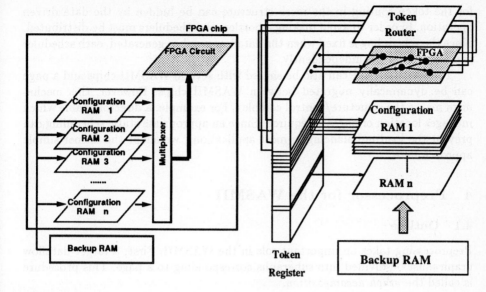

Fig. 1. FPGA structure for the Virtual Hardware

Fig. 3. WASMII chip

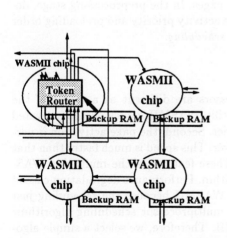

Fig. 2. Multi-chip WASMII with local Backup RAM.

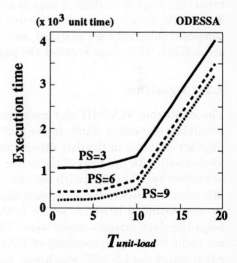

Fig. 4. The curve of T vs $T_{unit-load}$ ($NW = 1$)

for the token routing in the mesh structure can be hidden by the data driven operation. In order to avoid making a bottleneck, schedulers must be distributed. Since the scheduling is fixed when the dataflow graph is generated, each scheduler can execute its job independently.

The backup RAM can also be shared with several WASMII chips and a page can be dynamically migrated between WASMII chips. However, this mechanism makes the structure/control complex. For example, a directory table which manages location of pages is required. Since an appropriate static scheduling can prevent the load unbalancing in most applications, we adopt the former simple approach here.

4 Preprocessor for the WASMII

4.1 Outline

Preprocessing takes an important role in the WASMII. First, a target dataflow graph must be divided into subgraphs corresponding to a page. This procedure is called the *graph decomposition*.

Next, the execution priority of decomposed subgraphs is calculated as well as the execution order of nodes in a subgraph. Although the execution of WASMII is basically done in the data driven manner, the following two operations are managed according to the order or priority assigned in advance: (1) Preloading: a page is loaded from the backup RAM according to the order decided in advance; (2) Page activation: a page is selected according to the priority assigned in advance, if there are multiple activited pages. In the preprocessing stage, decomposed subgraphs are analyzed, and the activity priority and preloading order are decided. This stage is called the *page scheduling*.

4.2 Algorithm

The multi-chip WASMII and multiprocessors are different as a target of the scheduling algorithm. First, in the multi-chip WASMII, nodes on the activated page are executed in the date driven manner. Second, the page activation is performed only with the delay of the multiplexer. This speed is much faster than that of process switching in multiprocessors. These features of the multi-chip WAS-MII relax requests to the scheduling algorithm. Performance degradation caused by misscheduling is not so severe in the WASMII because the scheduling just helps the data driven computation. The multiprocessor scheduling algorithms are useful for the preprocessing of WASMII. Therefore, we select a simple algorithm called the LS-M[5] which was designed for problems with an assumption that the task processing time are equal, and modify it for the WASMII system. By using this scheduling, node assignments to a processor and the order of execution in the processor are determined. For further details of the LS-M, literature [5] will be referred to.

In a multi-chip WASMII system with n chips, the maximum available parallelism of the system, MP (the Maximum Parallelism) is represented by $PS \times n$

where *PS* (Page-Size) is the maximum number of tasks in a page. When the LS-M is applied to the multi-chip WASMII system, an operational unit which is realized on the WASMII chip is corresponding to a processor. Therefore, number *MP* is corresponding to the number of processors in common multiprocessors. The goal of the scheduling is to select appropriate operational units (processors) to which tasks are assigned, and to form pages for a WASMII chip.

Algorithm 1. *We define that $N(p)$ is a set of tasks assigned to processor p; $I(t)$ is the order number of the task t in the mapped processor; And ATS_i is the ith allocation task set where $ATS_i = \{t(I(t) = i)\}$. Then, in ATS_i, there may be tasks which receive tokens from other tasks in ATS_{i+1}. We call such a task the* premature task. *If the premature task is paged together with other tasks in ATS_i, deadlock may occur. To avoid it, premature tasks are removed from ATS_i, and checked again in the next step. The algorithm iterates following steps.*

1. *Check ATS_i. If there is any premature task, move it to ATS_{i+1}.*
2. *Divide tasks in ATS_i into NW pages, and assign the sequential number j to each page. The page is identified as $page_{i,j}$.*

$\square$

By using this algorithm, a set of pages $PAGE = \{page_{i,j}\}$ including tasks are obtained. Here, i indicates the order of execution in the WASMII chip, and j is corresponding to the number of the WASMII chip to which the page is assigned.

5 Evaluation

5.1 Application programs of the WASMII

Programs which satisfy the following features are suitable for execution on the WASMII.

- Programs which take a long time to run and can be used many times with various parameters are suitable. It takes a long time (hours) to convert a program into the execution form for the WASMII. A program is first converted into a dataflow graph, and then the configuration information is generated as well as preprocessing described before.
- The target dataflow graph includes small loops or subgraphs whose structures are the same. Thus, the configuration data can be used again in the chip. Internal pages can be utilized effectively in such programs.

Here, following problems satisfied these features are used for evaluations:

- **ODESSA** [4][5] is a continuous system simulator which solves ordinary differential equations by Euler's method.
- **NEURO** [6] is a simulator of neural networks for pattern recognition with the back propagation.
- **Production system** [7] transforms a program written in OPS5 to the dataflow graph including Rete network for quick matching.

These programs iteratively run for a long time, and there are a lot of subgraphs whose structure are the same in these programs. By using the configuration data inside the WASMII chip again, the performance will be enhanced. Details of applications are shown in Table 1.

Table 1. Target problems

Problem	Num. of tasks	Weight of tasks	Parallelism	Num. of task types
ODESSA(50)	297	10	148	4
NEURO(3x3)	216	10,20,40	162	6
OPS5(wine)	271	6,30	68	2

5.2 Evaluation by computer simulation

The following parameters are used in the execution level simulation:

- The weight of tasks: w_t ($w_t = 10$).
- The page size (the maximum number of tasks in a page): PS.
- The time for switching the multiplexor for activating a page: $DR \times w_t$ ($DR = 0.5$).
- The time for replacing a page from backup RAM: $T_{unit-load} \times PS \times w_t$.
- The time for transfer a token inside a WASMII chip: $DI \times w_t$ ($DI = 0.25$).
- The time for transfer a token to the neighboring chip: $DT \times w_t$ ($DT = 0.5$).
- The maximum number of pages inside of a chip: NR.
- The number of WASMII chips: NW.
- The maximum usable parallelism: $NW \times PS$ (100).
- The topology of an interconnection network: the nearest neighbor mesh (Figure 2: backup RAMs are not shared).

The simulation results are shown as the following.

Performance versus chip number: Figure 5 shows the execution time versus chip number of the multi-chip WASMII when the page size is five ($PS = 5$). The thick line shows the result when subgraphs are reused in the WASMII chip while the dotted line shows the result without reuse of subgraphs. In every graph, the execution time with reuse of subgraphs is about $\frac{1}{5} \sim \frac{1}{2}$ times as that without reuse. When the number of chips is small, the execution time is reduced rapidly with the chip number, but saturated with about 7 (NEURO,OPS5) or 10 chips(ODESSA). This comes from relatively small number of nodes in target programs (Table 1) and a large communication cost between chips. In both of Figure 5(b) (NEURO) and (c)(OPS5), the performance enhancement is saturated with smaller number of processors than that in Figure 5(a)(ODESSA) because the weight of tasks in the NEURO are not equal, and the maximum parallelism of problem OPS5 becomes smaller than the maximum parallelism of the system (MP).

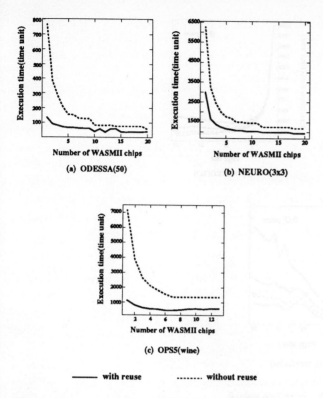

(a) ODESSA(50)

(b) NEURO(3x3)

(c) OPS5(wine)

——— with reuse   ·········· without reuse

Fig. 5. The curve of T vs. NW ($T_{unit-load} = 25 \times w_t$)

Execution time versus the cost of preloading: Figure 4 shows the execution time versus preloading cost factor ($T_{unit-load}$) when the number of chip is one. For observing the effect of scheduling, the reuse of subgraphs is prohibited in these results. In Figure 4, the execution time linearly increases after the preloading cost ($T_{load} = T_{unit-load} \times PS \times w_p$) reaches a certain time which is corresponding to the execution time of a page. This fact is reflecting that the preloading dominates the total performance. Note that, if the preloading cost is smaller than this limit, the execution time does not change. It demonstrates that the scheduling is appropriately done and preloaded page is usually hit.

The performance versus page size: Figure 6 and Figure 7 show the execution time versus the page size (PS) when the number of chips is 5 and the number of inside RAMs (NR) is 2. Pages are resued in Figure 6, while Figure 7 shows the result without reuse of pages. Comparing corresponding graphs, the effect of reuse is clearly demonstrated.

There are two turning points of the execution time. When the preloading cost (T_{load}) is smaller than the processing cost of a page in a WASMII chip, the preloading cost does not influence the execution time because the page is usually hit by the proper scheduling. We call the point where the preloading cost

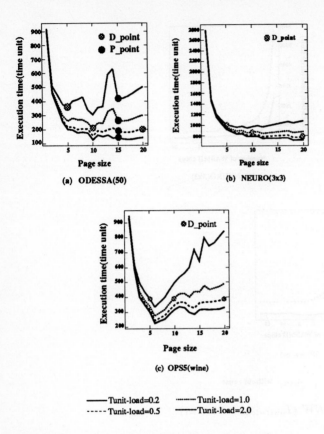

Fig. 6. The curve of T vs. PS with reusing used pages

is equal to processing cost of a page the **D_point**. In the area where the page size is smaller than the D_point, the execution time decreases even the page is not reused (Compare corresponding Figure 6 and Figure 7.)

If the page size becomes large and NR is larger than the whole graph of the target problem, every node in the graph is inside the chip. In this case, the execution time will be constant. We call this point the **P_point**.

If the page size is between the D_point and the P_point, the execution time is influenced wether subgraphs are reused or not. By comparing Figures 6 and corresponding Figures 7, it appears that the difference between both figures becomes great in this range.

We define the **reuse rate** as the following.

$$reuse\ rate = \frac{the\ number\ of\ reused\ pages}{the\ number\ of\ executed\ pages}$$

The reuse rate is clearly depends on the target graph and the page size. For general application problems, the reuse rate is randomly changed with the page size. However, the larger the page size is, the lower the reuse rate tends to be.

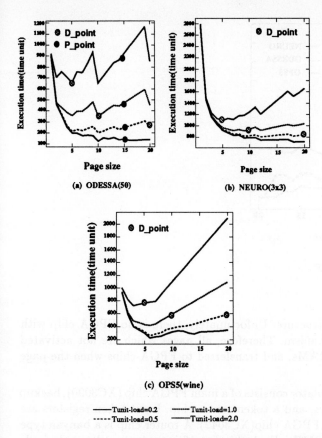

(a) ODESSA(50)

(b) NEURO(3x3)

(c) OPS5(wine)

———— Tunit-load=0.2   -------- Tunit-load=1.0
----- Tunit-load=0.5   ———— Tunit-load=2.0

Fig. 7. The curve of T vs. PS without reusing used pages

Figure 8 shows the relationship between the reuse rate and the page size. By the precise observation of Figure 8, the execution time is much influenced with the reuse rate. For example, from PS=8 to PS=10, the reuse rate of ODESSA is not desreased. From this influence, the execution time is reduced in this range (Figure 6(a)).

In ODESSA, since the parallelism is not so large as the problem NEURO, (See Table 1.) the execution time is sometimes not reduced if the reuse rate is increased with a larger page size. In NEURO, the execution time is constantly reduced when the page size is large. In OPS5, the reuse rate is small because the construction of the Rete network is relatively complex. Therefore, the execution time becomes large if the page size is beyond 6.

6   The WASMII emulator

In order to demonstrate the efficiency of the WASMII system, we are now developing a WASMII emulator. 4×4 array of WASMII chip emulators (Figure 9)

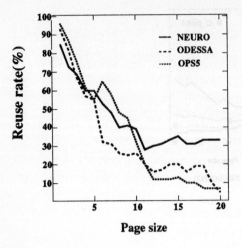

Fig. 8. The *reuse rate* vs *PS*.

are connected in a mesh structure. Unfortunately, there is no FPGA chip with the virtual hardware mechanism. Therefore, all pages which are not activated are stored in the backup RAMs, and transferred to FPGA chips when the page is activated.

Each WASMII chip emulator consists of a main FPGA chip (XC3090), backup RAM, input token registers, and a token router chip. Input token registers are realized with a small scale FPGA chip(XC3042). A router chip is a banyan type switch[3] which works at 50MHz. Each chip has 16 input/output lines. A single microprocessor board (the main CPU is 68040) connected with workstations via Ethernet works as a scheduler.

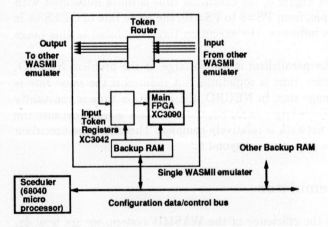

Fig. 9. The structure of the WASMII chip emulator

Now, three applications (Ordinary differential equation solver ODESSA, Production system MANJI[7], and Neural network simulator NEURO) generate a dataflow graph for the WASMII system. After the graph decomposition, the dataflow graph is converted into a program written in a hardware description language SFL. The corresponding logic is synthesized by the PARTHENON logic synthesis tool[1]. The logic is transferred to the Xilinx automatic design system and the configuration information is generated. The schedule information generated in the preprocessing system is transferred to the scheduler.

This emulator works at a high speed if there is a single page for each FPGA chip. If there are multiple pages, the replacing occurs, and the performance is severely degraded because it takes a long time to send the configuration information from the backup RAM.

7 Conclusion

A data driven computer WASMII is proposed on the basis of the virtual hardware, and its preprocessing system is introduced. Simulation results and analysis demonstrate that this system works effectively if the page loading time does not bottleneck the system.

A few years ago, WASMII (What A Stupid Machine It Is!) was hardly realizable computer as its name shows. However, quick development of the FPGA drastically changed the situation. Now, WASMII is a quite realistic computer Which may fill up the gap between software and hardware.

References

1. XILINX Corp.: Programmable gate array's data book. (1992)
2. Mitugi, S.: Rotarly computer and virtual circut. Proc. Annual Convention IPS Japan **44** (1992) 6-109
3. Amano, H., Zhou L., Gaye, K.: SSS (Simple Serial Synchronized)-MIN: a novel multi stage interconnection architecture for multiprocessors. Proc. IFIP Congress **20** (1992)
4. Ling, X.-P.: ODESSA: a OrDinary partical Equition Solving System by Analyzing on a sparse matrix parallel processing system $(SM)^2$. The M.D. thesis at Keio Univ. (1987)
5. Ling, X.-P., Amano, H.: A static scheduling system for a parallel machine $(SM)^2-II$. Proc. Conf. PARLE I LNCS 365 (1989) 118-135
6. Ling, X.-P., Amano, H., Anzai, Y.: An application of preprocessing system LS-M on a parallel computer $(SM)^2-II$—A Leaning Model. Proc. JSPP (1990) 401-408
7. Miyazaki, J., Amano, H., Aiso, H.: MANJI: A parallel machine for production system. Proc. Annual Hawaii Inter. Conf. System Sci. **20** (1987) 236-245

---

[1] PARTHENON is a logic synthesis tool developed by NTT Japan, and SFL is a hardware description language for it.

On the Performance of
Parallel Join Processing in
Shared Nothing Database Systems

Robert Marek

Erhard Rahm

University of Kaiserslautern, GERMANY

Abstract: Parallel database systems aim at providing high throughput for OLTP transactions as well as short response times for complex and data-intensive queries. Shared nothing systems represent the major architecture for parallel database processing. While the performance of such systems has been extensively analyzed in the past, the corresponding studies have made a number of best-case assumptions. In particular, almost all performance studies on parallel query processing assumed single-user mode, i.e., that the entire system is exclusively reserved for processing a single query. We study the performance of parallel join processing under more realistic conditions, in particular for multi-user mode. Experiments conducted with a detailed simulation model of shared nothing systems demonstrate the need for dynamic load balancing strategies for efficient join processing in multi-user mode. We focus on two major issues: (a) determining the number of processors to be allocated for the execution of join queries, and (b) determining which processors are to be chosen for join processing. For these scheduling decisions, we consider the current resource utilization as well as the size of intermediate results. Even simple dynamic scheduling strategies are shown to outperform static schemes by a large margin.

1 Introduction

Parallel database systems are the key to high performance transaction and database processing [DG92]. These systems utilize the capacity of multiple locally distributed processing nodes interconnected by a high-speed network. Typically, fast and inexpensive microprocessors are used as processors to achieve high cost-effectiveness compared to mainframe-based configurations. Parallel database systems aim at providing both high throughput for on-line transaction processing (OLTP) as well as short response times for complex ad-hoc queries. Efficient query processing increasingly gains importance due to the wide-spread use of powerful query languages and user tools. Next-generation database applications for engineering, VLSI design or multi-media support will lead to substantially increased query complexity [SSU91]. Since these complex queries typically access large amounts of data or/and perform extensive computations, in general the response time goal can only be achieved by employing parallel query processing strategies [Pi90]. Furthermore, performance should scale with the number of nodes: adding processing nodes ideally improves throughput for OLTP or response times for complex queries linearly.

Most research and development efforts on parallel database systems have concentrated on so-called *shared nothing* architectures [St86, DG92]. Shared nothing systems consist of multiple functionally homogenous processing nodes or processing elements (PE). Each PE comprises one or more CPUs and a local main memory, and runs local copies of application and system software like operating system and database management system (DBMS). Cooperation between PE takes place by means of message passing over a high-speed network. The characteristic feature of shared nothing systems is that the database is partitioned and distributed among all nodes so that every PE "owns" one partition. If a transaction (query) needs access to data owned by another node, a sub-transaction is started at the respective owner PE to access the remote data. In this case, a distributed two-phase commit protocol is also to be executed to guarantee the all-or-nothing property of the transaction [MLO86, ÖV91]. Existing shared nothing systems supporting parallel transaction processing include the products Tandem NonStop SQL [Ta89, EGKS90] and Teradata's DBC/1012 [Ne86] as well as several prototypes including Bubba [Bo90], Gamma [De90], EDS [WT91] and PRISMA/DB [WFA92]. With the exception of Tandem, these systems represent database machines (back-end systems) dedicated to database processing. The database operations or DML (Data Manipulation Language) statements submitted to the back-end system may originate directly from the end-user (ad-hoc queries) or from application programs running on workstations or mainframe hosts.

With respect to parallel transaction processing, we distinguish between inter- and intra-transaction parallelism. *Inter-transaction parallelism* refers to the concurrent execution of multiple independent transactions on the same database. This kind of parallelism is already supported in centralized DBMS (multi-user mode), e.g., in order to overlap I/O delays to achieve acceptable system throughput. To improve response time, intra-transaction parallelism is needed either in the form of inter-DML or intra-DML parallelism. *Inter-DML parallelism* refers to the concurrent execution of different DML statements (queries) of the same transaction. However, the degree of parallelism obtainable by inter-DML parallelism is limited by the number of database operations per transaction as well as by precedence constraints between these operations. Furthermore, the application programmer would have to specify inter-DML parallelism by means of adequate language features.

As a result, current parallel database systems support intra-transaction parallelism only in the form of *intra-DML parallelism*[1]. Relational database systems with their descriptive and set-oriented query languages (e.g. SQL) have made possible this kind of parallelism [DG92]. Intra-DML parallelism is implemented by the DBMS query optimizer, completely transparent for the database user and application programmer. For each query, the optimizer determines an (parallel) execution plan specifying the basic operators (e.g. scan, selection, join, etc.) to process the operation. The optimizer may support two types of intra-DML parallelism: inter- and intra-operator parallelism. *Inter-operator parallelism* refers to the concurrent execution of different operators in an execution plan, while *intra-operator parallelism* aims at parallelizing a single operator. In both cases, parallel processing is largely influenced by the database allocation. In particular, the database should be allocated such that operators or sub-operators on disjoint database portions can be processed in parallel on different PE. Typically, this is achieved by horizontally partitioning relations among several PE.

Despite the fact that several parallel database systems have been benchmarked and numerous performance studies on parallel query processing have been conducted (see section 2), we feel there is a strong need for further performance evaluations. This is because previous benchmarks and performance studies mostly assumed a number of best-case conditions that have an overriding effect on performance. One of the most questionable assumptions is the sole consideration of single-user experiments in most studies, frequently without even making this assumption explicit. Our research focus is to study the performance of parallel database systems under more realistic conditions and to identify shortcomings of current query processing approaches. The next step then is to develop better query processing strategies that work well under ideal and realistic conditions.

For this purpose, we have developed a comprehensive simulation system of a generic shared-nothing database system. In a previous paper, we have already presented performance results using this simulation model for the debit-credit workload as well as for real-life workloads represented by database traces [MR92]. For the present paper, we have extended our simulation model to study the performance of complex database queries, in particular join queries. In relational database systems, joins occur frequently and are the most expensive operations to execute, especially on large relations. We investigate join performance in single- as well as in multi-user mode. Our multi-user experiments clearly demonstrate the need for dynamic query processing and scheduling algorithms that take the current system state into account. Important scheduling decisions that should dynamically be drawn include determination of how many and which processors should be used for join processing. These decisions should be based on the size of intermediate results and current processor utilization. Our experiments show that even simple dynamic strategies outperform static schemes by a large margin.

The next section provides a survey of related performance studies. Sections 3 and 4 briefly describe our simulation system and the workload parameters, respectively. In section 5 we present and analyze simulation results for different configurations and scheduling strategies. Finally, we summarize the major findings of this investigation.

2   Related Work

Most benchmarks and performance studies of parallel database systems either concentrated on throughput for OLTP workloads or response time experiments for complex queries. For simple OLTP workloads such as debit-credit, it was shown that transaction rates can be linearly improved with the number of nodes [Ta88, Bo90, MR92]. The use of intra-transaction parallelism was found to be similarly effective with respect to decreasing the response time of complex queries,

---

1. In the case of ad-hoc queries there is only a single DML statement per transaction. Hence, intra-transaction parallelism is equivalent to intra-DML (intra-query) parallelism.

both in benchmarks [EGKS90, De90, WFA92] as well as in many analytical and simulation studies. However, the majority of the studies on intra-transaction parallelism is based on best-case assumptions like single-user mode, uniform data distribution, uniform load balancing, etc. Recently, researchers have begun to relax some of the uniformity assumptions by considering the effects of different forms of "data skew" [WDJ91, DG92]. However, these studies still assume single-user mode. This also holds for performance studies of different parallel join strategies (e.g. [SD89, Pa90]) and of schemes for processing N-way joins by means of inter-operator parallelism [SD90, MS91, CYW92].

While the single-user studies provided many significant insights, it is imperative to evaluate the effectiveness of intra-transaction parallelism in multi-user mode, i.e., in combination with inter-transaction parallelism. Assuming that a large system with hundreds of processors is exclusively reserved for processing a single query is clearly unrealistic since it would result in very poor cost-effectiveness. Furthermore, single-user operation would prevent meeting the throughput requirements for OLTP transactions. One problem with supporting multi-user mode ist that the current system load may significantly vary during query execution thus making dynamic scheduling strategies necessary. [GW89] already demonstrated that considerable performance gains can be realized by choosing dynamically among multiple query plans - depending on both system load and the size of intermediate results. However, they restricted their considerations to two alternative query plans (either B-tree scan and index nested loops join or file scans and hash join) and did not consider parallelization issues.

3 Simulation Model

Our simulation system models the hardware and transaction processing logic of a generic shared nothing DBMS architecture. The system has been implemented using the discrete event simulation language DeNet [Li89]. Our system consists of three main components: *workload generation, workload allocation* and *processing subsystem* (Figure 1). The workload generation component models user terminals and generates work requests (transactions, queries). The workload allocation component assigns these requests to the PE of the processing subsystem where the actual transaction processing takes place. In this section, we summarize the implementation of these components.

3.1 Workload Generation and Allocation

Database Model

Our database model supports four object granularities: database, partitions, pages and objects (tuples). The database is modeled as a set of partitions that may be used to represent a relation, a fragment of a relations or an index structure. A partition consists of a number of database pages which in turn consist of a specific number of objects. The number of objects per page is determined by a blocking factor which can be specified on a per-partition basis. Differentiating between objects and pages is important in order to study the effect of clustering which aims at reducing the number of page accesses (disk I/Os) by storing related objects into the same page. Furthermore, concurrency control may now be performed on the page or object level. Each relation can have associated clustered or unclustered B^*-tree indices.

We employ a horizontal data distribution of partitions (relations and indices) at the object level controlled by a relative distribution table. This table defines for every partition P_j and processing element PE_i which portion of P_j is allocated to PE_i. This approach models range partitioning and supports full declustering as well as partial declustering.

Workload Generation

Our simulation system supports heterogeneous workloads consisting of several transaction (query) types. In this paper we restrict ourselves to queries (transactions with a single DML statement), in particular join queries. Query types may differ in the structure of their operator trees, referenced relations, selection predicates etc. The simulation system is an open queuing model and allows definition of an individual arrival rate for each query type.

The join queries studied in this paper use three basic operators: *scan*, *sort* and *join*. These operators can be composed to query trees representing the execution plan for a query. The *scan* of a relation A using a predicate P produces a relational data output stream. The scan reads each tuple t of R and applies the predicate P to it. If P(t) is true, then the tuple is added to the output stream. We support relation scans as well as index (B^*-tree) scans. The *sort* operator reorders its input

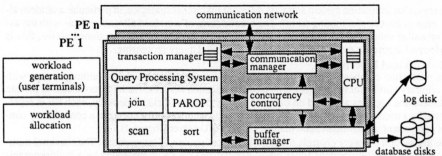

Figure 1: Gross structure of the simulation system.

tuples based on an attribute sort criteria. The *join* operator composes two relations, A and B, on some join attribute to produce a third relation. For each tuple t_a in A, the join finds all tuples t_b in B whose join attribute values are equal to that of t_a[2]. For each matching pair of tuples, the join operator inserts a tuple built by concatenating the pair into the output stream.

For our study we have implemented a representative parallel join strategy based on hash partitioning. It applies a hash function on the join attribute to partition both input relations (scan output relations) to a specific number of join processors (dynamic data redistribution). This hash partitioning guarantees that tuples with the same join attribute value are assigned to the same join processor. This approach has the advantage that it offers a high potential for dynamic load balancing since the number and selection of join processors constitute dynamically adjustable parameters. For local join processing we have implemented a sort-merge algorithm. At each join processor the input relations are first sorted on the join attribute. The sorted relations are then scanned and matching tuples are added to the output stream. The complete join result is obtained by merging the results of the distributed local joins.

In the query graphs of our model, parallelism is expressed by means of a so-called *parallelization* meta-operator (PAROP). This operator does not perform any semantic data transformations. Instead it implements inter- as well as intra-operator parallelism and encapsulates all parallelism issues[3]. In particular, the PAROP operator comprises two basic parallelization functions: a *merge* function which combines several parallel data streams into a single sequential stream, and a *split* function which is used to partition or replicate the stream of tuples produced by a relational operator.

We employ the PAROP operator to parallelize scan and join operators. For this purpose, PAROP operators are inserted into the query trees. With respect to intra-operator parallelism several strategies can be chosen to allocate parallel suboperations to processors. For scan operators, the processor allocation is always based on a relation's data allocation. For join operators, on the other hand, we support several static and dynamic allocation alternatives, e.g. random allocation or based on the PE's CPU utilization. More details will be given in section 5 together with the simulation results.

The example in Figure 2 illustrates the use of the PAROP operator. The query specifies that a join is to be performed between relations A and B and the result is to be printed. Relation A is partitioned into three fragments A_0, A_1, A_2 (residing on disjoint PE) and relation B into two fragments B_0, B_1. The two lower PAROP operators specify that the scan operations are parallelized according to this fragmentation. Furthermore, they indicate that the output streams of the local scans are to be split onto two join processors (according to some split function). Before the local joins are processed, the input streams have to be merged. The final PAROP operator specifies that the local join results are sent to and merged at an output (print) node.

Workload Allocation:
Two forms of workload allocation have to be distinguished. First, each incoming transaction (query) is assigned to one PE (acting as the coordinator for the transaction) according to a placement

---

2. We only consider equi-joins in this paper.
3. A similar operator-based parallelization model has been implemented in the Volcano prototype [G90].

strategy. Our simulation system supports different placement strategies, in particular a random allocation or the use of a routing table[4]. The second form of workload allocation deals with the assignment of suboperations to processors during query processing. As mentioned above, this is performed according to the chosen strategy for parallel query processing.

3.2 Workload Processing

The processing component models the execution of a workload on a shared nothing system with an arbitrary number of PE connected by a communication network. Each PE has access to private database and log files allocated on external storage devices (disks). Internally, each PE is represented by a transaction manager, a query processing system, a buffer manager, a concurrency control component, a communication manager and a CPU server (Figure 1).

The transaction manager controls the (distributed) execution of transactions. The maximal number of concurrent transactions (inter-query parallelism) per PE is controlled by a multiprogramming level. Newly arriving transactions must wait in an input queue until they can be served when this maximal degree of inter-transaction parallelism is already reached. The query processing system models basic relational operators (sort, scan and join) as well as the PAROP meta-operator (see above).

Execution of a transaction starts with the BOT processing (begin of transaction) entailing the transaction initialization overhead. The actual query processing is performed according to the relational query tree. Basically, the relational operators process local input streams (relation fragments, intermediate results) and produce output streams. The PAROP operators indicate when parallel sub-transactions have to be started and perform merge and split functions on their input data streams. An EOT step (end of transaction) triggers two-phase commit processing involving all PE that have participated during execution of the respective transaction. We support the optimization proposed in [MLO86] where read-only sub-transactions only participate in the first commit phase.

CPU requests are served by a single CPU per PE. The average number of instructions per request can be defined separately for every request type. To accurately model the cost of query processing, CPU service is requested for all major steps, in particular for query initialization (BOT), for object accesses in main memory (e.g. to compare attribute values, to sort temporary relations or to merge multiple input streams), I/O overhead, communication overhead, and commit processing.

For concurrency control, we employ distributed strict two-phase locking (long read and write locks). The local concurrency control manager in each PE controls all locks on the local partition. Locks may be requested either at the page or object level. A central deadlock detection scheme is used to detect global deadlocks and initiate transaction aborts to break cycles.

Database partitions can be kept memory-resident (to simulate main memory databases) or they can be allocated to a number of disks. Disks and disk controllers have explicitly been modelled as servers to capture I/O bottlenecks. Disks are accessed by the buffer manager component of the associated PE. The database buffer in main memory is managed according to a global LRU (Least Recently Used) replacement strategy.

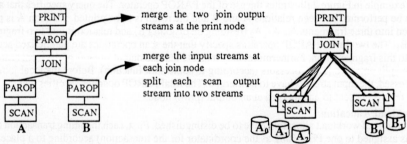

Figure 2: A simple relational query graph and the corresponding dataflow graph.

4. The routing table specifies for every transaction type T_j and processing element PE_i which percentage of transactions of type T_j will be assigned to PE_i.

The communication network provides transmission of message packets of fixed size. Messages exceeding the packet size (e.g. large sets of result tuples) are disassembled into the required number of packets.

4   Workload Profile and Simulation Parameter Settings

Our performance experiments are based on the query profile and database schema of the Wisconsin Benchmark [Gr91]. This benchmark has extensively been used for evaluating the performance of parallel database systems [EGKS90, De90, WFA92]. Although the Wisconsin Benchmark constitutes a single-user benchmark, we use it also for multi-user experiments.

Table 1 shows the major database, query and configuration parameters with their settings. Most parameters are self-explanatory, some will be discussed when presenting the simulation results. The join queries used in our experiments correspond to the Wisconsin *joinABprime* query [Gr91], but we support selections on both input relations. Each query performs two scans (selections) on the input relations A and B and joins the corresponding results. The A relation contains 1 million tuples, the B relation 100.000 tuples. The selections on A and B reduce the size of the input relations according to the selection predicate's selectivity (percentage of input tuples matching the predicate). Both selections employ indices (B*-trees), clustered on the join attribute. The join result has the same size as the scan output on B. Scan selectivity is varied between 0.1% and 10%, thus yielding join result sizes between 100 and 10.000 tuples.

The number of processing nodes is varied between 10 and 80, the number of join processors between 1 and 80 depending on the experiment. Both database relations are partitioned into an identical number of fragments and allocated on disjoint PE. Two declustering strategies are studied in the experiments with each relation allocated to either half of the PE or to a third of the PE.

The parameters for the I/O (disk) subsystem are chosen so that no bottlenecks occurred (sufficiently high number of disks and controllers). The duration of an I/O operation is composed of the controller service time, disk access time and transmission time. The parameter settings for the communication network have been chosen according to the EDS prototype [WT91].

Configuration	settings	Database/Queries	settings
number of PE (#PE)	10,20,30,60,80	relation A:	(200MB)
CPU speed per PE	20 MIPS	#tuples	1.000.000
		tuple size	200 bytes
avg. no. of instructions:		blocking factor	40
BOT	25000	index type	(clustered) B*-tree
EOT	25000	storage allocation	disk
I/O	3000	allocation to PE	1..#PE/2 (1..#PE/3)
send message (8 KB)	5000	relation B:	(20MB)
receive message (8 KB)	10000	#tuples	100.000
scan object reference	1000	tuple size	200 bytes
join object reference	500	blocking factor	40
sort n tuples	n $\log_2(n)$ * 10	index type	(clustered) B*-tree
		storage allocation	disk
buffer manager:		allocation to PE	#PE/2 + 1..#PE
page size	8 KB		(#PE/3 + 1..2#PE/3)
buffer size per PE	250 pages (2MB)	join queries:	
		access method	via clustered index
		input relations sorted	FALSE
disk devices:		scan selectivity	0.1%-10% (varied)
controller service time	1 ms (per page)	no. of result tuples	100-10000 (varied)
transmission time per page	0.4 ms	size of result tuples	400 bytes
avg. disk access time	15 ms	degree of parallelism	
		for join:	1-80 PE(varied)
communication network:		arrival rate	single-user,
packet size	128 bytes		multi-user (varied)
avg. transmission time	8 microsec	query placement	random (uniformly over all PE)

Table 1: System configuration, database and query profile.

5   Simulation Results

Our experiments concentrate on the performance of parallel join processing in single-user and multi-user mode. The single-user experiments have been performed to validate our simulation

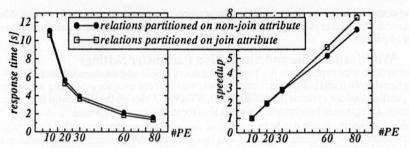

Figure 3: Influence of parallel query processing on response time and speedup.

system and to clarify the differences to the multi-user results. The base experiment described in section 5.1 analyses scalability of our join strategy in single-user mode. In sections 5.2 and 5.3 we investigate join performance for different degrees of intra-query parallelism in single-user and multi-user mode, respectively. Additionally, the performance impact of the size of intermediate results is analysed. Finally, we compare the performance of four workload allocation alternatives for parallel join processing in multi-user mode (5.4).

5.1 Base Experiment

The base experiment measures response time and response time speedup[5] of our parallel join strategy for the parameter settings of Table 1. The number of processing nodes (#PE) is varied between 10 and 80. The input relations A and B are both partitioned into #PE/2 fragments and allocated on disjoint nodes. The queries' join operators are executed on the PE holding relation A. Thus, both scan operators as well as the join operator are processed on #PE/2 nodes using intra-operator parallelism. Both scans are supported by indices and select 10% of the their input tuples. Two cases are considered depending on whether or not the join attribute corresponds to the par-titioning attribute of the relations. If the relations are partitioned on the join attribute, only the small relation B needs to be redistributed among the A nodes performing the joins. Otherwise, both relations are redistributed according to a hash function on the join attribute.

Figure 3 shows the obtained response time and speedup results. As expected, response times are better when the relations are partitioned on the join attribute because of the reduced communica-tion overhead. Still, the query response time is significantly reduced in both cases as more PE are added for query execution[6]. For both query types, we observe a near-linear response time speedup (speedup factors of 6.8 and 7.7 on 80 PE). This is favored by the large relation sizes and the con-siderable I/O overhead for accessing the database files on disks. So approximately 57% of the query response time is due to disk I/O for 80 PE (I/O activity occurs not only for the scan, but also during the join phase since the temporary relations could not always be kept in main memory). Since query execution is comparatively expensive, even 80 PE could be employed effectively. We also conducted the base experiment for memory-resident fragments. In this case the speedup val-ues were considerably lower, in particular for the joins on non-partitioning attributes. This is be-cause the communication overhead for redistributing the relations is more significant when no I/O delays occur.

Even for a disk-based database allocation, perfect linear speedup cannot generally be achieved over the entire range of processing nodes. This is because start-up costs for the distributed execu-tion of the (scan and join) operators increase with the number of PE involved, while the total amount of useful work remains the same. Furthermore, the communication overhead for redistrib-uting the scan output among the join processors increases quadratically with the number of pro-cessors. Therefore, the ratio between start-up and communication overhead, and the amount of useful work per PE deteriorates when the number of PE grows, thereby limiting the effectiveness

---

5. *Response time speedup* measures the improvement of complex query response times as more PE are added to execute the query. For N PE, the speedup is obtained by dividing the response time for the base case (10 PE in our experiments) by the response time result for parallel execution on N PE (N > 10) with the same database size [Gr91].
6. [De90] observed basically the same behaviour when running similar join queries on the Gamma database machine.

of parallel query processing. This is a general trade-off of parallel query processing and has been quantified in several previous studies [Bo90, DGSB90, MR92]. In the following experiments, these effects will be more pronounced than in the base experiment.

5.2 Degree of Join Parallelism in Single-User Mode

In this and the next subsection we study join performance for different degrees of intra-transaction parallelism and intermediate result sizes. For this purpose, we vary the number of join processors as well as the selectivity of the scan operators. For these experiments we use a constant system size of 80 PE and a declustering of both relations across 40 disjoint PE. Thus scan overhead for a given selectivity factor remains unchanged for the different configurations so that performance differences are due to join processing. The number of join processors is varied between 1 and 80 and the join PE are chosen at random.

Figure 4 shows the resulting response time and speedup results for different scan selectivities in single-user mode. We observe that increasing the number of join processors is most effective for

scan selectivity	number of join PE							response time speedup
	1	10	20	30	60	80		
10 %	6177	2082	1837	1797	1767	1736		scan selectivity 10%
1 %	677	281	**264**	266	279	286		scan selectivity 1.0%
0.1 %	182	**149**	151	158	172	178		scan selectivity 0.1%

response time [ms]   *#join processors*

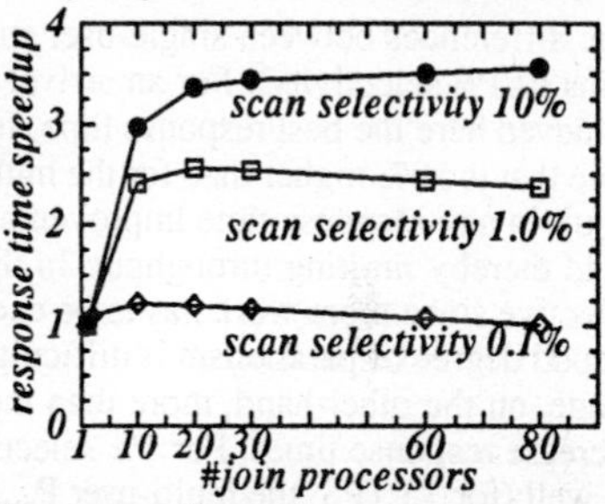

Figure 4: Influence of the size of intermediate results and the number of join processors on response time and speedup in single-user mode.

"large" joins, i.e. for high scan selectivity (10%). In this case, response times could continuously be improved by increasing the degree of intra-operator parallelism, although only slightly for more than 20 join processors. For small joins (selectivity 0.1%) response times improved only for up to 10 join processors. This is because the work per join processor decreases with the degree of intra-operator parallelism, while the communication overhead for redistributing the data increases. Thus even for large joins and despite single-user mode, comparatively modest speedup values are achieved. Of course, this is also influenced by the fact that the scan portion of the response times is not improved when increasing the number of join processors.

In the response time table of Fig. 4, the minimal response times are printed in bold-face to indicate the "optimal" degree of intra-query parallelism (minimum response time point P_{mrt}). In single-user mode when the entire system is at the disposal of a single query, the optimal degree of parallelism is solely determined by rather static parameters such as the database allocation, relation sizes and scan selectivity. Thus the query optimizer can determine the number of join processors without considering the current system state (no need for dynamic load balancing).

5.3 Degree of Join Parallelism in Multi-User Mode

For the multi-user experiment, we varied the arrival rate for our join query. The resulting response time results for different degrees of join parallelism and 1.0% and 0.1% scan selectivities are shown in Figure 5. The results show that multi-user mode significantly increases query response times. Furthermore, the effectiveness of join parallelism increasingly deteriorates with growing arrival rates. This is mainly due to increased CPU waits, because CPU requests (for communication as well as for object references) of concurrent queries have to be served by a limited number of processors. An important observation is that the optimal degree of join parallelism (P_{mrt}) for single-user mode does not yield the best response times in multi-user mode. In fact, for multi-user mode the optimal degree of join parallelism depends on the arrival rate and thus on the current system utilization. The higher the system load, the worse the single-user P_{mrt} point performs and the lower the optimal multi-user P_{mrt} becomes. This is because the communication overhead increases with the number of join processors which is the less affordable the more restricted the CPU resources are.

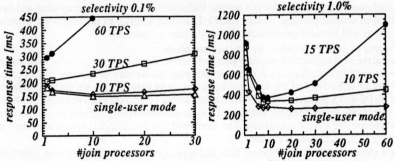

Figure 5: Influence of the system load and the number of join processors on response time.

The differences between single-user and multi-user results are particularly pronounced for small joins (0.1% selectivity). For an arrival rate of 60 TPS, join execution on a single join processor achieved here the best response time. In this case, the single-user P_{mn} of 10 results in a response time that is 50% higher than for the multi-user P_{mn} of 1. For 30 TPS, join parallelism also did not result in any response time improvement but only introduced unnecessary communication overhead thereby limiting throughput. In the case of 1% scan selectivity, join parallelism was more effective since more work has to be executed by the join processors. However, Fig. 5 shows that a good degree of parallelism is difficult to find since it is confined to a small range. In single-user mode, on the other hand, more than the optimal number of join processors did not significantly increase response times. For 1% selectivity, the multi-user P_{mn} differs from the single-user P_{mn} as well (for 15 TPS, the multi-user P_{mn} is 10 rather than 20).

Our experiment clearly demonstrates the need of dynamic load balancing and scheduling for parallel join processing in multi-user mode. The optimal degree of intra-query parallelism has to be chosen according to both the size of intermediate results and the current system load. In the next experiment we study the performance of a dynamic workload allocation strategy that selects the join processors based on the current system utilization.

5.4 Processor Allocation of Join Operator

While the processor allocation of scan operators is determined by the data distribution, there is more freedom for allocating parallel join operators. This is because the join is not performed on base relations but on intermediate data that can be distributed dynamically. Hence a join operator may be executed on any PE permitting a wide range of allocation strategies. In our last experiment, we study the performance of the following four join operator allocation strategies:

- **Strategy 1 "Minimize Data Transfer":**
  This strategy tries to minimize the communication cost for data transfers by allocating the join operators to those PE owning most of the data needed for join processing. The degree of join parallelism and the selection of join processors are determined by the data distribution. For our join query, strategy 1 means that the join operators are allocated on the processors holding fragments of the larger relation A.

- **Strategy 2 "Assign Join Operators to the Processors With Minimal Work for Scan":**
  This strategy aims at balancing the load by assigning join operators to processors where no scans have to be performed. If all processors hold fragments of the input relation, the join operators are assigned to those nodes with the smallest fragments.

- **Strategy 3 "Random":**
  This strategy does not care about any information on the database distribution or query profile. It tries to avoid that certain nodes become overloaded by simply distributing the join operators across all available PE at random.

- **Strategy 4 "Keep Overall CPU Utilization Balanced":**
  This strategy uses global information on the processing nodes' CPU utilization. The basic idea is to keep the overall CPU utilization balanced in order to avoid CPU bottlenecks. The join operators are assigned to those PE which currently offer the lowest CPU utilization[7].

Alternatives 1 to 3 represent *static strategies* since they do not consider the current system state; operator allocation is only based on static information such as the database distribution (strategies

1 and 2) or the number of PE (strategy 3). Strategy 4 is a dynamic approach since it considers the current CPU utilization for workload allocation.

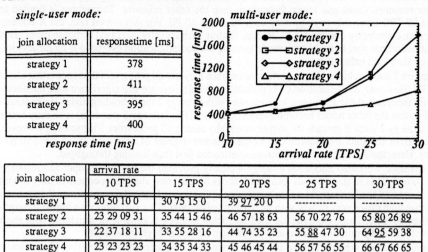

single-user mode:

join allocation	responsetime [ms]
strategy 1	378
strategy 2	411
strategy 3	395
strategy 4	400

response time [ms]

join allocation	arrival rate				
	10 TPS	15 TPS	20 TPS	25 TPS	30 TPS
strategy 1	20 50 10 0	30 75 15 0	39 97 20 0	------------	------------
strategy 2	23 29 09 31	35 44 15 46	46 57 18 63	56 70 22 76	65 80 26 89
strategy 3	22 37 18 11	33 55 28 16	44 74 35 23	55 88 47 30	64 95 59 38
strategy 4	23 23 23 23	34 35 34 33	45 46 45 44	56 57 56 55	66 67 66 65

cpu utilization [%] (global, nodes 1..20, 21..40, 41..60)

Figure 6: The influence of the workload allocation strategy and the system load on response time and processor utilization.

Using these strategies, we performed single-user as well as multi-user experiments on a 60 node shared nothing system. To provide some alternatives for operator allocation, we determined the data distribution as follows: relation A is distributed across the nodes 1 to 20 and relation B across nodes 21 to 40. Nodes 41 to 60 do not hold any data. Both scans select 1% of the relations tuples. To facilitate a comparison between the different allocation strategies, we employ a fixed degree of join parallelism in this experiment by always using 20 join processors. Strategy 1 uses the A-holding PE (1-20) for join processing, while strategy 2 selects the nodes 41-60 as join processors since they have no scan operations to perform. Strategies 3 and 4 may employ any PE of the system for join processing. The selection of the 20 join processors occurs at random (strategy 3) or based on the current CPU utilization (strategy 4).

Figure 6 plots response time results for single-user and multi-user mode. Furthermore, the average processor utilization for the multi-user experiments is shown. Each entry in this table consists of four numbers indicating the average CPU utilization of all PE, of the A-holding PE 1-20, of the B-holding PE 21-40, and of PE 41-60, respectively.

Single-user performance

As expected, the best single-user response times are achieved by strategy 1which minimizes communication overhead. Strategy 2 yields the highest response time since the joins are performed on nodes not holding any data leading to the highest communication and cooperation overhead. Strategies 3 and 4 offer response times in between of strategies 1 and 2. This shows that in single-user mode there is no need for dynamic load balancing since all PE have a low CPU utilization. This also explains the low differences between the four strategies (< 10%) indicating that in single-user mode selection of the join processors is less important than finding the right degree of join parallelism (section 5.2).

Multi-user performance

As the system load increases, the performance impact of the different allocation strategies becomes more visible. The average query execution time raises rapidly with increasing arrival rates,

---

7. For this purpose, we assume that information on the global CPU utilization is available when the join operators are allocated. This can be achieved by maintaining such information either at a designated PE or by periodically broadcasting it among all PE. The overhead for exchanging this information can be kept small by piggy-backing it to other messages used for query processing.

particularly in the case of the static strategies. Strategy 1 which performed best in single-user mode exhibits the lowest performance in multi-user mode. This strategy caused substantially higher response times and lower throughput than the other schemes. Throughput is limited to about 20 TPS since this strategy only uses 40 of the 60 PE. For this arrival rate, the A-holding nodes are completely overloaded (97%) thus leading to drastically increased response times. This result underlines that in multi-user mode limiting the communication overhead is by far less important than load balancing.

Strategies 2 and 3 achieved better performance since they use all processors thus supporting about 30 TPS. However, as the table on CPU utilization reveals there are still significant load imbalances with these two static strategies. In particular, with strategy 2 the B-holding nodes are underutilized so that the other nodes become overloaded at 30 TPS. Strategy 3 (random) is slightly better than strategy 2 since it spreads the join work equally among all processors. This strategy however, suffers from the load imbalances due to the different degrees of scan activity on the different nodes. Here, the A-holding nodes become overloaded first thus limiting throughput.

The dynamic workload allocation strategy 4 clearly provided the best throughput and response time results. This strategy avoids local bottlenecks by assigning the join operators to the PE with the lowest CPU utilization. As a result, resource utilization is kept balanced among all nodes and response time raises very slowly with increasing arrival rates. This also supports a higher throughput than 30 TPS. Thus, the dynamic load balancing strategy is capable of satisfying both short response times by utilizing intra-query parallelism as well as high throughput.

Although strategy 4 outperformed the static strategies, we observed an interesting phenomenon in our experiments which is inherent to dynamic load balancing strategies. We found out that strategy 4 tends towards assigning two consecutive queries' joins to the same processors, since the impact of the first query's activation on resource utilization does not appear immediately and since the information on CPU utilization is updated only periodically. Therefore, queries based on the same information about resource utilization will be assigned to the same processing nodes, thus impeding each other. By taking this effect into account, the dynamic strategy 4 can be further improved, e.g., by estimating changes in the resource utilization due to an assignment decision.

6 Summary

We have presented a simulation study of parallel join processing in shared nothing systems. In contrast to previous studies, we focussed on the performance behavior in multi-user mode since we believe this will be the operating mode where parallel query processing must be successful in practice. Multi-user mode means that only limited resources are available for query processing and that both response time and throughput requirements must be met. This necessitates dynamic scheduling strategies for assigning operators during query processing.

In contrast to scan operations, parallel join strategies offer a high potential for dynamic load balancing. In general, a join is not performed on base relations but on derived data obtained by previous scan operations. These intermediate results are dynamically redistributed among several join processors to perform the join in parallel. The number of join processors (degree of join parallelism) and the selection of these processors represent dynamically adjustable parameters.

Our experiments demonstrated that effectively parallelizing join operations is much simpler in single-user than in multi-user mode. In single-user mode the optimal degree of join parallelism is largely determined by static parameters, in particular the database allocation, relation sizes and scan selectivity. Determining where the join operators should be executed is also unproblematic since all processors are lowly utilized in single-user-mode. Thus, the join processors can also be selected statically so that communication overhead is minimized.

In multi-user mode, the optimal degree of join parallelism depends on the current system state and is the lower the higher the nodes are utilized. Using the optimal single-user degree of join parallelism in multi-user mode is therefore not appropriate and was shown to deliver sub-optimal performance (up to 50% higher response times in our experiments). Our results demonstrated that selection of the join processors must also be based on the current utilization in order to achieve both short response times and high throughput. Even a simple load balancing strategy based on the current CPU utilization was shown to clearly outperform static strategies. The best workload allocation strategy in single-user mode achieved the worst performance in multi-user mode. Thus, balancing the load is more important for selecting the join processors in multi-user mode than minimizing the communication overhead.

In future work, we will study further aspects of parallel query processing in multi-user mode that could not be covered in this paper. In particular, we plan to investigate dynamic scheduling strategies for mixed workloads consisting of different query and transaction types [RM93]. Furthermore, we will consider the impact of data contention (lock conflicts) and data skew on the performance of parallel query processing.

7 References

CYW92   Chen, M.; Yu, P.; Wu, K. 1992: Scheduling and Processor Allocation for Parallel Execution of Multi-Join Queries. *Proc. 8th IEEE Data Engineering Conference*, 58-67.

Bo90   Boral, H. et al. 1990: Prototyping Bubba: A Highly Parallel Database System. *IEEE Trans. on Knowledge and Data Engineering* 2(1), 4-24.

De90   DeWitt, D.J. et al. 1990: The Gamma Database Machine Project. *IEEE Trans. on Knowledge and Data Engineering* 2(1), 4-62.

DG92   DeWitt, D.; Gray, J. 1992: Parallel Database Systems: The Future of High Performance Database Processing. *Communications of the ACM* 35(6), 85-98.

EGKS90   Englert, S., Gray, J., Kocher, T., Shath, P. 1990: A Benchmark of NonStop SQL Release 2 Demonstrating Near-Linear Speedup and Scale-Up on Large Databases. *Proc. ACM SIGMETRICS Conf.*, 245-246.

GW89   Graefe, G; Ward, K. 1989: Dynamic Query Evaluation Plans. *Proc. 1989 SIGMOD Conf.*, 358-366.

G90   Graefe, G. 1990: Volcano, an Extensible and Parallel Query Evaluation System. University of Colorado at Boulder, Department of Computer Science.

Gr91   Gray, J. (Editor) 1991: The Benchmark Handbook. Morgan Kaufmann Publishers Inc.

Li89   Livny, M. 1989: DeNet Users's Guide, Version 1.5. Computer Science Department, University of Wisconsin, Madison.

MR92   Marek, R.; Rahm, E. 1992: Performance Evaluation of Parallel Transaction Processing in Shared Nothing Database Systems. *Proc. 4th Int. PARLE Conference*, LNCS 605, Springer, 295-310.

MLO86   Mohan, C., Lindsay, B., Obermarck, R. 1986: Transaction Management in the R* Distributed Database Management System. *ACM TODS* 11 (4), 378-396.

MS91   Murphy, M.; Shan, M. 1991: Execution Plan Balancing. *Proc. 1st Int. Conf. on Parallel and Distributed Information Systems*.

Ne86   Neches, P.M.1986: The Anatomy of a Database Computer - Revisited. *Proc. IEEE CompCon Spring Conf.*, 374-377.

ÖV91   Özsu, M.T., Valduriez, P. 1991: Principles of Distributed Database Systems. Prentice Hall.

Pa90   Patel, S. 1990: Performance Estimates of a Join. In: Parallel Database Systems (*Proc. PRIMSA Workshop*), Lecture Notes in Computer Science 503, Springer Verlag, 124-148.

Pi90   Pirahesh, H.et al. 1990: Parallelism in Relational Data Base Systems: Architectural Issues and Design Approaches. In *Proc. 2nd Int.Symposium on Databases in Parallel and Distributed Systems*, IEEE Computer Society Press.

RM93   Rahm, E.; Marek, R. 1993: Analysis of Dynamic Load Balancing for Parallel Shared Nothing Database Systems. Techn. Report, Univ. of Kaiserslautern, Dept. of Comp. Science, Febr. 1993.

SD89   Schneider, D.A., DeWitt, D.J. 1989: A Performance Evaluation of Four Parallel Join Algorithms in a Shared-Nothing Multiprocessor Environment. *Proc. ACM SIGMOD Conf.*, 110-121.

SD90   Schneider, D.A., DeWitt, D.J. 1990: Tradeoffs in Processing Complex Join Queries via Hashing in Multiprocessor Database Machines. *Proc. 16th Int. Conf. on Very Large Data Bases*, 469-480.

SSU91   Silberschatz, A.; Stonebraker, M.; Ullman, J. 1991: Database Systems: Achievements and Opportunities. *Communications of the ACM* 34(10), 110-120.

St86   Stonebraker, M. 1986: The Case for Shared Nothing. *IEEE Database Engineering* 9(1), 4-9.

Ta88   The Tandem Database Group 1988: A Benchmark of NonStop SQL on the Debit Credit Transaction. *Proc. ACM SIGMOD Conf.*, 337-341.

Ta89   The Tandem Database Group 1989: NonStop SQL, A Distributed, High-Performance, High-Availability Implementation of SQL. Lecture Notes in Computer Science 359, Springer-Verlag, 60-104.

WDJ91   Walton, C.B; Dale A.G.; Jenevein, R.M. 1991: A Taxanomy and Performance Model of Data Skew Effects in Parallel Joins. *Proc. 17th Int. Conf. on Very Large Data Bases*, 537-548.

WT91   Watson, P., Townsend, P. 1991: The EDS Parallel Relational Database System. In: Parallel Database Systems (*Proc. PRIMSA Workshop*), Lecture Notes in Computer Science 503, Springer-Verlag, 149-168.

WFA92   Wilschut, A.; Flokstra, J.; Apers, P. 1992: Parallelism in a Main-Memory DBMS: The performance of PRISMA/DB. *Proc. 18th Int. Conf. on Very Large Data Bases*, 521-532.

PROCESSING TRANSACTIONS ON GRIP,
A PARALLEL GRAPH REDUCER

G. AKERHOLT, K. HAMMOND, S. PEYTON JONES AND P. TRINDER

ABSTRACT. The GRIP architecture allows efficient execution of functional programs on a multi-processor built from standard hardware components. State-of-the-art compilation techniques are combined with sophisticated runtime resource-control to give good parallel performance. This paper reports the results of running GRIP on an application which is apparently unsuited to the basic functional model: a database transaction manager incorporating updates as well as lookup transactions. The results obtained show good relative speedups for GRIP, with real performance advantages over the same application executing on sequential machines.

1. INTRODUCTION

GRIP is a parallel processor designed for fast, efficient execution of pure functional programs. Good sequential compiler technology is combined with parallel runtime support to give good real-time performance. Pure functional languages form an attractive basis for parallel implementation, if a safe evaluation strategy such as parallel graph reduction is used:

- The principle of referential transparency ensures that all cached copies of a given object will have the same value when evaluated, whether or not they are shared, and no matter how many times they are evaluated. Thus, there can be no cache-coherency problems in a parallel functional implementation.
- The semantics of a functional program remains the same whether it is executed sequentially or in parallel. Thus, a parallel functional program may be debugged on a sequential machine without affecting its result. There can be no unexpected non-determinism in a parallel functional program.
- There is no possibility of deadlock. Parallel functional programs have exactly the same termination properties as their sequential counterparts.

This work is supported by the ESPRIT FIDE Project (BRA 3070), the SERC Bulk Data Type Constructors Project, the SERC GRASP Project and the Royal Society of Edinburgh. **Authors' address:** Computing Science Dept, Glasgow University, Glasgow, Scotland. **Email:** {akerholg, kh, simonpj,trinder}@dcs.glasgow.ac.uk

- Because there is no explicitly sequential evaluation order, it is easy to automatically partition a functional program for parallel execution.
- Automatic resource-control is much more straightforward, since there are no hidden dependencies between tasks.

A number of pragmatic issues remain, however, for example whether *good* partitions into tasks can be made without human intervention, or whether dynamic control decisions can be made sufficiently fast to allow scheduling of fine-grained parallelism on a machine such as GRIP. We have addressed some of these issues in earlier papers [HP92]. In this paper, we consider another important pragmatic issue: whether functional programs can be made to process large amounts of data in a manner which is competitive with imperative programs. We have chosen as our case-study a partial implementation of the well-known DebitCredit benchmark: a transaction-processing benchmark for databases, which involves updating the database. Given that sequential compilers for functional languages do not yet give performance which matches that of imperative languages, we do not expect our implementation to outperform a hand-coded imperative program for the same machine. We do, however, hope to obtain respectable performance compared with imperative implementations, and to obtain decent speedups from our parallel architecture. Choosing a widely-accepted benchmark allows tentative comparisons to be drawn with other architectures and models of computation.

While the results we obtain here apply principally to our novel GRIP architecture, there is some hope that the lessons learned here may also be of use to other parallel functional implementations, such as those for networks of transputers, or hypercubes. Although the GRIP model lessens the problems of locality through the use of a 2-level bus structure and fast heterogeneous communications hardware, the distinction between local and non-local memory accesses is still a crucial one.

The remainder of this paper is structured as follows. Section 2 describes the GRIP machine architecture. Section 3 describes the characteristics recorded during program execution on GRIP. Section 4 describes the DebitCredit-based application studied here. Section 5 gives the results gathered during the execution of the application. Section 6 concludes.

2. Machine Architecture

2.1. Overview. The GRIP architecture comprises a single bus-connected cluster of one to 20 printed circuit boards. A fully-populated board contains four processing elements (PEs) and one Intelligent Memory Unit (IMU), linked by a local bus. A fully-populated GRIP thus contains 80 PEs and 20 IMUs. The boards are connected using a fast packet-switched bus [Pey86], and the whole machine is attached to a Unix host using slower data links.

Each PE incorporates an MC68020 CPU, an MC68881 floating-point coprocessor, and 1Mbyte of private memory which is not accessible by any other hardware component.

The IMUs collectively constitute the global address space. They each contain 1M words of 40 bit-wide static memory, together with a microprogrammable data engine. The microcode interprets incoming requests from the bus, services them and dispatches a reply to the bus. In this way, the IMUs can support a variety of memory operations, rather than the simple READ and WRITE operations supported by conventional memories. The IMUs are the most innovative feature of the GRIP architecture, offering a fast implementation of low-level memory operations with great flexibility.

An internal bus was chosen specifically to make the locality issue less pressing. Communication is handled by sophisticated Bus Interface Processors (BIPs): one per board. Identical protocols are used for communication between remote components or those on the same board. Throughput and latency are essentially the same for both local and remote communication from functional programs [Mad91]. However, inter-component communication is still an order-of-magnitude slower than access to a PE's private memory. It is thus crucially important to minimise the number and frequency of remote accesses.

2.2. Graph reduction on GRIP. We start from the belief that parallel graph reduction will only be competitive if it can take advantage of all the compiler technology that has been developed for sequential graph-reduction implementations [Pey87]. Our intention is that, provided a thread does not refer to remote graph nodes, it should be executed exactly as a compiled program would be on a sequential machine.

Our graph reduction model is based on the Spineless Tagless G-machine [PS89]. The expression to be evaluated is represented by a graph of *closures*, held in dynamic heap memory. Each closure consists of a pointer to its *code*, together with zero or more *free-variable fields*. Closures in *(weak head) normal form* require no further evaluation, hence their code is usually just a return instruction[1]. Other closures represent unevaluated expressions, whose code will reduce the closure to its normal form. A closure is evaluated (or *entered*) by jumping to its code. A register records the current closure for update purposes, or for access to the free variables. When evaluation is complete, the closure is *updated* with (an indirection to) a closure representing its normal form.

A *thread* is a sequential computation whose purpose is to reduce a particular sub-graph to (weak head) normal form. In a parallel graph reducer, there will typically be many threads which could be executed. Idle PEs fetch new threads from this (distributed) pool of threads. A single PE may execute one thread at a time, or may multi-task between a number of threads.

---

[1] Closures in weak head normal form are functions, or constructors. In contrast to true normal forms, their arguments may be unevaluated.

Initially there is only one thread, representing the result of the program. When a thread encounters a closure whose value will be required in the future, it has the option of recording the closure for (possible) execution by other PEs. This is known as *sparking* the closure.

If the parent thread requires the value of the sparked closure while a child thread is computing it, the parent becomes *blocked*. When the child thread completes the evaluation of the closure, the closure is updated with its normal form, and the parent thread is *resumed*. If no PE has begun execution of the sparked closure when its value is required, the parent thread will evaluate the closure itself. Consequently a thread can only become blocked if it requires a result which some other thread is evaluating [PS89, HP90]. This is the *evaluate-and-die* model of evaluation for parallel functional languages. It is related to some other models such as lazy task creation [MKH91].

This blocking/resumption mechanism is the *only* form of inter-thread communication and synchronisation. Once an expression has been evaluated to normal form, then arbitrarily many threads can inspect it simultaneously without contention. The synchronisation provides the inter-transaction "locking" required by the functional database, as described in [Tri89]. A transaction demanding the result of a previous transaction is blocked until the previous transaction has constructed the value it requires.

2.3. IMU Operations. The following range of operations is supported by our current IMU microcode:

- Variable-sized heap nodes may be allocated and initialised.
- Garbage collection of global nodes is performed autonomously by the IMUs. Termination is ensured using an algorithm proposed by Baker [Bak78].
- Each IMU maintains a pool of executable threads, which may be exported to idle PEs.
- The blocking/resumption model is supported for access to global nodes.

2.4. Additional Configuration. Database applications require that the underlying machine supports permanent storage, typically in the form of disks. The existing GRIP machine has a simple stream-based disk interface, which is clearly inadequate for such an application. Pragmatics aside, it would be easy to extend the GRIP architecture to include more sophisticated disk storage. For example, a disk controller and disk could be added to each PE. Any PE could then access the data on any disk by sending a suitable request to the controlling PE. This architecture is depicted in Figure 1.

To simulate this architecture on the existing machine, a special primitive operation, *delay*, is used to model disk accesses. *delay n a* introduces a timed delay of n milliseconds for the current thread. To model the effect of contention for shared resources, such as disks, delays are queued on the PE addressed by a,

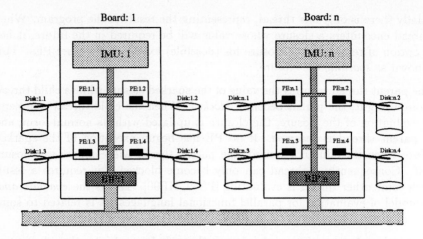

FIGURE 1. GRIP extended with disks and disk controllers

and are cumulative with any outstanding delays on that PE. We use a delay of 13ms for a disk read, and 14ms for a disk write, and assume a block size of 8K bytes, with a total capacity of 1G bytes per drive. These correspond to figures quoted for many small SCSI drives, e.g. Seagate ST41200N 1.2Gb (16.5ms) or Maxtor 1.7Gb (13ms).

3. DATABASE ARCHITECTURE

3.1. DebitCredit. The database application that has been implemented on GRIP is the processing part of the DebitCredit benchmark[Tpc89]. This section describes the significant features of this application. DebitCredit measures transaction processing capacity in a simple bank database. The full benchmark measures transactions passed over a network from a set of terminals and includes pricing information for the entire system. The application we describe only processes the transactions against the database: the so-called back-end processing. Network response times and equipment costs are not considered here.

The DebitCredit bank database comprises customer, teller, branch and history records. A single transaction is repeatedly executed against these records. The transaction adds an amount of money to an account (a negative amount is a withdrawal), the corresponding teller and branch records are similarly updated and a history record is generated. Various relationships exist between the records, for example the balance held at a branch should be the sum of all of the accounts at the branch. The benchmark specifies a set of atomicity, consistency, isolation and durability (ACID) tests. All except the durability test have been performed successfully for the program described here. Results are omitted for space reasons.

The essential metric measured in DebitCredit is the number of transactions processed in a second (tps). However, the database size does not remain constant as the tps rate increases. For each transaction-per-second the database must use 100,000 account records, 10 teller records and 1 branch record.

DebitCredit figures have been published for many machines. The figures reported in this paper are for only part of DebitCredit, involve simulated disk access and, as described in the next section, deviate from the specification in several respects. Hence they cannot be directly compared to a full implementation. However, for reference, the following figures are quoted by e.g. [Rob89, TPG88]: IBM 4381-P22, 22 TPS; DEC VAX 8830, 27 TPS; Tandem, 208 TPS.

3.2. Application Design.

3.2.1. *Persistent Functional Languages.* The transaction processor is designed using the principles first outlined in [AFHLT87] and prototyped in [AHPT91, Tri89], which assume the existence of a parallel persistent functional language. In most existing languages only certain types of data may be permanently stored. Much of the effort in writing programs that manipulate permanent data is expended in unpacking the data into a form suitable for the computation and then repacking it for storage afterwards. The idea behind *persistent* programming languages is to allow values of *any* type to be permanently stored. The length of time that an entity exists, or its persistence, is independent of its type.

In a persistent environment a class, or collection of 'similar' data items, can be represented as a data structure that persists for some time. Because of their large size, such structures are termed bulk data structures. Operations that do not modify bulk data structures, e.g. lookups, can be implemented efficiently in a functional language [HN91]. However, modifications to a data structure must be *non-destructive* in a pure functional language, i.e. a *new version* of the structure must be constructed and the original preserved. At first glance it seems to be prohibitively expensive to create a new version of a bulk data structure every time it is modified.

3.2.2. *Trees.* New versions of trees can be constructed cheaply, however. If *et* is the type of the data values at the leaves, and *kt* is the type of the keys, then a simplistic tree type can be written

$$bdt = Node\ bdt\ kt\ bdt\ |\ Tip\ et.$$

A function to update such a tree produces a new tree reflecting the update and a message reporting the success or failure of the operation.

$$update\ e'\ (Tip\ e) = (Ok\ e,\ Tip\ e'),\ \textbf{if}\ key\ e = key\ e'$$
$$= (Error,\ Tip\ e),\ \textbf{otherwise}$$

$$update\ e'\ (Node\ lt\ k\ rt) = (m, Node\ lt'\ k\ rt), \textbf{if}\ key\ e' \leq k$$
$$= (m, Node\ lt\ k\ rt'), \textbf{otherwise}$$
$$\textbf{where}$$
$$(m, lt') = update\ e'\ lt$$
$$(m, rt') = update\ e'\ rt$$

Let us assume that the tree contains n entities and is balanced. In this case its depth is proportional to $\log n$, hence the update function needs only to construct $\log n$ new nodes to create a new version of such a tree. Any unchanged nodes can be shared between the old and the new versions and thus a new *path* through the tree is all that need be constructed. The figure overleaf shows a tree which has been updated to associate a value of 3 with x.

A time complexity of $\log n$ is the same as an imperative tree update. The non-destructive update has a larger constant factor, however, as the new nodes must be created and some unchanged information copied into them. The functional update can be made more efficient using reference counting [Tri89], but the GRIP software does not currently support this optimisation. However, when non-destructive update is used, a copy of the tree can be kept cheaply because the nodes common to the old and new versions are shared, i.e. only the differences between the versions are required. The uses of cheap multiple versions of the database are described in [AFHLT87, Tri89]. Destructive update is also likely to introduce unwanted sequential dependencies (as its name suggests, single-threading imposes sequential access in order to allow destructive update). This is highly undesirable for our parallel application.

The DebitCredit branch, teller and account classes are each represented as trees, while the history is simply a sequence. Because the branch and teller classes are small enough they are stored entirely in primary memory, as binary trees with data (a single 100 byte record) only at the leaves. The account tree is too large to reside in primary memory, hence we use a 2-3 tree (i.e. a B-tree of order 3).

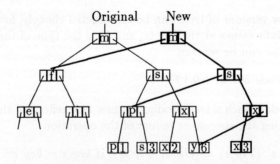

A disk-block access is simulated for each leaf access, as described in Section 2.4. This corresponds to an ideal 'warm start' in a conventional database, i.e. all of the index is in memory and only the data is disk resident. Each DebitCredit account record is 100 bytes and hence 80 records are retrieved from an 8Kb disk-block.

We choose a low-order B-tree to minimise the construction time required for the root node. This reduces a potential throughput bottleneck [Tri89]. Future work may include experimenting with the order of the B-tree.

3.2.3. *Transaction Manager.* A transaction is a function that takes the database as an argument and returns some output and a new version of the database as a result. Let us call this type, $bdt \rightarrow (output \times bdt)$, txt. Transactions are built out of tree manipulating operations such as *lookup* and *update*. Two functions that prove useful to construct a simple example transaction are *isok*, which determines whether an operation succeeded, and *dep* which increments the balance of an account. The arguments to *dep* are a some of money to deposit n and an entity whose components are an account number *ano*, the current balance of the account *bal*, the credit limit for the account *crl*, and the type of the account *class*.

$$isok \ (Ok \ e) = True$$
$$isok \ out = False$$

$$dep \ (Ok \ (Entity \ ano \ bal \ crl \ class)) \ n \ = \ Entity \ ano \ (bal + n) \ crl \ class$$

A transaction to deposit a sum of money in a bank account can be written as follows.

$$deposit \ a \ n \ d = update \ (dep \ m \ n) \ d, \textbf{if} \ (isok \ m)$$
$$= (Error, d), \textbf{otherwise}$$
$$\textbf{where}$$
$$m = lookup \ a \ d$$

The *deposit* function takes as its arguments an account number a, a sum of money n and a database d. If the *lookup* fails to locate the account an error message and the original database are returned. If the *lookup* succeeds, the result of the function is the result of updating the account. The update replaces the existing account entity with an identical entity, except that the balance has been incremented by the specified sum. Note that *deposit* is of the correct type for a transaction-function when it is partially applied to an account number and a sum of money, i.e. *deposit* a n has type $bdt \rightarrow (output \times bdt)$. The DebitCredit transaction, *dctrans* which is used for performance analysis is much more complicated than *deposit*. Its definition is given in [AHPT93].

Both *deposit* and *dctrans* have a common transaction form: some operations are performed on the database and if they succeed the transaction commits, i.e. returns the updated database. If the operations fail, the transaction aborts and returns an unchanged database. Transactions that may either commit or abort are termed *total*.

The database manager is a stream processing function. It consumes a lazy list, or stream, of transaction-functions and produces a stream of output. That is, the manager has type $bdt \rightarrow [txt] \rightarrow [output]$. A simple version can be written as follows.

$$manager \ d \ (f : fs) = out : manager \ d' \ fs$$
$$\textbf{where}$$
$$(out, d') = f \ d$$

The first transaction f in the input stream is applied to the database and a pair is returned as the result. The output component of the pair is placed in the output stream. The updated database, d', is given as the first argument to the recursive call to the manager. Because the manager retains the modified database produced by each transaction it has an evolving state. The manager can be made available to many users simultaneously using techniques developed for functional operating systems [Hen82].

3.2.4. *Concurrent Transactions.* Concurrency can be introduced between transactions by making the manager eager. This allows the current transaction to be evaluated in parallel with the remaining transactions. The original task evaluates the current transaction. The new task applies the manager to the remaining transactions. This proceeds recursively.

Unfortunately, total transactions can seriously restrict concurrency. This is because neither the original nor the updated database can be returned until the commit/abort decision has been taken. Consequently, no other transaction may access any other part of the database until this decision has been made. Total transactions have the form,

$$if \text{ predicate db } then \text{ transform db } else \text{ db.}$$

In most cases the bulk of the database will be the same whether or not the transaction commits. This common, or unchanged, part of the database will be returned whatever the result of the commit decision. If there were some way of returning the common part early then concurrency would be greatly increased. Transactions that only depend on unchanged data can begin and possibly even complete without waiting for the preceding total transaction to commit or abort.

The common parts of the database can be returned early using *fwif*, a variant of the conditional statement proposed by Friedman and Wise [FW78]. A more complete description of *fwif* and its implementation in a simulated parallel graph reducer can be found in [Tri89]. To define the semantics of *fwif* let us view every data value as a constructor and a sequence of constructed values. Every member of an unstructured type, e.g. 1, is a zero-arity constructor — the sequence of constructed values is empty. Using C to denote a constructor, the semantics can be given by the following reduction rules.

$$fwif \ True \ x \ y \Rightarrow x$$

$fwif\ False\ x\ y \Rightarrow y$

$fwif\ p\ (C\ x_0 \ldots x_n)\ (C\ y_0 \ldots y_n) \Rightarrow C\ (fwif\ p\ x_0\ y_0) \ldots (fwif\ p\ x_n\ y_n)$

To implement *fwif*, the predicate and the two conditional branches are evaluated concurrently. The values of the conditional branches are compared and common parts are returned. When a part is found not to be common to both branches, the evaluation of those branches ceases. Once the predicate is evaluated, the chosen branch is returned and the evaluation of the other is cancelled. This strategy amounts to speculative parallelism, the conditional branches being evaluated in the hope that parts of them will be identical.

The problems of speculative parallelism are well known. For example speculative tasks may consume resources and hence prevent more important tasks from completing. They, and any child tasks, may also be hard to kill if they are not required, or fail to terminate. Fortunately in the DebitCredit application the tasks being sparked by *fwif* evaluate functions like *update* which are relatively small, spark no additional tasks and are guaranteed to terminate as they traverse a finite data structure. Since most of the database is unchanged between transactions, the speculative work is likely to be used.

4. RESULTS

4.1. Performance on Parallel and Sequential Machines. The first set of results compares the absolute execution times of a fixed program running on a varying number of GRIP PEs with those for the same program executing on two common sequential machines. This program processes 400 transactions on a database configured for 50 DebitCredit TPS. Figure 2 plots the execution times for a 4-IMU GRIP (20Mb "slow" global heap) with between 2 and 15 PEs (this was the largest stable configuration at the time these results were obtained). Each PE has 600K available heap (the remaining 400K static RAM is occupied by program code, the operating system, and static data). Due to the size of the application, it could not be executed on a single GRIP PE. Offloading the in-memory index to global memory would bias the performance results, and give unrealistic super-linear speedups, which we wished to avoid.

The same figure also shows the execution times for an identical program executing on a Sun 3/50 (Motorola MC68020) and a Sun 4/60 (Sun Sparc). The Sun 3/50 uses the same processor at the same speed as GRIP; the Sun 4/60 is a commonly used modern machine. An 8M heap was used for the sequential machines: this gave the best overall time performance in both cases. The same compiler was used for all three machines. Disk accesses were simulated for GRIP using interrupt-timed delays, as described above. For the sequential versions, sequential disk access was simulated using count-down loops of an appropriate duration. The implementation of delays is the only difference between the programs. Results are averaged across 10 runs in each case.

A direct architectural comparison can be made between GRIP and the Sun

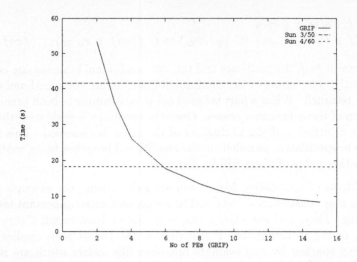

FIGURE 2. Execution Time Profile: 400 Transactions, 50 TPS Database

3/50. They use the same microprocessor (16MHz Motorola MC68020) to execute an essentially identical source program compiled by the same compiler. The machines differ in their memory architectures, in their communications subsystems, and in their virtual disk architectures, as described above. Absolute speedups over the Sun 3/50 are obtained with 3 or more PEs. Not all the overhead is due to communications and context-switching costs, however: a significant fraction of this overhead is caused by the relatively small local memory available to each GRIP PE (for example, decreasing the Sun 3/50 heap to 2Mb halves its overall performance).

The raw integer performance (given by SPECint89) of the Sparc-1 chip used in the Sun 4/60 is roughly 3 to 4 times that of the Motorola 68020. For this application, however, disk performance is at least as important as that of the processor. Consequently, the overall performance of the 4/60 is only twice that of the 3/50, in spite of using a RISC chip. Hence a GRIP with 6 or more PEs outperforms the Sun 4/60, and a 15-PE GRIP is more than twice as fast as a Sun 4/60. This is a primarily a consequence of our use of concurrency to exploit additional disks in the parallel machine.

To summarise, for this program, a 15-PE GRIP delivers good real-time performance compared with some common sequential machines.

4.2. Relative Speedup. The second set of results investigates the relative speedup as the number of processors is increased from 2 to 15. Figure 3 plots the same data as Figure 2, but in terms of the speedup relative to the two-PE case (the single PE data-point was unobtainable, but extrapolating from our data suggests a single PE would be roughly half the speed of a 2-PE system). That is, the program measured executes 400 transactions against a database configured for 50 DebitCredit TPS. We observe that the speedup is linear until

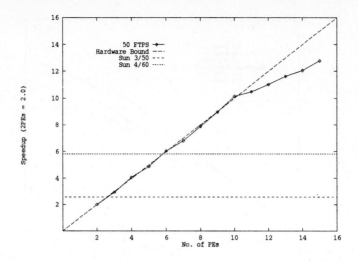

FIGURE 3. Speedup Graph: 400 transactions, 50 TPS Database

10 PEs are in use and degrades thereafter.

This degradation in speedup occurs as the software bound on parallelism is approached. The bound for a functional transaction processor has been shown to be the ratio between the time required to construct the root and make it available to other processors and the time required to process the transaction [Tri89]. Hence we would expect that, if the transactions became shorter, the software bound would be reached sooner.

The length of DebitCredit transactions is easily adjusted. Recall that the time to execute a transaction is proportional to the log of the size of the database. Furthermore, the benchmark specifies that the size of the database increases in proportion to the number of TPS. The largest database studied here is the 50 TPS database from the previous section, selected because a 15-PE GRIP achieves 48 FTPS (400 transactions in 8.36 seconds). The smallest database we consider is a 15 TPS database, chosen because a 2-PE GRIP achieves 14 FTPS. A good intermediate point is a 35 TPS database, chosen because an 8-PE GRIP achieves 36 FTPS.

Figure 4 plots the speedup curves for the 400 transaction program executed on 15 TPS, 35 TPS and 50 TPS databases respectively. As predicted, a program with shorter transactions (and hence a smaller database) reaches the software bound earlier. We note that considerable improvement is still obtained after the speedup becomes non-linear. In fact, none of the programs have actually reached a limit on speedup. This suggests that the DebitCredit execution time could be further reduced by increasing the number of processors beyond 15.

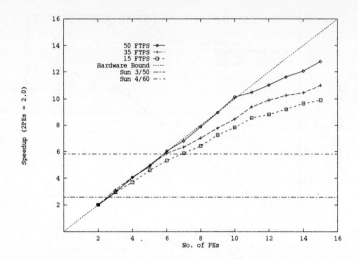

FIGURE 4. Parallel Speedup Graphs for Varying TPS

5. CONCLUSION

We have run a large data-intensive application on the parallel graph-reducer GRIP. Our application is written in the pure non-strict functional language, Haskell. It exploits the data-dependencies implicit in a functional program to provide inter-transaction concurrency and locking. This represents the first attempt that we are aware of to consider the problems of concurrency in a functional transaction processor, in the presence of update as well as lookup transactions. Our model allows the exploitation of concurrent hardware through the use of *fwif*: a primitive which allows early return of common parts of a data structure in the context of conditional expressions.

Our results show a clear improvement from the use of a parallel machine compared with the same application running on two popular sequential machines. We also obtain near-linear relative speedups between 2 and 10 PE on a 50-TPS database. Our GRIP results could be tentatively compared with those for the the full DebitCredit benchmark on a large sequential machine.

REFERENCES

[AFHLT87] Argo G, Fairbairn J, Hughes RJM, Launchbury EJ, and Trinder PW, "Implementing Functional Databases", *Proc Workshop on Database Programming Languages*, Roscoff, France (September 1987), pp. 87-103.

[AHPT91] Akerholt G, Hammond K, Peyton Jones SL, and Trinder P, "A Parallel Functional Database On GRIP", *Glasgow Workshop on Functional Programming*, Portree, Scotland (August 1991).

[AHPT93] Akerholt G, Hammond K, Peyton Jones SL, and Trinder P, "Processing Transactions on GRIP, a Parallel Graph Reducer", *Internal Report*, Dept. of Computing Science, Glasgow University (March 1993).

[AJ89]   Augustsson L and Johnsson T, "Parallel graph reduction with the $< \nu,$G$>$-machine", *Proc IFIP Conference on Functional Programming Languages and Computer Architecture, London, (September 1989)*.

[Bak78]   Baker HG, *"List processing in real time on a serial computer"*, Comm. ACM *21(4), (April 1978), pp. 280-294.*

[FW78]   Friedman DP, and Wise DS, *"A Note on Conditional Expressions"*, Comm. ACM *21(11), (November 1978).*

[HP90]   Hammond K, and Peyton Jones SL, *"Some Early Experiments on the GRIP Parallel Reducer"*, Proc 2nd Intl Workshop on Parallel Implementation of Functional Languages, Plasmeijer MJ (Ed), University of Nijmegen, *(1990).*

[HP92]   Hammond K, and Peyton Jones SL, *"Profiling Scheduling Strategies on the GRIP Parallel Reducer"*, Proc 4th Intl Workshop on Parallel Implementation of Functional Languages, Kuchen H and Loogen R (Eds), RWTH, Aachen, *(1992).*

[Hen82]   Henderson P. *"Purely Functional Operating Systems"*, in Functional Programming and its Application. Darlington J. Henderson P. Turner D.A. (Eds) Cambridge University Press *(1982).*

[HN91]   Heytens, M.L. and Nikhil R.S. *"List Comprehensions in AGNA, a Parallel Persistent Object System"* Proc FPCA 91, Cambridge, Mass. *(1991).*

[Mad91]   Madden, P.J. *"The Hardware Performance of the GRIP Multiprocessor"* MSc Thesis, Glasgow University, *(1991).*

[MKH91]   Mohr E, Kranz DA and Halstead RH, *"Lazy task creation - a technique for increasing the granularity of parallel programs"* IEEE Transactions on Parallel and Distributed Systems, *2(3), (July 1991).*

[PCSH87]   Peyton Jones SL, Clack, C, Salkild, J and Hardie, M *"GRIP – a high-performance architecture for parallel graph reduction"*, Proc FPCA 87, Portland, Oregon, ed Kahn G, Springer-Verlag LNCS, *(1987).*

[Pey86]   Peyton Jones SL, *"Using Futurebus in a Fifth Generation Computer"*, Microprocessors and Microsystems *10(2), (March 1986), pp. 69-76.*

[Pey87]   Peyton Jones SL, The Implementation of Functional Programming Languages, Prentice Hall, *(1987).*

[PS89]   Peyton Jones SL, and Salkild J, *"The Spineless Tagless G-machine"*, Proc FPCA 89, London, MacQueen (Ed), Addison Wesley, *(1989).*

[Rob89]   Robertson IB, *"Hope$^+$ on Flagship"*, Proc 1989 Glasgow Workshop on Functional Programming, Fraserburgh, Scotland, Springer Verlag, *(August 1989).*

[Tpc89]   Transaction Processing Performance Council (TPC), *"TPC BENCHMARK A, Draft 6-pr Proposed Standard"*, Administered by ITOM INternational Co, POB 1450, Los Altos, CA 94023, USA, *August 21, 1989.*

[TPG88]   The Tandem Performance Group, *"A Benchmark of NonStop SQL on the Debit-Credit Transaction"*, Tandem Computers Inc., 19333 Vallco Pky., Cupertino, CA. 95014, *1988.*

[Tri89]   Trinder PW, A Functional Database, Oxford University D.Phil. Thesis, *(December 1989).*

Arithmetic for Parallel Linear Recursive Query Evaluation in Deductive Databases

Jerome Robinson and Shutian Lin

Department of Computer Science, University of Essex, Colchester, CO4 3SQ, U.K.

Abstract: An arithmetic approach, such as the Level-Finding method described in this paper for evaluating linear recursive queries in deductive database systems provides great potential for parallel processing. It has advantages over other approaches using state-of-the-art parallel processing technology to improve processing speed. In the arithmetic approach, we identify two kind of parallelism, namely bridge node parallelism and formula parallelism. In this paper, the arithmetic foundations and algorithm to exploit formula parallelism were given. The algorithm is fully parallel.

1 Introduction

Deductive databases extend traditional database systems, using logic rules to deduce new facts from stored facts. Rules that use recursion are particularly useful because they specify a succession of repeated operations on data, providing a deductive program rather than a mere relational algebra expression. Users of traditional databases must embed relational queries into an imperative host language to obtain the iterative capabilities of recursive rules. Efficient evaluation of recursive rules is therefore essential in deductive database implementation. The problem is to devise a method that can use query constants to restrict data traffic during evaluation but at the same time ensure termination and completeness.

The Henschen-Naqvi method of evaluation [Henschen 84] like other Wavefront methods [Yu 87, Han 88, Lavington 88, Robinson 90] is efficient because it uses query constants to directly restrict the number of tuples involved in the iterative evaluation. A problem arising from this efficiency is that if cycles exist the derived data has insufficient information to decide termination. Naive and Semi-Naive are alternative evaluation strategies that find the Least Fixed Point of a relational algebraic function. They terminate correctly when no new tuples appear during an iteration. This simple termination condition works regardless of cycles in the EDB because in a fixpoint computation, if none of the arguments change then the result cannot change. The same does not apply to wavefront methods if the underlying data is cyclic. In that case a succession of iterations may produce nothing new, followed by an iteration providing new results. Wavefront methods are graph traversals and a path leading to new nodes may only become accessible once in each circuit of a data cycle. An example illustrates the problem:

The query ?-path(a,y). on recursively defined relation 'path':

    path(x,y) :- Link(x,y).
    path(x,y) :- Left(x,v), path(v,w), Right(w,y).

This is the 'same generation' rule cluster. The query asks for all nodes in graph 'Right' that are the same distance as node 'a' in graph 'Left' from a common Link tuple. Distance is measured by counting the number of arcs in a path between two nodes.

Using EDB relations: Left = { ab, bf, fg, ga }; Link = { bc }; Right = { cd, de, ec };
whose graph is:

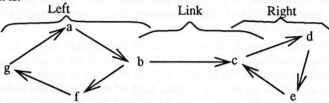

Results can only appear at iteration numbers 1,5,9,13,17,21, ... because only those
allow access to the Link path. New results appear at iterations 1,5, and 9. Continuing
after iteration 9 will produce no more new results.

Steps 1 to 5 produce a new tuple from at least one of the relations. Steps 6,7,8
produce no tuples that have not been seen before, but it would be wrong to stop after
step 6 (using the LFP termination condition) because new results arise at step 9. It
may be necessary to use cycles more than once to obtain all answers, but how do you
know when to stop ?

Section 2 answers that question. Section 3 discusses aspects of parallelism.
Section 4 provides fundamental theorems for the existence of formula parallelism,
optimisation, and duplication result identification. Section 5 presents an algorithm for
exploiting formula parallelism. Section 6 concludes the paper.

2.1 The Solution

If wavefront methods are used with cyclic data then auxiliary information about the
structure of the underlying data graph is needed, to identify accessible levels in Left
and Right. The levels are the integer values whose arithmetic forms the basis of the
new query evaluation strategy. The process of finding Level information can be used
as the query answering mechanism itself, rather than simply a control for relational
database operations: A node n in graph Right is an answer to the query if and only if
there is at least one level the same in sets $RS_a(b)$ and $RS_c(n)$. "$RS_p(q)$" denotes the
Recurrence Set of node q with respect to node p. This is the set of distances at which
node q will be encountered if graph traversal starts at node p.

Node b is a 'bridge node', identifiable from the node set in graph Left by two
criteria: i) it is reachable from node 'a', and ii) it occurs as a value of the first attribute
in relation Link. It appears during graph traversal at a number of levels (distances)
from node a. Its set of levels is infinite because there is a cycle on the path from a to b.
In general, for any graph structure in Left, for any simple path from query node 'a' to
bridge node 'b' the Recurrence Set will be either a single level or else an infinite
number of levels. (A 'simple path' is one in which no node appears more than once).
In the graph above, b occurs at levels {1, 5, 9, 13, ...}. It recurs at multiples of the
cycle length, 4, above a start level, 1. The infinite set of integers can be represented
compactly by formula. This allows infinite sets to be transferred rapidly between
processors by sending the formula instead of the values. The formula for node b with
respect to a above is 1(4), using a notation where v(w) means { v + k * w | k = 0, 1, 2,
... }.

[Wu 88] shows that any collection of cycles can be merged to a single virtual cycle,
formula v(w), plus a finite set of levels with values less than v-1. He also shows an
efficient way to obtain level formulae for complex structures of multiple cycles.

A formula is evaluated for each node pair <a,b> where 'a' is a query constant and
'b' a bridge node. Parallel evaluation on separate processors is possible since different

node pair calculations need no interaction.

A formula is evaluated for each node pair <a,b> where 'a' is a query constant and 'b' a bridge node. Parallel evaluation on separate processors is possible since different node pair calculations need no interaction.

For each bridge node, b, there is a set of RightOrigin nodes, c, obtained by selection using value b on relation Link. Each c node is the origin of a graph, ie the root of a (perhaps infinitely deep) tree. The set of nodes in Right is finite, however, and the reachable node set is even smaller. Each of these reachable nodes, n, will be output as an answer to the query if sets $RS_a(b)$ and $RS_c(n)$ have a level in common. Calculation of $RS_c(n)$ for each <c,n> pair can be done in parallel, and answer n can be output if the processor has the formula denoting b's level set.

2.2 The Algorithm

Algorithm-of-Level-Finding-method for query node 'a'
Begin {
    Determine the set, B, of bridge nodes; i.e. {reachable node} $\cap$ Π_1(Link).
    For each bridge node, b, b $\in$ B :
      {   Compute its Recurrence Sequence set, $RS_a(b)$, in Left.
         Obtain its corresponding set, H, of RightOrigin nodes, by selection from
         the Link relation, $\Pi_2(\sigma_{1=b}$ Link).
         For each h, h $\in$ H :
            {Obtain its set, R, of reachable nodes (by transitive closure in
            "graph Right" from origin node h).
            For each node, r, r $\in$ R :
               Compute $RS_h(r)$.
            If $RS_a(b) \cap RS_h(r) \neq \phi$
            Then r is an answer.   } } } end.

3.1 Managing Parallelism

The purpose of our research is to develop a parallel implementation of the Level-Finding evaluation strategy. The Level-Finding method has advantages when compared with other parallel systems: (i) the initial workload to be distributed is fairly well defined (by number of nodes and their simple path lengths), and (ii) redistribution of workload at runtime entails little overhead (no movement of code and minimal data transfer). Moreover, we expect the array of parallel processors to operate in conjunction with a database system whose work can overlaps that of the processor array. In a closely-coupled configuration an extended RDB, such as the IFS/2 [Lavington Parle92] able to perform iterative operations such as transitive closure, performs a preliminary operations on the EDB relations, to download only query-relevant tuples. It extracts and downloads the query subgraph from the base relations. This database creates download data as waves of tuples during a breadth-first graph traversal. A wave downloads as the next is created.

After deriving the Query Subgraph the database can identify Bridge Nodes, by Joining the derived relation and the Link EDB relation. This can alternatively be done during the iterative evaluation, by Joining each wave. Bridge nodes discovered during graph traversal are automatically classified by simple path length. This is useful when allocating work to processors, since each task is the recurrence sequence evaluation for a specified simple path. Each processor has a set of these tasks and a set of short paths is likely to finish before a set of long paths.

The database system could download the bridging subset of Link tuples. This allows processors to start path evaluation in Right when their work in Left is finished. However, better load balancing is possible, using information the database can produce: i) the set of <bridge node, RightOrigin node> tuples for each bridge node, and ii) the set of reachable nodes for each RightOrigin node.

Paths from RightOrigin nodes can be evaluated by a new set of processors (ie different from those working on the paths through Left to bridge nodes). However, at some stage the results of path evaluation in Left and Right for each bridge node must be brought together. Full interconnection between processors is not needed. Pairs of processors only need to be connected if they share a bridge node. Communication between them is simply the unidirectional transfer of a Recurrence Sequence formula.

Dynamic redistribution of workload is simple: Shifting a task from one processor to another requires only the transfer of a pair of node identifiers. The processor already contains the necessary graph data and program to identify a path between the two nodes and evaluate its Recurrence Sequence.

3.2 Comparison with other Methods

The popular Naive and Semi-Naive methods evaluate the Least Fixed Point (LFP) of the relational algebraic function defined by the recursive rule cluster. They avoid termination problems from cyclic data but are less efficient than wavefront methods. They must materialise the whole virtual relation rather than the subset relevant to the query. The query is finally answered by Selecting from the relation tuples with attributes matching the query constants. Loss of results by earlier Selection is discussed in [Agrawal, 88]. Rule rewriting methods, such as Magic Sets, magic counting, and its variants, attempt to emulate the efficiency of the wavefront methods. They are a processing phase before Naive or SemiNaive evaluation. Their purpose is to avoid irrelevant tuples generation during Naive or SemiNaive evaluation. However, they require the materialisation of an auxiliary relation. Since two virtual relations are now materialised instead of one, the benefits of rule-rewriting are not always realised. Sometimes the result is less efficient than the original.

Furthermore, LFP evaluation is inherently non-parallel since it requires every new tuple to be compared with all tuples derived so far. This is the mechanism to detect termination. Using multiple processors results in large communication overheads. Semi-Naive evaluation (more efficient than Naive when implemented on a single processor) suffers even more from this inter-processor communication problem than Naive, because it must do a Set Difference operation at every iteration, to derive the delta for the next iteration. This causes a synchronisation delay at every iteration, whereas Naive only uses Difference as an asynchronous termination detection scheme [Cacace 90]. In contrast, the cycle merging and path length calculating approach [Wu 88] is inherently parallel. If each processor has access to the base relations it has enough information to pursue one or more paths between query constant nodes and result nodes. Separate paths can be pursued in separate processors without interaction.

Although the discussion above referred to the two sided (same generation) rule form the arguments clearly apply in general to n-sided recursions. Further study will extend existing classifications of rule forms [eg Youn 88, Han 89] and show the exact application domain of the new method. The standard evaluation strategy for successful DDB languages is to select the most efficient method of evaluation for each particular query form/rule cluster combination. This approach is not yet available for systems with access to general-purpose multiprocessors, because there are not yet enough general multiprocessor methods to allow it. [Hulin 89, Van Gelder 86, Wolfson, 88] has included other work on this problem. A goal in devising methods for multiprocessor front-ends should be to produce a scheme compatible with the multiprocessor architecture on which other methods, including the most general, will work. Moreover, in order to be accessible to a wide range of users, the multiprocessor should be a readily- available configuration. This criterion applies to the parallel Level-Finding method.

3.3 Bridge Node and Formula Parallelism

From the algorithm of the Level-Finding method above it is evident that processing one bridge node is independent of the others. There is no interaction between different bridge node processes. The performance of bridge node parallelism and the easy load balancing it allows, is currently being assessed experimentally and will be reported in a later paper. At present we provide the theoretical basis for another aspect of parallelism inherent in the Level-Finding approach, namely *formula parallelism*. Recurrence sequence formulae can be processed in parallel using the algorithm specified in section 5.4. We now provide the arithmetic foundations for that algorithm.

4 Arithmetic Foundations of Formula Parallelism

4.1 Definitions and Notation

Definition 1: *(Divisibility)* An integer b is divisible by an integer a, not zero, if there is an integer x such that $b = ax$, and we write $a \mid b$. When b is not divisible by a, we write $a \!\!\mid b$.

Definition 2: *(Congruence)* If an integer m, not zero, divides the difference $a - b$, we say that a is congruent to b modulo m and write $a \equiv b \pmod{m}$. If $a - b$ is not divisible by m, we say that a is not congruent to b modulo m, and in this case we write $a \mathrel{!\!\equiv} b \pmod{m}$.

Definition 3: *(Residue)* If $x \equiv y \pmod{m}$ then y is called a residue of x modulo m. A set $x_1, x_2, \ldots, x_m$ is called a complete residue system modulo m if for every integer y there is one and only one x_j such that $y \equiv x_j \pmod{m}$.

Definition 4: *(Greatest Common Divisor)* The integer a is a common divisor of b and c in case $a \mid b$ and $a \mid c$. Since there is only a finite number of any nonzero integer, there is only a finite number of common divisors of b and c, except in the case $b = c = 0$. If at least one of b and c is not zero, the greatest among their common divisor is called the greatest common divisor of b and c and is denoted by $gcd(b, c)$. Similarly, we denote the greatest common divisor g of the integers $b_1, b_2, \ldots, b_n$, not all zero, by $gcd(b_1, b_2, \ldots, b_n)$.

4.2 Formula of Recurrence Sequence (RS) of a Bridge Node

For a given path from query constant node to a bridge node, the cycles on the simple path can be merged into a virtual cycle [Wu 88]. The virtual cycle length is the greatest common divisor of the cycles. The RS of a bridge node can be represented as a union of two sets. Set 1 is a finite number of integers, denoted as F_set. Set 2 is an infinite integer set, which is expressed as a formula $d + k*e$ denoted by $d(e)$, where $d \geq 0$ and $e > 0$. d is the recurrence start point, e is the virtual cycle length.

In summary, the RS of a bridge node with respect to the query constant node derived from a simple path can be represented as $F\_set \cup d(e)$, where the sets of integers F_set and $d(e)$ are disjoint with all values in $F\_set < (d - 1)$.

Suppose there are several simple paths, $p_1, p_2, \ldots, p_m$, from query constant node to a given bridge node, then the recurrence sequence of the bridge node is the union of all recurrence sequences derived from all of the simple paths.

In this section, theorems to support the *existence* of *formula parallelism* are presented. The main point here is that formulae for bridge node recurrence sequences can not always be merged into one formula.

Take the graph shown by Figure 1 as "graph Left", for example, the simple paths from a to b are p_1: <a, c, b> and p_2: <a, d, e, b>. The length of p_1, $|p_1|$, is 2. $|p_2| = 3$. The RS of b w.r.t. a generated from p_1 and p_2 are represented as { ϕ } $\cup$ 2(4) and { ϕ } $\cup$ 3(5) respectively.

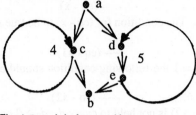

Fig. 1: "graph Left", a and b are query constant and bridge node respectively

The whole set of RS of b w.r.t. a is the union of the RS generated from two simple paths p1 and p2. That's, $RS_a(b)$ = { ϕ } $\cup$ 2(4) $\cup$ { ϕ } $\cup$ 3(5). This is the union of two formulae, 2(4) and 3(5), which denote two sets of integers. The two sets may have values in common, since the two formulae may both generate the same integer. Can a single formula $F\_set \cup d(e)$ be found which denotes the same set as 2(4) $\cup$ 3(5)?

Theorem 1: [Niven 91]

(1) $a \equiv b$ (mod m), $b \equiv a$ (mod m), and $a - b \equiv 0$ (mod m) are equivalent statements.

(2) if $a \equiv b$ (mod m) and $b \equiv c$ (mod m), then $a \equiv c$ (mod m).

(3) if $a \equiv b$ (mod m) and $c \equiv d$ (mod m), then $a + c \equiv c + d$ (mod m).

(4) if $a \equiv b$ (mod m) and $c \equiv d$ (mod m), then $a\,c \equiv c\,d$ (mod m).

(5) if $a \equiv b$ (mod m) and $d \mid m$, $d>0$, then $a \equiv b$ (mod d).

(6) if $a \equiv b$ (mod m) then $ac \equiv bc$ (mod m) for $c > 0$.

Theorem 2 [Wu 88]: let $m, n > 0$ and $gcd(m, n) = r$, then for any $t \geq 0$, $r*[(p-1)(q-1) + t] = k_1 * m + k_2 * n$, where $p = m/r$ and $q = n/r$, for some integers $k_1, k_2 \geq 0$.

Lemma 1: If $a \equiv b$ (mod m) and $a \equiv b$ (mod d), $d > 0$, then $d \mid m$.

Proof: Suppose $a \equiv b$ (mod m) and $a \equiv b$ (mod d), $d > 0$, then $d \,!!\, m$. According to definition 3 (congruence), the following equations are held:

$$a = m * k_1 + b \quad and \quad a = d * k_2 + b. \quad (k_1, k_2 = 0, 1, ..., n)$$

That's $m * k_1 + b = d * k_2 + b$. => $m * k_1 = d * k_2$. Take case of $k_1 = 1$, then $m = d * k_2$. Since $m, d > 0$, $d \mid m$ is held, which is contradictory with the initial assumption. Therefore, Lemma 1 is proved. ◆

Lemma 2: *If integers generated by formula $d_1(e_1)$ can be produced by an other formula $d(e)$, where $d_1, d \geq 0$, $e_1, e_2 > 0$, then $e \mid e_1$; and $d_1 \equiv d$ (mod e).*

Lemma 2 is easy to be proved by using theorem 1 and lama 1. ◆

Theorem 3: *There is no formula $d(e)$ where $d \geq 0$, $e>0$ that generates the identical sequence as the union of every two distinct formulae $d_1(e_1)$ and $d_2(e_2)$ where $d_1, d_1 \geq 0$, $e_1, e_2 > 1$.*

Proof: Assumption - A formula $d(e)$ can be found to generate identical recurrence sequence as the union of *every* two distinct formulae $d_1(e_1)$ and $d_2(e_2)$, where $d, d_1, d_2 \geq 0$ and $e > 0$, $e_1, e_2 > 1$.

According to Lemma 2, $e \mid e_1$ and $e \mid e_2$. therefore, e *is one of common divisors* of e_1 and e_2. Moreover, $d_1 \equiv d$ (mod e) and $d_2 \equiv d$ (mod e).

Theorem 1. (2). $d_1 \equiv d_2$ (mod e).

Let e be the greatest common divisor of e_1 and e_2, i.e. $e = gcd(e_1, e_2)$. According to the Theorem 2, there exists an integer k, $k = [(e_1/e - 1)(e_2/e - 1) + t]$, $t \geq 0$, such that $e * k = e_1 * k_1 + e_2 * k_2$. Take the case of $k_1, k_2 = 1$, integer, $e*k$, generated by the new formula can be represented as: $e * k + d = (e_1 + d_1) + (e_2 + d_2)$. It holds the following properties: $e * k + d \equiv e_1 + d_1 + d_2 \pmod{e_2}$ and $e * k + d \equiv e_2 + d_2 + d_1 \pmod{e_1}$.

Now, let us check if $e * k + d \in d_1(e_1)$ or $d_2(e_2)$. Suppose $e * k + d \in d_2(e_2)$, then $e * k + d \equiv d_2 \pmod{e_2}$. Theorem 1. (1). (2), $d_2 \equiv e_1 + d_1 + d_2 \pmod{e_2}$. Theorem 1. (1). $(e_1 + d_1 + d_2) - d_2 \equiv 0 \pmod{e_2}$.

That's, $e_1 + d_1 \equiv 0 \pmod{e_2}$.   ----- (eq - x)

Since $e_1, e_2 > 1$, (eq -x) is not held naturally. The condition for (eq - x) to be true is as follows:

$$e_2 \mid (e_1 + d_1).   ----- (eq - x1)$$

If $e * k + d \in d_1(e_1)$, for the case of $k_1, k_2 = 1$ the following condition should be held.

$$e_1 \mid (e_2 + d_2).   ----- (eq - x2)$$

The truth of equation either (eq - x1) or (eq - x2) is not held to every $d_1, d_2 \geq 0$ and $e_1, e_2 > 0$, such as, $d_1 = 2, d_2 = 3, e_1 = 4, e_2 = 5$. Therefore, some integers generated by the formula $d(e)$ are not in $d_1(e_1)$ nor $d_2(e_2)$. This is contradictory to the assumption. Therefore, theorem 3 is proved. ◆

4.3 Theorems for Merge of Formulae

Arithmetic theories to reduce number of formulae for the purpose of optimisation are presented in this section. Given a set of formulae, the **merge of formulae** here is the activity of reducing the number of formulae in the given formula set.

Theorem 4: *Given any two formulae $d_1(e_1)$ and $d_2(e_2)$, where $d_1, d_2 \geq 0, e_1, e_2 > 0$, if $e_2 \mid e_1$, and $d_1 \equiv d_2 \pmod{e_2}$, then the union of these two formulae can be merged into one formula $max\{d_1, d_2\}(e_2) \cup F\_set$, where F_set is a finite set of integers less than $max\{d_1, d_2\}$.*

Proof: Since $e_2 \mid e_1$, e2 > 0, applies to any integer, l, if $l \equiv d_1 \pmod{e_1}$, according to Theorem 1. (5), *then $l \equiv d_1 \pmod{e_2}$.*

Since $d_1 \equiv d_2 \pmod{e_2}$ and $l \equiv d_1 \pmod{e_2}$, according to Theorem 1. (2), $l \equiv d_2 \pmod{e_2}$. Therefore, the integers generated by formula $d_1(e_1)$ and $d_2(e_2)$ are congruent to $d_2 \pmod{e_2}$. Since the start point of integers in the union of $d_1(e_1)$ and $d_2(e_2)$ is the $max\{d_1, d_2\}$, the formula which generates the identical sequence as the union of $d_1(e_1)$ and $d_2(e_2)$ after the recurrence start point is $max\{d_1, d_2\}(e_2)$. The recurrence sequences less than the start point form the F_set. ◆

Theorem 5: *Given any two formulae $d_1(e_1)$ and $d_2(e_2)$, where $d_1, d_2 \geq 0, e_1, e_2 > 0$, if one of e_1 and e_2 is 1, then the sequence in the union of formulae $d_1(e_1)$ and $d_2(e_2)$ can be represented by $F\_set \cup d(1)$, where $d = d_i$ if $e_i = 1$ $(i = 1, 2)$.*

Proof: Suppose $e_1 = 1$, then $e_1 \mid e_2$. According to Theorem 1. (5), any integer l_2 generated by formula $d_2(e_2)$ holds $l_2 \equiv d_1(e_1)$, ie., for any integer $l_2 \geq d_1, l_2 = d_1 + k*e_1, (k = 0, 1,)$. If the integers less than d_1 exist, they are *in F_set,* the theorem 5 is proven. To apply theorem 5 to a given set *of n formulae, $\{d_i(e_i)\}$,* we have the conclusion that the union of the n formulae can be expressed by $F\_set \cup min\{d_1, d_2, ..., d_{nl}\}(1)$, where $F\_set = \{i \mid i < min\{d_1, d_2,...,d_{nl}\}\}$ and $i \in \cup d_i(e_i)$ }, d_i $(i=1$ to $nl)$ are those for which $e_i = 1$. ◆

Theorem 6: *Given a set of formulae SF, $\{d_i(e_i) \mid e_i \neq 1, i = 1, 2, ...\}$, divide SF into subsets, SFSs. Each subset is defined as: $SFS_i = \{d_j(e_j) \mid e_j = i, i$ is an integer$\}$. If $|SFS_i| = i$, and $d_j \not\equiv d_k \pmod{i}$ for $(j \neq k)$, then the given set of formulae can be merged into $F\_set \cup max\{ d_j \mid d_j(e_j) SFS_i \}(1)$.*

Proof: Suppose a subset SFS_w is such a set of formulae that meets the conditions of theorem 6. Let $x_1, x_2, ..., x_w$ represent the integers generated by formula $d_{w1}(e_{w1})$,

$d_{w2}(e_{w2})$, ..., $d_{ww}(e_{ww})$ respectively.

$$x_1 \equiv d_{w1}(\text{mod } w)$$
$$x_2 \equiv d_{w2}(\text{mod } w)$$
$$\cdots$$
$$x_w \equiv d_{ww}(\text{mod } w)$$

Since $d_{wi} \not\equiv d_{wk} (\text{mod } w)$, where $i \neq k$, for every integer x there is one and only one $d_{wj} (w \geq j \geq 1)$ such that $x \equiv d_{wj}(\text{mod } w)$. According to definition of residue system, the set of $d_{w1}, d_{w2}, \ldots, d_{ww}$ is a complete residue system *modulo w*. Therefore, for every integer x if $x > max\{d_{w1}, d_{w2}, \ldots, d_{ww}\}$, x can be generated by formula $max\{d_{w1}, d_{w2}, \ldots, d_{ww}\}$(1). The integers, which are less than $max\{d_{w1}, d_{w2}, \ldots, d_{ww}\}$ and in the union of formula form F_set. Based on theorem 5, theorem 6 is correct. The proof is complete. ◆

4.4 Theory for Identifying Duplicate Results

Duplication might occur when recurrence sequence formulae of a bridge node are processed in parallel. In this section, theorems needed to identify the duplicates are given.

Theorem 7: *(Cycle Intersection Theorem)* [Wu 88] Given $a, c \geq 0$ and $b, d > 0$. Then 1) $a(b) \cap c(d) \neq \phi$ if and only if $|a(b) \cap c(d)| = \infty$ and 2) $a(b) \cap c(d) \neq \phi$ if and only if $gcd(b, d)$ is a divisor of the absolute difference of a and c.

Theorem 7 provides a means to test whether two formulae generate common integers. If two formulae produce common integers, then the identity of those integers can be obtained using theorem 8 (The Chinese Remainder Theorem) below.

Now let us consider the situation of more than two formulae. Suppose we have r formulae. The simplest case of those r formulae generating the same integer x can be represented as the following congruences:

$$x \equiv a_1 (\text{mod } m_1)$$
$$x \equiv a_2 (\text{mod } m_2)$$
$$\cdots \quad\quad\quad \text{---- (cong - eq)}$$
$$x \equiv a_r (\text{mod } m_r)$$

Theorem 8: *(The Chinese Remainder Theorem)*. Let $m_1, m_2, \ldots, m_r$ denote r positive integers that are relatively prime in pairs, and let $a_1, a_2, \ldots, a_r$ denote any r integers. Then the congruences (cong - eq) have common solutions. If x_0 is one such solution, then an integer x satisfies the congruences (cong - eq) if and only if x is in the *form* $x = x_0 + k*m$ for some integer k. Here $m = m_1 m_2 \ldots m_r$.

x_0 can be found in the following way [Niven 91]: Writing $m = m_1 m_2 \ldots m_r$, m/m_j is an integer. $x_0 = \Sigma (m/m_j) b_j a_j$, where $b_j (m/m_j) \equiv 1 (\text{mod } m)$. Thus, find out all b_j ($j = 1, 2, \ldots, r$), x_0 will be obtained.

Theorem 7 gives necessary and sufficient condition for any two formulae to generate common integers. Theorem 8 identifies integers generated by more than 1 formula based on the hypothesis that the moduli m_i should be relatively prime. When m_i is not relative prime, the solution is: if x_0 is one of the solutions, then an integer x *is* a solution if and only if $x = x_0 + k * lcm(m_1, m_2, \ldots, m_n)$ for some integer k, where $lcm(m_1, m_2, \ldots, m_n)$ is the least common multiple of the m_i.

5 Exploitation of Formula Parallelism

As described in sections above, the recurrence sequences of a bridge node may be a union of several formulae which may not be reducible to a single formula $F\_set \cup d(e)$. The formulae associated with a bridge node can be processed in parallel -

different formulae on different processors.

The operation of processing formulae in parallel, in fact, is to traverse "graph Right" in parallel to retrieve the answers to the given query. If the "graph Right" for processing the given query is available to any processor then any formula can be processed by any processor, since the necessary information for retrieving answers is the levels generated by a formula and the graph from which the answers are retrieved. There is no communication between processors during formula processing.

The more formulae associated with a bridge node, the more parallelism we would be able to exploit. However, sometimes it might not be necessary to process all of them since some formulae may be implied by others. Therefore, before processing the formulae associated with a bridge node, it is useful to filter out formulae which do not contribute to the RS. This filtering work is supported by the theorems mentioned in section 4.3.

5.1 Algorithm of Merging Formula

Reviewing the theorems in section 4, if one of the given formulae is in the form $d(1)$, then all the formulae can be merged into $F\_set \cup d_x(1)$ according to theorem 5. Therefore, the first step of the algorithm is to identify any formula in the form $d(1)$. Also, in any step of processing, identification of formula $d(1)$ is important in order to save processing time, since during formula merging, a formula in form of $d(1)$ may be generated. If there is no formula $d(1)$ then the formulae implied by others will be checked.

It is a simple arithmetic calculation to check whether a formula $d_1(e_1)$ is implied by another formula $d(e)$. According to theorem 4, if two formulae $d_1(e_1)$ and $d_2(e_2)$ meet two conditions: (1) e_1 is divisible by e_2, and (2) $d_2 - d_1$ is divisible by e_2, then formula $d_1(e_1)$ is contained in formula $d_2(e_2)$. Thus, formula $d_1(e_1)$ can be removed from the formula set.

The complete residue system *modulo m* where *m* is an integer greater than 1, is an important concept in merging formulae. Once a complete residue system *modulo m* is found, the whole set of formulae can be merged into a formula in the form $d(1)$.

Even through there is no formula containing another formula in the given formula set, it might be the case that a subset of formulae makes up a complete residue system *modulo m*. A simple example is when the given formula set is { 0(3), 1(3), 2(3) }. The formulae in the given set don't contain each other. However they form the complete residue system of *modulo* 3. Thus, the whole set of formulae can be merged into the formula 0(1).

It is also an arithmetic operation to see if a set of formulae makes up a complete residue system. A necessary condition for this is that the number of formulae be equal to the modulus, i.e. the *e* in formula $d(e)$. If the necessary condition is met, then according to theorem 6 each pair of (d_i, d_j) where $i \neq j$ should be not congruent to each other under *modulus e*. If this second condition is satisfied, a complete residue system to *modulus e* has been found.

The formula merging algorithm can be described as the following procedure:
Algorithm_of_merging_formulae:
Begin {
    Search the set of formulae $d_i(e_i)$ SF, to obtain a set SF_1, with $e_i = 1$.
    If $SF_1 \neq \phi$
    Then merge the formulae into one formula;
    Else { Filter out unnecessary formulae;
           Check if there exists a complete residue system;
           If there is a complete residue system
           Then merge the formulae in SF into one formula. } } end

5.2 Duplicate Removal

Duplication of result values could occur when processing formulae on different processors, since a node in "graph Right" could satisfy more than one formula. If the result from parallel processing formulae involves further operations, duplicates would cause an endless-loop. Therefore, removal of duplicates is essential.

The reason duplication occurs is that an integer is generated by more than one formula. There are two solutions to removing duplicates: 1) filter out the duplicates in the answer sets; 2) identify in advance the Duplicate Integer Set (*DIS*) and retrieve the nodes at those levels from the "graph Right" only once from the nodes in "graph Right" at levels specified by the integers in set *DIS*.

Solution 1) is simple but will produce increased communication between processors and so reduce processing speed. With increasing size of individual answer sets, the load of message passing between processing elements will become severe.

Solution 2) has to identify the set of integers generated by more than one formula. It does not need communication between processing elements. Thus, solution 2) is preferable.

If two (or more) formulae create common integers then the number of integers is infinite. However, the infinite sequence of integers is in a regular pattern according to theorem 8 (The Chinese Remainder Theorem). In other words, the common integers generated can be represented by a formula in the same form as $x_0(m)$. This is an advantage since the newly generated formula can be processed in the same way as the original formulae.

It is simple to test whether two formulae will generate common integers by using theorem 7. If two formulae generate common integers, then the *constraining-formula* representing the common integers can be found using theorem 8. The constraining-formula is used to ensure that any common integer of two formulae is processed only once.

5.3 Constrained-Relationship Matrix (CRM)

The constrained-relationship Matrix is an n x n matrix, where n is number of formulae. Elements of a CRM take values 0 or 1. The value 0 for element CRM_{ij} indicates that the ith and jth formulae don't generate common integers. On the other hand, a 1 indicates the ith and jth formulae produce common integers. For example, if a given formula set is $\{1(3), 2(6), 1(8)\}$, then the constrained-relationship matrix of the formula set is as follows:

	1(3)	2(6)	1(8)
1(3)	x	0	1
2(6)	0	x	0
1(8)	1	0	x

It shows, for example, that formulae 1(3) and 1(8) will produce duplicate results whereas 1(3) and 2(6) will not. In a CRM matrix, element CRM_{ii} takes value x for obvious reasons.

5.4 Algorithm for Parallel Processing of Formulae

The algorithm for parallel processing of formulae consists of *distribution* and *manipulation* strategies. The *distribution* part assigns formulae to different processors for processing. The *manipulation* part is what each processor does to retrieve duplicate-free answers to the given query. In order to describe the algorithm clearly, let us make the following assumption:

A bridge edge is <b, g>; the recurrence sequence formulae of bridge node b with respect to the query-constant constitute set SF;

Distribution-part   /*Algorithm-of-parallel-processing-formulae*/

begin {
1. Merge formulae in set SF to produce set SF';
2. If | SF'| = 1   /* only one formula in set SF' */
   Then   Process formula;
   Else   { Create constrained-relationship matrix of SF';
              for(i=0; i<n; i++)
                 for(j=0; j<i-1; j++)
                    if(CRM$_{ij}$ == 1)
                 Put constraining-formula of *ith* and *jth* formulae in set CF$_i$;
              Send *ith* formula with its constraining-formula set CF$_i$ to a processor
                       for processing; }
       } end.

Manipulation-part (formula$_i$, CF$_i$)

begin {
1. Retrieve reachable node set RNSg from node g in "graph Right";
2. For each node n, n ∈ RNSg :
      { Calculate RS$_g$(n);
        If the formula of RS$_g$(n) generates common integer as formula i **and**
            NOT as any formula in its constrained formula set CF$_i$
        Then n is answer. }
      } end.

The manipulation part of the algorithm is modification of the algorithm we used in the Level-Finding approach. This algorithm is fully decomposable. During formula processing, no communication is required between the parallel processing elements.

6 Conclusion

The arithmetic approach used in the Level-Finding method for evaluating recursive queries in deductive database systems provides great potential of parallel processing. In this paper, we identified two kinds of parallelism, i.e. *bridge node parallelism* and *formula parallelism*. The arithmetic foundations and algorithm to exploit *formula parallelism* were given. The algorithm is parallel. No communication is necessary during processing each formula and termination is easily controlled.

The usual approach in efficient DDB systems is to select the most efficient evaluation strategy that will work with the current query. However, the existing repertoire of standard evaluation procedures lacks methods able to utilise a standard multiprocessor platform. The current paper makes a start at remedying that deficiency.

Although many operations on sets of tuples are inherently parallel, existing algorithms to implement those operations include features which prevent parallel processing. Features such as inter-processor data traffic and synchronisation delays degrade performance badly.

We have introduced a parallel strategy for evaluating an important (widely used) class of recursive queries in Deductive Databases, and provided new theoretical results to allow the efficient use of formula-level parallelism.

The magic sets method and its variants for cyclic data, magic counting [Sacca 87, Greco 92] are rule rewriting methods for Naive and Semi-naive evaluation. They are designed to improve the efficiency of Naive or Semi-naive evaluation by reducing the number of irrelevant tuples involved. But since those methods are not easily parallelised it is beneficial to seek alternative evaluation strategies. An advantage of graph traversal methods, including the Level Finding method, is their ability to use query constants directly, without the need for rule rewriting. A disadvantage is their lack of generality. However, chaining recursions include many of the most popular queries, so an efficient parallel evaluation strategy for them is useful in a DDB's repertoire of query processing methods, since overall performance depends on the most frequent forms of query.

Acknowledgements

It is a pleasure to acknowledge the stimulating research environment provided by the IFS research group at Essex University. Investigation of the Parallel Level Finding Method for recursive query evaluation is supported by SERC research grant GR/H/17701.

References

Agrawal, Rakesh; and Devanbu, Prem, "Moving Selections into Linear Least Fixpoint Queries", IEEE 4th Conference on Data Engineering, 1988, pp 452-461.

Cacace, Filippo; Ceri, Stefano; and Houtsma, Maurice A.W., "An Overview of Parallel Strategies for Transitive Closure on Algebraic Machines", Proc PRISMA 90, pp 48-66.

Greco, Sergio; and Zaniolo, Carlo, "Optimisation of Linear Logic Programs using Counting Methods", Proc EDBT 92 (LNCS 580), pp 72-87.

Han, Jiawei; Qadah, Ghassen, and Chaou, Chinying, "The Processing and Evaluation of Transitive Closure Queries", Intl Conf on Extending Database Technology - EDBT 88, Venice, 1988, pp 49-75.

Han, Jiawei, "Compiling General Linear Recursions by Variable Connection Graph Analysis", Comput. Intell. 5, pp12-31, 1989.

Henschen, Lawrence; and Naqvi, Shamim A, "On Compiling Queries In Recursive First-Order Databases", JACM, 31 (1), January 1984, pp 47-85.

Hulin, Guy, "Parallel Processing of Recursive Queries in Distributed Architectures", VLDB Conf 1989, pp 87-96.

Lavington, Simon; Robinson, Jerome; and Mok, Kai-Yau, "A High Performance Relational Algebraic Processor for Large Knowledge Bases", Proc VLSI for AI Conference, Oxford, 1988. Kluwer Academic, 1989, pp 133-143.

Lavington, S.H. Waite, M.E. Robinson, J. & Dewhurst N.E.J, "Exploiting Parallelism in Primitives operations on bulk data types", PARLE'92, Paris, June 1992.

Niven I., Zuckerman H. Montgomery H., "An Introduction to the Theory of Numbers", Fifth Ed. Published by Jojn Wiley & Sons, Inc. 1991.

Robinson, J.; Lavington, S., "A Transitive Closure and Magic Functions Machine", Proc 2nd Intl Symposium on Databases in Parallel & Distributed Systems, IEEE Press, July 1990, pp 44-54.

Sacca, Domenico; and Zaniolo, Carlo, "Magic Counting Methods", Proc ACM SIGMOD 1987, pp 49-59.

Van Gelder, Allen, "A Message Passing Framework for Logical Query Evaluation" Proc ACM SIGMOD 15 (2), 1986, pp 155-165.

Wolfson, Ouri; and Silberschatz, Avi, "Distributed Processing of Logic Programs", Proc ACM SIGMOD 88, pp 329-336.

Wu, Ching-Shyan; and Henschen, Lawrence, "Answering Linear Recursive Queries in Cyclic Databases", FGCS 88, Vol 2, pp 727-734.

Wu, Ching-Shyan, "An Algorithmic Approach for Handling Cyclic and Non-cyclic Linear Recursive Queries in Horn Databases," Ph.D thesis EECS, Northwestern Univ March 1988.

Youn, Cheong; Henschen, Lawrence J.; and Han, Jiawei, "Classification of Recursive Formulas in Deductive Databases", Proc ACM SIGMOD 88, pp 320-328.

Yu, C. Y.; and Zhang, Weining, "Efficient Recursive Query Processing using Wavefront Methods", IEEE 1987 Third Intl Conf on Data Engineering.

Computing the Complete Orthogonal Decomposition Using a SIMD Array Processor

E. J. Kontoghiorghes and M. R. B. Clarke

Dept. of Computer Science, QMW College,
Mile End Road, London E1 4NS, U.K.,
e–mail : {ricos, mike}@dcs.qmw.ac.uk

Abstract. In this paper we employ Householder transformations and compound Givens rotations to compute the Complete Orthogonal Decomposition of a rectangular matrix, using a SIMD array processor. Algorithms are proposed for the reconstruction of the orthogonal matrices involved in the decompositions and the estimated execution time of all parallel algorithms is obtained.

1 Introduction

Numerous parallel methods have been proposed to compute the QR decomposition of a matrix [1, 2, 6, 8]. Here we employ Householder transformations and compound Givens rotations to compute the Complete Orthogonal Decomposition (COD) of a rectangular matrix, using a SIMD array processor. We also propose methods for regenerating the orthogonal transformation matrices, when the data which define the Householder transformations is stored in the annihilated positions of the data matrix. The estimated execution time of all parallel algorithms on the AMT DAP 510 is obtained [7].

We divide the COD of a $m \times n$ ($m > n$) matrix A into two stages. In stage 1 the matrix A is reduced to lower trapezoidal form and in stage 2 the lower trapezoid is triangularized. Let $Q \in \Re^{m \times m}$, $P \in \Re^{n \times n}$ be orthogonal, $\Pi \in \Re^{n \times n}$ be a permutation matrix and the rank of A be k ($k < n$). The orthogonal decompositions of stages 1 and 2 are then

$$Q^T A \Pi = \begin{bmatrix} 0 & 0 \\ R_1 & R_2 \end{bmatrix} \quad \text{(stage 1)} \tag{1}$$

$$\begin{bmatrix} R_1 & R_2 \end{bmatrix} P = \begin{bmatrix} 0 & R \end{bmatrix} \quad \text{(stage 2)} \tag{2}$$

where $R_2 \in \Re^{k \times k}$ and $R \in \Re^{k \times k}$ are both lower triangular.

In the next sections we use the following notation. For $A = [a_{ij}] \in \Re^{m \times n}$ ($1 \le i \le m$, $1 \le j \le n$) and symmetric matrices $B_1, \ldots, B_m$, then $a_{\bullet k}$ and $a_{k \bullet}$ will denote the kth column and row of A respectively and $\prod_{i=1}^{m} B_i = B_1 B_2 \cdots B_m$. A zero dimension will denote a null matrix or vector and all vectors are considered to be column vectors except if transposed, i.e $a_{k \bullet}$ is a column vector and $a_{k \bullet}^T$ is a row vector.

2 Computing Stage 1

For the computation of the orthogonal decomposition (1), let $I_n^{(i, \mu)}$ be the matrix I_n with columns $n - i + 1$ and μ interchanged and $Q_i^T = I_m - \frac{1}{b_i} h^{(i)} h^{(i)^T}$ be an

m x m Householder matrix which annihilates the first $m - i$ elements of $a_{\bullet\, n-i+1}$ (pivot column), when it is premultiplied to A. If $A^{(0)} = A$, $V^{(0)} = [v_\varrho^{(0)}] \in \Re^n$ with $v_\varrho^{(0)} = \|a_{\bullet\, \varrho}\|^2$ and for $i = 1, \cdots, k$

$$
\left.
\begin{aligned}
\mu_i &= \max_\varrho \, (v_\varrho^{(i-1)}) \quad (1 \le \varrho \le n - i + 1) \\
A^{(i)} &= Q_i^T (A^{(i-1)} \, I_n^{(i,\,\mu_i)}) \\
&= \begin{bmatrix} R_{11}^{(i)} & 0 \\ R_{21}^{(i)} & R_{22}^{(i)} \end{bmatrix} \begin{matrix} m - i \\ i \end{matrix} \\
& \quad\;\; \begin{matrix} n - i & \;\; i \end{matrix} \\
V^{(i-1)} &= V^{(i-1)} \, I_n^{(i,\,\mu_i)} \\
v_j &= v_j - a_{m-i+1\,j}^2 \quad (j = 1, \ldots, n - i)
\end{aligned}
\right\}
\tag{3}
$$

then the matrices in (1) are equivalent to $[R_1 \; R_2] = [R_{21}^{(k)} \; R_{22}^{(k)}]$, $Q^T = \prod_{i=1}^k Q_{k-i+1}^T$ and $\Pi = \prod_{i=1}^k I^{(i,\,\mu_i)}$. The criterion used to declare rank$(A) = k$ is $v_{\mu_{k+1}}^{(k)} < \tau$, where τ is an absolute tolerance parameter and its value depends on the scaling of A [3, 5]. The value of τ is assumed to be given.

The permutation $A^{(i-1)} \, I_n^{(i,\,\mu_i)}$ interchanges columns μ_i and $n - i + 1$ of $A^{(i-1)}$, where column μ_i has the maximum Euclidean norm among all columns in $R_{11}^{(i-1)}$. This interchange method results in the diagonal of the lower triangular matrix $R_{22}^{(i)}$ be increasing in magnitude. The permutation matrix Π can be stored and computed using one of the two vectors $\xi, \zeta \in \Re^n$, where $\Pi = [e_{\zeta_1} \; \ldots \; e_{\zeta_n}] = [e_{\xi_1} \; \ldots \; e_{\xi_n}]^T$. With initial values $\zeta_i = \xi_i = i \, (i = 1, \ldots, n)$, a permutation $I_n^{(i,\,\mu_i)}$ is equivalent to swapping first the elements ζ_{n-i+1} and ζ_{μ_i} of ξ and then swapping the elements $n - i + 1$ and μ_i of ζ.

For the implementation of (3) on the DAP, we let $n = N$ ES, $m = M$ ES and $1 < M \le$ ES, where ES $= 32$ is the Edge Size of the AMT DAP 510. The time required to construct and apply a single Householder transformation, is given by $a_1 + b_1 \lceil \frac{m}{ES} \rceil \lceil \frac{n}{ES} \rceil$ for some constants a_1 and b_1. By applying Q_i^T only on the effected top $(m - i + 1)$ x $(n - i + 1)$ sub–matrix of A, the total execution time in msec. ([4]) for computing (1) when $\kappa = n$, is found to be $N(105.9 + 31.8M + 5.9N + 27.8MN - 9.2N^2)$.

3 Computing Stage 2

The computation of (2) using Householder transformations is similar to the computation of (1). For $\tilde{n} = n - k$, $R_1 = [\tilde{r}_{ij}]$ and $R_2 = [r_{ij}]$, let P_i be the n x n Householder matrix

$$
P_i = I_n - \frac{1}{c_i} \begin{bmatrix} \tilde{r}_{i\bullet} \\ \gamma_i \, e_i \end{bmatrix} [\; \tilde{r}_{i\bullet}^T \quad \gamma_i \, e_i^T \;]
\tag{4}
$$

where $\gamma_i = r_{ii} \pm s$, $s^2 = \|\tilde{r}_{i\bullet}\|^2 + r_{ii}^2$, $c_i = \gamma_i \, s$ and $I_k = [e_1 \ldots e_k]$. The application of P_i from the right of $[R_1 \; R_2]$ will annihilate the ith row of R_1 by affecting the whole matrix R_1 and only the ith column of R_2. After we have applied $P_1, \ldots, P_i$ $(1 \leq i \leq k)$ from the right of $[R_1 \; R_2]$, the first i rows of R_1 are zero and R_2 remains lower triangular. Thus, the orthogonal matrix P in (2) is defined as $\prod_{i=1}^{k} P_i$.

Now consider the use of compound disjoint Givens rotations (*cdgr*) to compute (2). Let $G_{ij} \in \Re^{n \times n}$ be a Givens matrix which annihilates $\tilde{r}_{ij}$ when it is applied from the right of $[R_1 \; R_2]$. The rotation $[R_1 \; R_2]G_{ij}$ effects only the two columns $\tilde{r}_{\bullet j}$, $r_{\bullet i}$ and thus, a compound rotation matrix can comprise at most $\min(\tilde{n}, k)$ disjoint Givens rotations, which can be applied simultaneously. The sequence of cdgr (*scdgr*) which we propose to computes (2) does not create any non zero elements above the main diagonal of R_2 and previously created zeroes of R_1 are preserved. The scdgr comprises $k + \tilde{n} - 1$ compound rotations and all elements of R_1 annihilated by any compound rotation lie on a diagonal.

In figure (1a) a number i ($1 \leq i < k + n$, $k = 16$, $n = 6$) denotes the elements of R_1 annihilated by the ith cdgr. Figure (1b) shows the ratio between the execution times required to compute (2) using the Given's and Householder methods (Given's/Householder), when $k = K$ ES, $\tilde{n} = \eta$ ES and $\tilde{n} \leq k$.

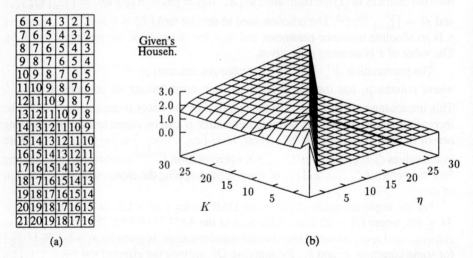

6	5	4	3	2	1
7	6	5	4	3	2
8	7	6	5	4	3
9	8	7	6	5	4
10	9	8	7	6	5
11	10	9	8	7	6
12	11	10	9	8	7
13	12	11	10	9	8
14	13	12	11	10	9
15	14	13	12	11	10
16	15	14	13	12	11
17	16	15	14	13	12
18	17	16	15	14	13
19	18	17	16	15	14
20	19	18	17	16	15
21	20	19	18	17	16

(a)   (b)

Fig. 1. scdgr and the execution time ratio of Given's / Householder methods to compute (2)

4 Reconstructing the Orthogonal Matrices

The reconstruction of the orthogonal matrix Q^T in (1) given $h^{(i)}$ and b_i of Q_i^T ($i = 1, \ldots, k$), is obvious and we will not discuss it here, but we consider the reconstruction of the orthogonal matrix P in (2). If $P^{(\lambda)} = \prod_{i=1}^{\lambda} P_i$, it can be shown by induction that $P^{(\lambda)}$ has the structural form

$$
\begin{bmatrix} A^{(\lambda)} & B^{(\lambda)} & 0 \\ 0 & 0 & I \end{bmatrix} \begin{matrix} \tilde{n} + \lambda \\ k - \lambda \end{matrix}
$$
$$
\;\;\;\; \tilde{n} \;\;\;\;\; \lambda \;\;\; k - \lambda
$$

where the bottom $\lambda \times \lambda$ sub–matrix of $B^{(\lambda)}$ is lower triangular. Further, if $P^{(0)} = I_n$ then it can be proven that $P^{(\lambda)} = P^{(\lambda-1)}P_\lambda$ is equivalent to

$$A^{(\lambda)} = \begin{bmatrix} A^{(\lambda-1)} \\ 0 \end{bmatrix} - x\,\tilde{r}_{\lambda\bullet}^{T}, \quad \text{and} \quad b_{\lambda\bullet}^{(\lambda)} = e_{\tilde{n}+\lambda} - \gamma_\lambda\,x \quad \text{for} \quad x = \frac{1}{c_\lambda}\begin{bmatrix} A^{(\lambda-1)}\,\tilde{r}_{\lambda\bullet} \\ \gamma_\lambda \end{bmatrix}$$

where now $I_n = [e_1 \ldots e_n]$. The latter defines the λth step of the algorithm.

On the DAP we divided the k steps needed to reconstruct P into μ phases, where $\eta = \lceil \frac{\tilde{n}+1}{ES} \rceil$, $\delta = \eta\,ES - \tilde{n}$ and $\mu = \lceil \frac{k-\delta}{ES} \rceil + 1$. The ith phase performs s_i steps, where $s_1 = \delta$, $s_i = ES$ for $i = 2, \ldots, \mu - 1$ and $s_\mu = k - \delta - (\mu - 2)ES$ if $\mu > 2$. At phases 1 to $\mu - 1$ the effected sub–matrix of A has number of rows a multiple of ES.

The execution time (in msec.) of the ith step is $a_0 + (a_1 + a_2\lceil \frac{\tilde{n}}{ES} \rceil)\lceil \frac{n+i}{ES} \rceil$, where $a = 0.78$, $a_1 = 0.21$ and $a_3 = 0.55$. Thus, for $n_i = \tilde{n} + \sum_{j=1}^{i} s_j$ the estimated time of reconstructing P on the DAP, excluding the overheads, is

$$\sum_{i=1}^{\mu} s_i\left(a_0 + (a_1 + a_2\lceil \frac{\tilde{n}}{ES} \rceil)\lceil \frac{n_i}{ES} \rceil \right) = \sum_{i=1}^{\mu} s_i\left(a_0 + (a_1 + a_2\lceil \frac{\tilde{n}}{ES} \rceil)(\eta + 1 - i) \right)$$

5 Discussion

The aim has been to present stable parallel algorithms for computing the complete orthogonal decomposition of a rectangular matrix. We considered aspects which either do not arise on a serial computer or do not seriously effect the performance of an algorithm. The execution time of all algorithms has been obtained. A comparison between the execution times of applying Householder transformations and compound disjoint Givens plane rotations to compute (2) on the SIMD AMT DAP 510, reveals the superiority in performance of using Householder reflections rather than Given's rotations, on the DAP.

References

1. G.S.J. Bowgen and J.J. Modi. Implementation of QR factorization on the DAP using Householder transformations. *Comp. Phys. comm.*, 37, 1985.
2. M. Cosnard, J.-M. Muller, and Y. Robert. Parallel QR decomposition of a rectangular matrix. *Numer. Math.*, 48, 1986.
3. G.H. Golub and C.F. Van Loan. *Matrix computations*. North Oxford Academic, 1983.
4. E.J. Kontoghiorghes and M.R.B. Clarke. Algorithms for the solution of the OLM on the DAP. Technical Report 602, QMW College, Dept. of Comp. Scien., 1992.
5. C.L. Lawson and R.J. Hanson. *Solving Least Squares Problems*. Prentice–Hall Englewood Cliff, 1974.
6. J.J. Modi and M.R.B. Clarke. An alternative Givens ordering. *Numer. Math.*, 43, 1984.
7. D. Parkinson, D.J. Hunt, and K.S. MacQueen. The AMT DAP 500. In *33rd IEEE Comp. Soc. Int. Conf.*, San Francisco, 1988.
8. A.H. Sameh and R.P. Brent. Solving triangular systems on a parallel computer. *SIAM jour. Numer. Anal.*, 14(6), 1977.

A Dynamic Load Balancing Strategy for Massively Parallel Computers

M. Cannataro[*], Ya. D. Sergeyev[§], G. Spezzano[*], and D. Talia[*]

[*]CRAI, Località S. Stefano, 87036 Rende, CS, Italy
[§]University of Nizhni Novgorod, Nizhni Novgorod 603600, Russia

Abstract

This paper describes a new load balancing algorithm, the probabilistic strategy with neighbourhood synchronization (PNS), for massively parallel computers. The proposed strategy differs from fully distributed approaches which require a high inter-processor communication overhead when the number of processors becomes large. This load balancing strategy uses only local information and takes into account the information lags in distributed systems for estimating the system load.

1 Introduction

Scheduling and load balancing strategies may play a considerable role to achieve an effective use of the computing power offered by massively parallel computers. Load balancing algorithms provide a distribution of processes to the computing nodes of a parallel computer attempting to balance the load on all nodes such that the whole throughput of the system is maximized [1].

The implementation of load balancing strategies on distributed-memory massively parallel computers (multicomputers) is very critical due to the large number of computing nodes and the overhead resulting from communications necessary to accomplish the application load balancing. Furthermore, most of the strategies which have been proposed are designed for coarse-grain distributed systems. They can not easily be adapted to multicomputers composed of a large number of medium-fine grain processors which support the execution of thousands fine-grain processes.

In some cases load balancing may result in a large increase of the execution time of parallel applications. Obviously, it is not possible to collect maximal state information with minimal communications. Load balancing strategies must make a compromise to solve this two-criteria problem.

In this paper a new dynamic load balancing strategy for distributed memory parallel computers is presented. This load balancing strategy is called Probabilistic strategy with Neighbourhood Synchronization (PNS). The PNS strategy uses only information from neighbours and takes into account the effect of information lags in multicomputer systems for estimating the system load and for task assignment decision.

2 The PNS strategy

This new load balancing strategy uses only load information from neighbours and takes into account the effect of information lags in distributed systems for task assignment. This means that dynamic status information of processors among which we choose one for executing a new task is not immediately available because a status information measured at time t on a node i will arrive an a node j at time $t+t_m$, where t_m is the time required to pass the distance between i and j. Thus, a status information collected by a node producing the load balancing decision may be obsolete. Then, if the flow of task arrivals has no regularity (or we don't know it) decision taken on the basis of currently available information will be non optimal. To cope with this problem we defined a probabilistic strategy based on the combination of two simple ideas :

i) A new task must be sent with higher probability to a processor with a short task queue and with lower probability to a processor with a long queue.

ii) A new task must be sent with higher probability to a processor about which we have more recent state information and with lower probability to a processor which we have more obsolete information about.

To describe PNS let us introduce the following notation and definitions:

- P, the number of processors (nodes) in the multicomputer.
- A, the node where a decision on the assignment of a new task to a node is to be taken.
- $W(A)$, the neighbourhood of A such that $A \in W(A)$. The neighbourhood may be defined in different ways depending on the topology of the system we are using.
- $N = N(W(A))$, the number of processors belonging to $W(A)$, $N \leq P$.
- $M = N - 1$, the number of neighbours belonging to $W(A)$ without A.
- $\tau(i)$, $1 \leq i \leq P$, the period at which every node i sends its load information to all nodes belonging to $W(i)$.
- $T(i)$, $1 \leq i \leq M$, the time of the last arrival onto the node A of the message with an information about load of node i. For node A, we define $T(N)=T(A)$ as the starting time of the load balancing procedure (i.e., node A is identified by the number N in $W(A)$).
- $l(i)$, $1 \leq i \leq M$, the length of task queue on the processor i (this information is hold in a message sent from a node i to the node A), $l(A) = l(N)$.
- $t_m(i)$, $1 \leq i \leq M$, the time required to pass the message containing $l(i)$ from a node i to node A.
- $t_a(i)$, $1 \leq i \leq M$, the time required to activate a task from the node A to a generic node i, if the node i will be obtained as a result of the load balancing procedure.
- $t(i) = T(A) - (T(i) - t_m(i) - t_a(i))$, $1 \leq i \leq M$, the time of synchronization of node A with a node $i \in W(A)$. It represents the obsolescence of $l(i)$ on node A. It is obtained as the difference between the time of $l(i)$ measurement on a node i and the time of arrival of a task from the node A to the node i, if this one will be obtained as a result of load balancing procedure executed on the node A. It is obvious that $t(A) = t(N) = 0$.
- $\alpha(i)$, $1 \leq i \leq N$, the utilization degree of synchronized times, $0 \leq \alpha(i) \leq 1$.
- $\Delta l(i)$, $1 \leq i \leq N$, the difference between the maximum queue length and the length $l(i)$ taking into account the obsolescence of $l(i)$.
- $p(i)$, $1 \leq i \leq N$, the probability to assign a task to the processor i.

2.1 The Algorithm

Each time on a node A a new task must be scheduled, the scheduler performs the steps as follows:

Step 1. Calculate the times of synchronization $t(i)$ for each node i such that $1 \leq i \leq M$.

Step 2. Calculate the values

$lmax = max \{ l(i): 1 \leq i \leq N \}$ and

$tmax = max \{ t(i): 1 \leq i \leq N \}$,

Step 3. For each node i such that $1 \leq i \leq N$, calculate the difference between the maximum queue length and its queue length $l(i)$ taking into account the obsolescence of $l(i)$:

$\Delta l(i) := (lmax - l(i)) (1 - \alpha(i) t(i) / tmax)$, where $0 \leq \alpha(i) \leq 1$.

Step 4. For each node i such that $1 \leq i \leq N$, compute the probability

$$p(i) := \Delta l(i) / S; \qquad \text{where } S = \sum_{k \in W(N)} \Delta l(k)$$

if $S = 0$, then set $p(A) = 1$.

Step 5. The result of the load balancing procedure is obtained by a randomized choice with probabilities $p(i)$ computed on step 4, on a random variable $X \in \{1 .. N\}$.

In the proposed algorithm the synchronization between node A and its neighbourhood is carried out using the synchronization times $t(i)$. When the queue information is not obsolete (there exists at least one such case - when we take load balancing decision on the node A, so $t(A) = 0$), the synchronized queue length calculated on Step 3 represents precisely the difference between the maximal queue length taking place in $W(A)$ and the length $l(i)$.

When the information about the load state of a node i is obsolete ($t(i) > 0$), we decrease the probability to send a task to the node i (see Steps 3, 4). Obviously, the probability of the assignment of a task to a processor with queue length equal to $lmax$ is zero. By means of the $\alpha(i)$ parameter it is possible to adjust the degree of influence of synchronization times on the result of the load balancing procedure. In case $\alpha(i) = 0$, $1 \leq i \leq N$, we use no information about the times of the load measurement. In case $\alpha(i) = 1$, we use this information in the strongest manner.

On Step 4 we use a simple probabilistic mechanism to avoid the following situation. Suppose that a node i has the smallest queue length in the system. During an interval, at least a period $\tau(i)$, all its neighbours send new tasks to this node and its load increases rapidly. At the same time, the load of the neighbours remains the same or decreases (because of termination of some task). Thus, we have an unbalanced situation again. Introducing Step 4 permits to distribute new tasks more uniformly.

The five steps of the PNS algorithm may be implemented using three different schemes, as follows.

- The *one-hop scheme*. According to this scheme the load balancing procedure takes the assignment decision only one time, so a task is sent to run in the target node.

- The *multi-hop scheme*. In this scheme PNS works using the parameters *min_hops* and *max_hops* as the Adaptive Contracting within Neighbourhood algorithm. Every hop of the multi-hop scheme is executed using the one-hop PNS and a new assignment decision may be taken. The notion of $W(A)$ may change from hop to hop (e.g., the cardinality of $W(A)$ can be decreased depending on the number of hops traveled);

- The *scheme with saturation control*. The main idea of this scheme is to forbid task assignment to processors with a load greater than a saturation threshold known a above. It may be applied in different ways.

3 PNS implementation

The one-hop PNS strategy has been implemented on a multicomputer composed of 32 T800 Transputers. We have compared the PNS strategy with a randomized strategy. In reference [2] a complete description of these experiments is given.

With respect to the random strategy, the PNS response time is preferable when the radius of the neighbourhood is less than 3, for every value of τ. In particular, it decreases when increasing τ. This effect is due to the lower frequency of data exchange that reduces the communication overhead. For the maximum process queue, the PNS values are still better for all values of τ when the radius is greater than one, and also for radius equal to one if a sufficiently short period is chosen. Obviously, reducing the period improves the knowledge of the system load and then results in a better task distribution.

4 Conclusions

In this paper we presented a new dynamic load balancing strategy for multicomputer systems called PNS. This strategy uses on each node of a multicomputer only status information collected from its neighbour nodes and it takes into account the information lags in distributed systems for estimating the system load.

The performance results have shown that the PNS strategy schedules the processes guarantying a locality-based computation with an information policy which takes into account the obsolescence of load information. This results in a better response time and a more balanced load distribution of our strategy respect to the randomized strategy. In particular, the PNS strategy yields a good performance when medium grained processes must be scheduled.

The behaviour of the load balancing algorithm can be tuned varying the dimension of the neighbourhood, the period of information exchange and the utilization degree of the information obsolescence. This characteristic allows to realize an adaptive strategy if these parameters are varied respect to the system load.

Acknowledgments
This research has been partially supported by "Progetto Finalizzato Sistemi Informatici e Calcolo Parallelo" of C.N.R. under grant no. 92.01669.69.

References

[1] T.L. Casavant and J.G. Kuhl, "A Taxonomy of Scheduling in General-Purpose Distributed Computing Systems," *IEEE Transactions on Software Engineering*, vol. SE-14, no. 2, pp. 141-154, Feb. 1988.

[2] M. Cannataro, Ya. D. Sergeyev, G. Spezzano, and D. Talia, "Probabilistic Load Balancing Strategy with the Neighbourhood Synchronization", Technical Report, CRAI, no. 92-03, Feb. 1992.

Issues in Event Abstraction

Thomas Kunz

Institut für Theoretische Informatik
Technische Hochschule Darmstadt

Abstract. Debugging distributed applications is very difficult, due to a number of problems. To manage the inherent complexity of distributed applications, for example, the use of abstractions is proposed. Event abstractions group sets of events into one higher–level event. Only event sets with certain properties guarantee proper abstraction. This paper examines two specific event set structures in more depth: complete precedence abstractions and contractions. Its main results are as follows. First, it is shown how the algorithmic detection of complete precedence abstractions can be simplified. Second, an additional structural requirement for contractions is derived to ensure their complete timestamping.

1 Introduction

Debugging distributed applications is commonly thought to be very difficult [3]. One of the problems is that distributed applications are inherently more complex than sequential ones. This problem is usually dealt with by debugging at different levels of abstraction, see [1]. This extended abstract discusses some of the issues relevant to event abstraction, where a set of events is grouped into one higher–level, abstract event. Due to space limitations, only systems with asynchronous interprocess communication will be dealt with. A more detailed treatment, including proofs for all theorems and a discussion of synchronous interprocess communication, can be found in [4].

2 Basic Definitions

The *happened before* ($\rightarrow$) relation defined in [5] is of particular importance for the analyses of distributed applications. An event a cannot influence another event b if it does not happen before that event. The *happened before* relation captures the notion of potential causality and the partial order induced by $\rightarrow$ is sometimes referred to as causality order or causality graph.

Each event e is assigned a timestamp T_e, usually an integer or a vector of integers. These timestamps are used to determine the $\rightarrow$ relation quickly (instead of tracing a path through the causality graph). Many timestamping techniques have been proposed in the literature. This abstract uses the vector timestamps proposed by [7]. For individual events, the following two timestamp tests can be used to derive the $\rightarrow$ relation:

Timestamp Test 1: $a \rightarrow b$ iff $T_a[i] \leq T_b[i]$ for all timestamp vector elements i.
Timestamp Test 2: $a \rightarrow b$ iff $T_a[p] \leq T_b[p]$, where event a occurs in process p.

3 Proper Abstraction

In the most general sense, *events* are atomic entities which cause changes to the state of an application. In distributed debugging, process creation and termination as well as all events related to interprocess communication are of particular interest. Each run of a distributed application produces a stream of these events. This is typically depicted in a diagram similar to Fig. 1. Each process is drawn as a line, events are drawn as circles. Time progresses from left to right, the layout of the events mirrors the underlying $\to$ relation.

Event abstractions are formed by grouping sets of events into one abstract event. There are two difficult problems involved in the abstraction process. First, it is far from obvious what abstractions should be formed to represent the overall program behaviour in a meaningful way [6]. Second, arbitrary abstractions may not reflect the $\to$ relation between events correctly at higher abstraction levels. Violations of the *happened before* relation at higher abstraction levels lead to a wrong or misleading representation of the overall program behaviour and will seriously impede the debugging process. Work reported in [2, 7] shows that only abstract events with specific properties guarantee proper abstraction, e.g. do not violate the $\to$ relation. The two more powerful abstract event structures identified in [7] are *complete precedence abstractions* and *contractions*.

Our research aims to analyze the event stream generated by the execution of a distributed application to automatically derive abstractions. Abstract events are essentially sets of more primitive events. Therefore, an automatic event abstraction algorithm will generate event sets and check whether a particular event set is suited as abstraction. However, generating all possible event sets is slow and inefficient. In a system with only 20 events, for example, 4845 different event sets of size 4 exist, but only very few will form useful abstractions. And real–life distributed applications produce event streams with thousands of events. So an important question we have to address is how to reduce the number of event sets generated without ignoring relevant event sets.

4 Complete Precedence Abstractions

Informally, let an event i^A (o^A) be an *input event* (*output event*) for a set of events A if it has an immediate predecessor (successor) according to the $\to$ relation outside A. A *complete precedence abstraction* is defined as follows:

Definition 1. A set E of events is called a *complete precedence abstraction* iff $\forall i^E, o^E : i^E \to o^E$.

Theorem 2. *A complete precedence abstraction E is dense:*
$\forall a, b \in E : a \to c \to b \Rightarrow c \in E$.

The density property is a very strong structural property, drastically reducing the number of event sets that have to be generated by an event abstraction algorithm. Consider the example shown in Fig. 1.

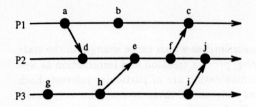

Fig. 1. A sample application execution

In this example, 36 distinct event sets of size 3 containing the event a exist. However, only the following 7 event sets are dense: $\{a, b, c\}$, $\{a, b, d\}$, $\{a, d, e\}$, $\{a, d, g\}$, $\{a, d, h\}$, $\{a, d, i\}$ and $\{a, g, h\}$. The event set $A = \{a, e, f\}$, for example, is not dense: $a \rightarrow d \rightarrow e \wedge a, e \in A, d \notin A$. A second possibility to reduce the number of event sets generated even further is presented in [4].

5 Contractions

Definition 3. An *input point* I_n^A (*output point* O_n^A) of a set of events A is a subset of the set of input events I^A (output events O^A). The indices are used to differentiate between multiple input/output points. Typically, we assume that all input/output events belong to exactly one input/output point: $I_n^A \cap I_m^A = \emptyset$ for $n \neq m$ and $\bigcup I_n^A = I^A$ ($O_n^A \cap O_m^A = \emptyset$ for $n \neq m$ and $\bigcup O_n^A = O^A$).

Definition 4. A set A of events is a *contraction* if, for every possible pair of an input point I_n^A and an output point O_m^A, there exists an input event $i^A \in I_n^A$ and an output event $o^A \in O_m^A$ such that $i^A \rightarrow o^A$.

To guarantee proper abstraction, contractions can only be connected according to the rules given in [7]. It can be shown that in systems with only asynchronous interprocess communication, contractions are dense. Contrary to complete precedence abstractions, this property is lost when synchronous interprocess communication is allowed too, makeing contractions harder to detect in such a case.

Another difference to complete precedence abstractions is that the contraction timestamps calculated with the algorithm given in [7] are *incomplete*: $E_1 \rightarrow E_2 \Rightarrow T_{E_1} \leq T_{E_2}$ but the converse is not necessarily true. Timestamps were introduced primarily to deduce the $\rightarrow$ relation quickly. Only *proper* contractions allow for *complete* timestamping, e.g. the derivation of the $\rightarrow$ relation from the contraction timestamps.

Definition 5. A contraction E_1 is called *proper* with respect to another contraction E_2 iff the following condition is fulfilled: $\exists a : (a \not\rightarrow E_2 \wedge \forall O_n^{E_1} : a \rightarrow O_n^{E_1})$. The event a is called *characteristic* event.

Theorem 6. *The timestamping of arbitrary contractions E_i is complete if and only if each E_i is proper with respect to all other events in the event stream that do not succeed it.*

To determine the *happened before* relation between two arbitrary *proper* contractions E_1 and E_2, the following timestamp test can be used: $T_{E_1} \leq T_{E_2} \Rightarrow E_1 \rightarrow E_2$.

6 Conclusions and Outlook

The research outlined in this extended abstract produced the following results to date. First, Theorem 2 provides the ground for an efficient algorithm to detect complete precedence abstractions. Second, Theorem 6 states the general criteria for complete timestamping of contractions.

The previous discussion implicitly assumed that an abstraction is always formed by replacing a set of events with a *single* abstract event. Another approach is pursued in [8]. The authors discuss a system for program visualization in which an abstract event (or supernode, in their terminology) can be represented by more than one node. Following this idea, the two problems discussed earlier (correct *and* meaningful representation of overall program behaviour) can be attacked independently. The set of events forming an abstract event is determined by an attempt to characterize some *meaningful* units of work. The display of this abstract event at higher abstraction levels is determined by the results in [2, 7] and this paper. These results control the display of the event set with fewer nodes so that the $\rightarrow$ relation is preserved at higher abstraction levels and the created supernodes can be timestamped completely.

References

1. Peter Bates. Distributed Debugging Tools for Heterogeneous Distributed Systems. In *Proceedings of the 8th International Conference on Distributed Computing Systems*, pages 308–315, San Jose, California, June 1988.
2. Wing Hong Cheung. *Process and Event Abstraction for Debugging Distributed Programs*. PhD thesis, University of Waterloo, Ontario, Canada, September 1989. Also available as Technical Report T-189, Computer Communications Network Group, University of Waterloo.
3. Wing Hong Cheung, James P. Black, and Eric Manning. A Framework for Distributed Debugging. *IEEE Software*, pages 106–115, January 1990.
4. Thomas Kunz. Event Abstraction: Some Definitions and Theorems. Technical Report TI-1/93, Technical University Darmstadt, February 1993.
5. Leslie Lamport. Time, Clocks, and the Ordering of Events in a Distributed System. *Communications of the ACM*, pages 558–565, July 1978.
6. Cherri M. Pancake. Debugger Visualization Techniques for Parallel Architectures. In *Proceedings of COMPCON*, pages 276–284, San Francisco, February 1992.
7. James Alexander Summers. Precedence-Preserving Abstraction for Distributed Debugging. Master's thesis, University of Waterloo, 1992.
8. Dror Zernik, Marc Snir, and Dalia Malki. Using Visualization Tools to Understand Concurrency. *IEEE Software*, pages 87–92, May 1992.

Modelling Replicated Processing

Maciej Koutny   Luigi V. Mancini   Giuseppe Pappalardo
Dept. of Computing Science   DISI, Genova University   Reggio Calabria University
Newcastle University, UK   Italy   Italy

1   Introduction

In the traditional "state machine" approach [4] to replicating distributed systems, the replicas of a module within a system node are required to receive the same input sequences. However, this does not provide a full notion of correctness for such systems, and little work has appeared yet on this problem.

Our approach here (extending [2,3]) is to introduce an *implementation relation* that must hold between a target or *base* system and its intended replicated implementation. Moreover, such a relation is defined independently of replication. This enables a uniform treatment both of other implementation techniques than replication, and of different fault assumptions for replication (e.g. fail-stop or byzantine faults with majority voting [4]).

Implementation relations are defined in terms of *extraction patterns* through which the behaviour of an implementation is related to that of the base system. We introduce two operational criteria for an implementation relation to be acceptable: *realisability* of the base process through its implementation, and *compositionality*, which requires that, if the systems in a set implement each a base system, their composition should implement the composition of the base systems.

The work is carried out in the CSP trace/failure/divergence model [1], which enables the treatment of nondeterminism (including deadlock properties) and a natural formulation of the classes of input faults tolerated by a process; furthermore, a fault-tolerant system may be usefully viewed as an indeterminate member of a set of CSP processes. Due to space limitations, no formal proofs are included.

We assume the reader is familiar with the basic concepts of CSP [1], like *processes*, *channels*, *actions* of the form $c!v$ (where c is a channel) and *traces*.

Some notation employed in the sequel follows: αc (the valid actions—or *alphabet*—of channel c), αC ($\bigcup_{c \in C} \alpha c$), $\langle a_1, \ldots, a_n \rangle$ (trace whose ith element is a_i), $Pref(T)$ (prefix-closure of a trace set T), $t \lceil C$ (t with actions not at channels in C deleted), $t \downarrow C$ ($\langle v_1, \ldots, v_k \rangle$, if $t \lceil C = \langle c_1!v_1, \ldots, c_k!v_k \rangle$), $t \leq u$ (t is a prefix of trace u, this is extended component-wise to trace vectors).

A CSP process P is characterised by its *alphabet* αP to which its actions must belong, its *divergences* δP (traces after which P behaves chaotically), and *failure set* φP; if $(t, R) \in \varphi P$, P is said to *refuse* the action set R after doing the trace t. The set of channels of P is denoted by χP and is partitioned into the input channels ιP and the output channels ωP. The *network* formed by processes $P_1, \ldots, P_n$ is modelled by the process $P_1 \# \ldots \# P_n$.

We say that P is *input-guarded* w.r.t. two prefix-closed trace sets U and V (denoted $P \in IG(U, V)$) if: **(IG1)** $t \in \tau P$ and $t \lceil \iota P \in U$ implies $t \lceil \omega P \in V$, and **(IG2)** if $T \subseteq \tau P$ and $T \lceil \iota P \subseteq U$ then $|T| = \infty$ implies $|T \lceil \iota P| = \infty$. The base processes we consider belong to the class GIO of *general input-output processes* [3]. $P \in GIO$ iff it is (1) input-guarded wrt $\alpha \iota P^*, \alpha \omega P^*$, and (2) always ready to accept any input, i.e. formally: $R \cap \alpha \iota P = \emptyset$, for all $(t, R) \in \varphi P$. These are rather mild restrictions, and identify a wide range of processes (e.g. a nondeterministic *merger*). To ease the discussion, we fix the processes P, K, L in Figure 1. It can be shown that if K, L are GIO so is $K \# L$.

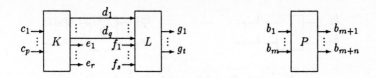

Figure 1: Three generic processes

	$idp(c)$	$fs = fs(c, C, NF)$	$mv = mv(c, C, NF)$ $\|NF\| > \frac{1}{2}\|C\|$
$t \in dom \Leftrightarrow$	always	$b, d \in C \Rightarrow t{\downarrow}b \leq t{\downarrow}d \lor t{\downarrow}d \leq t{\downarrow}b$ $b, d \in NF \Rightarrow t{\downarrow}d = t{\downarrow}b$	$b, d \in NF \Rightarrow t{\downarrow}b = t{\downarrow}d$
$extr(t) =$	t	$\max\{u \mid \exists b \in C : u{\downarrow}c = t{\downarrow}b\}$	$\max\{u \mid \kappa_u > \frac{1}{2}\|C\|\}$
$R \in ref(t) \Leftrightarrow$	$\alpha c - R \neq \emptyset$	$\alpha NF - R \neq \emptyset$	$\alpha NF - R \neq \emptyset$
$inv(c!v) =$	$\langle c!v\rangle$	$\langle e!v\rangle$	$\langle e_1!v, \ldots, e_{\|NF\|}!v\rangle$

Table 1: Basic kinds of extraction patterns

2 Extraction Patterns

An *extraction pattern* relates the interface of a replicated process to that of the base process it is intended to implement. Let C be a set of channels and c a channel. An extraction pattern ep over C and c is a quadruple $(dom_{ep}, extr_{ep}, ref_{ep}, inv_{ep})$. Among all the possible (potentially faulty) traces at C, those in $Pref(dom_{ep})$ are intended to represent the 'acceptable' ones and those in dom_{ep} the 'finished' ones. $extr_{ep}$, is a partial monotonic mapping from $Pref(dom_{ep})$ to the traces over c; it is intended to return traces of a base process from the redundant and noisy traces of its implementation. ref_{ep} is needed to ensure that communication over C does not introduce deadlocks which would not arise between base processes. inv_{ep} is an inverse mapping of $extr_{ep}$, used to ensure that each possible trace over c has its counterpart in the traces over C. We define $\chi_{ep} = C$, $\omega_{ep} = \{c\}$.

As shown in [3], given a *vector* of extraction patterns $\vec{ep} = (ep_1, \ldots, ep_k)$ (with $\chi_{ep_i} \cap \chi_{ep_j} = \emptyset$ and $\omega_{ep_i} \neq \omega_{ep_j}$, for all $i \neq j$), it is possible to define suitable $dom_{\vec{ep}}$, $Dom_{\vec{ep}}$, $\chi_{\vec{ep}}$, $\omega_{\vec{ep}}$, $ref_{\vec{ep}}(t)$, $extr_{\vec{ep}}$, $inv_{\vec{ep}}$. The concatenation of two vectors of extraction patterns is denoted $\vec{ep}' \bullet \vec{ep}''$.

Table 1 shows three basic kinds of extraction patterns. The identity extraction pattern $idp(c)$ is needed to formulate the realisability result. The other two extraction pattern, fs and mv, can be used to model replication based on fail-stop components and majority voting respectively [4]. In the table the following assumptions are made. C is $\{c\}$ for $idp(c)$, and any channel set with the same message set as c for $fs(c, C, NF)$, $mv(c, C, NF)$; $NF \subseteq C$ is intended to contain channels guaranteed to carry non-faulty data. For fs, e is a fixed channel in NF. For mv, $e_1, \ldots, e_{\|NF\|}$ is a fixed enumeration of the channels in NF, and $\kappa_u = \|\{b \in C \mid u{\downarrow}c \leq t{\downarrow}b\}\|$.

3 Replication in Networks of Processes

Suppose that a replicated system Q is intended as an implementation of the base process P (see Figure 2). Q's communication on the channel set χ_{ep_i} will be related to P's communication on channel ω_{ep_i} (i.e. b_i) through the extraction pattern vectors $\vec{in} = (ep_1, \ldots, ep_m)$ and $\vec{out} = (ep_{m+1}, \ldots, ep_{m+n})$, so that $\iota Q = \chi_{\vec{in}}$, $\omega Q = \chi_{\vec{out}}$ (see Figure 2).

Figure 2: P and its implementation Q

To be a correct implementation of P, Q has to satisfy the following properties, formalized as I1-I3 below. Firstly, if input to Q is interpreted by $\vec{in}$, then output from it should be interpreted by $\vec{out}$ (see I1-IG1). Secondly, Q should not introduce divergence when connected to another process and supplied with valid input: this is ensured by forbidding infinite uninterrupted communication on the output channels of Q (see I1-IG2). Property I2 below ensures, if satisfied by every process in a network, that the network is deadlock free; for this purpose, the *ref* component of extraction patterns is used to bound the input refusals of the replicated process Q (I2(a)), and also the output refusals of Q unless the output of Q is 'finished' (I2(b)). Finally, we ensure that the purely functional behaviour of P (i.e. that given by its traces) can be realised by Q (I3). Thus:

A process Q is an implementation of P, using extraction patterns $\vec{in}$ and $\vec{out}$ (denoted $Q \in I(P, \vec{in}, \vec{out})$), if $\iota Q = \chi_{\vec{in}}$, $\omega Q = \chi_{\vec{out}}$ and:

I1 $Q \in IG(Dom_{\vec{in}}, Dom_{\vec{out}})$.

I2 If $(t, R) \in \varphi Q$ and $t\lceil \iota Q \in Dom_{\vec{in}}$ then

    (a) $\alpha\iota Q - R \notin ref_{\vec{in}}(t)$

    (b) $\alpha\omega Q \cap R \notin ref_{\vec{out}}(t) \Rightarrow t\lceil \omega Q \in dom_{\vec{out}} \wedge (extr_{\vec{in}\bullet\vec{out}}(t), \alpha\omega P) \in \varphi P$.

I3 $inv_{\vec{in}\bullet\vec{out}}(\tau P) \subseteq \tau Q$.

Note that different extraction patterns are allowed on different channels of Q. This is essential to model heterogeneous networks of replicated processes.

As discussed in the introduction, the I relation should enjoy compositionality and realisability. This is ensured by the next two theorems respectively.

Theorem 1 Let K and L be GIO processes as in Fig. 1. Assume that, for $b \in \chi K \cup \chi L$, $ep(b)$ is an extraction pattern with $\omega_{ep(b)} = b$, and for all $c \neq b$, $\chi_{ep(b)} \cap \chi_{ep(c)} = \emptyset$. Define the vectors of extraction patterns $\vec{ep}_x = (ep(x_1), \ldots)$ for $x = c, d, e, f, g$. If $K_0 \in I(K, \vec{ep}_c, \vec{ep}_d \bullet \vec{ep}_e)$ and $L_0 \in I(L, \vec{ep}_d \bullet \vec{ep}_f, \vec{ep}_g)$, then $K_0 \# L_0 \in I(K\#L, \vec{ep}_c \bullet \vec{ep}_f, \vec{ep}_e \bullet \vec{ep}_g)$.

Theorem 2 Let $\vec{in}$ and $\vec{out}$ be vectors of identity extraction patterns. Then $Q \in I(P, \vec{in}, \vec{out})$ implies $\tau Q = \tau P$ and $\{t \mid (t, \alpha\omega P) \in \varphi P\} \subseteq \{t \mid (t, \alpha\omega Q) \in \varphi Q\}$.

To see why this is an adequate notion of realisability, note that, if $Q' \in I(P, \vec{in}', \vec{out}')$ with $\vec{in}'$ and $\vec{out}'$ general extraction patterns, compositionality easily allows $Q \in I(P, \vec{in}, \vec{out})$ to be constructed (using the extractors and disturbers of [2]). Moreover, the thesis of the above theorem entails that, given an arbitrary GIO process *Rec* as an environment that receives the results produced by Q or P, $Q\#Rec$ and $P\#Rec$ produce the same traces and $Q\#Rec$ is more deterministic than $P\#Rec$ and hence a (better) replacement for it according to the philosophy of [1].

Using induction, compositionality is easily proved for process networks, under the proviso of acyclicity (due to the hypothesis of Theorem 1 illustrated in Figure 1).

Because of the divergence which—though absent in the base network—may arise from a cycle of faulty implementations, the treatment of cyclic networks requires the following stronger notion of replication. Let $P \in GIO$ and $Q \in I(P, \vec{in}, \vec{out})$; we say that Q is a *strong* implementation of P, and write $Q \in SI(P, \vec{in}, \vec{out})$, if:

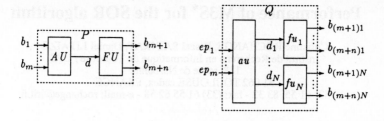

Figure 3: A base process P and its replicated implementation Q

$T \subseteq \tau Q$ is infinite and $T\lceil \iota Q \subseteq Dom_{\vec{in}}$ implies $extr_{\vec{in}}(T)$ is also infinite.

This condition strengthens I1-IG2 (it is a sort of IG2 relative to extraction).

To prove compositionality, we need another pair of generic GIO processes K and L like those shown in Figure 1, with the addition of a channel set from L to K. We must require K and L to be *compatible* (in the sense of [2]) for $K\#L$ to be a GIO process (this is false in general). This yields a compositionality result analogous to Theorem 1. The realisability result follows immediately from Theorem 2.

We now show how to implement a replication Q of a base process P by assembling N copies of P. P is assumed to contain an *arbiter unit* AU which receives messages on input channels $b_1, \ldots, b_m$ and forwards them along channel d, to the *functional unit* FU (Figure 3). We assume that AU is GIO, and FU is a deterministic process described by an input/output function, as in [2].

To construct Q we assemble an implementation au of AU with N (possibly faulty) copies of FU, as shown in Figure 3. Input to au is consistent with an (arbitrary) vector of extraction patterns $\vec{ep} = (ep_1, \ldots, ep_m)$. Output from au is more constrained; it is sent along channel $d_1, \ldots, d_N$, of which the ith feeds the replica fu_i of the functional unit. Without loss of generality, we assume that the first M channels (for $\frac{1}{2}N < M \leq N$) carry non-faulty output. Thus, we shall interpret the output of au by the extraction pattern $mv(d, \{d_1, \ldots, d_N\}, \{d_1, \ldots, d_M\})$ and that of Q by the extraction patterns $mv_j = mv(b_{m+j}, \{b_{(m+j)1}, \ldots, b_{(m+j)N}\}, \{b_{(m+j)1}, \ldots, b_{(m+j)M}\})$ (see Table 1).

We can now state that if au implements (resp. strongly implements) AU so does Q with P, provided the faulty functional units cannot issue infinite uninterrupted output.

Theorem 3 Let $\vec{mv} = (mv_1, \ldots, mv_n)$. Assume that, for $i \in \{M+1, \ldots, N\}$, if $T \subseteq \tau fu_i$ is infinite and $T\lceil d_i \subseteq \tau au\lceil d_i$ then $T\lceil d_i$ is infinite. Then: (1) if $au \in I(AU, \vec{ep}, mv)$ then $Q \in I(P, \vec{ep}, \vec{mv})$, and (2) if $au \in SI(AU, \vec{ep}, mv)$ then $Q \in SI(P, \vec{ep}, \vec{mv})$.

Acknowledgement: The authors were supported by the Esprit WG Caliban and the Italian CNR and MURST.

References

[1] Hoare, C.A.R.: Communicating sequential processes, (1985).

[2] Koutny, M., Mancini, L., and Pappalardo, G.: Formalising Replicated Distributed Processing. Proc. of 10th Symposium on Reliable Distributed Systems, 108-117 (1991).

[3] Koutny, M., Mancini, L., and Pappalardo, G.: Replication in Acyclic Networks of Communicating Processes, TR 378, Computing Laboratory, Newcastle University (1992).

[4] Schneider, F.B.: Implementing Fault-tolerant Services Using the State Machine Approach: A Tutorial. ACM Comput. Surveys 22(4), 299-319 (1990).

Performance of M3S* for the SOR algorithm

Christine ROCHANGE, Pascal SAINRAT, Daniel LITAIZE
Institut de Recherche en Informatique de Toulouse / UPS
118, route de Narbonne
31 062 TOULOUSE cedex, FRANCE
tel: (33) 61 55 83 32 - fax: (33) 61 55 62 58 - e-mail: rochange@irit.fr

M3S is a shared-memory multiprocessor based on two original features: 1) the shared memory is organized in serially-multiported modules, 2) each processor module is connected to each memory module by a private very-high-speed serial link (>1Gbits/s). In this way, the classical shared-bus bottleneck is avoided and the possible conflicts are distributed among the memory modules. We present an evaluation of the performance of M3S. This study relies on the throughput model proposed by M.Dubois in [Dubo88]. Experiments are carried out considering the execution of the Successive Over Relaxation algorithm. The conclusions of our study is that, thanks to its large communication bandwidth, M3S provides a high throughput, in terms of number of tasks executed per second.

1 Introduction

Analytical models are often used to evaluate the performance of multiprocessors. However, models based on Markov chains or on Generelized Timed Petri Nets have proved themselves expensive to evaluate. Queuing networks can easily be resolved by the Mean Value Analysis technique, but they require a detailed knowledge of the system under study. In [Dubo88], Dubois proposes a very simple throughput model that can be applied for a rapid and rough estimation of the performance of a multiprocessor. In this paper, we use this model to evaluate the M3S machine that is developed in our laboratory.

M3S is a shared-memory multiprocessor where each processor module is connected to each multiported memory module by a private high-speed serial link. M3S is described in section 2. Section 3 presents the throughput model. We apply this model to M3S in the case of a particular multitasked algorithm, the Successive Over-Relaxation algorithm (section 4). Concluding remarks are presented in section 5.

2 Presentation of M3S

 The structure of M3S* is presented in Fig. 1. It is a shared-memory multiprocessor based on two original features:

• Each processor module is connected to each memory module by a serial link. The main advantage of a set of serial links is that it induces no network bottleneck. The throughput on these serial links is high (2 Gbits per second for each). So, it is possible to have, on a single link, a transfer rate at least as high as the one obtained with a shared bus.

• The shared memory is multiported. Each serial link is associated to a shift register. A block is transferred between the RAM and a shift register in a single memory cycle. In this way, the main memory provides a sufficient bandwidth to avoid a new bottleneck at the memory level.

A further detailed description of the M3S multiprocessor is in [SMRL92].

---

*M3S is the French acronym for "Serial Multiported Memory Multiprocessor".

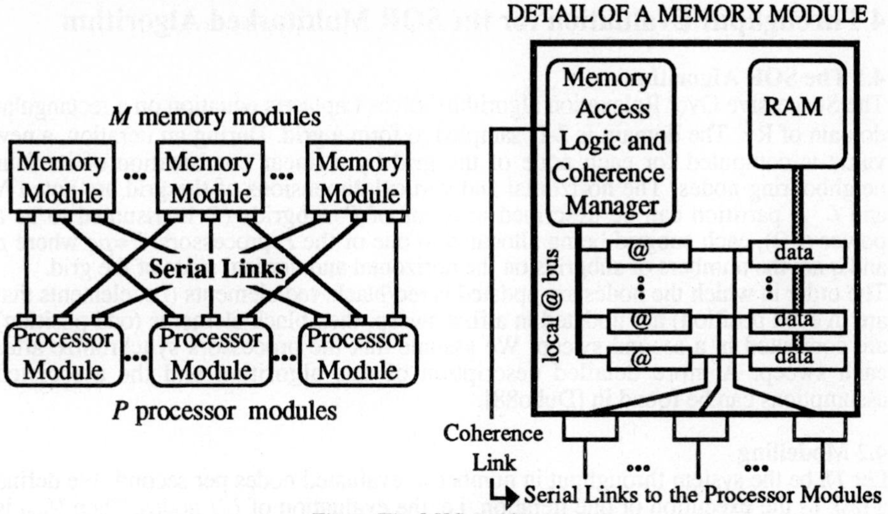

DETAIL OF A MEMORY MODULE

M memory modules

P processor modules

Fig. 1. The M3S architecture

The sequential data consistency is hardware-enforced according to a classical directory scheme. This scheme allows clean blocks to reside in many caches, but disallows dirty blocks from residing in more than one cache.

Because of the half-duplex mode of the serial links of the communication network and to avoid contention, the coherence-related messages are sent by a memory module to the processor boards through a specialized separate serial way called Coherence Link, which is private to this memory module but shared by all the processor modules.

3 Presentation of the Throughput Model

The system throughput Th is defined as the number of tasks executed per second.

We can evaluate two throughput upper bounds: the first one depends on the communication bandwidth, the second one depends on the computation bandwidth.

3.1 Throughput Limitation due to the Communication Bandwidth

The *communication bandwidth* N_{net} of a task is the number of network cycles needed to execute the task. In M3S, a network cycle is defined as the transfer time of a cache block on a serial link.

If Bw is the network bandwidth (expressed in units of network cycle per second), an upper bound of the system throughput is given by $Th \leq Bw / N_{net}$

3.2 Throughput Limitation due to the Computation Bandwidth

The *computation bandwidth* of a task is its execution time in the absence of conflicts on the network. It can be expanded in the sum of the compute time T_{ex} (total execution time when all the accesses are done in the cache) and the latency time T_l (total time during which the processor is blocked because of the network accesses). If there are P processors, a throughput upper bound is given by $Th \leq P / (T_{ex} + T_l)$

If R, W, I are the numbers of reads, writes and invalidations , and T_r, T_w, T_{inv} are the read,write and invalidation latency times, we can state :
$$T_l = RT_r + WT_w + IT_{inv}$$

4 Throughput Evaluation for the SOR Multitasked Algorithm

4.1 The SOR Algorithm

The Successive Over Relaxation algorithm solves Laplace's equation on a rectangular domain of R^2. The domain is 2-D sampled to form a grid. During an iteration, a new value is computed for each node of the grid by a linear combination of its four neighbouring nodes. The horizontal and vertical dimensions of the grid are noted N and L. A partition can be described in terms of P subgrids (P is assumed to be a power of 2), each subgrid being allocated to one of the P processors. $P=pq$ where p and q are the numbers of subgrids on the horizontal and vertical sides of the grid.

The order in which the nodes are updated is red/black: red elements (i.e. elements that are in even position) are updated in a first sweep, then black elements (odd position) are computed in a second sweep. We assume that the processors synchronize after each sweep. A more detailed description of this algorithm and the associated assumptions can be found in [Dubo88].

4.2 Modelling

Let Th be the system throughput in number of evaluated nodes per second. We define a task as the execution of one iteration, i.e. the evaluation of LN nodes. Then N_{net} is the communication bandwidth per iteration. If Bw is the network bandwidth, we obtain $Th \leq Bw\, L\, N\, /\, N_{net}$ which gives a throughput bound as a function of the communication bandwidth of the application.

Another bound is obtained in function of the computation bandwidth. If T_{ite} is the total execution time of one iteration, we have: $Th \leq LN\, /\, T_{ite}$

4.3 Evaluation of the Amount of Shared Data

The U set of all the grid points is divided into 4 subsets U_0, U_1, U_2, U_3 where U_0 is the set of boundary points, U_1 is the set of points that are not shared, U_2 is the set of the nodes that are shared by 2 processors and U_3 is the set of the nodes that are shared by 3 processors. The number of points in each set is:

$|U_0| = 2(N+L)$ $|U_3| = 4(p-1)(q-1)$

$|U_2| = 2(p-1)L + 2(q-1)N - 2|U_3|$ $|U_1| = LN - |U_2| - |U_3|$

4.4 Throughput as a Function of the Communication Bandwidth

The communication bandwidth is $N_{net} = RC_r + WC_w + IC_{inv}$ where R, W, and I are the numbers of reads, writes and invalidations per iteration of the main loop, expressed in units of network cycle.

We consider here that the caches are large enough to capture the locality of the main loop. The misses are then due to invalidations.

We can easily compute: $I = |U_2| + |U_3|$ $R = |U_2| + 2|U_3|$ $W = |U_2| + 2|U_3|$

4.5 Throughput as a Function of the Computation Bandwidth

T_{ite} is the total execution time of an iteration in the absence of conflicts on the network. As all the processors synchronize after each sweep loop, the total time of an iteration will be the maximum of all the subgrid iteration times. The number of subgrids is assumed to be greater than 16, thus the maximum iteration time corresponds to a processor associated with a subgrid at the center of the main grid:

$T_{ite} = t_0 + (LN/P)t_1 + rT_r + wT_w + iT_{inv}$

where t_1 is the time for a processor to update one iterate, when all the operands are in the cache, t_0 is a fixed overhead time and r, w, i are the numbers of reads, writes and invalidations during which the processor is blocked

We have: $i = 2[L/q + N/p] - 4$ $r = 2[L/q + N/p]$ $w = 2[L/q + N/p]$

4.6 Results

We consider a grid size of 256×256. The throughput is computed as $Th = $ Min $(Bw$ LN / N_{net}, $LN / T_{ite})$ and expressed in MFLOPS (the evaluation of a node requires 6 floating operations,). The size of a block is 64 bits. We consider processors with a power of 10 MFLOPS ($t_0 = 1\mu s, t_1 = 0.6\mu s$). The transfer rate on a serial link is assumed to be 2Gbit/s. We also assume: $C_r = C_w = 1.5$, $C_{inv} = 0.5$, $T_r = 0.06\mu s$, $T_w = 0.015\mu s$, T_{inv} $0.045\mu s$ The throughput of M3S for the execution of the SOR algorithm is plotted as a function of the number of processors in Fig. 2.

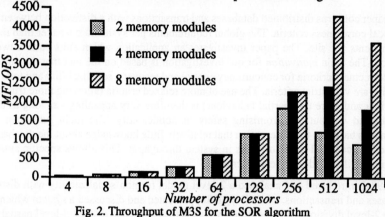

Fig. 2. Throughput of M3S for the SOR algorithm

4.7 Discussion

As the number of processors increases, we can distinct two parts on the throughput diagram. In the first part, the throughput is limited by the computation bandwidth, and thus increases with the number of processors. In the second part, the memory bandwidth is too small so the throughput is limited by the communication requirements and decreases. Adding memory modules increases the memory bandwidth, and thus allows the connection of a larger number of processors to obtain a higher throughput. With 8 memory modules and 512 processors, the throughput is close to 4.5 GFLOPS. Note that, since the network is composed of point-to-point links, this number of processor can reasonnably be considered.

5 Conclusions

The aim of this study was to estimate the performance of the M3S multiprocessor by using the throughput model proposed by Dubois in [Dubo88]. The results showed that the network of the M3S leads to a huge overall throughput. A large number of memory modules gives a high communication bandwidth, which permits the use of many processors. The computational power is then increased without being limited by the communication requirements. In this way, a large system throughput can be expected.

References

[Dubo88] M. Dubois, *Throughput Analysis of Cache-Based Multiprocessors with Multiple Buses*, IEEE Trans.on Comp., Vol.37, n°1, Jan. 1988.
[SMRL92] P. Sainrat, A. Mzoughi, C. Rochange, D. Litaize, *The Design of the M3S : a Multiported Shared-memory Multiprocessor*, Proc. of Supercomputing'92, Minneapolis, Nov. 1992.

Multi-Criteria:
Degrees of Recoverability in Distributed Databases

Dr. Techn. Mads Nygård, Sintef Delab
The Norwegian Institute of Technology, Trondheim

Abstract

This paper concerns distributed databases and transactions with a distinction between global and local correctness criteria. The global requirements per system are weaker than the local requirements per site. The paper investigates an application which suits such a two-level division. The main *motivation* for our investigation is based on the fact that the commonly used correctness criteria for concurrency control and recovery, serializability and total recoverability, are very strict criteria. The use of more relaxed criteria (allowing more true parallel behaviour and more true partial behaviour) is therefore very appealing - as long as this can be achieved without compromising safety or applicability. The main *paradigm* in our approach is based on the observation that relatively little knowledge about the databases and transactions can lead to major gains in system throughput. This allows specific systems to have more tailor-made correctness criteria.

[Nygå93a] introduced and analysed a 2-level model for non-serializability with distributed databases and transactions, while [Nygå93b] presented and discussed a system which suited such a 2-level division. Here the primary *goal* is to analyse and discuss n-level partial recoverability with distributed databases and transactions. The secondary *goal* is to integrate this with the 2-level model/system introduced in the above mentioned papers. Hence we both present a model and apply it to the given system.

We analyse the span between total recoverability per site and total recoverability per system. This requires local total recoverability but allows global partial recoverability. We discuss both single-level and multi-level recovery criteria. We relate and compare the resulting concepts to other established and proposed criteria. Our notions are brand new. We consider step-wise committing transactions. Our main point is not that *partial commitment* is being used, but rather to *discuss* how it should be *controlled*. The main result is a set of recovery rules which may be combined in an orthogonal way. The concepts and notions seem especially appropriate for systems/models which make use of added priority ruling.

The *appropriate choices* with respect to recovery for the application from [Nygå93b] corresponds to a *2-level criterion* - with one part stemming from the existence of intra-site integrity-constraints and value-dependencies and the other part stemming from the superimposition of priority which originates from the designated criteria for concurrency control. Effectively, knowledge about some missing integrity constraints in a distributed database opens the way for non-serializability and partial recoverability globally - and knowledge about some existing overall goals of distributed transactions leads the way to the add-on to serializability and total recoverability locally.

1   Context

For many distributed databases the type of global integrity constraints implied by the databases collectively is under discussion. Any such constraints come in addition to the local integrity constraints implied by the databases separately. By integrity constraints we mean any associated rules which couple the given database items in some way. Likewise, for many distributed transactions the type of global semantic requirements induced by the transactions per system is under discussion. Any such requirements come in addition to the local semantic requirements induced by the transactions per site. By semantic requirements we mean any overall information describing the assumed transaction results in some way. It is a fact that in some distributed databases global integrity constraints do exist but are weaker than the local integrity constraints. It is also a fact that in some distributed transactions global semantic requirements do exist but are weaker than the local semantic requirements.

Our specialized type of distributed database, the *skeleton-database*, represents sets of close substitutes for diverse articles. Effectively we investigate an organized coupling of cooperating databases. Each specific database contains a complementing set of article-offers - and the different databases contain substituting sets for these article-offers. Further, the databases may be accessed simultaneously in the sense that article-offers in one database may be "held" while article-offers in another database are checked - and the accesses to all participating databases in a skeleton-database will be collectively controlled. Our approach allows non-serializability and partial recoverability without compromising safety or applicability. We arrive at multi-level correctness criteria with respect to both consistency preservation and atomicity assurance.

Our specialized type of distributed transaction, the *wander-transaction*, traverses a skeleton-database trying to seize an optimal set - complying with any combined conditions on the attribute-values - of specific articles. Actually we discuss a traversing race among competing transactions. A transaction may require diverse articles of several types - and several articles of a single type. And a transaction/buyer may acquire articles directly - i.e. it corresponds to an on-line read-and-write service and not only an off-line read-only service. Further, a buyer may consider more static attributes like quality and price - as well as more dynamic attributes like no-left and who-purchased. Our concept allows transactions to build up priority during their traversing race. We show how acquiring an article-offer early may increase the priority of the corresponding buyer - while checking an article-offer later may decrease the priority of the corresponding buyer.

Wander-transactions accessing a skeleton-database allow breaks with both the common serializability criterion and the common total recoverability criterion. The designated criteria with respect to concurrency control - with one part stemming from the need to preserve integrity constraints in the local databases and the other part stemming from the need to observe overall goals of the global transactions - have been extended with a priority rule.

2 Basic Example

Here we only consider the simplest case; i.e. with one item per site. In general there are several items per site, and the different sites must not necessarily have entries for exactly corresponding sets of items. Imagine a skeleton-database containing the following three item-variants x, y and z:

x:	y:	z:
Quality = 80%	Quality = 85%	Quality = 90%
Price = 5 $	Price = 10 $	Price = 15 $
No-Left = 1	No-Left = 1	No-Left = 2
Who-Pur. = -	Who-Pur. = -	Who-Pur. = -

The item-variants represent the one and only item-type occurring at the three different sites. Or to put it another way: each specific quadruple corresponds to a specific department store's offer of the single article-kind. The four corresponding attributes of an article-offer have been introduced and discussed in [Nygå93b]. Imagine also the following two wander-transactions T_2 and T_1:

$$T_2: \text{Acquire One: Low-Price} \ \& \ \text{Quality} \geq 77.5 \ \%$$
$$\& \text{Acquire One: Low-Price} \ \& \ \text{Quality} \geq 82.5 \ \%$$

$$T_1: \text{Acquire One: Low-Price} \ \& \ \text{Quality} \geq 77.5 \ \%$$

The item-variants that the two wander-transactions will acquire if executed in isolation are T_2: $x + y$ and T_1: x. A possible schedule corresponding to the two wander-transactions being executed in parallel is:

$$
\begin{aligned}
H_1 = \\
T_2&: R_2(x)W_2(x) \qquad\qquad\qquad R_2(y)R_2(z)W_2(z) \ \ C_2 \\
T_1&: \qquad\qquad R_1(x)R_1(y)W_1(y) \qquad\qquad\qquad C_1
\end{aligned}
$$

The results stem from the facts that initially there is only one instance left of both item-variant x and item-variant y. When T_1 would like to acquire x, there is none left, and it has to settle with y. Further, when T_2 would like to acquire y, there is none left, and it has to settle with z. The item-variants that the two wander-transactions will acquire if executed in the H_1-schedule are T_2: $x + z$ and T_1: y.

In this schedule the local concurrency control requirements are observed - i.e. the write-read, read-write and write-write conflicts induce serializability per site. But the global concurrency control requirement is not observed - i.e. the write-read conflicts do not induce serializability per system. Hence the schedule would not be allowed by our combined criteria for concurrency control. According to the priority rule - with the write-read conflict on item x occurring first - the intermediate result is *"Aborting T_1"*, and this shall be enforced when $R_2(y)$ occurs. After later *"Rescheduling T_1"*, the final result with respect to the item-variants that the two wander-transactions will acquire is T_2: $x + y$ and T_1: z.

3 Basic Discussion

An initial reliability rule is defined as follows: *Before one can read another's written value - i.e. grant $R_1(x)$, that other must at least have partially committed that site - i.e. have requested $C_{X,2}$.*

Let us return to our basic example. The H_1'-schedule includes the partial commitment of T_2 at site X (containing item x) before the $R_1(x)$-operation, and includes the partial commitment of T_1 at site Y (containing item y) before the $R_2(y)$-operation:

$$
\begin{aligned}
H_1' = \\
T_2&: R_2(x)W_2(x)C_{X,2} \qquad\qquad\qquad R_2(y) \ ... \\
T_1&: \qquad\qquad R_1(x)R_1(y)W_1(y)C_{Y,1} \qquad ...
\end{aligned}
$$

In this schedule the reliability rule is observed, but the concurrency rules are not observed.

First, we consider two different situations termed a) and b). In *situation a)* we assume that $R_1(x)$ has not been committed. Then the priority rule says that T_1 will be aborted when $R_2(y)$ occurs - as T_2 has priority. In *situation b)* we assume that $R_1(x)$ has been committed too. Then the only option is that T_2 must be aborted when $R_2(y)$ occurs - though T_2 has priority.

Second, we consider two different effects termed I and II. For *effect I* we pretend that $C_{Y,1}$ has not occurred. This applies to both situations a) and b) above. When $R_2(y)$ is requested, the reliability rule says that it may not be granted until $C_{Y,1}$ occurs. But the concurrency rules also say that as soon as this happens, the actual occurrence of $R_2(y)$ must lead to an abortion of one of the transactions. Therefore the pure request of $R_2(y)$ will be allowed to invoke the abortion of T_1 - as T_2 has priority; i.e. even without an occurrence of $C_{Y,1}$. The result is that y will be given to T_2 *instead of* T_1. Remember that y is an item whose single occurrence will be wanted by both transactions. This result is definitely better in situation b) where T_2 had to be aborted, and it is even better in situation a) where T_2 was not aborted but had to let y go.

For *effect II* we include in the H_1'-schedule the race for an item u whose single occurrence will be wanted by both transactions. This applies to both situations a) and b):

$$H_1'(a') =$$
$$T_2: R_2(x)W_2(x)C_{X,2} \qquad\qquad\qquad R_2(y)R_2(u) \dots$$
$$T_1: \qquad\qquad R_1(x)R_1(y)W_1(y)C_{Y,1}R_1(u)W_1(u) \qquad\qquad \dots$$

$$H_1'(b') =$$
$$T_2: R_2(x)W_2(x)C_{X,2} \qquad\qquad R_2(u)W_2(u) \quad R_2(y) \qquad \dots$$
$$T_1: \qquad\qquad R_1(x)R_1(y)W_1(y)C_{Y,1} \qquad\quad C_{X,1} \quad R_1(u) \dots$$

In situation a´) - corresponding to a), we have indicated that T_1 is checking and acquiring u before T_2 will check it. In situation b´) - corresponding to b), we have indicated that T_2 is checking and acquiring u before T_1 will check it. As $R_1(x)$ is supposed to be uncommitted in a) there is no $C_{X,1}$ in a´). But as $R_1(x)$ is supposed to be committed in b) there is a $C_{X,1}$ in b´).

From the discussions of the H_1'-schedule we know that some transaction must be aborted already when $R_2(y)$ occurs in both situations a´) and b´). This is still due to non-observation of the concurrency rules - even though there is observation of the reliability rule. As before, T_1 will be aborted in a´). The net effect is that *u* will be given to T_2 *instead of* T_1. Further, as before, T_2 must be aborted in b´). The net effect is that *u* will be given to T_1 *instead of* T_2. In both situations a´) and b´) the change-over of item u happens even though $C_{Y,1}$ has occurred so that item y remains with transaction T_1. See the discussions of effect I.

In situations b) and b´) we saw that transaction T_2 had to be aborted even though it had priority over transaction T_1. This "unfair" result may be counter-effected by adding *another reliability rule* to the initial reliability rule - making commit-granting depend on priority-level and waiting-time. This *will superimpose priority* so that we end up with a 2-level recovery criterion - like we already have a 2-level concurrency control criterion.

4   Conclusion

Here we have elaborated on n-level partial recoverability with distributed databases and transactions. The material has been discussed and analysed basically connected to the special 2-level scenario for non-serializability presented in [Nygå93b], but it is equally applicable for the general 2-level model for non-serializability introduced in [Nygå93a].

References

[Nygå93a]   M. Nygård:
"BINMOD: A Model for Non-Serializability in Distributed Databases";
BNCOD 11 - 11th British National Conference on Databases.

[Nygå93b]   M. Nygård:
"Article-Acquisition: A Scenario for Non-Serializability in a Distr. Database";
PARLE'93 - 1993 Parallel Architectures and Languages Europe Conference.

Deadlock-Free Adaptive Routing Algorithms for the 3D-Torus: Limitations and Solutions *

Pedro López   José Duato

Dept. de Ingeniería de Sistemas, Computadores y Automática
Facultad de Informática. Universidad Politécnica de Valencia
P.O.B. 22012. 46071 - Valencia, Spain

Abstract. In this paper, a deadlock-free adaptive routing algorithm, obtained from the application of the theory proposed in [4] to the 3D-torus, is evaluated under different load conditions and compared with other algorithms. The results show that this algorithm is very fast, also increasing the network throughput considerably. Nevertheless, this adaptive algorithm has cycles in its channel dependency graph. As a consequence, when the network is heavily loaded messages may temporarily block cyclically, drastically reducing the performance of the algorithm. Two mechanisms are proposed to avoid this problem.

1 Introduction

Second generation multicomputers use wormhole routing [3]. With this mechanism, the message latency is largely insensitive to the distance in the message-passing network. Hence, more wirable network topologies can be considered. Several studies [1] show that 3D networks are the best choice in many cases. Although there is a more advanced flow control technique known as "mad postman" [6], it only improves performance significantly over wormhole when channels are narrow. Low dimensional networks allow the use of wide channels, making this technique very similar to wormhole.

Dally [3] has proposed a methodology to design deterministic deadlock-free routing algorithms. He defines a channel dependency graph and establishes a total order among channels. Routing is restricted to visit channels in decreasing or increasing order to eliminate cycles in the channel dependency graph. Although this restriction avoids deadlocks, traffic jams may increase, especially in heavily loaded networks. In order to avoid congested regions of the network, an adaptive routing algorithm can be used. In [4], a theory for the design of deadlock-free adaptive routing algorithms has been proposed, for store-and-forward and wormhole routing.

In this paper we evaluate the performance of an adaptive routing algorithm obtained by applying the former design methodology to the 3D-torus. This algorithm is compared with other algorithms for the 3D-torus under different load conditions.

*This work was supported in part by CICYT under grant number TIC91-1157-C03-03

2 Routing algorithm

The design methodology proposed in [4] starts from an existing deadlock-free routing algorithm. We have chosen the deterministic algorithm proposed in [3] for the k-ary n-cube, applied to the 3D-torus. It uses two virtual channels per physical channel.

Next, it adds some new virtual channels to each physical channel. The new channels can be used in any way, provided that messages follow a minimal path. The old channels can only be used according to the basic routing algorithm. In our algorithm, each physical channel has been split into $p = k + 2$ virtual channels. Thus, there are k new virtual channels per physical channel. The routing function can be stated as follows: Route over any useful dimension using the new channels. Alternatively, route in the same way as the deterministic algorithm using the old channels. This adaptive algorithm forwards messages following any minimal path.

We have chosen a selection function [4] that uses the new channels whenever possible, to exploit the flexibility of crossing the dimensions out of order. Based on local information, it minimizes the multiplexing of physical channels, assigning priorities cyclically among the virtual channels crossing different dimensions.

In what follows, this algorithm will be referred to as the *adaptive.k-2* algorithm, k being the number of added virtual channels. The number 2 represents the original channels. The deterministic algorithm was evaluated as well under the same conditions for comparison purposes. We will refer to this algorithm as the *deterministic.0-2* algorithm.

Additionally, a third algorithm obtained by applying the virtual channel flow control proposed in [2] was evaluated. It splits each virtual channel of the deterministic algorithm into v virtual channels, and routes messages in the same way as the deterministic one, but it can use any of the v virtual channels instead of only one. This algorithm will show the effect of channel multiplexing alone and will be referred to as the *deterministic.0-p* algorithm, p being the total number of virtual channels per physical channel, that is, $2v$.

3 Simulation results

The evaluation methodology is based on the one presented in [5]. The most important performance measures are delay and throughput. Delay is the additional latency required to transfer a message with respect to an idle network. Throughput is defined as the saturation traffic. Traffic is the flit reception rate.

Although we evaluated several network sizes, we will only show the results for a network with 512 nodes. Fig. 1 shows the results obtained by the *deterministic.0-2*, *deterministic.0-6*, and *adaptive.4-2* algorithms. We have chosen 6 virtual channels per physical channel because the adaptive algorithm with this number of links was the one which achieved the best results. For larger networks, more virtual channels are needed.

As can be seen, the adaptive algorithm achieves a reduction in message delay with respect to other algorithms. In addition, the adaptive algorithm provides

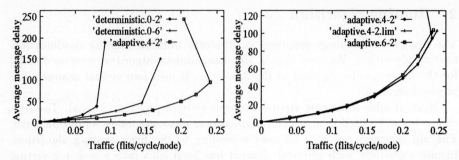

Fig. 1. Average message delay versus traffic for 512 nodes. Message length is 16 flits.

a throughput higher than the deterministic ones. Nevertheless, there is some performance degradation when the *adaptive.4-2* algorithm reaches saturation. This effect has also been observed with the adaptive algorithm in larger networks. It must be noticed that the curves are not functions, because both the average message delay and the traffic are measures. The independent variable is the flit generation rate. The delay for the adaptive algorithm grows with network traffic, until traffic reaches a certain point, from which the delay grows very fast but the traffic decreases. The higher the size of the network, the lower the value of traffic reached when this effect appears.

We speculate that this situation arises because the adaptive algorithm has cyclic dependencies between channels. Deadlocks are avoided by providing a channel subset free of cyclic dependencies that will drain those messages involved in cyclic dependencies. If the number of virtual channels per physical channel is insufficient, channel contention increases the number of blocked messages when traffic is high. Moreover, it is possible to reach a situation such that messages block cyclically faster that they are drained. This situation leads to two effects. On the one hand, some messages are blocked for long, increasing message delay considerably. On the other hand, most of the channels that can be used to cross the dimensions out of order are occupied by blocked messages, increasing contention and reducing throughput.

Nevertheless, it is possible to remove this problem. A solution is to add more virtual channels, as we can see in the curve belonging to the *adaptive.6-2* algorithm. Notice that by adding more virtual channels, channel contention decreases, and so does the probability of blocking cyclically, delaying or removing the performance degradation of the adaptive algorithm. This solution leads to a more complex switch implementation, and also increases message delay.

Another solution to the problem is to limit the traffic injected into the network, keeping the same number of virtual channels, in order to guarantee that the point of performance degradation will not be reached. This, of course, will increase the delay of those messages that are not injected into the network at once, but the average delay may be lower than the one obtained by the same adaptive algorithm without the injection limitation mechanism. The *adaptive.4-2.lim* algorithm shows the results achieved when at each node we impose the condition of having at least 6 free virtual channels to inject a message into the network. Notice that we estimate the amount of traffic in the network using only this local information. If the condition is not satisfied, the message is buffered until this situation changes. The number of free output channels required to inject a message has been determined empirically. Additionally, in order to guarantee the absence of livelock, this limitation mechanism has been combined with a time-out mechanism, injecting messages when the time they have been waiting is greater than a given threshold.

Finally, it is also interesting to analyse the throughput of the algorithms. The use of virtual channels in the deterministic algorithm increases throughput by a factor of 1.8 and the adaptive algorithm with limited injection increases throughput over the deterministic algorithm by a factor of 2.5. Therefore, the use of highly adaptive routing algorithms is interesting, even considering the additional cost of solving the above mentioned drawbacks.

4   Conclusions

The evaluation of a new adaptive routing algorithm for the 3D-torus shows an important reduction in message delay with respect to deterministic routing algorithms, even when virtual channels are used. The adaptive algorithm behaves better for any value of the flit generation rate and for all the network sizes we have analysed.

However, when traffic is intense, messages block cyclically for long periods, increasing message delay and reducing throughput significantly. This effect is especially noticeable for large networks. As shown, adding more virtual channels solves the problem. Nevertheless, by doing so, we also increase message delay.

In order to solve the problem in a more efficient way, we have proposed a simple mechanism to limit the injection of messages into the network. This mechanism does not affect messages in transit and it only requires local information (the number of free output channels).

References

1. A. Agarwal, Limits on interconnection network performance, *IEEE Trans. Parallel and Distributed Systems*, Vol. 2, No. 4, pp. 398-412, October 1991.

2. W.J. Dally, Virtual-channel flow control, *IEEE Trans. Parallel and Distributed Systems*, Vol. 3, No. 2, pp. 194-205, March 1992.

3. W.J. Dally and C.L. Seitz, Deadlock-free message routing in multiprocessor interconnection networks, *IEEE Trans. Computers*, Vol. C-36, No. 5, pp. 547-553, May 1987.

4. J. Duato, On the design of deadlock-free adaptive routing algorithms for multicomputers: design methodologies, *Proc. PARLE'91*, June 1991.

5. J. Duato, Improving the efficiency of virtual channels with time-dependent selection functions, *Proc. PARLE'92*, June 1992.

6. C.R. Jesshope, P.R. Miller and J.T. Yantchev, High performance communications in processor networks, *Proc. 16th Int. Symp. Computer Architecture*, May-June 1989.

Convergence of Asynchronous Iterations of Least Fixed Points

(Extended Abstract)

Jiawang Wei

GMD* Research Laboratory at the University of Karlsruhe,
Vincenz-Prießnitzstr.1, D-7500 Karlsruhe 1,
F.R. Germany

Abstract. This paper proves the convergence of parallel asynchronous
iterations of least fixed points of monotone functions on finite-chain partially ordered sets. This provides a basis for efficiently parallizing normal sequential iterative algorithms for computing least fixed points. A
detailed version of the paper can be found in [Wei93].

1 Introduction

We consider the problem of computing in parallel the *least fixed point* of a mono-
tone function F on a partially ordered set $(\mathbf{P}^n, \leq)$. Suppose $(\mathbf{P}, \leq)$ is a *finite
chain partially ordered set*, i.e., $\mathbf{P}$ has a least element (denoted as $\bot$), and every
chain of it is finite. It is well known that the least fixed point of F, $\mathbf{lfixp}(F)$,
exists and $\mathbf{lfixp}(F) = \bigsqcup\{F^i(\mathbf{0})|i \geq 0\}$, where $\mathbf{0} = (\bot, \bot, \cdots, \bot)$ is the least
element of $\mathbf{P}^n$, and $\bigsqcup$ is the least upper bound operation on $\mathbf{P}^n$. $\{F^i(\mathbf{0})\}_{i\geq 0}$
is actually a converging sequence of approximations of $\mathbf{lfixp}(F)$. This leads to
an obvious iterative algorithms for computing $\mathbf{lfixp}(F)$: starting at $F^0(\mathbf{0}) = \mathbf{0}$,
computing the iterands $F^{k+1}(\mathbf{0}) = F(F^k(\mathbf{0}))(k \geq 0)$ until reaching a l such that
$F^{l+1}(\mathbf{0}) = F^l(\mathbf{0})$, then $\mathbf{lfixp}(F) = F^l(\mathbf{0})$.

This naive iteration algorithm can be implemented in a parallel or distributed
system by having multiple processes compute the components of the iterands in
parallel. In *synchronous iteration*, these processes synchronize with each other
on the completion of computing each iterand before starting with the next. Such
a lock-step synchronized parallel iteration, though correct, are not efficient in
general due to such global synchronizations [Kun76, ÜD90]. In *asynchronous
iteration*, a process simply continues computing its assigned component(s) by
taking the currently available and possibly outdated approximation, without
synchronizing with and waiting for the other processes at each iteration step.
Asynchronous iterations are usually more efficient [Kun76, C+92]. However, the
correctness or convergence of asynchronous iterations is harder to guarantee.

In this paper, we prove the convergence of general asynchronous iterations
of least fixed points of monotone functions on finite chain partially ordered sets.

---

* Gesellschaft für Mathematik und Datenverarbeitung mbH

The whole process of an asynchronous iteration is described by a sequence of 'snapshots' of the iteration, and the sequence is shown to converge to the least fixed point. Since monotone and finite chain are quite weak requirements, our result provides a basis for efficiently parallizing many discrete problems, e.g., program flow analysis [KU76, NN92] in compiler code optimization, consistent labelling problem in artificial intelligence and computer vision [ÜD90], and many other combinatorial optimization problems, such as transitive closure, all-pair shortest paths, minimum spanning tree, etc..

2 Model for Parallel Asynchronous Iterations

In what follows N stands for the set of nonnegative integers and N^+ the set of natural numbers. $I = \{1, 2, \cdots n\}$. i, j range over I and k, l, m, u, v range over N. $\mathbf{x}|_i$ denotes x_i, the i-th component of $\mathbf{x}$, and $F_i(\mathbf{x})$ denotes $F(\mathbf{x})|_i$ for $\mathbf{x} \in \mathbf{P}^n$.

We model a parallel asynchronous iteration process by a sequence $\{\mathbf{x}(k)\}_{k \in N}$ in $\mathbf{P}^n$. $\mathbf{x}(k)$ is actually a snapshot of the iteration process at time k, which is intended to be an approximation of the desired least fixed point obtained at that moment. Here *time* means *logical time* and the logical clock is increased whenever a new component value is generated. The generality of this approach is discussed at length in [ÜD90]. In a shared memory implementation, a shared vector, initialized with $\mathbf{0}$, is set, from which each process takes the currently available approximation of the least fixed point and to which each process writes its newly computed component value(s). In this case $\mathbf{x}(k)$ is naturally the content of the vector at logical time k. In a distributed memory implementation $\mathbf{x}(k)$ would be an abstraction of the message queues at logical time k.

Definition 1 (Parallel Asynchronous Iteration) *An asynchronous iteration of the least fixed point of F is a sequence $\{\mathbf{x}(k)\}_{k \in N}$ in $\mathbf{P}^n$ defined inductively as follows:* $\mathbf{x}(0) = \mathbf{0}$; $\mathbf{x}(k) = (x_1(k), \cdots, x_n(k))$ *for $k > 0$ is:*

$$x_i(k) = \begin{cases} x_i(k-1) & \text{if } D(k) \neq i \\ F_i(x_1(s_1(k)), \cdots, x_n(s_n(k))) & \text{if } D(k) = i \end{cases}$$

where $D : N \to I$ is a function, $C = \{(s_1(k), \cdots, s_n(k))\}_{k \in N^+}$ is a sequence of elements in N^n. In addition, C and D are subject to the following conditions, for all $i \in I$:

(a) $\forall k \in N^+ : s_i(k) \leq k - 1$.

(b) $s_i(k)$, considered as a function of k, tends to infinity as k tends to infinity.

(c) $\{k \in N | D(k) = i\}$ is an infinite set.

This asynchronous iteration will be denoted as (F, C, D), and is said convergent if there exists $m \in N$, such that for all $k \in N$, if $k \geq m$ then $x(k) =$ $\mathbf{lfixp}(F)$.

In the definition $x_i(k) = F_i(x_1(s_1(k)), \cdots, x_n(s_n(k)))$ while $D(k) = i$ shows that the process that generates a new x_i at time k has taken the value of x_1 at time $s_1(k)$, x_2 at time $s_2(k)$, $\cdots$, x_n at time $s_n(k)$ to compute this new x_i. The *chaotic iteration* techniques [CC77, WZ91] for efficient sequential implementation of least fixed point iteration is just a special case of asynchronous iteration when for all $k \in N^+$ and $i \in I$, $s_i(k) = k - 1$.

(a) ensures that only the past value can be used. (b) guarantees that any old value can only be used for a finite number of times, some newly generated values will eventually be used. This is a quite weak assumption on the execution environment. In a shared memory multiprocessor system this permits a loose coherence of caches, and in a distributed system this allows unreliable communications. (c) states that every component must be updated an infinite number of times, which ensures fairness.

Fact 1 *(b) and (c) hold if and only if there exists an increasing sequence of integers $\{\phi(k)\}_{k \in N}$, such that*

- $\phi(0) = 0$,
- $\forall k \in N : \{D(l)|\phi(k) \leq l < \phi(k+1)\} = I$.
- $\forall k \in N^+, i \in I : l \geq \phi(k) \Rightarrow s_i(l) \geq \phi(k-1)$.

This fact is obvious [ÜD90]. $\{\phi(k)\}_{k \in N}$ is called a *pseudocycle sequence* of (F, C, D).

3 Convergence of Asynchronous Iterations

Let (F, C, D) be an arbitrary asynchronous least fixed point iteration, $\{\phi(k)\}_{k \in N}$ be a pseudocycle sequence of it.

Lemma 1 *For all $k \in N$, $\mathbf{x}(k) \leq F^k(0) \leq \text{lfixp}(F)$.*

Proof. We prove at first $\forall k \in N : \mathbf{x}(k) \leq F^k(0)$ by induction on k.

Basis $k = 0$. Obviously $\mathbf{x}(0) = 0 = F^0(0)$ by definition.

Induction Suppose for all $0 \leq l < k$, $\mathbf{x}(l) \leq F^l(0)$, we prove that $\mathbf{x}(k) \leq F^k(0)$ holds, i.e., for all $i \in I$, $\mathbf{x}(k)|_i \leq F^k(0)|_i$. Case (i) $i \neq D(k)$. By the induction hypothesis, $x_i(k) = x_i(k-1) = \mathbf{x}(k-1)|_i \leq F^{k-1}(0)|_i \leq F^k(0)|_i$. Case (ii) $i = D(k)$. Note that for all $j \in I$, $s_j(k) \leq k - 1 < k$, so $\mathbf{x}(s_j(k)) \leq F^{s_j(k)}(0) \leq F^{k-1}(0)$ by the induction hypothesis, hence $x_j(s_j(k)) = \mathbf{x}(s_j(k))|_j \leq F^{k-1}(0)|_j$, therefore $x_i(k) = F_i(x_1(s_1(k)), \cdots, x_n(s_n(k))) \leq F_i(F^{k-1}(0)) = F(F^{k-1}(0))|_i = F^k(0)|_i$ by the monotonity of F.

To sum up, we have for all $k \in N$, $\mathbf{x}(k) \leq F^k(0)$, hence $\mathbf{x}(k) \leq F^k(0) \leq \bigsqcup\{F^i(0)|i \geq 0\} = \text{lfixp}(F)$. □

This lemma shows also that for any k, if $\mathbf{x}(k)$ is a fixed point of F, then it *is* the least fixed point of F, even if (b) and (c) in Definition 1 are removed.

Lemma 2 *For all $m, k \in N$, if $m \geq \phi(2k)$ then $\mathbf{x}(m) \geq F^k(0)$.*

Proof. We prove it by induction on k.

Basis $k = 0$. Obviously for all $m \geq \phi(0) = 0$, $\mathbf{x}(m) \geq \mathbf{0} = F^0(\mathbf{0})$.

Induction Suppose for all $0 \leq l < k$, if $m \geq \phi(2l)$ then $\mathbf{x}(m) \geq F^l(\mathbf{0})$, we prove now for all $m \geq \phi(2k)$, $\mathbf{x}(m) \geq F^k(\mathbf{0})$, i.e., for all $i \in I$, $\mathbf{x}(m)|_i \geq F^k(\mathbf{0})|_i$.

For $i \in I$, by Fact 1, there must be some $v \in N$, $\phi(2k-1) \leq v < \phi(2k)$, such that i is updated at v, that is, $D(v) = i$. Suppose u is the maximum element in the set $\{v \in N | \phi(2k-1) \leq v \leq m \wedge D(v) = i\}$. Now it is easily seen from Definition 1 that $\mathbf{x}(m)|_i = \mathbf{x}(u)|_i$ since $D(v) \neq i$ for all $u < v \leq m$. So we just need to show that $\mathbf{x}(u)|_i = x_i(u) \geq F^k(\mathbf{0})|_i$. Recall that $x_i(u) = F_i(x_1(s_1(u)), \cdots, x_n(s_n(u)))$ because $D(u) = i$. Since $u \geq \phi(2k-1)$, by Fact 1 we have for all $j \in I$, $s_j(u) \geq \phi((2k-1)-1) = \phi(2(k-1))$, so by the induction hypothesis, $\mathbf{x}(s_j(u)) \geq F^{k-1}(\mathbf{0})$, hence $x_j(s_j(u)) = \mathbf{x}(s_j(u))|_j \geq F^{k-1}(\mathbf{0})|_j$, therefore by the monotonity of F we get $x_i(u) = F_i(x_1(s_1(u)), \cdots, x_n(s_n(u))) \geq F_i(F^{k-1}(\mathbf{0})) = F^k(\mathbf{0})|_i$.

In summary, the lemma is proved. $\qquad\qquad\qquad\qquad\qquad\qquad\qquad\qquad\quad\Box$

Theorem 1 (Convergence) *Let $(\mathbf{P}, \leq)$ be a finite-chain partially ordered set, $F : \mathbf{P}^n \to \mathbf{P}^n$ be a monotone function, then every asynchronous iteration (F, C, D) converges to the least fixed point of F. In fact, there is $m \in N$, such that for all $l \in N$, if $l \geq m$ then $\mathbf{x}(l) = \mathbf{lfixp}(F)$.*

Proof. Let $\mathbf{lfixp}(F) = F^u(\mathbf{0})$ for some $u \in N$. By Lemmas 2 and 1 we have $\mathbf{lfixp}(F) = F^u(\mathbf{0}) \leq \mathbf{x}(\phi(2u)) \leq \mathbf{lfixp}(F)$, hence $\mathbf{lfixp}(F) = \mathbf{x}(\phi(2u))$. Now let's take $m = \phi(2u)$. For all $l \in N$, if $l \geq m = \phi(2u)$, again by Lemma 2 and Lemma 1, we get $\mathbf{lfixp}(F) \geq \mathbf{x}(l) \geq F^u(\mathbf{0}) = \mathbf{lfixp}(F)$, i.e., $\mathbf{x}(l) = \mathbf{lfixp}(F)$. $\quad\Box$

References

[C+92] D. Conforti et al. A model of efficient asynchronous parallel algorithms on multicomputer systems. *Parallel Computing*, 18:31–45, 1992.

[CC77] P. Cousot and R. Cousot. Automatic synthesis of optimal invariant assertions: Mathematical foundations. *SIGPLAN Notices*, 12(8):1–12, 1977.

[KU76] J.B. Kam and J.D. Ullman. Global data flow analysis and iterative algorithms. *Journal of the ACM*, 23(1):158–171, 1976.

[Kun76] H.T. Kung. Synchronized and asynchronous parallel algorithms for multiprocessors. In J. F. Traub, editor, *Algorithms and Complexity: New Directions and Recent Results.*, pages 153–200. Academic Press, 1976.

[NN92] H. R. Nielson and F. Nielson. Bounded fixed point iteration. In *Proc. ACM Symp. on Principle of Programming Language*, pages 71–82, 1992.

[ÜD90] A. Üresin and M. Dubois. Parallel asynchronous algorithms for discrete data. *Journal of the ACM*, 37(3):588–606, 1990.

[Wei93] J. Wei. Parallel asynchronous iterations of least fixed points. *accepted in Parallel Computing*, 1993.

[WZ91] J. Wei and Z. Zhang. Convergence of chaotic iterative least fixed point computations. *Intern. J. Computer Mathematics*, 40:231–238, 1991.

LU–Decomposition on a Massively Parallel Transputer System

Stefan Lüpke

Technische Informatik 2
Technische Universität Hamburg–Harburg
Harburger Schloßstraße 20
2100 Hamburg 90, Germany

Abstract. Two algorithms for LU–decomposition on a transputer based reconfigurable MIMD parallel computer with distributed memory have been analyzed in view of the interdependence of granularity and execution time. In order to investigate this experimentally, LU–decomposition algorithms have been implemented on a parallel computer, the Parsytec SuperCluster 128. The results of this investigation may be summarized as follows. The LU–decomposition algorithms are very efficient on the parallel computer, if the ratio between problem size and number of processors is not too small. No loss of efficiency is to be expected, if the number of processors is increased only proportionally to the number of elements in the matrix being decomposed.

The parallel computer Parsytec SuperCluster 128 (SC 128) is a massively parallel transputer system with distributed memory and 128 processors of type T805 plus some special purpose processors [10].

In the SC 128 the transputers are connected by a statically reconfigurable interprocessor network built from 12 Network Configuration Units (NCUs) [10, 11]. Each NCU is a 96×96 crossbar switch for link connections. Software running on the SC 128 must be based on message passing.

Examplary parallel LU-decomposition algorithms have been implemented on this parallel computer to investigate parallel algorithms [7].

These algorithms decompose a matrix M into a lower triangular matrix L and an upper triangular matrix U with $M = L \cdot U$. One of the matrices L and U is unit upper/lower triangular. The parallel algorithms are derived from the algorithms of Crout and of Doolittle, which differ in the choice of the unit triangular matrix only [1, 2, 4, 8, 9].

The Processor Network

All algorithms described in this paper require a processor network with a torus structure of $p \times p$ processors. An ideal torus structure occupies all four links of each transputer and allows no entry into the processor network. Therefore, an additional transputer must be inserted into one of the link connections. A free link of this transputer provides the entry into the processor network. During execution of the algorithms this additional transputer only passes through data according to the torus structure. The (i, j)-element of each matrix is stored on the processor in row $((i-1) \bmod p) + 1$ and column $((j-1) \bmod p) + 1$ of the torus structure.

The Algorithms

Crout's method has been parallelized reordering independent operations [7]. In this paper the algorithm is called parallel Crout-Algorithm. Each processor computes all elements of L and U placed on it. Considering the choosen distribution of data this results in nearly symmetrically distributed load of the processors.

A second parallel LU-Decomposition algorithm has been derived from a block version of Crout's method. The problem is partitioned into subproblems which are multiplications of submatrices and LU-decompositions of the submatrices with inversion of the resulting triangular submatrices. The subproblems are executed sequentially, but each subproblem is parallelized itself. The multiplication of submatrices is parallelized using an extension of the Cannon-Algorithm (designed for systolic arrays [3]), which allows more than one matrix element per processor [7]. The LU-decomposition is done by recursively calling this parallel LU-decomposition algorithm with smaller block size, until an elementary block size of $p \times p$ is reached. Then the parallel Crout-Algorithm and a subsequently parallel inversion of the resulting triangular submatrices is applied to the submatrices of size $p \times p$.

Because of the required inversion of the resulting triangular submatrices, the parallel algorithm has been designed to calculate not only the LU-decomposition, but additionally the inversion of the resulting triangular matrices. Accordingly in this paper the algorithm is called partitioned LU-decomposition with inversion. A second version of the algorithm has been implemented, which in this paper is called partitioned LU-decomposition without inversion. This version eliminates all operations that are necessary for the computation of L^{-1} and U^{-1} but not for the LU-decomposition itself. If the application requires L^{-1} and U^{-1}, the first version of the algorithm must be preferred.

Provided that the size of the matrix being decomposed is not too small, the algorithms applied on elementary submatrices of size $p \times p$ insignificantly affect the total efficiency of the partitioned LU–decomposition.

In case of a large matrix being decomposed the LU–decomposition is mainly reduced to matrix multiplications in view of computing and communicating costs by recursive matrix subdivision. The matrix multiplications have been parallelized with symmetrical load distribution, therefore no dynamic load balancing is required.

The subdivision of the matrices does not require any interprocessor communication. Therefore, in the partitioned LU–decomposition algorithm communication is only required by the matrix multiplication algorithm and by the elementary algorithms for LU–decomposition and inversion of triangular submatrices of size $p \times p$.

Results of the Experiments

The algorithms have been implemented using the programming language
OCCAM [13, 14] in the Multitool development environment [12]. Figure 1 shows
the interdependence between efficiency (speed-up/number of processors) of the
algorithms and number of elements of matrix M per processor ($\frac{n \times n}{p \times p}$ for a $n \times n$
matrix M) for different sizes of the processor network. The speed-up is measured
in comparison with the original algorithm of Crout executing sequentially on a
single processor node.

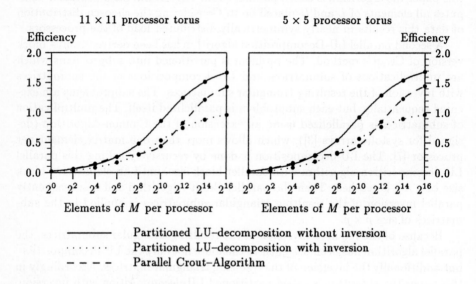

Fig. 1. Efficiency of the algorithms

Very small changes of the program source code may effect significant changes
in execution time due to the special RISC architecture of transputers. The instruction set of the transputer may be more suited for the parallel algorithm
than for the sequential algorithm. Therefore, the efficiency of the implemented
algorithms exceeds 1 in some cases.

Comparing the diagrams of figure 1, we got the following results:

- The efficiency is very high, if the ratio between the number of rows (columns)
  in the matrix and the number of rows (columns) of processors in the network
  is not too small.
- The efficiency of the algorithms is nearly independent of the number of
  processors, if the number of matrix elements per processor is constant.
- No loss of efficiency is to be expected, if the number of processors is only
  increased proportionally to the number of elements in the matrix being decomposed.

- The partitioned algorithm is faster than the parallel Crout–Algorithm for most matrix sizes. When decomposing large matrices the execution time of the two algorithms differ only marginally, because in case of large matrices the communication overhead contributes insignificantly to the execution time.

Acknowledgement

We would like to thank the Deutsche Forschungsgemeinschaft (DFG) for sponsoring this research project, especially for financing the SuperCluster 128 used for the experiments described in this paper.

References

1. Kai Hwang, Yeng-Heng Cheng, *Partitioned Matrix Algorithms for VLSI Arithmetic Systems*, IEEE Transactions on Computers, Vol. C–31, No. 12, 1982
2. Thula Vogell, *Entwicklung der Grundlagen einer Theorie paralleler partitionierter Algorithmen unter besonderer Berücksichtigung partitionierter Netzwerkalgorithmen*, KFA Jülich, ISSN 0366–0885, 1986
3. F. Hoßfeld, *Parallele Algorithmen*, KFA Jülich, ISSN 0343-7639, 1981
4. P. D. Crout, *A short method for evaluating determinants and solving systems of linear equations with real or complex coefficients*, Proc. American Inst. Elec. Eng., vol. 40, 1941
5. J. H. Goncalves Romero, *A Comparative Study of Two Wavefront Implementations of a LU Solver Algorithm*, CONPAR 90 — VAPP IV Proceedings, Springer Verlag, 1990
6. Gene H. Golub, Charles F. Van Loan, *Matrix Computations*, 2nd edition, The John Hopkins University Press, 1989
7. S. Lüpke, *Parallele Algorithmen der linearen Algebra und Netzwerkkonfigurationen für einen massiv parallelen Rechner mit verteiltem Speicher*, Diplomarbeit, TU Hamburg-Harburg, Technische Informatik 2, 1991
8. E. Kreyszig, *Advanced Engineering Mathematics*, John Wiley & Sons, 1988
9. W. H. Press, B. P. Flannery, S. A. Teukolsky, W. T. Vetterling, *Numerical Recipes*, Cambridge University Press, 1986
10. Parsytec GmbH, *SuperCluster Technical Documentation*, 1989
11. Parsytec GmbH, *Network Configuration Manager Software Documentation*, 1990
12. Parsytec GmbH, *Multitool 5.0 Manual, Technical Documentation*
13. G. Jones, M. Goldsmith, Inmos Limited, *Programming in occam 2*, Prentice Hall, 1988
14. Inmos Limited, *occam 2 Reference Manual*, Prentice Hall, 1988

PSEE: Parallel System Evaluation Environment

E.Luque, R.Suppi and **J.Sorribes**

Departament d'Informàtica - Universidad Autònoma de Barcelona

08193- Bellaterra-Spain- Fax: +3435812478. e-mail:iinfd@ccuab1.uab.es

Abstract.

Programs for parallel computers of distributed memory are difficult to write, understand, evaluate and debug. The design and performance evaluation of algorithms is much complex than the conventional sequential one. This short paper describes the PSEE (Parallel System Evaluation Environment), an interactive graphical environment, which permits to study the behaviour of parallel distributed memory systems. PSEE is an easy-to-use environment that enables parallel distributed memory systems programmers take decisions about the behaviour program and parallel computer in terms such as: scalability, tuning and performance of the underlying parallel machine.

1. Introduction.

Parallel computers, quite apart from technological developments, offer a long term possibility to improve the performance of computer systems. In theory, it is easy to argue that a parallel system is faster than a monoprocessor one. However, when processors are not properly coordinated, a multiprocessor machine may take longer to finish a job than a monoprocessor one. The use of an algorithm on a monoprocessor will differ in speed by no more than a constant factor from one manufacturer's to another's (usually), but in parallel machines, we have no such guarantees. Moreover, programs for one multiprocessor are rarely portable to other multiprocessor, so that for each algorithm and each architecture, the application of the algorithm must be repeated.

We have developed an integrated and interactive environment, PSEE (Parallel System Evaluation Environment) to give tools to study the behaviour of parallel distributed memory systems under variable conditions. It allows parallel programming, simulation and performance evaluation of parallel algorithms in parallel architectures [1,2].

2. PSEE Software Structure.

The PSEE environment is organized around three main tools: Parallel Programming Tool, Behaviour Simulator for Link Oriented Parallel Systems, and Data Filters and Visualization Tool. Through the **Parallel Programming Tool**, the user translates applications written in a parallel-high-level source language into a sequential code to be executed on a single processor. From the user code, the parallel programming tool generates also a graph (date type) representation. This graph is a machine - independent intermediate representation that can be mapped and executed (simulated) onto different architectures. The **Behavioural Simulator** is a simulation system that uses dataflow graphs to model the user's program and parallel architecture. This is a discrete event simulator with a graphical interface, oriented to reduce the user training and the development cycle. The simulator produces a full simulation trace (stamped time file type). The **Data Filters and Visualization Tool** allows to the user the evaluation of the performance from trace files, generating a set of performance measurements.

3. Parallel Program and architecture model.

We have selected a dynamic data flow programming approach. This modelling formalism is called Weighted Behavioural Directed Graph (WBG). As in any standard directed graph, nodes in a WBG model sequential code segments, and arcs represent dependence relations between nodes. A WBG node is characterized (in static form) by its computing "volume," and "class," which defines its behaviour. The "volume" parameter models node granularity (sequential code size). The "class" parameter defines the node's execution behaviour. Several classes are defined: Standard (sequential code segments), Macro, Input, Output (Hierarchical Representation), Call, Return (Dynamic Properties). The condition for node activation (firing rule) is handled by an input policy. Typical input policies are the "and" policy (at least one token on each input arc) and the "or" policy (a token in any input). There is also an output policy specification, which establishes the token output distribution after node execution.

Architecture model has the "class" parameter used to define hardware modules (processors, I/O processors, switches). Each architecture node has a parameter that models its speed relating to other members of its class. Arcs of the architecture graph have included parameters such as source-destination, and communication speed. They have a user defined buffer, allowing token queuing [2].

4. Parallel Programming Tool.

Parallel Programming Tool (PPT) is a program generator and program evaluation tool. This tool is oriented to obtain the main program characteristics and verify the correct functional operation of an algorithm designed in parallel form. The algorithm is executed in a sequential way on a single processor environment, maintaining data coherency.

The program generator is designed for lexical processing of character input streams. It accepts a high-level problem oriented specification and produces a program in a conventional language. The user supplies the additional code (extra primitives) to express the explicit parallelism with token passing. PPT generates a conventional code with the sequential user program, and control procedures to simulate, when is executed on a single processor, the execution on a multiprocessor. The execution of this code generates information such as: time of execution, communication volumes, context changes time, algorithm behaviour, conventional user output. Moreover, creates a synthetic program graph (input to Behaviour Simulator). The program generator accepts a user program with following extra primitives: Subroutine, Token, Varhold, Activa, and Init_token.

The basic declaration is the 'subroutine' and involves the sequential source code (one node) and the messages are sent by one subroutine to another using a token statement. The statement Varhold enables the use of static variables and the Activa operator returns the subroutine activation count (number of node's executions). The Init_token statement enables the start of parallel program execution.

5. Behaviour Simulator.

The simulation environment for synthetic programs (WBG) is based on a discrete event's simulator.

In simulation run time, measures on the system parameters are made. To get conclusions about system performance, this information is post-processed and presented in graphical form through the Data Filters & Visualization Tool to provide global and local vision of the system performance.

In addition, to the program and architecture modelling, the simulator requires the specification of two system features: task assignment and token routing policies. The solution adopted here is to specify the scheduler and the router by an algorithm written in a high level language. The default configuration includes for static allocation: hand scheduling, CP (Critical Path), CP/MISF (Critical Path with the most successor first) and a policy based in the simulating annealing algorithm. The default routing policies are: hand routing and routing to minimize the route-steps.

6. Visualization Tool: Performance evaluation.

The complexity of parallel systems involves a great difficulty to find an optimum stable point of operation for every algorithm and each architecture. The system tuning requires analysis and visualization of great volume of information, as well as detailed system knowledge [1]. The Data Filter & Visualization Tool is a window's environment with users' defined filters. The information shown by the instrument windows is processed (compress) to provide a better understanding on the system behaviour. The information processing consists of statistical calculations the information is presented through dot, tendency and bars diagrams. The user can combine results from several sessions in a single screen as well as visualization of statistics results. The system offers several defined filters. The current possibilities to visualize trace information are the following: available and exploited concurrency, communications and routing load, link overload and Gantt charts.

The interactive PSEE environment has been designed as an icon - directed paradigm, offering an interactive interface, based on animated graphics, windows and icons. This environment supports graphic interaction for edition (parallel program, algorithm graph and architecture graph), scheduling, clustering, routing, simulation, measurement and performance evaluation.

7. Future trends and conclusions.

In spite of the goodness of this tool, our work points several enhancements. These enhancements are based in a more fine modelling for both parallel system and parallel algorithm, and a new graphical representation format. Future work involves enhancements such as: A synthetic program description based on a graph description language and automatic generation of communication paths and source code. A functional model to the algorithm based in the independence between the sequential code of each node and its firing rules. The algorithm nodes model and token model represented by non constant values, given for distribution functions. Simulation's support of the operating system policies and scheduling algorithm onto a particular processor. Include the use of a hardware description language and a more detailed characterization of each processor, memory module and switching elements. Enhancement of the visualization model extended to support big information volumes, allowing event reorder and visualization through surfaces, level curves, and dimensional relations.

PSEE is an easy-to-use environment that enables parallel systems programmers take decisions about the behaviour program and parallel computer in terms as such: scalability, tuning and performance of the underlying parallel machine. PSEE is being used in development of application programs, it is being evaluated and improved.

8. References.

1. Proceedings of Working Conference on Programming Environments for Parallel Computing. International Federation for Information Processing - IFIP - . Edinburhg. UK. April 1992.
2. E. Luque, R. Suppi and J. Sorribes "Designing Parallel Systems: A Performance Prediction Problem" Microprocessors and Microsystems Vol. 16 No 1. pp. 25-35. 1992.

This software (PC - DOS version) is available for formal request of Technical Institutions or Schools (free distribution). Address request to: Remo Suppi. This work was supported by CICYT under contract number TIC 056/89.

Implementation of a Digital Modular Chip for a Reconfigurable Artificial Neural Network

Simin Pakzad and Paul Plaskonos

Department of Electrical and Computer Engineering
Pennsylvania State University
University Park, PA 16802

Abstract

Artificial Neural Networks (ANNs) are fast becoming an integral part of today's computing arsenal [4]. This paper discusses the issues involved in the design of a *General Purpose Reconfigurable Artificial Neural Network* (GPRNN). The IBM fabricated *Basic Neural Unit* (BNU) is used as a building block for the GPRNN. As a first step, a fully reconfigurable 2-BNU VLSI circuit is designed, implemented and tested.

1 Introduction

ANNs constitute a radically different approach to computation: based upon modern neurophysiology, a simplified model of the human neuron is organized into networks similar to those found in the brain [5]. In the process of developing a digital GPRNN, a modular ANN chip has been designed and fabricated. This paper reports on this ANN chip, namely the IBM fabricated Basic Neural Unit (BNU). The architecture of the BNU, which stresses modularity, is provided. The functionality of the chip will be shown. Next, the hardware of a small scale GPRNN which supports the coupling of two BNUs into a fully reconfigurable 2-BNU network is presented. Test results are provided to show the functionality of this circuitry in each of its three configurations. Lastly, some design issues for a large scale reconfigurable GPRNN are discussed.

2 Basic Neural Unit -The Building Block of the GPRNN

The BNU, which is based on the weight centered approach, is a 10 input - 3 output, single weight-layer chip capable of holding 30 weight values (10 per output neuron) fabricated by IBM [2]. A block diagram of a BNU's internal structure is shown in figure 1.

BNUs can be *coupled vertically* (or *stacked*) and partial values can be passed between chips; essentially increasing the number of inputs on a layer by 10 (figure 3(a)). This is accomplished through a presetable accumulator.

The three partial sums of BNU1, after ten activation value iterations have been performed, would be loaded into the corresponding accumulator of BNU2. After ten more activation iterations the final output would be available at the output of BNU2. In this manner, the number of weights and activation values for a layer of neurons can be increased. In essence, a $10n \times 3$ network can be generated, by stacking n BNUs.

BNUs *coupled horizontally* (or *cascaded*), on the other hand, increase the number of outputs as seen in figure 3(b). All six output neurons in these two BNUs receive the same activation values, but different weight values. In this manner, a 10×6 network is created (with all BNUs on the same level). In general, any $10 \times 3n$ network can be constructed by horizontal connection of n BNUs.

Numbers are represented in 2s complement format, and the most significant bit (MSB) of the output from the BNU is the sign bit. Hence, adding more layers is a matter of serially passing the complement of the MSB from each output to the next layer when utilizing the hard-limiter thresholding model. This can be accomplished

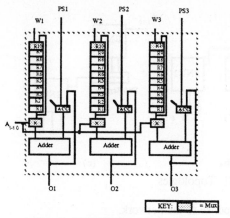

| PS1 | PS2 | PS3 |

Fig. 1. BNU's Internal Structure

Fig. 2. 2-BNU Platform

by loading these bits into a shift register and then serially passing them to the next layer. Figure 3(c) shows this configuration.

It is clear that by utilizing these properties any size network can be realized out of BNUs.

3 Building a Fully Reconfigurable 2-BNU ANN

A 2-BNU circuit has been constructed [3]. The 2-BNU ANN system is capable of dynamically configuring the BNUs connections to realize their three possible combinations. A block diagram of this circuit is shown in figure 2. The means by which each of the three topologies is realized by a 2-BNU network is described next.

10x6 Network: BNUs are connected to the same activation line (figure 3(b)). The ten activation values are passed. A six bit output is created by utilizing the MSB from each of the output neurons. These vales are then passed to the Output Register, and finally to the computer.

10x3x3 Network: In this configuration, shown in figure 3(c), BNU1 corresponds to the first weight-layer and performs the weighted summation of the input activation values. BNU2 receives the activation values from BNU1 and processes the data further based on its own set of weights.

20x3 Network: Partial sums from one set of 10 activation values must be passed to the next level BNU as in figure 3(a). The partial sums from BNU1 are passed to BNU2. Each of the three 8-bit accumulator values are loaded in parallel into the PASSER which transfers them to the accumulators of BNU2. The second set of 10 activation values are sent to BNU2 and the three bit output is then available for the output register.

4 Verification of the BNU and 2-BNU Circuitry

The 2-BNU network is fully reconfigurable. It can electronically alter the platform to connect the two BNUs in each of the three possible configurations (i.e. 10x6, 10x3x3, and 20x3 networks). Testing of the 2-BNU circuit involves demonstrating the functionality of the 2-BNU network in each of its three topologies.

The differences in generalizing power among the three configurations are not pronounced. Tests have been performed which demonstrate the contrast between them. These experiments involved teaching the network a series of alpha-numeric patterns

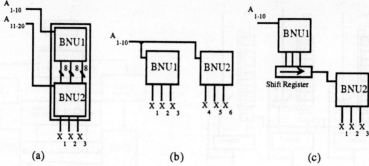

Fig. 3. 2-BNU Topologies

(of varying size) and the proper output response to the network.

The 10x6 configuration is different from the other two configurations by virtue of its six output neurons. To show that this network is capable of classifying patterns into more than eight groups, the network was taught 12 patterns. Once trained, the network was able to recall the 12 learned patterns. However, because of the high number of patterns, it was very susceptible to noise - altering a single bit of an input pattern resulted in only 18.4% correct response. In another experiment, the 10x6 network was taught only four patterns. As expected, its tolerance for noise was much greater - achieving 91.3% correct response for one bit of noise.

The 10x3x3 network has an additional layer of weights. These weights provide for the processing of the XOR logic function which single weight-layer networks are not capable of learning [1]. Results from a four pattern test similar to the 10x6 test show slightly higher accuracy response (93.3%).

The 20x3 network differs from the other three patterns because of its 20 inputs. Alpha-numeric patterns were again used as input patterns. The results from this test demonstrate that four patterns can be recalled and that this network, because of its large input space, is much less noise sensitive than either the 10x6 or the 10x3x3 networks - 97.4% accuracy response for 1 bit of noise, 90.7% accuracy for 2 bits.

5 GPRNN Design Issues

In this section, some issues crucial to the design of a large scale GPRNN will be discussed.

5.1 General Topological Rules

The 24 fabricated BNU chips can achieve a wide variety of configurations. The mathematical principles which govern realizable topologies are shown next.

Define: i = weight-layer number, I_i = number of inputs of layer i, O_i = number of outputs of layer i, V_i = the number of BNU chips stacked vertically to achieve I_i, H_i = the number of chips cascaded horizontally to achieve O_i, L = number of layers of weights, C_i = number of BNU chips required by weight-layer i, C_T = total number of chips required to realize a network.

The total number of chips required by a network is the sum of the chips required by each of its layers, hence:

$$C_T = \sum_{i=1}^{L} C_i = \sum_{i=1}^{L} \left\lceil \frac{I_i}{10} \right\rceil \times \left\lceil \frac{O_i}{3} \right\rceil \qquad (1)$$

5.2 Realizable Configurations

Procedure for defining the ranges of a 24-BNU GPRNN: Using equation 1 and the fact that we have only 24 IBM BNUs at our disposal ($C_T \le 24$), single layer networks can be shown to range from high input 240x3 , to high output 10x72 , and many different configurations in between (e.g. 120x6, 80x9, 60x12, 40x18, 20x36 networks).

The following topological extremes can be realized by a two layer network: a 230x3x3 high input network , a 10x3x69 high output network, and a 10x54x3 network. Some more reasonable configurations include: 100x6x12, 70x9x9, 50x9x27, 30x21x3, and 20x18x18 networks. 24 BNU chips allow for the realization of networks with a larger number of layers. Some possible topologies are 30x12x12x6, 50x9x12x6, 20x12x12x9x6, and 20x15x9x9x15.

Connecting a large number of BNU chips in the manner discussed in this paper would mean virtually any network is possible as long as there are enough chips and board space.

5.3 Space Requirements

The GPRNN is being designed to be utilized in an IBM PC. Implementation of this specialty hardware in such an environment will utilize the power of both hardware organizations. The mobility, universality, expandability, and installation ease provided by the PC, as well as the parallel processing capabilities of the specialty hardware will be exploited to the fullest.

Since it is being implemented in a PC environment, BNUs, which comprise a GPRNN, will be mounted on IBM PC prototyping cards. We estimate that five such cells can be mounted on a card. In order to mount all 24 BNUs, only five cards are necessary. These cards can be easily coupled to the PC through the bus expansion slots provided by an expansion unit.

6 Conclusion

In this paper we report on the design of a Basic Neural Unit (BNU). Its capability to be utilized as a building block of a large scale reconfigurable neural network has been demonstrated. This has been shown by constructing a 2-BNU network which can be dynamically reconfigured into any of its three realizable topologies.

Currently, we are engaged in the design and development of a large scale reconfigurable BNU-based neural network. Some of the technological constraints encountered in the design process of this larger network are briefly discussed. Upon completion of this system, performance evaluations will be undertaken.

7 References

[1] J.E. Dayhoff, "Neural Network Architectures: An Introduction." Van Nostrand Reinhold, New York NY, 1990.
[2] B. Jin, S. Pakzad and A.R. Hurson, "Application of Neural Networks in Handling Large Incomplete Databases." Proc. 1991 int. Conf. on Parallel Processing, pg. 404-408.
[3] P. Plaskonos, S. Pakzad, B. Jin, and A.R. Hurson, "Design of a Modular Chip for a Reconfigurable Artificial Neural Network." To be published in: Proc. Conf. on Developing and Managing Intelligent Systems Projects, March 1993.
[4] P. Treleaven, M. Pacheo and M. Vellasco, "VLSI Architechtures for Neural Networks.", IEEE Micro, Dec.1989, pg. 8-27.
[5] P.D. Wasserman and T. Schwartz, "Neural Networks, Part I." IEEE Expert, Winter 1987, pg. 10-14.

Article-Acquisition:
A Scenario for Non-Serializability in a Distributed Database

Dr. Techn. Mads Nygård, Sintef Delab
The Norwegian Institute of Technology, Trondheim

Abstract

This paper applies a model for distributed databases and transactions with a distinction between global and local correctness criteria. The global requirements per system are weaker than the local requirements per site. The paper presents an application which suits such a two-level division. The main *motivation* for our investigation is based on the fact that the commonly used correctness criteria for concurrency control and recovery, serializability and total recoverability, are very strict criteria. The use of more relaxed criteria (allowing more true parallel behaviour and more true partial behaviour) is therefore very appealing - as long as this can be achieved without compromising safety or applicability. The main *paradigm* in our approach is based on the observation that relatively little knowledge about the databases and transactions can lead to major gains in system throughput. This allows specific systems to have more tailor-made correctness criteria.

Our specialized type of distributed database, the *skeleton-database*, represents sets of close substitutes for diverse articles. Effectively we investigate an organized coupling of cooperating databases. Each specific database contains a complementing set of article-offers - and the different databases contain substituting sets for these article-offers. Further, the databases may be accessed simultaneously in the sense that article-offers in one database may be "held" while article-offers in another database are checked - and the accesses to all participating databases in a skeleton-database will be collectively controlled. Our approach allows non-serializability and partial recoverability. We arrive at multi-level correctness criteria with respect to both consistency preservation and atomicity assurance.

Our specialized type of distributed transaction, the *wander-transaction*, traverses a skeleton-database trying to seize an optimal set - complying with any combined conditions on the attribute-values - of specific articles. Actually we discuss a traversing race among competing transactions. A transaction may require diverse articles of several types - and several articles of a single type. And a transaction/buyer may acquire articles directly - i.e. it corresponds to an on-line read-and-write service and not only an off-line read-only service. Further, a buyer may consider more static attributes like quality and price - as well as more dynamic attributes like no-left and who-purchased. Our concept allows transactions to build up priority during their traversing race. Acquiring an article-offer early may increase the priority of the corresponding buyer - while checking an article-offer later may decrease the priority of the corresponding buyer.

Wander-transactions accessing a skeleton-database allow breaks with both the common serializability criterion and the common total recoverability criterion. Our main emphasis here is on the non-serializability aspect. The primary *goal* of this work is to designate correctness criteria for controlling local and global parallelism. The secondary *goal* of this work is to specify priority rules for handling local and global criteria breaks. Wander-transactions accessing a skeleton-database experience dynamic priorities. Our resulting concept, *priority serializability*, gives increased parallelism without reduced safety.

1 Introduction

For many distributed databases the type of global integrity constraints implied by the databases collectively is under discussion. Any such constraints come in addition to the local integrity constraints implied by the databases separately. By integrity constraints we mean any associated rules which couple the given database items in some way. Likewise, for many distributed transactions the type of global semantic requirements induced by the transactions per system is under discussion. Any such requirements come in addition to the local semantic requirements induced by the transactions per site. By semantic requirements we mean any overall information describing the assumed transaction results in some way. It is a fact that in some distributed databases global integrity constraints do exist but are weaker than the local integrity constraints. It is also a fact that in some distributed transactions global semantic requirements do exist but are weaker than the local semantic requirements. This opens up for non-serializability globally and partial recoverability globally - on top of serializability locally and total recoverability locally.

2 Alternative Database and Transaction Types

Imagine a collection of separately run department stores with corresponding types of articles. The current available qualities, prevailing prices, remaining quantities and confirmed reservations of articles naturally vary among the department stores. Their article information will have to exist in n variants and may have to be stored at n sites. A typical database corresponding to three department stores offering three specific articles is illustrated in Fig. 1.

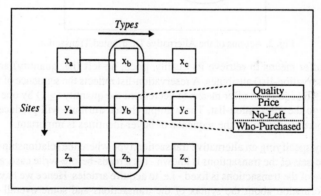

Fig. 1. Complementing Sets of Article-Offers at Single Sites &
A Substituting Set of Article-Offers of a Specific Type.

Here x, y and z specify different occurrences of sites, while a, b and c specify different types of items. So y_a, y_b and y_c represent different item-types available as article-kinds at a unique site or department store. We talk about a complementing set of article-offers. Further x_b, y_b and z_b represent a unique item-type available as article-variants at different sites or department stores. We talk about a substituting set of article-offers. Consider the article-information as a distributed database consisting of a set of local databases. Each set of items connected with horizontal lines corresponds to the intra-base view, while the set of items encircled by a vertical oval corresponds to an inter-base view. The different local databases of this non-replicated global database are not interrelated by normal integrity constraints. But within each local database there may be any kind of integrity constraints relating the local items in some way.

We are actually specifying an alternative database type where some integrity constraints - i.e. those between the separate local databases in a global database, are completely missing. Hence we have complete knowledge about a well-defined part of the integrity constraints. The non-existence of integrity constraints between clearly identifiable database parts is easy to represent and manipulate. We choose to call a global database of this type a *skeleton-data-base*.

Imagine also a simple but interesting operation requiring the cheapest article-variant of type B. The corresponding transaction should, after first checking (i.e. retrieving) some or all of the available article-offers, then acquire (i.e. update) the one article-offer fulfilling the given condition in the best way. This is illustrated in Fig. 2. Here the operation checks the current offers by retrieving all existing variants of the specified article-kind, finds one cheapest offer by comparing the prices and consulting the quantities, and acquires the best offer with at least one instance left by updating this variant of the article-kind.

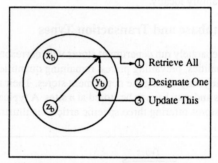

Fig. 2. Actions of the Alternative Distributed Transaction.

To check an offer means to retrieve its quality, price, no-left (i.e. quantity) and who-purchased (i.e. reservation-list) attributes. A reservation-list reflects the sequence of reservations already made. To acquire an offer means to decrement the quantity (≥ 1) by one and add the buyer-identity to the reservation-list. The who-purchased attribute will produce a delivery-list for the department store, so the sequence of buyer-identities is important.

We are actually specifying an alternative transaction type where the relationship between the read- and write-sets of the transactions is known - i.e. a reads-before-write case, and the functional objective of the transactions is fixed - i.e. to acquire articles. Hence we have both some high-level information about the syntax of the transactions and some overall information about the semantics of the transactions. We are separately concentrating on a specific type of transaction. We choose to call a transaction of this type a *wander-transaction*.

3 Inherent Freedom and Constraints

The normal correctness criterion for *concurrency control* corresponds to the one-after-the-other effect. Such *serializability* means that the effect of handling several transactions being run in parallel should be as if they were executed in some, unknown, serial order.

The lack of some integrity constraints in a skeleton-database leads to a certain degree-of-freedom in synchronizing accesses to such databases. The existence of some semantic information about a wander-transaction then fixes a specific point in this solution span for synchronization of such transactions. Consider for example using locking as a concurrency control mechanism. Is 2PhaseLock synchronization then necessary for wander-transactions accessing a skeleton-database? The answer is no! It is quite adequate to always hold the best offer currently found and constantly free already obsolete offers. Holding corresponds to locking and freeing to unlocking. Carrying out this principle recursively means that eventually an article is locked after another is unlocked. Hence 2PhaseLocking is violated.

Our aim is to arrive at relaxed concurrency control for all wander-transactions. We require normal serializability between the group of "selling transactions" and the group of "buying transactions" - and within the group of "selling transactions". It is within the group of "buying transactions" that we may allow some non-serializability. The designated criteria are 2-level. One part stems from the need to preserve integrity constraints in the local databases and requires that all the write-read, read-write and write-write conflicts have to induce serializability per site. The other part stems from the need to observe overall goals of the global transactions and requires that only the write-read conflicts have to induce serializability per system. The designated criteria have been extended with a priority rule. Each write-read conflict results in the writing transaction gaining priority over the reading transaction. [Nygå93a] has introduced such aspects.

The normal correctness criterion for *recovery* corresponds to the all-or-nothing effect. Such *total recoverability* means that the effect of dealing with a transaction being interrupted in the middle should be as if it was finished totally - or as if it was not started at all.

Wander-transactions accessing a skeleton-database may apply partial commitment instead of total commitment. This means that at selected points during its execution a given transaction may commit its hitherto purchased items - instead of having to commit all its purchased items together at the end. Each purchase corresponds to a single write, so committing a set of purchases corresponds to committing a set of writes. A reason for applying partial commitment instead of total commitment is that at given points a specific transaction may be able to live with the items acquired by then - without necessarily having to get hold of the remaining required items. Allowing such step-wise committing transactions does not mean that corresponding subtransactions become totally independent. Actually these will be priority-connected: early writes in a specific transaction build up priority for later writes in the same transaction. Further, early commits secure purchases from being aborted if the transaction waits too long.

Our point is not that partial commitment is to be used, but rather to discuss how it should be controlled. This exploits the priority rule - making commit-granting depend on priority-level and waiting-time. [Nygå93b] has covered these aspects.

4   Conclusion

To sum up, knowledge about some missing integrity constraints in a distributed database opens the way for global non-serializability - and knowledge about some existing overall goals of distributed transactions leads the way to the add-on to local serializability.

References

[Nygå93a]   M. Nygård:
             "BINMOD: A Model for Non-Serializability in Distributed Databases";
             BNCOD 11 - 11th British National Conference on Databases.

[Nygå93b]   M. Nygård:
             "Multi-Criteria: Degrees of Recoverability in Distr. Databases";
             PARLE'93 - 1993 Parallel Architectures and Languages Europe Conference.

AN EMPIRICAL STUDY OF VISION PROGRAMS FOR DATA DEPENDENCE ANALYSIS

LUIS ANGEL BARRAGAN, and ARMANDO ROY

Dpto. Ingeniería Eléctrica e Informática. Universidad de Zaragoza

Maria de Luna 3, 50015 Zaragoza (Spain)

1.The Experiment.

We attempt to study how helpful automatic program restructuring can be for image processing programs. The key to the success of the automatic restructuring, is to have accurate data dependence information. That is why, we concentrate on the suitability of data dependence tests in actual low level vision applications.

We have chosen a set of algorithms that cover a wide range of applications in low level image processing: Gray-level processing, morphological operators, FIR filters and Transform Techniques. Our measurements have been done on key modules (Kernels) extracted from the real programs, in this case this modules are basic blocks of loops.

Algorithm	Description
COMP	Calculates the complementary image.
CONVOL2D	Convolves an image with a filter kernel.
DCT2D	Discrete cosine transform in two dimensions.
DILATION	Calculates the dilation of an image.
EDETECT	Performs edge detection.
EROSION	Calculates the erosion.
FLATTEN	Level the histogram.
HISTOGRAM	Finds the histogram.
IDCT2D	Performs the inverse discrete cosine transform.
NONLIN2D	Nonlinear filtering.
SMOOTH	Convolves an image with a Gaussian filter.
THRESHOLD	Produces a binary image.

Table 1: Analyzed applications.

The above programs are user-written programs coded in sequential C, and their behaviour may be different from those of library programs. Due to restrictions of the analyzer, they are also subjected to some restrictions: loops do not contain function calls and there is not aliasing. In some cases, in-line expansion has been done by hand. The main data structures are two-dimensional arrays holding discretized values. These include images and convolution windows. The image size is statically allocated to be 512-by-512. The convolution window size is a compile time constant. The 40% of variables are scalars, mainly temporary variables that can be promoted to arrays by scalar expansion, reducing the number of dependences and increasing the potential for parallelism discovery. The 10% are one-dimensional arrays holding the histogram of the image. None of the array references have more than two dimensions.

2. Features of Array Subscripts.

First of all, this empirical study evaluates the complexity of array subscripts in real programs. In [SLY90], three factors are identified that could potentially weaken the results of current data dependence test algorithms. We have evaluated these factors and the main conclusions are shown below.

Linearity of Array Subscripts. All algorithms for data dependence test that we have implemented, operate on linear subscript expressions. In case of nonlinearity, to err on the safe side, they must assume that a data dependence exists on this dimension. All of the two-dimensional array references and the 60% of one-dimensional array references are linear. The main cause for a subscript expression to be nonlinear is that it contains a symbolic variable whose value is unknown at compile time.

Coupled Subscripts. In our programs, we did not find two-dimensional array references to have coupled subscripts. Then, single-dimension tests become as exact as multidimensional tests.

Coefficients of subscript expressions. The percentage of dimensions with subscript expressions in which some coefficients have absolute value greater than 1 is very small (0.57%). Then [Bane76], real dimension by dimension tests are as exact as an integer dimension by dimension test. In our case, this conclusion also applies to multidimensional array references because there is no coupled subscripts.

3. Test Efficiency.

Different test algorithms have different complexity and capability. That is why, these tests algorithms have been applied hierarchically in many Parallelizing Compilers like Parafrase. But, which arrangement of the test sequence achieve the best efficiency? We propose the arrangement that minimize a cost function, mainly running time:
$$C=t_1+t_2(1-p_1)+t_3(1-p_2)+...+t_n(1-p_{(n-1)}) \quad \text{(ec. 2.1.)}$$
where t_i is the average running execution time of the ith test applied in the hierarchy and p_i is the detection rate of the first i tests. Our main goal is discover the maximum number of independences in order to increase the potential parallelism. We will never sacrifice the possibility of detecting an independence for decreasing the execution time. A test will take part of the hierarchy provided that its application domain is not a proper subset of the hierarchy application domain and/or its accuracy is higher in some domain.

We have evaluated usage frequency and independence detection rate of some tests algorithms: GCD, Exact, Banerjee, Interval and Lambda when they are applied alone on the Kernels of Table 1. They are applied on linear array references.

-GCD test. The test is only used if the constant term of the subscript expressions tested is no zero. The 9% of times it could be applied. It could not detect

any independence. As we saw above most coefficients of loop indexes in subscript expressions are either 1 or -1. Then the gcd is very likely to be 1.

-*Exact Test* [ZiCh91]. It is applied when the separability condition holds and the loop bounds are compile-time constants. It was applied 365 times (i.e. 71%) and detected 179 independences. This represents an independence detection rate of 51%.

-*Banerjee Test* [Bane88]. The test is applied when the loops bounds are known at compile time. It was applied all the times. Its application range is the greater because its application conditions are the least restrictives. The independence detection rate is 42%. In absolute terms, it has detected the greater number of independences. Because of special features of subscript expressions analyzed above, this test can be considered as exact.

-*Interval-Test* [KKP91]. It is applied when the coefficient list with constant loop bounds is no null. It was applied 418 times (i.e. 69%). However it did not detect any independence. This is because this test as well as the GCD test only considers the case of dependence with a direction vector of the form $(*,*,...,*)$. We have known about a later work done by the same autors [PPK91] in which the Interval-Test is generalized to check for data dependence subject to an arbitrary direction vector. We have already implemented it and the results are outstanding.

-λ-*Test* [LYZ91]. It is applied when there are multidimensional array references. We have implemented it to solve the case of two-dimensional array references. Since, as we have said above, there is no array references with more than two dimensions in the analyzed kernels. To apply the test the loop bounds must be compile time constants. It was applied all the times and its detection independence rate was 76%.

- *The Test Sequence*. Here the data dependence tests are applied hierarchically. First we apply the dimension by dimension tests to all dimensions of a pair of multidimensional array references then if independence has not been proven in any dimension the multidimensional λ-Test is applied.

1) It is applied the GCD test. Since two multidimensional array references are independent if they are independent in any dimension, if independence is proven the sequence terminates. Otherwise the sequence goes on.

2) The Exact Test is applied. If dependence is proven the sequence terminates and other dimension is tested. In case dependence is proven in each individual dimension of the multidimensional array it is unclear if there is dependence when all dimensions are considered simultaneously. That is why we proceed to the multidimensional Test.

3) If Test (1) does not succeed and Test (2) does not apply the Banerjee Test is applied. If independence is proven the test terminates, otherwise it goes on with the next one.

4) The I-Test is applied. A returned value of yes means that independence is proven and the test terminates, and a returned value of no means that dependence is proven and we proceed to apply the multidimensional Test as we have explain in (2). If the I-Test returns a value of uncertain to err on the safe side, a dependence must be supposed.

5) The multidimensional λ-Test is applied when independence has not been proven by test (1)-(4) in any dimension.

4. Discussion of Results.

Table 2 shows the number of detected independence levels between one-dimensional array reference pairs and two-dimensional array reference pairs. We measured that the Banerjee test is the fastest one. From data shown below in Table 2, it is also the test with a greater independence detection capability. In all cases, the independences detected for the other algorithm tests when applied alone, were a subset of the ones detected for itself. Even the use of the hierarchy does not improve the independence results obtained by the only use of the Banerjee Test.

Tests	DimVar=1	DimVar=2
GCD	0	0
EXACT	6	180
BANERJEE	8	202
I-TEST	0	0
λ-TEST	No applicable	202
SEQUENCE	8	202

Table 2: Number of detected independences.

From these results it is clear that there is none hierarchy more efficient that apply the Banerjee test in all cases. This is in this way, because of the special features of the subscripts expressions that appear in the analyzed Kernels.

REFERENCES

[Bane88]   U. Banerjee. *"Dependence Analysis for Supercomputing"*. Norwell, Kluwer Academic, 1988.

[KKP91]   X. Kong, D. Klappholz, K. Psarris. *"The I-test: An Improved Test for Automatic Parallelization and Vectorization"*, in IEEE Transactions on Parallel and Distributed Systems, Vol. 2, No. 3, July 1991.

[LYZ91]   Z. Li, P. Yew, and C. Zhu. *"An efficient Data Dependence Analysis for Parallelizing Compilers"*, in IEEE Transactions on Parallel and Distributed Systems, Vol. 2, No. 3, July 1991.

[PKK91]   K. Psarris, X. Kong, D. Klappholz. *"Extending the I-Test to Direction Vectors"*, in Proc. of the Int. Conf. on Supercomputing, Cologne, Germany, June 1991.

[SLY90]   Z. Shen, Z. Li and P. Yew. *"An empirical study of Fortran Programs for Parallelizing Compilers"*, in IEEE Transactions on Parallel and Distributed Systems, Vol. 1, No. 3, July 1990.

[ZiCh91]   H. Zima, B. Chapman. *"Supercompilers for Parallel and Vector Computers"*. Addisson-Wesley 91.

Cyclic Weighted Reference Counting without Delay

Richard E. Jones[1] and Rafael D. Lins[1,2]

[1] University of Kent at Canterbury, Canterbury, U.K., CT2 7NF
[2] Dept. de Informática, U.F.P.E., Recife, Brazil

1   Introduction

Many algorithms for storage reclamation in loosely-coupled systems have been based on mark-scan garbage collection. This is an expensive process for distributed systems requiring substantial communication and termination detection. Reference counting suggests itself as an attractive method but is unable to reclaim cycles. Parallel systems complicate matters as care must be taken to avoid reclaiming live objects (e.g. if reference counting operations are executed out of order). We present a scheme based upon weighted reference counting but able to reclaim cycles. Cycles are handled by by garbage collecting subgraphs, concurrently with useful processing. Three colours and a secondary reference count per cell are required. For computations that do not create cycles, our scheme has the same communication overheads as weighted reference counting.

Weighted Reference Counting (WRC) makes reference counting practical for use in loosely-coupled architectures [1, 5] by sending messages only when references are deleted. A *weight* is associated with each pointer and a cell's reference count field contains the total weight of all pointers that refer to the cell. We denote a pointer from a cell R to cell S by <R,S>, its weight by Weight(<R,S>) and the reference count of cell S by RC(S). We describe the algorithms in this paper in terms of three primitive operations: New, Copy and Delete.

New(R) gets a fresh cell U from the free-list, initialises its RC and the weight of <R,U> to some fixed value. Copy(R,<S,T>) duplicates the pointer <S,T> by splitting its weight equally between <R,T> and <S,T>, thereby avoiding communication with T to change its RC. Indirection cells are used when copying pointers of weight 1. Delete (<R,S>) must send a message to the target S to decrement its RC by the weight of <R,S>. This is the only operation that requires communication: messages do not need to be synchronised.

Lazy Cyclic Reference Counting (LCRC) combines reference counting with lazy four-colour mark-scan garbage collection [2]. New and Copy are similar to those of the standard algorithm, as is the deletion of the last reference to an object.

Research sponsored by the British Council HED link, CNPq (Brazil) grants No 40.9110/88.4 and 46.0782/89.4, and CAPES (Brazil) grant 2487/91-08

Extended version of this paper is available by anonymous ftp from unix.hensa.ac.uk in /pub/misc/ukc.reports/comp.sci/reports/28-92.

However, if the target of a deleted pointer is shared then it may be part of an isolated, garbage, cycle. It is painted black and a reference to it is placed on a *control queue*. No further action is taken until either the free-list becomes empty or the control queue is full.

When either of these events occur, cells are popped from the control queue until a black one is found. Cells in the transitive closure of this cell are then marked and scanned to find any references from cells external to this subgraph. If none are found the subgraph is garbage and is returned to the free-list. Garbage collection proceeds in three phases. In the first phase all cells in the closure are painted *red*. Each time a cell is visited its RC is decremented. On completion only those cells that are the target of an external reference will have non-zero RCs. The task of the second phase is to discover any such cells. They and their descendants are re-painted *green* and their RCs are corrected. All other cells are painted *blue*. The last phase returns blue cells to the free-list.

Plainfossé and Shapiro [4] emphasised that an earlier version[3] of our algorithm was not truly concurrent. We now remove this deficiency.

2   The Algorithm

Our new algorithm combines the benefits of WRC—low communication overheads—and LCRC—efficient handling of cycles. Pointers have weights, cells one of three colours *green, red, blue*—the meanings are the same as LCRC—and a second reference count (SRC) used only by the garbage collector. New behaves in the same way as in WRC and in LCRC but care is taken to simulate the effect of any garbage collection phase that might be in operation by colouring the new cell the same as its parent and setting SRC to 0.

```
New(R) = allocate(U)
         RC(U) = W
         Weight(<R,U>) = W
         colour(U) := colour(R)
         SRC(U) := 0
```

Copy(R,<S,T> is similar to WRC unless S is currently subject to garbage collection; we discuss this problem later.

```
Copy(R,<S,T>) = if Weight(<S,T>) > 1 {
                    Weight(<S,T>) := Weight(<S,T>)/2
                    Weight(<R,T>) := Weight(<S,T>)
                    if red(S) {send retract(<S,T>) to T}}
                else {allocate(U)
                    RC(U) := W
                    SRC(U) := 0
                    colour(U) := colour(S)
                    Weight(<U,T>) := 1
                    Weight(<S,U>) := W/2
                    Weight(<R,U>) := W/2
                    insert(U, control_set)}
```

Delete(<R,S>) sends a message to S to reduce its RC by the weight of <R,S>. If S was shared it becomes a candidate for garbage collection and is added to the control set.

```
Delete(<R,S>) = send Delete(<R,S>) to S
                remove <R,S>

Handle_Delete(<R,S>) = RC(S) := RC(S) - Weight(<R,S>)
                       if RC(S) = 0 {
                           for <S,T> in Sons(S) {
                               send Delete(<S,T>) to T}
                           green(S)
                           free(S)}
                       else {insert(S, control_set)}
```

The control set is used to delay mark-scan in the hope that it will prove unnecessary (either the cell's last reference will have been deleted or scan_green will prove that it is still active) and for communication between mutators and collectors. The garbage collector gc removes items from the control set and collects from the subgraph of which these are the roots. Other processors may also wish to garbage collect so care must be taken to avoid interference thereby losing colour and weight information. In the mark_red phase, any processor that wishes to do so is allowed to initiate marking; no processor is allowed to start either scanning or collecting until the end of the phase. Only a subset of processing elements need be involved in this garbage collection at any time. Rules for the other phases are similar.

```
gc() = S := pop(control_set)
       RENDEZVOUS; mark_red(S)
       RENDEZVOUS; scan(S)
       RENDEZVOUS; collect_blue(S)
```

mark_red traces the transitive closure of its starting point. As each pointer is traversed, the SRC of its target cell is decremented by the weight of the pointer. On completion, red cells will only have a non-zero SRC if there are references to them from cells external to the subgraph that have not been visited by this, or another, mark_red. We emphasise that only a subset of the graph is marked: this may span processing elements.

```
mark_red(S) = if not red(S) {
                  redden(S)
                  SRC(S) := RC(S)
                  for <S,T> in Sons(S) {send mark_red(<S,T>) to T}}

Handle_mark_red(<S,T>) = if not red(T) {
                             redden(T)
                             SRC(T) := RC(T) - Weight(<S,T>)
                             for <T,U> in Sons(T) {
                                 send mark_red(<T,U>) to U}}
                         else {SRC(T) := SRC(T) - Weight(<S,T>)}
```

Copying a pointer from a red cell a subtle problem. mark_red has decremented the target's SRC by the weight of the pointer, but this value has now been halved. retract is used to preserve the invariant. This requires point to point messages to be delivered in order.

715

```
Handle_retract(<S,T>) = RC(T) := RC(T) + Weight(<S,T>)/2
```
Having removed the effect of internal pointers, scan is called to search for cells with external references which are be considered to be roots of active subgraphs and are re-painted green by scan_green. Cells not visited by scan_green are garbage and are marked blue.

```
scan(S) = if red(R) {
               if RC(S) > 0 {scan_green(S)}
               else {blue(S)
                     for <S,T> in Sons(S) {send scan(T) to T}}}

Handle_scan(T) = scan(T)

scan_green(S) = if not green(S) {
                    green(S)
                    for <S,T> in Sons(S) {
                        send scan_green(<S,T>) to T}}

Handle_scan_green(<S,T>) = scan_green(T)
```
Finally collect_blue returns blue cells to the free-list. Pointer from blue cells are Deleted.

```
collect_blue(S) = if blue(S) {
                      for <S,T> in Sons(S) {
                          send collect_blue(<S,T>) to T
                          remove <S,T>}}
                  free(S)

Handle_collect_blue(<S,T>) = if blue(T) {collect_blue(T)}
                             else {Handle_Delete(<S,T>)}
```
When a cell is returned to the free-list, it is removed from the control set. Since cells are only added to the control set by Delete which requires communication anyway they can be added to their local control set.

References

1. D.I. Bevan. Distributed garbage collection using reference counting. In *PARLE'87*, LNCS 259:176–187, Springer Verlag, 1987.
2. R.D. Lins. Cyclic reference counting with lazy mark-scan. *Information Processing Letters*, 44(4):215–220, 1992.
3. R.D. Lins and R.E. Jones. Cyclic weighted reference counting. Proceedings of WP&DP'93, K. Boyanov (editor), North-Holland, 1993.
4. D.Plainfossé and M.Shapiro. Experience with fault-tolerant garbage collection in a distributed Lisp system. In *IWMM*, LNCS 637:116–133, Springer Verlag, 1992.
5. P. Watson and I. Watson. An efficient garbage collection scheme for parallel computer architectures. In *PARLE'87*, LNCS 259:432–443, Springer Verlag, 1987.

Parallel Optimisation of Join Queries Using an Enhanced Iterative Improvement Technique

Maria Spiliopoulou, Yiannis Cotronis, Michalis Hatzopoulos

Department of Informatics, University of Athens, Panepistimiopolis, TYPA
Buildings, GR-157 71 Ilisia, Athens, Greece

Abstract. A parallel optimisation technique for large join queries is presented.
The technique processes the search space of query execution plans twice: the
first scan is based on iterative improvement; the second scan uses the results of
the first one to reduce the search space, in order to find an optimal solution
faster. Two scheduling algorithms are studied for the imple-mentation of the
technique. Experiments showing the behaviour of the technique are presented.

1 Introduction

Information retrieval in complex applications involves large join queries, for the optimisation of which researchers study methods with overhead increasing polynomially
to the query size: iterative improvement, simulated annealing and their combinations
yield the best results [2, 3, 6, 7]. These techniques find one local minimum per "start
state" in the "search space" [3], and then select the smallest local minimum as the
global one. This process can be parallelised by processing start states independently.

Parallel query execution is widespread; parallel query optimisation is less studied.
In this study, we propose a parallel variation of Iterative Improvement, the "two-
phase II-technique", showing that optimisation can be improved by parallelism, both
by reducing its overhead and by improving the quality of the optimal plan it produces.

2 An Enhanced Variation of Parallelised Iterative Improvement

Acccording to the terminology of [3, 6], the search space of our model consists of the
possible join trees for a query. The initial state is the unoptimised tree produced from
the user query; start states are produced by random transformations on this state. For
each start state, the technique performs an "optimisation run", i.e. it finds a local minimum by executing a series of moves [4]. The termination criterion is an upper limit T
on the total duration of the process. $T:=T(n):=C*n^3$, since the technique processes n
start states, where n is the "query size", i.e. the number of joins on the tree. The
technique performs two scans (in 2 phases) over the search space in parallel mode.We
assume a MIMD machine with p+1 processors: p ones execute the n "LM-constructors", i.e. the optimisation runs, while the last one acts as "coordinator" among them.

In Phase 1, LM-constructors are initiated for all start states and run for a time span
$T1 = c1 * n^3$, where $c1 < C$. By the end of Phase 1, local minima have been computed
for some start states, while the remaining start states have ended in "pending states",
i.e. their runs were interrupted upon expiration of T1. The coordinator sorts the
pending states in ascending order according to the coefficient of the speed of reaching
the PGM cost from a pending state PS. Let dMoves be the number of downhill moves
performed during the optimisation run, and let PScost, StScost, PGMcost be the cost
of the pending state, its start state and the PGM, respectively. Then:

speed_coef = dMoves * (PScost - PGMcost) / (StScost - PScost)

In Phase 2, LM-constructors are initiated to process the pending states in passes of p runs. The time span is $T2 = c2 * n^3$, where $c2 < C-c1$. Upon expiration of T2, all final states are returned to the coordinator, and the state with the lowest cost is the Global Minimum.The aim of Phase 2 is to improve the quality of a potential global minimum already available. So, the pending states selected for it must be the best candidates to produce a final state with lower cost than PGM. For this selection we use as criterion the speed of cost decrease in an optimisation run, taking into account the distance between the cost of the state finally reached and the PGM.

3 Parallel Versions of the Two-Phase Iterative Improvement

For the proposed technique, we consider a software-reconfigurable discless back-end transputer machine.We use a star of stars configuration, placing the coordinator in the center of the central star [5]; for query execution we use a different configuration [4].

At the beginning of Phase 1, the coordinator forwards the intial state and a para-meter for the construction of each start state to its neighbours, which keep a number of start states and forward the rest to their further neighbours. The execution of an optimisation run begins as soon as the start state is created by the processor. During time T1, the processors return local minima to the coordinator. As local minima are not processed further, any processor P1 across the route towards the coordinator may discard a local minimum received by a neighbour P2, if the state currently processed by P1 has already lower cost. So, communication during Phase 1 is reduced and localised. The same holds for the gathering of results at the end of Phase 2.

In order to make best use of the available parallelism, we simulated some alternative scheduling policies for the LM-constructors on the p processors, drawing analogies from other scheduling policies we have developed [1].

The Synchronous Approach. In Phase 1, all start states are loaded on the p proces-sors: all runs are executed together, and each processor performs multitasking with time slicing. As runs are completed, the freed resources are given to the remaining runs on the same processor. This approach has the advantage that all start states are processed simultaneously and results for all of them are used for the ordering of pending states. The impact of long runs is limited to the processors they are loaded on; the progress of other runs is not directly impedded. Moreover, our experiments have shown that some optimisation runs produce local minima very fast, whereas they quit and free their resources. This approach is not appropriate for Phase 2, because the simultaneous execution of all runs spoils the notion of ordering of pending states.

The Asynchronous Approach. In Phase 2, the coordinator sends the first p pending states to the p processors. Each processor performs one run to completion or until the time limit is reached. Upon completion of a run, the processor returns its results to the coordinator and processes the next pending state. Since each processor uses all resources for each single run, some local minima are certainly produced within the time span. Moreover, since pending states are ordered, long runs at the beginning of the queue preventing the execution of runs at its end, do not affect the final result.

This approach is not appropriate for Phase 1: if p or more long runs occur, it is not ensured that all start states will be processed before reaching the time limit. Then the remaining start states must be processed before the pending states in Phase 2. So, the results used in Phase 2 are not drawn from all runs, and Phase 2 itself is delayed.

4 Performance Results of the Parallel Two-Phase II-Technique

In our experiments, the query size was varied between 20 and 40. We present analytical results for $n=31$ joins. The number of processors is kept constant, since its value affects C. For the time span $T=C*n^3$, we set C according to previous measurements [4] after some tuning for the current series of query sizes. For $T1 = c1*n^3$, we set $c1 = (2/3) * C$ after experimenting on snapshots of Phase 1.

The speed coefficients for the pending states by the end of Phase 1 are shown in Fig. 1 in ascending order; the further to the right a pending state appears, the smaller is the possibility that its run will be completed before T2 expires. The enumeration of the optimisation runs corresponds to the values of the start parameter used to produce the start states. Start state 13 has produced the PGM and has a zero speed coefficient.

For $T2 = c2*n^3$, we set $c2 = (C-c1)/2$, i.e. $c2 = (1/5) * C$. In order to demonstrate the behaviour of pending states during Phase 2, we allowed the runs of all pending states to complete, so that Fig. 2 contains the final state each of them would reach.

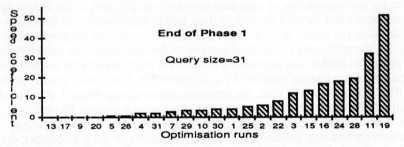

Fig. 1. Expected number of moves towards the PGM per optimisation run

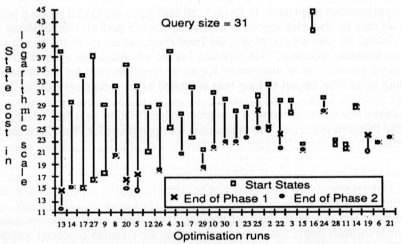

Fig. 2. Evolution of optimisation runs in Phase 1 and Phase 2

The previous assumption was withdrawn for the results on all queries shown in Fig. 3. The initial cost per query size corresponds to the start state which produced the global minimum; the FGM is the final global minimum that would have been produced by Phase 1 in a time span T. Since $T1 + T2 < T$, time savings are ensured.

Thus, the experimental results on a series of queries have confirmed the positive impact of Phase 2 on the base iterative improvement technique, and have shown a judicious usage of parallelism for the simultaneous execution of LM-constructors on Phase 1 and the queued execution of p LM-constructors at a time on Phase 2.

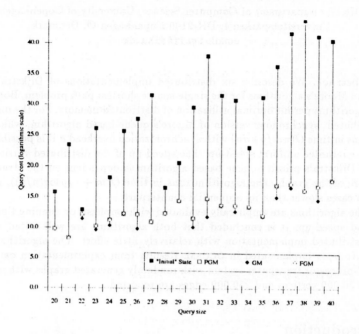

Fig. 3. Evolution of Query Cost by the Two-Phase II-Technique

References

1. J.Y.Cotronis, P.E.Lauer "Two Way Channel with Disconnect", Proc. on the Analysis of Concurrent Systems , LNCS Vol.207, 184-198, 1985
2. Y.E.Ioannidis, Y.C.Kang "Randomized Algorithms for Optimizing Large Join Queries", Proc. ACM-SIGMOD Intl. Conf. on Management of Data (Atlantic City, NJ), 312-321, 1990
3. Y.E.Ioannidis, Y.C.Kang "Left-deep vs. Bushy Trees: An Analysis of Strategy Spaces and its Implications on Query Optimization", Proc. ACM-SIGMOD Intl. Conf. on Management of Data (Denver, Colorado), 168-177, 1991
4. M.Spiliopoulou "Parallel Optimisation and Execution of Queries towards an RDBMS in a Parallel Environment Supporting Pipeline", Ph.D.thesis, University of Athens, Department of Informatics, March 1992 (on Greek)
5. M.Spiliopoulou, M.Hatzopoulos, C.Vassilakis "Using Parallelism and Pipeline for the Optimisation of Join Queries", Proc. Parle'92 Conf. (Paris, France), LNCS Vol.605, 279-294, 1992
6. A.Swami, A.Gupta "Optimization of large join queries", Proc. ACM-SIGMOD Intl. Conf. on Management of Data (Chicago, Illinois), 8-17, Sept. 1988
7. A.Swami "Optimization of large join queries: Combining heuristics and combinatorial techniques", Proc. ACM-SIGMOD Intl. Conf. on Management of Data (Portland, Oregon), 367-376, June 1989

Precis: Distributed Shortest Path Algorithms

Jesper Larsson Träff

DIKU – Department of Computer Science, University of Copenhagen
Universitetsparken 1, DK-2100 Copenhagen Ø, Denmark
email: traff@diku.dk

Abstract. We describe six distributed implementations of Dijkstra's and Moore's algorithms for the single-source shortest path problem. Both algorithms permit optimal utilization of distributed memory. For the distributed, synchronous version of Moore's queue-based algorithm, which runs in time $O(nm/p+\sigma n)$ with synchronization overhead σ it is possible to guarantee uniform speed-up .The speed-up of the distributed version of Dijkstra's priority-queue based algorithm is dependent on the structure of the graph. The algorithm runs in time $O(m + n/p \log(n/p))$, in no cases slower than its sequential counterpart.
The algorithms are empirically evaluated with emphasis on running time and speed-up. It is concluded that both algorithms are well suited to distributed implementation with relatively little effort. The algorithms have been implemented in OCCAM. Results from experimentation on a 17-processor transputer system with randomly generated graphs with up to 20,000 vertices and 250,000 edges are reported.

1 Introduction

The single-source shortest path problem is an important, well-studied optimization problem. Very fast sequential algorithms exist, hence the problem presents special challenges to algorithms for distributed systems. Parallel algorithms for various machine models have been proposed (see [Tra93b] for references) but only rarely for distributed systems. Our work indicates that existing sequential algorithms can be modified to perform well on a distributed system.

A tightly coupled distributed system consists of a fixed number p of identical, interconnected processors with no shared memory, which exchange information by explicitly passing messages. There are (at least) two requirements to distributed algorithms for such systems. First, utilization of available storage should be close to optimal, making it possible to solve problems p times larger on a p-processor system than on a single-processor system. This requirement implies that all large data structures have to be evenly distributed and that only limited replication of data can be tolerated. Second, a distributed algorithm must on average exhibit speed-up greater than 1 and in no cases run slower than the corresponding sequential algorithm.

Experiments with three distributed versions of Dijkstra's and Moore's algorithms implemented in the CSP-based language OCCAM have been carried out on a 17-processor transputer system. All algorithms are space optimal, and the best versions – the distributed minimal Dijkstra algorithm and the synchronized Moore algorithm – exhibit speed-up of about 4 on 16 processors.

2 Problem, algorithms and distributed data structures

Given a weighted, directed graph $G = (V, E, c)$, $E \subseteq V \times V$, $c : E \to \mathbf{R}$, and a source vertex $s \in V$, the single-source shortest path problem consists in finding the shortest paths from s to all other vertices of G.

Dijkstra's and Moore's algorithms iteratively maintain tentative distances from s to the other vertices of G. Each iteration selects a vertex and updates the tentative distances to all adjacent vertices. Dijkstra's algorithm greedily selects a vertex whose tentative distance is smallest using a priority queue, whereas Moore's algorithm processes vertices in first-in, first-out fashion using an ordinary queue. Dijkstra's algorithm processes each vertex once. In Moore's algorithm each vertex may enter the queue n times.

The graph is represented as adjacency lists and the edges are distributed evenly among the processors subject to the following: if vertex v is stored at processor i so are all edges $(v, w) \in E$. A mapping $\pi : V \to \{1, \ldots, p\}$ computable by all processors tells where each vertex is stored. For such *vertex distributed graphs* each processor needs to maintain only a fragment of the queue of size n/p, amounting to a storage demand of $O(m/p + n/p)$. Hence storage utilization is optimal. Algorithms based on a different distribution of the graph are presented in [Tra93a].

All processors run the same program, derived from the sequential algorithms as described in the next sections. Whenever vertex v is selected by processor i, updates on adjacent vertices w for which $\pi(w) \neq i$ have to be sent to processor $\pi(w)$. The algorithms differ in *how* and *when* this is done.

3 Dijkstra's algorithm: distributed priority queue

Global minimum algorithm: In this version the graph and priority queue are distributed, but the computation is not: only one processor which has a vertex of smallest tentative distance is allowed to perform updates. Processor i possess the global minimum if the locally smallest tentative distance is less than or equal to the smallest distance update sent to all other processors. When this condition no longer holds, control is passed to the processor to which the smallest update was sent. Extra storage requirement is $O(p)$, running time is $O(m + n/p \log(n/p))$ and no speed-up is possible in practice. If all updates to vertices of processor j are sent in chunks (of size at most n/p) the total number of messages is $O(pn)$. **Distributed algorithm:** In the version above only one processor is active at a time. However, correctness is not violated by letting *all* processors select vertices and perform updates concurrently. This *relaxation* brings out parallelism inherent in the problem, since it may happen that several vertices, although not globally smallest will nevertheless have their correct tentative distance. If selected in parallel these will all produce correct updates. Under reasonable assumptions about the distributed system, the total number of messages becomes $O(np^2)$. It can be proved that the complexity is not changed, but the algorithm suffers from a large number of messages. Uniform speed-up cannot be guaranteed, since all but one processor may do work which at a later time has to be redone. Vertices which are processed more than once are called *ghost vertices* and correspond to work which would not have been done by the sequential algorithm. **Distributed minimal algorithm:** The number of messages can be reduced by postponing the time at which updates are sent to the latest possible instant such that the complexity is not increased: when the selected vertex is not globally smallest updates have to be sent. This is achieved by combining the above two algorithms: all processors are allowed to perform updates, but only one which has a vertex of smallest tentative distance is allowed to send it's updates to other processors. A drawback is a relatively complicated protocol to keep track of the global minimum, but this can be relaxed such that the decision to send is taken using only local information. This algorithm is called *distributed minimal*. There is no extra storage requirement and the number of messages is again $O(np)$. The idea is similar to the token-algorithms of [CHL93], the difference being that the decision to pass on a token is independent of the shortest-path computation.

4 Moore's algorithm: distributed queue

Distributed algorithm: The distributed Moore algorithm is similar to the distributed Dijkstra algorithm, but since the algorithm performs n passes over the queue, the number of messages (again under reasonable assumptions about the system) becomes prohibitive, $O(n^2p)$ (even worse it is not even possible to guarantee polynomial running time, since a vertex may enter a queue more than n times).

Synchronous algorithm: Moore's algorithm performs up to n passes over the queue and at each pass all vertices can be processed independently. In the synchronous algorithm each processor performs updates until it's queue is empty. The processors then synchronize by exchanging the updated vertices. Running time of this algorithm is $O(n(m/p) + \sigma n)$ where the *synchronization time* σ is proportional to $p(n/p) = n$.

Asynchronous algorithm: The asynchronous version is an in-between the two previous algorithms, which alleviates the deficiency of the distributed algorithm by postponing update-propagation until the local queue is empty.

5 Experimental results

A series of experiments with the six distributed algorithms have been carried out. Randomly generated graphs of the following types have been used: complete graphs with 250 and 500 vertices, sparse graphs with 5000 and 10000 vertices and out-degree between 17 and 25 (about 100,000 to 200,000 edges), and very sparse graphs with 20000 vertices and up to 130,000 edges (out-degree between 4 and 9). All graphs have integer weights in the interval $[1, 500]$. Experiments with graphs with special structure (planar, road-maps, etc.) are still due.

Running times $T(p)$ are given in seconds as a function of the number of processors. The tables also list the number of messages ("mess.") and the number of ghost vertices (and, for the global minimum algorithm, the number of minimum-messages).

5.1 Results for Dijkstra's algorithm

$|V|$	Global minimum $T(16)$	mess.	min.	Distributed $T(16)$	mess.	ghost	Distributed minimal $T(1)$	$T(2)$	$T(4)$	$T(8)$	$T(16)$	mess.	ghost
250	4.8	2172	183	1.1	3584	28	1.3	0.8	0.5	0.5	0.7	1851	75
500	9.1	2365	172	2.3	6653	17		2.6	1.5	1.0	1.1	1973	47
5000	44.7	26841	2160	12.3	49077	223	7.0	4.4	3.1	2.8	3.6	12138	215
10000	67.7	38307	2769	24.4	97552	390		9.0	5.9	4.8	5.6	17571	273
20000	114.4	64031	7498	25.6	96795	752	22.6	13.5	8.8	8.0	9.9	29624	1292

5.2 Results for Moore's algorithm

$|V|$	Distributed $T(16)$	mess.	Asynchronous $T(16)$	mess.	Synchronous $T(1)$	$T(2)$	$T(4)$	$T(8)$	$T(16)$	mess.
250	2.0	7201	0.9	1040	3.6	2.1	1.2	0.8	0.8	1606
500	4.6	14608	2.3	1484		8.1	4.3	2.6	1.8	1680
5000	30.9	131887	4.6	5229	11.9	7.4	4.8	3.6	3.2	3984
10000	61.1	260943	8.2	6708		15.5	10.0	7.1	5.7	4467
20000	55.9	229682	9.5	12593	21.2	14.0	9.0	5.9	4.5	4784

6 Discussion

The distributed minimal algorithm based on Dijkstra's algorithm and the synchronous and asynchronous versions of Moore's algorithm qualify as acceptable distributed algorithms. A full treatment can be found in the report [Tra93b].

References

[CHL93] Jens Clausen, Bjarne Hansen, and Per S. Laursen. *Distributed Shortest Path Algorithms Based on Token Passing.* Technical Report, Department of Computer Science, University of Copenhagen (DIKU), 1993.

[Tra93a] Jesper Larsson Träff. *A comparison of two distributed algorithms for the single-source shortest path problem based on Dijkstra's algorithm.* Technical Report, Department of Computer Science, University of Copenhagen (DIKU), 1993.

[Tra93b] Jesper Larsson Träff. *Distributed Data Structures in Distributed Shortest Path Algorithms.* Technical Report, Department of Computer Science, University of Copenhagen (DIKU), 1993.

A DISABLING OF EVENT STRUCTURES

Nikolay A.ANISIMOV

Institute of Automation and Control Processes
Far East Division of the Russian Academy of Sciences
5 Radio Street, Vladivostok, 690041, Russia

E-Mail: *anisimov@iapu2.marine.su*

Abstract. It is well-recognized that event structures are a very suitable model for defining a true concurrency semantic for parallel algebraic languages like CCS and CSP. To define such a semantics in a denotational style a set of operations on the domain of event structures has been introduced. In this paper we add a new operation to this set. It corresponds to a well-known disabling operation in LOTOS, a specification language for distributed systems. A refinement operation is used which simplifies the whole definition. The problem of adequacy of the new operation is discussed. In particular, its consistency is proved by demonstrating how the original interleaving semantics is retrieved from the new one.

1. INTRODUCTION

At present, there are two main approaches to the description and verification of concurrent systems usually called *interleaving* and *true concurrency*. The first one is characterized by a well established theory and algebraic nature which enable us to describe and verify concurrent systems in a compositional fashion. Unfortunately, concurrency is treated in a quite restricted way as a non-deterministic choice which is insufficient for many applications. There are several algebraic theories, e.g. CCS, TCSP, ACP, etc., which will be referred to as CCSP [Ol] in the following.

The second approach based on the Petri net theory allows one to treat concurrency in a more explicit and natural way. However, the Petri net theory has no properties of compositionality and modularity. Several efforts were recently made to combine the two approaches by defining for CCSP-like languages non-interleaving semantics based on Petri nets or related models. Thus branch of concurrency theory is of great importance because CCSP-like languages give rise to some parallel languages of practical significance like OCCAM and LOTOS.

Event structures which were first introduced in [NPW] play a key role in defining true concurrency semantics of CCSP-like languages. They are very suitable for describing concurrent processes, permitting to explicitly describe concurrency, causality and conflict relations. They are more mathematically tractable then Petri nets but, at the same time have close relations to them. A set of CCSP-like operations on the domain of event structures has been defined in order to provide CCSP with a true concurrency semantics in a denotational fashion. Most of them, namely prefixing, choice (sum), hiding, parallel composition are easily defined.

At the same time, another important operation in process algebras that is widely used for the specification of distributed systems and communication protocols in particular. First, we should point out a disabling operation of LOTOS, a language for the specification of distributed and parallel systems. The disabling operation has the following syntax: B1 [>B2 where B1 and B2 are behavior expressions. The semantics of disabling was originally defined in an interleaving form by the following inference rules:

$$\frac{B1\text{-}a\rightarrow B1'}{B1\,[>B2\text{-}a\rightarrow B1'\,[>B2},a\neq\surd\ ;\quad \frac{B1\text{-}\surd\rightarrow B1'}{B1\,[>B2\text{-}\surd\rightarrow B1'}\ ;\quad \frac{B2\text{-}a\rightarrow B2'}{B1\,[>B2\text{-}a\rightarrow B2'} \quad (1.1)$$

Here B-a→B' denotes an execution of action *a* evolving B to B', √ is a special action indicating a successful termination. Thus a process B1[>B2 can behave like B1. But at any time (except the case when B1 is successfully terminated) the process B1[>B2 can start to behave like B2 excluding B1.

Another similar operation called *mode transfer* has been introduced within the framework of an axiomatic approach of ACP [Be], enabling us to transform any process expression containing a mode transfer operation into an equivalent one without this operation likewise the well-known Expansion theorem for the operation of parallel composition.

Thus one can conclude that the disabling operation may be easily defined within the framework of interleaving approach. As in the case with the parallel composition operation, the disabling is not a basic one and, in fact, a shorthand of a sequence of basic operations. But it is not the case with the true concurrency approach where a concurrency relation is defined in an explicit way. In this paper we give the definition of disabling operation of event structures. This paper is a shorten version of the report [An].

2. BASIC NOTIONS

This section outlines some well-known definitions concerning labelled event structures (LES, for short). We will use an earlier version of LES [NPW] sometimes called prime event structures with binary conflict relation. Let *Act* be an alphabet and special symbol √∈*Act* denotes a successful termination. We take this action into account in order to be as close to LOTOS as possible.

2.1 Definition. A *labelled event structure* (over an alphabet *Act*) is a tuple $E=<E,\leq,\#,l>$ where

- E is a set of *events*;
- $\leq \subseteq E\times E$ is a partial order (the causality relation) satisfying the principle of *finite causes*: $\forall e\in E:\{e'\in E\,|\,e'\leq e\}$ is finite;
- $\# \subseteq E\times E$ is an irreflexive, symmetrical relation (the conflict relation) satisfying the principle of *conflict heredity*:
  $$\forall e_1,e_2,e_3\in E:\ e_1\#e_2\leq e_3 \Rightarrow e_1\#e_3$$
- $l:E\to Act$ is a labelled function. ♦

A class of all LES's will be denoted as **E**.

2.2 Definition. Let $E=<E,\leq,\#,l>$ be some labelled event structure and $X\subseteq E$. Then

- X is *left-closed* if $e_1\leq e_2\in X \Rightarrow e_1\in X$;
- X is *conflict-free* if $\#\cap(X\times X)=\varnothing$.

A *configuration* of E is a left-closed, conflict-free subset of E. Let $C(E)$ denote the set of all finite configurations of LES E. ♦

Let $C_\sqrt{}(E)=\{X\in C(E)\,|\,\sqrt{}\in X\}$ be the set of all configurations corresponding to all non-terminal states of LES E, i.e. such states which can be reached without executing the √-action.

In the following, we will use a notion of a refinement of LES's [GlGo]. But, at first, some auxiliary notions are given. Denote the empty LES as $0=<\varnothing,\varnothing,\varnothing,\varnothing>$.

2.3 Definition. A *refinement* is a function $r:Act\to\mathbf{E}\backslash\{0\}$. For event structure E and refinement r the event structure $r(E)$ is defined by

- $E_{r(E)}=\{(e,e')\,|\,e\in E_E,e'\in E_{r(l_E(e))}\}$

- $(e_1,e_1') \leq_{r(E)} (e_2,e_2')$ *iff* $e_1 < e_2$ *or* $(e_1=e_2$ *and* $e_1' \leq_{r(l_E(e))} e_2')$
- $(e_1,e_1') \#_{r(E)} (e_2,e_2')$ *iff* $e_1 \#_E e_2$
- $l_{r(E)} (e,e')=l_{r(l_E(e))} (e')$ ◆

2.4 Definition. Let $E=\langle E,\leq,\#,l\rangle$ be a LES over the alphabet *Act*. Then
$C\text{-}^a{\rightarrow}C'$ *iff* $C,C'\in C(E)$, $C\subseteq C'$, $a\in Act$, $C'\backslash C=\{e\}$, $l(e)=a$;
  We will write $C\text{--}{>}C'$ if $\exists\ a_1,a_2,...,a_n\in Act,C_1,...C_{n-1}\in C(E)$ such that
$C\text{-}^{a1}{\rightarrow}C_1\text{-}^{a2}{\rightarrow}...C_{n-1}\text{-}^{an}{\rightarrow}C'$ ◆

  In fact, we have defined a relation: $\rightarrow\subseteq C(E)\times Act\times C(E)$.

3. A DISABLING OF EVENT STRUCTURES

Now we are ready to define a disabling operation on labelled event structures. The main idea of this definition is quite simple. Namely, for each configuration of the first LES we add a new event labelled by special symbol "*" to set of events and then refine all such events by the second LES.

3.1 Definition. Let $E_1=\langle E_1,\leq_1,\#_1,l_1\rangle$ and $E_2=\langle E_2,\leq_2,\#_2,l_2\rangle$ be labelled event structures. Then the disabling of these LES's is defined to be the LES $E=E_1[>E_2$ that is built as follows:

  $E = r(E')$ where $E'=\langle E',\leq',\#',l'\rangle$,
- $E' = E_1 \cup C_\sqrt{}(E_1)$;
- $\leq' = \leq_1 \cup \{(e_1,e_2)\,|\,e_2\in C_\sqrt{}(E_1),e_1\in e_2\}$;
- $\#' = \#_1 \cup \{(e_1,e_2),(e_2,e_1)\,|\,e_2\in C_\sqrt{}(E_1),e_1\notin e_2\}$
      $\cup \{(e_1,e_2),(e_2,e_1)\,|\,e_1,e_2\in C_\sqrt{}(E_1),e_1\neq e_2\}$;
- $l' = l_1 \cup \{(e,*)\,|\,e\in C_\sqrt{}(E_1)$ where $*\notin Act\}$;
- $r = \{(a,E_a)\,|\,a\in Act\} \cup \{(*,E_2)\}$ ◆

  In other words, we form E' by adding the set of extra events $C_\sqrt{}(E)$ labelled by the new symbol "*" to set of evens, each such an event being in a causal relation with all events contained in it and in a conflict relation with others. Then, we refine all the extra events by E_2.

4. ANALYSIS OF DISABLING OPERATION

When one suggests a new semantics for some language he/she has to demonstrate its consistency with the original semantics of this language. In this particular case when a more general "true concurrency" semantics for CCSP-like language is defined two main criteria of adequacy should be satisfied [Ol]:

i)   the original interleaving semantics of CCSP should be retrievable from a new one
         and

ii)   the *true concurrency* semantics should capture all and only all the parallelism
         presented in the step-semantics of CCSP.

Thus, it is clear what means the adequacy of the new semantics. But, however, we are interested in one operation only and have to show its adequacy. To do this we first should rewrite the criteria of adequacy.

  Operational interleaving semantics of CCSP-like languages including LOTOS is usually defined by means of labelled transition systems. Rewrite their definitions in our settings.

4.1 Definition. A labelled transition system (LTS, for short) over an alphabet *Act* is a tuple $L=<S,\rightarrow,s_0>$ where

- S is a set of states;
- $\rightarrow \subseteq S \times Act \times S$ is a transition relation;
- $s_0 \in S$ is an initial state.

Let L be a class of LTS ♦

Let P be a class of all CCSP-processes, i.e. terms built by operations of CCSP. The original semantics of CCSP-like languages are usually given in Plotkin's operational style as a mapping $\xi_I : P \rightarrow L$ where for each process $P \in P$ a LTS $\xi_I(P)=<P,\rightarrow,P>$ is defined. Here a relation $\rightarrow$ is defined by structural induction on process terms with the aid of inference rules like (1.1) in the introduction.

The denotational approach to the definition the CCSP semantics based on labelled event structures is to define a mapping usually called a valuation $\xi_E : P \rightarrow E$ that, however, is built by quite different way. For each n-ary CCSP-operator $op_{CCSP}(P_1,...,P_n)$ we define a similar operator on the domain of event structures $op_{LES}(E_1,...,E_n)$. A valuation ξ_E is defined by the set of rules of the form:

(*) $\qquad \xi_E[op_{CCSP}(P_1,...,P_n)] = op_{LES}[\xi_E(P_1),...,\xi_E(P_n)]$

The retrievability of original semantics from a new one means that there exists a mapping $\xi_{EI} : E \rightarrow L$ such that for each process $P \in P$ we have $\xi_{EI}[\xi_E[op_{CCSP}(P_1,...,P_n)]] = \xi_I[op_{CCSP}(P_1,...,P_n)]$. Using equation (*) we can rewrite it as follows

(**) $\qquad \xi_{EI}[op_{LES}[\xi_E(P_1),...,\xi_E(P_n)] = \xi_I[op_{CCSP}(P_1,...,P_n)]$

It is clear that if all operations op_{LES} satisfy this equation then the semantics will have the property of retrievability. So equation (**) will be used as a criterion of operation retrievability.

A mapping ξ_{EI} can be naturally defined by interleaving observation of LES: $\xi_{EI}(E)=<C(E),\rightarrow,\varnothing>$ where relation $\rightarrow \subseteq C(E) \times Act \times C(E)$ is the same as that introduced in definition 2.4. Thus in order to prove a retrievability criterion of disabling operation we have to check the following condition: $\xi_{EI}[\xi_E(P_1) [> \xi_E(P_2)] = \xi_I[P_1 [> P_2]$.

4.2 Theorem *(retrievability).* Let $P_1, P_2 \in P$ be two CCSP-processes with operational LTS semantics $L_1 = \xi_I[P_1]$ and $L_2 = \xi_I[P_2]$. Let $E_1 = \xi_E[P_1]$ and $E_2 = \xi_E[P_2]$ be their LES semantics. Assume also the semantics are retrievable, i.e. $\xi_{EI}[\xi_E[P_1]] \approx \xi_I[P_1]$ and $\xi_{EI}[\xi_E[P_2]] \approx \xi_I[P_2]$. Then $\xi_{EI}(\xi_E[P_1] [> \xi_E[P_2]) \approx \xi_I(P_1 [>P_2)$.

Here the relation $\approx$ is a well-known bisimulation relation. The second criterion of adequacy ii) can be proved by a similar way where interleaving expressions should be substituted by step ones including inference rules (1.1), see [An].

REFERENCES

[An]   Anisimov N.A. A Disabling of Event Structures. Internal Report CN-92-01. *Institute of Automation & Control Processes,* Vladivostok, January 1992.

[Be]   Bergstra J.A. A Mode Transfer Operator in Process Algebra. Report P8808, University of Amsterdam, *Programming Research Group,* 1988.

[GlGo] Van Glabbeek, R.J, Goltz U. Equivalence Notions for Concurrent Systems And Refinement of Actions. LNCS, 379, 1989, pp.237-248.

[NPW]   Nielsen M., Plotkin G., Winskel G. Petri Nets, Event Structures and Domains. LNCS, 70, 1979, pp.266-284.

[Ol]   Olderog E.-R. Operational Petri Nets Semantics for CCSP. LNCS, 266, 1987, pp.196-233.

Barrier Semantics in Very Weak Memory

Arnold Pears[1] and Rhys Francis[2]

[1] Dept. of Comp. Sci. and Comp. Eng., La Trobe University, Australia
[2] High Performance Computing, CSIRO, DIT, Australia

Abstract. The fundamental model of memory requires each read to an address to return the most recent value written to the same address. This model becomes a consistency requirement for parallel shared memory machines, and is taken as a necessary property for correct algorithm execution. In Distributed Shared Memory (DSM) systems the presence of processor memory caches means that the processors may develop historical and therefore different views of the distributed memory. The paper examines the relationship between synchronisation and consistency, proposes that synchronisation should enforce consistency, and examines the consequences using barriers as an example. A typical shared memory MIMD program is shown to execute correctly without normal consistency, and the experiment suggests that the relationship between synchronisation and consistency bears further investigation.

1 Introduction

DSM systems support the appearance of shared memory execution on multi-computer hardware. An overview of such systems and a comparison of design issues and facilities can be found in Nitzberg and Lo[3]. This paper concerns systems where the single address space implementation allows processors to address memory locations directly from any node of the machine. Memory consistency is achieved using cache based protocols.

In such systems a read on one processor can occur after a write to the same address on another processor, and receive a value other than the one just written (see figure 1). These read-write inconsistencies can never be eliminated if caches can hold shared values, hence multicomputers must use weak consistency.

If we accept this incoherent view of memory what is its effect on shared memory programs? MIMD programs rely on the implicit consistency implemented by multiprocessor synchronisation to ensure that values have been calculated prior to their use, wherever they may have been calculated.

In systems with weakly coherent memory, synchronisation must be extended to unify processor views of memory as well as coordinate execution schedules. Thus, synchronisation is an event where the threads of a program agree on their execution locations and their views of the program's data.

We define a very weak memory which allows writes to complete before all related network traffic has completed, or before such traffic has even been generated. The price is that processors can now disagree on their views of the temporal ordering of events in a processor's history.

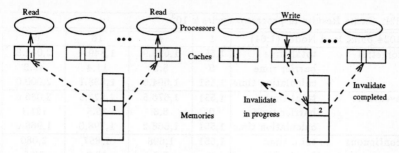

Fig. 1. Inconsistent Views of Memory

2   Establishing Consistency

Continuous consistency is the standard form of weak consistency proposed for multicomputers. It ensures that all processors see the same sequence of writes for each individual processor and that any view of the interleaving of writes between processors could have been generated by a sequential execution of the program.

Eventual consistency assumes that processors joining a barrier will eventually have a consistent view of memory. In effect, eventual consistency requires that the invalidates for all writes be generated and completed in order for the barrier to be satisfied. It is neither efficient nor necessary to generate all the invalidates at the barrier. Instead, invalidation traffic is distributed over the execution time by emitting invalidations when writes occur.

Forgetful consistency assumes that each thread can issue a command that allows it to forget any shared information stored in its cache. Shared cache lines are tagged to indicate shared or unshared status, and a selective flush operation removes all entries marked as shared. Program directed cache flushing has been used in software managed consistency systems such as those proposed by Veidenbaum[7].

One implication of this proposal is that machines relying on selective flushing do not require directories, or invalidation messages and their associated control logic.

3   Experiments

This paper uses the Odin architecture model for the experiments. Odin provides DSM using a mixture of hardware and operating system support. Each node consists of a processor, cache, local memory, link controller, and memory addressing and protection hardware. Caches provide local copies of the program code and data which are being referenced by the threads executing on each node. Further details can be found in [4].

The results are generated using DiST[5,2], which provides accurate and realistic execution driven multicomputer simulation. The experiments assume a wormhole routed hypercube interconnection network, in which the processors of

32K Cache Results in processor cycles x 10^3					
1024 point load Nodes (1:64)		1	4	16	64
forgetful	total time	1,551	1,699.9	1,849.4	2,042.3
	barrier time	0	5.3	11.4	42.3
	calculation time	1,551	1,694.6	1,838.1	2,000.0
eventual	total time	1,551	1,676.5	1,823.5	2,086.6
	barrier time	0	8.3	25.5	121.1
	calculation time	1,551	1,668.2	1,798.0	1,965.5
continuous	total time	1,551	1,698	1,857	2,080
	barrier time	0	5.8	13.8	50.5
	calculation time	1,551	1,692.0	1,843.4	2029.3
cost of refill		0 (0%)	26.4 (1.6%)	40.1 (2.2%)	34.5 (1.7%)

128 Cache Results in processor cycles x 10^3					
1024 point load Nodes (1:64)		1	4	16	64
forgetful	total time	1,491	1,696	1,843.9	2,037.9
	barrier time	0	3.8	9.4	40.9
	calculation time	1,491	1,692.2	1,834.5	1,997
eventual	total time	1,491	1,623.4	1,769.8	1,967.1
	barrier time	0	7.9	28.2	124.9
	calculation time	1,491	1,615.6	1,741.6	1,842.2
continuous	total time	1,491	1,645.4	1,803.1	1,962.8
	barrier time	0	6.9	17.2	54.8
	calculation time	1,491	1,638.5	1,785.9	1,908
cost of refill		0 (0%)	76.6 (4.5%)	92.9 (5%)	154.8 (7.6%)

Fig. 2. Experimental Results

each node cycle at 4 times the memory cycle rate and 8 times the network cycle rate.

The shared memory program used solves the shallow wave equation using a synchronised finite difference scheme[6]. The program's coarse grain parallelism only passes updated values between stages across barrier synchronisation.

Figure 2 presents the experimental results. Additional results may be found in [4]. The problem size was scaled to the machine size to ensure that the ratio of data set size to cache size remains constant from small to large machines. The cost of refilling the processor caches for the *forgetful* model is calculated and presented at the bottom of each table

The tables show that *continuous* consistency is generally slightly faster in execution than either of the other two schemes. However, the performance loss of *forgetful* caching for a 64 node machine is only 2% of the total execution time.

The increase in the calculation and barrier times with machine size is due to the increase in message latency and contention as the number of nodes grows. The *eventual* barrier implementation also generates frequent requests to un-cached addresses to test for barrier completion. This allows processors to generate additional network traffic while previous invalidation traffic is still active. As a result, network usage is heavy at the barrier causing network saturation and significant growth in message latencies.

4 Conclusions

This paper postulates that programs written with explicit synchronisation have a consistency requirement related to the type of synchronisation that they use. For barrier synchronised algorithms, the consistency requirement is that the barrier can only be joined when all outstanding writes have completed and all relevant processors have been notified of the writes. The experiments demonstrate two implementations which satisfy this requirement and within those implementations show correct execution of a typical MIMD program on the resulting incoherent memory model.

This paper is a report on work in progress and as such the experiment raises several questions.

Is it reasonable that all synchronisation within a program be explicitly identified, perhaps by the use of identifiable constructs?

Can consistency requirements be defined for synchronisation constructs other than the barrier and can these consistency requirements be implemented in a reasonable way?

Is the appeal to sequential consistency prevalent in memory consistency research actually required in practical MIMD programs?

If *Forgetful* consistency reduces hardware complexity why should designers chose to implement more complex consistency schemes in machines targeted to high performance scientific codes?

References

1. M. Dubois, and C. Scheurich, "Memory Access Dependencies in Shared–Memory Multiprocessors", Dept. of Elec. Eng., Univ. of Southern California, Los Angeles, CA, *IEEE Trans. on Software Eng.*, Vol. 16, No. 6, June 1990, pp. 660-673.
2. R.S. Francis, I.D. Mathieson, and A.N. Pears, "Compiler Integrated Multiprocessor Simulation", *Int. J. in Comp. Sim.*, Vol 1, No 2, pp. 169-188, 1991.
3. B. Nitzberg, and V. Lo, "Distributed Shared Memory: A Survey of Issues and Algorithms", *IEEE Comp.*, Aug 1991, pp. 52-60.
4. A.N. PEARS, and R.S. FRANCIS, "How Much Consistency is a Good Thing?", *Proc. of the Aust. Comp. Sci. Conf. ACSC-16*, Brisbane. Aust., Feb 3–5, 1993.
5. A.N. PEARS, and R.S. FRANCIS, "Execution Driven Multicomputer Simulation: The DiST Experience.", *2nd Int. Conf. on Modelling and Simulation*, Melb. Aust., July 12-14, 1993, To Appear.
6. R. SADOURNY, "The Dynamics of Finite-Difference Models of the Shallow Water Equations", *Journal of Atmos. Sci.*, Vol 32, 1975, pp. 680-689.
7. A.V. Veidenbaum, "A Compiler–Assisted Cache Coherence Solution for Multiprocessors", *Proc of ICPP*, 1986, pp. 1029-1036.

Using Hammock Graphs to Eliminate Nonstructured Branch Statements

Fubo Zhang and Erik H. D'Hollander

University of Ghent, Department of Electrical Engineering
B-9000 Ghent, Belgium

Abstract. The detection of parallelism is based on the dependence analysis of the program. One of the key problems is to partition the program into independent subtasks in the presence of control statements (MIMD). In this paper the nonstructured control statements are converted into structured ones. In this way, a large block of statements is obtained, and the control dependences of the program are easily converted into manageable parallel tasks.

1 Introduction

The parallelism in a program is detected by analyzing the interstatement *dependences*. In a Fortran program, control dependences arise in block-if, DO and branch statements. Although the data dependence techniques have been developed for a long time [1, 3], nonstructured control dependences have not received a lot of attention, because control dependences involving goto statements are not easily handled. In previous works, Allen, J.R [1, 2], proposed a method to eliminate nonstructured branches by using a *guard command* for each statement. Since guard commands keep the backward branches in the program there are unclear control regions in the resulting program, which is not the case for a block-structured program.

A new approach is proposed in this paper, which converts nonstructured control statements into nested block-if's and iterative structures. The advantages of this conversion are the following. First, the program is converted into a set of nested control structures. This makes it possible to schedule and distribute the tasks[4]. Secondly, by grouping and structuring the statements, the task-granularity of the program is enhanced. Finally, because the resulting program has a properly nested structure, *artificial dependences* are eliminated easily and additional parallelism may be extracted within each of the nested program segments.

This paper describes the approach of using hammock graphs to eliminate nonstructured branch statements. Informally, a hammock graph represents a region of the program bounded by two statements. All possible execution trajectories must enter the hammock graph at its beginning statement n_0 and leave it at the end statement n_e. Consequently, any transformation which is valid for the hammock graph is valid for the whole program. In this paper we will select minimal hammock graph?? of a branch statement and convert the branch statements inside this graph into structured control statements. The elimination of multiple *interacting* branches is done by three types of code transformations: Forward Copy, Backward Copy and Cut .

2 The conversion of branch statements

A branch can be classified into three types[2]: *forward branch, backward branch* and *exit-jump branch*. If a forward or backward branch occurs within a loop, we assume that its target is at the same loop level, otherwise one has an exit-jump branch.

Forward branches

If a forward branch $s1$ interacts with other branches which occur after branch $s1$, there exists a *minimal hammock graph* [5] $MHG_{s1} = < N', E', s1, s6, s1 >$ (see program (a)). The *shared* statements of $s1$ are the statements between the target of $s1$ and the terminal node $s6$. The *forward copy* duplicates the shared statements as the *true* part of the forward branch $s1$. The statements on the path from $s1$ to $s6$, excluding $s1$ and $s6$, are put into the *false* part of $s1$. Consider the following program(a).

```
s1    IF (J.LT.N) GOTO 60 --+              s1    IF (J.LT.N) THEN
s2       A = B+I              |             s4'       A = B+A
s3    IF (A.GT.10) GOTO 80 -|--+            s5'       B = B-1
s4 60    A = B+A  <----------+  |           ELSE
s5       B = B-1                |           s2        A = B+I
s6 80 B = A-5     <------------+            s3        IF (A.LE10)) THEN
                                            s4 60         A = B+A
                                            s5            B = B-1
                                                       ENDIF
                                                    ENDIF
                                            s6 80 B = A - 5
        (a)                                       (b)
```

The two forward branches $s1$ and $s3$ interact. The shared statements $s4, s5$ are duplicated into $s4', s5'$ as the true branch of $s1$ and statements $s2, s3, s4, s5$ as the false branch of $s1$ (see program (b)). After the Forward Copy, both block-if's are hammock graphs.

Backward branches

For the purpose of representing the structured control statements, two structured control statements, *while* and *repeat*, are introduced. Assume a backward branch i_b interacts with other forward or backward branches. Furthermore suppose i_b is an initial backward branch, then there exists a *minimal hammock graph* MHG_{i_b}. A backward branch is equivalent to a repeat statement. Since the body of a repeat statement is executed at least once, it is possible to convert the repeat statement into a while statement. This is done by duplicating the body in front of the loop, changing the repeat statement into a while statement and adjusting the loop condition. The benefit of this operation is that the targets of the incoming branches are also moved outside the while loop; therefore no branches point into the loop body. This process of converting backward branches is known as *Backward Copy*.

The following code is an example of a *Backward Copy*

```
s1    IF (A.GT.10) GOTO 60--+        s1    IF (A.GT.10) GOTO 60 -+
s2 80    B = B+10 <----------|--+    s2' 80   B = B+10              |
s3       A = B+A          |  |       s3'      A = B+A               |
s4 60    sum = sum+A <-------+  |    s4' 60   sum = sum+A <-------+
s5    IF (sum.LT.100) GOTO 80---+    s5    WHILE (sum.GE.1000) DO
                                     s2       B = B+10
                                     s3       A = B+A
                                     s4       sum = sum+A
                                           ENDWHILE
        (c)                                   (d)
```

The backward branch $s5$ creates an iterative structure with the loop body $s2, s3$ and $s4$. This is a 'repeat' iterative structure (see program (c)) and the statements of $s2, s3$ and $s4$ are duplicated to the front of target $s2$ which are denoted $s2', s3'$ and $s4'$. Then the labels of 60 and 80 are moved to new statements. Finally, the branch $s5$ is moved to the front of its target $s2$ and converted into a *while* loop over statements $s2, s3$ and $s4$ (see the program (d)).

Exit-jump branches

```
s1 80 B = B+10   <--------------+              REPEAT
s2    IF (A.LE.0.0) GOTO 60 --+ |    s1 80    B = B+10
s3       A = B+A            | |      s2       IF (A.LE.0.0) THEN
s4       sum = sum+A        | |      s2'         br1 = .TRUE.
s5    IF (sum.LT.100) GOTO 80-|-+    s2''         EXIT
      ...                     |               ENDIF
                              |      s3       A = B+A
s6 60 A = A+10   <------------+      s4       sum = sum+A
                                     s5       UNTIL (sum.GE.100)
                                           IF (.NOT.br1) THEN
                                              ...
                                           ENDIF
                                     s6 60 A = A+10
        (e)                                   (f)
```

Unlike the other branches, an exit-jump branch will terminate the execution of one or more loops. *Backward Copy* can not eliminate the exit branches from the loop, because when the statements are duplicated, the original exit-jump branches remain in the loop. Therefore the *Cut* conversion is used to solve this problem. Program (e) and (f) describe this method:

The backward branch $s5$ results in an iterative structure. The termination of the loop does not only depend on the value of $s5$'s expression, but also on the forward branch $s2$ (see program (e)). A new temporary variable br1 is introduced to register the value of the forward expression. The forward branch is *cut* into two forward branches. The first is an exit statement: when a jump happens $br1 =$.TRUE. and the exit statement transfers the control to end of the loop. The second is a forward branch which is appended after the loop and transfers the control to the proper targets according to the logical variable br1. The resulting program is given in program (f).

3 Conclusion

The detection of parallel tasks is hampered frequently by unstructured control statements such as if-goto's or simply goto's. We have shown that a systematic detection of hammock graphs in the flowgraph of the program allows to convert all these control constructs into block-structured code segments with a single locus of control. It is shown that nonstandard Fortran-77 instructions such as *while* or *repeat* loops, and the *exit* statement are essential for a parallel code generator. It is proven that the algorithms for forward, backward and exit branches reshape the program into blocks of a larger granularity in which the scope of the control statement is clearly defined. Consequently the converted program inherits the parallelism of the original program and makes it visible as independent subtasks.

References

1. Allen, J.R. 1983. Dependence Analysis for subscript Variables and Its Application to Program Transformations. Ph.D. Dissertation, Department of Mathematical Sciences, Rice University, Houston, Texas(April).
2. Allen, J.R., Kennedy, K., Porterfield, C., and Warren, J. 1983. Conversion of Control Dependence to Data Dependence. In *Conference Proceedings – The 10th Annual ACM Symposium on Principles of Programming Languages* (Austin, Texas, January 24-26), ACM Press, pp.177-189.
3. Banerjee, U., 1988. *Dependence Analysis for Supercomputing.* The Kluwer international series in engineering and computer science. Parallel processing and fifth generation computing. ISBN 0-89838-289-0. Kluwer Academic Publishers, 1988.
4. Erik D'Hollander. Computer Aided Dataflow Analysis for the Conversion of Sequential Programs into Parallel Form. *Algorithm and Applications on Vector and Parallel Computers.* Edited by H.J.J te Riele, Th.J.Dekker and H.A.van der Vorst. ©Elsvier Science Publishers B.V.(North-Holland), 1987. pp.75-102.
5. Fubo Zhang and Erik H. D'Hollander. 1993. Using Hammock Graphs to Eliminate Nonstructured Branch Statements. *LEM Internal Report* DG 93-31.

Performance Modeling of Microkernel Thread Schedulers for Shared Memory Multiprocessors

Wim Van de Velde, Johan Opsommer, Erik H. D'Hollander

University of Ghent,
Department of Electrical Engeneering,
Parallel Processing Group
St.-Pietersnieuwstraat 41, B-9000 Ghent, Belgium

Abstract. The scheduling policy of a microkernel significantly affects the parallel execution of fine-grained programs. In this study several thread management alternatives were implemented on a shared memory system with 6 processors. The speedup and execution behaviour was monitored for programs with a varying degree of granularity and parallelism. Then for each scheduling policy a suitable queueing network was developed and identified with the observed execution using the QNAP2 queueing network software package. Because of the close agreement between the predicted and the observed behaviour, the models allowed to compare the scheduling policies, pin-point the bottlenecks in the algorithm and the shared data structures, and improve the scheduling discipline significantly.

1 Introduction

The rapid power surge of very fast RISC processors increases the use of shared memory multiprocessors for computationally intensive calculations. In this type of applications a single program is split up into many parallel executable tasks and their interaction is represented by a taskgraph.

It is well known that the execution of each task as a seperate process creates an intolerable overhead due to process creation and kernel activity. In response to the fast context-switch requirements, modern multiprocessor operating systems execute multiple tasks within one process. A task is associated with a thread and all threads share the same address space of the process to which they belong. Moreover, the creation, termination and synchronization of threads is much faster than similar operations on processes. As a consequence, the introduction of threads favoured the parallel execution of fine-grained taskgraphs.

This paper addresses the selection of an optimal kernel scheduling policy which maximizes the speedup of highly interactive taskgraphs.

2 Thread scheduling techniques

Tasks ready for execution are placed in a *ready list* (fig. 1). This list is a data structure available to all processors. The various thread scheduling techniques differ in the way the ready list is structured and manipulated.

- *Global Ready List.* In this case the ready tasks are stored in a single list (fig. 1.a). When a processor becomes idle, its microkernel scheduler locks the ready list, selects the next task in the list and unlocks the list. Then the processor leaves the kernel and executes the task. This approach doesn't scale with a growing number of processors because the idle processors will queue-up in front of a locked ready list.

- *Local Taskbuffer.* In the previous case a finishing task first puts n successor tasks on the ready list and retrieves one task from the ready list. A significant improvement is to keep one ready task in a local task buffer and emitting the $n-1$ remaining ready tasks (fig. 1.b). This is especially useful for a chain of sequential tasks, because then the processor continues with the next task without contending for the shared ready list.

- *Multiple Global Ready Lists.* Another way to alleviate the contention for a single global ready list is to provide multiple lists, each protected by a separate lock (fig. 1.c). In this implementation initially a processor selects an arbitrary list, and skips to the next list when the previous one is locked. The first free list becomes the preferential list for the next accesses as long as it is unlocked and contains ready tasks.

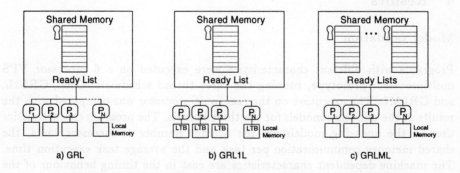

Fig. 1. Scheduler data structures a) GRL: global ready list, b) GRL1L: global ready list with one local task buffer (LTB), c) GRLML: multiple global ready lists.

3 Queueing models

The dynamic operation of the various schedulers is modeled by closed queueing networks using *resource contention*. In contrast to the usual queueing modeling approach, the CPU and the memory are represented as *resources* instead of service stations [4]. In this way the customers are requesting resources, the shared resources can be modelled in great detail as independent modular entities. The only service station in the model is the *task server*. The customer task requires to hold one or several resources while being served. The service is described by a sequence of steps, which reflect the phases of scheduling, execution and synchronization of a single task. The resource entities describe the timing, scheduling and the allocation behaviour of the CPU's, the bus, the shared memory and the global ready lists. A typical description of a ready list access follows:

```
/STATION/ NAME = bus_resource;
          TYPE = RESOURCE;      & resource declaration

rl_lock;                        & procedure to lock the ready list
   CST(computing_time);         & time spend on local computations
   P(bus_resource);             & grab the bus
      CST(bus_time);            & time spend on bus transactions
   V(bus_resource);             & release the bus
rl_unlock;                      & procedure to unlock the ready list
```

The different scheduling strategies were modeled using the QNAP2 queueing analysis package [2] and evaluated on the VPS multiprocessor prototype. A detailed description of the models can be found in [5].

4 Results

Model validation

Programs with different characteristics were executed on a 6 processor VPS multiprocessor prototype, running the three thread schedulers: GRL, GRL1L, and GRLML. The execution on the real multiprocessor was compared with the results of the queueing models for the three kernels. The program characteristics used in the queueing models are the average number of successor tasks, the shared memory communication per task and the average task execution time. The machine dependent characteristics are cast in the timing behaviour of the semaphore primitives and the shared memory operations. Using measured task and machine characteristics, the deviation between the real and the simulated execution of all programs is 3.5% on the average, with a maximum of 11.7%.

Figure 2 represents the results for a Gauss-Jordan linear system solver, comparing the model with the observed execution of the three kernels.

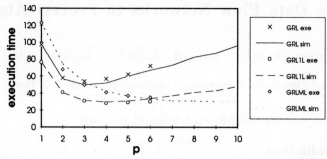

Fig. 2. Execution time for the Gauss-Jordan linear system solver. Marks indicate the observed times (exe), lines represent the simulation results (sim). Times are in ms.

Evaluation of the thread schedulers and the modeling approach

The measurement and simulation results for the program (fig. 2) both indicate the superiority of the kernel with a local taskbuffer GRL1L over a single global task list, GRL. Using a local taskbuffer always gives an advantage over a shared global list, because in this way a processor bypasses a critical shared resource by storing locally the next task it will execute.

Both kernels GRL and GRL1L don't scale very well with an increasing number of processors, because the contention overhead for the shared resources outweighs the benefits of a parallel execution.

The multiple lock kernel GRLML is more robust and scalable. While it takes longer to access multiple locked ready lists, the ready list doesn't saturate when the number of processors grows. The multiple locked ready lists also prove to be less demanding on the shared bus.

The modeling approach has two major advantages: the behaviour of the scheduler is explained in terms of program and machine characteristics and the simulation allows to deal with more processors than physically available.

References

1. Anderson T.E., Lazowska E.D., Levy H.M., *The Performance Implications of Thread Management Alternatives for Shared-Memory Multiprocessors*, IEEE Trans. on Computers, Vol. 38, 12, pp. 1631-1644, 1989.
2. Bull/INRIA, *QNAP2 Users Guide*, Simulog, pp. 315, 1992.
3. Gupta A., Tucker A., Urushibara S., *The Impact of Operating System Scheduling Policies and Synchronization Methods on the Performance of Parallel Applications*, ACM, pp. 120-132, 1991.
4. Onyuksel I. H. +, *Performance analysis of single-bus multiprocessor modeled as Markovian Queuing network*, IEEE Trans. on Computers, Vol. 39, Jul, pp. 975-980, 1990.
5. Van de Velde W., Opsommer J., D'Hollander E.H., *Implementation and Evaluation of Thread Schedulers for Shared Memory Multiprocessors*, Internal Report, DG93-4, 1993.

From Data Flow Networks to Process Algebras

Cinzia Bernardeschi[1],   Andrea Bondavalli[2],   Luca Simoncini[1]

[1] Department of Information Engineering, University of Pisa,
Via Diotisalvi 2, Pisa, Italy.

[2] CNUCE-CNR, Via S. Maria 36, Pisa, Italy.

1   Introduction

Data flow networks are a paradigm for concurrent computations in which a collection of concurrently and asynchronously executing nodes communicate by sending data over FIFO communication channels. The need to deal with data and the asynchronous communication make reasoning about the semantics of nondeterministic networks very difficult [2].

Let V be the set of data items, V* is the set of finite sequences of data item in V.

Definition: A data flow node P is a tuple <Ip, Op, Sp, Rp> where Ip is the set of incoming channels and Op is the set of outgoing channels with $(Ip \cap Op) = \varnothing$; Sp is the set of states; s^0p is the initial state, $s^0p \in Sp$; Rp is the set of firings. A firing is a tuple <s, χ_{in}, s', χ_{out}> where s, s'$\in$Sp, χ_{in} is a mapping from Ip to V* and χ_{out} is a mapping from Op to V*.

The meaning of a firing <s, χ_{in}, s', χ_{out}> is: when the node is in state s and the content of each incoming channel a$\in$Ip starts with the sequence $\chi_{in}(a)$, then these sequences may be consumed, while the node change its state to s' and the sequence $\chi_{out}(b)$ is produced on each outgoing channel b$\in$Op. A firing may require/put data only on a subset of the input/output channels of a node.

Definition: A data flow network N consists of a set P_N of nodes such that in P_N each channel occurs at most once as incoming channel and at most once as outgoing channel. The network is obtained connecting input channels to output channels with the same name.

The channels of the network are of three different types: *input* channels (I_N) to transmit data items from the environment to a node, *output* channels (O_N) to transmit data items from a node to the environment and *internal* channels to transmit data items from a node to another node of the network. The evolution of the network is determined by transitions: i) a firing of a node, ii) the arrival of a data item to an input channel, iii) the output of a data item from an output channel. The semantic of the network is denoted by the set of its traces [4]. A *trace* is a linearly ordered sequence of events (data items) that may appear on its input and output channels during a computation.

In this paper we model data flow networks by the Lotos (Language of Temporal Ordering Specification) [1], [3] formal specification language. The model is derived by defining a transformation that maps each node of the network into a process in the process algebras (composed by a set of subprocesses) and then putting these processes in parallel with synchronisation on the common actions to obtain the global behaviour of the network. We prove that given a data flow network N, the observable behaviour of the Lotos specification obtained by the transformation corresponds to the traces of the network in the Jonsson's *traces* semantic model [4]. The main contribution of the paper is thus to provide a framework where the theory and tools developed for the formal specification language can be applied to reason on and analyse data flow networks.

2 From Data Flow to Processes

Let DF be the set of data flow networks, DFP the set of data flow nodes and L the set of Lotos expressions, we first give the transformation for data flow nodes γp:DFP→L, and then we describe the entire transformation γ:DF→L. Without loss of generality, we restrict to networks composed by nodes whose firings satisfy the following condition: all the firings of a node that require data from a given channel, require the same number of data tokens from that channel.

2.1 Transformation γp for data flow nodes

Let P be a data flow node, we define the following actions in Lotos (all Lotos entities are in italic):

Ip={*ch* | *ch*∈*Ip*} and *Op*={*ch* | *ch*∈*Op*}: ∀ *ch*∈*Ip*∪*Op*, *ch* is an action meaning that a data item is put on channel ch; if *ch*∈*Ip* action *ch* corresponds to an input action from the environment,

Ip#={*ch#* | *ch*∈*Ip*} and *Op#*={*ch#* | *ch*∈*Op*}: ∀ *ch*∈*Ip*∪*Op*, *ch#* is an action meaning that a data item is taken from channel ch; if *ch*∈*Op* the action corresponds to an output action to the environment;

SYNCp={*sync_ch* | *ch*∈*Ip*}: ∀ *ch*∈*Ip*, *sync_ch* is a synchronisation action performed by the *channel process* and the *node process* meaning that all required data items are available on channel ch,

FIREp={*fireF* | *F*∈*Rp*}: ∀ *F*∈*Rp*, *fireF* is an action internal to the node process stating the choice of firing F (which must be one of the enabled firings).

Channel Processes. Each output channel is mapped into a *FIFO* process that only implements the FIFO buffer functionality. Each input channel is mapped into a *channel process CP* which, in addition to the FIFO buffer functionality, implements a synchronisation mechanism with the node (*FIFO* and *SYNC* processes). This is necessary to perform the phase of testing data availability over channel for choosing one executable firing. The *FIFO* process sends data to the *SYNC* process. If n is the number of tokens required on the channel, the *SYNC* process after having received n data from the *FIFO* process, synchronises with the receiving *node process* (on the SYNC_ch gate) to signal that all data required on the channel are available. After that, *SYNC* is ready to send data items to the receiving *node process*, and to start again to get other data from the *FIFO* process.

Node Processes. Let *P* be the name of the *node process* associated to the node P. *P* has as many gates as the set of channels of the node plus one synchronisation gate for each input channel: {*Ip#*∪*SYNCp*∪*Op*}. The *node process* is composed of two subprocesses: a testing subprocess *TEST*, to test data availability for the set of firings and an execution subprocess *EXEC* that has the same set of states as the node P and chooses one of the enabled firings executing it. The process *TEST* is defined as the parallel execution of a set of processes each testing data availability on a single input channel (*TESTinp_i*, inp_i∈Ip). At most one firing each time may be executed so *EXEC* synchronises with *TEST* to select one of the enabled firing. If more firings are enabled at a time then a nondeterministic choice is applied to execute one firing. For each firing F_k of the data flow node there is a corresponding process *EXEC_F_k*. After having selected the firing F_k, *EXEC* calls *EXEC_F_k* process. The process *EXEC_F_i*

i) gets the data items required from each input channel ch such that ch∈Ip $|_{F_i}$;

ii) executes an internal computation and puts new data tokens on all output channels ch such that ch∈Op $|_{F_i}$; and iii) executes the *EXEC* process again with the new state s' of the node after the firing.

The specification γp(P) for a node P is obtained by composing *channels processes* and the *node process* in parallel with synchronisation on the common actions and hiding all the actions that do not correspond to the external behaviour of the node:

γp(P) = process *SnP[Ip, Op#]* :noexit :=

hide *SYNCp, Ip#, Op* in

$((CP[a_1, a_1\#, sync\_a_1]$ ||| ... $<\forall a_i \in Ip>$ ... ||| $CP[a_k, a_k\#, sync\_a_k])$

|[*SYNCp, Ip#*]| $P[Ip\#, SYNCp, Op]$ $(s^0p))$

|[*Op*]| $(FIFO[b_1, b_1\#]$ ||| ... $<\forall b_j \in Op>$ ... ||| $(FIFO[b_h, b_h\#])$)

endspec (* *SnP* *)

2.2   Transformation γ for the Network

We build the specification of the network by taking the *SnP* processes obtained by γp(P) ∀P∈P_N. We cannot just put these processes in parallel with synchronization on gates with the same name. In fact, output of data items on a channel ch of node Q are represented by the action *ch#* in *SnQ*, while input of a data item from input channel ch of node R are represented by the action *ch* in *SnR*. In particular an ouput channel ch of a node Q is mapped in *SnQ* as *FIFO[ch, ch#]* in order to realise the buffering of output data items while an input channel ch of a node R is mapped in *SnR* as *CP[ch, ch#, sync_ch]* which at its turn is able to buffer data. ∀P∈P_N we define Op*={ch | ch∈Op and ∃R∈P_N, ch∈I_R} the set of output channels of P that are also input channels of another node of N and Op∧= Op-Op*. For all the channels ch∈Op* we remove the *FIFO* process in the specification *SnP*, thus obtaining *SnP'*. Let define *Op*={ch | ch∈Op*}*, *Op∧={ch | ch∈Op∧}*, *Op*#={ch# | ch∈Op*}* and *Op∧#={ch# | ch∈Op∧}*. The global specification of N is now obtained putting the obtained *SnP'* processes in parallel with synchronization on gates with the same name and hiding all the actions which corresponds to internal channels of the network:

γ(N) = specification *netN[I_N, O_N#]* :noexit

    hide ($\cup_{P∈P_N}$ *Op**) in

    $SnQ'[I_Q, O_{Q}*, O_{Q}\#]$|[@]| ... $<\forall P∈P_N>$ ... $SnR'[I_R, O_R*, O_R\#]$
    endspec (* *netN* *)

The Lotos specification of all the processes of the transformation and the proof of the following theorem, which shows that the observable behaviour of the Lotos specification obtained by γ(N) correspond to the traces of the network N in the Jonsson's *traces model*, is in [5]:

743

Theorem: Let N be a data flow network composed by a set of nodes P_N and $\gamma(N)$ its transformation. The observable behaviour of $\gamma(N) = netN[I_N, O_N\#]$ is the same as the traces of N where actions in I_N, correspond to input events on channels belonging to I_N and actions in $O_N\#$ correspond to output events on channnels belonging to O_N.

A simple data flow network and the graphical representation of the specification derived by applying the transformation are reported in Fig. 1.

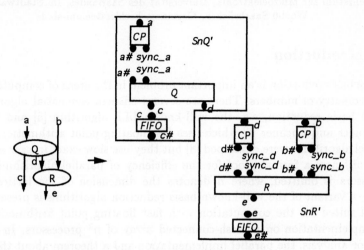

Fig. 1. Transformation of a data flow network

3   Conclusion

We have defined a transformation γ from data flow networks to process algebras specifications. The behaviour of $\gamma(N)$ in terms of the interleaving of observable actions corresponds to the traces of network N in the *traces model*. This opens the possibility of applying the tools and the theory developed for the process algebras to analyse data flow networks. An important field is verification where the tools of the process algebras can be significantly applied to prove networks equivalence.

References

[1]   T. Bolognesi, E. Brinskma, "Introduction to the ISO specification language LOTOS", "The formal description technique LOTOS", Elsevier Science Publishers B.V. (North-Holland), 1989, pp. 23-73.

[2]   J. Brock, W. Ackerman, "Scenarios: A Model of Non-determinate Computation", "LNCS 107", Springer-Verlag, 1981, pp. 252-259.

[3]   ISO, "LOTOS - A Formal Technique Based on the Temporal Ordering of Observational Behaviour", Open Systems Interconnection, July 1988.

[4]   B. Jonsson, "A Fully Abstract Trace Model for Data Flow networks", Journal of ACM, Vol. 36, pp. 155-165, 1989.

[5]   C. Bernardeschi, A. Bondavalli, L. Simoncini, "A Semantic Model of Data Flow Networks based on Process Algebras", CNUCE Internal Report C93-03, March 1993.

Parallel Complexity of Lattice Basis Reduction and a Floating-Point Parallel Algorithm

Christian Heckler and Lothar Thiele

Lehrstuhl für Mikroelektronik, Universität des Saarlandes, Im Stadtwald 13,
W6600 Saarbrücken, Germany, heckler@ee.uni-sb.de

1   Introduction

Lattice basis reduction is an important problem in the areas of computer algebra and geometry of numbers. There are several efficient sequential algorithms for lattice basis reduction, e.g. the well-known LLL algorithm [5] and a variant of Schnorr and Euchner [6] which uses fast floating-point arithmetic. Recently, parallel algorithms were developed [8] but they use slow exact integer arithmetic and until now a formal proof for the efficiency of parallel algorithms with n^2 processors is omitted, where n denotes the dimension of the lattice. In this paper, a variant of the well-known basis reduction algorithms is presented that is well suited for the computation with fast floating point arithmetic and for the implementation on a mesh-connected array of n^2 processors. In addition, an error analysis, the parallel implementation and a theorem about the parallel efficiency is provided.

2   Foundations of Lattice Basis Reduction

Basic concepts and sequential algorithms for lattice basis reduction are e.g. described in [5, 6]. Here, we only give our notation and some basic results.

Let $b_1, b_2, \ldots, b_n \in \mathbf{R}^n$ be n linearly independent vectors. Then $L = L(b_1, \ldots, b_n) = \{\sum_{i=1}^{n} \lambda_i b_i | \lambda_i \in \mathbf{Z}, i = 1, \ldots, n\}$ is called the lattice with basis $(b_1, \ldots, b_n)$. $(b_1^*, b_2^*, \ldots, b_n^*)$ denotes the associated Gram-Schmidt orthogonalization, i.e. $b_1^* = b_1$, $b_i^* = b_i - \sum_{j=1}^{i-1} \mu_{i,j} b_j^*$ for $i = 2, \ldots, n$ where $\mu_{i,j} = \frac{b_i^T b_j^*}{||b_j^*||^2}$. Let be $\mu_{i,i} = 1$ and $\mu_{i,j} = 0$ for $i < j$ and $M = (\mu_{i,j})_{1 \le i,j \le n}$ the matrix of the Gram-Schmidt coefficients. Then we can write the above equations as $(b_1, \ldots, b_n) = (b_1^*, \ldots, b_n^*) M^T$. In order to find short vectors the definition of a *reduced basis* was introduced [5].

Theorem 1 Reduced Basis [5]. *Let L be a lattice in $\mathbf{R}^n$ and $(b_1, \ldots, b_n)$ be a reduced basis of L. Then $||b_1|| \le 2^{\frac{n-1}{4}} (\det L)^{\frac{1}{n}}$.*

Theorem 2 Sequential Time Complexity [5]. *The LLL algorithm [5] terminates after at most $n^2 \log B$ swaps[1], if we start with an integral basis. At most $O(n^4 \log B)$ arithmetic operations are needed in order to find a reduced basis.*

---

[1] In the following, log denotes the logarithm with basis $\frac{4}{3}$ and B is defined as $B := \max_{i=1,\ldots,n} ||b_i||^2$.

3 A New Variant of Lattice Basis Reduction Algorithm

An efficient parallel implementation of the LLL-algorithm and the floating point variant of Schnorr and Euchner [6] on a ring of n processors can easily be derived. See [8] for the LLL-algorithm and [2] for the Schnorr-Euchner variant. In contrast to the case of n processors, these algorithms seem not to be parallelizable with n^2 processors. The crucial idea for a parallel algorithm is to compute the Gram-Schmidt orthogonalization and the size-reduction of the whole matrix and to execute all possible swaps for even indices in one phase and for odd indices in the next phase (the concatenation of such two phases is called 'all-swap phase').[2] An algorithm based on that strategy is called 'all-swap algorithm'. In order to avoid the slowness of exact integer arithmetic, we follow the idea of Schnorr and Euchner [6] of using floating point arithmetic. Only the lattice basis $(b_1, \ldots, b_n)$ is computed in exact representation. The values of $\|b_i^*\|^2$ and $\mu_{i,j}$ are stored in floating point format. The following measures are taken in order to minimize the floating point errors: First, unlike in the LLL algorithm the Gram-Schmidt orthogonalization is computed in each phase of the algorithm. Thus, rounding errors in the matrix M are corrected in each phase. Second, the Gram-Schmidt orthogonalization is computed by means of Givens rotations. Unlike the original Gram-Schmidt procedure, the orthogonalization with Givens rotations is parallelizable with n^2 processors and is numerically stable. Givens rotations are used in order to compute an orthogonal matrix Q with $Q(b_1, \ldots b_n) = R$, where R is upper triangular. Therefore, it holds $(b_1, \ldots, b_n) = Q^{\mathrm{T}} R$ and $\|b_i^*\|^2 = r_{i,i}^2$. M^{T} is computed from R by dividing each row i by $r_{i,i}$. In order to avoid wrong swaps on account of faulty data, an error analysis due to Wilkinson [9] and Gentleman [1] is used and formalized in Theorem 3.[3] If no swap is possible because of the rounding errors, one exact Gram-Schmidt computation has to be executed.

Theorem 3. *Let be $u = \frac{1}{2} b^{-r+1}$, where b denotes the basis and r the precision of the floating-point representation. Using the floating-point error model of Wilkinson [9], a swap will result in a better basis, if the condition $\|b_j^{*}\|^2 > 2\|b_{j+1}^{*'}\|^2$ is valid for the disturbed values and $n^3 B u^2 \ll \|b_j^{*}\|^2$ for $u \ll 1$, $n \in \mathbb{N}$ and $n \cdot u \ll 1$.*

Algorithm 4.

All-Swap Floating Point Lattice Basis Reduction Algorithm
input: $b_1, b_2, \ldots, b_n$ a basis in exact representation
output: $b_1, b_2, \ldots, b_n$ a reduced[4] basis
method:

  ordering $\leftarrow$ odd;
  while (any swap is possible) do

---

[2] Villard [8] had a similar idea, but he uses exact arithmetic.
[3] A detailed error analysis is given in [3].
[4] Reduced up to floating-point errors. It can happen, that the resulting basis does not exactly satisfy the conditions of a reduced basis.

$MT \leftarrow$ floating-point$(b_1, \ldots, b_n)$;
Compute the Gram-Schmidt orthogonalization by
Givens rotations on MT;

Compute the size reduction of the basis $(b_1, \ldots, b_n)$ and
the Gram-Schmidt coefficients MT;

if (ordering = odd) then
  swap b_i and b_{i+1} for every odd index i with $||b_i^*||^2 > 2||b_{i+1}^*||^2$,
  if the condition of Theorem 3 is satisfied;
  ordering $\leftarrow$ even;
else
  swap b_i and b_{i+1} for every even index i with $||b_i^*||^2 > 2||b_{i+1}^*||^2$,
  if the condition of Theorem 3 is satisfied;
  ordering $\leftarrow$ odd;
fi;
od.

Practical Results: The algorithm has been tested on a Sun Sparcstation 10 for random unimodular lattices (see Table 1) and subset sum lattices which are constructed due to [6]. The tests show that many swaps can be executed in parallel.

Table 1. Results for unimodular transformed lattices

n	B	all-swap phases	swaps	swaps per phase	CPU-time [sec]
5	$1.98 \cdot 10^{45}$	34	101	3	0.5
10	$5.18 \cdot 10^{64}$	104	786	7.6	15.56
20	$4.1 \cdot 10^{62}$	239	3765	15.75	303
30	$2.8 \cdot 10^{75}$	518	12012	23.2	2202
40	$2.3 \cdot 10^{82}$	800	23422	29.3	7324
50	$2.11 \cdot 10^{92}$	1018	36844	36.2	16870
60	$1.4 \cdot 10^{102}$	1519	66190	43.6	41209

4 Parallel Implementation on a Mesh-connected Array and Time Complexity

One phase of Algorithm 4 consists in two main steps: the orthogonalization of MT using Givens rotations and the size-reduction. Both steps are parallelizable on a mesh-connected processor, see e.g. Schwiegelshohn and Thiele [7]. Thus, the following theorem holds[5]:

---
[5] A more exact description can be found in [3].

Theorem 5. *One phase of the all-swap basis reduction algorithm can be executed in $O(n)$ parallel steps of arithmetic operations on a mesh-connected processor array with $O(n^2)$ processors cells.*

In order to show the efficiency of the parallel algorithm, a theorem on the number of swaps that have to be executed to find a short vector using all-swap algorithms is provided.[6] The proof can be found in [4, 3].

Theorem 6. *After at most $n \log B$ all-swap phases the vector b_1 of the resulting lattice basis satisfies $\|b_1\| \leq \frac{4}{3} c^{\frac{n-1}{4}} (\det L)^{\frac{1}{n}}$ with $c = \frac{32}{9}$.*

This is almost the same bound as in Theorem 1. Summing up, a speedup of n^2 (with respect to arithmetic operations[7]) in comparison with the LLL algorithm can be achieved.

Corollary 7. *A short vector of a lattice can be found in $O(n^2 \log B)$ parallel arithmetic operations using a network of n^2 processors.*

References

1. W. M. Gentleman. Error analysis of QR decompositions by Givens transformations. *Linear Algebra and Its Applications*, 10:189–197, 1975.
2. C. Heckler. *Parallele seminumerische Algorithmen.* PhD thesis, Universität des Saarlandes, Saarbrücken, Germany, 1993. In preparation.
3. C. Heckler and L. Thiele. A parallel lattice basis reduction for mesh-connected processor arrays and parallel complexity. to appear.
4. C. Heckler and L. Thiele. On the time complexity of parallel algorithms for lattice basis reduction. Technical Report 05/1993, SFB124, Universität Saarbrücken, Germany, 1993.
5. A.K. Lenstra, H.W. Lenstra Jr., and L. Lovasz. Factoring polynomials with rational coefficients. *Math. Ann.*, 261:515–534, 1982.
6. C.P. Schnorr and M. Euchner. Lattice basis reduction: Improved practical algorithms and solving subset sum problems. In *Proceedings of the FCT'91 (Gosen, Germany), LNCS 529*, pages 68–85. Springer, 1991.
7. U. Schwiegelshohn and L. Thiele. A systolic array for cyclic-by-rows Jacobi algorithms. *Journal of Parallel and Distributed Computing*, 4:334–340, 1987.
8. G. Villard. Parallel lattice basis reduction. In *International Symposium on Symbolic and Algebraic Computation, Berbeley California USA*, pages 269–277. ACM Press, 1992.
9. J. H. Wilkinson. *Rounding Errors in Algebraic Processes.* Prentice-Hall, Englewood Cliffs, 1963.

---

[6] Note: This theorem is true for exact arithmetic. An exact computation of the Gram-Schmidt orthogonalization is parallelizable in a similar way as shown above.

[7] Note: In order to execute the size-reduction in parallel, columns are computed with non-reduced columns. Thus, the numbers can grow more than in the original LLL algorithm. However practical results of [8] show that this phenomenon cannot be observed.

Computer Vision Applications Experience with Actors[*]

Francesca Arcelli   *Massimo De Santo*   *Michele Di Santo*

Dipartimento di Ingegneria dell'Informazione e Matematica Applicata
Università di Salerno - 84084 Fisciano (Salerno), Italy
E-.mail: {arcelli, desanto, disanto}@udsab.dia.unisa.it

Antonio Picariello

Istituto Ricerche sui Sistemi Informatici Paralleli - CNR
Via P. Castellino, 111 - 80131 Napoli, Italy

Abstract. The paper reports some initial experience in the use of the Actor Model for solving a complex Computer Vision problem: the segmentation of cursive script characters. Our goal is to show how an application programmer can express the different kinds of parallelism present in the problem, emphasizing the advantages obtained by the use of the Actor Model, both from the concurrency and the object-oriented design points of view.

1 Introduction

In the search of the right software framework for *parallelism*, many researchers are promoting the adoption of the *object-oriented methodology*. The motivations are at least the following:

• The methodology encourages the design and implementation of a program as a set of autonomous components, emphasizing modular structure, data abstraction and code reuse, and has already demonstrated some measure of success in the development of complex and large-scale sequential programs.

• By means of dynamic creation and reconfiguration of objects, object-based models and languages support applications whose structures are not statically determinate, but tend to evolve dynamically and unpredictably both in shape and size. These applications - such as combinatorial optimization, theorem-proving, symbolic and algebraic manipulation, image understanding, query processing and inference database systems - will come into pre-eminence in the coming years, when the application of parallel architectures will grow in diversity and scientific computation will no longer be so dominant.

• Objects mesh nicely with parallelism, since their logical autonomy makes them a natural unit for parallel execution.

Among the object-based models of parallel computation, the *actor model* [1] is the best known. It captures the essence of parallel computation in distributed systems at an abstract level and provides a flexible basis for parallel, distributed programming. In fact, the actor model has recently become the basis for a number of parallel programming languages [2-5], even though, due to the relative youth of the field, there is a scarcity of efficient implementations and of reported experience for

---

[*] This work was supported in part by CNR "Progetto Finalizzato Sistemi Informatici e Calcolo Parallelo" and by MURST (40% and 60% funds).
An extended version of this paper is available from the authors.

significant applications. So actors have yet to establish themselves as a practical tool for the development of parallel software.

In the framework of a project currently under development at the University of Salerno, aiming at designing, implementing and evaluating a parallel object-oriented language based on the actor model, in order to gain a better understanding of the model and of its merits, we began to use actors in the programming of parallel applications. Among the previous mentioned application fields we choose *computer vision* (CV). The motivations can be synthesized by saying that CV problems are complex, computationally intensive and exhibit a high degree of inherent parallelism. Moreover, if we consider the three levels which some widely-accepted characterizations of CV identify in the automated vision process[1], we can appreciate the variety of different forms of parallelism involved. So, we were convinced not only to use CV as a test bed for the actor model, but also to define some initial ideas about a parallel object-oriented programming framework for CV.

In this paper we describe an initial experiment of writing parallel code for solving a complex CV problem: the *segmentation of cursive script characters*. Our goal is to show how an application programmer can express the different kinds of parallelism present in the problem, emphasizing the advantages obtained by the use of the actor model, both from the concurrency and the object-oriented design points of view.

2 Object-Oriented Parallel Programming with Actors

The actor model of computation is based on the idea that the world is inherently parallel, and parallel systems in the world can be modelled as systems of parallel objects, known as *actors*. Parallelism in actors is obtained essentially by allowing an actor to *send a message* and then to proceed in parallel with the receiver. Actors are created dynamically and their *mail addresses* can be transmitted via messages. The communication mechanism is *asynchronous*. Incoming messages are buffered in an unbounded *mail queue*. The processing of a message by an actor gives rise to the selection of a *method* and to its execution by using the information in the message and in the current *behavior* (including methods and data local to the actor). In particular, during method execution an actor may make simple (based on local data) decisions, create more actors, send messages to itself or to other actors, and specify its *replacement behavior*. Replacements implement local state changes which can span from simple changes in the values of state variables to radical changes in the set of state variables and in the methods. In order to maintain their internal consistency, actors offer a very simple and implicit *synchronization mechanism*; in fact they do not share data and can process new messages only when their replacement behaviors have been evaluated.

Mechanisms and primitives of the actor model form a simple but powerful set to build a wide range of higher-level abstractions and parallel programming paradigms.

---

[1] (i) *Low Level Processing* (LLP) interested in treating iconic pictorial data structures in order to "organize" and "filter" their information contents; (ii) *Intermediate Level Processing* (ILP) having the aim of transforming iconic data structures into structures which are more synthetic and more convenient for reaching the ultimate goals of the process; (iii) *High Level Processing* (HLP) which is expected to achieve complex results such as recognition of objects in a scene.

However, to turn the model into a truly general-purpose parallel programming language some more constructs must be added. Among the many possible extensions, we consider here only the following three:

- *Inheritance*: Originally actors are not arranged in a hierarchy, but inheritance is an important form of reusability which should be added.
- *Type-checking*: Type-checking is an important topic in assuring program robustness, so actors should offer some level of type-checking, even though it is certainly difficult to conciliate it with the fact that an actor may become a different kind of actor.
- *Aggregations*: When the number of actors in a system becomes too high, it is essential to introduce some structure to the computation, avoiding at the same time the bottleneck consequent to the construction of abstractions made up of hierarchies of serializing actors. In particular, in this paper we adopt Chien's Concurrent Aggregates (or *groups*) which support expression of data parallelism and allow us to manage complexity and to guarantee unlimited potential for concurrency [4].

3 A Case Study: Cursive Script Segmentation

The case study briefly presented in this section is a *cursive script segmentation* (CSS) algorithm based on a new approach to character segmentation [6]. Starting from a pixel matrix corresponding to the original input image, the algorithm has first to detect the text lines present in the image, then to find the words which form the lines and finally to search for the characters inside each word. The algorithm generates a variable number of sub-matrices, corresponding first to the text-lines and then to the words detected in the image. For each word a complex set of computations is needed to perform characters-in-word detection.

In order to discuss the advantages an application programmer can achieve by designing actor-based solutions for CV needs, we have selected two subtasks, namely the *subdivision of the image in lines of text* and the *removal of skeleton distortions*.

The first subtask was chosen because it allows to exemplify the way an actor programmer can manage the data parallelism typical of LLV processing. The adopted solution uses two groups, *Pixels* and *Rows*, both dynamically created according to the number of pixel columns and rows in the image. Each actor in *Pixels* knows its gray level (classified as "background" or "text") and its position in the image. So, each background actor sends a message about its state to the next one along its row. The first text actor receiving such a message assumes that its row is a "text-row" and informs *Rows*. If no text actor is present in a row, the last background actor will inform *Rows* that it is located in a "background row". The group *Rows* uses the information received by *Pixels* to detect the lines of text. Each background row actor sends a message about its state to the next row. When a text row actor receives this message, it knows that a background/text transition has just occurred, so it will propagate a message containing a counter, initialized to zero, and incremented every time a text actor receives it. A background row receiving this counter message knows, on the contrary, that a text/background transition has occurred and that the detection of a line of text is complete. The described elaboration occurs in parallel for each row of the image. Moreover, the asynchronous message passing mechanism makes possible the parallel detection of the lines of text without any synchronization constraints. The solution found for this subtask confirms that the actor model allows the programmer to describe the behaviour of data-driven dynamic parallelism. Furthermore, the reuse at low-cost of detected programming patterns is possible: in fact, the mechanism introduced to solve text-lines detection can be simply reused in a "specular" way to detect "words" in text-lines.

The second subtask belongs to the so-called *feature extraction phase*. For each detected "word" it is possible to start a set of computations to extract and analyse *skeleton* and *contour* information (the "features"), which will be used in an integrated manner to detect characters-in-word. As well-known from current literature [7], every skeletonization procedure introduces a certain amount of unwanted distortions on the skeleton of the pattern it is working on. Designing a procedure to remove these distortions is a particularly critical task due to the sophisticated use one has to make of skeleton information. Starting from a polygonal approximation of the skeleton of a pattern, it is possible to regard the skeleton itself as a graph. Our original parallel algorithm [6] tries to remove distortions by merging vertices of the graph (*merge operation*) or by moving their geometrical positions (*normalization operation*). The vertices of the graph are represented by actors which are classified as *normal* or *branch* vertices (connected to no more or to more than two adiacent vertices); *inheritance* is used for defining a hierarchy of vertices from a basic vertex class. Vertex-actors cooperate to generate a new undistorted skeleton graph. During this process, the set of actors can dynamically change its configuration and each actor can change its state information or can even die. In this subtask we are in presence of data structures (graphs) which are built by means of active entities that are much more complex than pixel actors studied in the first examined subtask. Second, the interaction among these active entities is based on the irregular, dynamic links which are established among the vertices of the graph. The nature of the graph is in turn dynamic, in the sense that vertices can die, their death changing the topology of the graph.

References

1 G. Agha, "*Actors, A Model of Concurrent Computation in Distributed Systems*", MIT PRESS, 1986.

2 A. Yonezawa (ed.), *ABCL: An Object-Oriented Concurrent System*, The MIT Press, Cambridge, Mass., 1990.

3 C. Tomlinson, W. Kim, M. Schevel, V. Singh, B. Will and G. Agha, "Rosette: An Object-Oriented Concurrent System Architecture", *ACM Sigplan Notices*, 24(4), 1989.

4 A. A. Chien, *Concurrent Aggregates: An Object-Oriented Language for Fine-Grained Message-Passing Machines*, PhD Thesis, Massachussets Institute of Technology, 1990.

5 C. Houck and G. Agha, "A High-Level Actor Language and Its Distributed Implementation", *21st International Conference on Parallel Processing (ICPP '92)*, St. Charles, IL, 1992.

6 F. Arcelli, A. Chianese, M. DeSanto and A. Picariello, "Approaching Character Segmentation with Parallel Contour/Skeleton Analysis", *SCIA93*, Tromsoe, Norway, May 1993.

7 G. Boccignone, A. Chianese, L. P. Cordella and A. Marcelli, "Using Skeleton for OCR", *Prog. in Image Anal. and Proc.*, V. Cantoni et al. (eds.), World Scientific 1989.

Grid Massively Parallel Processor

V.P. Il'in, Ya.I. Fet

Computing Center, Siberian Div. of the Russian Academy of Sci.,
Novosibirsk, Russia
e-mail: fet@comcen.nsk.su

1 Introduction The Grid Massively Parallel Processor (GMPP) is a specialized supercomputer intended for solution of large-scale numerical problems by grid methods for partial differential equations of various types: elliptic, parabolic, hyperbolic and mixed systems; stationary and nonstationary, linear and nonlinear; using different kinds of grids, stencils, approximations, and matrix algorithms. Such mathematical topics cover a wide range of applied problems of diffusion, heat-conductivity, thermoelasticy, electrophysics, geophysics, aero- and hydrodynamics, a.s.o.

The GMPP is a multiprocessing computing complex of pyramidal architecture. At the first level of the pyramid an array of PE's is situated. Each PE of this array corresponds to an appropriate node of the grid and serves for computing the values of the grid function at this node. At the second level the devices of shared destination are located, namely, specialized functional processors, buffer memory units, and controllers. Each of these devices is used by a cluster of nearest PE's of the first level array. The third level is the main control unit, which organizes operation of the whole system. The GMPP may be connected with one or several host-computers. The important feature of GMPP distinguishing it from other similar computers is the use of specialized cellular arrays as basic building blocks. This paper focuses attention on two subsystems of GMPP, the Interconnection Network and the Functional Module.

2 Mathematical Motivations The grid algorithms are considered as a class of numerical methods, such as finite difference, finite element or finite volume methods, which are based on discretization and algebraization of PDE's or equivalent variational statements.

The most labor-consuming stages of numerical solution are (see [1], [2]): implementation of numerical time integration (for nonstationary problems) by explicit and implicit methods; solving of large linear algebraic systems for grid functions; recalculation of matrix coefficients in realization of time dependent or nonlinear iterations; because these stages are connected with multiple uniform calculations on the chosen grids and approximations.

The elementary stage of grid method implementation is written in the form

$$u_k^{n+1} = \sum_{l \in \omega_k} a_{kl} u_l^n + f_k \qquad n = 0, 1, \dots \qquad (1)$$

where k is the number of the current grid point, ω_k the set of neighboring nodes, and n is the number of the iteration or time step.

In general, the considered classes of numerical tasks and algorithms can be formulated in the following way: multiple computations by the formula (1) for a large number of grid points with a limited set of local communications; a variety of grid stencils in the sense of the number of neighboring nodes and the topology of interconnections; existence of functional dependencies which are realized efficiently by various approximations; presence of subdomains, where the types of relation (1) are changed as regards to the number of terms in the right side, the interconnection topology and the form of functional dependencies; necessity of arithmetic operations with sufficiently high accuracy.

The described structure of computational process prompts to the possible efficient mapping of its basic stages into the architecture of a multiprocessing computing system with specialization of particular components. Such system may retain sufficient universality, in the sense of its broad applicability.

The main principles of implementation of GMPP are:

- using of a large number of identical PE's, performing floating-point operations on high-capacity numbers according to the formulas of type (1);
- organization of local interprocessor communications of various topologies and various number of neighbors with combined hardware and software support of reconfiguration of grid stencils;
- using of dedicated functional modules to realize the spline-interpolation computations with required accuracy, ensuring resetting of different clusters of grid nodes when implementing block algorithms of decomposition or splitting type.

3 Homogeneous Structures

As mentioned above, in GMPP specialized homogeneous structures are used as building blocks. A well-known example of such structure is the content-addressed memory with its special (basic) operation "equality search". Some other specialized structures realizing other basic operations are also known. We call these cellular arrays Distributed Functional structures (DF-structures). For further discussion on GMPP consider two DF-structures implementing the basic operations "compression" (λ - structure) and "nearest neighbor search" (ε - structure) [3].

λ - *structure* is a two-dimensional homogeneous array, each cell of which realizes logical functions

$$z' = zt \qquad (2)$$
$$t' = z \vee t \qquad (3)$$
$$g' = g \vee z\neg tf \qquad (4)$$
$$f' = f \qquad (5)$$

where z, z', t, t', g, g', correspondingly, are input and output signals of the horizontal channel z and vertical channels t and g; f-f' is a horizontal bus.

Let an arbitrary binary vector be applied to the inputs z of the left boundary of the λ - structure. Consider the first (left) column. The variable t , in accordance with (3) retains its initial value "0" in the vertical channel t of this column only till $z=0$. In some k-th cell, where $z=1$ is encountered for the first time, the value of t changes to "1", which cannot change till the lower boundary. However, the k-th cell receives yet the signal $t=0$. Hence, it is the only cell in the whole column where the combination $z\neg t = 1$ is present.

Note that the horizontal channel z of the k-th cell is closed by the signal $t=0$; thus, in accordance with (2), the first "one" of the given vector does not propagate further along the current row. In all cells lower than k-th , $t=1$, so that $z'=z$. Hence, to the inputs of the second column a duplicate of the given vector is applied, with the exception of its first "one".

Similar transformations are performed in the second column, the third column, a.s.o.

Let now the inputs f of the left boundary of λ - matrix be the inputs of an interconnection network, and the outputs g' of the lower boundary its outputs. An N-bit binary control vector Z is applied bit-wise to the left boundary inputs z, in which M necessary input channels are indicated by "ones". In each cell of the matrix, where the condition $z\neg t = 1$ is fulfilled, in accordance with (4), g' = f. Hence, the specified M inputs f will be connected ("compressed") with the first M outputs g' of the lower boundary.

ε - *structure* is a one-dimensional homogeneous array (column), the i-th cell of which realizes logical functions

$$z_i' = z_i (a_i \lor \neg t_i) \qquad (6)$$
$$v_i' = v_i \lor z_i a_i \neg t_i \qquad (7)$$
$$t_i' = t_i \qquad (8)$$
$$w_i = \neg v_{i-1} \, 'v_i' \qquad (9)$$

where z_i, v_i are the current values of the signals in the horizontal channels z and v; z_i', v_i' are new values of these signals, produced in the present clock period; a_i is the input variable; t-t' is a vertical bus; w_i is the resulting flag.

Let the initial array A be placed in a "vertical" memory with sequential access to the bit-slices. Connect the outputs of this memory with corresponding inputs a_i of the ε - column. Then, during the interrogation of the memory, the bit-slices of the array A are sequentially fed to the inputs a_i. Apply simultaneously the corresponding bits of a comparand T to the bus t-t' . As shown in [3], the functions (6), (7), (8) ensure that, after the termination of the interrogation cycle, all the rows of the initial array A, containing $A_i > T$, will be marked by signals $v_i'=1$.

4 Distributed Interconnection Network

In GMPP a specialized interconnection network based on the λ - structure is used, allowing flexible programmable reconfiguration of grids and stencils.

The network is organized as follows. Each PE has its own Local Interconnection Module (LIM), consisting of a λ - structure of size p x q , and a Control Unit. The p inputs of the λ - structure are connected with the outputs of p neighboring PE's, corresponding to the necessary set of standard stencils. The q outputs are connected with q general purpose registers of the proper PE.

The Control Unit of the LIM contains a Standard Stencil Register (SSR), a Standard Stencil Memory (SSM), and a Control Vector Register (CVR). In SSM a set of p-bit control vectors is stored. Each of them has a definite number of "ones" defining the pattern of corresponding stencil. For rapid changing of stencils over the whole system or over some clusters, it is sufficient to write the code of new stencil from the controller (or from the host) into SSR's of necessary LIM's. Then, immediately, each LIM produces at the outputs of its SSM the corresponding control vector, and the

λ - network connects the inputs of the proper PE with the outputs of those neighboring PE's which correspond to the new stencil.

5 Table Look-Up Functional Module (TFM)

The TFM is a specialized processor for computation of functions, based on the known table interpolation methods.

As a rule, in table look-up computations a uniform division of the approximation interval is used. As the maximal error on the whole interval is determined by the maximal of errors in all subintervals, the number of subintervals has to be essentially enlarged to diminish it. That is why, the memory volume should be unacceptably increased to achieve the required accuracy.

One can reduce the memory volume by equalizing errors in subintervals. As a result, the interval of approximation is subdivided into uneven subintervals. The search of a subinterval becomes, for conventional memories, a rather troublesome problem. In GMPP an ε - structure is used to speed-up those searches.

The TFM consists of a vertical memory M1 in which the nodal values of the argument x_i are stored, a memory M2 (of conventional type) in which the corresponding values of interpolation coefficients are located, and an ε - column of corresponding size. The current value ξ of the argument is fed into the comparand register CR. Since the set of nodal values is stored in an ordered (say, ascending) form, all the "lower" rows, where $x_i > \xi$ produce the signals $v_i = 1$, while all the "upper" rows the signals $v_i = 0$. Then, in accordance with (9), the resulting flag $w_i = 1$ will be produced in the only cell, corresponding to the proper subinterval. This flag is used to generate the address in M2 of proper interpolation coefficients.

Since TFM is a rather complicated device (compared to the PE), the use of a separate TFM in each node is not acceptable. Therefore in GMPP parallel multiport TFM's are used, located on the middle level of the pyramid. Each of them co-operates with a cluster of nearest PE's.

The basic idea of a parallel TFM is quite simple. During the interrogation of memory M1, at its outputs appear the sequence of all bits of nodal argument values. This effect allows to use several ε - columns working concurrently. The bit-wise inputs a_i of all these columns are connected in parallel to the outputs of corresponding rows of M1, whereas the common comparison input is connected to the output of proper current argument shift register. After finishing of the interrogation cycle, at the outputs of each ε - column, a unique signal is produced indicating the corresponding subinterval.

References

[1] Il'in V.P. *Iterative incomplete factorization methods.* World Scientific Publ. Co., Singapore, 1992.

[2] Marchuk G.I., and Il'in V.P. Parallel computations in grid methods for solving mathematical physics problems. *Proc. IFIP Congress 1980.* Amsterdam: North-Holland, 1980. pp.671-676.

[3] Fet Ya.I. *Parallel processing in cellular arrays.* Research Studies Press, Taunton, 1993 (in press).

APPLAUSE: Application & Assessment of Parallel Programming Using Logic

Liang-Liang Li, Mike Reeve, Kees Schuerman & André Véron[1]
Jacques Bellone & Claudine Pradelles[2]
Angelos Kolokouris[3]
Takis Stamatopoulos[4]
Dominic Clark, Chris Rawlings & Jack Shirazi[5]
Giuseppe Sardu[6]

[1] European Computer-Industry Research Centre
Arabellastrasse 17, 8000 Munich 19, Germany
[2] Dassault Aviation, Toulouse, France
[3] Expert Systems International, Athens, Greece
[4] University of Athens, Greece
[5] Imperial Cancer Research Fund, London, UK
[6] Systems & Management, Rome, Italy

Abstract. The APPLAUSE ESPRIT Project is building major applications using the ElipSys parallel constraint logic programming system developed at ECRC. Two major aims of the project are to advance the state of the art in four commercially significant application areas and to promote the use of ElipSys-like languages among applications developers. This brief paper gives an outline of ElipSys and an overview of the applications being developed within the APPLAUSE Project.

1 Project Overview

The APPLAUSE ESPRIT III Project (6708), the Application and Assessment of Parallel Programming Using Logic, is building major applications using the Elip-Sys parallel constraint logic programming system developed at ECRC (European Computer-Industry Research Centre). It brings together end-users, applications developers and technology providers. APPLAUSE is a three year project and it began in May 1992. The aims of the project are manifold, the major ones being:

- to advance the state of the art in four commercially significant application areas;
- to build a corpus of expertise in using ElipSys-like languages amongst applications developers;
- to generate training material to introduce applications developers to ElipSys-like languages;
- to assess the advantages (and disadvantages) of ElipSys-like languages.

2 ElipSys

ElipSys is a programming system designed to allow the performance potential of large-scale parallel machines to be exploited in the field of search-based applications, such as planning & scheduling and decision support.

ElipSys is based on constraint logic programming. Pure logic programming is recognized as a convenient paradigm for stating and describing search applications and combinatorial problems. It is only relatively recently that it has been complemented with constraint handling, a feature that makes realistic search-based applications tractable. Sequential constraint logic programming systems have been successfully applied to a number of operations research and combinatorial applications. Performances comparable to, and sometimes better than, traditionally coded applications have been exhibited. The paradigm also significantly enhances the flexibility of programming and programmer productivity.

ElipSys enables a search-based application to be parallelized by enabling different processors to be used for exploring the different branches of the search tree, which are normally traversed sequentially a branch at a time.

The ElipSys internal execution model has been designed for maximum portability between different parallel platforms. It uses a hybrid scheme based on shared memory and message passing.

- Shared memory is used exclusively to implement internal static and dynamic data areas. On distributed memory machines, the shared memory concept is supported by virtual shared memory. Thanks to the well defined structure of an ElipSys computation (tree search), the memory reference patterns are such that the usual impediments to the use of virtual shared memory can be minimised. For instance non-strongly coherent memory can be used, or the internal load balancing mechanism of ElipSys can adopt more or less strong policies for improving the locality of reference.
- Message passing is used for synchronization and control purposes between the processors. Depending on the platform, message passing can be implemented using either shared memory, OS primitives or hardware supported mechanisms.

ElipSys yields performance improvements ranging from linear to super-linear. They depend on the type of application and the kind of tree search the applications performs. In all cases the search trees must be bushy enough to let the effect of sharing work overwhelm the overheads of parallelization and load balancing. Linear speed-ups are to be encountered when search trees have to be entirely explored, for example when the optimal solution is sought. Super-linear speed-ups might appear when search trees need only be partially explored, as for instance during branch-and-bound search, where one is satisfied with any solution.

ElipSys is currently available on a wide range of machines. It runs on Sun workstations, in sequential and pseudo-parallel mode. The shared memory machines it has been ported to are the Sequent Symmetry and SPARC-based multi-processors from Sun and ICL. ElipSys has also been ported to the KSR-1 distributed memory machine, on which it makes effective use of the hardware supported shared virtual memory.

3 Applications Using ElipSys

3.1 Manufacturing Planning: Dassault Aviation

Dassault Aviation is using ElipSys to enhance and extend the PLANE manufacturing planning system, currently implemented using the CHIP constraint programming system also developed at ECRC. PLANE is an aid for the planning of long term (5 to 10 years) production schedules for a collection of assembly lines manufacturing a mix of different aircraft types. The aim of the system is to pace the assembly lines, under a given set of two-dimensional constraints, so as to minimize the combination of the stock costs and the production rate changes. The first dimension consists of precedence constraints between the assembly lines and the second of disjunctive and precedence constraints on the production rate changes. The combinatorics of the problem is the main computational issue and these arise when the system has to decide for which aircraft it is wise to change the production rate and how to change it, e.g. in the most difficult case to choose one aircraft from the 250 that may be involved and to choose one value for the production rate among 90 possible values.

A port and enhancement of PLANE on ElipSys, known as PSAP (Planning System for Aircraft Production), will use the features of ElipSys to explore disjunctive constraints, labelling strategies and search heuristics in parallel.

3.2 Tourist Advice: Expert Systems International & the University of Athens

MaTourA is a Multi-agent Tourist Advisor being built by Expert Systems International (ESI) and the University of Athens as a demonstrator for the Greek National Tourist Organization. The purpose of the system is to support travel agencies in constructing personalized tours, selecting predefined package tours and accessing basic tourist information.

MaTourA consists of a set of specialized autonomous agents. Some of these agents handle information related to activities, events, sites, accommodation, transportation, ticketing, and so on. Other agents are responsible for more complicated tasks, such as the construction of personalized tours that satisfy constraints imposed by the tourist. These tours are actually instantiated Daily Plan Templates (DPTs) which are given by the user. In order for an agent to solve a specific problem, it may require the services offered by other agents. In such a case, it send a requests to the appropriate "expert" agents, which, after the required computation is carried out, send back their responses (results). The agents of MaTourA work in a physically distributed environment and not all will be implemented in ElipSys.

The system provides an interface which helps the user to state his/her problem via a well designed dialog procedure. A training facility will allow even casual users to use MaTourA.

3.3 Molecular Biology: Imperial Cancer Research Fund

The Imperial Cancer Research Fund (ICRF) is addressing a number of challenging problems in protein structure analysis and molecular genetics. These can both be characterized as combinatorially complex and computationally intensive.

The rationale for the use of CLP methods is the observation that many aspects of scientific activity can be viewed as attempts to produce the most general consistent interpretation of a broad range of possibly heterogeneous but interrelated data.

Additionally it should be emphasized that since molecular biology is a broad field of scientific endeavour, encompassing many distinct types of problem-solving requirements, an important aim of the project is the development of a generic schema for both identifying problems that are amenable to solutions that exploit parallel CLP and providing an implementation methodology.

The potential advantages arising from the use of ElipSys occur both: as a result of the existence of a priori constraints (e.g. rules that govern protein folding and prior knowledge of local gene order) which can be used to prune the search tree; and the remaining, possibly massive, search spaces which can be searched in parallel.

The specific systems initially being developed are a system for the prediction of protein topologies from secondary structure assignments and topological folding rules, and a system for generating a physical genetic map from hybridization fingerprinting data to support the human genome mapping work of Hans Lehrach's laboratory at the ICRF.

3.4 Environmental Monitoring and Control: Systems & Management

Systems & Management is developing a knowledge based decision support system (DSS) concerned with the monitoring and control of pollution in the Venice Lagoon as a demonstrator for the Venice Water Magistracy. It is aimed at assisting the authorities in two major aspects: the correct evaluation of the state of the pollution and the planning of technical interventions aimed at restoring an acceptable state at acceptable costs.

The DSS includes a relational database describing the emissions and a hydro-dynamic model of the lagoon able to plot the distribution of polluting substances. These modules are integrated through a knowledge based core, seen as the interpretive model of the analysis and decision making activities, which is being developed in ElipSys. The constraints and parallelism features of ElipSys are seen as complementary means to attack the combinatorial aspects of the evaluation and decision-making processes.

A complete modelization must consider up to 20,000 (registered) pollution sources and tens of dangerous substances. The system should provide an early prediction of potentially dangerous combinations by considering the combinatorial explosion of possible effects. Finally, it should enumerate a suitable mix of technical instruments to be applied to pollution sources to restore acceptable states at affordable costs.

4 Conclusion

By bringing together end-users, applications developers and technology providers, the APPLAUSE Project is building novel sophisticated applications designed to advance the state of the art in four commercially significant application areas. By using the ElipSys parallel constraint logic programming system, developed at ECRC, the project will provide a basis for other applications developers to assess the suitability of ElipSys-like systems for their tasks.

Acknowledgements

The APPLAUSE Project is partially funded by the ESPRIT Programme of the Commission of the European Communities as ESPRIT Project 6708.

EPOCH - European Parallel Operating System based on Chorus
- Esprit EP 6059 -

Lothar Borrmann *(Siemens AG)*, Erol Gelenbe *(EHEI)*,
Isabella Hofstetter *(IAO)*, Petro Istavrinos *(Siemens AG)*,
Karl Klaus *(SNI AG)*, Mike Ward *(ICL)*

1   Introduction

Parallel MIMD machines are now becoming established in the marketplace. So far, these machines are typically used for numerical applications. There is growing interest however in using parallel machines for commercial systems, with a particular focus on transaction processing and database systems. Commercial users have different requirements compared to scientific users. Features such as availability and data integrity are vital. Ease of use, for the system manager and for the programmer, is essential. Conformance to standards is also important as it provides a sound transition route for existing commercial applications, thereby protecting the large investment in existing software. Additionally it facilitates the porting of new applications.

EPOCH will provide a commercially usable parallel operating system based on *Chorus/MiX*. It builds on the operating system work of the Esprit project *EDS* (EP 2025) giving it additional commercial capability by enabling current commercial applications to be ported. It also integrates system management facilities from the *COMANDOS* project (EP 2071).

The EPOCH work will provide:

- A Unix SVR4 base operating system
- Unix enhancements giving:
  - a fully coherent distributed file system
  - high data integrity
  - distributed shared memory
  - single image view at the programmer's interface
  - dynamic load balancing
- High performance inter-process communication
- Advanced system management facilities
- Portability over a wide range of parallel architectures
- Conformance to international standards
- Support for the ORACLE and INGRES database systems and SNI's UTM transaction monitor

2   Hardware Platforms

The EPOCH operating system is targeted at a wide range of parallel
systems. The systems we are envisaging are made up of processing nodes
interconnected by a communication network. No physically shared memory
is required between nodes but each node may individually be a shared-
memory multiprocessor. Each node has access to background storage
devices, such as disks.

A first example is ICL's parallel platform derived from an architecture
developed in the *EDS* project. It consists of up to 256 processing elements
interconnected by a high-performance Delta net. Each node has two CPUs,
one for application programs and another one dedicated to system support
tasks like message passing. (Fig. 2)

The second example is a high-end parallel UNIX system based on SNI's
shared memory multiprocessors (Fig. 1). A third case is a development
platform consisting of a number of 486 PCs interconnected by a LAN.

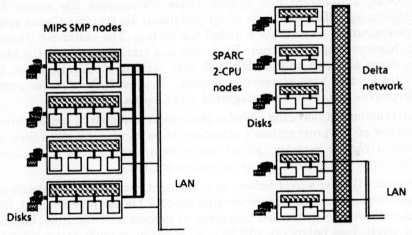

Fig. 1: SNI's Clustered System   Fig. 2: ICL's Parallel Machine

3   Architectural Outline of the Operating System

The software architecture is based on the *Chorus microkernel*. Together
with the microkernel, each node in the EPOCH system will run an
enhanced *Chorus/MiX* subsystem to implement *UNIX* functionality.

The microkernel provides the basic abstractions for the distributed
operating system, such as local process control, global unique identifiers,
local and remote interprocess communication and basic virtual memory
management functions. The *MiX subsystem* on top of the microkernel offers
a SVR4 interface. It is implemented by a number of privileged processes
executing in kernel address space. The current MiX system does not offer
any distributed facilities.

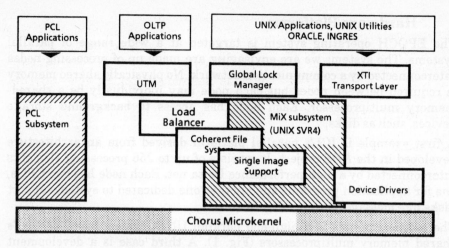

Fig. 3: Operating System Architecture

In EPOCH, a *Coherent File System* offers transparent file access for applications (eg. RDBMS). Parts of the individual file systems of each node are cross-mounted to emulate a global file system. The enhanced Chorus Object Manager supports remote file access in a transparent way. Caching at the client side can be disabled such that caching mechanisms can be controlled by data base systems as desired. To provide for *data integrity*, the *Veritas* file system has be integrated with Chorus.

Special functionality is being added to the system to support a *single system image* view at the programmer's interface. In particular, features such as *distributed shared memory*, *global semaphores*, *remote fork* and *global process control* will be provided as extensions of Unix.

The system will offer a *load balancing* component with special emphasis on high performance transaction processing aspects. On the process level, the system will provide static load balancing at process creation time. On the higher levels, load balancing will be carried out by module assignment to processing elements.

Additionally, EPOCH will support *PCL (Process Control Language)*, which was designed in the EDS project to provide support for parallel applications. PCL will implemented as a separate, portable subsystem.

4   System Management

When moving to parallel systems in a commercial environment, the additional complexity introduced must be minimised to keep the system usable. The burden of system administration can be alleviated by presenting a unified view of the parallel machine. Each visible component such as the hardware or the MiX system will be presented as a *Managed Object*, having a set of attributes and a set defined of operations.

The EPOCH System Management Architecture comprises *system observation, system modification, decision support* and *modification of the managed system*. Observation information is presented to the decision making application for future modification to the managed system. Modification can be either by changing the managed object or by altering the resource being managed. Tools will be provided for all areas. These tools will comprise a Configuration Tool, a Modification Service, a Modification Editor, a Logging Service, an Observation Service, an Information Analysis Tool, a Workload Modelling Tool, an Event Handling Tool and a Visualisation Tool.

5   Commercial Application Support

The EPOCH system will prove its suitability for commercial use by running three widely used commercial packages, Oracle, Ingres and UTM. The former two products are well known data base systems while UTM is a commercial transaction monitor by Siemens Nixdorf.

UTM supports distributed transaction processing in homogeneous and inhomogeneous environments. It allows interworking of EPOCH systems with other commercial systems, Unix as well as mainframes. UTM co-operates with data bases via the XA interface as defined by X/Open.

Porting of the data base systems is mostly accomplished outside of the EPOCH project within separate commercial agreements. The project however is to provide all support needed on the system side. For the parallel version of Oracle, this includes a Global Lock Manager (GLM). This distributed server is needed by Oracle to keep its data base caches in a coherent state. The interface between GLM and Oracle is a set of primitives defined by Oracle. The implementation of the GLM is crucial for the performance of the overall system. GLM performance itself depends not only on the distributed locking scheme used but also on the efficiency of the underlying communication system.

Another function needed is the distributed X/Open Transport Interface (XTI-D), which performs the task to forward a client message as early as possible to that EPOCH server instance, which was identified by the load balancer as the optimal processing instance for the included commission.

6   Consortium Information

The main partners of EPOCH are Siemens AG and ICL. IAO (part of Fraunhofer Gesellschaft) focusses on System Management as an associate of ICL. EHEI (École des Hautes Études Industrielles) do the load balancing work and SNI (Siemens Nixdorf Informationssysteme AG) are involved in supporting the commercial applications, both as associates to Siemens. Finally, as a subcontractor of ICL, Chorus Systèmes contribute enhancements of their system. For further information contact the project manager, Petro Istavrinos <istavrinos@zfe.siemens.de>.

Pythagoras Project Overview (EP7091)

K.-F.Wong, M.H.Williams, S.Leunig, M.L.Kersten, M.Jean-Noel, B.Finance,
B.Dageville, M.Couprie, P.Broughton, D.Boudigue, B.Bergsten and F.Andres

The Pythagoras Consortium**

Database vendors and researchers introduce new or extended database systems that provide advanced functionality (e.g. deductive databases) and/or high performance (e.g. using parallelism). Due to their complexity existing performance assessment tools and techniques (e.g. analytical models and benchmarks) are no longer suitable. It is this observation that underpins the goal of the Pythagoras project; namely, to develop the tools and methodologies to predict, evaluate and tune the performance of advanced information servers. The project is organized around three research areas: benchmarking, performance evaluation methods, and performance evaluation tools.

Among its novelties are the development of a benchmark for GIS, studies of the effectiveness of query optimization and data placement, and the development of tools to aid the DBMS developer and user in their quest to provide better services. The remainder of this paper outlines the Pythagoras activities.

(I) Case Studies and Benchmarks ¿From a user perspective, next generation DBMSs are valuable only if they indeed provide the functionality required by advanced applications at a reasonable performance level. Therefore, the Pythagoras project aims at the development of enhanced benchmarks. They are summarized below.

GIS - Geographic Information System. A geographical application is being developed, to form the nucleus of a benchmark for geographical information systems. This application is demonstrated on GeoSabrina, a relational DBMS extended with ADTs that support easy integration of a geographic domain and its associated operators inside the server. The representation of the geometric map relationships are hidden from the end-user through two ADT's in the DBMS kernel:

- At the outer level, an ADT deals with regions, lines and points, whose operations are visible to the end-user in terms of geographical operations. The three classes of geographic operators are : spatial retrieval, such as POINT LOCATION and SPATIAL RANGE SEARCHING; spatial join operators such as OVERLAPPING MAPS and ADJACENCY; and computation operators such as DISTANCE, AREA, LENGTH.
- At the inner level, an ADT deals with elementary faces, edges and nodes of the topology. At this level, a set of procedures is defined to access the geographical data representation. They are used in the implementation of the geographical operators. The collection of procedures can be extended with little effort, so as to support applications functionality yet unforeseen.

** For further information contact Martin Kersten, CWI, Kruislaan 413, 1098 SJ Amsterdam, The Netherlands, mk@cwi.nl .

Business Applications. Instead of developing a new benchmark from scratch, we focus on extensions of the Transaction Processing Council benchmark proposals, such that they better reflect the system characteristics encountered at our customer sites. Moreover, the extensions proposed highlight the potential of parallel platforms (e.g. the scalability of parallelism and use of object orientation).

Existing commercial work loads from customers of the Pythagoras' industrial partners - namely ICL (UK) and IFATEC (France) - are being selected for study and a detailed analysis of their performance using a modern database system is undertaken. Both mainframe and parallel MIMD based applications and their future needs are being studied and their important characteristics identified. Special attention is given to the impact of client-server architecture to support transaction processing on a current mini or mainframe platform.

Performance tests will be developed to exhibit the important characteristics identified and they are evaluated using systems and platforms available to the Pythagoras' industrial partners. Examples include the EDBS, Ingres, Oracle and IDEA (EP6333) systems on the sequential and parallel platforms.

(II) Techniques and Methods ¿From the perspective of system developer and DBA, improved knowledge is required on the effectiveness of baseline technology employed in advanced database systems. This knowledge drives the development of new system implementation technology, but also guides users in proper data management. The research activities are summarized below.

Architecture Classification. In this activity, the performance impact of the different system architectures, such as NORMA (NORmalized Memory Access) and NUMA (Non-Uniform Memory Access), to applications is being studied. To achieve the classification, key performance critical features, such as user/server communications, intra-server communications, I/O, CPU, etc., are being abstracted from the architectures and application work loads; and they are being analysed both analytically and by simulation (using the Pythagoras tools). The results is a set of guidelines for designers to determine architectural choices for different classes of database applications.

Query Optimization. The query optimizers in many database processing systems are rule-based. The rules are derived from the algebraic properties of the underlying data model and heuristics based on simple cost models to select an optimal plan of execution. A continual research challenge is to improve query optimization for new application domains by extending the data model, rules, and heuristics.

Our prime goal is to develop a technique to assess the effectiveness of a given query optimizer. In other words we wish to be able to develop an approach which provides answers to questions such as the following: what rules are most effective for a given application domain and a given DBMS architecture? How effective is query optimization work divided between Clients and Servers? Is the query optimizer accurate in choosing an evaluation plan for highly complex queries? These problems are studied both from the viewpoint of the underlying theory and through semi-automatic techniques to exercise a given optimizer using a static description of the target database environment together with a query language, or application building blocks. The prime focus is on the query optimizers for the shared-nothing database servers EDS and shared-memory database server DBS3.

Data Placement. In parallel databases, the issue of "is the data in the right place, in the right form, at the right time and, if not, how much does it cost to get it" is performance critical. This is a particularly important issue in shared-nothing parallel database systems (as opposed to shared memory systems). Basically it is concerned with the division of data into suitable fragments, the clustering of fragments into appropriate groups and the allocation of these to different nodes in the system. It is planned to embed several techniques into the PARADES simulator and to compare their performance on particular architectures for the applications considered in this project.

Analytical Methods. The objective is to derive in a semi-automatic way an analytical performance cost model for query processing and data placement suitable for various parallel platforms. Based on an abstraction of the key aspects from the architectures and databases, several case studies will be undertaken to identify the prime performance factors, such as user/server communication, intra-server communication, I/O, CPU, etc.. In line with the other activities in this project, we focus on shared-memory (DBS3) and shared-nothing parallel database servers (EDS). As a result of this activity, a parameterized analytical Performance Quality Prediction (PQP) model is defined and incorporated in the performance evaluation tool APE.

(III) Engineering Tools Performance suites and studies are complemented by a set of tools that provide direct benefits to the DBMS designer and DBA. The tool set encompasses a low- and high-level simulator, an analytical performance evaluator, and a Software Testpilot to automate performance assessment sessions. Prototype tool implementations are delivered at an early stage to improve early feedback to the previous activities.

Adaptive Performance Evaluator (APE). Parallelization of extended RDBMS adds to the complexity of physical database designs as well as to that of query optimization. A parallel query optimizer faces a much larger search space, and needs to anticipate congestion and bottlenecks. A poor decision can lead to low resource utilization and poor performance. APE is being designed to overcome these problems. This tool can be used as an advanced database administration tool: e.g. the analyses performed by APE can advice a administrator to modify the data distribution and/or indexing strategies of the physical database schema in order to achieve the maximum performance. Advanced database system designers can use it to determine the optimal software/hardware architectures for a specific work load under certain efficiency requirements. Furthermore, for a fixed architecture, the analytical formulae in APE can be used as the cost formulae for the physical query compiler-optimizer. The analytical methods developed in Pythagoras are extensively used in the design of APE. APE is linked with the Software Testpilot to form an automatic cost model calibration tool.

PARAllel DatabasE Simulator (PARADES). This activity aims to develop a simulation tool for building a parallel DBMS simulation program. It is being designed to permit maximum flexibility and it will cater for variations in the application program, the execution mechanisms of the database operations and the data placement strategy, as well as a variety of system variables. PARADES adopts an event-driven simulation approach coupled with behavioural modeling techniques similar to the approach described in. This approach allows designers to model the target system closely and it permits simulation at different system levels of execution granularity.

SMART2. At present, the OLTP performance figures are frequently used for comparing the efficiency between different commercial DBMSs. It will unquestionably remain one of the prime applications in future advanced database systems. The OLTP and distributed performance predictor being developed is, in fact, an enhanced version of an existing commercial database simulation tool, called SMART, which is primarily used to estimate the performance of commercial relational database applications running under Oracle V6. This enhanced tool, SMART2, provides both a model of client-server architecture and a model of the local network. In addition, it captures the facilities brought by the new generation of commercial relational DBMS (e.g. ORACLE7) in distributed applications, e.g. 2-phase commit protocols. Finally, SMART2 provides the means to predict the performance of a DBMS on current parallel computers using a model of process and thread management¿. It supports modeling a real load distribution on multi-cpu servers and multi-site servers.

DBMS Testpilot. A major step in putting a database server on the market is to assure that the system will not collapse under the actual data/user load. One should obtain certification on the performance quality of a reasonable range of system parameters. Furthermore, new database servers often contain system implementation errors and bottlenecks which cannot be identified even during system construction and beta testing. These harmful sources must be located as early as possible before a design is put into production. The Software Testpilot is a tool designed to aid the DBMS engineer and user to explore a large work load search space to find the slope, top, and knees of performance figures quickly. The approach taken is based on specifying the abstract work load search space, a small interface library with the target system, and a functional description of the expected performance behavior. Thereafter, the Software Testpilot selects work load parameter values and executes the corresponding DBMS experiments, such that the performance characteristics and quality weaknesses are determined with minimal cost (i.e. time). Note that the prototype Software Testpilot is already linked with APE to obtain an effective calibration tool and an Ingres back-end for performance assessment.

Conclusion The Pythagoras project described here is well on course. At present (the end of first year), the specifications of the benchmark programs are being defined, some results have already been produced from the "techniques and methods" activities and in the engineer tools front, the first prototypes of APE, PARADES and Software Testpilot are available and they will be demonstrated as part of the first year deliverables.

Authors Index

Springer-Verlag
and the Environment

We at Springer-Verlag firmly believe that an international science publisher has a special obligation to the environment, and our corporate policies consistently reflect this conviction.

We also expect our business partners – paper mills, printers, packaging manufacturers, etc. – to commit themselves to using environmentally friendly materials and production processes.

The paper in this book is made from low- or no-chlorine pulp and is acid free, in conformance with international standards for paper permanency.

Lecture Notes in Computer Science

For information about Vols. 1–610
please contact your bookseller or Springer-Verlag

Vol. 650: T. Ibaraki, Y. Inagaki, K. Iwama, T. Nishizeki, M. Yamashita (Eds.), Algorithms and Computation. Proceedings, 1992. XI, 510 pages. 1992.

Vol. 651: R. Koymans, Specifying Message Passing and Time-Critical Systems with Temporal Logic. IX, 164 pages. 1992.

Vol. 652: R. Shyamasundar (Ed.), Foundations of Software Technology and Theoretical Computer Science. Proceedings, 1992. XIII, 405 pages. 1992.

Vol. 653: A. Bensoussan, J.-P. Verjus (Eds.), Future Tendencies in Computer Science, Control and Applied Mathematics. Proceedings, 1992. XV, 371 pages. 1992.

Vol. 654: A. Nakamura, M. Nivat, A. Saoudi, P. S. P. Wang, K. Inoue (Eds.), Prallel Image Analysis. Proceedings, 1992. VIII, 312 pages. 1992.

Vol. 655: M. Bidoit, C. Choppy (Eds.), Recent Trends in Data Type Specification. X, 344 pages. 1993.

Vol. 656: M. Rusinowitch, J. L. Rémy (Eds.), Conditional Term Rewriting Systems. Proceedings, 1992. XI, 501 pages. 1993.

Vol. 657: E. W. Mayr (Ed.), Graph-Theoretic Concepts in Computer Science. Proceedings, 1992. VIII, 350 pages. 1993.

Vol. 658: R. A. Rueppel (Ed.), Advances in Cryptology – EUROCRYPT '92. Proceedings, 1992. X, 493 pages. 1993.

Vol. 659: G. Brewka, K. P. Jantke, P. H. Schmitt (Eds.), Nonmonotonic and Inductive Logic. Proceedings, 1991. VIII, 332 pages. 1993. (Subseries LNAI).

Vol. 660: E. Lamma, P. Mello (Eds.), Extensions of Logic Programming. Proceedings, 1992. VIII, 417 pages. 1993. (Subseries LNAI).

Vol. 661: S. J. Hanson, W. Remmele, R. L. Rivest (Eds.), Machine Learning: From Theory to Applications. VIII, 271 pages. 1993.

Vol. 662: M. Nitzberg, D. Mumford, T. Shiota, Filtering, Segmentation and Depth. VIII, 143 pages. 1993.

Vol. 663: G. v. Bochmann, D. K. Probst (Eds.), Computer Aided Verification. Proceedings, 1992. IX, 422 pages. 1993.

Vol. 664: M. Bezem, J. F. Groote (Eds.), Typed Lambda Calculi and Applications. Proceedings, 1993. VIII, 433 pages. 1993.

Vol. 665: P. Enjalbert, A. Finkel, K. W. Wagner (Eds.), STACS 93. Proceedings, 1993. XIV, 724 pages. 1993.

Vol. 666: J. W. de Bakker, W.-P. de Roever, G. Rozenberg (Eds.), Semantics: Foundations and Applications. Proceedings, 1992. VIII, 659 pages. 1993.

Vol. 667: P. B. Brazdil (Ed.), Machine Learning: ECML – 93. Proceedings, 1993. XII, 471 pages. 1993. (Subseries LNAI).

Vol. 668: M.-C. Gaudel, J.-P. Jouannaud (Eds.), TAPSOFT '93: Theory and Practice of Software Development. Proceedings, 1993. XII, 762 pages. 1993.

Vol. 669: R. S. Bird, C. C. Morgan, J. C. P. Woodcock (Eds.), Mathematics of Program Construction. Proceedings, 1992. VIII, 378 pages. 1993.

Vol. 670: J. C. P. Woodcock, P. G. Larsen (Eds.), FME '93: Industrial-Strength Formal Methods. Proceedings, 1993. XI, 689 pages. 1993.

Vol. 671: H. J. Ohlbach (Ed.), GWAI-92: Advances in Artificial Intelligence. Proceedings, 1992. XI, 397 pages. 1993. (Subseries LNAI).

Vol. 672: A. Barak, S. Guday, R. G. Wheeler, The MOSIX Distributed Operating System. X, 221 pages. 1993.

Vol. 673: G. Cohen, T. Mora, O. Moreno (Eds.), Applied Algebra, Algebraic Algorithms and Error-Correcting Codes. Proceedings, 1993. X, 355 pages 1993.

Vol. 674: G. Rozenberg (Ed.), Advances in Petri Nets 1993. VII, 457 pages. 1993.

Vol. 675: A. Mulkers, Live Data Structures in Logic Programs. VIII, 220 pages. 1993.

Vol. 676: Th. H. Reiss, Recognizing Planar Objects Using Invariant Image Features. X, 180 pages. 1993.

Vol. 677: H. Abdulrab, J.-P. Pécuchet (Eds.), Word Equations and Related Topics. Proceedings, 1991. VII, 214 pages. 1993.

Vol. 678: F. Meyer auf der Heide, B. Monien, A. L. Rosenberg (Eds.), Parallel Architectures and Their Efficient Use. Proceedings, 1992. XII, 227 pages. 1993.

Vol. 683: G.J. Milne, L. Pierre (Eds.), Correct Hardware Design and Verification Methods. Proceedings, 1993. VIII, 270 Pages. 1993.

Vol. 684: A. Apostolico, M. Crochemore, Z. Galil, U. Manber (Eds.), Combinatorial Pattern Matching. Proceedings, 1993. VIII, 265 pages. 1993.

Vol. 685: C. Rolland, F. Bodart, C. Cauvet (Eds.), Advanced Information Systems Engineering. Proceedings, 1993. XI, 650 pages. 1993.

Vol. 686: J. Mira, J. Cabestany, A. Prieto (Eds.), New Trends in Neural Computation. Procedings, 1993. XVII, 746 pages. 1993.

Vol. 687: H. H. Barrett, A. F. Gmitro (Eds.), Information Processing in Medical Imaging. Proceedings, 1993. XVI, 567 pages. 1993.

Vol. 688: M. Gauthier (Ed.), Ada - Europe '93. Proceedings, 1993. VIII, 353 pages. 1993.

Vol. 689: J. Komorowski, Z. W. Ras (Eds.), Methodologies for Intelligent Systems. Proceedings, 1993. XI, 653 pages. 1993. (Subseries LNAI).

Vol. 690: C. Kirchner (Ed.), Rewriting Techniques and Applications. Proceedings, 1993. XI, 488 pages. 1993.

Vol. 691: M. Ajmone Marsan (Ed.), Application and Theory of Petri Nets 1993. Proceedings, 1993. IX, 591 pages. 1993.

Vol. 692: D. Abel, B.C. Ooi (Eds.), Advances in Spatial Databases. Proceedings, 1993. XIII, 529 pages. 1993.

Vol. 694: A. Bode, M. Reeve, G. Wolf (Eds.), PARLE '93. Parallel Architectures and Languages Europe. Proceedings, 1993. XVII, 770 pages. 1993.

Lecture Notes in Computer Science 694

Edited by G. Goos and J. Hartmanis

Advisory Board: W. Brauer   D. Gries   J. Stoer